BUSINESS LAW

ɔks are to be returned on or before
the last ᵈᵃᵗᵉ below.

BUSINESS LAW
Second edition

Ewan MacIntyre

PEARSON
Longman

Harlow, England • London • New York • Boston • San Francisco • Toronto
Sydney • Tokyo • Singapore • Hong Kong • Seoul • Taipei • New Delhi
Cape Town • Madrid • Mexico City • Amsterdam • Munich • Paris • Milan

Pearson Education Limited
Edinburgh Gate
Harlow
Essex CM20 2JE
England

and Associated Companies throughout the world

Visit us on the World Wide Web at
www.pearsoned.co.uk

First published in Great Britain in 2001
Second edition published 2005

ISBN 0 582 89422 0

British Library Cataloguing-in-Publication Data
A catalogue record for this book is available from the British Library

10   9   8   7   6   5   4   3   2   1
10   09   08   07   06   05

Typeset in 10/12 pt Sabon by 30
Printed and bound by Mateu Cromo, Spain

The publisher's policy is to use paper manufactured from sustainable forests.

CONTENTS

PREFACE

Changes in the law

Since the first edition of this book was published in 2001 the law has continued to change at a relentless pace. The major changes which this edition incorporates are set out below.

The following new legislation is considered in detail:

■ The Electronic Commerce Regulations 2002
■ The Sale and Supply of Goods to Consumers Regulations 2002
■ The Enterprise Act 2002 (on insolvency, competition and enforcement of consumer law)
■ The Employment Act 2002
■ The Employment Equality (Religion or Belief) Regulations 2003
■ The Fixed Term Employees (Prevention of Less Favourable Treatment) Regulations 2002
■ The Employment Equality (Sexual Orientation) Regulations 2003
■ The Paternity and Adoption Leave Regulations 2002
■ The Copyright and Related Rights Regulations 2003

New cases are included throughout the text, including the following decisions of the House of Lords and Privy Council:

■ *Transco plc v Stockport MBC* [2004]
■ *Fairchild v Glenhaven Funeral Services Ltd* [2002]
■ *Lister v Hesley Hall* [2001]
■ *Farley v Skinner* [2001]
■ *Attorney General v Blake* [2001]
■ *Royal Bank of Scotland v Etridge (No. 2)* [2001]
■ *R v Attorney General* [2003]
■ *Shogun Finance Ltd v Hudson* [2003]
■ *Wilson v First County Trust Ltd (No. 2)* [2003]
■ *Dubai Aluminium Co Ltd v Salaam* [2003]

Other substantial additions to this edition include:

■ A new chapter on the law of torts
■ A detailed consideration of the Limited Liability Partnerships Act 2000
■ Company administration and administrative receivership, assessing the likely impact of the new insolvency regime
■ The reforms made by the Treaty of Nice
■ Competition law
■ The Commercial Agents Regulations 1993
■ The Banking Code
■ The Computer Misuse Act 1990
■ The impact of the Human Rights Act 1998

The aim of this book

This book aims to provide a comprehensive treatment of business law in a way which is both interesting and easily understood. The text covers most areas which could be classified as business law in an academically rigorous way. More specifically this text aims to be:

- **Comprehensive** in its scope, covering not only the more traditional business law subjects, but also the English Legal System, Employment, Consumer Credit, Intellectual Property, Trade Descriptions, Misleading Price Indications, Competition Law and Product Safety.
- **Holistic** in its approach. In every chapter there are numerous cross-references to other sections of the text, demonstrating the inter-relationship between the various subject areas.
- **Thorough** in its treatment of the law. Despite the easily readable style of the text, difficult issues are dealt with thoroughly even in areas where the law is highly technical.
- **Easy to read**. The style of the text is straightforward and accessible. The policy behind the law is explained, making comprehension of the law much easier.
- **Well structured**. In every chapter the text frequently reminds the reader of the main issues involved and the context of the particular subject being considered.
- **Up to date** in its treatment of the law. The text reflects the changes made by recent cases, and legislation and above all by EC law. The accompanying web sites will deal with changes to the law and keep the text as up to date as possible.

Who should use this book?

This book is intended to be suitable for a wide variety of students who study Business Law; for example:

- **Undergraduates** who study one or more law modules as part of their accountancy, business studies or business-related degrees.
- Students on **professional courses**, such as ACCA, CIMA, ILEX, ICAEW, IComA and ICSA.
- **HNC/D students**.
- **Postgraduate students** who need a thorough grounding in business law.

Distinctive features

Clear structure

The book is very clearly structured. The text in each chapter is broken up with several sets of 'Check your Understanding Questions.' These are designed to keep the reader firmly focused on the the main issues with which the text deals. 'Key Points' at the end of each chapter have the same aim. The text is detailed, but the reader is frequently reminded of the context and structure of the material.

Multiple choice and summary questions

Each chapter ends with a selection of multiple choice and summary questions. These questions are designed to be intellectually demanding and to give the reader the chance to apply the law contained in the preceding chapter to problem situations. The answers to the questions can be found in the special lecturer's edition of the book.

Student and lecturer web sites

Several areas of business law are changing very rapidly. None of the areas remain static. The student web site will point students to important changes in the law. There will be a brief summary of new cases and new legislation, along with an explanation of how these changes fit in with the book. The student web site will also contain a brief overview of each chapter and additional multiple choice questions. The answers to the multiple choice questions are 'justified' so that students can refer to the text and see why the answer is as it is. The lecturers' web site will contain a brief overview of each chapter, power point slides and more detailed comment on changes in the law and how these changes affect the material in the book.

Selected further readings

At the end of the book there is a short bibliography, suggesting further reading for those who want to know more about a particular subject area.

Acknowledgements

I would like to thank Judith Ward, Michael Ottley, Beth Chadwick, Andrew Bell, Austin Garwood-Gowers and Sylvia Hargreaves for their help in reviewing the draft material or helping me to deal with some of the more difficult issues.

TABLE OF CASES

TABLE OF STATUTES

TABLE OF STATUTORY INSTRUMENTS

TABLE OF EUROPEAN LEGISLATION

Chapter 1

THE LEGAL SYSTEM

Introduction

We begin this chapter by considering the characteristics of the English legal system, most of which have their origins in the Middle Ages. The distinguishing features of the English legal system have been modified over the years, but it is nevertheless questionable whether they are best suited to the needs of the twenty-first century. Having examined the characteristics peculiar to the English legal system, we then consider the ways in which the law can be classified. We contrast public law and private law; civil law and criminal law; and common law and equity.

The main focus of this chapter is on the different sources of law. We first examine legislation, considering how both statutes and delegated legislation are passed and the way in which legislation is interpreted. Rather more time is spent considering the doctrine of judicial precedent, which holds that principles of law formulated in senior courts are binding upon other courts. We consider both the hierarchy of the courts and the way in which the system of judicial precedent operates.

European Community (EC) law is becoming ever more influential in the United Kingdom. We therefore examine the EC institutions, the EC Treaties, the different types of EC legislation and the role of the European Court of Justice. We conclude the chapter by considering the European Convention on Human Rights. The Human Rights Act 1998 has incorporated the Convention on Human Rights into English law. Although Parliamentary sovereignty has been preserved, the 1998 Act is expected to have a profound effect on English law. All businesses are likely to be affected, particularly those which provide a function of a public nature.

1.1 · Features of the English legal system

The English legal system is unlike that of any other European country. An outline knowledge of the features which make the English system so distinct is essential to an understanding of English law and the English legal process.

1.1.1 Antiquity and continuity

English law has evolved, without any major upheaval or interruption, over many hundreds of years. The last successful invasion of England occurred in 1066, when King William and his Normans conquered the country. King William did not impose Norman law on the conquered Anglo-Saxons, but allowed them to keep their own laws. These laws were not uniform throughout the kingdom. Anglo-Saxon law was based on custom and in different parts of the country different customs prevailed.

In the second half of the twelfth century King Henry II introduced a central administration for the law and begun the process of applying one set of legal rules, 'the common law', throughout England. Since that time, English law has evolved piecemeal. For this reason the English legal system retains a number of peculiarities and anomalies which find their origins in Mediaeval England.

The world history of the past few hundred years has been a litany of revolution and conquest. The new rulers of a country tend to start afresh with the law. In the Soviet Union the communists introduced Soviet law, in France Napoleon introduced the Napoleonic code, in the United States the founding fathers wrote the American Constitution. But England is one of the very few countries to have survived the last nine hundred years with no lasting revolution from within or foreign conquest from abroad. Some English laws and legal practices have evolved continuously since the time of King Ethelbert, who became king of Kent in the year 560. The Norman conquest was a major upheaval, but even that was not a fresh beginning for the law.

English law does not become inoperative merely because of the passage of time. When we study the law of contract we shall see that two ancient cases, *Pinnel's Case* (1602) 5 Co Rep 117a and *Lampleigh v Brathwaite* (1615) Hob 105, are still important precedents. Although these cases have been refined and developed by subsequent cases, there would be no reason why a modern lawyer should not cite them in court. In the same way, statutes remain in force indefinitely or until they are repealed. A statute loses none of its authority merely because it has lain dormant for many years. In *R v Duncan* [1944] KB 713, for example, a defendant was convicted of fortune telling under the Witchcraft Act 1735, even though the statute had long since fallen into disuse.

Occasionally a litigant springs a major surprise by invoking an ancient law. In 1818 the defendant in *Ashford v Thornton* (1818) 1 B & A 405, who was accused of murder, claimed the right to have his case settled by battle. Trial by battle had been a method of resolving disputes shortly after the Norman Conquest but had fallen into disuse before the end of the thirteenth century. In *Ashford v Thornton*, the offer of trial by battle was declined and so the defendant was discharged. The Appeals of Murder Act 1819 was hurriedly passed. Until Parliament passed this Act trial by battle still existed as a possible means of settling some types of legal disputes.

1.1.2 Absence of a legal code

In most European countries the law has been codified. This means that the whole of the law on a particular subject, for example the law of property, can be found in one document or code. As we shall see, the bulk of English law has been made by judges in individual cases. Rules of law made by senior judges must be followed in later cases. In the majority of cases brought before an English court a lawyer who is trying to establish a legal principle will cite earlier cases to prove that the principle exists and that it should be applied in the current case. Often a statute, an Act of Parliament, will provide the main legal rules applicable to a particular case. A statute ranks higher as a source of law than the previous decision of any court. But even where a statute does apply to a particular case, the court is likely to be guided as to the meaning of the statute by earlier cases which have considered its meaning.

In general, the important cases on a particular area of law are not reported in one special volume of law reports devoted to a particular area of law, such as the law of contract. (There are exceptions, specialist law reports can be found on some areas of law such as employment law or road traffic law. The system of law reporting is examined in the following chapter at 2.9.) Generally, cases are reported as they are decided and are therefore to be found in the law report volume devoted to the year in which the case was decided. As lawyers and students are only too well aware, it can be very difficult to find all the cases relevant to a particular legal issue.

Occasionally, Parliament codifies an area of law with a statute such as the Partnership Act 1890. Such an Act aims to take all the relevant case law on a particular subject and to codify it into one comprehensible statute. The Law Commission, an important law reform institution set up in 1965, has the codification of appropriate areas of law as one of its objects. But as we shall see, the vast majority of English law remains uncodified. Nor does Britain have a written constitution, as most other democratic countries have.

1.1.3 The law making role of the judges

In most European countries the judges interpret the legal code. In doing this they do not themselves deliberately set out to create law. Later in this chapter, when we study the doctrine of judicial precedent, we shall see that the English courts are arranged in an hierarchical structure and that courts lower down the hierarchy must follow the previous decisions of courts which are higher up. Senior English judges therefore have a dual role. First, they interpret the existing law, which is to be found in legislation and previous decisions of higher ranking courts. Second, they create the law by making legal principles which courts lower down the hierarchy are bound to follow.

1.1.4 Importance of procedure

In the Middle Ages a legal right could only be enforced by means of a writ. (An order signed by the King, requiring a defendant to appear in court to answer the claim being made.) There were few types of writ and, if a claim could not be brought within the confines of one of the writs then no remedy was available. To some extent lawyers were people who knew the procedure of obtaining a remedy, rather than people who knew the substantive principles of the law. A person with a perfectly just claim would need a lawyer to fit the claim within the procedures of one of the writs. If the correct procedure was not rigidly adhered to, then the claim would fail, even if the substance of the claim was perfectly valid. To some extent this is still true today. If a litigant fails to follow the correct procedure it is possible that his claim will be struck out. Recent reforms of the judicial process, which we consider in Chapter 2, have attempted to reduce the importance of procedure. However, in cases which involve a substantial claim there is no doubt that procedure remains very important.

1.1.5 Absence of Roman law

The Romans occupied England from 55 BC to AD 430. Roman law was extremely sophisticated by the standards of its day. The other European countries which were part of the Roman Empire have retained elements of Roman law. But English law has almost no Roman law influence, although Roman law is still taught as an academic subject at some English universities. Scotland was not conquered by the Romans, but Scots law has more of a Roman law influence than English law. This influence has been brought about by the traditional alliance of France and Scotland. During the Renaissance, when the modern European world began to develop, Scotland and Continental Europe saw a revival of interest in Roman law. This interest was largely absent in England.

1.1.6 The adversarial system of trial

The English system of trial is adversarial. This means that the lawyers on either side are adversaries, who 'fight' each other in trying to win judgment for their client. The judge supervises the battle between the lawyers, but does not take part. Today the battle is metaphoric, one party's lawyers try to establish that there is a case, the other party's lawyers deny this by whatever means permissible. In the early Middle Ages the battle could be real enough, as certain types of dispute were resolved with a Trial by Battle. In such a trial the parties would fight each other, both armed with a leather shield and a staff and it was thought that God would grant victory to the righteous litigant. If either of the parties was disabled, or too young, or too old, he could hire a champion to fight for him. This was no doubt considerably more entertaining than a modern trial, but eventually it came to be realised that it was not the best way to achieve justice. Lawyers therefore replaced the champions. But the idea of a battle survived and a trial is still a battle between the lawyers, even if the shields and staffs have given way to witnesses and precedents.

Most other countries have an **inquisitorial** system of trial where the judge is the inquisitor, determined to discover the truth. A French examining magistrate, for example, has enormous powers. He takes over the investigation of a criminal case from the police. He can interrogate whoever he wishes. He can compel witnesses to give evidence and can surprise witnesses with other witnesses, hoping that the confrontation will point the finger of guilt. In a civil case, too, a French judge will take a much more interventionist approach than an English judge and it is the judge, rather than the lawyers, who manage the case.

When a French case reaches court it is often all but decided. By contrast, no one can ever be certain of the outcome of an English trial. The lawyers will fight for their clients on the day and either side might win. The judge should be disinterested in the outcome, merely ensuring that the lawyers fight by the rules.

An important aspect of the adversarial system of trial is that it is the task of the lawyers to bring the relevant legal rules to the attention of the court. If a lawyer in court makes a perfectly true statement of law, such as the statement that all goods sold in the course of business must be of satisfactory quality, he must provide authority for this statement. This means that the lawyer must quote the case, or in this instance the statute, which made the law. Similarly, students must cite authorities. At all levels of study, a statement of law with no authority to back it up is not regarded highly.

Two other features of the English legal system, both of which are examined in Chapter 2, are worth mentioning here. First, the legal profession is divided, lawyers being either barristers or solicitors. Second, in almost all criminal trials the innocence or guilt of the accused is decided by laymen, rather than by lawyers or judges. If the accused is tried in the Crown Court it will be a jury who decides whether the accused is guilty. If the crime is tried in the magistrates' court it is generally a bench of lay magistrates who make this decision.

Commonwealth and former Commonwealth countries, such as Australia, Canada and New Zealand, have retained the adversarial system of trial and most other features of the English legal system. In the United States of America trials are adversarial and some features of the English legal system have been retained. As we shall see both in this chapter and Chapter 2, there is now considerable pressure to change many of the traditional features of the English legal system, which are increasingly perceived to be ill-suited to the needs of the twenty-first century.

1.2 · Classification of English law

English law can be classified in three main ways: as **public law** or **private law**; as **common law** or **equity**; or, as **civil law** or **criminal law**. Each of these classifications is worth considering in some detail. It is also worth considering the distinction between law and fact.

1.2.1 Public law and private law

Public law is concerned with decisions made by bodies which are governmental in nature. Private law is concerned with the legal relationships of individual citizens. Criminal law, for example, is regarded as public law. Citizens are prosecuted by the State. The law of contract, on the other hand, is private law. A person who sues for breach of contract acts as one individual suing another individual. The State provides a framework for such a dispute to be resolved. That is to say, it provides the courts and the judges, but it plays no part in bringing or defending the action.

There are three main areas of public law. Constitutional law is concerned with the workings of the British Constitution, deciding such matters as the powers of Government Ministers. Criminal law makes certain types of behaviour criminal offences, giving the State the power to prosecute and punish those who commit such offences. Administrative law deals with disputes between citizens and Government agencies, such as the Department of Health and Social Security.

Private law is also called civil law and can be broadly broken down into five main areas; contract, tort, property, trusts and family law.

1.2.2 Common law and equity

The term common law is used in three distinct senses. First, it is used to distinguish countries which have adopted the features of the English legal system from those countries which have not. The features of the English legal system were explained at the beginning of this chapter. Countries which adopt these features are said to have a common law system. Countries which adopt the central European system are said to have a civil law system. Second, the term common law denotes that body of law which was made by the judges in the King's (or Queen's) courts, rather than the body of law made by the judges in the courts of equity. Third, common law means judge-made law as distinct from statute law.

It is, perhaps, unfortunate that the term common law is used in three different ways. However, the context in which the term is used will generally make apparent the sense in which the term is used. Here we are considering the difference between the law made by the judges in the King's courts and the law made by the judges in the courts of equity. To understand this distinction and to understand the meaning of equity, we must know something of the historical development of the law.

A hundred years after the Norman conquest, Henry II began the process of applying one set of legal rules, the common law, throughout the country. The King's representatives travelled from London to the provinces, checking on the procedures in the local courts. Gradually these representatives became judges rather than administrators. When they arrived they would try the cases which had been waiting for them (a system which survived into the 1970s). The decisions of these first travelling judges began to be recorded. Subsequent judges followed the earlier decisions, in order to provide a uniform system of law. Gradually one set of legal rules became common to the whole country and it therefore became known as the common law.

The common law grew to have several defects. First, legal actions could only be commenced through the issuing of a writ. By the middle of the thirteenth century there were around 50 writs, to cover different types of cases. In the reign of Henry III, after political pressure from the barons, the Provisions of Oxford in 1258 ruled that new types of writs should not be created. The development of the common law was very much hindered by this. Sometimes existing writs could be stretched to cover new situations, but more often they could not.

A second defect of the common law was that procedure was extremely hidebound. If a writ contained the slightest defect in its wording it was rendered useless. There were also problems with fictitious defences. Originally the truth of these defences had been checked by the King's knights, but later the defences became very effective delaying tactics.

A third major defect of the common law was that it had only one civil remedy at its disposal, the payment of damages. In some cases, such as those where a nuisance was being continually committed, the payment of damages was not much of a remedy. What the litigant really wanted was that the defendant be ordered to stop committing the nuisance.

In the Middle Ages people who could not gain a remedy under the rigid rules of the common law could petition the Chancellor, the highest ranking clergyman, to ask him to intercede.

The Church was the one mediaeval institution where men of ability could better themselves. Generally speaking, only clergymen could read and write. Clergymen were trained in Canon Law. This was based on God's law and on the laws of conscience and therefore contained an element of natural justice. The Chancellor could order litigants to appear before him, without the use of writs. There were no complex rules of evidence or procedure and the Chancellor could order justice to be done in various ways. In particular, he could issue injunctions which ordered a person to behave in a certain way. This justice dispensed by the Chancellor became known as equity.

Equity was not designed to be a rival system to the common law system. Originally it was intended to supplement the common law, to fill in the gaps. But gradually equity developed into a rival system and gradually it became just as hidebound as the common law.

For several hundred years, until the Judicature Acts of 1873 and 1875, England had two separate systems of courts and laws. The systems did not always deal with separate matters. In the *Earl of Oxford's Case* (1615) 1 Rep Ch 1 it was decided that if common law and equity conflicted then equity had to prevail.

The Judicature Acts 1873–1875 merged the two systems of law. These Acts created the modern court structure, designed to apply both common law and equity side-by-side in the same courts. This has not meant that equity has ceased to exist. Equity still plays an important part in English law. The administration of common law and equity may have been fused, but the separate rules of each branch of the law have lived on. Equitable remedies remain discretionary and can be withheld from those who have behaved inequitably (unfairly). This was reflected in the maxim, 'He who comes to Equity must come with clean hands'. An example can be seen in *Falcke* v *Gray* (1859) ER 4 Drew 651 in Chapter 7 at 7.2.4.

Any court can now apply both legal and equitable rules. However, barristers still regard themselves as either common law barristers, dealing with contract, tort or crime, or Chancery barristers, dealing with trusts and property.

1.2.3 Civil law and criminal law

The distinction between civil and criminal liability is fundamental to English law. The courts themselves are divided into civil courts and criminal courts and the two sets of courts have quite different purposes. The civil courts are designed to **compensate** people who have been caused loss or injury by the wrongful acts of other people. The criminal courts are designed to **punish** people who have committed a criminal offence.

Table 1.1 shows the essential differences between civil and criminal law.

Despite the differences shown in Table 1.1, it is quite possible that the same wrongful act will give rise to both civil and criminal liability. For example, if a motorist injures a pedestrian by dangerous driving then both a crime and a tort (a civil wrong) will have been committed.

The State might **prosecute** the driver for the crime of dangerous driving and if found guilty the driver will be punished. (Probably by a driving ban and possibly by a fine or imprisonment.) The **injured pedestrian** might **sue** the driver in the civil courts for the tort of negligence. If the driver is found to have committed this tort then damages will be sought to compensate for the pedestrian's injuries.

The different functions of the civil and criminal courts can be further demonstrated if we consider what would have happened if the driver's behaviour had been much worse.

Let us now assume that the driver was very drunk, driving very badly and had killed the pedestrian. Under the criminal law the driver would be charged with the more serious offences of causing death by dangerous driving and of driving with excess alcohol. The purpose of charging the driver with these more serious offences would be to give out a more serious punishment. If convicted the defendant would almost certainly be imprisoned.

However, the civil courts would not order the defendant to pay more damages merely on account of worse behaviour. In fact, if the pedestrian was killed the damages might well be less than for a bad injury. If the pedestrian was injured in such a way that nursing care would be required for life, damages might well exceed a million pounds, as they would take account of the cost of the nursing care, pain and suffering and loss of earnings, if appropriate. If the driver was killed instantly no damages would be paid in respect of nursing care or pain and suffering. A pedestrian who was not injured at all could bring no claim for damages.

This example demonstrates the different purposes which the two sets of courts are trying to achieve. The criminal courts are designed to punish bad behaviour. The worse the behaviour, the more severe the punishment. The civil courts are not concerned with the heinousness of the defendant's behaviour, they are concerned with compensating a person for injuries suffered as a consequence of the defendant's wrongdoing. The more severe the injuries, the higher the compensation.

Table 1.1   Essential differences between civil and criminal law

	Criminal	*Civil*
Purpose of the case	To punish a wrongdoer.	To compensate a person who has suffered loss or injury or to prevent unlawful acts.
The parties	The State prosecutes a person (the defendant) e.g. *Regina (Queen)* v *Smith*.	An individual (the claimant) sues an individual (the defendant) e.g. *Smith* v *Jones*.
The outcome	The defendant is either acquitted or convicted.	The claimant either wins the case or does not.
The consequences	If convicted, the defendant will be sentenced.	If the claimant wins he will be awarded a remedy.
The courts	The case is first heard in either the magistrates' court or the Crown Court.	The case is first heard in either the county court or the High Court.
The costs	Legal aid is usually available to the defendant. If convicted, he must pay towards the costs.	Generally, the loser pays both sides' costs. Insurance against losing is encouraged. Legal aid may be available to the very needy.
The facts	Decided by bench of magistrates (occasionally by a stipendiary magistrate) or by the jury.	Decided by the judge.
The law	Decided and applied by the judge or by the magistrates on the advice of the legally qualified clerk.	Decided and applied by the judge.
Burden and standard of proof	The prosecution must prove the defendant's guilt beyond reasonable doubt.	The claimant must prove his case on a balance of probabilities.
Examples	Murder, theft, applying false trade descriptions or giving misleading price indications, failure to observe health and safety provisions.	Negligence, trespass, breach of contract, disputes as to ownership of property.

As we have seen, crimes which cause injury to a victim will also give rise to a civil action. But 'victimless' crimes will not. Possessing a dangerous drug, for example, is a crime and the possessor of the drug might be prosecuted by the State. But the fact that a person possesses the drug does not directly injure anyone else, and so no one will have any right to sue him. Although the criminal courts have as their purpose the punishment of offenders, rather than the compensation of the injured, they do have the power to make compensation orders. Section 35 of the Powers of Criminal Courts Act 1973 gives magistrates the power to make compensation orders of up to £5 000 per offence. The compensation is paid by the perpetrator of the crime. The Crown Court is given the power to make a compensation order of any amount, although it is required to have regard to the defendant's means. If a court does not make a compensation order in a case in which it is empowered to do so, it must give reasons for not making the order when passing sentence. An award made in the magistrates' court does not preclude a later civil claim by the victim of the crime. Compensation orders can generally not be ordered when the offence is a motoring offence. The Criminal Injuries Compensation Authority can also award compensation to victims of violent crime, but any award is reduced by the amount of any compensation ordered by a criminal court. The Board has reference to a list of suggested awards for various types of injury. For example, the suggested award for the loss of a front tooth is currently £1 500, and for the loss of one eye £25 000.

Most civil wrongs are not crimes. If a person breaks a contract or trespasses on another's property that person might well be sued, but in general will have committed no crime.

The burden of proof is placed upon the party who must prove the case. In criminal cases the burden is placed upon the prosecution. In civil cases the burden is placed on the claimant. The standard of proof is concerned with the extent to which the case must be proved. In criminal cases the prosecution must prove the guilt of the accused beyond reasonable doubt. In a civil case the claimant must prove the case on a balance of probabilities.

1.2.4 The distinction between law and fact

In general, civil cases require the claimant to prove not only the facts which give rise to the claim, but also the principles of law which provide a remedy in respect of the facts proved. So a pedestrian run over by a car will first need to prove that the defendant did run him over and will also have to prove that the law of negligence provides him with a remedy in respect of this. Generally, the criminal law also requires the prosecution to prove both fact and law. The prosecution must prove beyond a reasonable doubt that the defendant did the act for which he is being prosecuted and must also prove that such an act amounts to a criminal offence.

It can be important to distinguish law and fact for three main reasons. First, only statements of law can become precedents. (Judicial precedent is examined below at 1.3.2.) Second, in many cases an appeal may only be possible on a point of law. In other cases an appeal on the law would go to one court, whereas an appeal against a finding of fact would go to a different court. Third, in a criminal trial conducted in the Crown Court the jury's function is to determine the facts, whereas the correct application of the law is the function of the judge.

Often it is obvious enough whether or not a question is one of law or fact. The well-known case *Carlill v The Carbolic Smoke Ball Company* [1893] 1 QB 256, which is set out in Chapter 3 at 3.1.2, can be used as an example. Whether or not Mrs Carlill really did use a smoke ball and whether she really did catch flu were questions of fact. Whether or not the advertisement was an offer or an invitation to treat was a question of law.

Sometimes it must be decided whether certain facts fit within a definition made by a statute, or fit within a rule made by the common law. These questions can be regarded as a question of mixed law and fact, or law and degree as they are sometimes known. For example, in *Cozens v Brutus* [1975] AC 854 the defendant was charged with using insulting behaviour whereby a breach of the peace was likely to be occasioned, contrary to s.5 of the Public Order Act 1936. The defendant had interrupted the Wimbledon tennis tournament by blowing a whistle, sitting down on the court and attempting to hand a leaflet to the players. The magistrates held that the defendant's behaviour had not been insulting. The Court of Appeal considered that whether or not the defendant's behaviour was insulting was a question of law and went on to define the meaning of insulting in this context. As they regarded the magistrates' finding as provisional, they sent the case back to the magistrates to continue the hearing. The House of Lords reversed the decision of the Court of Appeal and held that whether or not the defendant's behaviour had been insulting was a question of fact. It had therefore been properly decided by the magistrates and so no appeal against their finding could be made.

The conflicting decisions of the Court of Appeal and the House of Lords demonstrate the difficulty of classifying some questions as either questions of law or questions of fact. In deciding such matters the courts will, of course, try to reach the correct conclusion. However, there is perhaps a tendency to classify such questions as matters of fact to reduce the number of precedents being made and to reduce the number of appeals which will be allowed.

Test your understanding

1 What is meant by the adversarial system of trial?

2 What is meant by the distinction between common law and equity? Does the distinction still exist?

3 What are the different purposes of a civil and a criminal case?

4 Upon whom is the burden of proof placed in civil and criminal cases? What standard of proof is required?

5 For what three reasons might it become important to distinguish law and fact?

Answers

1 Under the adversarial system of trial the lawyers act as adversaries. One party's lawyers try to establish a case, the other party's lawyers use whatever means permissible to deny that there is a case.

2 The distinction between common law and equity is concerned with whether legal rules originated in the King's (or Queen's) courts or whether they originated in the courts of equity. The two systems of common law and equity have been merged but the distinction is still significant today. Some matters are still equitable and in such cases equitable rules and principles will be applied. Any court can apply both common law and equitable rules.

3 A criminal case has the purpose of punishing a wrongdoer who has committed a criminal offence. A civil case has the purpose of compensating a person wrongly caused to suffer a loss or injury.

4 In civil cases the burden of proof is on the claimant, in criminal cases it is on the prosecution. The civil standard of proof requires the claimant to prove his case on a balance of probabilities. The criminal standard of proof requires the prosecution to prove the accused's guilt beyond reasonable doubt.

5 The distinction between law and fact can be important because: only statements of law can become precedents; an appeal may only be available against a statement of law, or the appeal might have to be made to different courts depending upon whether it was against a statement of law or a statement of fact; and in Crown Court cases the jury decide the facts, whereas the judge decides the law.

1.3 · Sources of English law

1.3.1 Statutes

Acts of Parliament are called statutes. The theory of parliamentary sovereignty holds that Parliament had the power to enact, or revoke, any new law it pleases and that the courts cannot question the validity of this law. Even Parliament itself cannot limit the power of a successive Parliament. In *British Railways Board* v *Pickin* [1974] AC 765, for example, a claimant whose land had been compulsorily purchased under the British Railways Act 1968 tried to argue that the statute was invalid. The 1968 Act was a private Act, which had been passed unopposed and the claimant argued that Parliament had been fraudulently misled into passing it. The House of Lords, the highest court in the land, ruled that such an argument could not be raised in any court.

The United Kingdom joined the European Economic Community, now called the European Community, in 1973. It is arguable that membership of the European Community means that the United Kingdom Parliament is no longer truly sovereign. This matter is considered below at 1.4.4.

1.3.1.1 How is a statute passed?

The Government of the day is formed by the political party which wins a majority of the seats in the House of Commons. Government Departments, such as the Department of Trade and Industry, propose legislation for approval. Parliamentary draftsmen (lawyers who specialise in drafting legislation) then draw a Bill up and the Bill starts its parliamentary journey.

To become a statute the Bill must pass through both Houses of Parliament, that is to say the House of Commons and the House of Lords and then gain the Royal Assent. Many Bills achieve this without significant alterations. Others have to be amended to gain Parliamentary approval and some Bills fail to become statutes at all.

Bills usually start in the House of Commons. The initial stage is the **First Reading**. This merely gives the title of the Bill and announces the date of the Second Reading. At the **Second Reading** the principles of the Bill are debated. If the Bill passes this stage, on account of more MPs having voted in favour of it than against it, it is referred to a **standing committee** which considers the details of the Bill and recommends amendments. Any such amendments are considered by the House of Commons at the **report stage**, after which the Bill then proceeds to the **Third Reading**. Like the First Reading, this is a short stage where only minor amendments to the content of the Bill, rather than amendments to the general principle of the Bill, can be made.

The Bill is then sent to the House of Lords, where the whole process is repeated. The wording of the Bill must be the same for both Houses. If the House of Lords disagrees with the wording or refuses to pass the Bill, the Parliament Acts 1911 and 1949 can be invoked. The effect of these Acts will be that the Bill can go ahead without House of Lords approval, after a delay of one year. (This happens very rarely.) A Money Bill, which would contain only financial provisions, can become a statute without being passed by the House of Lords after a delay of only one month.

After passing through both Houses of Parliament, the Bill will then receive the Royal Assent. It is a Convention that the Queen does not withhold consent and no monarch has done so since 1707. (The Queen does not give assent personally but through the Lord Commissioners or by notification to both Houses of Parliament.)

Once the Bill has received the Royal Assent it becomes a statute (an Act) which the courts must enforce either from a date agreed by Parliament, or until an order is passed by the relevant Secretary of State.

Almost all Bills are introduced into Parliament by the Government of the day. A Government with a large majority has enormous power to ensure that Bills it proposes become enacted. The system is subject to the criticism that the Government can ignore not only the wishes of opposition MPs but, if its majority is large enough, can also ignore the wishes of many of its own MPs. However, not all Bills are introduced by the Government. Every year a ballot is held to identify 20 MPs who may attempt to introduce **Private Member's Bills**. In fact, only an MP who was close to winning the ballot will have a reasonable chance of seeing his Private Member's Bill become the law. The Abortion Act 1967, which liberalised the law on abortion, was introduced as a Private Member's Bill by David Steel MP.

1.3.1.2 Codifying, consolidating and amending Acts

We have seen that, in general, English law is not codified. However, certain areas of law have been the subject of a **codifying Act**. Such an Act attempts to put all the existing law on a particular subject, whether common law or statutory, into one comprehensive statute. In doing this the law may be changed and if the Act is inconsistent with the law which it codified, the Act prevails. The major codifications in English law have been the Bills of Exchange Act 1882, the Partnership Act 1890, the Sale of Goods Act 1893, and the Theft Act 1968.

A **consolidating Act** re-enacts all the law on a given area, so that the law contained in several existing statutes is re-enacted as one new statute. Minor changes to the law may be made, but the purpose of a consolidating Act is not to change the law, but to make it more easily accessible. The Companies Act 1985 was a consolidating Act. It re-enacted the 1948 Companies Act, including several other amending Acts which had altered the 1948 Act. An **amending Act** changes one or more sections of an existing Act.

■ Example

The effects of the three types of Act can be considered by looking at the history of sale of goods law. Prior to 1893 sale of goods law was almost entirely common law, that is to say it was made by the courts in innumerable cases. In 1893 the Sale of Goods Act, a codifying Act, codified the common law.

No real changes were made until 1973, when the 1893 Act was amended very slightly to make it more appropriate to the needs of consumers. These minor changes were made by an amending Act, the Supply of Goods (Implied Terms) Act 1973. In 1977 the Unfair Contract Terms Act made more amendments. In 1979 the Sale of Goods Act 1979, a consolidating Act, was passed. This Act, which is the Act currently in force, consolidated the 1893 Act and the amendments which had been made to it. Three amending Acts have been passed since 1979: the Sale of Goods (Amendment) Act 1994; the Sale and Supply of Goods Act 1994; and the Sale of Goods (Amendment) Act 1995. The amendments achieved by these Acts are incorporated into the Sale of Goods Act 1979.

Parliament has the power to repeal any statute. As we saw earlier, a statute remains in force until it is repealed even if it has become obsolete.

1.3.1.3 Delegated legislation

Delegated legislation is the name given to legislation passed otherwise than as a statute. Most delegated legislation is concerned with relatively narrow, technical matters. However, it is arguable that delegated legislation is a more important source of law than statute. This argument is based on the fact that nowadays there is far more delegated legislation than statute law. Once delegated legislation is enacted, it generally has the same force as the statute which enabled it to be enacted.

Delegated legislation can take several forms. The most important form is a **statutory instrument**. This legislation is not passed as a statute. Instead, a statute called an enabling Act is passed and this enabling Act gives a Government Minister the power to introduce the legislation. The statutory instrument will contain a preamble which sets out the authority under which it was passed. It will also contain a statutory note which sets out its purpose and its scope. Statutory instruments are made in the name of a Minister but are drawn up by the legal department of the relevant Ministry. The Deregulation and Contracting Out Act 1994 allows Ministers to change certain Acts of Parliament, by way of statutory instrument, without going through the normal parliamentary procedure. The 1994 Act is used to repeal or amend provisions in primary legislation which impose a burden on business or others. In later chapters we shall see that legislation of considerable importance, such as the Commercial Agents (Council Directive) Regulations 1993, takes the form of statutory instrument rather than the form of a statute. Many statutory instruments, such as the 1993 Regulations, are used to implement EC Directives. (Directives are examined later in this chapter at 1.4.2.4.)

Orders in Council are made by the Privy Council. The Council is made up of eminent Parliamentarians and the Government of the day can use it to introduce legislation without going through the process of enacting a statute. Orders in Council can be used to implement emergency legislation, where there would not be time to have formal debates in the Houses of Parliament. Orders in Council are also used to give effect to provisions of the European Community which do not have direct effect, to shift responsibilities between Government departments or in relation to matters which affect the constitution. Many statutes only become operative when an Order in Council provides that they should, the power exercised by the Order in Council being contained in the statute itself.

Bye-laws made by local authorities and other public bodies are another type of delegated legislation. These are used to introduce local rules of minor importance. The power to enact bye-laws is given by an enabling Act, such as the Local Government Act 1972.

Delegated legislation has certain advantages and disadvantages. The advantages usually claimed are that it can be enacted without using up Parliamentary time, that it makes use of particular expertise held by those who enact it, and that it is flexible enough to deal speedily with changing circumstances and emergencies. These claims in general seem to be true. Parliament often does not have time to pass all of its legislative programme, even though the vast majority of this is already contained in statutory instruments. In 1999 several thousand statutory instruments were passed, but only 35 Public Acts. It is also true that MPs are not particularly knowledgeable about the details of the types of matters which are enacted by statutory instrument. These matters are often extremely technical, dealing with a huge variety of matters, such as the safe storage of hazardous materials, or the intricacies of housing benefit. A separate justification is that if there were to be a true emergency, such as a major leak of radiation, legislation might be needed quickly and there would not be the time to pass a statute and have debates in the Houses of Parliament. Also, the type of matter which arises from time to time, such as financial eligibility for housing benefit, are obviously better dealt with by delegated legislation than by statute. The same is obviously true of local bye-laws. MPs have no real interest in areas other than the areas which they represent, or in which they live, and could not therefore determine whether or not a bye-law was needed.

Delegated legislation is also criticised on several grounds. First, there is the danger that the Government can pass legislation setting out new principles by abusing the process of delegated legislation. Second, some delegated legislation gives Ministers the power to alter statutes, possibly including the very enabling Act which conferred the power to make the delegated legislation in question. In *Hyde Park Residence Ltd* v *Secretary of State for the Environment, Transport and the Regions* [2000] 1 PLR 85 the Court of Appeal held that although it was possible for one statute to confer a power to amend another statute by delegated legislation, this power should be construed narrowly and strictly. Third, it is possible that the enabling Act states that the delegated legislation should not be subject to judicial review by the courts, or that it is worded so widely that the courts would not be able to say that its powers had been exceeded. (Judicial review is considered in Chapter 2 at 2.6.1.)

Certain controls over delegated legislation do exist. Ministers are often required by the enabling Act to consult various bodies before enacting delegated legislation. Statutory instruments must be published and made available for sale to the public. In addition to these controls, delegated legislation is controlled both by Parliament and by the courts. Although some non contentious statutory instruments just become law on the date stated in them, most are required by their enabling Acts to be laid before both Houses of Parliament. If this process is subject to the negative resolution procedure the legislation must be laid before both Houses for 40 days, during which time either House can pass an annulment or negative resolution, which will cause the statutory instrument to be rendered ineffective. Any MP can put forward a motion for annulment. The affirmative resolution procedure requires the instrument to be laid before one or both Houses for a specified time, usually 40 days, after which time an affirmative resolution agreeing to the instrument must be passed or the instrument will have no effect. Delegated legislation to deal with politically contentious or emergency matters generally requires this procedure. However, the majority of delegated legislation is subject only to the negative control. It is most unusual for either House of Parliament to have the power to amend a statutory instrument. They either allow it to be passed or annul it.

The courts have the power, through the process of judicial review, to declare a statutory instrument *ultra vires* on the grounds that it tries to exercise a power greater than that conferred by the enabling Act. It is presumed that an enabling Act does not confer the power to raise tax; or to retrospectively alter the law; or to prevent a person from having access to the courts; or to take away civil liberties. However, if the enabling Act was sufficiently clear it could confer these powers. A statutory instrument can only be declared invalid on the grounds of being unreasonable if the objectives of the instrument were so outrageously unreasonable that Parliament could not have intended that the powers created by the enabling Act would be used in the way in which they were used. The courts can also declare a statutory instrument *ultra vires* on the grounds that some mandatory procedure, such as mandatory duty to consult, was not adhered to.

Below (at 1.4) we examine the effect of European Community legislation, much of which is implemented into UK law by statutory instrument under s.2(2) of the European Communities Act 1972.

1.3.1.4 Interpretation of statutes

The three approaches

When considering the meaning of legislation, a court might adopt one of three approaches. These approaches are often called rules – the literal rule, the golden rule and the mischief rule. The rules contradict each other to a certain extent and it cannot be certain which rule a court will apply. The courts will tend to use whichever of the approaches seems best suited to achieving justice in the case it is hearing.

When the **literal rule** is applied words in a statute which are not ambiguous are given their ordinary, literal meaning, even if this leads to a decision which is unjust or undesirable. An example of this approach can be seen in *Inland Revenue Commissioners v Hinchy* [1960] AC 748, in which the House of Lords was considering the effect of the Income Tax Act 1952. Section 25(3) of the Act stated that a person found guilty of tax avoidance should 'forfeit the sum of £20 and treble the tax which he ought to be charged under this Act'. Hinchy's lawyers argued that this meant a £20 fine and treble the amount of tax which had been avoided. Unfortunately for Hinchy, the House of Lords decided that the literal meaning of s.25(3) was that a tax avoider should pay a £20 fine and treble his whole tax bill for the year.

The outcome of the case was that Hinchy had to pay slightly over £438, even though the amount he had avoided was only £14.25. This was obviously a severe blow for Hinchy. (In 1960, £438 could be a year's pay for an unskilled worker.) But the implications for other tax avoiders were terrifying. Under the system of precedent, all other English courts are bound to follow precedents formulated in the House of Lords. So other tax avoiders appearing before the courts would have to be fined on the same basis as Hinchy had been fined. A court hearing the case of a wealthy businessman, who rightly paid £1 000 000 tax in the year but avoided paying £5, would be bound to fine him £3 000 035!

It is almost certain that the meaning applied by the House of Lords was not what Parliament had in mind when the Income Tax Act was passed. The statute was badly worded. The blame for this must lie with the Parliamentary draftsmen. But at the same time it must be realised that they have a near impossible task. Skilled lawyers though these draftsmen are, they cannot possibly foresee every interpretation of the statutes they prepare. But once the statute has become law, any lawyer in the land might be looking for an interpretation which would suit his client. In *Hinchy's* case the Revenue lawyers, with typical ingenuity, spotted a literal meaning that had not been apparent before. The House of Lords gave the words in the statute their literal meaning, holding that the words of the statute were not ambiguous. When the literal rule is applied the court is seeking not what Parliament meant to say when it enacted the statute, but rather the true meaning of the words which Parliament used.

If Parliament considers that the application of the literal rule by a high-ranking court causes a statute to be interpreted in a way which is contrary to what was intended when the statute was enacted, it can pass an amending Act to remedy the situation.

There has been a movement away from the literal approach in recent years. In *McMonagle v Westminster City Council* [1990] 2 AC 716 the House of Lords unanimously indicated that the literal rule would not be applied where to do so would produce an absurd result. In such a case the **golden rule**, also known as the purposive approach, would be applied. When the golden rule is used a judge gives the words in a statute their ordinary, literal meaning as far as possible, but only to the extent that this would not produce an absurd result. Where the words of a statute are ambiguous, the golden rule is also used to prefer the meaning which would give the least absurd or undesirable result.

The idea that when faced with an ambiguity the court should prefer the outcome which is not absurd to the one which is absurd seems obviously to be correct. An example of the golden rule being used in this way can be seen in *Adler v George* [1964] 2 QB 7. The defendant had got into an RAF station, which was classified as a prohibited place by the Official Secrets Act 1920. He was arrested and charged with obstructing a member of the armed forces 'in the vicinity of a prohibited place', contrary to s.3 of the 1920 Act. The defendant argued that as he was actually inside the prohibited place he was not in the vicinity of it and should not therefore be convicted. The Divisional Court rejected this argument and held that the proper construction of s.3 was to read the words 'in the vicinity of' as 'in or in the vicinity of'. Lord Parker CJ gave the only judgment of the court and said that it would be absurd to read the section as the defendant had argued that it should be read.

When the words of the statute are not ambiguous but would, if interpreted literally, produce an absurd result, the golden rule is sometimes seen as an extension of the literal rule. First, the court considers the literal rule. Seeing that the literal rule would lead to a manifestly absurd result and wishing to avoid this result, the court chooses to apply the golden rule and give the statutory words a meaning other than their normal meaning. The following case provides an example. In *R* v *Allen* (1872) LR 1 CCR 376 the defendant was charged with bigamy. He had married another woman even though his first wife was still alive and he was not divorced from her. Section 57 of the Offences Against the Person Act 1861 provided that a person should be guilty of bigamy if 'being married, [he or she] shall marry any other person during the life of the former husband or wife'. The defendant argued that he was not guilty of the offence as he had not legally married the second wife, because you cannot legally get married if you are already married. He claimed that he had only gone through a ceremony of marriage with the second woman. The court gave the word 'marry' in s.57 the meaning of going through a ceremony of marriage, rather than the meaning of contracting a legal marriage, and therefore convicted the defendant. Had they not done this bigamy would have been impossible to commit.

The oldest of the three main rules of statutory interpretation is the **mischief rule**. In *Heydon's Case* (1584) 3 Co Rep 7a it was established that before applying the mischief rule the court should ask itself four questions. First, what was the common law before the Act was passed? Second, what mischief or problem did the Act seek to rectify? Third, what remedy had Parliament decided upon to cure the mischief? Fourth, what was the reason for providing the remedy? Having considered these four questions, a court would be guided as to how the statute should be interpreted. This rule is only to be used when a statute is ambiguous, it should not be used to deal with a clear, but absurd, meaning. The following case provides an example of the rule.

■ *Smith* v *Hughes* [1960] 1 WLR 830

Two prostitutes, standing either on a balcony or behind the windows of their house, attracted passers by to invite them into the house. They did this by tapping on the balcony rail or the window panes. They were charged under s.1(1) of the Street Offences Act 1959, which made it an offence to solicit 'in a street or public place' for the purposes of prostitution. The defendants argued that they were not guilty as they had not been in the street or in a public place when they had been soliciting customers.

Held. Applying the mischief rule, the defendants were guilty. It did not matter that they were not literally in the street when soliciting, if the solicitation was projected to and aimed at somebody who was walking in the street.

COMMENT Lord Parker CJ, 'For my part, I approach the matter by considering what is the mischief aimed at by this Act. Everybody knows that this was an Act intended to clean up the streets, to enable people to walk along the streets without being molested or solicited by common prostitutes. Viewed in that way, it can matter little whether the prostitute is soliciting while in the street or is standing in a doorway or on a balcony, or at a window, or whether the window is open or shut or half open; in each case her solicitation is projected to and addressed to somebody walking in the street. For my part, I am content to base my decision on that ground and on that ground alone.'

The mischief rule was extensively used by Lord Widgery CJ in deciding early cases on the Trade Descriptions Act 1968. (See, for example, *Wycombe Marsh Garages Ltd* v *Fowler* [1972] 1 WLR 1152, in Chapter 22 at 22.2.2.1.)

In *Inco Europe Ltd* v *First Choice Distribution* [2000] 1 WLR 561 Lord Nicholls, giving the only speech of the House of Lords, considered the circumstances in which the court could read words into a statute to correct an obvious drafting error. Lord Nicholls said:

'This power is confined to plain cases of drafting mistakes. The courts are ever mindful that their constitutional role in this field is interpretative. They must abstain from any course which might have the appearance of judicial legislation. A statute is expressed in language approved and enacted by the legislature. So the courts exercise considerable caution before adding or omitting or substituting words. Before interpreting a statute in this way the court must be abundantly sure of three matters:

(1) the intended purpose of the statute or provision in question;

(2) that by inadvertence the draftsman and Parliament failed to give effect to that purpose in the provision in question; and

(3) the substance of the provision Parliament would have made, although not necessarily the precise words Parliament would have used, had the error in the Bill been noticed.

The third of these conditions is of crucial importance. Otherwise any attempt to determine the meaning of the enactment would cross the boundary between construction and legislation.'

Lord Nicholls went on to say that even if the three conditions were satisfied the court might nevertheless sometimes find itself inhibited from interpreting the statutory provision in accordance with what it was satisfied was the underlying intention of Parliament. This might be the case if the alteration in language would be too far reaching, or if the subject matter of the statutory provision called for strict interpretation of the statutory language, as in penal legislation.

Minor rules of statutory interpretation

Other, less important, rules of statutory interpretation are applied by the courts. The *ejusdem generis rule* (of the same kind rule) means that general words which follow specific words must be given the same type of meaning as the specific words. For example, the Betting Act 1853 prohibited betting in any 'house, office, room or other place'. In *Powell* v *Kempton Racecourse Company* [1899] AC 143, the House of Lords held that the Act did not apply to betting at a racecourse. The specific words, 'house, office, room', were all indoor places and so the general words, 'or other place', had to be interpreted as applying only to indoor places.

The rule *expressio unius est exclusio alterius* (to express one thing is to exclude another) means that if the statute lists specific words and these are not followed by any general words, then the statute only applies to the specific words listed. For example, in *R* v *Inhabitants of Sedgeley* (1831) 2 B & Ad 65, a statute which raised taxes on 'Lands, houses, tithes and coal mines', did not apply to other types of mines such as the mine in question, a limestone mine.

Aids to construction of statutes

When considering the meaning of a statute, a court may consider certain aids to construction. These aids are usually labelled either intrinsic aids, which are part of the statute itself, or extrinsic aids, which are not part of the statute itself. Intrinsic aids would include interpretation sections of the Act, which state the meaning of words used in the Act. The Act's title and punctuation are also of relevance as intrinsic aids. (See, for example, Lord Keith's use of the long title of the Trade Descriptions Act 1968 in *Davies* v *Sumner* [1984] 3 All ER 831, which is set out in Chapter 22 at 22.2.2.1.) It is not clear to what extent marginal notes and headings are to be regarded as aids to construction of the statute. It is probable that both can be considered.

Extrinsic aids to interpretation include dictionaries, previous statutes concerning the same subject matter, and the Interpretation Act 1978. Despite the name of this Act it is concerned with relatively minor matters such as; unless there is an indication to the contrary, the singular includes the plural; and, when a statute refers to the masculine it also includes the feminine.

Until recently, a judge interpreting a statute was not allowed to consider the speeches which MPs made when the statute was being debated. However, in the following case, a landmark decision, the House of Lords held that Hansard could be consulted if this was the only way to solve an ambiguity.

■ *Pepper (Inspector of Taxes)* v *Hart* [1992] AC 593 (House of Lords)

Masters at a fee-paying school were entitled to have their sons educated at the school at one fifth of the usual price. During the years in question the school was never full and so no pupils were turned away in consequence of this right. Section 61 of the Finance Act 1976 provided that masters who took advantage of the scheme should be taxed on the cash equivalent of the benefit they had received. The masters contended that the cash benefit was the marginal cost of admitting their sons and therefore practically nothing. The Revenue argued that the cash equivalent could be found for each pupil by dividing the whole costs of running the school by the number of pupils attending the school. The statute was ambiguous as to which meaning was correct.

Held. The masters should only be taxed at the marginal cost of their sons attending the school. This was the intention of Parliament, as could be discovered by consulting Hansard. The rule that Parliamentary material could not be considered by a court should be relaxed if (i) the legislation was either ambiguous or obscure, or led to absurdity, and (ii) the material relied upon consisted of statements made by the relevant Minister, or promoter of the Bill, or other material such as was necessary, and (iii) the statements relied upon were clear.

Presumptions

There are certain presumptions which a court may make when in doubt as to the meaning of a statute. These are: a presumption against changing the common law (so a statute does not change the common law in any particular way unless it makes clear that it does); a presumption against ousting the jurisdiction of the courts (only if clear language is used is a statute to be read as taking away the right to take a case to court); a presumption that citizens will not have their liberty, property or rights taken away; presumption against criminal liability without *mens rea* (for the meaning of *mens rea* see Chapter 22 at 22.1); a presumption that a statute does not bind the Crown; a presumption against a statute having retrospective effect; and, a presumption that Parliament does not intend a statute to conflict with international law.

Test your understanding

1 What three procedures must be satisfied before a Bill becomes a statute?

2 What is the meaning of a codifying Act, a consolidating Act and an amending Act?

3 What is delegated legislation? What are the main types of delegated legislation?

4 What are the three main rules of statutory interpretation? What is the effect of these rules?

5 What is the effect of the *ejusdem generis rule* and the rule *expressio unius est exclusio alterius*?

6 What intrinsic and extrinsic aids can be used to assist in interpreting a statute?

Answers

1 In order to become a statute a Bill will need to pass through both Houses of Parliament and gain the Royal Assent.

2 A codifying Act puts all the existing law into one comprehensive statute, perhaps making some changes to the law at the same time. A consolidating Act re-enacts several existing statutes into one new Act. An amending Act makes minor amendments to an existing Act.

3 Delegated legislation is legislation passed otherwise than by statute. Statutory instruments are introduced by Government Ministers, the power to create the instruments having been conferred by an enabling Act. Orders in Council are introduced by the Privy Council, which is made up of eminent parliamentarians. Bye-laws are local laws passed by local authorities.

4 The three main rules of statutory interpretation are the literal rule, the golden rule and the mischief rule. The literal rule holds that if the words in a statute are not ambiguous they should be given their ordinary literal meaning. The golden rule requires a judge to give the words in a statute their ordinary, literal meaning as far as possible, but only to the extent that this would not produce an absurd result or, where the words are ambiguous, to prefer the meaning which would give the least absurd or undesirable result. The mischief rule allows the court to be guided by the 'mischief' or problem which the statute sought to address.

5 The *ejusdem generis rule* is where specific words are followed by general words, the general words must be given the same type of meaning as the specific words. The rule *expressio unius est exclusio alterius* is to the effect that where specific words are not followed by any general words then the statute only applies to the specific words included.

6 Intrinsic aids to interpretation include interpretation sections, the Act's title and punctuation and probably also marginal notes and headings. External aids include dictionaries, previous statutes on the same subject and the Interpretation Act 1978. In the limited circumstances specified in *Pepper* v *Hart*, Parliamentary materials may be considered.

1.3.2 Judicial precedent

The doctrine of judicial precedent, or *stare decisis*, holds that judges in lower-ranking courts are bound to follow legal principles previously formulated by judges in higher-ranking courts. As so much of the law in this book is derived from precedent, it seems important to examine the system in some detail.

1.3.2.1 The hierarchy of the courts

The courts are arranged in an hierarchical structure. The structure of the courts is considered in more detail in Chapter 2. Here it is enough to outline the five levels in the hierarchy.

The House of Lords

The House of Lords is the most senior of the English courts. The court is comprised of 12 judges, known as Law Lords (or, more properly, as Lords of Appeal in Ordinary), five of whom usually sit in any one case. Lady Hale became the first female member of the House of Lords in October 2003. The House of Lords is not bound to follow any previous precedents. Furthermore, the decisions of the House of Lords are absolutely binding on all courts beneath it. Until 1966 the House of Lords was bound to follow its own previous decisions. However, in 1966 a Practice Statement was made by Lord Gardiner on behalf of the other Law Lords. This statement said that the House of Lords recognised that if the doctrine of precedent was too rigidly adhered to, the development of the law might be hindered and injustice might be caused in a particular case. The House of Lords would therefore normally treat their own decisions as binding, but would depart from them where it appeared right to do so. In doing this the Lords would bear in mind the danger of disturbing agreements previously entered into. In practice, the House of Lords only rarely departs from one of its own previous decisions. Sometimes seven judges sit rather than five. However, a later sitting of the court can still refuse to follow the decision made by the seven member court.

The Law Lords also hear appeals from the courts in Her Majesty's dominions and from some Commonwealth countries. When the Law Lords sit in this particular capacity they are known as the Privy Council. Countries from which appeals are still heard by the Privy Council include Barbados, Bermuda, the Falkland Islands, Gibraltar and Jamaica. Technically, decisions of the Privy Council are not binding on English courts. However, in practice they are usually regarded as having the same authority as House of Lords decisions. (An example of this can be seen in Chapter 12 at 12.2.4, where the Privy Council decision in *The Wagon Mound* [1961] AC 388 is generally taken to have overruled the long standing Court of Appeal decision in *Re Polemis* [1921] 3 KB 560.)

It seems likely that the House of Lords is soon to be replaced by a new Supreme Court, a matter considered in Chapter 2 at 2.1.4.1.

The Court of Appeal

The Court of Appeal is the next rung down the ladder. Its decisions are binding on all lower courts. They are also binding on future Court of Appeal judges. In terms of precedent the Court of Appeal is the most important court, hearing many more appeals than the House of Lords. However, the House of Lords hears cases of greater public importance and there is no doubt that its decisions have the greatest authority.

Following Lord Gardiner's Practice Statement of 1966, the Court of Appeal made several attempts to depart from its own previous decisions. However, the Practice Statement itself stated that it was not meant to apply to any court other than the House of Lords. It is plain, therefore, that the Court of Appeal is bound by its own previous decisions, the only exceptions to this principle having been formulated in *Young* v *Bristol Aeroplane Co Ltd* [1944] KB 718. In that case it was decided that the Court of Appeal could only depart from its own previous decisions in three circumstances.

(1) Where there were two conflicting earlier Court of Appeal decisions it could decide which one to follow and which one to overrule.
(2) If a previous Court of Appeal decision had later been overruled by the House of Lords the Court of Appeal should not follow it.
(3) A previous Court of Appeal decision should not be followed if it was decided through lack of care, ignoring some statute or other higher-ranking authority such as a previously decided House of Lords case.

Although the principles set out apply to both the Civil and Criminal Divisions of the Court of Appeal, it is generally recognised that the Criminal Division has slightly wider powers to depart from its own previous decisions. It can do so where justice would otherwise be denied to an appellant. Generally, the Court of Appeal is comprised of three judges known as Lord Justices of Appeal. Sometimes a full court of five judges sit in the Court of Appeal. A full court of the Court of Appeal has no greater power to depart from its own previous decisions than an ordinary court.

Divisional Courts

Each of the three divisions of the High Court has a Divisional Court, staffed by three High Court judges. In certain areas of business law the Queen's Bench Divisional Court makes a large number of significant precedents. This court hears appeals from lower courts, as explained in Chapter 2. Decisions of the Divisional Courts are binding upon other sittings of the Divisional Court (subject to the *Young* v *Bristol Aeroplane Co Ltd* exceptions), on High Court judges sitting alone and on all inferior courts. Decisions of the Divisional Court are not binding upon the Employment Appeal Tribunal (EAT). (The jurisdiction of the EAT is explained in Chapter 20 at 20.0.) Divisional Courts are bound by the decisions of the House of Lords, the Court of Appeal and by previous decisions of Divisional Courts. In criminal cases a Divisional Court may depart from the decision of a previous Divisional Court where it would cause injustice not to do so.

The High Court

Judges sitting in the High Court are bound by decisions of the House of Lords and the Court of Appeal. High Court decisions are binding upon all lower courts. High Court judges are not bound by the decisions of other High Court judges. However, High Court judges do tend to follow each others' decisions as not to do so can lead to uncertainty, particularly as regards decisions made and agreements reached on the strength of the earlier judgment.

Inferior courts

The decisions of inferior courts (the Crown Court, the county court and the magistrates' court) are not binding on any other courts. Judges sitting in these courts do not make binding precedents.

All English courts must take into consideration decisions made by the European Court of Human Rights. The effect of this is considered below at 1.5. The European Court of Justice does not use a system of precedent. However, the decisions of this court are binding upon all English courts, a matter considered below at 1.4.

1.3.2.2 The binding part of the case

The *ratio decidendi*, loosely translated from the Latin as the reason for the decision, is the part of the judgment which is binding on other courts. The *ratio decidendi* might be described as any statement of law which the judge applied to the facts of the case and upon which the decision in the case is based. The ratio of a case will be decided by future courts when they are considering whether or not they are bound by the ratio. Cases may contain more than one ratio.

Statements of law which did not form the basis of the decision are known as ***obiter dicta*** (literally, other things said). Obiters can arise as statements of law based on facts which did not exist. It commonly happens that judgments state what the law would have been if the facts had differed in some material way. Statements of law which were wider than was necessary to deal with the facts of the particular case are also *obiter dicta*. Examples of obiters can be found in most cases. Obiters are not binding on lower courts, no matter which court made the obiter. However, if the judges in a superior court strongly express an obiter then a lower court judge would almost certainly follow this in the absence of a binding precedent.

Courts to which appeals are made (appellate courts) usually have more than one judge sitting. Fortunately, it is an odd number of judges rather than an even number. A majority of judges will therefore decide for one of the parties or for the other. If the decision is unanimous, for instance the Court of Appeal decides 3 : 0 for the defendant, then the ratio of the case can be found in the judgments of any of the three judges. If the Court reaches a decision by a majority of 2 : 1, then the ratio must be found in the decisions of the two judges in the majority. The decision of the judge in the minority may be persuasive as obiter, but it cannot form a ratio which will bind future courts.

■ **Example**

If you read the case of *Carlill* v *The Carbolic Smoke Ball Company* [1893] 1 QB 525 (Court of Appeal), which is set out in Chapter 3 at 3.1.2, you will see that it concerned whether or not an advertisement made by the company was an offer which could be accepted by a member of the public buying a smoke ball, using it and catching flu. The Court of Appeal held that the advertisement was an offer and that the claimant was entitled to the £100 reward as she had accepted the offer and thus created a contract between herself and the company. This famous case can be used to demonstrate several points.

First, the ratio of the case will be decided by later courts. However, it seems fairly safe to say that the ratio is something like: 'Newspaper advertisements offering rewards to members of the public who perform certain well-defined actions can amount to contractual offers, which can be accepted by members of the public who perform those actions, as long as the advertisement was not too vague to be understood by an ordinary member of the public.' Further ratios might be that an offer can be made to the whole world and that the offer of a unilateral contract can be accepted without notification of acceptance, merely by performing the action requested by the offeror. An example made by Bowen LJ, concerning a reward offered for a lost dog, was clearly *obiter dicta* as it was based on facts which did not arise. As this case was decided in the Court of Appeal, the *ratio decidendi* of the case would be binding upon later sittings of the Court of Appeal and upon all inferior courts, but not upon the House of Lords. Bowen LJ's obiter could be persuasive if a court was considering a case concerning a reward for finding a lost dog or more generally by way of analogy.

A higher-ranking court can **overrule** a ratio created by a lower ranking court. The House of Lords, for instance, could overrule *Carlill*'s case later this year and hold that newspaper advertisements cannot be offers. (This is most unlikely, it is merely an example.) If the House of Lords were to overrule the decision then the ratio of *Carlill*'s case would be deemed to have been wrongly decided. When overruling a case, the superior court specifically names the case and the rule of law being overruled. A statute may overrule the ratio of a particular case, but the statute will not mention the case concerned.

Many cases are **reversed** on appeal. Reversing is of no legal significance. It merely means that a party who appeals against the decision of an inferior court wins the appeal. No rule of law is necessarily changed. For example, in the fictitious case *Smith* v *Jones*, let us assume that Smith wins in the High Court and Jones appeals to the Court of Appeal. If Jones's appeal is allowed, the Court of Appeal have reversed the judgment of the High Court.

Disadvantages of the system of precedent

In addition to the 12 Law Lords, the five Heads of Divisions, and the 36 Lord Justices of Appeal, there are currently 107 High Court judges. Every word of every judgment made by a High Court judge might contain a precedent which would be binding on future judges. Plainly, it is an impossible task for anyone to be aware of all of these potential precedents. In fact, so many High Court judgments are made that most are not even reported in the law reports.

Law reporting is not a Government task but is carried out by private firms. The law reporters are barristers and they weed out the vast number of judgments which they consider to be unimportant. Even so, as students become aware when they step into a law library, the system of precedent does mean that English law is very bulky. There are so many precedents that it can be very hard for a lawyer to find the law he is looking for. The fact that major law reports are now available on the Internet has made them more easily accessible to those with the appropriate technology.

Precedent suffers from another disadvantage and that is that bad decisions can live on for a very long time. As we have seen, before 1966 a House of Lords decision was binding on all other courts, including future sittings of the House of Lords. If a bad House of Lords decision was made, then before 1966 it could be changed only by Parliament, which was generally far too busy to interfere unless grave injustice was being caused.

A third disadvantage is that the vast number of precedents can take away the very certainty which the system is said to promote. This is particularly true when appellate courts apply the law creatively to achieve justice in the particular case in front of them.

These disadvantages of the system of precedent are thought to be outweighed by the advantages of the system. One final criticism which might be made is that under the system of precedent judges make most of the law. Most laymen might be surprised to find that this is the case and might question whether it ought to be. Some have argued that as regards decisions which might be classed as 'political' the judges are not the most appropriate body to create the law. However, it seems hard to imagine that anyone other than the judiciary could so effectively create law of a technical nature, such as the law of contract, and so effectively allow it to respond to the changing needs of business.

Advantages of the system of precedent

The first advantage is that the device of **distinguishing** a case means that the system of precedent is not entirely rigid. A judge who is lower down the hierarchy can refuse to follow a precedent if he distinguishes it on its facts. This means that the judge will say that the facts of the case he is considering are materially different from the facts of the case by which he appears to be bound. This device of distinguishing gives a degree of flexibility to the system of precedent. It allows judges to escape precedents which they consider inappropriate to the case in front of them.

A second and more important advantage of precedent is that it causes high quality decisions to be applied in all courts. Judges in appellate courts have the time and the experience to make very good decisions, often on extremely complex matters. These decisions can then be applied by much busier and less experienced lower court judges, who do not have to give the same consideration as to whether the principles of law involved are right or wrong.

It must be realised that the House of Lords, the highest English court, is nowadays a quite different institution from the Parliamentary House of Lords. Historically, it has been possible for people of no great ability, whether through inheritance or public service, to gain entry to the Parliamentary House of Lords. It is nowadays impossible for any but the very able to become Law Lords.

The way in which a person might become a Law Lord demonstrates that only those of the highest ability could achieve it. Until recently, judges were chosen only from the ranks of barristers. Now solicitors too can become judges. The Bar is a career, rather like acting, which has extremes of success and very many talented young people enter it. If a barrister gains promotion and becomes a circuit judge he will sit in the Crown Court or the county court. This is an honour and an achievement. Even so, a circuit judge will make no law. He will supervise proceedings, decide who wins civil cases, award damages and sentence those convicted in the Crown Court. But no matter how brilliant a circuit judge's analysis of the law might be, it will not form a precedent.

High Court judges are a different matter. There are only 107 of them and they make the law of England from the very first case in which they sit. Every word they speak is open to scrutiny by the other judges, by lawyers and by academics. If they were not very able, this would soon be noticed.

About 50 judges are promoted beyond the High Court to the House of Lords or Court of Appeal. These days it seems unthinkable that any but the very able should go this far.

It is not only on the grounds of ability that the House of Lords ought to come to very high quality decisions. Unlike lower court judges, the Law Lords do not decide a case there and then. They hear the facts and the arguments in the case and then reserve their judgment. They talk to each other informally to see whether there is a consensus of opinion. If there is a consensus one of the judges is chosen to write the judgment. If there is no consensus the minority will write their own dissenting judgments. In a particularly difficult case the process of writing the judgment can take a very long time.

English Commercial Law is very often adopted by merchants of different nationalities when they contract with each other. In the event of a dispute they consult English lawyers and settle their cases in the English courts or in front of English arbitrators. The earnings to the United Kingdom from these disputes amount to a considerable invisible export. English law would not be adopted in this way if it were not thought to be the most suitable system of law for resolving commercial disputes. The main reason why it should be thought the most suitable is the system of precedent allows for excellent updating of the law in a way which can keep up with changing business trends.

A third major advantage of the system of precedent is that it is consistent and certain. Lawyers can predict the outcome of most cases, as almost any legal problem will have been previously considered by the courts and a precedent made. This certainty enables the vast majority of cases to be settled without the need to go to court. (The practical importance of this is explained in the following chapter at 2.4.)

Impact of the Human Rights Act 1998

Later in this chapter, at 1.5.1, the Human Rights Act 1998 is considered. As we shall see, s.3(1) of this Act requires that, so far as it is possible to do so, all legislation must be read and given effect in a way which is compatible with the Convention rights. In *R v A* [2001] 2 AC 45 Lord Steyn said that a declaration of incompatibility was a measure of last resort and to be avoided unless it was plainly impossible to do so. In *Re S and others* [2002] UKHL 10 Lord Nicholls said that use of s.3(1) was obligatory and that it was not an optional rule of construction. The new approach seems to be first to ask if the Act in question is incompatible with a Convention right. If so, to then ask whether any incompatibility could be avoided by using the purposive approach, the mischief rule or *Pepper* v *Hart*. Finally, the Act in question must be read in accordance with s.3(1) of the Human Rights Act, unless there was evidence that Parliament had intended to legislate in a way which was contrary to the Human Rights Act.

Alternatives to the system of precedent

Most other countries do not use a system of precedent. France, which is fairly typical of European countries, has a codified system of law known as a civil law system. The civil law is contained in the various Civil Codes. French judges, who are civil servants rather than lawyers, do not feel compelled to interpret the Codes according to previous decisions until those decisions have for some time unanimously interpreted the Codes in the same way. Scotland has a mixed legal system. It is based on the civil law system, but has strong common law influences. In Scotland the system of precedent is used, but a precedent does not have quite the same force as in England.

Test your understanding

1 What is meant by the doctrine of judicial precedent?

2 What are the five main levels of the courts, for the purposes of precedent?

3 What is meant by *ratio decidendi* and *obiter dicta*? What is the significance of the distinction?

4 What is meant by overruling, reversing and distinguishing?

Answers

1 The doctrine of judicial precedent requires lower-ranking courts to follow legal principles previously formulated in higher-ranking courts.

2 The House of Lords is the highest ranking court. Its precedents bind all lower courts but not future sittings of the House of Lords. The Court of Appeal ranks below the House of Lords. Decisions of the Court of Appeal are binding on all inferior courts and, almost always, upon future sittings of the Court of Appeal. Decisions of Divisional Courts of the High Court are binding upon future sittings of the High Court and upon inferior courts. Decisions of ordinary courts of the High Court are binding upon inferior courts but not upon other High Court judges. Decisions of inferior courts are not binding.

3 The *ratio decidendi* of a case could be defined as any statement of law which the judge applied to the facts of the case and upon which the decision in the case is based. *Obiter dicta* would include other statements of law made by the judge. Only the *ratio decidendi* of a case can be a binding precedent. *Obiter dicta* can be of persuasive authority only.

4 When a precedent is overruled it is changed by a higher-ranking court or by a statute. A case is reversed when an appeal is successful so that the party who won in the lower court loses the appeal. An apparently binding precedent can be distinguished by a judge who refuses to follow it on the grounds that the facts of the case he is considering are materially different from the facts of the case he is distinguishing.

1.4 · European Community law

In 1952 the European Coal and Steel Community was set up with the object of preventing any European country from building up stockpiles of steel and coal, the means of waging war. Following the success of this, the European Economic Community (the EEC) came into existence in 1957. The six original Member States signed the Treaty of Rome, which was also known as the EEC Treaty. These six original countries were Germany, France, Italy, Belgium, the Netherlands and Luxembourg. Part of the founding philosophy of the Community was to provide an appropriate response to the Soviet Bloc countries to the East, but the motivation was also more pragmatic in that there seemed to be obvious advantages to the creation of a free market in Europe. At the time of writing there are 15 Member States, the original six having been joined by Denmark, Greece, Spain, Ireland, Austria, Portugal, Finland, Sweden and the United Kingdom. The Treaty of Nice will allow another ten countries to join in May 2004.

The United Kingdom joined the EEC in 1973. In order to be admitted as a member, the UK Parliament passed the European Communities Act 1972. This statute agreed that Community law should be directly effective in UK courts. In 1992 the Treaty on European Union (the Maastricht Treaty) renamed the EEC as the European Community (the EC). It is now therefore convenient to refer to the Community as the EC, rather than as the EEC, even when considering matters before the Maastricht Treaty.

In 1986 the EC consisted of 12 Member States, all of whom signed the Single European Act. This Act was designed to remove all barriers to a single market by 1992. In addition, the Act introduced a system of qualified majority voting in the European Council, thereby reducing the power of any single State to block developments. The Act also strengthened the powers of the European Parliament and created a Court of First Instance to work beneath the European Court of Justice.

In 1992 the Treaty on European Union (the Maastricht Treaty), was signed by all 15 Member States. The Treaty was more of a statement of political intention than a statement of precise obligations. It proposed cooperation on matters other than purely economic matters, envisaging the creation of a European Union with the three following **pillars**: the European Community; a common foreign and security policy; and cooperation in the fields of justice and home affairs. Also, the European Parliament was given greater power to legislate and a timetable was set for economic and monetary union.

The Treaty of Amsterdam was signed in October 1997 and came into force in May 1999. This Treaty aimed for closer political cooperation between Member States. It incorporated much of the Justice and Home Affairs pillar into the EC Treaty and gave Member States a greater power to veto proposals which would affect their vital national interests. It again increased the power of the European Parliament and gave the Community greater power to fight fraud, to prevent discrimination and to protect the environment. It also renumbered the articles of the EC Treaty.

The Treaty of Nice came into force in February 2003 and allows ten more countries to join as from 1 May 2004. These countries are: Cyprus, the Czech Republic, Estonia, Hungary, Latvia, Lithuania, Malta, Poland, Slovakia and Slovenia. Bulgaria and Romania are scheduled to join in 2007. Turkey has also applied to join but is regarded as not yet ready to do so.

1.4.1 The Institutions of the European Community

The original EEC Treaty set up four principal **institutions**. These institutions are now known as: the Council of the European Communities; the European Commission; the European Parliament; and the European Court of Justice. The first three of these are considered immediately below. The European Court of Justice is considered below at 1.4.3. In addition, there is a Court of Auditors and two advisory bodies: the Economic and Social Committee and the Committee of the Regions. The Court of Auditors monitors the Community's accounts. When the Treaty of Nice is fully effective, each Member State will have one national as a member of the Court. The Economic and Social Committee gives advisory opinions to the institutions. The Committee of the Regions is a consultative body which promotes the interests of the regions at European level. Both of these committees have 344 members. Each Member State has between six and 24 representatives, depending upon the size of the State.

1.4.1.1 The Council of the European Communities

The Council of the European Communities, generally known as the Council, is not a permanent body. It consists at any given time of one Minister from the Government of each Member State, and the President of the European Commission. Which Government Ministers will constitute the Council of Ministers depends upon the nature of the measures which the Council is considering. For example, if the measures relate to agriculture then it will be the relevant Ministers of Agriculture. Often the Council is made up of heads of Government or the Member States' Foreign Ministers.

The Council is the main policy-making body of the EC. It passes legislation, generally by a system of qualified majority voting. However, a Treaty might require unanimity for votes on certain matters such as the common and foreign security policy, police and judicial cooperation in criminal matters, asylum and immigration policy, economic and social cohesion policy or taxation. Under this system each country is allocated a certain number of votes in relation to its population. The United Kingdom is one of four countries having the maximum voting weighting of ten votes. There are 87 votes in total, and 62 votes are required to obtain a qualified majority. It follows that a measure can only be blocked by a minority of 26 votes. At least three States would therefore be needed to block a vote. The required majority of 62 votes needs a minimum of eight States voting in favour.

Article 11 of the Treaty of Amsterdam allows any Member State to argue that unanimity, rather than a qualified majority vote, should be required on any particular proposal. When such an argument is raised, the Council will delay taking a vote in order to enable the dissenting State to gain the support of other Member States. However, if it is unsuccessful in this the issues will anyway be resolved by a qualified majority vote. It is also possible, under the Luxembourg Accord, for a Member State to argue that a unanimous vote rather than qualified majority voting is necessary where the very important interests of a Member State are at stake. However, the other States may override the request for unanimity and no Member State whose wishes have been overridden in this way has ever taken the matter before the European Court of Justice (ECJ).

Two committees assist the Council. The Committee of Permanent Representatives (COREPER) prepares the work of the Council and performs other administrative functions. This committee is comprised of senior diplomatic representatives of the Member States. The Economic and Social Committee (ECOSOC) has a consultative role.

Reforms made by the Treaty of Nice

Once the twelve new Member States have been admitted it is feared that if a unanimous vote of all Member States is required then the EC would be paralysed. In respect of 30 Treaty Articles which previously required a unanimous vote qualified majority voting will be allowed. As from 1 January 2005, the voting rights attached to each Member State will be altered, as shown in Table 1.2.

Countries with small populations have more votes per person than countries with larger populations. (For example, Malta with a population of under half a million has three votes, whereas the UK with a population in excess of 60 million has 29 votes.) A qualified majority vote will be passed if a decision reaches a certain number of votes (the number will alter as new Member States accede) and if the vote was approved by a majority of Member States. However, to protect the States with large populations, any Member State can ask for confirmation that the qualified majority represented at least 62% of the total population of the EC. If it did not then the decision will not be adopted.

1.4.1.2 The European Commission

Twenty individual commissioners are appointed by the Member States to serve in a full-time capacity for a term of four years. When these commissioners act collectively they are known as the European Commission, which is generally abbreviated to the Commission. The Commission is supported by large executive and administrative systems. Some States have one commissioner whilst others, such as the United Kingdom, have two. The commissioners are expected to act completely independently of their Member States but in practice tend to guard the independence of their Member States. They are selected on political grounds, and all UK commissioners have previously played a leading role in UK politics.

The most powerful position in the EC is the President of the Commission. The President is the figurehead of the EC and has a strong political influence upon it. The Member States select the President after consultation with the European Parliament.

The Commission is involved in broad policy-making. It prepares specific proposals to be submitted to the Council. It drafts secondary legislation (see 1.4.2) in accordance with powers which have been delegated to it. The Commission ensures that the Treaties are observed and has the power to initiate proceedings against Member States which infringe the Treaties. It commissions research and prepares reports on matters which concern the Community and negotiates with non-Member States on these matters. It also prepares the draft Community budget.

Table 1.2 Voting rights of Member States

Old State		New Member States	
Belgium	12	Bulgaria	10
Denmark	7	Cyprus	4
Germany	29	Czech Rep.	12
Greece	12	Estonia	4
Spain	27	Hungary	12
France	29	Latvia	4
Ireland	7	Lithuania	7
Italy	29	Malta	3
Luxembourg	4	Poland	27
Netherlands	13	Romania	14
Austria	10	Slovakia	7
Portugal	12	Slovenia	4
Finland	7		
Sweden	10		
United Kingdom	29		

Reforms made by the Treaty of Nice

The current system of appointing commissioners would mean that once the new States had been admitted there would be 33 commissioners. The Treaty of Nice provides that from 2005 there will be a maximum of one commissioner from each Member State. Once there are 27 Member States a ceiling on the number of commissioners will be imposed. This ceiling will be less than 27, the exact number having to be fixed by a unanimous decision of the Council. A rotation system will then operate so that each State is fairly represented. As the Commission will be much larger than was originally envisaged, the President of the Commission is to be given greater powers. These will include the power to demand any commissioner's resignation, subject to the Commission's approval.

1.4.1.3 The European Parliament

Members of the European Parliament are elected directly by Member States, using a system of proportional representation. It is perhaps surprising that the European Parliament does not have the power to initiate and pass legislation, these powers lying with the Council and the Commission. One of the Parliament's most significant powers is to approve or amend the EC budget. The Commission prepares a draft budget, which is submitted to the Council and then to the Parliament. The Parliament must approve, amend or reject the budget within 45 days. When the budget is amended the Council is given 15 days to consider the amendments. If no challenge is made to the amendments then the budget is deemed to have been accepted as amended. If the Council does challenge the amendments, the budget is re-submitted to the Parliament. The Parliament then has 15 days to amend or reject the modifications made by the Council. This must be done by a 60% majority and a majority of members must vote. If no such vote is passed, the Council's modifications are adopted as the budget.

The Parliament must approve the accounts of the Commission and must also approve new appointments to the Commission. Article 201 of the EC Treaty gives the Parliament the power to pass a vote of censure to dismiss the Commission. Such a vote must be passed by a two-thirds majority. In January 1999 a vote to remove the Commission on account of nepotism and corruption failed. 232 MEPs voted for removal, 293 voted against. However, the whole of the Commission resigned in March 1999, on publication of a report made by an investigative committee.

Initially the Parliament had few real powers. It had to be consulted about EC legislation but had no powers to block any legislation. The Parliament has now been given more power by two Articles. Article 251 of the EC Treaty gives the Parliament a right of veto in limited areas concerning the competence of the Community. This right is subject to the Parliament making every effort to compromise. Article 252 gives the Council an overriding power to legislate, but only after it has re-examined amendments put forward by the Parliament. Although this allows the Parliament to be overridden, there are substantial procedural safeguards. There will therefore be extensive negotiations with the Parliament in order to try to gain consensus.

Reforms made by the Treaty of Nice

The Treaty of Nice enhances the power of the European Parliament. The co-decision procedure extends the Parliament's power to legislate to more areas. The Parliament is also given more power over the funding of political parties at European level. The Treaty limits the number of MEPs to a maximum of 732. Table 1.3 shows how seats in the European Parliament are to be allocated between Member States.

1.4.2 Sources of community law

1.4.2.1 Applicability and effect

In order to understand the effect of EC law it is necessary to understand the distinction between the terms 'direct applicability' and 'direct effect'. If EC legislation is directly applicable, it automatically

Table 1.3 Allocation of seats in the European Parliament

Old State		New Member States	
Belgium	22	Bulgaria	17
Denmark	13	Cyprus	6
Germany	99	Czech Rep.	20
Greece	22	Estonia	6
Spain	50	Hungary	20
France	72	Latvia	8
Ireland	12	Lithuania	12
Italy	72	Malta	5
Luxembourg	6	Poland	50
Netherlands	25	Romania	33
Austria	17	Slovakia	13
Portugal	22	Slovenia	7
Finland	13		
Sweden	18		
United Kingdom	72		

forms part of the domestic law of Member States. However, this would not necessarily mean that claimants could directly rely upon the legislation in the domestic courts of their own countries. In order for such reliance to be possible, the legislation would have to be capable of having direct effect. Where EC legislation has direct effect an individual can directly rely upon the legislation, either as a cause of action or a defence, in the domestic courts of his country. Treaty Articles are always directly applicable, as are EC Regulations, but as we have seen this does not necessarily mean that they have direct effect.

No EC legislation can have direct effect unless it satisfies the criteria laid down by the European Court of Justice in *Van Gend en Loos* v *Nederlands Administratie der Belastingen* [1963] ECR 1. These criteria will only be satisfied if the legislation is sufficiently clear, precise and unconditional. Many Treaty Articles do not meet these criteria as they are mere statements of aspiration. Even if Community legislation does meet the *Van Gend* criteria, it may have only direct vertical effect, rather than direct horizontal effect. If it has direct vertical effect it can be invoked by an individual against the State and against emanations of the State, such as health authorities. A provision which has direct horizontal effect can be invoked between private parties.

1.4.2.2 Treaty Articles

The EC Treaty, the Treaty of Rome as amended, has over 300 Articles. These are directly applicable. Whether or not a Treaty Article also has direct effect depends upon whether it satisfies the criteria in *Van Gend*. As we have seen, some will not satisfy these criteria as they are merely statements of aspiration.

Some of the articles are much more significant than others. Article 141 of the EC Treaty (formerly Article 119) requires Member States to ensure and subsequently maintain the application of the principle that men and women should receive equal pay for equal work. The effect of this Article has been highly significant, as we shall see in Chapter 21, and has caused the Sex Discrimination Act 1975 to be amended to make sure that the Article is not contradicted. Although Article 141 is addressed to Member States, individuals have successfully invoked it.

Some Treaty Articles have both direct horizontal and vertical effect, others have only direct vertical effect. Whether or not they have direct horizontal effect will depend upon the wording of the Article and the interpretation of the Article by the ECJ. For example, Article 28 of the EC Treaty, which prohibits restrictions on the free movement of goods, only has direct vertical effect. It can therefore only be invoked by an individual against the State or against an emanation of the State. One private company could not invoke Article 28 against another private company which was not an emanation of the State.

1.4.2.3 Regulations

Regulations are binding in their entirety and are directly applicable in all Member States without any further implementation by Member States. A regulation may specify the date on which it is to come into effect. If it does not do this, it will come into effect 20 days after the date of its publication in the Official Journal of the Community. Regulations may be directly invoked, both vertically and horizontally, providing the *Van Gend* criteria are satisfied. If these criteria are not satisfied, a Regulation may have indirect effect.

1.4.2.4 Directives

Directives are addressed to the governments of Member States and must be published in the Official Journal of the Community. Directives are not directly applicable. It is therefore left to each individual Member State to implement the objectives of the Directive in a manner and form that is best suited to its own particular political and economic culture. All Directives are issued with an implementation date and Member States are under a duty to implement by this date. If the Directive is not implemented by the due date, the Commission has the power to take proceedings against the Member State in question.

Before the implementation date has been reached, Directives have no effect at all. However, in the Wallonie ASBL case [1997] ECR I-7411 the European Court of Justice held that a Member State should not enact legislation or implement measures that significantly conflict with the objectives of a Directive that has yet to meet its implementation date. Generally, the UK Government will implement EC Directives by delegated legislation. Several statutory instruments which we consider in this book, such as the Commercial Agents (Council Directive) Regulations 1993, were enacted to give effect to Directives. (It is slightly confusing that these statutory instruments are usually called Regulations, given that EC Regulations are a quite different matter.) Once an EC Directive has been implemented by UK legislation then, obviously, an individual can invoke the domestic legislation against another individual. For example, the Commercial Agents (Council Directive) Regulations 1993 are regularly invoked by individuals against individuals.

There can, however, be a problem if the UK Government either fails to implement a Directive at all, or does not implement the Directive properly. Once the implementation date has been reached, whether or not the Directive has direct effect depends first on whether the Directive satisfies the *Van Gend* criteria, and second upon the relationship between the parties involved. Where the parties to a legal action are in a vertical relationship (for example, patient and health authority), the Directive is capable of having direct effect. Where the parties are in a horizontal relationship (for example, a consumer suing a shop), the Directive does not have direct effect. In other words, Directives which should have been implemented are capable of having direct vertical effect, but not direct horizontal effect. However, when dealing with a case between two individuals the domestic courts are under a duty, by virtue of Article 10 of the EC Treaty, to attempt as far as possible to give indirect effect to the EC Directive which should have been implemented. This means that they have to try to interpret the domestic legislation so as to give effect indirectly to the objectives of the Directive.

In situations where it is not possible for the domestic court to give direct or indirect effect to an EC Directive, the remedy of last resort is for the aggrieved individual to sue the Member State for failure to implement. If found to be in breach, the Member State could be ordered to pay compensation to the aggrieved individual. This right was set out in the following case.

■ *Francovich and Bonifaci v Republic of Italy* [1993] 2 CMLR 66 (European Court of Justice)

Mr Francovich's employer went into liquidation, while owing money to Mr Francovich and others. An EC Directive required Member States to set up compensation funds to deal with this type of situation. However, Italy had not set up such a fund. The Directive in question was not sufficiently precise to have direct effect. Mr Francovich asked for damages against Italy to compensate for its failure to set up a fund.

Held. Article 10 impliedly allowed for an individual to be compensated on account of an EC Directive not having been implemented, but only if three conditions were satisfied. First, the Directive must relate to rights conferred upon an individual.

Second, the contents of those rights must be identifiable from the Directive's provisions. Third, a causal link must exist between the State's failure to implement the Directive and the loss suffered by the individual.

In *Brasserie du Pêcheur SA* v *Germany* [1996] ECR 1-1029 the ECJ refined the *Francovitch* criteria in the following way. First, the rule of law in question must confer rights upon individuals. Second, the breach must be sufficiently serious. Third, there must be a direct causal link between the breach and the damage. That the breach should have been sufficiently serious, means that the Member State must have 'manifestly and gravely' disregarded the limits on its discretion. In deciding whether or not this had happened, account will be taken of the following matters: the clarity of the legislation in question; whether the rule in question allowed any measure of discretion; whether the failure to implement and the damage caused were deliberate; whether the error had been induced by the acts or words of the Council or the Commission; whether the error was contrary to settled ECJ case law; and the speed with which the error was corrected.

The legal effect of the Treaties, Regulations and Directives is shown in Figure 1.1.

1.4.2.5 Decisions

Decisions are addressed to one or more Member States, to individuals or to institutions. They are binding in their entirety, without the need for implementation by Member States, but only on those to whom they were addressed. They do not need to be published in the Official Journal. Decisions can only be invoked against the person to whom they are addressed. In practice, decisions are of little practical importance.

1.4.2.6 Recommendations and opinions

The Commission has the power to make recommendations and opinions. These have no binding legal force. However, where a Member State passes legislation to comply with a decision or an opinion a national court may refer a case to the ECJ to see whether or not the decision or opinion applies and how it should be interpreted.

1.4.3 The European Court of Justice

The European Court of Justice (ECJ) is made up of 15 judges and nine advocates-general. The judges and advocates are appointed by common consent of the Member States and hold office for a six-year term which may be renewed. Each Member State nominates one judge and Britain, France, Germany, Italy and Spain also nominate an advocate-general. The other advocates-general are nominated by the remaining ten smaller Member States. A rotation system is used, so that an advocate-general nominated by one of the smaller nations retires after six years, to be replaced by the nominee of a different smaller State.

The decisions of the court are signed by all the judges, without any indication that some may have dissented. 80% of cases are referred to one of the six chambers where either three or five judges sit. A plenary session of the court will have nine or more judges, and disputes involving Member States tend to be heard by plenary session. The number of judges sitting is always odd, so that a majority decision can always be reached. The more important the issues thought to be involved, the greater the number of judges sitting. The judgments of the court are available free on its web site, but cases typically take between 18 months and two years to be heard.

The advocates-general must act with complete impartiality and independence, in open court, making reasoned submissions on cases brought before the Court. They do not therefore argue the case for either of the sides involved. Each case has an advocate-general assigned to it. The advocate-general makes a summary of the facts, an analysis of all the relevant Community law and a recommendation as to what the decision of the court should be. The parties cannot comment on this and the judges deliberate upon it in secret. The Court has no obligation to agree with the advocate-general's recommendation.

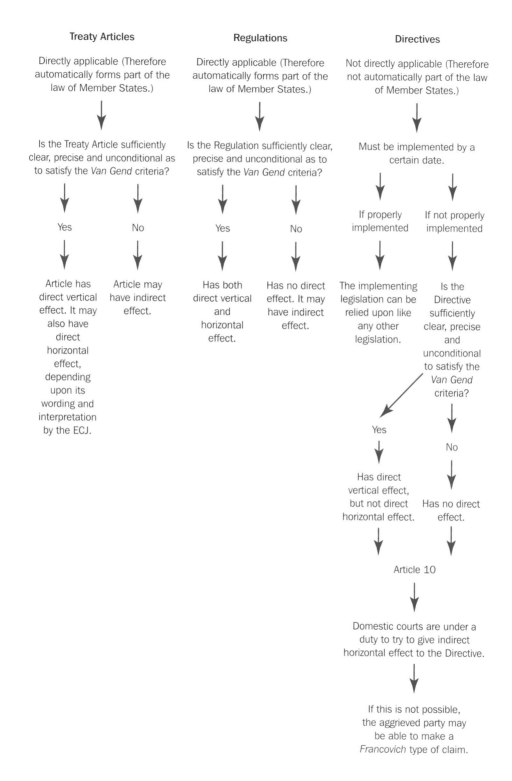

Figure 1.1 The legal effect of Treaty Articles, Regulations and Directives

The judges speak in French, without translators, when deliberating. When ready to vote the most junior judges vote first and then the other judges vote in order of reverse seniority. The court does not use a system of precedent. It can and does depart from its own previous decisions.

Certain matters may be referred to the Court of First Instance rather than to the European Court of Justice. This Court of First Instance operates in a very similar way to the way in which the ECJ operates. Article 51 of the EC Treaty provides an automatic right of appeal on a point of law from the Court of First Instance to the ECJ.

1.4.3.1 Jurisdiction of the ECJ

Apart from hearing appeals from the Court of First Instance, the ECJ has three separate heads of jurisdiction.

First, it can express an authoritative opinion on EC law, if requested to do so by a national court. Once the ruling has been made by the ECJ the case returns to the court which asked for the ruling so that that court can apply the ruling. Article 234 of the EC Treaty allows a national court to request an authoritative ruling as to three types of matters: the interpretation of the EC legislation; the validity and interpretation of acts of institutions of the Community; and on the interpretation of statutes of bodies established by an act of the Council, where those statutes so provide. Any national court or tribunal may refer a matter within Article 234 to the ECJ if it thinks this necessary to give judgment. Most of the ECJ's work involves preliminary rulings. In Chapter 20 we shall consider several cases in which a national court sought a preliminary ruling as to the interpretation of EC legislation from the ECJ. The ruling is sought by the court, not by the parties to the case. Although a national court has a discretion to seek a preliminary ruling, a court of final appeal has an obligation to do so where a relevant point of EU law is at issue and where there has been no previous interpretation of the point by the ECJ. However, there is no such obligation where the point is so obvious as not to require a ruling.

The second area of jurisdiction arises under Article 230 of the EC Treaty, which allows the ECJ to review the legality of acts adopted by the European Parliament or other Community institutions. This is similar to the process of judicial review whereby the High Court ensures that the Government and others do not exceed their powers.

The third area of jurisdiction arises under Article 226, which allows the ECJ to bring actions against Member States to make sure that they fulfil their Community obligations. Article 227 allows Member States to take other Member States to the ECJ for failure to live up to their Treaty obligations.

1.4.3.2 Reforms made by the Treaty of Nice

The Treaty of Nice envisages that the ECJ will share tasks with the Court of First Instance in a more effective way in order to cut down on the backlog of cases. It also envisages that specialised Chambers will be created to deal with particular types of disputes, such as those between EC officials. Each Member State will continue to appoint one judge and sometimes the full plenary session will sit. However, 13 judges may instead sit in a Grand Chamber.

1.4.4 Supremacy of EC law

EC law can only be effective if it overrides national law. If every Member State were free to pass legislation which conflicted with EC legislation, the EC would be rendered ineffective. In *Costa* v *ENEL* [1964] ECR 585 the ECJ stated that the EEC Treaty had become an integral part of the legal systems of Member States and that the courts of Member States were bound to apply the Treaty. It also stated that Member States had, by signing the Treaty, limited their sovereign rights, within limited areas, and created a body of law which bound both their citizens and themselves. The case specifically decided that Italian legislation which was incompatible with Community law, and which had been passed after Italy had signed the Treaty, could have no effect.

In *R* v *Secretary of State for Transport, ex parte Factortame (No. 2)* [1991] 1 AC 603, Spanish companies sought judicial review of the Merchant Shipping Act 1988, which they claimed breached two Articles of the EC Treaty. The companies asked for an injunction to suspend that part of the Act which was in breach of the relevant Treaty Article. The House of Lords held that injunctions could not be effective against the Crown and refused to grant the injunction. However, the case was referred to the ECJ, which held that UK limitations on the availability of remedies should be over-ruled and that the injunctions should be available. Subsequently, the House of Lords immediately suspended the operation of the offending part of the Act. A few years after *Factortame* in *Equal Opportunities Commission* v *Secretary of State for Employment* [1994] 1 All ER 110, the House of Lords suspended the operation of a section of the governing employment legislation on the grounds that it was in breach of the EC Equal Treatment legislation. However, it should be noted that this power of UK courts to suspend conflicting domestic legislation will only be used sparingly in cases involving serious breaches of directly effective EC legislation.

Whilst the United Kingdom remains a member of the EC it is therefore arguable that it has surrendered Parliamentary sovereignty. However, two points should be noted. First, other Treaties such as those which provided that the United States had direct command over US soldiers based in the United Kingdom, have at some time or other meant that the United Kingdom did not have true Parliamentary sovereignty. Second, the UK Parliament could vote to repeal the European Communites Act 1972 and leave the EC. It must be said, however, that this option becomes increasingly unlikely and would become virtually impossible if full monetary union were ever achieved.

Test your understanding

1 What is the role of the Council of the European Communities?

2 What is the role of the European Commission?

3 What is the role of the European Parliament?

4 What is meant by EC legislation being directly applicable?

5 What is meant by EC legislation having direct effect?

6 What is the difference between direct vertical effect and direct horizontal effect?

7 Are Articles of the EC Treaty and Regulations directly applicable? Do they have direct effect?

8 What is the legal effect of a Directive both before and after implementation?

9 Can an individual sue a Member State on account of a Directive not having been correctly implemented?

10 What is the jurisdiction of the European Court of Justice?

Answers

1 The Council, which is not a permanent body but is made up of the relevant Ministers from Member States, is the main policy-making body of the EC. It passes legislation by a system of qualified majority-voting.

2 The European Commission is a permanent institution which makes broad EC policy, drafts secondary legislation and ensures that the Treaty is observed. It also prepares reports on EC matters and negotiates with Member States on these matters.

3 The European Parliament does not pass legislation but has important powers in its capacity as part of the legislative process. It has the power to approve or amend the EC budget, to approve the accounts of the European Commission and to dismiss the entire Commission.

4 If EC legislation is directly applicable it automatically forms part of the domestic law of member States.

5 EC legislation which has direct effect can be relied upon directly by an individual in a legal action in the domestic courts.

6 If EC legislation has only direct vertical effect, it can only be relied upon by an individual against the State or against an emanation of the State. If the legislation has direct horizontal effect, one individual can invoke it against another individual.

7 Articles of the EC Treaty and Regulations are directly applicable. Whether or not they have direct effect will depend upon whether or not they satisfy the *Van Gend* criteria of being sufficiently clear, precise and unconditional.

8 Before its implementation date, a Directive has no legal effect (subject to the *Wallonie* principle). Once it has been implemented, the UK legislation which implemented the Directive can be relied upon like any other UK law. If the Directive is not properly implemented by the implementation date it can have direct vertical effect, but not direct horizontal effect. Domestic courts are under a duty to try to give indirect effect as far as possible.

9 As a last resort this can be allowed, if the criteria set out in the *Francovich* case (as refined by the *Brasserie de Pêcheur* case) are satisfied.

10 The ECJ expresses authoritative rulings on the interpretation of EC legislation when such interpretations are sought by national courts. It reviews acts adopted by the European Parliament and the other EC institutions. It can also hear cases which the Commission brings against Member States to make sure that they fulfil their EC obligations.

1.5 · The European Convention on Human Rights

1.5.1 The Human Rights Act 1998

The Human Rights Act 1998 came into effect in October 2000. This Act incorporates the Convention on Human Rights into UK law. However, the implementation is not complete as Parliamentary sovereignty is preserved. Section 2(1) of the Act states that a court or tribunal which is determining a question which has arisen in connection with a Convention right must take into account both the Convention and decisions of institutions of the Convention, such as the Court of Human Rights.

Section 3(1) of the Act requires that, so far as it is possible to do so, all legislation must be read and given effect in a way which is compatible with the Convention rights. This can be regarded as a new rule of statutory interpretation and it is not to be applied only where a statute is ambiguous. Section 4 allows any precedent-making courts (the High Court, Court of Appeal and House of Lords) to make a declaration of incompatibility in any legal proceedings in which a court determines whether or not UK legislation is compatible with a Convention right. Such a declaration of incompatibility does not affect the validity of the legislation in question, and is not binding on the parties to the litigation. Where a declaration of incompatibility is made, the relevant Minister has the option to revoke the offending legislation, or amend it so that it is no longer incompatible. Section 10 gives the Minister power to do this by remedial order so as to achieve the change by a 'fast-track' procedure. However, the Minister will revoke or amend the legislation only if he considers that there are compelling reasons for doing either of these things. As the Minister can leave the incompatible legislation in place, Parliamentary sovereignty is preserved. The relevant Minister has the same power to revoke, amend or leave primary legislation in place following an adverse ruling from the European Court of Human Rights. If secondary legislation is found to be incompatible with Convention rights, any domestic court can declare the legislation invalid, unless the Parent Act provides that the secondary legislation is to prevail even if it is incompatible. If the Parent Act does not allow the legislation to be declared invalid, a court is restricted to making a declaration of incompatibility. The process of judicial review (see Chapter 2 at 2.6.1) can also cause secondary legislation which is invalid to be declared *ultra vires* the parent Act (see 1.3.1.3, above).

Since the Act came into effect, positive consideration must be given as to whether new legislation is compatible with the Convention. Before the Second Reading of a Bill in Parliament the relevant Minister will have to make a written statement to Parliament, either stating compatibility with the Convention or stating incompatibility. If stating incompatibility, the Minister will need to state the Government's intention to proceed with the legislation anyway. The Minister does not need to state the way in which the legislation is incompatible. Obviously, stating incompatibility might lead to political difficulties.

Section 6(1) provides that it is unlawful for a public authority to act in a way which is incompatible with a Convention right. However, this is not the case if the public authority could not have acted differently as a result of primary UK legislation. Section 6(1) will have a considerable impact on many UK businesses, as s.6(3) defines a public authority as including not only a court or a tribunal, but also any person certain of whose functions are functions of a public nature. Therefore, businesses such as private nursing homes, private schools, security firms and housing associations will all be subject to the effect of s.6(1).

Section 7 creates a new public tort which allows individuals to bring legal proceedings against public authorities breaching Convention rights. It is only the 'victim' of a breach of Convention rights who has the standing to bring proceedings under s.7. Where proceedings are brought a court may order such remedies as it considers just and appropriate.

Section 13(1) provides that if a court's determination of any question arising under the Act might affect the exercise by a religious organisation of the Convention right to freedom of thought, conscience and religion, it must have particular regard to the importance of that right.

An outline of the effect of the Human Rights Act can be seen in Figure 1.2.

1.5.2 The European Convention on Human Rights

We have seen that the Human Rights Act incorporates the Convention on Human Rights into UK law. It is therefore necessary to consider the effect of the Convention.

Article 1 provides that the contracting States should ensure that everyone within their jurisdiction is given the rights and freedoms set out by the Convention. The rights will therefore have to be extended to citizens and non-citizens, including illegal immigrants.

Article 2 provides that everyone's right to life shall be preserved by law, except in carrying out a death sentence properly passed by a court.

Article 3 provides that no one shall be subjected to torture or to inhumane or degrading treatment or punishment. In *Ireland v UK* (1978) 2 EHRR 25 the Court of Human Rights found that the UK's interrogation of suspected terrorists was inhumane and degrading, although it fell short of being torture. In *D v UK* (1997) 24 EHRR 423 it was held that deporting a person with Aids to a country where there would be no treatment and where he would be destitute breached Article 3. In *Tyrer v UK* (1978) 2 EHRR 1 it was held that birching on the Isle of Man breached Article 3.

Article 4 provides that no one should be held in slavery or servitude or be required to perform forced or compulsory labour. There are exceptions for prisoners, the military, for work done as part of normal civic obligation, or service required in the case of an emergency or calamity threatening the life or well-being of the community.

Article 5(1) provides that everyone has the right to liberty and security of person. No one is to be deprived of their liberty except in the following circumstances: after conviction by a court; upon arrest; to prevent the spread of infectious diseases; in order to treat the mentally ill; or in the case of alcoholics, drug addicts or vagrants. Article 5(2) gives anyone arrested the right to be informed promptly, in a language which he understands, of the reason for the arrest and the charges against him. Article 5(3) requires that those arrested are brought promptly before a judge. If anyone is arrested in contravention of Article 5 he is given an enforceable right to compensation.

Article 6(1) guarantees the right to a fair trial. The trial must be a public hearing within a reasonable time of arrest by an independent and impartial tribunal established by law. Judgment has to be pronounced publicly. Article 6(2) holds that everyone charged with a criminal offence is presumed innocent until found guilty according to the law. Article 6(3) sets out the minimum rights of those charged with a criminal offence. These include: prompt information as to the details of the charge; adequate time and facilities to prepare a defence; the right to choose a lawyer and to be given free legal assistance if the interests of justice demand this; to have the same rights to require witnesses to attend as is enjoyed by the prosecution; to have the prosecution witnesses cross examined; and to have the free assistance of an interpreter if one is needed.

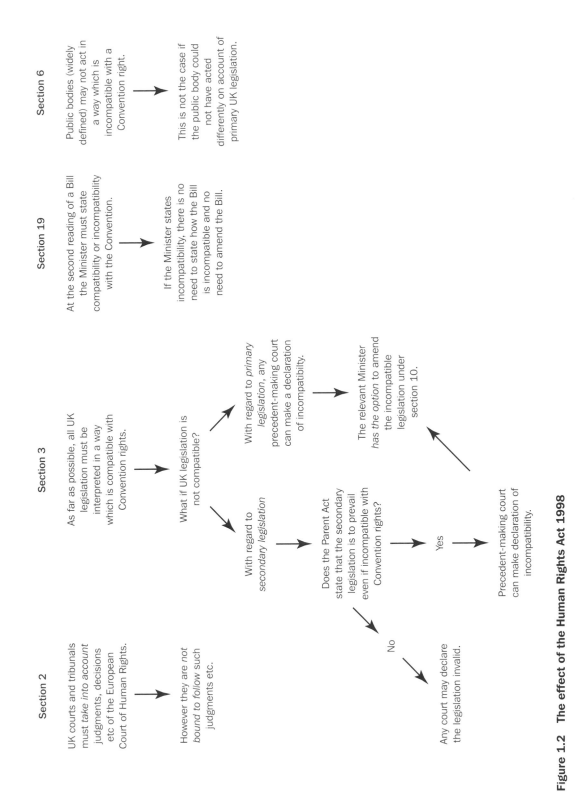

Section 2

UK courts and tribunals must take *into account* judgments, decisions etc of the European Court of Human Rights.

However they are *not bound to follow* such judgments etc.

Section 3

As far as possible, all UK legislation must be interpreted in a way which is compatible with Convention rights.

What if UK legislation is not compatible?

With regard to *primary legislation*, any precedent-making court can make a declaration of incompatibilty.

The relevant Minister *has the option* to amend the incompatible legislation under section 10.

With regard to *secondary legislation*

Does the Parent Act state that the secondary legislation is to prevail even if incompatible with Convention rights?

No

Any court may declare the legislation invalid.

Yes

Precedent-making court can make declaration of incompatibility.

Section 19

At the second reading of a Bill the Minister must state compatibility or incompatibility with the Convention.

If the Minister states incompatibility, there is no need to state how the Bill is incompatible and no need to amend the Bill.

Section 6

Public bodies (widely defined) may not act in a way which is incompatible with a Convention right.

This is not the case if the public body could not have acted differently on account of primary UK legislation.

Figure 1.2   The effect of the Human Rights Act 1998

Article 7 provides that no one should be guilty of a criminal offence which did not exist at the time when the act was committed, unless the act was criminal according to the general principles of law recognised by civilised nations.

Article 8(1) provides that everyone has the right to respect for his private and family life, his home and his correspondence. However, Article 8(2) provides that public authorities may interfere with this right on the following grounds: in the interests of national security, public safety or the economic well-being of the country; for the prevention of disorder or crime; for the protection of health or morals; or for the protection of the rights and freedoms of others.

Article 9 gives the right to freedom of thought, conscience and religion. However, this right is balanced against the rights of others to free expression, which includes criticism of religious beliefs and practices.

Article 10(1) gives a right to freedom of expression. This does not prevent the State from requiring broadcasters to hold licences, but does insist upon freedom to hold opinions, and to receive and impart information and ideas without interference by public authority. Article 10(2) provides that the freedoms set out in Article 10(1) carry duties and responsibilities and therefore may be subject to formalities, conditions, restrictions or penalties as are prescribed by law and as are necessary in a democratic society for the following reasons: to secure the interests of national security, territorial integrity or public safety; to prevent disorder or crime; to protect public health or morals; to protect the reputation or rights of others; to prevent the disclosure of confidential information; or to maintain the authority and impartiality of the judiciary.

Article 11 gives the right to freedom of peaceful assembly and to freedom of association with others, including the right to form and join a trade union. This right does not apply to the armed forces or the police. Restrictions are also allowed in the interests of national security or public safety, to prevent disorder or crime, to protect health or morals, or for the protection of the rights and freedoms of others.

Article 12 gives members of the opposite sex the right to marry and form a family if they are of marriageable age.

Article 13 provides that anyone whose rights and freedoms as set out in the Convention are violated shall have an effective remedy before a national authority even if the violation was committed by a person acting in an official capacity.

Article 14 provides that the rights set out in the Convention shall be secured without discrimination on any ground.

Article 15 allows derogation from the Convention in time of war.

Two Protocols, the First and the Sixth have also been incorporated into UK law by the Human Rights Act 1998.

The First Protocol, Article 1 provides that every natural or legal person is entitled to peaceful enjoyment of his possessions. Nobody should be deprived of his possessions except in the public interest and subject to provisions provided for by law.

The First Protocol, Article 2 provides that no-one should be denied the right to education.

The First Protocol, Article 3 provides that States must agree to conduct free elections at regular intervals by secret ballot so as to allow the people to freely choose the legislature.

The Sixth Protocol outlaws the death penalty.

The UK has been allowed one derogation from the Convention under Article 15(3) with regard to Article 5 of the Convention. This allows the authorities to detain anyone suspected of terrorist offences in line with the provisions of the Prevention of Terrorism (Temporary Provisions) Act 1989.

1.5.2 The Court of Human Rights

It is important to realise that this court, which sits in Strasbourg, is quite separate from the European Court of Justice, which sits in Luxembourg. The ECJ is the supreme court of the European

Community and its decisions are binding upon the Member States of the European Community. The Court of Human Rights hears cases concerning breach of the Convention on Human Rights. Forty States have signed the Convention and although this includes all of the Member States of the European Community, it also obviously includes other States which are not EC members.

There are 40 judges in the plenary Court of Human Rights. One judge represents each signatory State. The plenary court sets up Chambers to hear complaints. These Chambers are made up of seven judges plus an additional one who represents the State against which the complaint is being made. Each Chamber sets up Committees of three judges to consider applications and to dismiss as early as possible those which are completely unfounded. An individual with a complaint applies to a judge, known as a rapporteur, who passes the complaint on to a Committee or Chambers. Particularly difficult cases can be passed on to a Grand Chamber of 17 judges. The Grand Chamber also acts as an appeal court. Judges hold office for six years, with half being replaced every three years.

Article 35 of the Convention provides that an applicant to the court must prove:

(1) that the complaint involves a breach of the Convention by a country which has ratified it;
(2) that the breach occurred within the jurisdiction of that country; and
(3) that all domestic remedies have been exhausted and that the application to the Court has been made within six months of these remedies having been exhausted (it is possible, however, for the Court to proceed on the basis that domestic remedies are deemed to be exhausted on account of their being unsatisfactory).

It can be seen that the Court of Human Rights is very much a court of last resort. The decisions of the Court are delivered in open court. Although the decision is binding on the State to which it is addressed, the Court cannot enforce it. The Court can, however, order 'just satisfaction', which could order the payment of compensation and costs. In *McCann* v *UK* (1995) 21 EHRR 97, which involved IRA members being shot dead by the SAS in Gibraltar, the United Kingdom was ordered to pay the legal costs of the relatives of the dead IRA men. These costs amounted to £38 000.

The Court does not use a system of precedent. It does, however, adhere to a doctrine of proportionality, meaning that every formality, condition, restriction or penalty must be proportionate to the end which is trying to be achieved. In interpreting the law the Court adopts a broad, purposive approach rather than a technical 'letter of the law' approach.

1.5.4 The impact of the Human Rights Act

Lord Falconer, the Lord Chancellor, in a speech given in December 2003, said that only ten declarations of incompatibility had been made in the three years since the Act came into force. He also said that the Government intended to create a new Commission for Equality and Human Rights, in order to put human rights at the heart of the new politics of equality. He did not think that the Act had harmed Britain or made lawyers rich, as many had predicted it would. Rather, he thought that our fundamental rights on matters such as liberty, security, privacy and freedom of speech had been written down and made enforceable in a meaningful way. He thought that the Act had made a practical difference to ordinary people's lives and cited three cases which demonstrated this. In *R (on the application of C)* v *Mental Health Review Tribunal* [2001] EWCA Civ 110, a rule that compulsorily detained mental patients could not have their cases reviewed until eight weeks after the date of application was incompatible with Article 5. In *R (Bernard)* v *Enfield London Borough Council* [2002] EWHC 2282 (Admin), a severely disabled woman in a wheelchair had been housed in deplorable conditions where she could not keep herself clean or use the toilet for twenty months. The High Court considered Article 8 and the woman was rehoused and received compensation. In *R (Robertson)* v *City of Wakefield Metropolitan Council* [2001] EWHC Admin 915 a person won the right to have his name removed from the electoral register so that he no longer received junk mail. After describing these three cases, Lord Falconer said that the Act had achieved a great deal in cases which did not go to court by inspiring good practice and a sharper focus on individual rights. He also stressed that public authorities must act **proportionately** when interfering with rights. He gave an example of an unnamed local council which had intended to cut of all the branches of an ancient and beautiful walnut tree, the branches of which were hanging over a council car park, before it realised that it had to act proportionately and then cut off only the one branch which needed to be cut off.

In the business context, employment law is likely to be affected in a significant way. Article 8 may give workers the right to take time off to fulfil their family life. Electronic spying on employees is also likely to be contrary to Article 8. Article 9 might give workers the right to time off work to observe religious duties. Article 10 might prevent an employer from insisting on the wearing of a uniform or insisting on a dress code. There is no exemption from the Act for partnerships or companies. In some circumstances company directors are obliged by statute to cooperate fully with investigators, and this might breach Article 6. In 1996 the Court of Human Rights found that the rights of Ernest Saunders, who was convicted and imprisoned as a result of the Guinness fraud trial in 1990, had been breached because he was not given the right to silence. However, the Court did not award Saunders any compensation.

In Chapter 14 at 14.1.3.6 the decision of the House of Lords in *Wilson* v *First County Trust Ltd* [2003] UKHL 40 is set out in detail. In this important case the Court of Appeal had declared that to exclude a judicial remedy by virtue of s.127(3) of the Consumer Credit Act (CCA) 1974 was incompatible with the defendant's rights under Articles 6 and 1 of the First Protocol to the Convention. (Section 127(3) CCA 1974 rendered some improperly executed credit agreements unenforceable.) However, the House of Lords reversed this decision, holding that s.127(3) was not incompatible with Article 6. Parliament had decided that it was appropriate to render some improperly executed agreements completely unenforceable, even if this meant the unjust enrichment of a debtor at the expense of a creditor acting in good faith. Section 127(3) was a proportionate way to achieve this policy and so it was not incompatible with Article 6 or Article 1 of the First Protocol. The House of Lords thought that when deciding whether a statute was compatible with Convention rights, the court needed to find the policy objective of the legislation and decide whether the means of achieving the policy was proportionate to any adverse effects of the legislation.

Test your understanding

1 Which courts have the power to make a declaration of incompatibility? What is the effect of such a declaration?

2 Can new UK legislation be passed by parliament if it is incompatible with the Convention?

3 What is the position of public authorities under the Human Rights Act?

4 In what circumstances can an individual bring a case before the Court of Human Rights?

Answers

1 Any precedent-making court can make a declaration of incompatibility during legal proceedings. Such a declaration would be to the effect that UK legislation is incompatible with a Convention right. The relevant Minister may revoke or amend the legislation in question, but has the power to leave it unamended.

2 Parliament still has the power to pass legislation which is incompatible with the Convention. However, before the second reading of a Bill the relevant Minister will have to make a written statement saying whether or not the legislation is compatible or incompatible.

3 It is unlawful for public authorities to act in a way which is incompatible with a Convention right. (Unless this was unavoidable as a result of UK legislation.) Public authorities are defined so as to include any person certain of whose functions are of a public nature. Individuals are given the power to bring proceedings against public authorities which breach Convention rights.

4 An individual can only bring a case before the Court of Human Rights as a last resort. The complaint must involve a breach of the Convention by a country which has ratified the Convention. All domestic remedies must have been exhausted and the complaint must be brought within six months of these remedies having been exhausted.

Key points

General matters

■ Many of the features of the English legal system have their roots in mediaeval England.

■ English law has not been codified to a great extent.

■ The English system of trial is adversarial. The lawyers representing one party try to prove the case. The lawyers representing the other party use whatever means permissible to prevent the case from being proved.

■ Law which originated in the King's or Queen's courts is known as common law and is contrasted with law which originated in the courts of equity, which is known as equity.

■ Any court can now apply both common law and equitable principles.

■ The criminal law is designed to punish wrongdoers who have broken the criminal law. The civil law is designed to compensate those who have been caused loss or injury by the wrongdoing of another.

■ In criminal cases the prosecution must prove the accused's guilt beyond reasonable doubt. In civil cases the claimant must prove his case on a balance of probabilities.

■ It can be important to distinguish between law and fact for three reasons: only statements of law can become precedents; an appeal may only be possible against a question of law, or may be required to be made to a different court depending upon whether the appeal is against a finding of law or fact; and, in Crown Court trials the judge decides the law but the jury decide the facts.

Legislation

■ Bills are introduced into Parliament by the Government. (A very small number of bills are introduced by individual MPs.)

■ To become a statute, a Bill must pass through both Houses of Parliament and gain the Royal Assent. A Bill which does not pass through the House of Lords can be enacted without approval of the House of Lords after a delay of one year.

■ A codifying Act reduces the existing law to one comprehensive statute. A consolidating Act re-enacts as one Act several pieces of legislation which concern the same subject. An amending Act alters some of the sections of an existing Act.

■ Delegated legislation is passed other than as a statute. Once passed it has the same effect as a statute. Statutory instruments are introduced by Government Ministers upon whom power has been conferred by an enabling Act. Orders in Council are introduced by the Privy Council. Bye-laws are passed by local authorities.

■ The literal rule of statutory interpretation requires that unambiguous words in a statute are given their ordinary, literal meaning.

■ The golden rule allows the court to avoid giving the words in a statute a meaning which is manifestly absurd. It also allows a court to prefer the less absurd or undesirable interpretation when the words of a statute are ambiguous.

■ The mischief rule allows a court to be guided by consideration of the problem which the statute sought to rectify.

■ The *ejusdem generis* rule is that where general words in a statute follow specific words the general words must be interpreted as having the same type of meaning as the specific words.

■ The rule *expressio unius est exclusio alterius* means that where a statute lists specific words which are not followed by any general words then the statute applies only to the words listed.

■ In the very limited circumstances set out in *Pepper* v *Hart* a court may consider Parliamentary material when interpreting a statute.

Judicial precedent

■ The doctrine of judicial precedent holds that the decisions of higher-ranking courts are binding upon lower-ranking courts.

■ The courts are arranged in an hierarchical structure. The decisions of the House of Lords bind all inferior courts. Decisions of the Court of Appeal bind all inferior courts and, almost always, future sittings of the Court of Appeal. Decisions of the Divisional Court of the High Court bind other High Court judges sitting alone and all inferior courts. They also generally bind future sittings of the Divisional Court. Decisions of High Court judges sitting alone bind inferior courts but do not bind other High Court judges.

■ The binding element in a case is the *ratio decidendi*, which might be defined as any statement of law which the judge applied to the facts of the case and upon which the decision in the case is based.

■ Statements of law made by a judge which are not part of the *ratio decidendi* are known as *obiter dicta*. These are of persuasive authority only.

■ A statute or a higher court may overrule a decision, in which case the overruled decision ceases to operate as a precedent.

■ A decision is reversed when an appellate court allows an appeal. No rule of law is necessarily changed.

■ A judge can refuse to follow a precedent by distinguishing it, that is by saying that the facts of the case in front of him are materially different from the facts of the case which created the precedent.

The European Community

■ The United Kingdom became a member of the EC in 1973. The European Communities Act 1972 provided that Community law should be directly applicable in the UK courts.

■ The Council of the European Communities is the main policy-making body of the EC. Membership of the Council varies, being made up of relevant Ministers of the Member States.

■ Each Member State has one Commissioner and some of the larger States have two. (However, after the Treaty of Nice is fully effective, each Member State will have a maximum of one.) The Commission makes broad EC policy and drafts secondary legislation. It also ensures that Member States adhere to the Treaties.

■ The European Parliament does not pass legislation. It has a consultative role which is becoming increasingly powerful.

■ Treaty Articles and EC Regulations are directly applicable. This means that they automatically form part of the domestic law of Member States.

■ EC legislation can only be relied upon by an individual in a legal action if it has direct effect. It will only have direct effect if it satisfies the *Van Gend* criteria of being sufficiently clear, precise and unconditional.

■ EC legislation which has only direct vertical effect may only be invoked by an individual against the State or against an emanation of the State. Legislation which has direct horizontal effect may be invoked by one individual against another.

■ Before their implementation date, Directives have no effect (subject to the *Wallonie* principle). After their implementation date they can have direct vertical affect but not direct horizontal effect. This is only likely to be of importance where they are not properly implemented by UK legislation.

■ The European Court of Justice expresses authoritative opinions on EC law when requested to do so by the national courts of Member States.

The European Convention on Human Rights

■ The United Kingdom signed the European Convention on Human Rights in 1951.

■ The Human Rights Act 1998 incorporates the Convention into UK law, but preserves Parliamentary sovereignty.

■ When determining a question which has arisen in connection with a Convention right, a UK court must take into account any decisions of the European Court of Human Rights.

■ As far as it is possible to do so, UK legislation must be read and given effect in a way which is compatible with the Convention rights.

■ A precedent-making court can make a declaration that UK legislation is incompatible with a Convention right. The relevant Minister would then have to consider amending or revoking the UK legislation, but would have the power to leave the legislation in place.

■ New legislation requires positive consideration by the relevant Minister as to whether or not it is compatible with the Convention. However, the Government may still introduce legislation which is incompatible with the Convention.

■ A public authority may not act in a way which is incompatible with a Convention right. However, this is not the case if the public authority could not have acted differently on account of UK legislation. Individuals are given the power to sue public authorities which breach this duty.

■ The major rights set out in the Convention are: the right to have one's life preserved by law; the right not to be subject to torture or inhumane or degrading punishment; the right not to be held in slavery or servitude or required to perform forced or compulsory labour; the right to liberty and security of the person; the right to a fair trial; the right not to be made retrospectively guilty of a criminal offence; the right to respect for private and family life; the right to freedom of thought, conscience and religion; the rights to freedom of assembly and freedom of association with others; and, the right to marry a member of the opposite sex.

■ An individual can only bring a case before the Court of Human Rights after all domestic remedies have been exhausted.

■ Protocols have added that every natural or legal person is entitled to peaceful enjoyment of his possessions, that no-one should be denied the right to education, that States must agree to conduct free elections at regular intervals by secret ballot so as to allow the people to freely choose the legislature and that the death penalty is outlawed.

Summary questions

1 Explain the process by which a statute is enacted.

2 Using the newspapers or the Internet, find a recent statute, a recent statutory instrument and a recent rule of law made by a court. In each case, outline the process by which the law in question was made.

3 Explain the three main rules of statutory interpretation.

4 Outline the way in which the system of precedent operates. Do you think that the advantages of the system outweigh the disadvantages?

5 Explain the difference between EC law being directly applicable and its being directly effective.

6 Explain the impact of the Human Rights Act 1998 on UK law. Find a case concerning the Act in either a newspaper or on the Internet. Which articles of the Convention did the case concern? Describe the outcome of the case or, if it has not yet been decided, state what you think the outcome of the case might be.

Multiple choice questions

1 Which one of the following statements is not true?

  a Principles of law may still be classified as equitable, but both common law and equitable principles can now be applied by all courts.

  b Equitable remedies are discretionary and can be withheld from those who have acted inequitably.

  c In a criminal trial the prosecution must prove the accused's guilt beyond reasonable doubt. In a civil trial the claimant must prove his case on a balance of probabilities.

  d An act committed by a person cannot give rise to both civil and criminal liability.

2 Which one of the following statements is not true?

  a The power to pass a statutory instrument is conferred by an enabling Act.

  b Once properly passed, a statutory instrument can give a Minister the power to alter a statute without the need to pass an amending Act.

  c The courts have no power to declare either a statute or a statutory instrument void.

  d Some Acts of Parliament are introduced as Bills by individual MPs, rather than by the Government of the day.

3 Which one of the following statements is not true?

  a All deliberate statements of law made by the House of Lords when deciding a case will be binding upon all inferior courts.

  b The Court of Appeal is almost always bound by its own previous decisions.

  c The Decisions of the Divisional Court are binding on High Court judges sitting alone, but the decisions of High Court judges sitting alone are not binding upon other High Court judges.

  d Circuit judges do not make precedents.

  e A court which distinguishes a case refuses to follow an apparently binding precedent on the grounds that the facts of the case which created the precedent are materially different from the facts of the case it is considering.

4 Consider the following statements.

  i The European Parliament enacts EC legislation, but its power to do this is very much subject to the control of the European Commission and the European Council.

  ii EC legislation which is directly applicable in Member States cannot always be relied upon by an individual in a legal action.

  iii Whether EC legislation has direct vertical effect will depend upon whether it is sufficiently clear, precise and unconditional as to satisfy the *Van Gend* criteria.

  iv Regulations which are directly applicable will have only direct vertical effect, whereas Treaty Articles which are directly applicable will always have direct vertical and horizontal effect.

  v Only the House of Lords can refer a case to the European Court of Justice, which acts as a final court of appeal on issues of EC law.

Which of the above statements are true?

  a i, ii and iv only.

  b ii and iii only.

  c ii, iv and v only.

  d ii, iii and v only.

5 Which one of the following statements is not true?

  a The European Court of Human Rights is the highest court of the European Community.

b New legislation which is incompatible with a Convention right can still be passed by the UK Parliament.

c It is now possible for a person to sue a public authority for breach of a Convention right.

d Even if a precedent-making court makes a declaration of incompatibility, the relevant Minister will not need to ensure that the UK legislation is amended so as to become compatible with Convention rights.

Task 1

Your employer has asked you to draw up a report, briefly explaining the following matters:

a The different senses in which the expression 'common law' is used.

b How statutes and delegated legislation are passed.

c The main rules of statutory interpretation.

d The way in which the system of judicial precedent operates.

e The ways in which EC law is created and the effect of EC law in the UK.

f The effect of the Human Rights Act 1998.

Chapter 2

THE COURTS AND LEGAL PERSONNEL

Introduction

In this chapter we first consider the jurisdiction and composition of the civil and criminal courts. In Chapter 1 we saw that certain courts exist to resolve civil disputes whilst others hear criminal cases. In this chapter we consider the role and composition of the various courts in more detail.

We then consider civil procedure. As a result of the Woolf reforms coming into effect, civil procedure has changed significantly in the past two years. An understanding of the new procedure is essential to a business which is considering litigation. We also examine the various methods of alternative dispute resolution, by which businesses can resolve disputes without litigation. Criminal procedure is considered in outline only, as it is of much less significance in a business context.

We then briefly consider the personnel of the law, examining the various roles of the judiciary, magistrates, lawyers and juries. At the conclusion of this chapter the systems of law reporting and law reform are explained in outline.

2.1 · The civil courts

The civil courts are arranged in an hierarchical structure. If a civil dispute reaches the stage of litigation it will commence either in the county court or in the High Court. An appeal against the decision of the county court can be made to a High Court judge. An appeal against a decision of the High Court can be made to the Court of Appeal, and from there to the House of Lords. An outline of the structure of the civil courts is shown in Figure 2.1.

2.1.1 County courts

There are around 220 county courts in England and Wales, and at least one circuit judge and one district judge is assigned to each court. A business dispute is likely to involve a claim for breach of contract or a claim in tort. As regards both of these matters the county court has unlimited jurisdiction to hear the case. The High Court also has unlimited jurisdiction to hear contract and tort cases as long as the case involves a claim for a sufficiently large sum of money. However, if the claim includes a claim for personal injuries the claim must be for at least £50 000. The value of the action is the amount which the claimant reasonably expects to recover. In cases in which there is no claim for personal injuries, two prima facie rules apply in the allocation of cases between the county court and the High Court. First, that cases in which the claim is for less than £25 000 should be heard in the county court. Second, that cases in which the claim is for over £50 000 should be heard in the High Court.

Even where a claim is for a large enough sum of money to make litigation in the High Court a possibility, there is a presumption that a claim should be made in the county court rather than the High Court. This presumption might be rebutted on one of two main grounds. First, a claim might

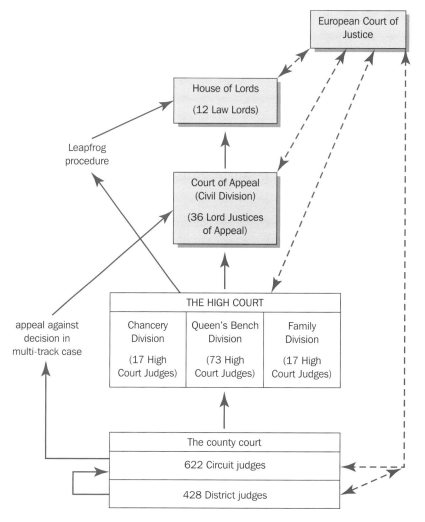

Figure 2.1   An outline of the structure of the civil courts

be brought in the High Court if the claimant believed that the case was sufficiently complex to warrant this. Second, the case might be brought in the High Court if the outcome of the case was of importance to the public in general. (This last reason reflects the fact that the decisions of the High Court can amount to binding judicial precedents, whereas decisions of the county court cannot. See Chapter 1 at 1.3.2.1.)

As well as jurisdiction in contract and tort cases, as described above, the county court can hear equity actions (such as those involving a trust or a will) where the value of the trust or estate is not more than £30 000. It hears claims for salvage which do not exceed £15 000, as well as certain divorce matters, and certain bankruptcy and insolvency matters. Claims to enforce regulated consumer credit agreements must be commenced in the county court.

Generally the district judge, who is junior to the circuit judge, will hear uncontested cases, as well as claims for mortgage repossessions and cases which are allocated to the small claims track. (Below at 2.3.1 we shall see that straightforward claims for not more than £5 000 are generally allocated to the small claims track.) The circuit judge hears the more complex claims and those in which the amount claimed is greater. If the amount claimed is over £15 000 the case should be heard by a circuit judge. If it is between £5 000 and £15 000 the case might be heard by either a district judge or a circuit judge. There are currently 622 circuit judges and 428 district judges. Appeals from a district judge are made to a circuit judge. Appeals from a circuit judge are to the High Court. However, in two exceptional circumstances an appeal from a circuit judge can be made to the Court of Appeal. First, where the appeal is a second appeal, that is to say where the decision of the circuit judge is on an appeal from a district judge. Second, where the decision is a final decision (that is to say a decision which determines the entire proceedings) on a multi-track case. (See below at 2.3.)

County court judgments are registered with the Registry of County Court Judgments and the register can be inspected by members of the public. A commercial creditor is likely to inspect it before making a loan. Once a county court judgment has been satisfied the judgment debtor's name will be removed from the register. If the judgment was satisfied within one month of judgment the entry on the register is cancelled altogether. If the judgment is satisfied later than one month after the date of judgment it can be noted as satisfied, but an entry will remain on the register. All entries are removed altogether six years after the date of judgment.

The county court does not have the responsibility of enforcing its judgment. It leaves this to the person in whose favour the judgment was given, the judgment creditor. However, the creditor can apply for oral examination of the judgment debtor in which case the debtor may be brought before the court to explain his financial position. Non-attendance is punishable by imprisonment.

County court judgments may be enforced in several ways. A warrant of execution against the debtor's goods allows bailiffs to take those goods, sell them and pay the judgment creditor out of the proceeds. The debtor can prevent this from happening by paying the amount due. A warrant of execution can generally be taken out without the court's permission, by filling in the appropriate form and paying the appropriate fee. Third party debt orders require a third party who owes money to the judgment debtor to pay the judgment creditor. These proceedings might be taken against an amount held in a bank account. An attachment of earnings order will require the judgment debtor's employer to make regular deductions from his earnings and pay these amounts into court. A charging order over land (including the debtor's house) can sometimes be made and in effect this gives the judgment creditor a mortgage over the judgment debtor's land. The creditor will then be entitled to be paid in preference to most other creditors when the land is sold, and may apply for an order that the land is sold. Despite all these methods of enforcement, many county court judgments are not satisfied. Winning the case is only half the battle. The other half is getting paid.

Judgment debtors have the right to apply for an administration order if their total indebtedness is less than £5 000. Under such an order a list of all the debtor's creditors is drawn up. This list shows the amount owing to each creditor and the debtor is ordered to pay the whole amount owing by instalments.

2.1.2 The High Court

The High Court is divided into three divisions: the Queen's Bench Division, the Chancery Division and the Family Division. Each Division hears different types of actions. The Family Division is, as the name suggests, concerned with family matters and is of little interest in a business context. The Chancery Division deals with matters which originated in equity, such as bankruptcy, mortgages, trusts, wills, company law and partnership law. It includes two specialist courts, the Companies Court and the Patents Court. The Companies Court deals with company liquidation. The Queen's Bench Division deals with contract and tort cases and includes three specialist courts, the Commercial Court, the Technology and Construction Court and the Admiralty Court. Despite these allocations, any of the three Divisions can transfer a case to another Division. The Commercial Court hears cases involving import and export of goods, banking, insurance and financial services and can hear any case arising out of trade or commerce in general. The Commercial Court has its own specialist procedures, which are set out in a practice direction and in the Commercial Court Guide. These procedures are less formal than those generally used in the High Court, the rules of evidence being somewhat less rigid. The Technology and Construction Court deals with specialist matters relating to building work, engineering work, professional negligence claims which are not made against the medical profession or lawyers, claims concerning computers and other cases which involve complex scientific or technical questions of fact.

Generally only one judge sits in a High Court case. Slightly junior judges, known as Masters, hear some of the less complex High Court cases. Appeals from the High Court go the Court of Appeal and from there to the House of Lords. As regards both appeals, permission must be gained. Appeals from a Master go first to a High Court judge and then to the Court of Appeal, although it is quite likely that permission for this second appeal will not be granted.

The High Court hears appeals from circuit judges in the county court. It also hears appeals from two criminal courts, the magistrates' court and the Crown Court. When these criminal appeals are heard they are heard by two or three High Court judges and these Courts are known as Divisional Courts. The Queen's Bench Divisional Court is of particular significance in relation to statutes which impose criminal liability on business, such as the Trade Descriptions Act 1968 and the Consumer Protection Act, Parts II and III. The Divisional Court hears appeals by way of case stated from the magistrates' court, tribunals or the Crown Court. An appeal by way of case stated can only be made against a decision of law made by the lower court. These appeals are generally made against decisions taken in the magistrates' court, but can be against decisions of the Crown Court if the case was one which was originally tried in the magistrates' court. The justices' clerk sends a draft case to the parties, and this may be amended after representations from the parties. The case states the facts of the case, the ruling given by the lower court and the question of law for the Divisional Court to consider. The Divisional Court can uphold the decision, reverse it, amend it or send it back to the lower court to make the decision which it thinks fit. The law made in this way is of greater value than the law made by ordinary High Courts. The decisions of ordinary sittings of the High Court are binding upon inferior courts, but not upon other High Courts. The decisions of the Divisional Court are binding upon other Divisional Courts, ordinary sittings of the High Court and inferior courts. The Chancery Divisional Court and the Family Divisional Court also hear appeals, but these are generally less significant in a business context.

We considered the jurisdiction of the High Court when considering the jurisdiction of the county court. There are currently 107 High Court judges, 73 of these sit in the Queen's Bench Division, 17 in the Chancery Division and 17 in the Family Division.

2.1.3 The Court of Appeal (Civil Division)

The Court of Appeal is split into two divisions: the Civil Division and the Criminal Division. The Court of Appeal (Civil Division) hears appeals from the High Court, but does not hear appeals from the Divisional Courts. Permission to appeal must be granted. Appeals from a Master in the High Court go first on appeal to a High Court judge and only then is there an appeal to the Court of Appeal.

A 'leapfrog' appeal can be made direct from the High Court to the House of Lords if all parties consent, and the House of Lords gives permission. In addition, the High Court judge must issue a certificate stating that the case involves an important point of law involving the interpretation of legislation or the case concerns a matter which has already been fully considered by the Court of Appeal or House of Lords. (In which case neither the High Court nor the Court of Appeal would have the power to refuse to follow the earlier decision.) There is also a new leapfrog procedure whereby any appeal to a circuit judge or a High Court judge, from a district judge or a Master, can be referred straight to the Court of Appeal. This can be done if the judge who was to hear the appeal, or the Master of the Rolls, considers that it raises an important point of principle or practice or that there is some other compelling reason why the Court of Appeal should hear it.

There are 36 Lords Justices of Appeal, as Court of Appeal judges are known. Usually three judges sit when an appeal is heard, although sometimes a full court of five judges is invoked. Different batches of three judges sit as the Court of Appeal at the same time. The Master of the Rolls presides over the Civil Division of the Court of Appeal.

2.1.4 The House of Lords

The House of Lords is the supreme appellate court in Great Britain and Northern Ireland. The court is staffed by 12 Lords of Appeal in Ordinary (Law Lords), five of whom sit to constitute the court. The House of Lords hears appeals from the Court of Appeal. Before such an appeal can be made leave to appeal is needed. The Court of Appeal hears such an application for leave to appeal and refers it to an Appeal Committee of three Law Lords. This Committee can allow the barrister representing the appellant to make an oral argument. In 2003, 107 appeals were presented to the House of Lords, 78 of these coming from the Civil Division of the Court of Appeal. The House of Lords also hears appeals from the Scottish Court of Session and, occasionally, from the High Court when the leapfrog procedure is invoked.

Appeals to the House of Lords are generally heard by five Law Lords. If the case is considered to be of particular importance seven judges may sit, as happened in *Pepper* v *Hart* which was considered in the previous chapter at 1.3.1.4. Although the barristers involved in the appeal wear wigs and gowns, the Law Lords wear ordinary suits rather than judicial robes. Typically, a case takes about two days to hear. The Law Lords always reserve their judgment, so they do not give a decision at the end of the case but at some later date. The individual judgments of the Law Lords are known as opinions. In the interests of clearly establishing a *ratio decidendi*, it is considered desirable that the Law Lords do not individually deliver judgments which are essentially similar but expressed in different ways. Often the Lords delegate the task of delivering the judgment to one of their number. Commonly one Law Lord delivers the decision of the majority, while the judge or judges in the minority deliver their opinions separately. Judgments of the House of Lords are published on the Internet at www.parliament.UK.

2.1.4.1 A new Supreme Court

In June 2003 the Government announced its intention to replace the House of Lords with a new Supreme Court which would be free from the second house of Parliament and which would remove the Lords of Appeal in Ordinary from the legislature. The motive is to increase the judiciary's independence from both the legislature and the executive. It is proposed that the new court will be the Supreme Court of all of the United Kingdom; England, Wales, Scotland and Northern Ireland. A consultation paper was issued by the Department of Constitutional Affairs in June 2003. It proposed that the existing members of the House of Lords should be the first members of the Supreme Court and that the most senior Law Lord would become the first President of the Court.

The primary purpose of the Supreme Court would be to give rulings on difficult points of law but it would not have the power to overturn legislation, as the US Supreme Court has. The consultation paper seeks views on the size of the Supreme Court and whether it should include part-time members, what the new members should be called and how to ensure that Scotland and Northern Ireland have proper representation. It also seeks views on how members should be appointed, envisaging that it might be appropriate for suitably qualified people to openly apply. The initial proposals are either that Ministers alone should make the appointments, after consultation with the senior judiciary, or that a recommending Judicial Appointments Commission should be set up. The members of this Commission would be appointed by the Lord Chancellor, after consultation with the Home Secretary.

The new proposed Supreme Court seems, likely to replace the House of Lords but it is not easy to predict precisely when this will happen. This is especially true as six current members of the House of Lords have gone on record as saying that the change will be expensive and unnecessary, a view echoed by several leading politicians.

2.1.5 **The Judicial Committee of the Privy Council**

The Judicial Committee of the Privy Council is the final court of appeal for 30 Commonwealth and ex-Commonwealth countries, including New Zealand and Jamaica. The origins of this court can be traced back to the Middle Ages, when the King would consult advisors known as the Privy Council. The Judicial Committee Act 1933 created the Judicial Committee of the Privy Council, as a court in which senior judges should hear legal appeals.

The Judicial Committee of the Privy Council is, in effect, made up of Law Lords. Five of these Law Lords sit in a case, sometimes accompanied by a judge from the country where the appeal originated. The judgment of the Council is usually delivered as one opinion. Prior to 1966 dissenting opinions were not allowed. It is still the case today that there will not be more than one dissenting opinion published, even if two of the Law Lords dissent. Although technically of persuasive value only, decisions of the Privy Council are generally treated as House of Lords decisions. The Privy Council heard 103 appeals in 2002.

The Privy Council also has jurisdiction to hear appeals concerning misconduct of doctors, dentists, opticians and vets.

2.1.6 **The European Court of Justice**

In the previous chapter, at 1.4.3.1, we saw that the ECJ can express an authoritative opinion on EC law, if requested to do so by a national court, and that once the ruling has been made by the ECJ the case returns to the court which asked for the ruling so that that court can apply the ruling. We saw that Article 234 of the EC Treaty allows a national court to request an authoritative ruling as to only three types of matters: the interpretation of the EC legislation; the validity and interpretation of acts of institutions of the Community; and the interpretation of statutes of bodies established by an act of the Council, where those statutes so provide. Any national court or tribunal may refer a matter within Article 234 to the ECJ if it thinks this necessary to give judgment. We also saw that a court of final appeal has an obligation to seek a preliminary ruling where a relevant point of EU law is at issue and where there has been no previous interpretation of the point by the ECJ. (Unless the point is so obvious as not to require a ruling.)

2.1.7 **Appeals**

The basic appeal structure is as follows.

From a district judge to a circuit judge and from there to the Court of Appeal. From a circuit judge to a High Court judge. (Unless the decision of the circuit judge was an appeal from a district judge or a final decision on a multi-track case, in which the appeal is to the Court of Appeal rather than to a High Court judge.) The Court of Appeal hears appeals from High Court judges (but not from Divisional Courts of the High Court) although it is possible for a 'leapfrog' appeal to be made direct to the House of Lords. The House of Lords hears appeals from the Court of Appeal. The Privy Council hears appeals from the highest courts in some 30 Commonwealth or ex-Commonwealth countries.

In all but a few exceptional cases, permission to appeal is required. Permission to appeal from a decision of either the county court or the High Court is usually sought orally from the lower court which made the decision or from the court to which an appeal would lie. If the lower court refuses permission, permission may be sought from the court to which the appeal would lie. When the appeal court refuses permission to appeal it gives reasons for the refusal. The appellant can then ask the same court for an oral hearing to reconsider this decision but this may be made to the same judge as refused the appeal. This is almost always the end of the matter. However, the court which heard the appeal has the power to allow a further appeal to the Court of Appeal if the appeal raises an important principle of law or procedure or if there is some other compelling reason for the Court of Appeal to hear it. In exceptional circumstances the Court of Appeal or the High Court, but not the county court, can re-open proceedings if three conditions are satisfied: first, that it is necessary to do this to avoid real injustice; second, the circumstances are exceptional and make it appropriate to re-open the appeal; third, no alternative effective remedy is available. The Court of Appeal hears applications to appeal to the House of Lords and refers them to an Appeals Committee of three Law Lords.

In all civil cases an appeal is allowed, and the decision of the lower court reversed, only where either the decision was wrong or where the decision was unjust because of a serious procedural or other irregularity in the lower court proceedings.

Generally, the appeal court reviews the case rather than rehears it.

2.2 · The criminal courts

Criminal trials are conducted in either the magistrates' court or the Crown Court. Criminal offences are classified into three bands, according to their seriousness. Offences triable only on indictment are the most serious offences, such as murder, and these can only be tried in the Crown Court. The most minor offences, such as the majority of motoring offences, are triable only summarily and must be heard by the magistrates' court. Other offences, such as theft, are 'either way' offences, and may be tried either in the magistrates' court or in the Crown Court. The magistrates will decide whether they think the case should be tried summarily by the magistrates' court or on indictment in the Crown Court. Generally, the magistrates will opt for summary trial unless the offence is so serious that the sentences which could be passed by the magistrates' court would not be sufficiently severe. If the magistrates decide upon summary trial they must then ask the accused whether or not he consents to this or whether he wishes to opt for jury trial. They must explain to the accused that if he opts for summary trial he may nevertheless be sent to the Crown Court for sentence if the accused's character and history are subsequently found to be such that a sentence greater than that which could be passed by the magistrates is justified.

An outline of the structure of the criminal courts is shown in Figures 2.2 and 2.3.

2.2.1 The magistrates' court

There are slightly more than 100 district judges (magistrates' court) and over 30,000 lay magistrates. The district judges (magistrates' courts) are full-time judges who used to be called stipendiary magistrates. Magistrates' courts dispose of over 97% of criminal cases. Lay magistrates are not legally qualified. They sit as a Bench, usually comprising three magistrates, whereas district judges (magistrates' courts) sit on their own. In a criminal case it is the job of the magistrates to decide the facts, that is to say whether the defendant is guilty or not guilty. If the defendant is guilty the magistrates also pass sentence upon him, although sometimes they commit him to the Crown Court for sentence. Lay magistrates should seek the advice of the clerk of the court, also known as a Justice's clerk, in order to ascertain matters of law, sentencing or procedure. Magistrates' clerks are lawyers who pursue a career as clerks. They may offer advice to the magistrates even when the magistrates have not sought it.

As well as hearing summary offences and most either way offences, magistrates' courts also have other duties. After a defendant's arrest they decide whether he should be given bail or remanded in custody. They conduct the committal proceedings if the defendant is to be committed to the Crown Court for trial. They have jurisdiction in some civil areas which affect children and families. They hear applications for various types of licences, such as liquor licences and also deal with some types of civil debts, such as arrears of council tax. The Crime and Disorder Act 1998 has recently empowered them to pass Anti Social Behaviour Orders against offenders aged 10 or over.

Magistrates may commit those summarily convicted of an either way offence to the Crown Court for sentence if they feel that a punishment which is greater than they can impose is warranted. Magistrates may impose a fine of up to £5 000 and may pass sentences of up to six months in prison in respect of any one offence. Where the offences are triable either way, magistrates can pass two consecutive six month sentences, so that the defendant is sentenced to a total of 12 months in prison.

Defendants have a right to appeal against conviction or sentence to the Crown Court but must be made aware that the Crown Court may increase the sentence passed by the magistrates, as long as this does not exceed the maximum sentence which the magistrates could have passed. If the appeal is against conviction, which is only possible if the defendant pleaded not guilty in the magistrates' court, the case is re-heard in the Crown Court. Such an appeal could be against the facts or the law. If the appeal is against sentence the prosecution generally outlines facts admitted or found by the magistrates, although a complete re-hearing of the case is possible. However, if the appeal concerns a point of law it may be made to the Divisional Court by way of case stated, which is explained below at 2.2.3.

2.2.2 The Crown Court

As explained earlier, the Crown Court conducts all trials of indictable offences and some trials where the crime was an either way offence. Generally, the Crown Court is staffed by a circuit judge, although sometimes a High Court judge sits. Offences range through four degrees of seriousness. Class 1 offences, such as murder, are almost always tried by a High Court judge. Class 2 offences, such as rape, are also generally tried by a High Court judge. Class 3 offences, such as causing death by dangerous driving, may be tried by either a High Court judge or by a circuit judge. Class 4 offences, such as grievous bodily harm or an either way offence, are tried by a circuit judge.

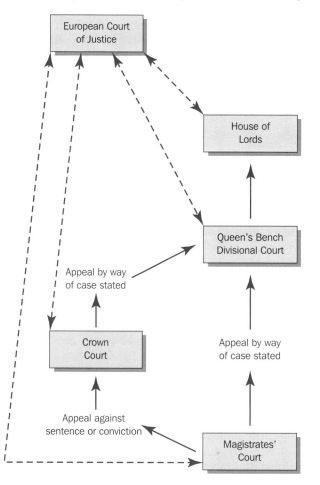

Figure 2.2   Structure of the criminal courts as regards summary offences

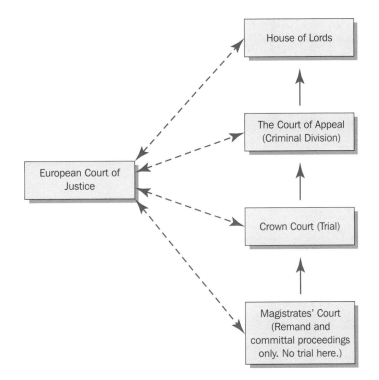

Figure 2.3 Structure of the criminal courts as regards indictable offences

The Crown Court may pass sentence on those summarily convicted of an either way offence if the magistrates commit to the Crown Court for sentence. Such a committal would generally be heard, like an appeal from the magistrates' court against sentence or conviction, by a circuit judge and two magistrates.

When a case is tried in the Crown Court the jury decide the facts, that is to say whether or not the defendant is guilty or not guilty. The judge sums up to the jury the matters which they should take into consideration in reaching their verdict. The judge also supervises the running of the trial, for instance deciding whether or not certain matters are admissible as evidence. If the defendant is found guilty, the judge passes sentence, although there is often a considerable delay while various reports are being made. Appeals against conviction or sentence are made to the Court of Appeal (Criminal Division).

2.2.3 The Divisional Court

The Queen's Bench Divisional Court hears appeals by way of case stated from the magistrates' court. It can also hear appeals by way of case stated from the Crown Court if the case was first tried in the magistrates' court and then appealed to the Crown Court. The appeal can only be on a point of law or on an argument that the magistrates exceeded their powers. Such cases are heard by two or more judges, at least one of whom will usually be the Lord Chief Justice or a Lord Justice of Appeal. If the prosecution appeals, the Divisional Court can order the magistrates' court to convict a defendant who was acquitted by the magistrates. Many cases heard by way of case stated become important precedents. This is particularly true where statutes such as the Trade Descriptions Act 1968 regulate business by making certain behaviour a criminal offence. An appeal from a Divisional Court goes to the House of Lords.

2.2.4 **The Court of Appeal (Criminal Division)**

The Criminal Division of the Court of Appeal is presided over by the Lord Chief Justice. This court hears appeals from the Crown Court, either against conviction or against sentence. Section 2 of the Criminal Appeal Act 1996 allows an appeal to the Court of Appeal (Criminal Division), against conviction in the Crown Court, on only three grounds: that the jury's verdict should be set aside as having been unsafe and unsatisfactory; that a wrong decision was taken as to a question of law; or that there was a material irregularity in the course of the trial. Appeals against acquittal can be made. These appeals might result in the law being amended, but will not mean that the defendant who was acquitted is subsequently convicted. When an appeal against sentence is made, the Court of Appeal may impose a greater sentence than that imposed by the Crown Court.

2.2.5 **The House of Lords**

The House of Lords hears appeals from the Court of Appeal (Criminal Division) and from the Queen's Bench Divisional Court. The Court of Appeal will need to certify that the case involves a point of law of general public importance. In addition, either the Court of Appeal or the House of Lords must grant permission for the appeal to be made on the grounds that it is a case which ought to be made to the House of Lords. The Privy Council's jurisdiction, explained above at 2.1.5, covers criminal appeals as well as civil appeals.

Test your understanding

1 In which two courts might a civil case be tried?

2 How will it be decided which of the two courts is the appropriate court to try the case?

3 From which courts does the Court of Appeal (Civil Division) hear appeals?

4 From which civil courts does the House of Lords hear appeals?

5 In which two courts might a criminal case be tried? How will it be decided in which court the case should be tried?

6 What is an appeal by way of case stated?

7 To which court is an appeal against conviction by the magistrates' court, or against the sentence imposed by the magistrates' court, made?

8 From which courts do the Court of Appeal (Criminal Division) and the House of Lords hear criminal appeals?

Answers

1 A civil case might be tried in either the county court or the High Court.

2 The county court has unlimited jurisdiction to hear contract and tort cases, as does the High Court, subject to the claim being for a large enough sum of money. If the claim is sufficiently large the claimant can issue his claim in either court. However, there is a presumption that the case will be heard in the county court, this presumption being rebuttable if the case is particularly complex or of particular importance to the general public.

3 The Court of Appeal (Civil Division) hears appeals from the High Court. It also hears appeals from the county court, but only if the appeal was against a final decision in a multi-track case or if it was itself an appeal from a district judge.

4 The House of Lords hears appeals from the Court of Appeal (Civil Division) and, very occasionally, from the High Court when the leapfrog procedure is invoked.

5 Criminal cases might be tried in either the magistrates' court or in the Crown Court. Summary offences are tried in the magistrates' court, as are the majority of either way offences. The Crown Court tries indictable offences and some either way offences.

6 The Queen's Bench Divisional Court can hear appeals by way of case stated from the magistrates' court or from the Crown Court if the case was appealed to the Crown Court from the magistrates' court. The appeal can only be made on a point of law or on the grounds of the magistrates having exceeded their powers.

7 The Crown Court hears appeals against conviction by the magistrates and against sentences imposed by the magistrates.

8 The Court of Appeal (Criminal Division) hears appeals from the Crown Court. The House of Lords hears appeals from the Court of Appeal (Criminal Division) and from the Queen's Bench Divisional Court.

2.3 · Procedure in the civil courts

In 1999 the Woolf reforms radically overhauled procedure in the civil courts. The reforms were brought about to give effect to the Woolf Report, which was produced by a committee chaired by Lord Woolf, the Master of the Rolls. This report found that the civil justice system was slow, expensive, bound by archaic procedures, excessively complicated and generally ill-suited to the needs of clients. These critical views were shared by a majority of those who had litigated in the courts. The adversarial culture of litigation meant that unnecessary delays and the deliberate running up of expenses were often used as a tactic to defeat the other side. In many types of disputes expensive expert witnesses were routinely produced by each side. Rather than helping the court to resolve a technical problem, these experts were seen as on the side of one or other of the parties and were subjected to partisan pressure by the other party's lawyers.

Lord Woolf's Report concluded that civil justice was in a state of crisis and therefore made recommendations for sweeping change. These changes have been brought about by the Civil Procedure Act 1997 and the Civil Procedure Rules 1998. The overriding objective of the new rules is to enable the court to deal with cases justly.

One of the main features of the reforms is that the management of the case is removed from the hands of the litigants and passes to the judge. Under this new system of judicial case management the judge will first determine which of the three new tracks the case is to be on; the small claims track, the fast track or the multi-track. The judge will also set time scales by which certain procedures must have been completed. The judge's active management of the case requires him to do the following things: encourage cooperation between the parties to the case; encourage the parties to settle the case or part of the case; identify the true points at issue as early as possible and ensure that issues which do not require litigation are disposed of before the case is tried; decide the order in which issues will be resolved; consider whether the taking of any step is justified by the costs which this would involve; and to ensure that the case proceeds quickly and efficiently. Technology should be used wherever appropriate. As many aspects of the case as possible should be dealt with on the same occasion and the case may be dealt with without the parties having to attend court. If the case is to reach court, the judge sets out timetables for the hearing and supervises the control of the case. The courts have the power to decide the issues on which evidence will be allowed. They also have the power to decide the nature of evidence which is to be allowed and the way in which the evidence may be presented.

The judges have been trained to become unsympathetic to the old style of litigation. The court can ask a party to clarify a matter or provide additional information about it. It can shorten the time by which procedures must be completed. The time limits set by the court are rules not targets. In appropriate circumstances the judge can also increase time limits. The judge can identify preliminary issues which should be tried first and can dismiss a case or give judgment as soon as a certain preliminary issue has been decided. In many cases the parties will themselves settle the case after one preliminary issue has been decided.

Orders made by the court may be subject to conditions, such as the payment of money into court. If these conditions are not complied with the party in default may have his case struck out. Claims and defences which have no reasonable chance of success can be struck out. They can also be struck out if either a rule, a practice direction or a court order has not been complied with. Lesser sanctions are also available to the court. It may order a party in default to pay all or part of the costs of the case, refuse to allow interest on damages where the claimant is at fault, or order that interest is paid at a higher rate where the defendant is at fault. Procedural errors are not to invalidate any part of the proceedings unless the court exercises its discretion to order that they should. Furthermore, accidental errors or omissions can be corrected at any time and the court may do this on its own initiative.

The parties to a dispute are now actively encouraged to consider alternative dispute resolution (ADR). Moreover, the judge not only encourages the parties to seek ADR, but may also stay (suspend) the proceedings so that the parties can try to resolve their dispute by an alternative method. We examine the various methods of ADR below at 2.4.

As regards claims for clinical negligence and personal injury, two new pre-action protocols have been drawn up. These protocols require that at the start the parties should identify three matters: the issues in dispute, the evidence available and how the disputed points should be resolved. The idea is that litigation is to be a last resort. A party who does not follow the letter and spirit of the protocols can be subject to a sanction – even in a kind of case (such as breach of contract) where there is not (yet) a protocol.

Perhaps the most significant of the new reforms is that cases will be allocated to one of the three tracks. Earlier we considered the jurisdiction of the county court and the High Court. The High Court only takes multi-track cases. The county court takes all fast track cases and small claims, as well as some multi-track cases. A claim which is being defended will be allocated by the court to either the small claims track, the fast track or the multi-track. Generally, this allocation will be made by a Master or a district judge on the basis of a questionnaire completed by the parties. Each of the three tracks needs to be considered in turn. Before considering them, however, it is worth stressing the point that litigation should always be a last resort for any business. It is expensive, time consuming, uncertain and very likely to destroy any business relationship which exists with the other party.

Making a claim

Once it has become apparent that a business dispute is not going to be resolved informally, one of the parties may initiate legal proceedings by issuing a claim against the other. First, a final letter should be sent to the other party, warning that a claim will be made if a satisfactory response to the claimant's demands is not received by a certain date. A claim is commenced by filling in a claim form. This is done whether the amount of money claimed is specified or unspecified and whether the claim is for a court order rather than for money. The form will require the claimant to state the value of the amount claimed. The particulars of the claim can either be attached to the claim itself or can be served on the defendant separately. These particulars set out a concise statement of the facts upon which the claimant is relying, and a statement of truth that the claimant believes the facts to be true. It is advisable for the claimant to state the remedy which he is seeking but it is not absolutely necessary to do this as the court may award a successful claimant any remedy to which he would be entitled.

The claim, the particulars and a response pack are served on the defendant, who must generally respond within 14 days or judgment can be given against him. If the defendant does respond, the response might take several forms. First, the defendant might pay the claim in full. Second, the defendant might file an acknowledgement of service if he cannot file a defence within 14 days or wants to dispute the court's jurisdiction to hear the case. The filing of an acknowledgement of service will give the defendant another 14 days in which to respond. Third, the defendant might admit some or all of the claim. If the admission is only partial he will also file a defence. If the claim is for an unspecified amount of money the defendant might offer a certain sum in satisfaction of the claim and might offer to pay this amount by instalments. Where a claim is admitted but the claimant does not accept the amount offered, or the rate at which this amount is to be paid, the claimant may nevertheless ask that judgment is entered in his favour. If this is done, the court will determine the amount of damages at a later hearing. Fourth, the defendant might file a defence. A defence must be specific as to the reason why specific allegations are denied, which allegations the claimant will have to prove, which allegations are admitted and any reason for disputing the value of the claim. The defendant might also make a counter claim against the claimant, either as part of a defence or while admitting the claim.

The responses which the defendant might make, and the effect of these responses, is shown in Figure 2.4. Once a claim has been filed the court moves on to the process of allocating the claim to one of the three tracks.

2.3.1 The small claims track

Cases other than personal injury cases are likely to be allocated to the small claims track if they satisfy three criteria. First, they must be straightforward claims for not more than £5 000. (This amount can be greater if both parties agree to allocation to the small claims track.) Second, the case should not involve a substantial amount of preparation before the hearing. Third, the case should not be one where large legal costs will be incurred.

The third requirement reflects the fact the small claims procedure has been designed so that the parties have the option of conducting their own case without legal representation. However, litigants on the small claims track can be represented by lawyers if they so wish.

Special rules apply to personal injury cases and to landlord and tenant disputes. Personal injury cases will only be allocated to the small claims track where the total amount of the claim is not more than £5 000 and the claim for general damages for personal injuries is not more than £1 000. Claims concerning landlord and tenant are of little significance for the purposes of this book. In broad terms, an allocation will only be made to the small claims track where the tenant is claiming damages of not more than £1 000 or where he is asking that the landlord be ordered to complete repairs which will cost not more than £1 000.

Generally, a small claims case will involve only one hearing in front of a district judge. The parties will be required to file and serve copies of all relevant documents, including any expert's report. However, expert evidence cannot be admitted in a small claim hearing unless the court consents and such consent would not usually be granted. The originals of documents must be brought to the hearing. The judge can hold a preliminary hearing, although this is discouraged. A preliminary hearing might be used to clarify a claim or to dispose of a claim which has no real chance of success. On rare occasions, the judge may decide the case by a 'paper disposal', without any hearing at all.

The district judge has considerable leeway as to the proceedings at the hearing. The hearing is informal and the strict rules of evidence do not apply. The judge will probably appoint each side the same amount of time to present their evidence and give an immediate decision at the conclusion of the case.

Generally each side will pay its own costs. The only costs recoverable will usually be the costs involved in issuing the claim. However, the district judge has a discretion to allow costs for travelling expenses, loss of earnings and an expert's fee. The amount of costs for the expert's fee cannot exceed £200 (and the emphasis is very strongly against experts appearing in small claims hearings) and the amount of costs for lost earnings cannot exceed £50 per day. If a party behaves unreasonably the court can penalise him by ordering him to pay costs.

Appeals against small claims decisions can be made to a circuit judge, but such appeals are most unusual. The appeal cannot be made on fact, but only on the grounds that there was a mistake of law or a serious irregularity in the way in which the case was conducted. Where an appeal is made, the circuit judge will give a decision and will not order a rehearing of the case.

2.3.2 The fast track

Cases other than landlord and tenant cases, or claims which include a claim for personal injury, will generally be allocated to the fast track if the claim is for not more than £15 000 and there is not a substantial amount of pre-hearing preparation. However, these cases will not be allocated to the fast track if they are expected to last for longer than one day or if there is likely to be a substantial amount of oral expert evidence at the trial. We saw earlier that a claim of not more than £5 000 is not allocated to the small claims track if it involves a claim for personal injuries of over £1 000. Such cases are

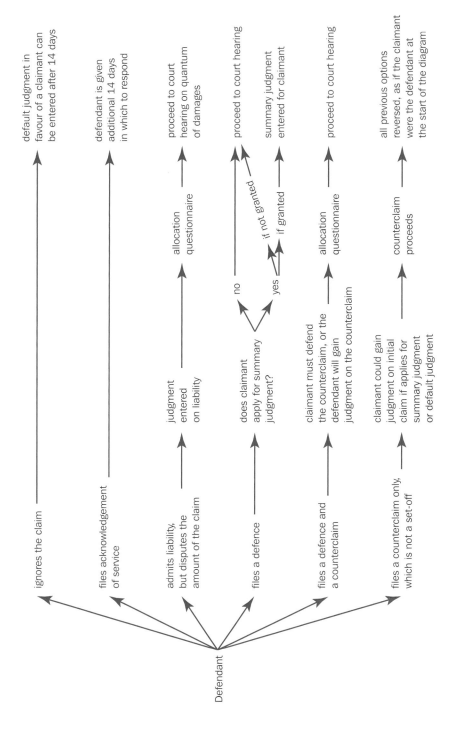

Figure 2.4 An outline of the effect of the defendant's responses to a claim which has been served

allocated to the fast track. We also saw that some claims for less than £1 000 by a tenant against a land-lord were not allocated to the small claims track. These too are allocated to the fast track.

It is expected that a fast track case will be completed 30 weeks after allocation. Upon allocation to the fast track the court will set out a timetable for matters such as disclosing documents, exchanging witness statements and expert's reports, the sending of listing questionnaires by the courts so that the date and length of the trial can be fixed, the completing of these questionnaires and the hearing itself. Financial penalties can be imposed on parties who do not adhere to the timetable. Postponement of the trial is a possibility, but is very much a last resort.

A one day fast-track trial actually runs for five hours. The judge will begin with a certain amount of reading time and then brief opening speeches will be made by the lawyers. The majority of the time, perhaps about three hours, will be for examination of witnesses by the two sides. Both the defendant and the claimant will make closing submissions to the judge, who will prepare and deliver judgment and assess the costs.

If extensive oral expert evidence is needed, a case is not suitable for the fast track. In a fast track trial each party can be allowed one expert per issue, with a maximum of two issues. However, the court will appoint an independent expert, instructed jointly by both parties, wherever possible and will strive to cut down on expert evidence. Generally, expert evidence would be found in written reports rather than given orally at the trial.

2.3.3 The multi-track

Claims which are not suitable for the small claims track or the fast track are allocated to the multi-track. This usually means cases where the amount claimed is substantially over £15 000, or cases which are likely to take more than one day in court or in which there will be substantial expert evidence. In addition, a claim will be allocated to the multi-track where the court is likely to have to decide a substantial question of fact. A multi-track case is heard either by a circuit judge or a High Court judge.

As the name suggests, the multi-track allows the court considerable flexibility in dealing with the claim. The case will be judicially managed but there is no standard procedure. Whereas a fast-track case is likely, but not certain, to follow a pre-arranged procedure, multi-track cases adopt the pro-cedure to meet the needs of the case. A party may indicate in the allocation questionnaire that he thinks that it will be necessary to have a case management conference, which is similar to an ordinary business meeting. At such a conference a judge, usually a Master or a district judge, will try to identify the issues in dispute. The lawyers attending the meeting must be familiar with the case. They must also have the authority to deal with matters which arise. The court has the power to order the clients to attend. We have already seen that case management would, among other things, encourage the parties to co-operate with each other in the conduct of the proceedings, fix timetables for the case and give directions to ensure the speedy and efficient progress of the trial. The claimant may be asked to provide a case summary, which should generally not be of more than 500 words and which the defendant can be asked to agree to. The summary might set out the issues of fact which are agreed, the issues of fact which are in dispute, and the evidence which will be needed in order to ascertain the facts.

The judge can alter the standard rules on disclosure of documents so as to fit the needs of the par-ticular case. The judge will also determine the extent to which experts are needed. In many multi-track cases it would not be appropriate to insist upon one expert appointed by both sides.

If the case involves complex issues the court may order a pre-trial review. This would usually take place about one or two months before the trial and would be presided over by the trial judge. This review would consider whether any preliminary issues could be sorted out, and then analyse how the trial should run. The order in which issues are to be decided should be set out. Information technology requirements should be set out, as well as the order of witnesses and the way in which the trial docu-ments will be organised. The clients should attend, along with the lawyers who will argue the case.

After the trial itself, the judge may either deliver the judgment, or may reserve judgment until a later date. The assessment of costs will be made after the judgment is given. An appeal from a decided multi-track case goes to the Court of Appeal, whether the case was heard by a circuit judge or a High Court judge.

2.3.4 Funding of litigation

The costs of legal representation are generally not recoverable in respect of a claim made on the small claims track. As from April 2000, legal aid became unavailable for most personal injury claims, having been replaced by a 'no win, no fee' scheme. The idea of the scheme is that the insurance industry will fund litigation and it is hoped that this will make litigation available to all people. Previously there was a well-founded criticism that litigation was only an option available to the very rich or to those who were sufficiently needy to qualify for legal aid.

'No win, no fee' systems had existed in personal injury claims since 1998, but before the 2000 reforms the system had several inadequacies. A party did not have to pay his solicitor if he did not win the case, but would have to pay an increased fee, which might be up to double the usual fee, if he won the case. This premium came out of the damages awarded. A party who won and therefore had to pay his lawyer an increased fee, would hope to recover some or all of the cost of this from the other party.

It is now envisaged that both sides will take out insurance to cover the legal costs of the other side, should they lose the case. Damages awarded to the winner will therefore be received in full, as the loser's insurance will include payment of the winning lawyer's 'success fee'. Insurers will set up panels of solicitors who can take on cases which the insurers fund. Critics of the new system fear that it will cause an explosion in personal injury litigation. However, the fact that the insurers have to be satisfied that a prospective litigant has a viable case is likely to avoid this. Insurance companies do not like to back losers.

Legal aid remains available for some other types of actions, but not for the following matters:

- disputes concerning personal injuries other than clinical negligence;
- conveyancing and boundary disputes;
- the making of wills;
- matters of trusts law;
- actions for defamation and malicious falsehood;
- death or damage to property;
- matters of company and partnership law; and
- other matters arising out of the carrying on of a business.

2.4 · Alternative dispute resolution

Litigation should always be a last resort for a business. The disadvantages are manifest. The first and most obvious problem is that the whole process is likely to prove costly. If the case is lost, the loser will have to pay not only his own legal costs but also the costs of the other party. Even if the case is won full legal costs are not always recovered. Costs incurred in attending court as a witness are recoverable, but costs in respect of time spent instructing a solicitor are not. There is also the danger, particularly when the case concerns securing the payment of a debt, that the other side will become insolvent. It is bad enough that even though the case is won the bill is not paid. It is worse still that legal costs have been incurred and these too are not recoverable. In such circumstances it will generally be much better to compromise and get paid something.

A second problem is that litigation is complex. Despite the new rules of procedure the litigants may not always be fully aware of how the case is proceeding. Litigating is also a major worry and the stress involved can mean there are risks to health as well as financial risks. Nor is litigation speedy.

It may be quicker than it was before the recent reforms, but a fast track case will only be resolved some six months after allocation and a multi-track is likely to take considerably longer.

A third problem is that litigation creates lasting ill-feeling. If a business sues a customer then, win or lose, this is likely to be the end of the business relationship. If the dispute can be settled amicably the parties may continue to do business with each other.

Yet another disadvantage is that litigation takes place in open court. A typical case might involve a claim for the price of goods, where the buyer alleges that the goods were not of satisfactory quality. The seller will not want the allegations to be aired in open court. Nor will the buyer want it to be publicly claimed that he does not pay his bills. Alternative dispute resolution can avoid this bad publicity.

Before considering arbitration, mediation and conciliation, it should be realised that the vast majority of disputes are settled by the parties themselves. Generally, there will be an exchange of correspondence and, perhaps after a period of negotiation, the claimant will agree to withdraw the action in return for the defendant paying a sum of money or agreeing to other conditions.

2.4.1 Arbitration

When the parties to a dispute agree to refer the dispute to arbitration they agree that their dispute should be resolved by an arbitrator rather than by a court. Having made such an agreement the parties are stuck with it. In commercial disputes arbitration may be very similar to litigation, especially if the arbitrator is a judge or a Master from the Commercial Court. The rules of procedure may be very similar to those of the High Court and the lawyers representing the parties may be required to act much as they would in the High Court. All of this means that the proceedings might not be much cheaper than litigation, if it is cheaper at all. The big advantage is that the case would be resolved in private. The procedure might also be speedier than litigation.

The Arbitration Act 1996 was needed because prior to the Act coming into effect three separate Arbitration Acts, the 1950, 1975 and 1979 Acts were all in force and it was extremely difficult to know exactly what the law on arbitration was. Arbitrators were also very prone to a challenge by one of the parties, which would bar them from hearing the case. This was particularly the case where they tried to settle the case in a proactive way. Consequently, the High Court rules of procedure and evidence tended to be followed slavishly to prevent a challenge. Challenges to an arbitrator's jurisdiction to hear the case were an extremely common delaying tactic. The arbitrator could not decide upon his own jurisdiction and so a lengthy referral to a court was necessary.

The new Act has mandatory sections and non-mandatory sections, out of which the parties may contract.

Section 1 of the Arbitration Act 1996 provides that:

'The provisions of this Part are founded on the following principles and shall be construed accordingly–
(a) the object of arbitration is to obtain a fair resolution of disputes by an impartial tribunal without unnecessary delay or expense;
(b) the parties should be free to agree how their disputes are resolved, subject only to such safeguards as are necessary in the public interest;
(c) in matters governed by this Part the court should not intervene except as provided by this Part.'

Section 33(a) requires that the arbitrator should act fairly and impartially as between the parties, giving each party a reasonable opportunity of putting his case and dealing with that of the opponent. Section 33(b) makes it plain that the arbitrator has no need to follow High Court procedures. It requires that the arbitration adopts procedures suitable to the circumstances of the particular case, avoiding unnecessary delay or expense, so as to provide a fair means for the resolution of the matters falling to be determined. Section 33 is mandatory, but s.34, which is non-mandatory, allows the arbitrator to decide all procedural and evidential matters.

There are now fewer challenges to the arbitrator's jurisdiction and unjustified challenges are not dealt with sympathetically. Section 34, a non-mandatory section, allows the arbitrator to decide upon his own jurisdiction to hear the case. Section 34 also allows the arbitrator to use an inquisitorial approach to deciding the facts and the law.

A mandatory section, s.44, requires that the parties shall do all things necessary for the proper and expeditious conduct of the arbitral proceedings. This includes complying without delay with procedural and evidential matters and, where it is necessary to gain a preliminary judgment of a question of law from a court, getting such a judgment without delay.

Section 9 allows a party to apply for a stay of the proceedings if the other party brings court proceedings in respect of a matter which it has been agreed should be resolved by arbitration. The court will grant a stay unless satisfied that the arbitration agreement is null and void, inoperative or incapable of being performed.

Section 65, which is non-mandatory, allows the arbitrator to determine that the costs of the proceedings should be limited to a certain amount.

An agreement may be referred to arbitration either by the court, or by an Act of Parliament, or by the parties themselves. The parties may refer the dispute to arbitration by a term of a contract which is in dispute, or by agreement once a dispute has arisen. A court may refer one specific point to arbitration or may refer the whole case, if the parties agree to this or if the case will involve lengthy examination of scientific documents. Several Acts of Parliament refer disputes to arbitration. Legal aid is not available in respect of arbitration proceedings. This may prove a considerable hindrance to those of limited means.

2.4.2 Mediation

As regards litigation and arbitration the dispute is resolved for the parties by an independent body. Mediation is different, in that the parties themselves agree to any resolution of the dispute. The mediator's role is to try and facilitate such an agreement. There are no fixed rules as to how mediation might operate. Generally, however, the parties would first present an outline of their case to each other, in the presence of the mediator and reply to the other party's case. The mediator will set out the rules, trying to keep matters simple and striving to identify the key issues in dispute. Then the two sides will probably repair to different rooms and the mediator will spend time with one group, before passing on the position of that party to the other party. A large number of such visits might need to be made and ideally the parties should move closer to agreement until they finally agree to settle. If the mediator is a solicitor a Law Society Code in the Professional Conduct Book can be adopted. It is not always the case that those taking part in mediation are genuinely attempting to settle the case. They might merely be trying to find out the strengths and weaknesses of the other party's case. Mediators report that many disputes which are not settled during the mediation are settled shortly afterwards. The Court of Appeal and the Commercial Court both have mediation schemes and Court Annexed Mediation Schemes are available in London and five provincial cities.

2.4.3 Conciliation

Conciliation is similar to mediation except that the conciliator actually suggests a basis for settlement to the parties. In Chapter 19 we shall see that ACAS attempts to conciliate between the parties before an employment dispute is taken to an employment tribunal.

Both mediation and conciliation suffer from the problem that they may well prove futile in that no settlement will be reached or become any closer.

2.4.4 Other types of ADR

Other types of ADR include: Neutral Evaluation by a third party who gives a non-binding view of the case; Expert Determination, which allows an independent expert to decide an issue; Neutral Fact Finding, whereby a neutral expert comes to a non-binding decision on a complex, technical issue of fact; and Med-AB, which is a combination of mediation and arbitration – first the parties mediate but if this is not successful they take the dispute to arbitration.

2.4.5 Tribunals

Various Acts of Parliament have established tribunals to hear certain types of cases. These tribunals hear very many more cases than are heard by the county court or the High Court. Tribunals might exercise administrative or judicial functions. Those exercising a judicial function act in the same way as a court.

It is not possible to take a dispute to a tribunal unless the dispute concerns the particular type of matter with which the tribunal deals. If the dispute does concern such a matter then a dispute cannot be taken before the ordinary courts, but must be dealt with by the relevant tribunal. The matters with which the major tribunals deal can be deduced from their names. The major tribunals are:

- Employment Appeal Tribunal (an Agency of the Department of Trade and Industry);
- Finance and Tax Tribunals;
- Immigration Appellate Authority;
- Immigration Services Tribunal;
- Lands Tribunal;
- Pensions Appeal Tribunals;
- Review of Tribunals;
- The General Commissioners of Income Tax (Tax Appeal Tribunal);
- The Social Security Commissioners and Child Support Commissioners;
- Transport Tribunal.

In the study of business law the tribunals of real significance are the employment tribunals and the Employment Appeal Tribunal. The nature of these tribunals is explained in Chapter 20. The procedure used in an employment tribunal is examined in Chapter 21 at 21.15.

Typically a tribunal will consist of three members, one of whom, the chairman, will be legally qualified. The two lay members will have some expert knowledge of the area of law with which the tribunal deals and the chairman will tend to specialise in that area of law. For example, in the employment tribunal the two lay members would typically be nominated by a trade union official and by an employer's association, and the chairman would be a lawyer who specialises in employment law.

Several advantages are claimed for tribunals. First, cases can be brought before a tribunal on a certain date and the waiting time for the case to begin is likely to be much shorter than it would be for a court case. Second, the costs in tribunals are likely to be much lower than court costs, as the parties can represent themselves. There are often no court fees and the losers usually do not have to pay the costs of the winner. Third, the proceedings are informal and this allows the parties to express themselves personally or to get a lay person who they feel really understands their case, such as a trade union official, to present the case. Fourth, tribunal members have technical expertise of a practical nature and can bring this to bear on the case. Fifth, it is possible that in certain circumstances a tribunal might sit in private.

These advantages must be viewed in the light of certain disadvantages. First, the lack of court procedure and, perhaps, of legal representation might mean that the high standards of justice which one would expect in court proceedings are not found in tribunal proceedings. Second, an appeal from a tribunal can sometimes be made to another tribunal or to a Minister, rather than to a court of law. Third, the lack of legal aid may mean that some claimants cannot find anyone to represent them effectively.

Tribunals are controlled by the courts and by the Council on Tribunals. A claim of judicial review may be brought before the High Court, arguing that a tribunal has exceeded its powers or has not adhered to the rules of natural justice. The courts also have the power to reverse the decisions of tribunals which did not correctly apply the law. The Council on Tribunals supervises tribunals generally and publishes an annual review in which criticism of tribunals can be made.

Test your understanding

1 What is the overriding objective of the changes made by the Civil Procedure Act 1997 and the Civil Procedure Rules 1998?

2 To what three tracks might a case be allocated? Who makes this allocation?

3 What are the alternatives open to a defendant upon whom particulars of claim have been served?

4 How does the 'no win, no fee' scheme help to fund personal injury cases?

5 What are the main disadvantages of litigation perceived to be?

6 What is arbitration?

7 What are mediation and conciliation?

8 What is a tribunal?

Answers

1 The overriding objective of both the Act and the Procedure Rules is that the courts should be enabled to deal with cases justly.

2 A case might be allocated to the small claims track, to the fast track or to the multi-track. This allocation will be done by a Master or a district judge, who will take into account the size of the claim, the complexity of the case and the amount of expert evidence which may be needed.

3 The defendant may ignore the claim (and thereby lose the case); admit the claim in full; admit part of the claim; admit the claim but dispute the amount claimed; gain an extra 14 days by filing an acknowledgement of service; or file a defence and/or a counterclaim.

4 The scheme means that a party will not be liable to pay his lawyer if he does not win the case. However, the loser is likely to have to pay the costs of the successful party and should insure against such a possibility.

5 Litigation has the disadvantages of being costly, lengthy, complex, stressful, likely to destroy any business relationship with the other party and conducted in public.

6 Arbitration is the process in which disputes are resolved by an arbitrator rather than by a court. A dispute may be referred to arbitration by the parties themselves, by a term of a contract between the parties, by a court or by an Act of Parliament.

7 Mediation and conciliation do not involve a third party having the power to resolve a dispute. Mediation allows a third party to communicate between the parties, in an attempt to get them to agree to a resolution. Conciliation envisages that a third party will suggest the basis on which a dispute might be resolved.

8 A tribunal is a body which, although technically not a court, acts as a court to resolve certain types of disputes within its ambit. Generally, a tribunal is made up of a legally qualified chairman and two lay members who have expert knowledge of the appropriate field.

2.5 · The legal profession

Unlike other European countries, England has two different types of lawyers – barristers and solicitors. There are currently about 11 000 practising barristers, about 3 000 of whom are women, and it is their main job to argue cases in court. However, the role of the practising barrister is much wider than merely acting as an advocate. Barristers spend a considerable amount of time giving written opinions, in which they state what they consider the law to be. They also draft statements of case, the formal documents which the parties must exchange before a case is heard in court. Barristers tend to specialise either in criminal law or in a particular branch of civil law. They have rights of audience in all civil and criminal courts. Until 1990 barristers had an exclusive right to be heard in senior courts, but now solicitors may also have rights in such courts.

About 1150 barristers are known as Queen's Counsel. These senior barristers generally appear in court with a junior barrister assisting them. They are appointed by the Queen, on the advice of the Lord Chancellor. Queen's Counsel, or QCs as they are usually known, can charge higher fees than other barristers, in recognition of their expertise. Currently only about 6% of QCs are women. In July 2003 the Department of Constitutional Affairs issued a Consultation Paper asking whether the system of Queen's Counsel should be abolished. It seems quite likely that it will be abolished in the near future.

Barristers are not allowed to form partnerships. Instead, they operate from chambers, which are offices where several barristers are allocated work by a barrister's clerk, who also negotiates the barrister's fees. A barrister can only be hired by a solicitor and can only meet the client he represents if the client's solicitor is also present. This prevents impropriety and should also mean that the barrister keeps an objective view of the case. Under the 'cab rank' rule a barrister, like a taxi, is supposed to provide his services to any client. Theoretically therefore, any barrister is available to any client whose solicitor asks that the barrister should be engaged. This is not always true as some barristers fees are beyond the means of many clients and because barrister's clerks, who arrange what cases a barrister can take, are skilled at deflecting unwanted cases. It often happens that when a particular barrister has been engaged he is not available when the case starts because another case in which he is appearing has not finished in time. The client is then allocated a different barrister. Many barristers do not practise, but work in industry or commerce or for local government or the Civil Service.

Barristers must wear wigs and gowns in court, or the judge cannot 'see' or 'hear' them. This, like many other aspects of the Bar, seems somewhat out of date. (It is still part of a barrister's training that he should eat a certain number of dinners at one of the four Inns of Court in London.) In May 2003, the Lord Chancellor's Department (now the Department of Constitutional Affairs) issued a working paper seeking views on whether the clothes which barristers and judges wear in court should be made less formal. Complaints against barristers can be made to a Professional Complaints and Conduct Committee. In addition, the General Council of the Bar could debar a barrister who was guilty of serious professional misconduct and could thereby prevent him from practising.

There are about 100 000 solicitors, about three-quarters of whom hold a practising certificate. About 35% of solicitors are women, a percentage which is increasing annually. Solicitors are the first point of contact for a client with a legal problem. Unlike barristers, solicitors can form partnerships and some of the partnerships are very large.

A solicitor in a one-person business should have a good idea of most areas of law and should know where more information could be found if needed. In the larger firms solicitors would tend to specialise in one particular area of law. Solicitors routinely give their clients legal advice, enter into correspondence on their behalf, draft wills and draw up documents which transfer ownership of land.

Until 1990, solicitors were only allowed to argue cases in the magistrates' court and the county court. Now the barrister's monopoly right to appear in the Crown Court and appellate courts has been removed by statute, and solicitors who have gained the necessary advocacy qualifications can represent clients in any court. About 1 800 have this right and seven have become QCs. However, barristers still perform the vast bulk of advocacy work in these courts. Whereas solicitors have gained rights of audience since 1990, they have lost their monopoly rights to perform conveyancing and to obtain grants of probate. The Administration of Justice Act 1985 allowed licensed conveyancers to practise. It was widely predicted that this would be disastrous for many small firms of solicitors, but this does not seem to have been the case.

In explaining the different roles of the two branches of the legal profession, an analogy is sometimes made with the medical profession. Solicitors, it is said, are like family doctors. They are the first people to approach with a problem and they can almost always resolve the problem. Barristers are considered more like surgeons; they perform a specialist task, but in far fewer cases.

Complaints against solicitors can be made to the Office for the Supervision of Solicitors which was set up by the Law Society to deal with complaints about solicitors. The OSS can impose minor sanctions against solicitors and may also present a case to the Solicitors Disciplinary Tribunal. This tribunal has the power to strike a solicitor off, so that he may no longer practise. When acting as advocates, solicitors enjoy the same protection against claims for negligence as is enjoyed by barristers. The Legal Services Ombudsman has the power to investigate complaints that a professional body relating to a legal professional has not adequately investigated a complaint.

As well as barristers and solicitors, there are over 20 000 legal executives, who are members of the Institute of Legal Executives. If legal executives pass the necessary exams they can have rights of audience in some courts. They generally carry out routine work of a legal nature but increasingly do the type of work formerly carried out by a solicitor.

2.6 · The judiciary

The Lord Chancellor, who is a member of the Cabinet, is the head of the judiciary. He also sits as a judge in the House of Lords. However, the office of Lord Chancellor is soon to be abolished, probably in 2005, in the interests of the separation of powers between the executive, the legislature and the judiciary. Already the Lord Chancellor's Department has become the Department of Constitutional Affairs. The Office of Lord Chancellor will be replaced by a Secretary of State for Constitutional Affairs, the main duties of whom will be: to ensure that there is an efficient and effective system in place to support the carrying on of business in the courts; to account to Parliament for the overall efficiency and effectiveness of the administration of the court system; to support the judiciary, so that they can fulfil their functions to dispense justice; and to ensure that the public interest is protected in decisions taken on matters affecting the judiciary. The Secretary of State for Constitutional Affairs will not sit as a judge. The next most senior judge is the Lord Chief Justice of England, who is the head of the Court of Appeal (Criminal Division) and the head of the High Court. When the office of Lord Chancellor is abolished, the Lord Chief Justice is to become 'President of the Courts of England and Wales'. (However, the most senior Law Lord will be the Head of the new Supreme Court.) There will also be a new post of 'Head of Criminal Justice', which will be held by the Lord Chief Justice or his nominee. The Master of the Rolls, who will be the second most senior judge, will be 'Head of Civil Justice'. The President of the Family Division of the High Court will become 'Head of Family Justice'. The Vice-Chancellor will become the 'Chancellor of the Chancery Division'.

Apart from the judicial offices outlined in the previous paragraph, there are five main levels in the judicial hierarchy. Lords of Appeal in Ordinary, usually known as Law Lords, sit as judges in the House of Lords. As we saw in the previous chapter, precedents made by the House of Lords are binding upon all English courts. Lords Justices of Appeal sit in the Court of Appeal. As decisions of the Court of Appeal are generally binding on future sittings of the Court of Appeal, and are binding on all inferior courts, the Court of Appeal is perhaps the most significant court in terms of creating the law. There are currently 36 Lords Justices of Appeal and 12 Law Lords. There are also 107 High Court judges, who sit in the High Court and sometimes in the Crown Court.

It is convenient to consider the judges who sit in the High Court, the Court of Appeal and the House of Lords as distinct from judges who sit in lower courts. The High Court is generally not an appellate court, but a court of first instance. However, in deciding a case a High Court judge is likely to be very aware of any precedent he is making, as well as being aware of his duty to try the case fairly. The Court of Appeal and House of Lords do not try cases but only hear appeals. The further up the hierarchy the judge is sitting the more importance he is likely to attach to the precedent which he is creating.

There are currently 622 circuit judges who try criminal cases in the Crown Court and civil cases in the county court. In the Crown Court these circuit judges are assisted by some 1 342 recorders and assistant recorders. In the county court they are assisted by 428 district judges and over 750 deputy district judges. Circuit judges, recorders and district judges do not create precedents. Their role is therefore confined to trying the cases which they hear. They supervise the proceedings in court, and in civil cases decide the facts of the case if they are in dispute and award damages and costs. In criminal cases in which a judge sits the facts will be decided by the jury, but the judge will supervise the proceedings. He will also pass sentence if the accused is convicted and sum up the law to the jury, so that they can reach the correct verdict.

Judges are appointed from the ranks of successful lawyers. Prior to 1990 only barristers could become judges, but now solicitors who have acted as advocates in the higher courts are also eligible. Judges are well paid. The Lord Chief Justice currently earns a salary of £205 242, High Court judges earn £150 878 and circuit judges in the provinces earn £113 121. These salaries are necessary to tempt suitably qualified lawyers to become judges and to ensure that judges maintain their independence when hearing cases.

Judges must now retire at 70 and are subject to training organised by the Judicial Studies Board. The judgment of any precedent making judge could well be scrutinised by academics, lawyers and other judges. In the light of this scrutiny, if a senior judge were not up to the high standard required this would soon become apparent.

97% of all criminal cases are decided in the magistrates' court, rather than in the Crown Court. Most magistrates are lay magistrates, meaning that they are not legally qualified. However, there are currently 105 District Judges (Magistrates' Courts), formerly known as stipendiary magistrates and over 150 Deputy District Judges (Magistrates' Courts). Only lawyers can qualify as District Judges (Magistrates' Courts), who are paid a salary of £90 760 if they work outside London.

There are around 30 000 lay magistrates, who are not paid a salary. Although they are not legally qualified, upon appointment lay magistrates do receive training on matters such as decision making, stereotyping and avoiding prejudice. Magistrates generally sit as a bench of three, and are advised about the law by the legally qualified clerk of the court. As well as deciding whether or not a person accused of a crime is granted bail, magistrates try cases, deciding whether an accused is innocent or guilty and pass sentence on those who are convicted. They also conduct committal proceedings when a defendant is committed for trial to the Crown Court. Lay magistrates must live or work in the area in which they serve, must have a good knowledge of the local community, must be of good character and have personal integrity. Generally, they must be between the ages of 27 and 65. Most people are eligible to become magistrates, but those in the police or the armed forces are not.

2.6.1 Judicial review

Judicial Review is a legal procedure which allows the Administative Court in London to examine whether a public law decision, or the exercise of discretionary power by a public body, is legal. The definition of public body for these purposes is quite wide. It includes Government Ministers and has been held to cover decisions of private bodies which make decisions that affect the public.

An application for judicial review will be subject to an initial filtering process. The applicant (who can be either a person directly affected by a public law decision, or a pressure group representing people who are affected) has first to apply for permission to proceed. On the application for permission to proceed the judge will be checking for the existence of the following criteria:

(a) Whether the decision itself is amenable to judicial review.
(b) Whether there is either express or implied exclusion of judicial review (i.e., whether Parliament has specifically enacted that such a decision should not be reviewed).
(c) Whether the applicant has a sufficient legal interest to sue.
(d) Whether there are grounds for judicial review.

With regard to the last criterion the grounds for judicial review were set out by Lord Diplock in *CCSU v Minister for the Civil Service* [1985] 1 WLR 1174, commonly referred to as the GCHQ case. Lord Diplock stated that there are three main grounds for review: illegality, irrationality and procedural impropriety. It is important to bear in mind, however, that the grounds are not mutually exclusive.

Where the Administrative Court finds that a decision is not legal (on any one or more of the above grounds) the court can grant one or more of the following remedies:

(a) a quashing order, formerly known as *certiorari* – an order that acts to quash the original decision;

(b) a mandatory order, formerly known as *mandamus* – an order that compels the decision-maker to do something;

(c) a prohibiting order, formerly known as *prohibition* – an order which prevents a decision-maker from embarking on a course of action which is not legal;

(d) *make a declaration* – this is nothing more than the court stating the legal position between the parties;

(e) *award damages* – but only where there are also private law issues involved or it involves a case under the Human Rights Act 1998; and

(f) *issue an injunction* – although an order for *mandamus* is more common in judicial review proceedings.

Judicial review has become increasingly important in recent years as the number of applications has increased dramatically. Businesses are increasingly either applying for judicial review or are subject to judicial review proceedings. A business might apply, for example, on the grounds that a decision taken by a Government Minister affects the running of the business. Even private companies may be subject to judicial review proceedings if their decisions have an effect upon the public. It is important to remember that judicial review is not concerned with the merits of the decision in question, it is concerned with whether or not that decision was legally taken.

2.7 · Juries

In the Crown Court the jury decides whether the accused is guilty or not guilty. This decision is based on the judge's summing up, which explains the relevant law to the jury. It is therefore said that juries decide the facts of the case. A judge can direct a jury to acquit an accused, but cannot direct them to convict. Juries do not give an explanation for their decisions. If a jury acquits, an appeal cannot overturn this acquittal. This enables juries to bring in 'perverse acquittals' if they think that the circumstances of the case so demand. Jurors may sometimes be discharged during a trial if they become ill or otherwise incapable of continuing to serve, but the number of jurors must not fall below nine. Majority verdicts are acceptable, but at least ten out of eleven or twelve jurors must agree, or at least nine out of ten. A jury which falls to nine members cannot give a majority verdict. The judge should not readily accept a majority verdict but should first urge the jury to try to reach a unanimous verdict. If the jury is unable to reach a verdict the case may be retried with a different jury.

Citizens between the ages of 18 and 70, who are on the electoral roll and have lived in the United Kingdom for five years, can be required to serve as jurors and can be fined up to £1000 for failing to serve. Certain people such as judges, policemen, lawyers and ministers of religion are exempt from jury service. Persons who have been sentenced to a term of imprisonment of more than five years are permanently disqualified. Those who received lesser sentences may be temporarily disqualified. Other people, such as doctors, members of the armed forces and MPs are excused from jury service as of right. The court can exercise a discretion to excuse others if they show a good reason why this should happen. However, a recent consultation paper proposes that the number of people who are exempt should be reduced. The defence has a right to challenge up to three jurors, without giving any reason. The defence can challenge any number of jurors if it gives a good reason. As well as a right to challenge for a good reason, the prosecution can ask jurors to stand by, which in effect excludes them from sitting in the case. This procedure is only used in very limited circumstances.

Juries play little part in civil cases. This was not always so. In several cases which we consider in this book the appellate court was considering whether or not to overturn the decision of a jury sitting in a civil court. Section 69 of the Supreme Court Act 1981 now limits civil jury trial to cases of defamation, malicious prosecution and false imprisonment and cases where fraud is alleged. The judge has a power to deny the right to jury trial even in these cases if the examination of scientific or technical documents would make a jury inappropriate. Where a jury is used in a civil case the jury also awards damages. The excessive amounts awarded in some defamation cases has led to considerable criticism and the Court of Appeal may now substitute the amount of damages which appears proper for the amount awarded by the jury, without the need for a new trial.

2.8 · Law reform

Parliament and the judiciary are, of course, the main reformers of the law. The system of precedent operates in a relatively haphazard way. It depends upon appropriate cases being brought in front of courts which have the power to make new rules of law. For this reason certain law reform bodies do exist. The most significant of these is the Law Commission. Its role is to keep under review all the law with which it is concerned, with a view to its systematic development and reform. In particular it should attempt to codify the law, to eliminate anomalies, to suggest the repeal of outdated and unnecessary Acts, to reduce the number of separate Acts and to generally simplify and modernise the law. The chairman of the Law Commission is a High Court judge and the five full-time commissioners are lawyers seconded for five years at a time. Other lawyers act as part-time commissioners. Reforms suggested by the Law Commission can be enacted by Parliament either in part or in whole. However, many reforms suggested are never enacted at all. The Contracts (Rights of Third Parties) Act 1999, considered in Chapter 4 at 4.2.2.2, provides an example of an Act which enacted a Bill proposed by the Law Commission.

The Law Reform Committee is a part-time body which considers the reform of civil matters referred to it by the Lord Chancellor. The Committee does not meet regularly, but its reports have tended to be very thorough. The Criminal Law Revision Committee examines matters of criminal law when asked to do so by the Home Secretary. It too is part-time, but its reports have led to the passing of significant legislation, such as the Theft Act 1968.

Royal Commissions have been set up to consider various administrative reforms. The Woolf Committee, which proposed the changes to legal procedure outlined above at 2.3, provides a good example. It should also be borne in mind that when the Government is proposing legislation it may first produce its suggestions in a green paper, which invites discussion and comment. After receiving these comments the Government publishes a white paper, in which definite proposals are set out. In this way suggestions as to the reform of the law are invited from a wide body of persons.

2.9 · Law reporting

The system of judicial precedent is dependent upon a good system of law reporting. The first law reports are contained in the Year Books, which reported on cases between 1275 and 1535. These reports are very scanty and are never quoted in court. The Private Reports made between 1535 and 1865 vary tremendously in quality, depending upon who the reporter was. Since 1865 the Modern Reports have been published by the Incorporated Council of Law Reporting for England and Wales. The Council is not a Government agency, but a non-profit-making charitable organisation. Since 1891 the Council's reports have been known as the Law Reports, which are divided into four series. A series known as Appeal Cases report the decisions of the House of Lords and the Privy Council. The other series are known as Queen's Bench, Family Division or Chancery Division. The areas which these reports cover is self-explanatory, although they are not restricted to decisions of the relevant Divisions of the High Court, but may also cover appeals in the Court of Appeal or House of Lords.

Throughout this book case references are shown. Since 1891 the Law Reports have shown the year in which the case was reported in square brackets. In Chapter 1 we considered *Adler v George* [1964] 2 QB 7. In order to find this law report it is first necessary to find the Queen's Bench Law Reports. Then to find volume 2 of the 1964 reports. The case is reported on page 7 of Volume 2. A law report will indicate the court in which the case was heard. (*Adler* v *George* was heard in the Queen's Bench Division Court of the High Court.) It will indicate the judges who heard the case (Lord Parker CJ, Paul and Widgery JJ). Then the facts of the case and the decision are set out very briefly. After a fairly detailed description of the facts and the arguments put forward, the judgments of the various judges are set out. The Council also puts out a series of Weekly Law Reports, which appear more quickly than the Law Reports.

Since 1936 Butterworths (now Lexis Nexis UK) have published the All England Law Reports. These do not set out the arguments put forward by the lawyers. Important cases decided prior to 1936 are set out in 36 other volumes of the All England Law Reports. Specialist reports published by various bodies deal with various specialist matters. There are, for instance, Road Traffic Reports, Industrial Relations Law Reports and Reports on Tax Cases.

Many of the decisions made in the higher courts are not reported. Unreported cases of the Court of Appeal can be found in a Butterworth data base known as Lexis. Such cases can only be cited in the House of Lords with permission from that court. Unreported cases of the House of Lords can be found in the Record Office of the House of Lords. The law reporters decide whether or not a case is worthy of being reported.

Test your understanding

1 What are the main roles of practising barristers?

2 What are the main roles of solicitors?

3 Can a member of the public directly engage a barrister to argue a case in court?

4 Which judges make precedents?

5 What is the difference between lay magistrates and District Judges (Magistrates' Courts)?

6 What is judicial review?

7 What is the function of a jury? In which courts are juries used?

8 What are the official law reform bodies.

9 What are the Law Reports?

Answers

1 Barristers act as advocates in all courts. They also draft opinions and statements of case.

2 Solicitors act as the first point of contact for a person seeking professional legal advice. They advise clients, enter into correspondence on their behalf, draft wills, draw up documents which transfer ownership of land and, if necessary, engage the services of a barrister. Solicitors may act as advocates in the magistrates' court and the county court and also in higher courts if they gain the qualifications needed to do this.

3 Barristers can only be engaged through solicitors. The public may not engage them directly.

4 Only High Court judges, Court of Appeal judges and Law Lords make precedents. Circuit judges try cases but do not make precedents.

5 A District Judge (Magistrates' Court) is a professional magistrate who tries case on his own. Lay magistrates are not legally qualified and sit with other magistrates as a bench when deciding cases.

6 Judicial review is the process by which the High Court considers whether a decision of public law or the exercise of a discretionary power by a public body was legally taken.

7 In the Crown Court juries decide whether the accused is guilty or not guilty. The decision is based on the judge's summing up of the law. Juries are very rarely used in civil cases.

8 The Law Commission, which has some full-time commissioners, keeps certain areas of the law under review, with a view to systematic development and reform. The Law Reform Committee is a part-time body which considers civil law matters which have been referred to it by the Lord Chancellor. The Criminal Law Revision Committee is a part-time body which has a similar role as regards matters of criminal law referred to it by the Home Secretary.

9 The Law Reports are published by the Incorporated Council for Law Reporting for England and Wales. They report cases in four series. The All England Law Reports report major decisions on any subject. Specialist law reports also exist.

Key points

The structure of the courts

- A civil case might be tried in the county court or in the High Court.

- There is a presumption that a case over which both the county court and the High Court have jurisdiction will be heard in the county court. This presumption can be rebutted if the case is particularly complex or involves issues of importance to the general public.

- The Court of Appeal (Civil Division) hears appeals from the High Court. The High Court hears most appeals from the county court

- The House of Lords hears appeals from the Court of Appeal (Civil Division). It also very occasionally hears appeals from the High Court when the leapfrog procedure is invoked.

- Indictable offences are tried in the Crown Court. Summary offences are tried in the magistrates' court. Either way offences can be tried in either the Crown Court or the magistrates' court.

- When a case is first tried in the magistrates' court appeals on points of law can be made by way of case stated to the Divisional Court.

- An appeal against sentence or conviction lies from the magistrates' court to the Crown Court.

- The Court of Appeal (Criminal Division) hears appeals from the Crown Court.

- The House of Lords hears appeals from the Divisional Court and from the Court of Appeal (Criminal Division).

Procedure in the courts

- The Civil Procedure Act 1997 and the Civil Procedure Rules 1998 have radically changed civil procedure, in an attempt to enable the courts to deal with cases justly.

- The judge has now become the case manager, with wide powers to run the case. Before the reforms the case was to a large extent run by the litigants.

- Civil cases will be allocated to one of three tracks (the small claims track, the fast track or the multi-track), depending upon the amount of the claim, the complexity of the case and the need for expert evidence.

- A defendant upon whom a claim has been served may ignore it (and therefore have judgment entered against him), admit the claim in full, admit part of the claim, file an acknowledgement of service (thereby getting an extra 14 days in which to reply), file a defence and/or file a counterclaim.

- Claims on the small claims track will be heard in the county court, generally by a district judge.

- Fast track claims should be decided within 30 weeks of allocation.

- All cases will be subject to extensive case management by the judge.

- Legal aid has been abolished as regards personal injury claims. Such claims can be pursued on a 'no win, no fee' basis. The parties should therefore insure themselves against having to pay the other side's costs.

Alternative dispute resolution

- Litigation has several disadvantages. It is costly, slow, complex, worrying and conducted in public. It is also likely to finish any business relationship with the other party.

- Disputes may be referred to arbitration by the parties, by a court or by an Act of Parliament. If a dispute is referred to arbitration it is resolved by an arbitrator rather than by a court.

- A mediator communicates between the parties, trying to get them to resolve their dispute. Conciliation involves a conciliator suggesting to the parties the basis on which they might settle their dispute.

- Tribunals hear disputes on specialist matters, and these types of disputes must be referred to the appropriate tribunal rather than to the ordinary courts. Generally, a tribunal is made up of a legally qualified chairman and two lay members.

Miscellaneous matters

- The legal profession is split into barristers and solicitors.

- Barristers act as advocates in all courts, draft opinions and draft statements of case.

- Solicitors act as general legal advisors. They can act as advocates in the magistrates' court or the county court. If qualified they can act as advocates in higher courts.

- High Court judges, Court of Appeal judges and Law Lords make precedents. Circuit judges do not.

- District Judges (Magistrates' Courts) are salaried, legally qualified magistrates. Lay magistrates are not legally qualified and sit as a bench of three.

- Judicial review is the process by which the Administrative Court considers the legality of decisions of public law and the legality of a discretionary power exercised by a public body.

- Juries decide whether or not the defendant in a Crown Court trial is guilty or not guilty.

- The Law Commission is a law reform body with full-time members. The Law Reform Committee and the Criminal Law Revision Committee are part-time law reform bodies.

- Law reporting is not done by the Government. The most significant law reports are the All England Law Reports and the Law Reports of the Incorporated Council of Law Reporting for England and Wales.

Summary questions

1 A Ltd is suing B Ltd, claiming contract damages of £25 000. B Ltd is contesting the claim. The claim is not in respect of any personal injuries. In which courts might the case be tried? To which courts might an appeal be made, if all possible appeals were made?

2 Explain the considerations which will be taken into account in deciding the appropriate track for the hearing of a case. As regards each track, outline the procedures which are likely to be followed from allocation to conclusion of the case.

3 Explain the way in which a dispute can be referred to arbitration and the powers which an arbitrator has. How do mediation and conciliation differ from arbitration?

4 By scanning the newspapers or the Internet, find a recent case in which an application for judicial review was made. Outline the grounds on which the application was made and the outcome of the application.

Multiple choice questions

1 Which one of the following statements is not true?

a If a claim can be brought in either the county court or the High Court, there is a presumption that it should be heard in the High Court.

b An appeal from a Master who is sitting as a High Court judge will be made to a High Court judge, rather than to the Court of Appeal.

c If an offence is classed as triable either way, an accused has the right to insist upon trial in the Crown Court.

d Lay magistrates are trained, but they can be appointed even if they have no special knowledge of the law.

2 Which one of the following statements is not true?

a If a defendant upon whom particulars of claim are served does not respond within 14 days, judgment can be entered against him.

b If the defendant files an acknowledgement of service he will be given a further 14 days to respond to the claim.

c An appeal from a district judge's ruling on the small claims track will be made to the Court of Appeal.

d A fast-track case will generally be concluded within 30 weeks of allocation.

3 Which one of the following statements is not true?

a Legal aid is no longer available in some personal injury cases.

b If a party tries to bring legal proceedings in respect of a matter which it has been agreed should be resolved by arbitration, the court will stay the proceedings unless the arbitration agreement was either null and void, inoperative or incapable of being performed.

c Tribunals act as specialist courts, hearing certain types of disputes which must be taken to the appropriate tribunal rather than to the ordinary courts.

d A mediator will suggest the basis on which a dispute might be resolved and try to get the parties to agree to be legally bound by the suggested resolution.

4 Consider the following statements

i A member of the public cannot directly engage a barrister to represent him, but must engage the barrister through a solicitor.

ii Barristers can be appointed judges but solicitors cannot.

iii The process of judicial review allows the Administrative Court to consider the merits of decisions taken by public bodies.

iv Juries can acquit a defendant even if they are sure that he is guilty.

v Not all decisions of the precedent-making courts are reported.

Which of the statements are true?

a i, iii and iv only.

b ii and iii only.

c i, iv and v only.

d All of the statements.

Task 2

Your employer has asked you to write a report, explaining briefly the following matters.

a The different courts in which a civil dispute might start and the courts to which an appeal might subsequently be made.

b The three tracks to which a civil case might be allocated and the principles of case management which the courts will apply.

c The main methods of dispute resolution which can be used as an alternative to going to court.

Chapter 3

FORMATION OF CONTRACTS – OFFER AND ACCEPTANCE

Introduction

A contract is a legally binding agreement. Every business will need to make contracts at one time or another, and most businesses will make very many. A manufacturing business, for example, will need to make many contracts both to buy its means of production and to sell its finished product. Further contracts may well be needed to employ staff, or to advertise, or to dispose of unwanted assets. As soon as a contract is made it is binding on the parties. They must must stick to what they have agreed or take the legal consequences.

It is not only between two or more businesses that contracts are made. Many contracts, perhaps the majority, are made by members of the public when they buy everyday goods and services. Every time a person buys a bar of chocolate, or gets on a bus, or buys a cup of tea, that person makes a contract. It might be hard to see how such everyday agreements fit within the definition of a contract as a legally binding agreement. Surely the courts would not force a shop to stick to an agreement to sell a bar of chocolate? As we shall see, they would not. But if the bar of chocolate was defective, perhaps injurious to health, then in order to sue the shop for damages the customer would need to prove that the sale of the chocolate by the shop constituted a contract. A court would have little difficulty in deciding that it did.

Several points about the nature of a contract are worth noting at this early stage. First, contracts are formed by agreement between the parties to the contract. A person cannot become liable under a contract unless it can be inferred that he chose to enter into a legally binding agreement. Second, a contract is a bargain under which both sides give some benefit to the other. The rights acquired under the contract are exchanged for the benefits given, and an agreement under which a person gratuitously promises a benefit to another is a gift and not a contract. Third, contractual liability is strict. In order to make a person liable for breach of contract it is always necessary to prove that the terms of the contract were not honoured, but it is not always necessary to show that this failure involved any element of fault. Fourth, damages for breach of contract aim to compensate for all foreseeable losses which flowed naturally from the breach.

3.1 · Offer

Almost all contracts are made through the process of offer and acceptance. One of the parties (the offeror) makes an offer by proposing a set of terms with the intention that these terms will form a legally binding agreement if they are accepted by the party to whom they are proposed, the offeree. If the offeree accepts, by indicating that he too is willing to be bound by the terms proposed, a contract will result. The offer can be written or spoken, or it can be inferred from the conduct of the offeror. When goods are bought at auction both the offer and the acceptance are made by conduct. The sale of a lot at auction can provide a good initial example of how an offer is made and of how it is accepted.

Let us assume that Mrs Ashley buys an antique vase at an auction conducted by Mr Bower. Mrs Ashley, if she is sensible, will have examined the vase beforehand or at least have seen it described in a catalogue. Neither the examination nor the description in the catalogue amount to an offer.

When the auctioneer comes to the lot in question, let us call it Lot 1, he probably makes a brief description of it to make sure that the bidders know which lot is up for sale. Then the auctioneer asks for bids. He usually suggests a price. None of these actions of the auctioneer amount to an offer.

When one of the bidders signifies that he is making a bid (by raising his hand, or nodding, or making whatever other gesture the auctioneer recognises) this, at last, is an offer. It is the first move of legal significance and as such it is not a move to be made lightly. If the offer is accepted then the bidder will have made a contract to buy Lot 1 and will be legally bound by that contract.

The auctioneer will be in no hurry to accept the first bid. Let us assume that several higher bids are made, but that eventually Mrs Ashley makes a bid of £100 and that this appears to be the highest bid which is going to be made. The auctioneer will probably repeat the figure £100 several times and then, after a slight delay, he will bang his hammer on the table.

At the precise moment that the auctioneer's hammer hits the table the acceptance is made and the contract is concluded.

While the hammer was descending towards the table Lot 1 still belonged to the person who had asked the auctioneer to sell it. But as soon as the hammer hit the table the contract was made. As the contract was for the sale of specific goods in a deliverable state, ownership of Lot 1 would immediately be transferred from the person who put the vase into the auction to Mrs Ashley.

The fact that the contract has now been made has important legal consequences. Mrs Ashley is now free to do as she pleases with Lot 1, but she is no longer free to change her mind and say that she does not want to buy it. (Nor, of course, can the auctioneer say that he no longer wants to sell.) If Lot 1 is damaged **after** the contract has been made then it is Mrs Ashley whose property has been damaged and it is she, not the seller, who would have the right to sue the person causing the damage. If the lot had been damaged **before** the hammer hit the table, no contract would yet have been made and it would have been the seller on whose behalf the auctioneer was acting whose property would have been damaged.

This example of the sale of a lot at an auction is a useful one because the offer and acceptance are well-established and easy to recognise. The classical approach to the formation of contracts holds that every other type of contract is made when an offer is accepted. However, it is not always so easy to see what the offer and acceptance were. In exceptional cases a court may hold that a contract existed even though it is not possible to identify a definite offer and a definite acceptance. But this can only happen if the court is satisfied that the parties reached agreement on all material points.

3.1.1 Invitation to treat

The word treat has several meanings. In the context of the law relating to offer and acceptance it means to negotiate. An invitation to treat is therefore an invitation to negotiate, or an invitation to make a deal. The main significance of an invitation to treat is that it is not an offer.

Making an offer carries an element of risk. A business, for example, should not offer to sell an asset for £1 000 unless it is quite sure that this is what it wants to do. If the person to whom the offer was made, the offeree, were to accept the offer then the business would have to hand the asset over in return for the money or accept the legal consequences. But it would be quite safe for the business to make an invitation to treat. It might do this by inquiring of another how much he would be prepared to pay for the asset. Whatever the reply, the business could not be forced to sell.

In deciding whether or not one party made an offer to another a court will be guided by the intentions of the parties. These intentions will be deduced from all the circumstances of the case.

3.1.2 Advertisements

The legal status of advertisements is of considerable importance. If an advertisement amounts to an offer, then people who respond in such a way that they accept the offer will have made a contract. If an advertisement is only an invitation to treat, as is usually the case, a response to the advertisement cannot form a binding contract. In the following case the court had to decide whether an advertisement which described goods, and the price for which they could be purchased, was an offer or an invitation to treat.

■ *Partridge* v *Crittenden* [1968] 1 WLR 1204

The defendant was charged with unlawfully offering for sale a bramblefinch contrary to s.6(1) of the Protection of Birds Act 1954. The defendant had placed an advertisement in the classified section of a magazine. This advertisement had said, 'Quality British … bramblefinch cocks, bramblefinch hens … 25 s. each'. The words 'offers for sale' were not directly used in the advertisement. A customer posted a cheque for 25 shillings, requesting a bramblefinch hen. Such a bird was sent to the customer in a box by British Rail.

Held. The defendant was not guilty. His advertisement was an invitation to treat, not an offer. The defendant had not therefore 'offered for sale' a wild bird.

COMMENT (i) The defendant would have been guilty of a different crime, that of selling a wild bird. Fortunately for him, this was not the crime with which he was charged.

(ii) This case is of course a criminal case, as are several of the cases which follow. In order to decide whether or not a criminal offence has been committed it is often necessary to consider the civil law. This is particularly true of crimes which are committed by selling or offering for sale.

(iii) Lord Parker, who gave the leading judgment, indicated that he felt that the defendant ought to be guilty of the offence. However, this had no influence on his decision as to whether or not the advertisement amounted to an offer. Lord Parker's primary concern was with the consequences of the decision he was making. If, in their desire to convict the defendant, Lord Parker and his fellow judge had decided that the advertisement was an offer, then under the doctrine of judicial precedent every junior judge would have become obliged to follow this decision when considering similar advertisements. (The doctrine of judicial precedent is examined in Chapter 1 at 1.3.2.) Lord Parker demonstrated how undesirable the consequences of this might be by quoting with approval the following example concerning a wine merchant sending out a wine list to customers. The example was originally made by Lord Herschell in *Grainger and Son* v *Gough* [1896] AC 325:

> 'The transmission of such a wine list does not amount to an offer to supply an unlimited quantity of the wine described at the price named, so that as soon as an order is given there is a binding contract … If it were so, the merchant might find himself involved in any number of contractual obligations to supply wine of a particular description which he would be quite unable to carry out, his stock of wine of that description being necessarily limited.'

Although the advertisement in *Partridge* v *Crittenden* was classified as an invitation to treat, some advertisements do amount to offers. If the general rule that advertisements are only invitations to treat were to be applied rigidly to all advertisements then this would lead to unfairness, as the following case demonstrates.

■ *Carlill* v *The Carbolic Smoke Ball Company* [1893] 1 QB 525 (Court of Appeal)

The defendant claimed that the smoke balls which they manufactured cured many illnesses and made it impossible to catch flu. They advertised the smoke balls heavily, stating that if anyone could show that they had correctly used a smoke ball yet still caught flu they would be paid £100 reward. The advertisement also stated that the defendant had deposited £1 000 in a Regent Street bank, 'shewing our sincerity in the matter'. The claimant, Mrs Carlill, bought one of the smoke balls on the strength of the advertisement. Despite using the smoke ball properly, the claimant still caught flu. She claimed the £100 reward. The defendants refused to pay on several grounds.

First, it was claimed that the advertisement was a mere sales puff rather than an offer. Second, it was contended that a contract could not be made with the whole world. Third, it was argued that the defendant's promises were too vague to be an offer.

Held. The claimant had made a contract with the company and was entitled to the £100 reward. The advertisement constituted an offer of a unilateral contract which was made to the whole world. The offer stipulated that acceptance could be made by using a smoke ball in the correct manner and catching flu. The claimant had fulfilled these requirements and had therefore accepted.

COMMENT (i) A sales puff is a statement which promotes a product in a way which is not intended to be taken to amount to a definite promise. Modern examples can be seen in the claims made by manufacturers of washing powders that their product washes whitest. The defendant's reference to the £1 000 having been deposited in the Regent Street bank indicated to the court that the promise of the reward was not a mere sales puff.

(ii) The case illustrates that an offer can be made to the whole world. In reward cases this is not uncommon. Offers are more usually made to one person or to a group of people. An offer can only be accepted by an offeree, a person to whom it was made (or by an agent acting on an offeree's behalf). The defendant's argument that if the court found for Mrs Carlill this would have meant that a contract was made with the whole world was exposed as a fallacy by Bowen LJ. The offer was made to the whole world but this did not of course mean that a contract was made with the whole world. A contract was only made with that limited portion of the public who accepted the offer.

(iii) The offer was not considered too vague. Bowen LJ reached this conclusion by giving the advertisement its plain meaning as the public would understand it.

3.1.3 Offers of unilateral contracts

Almost all contracts are bilateral (two-sided) because both sides make a contractual promise to the other. If, for example, a farmer telephones a dealer and makes a contract to buy a new combine harvester, this is a bilateral contract. The dealer has promised to sell the combine harvester to the farmer and the farmer in return has promised to pay the price agreed.

However, a person who makes an offer of a unilateral contract agrees to be bound if the offeree performs some act, rather than if the offeree promises to perform some act. Although the offeror does not always spell it out so specifically, in effect he says, 'If you do one thing, then I promise that I will definitely do another'. The contracts are called unilateral (one-sided) because only one of the parties, the offeror, makes a promise. The offeree cannot accept by promising to do the act requested, but only by actually doing it. In *Carlill*'s case, the Smoke Ball Company promised that if Mrs Carlill, or anyone else, used a smoke ball and caught flu they would be paid the reward. But Mrs Carlill did not promise that she would catch flu, and presumably did not even intend to do so. She accepted by performing the acts requested – using a smoke ball and catching flu.

A further peculiarity of unilateral contracts is that acceptance of the offer does not need to be communicated to the offeror. Mrs Carlill did not need to tell the company that she intended to accept the offer. Indeed, her saying this would not have amounted to acceptance. The only way in which she could accept was by fulfilling the requirements of the offer. That is to say she could only accept by using a smoke ball as directed and catching flu. The company would not have been aware of her acceptance until she claimed the reward. As we shall see later in this chapter, a bilateral contract is generally not legally binding until the acceptance is received by the offeror.

3.1.4 Goods in shops

In order to analyse when a contract is concluded by a customer in a shop it is necessary to consider separately those shops which operate a self-service system and those which do not. As regards shops which do not operate a self-service system Somervell LJ, in *Pharmaceutical Society of Great Britain v Boots Cash Chemists (Southern) Ltd* [1953] 1 QB 401, explained the position in the following way:

> 'in the case of an ordinary shop, [one in which there is no self-service] although goods are displayed and it is intended that customers should go and choose what they want, the contract is not completed until, the customer having indicated the articles which he needs, the shopkeeper, or someone on his behalf, accepts that offer.'

The other members of the Court of Appeal seemed to regard this point of view as self-evidently correct, although none of them identified the precise way in which the shopkeeper accepts the offer.

It is well established that the display of goods in a shop window amounts only to an invitation to treat and not to an offer.

■ *Fisher v Bell* [1961] 1 QB 394

The defendant displayed a flick knife in his shop window. A ticket behind the knife said, 'Ejector knife – 4s'. The defendant was charged with the criminal offence of offering the knife for sale, contrary to s.1(1) of the Restriction of Offensive Weapons Act 1959.

Held. The defendant was not guilty of the offence. The display of the knife amounted not to an offer to sell, but only an invitation to treat.

Lord Parker: '... the display of an article with a price on it in a shop window is merely an invitation to treat. It is in no sense an offer for sale the acceptance of which constitutes a contract. That is clearly the general law of the country.'

In the following case the Court of Appeal considered the position as regards self-service shops.

■ *Pharmaceutical Society of Great Britain v Boots Cash Chemists (Southern) Ltd* [1953] 1 QB 401 (Court of Appeal)

The defendants were charged with the criminal offence of selling a listed drug other than by or under the supervision of a registered pharmacist, contrary to s.18 of the Pharmacy and Poisons Act 1933. The defendants operated a self-service shop where the goods for sale were displayed on shelves around the walls. Customers entering the shop picked up whatever goods they wished to buy and took them to a cashier near the exit. The goods displayed, including listed drugs, were wrapped in packages with the prices marked on them. A registered pharmacist was present near the cash desk and could prevent a customer from buying any listed drug. The prosecution contended that the sale of the displayed goods was completed when the customers put the goods into their baskets. If this contention was correct then the offence would have been committed whenever customers put listed drugs into their baskets because at this stage no pharmacist supervised or made the sale.

Held. The defendants were not guilty. The display of goods on the supermarket shelves amounted to an invitation to treat rather than to an offer to sell. The customers' action in taking the goods from the shelves and placing them in their baskets constituted an offer to buy. The customers' offer to buy was accepted when the cashier took the purchase price. This contract took place under the supervision of a pharmacist and so no offence was committed.

Test your understanding

1 How does an offeror make an offer?

2 What is the significance of an offer being accepted?

3 What is an invitation to treat?

4 What is a bilateral contract?

5 How is the offer of a unilateral contract made?

Answers

1 An offeror makes an offer by proposing a set of terms with the intention that these terms will form a legally binding agreement if they are accepted by the person to whom they are proposed, the offeree.

2 As soon as an offer is accepted a contract is made.

3 An invitation to treat is an invitation to negotiate or an invitation to bargain. It is not an offer.

4 A bilateral contract is one under which both sides exchange promises.

5 The offer of a unilateral contract is made when the offeror gives a definite promise to be bound if the offeree performs some specified action.

3.2 · Acceptance

As soon as an offer is accepted, a contract comes into existence and both sides are legally bound. An acceptance can be made by words or conduct. Unless the offer was of a unilateral contract, the acceptance must be communicated to the offeror and the contract is not completed until this communication is received. This important principle is clearly demonstrated by the following case.

■ *Entores Ltd* v *Miles Far East Corporation* [1955] 2 QB 327 (Court of Appeal)

The claimants, in London, telexed an offer to purchase copper cathodes to the defendants in Holland. The defendants telexed acceptance back to London. Later, when sued for breach of contract in England, the defendants argued that the contract was not made in England and was not therefore within the jurisdiction of the English courts. The defendants claimed that the acceptance was effective as soon as it was typed out on the telex machine in Holland and that the contract was therefore made in Holland. The claimants argued that the acceptance was not effective until it was printed out in London, and that the contract was therefore made in England.

Held. English law applied. Where a contract is made by instantaneous communication the contract is complete only when the acceptance is received by the offeror.

Lord Denning: 'Suppose, for instance, that I shout an offer to a man across a river or a courtyard but I do not hear his reply because it is drowned by an aircraft flying overhead. There is no contract at that moment. If he wishes to make a contract, he must wait until the aircraft is gone and then shout back his acceptance so that I can hear what he says. Not till I have heard his answer am I bound.'

COMMENT (i) Lord Denning also explained that an acceptance by telephone would not be effective until it was heard by the offeror, but that this was only the case if the offeree knew that the acceptance had not been heard. He suggested that if the offeror did not make it known that he had not heard the acceptance then a contract would come into existence because the offeror would be estopped (prevented) from saying that he had not received the message. He also thought that this would be the case if the ink ran out on a printer receiving the acceptance and the offeror did not ask for the message to be repeated.

(ii) The decision in *Entores* was approved by the House of Lords in *Brinkibon Ltd* v *Stahag Stahl und Stahlwarenhandelsgesellschaft mbH* [1983] 2 AC 34.

As an acceptance of an offer of a bilateral contract is only effective when it is received, it follows that the acceptance must take the form of some positive action. A person cannot accept a contract by saying nothing and doing nothing, even if the offeror has stipulated that acceptance should be made in this way.

■ *Felthouse* v *Bindley* (1862) 11 CBNS 869

The claimant's nephew thought that he had sold a horse to the claimant for 30 guineas (£31.50). The claimant thought that he had bought the horse for £30. Realising that the mistake meant there was no contract, the claimant wrote to his nephew offering to split the difference. The claimant's letter stated, 'If I hear no more about him, I consider the horse mine at £30 15 shillings.' The nephew wanted to sell at this price so he did not reply. Six weeks later an auctioneer sold the horse by mistake. The claimant sued the auctioneer in tort for selling his property. The auctioneer's defence was that the horse still belonged to the claimant's nephew and that the wrongful sale of the horse was therefore nothing to do with the claimant.

Held. The auctioneer was not liable. The claimant's offer to buy the horse for £30 15 shillings had never been accepted and so the horse still belonged to his nephew.

Some businesses try to sell their goods by sending them to people who have not requested them, and then following up with aggressive demands for payment or the return of the goods. *Felthouse* v *Bindley* makes it plain that the recipients cannot be deemed to have accepted the goods merely because they do not return them. Section 2 of the Unsolicited Goods and Services Act 1971 makes it a criminal offence to demand payment for unsolicited goods sent to a business. (Goods are unsolicited if they are sent to a person who has not made a prior request for them. Furthermore, reg.24 of the Consumer Protection (Distance Selling) Regulations 2000 provides that a consumer recipient of unsolicited goods may treat the goods as an unconditional gift if three conditions are fulfilled. First, the goods must have been sent with a view to the recipient acquiring them. Second, the recipient must have no reasonable cause to believe that the goods were sent with a view to their being acquired for a business purpose. Third, the recipient must have neither agreed to acquire them or return them. Regulation 24 also makes it a criminal offence to demand payment for such goods.) Surprisingly, the legislation has not eradicated the practice of demanding payment for unsolicited goods. It seems that the basis of such 'selling' is that the goods sent are so worthless and the prices demanded so high, that the sender of the goods makes a profit if even a small percentage of customers pay up. The criminal side of the legislation seems rarely to be enforced. Section 3 of the 1971 Act allows a business to refuse to pay a charge for being included in a trade directory, or to recover any payment made for being included, unless a signed order is made on the stationery of the business to be included in the directory.

3.2.1 The postal rule

As we have already seen, it can be extremely important to know exactly when an acceptance becomes legally effective. Before the acceptance is made the offeror can call the offer off, but once the acceptance has been made this is no longer possible.

When an offer is accepted by letter or telegram, the effect of the postal rule has to be considered. The rule, which holds that the acceptance of an offer by post is effective as soon as the letter or telegram is properly posted, originated in the early nineteenth century. In order to understand the current effect of the rule it is necessary to examine several cases in their historical context.

■ *Adams* v *Lindsell* (1818) 1 B & Ald 681

On Tuesday 2 September 1818 the defendants sent a letter to the claimants, offering to sell wool and requiring an answer by return of post. The defendants misdirected the letter and this caused it to be delivered at 7 pm on Friday 5 September. If the letter had not been misdirected it would have arrived on 3 September. The claimants posted an acceptance on 5 September. As this letter of acceptance was carried via London, it was not received by the defendants until 9 September. If the defendants had not misdirected the letter containing their offer then a reply by return of post would have arrived on 7 September. As they had not received an acceptance by 7 September, the defendants sold the wool to a third party.

Held. There was a good contract on 5 September when the letter of acceptance was posted.

COMMENT (i) To some extent the court was influenced by the fact that it was the defendants' fault that the letter had been misdirected.

(ii) In *Household Fire Insurance Co v Grant* (1879) 4 Ex D 216 the Court of Appeal applied the postal rule in a case where the letter of acceptance was permanently lost in the post. The defendant's letter agreed to buy 100 shares in a company. He paid 5% of the price of £100. A letter accepting his offer was posted but never received. The company went into liquidation. A good contract was formed when the letter was posted and the defendant was therefore obliged to pay the remaining £95.

(iii) In *Henthorn v Fraser* [1892] 2 Ch 27 the Court of Appeal held that the rule would operate not only where the offer was sent by post, but whenever it would reasonably be expected that an acceptance would be made by post. Lord Herschell said that an acceptance would be effective when posted, 'where the circumstances are such that it must have been within the contemplation of the parties that, according to the ordinary usages of mankind, the post might be used as a means of communicating the acceptance of an offer'.

In order for the rule to apply the letter of acceptance must have been properly addressed and properly posted.

■ *Re London and Northern Bank, ex parte Jones* [1900] 1 Ch 220

The claimant applied for shares in a company. On 26 October 1898 he wrote a letter withdrawing his application. This letter of revocation was received by the company at 8.30 am on 27 October and read at 9.30 am. At 7 am on 27 October the company had handed a letter of acceptance to a postman, paying him a small fee for taking this and other letters. This letter of acceptance was delivered to the claimant in Sheffield at 7.30 pm on 27 October. (If the postman had handed the letter into the London General Post Office before 7.30 am it would have been delivered in Sheffield at about 5.30 pm.) The claimant sued to have his name removed from the company register. He argued that as his offer had been revoked before it was accepted he had never made a contract to buy the shares.

Held. The letter of revocation was received before the letter of acceptance became effective and so there was no binding contract. Postmen are not authorised to take letters for posting and do not do so as agents of the Post Office. Therefore, the company could not prove that the letter of acceptance was properly posted before 9.30 am. Cozens-Hardy J: 'I cannot, therefore, regard the postman as anything better than a boy messenger employed … to post the letters, and the mere fact of handing the letter to the postman … was not a posting of the letter.'

COMMENT (i) The case also illustrates the well accepted position that letters of revocation are never effective upon posting. The postal rule has never applied to letters of revocation, but only to letters of acceptance.

(ii) Cozens-Hardy J said that the postal rule was made because the Post Office is considered the common agent of both parties. The fact that the rule does not apply to letters of revocation makes this proposition highly dubious.

In *Holwell Securities v Hughes* [1974] 1 WLR 155 the Court of Appeal reviewed the postal rule. On 19 October 1971 Dr Hughes had given Holwell Securities an option to purchase his house for £45 000. The option was said to be exercisable 'by notice in writing' to the defendant within six months. On 14 April 1972 Holwell Securities posted a letter exercising the option, but the letter was never delivered. No further communication was made until the option expired on 19 April. Holwell Securities sued for specific performance (a court order requiring Dr Hughes to sell the house to them). They argued that the postal rule applied, and that a contract was therefore created as soon as their letter was posted. The Court of Appeal held that the rule did not apply and so there was no contract. The express terms of the offer ('by notice in writing') indicated that the acceptance had to reach the offeror and this made the postal rule inappropriate. Lawton LJ also stated that the rule would not apply where it would 'produce manifest inconvenience and absurdity'. He went on to say: 'In my judgment, the factors of inconvenience and absurdity are but illustrations of a wider principle, namely, that the rule does not apply if, having regard to all the circumstances, including the nature of the subject-matter under consideration, the negotiating parties cannot have intended that there should be a binding agreement until the party accepting an offer or exercising an option had in fact communicated the acceptance or exercise to the other.'

If the offeror stipulates that acceptance should be made in a particular manner then any method of acceptance which is equally expeditious is likely to be valid, unless the offeror made it plain that the offer had to be accepted in the precise way stipulated. Even if the offeror does insist that acceptance can only be made in the precise way stipulated, this requirement can be waived by the offeror's conduct.

3.2.2 Counter offer

Acceptance of an offer must be unqualified and unconditional. A response which proposes a material alteration of the terms of the offer will amount to a counter offer. The effect of such a counter offer will be to revoke the original offer.

■ *Hyde* v *Wrench* (1840) 3 Beav 334

On 6 June 1840 the defendant offered to sell his farm to the claimant for £1000. The defendant asked for a reply by return of post as he had another buyer in mind. The claimant's agent called on the defendant and offered £950 for the farm on the claimant's behalf. The defendant replied that he would need to think about this and assured the agent that he was not carrying on negotiations to sell to anyone else. On 27 June the defendant wrote to the claimant's agent declining the offer of £950. On 29 June the claimant wrote back accepting the original offer to sell the farm at £1000. The defendant refused to sell at this price.

Held. There was no contract. The claimant's counter offer of £950 had revoked the defendant's original offer.

COMMENT It might seem strange that the counter offer was held to have revoked the original offer, but this must be the correct decision. If a business offers to sell an asset for a certain price and this offer is rejected by the offeree making a counter offer, the business is likely to sell the asset to someone else. It would be very harsh if the offeree, having refused the original offer, could now accept it and make the offeror liable for breach of contract.

The following case shows a modern example of the counter-offer rule.

■ *Pickfords Ltd* v *Celestica Ltd* [2003] EWCA Civ 1741 (Court of Appeal)

The defendants hired the claimants to move business property from Stoke-on-Trent to Shropshire. On 13 September 2001 the claimants faxed an offer to do the work at a certain price per unit plus additional costs such as insurance. (The first offer.) On 27 September the claimants sent a second offer to do the work for a fixed price, including insurance. On 15 October the defendants faxed a 'confirmation', which stated that the cost of the work would be capped at £10000. The work was performed and the defendants paid the price based on the first offer. The claimants argued that the price should have been as per the second offer because the defendants had accepted this.

Held. The second offer was materially inconsistent with the first offer and therefore revoked it. It was clear that the defendant intended to accept the first offer because reference to a ceiling price could not mean that they were accepting the second offer, which was a set fixed price. However, because the first offer had been revoked the defendant's 'confirmation' fax was a counter offer on the same terms as the first offer, with the additional term that the price should be capped at £10000. By carrying out the removal work the claimants had accepted this counter offer.

3.2.3 Auctions

Earlier in this chapter we saw that when goods are sold by auction the various bidders make a series of offers, and that the auctioneer accepts the highest offer by banging his hammer. Section 57(1) of the Sale of Goods Act 1979 states that each lot is taken to be the subject of a separate contract of sale. Section 57(2) confirms that a sale is complete when the auctioneer announces this by banging his hammer, or by some other customary manner, and that until this time any bid can be retracted.

A sale by auction may be notified to be subject to a reserve price, beneath which the goods will not be sold, and the seller of the goods may also expressly reserve a right to bid for them (s.57(3)). However, if the sale by auction is not notified to be subject to the right to bid by or on behalf of the seller, it is not lawful for the seller to bid, or to employ any person to bid for him, or for the auctioneer to take any such bid (s.57(4)). A sale which contravenes s.57(4) can be treated as fraudulent by the buyer (s.57(5)).

When an auction is advertised as being 'without reserve' this means that if the auction of a particular lot actually starts the auctioneer makes an offer of a unilateral contract, promising that he will sell to the highest genuine bidder, no matter how low that bid might be. This offer of a unilateral contract can be accepted by making the highest bid. Such a bid would not conclude a contract of sale between the bidder and the owner of the goods. It would make the auctioneer liable to the highest bidder on a collateral contract.

In *Barry v Davies (T/A Heathcote-Ball & Co)* [2000] 1 WLR 1962 (Court of Appeal) two machines were put up for auction without a reserve price. The machines were each worth £14 521 new and the auctioneer tried to get a bid of £5 000. The claimant bid £400 for the machines but the auctioneer refused to accept the bid. After the auction the machines were sold to a third party for £3 000. It was held that the auctioneer had breached a collateral contract with the claimant and the claimant was awarded damages of £27 600. (This was the difference between what the claimant had bid and the amount he would have had to pay to buy the machines elsewhere.) The auctioneer's promise that the machines would be sold without reserve was the offer of a unilateral contract, given in exchange for the claimant's attending the auction and making the highest bid.

If an auctioneer advertises that goods will be sold 'without reserve' this does not amount to a promise that the goods will be included in the auction or that the auction will definitely take place.

■ *Harris v Nickerson* (1873) LR 8 QB 286

An auctioneer advertised in the London newspapers that office furniture was to be sold by auction in Bury St Edmunds. The advertisement stated that the highest bidder would get the goods. The claimant travelled to Bury St Edmunds from London, and bought several lots. However, the office furniture which he intended to buy was not included in the auction. The claimant sued for the expenses which he had incurred.

Held. The claimant had no remedy. The advertisement was merely an invitation to treat and did not amount to a definite offer. It amounted to a declaration of intention rather than a promise to put the goods up for sale.

It must be remembered that most lots at auction do have a reserve price. If this is the case then the auctioneer will take bids in the normal way, but will refuse to sell if the highest bid does not reach the reserve price.

For example, if a painting is put up for auction with a reserve price of £50 then the auctioneer will not sell to the highest bidder unless his bid is £50 or higher. The auctioneer will usually state in advance that a particular lot is subject to a reserve, without disclosing what the reserve is. If the highest bid does reach the reserve the auctioneer will sell the goods. If the highest bid does not reach the reserve the auctioneer will say so and refuse to sell.

3.2.4 Tenders

Both goods and services can be bought or sold by tender. As well as being an effective way of contracting at the best price it is a business method particularly favoured by organisations (such as local authorities) which must show that a contract was not gained as a result of favouritism or corruption. The way in which the contract is formed can be understood by reference to an example.

Let us assume that a local authority needs a supply of school desks and that it places advertisements which invite tenders to supply the desks. Whether this advertisement will amount to an offer or an invitation to treat will depend entirely on the words which are used.

If the advertisement merely asks for tenders to supply 1 000 desks of a certain description, then it will amount only to an invitation to treat. A tenderer who responds by submitting a tender to supply the desks at £40 each would be making an offer. The local authority might accept this offer, but it would not be bound to do so.

Sometimes, however, the invitation to tender can itself be an offer. Let us suppose that an invitation to tender invites bids for the sale of certain goods, and states that the highest bid will definitely get the goods. The invitation to tender would amount to the offer of a unilateral contract. The tenderer who submits the highest price would be deemed to have accepted the offer and to have made a contract to buy the goods. These principles are clearly demonstrated by the following case.

■ *Spencer v Harding* (1870) LR 5 CP 561

The defendants advertised that they would sell certain goods by tender. The advertisement began, 'We are instructed to offer to the wholesale trade for sale by tender the stock-in-trade of Messrs. G. Eilbeck and Co ...' and went on to state where the goods could be viewed, the time at which the tenders would be opened and that payment would have to be in cash. The claimant submitted the highest tender but the defendants refused to sell to him.

Held. The defendants did not have to sell. Their advertisement asking for tenders was only an invitation to treat. The claimant had made an offer but the defendants had no obligation to accept this. However, Willes J stated that the invitation for tenders would have been the offer of a unilateral contract if it had gone on to say, 'and we undertake to sell to the highest bidder'.

Many advertisements invite tenders to supply such goods as the invitor might require within a certain time. A tenderer who puts in a price at which the goods will be supplied for the whole period of time makes what is known as a standing offer.

Such an offer can be accepted many times, and each acceptance leads to a new contract. However, the offer is only accepted when the person who invited tenders actually orders goods, and the offer can be withdrawn before any particular order is made.

■ *Great Northern Railway Company v Witham* (1873) LR 9 CP 16

The claimants' advertisement asked for tenders to supply goods 'such as they may think fit to order' in a one year period. The defendant put in a tender stating the price at which he would supply such quantities as the claimants might order within the period. The claimants accepted this tender. After filling several orders the defendant, within the year, refused to fill one. The claimants argued that the defendant had made a contract to fill the order.

Held. The defendant had made a contract to fill that particular order. He had made a 'standing offer' and each time the claimants made an order they accepted this offer.

COMMENT The defendant could have withdrawn his offer as regards future orders, even if the orders were made within the one year period. Such a revocation of the standing offer would be effective when it was received. (Revocation would be allowed because the defendant had been given no consideration in return for keeping the offer open, that is to say he had been given nothing of any value in return for doing so.) (Consideration is considered in detail in Chapter 4.)

In *Harvela Investments Ltd* v *Royal Trust Co of Canada Ltd* [1986] AC 207 the House of Lords had to consider whether or not to allow 'referential tenders'. Such tenders state their price by reference to other tenders. In the *Harvela* case two people wishing to buy shares were asked to put in a tender indicating the price they would pay. The seller promised that the two tenders would be opened at the same time and that the highest bid would get the shares. The defendant put in a tender agreeing to pay $2 100 000 or $101 000 in excess of any other offer. The other tender was for $2 175 000. The House of Lords held that the referential tender was invalid because it defeated the whole object of fixed competitive tendering, the idea of which is that the amounts tendered are confidential and unknown to the other tenderers. The seller had shown a clear intention to sell and if both sides made a referential bid this intention would have been defeated. The seller was not therefore entitled to accept the referential tender. The tender of $2 175 000 was therefore successful.

In certain circumstances the mere fact of inviting tenders may give rise to a binding contractual obligation to consider tenders properly submitted.

■ *Blackpool & Fylde Aero Club Ltd* v *Blackpool Borough Council* [1990] 3 All ER 25

The defendants owned and managed an airport. Revenue was raised by letting this out to air operators who conducted pleasure flights. The claimant club had held the concession for several years. The defendants sent invitations to tender to the claimant club and to six other parties who were connected with the airport. Tenders were to be submitted in envelopes supplied and were not to bear any mark indicating who the tenderer was. The defendants stated that only tenders received by 12 noon on 17 March 1983 would be considered. The claimants' tender was put into the defendants letter box at 11 am 17 March. However, the letter box was not emptied at noon as it should have been. The claimants' tender was regarded as late and was not considered. The claimants sued for damages for breach of contract, arguing that the council had promised that if a tender was received before the deadline it would be considered.

Held. The claimants were entitled to damages. In certain circumstances an invitation to tender could create binding obligations to consider conforming tenders. The circumstances of the case indicated that any of the seven potential tenderers who submitted their tender in the correct way had a contractual right to have their tenders opened and considered along with any other tenders which were considered.

3.3 · Certainty

A contract will only come into existence if the offer which is accepted contains all of the essential terms of the contract. A court must be able to identify, with certainty, exactly what has been agreed. It is a well-established principle that a court will not write a contract for the parties. In deciding whether or not an agreement is sufficiently certain to amount to a contract the courts do not consider the subjective views of the offeror and offeree. Rather they take an objective view by asking whether the reasonable person would have thought that the agreement was sufficiently certain.

The advantage of this objective approach can be demonstrated by considering an example. Let us suppose that there is a dispute between X and Y. X made an offer which Y accepted. Later X claims that there is no contract because the meaning of what was agreed is uncertain. Y maintains that the essential terms were agreed with certainty and that there is a contract which X must perform. There is little point in a court considering the subjective opinions of X and Y as to whether or not the agreement was sufficiently certain. Maybe both of the parties genuinely do believe what they maintain. If not, it is perfectly possible that they will be prepared to give evidence in court that they do believe it. Plainly, therefore, many disputes could not be resolved by looking at the subjective opinions of the parties themselves. Instead the courts use the reasonable person to look for the objective meaning of the contract. Reference to the reasonable person allows the court to ask not what the parties to the contract actually meant, but what they appeared to mean. If the contract appeared to the reasonable person to be certain then it will be certain. If it did not appear to the reasonable person to be certain then it will not be.

■ *Scammell and Nephew Ltd* v *Ouston* [1941] AC 251 (House of Lords)

A firm of furnishers wanted to acquire a new van on hire-purchase. Scammell agreed to supply a van priced at £286, allowing the firm £100 for an old van which was traded in. The agreement stated that 'this order is given on the understanding that the balance of the purchase price can be had on hire purchase terms over a period of two years'. After some disagreements Scammells refused to supply the van, claiming that the agreement was not certain enough to amount to a contract.

Held. There was no contract between the parties. The agreement as to hire-purchase terms was so vague that it could not be given a definite meaning. The parties would need to reach further agreement before there could be a completed contract.

■ *Sudbrook Trading Estate Ltd* v *Eggleton* [1983] AC 444 (House of Lords)

A lease gave the tenant an option to buy the land absolutely, 'at such price, not being less than £12 000, as may be agreed upon by two valuers one to be nominated by the lessor and the other by the lessee and in default of such agreement by an umpire appointed by the … valuers …'. The tenant exercised the option to purchase but the landlord refused to appoint a valuer.

Held. This was a good contract for sale of the land at a fair and reasonable price which was to be reached by applying objective standards. If the machinery which the parties had set up to ascertain the price broke down the court would substitute its own machinery to find a fair and reasonable price.

In contracts to sell goods or to supply services a contract can exist even if the price has not been agreed. Section 8(1) of the Sale of Goods Act 1979 provides that the price in a contract of sale of goods may be fixed by the contract, or may be left to be fixed in a manner agreed by the contract, or may be determined by the course of dealing between the parties. Section 8(2) provides that where the price is not determined by any of these methods the buyer must pay a reasonable price. Section 15(1) of the Supply of Goods and Services Act 1982 makes a similar provision where the contract is for the supply of a service.

Once an agreement has started to be performed the courts are much more likely to hold that there is a contract. It is not absolutely essential to do this because in the absence of a contract a party who had received valuable benefits could be ordered to pay for them on a *quantum meruit* basis. (This would mean that the person who had supplied the goods or services would be paid a reasonable price or remuneration.) However, the fact of the agreement having been partly performed is a strong indication that the parties intended to create a contract.

■ *Percy Trentham Ltd* v *Archital Luxfer Ltd* [1993] 1 Lloyd's Rep 25 (Court of Appeal)

The claimants, who were building engineers, were engaged by MMI Ltd as the main contractors to build industrial units in two phases. The defendants were manufacturers and installers of aluminium doors and windows. The defendants did the window work for the claimants in phases 1 and 2, and the claimants paid the defendants for this work. The claimants found defects with the defendants' work in both phase 1 and phase 2. They claimed damages for breach of contract. The defendants denied that their dealings with the claimants ever resulted in concluded contracts.

Held. There was a contract between the two parties as regards both phase 1 and phase 2. This contract was formed by conduct. The parties plainly intended to enter into binding contractual relations. The course of dealing between the parties entitled the claimants to performance of the work and the defendants to be paid.

Steyn LJ: 'English law generally adopts an objective theory of contract formation. That means that in practice our law generally ignores the subjective expectations and the unexpressed mental reservations of the parties. Instead the governing criterion is the reasonable expectations of … sensible businessmen … The fact that the transaction was performed on both sides will often make it unrealistic to argue that there was no intention to enter into legal relations. It will often make it difficult to submit that the contract is void for vagueness or uncertainty. Specifically, the fact that the transaction is executed makes it easier to imply a term resolving any uncertainty, or, alternatively, it may make it possible to treat a matter not finalised in negotiations as inessential.'

COMMENT Steyn LJ also made the following points. (i) Although the vast majority of contracts would be formed through offer and acceptance this would not necessarily be the case where a contract came into existence by performance.

(ii) If a contract only comes into existence as a result of performance it will frequently be possible to imply that the contract retrospectively covers pre-contractual performance.

(iii) When a transaction has been partly performed this will give rise to similar considerations as those which apply when the contract has been fully performed.

3.3.1 Meaningless terms

Many written contracts contain meaningless terms. As the following case shows, it would be poor policy to allow a person to escape from a contract merely because he had discovered such a term.

■ *Nicolene Ltd* v *Simmonds* [1953] 1 QB 543 (Court of Appeal)

The claimants wrote to the defendant ordering 3000 tons of reinforced steel bars and asked for written confirmation of acceptance of the order. The defendant wrote back from his private address thanking the claimants for the contract. However, this letter said 'As you have made the order direct to me, I am unable to confirm on my usual printed form which would have the usual force majeure and war clauses, but I assume that we are in agreement that the usual conditions of acceptance apply.' Later the defendant argued that there was no contract as complete agreement had not been reached with regard to the usual conditions of acceptance.

Held. As there were no usual conditions of acceptance the words were meaningless and could be ignored. There was therefore a complete and enforceable contract between the parties.

Denning LJ: 'In my opinion a distinction must be drawn between a clause which is meaningless and a clause which is yet to be agreed. A clause which is meaningless can often be ignored, whilst still leaving the contract good; whereas a clause which has yet to be agreed may mean that there is no contract at all, because the parties have not agreed on all the essential terms …'

COMMENT Lord Denning pointed out that if meaningless clauses were allowed to negate a contract, 'You would find defaulters all scanning their contracts to find some meaningless clause on which to ride free.'

It should be noted that in this type of case either the previous dealings of the parties or trade custom could have a strong influence on the court's decision. If, for example, Nicolene Ltd and Simmonds had dealt with each other on several previous occasions there might have been little difficulty in deciding what the usual conditions of acceptance were. Similarly, if Ouston had several times taken vans from Scammell Ltd on hire-purchase then the court might well have decided that 'on hire-purchase terms' was definite enough for the reasonable person to say what had been agreed.

Many agreements, especially those to sell land and houses, are expressed to be made 'subject to contract'. Generally it is accepted that the use of these words mean that no contract has yet been concluded.

3.4 · Offer and acceptance when dealing with machines

It has become common for people to buy goods (or tickets which entitle them to services) from machines. At first sight this seems to cause considerable difficulty in finding the offer and the acceptance. The customer cannot make both the offer and the acceptance so the machine, on behalf of the supplier of the goods or services, must make either the offer or the acceptance.

In *Thornton* v *Shoe Lane Parking Ltd* [1971] 2 QB 163 (Court of Appeal) Lord Denning MR analysed the position when a customer in a multi-storey car park is given a ticket by a machine on entry to the car park. He concluded that the contract was completed not when the customer received the ticket, but as soon as the customer became irrevocably committed to the contract, that is to say, as soon as he put his money into the machine.

Lord Denning MR stated:

'The customer pays his money and gets a ticket. He cannot refuse it. He cannot get his money back. He may protest to the machine, even swear at it. But it will remain unmoved. He is committed beyond recall. He was committed at the very moment when he put his money into the machine. The contract was concluded at that time. It can be translated into offer and acceptance in this way: the offer is made when the proprietor of the machine holds it out as being ready to receive the money. The acceptance is made when the customer puts his money into the slot.'

Thornton v *Shoe Lane Parking* will be considered in more detail in Chapter 5. It will be seen there that the significance of the contract being formed before the ticket was received was that words on the ticket were therefore too late to be incorporated into the contract.

Earlier in this chapter, at 3.2, we considered *Entores* v *Miles Far East Corporation* [1955] 2 QB 327 (Court of Appeal) and saw that an acceptance by telex is effective when it is received. We also saw that Lord Denning took the view that an acceptance by telex, like a personal communication, will not be effective if the person making it knows that it has not been received. Lord Denning also indicated that if it was the fault of the offeror that the acceptance was not received, for example if his telex machine had run out of ink, then the acceptance could be regarded as received when it should have been received. In *Brinkibon Ltd* v *Stahag Stahl und Stahlwarenhandelsgesellschaft mbH* [1983] 2 AC 34 the House of Lords approved the decision in *Entores*.

Lord Wilberforce, dealing with communication by telex, made it plain that the courts will take a pragmatic, flexible approach.

'The message may not reach, or be intended to reach, the designated recipient immediately: messages may be sent out of office hours, or at night, with the intention, or on the assumption, that they will be read at a later time. There may be some error or default at the recipient's end which prevents receipt at the time contemplated and believed in by the sender … And many other variations may occur. No universal rule can cover all such cases; they must be resolved by reference to the intentions of the parties, by sound business practice and in some cases by a judgment where the risks should lie.'

It does seem fairly certain that if an acceptance by telex or fax is received during office hours it is effective when received and not when it is noticed. But what if the recipient machine is turned off? It is not possible to answer such a question with certainty, but in *Brinkibon* Lord Fraser said, 'Once the message has been received on the offeror's telex machine, it is not unreasonable to treat it as delivered to the principal offeror, because it is his responsibility to arrange for prompt handling of messages within his own office.' Lord Fraser also made the point that the acceptor by telex can generally tell if his message has not been received, whereas the offeror would not know that an unsuccessful attempt had been made to send an acceptance.

3.4.1 **Offer and acceptance made over the Internet**

As yet there have been no significant decisions by the courts as to when a contract is concluded over the Internet. There are two main ways in which such a contract might be formed. First, a contract could be made by exchange of emails. Second, a customer might visit a web site and buy goods or services described there.

The position where emails have been exchanged should be catered for by the common law rules already considered in this chapter. The courts will take an objective view of an email and consider whether it was an offer or an invitation to treat. An offer might or might not be of a unilateral contract. In the same way the courts will consider objectively whether an email amounted to acceptance of an offer. The most likely difficulty will arise in deciding precisely when an acceptance by email is effective. The general principles laid down in relation to telex seems likely to be applied. However, email differs from communication by telex in that a person who sends an email does not immediately know whether or not it has been received. In some ways acceptance by email is more similar to acceptance by letter than acceptance by telex. However, it seems very unlikely that the postal rule will apply. The rule is anomalous and the approach of the courts has been to restrict its application rather than to expand it. It seems much more likely that the statement of Lord Wilberforce in *Brinkibon*, set out above, will apply to acceptance by email. This statement does not provide a cast iron answer applicable to all situations. It indicates that the court will be guided by the intentions of the parties, sound business practice and a judgment as to where the risks should lie.

In general, web sites which describe goods and services and the prices at which they are available will be making invitations to treat rather than offers. This would be particularly true if the material on the web site makes it plain that it is the customer who makes the offer and that his offer might or might not be accepted. The customer might make the offer by clicking on a button. Any acceptance would be effective when the customer was informed that his offer had been accepted. However, there is no reason why a web site should not make the offer of a unilateral contract. If this were the case then the contract would be concluded as soon as the customer had performed the stipulated act of acceptance (generally by clicking on an acceptance button).

As we have seen, the key question when dealing with the conclusion of contracts is the time when the acceptance is effective. The Electronic Commerce (EC Directive) Regulations 2002 are concerned with the formalities which must be complied with when a contract is made with an Internet services provider. They do not deal with the time at which the contract is concluded. However, Reg.11 provides that an offer made by a consumer to an Internet service provider, and an acknowledgement of having received such an offer, are to be effective when the person to whom they are addressed can access them. The Regulations do not deal with the time at which an acceptance is effective. However, there seems to be no reason why this too should not be when the person to whom it is addressed is able to access it. But this is not explicitly stated. In any event, as we shall see in Chapter 7 at 7.1.5 the question is often of little relevance in consumer contracts because the Consumer Protection (Distance Selling) Regulations 2000 give consumers the right to cancel concluded distance contracts.

3.5 · Acceptance of an offer of a unilateral contract

In *Carlill*'s case we saw that the offeree's motive for performing the act requested by the offeror is irrelevant. Presumably Mrs Carlill used the smoke ball to avoid catching flu, but this did not mean that she had failed to accept the offer. In *Williams* v *Carwardine* (1833) 5 C & P 566 a woman gave information leading to the conviction of a murderer. She did this because she thought she was about to die and she wanted to ease her conscience. Nevertheless, she was entitled to the reward which had been offered for the supply of information which led to the murderer's conviction.

Although the situation is not entirely clear, it seems that a person who claims to have accepted an offer of a unilateral contract does not need to have known of the offer at the time when the act which constitutes acceptance was begun. It is sufficient that the offeree has knowledge before the act is completed. So if Mrs Carlill had only heard of the reward shortly before she caught flu she would still have been entitled to claim that she had accepted the offer.

Test your understanding

1 At what point does an acceptance become effective so as to create a bilateral contract?

2 What is the effect of the postal rule? In what circumstances will the rule not apply?

3 What effect does a counter offer have on the offer to which it is a response?

4 What is the legal effect of advertising that an auction will be held at which goods will be sold without reserve?

5 In what circumstances will an invitation to submit tenders amount to an offer?

6 In ascertaining whether or not an agreement was sufficiently certain to constitute a contract, do the courts consider the objective meaning of what the parties agreed, or do they consider the subjective views of the parties themselves?

7 How will the presence of a meaningless term in a contract affect the validity of the contract?

Answers

1 An acceptance is effective when it is communicated to the offeror. As soon as acceptance is received by the offeror a contract is created. (Communication of acceptance is not necessary when the offer was of a unilateral contract.)

2 When the postal rule applies an acceptance by letter or telegram is effective as soon as it is properly posted. The rule will not be applied where to do so would produce a manifestly absurd result. Nor will it be applied if the circumstances indicated that the parties did not intend there to be a binding contract until acceptance of the offer was received.

3 A counter offer revokes the offer to which it is a response.

4 If an auction is advertised as being 'without reserve' this means that if the auction of a particular lot actually starts the auctioneer makes an offer of a unilateral contract, promising that he will sell to the highest genuine bidder, no matter how low that bid might be. However, the auctioneer does not make a definite offer that particular goods will be included in the auction or that the auction will actually take place.

5 An invitation to submit tenders will generally only be an invitation to treat. However, an invitation to submit tenders will amount to an offer if it states that the highest or lowest tender will definitely be accepted.

6 In ascertaining whether or not an agreement was sufficiently certain to constitute a contract the court considers the objective meaning of what was agreed.

7 A meaningless term will generally not affect the validity of a contract. If a term is meaningless it can generally be ignored.

3.6 · Termination of offers

We have seen that as soon as an offer is accepted a contract results. There are several ways in which an offer which has been made can later cease to exist. Before examining these methods it must be borne in mind that we are not here concerned with whether or not the obligations imposed by a contract have ceased to exist. If an offer ceases to exist, before it has been accepted, then no contract will ever come into existence. The obligations imposed by a contract will cease to exist once the contract has been discharged, a matter considered in Chapter 7.

3.6.1 Revocation

An offer can be revoked at any time before it is accepted. Once revoked, the offer no longer exists and acceptance of it is therefore no longer possible. A revocation is effective only when it is received by the offeree. Earlier in this chapter we saw that, the postal rule and offers of unilateral contracts apart, an acceptance of an offer is only effective when it is received by the offeror. So when an offeree claims to have accepted an offer which the offeror claims to have revoked, the court will need to discover whether or not the acceptance was received before the revocation was received. The following example demonstrates the two possibilities.

Let us suppose that farmer X has offered to sell 100 tons of potatoes to wholesaler Y, who has expressed interest but has not yet accepted. All of the terms of the proposed contract have been clearly identified and if Y were to accept a contract would immediately be created. Both X and Y go home and watch the News on the television. One of the news items announces that the price of potatoes is likely to increase because of disastrous weather in Europe. X decides that he no longer wants to sell his crop to Y at the price offered and resolves to revoke his offer. Y decides that he wants to make the contract and to let X know that the offer is accepted. Whether or not a contract will come into being will depend upon who communicates first. If Y receives X's revocation before X receives Y's acceptance, then there will be no contract. If X receives Y's acceptance before Y has received the revocation, then a contract will have been created.

Once an offer has been made, if the offeror makes a subsequent inconsistent offer this will revoke the original offer. *Pickfords Ltd* v *Celestica*, considered earlier in this chapter at 3.2.2, provides an example. In that case the Court of Appeal also stated that acting inconsistently with the original offer, to the knowledge of the offeree, could also revoke the original offer even if no words were used.

Revocation will generally be communicated to the offeree by the offeror or his agent. However, the following shows that an unauthorised third party can also communicate revocation as long as the offeree can regard the third party as reliable.

■ *Dickinson* v *Dodds* (1876) 2 Ch D 463 (Court of Appeal)

On Wednesday 10 June the defendant delivered a written offer to sell a house and outbuildings to the claimant. The offer stated that, 'This offer to be left over until Friday, 9 o'clock a.m. June 12, 1874.' On Thursday the defendant negotiated to sell the house to one Allen. One Berry found out about the negotiated sale and told the claimant. At 7 am on Friday morning Berry, acting as the claimant's agent, handed the defendant a letter of acceptance and explained its effect to him. The defendant had sold the house to Allan on the Thursday.

Held. There was no contract. As no consideration had been provided to keep the offer open, it could be revoked at any time. At the time when the claimant purported to accept the offer he knew that the defendant had changed his mind. Berry had effectively revoked the offer.

The old postal rule on acceptance of contracts has never applied to revocation of an offer but only to acceptance of an offer. Revocation of an offer is effective when received, whether posted or not, as the following case demonstrates.

■ *Byrne & Co* v *Van Tienhoven & Co* (1880) 5 CPD 344

On 1 October 1879 the defendants, who carried on business in Cardiff, posted an offer to sell 1 000 boxes of tin-plate to the claimants in New York. On 8 October the defendants posted a revocation of their offer. The defendant's offer was received by the claimants on 11 October and a telegram of acceptance was sent the same day. A letter of acceptance was also sent on 15 October. On 20 October the defendant's letter of revocation reached the claimants.

Held. A good contract came into existence on 11 October. The revocation was not effective until it was received on 20 October.

An offer, whether of a unilateral or a bilateral contract, can be revoked at any time before acceptance. However, some difficulty is caused by the fact that acceptance of the offer of a unilateral contract takes the form of performing an action, and frequently the performance of this action will take some considerable time. The following case suggests that the offer of a unilateral contract cannot be revoked once the offeree has started to perform the act which constitutes acceptance.

■ *Errington* v *Errington & Woods* [1952] 1 KB 290 (Court of Appeal)

A father bought a house for £750, paying £250 cash and borrowing £500 from a building society. The father told his daughter-in-law that if she paid the mortgage instalments she could have the house when the mortgage was paid off. The daughter-in-law did not agree to pay all of the mortgage instalments, but did begin to pay them as they became due. After the daughter-in-law had paid the mortgage instalments for some time, the father died leaving the house in his will to his widow. Soon afterwards the widow claimed possession of the house.

Held. The widow (who was in exactly the same position as her husband would have been in if he had still been alive) could not revoke the offer.

Denning LJ: 'The father's promise was a unilateral contract – a promise of the house in return for their act of paying the instalments. It could not be revoked by him once the couple entered on performance of the act, but it would cease to bind him if they left it incomplete and unperformed, which they have not done. If that was the position during the father's lifetime, so it must be after his death.'

COMMENT This case illustrates a general principle. However, in some circumstances it will be possible to revoke the offer of a unilateral contract even after the commencement of acceptance. (See the House of Lords decision in *Luxor (Eastbourne) Ltd* v *Cooper* [1941] AC 108 set out in Chapter 11 at 11.5.2.) In *Daulia Ltd* v *Four Millbank Nominees* [1978] 2 All ER 557 Goff LJ seemed to agree with Denning's view in *Errington* v *Errington and Woods*: 'there must be an implied obligation on the part of the [unilateral] offeror not to prevent the condition becoming satisfied, which obligation it seems to me must arise as soon as the offeree starts to perform. Until then the offeror can revoke the whole thing, but once the offeree has embarked on performance it is too late for the offeror to revoke his offer.'

The rule that revocation is effective only when it is communicated to the offeree causes some difficulty in reward cases where the offer of a unilateral contract is made to the whole world. It must be possible to revoke such an offer and the legal position seems to be that this can be achieved by advertising the revocation in the same way as the offer was advertised. So the Carbolic Smoke Ball Company's offer to pay the £100 reward could have been revoked by advertising the revocation in the same way as the offer was advertised. This revocation would be effective even as regards a person who had read the offer but had not read the revocation. It would not be effective as regards a person who had already begun to accept the offer by using the smoke ball in the correct way.

3.6.2 Rejection of offer

If an offeree communicates rejection of an offer then this terminates the offer. We saw an example in *Hyde* v *Wrench*, above at 3.2.2. The claimant's counter offer of £950 for the farm amounted to a rejection of the defendant's offer to sell for £1 000. It therefore terminated the offer.

A request for more information about an offer does not terminate the offer as it does not imply rejection of it. It can therefore be important to distinguish a request for more information from a counter offer.

■ *Stevenson, Jacques & Co* v *McLean* (1880) 5 QBD 346

At a time when the market price of iron was extremely volatile, the defendant offered to sell the claimants a quantity of iron for 40 shillings net cash per ton. The offer was made on Sunday 28 September and was to remain open until close of business on Monday 29 September. The claimants would have preferred to take the iron in instalments, paying as each instalment was received. At 9.42 am Monday 29 September the claimants sent a telegram, 'Please wire whether you would accept forty [shillings] for delivery over two months, or if not, longest time you would give'. The defendant did not reply to this telegram but on the same day sold the iron to someone else. At 1.25 pm the defendant telegraphed the claimants to tell them that this had been done. Before this telegram arrived the claimants sent a telegram accepting the defendant's offer. The defendant refused to deliver the iron and the claimants sued for non-delivery.

Held. There was a good contract to sell to the claimants at forty shillings per ton for immediate delivery, as originally offered. The claimants' first telegram had not been a counter offer, it was just a request for more information. Consequently it did not revoke the defendant's offer.

A counter offer attempts to introduce a new term. A request for information does not, rather it merely seeks to clarify what the offer is. When business contracts are made there are often a series of negotiations, proposals and enquiries. It can be very difficult to distinguish those which amount to a counter offer from those which do not.

3.6.3 Lapse of time

If an offer is stipulated as being open for a particular time then it will be open for that length of time unless it is revoked. In *Dickinson* v *Dodds*, for example, the offer would have remained open until

9 am on Friday had it not been revoked. Any acceptance before 9 am on Friday would have been effective, but any acceptance after that time would have been too late.

It might seem rather unfair that an offer which has been stipulated as being open for a particular time can then be revoked before the time limit has expired. Revocation is allowed because the person to whom the offer was made has provided no consideration in return for the offer being kept open. This will be better understood after reading the following chapter, in which the meaning of consideration is examined. Put simply, it means that if the offeree had promised any benefit, for example the payment of 10p, in return for keeping the offer open then this would have amounted to a contract to keep the offer open and so the offer could not then have been revoked. But because no consideration was given in return for the offer it was just a gratuitous promise and could therefore be revoked. In Chapter 4 we shall see that a promise for which nothing was received in return does not create a binding contractual obligation.

If an offer is not specified as being open for any particular length of time then it will remain open for a **reasonable time** the length of which will depend upon all the circumstances of the case. If, for instance, a businessman made two offers, one to sell a boatload of ripe bananas and the other to sell his business premises, the offers would not remain open for the same length of time.

3.6.4 Condition not fulfilled

An offer can be stipulated as remaining in force until the happening of a certain event. When a person offers to buy goods, for example, it is implied that the offer is conditional on the goods remaining in the same condition as when the offer was made until the acceptance is made. If the goods are damaged before acceptance then the offer will cease to exist.

It is also possible to make a contract which will only become operative if a condition is fulfilled. The contract will exist as soon as it is made, but until the condition is fulfilled the rights and obligations of the parties do not become operative. For example, it is possible to make a sale of goods on the terms that a third party will fix the price. The contract exists as soon as it is made, and if the third party does fix the price then both sides will be bound to perform their obligations under the contract. But if the third party cannot or does not make the valuation the agreement is frustrated (Sale of Goods Act 1979, s.9).

3.6.5 Death of offeror or offeree

The fact that the offeror has died before the offer is accepted will not necessarily prevent the offeree from accepting the offer. If the offer was to supply a personal service, such as to sing at a concert, then the offer cannot be accepted. If the offer was not to supply a personal service, such as an offer to sell a car, then the legal position is less clear. In *Bradbury* v *Morgan* (1862) 1 H & C 249 it was suggested that the offeree can accept the offer until he has notification of the offeror's death. If this point of view is correct then the offeror's personal representatives would need to perform the contract. The position is different where it is the offeree who has died. Although there is little authority on the matter, it seems likely that the personal representatives of an offeree who has died will not be able to accept any offer.

If one of the parties dies after the contract has been concluded then this will generally not prevent performance of the contract unless the party who died had contracted to supply personal services. This is a separate matter which is examined in Chapter 7 when we look at discharge of contractual obligations.

3.7 · Battle of the forms

Many businesses use standard form contracts when buying and selling. When a seller believes that the contract was made on his standard form of sale, and the buyer believes the goods were bought on his standard form of purchase, the courts have to decide which form applies. As the following case demonstrates, they do this by applying the ordinary rules of offer and acceptance.

■ *Butler Machine Tool Co Ltd* v *Ex-Cell-O Corporation Ltd* [1979] 1 All ER 965 (Court of Appeal)

On 23 May 1969 the claimants offered to sell a machine for £75 553, delivery to be made within ten months. The offer was made on the claimants' terms and conditions, which stated that these terms and conditions were to prevail over any terms and conditions in the buyer's order. One of the claimants' terms allowed for an increase in the contract price if the price of manufacture should increase before the date for delivery. On 27 May the defendants ordered a machine, saying that the order was made on their terms and conditions. These terms and conditions differed from the claimants' terms and conditions, and did not include a price variation clause. At the foot of the order was a tear-off slip which stated, 'We accept your order on the Terms and Conditions stated thereon'. On 5 June the claimants signed the slip and sent it back to the defendants, adding that the order 'is being entered in accordance with our revised quotation of 23rd May'. The machine was delivered, but the claimants then claimed an extra £2 892 under their price variation clause.

Held. The claimants were not entitled to the extra money as the contract was made on the defendants' terms and conditions. The claimants made an offer on 23 May. The defendants made a counter offer on 27 May. The claimants accepted this counter offer by signing and returning the defendants' acknowledgement slip on 5 June.

COMMENT The decision in this case shows that generally the party who fires the last shot wins, that is to say the person who submits the last counter offer wins as long as the circumstances indicate that the other party accepted this counter offer. Lord Denning MR was critical of the classical offer, counter offer, and acceptance approach. He considered it ill-suited to the needs of modern business. If both sides insist on firing the last shot then a contract will not come into existence at all as agreement will never be reached.

Test your understanding

1 At what stage will a revocation of an offer be effective?

2 At what stage will revocation of an offer of a unilateral contract no longer be possible?

3 For how long will an offer remain open?

4 How will the courts solve 'battle of the forms' cases?

Answers

1 A revocation of an offer will be effective once it is received by the offeree. This is the case whether or not the revocation was posted.

2 In all but exceptional cases it will not be possible to revoke an offer of a unilateral contract once an offeree has begun to perform the act requested in the offer.

3 Unless an offer is revoked, it will remain open for a stipulated time, or if no time was stipulated for a reasonable time.

4 The courts will solve 'battle of the forms' cases by applying the ordinary rules of offer and acceptance. Generally, the person who makes the last counter offer will win as long as it can be inferred that this was accepted by the other party.

Key points

Offer

- An offeror makes an offer by proposing a set of terms with the intention that these terms will form a legally binding agreement if they are accepted by the person to whom they are proposed, the offeree.

- An offer can be made by words or by conduct.

- An invitation to treat is an invitation to bargain and is not an offer.

- Advertisements are generally invitations to treat rather than offers. However, an advertisement which makes a definite promise can amount to the offer of a unilateral contract.

- A unilateral contract is offered when one party promises to be bound if the other party performs some specified act. The parties to a bilateral contract exchange promises.

- The display of goods in shop windows or on supermarket shelves does not amount to an offer to sell those goods.

Acceptance

- As soon as an acceptance is received by the offeror a contract will come into existence. When the offer is of a unilateral contract acceptance does not need to be communicated, as acceptance is completed by performing the act requested.

- An offer cannot be accepted by silence and inactivity.

- When the postal rule applies the acceptance of an offer (by letter or telegram) will be effective from the time when it is posted. The rule will only apply when the letter of acceptance was properly addressed and posted. The rule will not apply where it would cause manifest inconvenience and absurdity. Nor will it apply where the circumstances of the case indicate that the parties cannot have intended that there should be a binding contract until the acceptance was received.

- A counter offer will revoke the original offer.

- If a lot is put up for sale at auction 'without reserve' this amounts to the offer of a unilateral contract by the auctioneer promising that the highest genuine bid will be accepted. Advertising that an auction will be held without reserve does not amount to a definite offer that the auction will be held or that any of the lots will be put up for auction.

- An invitation to tender is generally only an invitation to treat. However, if the invitation promises that the highest or lowest tender will be successful then it can amount to the offer of a unilateral contract.

- A standing offer for which no consideration was received can be withdrawn at any time. However, orders placed prior to withdrawal will amount to acceptances of the offer and lead to the creation of contracts.

- When a seller asks for fixed competitive bids, a referential tender will not be valid and the seller will not be allowed to accept it.

- A contract will not come into existence unless the offer which is accepted contains all of the essential terms of the contract and the meaning of these terms can be ascertained with certainty.

- If an accepted offer contains a meaningless term this will not of itself mean that no contract is formed. The meaningless term can generally be ignored.

Termination of offers

- An offer cannot be accepted after it has terminated.

- An offer of a bilateral contract can be revoked at any time before it is accepted. The revocation will be effective from the time when it is received by the offeree.

- In all but exceptional cases it is not possible to revoke an offer of a unilateral contract once the offeree has begun to accept by performing the act requested.
- An offeree who rejects an offer will not subsequently be able to accept it.
- If no time limit is stipulated then an offer will remain open for a reasonable time. If no consideration is given for keeping an offer open then it can be revoked at any time, even if the offer was stipulated as being open for a particular time.

Summary questions

1 Which of the following would amount to an offer and which would amount only to an invitation to treat?

  a A supermarket advertises that it will give a free chicken to anyone who spends at least £20 in any one visit.

  b A business writes to a customer: 'You mentioned that you might want to buy our old fax machine. We have now bought a new machine. I've asked the office manager to put the old machine to one side, and you can have it for £100. If you do want the machine, let me know before the end of the month. If I don't hear from you before then I'll take it you don't want the machine and send it off to an auction.'

  c A wholesaler writes to his customers, 'I am selling off all last year's stock. If you place an order before the end of this month I will guarantee 25% discount on any old stock which I still have.'

  d A corner shop advertises its biscuits, 'Summer madness! Special offer for the month of June! Chocolate digestives only 25p! We will not be beaten on price or quality!'

  e A manufacturer of electric shavers advertises: 'Shaves as close as your blade or your money back.'

  f In a supermarket meat which is nearing its sell-by date bears a 'special offer' label, stating that the original price has been reduced by 25%.

2 If goods on supermarket shelves did generally amount to offers to sell, what undesirable consequences would follow?

3 A motorist drives into a self-service garage and fills his car with petrol. The motorist goes into the office where an attendant asks him for the price of the petrol. The customer pays the price. When was the contract formed?

4 Allen Ltd advertise a second-hand articulated lorry in a trade journal for £6 000. Bernard, a local haulier, phones Allen Ltd and says that he would very much like to look at the lorry but that he is off on a two-day trip to the Continent. The managing director of Allen Ltd says that if another buyer comes forward he will have to sell to that buyer. Bernard then says that he will pay £100 if Allen Ltd promise to keep open for three days an offer to sell the lorry to him for £6 000. The managing director agrees to this. Has any contract been made. If so, what are its terms?

5 A customer in a shop sees a cooker bearing a £56 price tag. The customer says that he will buy the cooker but the shop assistant says that the price tag should read £560. Can the customer insist on buying the cooker for £56?

6 Customers who buy from vending machines make contracts with the owner of the goods which the machines supply. Analyse the offer and acceptance position when a customer buys a can of soft drink from a vending machine. Would it make a difference that the machine did or did not have a coin refund?

7 In *Brogden* v *Metropolitan Railway* (1877) 2 AC 666 (House of Lords), a dispute arose as to whether a contract existed between a coalman and the railway and, if the contract did exist, what its terms were. The facts of the case can be reduced to the following four statements.

  a A company which had taken coal from B for many years sent B a written agreement regarding the future supply of coal.

  b B altered the document, signed it, and sent it back.

  c The company put the signed document in a drawer, where it stayed for two years.

d The company ordered coal, which B delivered, in accordance with the altered document.

Each of the four statements can be classified as one of the following; an offer, an invitation to treat, a counter offer, a revocation, a contract, or nothing at all.

Decide which of these each statement is. At least three of the cases quoted in this chapter can be used to justify your decisions. Which cases are they?

8 Company A wants to sell a second-hand machine tool to Company B. Both parties want to make the deal but they cannot agree about the price. Would the agreement be sufficiently certain to be a contract if the price was agreed to be:

  a A fair price.

  b A price to be fixed by C.

  c The price at which a similar machine tool is sold at an auction which is due to take place the following day.

  d A price which the parties will agree later.

9 A supermarket has a butchery counter. A customer asks for half a kilo of chuck steak. The assistant weighs a piece of meat and says that it is 480 grams. The customer says that this is all right, and then asks the assistant to mince the meat. The assistant minces it, puts it into a bag and sticks a price label on the bag. The customer pays for the meat at the till. Analyse this transaction in terms of offer and acceptance.

10 In *May and Butcher v R* [1934] 2 KB 17n (House of Lords), M and B agreed to buy tents from the Disposals Board. The price to be paid was described as follows: 'The price or prices to be paid … shall be agreed upon from time to time between the (Disposals Board) and the purchasers as the quantities of said old tentage become available for disposal.' A further clause said that all disputes arising under the contract should be referred to arbitration. Do you think that this agreement was sufficiently definite to amount to a contract? Would your answer be different if there had been a definite agreement to buy tents with no mention of the price to be paid?

Multiple choice questions

1 Y Co Ltd, a large department store, advertise their price promise which states that if any customer buys from them and, within 28 days, notifies them in writing that the same goods are on sale at a lower price in another local shop they can have all of the purchase price returned to them. On 1 March a shopper buys a camera from the store for £49.99. On 28 March the shopper posts a letter explaining that the same camera is on sale at another shop for £49.89. The letter arrives on March 30. Which **one** of the following statements is correct?

  a The store's price promise was only an invitation to treat. The shopper made an offer which the store can accept or reject.

  b The store's price promise was an offer which the shopper has validly accepted.

  c The store's price promise was an offer. However, the shopper's acceptance was too late to be effective.

  d The store's price promise was too vague to be an offer and would not apply to a 10p difference in price.

2 At an auction which had been advertised as being 'without reserve' X appears to have made the highest bid for Lot 7. The auctioneer is asking one last time for any higher bids. Assuming that no higher bid is made by anyone else, which **one** of the following statements is correct?

  a X can withdraw his bid. If X does not withdraw his bid the auctioneer can refuse to accept it without being in breach of contract.

  b X can withdraw his bid. If X does not withdraw his bid the auctioneer will be in breach of a collateral contract if he refuses to accept it.

  c X can withdraw his bid. If X does not withdraw his bid, the auctioneer is bound to accept it and X will then have bought Lot 7.

d X cannot withdraw his bid. If X does not withdraw, the auctioneer has no contractual obligation to accept the bid.

3 Xshire County Council place an advertisement in a newspaper asking for tenders to supply 'such paper as we might require over a 12 month period'. Y puts in a tender stating the price at which he is willing to supply the paper. Xshire County Council write to Y accepting his tender for the whole 12 months. Three months later Xshire County Council place an order which Y refuses to fill. Which **one** of the following statements is correct?

   a Y has made a contract to supply orders for any reasonable amount of paper ordered in the year.
   b Y has made a contract to supply any orders for paper placed within the year, no matter how many orders might be placed.
   c Y must fill the particular order which has been made. Y could then revoke his tender, and refuse to fill any more orders.
   d Y has only made an invitation to treat. Each time Xshire County Council place an order this amounts to an offer which Y can either accept or reject.

4 On 20 January X offered to sell his boat to Y. X said that he would have to receive a reply to his offer before 31 January. On 21 January Y telephoned X to ask if X would take a cheque. X replied that he wanted cash. On 29 January X sold the boat to Z, a third party. Y did not know about the sale of the boat and on 30 January he posted a letter, accepting X's offer. The letter did not arrive until 1 February. Which one of the following statements is correct?

   a There is no contract between X and Y. Y made a counter offer which revoked X's offer.
   b There is no contract between X and Y because the boat had already been sold to Z and this revoked X's offer.
   c There is a good contract between X and Y because Y posted the acceptance before the deadline.
   d There is no contract between X and Y because Y's acceptance was not received until after the deadline.

5 Consider the following statements.

   i In certain circumstances the mere fact of inviting tenders may give rise to a binding contractual obligation to consider tenders properly submitted.
   ii Revocation of a unilateral offer will always be effective if it is communicated to the offeror before the offeror has communicated acceptance.
   iii The postal rule can mean that acceptances by post, but not revocations, are effective when posted.
   iv An advertisement that an auction will take place without reserve does not amount to an offer that the auction will take place or that any particular goods will actually be included in the auction.

   Which of the above statements are true?

   a (i), (iii) and (iv) only.
   b (ii) and (iii) only.
   c (i) and (iv) only.
   d All of the statements.

6 A offers to sell his car to B for £3 000. Which of the following would terminate the offer?

   i B offers £2 400 for the car.
   ii B inquires if he can have three months' credit.
   iii A sells the car to C.
   iv B hears from a reliable source that A has sold the car to C.
   v B does not reply for two years.

   a (i), (ii), (iv) and (v) only.
   b (i), (iv) and (v) only.
   c (iii) and (v) only.
   d All of the alternatives.

Task 3

A friend of yours, a market trader, has always bought his goods from wholesalers. Your friend has heard that goods can sometimes be bought very cheaply at auction or by tender, and would like to know the legal position when buying in these ways.

Write a report, indicating:

a How a contract is made.
b The difference between an offer and an invitation to treat.
c The offer and acceptance position when buying at auctions.
d The offer and acceptance position when buying by tender.
e The extent to which offers can be withdrawn after they have been made.

Chapter 4

OTHER REQUIREMENTS OF A CONTRACT – INTENTION TO CREATE LEGAL RELATIONS · CONSIDERATION · FORMALITIES · CAPACITY

Introduction

In Chapter 3 we considered offer and acceptance. In this chapter we consider the two further requirements of a contract: intention to create legal relations and consideration. First we shall see that in order for a contract to be created the offer and acceptance must be made in circumstances which indicate that the parties intended to create legal relations. We shall then see that any party to the contract must provide some consideration in return for the benefits gained under the contract. Towards the end of the chapter we briefly consider those types of contract which can be validly created only if certain formalities are complied with. The chapter concludes by considering the validity of contracts made by minors and mentally disordered persons.

4.1 · Intention to create legal relations

In Chapter 3 we saw that a contract is made through the medium of offer and acceptance. But the acceptance of an offer will only give rise to a contract if the offeror and the offeree appeared to intend to create legal relations. If the parties did not appear to intend that their agreement should be legally binding then there will be no contract.

Let us assume for example that A says to B, 'I will sell you my shares in X Ltd for £10 000', and that B replies, 'I accept'. There is plainly an offer and plainly an acceptance of it. But whether or not the offer and acceptance would create a contract would depend upon the context in which the words were spoken. If A and B were businessmen, dealing at arm's length in a business context, a court would infer that they did intend to make a contract, and there would therefore be a contract. If A and B were friends, speaking the words lightheartedly, there would be no contract because it would be inferred that they did not intend to make a contract.

In ascertaining whether or not the parties intended that their agreement should be legally enforceable the courts take an objective view of the parties' intentions rather than trying to assess the actual intentions of the offeror and offeree. The question is not whether or not the parties actually did intend to enter into a legal relationship, it is whether they appeared to the reasonable person to have this intention. As Lord Devlin put it in *Parker v Clark* [1960] 1 WLR 286: 'The question [whether or not there is a binding contract] must, of course, depend upon the intention of the parties, to be inferred from the language they use and from the circumstances in which they use it.'

4.1.1 Business and commercial agreements

When deciding whether or not there is an intention to create legal relations, the courts divide agreements into two classes; business and commercial agreements on the one hand, and social and domestic agreements on the other. As regards business and commercial agreements, there is a presumption that the parties do intend to make a contract. As regards social and domestic agreements, there is a presumption that they do not. Either of these presumptions can be rebutted by evidence to the contrary.

So if an offer is made and accepted in a business or commercial context a court will start with the strong presumption that the parties did intend to make a contract. An offeror or offeree who wishes to rebut this presumption will need to introduce evidence which shows that there was in fact no intention to create legal relations.

■ ***Esso Petroleum Ltd*** v ***Commissioners of Customs and Excise*** [1976] 1 WLR 1 (House of Lords)

In order to promote their petrol, Esso advertised that they would give a World Cup coin to motorists who bought four gallons of petrol. The coins bore the likeness of one of the 30 footballers in the England squad for the 1970 World Cup. The Customs and Excise Commissioners claimed that the coins were goods on which purchase tax was payable. Schedule 1 to the Purchase Tax Act 1963 made coins of this type liable to purchase tax if they were 'produced in quantity for general sale'.

Held. There was a legally binding contract to supply a World Cup coin to a motorist who bought four gallons of petrol. There was an intention to create legal relations because the advertising took place in a business context and was designed to achieve commercial success.

COMMENT (i) Purchase tax was not payable because the agreement to supply the coin was not a sale. The motorists' consideration for the coins was not the payment of money but rather entering into a contract to buy petrol. (See the definition of a contract of sale of goods at 8.1.1.)
(ii) Two of the five Law Lords thought that there was no intention to create legal relations in respect of the coins.

Many claims made in advertisements, although made in a commercial context, do not amount to definite contractual promises because they are either too vague to be capable of being proved true or are too extravagant to be credible. So the claims by various manufacturers of washing powders that their product washes whitest will amount to no more than sales puffs.

If the parties to a commercial agreement make it quite plain that they do not intend their agreement to be a contract, this will override the presumption that they do intend to enter into legal relations.

■ ***Rose and Frank Co*** v ***Crompton Bros*** [1925] AC 445 (House of Lords)

Since 1905 the claimants had been supplied with the defendants' carbonising tissue paper, which the claimants finished and sold in America. The business between the two parties was very considerable and very profitable. In 1913 the claimants and the defendants both signed a document which expressed their willingness that the claimants should continue to be supplied with the defendants' products. Under this agreement the claimants were to be the defendants' sole agents in the United States for three years, with an option to extend that period for another three years. An 'Honourable Pledge Clause' stated, 'This arrangement is not entered into ... as a formal or legal agreement, and shall not be subject to legal jurisdiction in the law courts either of the United States or England, but it is only a definite expression and record of the purpose and intention of the ... parties concerned, to which they honourably pledge themselves with the fullest confidence, based on past business with each other, that it will be carried through ...' Later the agreement was extended until March 1920, but in 1919 the defendants terminated the agreement without notice. The claimants sued for breach of contract.

Held. The agreement was not a contract and could not therefore be sued upon. The Honourable Pledge Clause dominated the whole signed document and its ordinary and natural meaning was that the agreement should not be legally enforceable.

A letter of comfort is a letter written to give reassurance to a person who is considering extending credit to a third party. Such a letter may amount to a guarantee, in which case it will provide a definite promise to answer for the debt of the third party. A letter of comfort which does not amount to a guarantee may give rise to a contractual obligation, but this will depend upon whether an intention to create legal relations can be inferred from the language of the letter and all the surrounding circumstances.

■ *Kleinwort Benson Ltd* v *Malaysia Mining Corporation Bhd* [1988] 1 WLR 379 (Court of Appeal)

The claimant bank was unwilling to lend money to MMC Metals Ltd, a subsidiary of MMC Bhd. The bank was not satisfied with the creditworthiness of MMC Metals Ltd and asked MMC Bhd to guarantee the loan. MMC Bhd replied that it was not their policy to guarantee loans made to their subsidiaries. After some negotiations, MMC Bhd issued a letter of comfort which stated that it was MMC Bhd's policy to make sure that MMC Metals Ltd was 'at all times in a position to meet its liabilities to you'. The bank made the loan to MMC Metals Ltd which went into liquidation without repaying the debt. The bank sued MMC Bhd on the letter of comfort.

Held. The letter of comfort did not give rise to any contractual liability. The letter contained no contractual promise intending to give rise to a legal relationship. It was merely a statement of present intention.

COMMENT (i) The letter of comfort was carefully drafted so as not to give rise to a contractual promise. However, care should be taken when considering other letters of comfort. In every case the precise wording is likely to be the deciding factor.

(ii) The Court of Appeal distinguished *Edwards* v *Skyways Ltd* [1964] 1 All ER 494. In that case the claimant worked for the defendants as a pilot. He was made redundant, along with 15% of the work-force, and given three months' notice of termination of his employment. The claimant had the right either to withdraw pension contributions he had made, or to take the right to a pension which would become payable at retirement age. At a meeting between the defendants and the claimant's trade association, the defendants said that if the redundant employees withdrew their pension contributions the defendants would make *ex gratia* payments which would approximate to the defendant company's pension contributions. (The fact that the payment was *ex gratia* merely meant that it was made without admitting any legal liability on the defendants' part. It did not mean that the agreement should have no effect in law.) On the strength of the defendants' promise the claimant decided to withdraw from the pension fund and take his own contributions and the promised *ex gratia* payment. The defendants got into some financial difficulty and rescinded the promise to make the *ex gratia* payments. It was held that in a business context there was a strong presumption that an agreement was intended to create legal relations and that the defendants had not rebutted this presumption. Therefore the claimant was entitled to the *ex gratia* payment.

4.1.1.1 Terms which exclude the jurisdiction of the courts

In *Rose and Frank Co* v *Crompton Bros* we saw that it is possible to make a commercial agreement which will not amount to a contract, on account of the parties having expressly stipulated that the agreement should not have any legal effect. However, it is not permissible to make a contract on the basis that the contract will be exempt from the jurisdiction of the courts. Any term in a contract which tries to prevent a party putting an issue of law before a court will be void. (Arbitration, examined in Chapter 2 at 2.4.1 is the one exception to this rule.) An example of a term being held void on account of its attempting to exclude the jurisdiction of the courts can be seen in *Baker* v *Jones* [1954] 1 WLR 1005. In that case the rules of a weightlifting association made a contract between the association and its members. The association was governed by a central council, made up of officers of the association and certain members. One of the association's rules stated that in any dispute between the association and a member the decision of the association should be final, and neither party should be able to take the dispute to any court. A dispute arose as to whether the central council had improperly used the association's money and it was held that the rule giving the central council the sole right to interpret the rules was against public policy and therefore void. This case differs from a case such as *Rose and Frank Co* v *Crompton Bros* in that in *Baker* v *Jones* the rule in question applied to the method of resolving disputes, rather than to the legal effect of the agreement itself. It is permissible to make an agreement and insist that it will have no legal effect. It is not permissible to make a legally binding agreement and say that it should be interpreted by a body other than the ordinary courts.

4.1.2 Social and domestic agreements

When considering whether or not a social or domestic agreement amounted to a contract the courts presume that the parties did not intend to create legal relations. However, this strong presumption can be rebutted by the evidence. All of the circumstances of the case will be examined to deduce the apparent intentions of the parties.

■ *Jones v Padavatton* [1969] 1 WLR 328 (Court of Appeal)

Mrs Padavatton, a 34-year-old divorcee, was working as a secretary at the Indian Embassy In Washington DC, USA. She had a flat in Washington where she lived with her son. Her mother, Mrs Jones, lived in Trinidad. The mother agreed to pay her daughter $200 dollars a month if she would go to England and read for the Bar. The daughter left her job and went to England and enrolled as a student at Lincoln's Inn. The mother paid her daughter an allowance of £42 a month, which was the equivalent of $200 West Indian dollars. (The daughter had thought the agreement was for 200 USA dollars, worth about £70, a month.) Nothing was agreed as to the duration of the agreement. The agreement was subsequently varied so that the daughter, instead of receiving the allowance, was provided with a house where she could live rent free in part of the house and let the rest out to provide herself with money to live on. After a disagreement the mother gave her daughter notice to quit the house. The daughter maintained that under the varied agreement she had a contractual right to remain in occupation.

Held. The daughter was not entitled to remain in occupation. In family agreements there is a strong presumption that the parties do not intend to create legal relations. The facts of the case indicated that the housing arrangements were not made with the intention of creating a contract but were merely family arrangements.

COMMENT (i) Although the majority of the Court of Appeal, Danckwerts and Fenton Atkinson LJJ thought that there was no intention to create legal relations, Salmon LJ thought that there was. Salmon thought that the initial agreement had been a unilateral offer by the mother but that it was an implied term that the daughter should complete her studies within a reasonable time. As she was not close to completing her Bar exams five years after becoming a student Salmon LJ thought that the offer had lapsed.

(ii) Danckwerts and Fenton Atkinson LJJ also held that the agreement was far too vague and uncertain to amount to a contract.

In *Balfour* v *Balfour* [1919] 2 KB 571, the Court of Appeal established the principle that agreements between husband and wife are unlikely to be contracts unless there is very clear evidence that this was in fact the intention. In that case Lord Atkin said: '… one of the most usual forms of agreement which does not constitute a contract appears to me to be the arrangements which are made between husband and wife … they are not contracts because the parties did not intend that they should be attended by legal consequences … All I can say is that the small courts of this country would have to be multiplied one hundredfold if these arrangements were held to result in legal obligations.'

However, the principle set out in the *Balfour* case is very much weakened if the husband and wife are separated or are contemplating separation.

■ *Merritt* v *Merritt* [1970] 1 WLR 1121 (Court of Appeal)

A husband and wife married in 1941 and in 1949 built a house as their home. The house was in the husband's name but in 1966 the couple put the house in their joint names. Soon after this the husband left the wife and went to live with another woman. £180 was left owing on the building society mortgage. The husband and wife held a meeting in the husband's car where the husband agreed to pay the wife £40 a month so that she could keep up the mortgage instalments. The husband gave the wife the building society mortgage book. The wife insisted that the husband sign a statement saying that if she paid all the charges which arose in connection with the house until the mortgage was paid off he would transfer sole ownership of the house to her. The husband signed the agreement. When the wife had paid off the mortgage the husband reduced the payments to £25 a month. The wife applied for a declaration that the house now belonged to her and that the husband should immediately transfer ownership to her.

Held. The agreement which the husband and wife had made was binding upon them. As the couple were no longer living together, the presumption that they did not intend to make a contract was greatly reduced. A reasonable person looking at the agreement would have regarded it as intending to be binding.

COMMENT Lord Denning MR stressed that the courts do not seek the actual intentions of the parties, but their apparent intentions: 'In all these cases the court does not try to discover the intention by looking into the minds of the parties. It looks at the situation in which they were placed and asks itself: would reasonable people regard this agreement as intended to be binding?'

The following case examined whether an agreement between friends, a social agreement, amounted to a contract.

■ *Coward* v *MIB* [1963] 1 QB 359 (Court of Appeal)

In December 1953 Coward and his friend Cole were killed in a motorcycle accident. The motorcycle was owned and driven by Cole while Coward rode as a pillion passenger. The accident was caused by Cole's negligence. Coward's widow sued Cole's personal representatives and was awarded £7 850 19s. damages. This sum was not paid because Cole's insurance did not cover pillion passengers and Cole's estate was of no value. Coward's widow therefore sued the Motor Insurance Bureau who were bound to pay only if the insurance of the pillion passenger was compulsory. If Coward had been carried for 'hire or reward' then insurance of him would have been compulsory, but not otherwise. It was therefore argued by Coward's widow that Cole had made a contract to carry Coward on the bike. Coward had paid Cole a small weekly sum in exchange for being given a lift to work each day.

Held. There was no contract because neither party would have intended to enter into a legal contract.

COMMENT The facts of *Albert* v *Motor Insurers' Bureau* [1971] 3 WLR 291 (House of Lords) were very similar but the outcome was different. Q, the owner of the car in which the passenger was killed, was a docker who had given other dockers a lift to work for eight years. He would carry any docker who would pay and his services were well known although not advertised. The House of Lords decided that these passengers were carried under a contract, the test being whether there was a systematic carrying of passengers which went beyond the bounds of mere social kindness, that is to say whether the agreement was predominantly a business agreement rather than a social one. On the facts of the case this test was satisfied and it did not matter that neither the driver nor the passengers intended any contract to result.

Test your understanding

1 When an agreement is made in a business or commercial context what presumption do the courts make as to whether or not there was an intention to create legal relations?

2 When an agreement is made in a social or domestic context what presumption do the courts make as to whether or not there was an intention to create legal relations?

3 What is a letter of comfort?

4 What is the effect of a contractual term which excludes the jurisdiction of the courts?

Answers

1 When an agreement is made in a business or commercial context the courts will presume that the parties did intend to create legal relations. This presumption can be rebutted by the evidence.

2 When an agreement is made in a social or domestic context the courts will presume that the parties did not intend to create legal relations. This presumption can be rebutted by the evidence.

3 A letter of comfort is a letter designed to give reassurance. It might or might not give rise to contractual liability depending upon the words used and the circumstances of the case.

4 Any contractual term which excludes the jurisdiction of the courts will be void. (A term providing that disputes should be referred to arbitration is the only exception to this principle.)

4.2 · Consideration

An agreement cannot amount to a contract unless each party gives some 'consideration' to the other. The word 'consideration' is used here not in its everyday sense, but in the legal sense of a benefit. In bilateral contracts the consideration of both parties takes the form of a promise to do something in the future. The consideration of a person accepting a unilateral offer lies in performing the act specified, rather than in making a promise. In *Currie* v *Misa* (1875) LR 10 Ex 153 the following well-recognised definition of consideration was made: 'A valuable consideration, in the sense of the law, may consist either in some right, interest, profit or benefit accruing to one party, or some forbearance, detriment, loss or responsibility, given, suffered or undertaken by the other.' This definition might be abbreviated to say that consideration consists either in the giving of a benefit or the suffering of a loss. Usually it will amount to both. In a contract of sale of goods, for example, the buyer's consideration is the promise to pay the price. The giving of this promise is a benefit to the seller while at the same time it is a loss to the buyer.

It is the requirement that consideration must move to and from each party which distinguishes contracts from gifts. If a contract is made, each side gives a benefit to the other in return for a benefit received. If a gift is made, only one side gives a benefit.

Let us look at an example. A says to B, 'I will sell you my fax machine for £200', and B accepts. This is a contract, not a gift, because each party has given some consideration to the other. A's consideration is the promise to give B the fax machine. B's consideration is the promise to pay the money.

If, however, A had said, 'I will give you my fax machine', and B had replied, 'Thank you very much. I accept', there would be no contract. A would have given some consideration to B, but B would not have given any consideration in return.

A contract which is not made by a deed is known as a simple contract and it is in simple contracts that consideration must be given by both parties. An agreement made by deed is enforceable as a specialty contract without the need to prove that consideration was given by both parties. So a promise to make a gift would not be enforceable unless it was made by a deed. The way in which a deed is made is considered below at 4.3.

4.2.1 Executory, executed and past consideration

Executory consideration consists of a promise to do something in the future. The consideration is called executory because when the contract is made the promisor has not yet performed (executed) his consideration. If we examine a typical bilateral contract, for example *Nicolene Ltd* v *Simmonds* at 3.3.1 we see that the consideration of both parties was executory. The defendant promised that he would deliver the 3 000 tons of steel bars, and the claimants promised that they would pay for them.

Executed consideration occurs when one of the parties makes the offer or the acceptance in such a way that he has completely fulfilled his liability under the contract. The only contractual liability remaining is that of the other party. A seller of goods, for example, might offer to sell goods if the buyer sends cash with an order. If the buyer accepts this offer by sending the cash then his consideration is executed. Executed consideration is found in the acceptance of unilateral offers, where the acceptance is made by performing some action rather than by promising to do something in the future. For example, in *Carlill* v *The Carbolic Smoke Ball Company* [1893] Mrs Carlill's consideration was executed. She did not promise to use a smoke ball and catch flu, she just did it. The consideration of the smoke ball company, being a promise, was executory.

Past consideration is said to be no consideration. This means that a party cannot give as consideration some act which he has already performed, because to promise to do something which has already been done is to promise nothing at all. In some circumstances the rule can seem rather unfair, but it is a logical consequence of a contract being a bargain under which both parties exchange something of value.

■ *Re McArdle* [1951] Ch 669 (Court of Appeal)

In 1935 William McArdle died, leaving his estate to his wife for life and then on trust for his five children. One of William's sons, Monty McArdle, lived with his wife Marjorie in a bungalow which formed part of William's estate. In 1943 Monty and Marjorie carried out improvements and repairs to the bungalow which was called Gravel Hill. The cost of this work was £488 and it was paid for by Marjorie. In 1945 Monty and his brothers and sisters signed a document which contained the following terms: 'To Mrs Marjorie McArdle … In consideration of your carrying out certain alterations and improvements to the property known as Gravel Hill … we the beneficiaries under the will of William Henry McArdle hereby agree that the executors … shall pay to you … the sum of £488 in settlement of the amount spent on such improvements.' The money was to be paid when William McArdle's estate was distributed among the five children. When this time came Monty's brothers and sisters refused to agree to the payment.

Held. The agreement to pay the money was not enforceable as a contract. At the time of executing the agreement all of the work had been completed and so the consideration for the agreement was wholly past consideration.

Similarly, in *Roscorla* v *Thomas* (1842) 3 QB 324 a promise that a horse was 'sound and free from vice' was given after the contract to buy the horse had been made. The purchaser soon discovered that the horse was very vicious, but the promise was held to have no legal effect. No consideration had been received for the promise. The purchaser's consideration, promising to pay the purchase price of the horse, was past when the seller's promise that the horse was sound and free from vice was made. Nothing was therefore given in return for that promise.

However, a past act can amount to good consideration for a promise by another person if three conditions are satisfied. First, the act must have been performed at the request of the promisor. Second, both parties must all along have contemplated that payment would be made. Third, the payment given in return for the act would have to have been legally enforceable if it had been given before the act had been performed, that is to say all the requirements to form a contract would have to have been satisfied.

■ *Lampleigh* v *Brathwaite* (1615) Hob 105

The defendant had killed another man and he asked the claimant to go to the King and obtain a pardon. The claimant managed to get the pardon, a task which involved many days' labour in riding around following the King. Afterwards the defendant was so grateful that he agreed to pay the claimant £100 for the work he had done. Later the defendant refused to pay.

Held. The defendant had to pay the £100 because he had asked the claimant to get the pardon and because both parties would have contemplated that payment would be made.

COMMENT The principle of the case, that there was a good contract, remains unchanged. However, s.15(1) of the Supply of Goods and Services Act 1982 would now imply a term that if no price is fixed when a contract for the supply of a service is made, then the supplier should be paid a reasonable price (see Chapter 8 at 8.4.3.3).

4.2.2 Sufficient not adequate

It is a general principle of the law of contract that consideration must be 'sufficient' but need not be 'adequate'. In everyday usage the words sufficient and adequate have very similar meanings and this can make the principle seem rather puzzling. However, in this legal context the words 'sufficient' and 'adequate' have distinct meanings. Sufficient means of some recognisable economic value, however small. Adequate means of the same value as the other party's consideration.

By way of example, let us examine a contract to buy a new Ford Ka for its normal selling price of £9 000. The consideration given by the buyer is both sufficient and adequate, and so is the consideration given by the seller. That is to say that the buyer's promise to pay the money is generally thought to be worth much the same as the seller's promise to transfer ownership of the car.

If the contract had been to sell the new car for £1 then the buyer's consideration would have been sufficient, but would not have been adequate. However, as long as the seller had freely agreed to the deal, and as long as there was an intention to create legal relations, the inadequacy of the buyer's consideration would not matter. The deal would still be a contract. In *Thomas v Thomas* (1842) 2 QB 851, for example, the claimant was given a house and premises for life in return for paying £1 a year towards the ground rent and keeping the house in good repair. It was held that this amounted to a contract.

In *White v Bluett* (1853) 23 LJ Ex 36 the court had to consider whether a son's promise to his father that he would stop complaining amounted to sufficient consideration. The son had made out a promissory note in favour of his father in respect of money which the father had lent to him. The father had distributed his property in a way which the son considered unfair. The son agreed to stop complaining about this if the father agreed not to enforce the promissory note. The agreement was made but the father later sued the son on the promissory note. It was held that the father could do this because the son's promise to stop complaining could not amount to sufficient consideration. The promise could not be said to be of any economic value.

The rule that consideration does not need to be adequate seems to be based on two principles. The first principle is that it is impossible for the courts to attach definite values to goods and services. The value of a thing at any particular time depends on any number of circumstances. A second reason why the courts have never concerned themselves with the adequacy of consideration is that they have always taken the view that people are free to make any contracts they like. If a business uses this freedom to make bad contracts then the courts will not protect the business from its own stupidity. If the contracts made are sufficiently costly, then it is in the public interest that the business should cease to exist and be replaced by another business which is more astute.

4.2.2.1 Trivial acts

Even performing a trivial act is capable of amounting to sufficient consideration, as long as the performance of it can be regarded as conferring an economic benefit. This important principle can be extracted from the following case.

■ *Chappell & Co Ltd v The Nestlé Co Ltd* [1960] AC 87 (House of Lords)

As part of an advertising campaign, the Nestlé company was 'giving away' records to members of the public who sent 1/6d (7.5p) and three chocolate bar wrappers. Nestlé bought the records for 4d each from H. Co and made a slight profit on each sale. The wrappers sent in were thrown away. The records consisted of thin strips of cellulose acetate which were then mounted on cardboard discs which advertised Nestlé's chocolate. The copyright in the record was owned by the claimants, who were most unhappy with Nestlé's scheme because ordinarily records were sold for 6/8d (34p). Section 8 of the Copyright Act 1956 protected retailers against claims for breach of copyright if they paid 6.25% of the 'ordinary retail selling price' of the record to the copyright holders. If the ordinary retail selling price could not be ascertained Nestlés would have been in breach of the Copyright Act. Nestlé claimed that the ordinary retail selling price of the records was 1/6d, arguing that the wrappers were of no value and that sending them was not therefore part of the consideration. The claimants applied for an injunction to prevent further manufacturing of the records.

Held. The sending of the wrappers was part of the consideration. (If customers had sent 1/6d without the wrappers they would not have received a record.) Therefore, the copyright holder could prevent further manufacture and sale of the records.

COMMENT (i) Lord Reid had no doubt that the promotion of the scheme was designed to be an economic benefit to Nestlé Ltd: 'The Nestlé Co's intention can hardly be in doubt. They were not setting out to trade in gramophone records. They were using these records to increase their sales of chocolate ... The requirement that wrappers should be sent was of great importance to the Nestlé Co; there would have been no point in their simply offering records for 1s. 6d each.'

(ii) Lord Somervell made it plain that the adequacy of the consideration was not relevant as long as the consideration conferred some economic benefit: 'It is said that when received the wrappers are of no value to Nestlés. This I would have thought irrelevant. A contracting party can stipulate for what consideration he chooses. A peppercorn does not cease to be good consideration if it is established that the promisee does not like pepper and will throw the corn away … the whole object of selling the record … was to increase the sales of chocolate.'

(iii) If sending the wrappers was part of the consideration for the records then it logically follows that sending the wrappers could have been the whole of the consideration.

4.2.2.2 Privity of contract

The common law has always prevented a person who is not a party to a contract from suing on the contract. This is the case even if the contract was expressly made for the benefit of the person trying to sue. The rule is known as privity of contract. The contract is regarded as private between the offeror and the offeree and no other person can become liable under the contract or sue to enforce it. The following case provides a classic example of the rule.

■ *Tweddle* v *Atkinson* (1831) 1 B & S 393

The claimant married the daughter of William Guy. At the time of the marriage William Guy and John Tweddle, the claimant's father, agreed with each other that they would both pay the claimant a sum of money. William Guy promised to pay the claimant £200 and in return for this promise John Tweddle promised to pay the claimant £100. The agreement said that the claimant 'has full power to sue the said parties in any court of law or equity for the aforesaid sums hereby promised and specified'. William Guy died without having paid the £200 he had promised to pay. The claimant sued William Guy's personal representatives for the money.

Held. The claimant could not sue on the contract because he was not a party to it.

COMMENT William Guy had broken the contract which he had made with John Tweddle and John Tweddle could have sued him for breach of contract. However, John Tweddle would only have been awarded nominal damages for the breach of contract as it had caused him no loss. In *Jackson* v *Horizon Holidays Ltd* [1975] 1 WLR 1468 the Court of Appeal appeared to depart from this principle and awarded substantial damages to a man who had booked a holiday for himself and his wife. The holiday was disastrous and the trial judge awarded damages of £1 100 to compensate for the loss of enjoyment suffered by both the husband and his wife. The Court of Appeal allowed this award to stand, but gave different reasons for doing so. Lord Denning MR said that the husband could claim damages on behalf of his wife's vexation and discomfort as the contract was made for her benefit. This decision was severely criticised by the House of Lords in *Woodar Investment Developments Ltd* v *Wimpey Construction UK Ltd* [1980] 1 WLR 277. Lord Keith said that the decision in *Jackson* v *Horizon Holidays* did not 'lay down any rule regarding the recovery of damages for the benefit of third parties'. In the light of the criticism made by the House of Lords, the reasoning of Lord Denning must be regarded as incorrect. In the case of package holidays only, the Package Travel, Package Holidays and Package Tours Regulations 1992 now allow damages to be awarded for loss of enjoyment suffered by holidaymakers who did not make the contract.

The privity rule was affirmed by the House of Lords in the following case.

■ *Dunlop Pneumatic Tyre Co Ltd* v *Selfridge & Co Ltd* [1915] AC 847 (House of Lords)

Dunlop sold car tyres to Dew & Co, who were dealers in motor accessories. In return for being given a 10% discount on the price, Dew & Co agreed that they would obtain a written undertaking from any person to whom they resold the tyres that the tyres would not be sold on below a certain price. Dew & Co resold the tyres to Selfridge & Co. Dew & Co gave Selfridge & Co a discount on the price of the tyres in return for the written agreement not to sell the tyres on below the agreed price. Selfridge & Co sold the tyres on below the agreed price and Dunlop sued them on the written agreement not to do this.

Held. Dunlop could not sue Selfridge on the agreement as there was no contract between them. Dunlop had given no consideration to Selfridge & Co in return for the promise not to sell the tyres on below the agreed price. The discount which Selfridge & Co had been given in return for their agreement had been given by Dew & Co and not by Dunlop.

When a contract is made on behalf of a third party it is in some circumstances possible for the contracting party to obtain a decree of specific performance of the contract. If such a decree is obtained the third party may be able to enforce the performance of the contract.

■ *Beswick* v *Beswick* [1968] AC 58 (House of Lords)

A coal merchant assigned his business to his nephew in return for the nephew agreeing to pay the coal merchant £6 10s. for the rest of his life. The agreement also provided that if the coal merchant should predecease his wife the nephew would pay the widow £5 a week for the rest of her life. After the coal merchant died the nephew made only one payment to the widow. Then the nephew refused to make any more payments on the grounds of privity of contract. The widow sued for arrears of £175 and for an order of specific performance requiring future payments to be made. The widow sued not only in her personal capacity, but also as administratrix of her husband's estate.

Held. The widow did not succeed in her personal capacity. However, she did succeed in her capacity as administratrix of her husband's estate. The widow could only be awarded nominal damages because her husband's estate had suffered no loss as a consequence of the refusal to make the payments to the widow. However, the widow could have specific performance of the contract as she was, in effect, suing as her husband.

COMMENT This decision achieved justice in the case but is problematic. The remedy of specific performance is examined in Chapter 7 at 7.2.4, where we shall see that it is rarely ordered. In this case it could only be ordered because of the coincidence that the widow happened to be the administratrix of her husband's estate. If someone else had been the administrator they would have been unlikely to risk a legal action on the widow's behalf. Specific performance is not ordered to enforce personal service contracts. Nor is it usually ordered to enforce contracts of continuing obligation.

There are several well-established exceptions to the privity rule. Assignment can allow the benefit of a contract to be transferred to another person if certain procedures are followed. Agency allows one person to make a contract on behalf of another (see Chapter 11). When two parties create a contract a collateral contract may arise in favour of a third party (see Chapter 14 at 14.2). The privity rule does not apply in the law of trusts where a beneficiary under a trust is entitled to sue to enforce the trust. There are also several statutory exceptions to the rule. Over the years several attempts to evade the doctrine of privity have been made. The Contract (Rights of Third Parties) Act 1999 has modified the rule in some circumstances.

The Contracts (Rights of Third Parties) Act 1999

This Act does not abolish the privity rule, but does in some circumstances enable a third party to enforce a term of a contract. Section 1 sets out the two circumstances in which a third party may enforce a term of a contract made by the promisor and the promisee. 'The promisor' is defined by the Act as meaning the party to the contract against whom the term is enforceable by the third party. 'The promisee' is defined as meaning the party to the contract by whom the term is enforceable against the promisor. For example, let us assume that a shop sells a television to X, that the television is not of satisfactory quality, and that the Act operates to allow Y to sue the shop. The shop is the promisor, X is the promisee, and Y is the third party.

Section 1(1)(a) of this Act provides that a third party may enforce a term of a contract if the contract expressly provides that he may. For example, the contract between X and the shop might have expressly stated that Y was to be able to enforce the contract or that he could enforce certain terms of the contract.

Section 1(1)(b) allows a third party to enforce a term of a contract if the term purports to confer a benefit on him. However, s.1(2) provides that this will not be the case if on a proper construction of the contract it appears that the parties did not intend the term to be enforceable by the third party. The Law Commission, whose proposed Bill was enacted as this Act, considered that the effect of s.1(2) was to create a rebuttable presumption that a third party can enforce a term which objectively purports to confer a contractual benefit on him. If therefore a term in the contract between X and the shop had purported to confer a benefit on Y (for example by stipulating that the television should be delivered to Y at his home address), it would be presumed that Y could enforce the term but this presumption would be rebuttable.

Section 1(3) requires that, whether using the s.1(1)(a) route or the s.1(1)(b) route the third party must be expressly identified in the contract by name, as a member of a class or as answering a particular description. Express identification by name needs no explanation. Express identification by class could arise in many ways, for example if a contractual provision was made for the benefit of all the members of a particular club, or for the benefit of the promisee's brothers and sisters. Express identification of the third party as his or her answering a particular description could also arise in many ways, for example if a contractual provision was made for the benefit of 'my youngest brother' or for the benefit of the Sheriff of Nottingham. Although the third party must be expressly identified, he does not need to be in existence when the contract is entered into (s.1(3)). So enforceable rights could be conferred on unborn children or on companies which had not yet been incorporated.

When a benefit is conferred on a third party by the Act, the third party can avail himself of any remedy which would have been available to him if he had made the contract (s.1(5)). The third party can also avail himself of exclusion or limitation clauses (s.1(6)). Section 4 provides that s.1 does not affect any right of the promisee to enforce any term of the contract. So any rights conferred on the third party are additional to rights conferred on the promisee. However, s.5 protects the promisor from double liability. Section 5(a) provides that where the promisee has recovered any sum in respect of the third party's loss in respect of a term, any award to the third party by the court would be reduced to take account of this. Section 5(b) provides that where the promisee has recovered from the promisor a sum in respect of the expense to the promisee of making good to the third party the default of the promisor, any award to the third party by the court would be reduced to take account of this. So the overall effect of s.5 is that the promisor will not have to compensate twice for a loss to the third party.

Section 2(1) provides that where the third party does gain rights under s.1 to enforce a term of a contract, the parties to the contract may not generally rescind or vary the contract in such a way as to extinguish or alter the third party's rights without his consent. However, this is only the case if the third party has communicated his assent to the contract to the promisor, or if the promisor knows that the third party has relied on the term, or if the promisor should reasonably have foreseen that the third party would rely on the term and the third party has in fact relied upon it. The assent of the third party may be by words or conduct. If it is sent by post it is not to be regarded as communicated to the promisor until received by him (s.2(2)).

The parties to the contract will be able to rescind or vary it without the consent of the third party if an express term of the contract allows them to do this, or if an express term sets out the circumstances in which they will be able to do this (s.2(3)). The assent of the third party can be dispensed with if his whereabouts cannot be reasonably ascertained or if he is mentally incapable of giving his assent (s.2(4)). Section 2(5) allows the court, on application of the parties to a contract, to dispense with the third party's assent if it is satisfied that it cannot reasonably be ascertained whether or not the third party has in fact relied on the term. If the court does dispense with the third party's consent, s.2(6) allows it to impose such conditions as it thinks fit, including a condition requiring the payment of compensation to the third party.

Section 3 provides that if the promisor has any defences, or rights of set-off, arising from or in connection with the contract, these shall be as available against the third party as would have been available against the promisee. For example, a contract is made between B and C. B is to sell 50 bicycles to C, and a term of the contract provides that C should pay the price to D. B delivers only 30 bicycles to C. C accepts the 30 bicycles. C will not need to pay the whole contract price to D, but will only need to pay the price of 30 bicycles. Similarly, if B had induced the contract by making an actionable misrepresentation, or breached the requirement that the goods be of satisfactory quality, C could raise these matters as a defence against D. The promisor will also have available defences, rights of set-off and counterclaims which did not arise in connection with the contract, if these would have been available against the third party if the third party had been a party to the contract. For example, B agrees to sell 50 bicycles to C. A term of the contract provides that C is to pay the price of £5 000 to D. D owes £1 000 to C in connection with a contract made last month. C is entitled to set-off the £1 000 and pay D only £4 000.

Section 6 makes it plain that the Act does not alter the law relating to negotiable instruments. Nor does it confer rights on a third party in the case of any contract binding on a company and its members under s.14 of the Companies Act 1985.

Section 7(1) provides that s.1 does not affect any right or remedy of a third party that exists or is available apart from this Act. This allows common law development of third party rights and preserves existing exceptions to the doctrine of privity, whether they be common law or statutory.

Section 7(2) prevents a third party from relying on s.2(2) of the Unfair Contract Terms Act (UCTA) 1977 where the negligence consists of the breach of an obligation arising from a term of a contract. This is somewhat controversial because the third party is put in a worse position than the promisee would have been in. The promisee can use s.2(2) UCTA 1977 to challenge an exclusion or limitation clause on which the promisor intends to rely. The third party cannot use s.2(2) in this way. A third party could rely on s.2(2) UCTA if he was bringing his claim in tort. A third party who is injured or killed by negligence could still rely on s.2(1) UCTA, even where the negligence consists of the breach of an obligation arising from a term of a contract. Section 2(2) UCTA is considered in Chapter 5 at 5.6.1.1.

The limitation periods within which the third party must bring a claim are the same as if he had been the promisee.

4.2.2.3 Performing an existing duty

Whether or not it is good consideration to promise to perform a legal duty which has already arisen depends upon how that duty arose. The existing duty might have arisen under the general law, under a previous contract with a different person or under a previous contract with the same person. Each of the three situations needs to be considered in turn.

The duty was imposed by law

A promise by a person to do something which the general law of the land already obliges him to do will not amount to good consideration.

■ *Collins* v *Godefroy* (1813) 1 B & Ad 950

Godefroy caused Collins to be subpoenaed to go to court and give evidence in a court case which Godefroy was pursuing. (This meant that Collins was legally obliged to attend and give evidence.) Collins attended the court for six days but was not in fact called to give evidence. Collins then demanded 6 guineas (£6.30) as his usual fee for attending in court. Godefroy agreed to pay this, but later a dispute arose.

Held. Collins was not entitled to any payment. As Collins was obliged by the general law to attend and give evidence, he had given Godefroy no consideration for his promise to pay the money.

However, a promise to exceed a duty imposed by the general law will amount to good consideration.

■ *Glasbrook Bros* v *Glamorgan County Council* [1925] AC 270 (House of Lords)

During a coal strike a colliery manager asked the police for extra protection for his colliery and insisted that this could only be provided by billeting policemen on the colliery premises. The police superintendent claimed that this would not be necessary because a mobile force could provide adequate protection. The colliery manager then agreed to pay for extra police at a specified rate if they were billeted on the colliery premises. After the strike the colliery owners refused to pay the bill of £2 300, arguing that no consideration had been provided by the police even though the extra police had been billeted on the colliery premises.

Held. The colliery owners had to pay. The police had a discretion as to how and where best to deploy their forces. If the police believed that adequate protection could have been given by a mobile force then any greater protection could amount to consideration for the manager's promise.

COMMENT   In *Harris* v *Sheffield United Football Club* [1987] 2 All ER 838 this decision was followed. Extra police were needed inside the defendant's football ground as a result of violence at home matches. The police claimed £51 699 for providing special police services between August 1982 and November 1983. Section 15(1) of the Police Act 1964 was applied, requiring the club to pay. The Court of Appeal held that the club had requested the extra police presence because the extra presence was necessary to enable the club to play its matches safely. It was also held, following *Glasbrook*, that the extent of the police services provided was beyond that which the club was entitled to expect.

The duty arose under a previous contract with a different person

It is possible for a person to give the same consideration to two different people, thereby creating two valid contracts, as the following case shows.

■ *Shadwell* v *Shadwell* (1860) 9 CB (NS) 159

The claimant was engaged to marry Ellen Nicholl. In those days this was a contract, and if the claimant had broken off the engagement Ellen could have sued him. The claimant's uncle wrote to the claimant in the following way, 'I am glad to hear of your intended marriage with E.N.; and, as I promised to assist you at starting, I am happy to tell you that I will pay to you £150 yearly during my life and until your annual income derived from your profession of a Chancery barrister shall amount to 600 guineas. Your ever affectionate uncle, A.' The claimant married Ellen Nicholl and received the full allowance for twelve of the next 18 years and part of the allowance for one year. The claimant's income from his work as a Chancery barrister never exceeded 600 guineas. The uncle died without having paid five of the yearly sums. The claimant sued the uncle's personal representatives for the payments which had not been made.

Held. The claimant was entitled to the money. His promise to marry Ellen was good consideration in return for the uncle's promise to pay the money, even though he had already given exactly the same promise to Ellen Nicholl in his contract with her.

The principle that the same consideration can be given to two different persons can be important in a business context, as the following case demonstrates.

■ *New Zealand Shipping Co Ltd* v *A M Satterthwaite & Co Ltd* [1974] AC 154 (Privy Council)

Carriers made a contract with the owners of a drilling machine, agreeing to take the machine by sea to New Zealand. The contract provided that the owners of the machine could not sue the carriers, or the stevedores who unloaded the ship, unless the claim was brought within one year. While unloading the machine, the stevedores damaged it. More than one year later, the owners sued the stevedores. The stevedores relied on the agreement between the carriers and the owners. The owners argued that privity of contract meant that the stevedores could not rely on this agreement because they had provided no consideration to the owners.

Held. The owners' promise not to sue if the goods were damaged did form a contract between the owners and the stevedores. The stevedores provided consideration to the owners of the machine by unloading the machine. It was irrelevant that the stevedores had already promised someone else, the carriers, that they would unload the machine.

The duty arose under a previous contract with the same person

The position here is less clear. Until recently there was a well-established rule that it is not good consideration for a claimant to promise to perform an existing contractual duty owed to the defendant. Although this might seem unfair, the rule had a logical foundation.

Let us assume that A has promised B that he will service B's boiler for £100. The contract gives rights to B. If A does not perform, B could sue and get damages. Let us now assume that A says that he will not perform and that B, instead of suing, promises to pay an extra £50 if A goes ahead and does perform his contract. If A does service the boiler he can only claim £100. He will not be entitled to the extra £50 because he gave no extra benefit to B in return for the extra £50. This is because if, after the second agreement, A still did not service the boiler B could only sue him for the same damages as owing under the first agreement. In effect B has been given nothing for the extra £50.

This principle was clearly laid down in the following case.

■ *Stilk* v *Myrick* (1809) 2 Camp 317

The claimant signed ship's articles, agreeing to work as a sailor on a voyage for £5 a month. In the course of the voyage, at Crondstat, two of the eleven man crew deserted. The captain agreed that if replacements could not be found, and if the remaining crew worked the rest of the voyage, then the wages of the two deserters would be shared among the remaining crew members. The remaining crew agreed and worked the ship back to London. The captain then refused to pay the extra wages promised.

Held. The men were not entitled to the extra money, but only to the £5 a month originally agreed. They had already promised the captain that they would do their duty when they took their jobs. They could not give the same promise to the same person to create a new contract.

COMMENT   In those days there were of course no demarcation roles for sailors. Lord Ellenborough, explaining that the men had given no extra consideration, said: 'There was no consideration for the ulterior pay promised to the mariners who remained with the ship. Before they sailed from London they had undertaken to do all that they could under all the emergencies of the voyage. They had sold all their services till the voyage should be completed.'

If the claimant exceeds the duty owed to the defendant then this can amount to fresh consideration. This was the decision in a very similar case, *Hartley* v *Ponsonby* (1857) 7 E & B 872, where half of a ship's crew deserted and the captain promised extra money to those remaining if they completed the voyage. The jury found as a fact that it was unreasonable to carry on with the voyage with such a diminished crew. Therefore by agreeing to complete the voyage the remaining crew were giving more than they had originally promised and were entitled to the extra money. Lord Ellenborough, in *Stilk* v *Myrick* indicated that the men would have been paid the extra money if they had exceeded their duty. He said: 'If they had been at liberty to quit the vessel at Crondstat the case would have been quite different.'

This area of the law was recently considered by the Court of Appeal in the following case.

■ *Williams* v *Roffey Bros Ltd* [1990] 2 WLR 1153 (Court of Appeal)

The defendants had a contract to refurbish a block of flats. They employed Williams to do the carpentry work on 27 of the flats at a price of £20 000. After doing the carpentry on a few flats Williams realised that he had priced the job too low. He told the defendants that he could not afford to finish the job. The defendants were alarmed because if they did not finish the main contract on time they would have to pay huge penalty clauses to the owner of the block of flats. They therefore orally agreed to pay Williams an extra £575 per flat if he did the carpentry work as originally agreed. Williams did the carpentry work on eight more flats but was not paid all of the extra money which he had been promised. He therefore stopped work on the flats and sued for the amount he had not been paid.

Held. Williams was entitled to the extra money. By carrying on and doing the carpentry work as originally agreed he had helped the defendants avoid the penalty clause. This was a benefit to the defendants because it resulted in their gaining a commercial advantage. It therefore amounted to fresh consideration.

COMMENT (i) If the parties had abandoned their original contract and made a new one then there would have been no doubt that Williams would have been entitled to the extra money. (See Discharge by Agreement in Chapter 7 at 7.1.2.) However, there was no evidence that this is what happened.

(ii) The Court of Appeal did not overrule *Stilk* v *Myrick*, but claimed to have refined it. However, the principle of the two cases appears to be very similar. All three Court of Appeal judges thought that the defendants had been given a 'practical benefit' when the claimant agreed to carry on with the work. Russell LJ thought that fresh consideration was provided because under the agreement to pay more money per flat completed the 'previous haphazard method of payment' was replaced by a 'more formalised scheme involving the payment of a specified sum on the completion of each flat'. This gave the defendants more control over the carpenter's performance and, along with the fact that the defendants would not need to employ another subcontractor, was an advantage accruing to the defendant. Glidewell LJ thought that the defendants would have needed in practice to obtain a benefit or 'obviate a disbenefit'. He thought that on the facts this condition had been satisfied because: (a) the agreement sought to ensure that the claimant would continue work and not stop in breach of his subcontract; (b) the agreement enabled the defendants to avoid the penalty clause; and (c) the agreement prevented the defendants from having to go to the trouble and expense of finding another carpenter. (iii) When considering whether or not the performance of an existing duty already owed to the defendant amounts to good consideration, duress, economic duress or fraud might also be relevant. (Duress and economic duress are considered in Chapter 6 at 6.3.1.) There was no such concept as economic duress when *Stilk* v *Myrick* was decided. If there had been then the agreement to pay the extra money might have been avoided on the grounds of economic duress rather than invalid for lack of consideration.

The current position as to whether or not a promise to perform an existing duty can amount to good consideration is summarised by Figure 4.1.

4.2.2.4 Compositions with creditors

If an insolvent person owes money to more than one creditor, all of the creditors might make a composition agreement between themselves. Under such an agreement all the creditors would agree with each other that they would settle for less than they were owed.

Let us assume, for example, that an insolvent businessman owes £10 000 to A, £20 000 to B, and £20 000 to C. The businessman's assets only amount to £10 000. A, B, and C might agree with each other that they will each accept 20p in the pound on the debts owed. If they do agree this, then all three will make a contract with each other. Each of the creditors has promised the other two, 'I will accept 20p in the pound, if you will', see Figure 4.2.

If any creditor sued for the whole amount owing to him the other creditors could prevent the action from going ahead. But if all the creditors changed their minds and sued the businessman for the full debt (perhaps because he had come into some money) he could not prevent them from doing this, because he gave no consideration for the composition agreement.

4.2.2.5 Settling out of court

When a dispute is settled out of court a party who honestly and reasonably believes that he has a right to sue promises to give up that right in return for a payment from the other party. Such an agreement is a perfectly valid contract and there is no need to prove that the legal claim given up would have been successful. The vast majority of legal disputes are settled in this way and it is highly desirable that they should be. (Dispute resolution is considered in Chapter 2 at 2.4.)

For example, let us assume that Firm A's van has run over and injured B, who is demanding £50 000 compensation. Eventually the parties, through their solicitors, settle for a payment of £30 000. This is a contract. Firm A's consideration consists of the promise to pay the money. B's consideration is his promise not to bring proceedings in respect of the accident. No matter how much worse B's injuries might become, or how well he might subsequently recover, neither side can change their minds. (Unless Misrepresentation could be proved. See Chapter 6 at 6.1.)

How the promise to perform arose \ Extent to which performed	Performed	Exceeded
Duty arose under the general law	No consideration (*Collins* v *Godefroy*)	Good consideration (*Glasbrook Bros* v G.C.C.)
Duty arose under a previous contract with a third party	Good consideration (*Shadwell* v *Shadwell*)	Good consideration
Duty arose under a previous contract with the same person	Possibly good consideration (*Williams* v *R. B. Ltd*) Difficulties with *Stilk* v *Myrick*	Good consideration (*Hartley* v *Ponsonby*)

Figure 4.1 Whether a promise to perform an existing duty amounts to fresh consideration

4.2.3 Part payment of a debt

At common law a debt can be extinguished either by paying it in full, or by accord and satisfaction (agreement and consideration). For example, if A owes £10 000 to B the debt is extinguished if A pays £10 000, or if B agrees to accept anything else (perhaps A's delivery van) instead. As we have seen, consideration does not need to be adequate, and so the courts will not enquire whether a thing taken instead of the money was actually worth £10 000.

An ancient case, *Pinnel's Case* (1602) 5 Co Rep 117a, made the rule that payment of a lesser sum of money on the date when a greater sum is due cannot be consideration for the greater sum owed.

Let us assume, for example, that Firm X is owed £10 000 by Firm Y, which is having difficulty in paying. Firm X promises Firm Y that if it pays what it can, say £6 000, the debt will be extinguished. Firm Y accepts this offer and pays the £6 000. Firm X can still sue for the outstanding £4 000 because the lesser sum of money (£6 000) could not be consideration for the greater sum owed (£10 000).

This rule seems somewhat illogical when placed beside the rule that consideration must be sufficient but need not be adequate. In effect, the court is inquiring into the adequacy of the consideration because it is saying that £6 000 cannot be worth £10 000. In *Pinnel's Case* the claimant was owed £8 10 shillings. The defendant paid £5 2 shillings and 2 pence. The Court of Common Pleas held that this could not be consideration for the whole debt, even if both parties had agreed that it should be.

The justification for the rule in *Pinnel's Case* comes from the idea that the only thing which always has a quantifiable monetary value is money itself. We saw earlier in this chapter that the value of goods varies with all the circumstances. However, the one thing which always has a fixed monetary value is money itself, and so a lesser sum of money cannot in any circumstances be worth as much as a greater sum. In *Pinnel's Case* creditor accepts a lesser sum in full settlement from a third party this too will extinguish the debt.

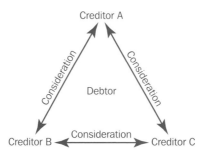

Figure 4.2   Compositions with creditors

The authority of *Foakes* v *Beer* (1884) 9 App Case 605 has been doubted at times. However, the decision protects creditors from unscrupulous creditors, as can be seen in *D & C Builders* v *Rees*, below. Furthermore, in *Re Selectmove* [1995] 2 All ER 534 the Court of Appeal made it plain that as *Foakes* v *Beer* was a House of Lords decision, only another House of Lords decision or legislation could change it. It was also made plain that as *Williams* v *Roffey Bros* (see above at 4.2.2.3) was a Court of Appeal decision it could not change *Foakes* v *Beer*. The crucial difference between the two cases is that *Williams* v *Roffey* concerned a promise to pay more than was contractually due, *Foakes* v *Beer* concerned a promise to accept less. *Foakes* v *Beer* would therefore seem to be good law as regards part payment of a debt. However, it is possible that promissory estoppel, considered immediately below, can apply to a promise to accept part payment of a debt, as the doctrine may have its origins in *Hughes* v *Metropolitan Railway* (1877) 2 App Case 439, a House of Lords case which pre-dated *Foakes* v *Beer* by seven years.

4.2.3.1 The doctrine of promissory estoppel

The effect of promises which seem to be supported by no consideration must now be viewed in the light of the doctrine of promissory estoppel, which was introduced in the following case.

■ *Central London Property Trust Ltd* v *High Trees House Ltd* [1947] KB 130

In 1937 a block of flats in central London was let to the defendants for £2 500 p.a. During the war years (1939–45) the flats could not be sublet because many people had moved away from central London. In 1940 the claimants therefore agreed to accept rent of £1 250 p.a. but without saying for how long this agreement should last. By the beginning of 1945 the flats were once again fully sublet, but the defendants were still paying the lower rent. In September 1945, in order to regulate the legal position, the claimants sued for the full rent from the time when the flats had become fully sublet and for the future.

Held. The claimants won, as both parties had anticipated, because the conditions which had given rise to the agreement no longer applied.

COMMENT (i) The actual decision in this case was not at all contentious. But in an *obiter* Denning J stated that if the claimants had sued for the full rent for the war years, as they were thinking of doing, they would not have won because of the doctrine of promissory estoppel. This doctrine would prevent a claimant from insisting on his strict legal rights, even if no consideration were received for the promise, if the following conditions were satisfied: (a) the claimant had made a promise not to insist upon his strict legal rights and this promise was intended to create legal relations; (b) the claimant knew that the promise was going to be acted upon; and (c) the defendant did act upon the promise.
(ii) Denning J suggested that *Foakes* v *Beer* might have been differently decided if the House of Lords had considered the effect of an earlier House of Lords case, *Hughes* v *Metropolitan Railway* (1877) 2 App Cas 439. In that case a tenant was obliged to repair the premises he occupied within six months or lose the lease. Shortly after the obligation to repair arose, the landlord began negotiations to buy

the lease from the tenant. The tenant therefore did no repairs until the negotiations broke down about ten weeks later, on 31 December 1874. The tenant could not complete the repairs within the original six month time limit but they were completed in June 1875. The landlord claimed the lease but the House of Lords held that the duty to repair was suspended until 31 December 1874. The tenant had completed the repairs within six months of this date and so the lease was not forfeited. Lord Cairns stated: 'It is the first principle on which all Courts of Equity proceed, that if parties who have entered into definite and distinct terms involving certain legal results … afterwards by their own act or with their own consent enter upon a course of negotiations which has the effect of leading one of the parties to suppose that the strict rights arising under the contract will not be enforced, or will be kept in suspense, or held in abeyance, the person who might otherwise have enforced those rights will not be allowed to enforce them where it would be inequitable having regard to the dealings which have thus taken place between the parties.'

It has long been accepted that estoppel can prevent the claimant from breaking his promise only where it would be inequitable (unfair) of him to do so.

■ *D & C Builders* v *Rees* [1966] 2 QB 617 (Court of Appeal)

The claimants, a small firm of builders, were owed £482 and 13 shillings for work they had done on the defendant's shop. Knowing that the claimants were in desperate financial difficulty, the defendant's wife intimidated them into accepting £300 in full settlement of the debt, telling them that if they did not take this they would get nothing. The claimants told the defendant's wife that they had no choice but to accept. The claimants took a cheque for £300 'in completion of the account'. Then the claimants sued for the remaining £182 13 shillings.

Held. Applying *Foakes* v *Beer*, the claimants won.

COMMENT (i) Lord Denning MR by now regarded his own judgment in the *High Trees* case as 'so obviously just that no one could well gainsay it'. (As we have seen, this view is not shared by everyone.) However, Lord Denning thought that promissory estoppel would arise only where it would be inequitable for the claimant to forget the promise he had made and to insist on his strict legal rights. Here it was not inequitable because the claimants had only made the promise as a result of the pressure they were put under.

(ii) The Court of Appeal decided that there was no true accord between the claimants and the defendant and that the agreement was therefore not binding. The law on economic duress has advanced very considerably in recent years, and if the case were to arise today the agreement to accept the lesser sum of money would plainly be voidable for economic duress.

(iii) It was in this case that the Court of Appeal emphatically rejected the argument that a payment of a lesser sum by cheque would amount to good consideration for the greater sum owed.

It is often said that promissory estoppel 'is a shield not a sword'. This means that it can be used only as a defence to being sued. It cannot be used to sue somebody with. It would therefore have been no use to the seamen in *Stilk* v *Myrick*. As the captain had never handed over the extra money promised, the seamen would have needed to sue the captain to get it. In the same way it would not have been of any use to the carpenter in *Williams* v *Roffey Bros*.

There is considerable doubt as to whether promissory estoppel acts so as to extinguishes rights or whether rights are merely suspended until they are introduced by giving reasonable notice. It seems likely that the doctrine will only suspend the promisor's legal rights unless it would be impossible for the promisee to resume his original position or unless the promisor indicated that he would permanently give up his rights. In the *High Trees* case Denning J seemed to think that the House of Lords in *Foakes* v *Beer* was not familiar with *Hughes* v *Metropolitan Railway*. This seems most unlikely, as the case arose only seven years earlier and two of the Lords sat in both cases. It seems more likely that *Hughes* v *Metropolitan Railway* was not considered relevant as it concerned the temporary suspension of a right whereas *Foakes* v *Beer* concerned the permanent extinction of a right. In *Tool Metal Manufacturing Co* v *Tungsten Electric Company* [1955] 2 All ER 657 the House of Lords held that an estoppel generally suspends rights rather than extinguishes them. But in some cases, such as *D & C Builders* v *Rees*, where the obligation was not a continuing one, a suspension of rights would be of very little use. The answer would seem to be that whether the rights are suspended or are extinguished will depend upon what exactly was promised and the context of the case.

Test your understandi/ng

1 What is meant by consideration in the law of contract?

2 What is meant by the rule that past consideration is no consideration? In what circumstances can a past act amount to good consideration?

3 What is meant by the rule that consideration must be sufficient but need not be adequate?

4 What is meant by privity of contract?

5 Can a third party ever sue to enforce a contract made on his behalf?

6 Is it good consideration to promise to perform a duty imposed by the general law?

7 Is it good consideration to promise to perform an existing contractual duty?

8 What is the rule in *Pinnel's Case*?

9 What is promissory estoppel?

Answers

1 Consideration consists either in the giving of a benefit or the suffering of a loss. An agreement will only amount to a contract if both parties give some consideration to the other. A contract is a bargain under which the parties exchange their respective considerations.

2 The rule that past consideration is no consideration means that a party cannot give as consideration some act which he has already performed. A past act can amount to consideration for a promise if the act was performed at the request of the promisor and if both parties all along contemplated that payment would be made.

3 The rule means that consideration must be of some recognisable economic value (sufficient), but it does not need to be equal in value to the other party's consideration (adequate).

4 Privity of contract holds that a person who is not a party to a contract can neither sue to enforce the contract nor be sued on the contract. There are several exceptions to this rule.

5 Generally, the common law will not allow a third party to sue to enforce a contract made on his behalf. The Contracts (Rights of Third Parties) Act 1999 may allow a third party to sue to enforce a term of a contract made on his behalf, but only if the third party was expressly identified in the contract. A term can be enforced by the third party if the term expressly provides that it may be enforced by him. If a term purports to confer a contractual benefit on a third party the term will be enforceable by the third party unless the parties to the contract did not intend it to be enforceable by the third party. There is therefore a rebuttable presumption that a third party can enforce a term which purports to confer a benefit upon him.

6 It is not good consideration to promise to perform a duty imposed by the general law.

7 A promise to perform an existing duty which arose under a contract with a third party can be given as good consideration. A promise to perform an existing duty which arose under a previous contract with the same promisee may possibly be good consideration if performance of the duty confers a benefit on the promisee.

8 The rule in *Pinnel's Case* is that a lesser sum of money paid on the date when a greater sum is owed cannot be good consideration for the greater sum.

9 Promissory estoppel is an equitable doctrine which prevents a claimant from breaking a promise not to insist on his strict legal rights if the promise was intended to create legal relations, if the claimant knew that the promise was going to be acted upon and if the defendant did act upon the promise. The doctrine only applies where it would be inequitable for the claimant to break his promise.

4.3 · Formalities

In general, contracts do not need to be made in any particular way. Most commercial contracts are made in writing but there is no legal requirement that this should be so. The types of formalities which sometimes are required are as follows.

4.3.1 Contracts which must be made by a deed

(a) A conveyance of a legal estate in land must be made by deed.
(b) The creation of a lease of **over** three years duration must be made by deed or no legal estate will be created.
(c) A promise of a gift is not enforceable unless made by deed.

The Law of Property (Miscellaneous Provisions) Act 1989 s.1(2) states that an instrument shall not be a deed unless it is made clear on its face that it is intended to be a deed by the party or parties making it, and it is validly executed as a deed. Section 1(3) explains that an instrument is validly executed as a deed by an individual only if:

(i)   the instrument is signed by the individual in the presence of a witness who attests the signature; or
(ii) the individual directs someone else to sign the instrument in his presence and in the presence of two witnesses who attest the signature; and
(iii) the instrument is delivered by the individual as a deed or by someone authorised to do so on his behalf. A person attests a document by signing it to show that he has witnessed the signature of another.

The Limitation Act 1980 provides that an action cannot be brought on a simple contract six years after the date when the right to bring the action arose. However, when the contract was made by deed an action cannot be brought 12 years after the right to bring the action arose. (See Time limits on remedies in Chapter 7 at 7.2.8.)

4.3.2 Contracts which must be in writing

Certain types of contracts must be in writing. The most important of these are contracts for the sale or other disposition of land and regulated consumer credit agreements.

4.3.2.1 Contracts for the sale or other disposition of an interest in land

Section 2(1) of the Law of Property (Miscellaneous Provisions) Act 1989 provides that contracts for the sale or other disposition of an interest in land can only be made in writing and only by incorporating all the terms which the parties have expressly agreed in one document or, where contracts are exchanged, in each. Both parties must sign the document. An exception exists for leases of land of three years or less, which can be made orally as long as the lease takes effect immediately. A contract which does not comply with s.2(1) will be void. Before the 1989 Act came into force contracts for the sale or other disposition of land had only to be evidenced in writing. If they were not so evidenced they were unenforceable, rather than void.

4.3.2.2 Regulated consumer credit agreements

Regulated consumer credit agreements are unenforceable without a court order unless they are in writing, and signed by the debtor or hirer. (See the improper execution of regulated agreements in Chapter 14 at 14.1.3.6.)

4.3.3 Contracts which must be evidenced in writing

Section 4 of the Statute of Frauds 1677 requires that contracts of guarantee, under which one person assumes secondary liability to settle the debts or liabilities of another, must be evidenced in writing and signed by the person giving the guarantee or they will be unenforceable. This does not mean that the contract performance of which is being guaranteed must be evidenced in writing. It is only the contract under which the guarantee is given which must be evidenced in writing.

For example, A buys a motorbike from a garage and B guarantees that he will pay the price if A fails to do so. The contract to sell the motorbike does not need to be evidenced in writing, the contract under which B gives the guarantee does.

By evidenced in writing it is meant that there must be some written evidence that the contract has been made. This evidence must contain all the material terms of the contract and must be signed or initialled by the person giving the guarantee.

An indemnity must be distinguished from a guarantee, as s.4 does not apply to indemnities. A person who indemnifies another assumes primary liability to settle the obligations of that person. If, in the example about the motorbike, B had told the garage to let A have the motorbike and he (B) would see that the garage was paid, this would have been an indemnity rather than a guarantee.

4.3.4 The Electronic Commerce (EC) Regulations 2002

Regulation 9(1) of the Electronic Commerce (EC Directive) Regulations 2002 requires Internet service providers to provide clear, comprehensible and unambiguous information before any offer is made by a recipient of the Internet service. The information must set out: (a) the different technical steps to conclude the contract; (b) whether or not the contract will be filed by the service provider and whether it will be accessible; (c) the technical means of identifying and correcting input errors prior to the placing of the order; and (d) the languages offered for the conclusion of the contract. Regulation 9(2) requires the service provider to indicate relevant codes of practice to which he subscribes and to give information on how these can be consulted electronically. Regulation 9(1) does not apply if the service provider makes the offer. Neither reg.9(1) nor reg.9(2) will apply if the recipient is not a consumer and it has been agreed that the regulation will not apply. Nor will either regulation apply if the contract is concluded exclusively by exchange of email. However, reg.9(3) applies to all contracts concluded by electronic means if the service provider provides terms and conditions which apply to the recipient. In such cases the service provider must make the terms and conditions available to the recipient in such a way that allows him to store and reproduce them.

Regulation 11 deals with placing of the order.

> '(1) Unless parties who are not consumers have agreed otherwise, where the recipient of the service places his order through technological means, a service provider shall –
> (a) acknowledge receipt of the order to the recipient of the service without due delay and by electronic means; and
> (b) make available to the recipient of the service appropriate, effective and accessible technical means allowing him to identify and correct input errors prior to the placing of the order.'

This regulation does not apply where the contract is concluded exclusively by exchange of email. However, it does apply to the typical situation where the website is an invitation to treat and the consumer makes the offer. The service provider cannot accept the offer without acknowledging receipt of the offer and giving the consumer the chance to correct errors. If the consumer is not given the chance to correct errors then the consumer can rescind the contract (reg.15). If reg.9(1) or 11(1)(a) is breached the recipient can sue for damages for breach of statutory duty (reg 13).

Regulation 11(2) provides that, for the purposes of reg.11(1)(a), an offer, and acknowledgement of receipt of it, will be deemed to be effective when the parties to whom they are addressed are able to access them.

4.4 · Capacity

Generally speaking, everyone has the capacity to make any contract they please. But minors, mentally disordered persons and drunkards do not have full capacity.

4.4.1 Minors

The Family Law Reform Act 1969 s.1 defines a minor as a person who has not yet reached the age of 18. Contracts made by minors fall into three categories.

4.4.1.1 Valid contracts

The Sale of Goods Act 1979 s.3(2) provides that where necessaries are delivered to a minor he must pay a reasonable price for them. Section 3(3) defines necessaries as 'goods suitable to the condition in life of the minor or other person concerned and to his actual requirements at the time of sale and delivery'. Three points should be noted. First, the obligation is to pay a reasonable price which may well differ from the price agreed in the contract. Second, the obligation only exists if the goods were sold and delivered to the minor. Third, goods can be necessary goods even though they are not necessities of life. In *Nash* v *Inman* [1908] 2 KB 1 a Savile Row tailor sued a wealthy Cambridge student for clothes supplied. The clothes included 11 fancy waistcoats. The Court of Appeal held that the clothes were not necessaries and that the minor did not therefore have to pay for them. It was not the case that such clothes could not possibly be necessaries for a wealthy student but rather that the student in question was already adequately supplied with clothes of this type. The provisions of the Sale of Goods Act 1979 apply only to goods. The common law requires minors to pay a reasonable price for necessary services supplied.

A minor can also validly make a contract of employment as long as the contract is overall beneficial to the minor. It is the overall effect of the contract when made which must be considered. A contract which turned out to be against the minor's interests can be binding if it was overall beneficial when made.

■ *Clements* v *London and North Western Railway Company* [1894] 2 QB 482 (Court of Appeal)

The defendant, a minor, took a job as a railway porter and agreed to become a member of an insurance society formed by the railway employees. Joining this society meant giving up rights against the employer under the Employers' Liability Act 1880. The insurance society gave the members very wide protection against injuries, whether these were caused by the employers' negligence or not and allowed for payment without the need for litigation. However, as regards certain types of claims the amounts payable under the insurance scheme were less than those which could be claimed under the Act. The minor was injured by the employers' negligence and wished to sue under the Act.

Held. The minor could not sue under the Act as he was bound by the agreement he had made. The contract taken as a whole was beneficial to the minor and it was therefore binding upon him.

The same rules apply to contracts which are analogous to contracts of employment. In *Chaplin* v *Leslie Frewin (Publishers) Ltd* [1966] Ch 71 the Court of Appeal had to decide whether a minor was bound by an agreement he had made to have a book published. The minor was the son of Charlie Chaplin, the famous actor, and when he claimed National Assistance benefits several publishers proposed that he should write a book about his bohemian life. The minor made contracts to have his life story ghost written and for a publisher to have exclusive rights to publish and sell the book. The minor was paid an initial advance of £300. A further £100 advance was paid when the book was almost ready for publication. The minor then changed his mind about the book and applied for an injunction to prevent publication. The Court of Appeal held that the contract was binding upon the minor because it was analogous to a contract of employment and at the date when the contract was made it was beneficial to him because it would allow him to support his family. Lord Denning MR dissented on the grounds that the contract was not beneficial to the minor as it was scandalous, brought shame on himself and others, invaded family life and exposed the minor to claims for libel.

4.4.1.2 Voidable contracts

Contracts giving a minor an interest of a permanent nature, which impose a continuing liability on a minor, are voidable by the minor either before he reaches 18 or within a reasonable time of his having done so. By voidable it is meant that the minor has the option to avoid (call off) the contract. If the minor does avoid the contract he is absolved from future liability. Whether or not the minor can be sued for liabilities which have already arisen at the time the contract is avoided is a matter of some uncertainty.

The main types of contract which are voidable by a minor are:

(a) Contracts of partnership.
(b) Contracts to buy shares.
(c) Contracts to take a lease of land.

4.4.1.3 Void contracts

Contracts other than those classed as valid or voidable are not binding on a minor. However, a minor will only be able to recover any money paid or property delivered under such a contract if there has been a total failure of consideration. That is to say only if the minor has received no benefit at all under the contract.

A loan made to a minor will not be enforceable unless the minor, having reached the age of majority, makes a new agreement to pay it. This new agreement does not need to be supported by any consideration.

The Minors Contracts Act 1987 s.3(1) allows a court to order a minor to return property gained under a void contract, or property representing that gained, if the court considers it just and equitable to do so. Obviously such an order would not be made if the minor had paid for the property supplied. If the minor no longer has the property supplied, or other property representing that gained, then he will be under no obligation to pay any compensation to the supplier. If the minor sells non-necessary goods on to a third party acting in good faith for value, the third party will gain complete title to the goods and the person who supplied them to the minor will not therefore be able to recover them. Section 2 of the Act allows a person who has guaranteed a contract which is unenforceable against the minor to be sued on the guarantee.

4.4.2 Drunkards and mental patients

Like minors, drunkards must pay a reasonable price for necessary goods delivered and necessary services supplied. Other contracts will be voidable if the drunkard did not know what he was doing when he made the contract, and the person with whom he made the contract was aware of this. If the drunkard ratifies a voidable contract upon becoming sober he will be liable on it. The same rules apply to mentally disordered persons who have not been certified as insane. If a patient is certified as insane under the Mental Health Act 1983 then his property becomes controlled by the court and any attempt he makes to dispose of his property will be void.

4.4.2.1 Corporations

The capacity of corporations to make contracts is considered in Chapters 16 and 17 at 16.1.5 and 17.1.8.

Test your understanding

1 What types of contracts must be made by a deed?

2 Name two classes of contracts which will be void if they are not made in writing.

3 What type of contract must be evidenced in writing?

4 What type of contracts will be binding upon a minor?

5 What type of contracts are voidable if made by a minor?

Answers

1 A deed is necessary to convey a legal estate in land. A lease of over three years' duration must also be made by a deed or no legal estate will be created. A promise of a gift will not be enforceable unless made by a deed.

2 Contracts for the sale or other disposition of an interest in land must be made in writing. Regulated consumer credit agreements will be unenforceable without a court order if not made in writing and signed by the debtor.

3 Contracts of guarantee must be evidenced in writing or they will be unenforceable.

4 A minor will be bound to pay a reasonable price for necessary goods delivered or necessary services supplied. Beneficial contracts of employment, and analogous contracts, will also be binding upon a minor.

5 Contracts of a permanent nature, which impose a continuing liability on a minor, are voidable by the minor.

Key points

Intention to create legal relations

- A contract will only come into being if it can be objectively inferred that the parties intended to create legal relations.

- When considering business and commercial agreements the courts will presume that the parties did intend to create legal relations. This presumption can be rebutted by the evidence.

- When considering social and domestic agreements the courts will presume that the parties did not intend to create legal relations. This presumption can be rebutted by the evidence.

- A letter of comfort might or might not amount to a contractual promise, depending upon its wording and upon all the surrounding circumstances.

- A term in a contract which seeks to exclude the jurisdiction of the courts will be void as against public policy. (This is not the case as regards terms which provide for reference of disputes to arbitration.)

Consideration

- An agreement will only amount to a contract if both parties give some consideration to the other.

- Consideration consists either in the giving of a benefit or the suffering of a loss.

- Executory consideration consists of a promise to do something in the future. Executed consideration occurs when one of the parties makes the offer or the acceptance in such a way that he has completely fulfilled his liability under the contract.

- Past consideration is no consideration for a promise unless the past act was performed at the request of the promisor and both parties all along contemplated that payment would be made.

- The performance of a trivial act can amount to good consideration if performance of the act conferred an economic benefit on the promisee.

- The doctrine of privity of contract holds that a person who is not a party to a contract may not sue to enforce the contract or be sued upon the contract. There are several well established exceptions to the rule.

■ The Contracts (Rights of Third Parties) Act 1999 allows a third party who is expressly identified in a contract to sue to enforce a term of a contract if the term expressly states that he may. An expressly identified third party may also sue to enforce a term which confers a benefit upon him if this is what the parties to the contract intended.

■ It is not good consideration to promise to perform a duty which arose under the general law.

■ The same consideration can be given to two different people, thereby creating two valid contracts.

■ It is possible that it can be good consideration to promise to perform an existing duty which arose under a previous contract with the same person, but only if this promise confers an economic benefit on that person.

■ At common law a lesser sum of money paid on the date due cannot be consideration for a greater sum owed.

■ A lesser sum of money can be good consideration for a greater sum owed if, at the creditor's request, it is paid early or in a different place.

■ Promissory estoppel is an equitable doctrine which will prevent a claimant from breaking a promise not to insist on his strict legal rights if the promise was intended to create legal relations, if the claimant knew that the promise was going to be acted upon and if the defendant did act upon the promise.

■ Promissory estoppel will only prevent a claimant from breaking his promise where it would be inequitable for him to break it.

Formalities

■ Generally, no formalities are needed to make a contract.

■ A conveyance of a legal estate in land must be made by a deed. The creation of a lease of over three years' duration must be made by a deed or no legal estate will be created.

■ Contracts for the sale or other disposition of land must be made in writing or they will be invalid. Regulated consumer credit agreements must be made in writing and signed by the debtor or hirer or they will be unenforceable without a court order.

■ Contracts of guarantee must be evidenced in writing or they will be unenforceable.

Contractual capacity

■ Minors must pay a reasonable price for necessary goods delivered or necessary services supplied.

■ Contracts of a permanent nature, which impose a continuing liability on a minor, are voidable by the minor.

■ Minors are not bound by contracts to buy non-necessary goods or services. Nor are they bound to repay loans which they took out while minors.

Summary questions

1 Is there likely to be an intention to create legal relations in the following circumstances:
   a When a student enrols at a university?
   b When magazine readers enter competitions to win prizes?
   c When work mates jointly buy a lottery ticket?
   d When supermarkets promote 'Club Card' schemes, which give customers free spending vouchers for every £100 they spend?

2 In *Appleson v H. Littlewood Ltd* [1939] 1 All ER 464 a punter claimed to have won £4 335 on the football pools but the defendants refused to pay. The pools form which the claimant had completed contained the rules and conditions. Rule 2 said, 'It is a basic condition of the sending in and the acceptance of this coupon that … any agreement entered into or payment made by or under it shall not be attended by or give rise to any legal relationship, rights, duties or consequences whatsoever or be legally enforceable or the subject of litigation, but all such arrangements, agreements and transactions are binding in honour only'. The defendants claimed that the sending in of the coupon and the acceptance of it could not possibly amount to a contract. Do you think that the Court of Appeal agreed?

3   Look again at *Carlill* v *The Carbolic Smoke Ball Company* (p.74 above). Analyse the consideration given by Mrs Carlill and by the Smoke Ball Co. When Mrs Carlill claimed the reward, was the consideration of the parties executed or executory?

4   In *Midland Bank Trust Co Ltd* v *Green* [1981] AC 513 (House of Lords) a farmer, for good reasons of his own, sold his farm to his wife for £500 even though the farm was valued at over £40 000. Was this a good contract?

5   A householder is just about to leave for work when he notices that a pipe in his house has burst. He rings an emergency plumber and arranges for the plumber to pick the keys up from his next-door neighbour and fix the pipe. The plumber repairs the pipe and leaves a bill. Can the householder refuse to pay the plumber on the grounds that the work was already done before any price was mentioned?

6   The president of the local bowls club employs a painter to paint the clubhouse for £600. The painter later finds a job which will pay him more and tells the president that he is not going to do the work. A wealthy club member promises the painter an extra £250 if he goes ahead with the contract, as originally agreed. The painter performs the contract. To how much money, if any, will the painter be entitled?

7   A builder makes a contract with Arthur whereby he is to repair Arthur's house for £500. The builder then decided that he has priced the job too low and tells Arthur that he will not do the work unless he is paid more money. Arthur agrees to pay an extra £250 and the builder carries out the repair. To how much money, if any, will the builder be entitled?

8   John and Mary work together running a seaside tea shop and are paid an hourly wage. One day their employer phones John to tell him that Mary is ill and will be unable to work for the rest of the week. The employer tells John that he will have to run the tea shop single handed. With difficulty, John manages to do this for the rest of the week. At the end of the week the employer tells John that he will be paid double wages for the period when he worked on his own. The employer is now refusing to pay the extra money. Advise John as to whether or not he will be entitled to the extra sum.

9   In *Williams* v *Roffey Bros Ltd* the contractor who had priced the carpentry work too low was entitled to recover the extra money he was promised.

   a   Is it good policy to allow sub-contractors who have priced the job too low to demand more money from the main contractor?
   b   Would the main contractors, Roffey Bros Ltd, have been able to demand more money if they realised that they had priced the main job, the refurbishment of the flats, too low?

10   George, a builder, owes £36 000 to Builders Merchants Ltd. George explains that he has not been paid by a customer who has become bankrupt and that this means that he cannot pay his bill to Builders Merchants. The manager of Builders Merchants agrees to accept £27 200 in complete satisfaction of the debt. Now the manager of Builders Merchants has heard that George has won £1 million on the National Lottery. Advise Builders Merchants Ltd as to whether or not they will be able to sue for the £8 800 of the original debt which they agreed to forgo.

11   Mary's daughter, Samantha, comes over to England from Australia for Mary's fiftieth birthday. Samantha buys Mary a new television as a birthday present. Mary does not use the television until Samantha has left the country. When Mary does use the television she finds that it does not work. Mary returns the television to the shop from where it was bought, explaining that Samantha bought it as a birthday present. The shop refuses to give Mary any remedy. Samantha will not be returning to England in the foreseeable future. Has Mary any contractual remedy against the shop?

Multiple choice questions

1 A supermarket advertises that any customer who spends £100 on wine will receive a free gallon of petrol. A customer who relied on this promise and who spent £100 on wine is refused the petrol. Which one of the following statements is true?

   a There will be no contract as there was no intention to create legal relations.

   b There will be no contract as the customer provided no consideration for the petrol.

   c The customer will be entitled to the petrol as there was a good contract.

   d The customer will not be entitled to the petrol because when he claimed the petrol his consideration was past.

2 A solicitor claims that his wife, an accountant, made a contract to sell him her car for £4 500. Which one of the following statements is true?

   a A court would presume that the parties did not intend to make a contract unless the evidence clearly showed that they did.

   b A court would presume that the parties did intend to make a contract unless the evidence clearly showed that they did not.

   c It is not possible for a husband and wife to make a contract with each other.

   d The agreement could not amount to a contract unless it was evidenced in writing.

3 A Co Ltd offers a reward of £10 000 to anyone who supplies information which leads to the arrest and conviction of arsonists who set fire to their factory. Bill supplies the necessary information and claims the reward. After Bill has done this, but before A Co Ltd has paid, which one of the following statements is true?

   a Bill's consideration is past and therefore amounts to no consideration.

   b The consideration given by both sides is executory.

   c The consideration given by A Co Ltd is executed, the consideration given by Bill is executory.

   d The consideration given by A Co Ltd is executory, the consideration given by Bill is executed.

4 A building firm sells an old lorry for a quarter of its market value. Which one of the following statements is true?

   a The buyer's consideration is neither sufficient nor adequate and so there is no contract.

   b The buyer's consideration is sufficient and adequate and so there is a contract.

   c The buyer's consideration is adequate but not sufficient and so there is no contract.

   d The buyer's consideration is sufficient but not adequate and so there is a contract.

5 A joiner agrees with a builder that he will install all the windows in four houses which the builder is constructing for a price of £2 000. The joiner finds that he has priced the job too low and tells the builder that he cannot afford to do the job. The customer for whom the houses are being built, tells the joiner that he will pay an extra £1 000 if the joiner performs the job as agreed, which the joiner does. Which one of the following statements is true?

   a Neither the builder nor the customer need pay because the joiner broke his contract when he refused to install the windows as originally agreed.

   b The builder will need to pay the £2 000, but the customer will not need to pay the £1 000.

   c The customer will need to pay the £1 000, but the builder will not need to pay the £2 000.

   d The builder will need to pay the £2 000 and the customer will need to pay the £1 000.

6 Which one of the following statements is not true?

   a The Contracts (Rights of Third Parties) Act 1999 allows a third party who is expressly identified in the contract to enforce a term of a contract if the term expressly provides that he may enforce it.

   b The Contracts (Rights of Third Parties) Act 1999 allows a third party who is expressly identified in the contract to enforce a term of a contract if the term purports to confer a benefit upon him.

c When the Contracts (Rights of Third Parties) Act 1999 confers a benefit on a third party, the third party can avail himself of any remedy which would have been available to him if he had made the contract.

d Where a third party does gain rights under s.1 of the Contracts (Rights of Third Parties) Act 1999, the parties to the contract can never alter the contract in such a way as to alter the third party's rights without his consent.

7 A landlord lets a house for one year for a rent of £4 000. The tenant intimidates the landlord into accepting half rent, threatening that if the landlord does not accept this the tenant will refuse to leave when the lease is up. The lease has now expired and the tenant has now left the house. The landlord is suing for the half of the rent which was withheld. Which **two** of the following statements are true?

a *Foakes* v *Beer* supports the landlord's case.

b *Foakes* v *Beer* supports the tenant's case.

c Promissory estoppel would not prevent the landlord from breaking his promise, as it would not be inequitable for him to break his promise.

d The tenant could not rely on promissory estoppel because it is a shield not a sword.

8 A tenant orally agrees to lease a business unit for one year. The tenant pays two months' rent in advance and takes immediate possession. Which **one** of the following statements is true?

a The lease is invalid because it was not made by a deed.

b The lease is invalid because it was not in writing.

c The lease is invalid because it was not evidenced in writing.

d The lease was validly formed.

9 Adrian, who is 17, buys a much needed pair of shoes from a mail order catalogue for double their normal price. Adrian has received the shoes but has not yet paid for them. Which one of the following statements is true?

a Adrian must pay the agreed price.

b Adrian must pay a reasonable price for the shoes.

c Adrian can avoid the contract within a reasonable time.

d The contract is void.

Task 4

From Chapter 3, choose three cases in which the court decided that there was a contract. As regards each case, indicate:

a The consideration given by both parties.

b Any formalities with which the parties would have to comply.

c The factors which would have persuaded the court that there was an intention to create legal relations.

Chapter 5

CONTRACTUAL TERMS

Introduction

The terms of the contract define the obligations and promises contained in the contract. Terms which state the obligations in words, whether written or spoken, are known as express terms. However, not all words exchanged between the parties amount to terms of the contract. Some statements may amount only to representations, which are not part of the contract because the parties did not intend them to be contractually binding. In addition to the express terms, a contract may also contain implied terms. These terms may be implied either by the courts or by a statute.

A party who does not adhere to a term of a contract is said to have breached the term. Whenever a term is breached this will give rise to an action for damages for breach of contract. Sometimes the injured party will claim that breach of a term also allows him to treat the contract as repudiated, in which case the injured party will be absolved from any further obligation to perform the contract. Whether or not breach of a term will allow the injured party to do this will depend upon what type of term was breached. If the breached term can be classed as a condition, a very serious term which went to the root of the contract, the injured party will be able to treat the contract as repudiated. If the breached term can be classed only as a warranty, a term which was not serious enough to go to the root of the contract, then the injured party will not be entitled to treat the contract as repudiated. However, some terms are classed as innominate terms, rather than as conditions or warranties. Whether or not breach of an innominate term will allow the injured party to treat the contract as repudiated will depend upon the severity of the consequences of breach of the term.

Exclusion or exemption clauses are terms in contracts which try to exclude or exempt a party's liability for breach of contract. The Unfair Contract Terms Act 1977 has limited the effect of exclusion and exemption clauses to a considerable degree. The Unfair Terms in Consumer Contracts Regulations 1999 have provided additional protection to consumers faced with unfair terms.

5.1 · Nature of contractual terms

The terms of the contract define the contractual promises which the parties exchanged when they made the contract. If any term is breached the injured party will always have a remedy for breach of contract.

Terms are incorporated into contracts in one of two ways; they can either be expressed or implied. Express terms are specifically agreed upon by the parties. Implied terms are put into the contract, either by the courts or by a statute, without the parties needing to agree them (see Figure 5.1).

5.2 · Express terms distinguished from representations

In Chapter 3 we saw that a contract is formed when an offer is accepted. The express terms of the contract are contained in the offer. By accepting the offer, the offeree agrees to the terms proposed by the offeror. These terms then become contractually binding.

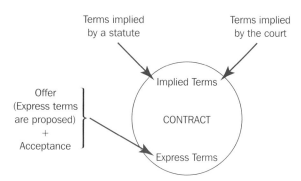

Figure 5.1 Express and Implied Terms

Although it is simple to state that the express terms of the contract are contained in the offer which has been accepted, it can often be very difficult to tell precisely what terms were agreed. When parties negotiate before making a contract, assurances and promises are often made over a period of time. Some of these statements will be incorporated as terms of the contract, but others will amount only to representations. If a representation is subsequently shown to be untrue there is no breach of contract. (In certain circumstances, a remedy for misrepresentation may be available, a matter considered in the following chapter.) In addition, some statements may be neither terms nor representations but mere sales puffs.

The following example may clarify the distinction between terms, representations and sales puffs. Let us assume that X makes an oral contract to buy a car from Y. X asks Y about the car's age, its mileage, and whether it has given any trouble. After receiving satisfactory replies to these questions X offers a price of £6 000 and this offer is accepted by Y. A contract has been made and two express terms are quite evident. X has agreed to pay £6 000 to Y, and Y has agreed to transfer ownership of the car to X. These two matters are terms of the contract because it is evident that X and Y intended them to be contractually binding. But the effect of the assurances given by Y is less clear. If X made it plain that he would only buy the car if it had a valid MOT certificate, and Y assured him that it did, then it would be a term of the contract that the car had a valid MOT certificate. It would have been implicit in X's offer to buy the car for £6 000 that Y's promise that the car had a valid MOT certificate was a part of the bargain. But a statement by Y that he had himself bought the car two years ago for £4 000, which seemed to make little impression on X, would not be a term of the contract. The reasonable person would infer that the parties did not intend the statement to be a part of the contract. Such a statement, being a statement of fact which did not amount to a term of the contract, would merely be a representation. A statement by Y that the car was a bargain at the price would amount to nothing more than a sales puff. The reasonable person would not think that such a statement was intended to amount to a term of the contract. Nor could the statement be taken as a representation, as it did not amount to a statement of definite fact.

In deciding whether or not a statement is a term of a contract, the courts consider whether the parties appeared to intend that the statement should be a term. It is important to realise that the courts are not concerned with the parties' actual intentions but with their apparent intentions. Over the years several tests which assist the courts in determining the parties' intentions have developed.

5.2.1 The relative degrees of the parties' knowledge

It is often the case that one of the parties to the contract has considerably more knowledge than the other about the subject matter of the contract, so that this knowledge will put him in a better position to know whether or not a particular statement is true. A garage owner, for example, will know considerably more about cars than most customers. Statements made by a party with considerably more knowledge are likely to be classified by the courts as terms, whereas statements made by a party with considerably less knowledge are likely to be classified as representations. The following two cases demonstrate these principles.

■ *Oscar Chess Ltd* v *Williams* [1957] 1 WLR 370 (Court of Appeal)

The defendant, a private motorist, traded in his car to the claimant, a car dealer, in order to acquire a new Hillman Minx. The defendant told the dealer that the car he was trading in was a 1948 model. The defendant believed this to be the case because when he had taken the car on hire-purchase, the previous year, the registration book had shown the year of registration as 1948. The dealer looked the car up in Glass's guide and offered £290 for it, an offer which was accepted by the defendant. Eight months later the dealer discovered that the car was a 1939 model. The dealer sued for breach of contract.

Held. The defendant was not liable for breach of contract because his statement was a representation rather than a term. The defendant knew little about cars whereas the claimant had considerable knowledge and expertise. The defendant could not be taken as having made a definite promise that the car was a 1948 model.

COMMENT (i) In the following chapter we shall see that a representation may become an actionable misrepresentation, thereby providing the injured party with a remedy. The remedy available will depend upon whether the misrepresentation was made fraudulently, negligently or innocently. When a term is breached the state of mind of the party who made the promise is irrelevant. The fact that a term has been breached will amount to breach of contract whether the maker of the term knew that the promise embodied in the term was untrue, whether he ought to have known that it was untrue or whether he could not possibly have known.

(ii) The statement made by the defendant would have amounted to an innocent misrepresentation. Before the Misrepresentation Act 1967 came into force a person to whom a non-fraudulent misrepresentation was made could not claim damages. An innocent misrepresentation could give rise to a right to rescind the contract. In this case the claimant could not rescind because his claim to do so came too long after the misrepresentation was made. (Misrepresentation is considered in Chapter 6.)

■ *Dick Bentley Productions Ltd* v *Harold Smith Motors Ltd* [1965] 1 WLR 623 (Court of Appeal)

The claimant, a wealthy businessman, asked the defendant, a car dealer, to keep his eye open for a 'well vetted' second-hand British car, the history of which was known. The defendant found an apparently suitable car, a Park Ward coupé Bentley, and told the claimant that it had done only 20 000 miles since it had been fitted with a new engine and gearbox. This statement was repeated later the same day when the claimant brought his wife to look at the car. The car soon gave trouble and the claimant discovered that it had done 100 000 miles since the new engine had been fitted.

Held. The defendant was liable for breach of contract as his statement was a term. The defendant, with his greater knowledge of cars, could be taken to have promised that the car had only done 20 000 miles since the new engine had been fitted.

5.2.2 The reliance shown to be placed on the statement

If the party to whom the statement was made demonstrated that he considered the statement to be very important to him then the statement is likely to be a term.

■ *Bannerman* v *White* (1861) 10 CB NS 844

The defendant, a hop merchant, bought hops from the claimant, a farmer. The defendant intended to sell the hops to brewers of beer in Burton. These brewers had told the defendant that they would not buy any hops which had been treated with sulphur. The defendant therefore sent a circular to hop growers stating that he would not buy hops which had been treated with sulphur at any price. Before the contract was made the claimant assured the defendant that the hops which were being sold had not been treated with sulphur. Of the 300 acres of hops sold 5 acres had been treated with sulphur but the claimant had forgotten about this when giving the assurance. When the defendant found that some of the hops had been treated with sulphur he claimed to treat the contract as repudiated and refused to pay the price. The claimant sued for the price. The jury found as a fact that the statement that no sulphur had been used on the hops was intended to be a part of the contract.

Held. The jury's finding was confirmed on appeal. A term of the contract had been broken.

COMMENT (i) The statement was a term of the contract because the defendant had **demonstrated** how important it was to him. Anybody could later claim that they were thinking that a particular term was very important. The court takes an objective view as to the parties' intentions. This view is reached by considering all of the circumstances.

(ii) As the broken term was a condition of the contract the claimant was entitled to treat the contract as repudiated and therefore had a defence when sued for the price. (The difference between conditions, warranties and innominate terms is considered below at 5.4.3.)

5.2.3 The strength of the statement

A statement which is made very strongly is likely to be a term of the contract. A guarded statement is likely to be a representation.

■ *Schawel v Reade* [1913] 2 IR 81 (House of Lords)

The claimant inspected a horse owned by the defendant. The claimant made it plain that he wanted to buy a horse for stud purposes. The defendant told him, 'You need not look for anything; the horse is perfectly sound. If there was anything the matter with the horse I would tell you.' A price for the horse was agreed a few days later and the sale of the horse was concluded about a month later. After the conclusion of the contract the claimant discovered that the horse was quite unsuitable for stud purposes because it had an incurable hereditary eye disease.

Held. The defendant's statement was a term. It was intended to be a part of the transaction and the basis of the sale.

■ *Ecay v Godfrey* (1947) 80 Lloyd's Rep 286

The claimant, a Spanish diplomat, bought a boat called the Tio Pepe from the defendant for £750. The boat, which had once been a lifeboat, had recently been painted and looked in good condition. In fact the boat was in a very poor condition and barely seaworthy. The defendant said that the boat was sound but he also advised the claimant to have it surveyed before he bought it. The claimant wanted the boat in a hurry and so he bought it without having it surveyed.

Held. The defendant's statement that the boat was sound was a representation rather than a term. The statement was made in such a guarded way that it could not amount to a contractual promise that the boat was sound.

Even a very strong statement will not amount to a term if the parties understood that it was not to be a term. In *Hopkins* v *Tanqueray* (1854) 15 CB 130 the defendant's horse was sold at Tattersall's by public auction. Before the sale the defendant found the claimant looking at the horse's legs and told him, 'You have nothing to look for; I assure you that he is perfectly sound in every respect'. The claimant replied that he was satisfied with this statement and the following day bought the horse at the auction. Later the claimant discovered that the horse was not sound. Despite being a strong statement, it was held that the defendant's assurance could not be a term as both parties were well aware that horses sold at Tattersall's were sold without any terms as to soundness.

5.2.4 The time at which the statement was made

A statement which immediately prompts the making of the contract is more likely to be a term than a statement made a considerable time before the making of the contract. The shorter the delay between the making of the statement and the formation of the contract the more likely it is that the parties intended the statement to be a part of the contract. However, like the other tests, this one is not conclusive. For example, in *Schawel* v *Reade* the statement was held to be a term even though it was made a month before the contract was finalised. The very similar assurance in *Hopkins* v *Tanqueray* was not a term even though it was made the day before the sale of the horse. Neither are any of the other tests which the courts have evolved conclusive. All of the circumstances must be considered. In all of the post-1913 cases which we have considered the following words of Lord Moulton in *Heilbut, Symons & Co* v *Buckleton* [1913] AC 30 were considered by the various courts to be binding:

> 'It may well be that [various tests used to tell a term from a representation] may be criteria of value in … coming to a decision whether or not a [term] was intended; but they cannot be said to furnish decisive tests, because it cannot be said as a matter of law that the presence or absence of these features is conclusive of the intention of the parties. The intention of the parties can only be deduced from the totality of the evidence, and no secondary principles of such a kind can be universally true.'

5.2.5 Written contracts

Where the contract is written the parol evidence rule prevents extrinsic [outside] evidence from being introduced to add to or vary what was written. Consequently, the factors which we have considered above will not apply. The general rule is that what was written will be the entire contract and oral statements will not be included as part of the contract. However, there are a number of exceptions to the rule. The most important of these exceptions are as follows. The equitable remedy of rectification will be allowed to correct a written version of the contract if an oral contract had previously been made and the written version was intended merely to record what had been agreed but had recorded this incorrectly. Extrinsic evidence will be allowed to show that a contract was rendered invalid by some rule of law. Extrinsic evidence is also allowed to show that the contract was not to operate until a condition was fulfilled. Nor will the parol evidence rule prevent a party from introducing evidence of a custom. Finally, in some circumstances, it may be possible to introduce extrinsic evidence that what was agreed was not the whole contract.

Another matter to be considered is that an oral statement might be part of a collateral contract. Such a contract exists side by side with the main contract which is being made. For example, in *Webster* v *Higgin* [1948] 2 All ER 127 the claimant took a car on hire-purchase because the supplier said that he would guarantee that the car was in good condition. The written contract of hire-purchase which the claimant signed contained a clause excluding liability for the condition of the car. The car was in extremely poor condition. The claimant could not sue on the contract of hire-purchase because the assurance about the condition of the car could not be a term of that written contract and the exclusion clause would probably have prevented him from suing on any implied term as to the quality of the car. However, the claimant succeeded on a collateral contract which existed side by side with the main contract of hire-purchase. The terms of this collateral contract were that the defendant's guarantee about the condition of the car was given in return for the claimant's consideration in entering into the contract of hire-purchase. As the defendant's guarantee was not true the defendant had breached a term of the collateral contract. The claimant was therefore entitled to treat the contract of hire-purchase as terminated and recover all money already paid under it. (*Andrews* v *Hopkinson* [1957] 1 QB 229, which is set out in Chapter 14 at 14.2 provides another example of a collateral contract.)

5.2.6 Statements of opinion

A statement of pure opinion cannot itself amount to either a term or a representation. However, in certain circumstances, as the following case shows, a statement of opinion can nevertheless give rise to a term.

■ *Esso Petroleum Co Ltd v Mardon* [1976] QB 801 (Court of Appeal)

The defendant was persuaded to take over the tenancy of an Esso petrol station because of an assurance that the station would sell about 200 000 gallons of petrol a year within three years. The defendant had indicated that he thought a figure of 100 000 to 150 000 was a more realistic estimate. However, he was persuaded by the fact that the Esso representative who gave the figure of 200 000 gallons had 40 years' experience in the trade. The defendant managed the petrol station well but it became apparent that the station would never come close to selling 200 000 gallons a year. The defendant was sued by the claimants and counterclaimed for breach of warranty.

Held. It was not a term of the contract that the station would sell 200 000 gallons a year because this was only an opinion. However, there was an implied term, in the form of a collateral warranty, that this opinion had been made using reasonable care and skill. This collateral warranty had been broken and so the defendant was entitled to damages for breach of contract.

COMMENT (i) The statement was made before the Misrepresentation Act 1967 came into force. At that time there could be no claim for damages for a non-fraudulent misrepresentation. If the Act had been in force it would not have been necessary to imply the collateral warranty. (Misrepresentation, and the remedies available, are considered in the following chapter.)

(ii) The Court of Appeal also held that Esso were liable for the tort of negligent misstatement. (This tort is considered in Chapter 12 at 12.3.) However, such a claim would be unlikely to be pursued since the Misrepresentation Act 1967 came into force. Negligent misstatement must be proved by the person alleging it. When negligent misrepresentation is alleged the burden of proof is on the person making the misrepresentation to show that he had reasonable grounds for believing that the statement was true and actually did believe that the statement was true. The statement in this case, although an opinion, implied statements of fact which could amount to a misrepresentation. (See *Smith* v *Land and House Property Corporation* (1884) 28 ChD7 in Chapter 6 at 6.1.1.1.)

(iii) Section 1 of the Misrepresentation Act 1967 contemplates that a misrepresentation may later become a term of the contract. If this is the case then remedies will be available for either misrepresentation or for breach of contract.

Test your understanding

1 How do express terms arise? How do implied terms arise?

2 Upon what basis will a court decide whether or not an express statement is a term of a contract?

3 In deciding whether or not the parties intended a statement to be a term of the contract the courts are guided by various tests. What do the following matters indicate about the presumed intention of the parties:

   a One of the parties to the contract was much better placed than the other to know whether or not the statement was true?

   b The party to whom the statement was made indicated that the statement was vitally important to him?

   c The statement was made very strongly/weakly?

   d The contract was concluded a long time after the statement was made?

4 What is the parol evidence rule?

Answers

1 Express terms are specifically agreed upon by the parties. Implied terms are put into the contract, either by the courts or by a statute, without the parties needing to expressly agree them.

2 An express statement will be a term of a contract if the court infers that the parties intended the statement to be a term of the contract.

3 a If the maker of the statement was much better placed to know whether or not it was true, the statement is likely to be a term. If the person to whom the statement was made was much better placed to know whether or not it was true, the statement is likely to be a representation.

   b If the party to whom the statement was made indicated that he considered the statement to be vitally important to him then it is likely to be a term.

    c A statement which is made very strongly is likely to be a term. A statement made very weakly is likely to be a representation.

    d The longer the time lapse between the making of the statement and the making of the contract the more likely it is that the statement is not a term. The shorter the time lapse between the making of the statement and the formation of the contract the more likely it is that the statement is a term.

4 The parol evidence rule is that extrinsic (outside) evidence cannot be introduced to add to or vary a written contract. There are several exceptions to the rule.

5.3 · Implied terms

As well as the express terms agreed upon by the parties, most contracts also contain implied terms. These implied terms are inserted into the contract either by a statute or by the courts.

5.3.1 Terms implied by statute

The Sale of Goods Act 1979 implies terms into contracts of sale of goods and these terms are considered in detail in Chapter 8. However, it is important when considering the nature of implied terms to have an outline knowledge of the five major terms implied by the 1979 Act. First, it is implied that the seller has the right to sell the goods. Second, where there is a contract for the sale of goods by description there is an implied term that the goods will correspond with the description. Third, in a contract for the sale of goods by sample it is implied that the goods will match the sample in quality and that the bulk of the goods will not contain defects which were not apparent in the sample. The final major implied terms, which are probably the most important two, are only implied into contracts where the seller sells the goods in the course of a business. The two terms implied into such sales are that the goods sold are of satisfactory quality, and that the goods are reasonably fit for any purpose which the buyer expressly or impliedly made known to the seller.

In Chapter 8 we shall also see that the Supply of Goods (Implied Terms) Act 1973 and the Supply of Goods and Services Act 1982 imply terms into other types of contracts which cannot be classified as contracts of sale of goods. The terms implied into these contracts, under which goods are supplied but not sold, are virtually identical to the terms implied by the Sale of Goods Act. Where a contract is made to supply a service in the course of a business, the Supply of Goods and Services Act 1982 implies an important term that the supplier will carry out the service with reasonable care and skill. This term has no equivalent in the Sale of Goods Act 1979.

Because the three statutes imply the terms outlined above, the parties do not need to mention these terms when they make the contract. The implied terms are automatically put into the contract by the relevant statute. Indeed, in consumer contracts the terms implied by the Sale of Goods Act 1979, and the corresponding terms contained in the 1973 and 1982 Acts, cannot be removed from the contract even by an express term which states that they should be. An outline of the statutory implied terms is shown in Figure 8.4 in Chapter 8.

5.3.2 Terms implied by the courts

The courts imply terms into contracts either as a matter of fact or as a matter of law. Terms are implied as a matter of fact on the grounds that the parties to the contract intended the term to be a part of their agreement even though they did not agree the term verbally. Such terms are implied on the grounds that it is necessary and obvious that the term should be implied in order to give the agreement 'business efficacy'.

Mackinnon LJ in *Shirlaw v Southern Foundries* [1939] 2 All ER 113 (Court of Appeal) explained the circumstances in which a term will be implied by the courts as a matter of fact: ' ... that which in any contract is left to be implied and need not be expressed is something so obvious that it goes without saying.' Mackinnon went on to formulate his officious bystander test. Under this test the courts decide whether or not to imply a term by asking how the parties to the contract would have reacted if an officious bystander had suggested that the term should be expressly included in their contract. If the parties would in fact irritably have told the officious bystander that the term was so obviously included that it did not need to be mentioned, then the term would be implied by the courts. If the parties would not have reacted in this way, then the term would not be implied.

The test can be demonstrated by looking at the following case.

■ *The Moorcock* [1889] 14 PD 64 (Court of Appeal)

The defendants owned a wharf and a jetty on the River Thames. The claimants owned a steamship, the Moorcock. An agreement was made that the Moorcock should be moored alongside the defendant's jetty so that its cargo could be unloaded and another cargo loaded. If moored at this place the Moorcock would inevitably touch the bottom of the river at low tide. No charge was made for the steamship being moored at the jetty. However, the defendant benefited from its being moored there because the claimant paid for the use of cranes and the defendant was entitled to part of this payment as commission. At low tide the Moorcock was damaged because it settled on a ridge of hard ground beneath the mud.

Held. The defendants were liable for the damage to the steamship. The steamship would inevitably touch the bottom of the river at low tide, and so the defendants had impliedly promised that they had taken reasonable care to make sure that the bottom of the river adjoining the jetty was in such a condition that it would not damage the steamship.

This case arose half a century before Mackinnon LJ set out his version of the officious bystander test. Even so, we can see that an application of the test would have resulted in the same outcome. If the officious bystander had said to the two parties, 'Hadn't you better include a term that the jetty owner has taken reasonable care to ensure that the jetty is a safe place to moor a steamship?' they would both irritably have told him that such a term was so obvious that it did not need to be stated.

The officious bystander test will ensure that a term is not implied where one of the parties might not have agreed to the term in question. In *Shell (UK) v Lostock Garages* [1976] 1 All ER 481 the defendant made a written contract, agreeing to buy only Shell's petrol in return for a discount on the price. During a price war, Shell supplied all neighbouring garages more cheaply with the consequence that the defendant could only carry on his business at a loss. The defendant claimed an implied term that Shell would not 'abnormally discriminate' against him. The Court of Appeal refused to imply the term not only because it was too vague and uncertain, but also because there was no certainty that Shell would have agreed to it.

Despite having this power to imply terms, the judges have always used it sparingly. They have repeatedly made it plain that they are not prepared to make a contract on behalf of the parties.

As Lord Pearson said in *Trollope v NWRHB* [1973] 2 All ER 260 (House of Lords): 'The court does not make a contract for the parties. The court will not even improve the contract which the parties have made for themselves, however desirable the improvement might be … An unexpressed term can be implied if and only if the court finds the parties must have intended that term to form part of their contract … it is not enough for the court to find that such a term would have been adopted by the parties as reasonable men if it had been suggested to them … it must have been a term which went without saying, a term necessary to give business efficacy to the contract.'

As well as implying terms as a matter of fact, the courts also imply terms as a matter of law. These terms are not implied on the basis that the parties to the contract must have intended them to be included in their contract. They are implied on the basis that such a term is implied into this type of contract generally.

■ *Liverpool City Council* v *Irwin* [1977] AC 239 (House of Lords)

Liverpool City Council owned a tower block containing 70 flats. There were two lifts and a staircase. The tenancy agreements imposed a list of obligations on the tenants but did not impose any obligations on the City Council. The condition of the tower block deteriorated very badly because of vandalism and a lack of co-operation from the tenants. The lifts often failed, there was a lack of proper lighting on the stairs and the chutes down which rubbish was deposited were often blocked. Two tenants, a husband and wife, refused to pay rent as a protest. The City Council applied for an order to reclaim possession of their maisonette. The tenants counterclaimed that the City Council had breached an implied term giving the tenants a right to quiet enjoyment of the property.

Held. A term was implied that the City Council should keep the communal facilities in reasonable repair and usability. This term was not implied as a matter of fact, because the City Council would not have agreed to it. It was implied as a matter of law because such a term should generally be implied into leases of high-rise flats.

COMMENT (i) In the Court of Appeal Lord Denning had suggested that a term should be implied on the basis of it being reasonable to imply it. The House of Lords emphatically rejected this suggestion. (ii) The City Council had not in fact breached the implied term.

5.3.3 Customary terms

Terms will be implied by the courts on the grounds that they are customary in a particular trade, customary in a particular locality or customary between the parties. The courts impose such terms on the grounds that the parties, fully aware of the custom in question, must have intended the term to be a part of the contract.

Many trades have customs, and these customs will be implied into contracts made within the context of that trade. For example, in *British Crane Hire Corporation Ltd* v *Ipswich Plant Hire Ltd* [1975] QB 303 one of the parties urgently needed to hire a crane from the other. An oral contract was made, and this contract was deemed by the Court of Appeal to include the terms contained in 'the Contractors' Plant Association form'. Both parties were in the business of hiring out heavy earth moving equipment and both knew that whenever heavy plant was hired it was always done so under terms based on the Contractors' Plant Association form.

Similarly, customs of a particular locality will be implied into contracts made within that locality. In *Hutton* v *Warren* (1836) 1 M & W 466, for example, a Lincolnshire tenant farmer who was given notice to quit the farm had to be paid an allowance for seeds and labour because there was an agricultural custom to that effect in that area.

A particular term can become customary between the parties themselves, if they regularly make contracts which include the term. In *Kendall (Henry) & Sons* v *William Lillico & Sons Ltd* [1969] 2 AC 31 an oral contract for the sale of animal foodstuffs was made. Over the previous three years the parties had made three or four similar contracts a month with each other. The same written contract note, setting out terms and conditions, was always sent within a day of the oral contract being made. The House of Lords held that the oral contract was made subject to the terms and conditions contained in the written contract note. When the buyers placed an order they did so in the knowledge that the acceptance would be on these terms and conditions.

5.3.4 Exclusion of implied terms

In many circumstances the terms implied by statute cannot be excluded, as we shall see in Chapter 8. But terms implied by the court on the basis that they were obviously what the parties intended can always be excluded by an express term. If, for instance, the lease in *Hutton* v *Warren* had expressly stated that the tenant farmer would not get an allowance for seeds and labour, then he would not have received such an allowance. Similarly, terms will not be implied by the courts as a matter of law if the parties have expressly agreed that they should not be included.

5.4 · Types of terms

If any term is broken, the injured party will always be able to claim damages for breach of contract. In addition, the injured party might also be entitled to treat the contract as repudiated and therefore be entitled to refuse performance of the contract. Whether or not the injured party has the right to do this depends upon what type of term was broken.

5.4.1 Conditions and warranties

Traditionally, all contract terms were classified as being either conditions or warranties. A condition is an important term, one which goes 'to the root of the contract'. If a condition is broken then the injured party can not only claim damages but is also entitled to treat the contract as repudiated. This right to treat the contract as repudiated is available even if the consequences of the breach of condition were trivial.

A warranty is a term which did not seem vitally important when the contract was made. (A term which does not go 'to the root of the contract'.) If a warranty is broken the injured party can only claim damages. He is not entitled to treat the contract as repudiated. If the injured party does treat the contract as repudiated, and refuses to perform his side of the contract, he will himself be in breach of contract.

Two cases decided in 1876, both involving opera singers who had broken their contracts, have traditionally been used to demonstrate the difference between conditions and warranties.

■ *Bettini* v *Gye* (1876) 1 QB 183

Bettini was an opera singer who made a contract to give a series of performances over a three-month period. He fell ill and missed half of the six days' rehearsals which the contract demanded. His employer found a substitute and sacked Bettini. It was a term of Bettini's contract that he should attend all six days of the rehearsals, and there was no doubt that he had broken this term. His employers argued that this term was a condition and that they could therefore terminate the contract. Bettini argued that the term was a warranty and that, while this made him liable in damages, it did not give the employer the right to terminate the contract.

Held. The employer was not entitled to dismiss Bettini. The terms requiring him to attend the rehearsals were only warranties as they did not go to the root of the contract. (So the employer had himself broken a term of the contract, by sacking Bettini unjustifiably, and consequently had to pay damages to Bettini.)

■ *Poussard* v *Spiers* (1876) 1 QB 410

The facts of this case were substantially the same as those of *Bettini* v *Gye*, except that Madame Poussard became seriously ill five days before the first performance. As a result of this illness, she was unavailable for the first four performances of her three-month contract. The employers found it necessary to sack Madame Poussard because they could only find a replacement if they offered her the whole three months' work.

Held. The employers were entitled to terminate the contract and dismiss Madame Poussard. Missing the opening night amounted to a breach of condition.

5.4.2 Innominate terms

In 1962 Lord Diplock, in the following case, demonstrated that the existing classification of terms into either conditions or warranties could be fundamentally flawed. He invented a new type of term, the innominate term (the term with no name). Innominate terms are sometimes called intermediate terms.

■ *Hong Kong Fir Shipping Co Ltd* v *Kawasaki Kisen Kaisha Ltd* [1962] 1 All ER 474 (Court of Appeal)

A ship was chartered to the defendants for a 24-month period. The engines of the ship were in poor condition and the crew were inefficient. Because of these problems five weeks were lost during the first voyage and a further fifteen would be lost while repairs were carried out. However, after the repairs were completed and a new crew found the ship was seaworthy in every respect. At this time the ship was still available for the remaining 17 months of the contract. One of the terms said that the ship should be 'in every way fitted for ordinary cargo service'. Both sides agreed that this term had been broken. The defendants argued that the broken term was a condition and that breach of this term therefore entitled them to treat the contract as repudiated. The claimants sued for wrongful repudiation, claiming that the defendants were not entitled to treat the contract as repudiated because the term was only a warranty.

Held. The term that the ship should be 'in every way fitted for ordinary cargo service' could not be classified in advance as either a condition or a warranty. The term was an innominate term, and the contract could not be terminated because the defendants had not been deprived of 'substantially the whole benefit which it was the intention of the parties they should obtain'.

COMMENT (i) The term that the ship should be in every way fitted for ordinary cargo service covered very minor breaches (such as a rivet being missing) as well as very major breaches (such as the ship sinking). If the term was held to be a condition, this would lead to the absurd result that the whole contract could be terminated because one rivet was missing. If the term was held to be a warranty this would lead to the even more absurd result that the contract could not be terminated even if the ship sunk to the bottom of the ocean.

(ii) Under the charter the ship was hired at 47s. per ton. At the time when the defendants claimed to treat the contract as repudiated freight had fallen to 13s. 6d. per ton. This was almost certainly the defendants' real motive in claiming that they had the right to treat the contract as repudiated. However, the defendants' motive would not have any bearing on the court's decision as to whether or not the contract could be treated as repudiated.

5.4.3 Difference between conditions, warranties and innominate terms

In deciding whether or not a breach of an innominate term allows the injured party to terminate the contract, the court considers the effect of the breach. If the injured party is deprived of substantially the whole benefit of the contract, he can treat the contract as repudiated and claim damages. If he is not deprived of substantially the whole benefit, he can claim damages but not treat the contract as repudiated.

Under the traditional conditions and warranties approach the courts do not wait to see the effect of the breach. Instead they look back to the time when the contract was made, and look at all the circumstances of the case to decide how important the parties would have considered the term to be when they made the contract. If the parties would have intended the term to go to the root of the contract the term was a condition, if they would not have intended the term to go to the root of the contract the term was only a warranty.

Innominate terms have not replaced conditions and warranties. Some terms can now be classed as conditions or warranties, others are innominate terms. In outline, the current position is as follows.

The statutory implied terms are classified by the statutes themselves as either conditions or warranties. The more important statutory implied terms are conditions. Breach of a condition will allow the injured party to treat the contract as repudiated, breach of a warranty will not. However, s.15A of the Sale of Goods Act 1979, s.11A of the Supply of Goods (Implied Terms) Act 1973 and ss.5A and 10A of the Supply of Goods and Services Act 1982 provide that a buyer who does not deal as a consumer will have to treat breach of a statutory implied condition as a breach of warranty if the breach is so slight that it would be unreasonable for the buyer to reject the goods. (See Chapter 8 at 8.4.4.)

Terms other than the statutory implied terms will be treated as innominate terms unless the parties have expressly or impliedly agreed that breach of the term will or will not entitle the injured party to treat the contract as repudiated. If such an intention has been shown then the courts will give it effect and the term will be either a condition or a warranty. (Calling the term a condition or a warranty is not conclusive of such an intention, although it is an indication of it.) A rule of law might indicate that a particular term is to be treated as a condition or a warranty. Where none of the previously mentioned matters classify a term as either a condition or a warranty, the term will be an innominate term. If an innominate term is breached then the injured party can treat the contract as repudiated if he has been deprived of substantially the whole benefit of the contract.

Test your understanding

1 In what circumstances will a court imply a term as a matter of fact?

2 In what circumstances will a court imply a term as a matter of law?

3 In what three circumstances will a term be implied on the grounds of custom?

4 How will a court decide whether or not a term was a condition or a warranty?

5 What are the remedies available for breach of condition and breach of warranty?

6 What remedies are available for breach of an innominate term?

Answers

1 A court will imply a term as a matter of fact to give business efficacy to a contract. The term is implied because the court considers that the parties obviously intended the term to be a part of the contract.

2 A court will imply a term as a matter of law when the contract is of a type where such a term would generally be implied.

3 A customary term can be implied by the courts on the grounds that it is customary in a particular locality, or customary in a particular trade, or customary between the parties themselves.

4 In deciding whether a term is a condition or a warranty a court will look at all the evidence to see if the parties considered the term to be vitally important, a term which went to the root of the contract at the time when the contract was made. If the parties would have considered the term vitally important the term will be a condition. If the parties would not have considered the term to be vitally important it will only be a warranty.

5 Breach of a condition allows the injured party to treat the contract as repudiated and/or claim damages. Breach of a warranty allows the injured party to claim damages but not to treat the contract as repudiated.

6 Breach of an innominate term will always allow the injured party to claim damages. The injured party will be entitled to treat the contract as repudiated only if he was deprived of substantially the whole benefit of the contract.

5.5 · Exclusion clauses

Exclusion clauses, or exemption clauses as they are sometimes known, are contractual clauses which try to exclude or exempt one party's liability. Usually the liability in question will have arisen as a result of an express or implied term of the contract. However, exclusion clauses can also exclude liability arising in tort.

Exclusion clauses have sometimes operated very unfairly, as the following case shows.

■ *L'Estrange* v *Graucob* [1934] 2 KB 394 (Court of Appeal)

The claimant, a café owner, bought a new cigarette vending machine. She signed an order form which contained the main terms of the contract in ordinary size print. In small print, but still legible, a term stated that, 'Any express or implied, condition, statement or warranty, statutory or otherwise, not stated herein is expressly excluded'. The claimant did not read the order form and did not know of the exclusion clause. The vending machine did not work properly. The claimant sued for damages for breach of the statutory implied term, now contained in s.14(3) of the Sale of Goods Act 1979, that the machine should be fit for the buyer's purpose. There was no doubt that this term had been broken.

Held. The claimant's claim failed. The claimant had signed the order form and so she was bound by the exclusion clause.

Scrutton LJ: 'When a document containing contractual terms is signed … the party signing it is bound, and it is wholly immaterial whether he has read the document or not … The claimant, having put her signature to the document … cannot be heard to say that she is not bound by the terms of the document because she has not read them.'

The unfair way in which exclusion clauses can operate has been considerably reduced since the Unfair Contract Terms Act 1977 came into force. In addition, the courts may render an exclusion clause invalid, either by holding that the clause was not a term of the contract in question or by finding that the clause did not exclude liability for the particular breach which occurred.

5.5.1 Judicial control of exclusion clauses

The English courts have always been attached to the doctrine of freedom of contract, which holds that sane adults are free to contract on any terms they wish. In *Printing and Numerical Registering* Co v *Samson* (1875) LR 19 Eq 462 Sir George Jessel MR said:

> 'If there is one thing more than another which public policy requires it is that men of full age and competent understanding shall have the utmost liberty of contracting, and that their contracts when entered into freely and voluntarily shall be held sacred and shall be enforced by Courts of justice. Therefore, you have this paramount public policy to consider – that you are not lightly to interfere with this freedom of contract.'

The courts have traditionally taken the view that if parties to a contract freely agree to an exclusion clause, then it is not the role of any court to interfere with that agreement. However, the assumption that exclusion clauses are freely negotiated rather ignores the reality of the situation. In fact, exclusion clauses are inserted into contracts by the party with the greater bargaining power. In *L'Estrange* v *Graucob*, for example, the café owner would have had little choice but to agree to the exclusion clause. If she had refused to sign the order form then it is likely that she would not have been able to buy the vending machine.

Attached as they were to the notion of freedom of contract, the courts did nevertheless realise the unfairness of exclusion clauses and did therefore try to limit the effect of them. There were two main ways in which they might achieve this. First, they might decide that the clause was never incorporated into the contract. Second, they might interpret the clause in such a way that it did not exclude liability for the breach which subsequently occurred. Later in this chapter we will examine the effect of the Unfair Contract Terms Act 1977 and the Unfair Terms in Consumer Contracts Regulations 1999. But first we must examine judicial control of exclusion clauses. If an exclusion clause is not incorporated as a term of a contract then it will not be necessary to consider the effect of the 1977 Act or the 1999 Regulations, as the exclusion clause will not have any contractual effect.

5.5.1.1 Is the exclusion clause a term of the contract?

As we saw in *L'Estrange* v *Graucob*, a person who signs a contract will generally be bound by its contents. This is not the case however if the person signed because the effect of the document was misrepresented to him.

■ *Curtis* v *Chemical Cleaning and Dyeing Co* [1951] 1 All ER 631 (Court of Appeal)

The claimant took her white satin wedding dress to a dry cleaners. She was asked to sign a form, headed 'Receipt', and inquired what it said. She was told that the form protected the cleaners against certain specified types of damage, such as damage to beads and sequins. The claimant signed the form which in fact contained a term which stated, 'This article is accepted on condition that the company is not liable for any damage howsoever arising'. The wedding dress was badly stained and the cleaners relied on the exclusion clause.

Held. The cleaners could not rely on the exclusion clause because they had misrepresented its effect.

When both parties sign a written document it is relatively easy to say whether or not an exclusion clause is a term of the contract. If the clause is included in the signed document it is a term, if it is not included it is not. But in contracts which are not written and signed by the parties it is not so easy to say. Case law has decided that a party will be bound by an exclusion clause if it is contained in a document which the reasonable man would have thought to be a contractual document.

■ *Thompson v London, Midland and Scottish Railway Co* [1930] 1 KB 41 (Court of Appeal)

The claimant's niece bought her a railway ticket. The claimant could not read. If she had been able to read she would have been able to see that the front of the ticket said, 'Excursion. For conditions see back'. On the back of the ticket it was stated that the ticket was issued subject to the defendants' timetables and excursion bills. The excursion bills themselves referred to the conditions in the defendants' timetables. The timetable could be purchased for 6d and one of its conditions excluded liability for injuries caused by the defendants' negligence. While stepping out of the train, the claimant was injured by the defendants' negligence.

Held. The claimant was bound by the exclusion clause in the timetable. Even though she could not read she had sufficient notice of the exclusion clause.

COMMENT (i) The Court of Appeal overruled a jury which had found that passengers had not been given reasonable notice of the exclusion clause.
(ii) The Unfair Contract Terms Act 1977 s.2(1) now prevents the exclusion of liability for negligence which resulted in personal injury. However, this case is still an authority on the incorporation of exclusion clauses into contracts.

■ *Chapelton v Barry UDC* [1940] 1 KB 532 (Court of Appeal)

Deck chairs belonging to the defendants were piled up on a seaside beach near a notice which read, 'Barry Urban District Council. Cold Knap. Hire of deck chairs 2d per session of 3 hours'. The notice also said that tickets for the deck chairs should be obtained from the attendant and that the tickets should be retained for inspection. The notice did not contain any exclusion clause. The claimant hired two deck chairs from the attendant, paying 4d for two tickets. On the back of the tickets it stated that the defendants could not be liable for any accident or damage arising from the hire of the chair. The defendant did not read the tickets but put them in his pocket. The canvas on one of the chairs came away from the frame of the chair and this caused an accident which injured the claimant.

Held. The exclusion clause was not a part of the contract. The notice board set out the terms on which the deck chairs were hired. The ticket was not a contractual document, it was just a voucher or receipt for the money paid to hire the chair.

COMMENT Although this case appears very similar to *Thompson v LMS Railway*, the essential difference is that in this case the Court of Appeal thought that the ticket was not a document which a reasonable person would expect to contain contractual terms.

To be effective an exclusion clause must be a term of the contract, and as such it must have been agreed before the contract was made. A term cannot later be incorporated into the contract.

■ *Olley v Marlborough Court Hotel Ltd* [1949] 1 KB 532 (Court of Appeal)

A married couple booked into a residential hotel. They paid the bill in advance. Furs belonging to the wife were stolen from the hotel room. When sued for this loss the defendants sought to rely on a notice in the hotel bedroom, which stated, 'The proprietors will not hold themselves responsible for articles lost or stolen, unless handed to the manageress for safe custody. Valuables should be deposited for safe custody in a sealed packet and a receipt obtained'.

Held. The notice was too late to be effective. The contract had already been made before the couple had an opportunity to see the notice.

COMMENT In *Chapelton* the ticket was too late to be a part of the contract. Once a customer had taken a deck chair and sat upon it he had incurred liability to pay for the chair and had therefore already made the contract.

■ *Thornton v Shoe Lane Parking Ltd* [1971] 1 All ER 686 (Court of Appeal)

The claimant was badly injured in a car park operated by the defendants. The accident was partly caused by the defendants' negligence. The claimant had driven into the car park, passing a notice which said, 'All cars parked at owner's risk'. Inside the car park the claimant encountered a red light. When this light changed to green a machine issued the claimant with a ticket. The claimant did not read the ticket, which said that the ticket was issued subject to conditions displayed inside the premises. These conditions excluded liability for damage to goods and for injuries to customers. However, they could only have been discovered by driving into the car park and walking around. The defendants denied liability, relying on the conditions inside the car park to which the ticket referred.

Held. The exclusion clause to which the ticket referred was introduced too late to be a part of the contract. At the time of making the contract the claimant neither knew of the exclusion clause nor had reasonable steps been taken to draw it to his attention.

COMMENT (i) Lord Denning MR analysed that the contract had already been concluded when the customer received the ticket. It was concluded as soon as the customer was irrevocably committed to the contract. (See Chapter 3 at 3.4.)
(ii) The notice outside the car park was incorporated into the contract but it did not exclude liability for personal injuries.

A custom of a particular trade might incorporate an exclusion clause into a contract made within that trade. Similarly a course of dealing between the parties might have the same effect. (See *British Crane Hire Corporation Ltd v Ipswich Plant Hire Ltd* [1975] QB 303 and *Kendall (Henry) & Sons v William Lillico & Sons Ltd* [1969] 2 AC 31 at 5.3.3 above. In both cases exclusion clauses were implied into the contracts.)

In order for a term to be implied on the basis of a course of dealing between the parties the course of dealing must be well established. In *Hollier v Rambler Motors Ltd* [1972] 2 QB 71 the claimant had taken his car for repair at the defendants' garage three or four times in the previous five years. Each time a form containing an exclusion clause had been signed. The claimant made an oral contract to have the car repaired. The car was damaged. The Court of Appeal held that a course of dealing had not been clearly established and so the exclusion clause had not been incorporated into the oral contract. Salomon LJ said, 'I am bound to say that, for my part, I do not know of any other case in which it has been decided or even argued that a term could be implied into an oral contract on the strength of a course of dealing (if it can be so called) which consisted at the most of three or four transactions over a period of five years'.

In *McCutcheon v David MacBrayne Ltd* [1964] 1 All ER 430 the claimant sued a ferry company for damages when a ferry carrying his car from Islay to the Scottish mainland sank. The contract had been made by the claimant's brother in law, one McSporran, and no exclusion clause was signed. However, exclusion clauses had been displayed on the walls of the office where the contract was made and on the ferries. Over the previous years both the claimant and McSporran had used the defendants' ferries to transport sheep, sometimes signing the exclusion clause and sometimes not. The House of Lords held that there was no consistent course of dealing which would have the effect of incorporating an exclusion clause into the contract which McSporran made.

If an exclusion clause was accepted only because of an oral undertaking that it would not be enforced then it cannot be enforced.

■ *Evans & Son (Portsmouth) Ltd v Andrea Merzario Ltd* [1976] 1 WLR 1078 (Court of Appeal)

The claimants imported machines to England from Italy. Since 1959 the claimants had arranged the contracts of carriage with the defendants. The machines were liable to rust and so it was arranged that they would always be carried below deck. In 1967 containerisation was proposed so that in future the machines would be shipped in large containers. The claimants agreed to a new contract only after they were assured that their machines would still be carried below deck. There was nothing in the written contract about carrying the machines below deck. A container carrying one of the claimant's machines fell overboard. The defendants relied on exclusion clauses in their written contract which allowed the containers to be carried on deck.

Held. The oral assurance that the claimants' machines would be carried below deck was contractually binding. The defendants' exclusion clauses could not protect the defendants from liability for breach of the oral term because the printed conditions were repugnant to the oral promise and therefore overridden by it.

Earlier in this chapter we examined *Webster* v *Higgin* and saw that even where an exclusion clause is validly incorporated into a contract there may also exist a collateral contract of which the exclusion clause is no part. We examined the doctrine of privity in the previous chapter and saw that in general only the parties who made a contract will acquire rights under the contract. The doctrine might mean that a person may not be able to rely on an exclusion clause which is expressed to be for his benefit. In *Adler* v *Dickson and Another* [1955] 1 QB 158, for example, a shipping company's exclusion clause stated that the company was excluded from liability for negligence, even if this was caused by the company's employees or other persons directly or indirectly working for the company. The claimant was injured and sued the master and the boatswain of the ship in negligence. Although the clause did not directly confer protection on the company's employees Jenkins LJ held that even if it had done so it would have been ineffective on the grounds of privity of contract. However, in the light of the Contracts (Rights of Third Parties) Act 1999 it would seem that the company's employees could now rely on the exclusion clause. They were expressly identified in the contract and the exclusion clause purported to confer a benefit upon them.

5.5.1.2 Does the exclusion clause cover the breach which occurred?

Before the Unfair Contract Terms Act 1977 came into force the courts went to considerable lengths to limit the effect of exclusion clauses by interpreting them contra preferentum (strictly against the wishes of the party trying to rely on them). Generally these 'mental gymnastics', as Lord Denning called them, have been made unnecessary by the 1977 Act. However, the Act does not invalidate all exclusion clauses and so the contra preferentum rule can still be important. The following case shows the way in which a court could defeat an exclusion clause by strict interpretation of it.

■ *Andrews Bros Ltd* v *Singer & Co Ltd* [1934] 1 KB 17 (Court of Appeal)

The claimants agreed to buy 'new Singer cars' from the defendants. One of the cars delivered was not new. Section 13 of the Sale of Goods Act says that when goods are sold by description, 'there is an implied condition that the goods shall correspond with the description'. Relying on this, the claimants claimed damages. The defendants, in turn, relied on an exclusion clause which stated 'All conditions, warranties and liabilities implied by statute, common law or otherwise are excluded'.

Held. The exclusion clause did not apply. It was not an implied term that the cars should be new, it was an express term. The exclusion clause did not limit the effect of express terms.

5.6 · The Unfair Contract Terms Act 1977

The Unfair Contract Terms Act 1977 was passed because Parliament perceived that the judiciary were not adequately controlling exclusion clauses. The important sections of the Act, ss.2–7, apply only to business liability, which is defined by s.1(3) as:

'liability to breach of obligations or duties arising –
(a) from things done or to be done by a person in the course of a business (whether his own business or another's): or
(b) from the occupation of premises used for the business purposes of the occupier.'

5.6.1 The effect of the 1977 Act

5.6.1.1 Section 2 – Liability for negligence

Section 2(1) provides that a person cannot by reference to a contract term or to a notice exclude or restrict his liability for death or personal injury resulting from negligence.

Section 2(2) provides that liability for other types of loss or damage caused by negligence, such as damage to goods, cannot be excluded except in so far as the term or notice satisfies the Act's requirement of reasonableness. (Later in this chapter we shall examine the requirement of reasonableness.)

'Negligence' is defined by s.1(1) as:

'the breach –
(a) of any obligation, arising from the express or implied terms of a contract, to take reasonable care or exercise reasonable skill in the performance of the contract;
(b) of any common law duty to take reasonable care or exercise reasonable skill(but not any stricter duty);
(c) of the common duty of care imposed by the Occupiers' Liability Act 1957.'

It can be seen that in this context 'negligence' means not only the tort of negligence but also negligent performance of a contract and breach of the statutory duty of care which occupiers owe to lawful visitors. (See Chapter 12 at 12.5.)

■ *Smith* v *Eric S Bush* [1989] 2 All ER 514 (House of Lords)

The claimant applied to a building society for a mortgage to buy a house. The building society employed a firm of surveyors, the defendants, to make a survey of the house. The claimant paid £39 to the building society, who agreed to supply her with a copy of the surveyor's report. A disclaimer said that neither the building society nor the surveyors would be liable for any inaccuracies. The report, which also carried a similar disclaimer, said that the house was worth £16 500 and that no major building work was necessary. Eighteen months later the chimneys fell through the roof because two chimney breasts had been removed without proper supports being fitted. The claimant sued the defendants for negligence. The defendants relied on the disclaimer.

Held. The defendants were liable. The damage to property which had occurred was caused by the defendant's negligence. Section 2(2) therefore applied so that the disclaimer which excluded liability could only be effective in so far as it satisfied the Act's requirement of reasonableness. This requirement of reasonableness had not been satisfied.

COMMENT   If the falling chimneys had caused personal injury or death then s.2(1) would have rendered invalid any contract term which tried to exclude liability in respect of this.

Section 2 of the Act is very far reaching in its effect. For example, in most of the cases which we examined when considering judicial control of exclusion clauses the claimant's loss or injury was caused by the defendant's negligence. (This does not mean that the Act renders those cases irrelevant. They are still authorities on the circumstances in which an exclusion clause will be incorporated into a contract. It does show that litigation on exclusion clauses very often involves a claim for loss or injury caused by negligence. In such cases the effect of s.2 of the Act will have to be considered.)

5.6.1.2 Sections 6 and 7 – Exclusion of statutory implied terms

Earlier in this chapter we considered in outline the terms implied by the Sale of Goods Act (SGA) 1979, the Supply of Goods (Implied Terms) Act (SGITA) 1973 and the Supply of Goods and Services Act (SGSA) 1982. Section 6 of the Unfair Contract Terms Act (UCTA) 1977 deals with exclusion of the terms implied by SGA 1979 and SGITA 1973.

Section 6(1) provides that the implied terms as to the right to sell which are contained in SGA s.12 and SGITA s.8 cannot be excluded by any contract term.

Section 6(2) provides that as against a person dealing as a consumer liability for the terms implied by SGA ss.13–15, and liability for breach of the corresponding terms set out in SGITA ss.9–11, cannot be excluded or restricted by reference to any contract term. The terms set out in SGA ss.13–15 and SGITA ss.9–11 can be excluded or restricted where the buyer does not deal as a consumer, but only in so far as the term which excludes or restricts liability satisfies the UCTA's requirement of reasonableness.

Section 7 UCTA 1977 makes similar rules regarding the exclusion of the terms implied by the Supply of Goods and Services Act 1982. The implied terms as to the right to hire or transfer property in goods cannot be excluded by any contract term. Section 7(2) UCTA provides that as regards consumers the other terms which the Act implies cannot be excluded or restricted by reference to any contract term. Where the person to whom the goods are transferred does not deal as a consumer, the implied terms can be excluded or restricted by a term only in so far as that term meets the UCTA's requirement of reasonableness.

In order to fully understand the effect of ss.6 and 7 UCTA we therefore need to know exactly when a person is to be regarded as dealing as a consumer. Section 12(1) UCTA provides the answer:

'A party to a contract "deals as a consumer" in relation to another party if –
(a) he neither makes the contract in the course of a business nor holds himself out as doing so; and
(b) the other party does make the contract in the course of a business; and
(c) in the case of a contract governed by the law of sale of goods or hire-purchase, or by s.7 of this Act, the goods passing under or in pursuance of the contract are of a type ordinarily supplied for private use or consumption.
[But if the first party mentioned in subsection 1 is an individual paragraph (c) of that subsection must be ignored.]'

So when the contracting party is an individual, that is to say a living person rather than a company, only the two requirements in s.12(1)(a) and (b) apply. Where the contracting party is a company s.12(1)(c) must also be satisfied.

By way of example, let us assume that a shop buys a radio from a manufacturer and sells the radio to John, a bus driver, who later sells it to his friend, Mark. The shop does not deal as a consumer because it makes the contract in the course of a business. John does deal as a consumer. Mark does not deal as a consumer because John does not sell the radio in the course of a business of his. John would not have been a consumer if he had held himself out as acting in the course of a business when he had bought the radio.

In *R & B Customs Brokers Ltd* v *United Dominions Trust Ltd* [1988] 1 All ER 847 the Court of Appeal held that a company could deal as a consumer. The company bought a second hand car for a director to use both on company business and privately. A term of the contract which excluded the term in the buyer's favour implied by s.13 SGA 1979 could not be effective as the company was a consumer. This decision was reached because, although the company had bought two or three cars previously, the purchase of the car was not the type of transaction entered into sufficiently regularly to become an integral part of the company's business and the business of the company was not buying and selling cars. (This test is based on the test used to see whether a person is acting in the course of a business for the purposes of the Trade Descriptions Act 1968 – see Chapter 22 at 22.2.1. A different test is used to see whether a seller sells goods in the course of a business for the purposes of SGA 1979 s.14(2) and (3) – see *Stevenson* v *Rogers* in Chapter 8 at 8.2.4.)

Section 12(2) again distinguishes between individuals and companies. Section 12(2)(a) provides that a buyer is not to be regarded as dealing as a consumer if he is an individual and the goods are second-hand goods sold at public auction at which individuals have the opportunity of attending the sale in person. Section 12(2)(b) provides that a buyer who is not an individual should never be regarded as dealing as a consumer when he buys goods sold by auction or by competitive tender.

Section 13 SGSA 1982 provides that in a contract for the supply of a service where the supplier is acting in the course of a business there is an implied term that the supplier will carry out the service with reasonable care and skill. Sections 6 and 7 UCTA 1977 do not touch exclusion of this implied term. However, s.2(1) and (2) UCTA will apply to attempts to exclude liability for breach of the implied term. Section 1(1) UCTA makes this plain by stating that as regards UCTA 1977 'negligence' means the breach of any obligation, arising from the express or implied terms of a contract, to take reasonable care or exercise reasonable skill in the performance of a contract.

5.6.1.3 Section 3 – Excluding liability arising in contract

Section 3 UCTA 1977 protects two classes of people:

(a) those who 'deal as a consumer', and
(b) those who deal on the other party's written standard terms of business.

We have already identified the circumstances in which a person deals as a consumer. UCTA 1977 does not define written standard terms of business. However, written terms would seem to be standard where the same terms are used when supplying all customers of the business or where the same terms are always used when the two parties in question make contracts with each other. Where a person deals as a consumer it will not be necessary to decide whether or not the consumer deals on the other's written standard terms of business.

As against a person either dealing as a consumer or dealing on the other party's written standard terms, s.3 provides that, except in so far as the contract term satisfies the requirement of reasonableness, the other party cannot by reference to any contract term:

(a) exclude or restrict any liability of his in respect of a breach of contract; or
(b) claim to be entitled to render a contractual performance substantially different from that which was reasonably expected of him; or
(c) claim to be entitled, in respect of the whole or part of his contractual obligation, to render no performance at all.

This section will be useful when the breach of contract does not involve negligence (in which case s.2 provides adequate protection) and does not involve breach of a statutory implied term (in which case ss.6 and 7 provide protection). It might, for example, be useful where Business A contracts to have a building painted on Business B's standard terms, one of these terms stating that Business B cannot be liable if the painting is not completed on time. If the painting was completed very late, for reasons other than negligence, then s.3 would only allow the exclusion clause to exclude or restrict the liability of Business B in so far as the term satisfied the Act's requirement of reasonableness.

5.6.1.4 Section 4 – Indemnity clauses

In the previous chapter, at 4.3.3, we examined the nature of an indemnity. Section 4(1) UCTA 1977 provides that a person dealing as a consumer cannot by reference to any contract term be made to indemnify another person (whether a party to the contract or not) in respect of liability that may be incurred by the other for negligence or breach of contract, except in so far as the contract term satisfies the Act's requirement of reasonableness. In non-consumer contracts indemnity clauses are not touched by the Act, unless they are covered by one of the other sections. The following case shows how this can happen.

■ *Phillips Products Ltd* v *Hyland* [1987] 2 All ER 620 (Court of Appeal)

The claimants, who were in business, hired an excavator and a driver from a hire company. A term of the contract provided that the claimants had to indemnify the hire company for any damage caused by the driver. The driver damaged the claimants' buildings. The claimants sued the hire company, who relied on the indemnity clause.

Held. If the claimants had not been in business this would have been a consumer contract and the indemnity clause would not have applied, under s.4, because it would not have satisfied the Act's requirement of reasonableness. But because the contract was not a consumer contract s.4 did not apply. However, the defendant's negligence had damaged the claimants' property. Under s.2(2) a term can only exclude liability for damage to property caused by negligence in so far as the term satisfies the Act's requirement of reasonableness. The term providing that the claimants had to indemnify the hire company did not satisfy the Act's requirement of reasonableness and so it did not apply.

5.6.1.5 Section 5 – 'Guarantee' of consumer goods

In the context of s.5 'consumer goods' means goods of a type ordinarily supplied for private use or consumption. Section 5(1) provides that in the case of such consumer goods, where loss or damage arises from the goods proving defective while in consumer use, and results from the negligence of a person concerned in the manufacture or distribution of the goods, liability for the loss or damage cannot be excluded or restricted by reference to any contract term or notice contained in or operating by reference to a guarantee of the goods. For the purposes of s.5 consumer goods are in consumer use when a person is using them, or has them in his possession for use, otherwise than exclusively for the purposes of a business (s.5(2)(a)). This section is aimed at manufacturers' 'guarantees' which attempt to exclude liability owed to a consumer in tort. The section is not necessary where a manufacturer's negligence caused death or physical injury, because s.2(1) would not allow the exclusion clause to be effective. Section 5 therefore only covers damage to property caused by the manufacturer's negligence. It does however provide greater protection than s.2(2) in that s.5 applies even if the guarantee's exclusion would have satisfied the Act's requirement of reasonableness. Section 5 does not affect the position between the retailer and the consumer. The Sale and Supply of Goods to Consumers Regulations 2002 provide that a consumer guarantee given by a manufacturer now takes effect as a contractual obligation. The Regulations are considered at the end of this chapter at 5.8.

5.6.1.6 Section 8 – Excluding liability for misrepresentations

Section 3 of the Misrepresentation Act 1967, as substituted by s.8 UCTA 1977, provides as follows:

'If a contract contains a term which would exclude or restrict —
(a) any liability to which a party to a contract may be subject by reason of any misrepresentation made by him before the contract was made; or
(b) any remedy available to another party to the contract by reason of such a misrepresentation, the term shall be of no effect except in so far as it satisfies the requirement of reasonableness as stated in section 11(1) of the Unfair Contract Terms Act 1977; and it is for those claiming that the term satisfies that requirement to show that it does.'

It should be noticed that this section does not distinguish between those who deal as a consumer and those who do not.

5.6.1.7 The Act's requirement of reasonableness

We have seen that in several circumstances a term which excludes or restricts liability can be effective only in so far as it satisfies the Act's requirement of reasonableness.

Section 11(1) UCTA states that the requirement of reasonableness in relation to a contract term is 'that the term shall have been a fair and reasonable one to be included having regard to the circumstances which were, or ought reasonably to have been, known to or in the contemplation of the parties when the contract was made'.

The burden of proof is on the party claiming that a contract term or notice satisfies the requirement of reasonableness to show that it does (s.11(5)).

Section 11(2) states that in determining for the purposes of ss.6 and 7 whether a term satisfies the requirement of reasonableness regard shall be had to the particular matters specified in Schedule 2 to the Act. Schedule 2 gives five guidelines for the application of the reasonableness test. Regard should be had to any of these which appear relevant. The matters are:

(a) the strength of the bargaining position of the parties relevant to each other, taking into account (among other things) alternative means by which the customer's requirements could have been met;

(b)   whether the customer received an inducement to agree to the term, or in accepting it had an opportunity of entering into a similar contract with other persons, but without having to accept a similar term;

(c)   whether the customer knew or ought reasonably to have known of the existence and extent of the term (having regard, among other things, to any custom of the trade and any previous course of dealing between the parties);

(d)   where the term excludes or restricts any relevant liability if some condition is not complied with, whether it was reasonable at the time of the contract to expect that compliance with the term would be practicable;

(e)   whether the goods were manufactured, processed or adapted to the special order of the customer.

Although Schedule 2 is theoretically only to be used when the contract is to supply goods, the judge considered Schedule 2 in the following case, which concerned a defective service. It is now routine that reference to Schedule 2 will be made whenever a court has to consider the Act's requirement of reasonableness.

■ *Woodman* v *Photo Trade Processing Ltd* (1981) 131 NLJ 933

The defendants were given a reel of film to develop. On account of the defendants' negligence, most of the pictures were lost. The defendants relied on a clause which read: 'All photographic materials are accepted on the basis that their value does not exceed the cost of the material itself. Responsibility is limited to the replacement of the films.' The claimant had taken the pictures at a friend's wedding, where he had been the only photographer.

Held. The exclusion clause did not apply because it was not reasonable. In reaching this decision the judge had regard to the fact that the claimant had little choice but to agree to such a term, as most commercial film developers insisted on a similar term. Consequently, the claimant was awarded damages of £75.

5.6.1.8 Provisions against evasion of liability

Section 10 provides that a person is not bound by any contract term prejudicing or taking away rights of his which arose under, or in connection with the performance of, another contract. So if a consumer bought a computer system and also made a second contract under which the system was to be set up, the second contract could not deny the consumer rights which arose under the contract of sale.

Where an earlier section of the Act prevents the exclusion or restriction of liability, s.13 also prevents:

(a)   making the liability or its enforcement subject to restrictive or onerous conditions (for example, that defects in garden seeds should be notified within seven days of purchase);

(b)   excluding any right or remedy in respect of the liability, or subjecting a person to any prejudice in consequence of his pursuing any such right or remedy (for example, restricting the amount of damages payable to the cost of the goods bought);

(c)   excluding or restricting rules of evidence or procedure (for example, a term would not be able to insist that a buyer's signature would be taken as absolute proof that the goods bought conformed to the contract).

However, s.13(2) provides that an agreement in writing to submit present or future differences to arbitration is not to be treated as excluding or restricting any liability. Such clauses are therefore not affected by UCTA 1977.

An outline of the effect of the main provisions of UCTA 1977 is shown in Figure 5.2.

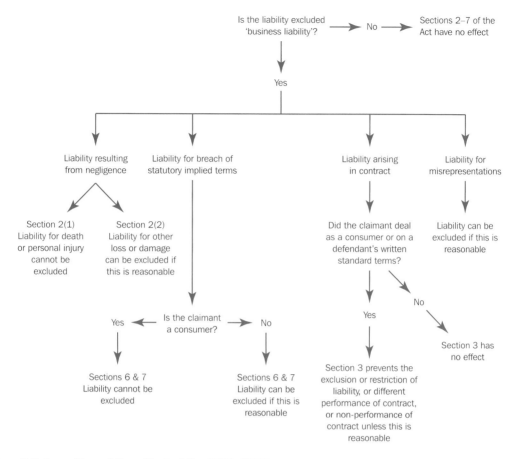

Figure 5.2 An outline of the effect of the UCTA 1977

5.7 · The Unfair Terms in Consumer Contracts Regulations 1999

The Unfair Terms in Consumer Contracts Regulations 1994 were passed to give effect to an EU directive. The regulations did not replace the Unfair Contract Terms Act, but run alongside it. The 1994 Regulations have been repealed and replaced by the 1999 Regulations. The changes made by the 1999 Regulations were very slight, relating mainly to which bodies were given the power to apply for injunctions to see that the Regulations were complied with.

5.7.1 Application of the Regulations

Regulation 4(1) states that the Regulations apply to unfair terms in contracts to supply goods or services if they are concluded between a seller or supplier and a consumer.

A consumer is defined as a natural person (and not therefore a company) who, in contracts covered by the Regulations, is acting for purposes which are outside his trade, business or profession. Sellers and suppliers are defined as legal persons who, in contracts covered by the Regulations, are acting for purposes relating to their trades, businesses or professions, whether publicly owned or privately owned.

The Regulations are not confined to exclusion and limitation clauses, but can consider the effect of any unfair term in a consumer contract. However, the Regulations will not allow assessment of a 'core' term which is written in plain and intelligible language (reg. 6(2)). A core term defines the main subject matter of the contract and the price for which it is bought.

5.7.2 Unfair terms

Regulation 5(1) states that: 'A contractual term which has not been individually negotiated shall be regarded as unfair if, contrary to the requirement of good faith, it causes a significant imbalance in the parties' rights and obligations arising under the contract, to the detriment of the consumer.'

Regulation 5(2) states that a term shall always be regarded as not having been individually negotiated where it has been drafted in advance and the consumer has therefore not been able to influence the substance of the term. Even if a specific term or certain aspects of it has been individually negotiated, the Regulations apply to the rest of the contract if an overall assessment of it indicates that it is a pre-formulated standard contract (reg. 5(3)). The burden of proof is on the seller or supplier to show that a term was individually negotiated (reg. 5(4)).

5.7.3 The requirement of good faith

A Schedule to the 1994 Regulations set out a list of matters to be taken into account when assessing whether or not the seller or supplier had acted in good faith. The 1999 Regulations contain no such list as under the 1999 Regulations a court will consider all relevant matters.

5.7.4 Assessment of unfair terms

Regulation 6(1) states that: 'Without prejudice to Regulation 12, the unfairness of a contractual term shall be assessed, taking into account the nature of the goods or services for which the contract was concluded and by referring, at the time of the conclusion of the contract, to all the circumstances attending the conclusion of the contract and to all the other terms of the contract or of another contract on which it is dependent.'

Regulation 12 allows the Director General of Fair Trading and other qualifying bodies to apply for an injunction to prevent the use of, or the recommendation of the use of, an unfair term.

5.7.5 Indicative list of terms which may be regarded as unfair

Schedule 2 to the Regulations specifies an indicative and illustrative list of terms which may be regarded as unfair. These include: terms which have the object or effect of excluding liability for death or personal injury caused by negligence (1)(a); making an agreement binding on consumers whereas the seller or supplier's obligations are subject to a condition which he can choose to realise (c); requiring a consumer who fails to fulfil his obligation to pay a disproportionately high sum in compensation (e); authorising the seller or supplier to dissolve the contract on a discretionary basis, where the same facility is not granted to the consumer (f); allowing the seller or supplier to terminate a contract of indeterminate duration without reasonable notice or serious grounds for determination (g); using hidden terms to irrevocably bind the consumer (i); altering the terms of the contract unless there is a valid reason specified in the contract (j, k and l); and requiring the consumer to take disputes to arbitration not covered by legal provisions (q). A complete list of all the indicative and illustrative terms can be found on the Office of Fair Trading's web site.

5.7.6 Effect of unfair term

Regulation 8(1) states that an unfair term in a contract concluded with a consumer by a seller or supplier shall not be binding on the consumer. Regulation 8(2) provides that the contract shall continue to bind the parties if it is capable of continuing in existence without the unfair term. So it seems that a blue pencil test will apply, and the rest of the contract should stand if it could do so unaffected once the unfair term had been crossed out with a blue pencil.

5.7.7 Construction of written contract

Regulation 7 reiterates the contra preferentum rule, providing that if there is a doubt about the meaning of a written term, the interpretation most favourable to the consumer shall prevail.

5.7.8 Prevention of continued use of unfair terms

Regulation 10(1) provides that it is the duty of the Director General of Fair Trading to consider any complaint made to him that any contract term drawn up for general use is unfair. However, the Director does not have to consider the complaint if he considers it frivolous or vexatious. The Director and other qualifying bodies may apply for an injunction to prevent the use of, or the recommendation of the use of, any unfair term drawn up for general use in contracts concluded with consumers (reg. 12(1)). Eleven qualifying bodies are listed, and these include the Director Generals of Gas, Electricity, Water and Telecommunications supplies, the Rail Regulator, all British weights and measures authorities and the Consumers' Association. A qualifying body must give the Director General of Fair Trading 14 days' notice of intention to apply for an injunction. However, if given sufficient undertakings about the continued use of an unfair term the Director General may choose not to seek an injunction (reg. 10(3)). An injunction may prevent not only the use of the particular unfair term, but also of any term having similar effect (reg. 12(4)).

The Office of Fair Trading have taken a very interventionist approach in threatening to apply for injunctions. Almost invariably the business concerned backs down. One unfortunate effect of this success is that there are very few, if any, reported cases on the interpretation of the Regulations, although the Office of Fair Trading do publish reports giving details on the cases in which they have been involved. Under the 1994 Regulations there were no other qualifying bodies which could apply for injunctions. In order to facilitate the investigation of complaints, traders can be ordered by the qualifying bodies or the Director General of Fair Trading to produce copies of their standard contracts and to give information about their use (reg. 13(3)).

5.8 · Consumer guarantees

The Sale and Supply of Goods to Consumers Regulations 2002 have introduced new rules on consumer guarantees. Goods supplied to consumers do not need to come with a guarantee. However, where goods sold or supplied are offered with a consumer guarantee, reg. 15(1) provides that the consumer guarantee takes effect at the time the goods are delivered as a contractual obligation. This contractual obligation is owed by the guarantor under the conditions set out in the guarantee statement and the associated advertising. The Regulations have therefore removed the need to prove a contract between the consumer and the manufacturer. (Prior to the Regulations taking effect there was some doubt as to whether or not such a contract could be proved.)

Regulation 2 defines a consumer as any natural person who is acting for purposes which are outside his trade, business or profession. A 'consumer guarantee' is defined as any undertaking to a consumer by a person acting in the course of his business, given without extra charge, to reimburse the price paid or to replace, repair or handle consumer goods in any way if they do not meet the specifications set out in the guarantee statement or in the relevant advertising. It should be noticed that the guarantor only has to do what he promised to do. Many guarantees are restricted to repairing goods and do not promise a refund if the goods are faulty. When a consumer buys defective goods the primary remedy will be against the retailer under the statutory implied terms. (See Chapter 8 at 8.2.) However, a guarantee can be particularly useful if the retailer has become insolvent or if the guarantee period is for several years. SGA 1979, and other equivalent statutes, require goods to be of satisfactory quality at the time of delivery. If the goods prove defective much later it can be difficult to prove that the goods were not of satisfactory quality at the time of delivery. Also, a buyer will be too late to reject, though not too late to claim damages, on account of having accepted the goods if he retains the goods for more than a reasonable time without intimating rejection of them. (See Chapter 10 at 10.4.3.) In the Regulations the 'supply' of goods includes supply by way of sale, lease, hire or hire-purchase.

The guarantee must be written in plain, intelligible English. The name and address of the guarantor must be supplied, along with the extent and duration of the guarantee and how to claim under it.

If the consumer so requests the guarantee must, within a reasonable time, be made available to him in writing or in another durable medium which he can access. This obligation to make the guarantee available is placed not only on the guarantor but also on any person who offers the goods to the consumer. Trading standards officers can enforce the rules on supplying the guarantee in the required form by way of injunction.

Test your understanding

1 In the light of the protection conferred by the Unfair Contract Terms Act 1977 and the Unfair Terms in Consumer Contracts Regulations 1999, why is it still necessary to analyse whether or not an exclusion clause is a term of a contract?

2 An exclusion clause can be incorporated into a contract if it was agreed upon by both parties or if the party affected by the clause had reasonable notice of it. At what time must the clause have been agreed upon or notice of it have been given?

3 As regards business liability, to what extent can a contract term exclude liability for negligence?

4 To what extent can a contract term exclude liability for breach of the terms implied by the Sale of Goods Act 1979 and the corresponding terms implied by the Supply of Goods (Implied Terms) Act 1973 and the Supply of Goods and Services Act 1982?

5 What types of contracts are affected by the Unfair Terms in Consumer Contracts Regulations 1999?

6 What is the main effect of the 1999 Regulations?

Answers

1 If an exclusion clause is not incorporated as a term of a contract then it cannot affect liability arising under the contract, in which case there is no need to consider the effect of the 1977 Act or the 1999 Regulations.

2 In order for an exclusion clause to be a term of a contract it must have been agreed upon, or reasonable notice of it have been given, before the contract was made.

3 As regards business liability, a contract term or notice cannot exclude liability for death or personal injury caused by negligence (UCTA s.2(1)). A contract term can only exclude liability for other types of loss caused by negligence in so far as the term satisfies UCTA's requirement of reasonableness (UCTA s.2(2)).

4 Liability for breach of the terms implied by SGA 1979, and the corresponding terms implied by SGITA 1973 and SGSA 1982 can never be excluded where the buyer deals as a consumer. Where the buyer does not deal as a consumer liability for breach of the implied terms can be excluded by a term which satisfies UCTA's requirement of reasonableness. However, liability for breach of the terms as to the right to sell can never be excluded.

5 The 1999 Regulations apply only to terms in contracts between a consumer and a seller or supplier.

6 The main effect of the 1999 Regulations is that consumers will not be bound by unfair terms, that is to say by terms which were not individually negotiated and which, contrary to the requirement of good faith, cause a significant imbalance between the rights and obligations under the contract to the detriment of the consumer.

Key points

Distinguishing terms and representations

- Express terms are expressly agreed by the parties. Implied terms are implied either by the courts or by statute.

- A promise which was intended by the parties to be a part of a contract will be a term of the contract.

- A representation is not a part of the contract because the parties did not intend that it should be.

- The courts have devised several tests to help to decide whether or not the parties to the contract intended a particular statement to be a term or not. The tests are not conclusive as the intentions of the parties can only be deduced from all the evidence.
- The parol evidence rule, to which there are several exceptions, holds that extrinsic (outside) evidence cannot be introduced to add to or vary a written contract.

Implied terms

- Terms can be implied into contracts either by statute or by the courts.
- Important terms are implied into contracts by the Sale of Goods Act 1979, the Supply of Goods (Implied Terms) Act 1973 and the Supply of Goods and Services Act 1982.
- Terms are implied by the courts as a matter of fact on the basis that the parties must have intended the term to be a part of the contract.
- Terms can be implied by the courts as a matter of law on the basis that such a term would generally be implied into a contract of the same type.
- The courts can imply terms on the basis that they are customary in a particular locality, customary in a particular trade, or customary between the parties.

Conditions, warranties and innominate terms

- A condition is a term which the parties intended to be vitally important so that it went to the root of the contract. A warranty is a term which the parties did not intend to be vitally important.
- If a condition is breached the injured party can treat the contract as repudiated and/or claim damages. If a warranty is breached the injured party can claim damages but cannot treat the contract as repudiated.
- Breach of an innominate term will allow the injured party to treat the contract as repudiated only if he was deprived of substantially the whole benefit of the contract. Breach of an innominate term will always allow the injured party to claim damages.

Exclusion clauses

- An exclusion or exemption clause is a term in a contract which tries to exclude or exempt liability for breach of contract. Exclusion clauses may also attempt to exclude liability for breach of a tortious duty.
- An exclusion clause will only be a term of a contract if it was agreed before the contract was made or if the party affected by the clause was given sufficient notice of the clause before the contract was made.
- An exclusion clause will be ineffective to the extent that its effect was misrepresented to the party affected by it.
- An exclusion clause can be incorporated into a contract by a course of dealing between the parties or by a trade custom.
- The important sections of UCTA 1977 apply only to business liability.
- Section 2(1) of UCTA will not allow a contract term to exclude liability for death or personal injury caused by negligence. Section 2(2) allows a term to exclude liability for other types of loss caused by negligence, but only in so far as the term satisfies UCTA 1977 requirement of reasonableness.
- As against a person dealing as a consumer, s.6 of UCTA prevents liability for breach of the statutory terms implied by SGA 1979 from being excluded by any contract term. As against a person not dealing as a consumer liability for breach of these terms can be excluded by a term which satisfies UCTA's requirement of reasonableness. (However, liability for breach of the term as to the

right to sell can never be excluded.) The position is the same as regards the corresponding terms implied by SGITA 1973 and SGSA 1982.

- Section 8 of UCTA 1977 only allows liability for misrepresentation to be excluded by a contract term in so far as the term satisfies the UCTA's requirement of reasonableness.
- The 1999 Regulations apply only to terms in contracts between a consumer and a seller or supplier.
- The 1999 Regulations provide that consumers will not be bound by unfair terms. These are defined as terms which have not been individually negotiated and which, contrary to the requirement of good faith, cause a significant imbalance between the rights and obligations under the contract to the detriment of the consumer.

Summary questions

1   John, a carpenter, sold his van to a small garage on 30 April. On 4 April John drove his van to the garage, where the garage owner gave it a cursory inspection. John said that the van was eight years old but a new engine had been fitted two years ago. In fact no new engine was fitted but John believed that his statement was true because he had been told, when he had bought the van six months ago, that a new engine had been fitted. The garage owner says that he definitely would not buy the van unless a new engine had been fitted. John assured him that it had been. No deal was struck that day. On 30 April John returned to the garage and after five minutes' negotiation about the price the dealer bought the van for £2 500. Before making the contract the dealer told John that if a new engine had not been fitted he would only have paid £1 300. Is John's statement about the new engine having been fitted likely to be a term or a representation?

2   At a typical self-service petrol station the customer drives in, fills his tank, and then pays the cashier. Assuming this to be the series of events, would an exclusion clause be a part of the contract if:

    a It was displayed at the entrance to the petrol station?
    b It was displayed on the petrol pump?
    c It was displayed above the cashier's till?

3   In *Thornton* v *Shoe Lane Parking* Lord Denning said that the exclusion clause on the ticket did not apply because it came after the contract was made. It follows that the offer and acceptance must have been concluded before the ticket was issued to the driver. What then was the offer, and what was the acceptance?

4   The Unfair Contract Terms Act 1977 and the Unfair Terms in Consumer Contract Regulations 1999 both give special protection to purchasers who deal as consumers. Would the following purchasers be regarded by either the Act or the Regulations as dealing as consumers?

    a John, a civil servant, buys a car from Mary, a teacher.
    b Mary buys a new car from a garage.
    c A garage buys 12 new cars from a motor manufacturer.
    d Jack, a self-employed builder, buys a cement mixer from Bill, a retired builder.
    e Bill soon regrets having sold his cement mixer. He is bored with retirement and decides to extend his kitchen. He buys a new cement mixer from a builder's merchant, and gets trade discount by pretending that he is still in business.

5   The Unfair Contract Terms Act has not outlawed standard form contracts. Such contracts are very commonly used.

    a Identify three types of contracts which are usually made by one party agreeing to the other's written standard terms.
    b Is it only consumers who agree to another's written standard terms?

6   Belinda pays £500 to go on a two-week pleasure cruise. Belinda breaks a leg, and her luggage is waterlogged when the captain of the ferry negligently crashes into a pier. In addition, the last four days of her holiday are lost and she has to return home early. Belinda signed a standard form contract when booking the holiday. What would be the effect of:

a A clause in the contract which said that the ferry operator was not to be liable for personal injuries?

b A clause which said that the operator would not be liable for damage to passenger's luggage?

c A clause which said that passengers could not be entitled to any refund or damages if their holiday ended early due to navigational accidents?

7 Assuming that in each case the exclusion clause had been a term of the contract, what would be the outcome of the following cases if they were to arise today?

a *Thompson v London, Midland and Scottish Railway Co.*

b *Chapelton v Barry UDC.*

c *Olley v Marlborough Court Hotel Ltd.*

d *L'Estrange v Graucob.*

Multiple choice questions

1 Which one of the following statements is not true? When reference is made to a statement, assume that the statement was one of fact made by one party to the contract to the other party to the contract.

a In considering whether or not a statement is a term of a contract, the courts will be guided by the apparent intentions of the parties to the contract.

b A very strong statement, made by a party who knows more about the subject matter of the contract than the party to whom the statement was made, will always be a term of the contract.

c If the contract was concluded very shortly after a statement was made, this is an indication that the statement was a term of the contract.

d There are no tests which can be conclusive in determining whether or not the parties to a contract intended a statement to be a term of the contract.

2 By which of the following methods can a term be implied into a contract?

i By a statute.

ii By a court, on the grounds that the term is customary in the locality.

iii By a court, on the grounds that the term would significantly improve the contract.

iv By a court, on the grounds of the previous dealings of the parties to the contract.

v By a court, on the grounds of business efficacy.

a By all of these methods.

b By i, ii, iii and v only.

c By i, ii, iv and v only.

d By i, ii, iii and iv only.

3 In *The Moorcock*, the court implied a term that the jetty was a safe place to moor a boat. On which one of the following grounds was the term implied?

a Because such a term was customary in the locality.

b Because the parties, as reasonable men, would have included the term if it had been suggested to them.

c Because the term was customary in the trade.

d Because the term was necessary to give the contract business efficacy.

4 Which of the following statements are true?

i If a condition is breached then the contract must be terminated.

ii A contract cannot be terminated merely because a warranty has been breached.

iii If an innominate term is breached then the injured party has the choice as to whether or not to terminate.

iv An injured party can terminate a contract if breach of an innominate term deprived him of substantially the whole benefit of the contract.

   a i, ii and iii.
   b i, ii and iv.
   c ii and iv only.
   d i and iii only.

5   If *Olley* v *Marlborough Court Hotel* were to come to court today, which one of the following statements would be true?

   a As the notice was not a term of the contract, the case would be decided exactly as it was in 1949.

   b As Mrs Olley would now be a consumer, UCTA 1977 would not allow the notice to exclude liability for negligence.

   c As Mrs Olley would now be a consumer, the 1999 Regulations would automatically invalidate any term of the contract which would operate to her detriment.

   d The effect of the notice was misrepresented and therefore the hotel could not rely on it.

6   If *L'Estrange* v *Graucob* were to come to court today, the café owner would win the case. On which one of the following grounds would she win?

   a The buyer would now be regarded as dealing as a consumer, and therefore no term could exclude the seller's liability for breach of the terms implied by SGA 1979.

   b The buyer would not be regarded as dealing as a consumer. But in non-consumer sales liability for breach of the terms implied by SGA 1979 can only be excluded if the term seeking to do so would satisfy UCTA 1977 requirement of reasonableness, which the term in question would not.

   c The Unfair Terms in Consumer Contracts Regulations 1999 would invalidate the exclusion clause on the grounds that it was not individually negotiated and, contrary to the requirement of good faith, caused a significant imbalance in the parties' rights and obligations under the contract.

   d As the buyer dealt on the written standard terms of the seller, the protection conferred by SGA 1979 implied terms could not be excluded under any circumstances.

7   Which one of the following statements is true of the Unfair Terms in Consumer Contracts Regulations 1999?

   a The Regulations will invalidate a contract under which a consumer has agreed to pay an exorbitant price for goods or services.

   b If a contract to which the Regulations apply contains a term which the Regulations classify as unfair, the whole contract shall not be binding on the consumer.

   c The Regulations only apply to contracts concluded between a consumer and a seller or supplier. However, in certain circumstances a company can be classified as a consumer.

   d The Regulations define an unfair term as one which has not been individually negotiated, and which, contrary to the requirement of good faith, causes a significant imbalance in the parties' rights and obligations under the contract to the detriment of the consumer.

Task 5

John, a schoolteacher, decides to renovate his house in the summer holidays. John hires an industrial sander for use on the floorboards of his house. Due to an electrical fault, the sander catches fire while in use. John is badly burnt, and the floorboards in his living room catch fire, causing extensive damage to the house. When hiring the sander, John signed a standard 'sales agreement'. This agreement stated that the hire company could not be liable for any loss or damage caused by defects in previously hired goods.

Write a report for John, indicating:

   a Whether John deals as a 'consumer', as defined by the Unfair Contract Terms Act 1977.

   b The protection given to consumers by the 1977 Act.

   c Whether John dealt on the hire company's 'written standard terms', as defined by the 1977 Act.

   d The extent to which the Unfair Terms in Consumer Contracts Regulations 1999 would protect John.

   e The overall effect of the agreement which John signed.

   f The overall effect of the agreement if John had not been a teacher, but had hired the sander for use in his trade as a builder.

Chapter 6

MISREPRESENTATION · MISTAKE · DURESS AND UNDUE INFLUENCE · ILLEGALITY

Introduction

In the previous three chapters we examined the formation of contracts and the nature of contractual terms. In this chapter we see that even if all of the requirements of a valid contract are to be found, the contract may nevertheless be voidable or void. A contract which is voidable comes into being and creates obligations between the parties. However, one of the parties has the option to avoid the contract, that is to say has the option to call it off. The party with the option to avoid the contract has no need to avoid it and may instead elect to treat the contract as binding. Once an election has been made, either to affirm the contract or to avoid it, this election will be irrevocable. A contract which is void is in fact a nullity and as such it confers no rights on either party.

A contract will be rendered voidable if it was made in reliance on an actionable misrepresentation, or was made under duress or was made on account of undue influence having been exerted. None of these three matters will make the contract void. Contractual mistake occurs when one or other of the parties makes the contract while labouring under a fundamental mistake as to some important matter. Depending upon the nature of the mistake, the agreement will either be void or it will be a valid contract unaffected by the mistake. A mistake will not make a contract voidable. Agreements can also be rendered void if they contravene public policy or if what was agreed is illegal.

The same set of facts which cause a contract to be voidable for misrepresentation commonly also give rise to an argument that the contract is void for mistake. We therefore consider mistake immediately after misrepresentation, and then go on to consider duress and undue influence. Illegal contracts and contracts which contravene public policy are considered at the end of the chapter.

6.1 · Misrepresentation

In Chapter 5 we examined the difference between terms and representations. We saw that a term is a part of the contract whereas a representation is not.

In some circumstances an untrue representation may amount to an actionable misrepresentation, and if this is the case then the party to whom the misrepresentation was made will have legal remedies. It is important to remember that these remedies are not the same as those available for a breach of contract. A breach of contract occurs whenever a term of the contract is breached. The remedies available for breach of contract are considered in the following chapter. An untrue representation which does not amount to an actionable misrepresentation will not give rise to any legal remedy for misrepresentation. We therefore need to define an actionable misrepresentation.

6.1.1 Definition of an actionable misrepresentation

An actionable misrepresentation is an untrue statement of fact made by one party to a contract which induced the other party to enter into the contract. We examine the two requirements of this definition in turn. The first requirement is that the untrue statement was one of fact. The second requirement is that this statement induced the other party to enter into the contract. A misrepresentation which does not satisfy these two requirements is not an actionable misrepresentation.

6.1.1.1 An untrue statement of fact

A statement of mere opinion, being a statement which is not capable of being objectively proved true or false, cannot amount to a misrepresentation.

■ *Bisset* v *Wilkinson* [1927] AC 177 (Privy Council)

In May 1919, 2 410 acres of land in the South Island of New Zealand were sold for £13 260. The purchaser knew that no person had ever previously carried on sheep farming on the particular unit of land which was sold. Soon after the land was sold, sheep farming became very unprofitable. Before the contract was made the vendor had told the purchaser that the unit of land could support 2 000 sheep. The purchaser found that the land could not support anything like this number.

Held. As the purchaser knew that the unit of land had never been used as a sheep farm, the statement that the farm would support 2 000 sheep was only a statement of opinion and could not amount to a misrepresentation.

In the above case the statement was regarded as being a mere statement of opinion. However, what sounds like a mere statement of opinion may impliedly contain a statement of fact, which is capable of objectively being proved either true or false.

■ *Smith* v *Land and House Property Corporation* (1884) 28 ChD 7 (Court of Appeal)

The claimants put a hotel up for auction. The auction particulars stated that the hotel was let to 'F. (a most desirable tenant), at a rental of £400 for an unexpired term of 27 and a half years'. The defendant company sent their secretary to the hotel and the secretary thought the hotel was doing little business and that trade in the locality was likely to decline. The defendant company authorised the secretary to bid up to £5 000 for the hotel. The hotel was not sold at the auction. However, immediately after the auction the company secretary bought the hotel on the company's behalf for £4 700. One month later F became insolvent. The defendants refused to complete the purchase. They claimed that the statement which described F as a most desirable tenant was a misrepresentation, because when the statement was made F was badly behind with his rent and the claimants were threatening him with legal action.

Held. The statement was a misrepresentation, as it was a statement of fact, not a statement of mere opinion. F was not a most desirable tenant. The statement that he was a most desirable tenant impliedly asserted that the claimants knew of no facts which would lead to the conclusion that he was not.

COMMENT (i) Bowen LJ explained the circumstances in which a statement of opinion can be a statement of fact in this way: 'It is often fallaciously assumed that a statement of opinion cannot involve a statement of fact. In a case where the facts are equally well known to both parties, what one of them says to the other is frequently nothing but an expression of opinion ... But if the facts are not equally well known to both sides, then a statement of opinion by one who knows the facts best involves very often a statement of a material fact, for he impliedly states that he knows facts which justify his opinion.'
(ii) The decision in this case was approved by the Court of Appeal in *Esso Petroleum Co Ltd* v *Mardon* (1976), which we examined in the previous chapter at 5.2.6.

Generally, a statement of intention cannot amount to a misrepresentation because it cannot amount to a statement of fact. However, when a person makes a statement of intention knowing that it is false, then the statement may be regarded as one of fact. In *Edgington* v *Fitzmaurice* (1885) 29 ChD 476, for example, a company issued a prospectus which invited people to lend money to the company by subscribing for debentures. The prospectus stated that the company intended to use the money raised by the debentures to alter company buildings, to buy horses and vans and to develop the company's trade. In fact the real purpose of issuing the debentures was to raise money to pay off the company's debts. The company argued that their statement in the prospectus could not amount to a misrepresentation as it was a mere statement of their intention, rather than a statement of fact. The Court of Appeal had little difficulty in disposing of this argument. Bowen LJ said that in order for fraudulent misrepresentation to be established, 'There must be a statement of existing fact: but the state of a man's mind is as much a fact as the state of his digestion'.

Statements of law cannot be actionable misrepresentations. So a statement that a contract cannot be effective unless it was made in writing would not amount to an actionable misrepresentation. This principle is probably based on the idea that knowledge of the law is equally accessible to both parties, through their legal advisors. It must be said that in some circumstances it can be very difficult to categorise a statement as either a statement of law or a statement of fact.

6.1.1.2 Silence as a misrepresentation

As a general rule, neither party to a contract is under any duty to disclose information to the other party. The old rule *caveat emptor* (let the buyer beware) applies. So remaining silent will generally not amount to making a misrepresentation. This is the case even when the party who remains silent knows that the other party would not have made the contract if aware of all the facts.

■ *Fletcher v Krell* (1873) 42 LJ(QB) 55

The claimant entered into a contract of employment to be a governess in Argentina for three years at a salary of £100 a year. When making the contract she concealed from the defendant the fact that she was divorced. When the employer discovered the truth he refused to employ the claimant.

Held. The claimant was entitled to damages for breach of contract. As she had not been asked whether or not she was divorced, she had no obligation to reveal that she had. Her failure to reveal that she was divorced could not amount to a misrepresentation.

COMMENT (i) In those days both parties would have known that the claimant would have had no chance of getting the job if the employer had discovered that she was divorced.
(ii) In *Smith v Hughes* (1871) LR 6(QB) 597 (House of Lords) Cockburn CJ said, 'The passive acquiescence of the seller in the self-deception of the buyer' would not entitle the buyer to avoid the contract. The facts of this case are set out below at 6.2.3.2.

There are four exceptions to the rule that silence cannot be a misrepresentation. Silence can amount to a misrepresentation if:

(a) there was a change of circumstances; or
(b) the silence concerned a material fact in a contract of insurance; or
(c) a fiduciary relationship existed between the parties; or
(d) the silence made a statement misleading.

These exceptions need to be examined individually.

A change of circumstances

If a person makes a statement which is true at the time when it is made but which, owing to a change of circumstances, becomes untrue before the contract is made, then it may be a misrepresentation not to reveal that the circumstances have changed.

■ *With* v *O'Flanagan* [1936] Ch 575 (Court of Appeal)

In January 1934 the defendant offered to sell his medical practice to the claimant for £4 000. The defendant stated that the practice had takings of £2 000 per annum. This statement was true when it was made. However, by the time the sale was completed on 1 May the practice was almost non-existent. The defendant had been ill and several locum doctors had stood in for him, but almost all of his patients had deserted the practice.

Held. The statement that the practice had takings of £2 000 per annum had to be treated as continuing until the sale was completed and did therefore amount to an actionable misrepresentation. By failing to correct the statement the defendant continued to make it.

Contracts of insurance

Contracts of insurance are contracts *uberrimae fidei* (of the utmost good faith). In such contracts everything which could influence a prudent insurer as to the price of the premium, or as to whether or not to take the risk, is a material fact. A person taking out insurance must reveal all material facts, whether asked about the matter in question or not.

■ *Lambert* v *Co-op Insurance Society Ltd* [1975] 2 Lloyd's Rep 485 (Court of Appeal)

In April 1963 the claimant insured her own and her husband's jewellery. There were no questions asked about previous convictions. At the time of taking out the policy the claimant knew that her husband had been convicted some years earlier of receiving 1 730 stolen cigarettes and had been fined £25. In December 1971 the claimant's husband was convicted of offences of conspiracy to steal, and of theft, and was imprisoned for 15 months. The claimant did not reveal these convictions to the insurance company either at the time of the conviction or when the policy was renewed in March 1972. In April 1972 the claimant made a claim of £311, representing the value of lost or stolen jewellery.

Held. The insurers could avoid the contract on account of the misrepresentation made by the claimant. The claimant had a duty to disclose the original conviction when applying for the insurance, and to disclose the later conviction when renewing it.

Although insurance contracts are the most important contracts of the utmost good faith, there are other such contracts such as contracts to allot shares in a company.

Where there is a fiduciary relationship between the parties

A fiduciary relationship is a relationship of great trust, where one of the parties can expect to trust the other implicitly. Examples of such relationships would include contracts between partners in a firm, between agent and principal and between promoters of a company and the company. The person of whom the trust is expected must reveal everything to the person with whom he makes the contract. If he does not do so, his silence will amount to a misrepresentation.

A relationship is fiduciary because of the nature of the relationship itself. A contract is of the utmost good faith because of the nature of the contract, i.e. that it is a contract of insurance.

When silence makes a statement misleading

Even a statement which is literally true can amount to a misrepresentation if the statement conveys a misleading impression on account of not being the whole truth.

■ *Nottingham Patent Brick and Tile Co* v *Butler* (1886) 16 QBD 778 (Court of Appeal)

In 1882 the claimants, a brick manufacturing company, agreed to purchase a plot of land from the defendant and paid a deposit of £610. Some 15 years earlier the land had become the subject of a restrictive covenant which prevented the land from being used to manufacture bricks. The defendant, during the negotiations, made mention of this covenant. The claimants' solicitor asked the defendant's solicitor whether or not any such covenant existed. The defendant's solicitor replied that he was not aware of any such covenant. The defendant again said that he thought there was a restrictive covenant. The claimants' solicitor asked if this was correct and the defendant's solicitor again said that he was not aware of any such covenant. The defendant's solicitor did not explain that the reason why he was not aware of any such covenant was that he had not read the title deeds and knew nothing of their contents.

Held. The defendant's solicitor's statement, although literally true, was a misrepresentation. It was not the whole truth and it conveyed a misleading statement of fact.

6.1.1.3 The statement must induce the making of the contract

A statement can only be an actionable misrepresentation if it was influential in inducing the other party to make the contract on the terms upon which he did make the contract. An untrue statement which did not induce the other party cannot be an actionable misrepresentation. The statement in question does not need to be the sole reason why the claimant made the contract, but it must at least be one of the reasons.

If a person makes a contract without checking the truth of a statement made to him, this suggests that the statement did induce him to make the contract. In *Redgrave* v *Hurd* (1881) 20 ChD 1, for example, a solicitor agreed to become a partner in a firm because he was told that the business had an income of £300 a year. The incoming partner was offered the chance to check the books but declined the offer. If he had checked the books he would have discovered that the income was only £200 a year. Upon discovering the truth, the incoming partner refused to go ahead with the agreement. When sued for breach of contract he successfully raised misrepresentation as a defence. He had no duty to check the truth of the statements made to him, and the fact that he did not check them indicated that they had induced him to enter into the contract.

If a person does check the truth of a statement made to him then he cannot later say that the statement induced him to make a contract. The fact of his checking the statement will prove that he did not rely on it. In *Attwood* v *Small* (1838) 6 Cl & Fin 232, for example, a vendor of a mine exaggerated its capacity. The purchaser got his own experts to check the vendor's statement and these experts mistakenly said that the vendor's statement was correct. Upon finding out that the mine had the reduced capacity, the purchaser claimed to rescind the contract for misrepresentation. He was not allowed to do so. The purchaser had relied on the statement of his own experts, not on the statement of the vendor.

Test your understanding

1 What is the difference between a voidable contract and a void contract?

2 What is the definition of an actionable misrepresentation?

3 Can silence amount to an actionable misrepresentation?

Answers

1 A voidable contract is a valid contract, but one of the parties has the option to avoid the contract (call it off). A void contract is a nullity, and confers no legal rights on either party.

2 An actionable misrepresentation is an untrue statement of fact made by one of the parties to a contract which induced the other party to make the contract.

3 Silence is not generally capable of amounting to an actionable misrepresentation. It can however do so, (i) where there has been a change of circumstances, (ii) where the contract is of the utmost good faith, (iii) where there is a fiduciary relationship between the parties or (iv) where the silence makes a statement misleading.

6.1.2 The different types of misrepresentation

Once it has become established that an actionable misrepresentation has been made, it becomes necessary to consider what type of misrepresentation it was. An actionable misrepresentation can be classified as either fraudulent, negligent or wholly innocent. The classification will depend upon the state of mind of the party who made the misrepresentation.

6.1.2.1 Fraudulent misrepresentation

In *Derry* v *Peek* (1889) 14 App Cas 337 the House of Lords defined a fraudulent misrepresentation as one made either knowing that it was false, or without belief in its truth, or recklessly careless as to whether it was true or false. For example, if X sells a car to Y and makes an actionable misrepresentation that the car has been fitted with a new engine, the misrepresentation would be fraudulent if X knew that the car had not been fitted with a new engine, or if X did not think that it had been, or if X had not the slightest idea whether or not it had been.

Whichever of the three states of mind is held by the maker of the misrepresentation, he must have acted dishonestly. Mere carelessness is not enough to amount to fraudulent misrepresentation. As dishonesty must be proved, the courts require a very strong standard of proof which is closer to the criminal standard (beyond a reasonable doubt) than to the ordinary civil standard (on a balance of probabilities). For this reason many claimants faced with what is probably a fraudulent misrepresentation choose to allege negligent misrepresentation instead. (See, for example, *Royscot Trust Ltd* v *Rogerson* [1991] 3 All ER 294, which is set out below at 6.1.4.)

Fraudulent misrepresentation amounts to the common law tort of deceit. The remedies available are to claim tort damages or to rescind the contract. The remedies available for misrepresentation are examined in detail at 6.1.3 and 6.1.4.

6.1.2.2 Negligent misrepresentation

Section 2(1) of the Misrepresentation Act 1967 provides that damages are available for a negligent misrepresentation. A negligent misrepresentation arises if two steps are satisfied.

First, the injured party must prove that he has suffered a loss because an actionable misrepresentation was made to him, and that this misrepresentation would have entitled him to damages if it had been made fraudulently. Second, the burden of proof is switched to the maker of the misrepresentation. He must prove that the misrepresentation was not made negligently, that is to say that he must prove that he did believe the misrepresentation was true, with reasonable grounds for such a belief, up until the time the contract was made. If the maker of the misrepresentation cannot prove this then negligent misrepresentation is established.

A negligent misrepresentation allows the injured party to rescind the contract and claim damages which will be assessed on a tort basis.

It should also be noticed that when a negligent misrepresentation is committed a common law action for negligent misstatement might also be possible. This action is available whether or not the misrepresentation was an actionable misrepresentation (i.e. whether or not it induced the making of the contract) and is examined in Chapter 12 at 12.3. An action for negligent misstatement is generally not pursued where it is possible to sue for damages under s.2(1) of the Misrepresentation Act because the burden of proof is on the claimant alleging negligent misstatement to prove four things: that a 'special relationship' existed between the parties; that a duty of care was owed; that the duty was breached; and that this caused a foreseeable loss.

6.1.2.3 Wholly innocent misrepresentation

We have seen that a misrepresentation will not be negligent if the party who made it can establish that he did believe that the misrepresentation was true, with reasonable grounds for such a belief, up until the time when the contract was made. If these matters are proved, then a wholly innocent, rather than a negligent, misrepresentation will have been made.

When considering the nature of a fraudulent misrepresentation we considered an example where X sold his car to Y and made a misrepresentation that the car had been fitted with with a new engine. We saw the circumstances in which this misrepresentation would be fraudulent. If X honestly believed that the car had been fitted with a new engine then the misrepresentation could not be fraudulent (this is a subjective test). The misrepresentation will be negligent unless X can prove two things:

that up until the time of the contract he did believe the car had been fitted with a new engine, and that there were reasonable grounds for this belief. If X can prove these two things then the misrepresentation will have been wholly innocent.

6.1.3 Rescission of the contract

All three types of actionable misrepresentation can give rise to rescission of the contract. In cases of fraudulent misrepresentation rescission is a right, subject to the rule that any equitable remedy is only available at the discretion of the court. A negligent or wholly innocent misrepresentation generally allows for rescission, but this is not a right. In cases of negligent or innocent misrepresentation s.2(2) of the Misrepresentation Act 1967 allows the court to award damages in lieu of rescission where it would be equitable to do so. It is most unusual for a court to exercise this power. The circumstances in which it might do so are considered below at 6.1.5.

As all three types of misrepresentation allow for rescission, a contract which has been made because of an actionable misrepresentation is said to be voidable. This means that the person to whom the misrepresentation was made has the option to avoid the contract (to rescind it) within a reasonable time. If the contract is avoided in this way then it is no longer binding and the parties are restored to their pre-contract positions. However, the contract is not rescinded unless the person to whom the misrepresentation was made communicates to the other party that he is rescinding the contract. Once this decision has been made he will be too late to change his mind. Later in this chapter we shall see that in certain circumstances a contract can be void. There the position is different, a void contract is a nullity.

In cases of fraudulent misrepresentation, especially where a rogue pays for goods with a bad cheque, it may not be possible to communicate rescission. The rogue will generally have disappeared by the time the fraud is discovered. Rescission can still be made in two ways. First, the innocent party might seize the goods which he sold, thus indicating an intention to rescind. Alternatively he might rescind by an overt act which shows an intention to rescind. An example of this can be seen in *Car and Universal Finance Co Ltd* v *Caldwell* [1965] 1 QB 525 at 9.3.3 below.

Misrepresentation may also be raised as a defence by a person being sued on a contract. When misrepresentation is raised as a defence there is no need for the defendant to show that he took any steps to avoid the contract. He can wait until sued and then rely on the misrepresentation as a reason to refuse to perform the contract.

6.1.3.1 Losing the right to rescind

The right to rescind can be lost if the person to whom the misrepresentation was made has affirmed the contract, or if it has become impossible to restore the parties to the pre-contract position or if a third party has acquired rights to the subject matter of the contract before it was rescinded. Each of these three bars to rescission needs to be examined in turn.

Affirmation

A person with a right to rescind affirms a contract, and therefore loses the right to rescind it, if he expressly or impliedly indicates that he intends to continue with the contract despite knowledge of his right to rescind. In a commercial contract the right to rescind can be lost through affirmation fairly easily.

■ *Long* v *Lloyd* [1958] 1 WLR 753 (Court of Appeal)

The claimant, a haulage contractor, bought a lorry because of several non-fraudulent misrepresentations, namely that the lorry was in first class condition, that it did 11 miles to the gallon and could be driven at 40 miles per hour. Two days after buying the lorry the claimant took it on a short trip and discovered that the dynamo did not work, that an oil seal was leaking, that one of the wheels was cracked and that the lorry was only doing five miles to the gallon. When the claimant complained about these defects the defendant agreed to pay half the cost of putting the dynamo right. The claimant agreed to this and got the dynamo fixed. The next day the claimant's brother took the lorry on a trip from Kent to Middlesbrough. The lorry broke down. The claimant wrote to the defendant rescinding the contract on the grounds that the oil seal leaked, that the lorry was only doing nine miles to the gallon on a long journey and could only do 25 miles per hour when loaded.

Held. The claimant had lost the right to rescind because he had affirmed the contract. He had done this by accepting the agreement to pay half the cost of fixing the dynamo and by sending the lorry to Middlesbrough. The first short journey was not affirmation as it was a reasonable examination of the lorry.

COMMENT (i) This case seemed particularly hard on the claimant as damages for non-fraudulent misrepresentation were not available prior to the Misrepresentation Act 1967.
(ii) The trial judge, Glyn-Jones J, did not find that the defendants had been fraudulent. This seems very surprising, but indicates the high standard of proof required before fraud is proved.

Mere lapse of time may be enough to indicate that a contract has been affirmed.

■ *Leaf v International Galleries* [1950] 2 KB 86 (Court of Appeal)

The claimant bought a painting from a gallery because of a non-fraudulent misrepresentation that the painting was by John Constable. Five years later the claimant discovered that the painting was not by Constable and tried to rescind the contract.

Held. The claimant was too late to rescind. The claimant had affirmed the contract by doing nothing for five years. Rescission for non-fraudulent misrepresentation must take place within a reasonable time.

COMMENT If the misrepresentation had been fraudulent then time would not have started to run against the claimant until he either knew of the misrepresentation or ought to have known of it (Limitation Act 1980 s.32). This is an important practical difference between fraudulent misrepresentation and non-fraudulent. Before the Misrepresentation Act 1967 came into effect there were only two classes of misrepresentations: fraudulent and non-fraudulent.

Inability to restore pre-contract position

In Chapter 5 we examined in outline the remedies available for breach of contract. We saw that a person may treat the contract as repudiated if a condition is breached or if the breach of an innominate term deprived him of substantially the whole benefit of the contract. A contract can be treated as repudiated for breach of condition, or for a breach of an innominate term which deprived of substantially the whole benefit of the contract, even if it is not possible to restore the parties to the positions which they were in before the contract was made. It is future performance that is excused.

When a contract is avoided the parties must be restored to their pre-contract positions. If this is not possible then rescission will generally not be possible. In *Clarke v Dickson* (1858) El Bl & El 148 Crompton J illustrated this by giving an example of a butcher who bought live cattle because a grazier had made a fraudulent misrepresentation about them. If the butcher only discovered the misrepresentation after the cattle had been slaughtered and butchered rescission would not be possible (although damages for the tort of deceit could be claimed). However, rescission is an equitable remedy and so if the subject matter of the contract cannot be restored in exactly the same condition as it was in before the contract was made the court may order rescission, along with a monetary payment to compensate for the slight change. In *Erlanger v New Sombrero Phosphate Co* (1878) 3 App Cas 1218, for example, the buyer of a phosphate mine had extracted phosphate from the mine by the time he found out that the seller had made a misrepresentation about the mine. The House of Lords did allow rescission and ordered the buyer to compensate the seller for the phosphate he had extracted.

Third party has acquired rights

Section 23 SGA 1979 states that: 'Where the seller of goods has a voidable title to them, but his title has not been avoided at the time of the sale, the buyer acquires a good title to the goods, provided he buys them in good faith and without notice of the seller's defect of title.'

The following case demonstrates the effect of s.23.

■ *Lewis* v *Averay* [1972] 1 QB 198 (Court of Appeal)

The claimant advertised his car for sale for £450. A rogue visited the claimant and agreed to buy the car. When the rogue wrote out a cheque for £450 the claimant demanded proof of identity. The rogue, who had been claiming to be Richard Greene a well known television actor, produced a Pinewood Studios pass. The pass, which was in Richard Greene's name, showed the rogue's photograph, and bore an official looking stamp. The claimant let the rogue take possession of the car and the logbook. In fact the cheque was from a stolen cheque book. The defendant had advertised that he would like to buy a car and the rogue, now in possession of the car which the claimant had sold to him, called upon the defendant. The rogue now pretended to be the claimant and showed the defendant the logbook in the claimant's name and address. The defendant bought the car for £200. The defendant then wrote to the claimant asking for the car's workshop manual and the fraud was discovered. The rogue was never traced.

Held. The contract was voidable for fraudulent misrepresentation. However, once the defendant bought the car in good faith he acquired complete ownership of the car by virtue of s.23 SGA 1979. The claimant could no longer rescind the contract and had lost ownership of the car.

COMMENT (i) If the claimant had avoided the contract before the rogue sold to the defendant then s.23 would have provided no help to the defendant. (See *Car and Universal Finance Co Ltd* v *Caldwell* in Chapter 9 at 9.3.3.)
(ii) The contract was not void for mistake. (See below at 6.2.3.)

6.1.4 Damages for misrepresentation

The measure of damages available in respect of an actionable misrepresentation differs according to the type of misrepresentation made.

6.1.4.1 Fraudulent misrepresentation

If a fraudulent misrepresentation is proved then this amounts to the tort of deceit and damages are assessed on a fraud basis. Such damages will attempt to put the parties into the position which they would have been in if the tort had never been committed and so all expenses and losses subsequently incurred will be recoverable.

■ *Doyle* v *Olby* [1969] 2 QB 158 (Court of Appeal)

The claimant bought an ironmongery business on the strength of a fraudulent misrepresentation that the business achieved its turnover without employing a travelling salesman. The claimant paid £4 500 for the business, the goodwill and the existing lease of the business premises. He paid £5 000 for the stock and took a longer lease of the business premises from the vendor at a greatly increased rent. In fact the vendor of the business had employed a travelling salesman and half of the business had been brought in through this salesman. The claimant could not afford a travelling salesman and so that half of the business was lost. The claimant carried on the business as best he could until the case was heard. The trial judge awarded £1 500 damages. This figure was reached either as the cost of employing a travelling salesman or as the amount by which the goodwill of the business was reduced by the misrepresentation.

Held. £5 500 damages were awarded for the tort of deceit. These damages compensated not only for the money which the claimant had put into the business but also for all losses and expenses which he had subsequently suffered.

Lord Denning MR: 'In contract, the damages are limited to what may reasonably be supposed to have been in the contemplation of the parties. In fraud, they are not so limited. The defendant is bound to make reparation for all the actual damages flowing directly from the fraudulent inducement.'

COMMENT (i) This decision was approved by the House of Lords in *Smith New Court Securities Ltd v Scrimgeour Vickers (Asset Management) Ltd* [1996] 4 All ER 769.

(ii) The trial judge has assessed damages on the basis of a breach of contract. Fraud damages will generally be higher although this will not always be the case as they do not compensate for loss of the bargain. The quantification of damages for breach of contract, which do take into account the loss of the bargain, is examined in the following chapter at 7.2.2.2.

(iii) In general, tort damages will be limited by remoteness of damage – damages only being claimable for losses which were reasonably foreseeable. (See Chapter 12 at 12.2.4.) There is no such limitation when damages are awarded for the tort of deceit. Lord Denning LJ in *Doyle* v *Olby* said that: 'It does not lie in the mouth of the fraudulent person to say that they [losses actually flowing from the deceit] could not have been reasonably foreseen.'

6.1.4.2 Negligent misrepresentation

Before the Misrepresentation Act 1967 came into force misrepresentations were classified as either made fraudulently or made non-fraudulently, and damages were not available for a misrepresentation which was not made fraudulently. (Unless damages could be claimed for the tort of negligent misstatement.) Section 2(1) of the 1967 Act does allow damages for negligent misrepresentation. The section states that where a person has committed a negligent misrepresentation he shall 'be so liable' as if the misrepresentation had been made fraudulently. In the following case the Court of Appeal assessed damages for a negligent misrepresentation on the tort of deceit basis.

■ *Royscot Trust Ltd* v *Rogerson* [1991] 3 All ER 294 (Court of Appeal)

The claimant was a finance company which provided finance for the first defendant (a consumer) to take a car on hire-purchase from the second defendant (a car dealer). The consumer had enough money to put down a deposit of £1 200, this representing 15.8% of the car's price of £7 600. The car dealer knew that the finance company would demand a deposit of 20%. The two defendants therefore falsified the price of the car to £8 000 and the amount of the deposit paid to £1 600. The balance to be paid therefore appeared to be £6 400, which was the true balance the consumer had agreed to pay. The consumer repaid instalments totalling £2 775 and then dishonestly sold the car to an innocent private purchaser. The finance company could not recover ownership of the car and so it sued the car dealer for negligent misrepresentation.

Held. Damages were awarded on the tort of deceit basis. The finance company was therefore able to recover all losses which flowed from their having entered into the contract, even unforeseeable losses, as long as these were not too remote. The finance company was therefore awarded £3 265. This figure was reached by subtracting the amount it had received from the consumer (£2 775) from the amount it had paid the dealer (£6 400).

COMMENT (i) Balcombe LJ said: 'In my judgment the wording of the subsection is clear: the person making the innocent [negligent] misrepresentation shall be "so liable", i.e. liable to damages as if the representation had been made fraudulently.'

(ii) *South Australia Asset Management Corp* v *York Montague Ltd* [1996] 3 All ER 365 was a case decided on negligent misstatement rather than on negligent misrepresentation. However, it has cast some doubt on the correctness of this case. Lord Steyn stated that he could not see why a person who had not behaved immorally should be treated as if he had committed fraud.

(iii) The case seems a clear example of fraudulent misrepresentation. However, the claimant opted for negligent misrepresentation because of the reduced standard of proof and because the burden of proof was thrown on to the defendants to show that they had not made an innocent misrepresentation.

(iv) The innocent private purchaser of the car gained ownership of it by virtue of the Hire Purchase Act 1964 Part III, which is considered in Chapter 9 at 9.3.6.

(v) At first instance the damages were assessed, on the basis of a breach of warranty, at £1 600. This figure was reached by attempting to put the finance company into the position which it would have been in if the dealer had revealed that the true deposit paid was £1 200. The finance company would have regarded this as 20% of the purchase price and would therefore have paid the dealer £4 800. The contract damages would therefore have been the difference between this figure of £4 800 and the actual amount handed over to the dealer (£6 400), which equals £1 600.

6.1.4.3 Wholly innocent misrepresentation

There is no right to damages for a wholly innocent misrepresentation. However, the court has a discretion to award damages under s.2(2) of the Misrepresentation Act 1967, the effect of which is considered immediately below.

6.1.5 Damages under s.2(2) Misrepresentation Act 1967

Section 2(2) of the Misrepresentation Act 1967 introduced the possibility of damages in lieu of rescission in cases of non-fraudulent misrepresentation (that is to say in cases of negligent or wholly innocent misrepresentation). However, the claimant has no right to such damages, rather the court has a discretion to award damages in lieu of rescission in the following circumstances. First, there must have been a non-fraudulent misrepresentation which would have entitled the claimant to rescind the contract. Second, the claimant must claim that the contract has been or ought to be rescinded. Third, the court must consider it equitable to award damages rather than award rescission. In deciding whether or not it is equitable to award damages the court will consider three matters: the nature of the misrepresentation; the loss which would be caused by the misrepresentation if the contract is upheld; and the loss which would be caused to the misrepresentor if rescission is allowed.

	Fraudulent	Negligent	Wholly Innocent
Definition	Made 1) Knowing that it was false. 2) Without belief in its truth. 3) Recklessly careless whether true or false. (*Derry* v *Peek*) Dishonesty must be proved	Injured party must prove defendant made an actionable misrep. The misrep will be negligent *unless* the defendant can prove i he did believe misrep was true ii with reasonable grounds for such a belief. Misrep. Act 1967 s.2(1)	Injured party must prove defendant made an actionable misrep. The misrep will be wholly innocent *if* the defendant can prove i he did believe misrep was true ii with reasonable grounds for such a belief. Misrep. Act 1967 s.2(1)
Remedies	A right to rescind. (Time does not run until fraud discovered.) + Damages for the tort of deceit	Usually rescission (But contract damages might be awarded in lieu – s.2(2) Misrep. Act 1967.) + Damages on tort of deceit basis	Usually rescission (But contract damages might be awarded in lieu – s.2(2) Misrep. Act 1967.) No right to damages

Rescission

Contract is affirmed ← lost if → Parties cannot be restored to pre-contract position

Third party has acquired rights

Figure 6.1 An outline of the types of actionable misrepresentation and the remedies available

It is only very rarely that a court does award damages under s.2(2). When such damages are awarded they will be assessed on a contract basis. That is to say that they will attempt to put the parties into the position which they would have been in if the misrepresentation had not been untrue. They will therefore be the difference in value between the contract price paid and what the price would have been if the misrepresentation had been true. Consequential losses will not be taken into account. In *William Sindell plc* v *Cambridgeshire County Council* [1994] 3 All ER 932 the Court of Appeal considered s.2(2). In 1988 a building company had bought land from the Council for £5m. The council had stated that they did not know of any matter likely to affect the use and enjoyment of the land. The sale was concluded in March 1989. Building work started 18 months later but by this time the land was only worth about £2.5m as the property market had collapsed. In October 1990 the builders found a nine inch foul sewer which had been under the land since 1970. The trial judge found that there had been a misrepresentation and allowed the builders to rescind the contract. The Court of Appeal (on a matter of land law which does not concern us) found that there had been no misrepresentation. However, the Court of Appeal went on to state that if there had been a wholly innocent misrepresentation then rescission would not have been allowed but instead damages would have been awarded under s.2(2). These damages would either have been the cost of remedying the defect or the lesser amount the land would have been worth at the time of the contract if the defect had been known. In reaching this decision the court considered that rescission would have been inappropriate because it would have meant the Council having to repay £8m (the purchase price plus interest) for land that was currently worth about £2m.

When damages are awarded under s.2(2) in a case of negligent misrepresentation these damages should be deducted from any amount awarded under s.2(1).

In the previous chapter, at 5.6.1, we examined the circumstances in which liability for misrepresentation can be excluded.

Figure 6.1 shows an outline of the different types of misrepresentations and the different remedies available for each.

Test your understanding

1 What is the definition of a fraudulent misrepresentation?

2 In what circumstances will a non-fraudulent misrepresentation be (i) negligent and (ii) wholly innocent?

3 What remedies are available in respect of a fraudulent misrepresentation?

4 What remedies are available in respect of a negligent misrepresentation?

5 What remedies are available in respect of a wholly innocent misrepresentation?

6 In what circumstances can damages be awarded under s.2(2) of the Misrepresentation Act 1967? How will these damages be assessed?

7 In what circumstances will the right to rescind the contract for misrepresentation be lost?

Answers

1 A fraudulent misrepresentation is an actionable misrepresentation made either knowing that it was false, or without belief in its truth or recklessly carelessly whether it was true or false.

2 A non-fraudulent misrepresentation will be a negligent misrepresentation unless the maker of the misrepresentation can prove that he had reasonable grounds for believing that it was true and did hold such a belief up until the time of the contract. If these matters can be proved then the misrepresentation will have been made wholly innocently.

3 A fraudulent misrepresentation makes the contract voidable and gives rise to an action for damages for the tort of deceit.

4 Section 2(1) of the Misrepresentation Act 1967 gives a right to damages for negligent misrepresentation. These damages are assessed on the tort of deceit basis. The contract will be voidable, but the court may award damages in lieu of rescission under s.2(2) of the Misrepresentation Act 1967.

5 There is no right to damages for wholly innocent misrepresentation. The contract will be voidable, but the court may award damages in lieu of rescission under s.2(2) of the Misrepresentation Act 1967. Such awards of damages are very rare.

6 Under s.2(2) of the 1967 Act damages may be awarded in lieu of rescission for either negligent or wholly innocent misrepresentation. These damages are assessed on the breach of warranty basis.

7 The right to rescind can be lost if the contract has been affirmed, if restitution is impossible or if a third party in good faith has acquired ownership of the subject matter of the contract.

6.2 · Mistake

In certain circumstances a contract may be void for mistake, in which case it will be a nullity. No legal rights will then be conferred upon the parties. Where goods are sold under a contract void for mistake ownership of the goods will not pass to the buyer. The buyer will therefore be able to recover any of the price paid on the grounds that there has been a total failure of consideration on the part of the seller. When we considered *Lewis* v *Averay*, earlier in this chapter, at 6.1.3.1, we saw that the innocent third party became the absolute owner of the car because he had bought it before the contract with the rogue had been avoided. The claimant, who had sold the car to the rogue, argued that the contract was void for mistake, rather than merely voidable for misrepresentation. If the contract had been void for mistake then the rogue would never have acquired any title to the car at all and he could not therefore have passed any title to the innocent third party. The claimant would have been entitled to regain possession of his car as it would all the time have belonged to him. Nor would it have mattered if the claimant had not realised that the contract was void for some considerable time, or if the car had been damaged and was no longer in the same condition as when sold. The bars to rescission have no application if the contract is void. As a contract which is void for mistake is a nullity, no contractual obligations arise under it and no property passes as a result of it.

There are several different ways in which the parties to a contract might be labouring under a fundamental mistake. Some of these have no effect at all on the validity of the contract, others make the contract void.

It is convenient when considering mistake to consider first the position where both parties make the same mistake (common mistake), then the position where the offeror thinks the contract is made on one set of terms while the offeree thinks it is made on another (mutual mistake) and finally the position where only one of the parties makes a mistake (unilateral mistake).

6.2.1 Common mistake

When common mistake occurs the parties to the contract do reach agreement, but they do so while both making the same fundamental mistake. Such a mistake can make the contract void, although it will not necessarily do so. The mistake which the parties make might be about the existence of the subject matter of the contract, the ownership of the subject matter or the quality of the subject matter. Each of these three possibilities needs to be considered in turn.

6.2.1.1 Mistake as to the existence of the subject matter

If, unknown to either of the parties, the subject matter of the contract does not exist at the time when the contract is made then the contract can be void for mistake.

■ *Scott v Coulson* [1903] 2 Ch 439

A contract for the sale of a life policy of assurance was made. At the time of the sale both parties thought that the assured person was alive. In fact the assured person was dead at the time of the contract.

Held. The contract was void for mistake.

Section 6 of the Sale of Goods Act 1979 provides that where there is a contract for the sale of specific goods and the goods without the knowledge of the seller have perished at the time when the contract is made, the contract is void. This section is examined in slightly more detail at 9.1.1.1.

Two points should be noticed about mistake on the grounds of non-existence of the subject matter of the contract. First, the contract might well stipulate that one or other parties bears the risk of the subject matter not existing, and if this is the case the contract will be valid even if the subject matter did not in fact exist. For example, if X hears that Y's warehouse has suffered a major fire he could validly contract to buy from Y any stock in the warehouse which had survived the fire. If it was later shown that all of the stock had been burnt the contract would not be void for mistake. It might also be possible to find that one party had impliedly assumed the risk of the subject matter not existing. This was emphasised repeatedly in *Great Peace Shipping Ltd* v *Tsavliris Salvage International Ltd* [2002] EWCA Civ 1407 (Court of Appeal). Lord Phillips MR, giving the only judgment of the Court of Appeal, said at para 75: 'Just as the doctrine of frustration only applies if the contract contains no provision that covers the situation, the same should be true of common mistake. If, on true construction of the contract, a party warrants that the subject matter exists, or that it will be possible to perform the contract, there will be no scope to hold the contract void on the ground of common mistake …'

A second important point to note is that the contract can only be void for mistake if the goods had ceased to exist at the time when the contract was made. If the goods should cease to exist after the contract was made, but before the buyer took delivery of them, then the contract would not be void for mistake.

6.2.1.2 Mistake as to ownership

If a seller of property does not in fact own the property at the time when it is sold then it is possible that the contract will be void for mistake. First, however, we should notice that the contract will not be void for mistake if the contract is for the sale of goods and the seller expressly or impliedly warrants that he does own the goods. In the previous chapter we mentioned s.12 of the Sale of Goods Act 1979, which states that in a contract of sale of goods there is an implied condition on the part of the seller that he has a right to sell the goods. (This matter is explored further in Chapter 8 at 8.2.1.) We also saw that SGITA 1973 and SGSA 1982 imply similar terms into contracts of hire-purchase, contracts of hire and contracts under which the property in goods is to pass. These terms as to the right to sell cannot be excluded by any contract term, and if they are breached the seller will be in breach of contract. However, these implied terms as to the right to sell do not apply where the terms of the contract, or the circumstances, show an intention that the seller should transfer only such title as he or a third party might have.

Mistake as to ownership is therefore only capable of making the contract void at common law where the contract is not one into which a statute implies a term that the seller has the right to sell. Such situations are relatively rare but an example can be seen in *Cooper* v *Phibbs* (1867) LR 2 HL 149. A agreed to take a lease of a fishery from B, but unknown to both parties A was already the tenant for life of the fishery and B had no ownership of it at all. The House of Lords held that the contract was voidable in equity. In *Bell* v *Lever Bros* [1932] AC 161 Lord Atkin thought that the case was correctly decided, except that the contract should have been void rather than voidable and it is now generally accepted that this view of the case is correct.

6.2.1.3 Mistake as to quality

It is unlikely that a common mistake as to the quality of what is being sold will have any effect upon the contract.

■ *Bell* v *Lever Bros* [1932] AC 161 (House of Lords)

In 1926 Lever Bros renewed Bell's contract of employment. The renewed contract was to run for five years and Bell was to be paid £8 000 a year. In 1929 Lever Bros wanted to make Bell redundant. A contract was entered into, giving Bell £30 000 as compensation for the early termination of his contract. In fact Bell could have been dismissed without the payment of any compensation because he had in the past broken his contract of employment by speculating in the employer's business. At the time of the making of the redundancy agreement Lever Bros were not aware that Bell had broken the company rules. The jury found that at the time of making the redundancy agreement Bell had either forgotten that he had broken the company's rules or did not appreciate that this breach could have caused him to be dismissed without paying any compensation.

Held. The mistake did not make the contract void.

Lord Atkin: 'A mistake [as to quality] will not affect assent unless it is the mistake of both parties, and is as to the existence of some quality which makes the thing without the quality essentially different from the thing as it was believed to be. Of course it may appear that the parties contracted that the article should possess the quality which one or other or both mistakenly believed it to possess. But in such cases there is a contract and the inquiry is a different one, being whether the contract as to the quality amounts to a condition or a warranty, a different branch of the law … A buys B's horse; he thinks the horse is sound and he pays the price of a sound horse; he would certainly not have bought the horse if he had known, as the fact is, that the horse is unsound. If B has made no representation as to soundness and has not contracted that the horse is sound, A is bound and cannot recover back the price. A buys a picture from B; both A and B believe it to be the work of an old master, and a high price is paid. It turns out to be a modern copy. A has no remedy in the absence of a representation or warranty.'

COMMENT (i) The House of Lords only reached this decision by a majority of 3 : 2. The Court of Appeal had held that the contract was void for mistake.
(ii) What was being bought were Bell's rights under his contract of employment. Both parties were mistaken as to the quality of this. They both thought that it was worth somewhere in the region of £30 000. In fact it was worth nothing.

In *Solle* v *Butcher* [1950] 1 KB 51 the Court of Appeal held that a mistake as to quality could render a contract voidable in certain circumstances. *Solle* v *Butcher* was overruled by the following case:

■ *Great Peace Shipping Ltd* v *Tsavliris Salvage International Ltd* [2002] 4 All ER 689 (Court of Appeal)

A ship, the Cape Providence, suffered structural damage in the South Indian Ocean. The defendants offered salvage services which were accepted by the ship's owners. The defendants found a salvage tug which would take five or six days to reach the ship. However, it was feared that the ship might have sunk by then so the defendants looked for a ship in the vicinity of the Cape Providence. A reliable source told the defendants that the claimant's ship, the Great Peace, was the closest and could reach the Cape Providence in about 12 hours. The defendants therefore made a contract under which the Great Peace was to supply salvage services and save the lives of the crew of the Cape Providence. The contract was to run for a minimum of five days. At the time of the contract the defendants thought that the two ships were 35 miles apart, whereas in fact they were 410 miles apart. It would have taken the Great Peace 39 hours to reach the Cape Providence. When the defendants found out about the mistake they told the claimants that they wanted to cancel the contract but not until they had found out if there was a closer ship which could provide salvage. A few hours later they found such a ship and cancelled the contract with the claimants. At first instance Toulson J found that the defendants were in breach of contract. The defendants appealed on two counts. First, they argued that the contract was void at common law on the grounds of common mistake. Second, they argued that the contract was voidable in equity.

Held The appeal was dismissed. (i) Contracts cannot be voidable in equity for common mistake. If there was such a rule it would amount to saying that the common law was wrong, rather than of adding to or mitigating the effect of the common law. (ii) The mistake as to the position of the Great Peace did not mean that the services which the Great Peace was to provide was something essentially different than what the parties had contracted for. If the closer salvage ship had not been discovered, the defendants would have wanted the contract to be performed. It was not impossible to perform the commercial venture which had been agreed.

Lord Phillips MR, giving the only judgment of the Court of Appeal, classified the mistake in this case as a common mistake such as occurred in *Bell* v *Lever Brothers*. The decision in *Solle* v *Butcher* was not reconcilable with *Bell* v *Lever Bros* and was therefore overruled. There is no equitable doctrine of common mistake. The law on common mistake did not arise on account of an implied term. (That the parties had impliedly agreed that in the circumstances which actually arose the contract should not be binding.) Rather, it arose from a rule of law that if the parties had agreed to do something which is impossible to perform, no contract would arise. However, by impossible to perform this did not mean literally impossible, but rather that 'it was impossible to perform the contractual adventure'. The true question was whether the mistake as to the distance apart of the two ships had the effect that the services which the Great Peace was in a position to provide 'were something essentially different from that to which the parties had agreed'. The Court of Appeal decided that they were not, particularly as the contract was not cancelled until a closer salvage ship had been found. Emphasising the common history of common mistake and frustration, Lord Phillips stressed that the doctrine of common mistake could not arise if one of the parties had assumed the risk that the subject matter existed or that it would be possible to perform the commercial venture. Generally, construction of the contract would indicate that one of the parties had assumed the risk and this was probably why there were so few cases where a common mistake rendered a contract void.

COMMENT Following this decision contracts will very rarely be void for common mistake. First, the courts will look hard for express or implied terms which allocate the risk. Second, the circumstances in which the contract will be essentially different from what was agreed will be rarely found. This is perhaps fortunate because, once the parties have begun to perform a contract which they take to be valid, the consequences of a court declaring the contract void can be very complicated.

6.2.2 Mutual mistake

The parties are said to have made a mutual mistake when they are at cross purposes, so that there never was any real agreement. The offer relates to one thing and it is accepted in the belief that it relates to a quite different thing. If the reasonable man could not infer that the view of either the offeror or the offeree were objectively what was intended, then the contract can be void for mistake. However, if the reasonable man could objectively infer that either meaning reflected the objective intention of the parties then there will be a good contract on these terms.

■ *Raffles* v *Wichelhaus* (1864) 2 H & C 906

There was a contract for the sale of cotton which was to arrive at Liverpool on the ship 'Peerless' from Bombay. In fact two ships called Peerless sailed from Bombay to Liverpool. The defendant was thinking of the Peerless which set off in October. The claimant was thinking of the Peerless which set off in December.

Held. There was no binding contract because there was no *consensus ad idem*, meaning that the parties never reached agreement.

COMMENT If the circumstances had objectively indicated that the parties' intention was that the cotton should be carried on either of the two ships, then there would have been a contract for the sale of cotton to be carried on that ship.

6.2.3 Unilateral mistake

A unilateral mistake occurs where only one of the parties makes a mistake. It is possible that a unilateral mistake as to either the identity of the other contracting party, or as to the terms of the contract, can render an agreement void.

6.2.3.1 Mistake as to identity

Mistake as to the identity of the other contracting party is generally important when that party turns out to be a rogue who pays with a bad cheque while pretending to be someone else. Earlier in this chapter, at 6.1.3.1, we examined *Lewis* v *Averay* (1972) and saw that such contracts are voidable for fraudulent misrepresentation. But we also saw that if the rogue sells the goods on to an innocent third party before the contract is avoided the third party will gain complete ownership of the goods by virtue of s.23 of the Sale of Goods Act 1979. In *Lewis* v *Averay* the claimant argued that the contract was void for mistake. This argument failed. If it had succeeded the defendant, to whom the rogue sold, would not have gained ownership of the car.

First, we consider the situation where the two contracting parties made a written contract without meeting face to face. Here the contract can be void for mistake, but only if the contracting party claiming mistake was mistaken as to the identity of the other party. It is not enough that he was mistaken merely as to the attributes of the other party. The following two cases demonstrate the difference between a mistake as to identity and a mistake as to attributes.

■ *Cundy* v *Lindsay* (1878) 3 App Cas 459 (House of Lords)

Blenkarn, a rogue, hired a room at 37 Wood Street, Cheapside. From this address he wrote to the claimants, who were linen manufacturers in Belfast. In the letter Blenkarn ordered handkerchiefs and he disguised his signature so that it looked like Blenkiron & Co. A highly respectable firm, W. Blenkiron & Son, carried on business at 123 Wood Street. The claimants sent a large quantity of linen goods to 'Messrs. Blenkiron & Co, 37, Wood Street, Cheapside'. Blenkarn sold the goods obtained to different purchasers. He sold 250 dozen handkerchiefs to the defendants, who bought them in good faith and who resold them in the ordinary course of their trade. The claimants sued the defendants for the tort of conversion. This action would only be successful if the contract between the claimants and the rogue was void for mistake.

Held. There was no contract between the claimants and the rogue. The contract was void for mistake because the claimants were mistaken as to the identity of the person with whom they were dealing. Consequently, the defendants were liable in the tort of conversion.

■ *Kings Norton Metal Co Ltd* v *Edridge, Merrett & Co Ltd* (1897) 14 TLR 98 (Court of Appeal)

A rogue called Wallis ordered goods from the claimants, who were metal manufacturers in Worcestershire. The letter appeared to come from Hallam & Co, Soho Hackle Pin and Wire Works, Sheffield. No such firm ever existed but the rogue's letter was very impressive. It showed a factory with a large number of chimneys and indicated that there were offices in Belfast, Lille and Ghent. The claimants sent goods to the rogue on credit. The rogue sold the goods which he had obtained on to the defendants, who bought them in good faith. The claimants sued the defendants for the conversion of the goods.

Held. The contract was not void for mistake. The claimants were not mistaken as to the identity of the person with whom they were dealing but only as to his attributes. They made the contract with the writer of the letter. As the contract between the claimants and the rogue was a good one, the defendants were not liable to the claimants in conversion.

COMMENT (i) A person's attributes concern his qualities or features. In this case the claimants thought they were dealing with a creditworthy, respectable buyer. In fact they were dealing with a dishonest rogue. The attributes which they ascribed to the buyer (creditworthiness and respectability) were not in fact held by him. This was not enough to make the contract void. In *Cundy* v *Lindsay* the claimants had knowledge of Blenkiron & Son. They were convinced that they were dealing with this firm and were therefore mistaken as to the identity of the person with whom they actually dealt. The contract was therefore void for mistake.

(ii) The contract, like all the other cases where a rogue buys goods with a bad cheque, would of course have been voidable for fraudulent misrepresentation. But this will not help the party contracting with the rogue if the rogue sells the goods on to an innocent third party before the contract is avoided.

(iii) In all of these cases the rogue could be sued by the innocent party for the tort of deceit. However, rogues are hard to trace and when they are traced they very rarely have the means to pay damages.

(iv) In *Shogun Finance Ltd* v *Hudson (FC)* [2003] 3 WLR 1371 (see below) the two dissenting Law Lords, Lords Millett and Nicholls, thought that *Cundy* v *Lindsay* should be overruled. The majority, Lords Hobhouse, Phillips and Walker, did not.

Where the parties do meet face to face a mistake as to the person will not make a contract void.

■ *Phillips* v *Brooks* [1919] 2 KB 243

A rogue called North entered the claimant's jeweller's shop and selected pearls at a price of £2 550 and a ring at £450. He wrote a cheque and said, 'You see who I am, Sir George Bullough', and gave an address in St James's Square. The rogue said that he had better not take the pearls until the cheque was cleared but that he would take the ring immediately as it was his wife's birthday the following day. The jeweller checked Sir George's address in a directory and then let the rogue take the ring away. The rogue, now calling himself Firth, pledged the ring to the defendant, a pawnbroker, for £350. The defendant acted in good faith.

Held. The contract was not void for mistake. The jeweller dealt with the person who came into the shop. Consequently, the defendant had a good title to the ring.

COMMENT A 1960 Court of Appeal case, *Ingram* v *Little* [1961] 1 QB 31, had indicated that in these circumstances a contract could be void for mistake. In *Lewis* v *Averay* in 1972 the Court of Appeal confirmed the correctness of the decision in *Phillips* v *Brooks*. In *Shogun Finance Ltd* v *Hudson (FC)* (see below) all five Law Lords considered *Phillips* v *Brookes* and *Lewis* v *Averay* to be correctly decided.

In the following case the House of Lords gave the authorities on mistake as to the person a very thorough review.

■ *Shogun Finance Ltd v Hudson (FC)* [2003] 3 WLR 1371 (House of Lords)

Hudson, the defendant, bought a Mitsubishi Shogun car from a rogue. The rogue had taken the car on hire-purchase from the claimant finance company, Shogun Finance Ltd. He had persuaded the finance company to enter into the hire-purchase agreement by pretending to be one Durlabh Patel, living at an address in Leicester. The rogue had visited a dealer who had the car in his showroom and had produced Durlabh Patel's driving licence, which he had improperly obtained. The dealer got the rogue to fill in one of Shogun Finance Ltd's standard hire-purchase forms, which the rogue did in the name of Durlabh Patel. The dealer then phoned through to Shogun Finance Ltd the details put on the form and also faxed through a copy of the agreement and a copy of Durlabh Patel's driving licence. Having checked the credit rating of Durlabh Patel by computer, the finance company telephoned the dealer and told him to let the rogue have the car. The rogue paid a 10% deposit, only part of which was paid in cash, and drove the car away. If the contract between Shogun Finance Ltd and the rogue was a valid contract of hire-purchase, then the defendant would become owner of the car by virtue of s.27 of the Hire Purchase Act 1964. (The effect of s.27 is set out in Chapter 9 at 9.3.6.) If there was no contract between Shogun Finance Ltd and the rogue, then the defendant could not become owner of the car. The crucial question therefore was whether or not the rogue entered into a valid contract with Shogun Finance Ltd.

Held (Lords Nicholls and Millett dissenting). There was no contract between the rogue and the finance company and so the defendant had no title to the car. The claimant, Shogun Finance Ltd, had remained owner of the car throughout.

Lord Hobhouse saw significance in the fact that the hire-purchase agreement was a written contract to provide credit. Unlike a sale of goods, where property might well have passed before the time for payment arrived (see Chapter 9 at 9.1.1) in a contract where credit is provided no contract comes into existence until the credit check has been satisfactorily conducted. The language in the written contract made it plain that Shogun Finance Ltd intended only to make the contract with 'the customer named overleaf'. Therefore, only Durlabh Patel, and not the rogue or anyone else, could have validly made the contract. Durlabh Patel obviously did not make the contract. There was no true agreement between Shogun Finance Ltd and the rogue because Shogun Finance Ltd believed it was accepting an offer from Durlabh Patel and the rogue had no honest belief or contractual intent whatsoever. The contract was not made face-to-face because the dealer was not the agent of Shogun Finance Ltd for the purposes of making the contract. Therefore, the principle in *Lewis* v *Averay* was not applicable. This contract was not a face to face sale of goods, but concerned the construction of a written contract to provide credit.

Lord Phillips approved *Cundy* v *Lindsay*. He thought that where there was some form of personal contact between parties conducting negotiations there should be a strong presumption that the parties intended to deal with each other. But he thought that there was no need for such a presumption where the dealings were conducted exclusively in writing.

Lord Walker concurred with the speech of Lord Hobhouse. He thought that the face-to-face principle in *Lewis* v *Averay* might be extended to the situation where the parties made the contract on the phone. However, he did not think it could cover a case where the contract was formed by written communication by post or email.

Lord Nicholls gave a strong dissenting judgment, indicating that *Cundy* v *Lindsay* should be overruled, in favour of the approach adopted in *Lewis* v *Averay*. He did not think that there should be a distinction between cases where the rogue and the seller met face to face and those where they did not. He thought that Shogun Finance Ltd, believing that the person in the dealer's showroom was Durlabh Patel, intended to make the contract with the person in the showroom. If this had not been the case, they would not have let the person in the showroom take the car away.

Lord Millett thought that there should be no distinction between cases where the parties met face to face and those where they did not. He thought that *Cundy* v *Lindsay* should be overruled and that there was a voidable contract between Shogun Finance Ltd and the rogue.

COMMENT (i) This decision seems to have left the existing authorities unaltered but the fundamental split in the opinions of the Law Lords suggests that the matter has not been finally resolved.
(ii) It might seem surprising that the dealer was not the agent of Shogun Finance Ltd, when making the contract. However, in *Branwhite* v *Worcester Works Finance Ltd* [1962] 1 AC 552 the House of Lords held that in a triangular transaction such as this (see Chapter 14 at 14.2.2) the dealer is not normally the agent of the finance company when making the contract. However, the dealer did act as the finance company's agent when making delivery of the car to the rogue.

A mistake as to the person can only make the contract void if the mistake mattered to the person who made it and if the mistake was known to the other contracting party. In *Mackie* v *European Assurance Society* (1869) 21 LT 102 the claimant asked a friend to take out an insurance policy on his behalf. The claimant believed that the contract was being made with a certain insurance society but in fact the friend made it with the defendant society. When sued on the policy, the defendants argued that this mistake as to identity meant that the contract was void. The contract was held to be valid because the identity of the insurers did not matter to the claimant.

6.2.3.2 Mistake as to the terms of the contract

If one of the parties knows that the other made the contract on the strength of a fundamental mistake as to the terms of the contract then the contract can be void for mistake.

■ *Hartog* v *Colin & Shields* [1939] 3 All ER 566

The defendants agreed to sell the claimants 30 000 Argentine hare skins. When selling large quantities, hare skins were either sold per piece (per skin) or per pound, there being roughly three pieces in a pound. The defendants mistakenly offered the skins at a certain price per pound whereas they meant to offer them at this price per piece. The claimants accepted the offer. All the earlier negotiations had been conducted on a per piece basis and Argentine hare skins are generally sold per piece.

Held. There was no contract. The claimants could not reasonably have supposed that the offer expressed the true intention of the defendants and must have known that it was made by mistake.

Singleton J: 'I am satisfied that it was a mistake on the part of the defendants or their servants which caused the offer to go forward in that way, and I am satisfied that anyone with knowledge of the trade must have realised that there was a mistake.'

The following case is different because the buyer was not mistaken about the fundamental terms of the contract, but only as to the quality of what he was buying.

■ *Smith* v *Hughes* (1871) LR 6 QB 597

The defendant, a racehorse trainer, bought oats from the defendant, a farmer. The defendant had shown a sample of the oats to the claimant who agreed to pay 34s. per quarter. The claimant thought that the oats were old oats, whereas in fact they were new oats. Oats were very scarce at the time, but even so 34s. a quarter was a very high price for new oats.

Held. The contract was not void for mistake, even if the claimant knew that the defendant thought he was buying old oats.

Cockburn CJ: 'The question is whether … the passive acquiescence of the seller in the self-deception of the buyer will entitle the latter to avoid the contract. I am of opinion that it will not.'

COMMENT If the seller had warranted that the oats were old oats then the outcome would have been different. There would have been a valid contract for the sale of old oats, which could not be performed by delivering new oats. This case differs from *Bell* v *Lever Bros* and *Great Peace Shipping* in that only one of the parties was mistaken as to the quality of the subject matter of the contract. This was a case of unilateral, but common, mistake.

6.2.4 *Non est factum* (It is not my deed)

If one of the parties signs a document whilst under a complete misapprehension as to its effect then the contract may be void on the grounds of *non est factum*.

■ *Saunders* v *Anglia Building Society* [1970] AC 1004 (House of Lords)

Mrs Gallie intended to leave her house to her nephew, Parkin, after her death but to remain in the house for the rest of her life. A friend of Parkin's, Lee, visited Mrs Gallie. In Parkin's presence Lee presented a document to Mrs Gallie for signature. Lee told Mrs Gallie that the document gave the house to Parkin. Mrs Gallie believed this and as her spectacles were broken she signed the document without reading it. In fact the document said that the house had been assigned to Lee and that he had paid for it. Lee then used the document to obtain a mortgage from a building society. Lee did not pay the mortgage instalments and the building society applied to repossess the house.

Held. The plea of *non est factum* was not available to Mrs Gallie because there was not a fundamental difference between what she signed and what she thought she signed. Either way the document was an assignment of her interest in the house.

The plea of *non est factum* will not be available to a person who was careless in signing the document.
  A person who signs a blank document is likely to be regarded as having been careless if incorrect figures are subsequently filled in (*United Dominions Trust Ltd* v *Western* [1976] QB 513 (Court of Appeal)).
  A plea of *non est factum* is only rarely successful. An example of a case in which it was successful is provided by *Foster* v *Mackinnon* (1869) LR 4 CP 704. An old man with feeble eyesight was tricked into signing a bill of exchange because he was told that it was a guarantee. The old man was not liable on the bill because he was completely mistaken as to its effect and he had not been careless in signing.

Test your understanding

1 What is the effect of a contract being held to be void for mistake?

2 The parties to a contract make a common mistake when they both make the same mistake. As to what three matters might this mistake be made? Could all three matters make the contract void?

3 The parties to a contract make a mutual mistake when they are at cross purposes so that there is never any real agreement. In what circumstances will such a mistake render the contract void?

4 When a unilateral mistake is made only one of the parties makes a mistake. As to what two matters might a unilateral mistake be made?

5 In what circumstances will a mistake as to the identity of the other contracting party make a contract void?

6 In what circumstances will a mistake as to the terms of the contract make a contract void?

7 In what circumstances will *non est factum* make a contract void?

Answers

1 A contract which is held to be void for a mistake is a nullity. It cannot give rise to contractual rights or obligations. If goods are sold under a contract which is void for mistake ownership will not pass to the buyer and the seller will have to refund the purchase price.

2 A common mistake might be either as to the existence of the subject matter of the contract, or as to its ownership or as to its quality. Mistake as to existence or ownership can make the contract void. Mistake as to quality is most unlikely to make the contract void.

3 A mutual mistake will render the contract void if it could not be objectively inferred that either of the views held by the parties, as to the terms of the contract, was what the parties intended. If either view could be inferred as objectively reflecting the intention of the parties then there will be a contract on those terms.

4 A unilateral mistake might be made either as to the identity of the other contracting party, or as to the terms of the contract.

5 Mistake as to the identity of the other contracting party will make a contract void if the parties made a written contract without meeting face to face, if the mistake was as to the identity of the other party and not just as to his attributes, and if the mistake was a material mistake which was known to the other party.

6 A unilateral mistake as to the terms of the contract will make a contract void only if the party who is not mistaken could not reasonably have supposed that the other party intended to contract on the terms which were agreed.

7 A person can escape a contract on the grounds of *non est factum* if he signed a document, without being careless in so doing, while under a complete misapprehension as to its effect.

6.3 · Duress and undue influence

Historically, the common law would hold a contract voidable for duress only if the contract was entered into as a result of the threat of unlawful physical violence. A threat to goods was not enough. In recent years a doctrine of economic duress has taken hold, under which a contract becomes voidable by a person who was coerced into making it in such a way that he did not really consent. If one of the parties to the contract exerted undue influence over the other the contract may be voidable in equity. The basis of both duress and undue influence is that one of the parties gave no real consent to the contract.

6.3.1 Duress

Traditionally, the common law only rendered a contract voidable on the grounds of duress if the contract was entered into on account of illegal physical violence or the threat of it. Such cases rarely come before the courts. If the victim is sufficiently frightened to enter a contract against his will, he almost always remains sufficiently frightened not to go to court to argue that the contract is voidable.

In recent years the doctrine of duress has become considerably wider as 'economic duress' has come to be recognised. Many types of economic duress are perfectly valid. For example, if a buyer knows that the seller must sell goods immediately in order to raise cash, then this knowledge might well allow him to buy the goods more cheaply than would otherwise be the case. However, this knowledge would not affect the validity of the contract entered into. In *Occidental Worldwide Investment Corporation* v *Skibs A/S Avanti (The Sibeon and the Sibotre)* [1976] 1 Lloyd's Rep 293 Kerr J rejected a claim of economic duress because, although there was commercial pressure, there was nothing under the law which could be regarded as 'a coercion of will so as to vitiate consent'. This last phrase has been adopted in several later cases as the definition of duress and so its meaning is worth clarifying. A person who is coerced into doing something is pushed into doing it, without regard to his wishes. If consent is vitiated it is destroyed so that consent does not really exist. So we might say that a person has entered a contract on account of duress where he has been pushed into the agreement in such a way that he did not really consent to it. Kerr J was merely putting the matter more succinctly when he said there must have been 'a coercion of will so as to vitiate consent'.

■ *North Ocean Shipping Co Ltd* v *Hyundai Construction Co Ltd, the Atlantic Baron* [1979] QB 705

A shipbuilding company agreed to build a ship for a certain price in US dollars, payment to be made in five instalments. The shipbuilding company agreed to open letters of credit so that the buyers could get their instalments back if the contract was not performed properly. After the first instalment had been paid the US dollar was devalued by 10%. The shipbuilding company demanded that the remaining instalments be increased by 10%. The buyers refused, paying the second and third instalments without the additional 10%. These instalments were returned. The shipbuilding company set a certain date and said that if the extra money was not paid by this date they would terminate the contract. The buyers needed the ship as they were negotiating to charter it out, very profitably, to a third party. They therefore agreed to pay the extra money 'without prejudice' and asked that there should be corresponding increases in the letters of credit. The shipbuilding company agreed to this in June 1973 and so the buyers paid the last instalment, including the extra 10%, without protest. The ship was delivered in November 1974. Only in June 1975 did the shipbuilders know that the buyers were claiming the return of the extra 10% paid in the last four instalments plus interest.

Held. The agreement of June 1973 was voidable for economic duress. However, the buyers had affirmed the contract by making the final payment without protest and by delaying making their claim until July 1975.

COMMENT (i) As duress, economic duress and undue influence can only make a contract voidable, rather than void, the right to avoid can be lost by affirmation, inability to restore the parties to their pre-contract position or the acquisition of rights by third parties. These bars to rescission were considered above, at 6.1.3.1, in relation to misrepresentation.
(ii) The case also raised the question of consideration. Had the shipbuilding company provided any additional consideration in return for the extra money? It was held that they had, in that they had increased their letters of credit by 10%, something which the original contract did not require them to do.

In *Pao On* v *Lau Yiu Long* [1980] AC 614 (Privy Council) Scarman LJ identified four matters to be taken into account in assessing whether or not economic duress had taken place. These four matters are as follows. Did the person claiming to have been coerced protest? Did that person have any other available course of action, such as a legal remedy? Was he independently advised? After entering the contract did he take steps to avoid it?

If the victim protested this would make economic duress more likely, as would the fact that there was no other course of action open to him. If he was independently advised, or if he delayed in taking steps to avoid the contract, these matters would indicate that the contract was not entered into as a result of duress. The effect of the four matters can be seen in the following case.

■ *Universe Tankships of Monrovia* v *International Transport Workers Federation* [1982] 1 AC 366 (House of Lords)

A ship which flew a flag of convenience arrived at Milford Haven. The ITF, a trade union, 'blacked' the ship to prevent it from leaving port because they considered that the wages payable to the crew were too low. The ITF demanded that the shipowners pay $80 000, threatening that if this was not paid the ship could not be allowed to leave port. The owners paid this sum under protest. Part of the $80 000 was paid to a seamen's charity, the

Seafarer's International Welfare Fund. Once the ship had sailed out of Milford Haven the shipowners sued to recover the money paid to the charity.

Held. The money was recoverable because the agreement to pay it had been obtained under economic duress.

In general, in order to amount to economic duress the threat must be to do an unlawful act, such as to break a contract, although possibly an immoral lawful act will suffice.

■ *Atlas Express Ltd* v *Kafco (Importers and Distributors) Ltd* [1989] 1 All ER 641

The defendants were a small company which imported basketware and distributed it to retailers. They made a contract with the claimants, a national carrier, under which the claimants were to distribute the basketware to Woolworths shops nationwide. A price of £1.10 per carton was agreed, the claimants' depot manager having estimated that each load would contain a minimum of 400 cartons and maybe as many as 600. The first load contained only 200 cartons and the claimants' depot manager told the defendants that unless they agreed to a minimum payment of £440 per load no more loads would be carried. The defendants agreed to this because they were heavily dependent on the contract with Woolworths and they could find no other carrier. Later the defendants refused to pay the new rate.

Held. The defendants did not have to pay the extra amount. If a person is forced to renegotiate a contract against his will, and had no alternative but to accept the new terms proposed, the consent to the new terms was vitiated by economic duress.

It is possible, although very unlikely, that a threat to perform a lawful act coupled with a demand for payment could amount to economic duress.

■ *CTN Cash and Carry Ltd* v *Gallagher Ltd* [1994] 4 All ER 714 (Court of Appeal)

The claimants, who ran six cash and carry warehouses in the north of England, bought large consignments of cigarettes from the defendants. The defendants arranged credit facilities for the claimants but they were free to withdraw these. By mistake the defendants delivered one consignment of £17 000 worth of cigarettes to the wrong warehouse. It was arranged that the defendants would take the cigarettes to the correct warehouse but before this happened the cigarettes were stolen. The defendants honestly believed that the cigarettes were at the claimants' risk at the time of the theft. (During the trial they discovered that this view was not correct.) The defendants insisted that the claimants pay for the cigarettes. The claimants refused, but then agreed to pay when the defendants made it plain that if they did not do so their credit facilities would be withdrawn. Later the claimants claimed to avoid the agreement to pay the £17 000, on the grounds of economic duress, and sued to get their money back.

Held. The claimants were not entitled to avoid the agreement. Although it is possible that a threat to perform a lawful act coupled with a demand for payment might amount to economic duress it would be extremely difficult to succeed in such a claim when the agreement was made between two commercial companies, especially where the person making the demand believed it to be valid.

COMMENT (i) The outcome of the case was described by Steyn LJ as unattractive 'inasmuch as the defendants are allowed to retain a sum which at the trial they became aware was not in truth due to them'. (The rules on the passing of the risk are considered in Chapter 9 at 9.1.4.)

(ii) The Court of Appeal made it plain that it would be highly undesirable if accounts settled in good faith could be reopened once the parties had fallen out with each other.

(iii) In *R* v *Attorney-General for England and Wales* [2003] UKPC 22, considered below, Lord Hoffmann delivered the judgment of the Privy Council and said that the fact that the threat is lawful does not necessarily make the pressure legitimate. He quoted with approval the following example of Lord Atkin's from *Thorne* v *Motor Trade Association* [1937] AC 797: 'The ordinary blackmailer normally threatens to do what he has a perfect right to do – namely, communicate some compromising conduct to a person whose knowledge is likely to affect the person threatened ... What he has to justify is not the threat, but the demand of money.'

6.3.2 Undue influence

Historically, the limits of duress were very narrow. The courts of equity therefore developed a doctrine of undue influence which can cause either gifts or contracts to be set aside. When considering undue influence a distinction can be drawn between cases where it is presumed and cases where it must be proved.

6.3.2.1 Actual undue influence

A person alleging actual undue influence must prove that he only entered into the contract, or made the gift, on account of undue pressure exerted by the other party. There is no need to prove any type of special relationship or any previous dealings between the parties. In *Williams* v *Bayley* (1866) LR 1 HL 200, for example, a colliery owner mortgaged his colliery to a bank because the bank indirectly threatened him that if he did not do this his son would be prosecuted for forgery. The House of Lords set the agreement aside because the colliery owner did not freely and voluntarily enter into it.

The person alleging the undue influence must prove that it was in fact exerted but does not need to show that the agreement consequently entered into was manifestly disadvantageous to him. In *CIBC Mortgages plc* v *Pitt* [1993] 4 All ER 433 (House of Lords) Lord Browne-Wilkinson said that actual undue influence is a species of fraud and that just as a person who perpetrated a fraud cannot argue that the transaction was beneficial to the person defrauded, so a person exercising actual undue influence cannot argue that the contract was beneficial to the person influenced. The agreement will be set aside (if the wronged party avoids the contract in the correct way) as a matter of justice, because the wrongdoer's conduct prevented the wronged party from exercising free will and a properly informed mind.

Actual undue influence is becoming less important as duress has become easier to establish. The boundaries between duress and actual undue influence are becoming increasingly blurred.

6.3.2.2 Presumed undue influence

Certain types of relationship give rise to an automatic presumption of undue influence. These well-established relationships include those of solicitor and client, doctor and patient, parent and child, guardian and ward, trustee and beneficiary, and religious advisor and disciple. Historically, if the influenced party alleged undue influence and could prove that the contract was manifestly to his disadvantage, the contract would be voidable unless the dominant party could prove that there was no undue influence. In *Allcard* v *Skinner* (1887) 36 ChD 145, for example, the claimant became a member of a Protestant religious group, the sisterhood of St Mary of the Cross. Over the years the claimant gave £7000 to the Lady Superior of the Sisterhood. One of the rules of the Sisterhood was that no member should seek outside advice without first getting permission from the Lady Superior. When the claimant left to become a Roman Catholic she would have been able to reclaim such of this money as was left on the grounds of presumed undue influence. (However, the claim was defeated because the claimant did not claim the money until six years after she had left the sisterhood.)

Following the decision of the House of Lords in *Royal Bank of Scotland* v *Etridge (No 2)* [2001] 4 All ER 449, the term 'manifest disadvantage' should no longer be used in this context. Instead, the transaction must be one which is not readily explicable by the relationship of the parties. So minor or seemingly normal transactions would not be presumed to have been brought about by undue influence. Lord Nicholls said: 'Something more is needed before the law reverses the burden of proof, something which calls for an explanation. When that something more is present, the greater the disadvantage to the vulnerable person, the more cogent must be the explanation before the presumption will be regarded as rebutted.'

Where the type of relationship is not within those set out in the previous paragraph, undue influence may still be presumed if the influenced party proves as a matter of fact that there existed a relationship of great trust and confidence between himself and the other party. There is no automatic presumption of undue influence between husband and wife, but in several cases a wife has proved that she placed great trust and confidence in her husband. It is also a requirement of presumed undue influence that the victim proves that the contract was not readily explicable by the relationship of the parties. Where a party can prove that the relationship was one of great trust and confidence, and that the contract was not readily explicable by the relationship of the parties, then the court will presume undue influence and it will be up to the other party to disprove that undue influence actually existed. Presumed undue influence can occasionally occur in the relationship between bank and customer, as the following case shows.

■ *Lloyds Bank v Bundy* [1975] QB 326 (Court of Appeal)

The defendant was an elderly farmer. He and his only son had banked with the claimant bank for many years. The son formed a company and opened a company account at the same branch of the bank. In 1966 the farmer mortgaged his farm to the bank for £1 500 in order to guarantee the company's overdraft. The bank's assistant manager and the son visited the defendant and suggested that he sign a further guarantee for £5 000 and a further mortgage of £6 000. After consulting his solicitor the farmer did this in May 1969. In December 1969 the son and the bank's new assistant manager visited the defendant again with a further guarantee of £11 000 and a further charge of £3 500 already written out and ready for the defendant's signature. The defendant signed these because he was told that if he did not his son's business would fail. The son's business did fail and the bank sought to repossess the farmer's only asset, the house which he had mortgaged. The new assistant bank manager said in evidence that the defendant relied on him implicitly to advise him about the transactions as bank manager. The defendant said that he always trusted the assistant manager and sat back and did what the manager said.

Held. The charge and the guarantee executed in December 1969 were set aside. There was such a relationship of confidentiality between the defendant and the bank that the court could intervene to prevent this from being abused. The bank had breached its fiduciary duty of care by not advising the defendant to get independent advice as to the wisdom of what he was doing.

COMMENT Lord Denning MR thought that the contract should be set aside on the grounds of inequality of bargaining power. At one time there did seem to be judicial support for such a theory. In recent years this support has become less marked.

The relationship between banker and customer is not one which usually gives rise to a presumption of undue influence. However, each case must be carefully examined on its facts.

A situation which has come before the courts fairly commonly is that in which a husband exerts undue influence over or makes a misrepresentation to his wife, who then agrees to give the matrimonial house or other assets as a security for a loan which is made to the husband's business. The wife can have the agreement set aside, as against the husband, if either undue influence or misrepresentation is proved. The more difficult question is whether or not she can have the loan set aside against the bank which lent the money. The House of Lords considered this matter in the following case.

■ *Barclays Bank plc v O'Brien and another* [1993] 4 All ER 417 (House of Lords)

A husband's company was given an overdraft by a bank. The overdraft was for £135 000, reducing to £120 000 after three weeks, and the overdraft was guaranteed by a second charge over the matrimonial home which was owned jointly by the husband and his wife. The bank manager arranged the documentation and told the bank staff that both husband and wife should be made fully aware of the nature of the transaction and should take independent legal advice. These instructions were not however followed by the bank staff. Both the husband and the wife signed the documents without reading them. The company's debt increased and the bank brought proceedings to possess the house. The wife argued that she had only signed because her husband had put undue pressure on her, and that her husband had misrepresented the effect of the charge, saying that the security was limited to £60 000 and would only last for three weeks. The trial judge gave judgment for the bank on the grounds that the husband had not unduly influenced his wife, and that although the husband had made a misrepresentation the bank could not be liable for this. The Court of Appeal held that the charge was enforceable against the wife only to the extent of £60 000 because the bank had not taken adequate steps to ensure that she had adequate comprehension of the effect of the charge. The bank appealed to the House of Lords.

Held. Where a wife agreed to stand surety for the debts of a company in which the husband had a direct financial interest but in which she did not have such an interest, and the creditor knew that they were husband and wife, the creditor could enforce the surety unless it was procured as a result of undue influence, misrepresentation or other legal wrong committed by the husband. Where the wife did enter into the transaction only because of the undue influence, misrepresentation or other legal wrong committed by the husband the creditor would be unable to enforce the security, on account of having constructive notice of the wife's right to set aside the transaction. In all but exceptional circumstances the creditor would not be fixed with constructive notice if he had warned the wife of the risks involved, at a meeting not attended by the husband, and advised her to get independent legal advice. On the facts of the case, the bank did know that the couple were husband and wife and should have been put on enquiry as to the circumstances when the wife agreed to stand surety. The legal charge on the home could be set aside because the bank had not warned the wife of the risks and had not advised her to obtain independent legal advice. The appeal was therefore dismissed.

COMMENT (i) The principles of the case apply not only to husband and wife but to any cohabitees. (ii) The charge was enforceable against the wife only to the extent of £60 000, the amount she believed to be the full extent of the charge.

In *Royal Bank of Scotland* v *Etridge (No 2)* [2001] 4 All ER 449 the House of Lords reviewed the situation where a wife charges the matrimonial home by way of security for a loan made to the husband's business. The following points were made.

(1) In undue influence cases the burden of proof will not shift to the dominant party, to prove that there was no undue influence, unless the transaction cannot readily be explained by the relationship of the parties. (The term 'manifest disadvantage' should no longer be used.) Generally, a wife's guarantee of her husband's business debts should not be regarded as a transaction which, failing proof to the contrary, can be explained only on the basis that it was procured by the husband's undue influence. Such transactions are not to be regarded, as a class, as prima facie evidence of the husband having exerted undue influence. However, there will be cases which do call for an explanation.

(2) Where the wife proposes to give her share of the matrimonial home as security for a loan to the husband or his company, the following guidelines apply to the bank and the solicitor acting for the wife:

   (i)   The bank is put on enquiry whenever a wife stands surety for a husband's debts (or a husband stands surety for a wife's debts). This is the case even if the bank does not know that the parties are cohabiting or that the wife trusts the husband implicitly. If the loan is made to a company it does not matter that the wife is a company officer or shareholder.

   (ii) When the bank has been put on enquiry, it only has to take reasonable steps to ensure that the wife understands what she is doing. There is no need for the bank to meet the wife personally. If a solicitor tells the bank that the wife has been properly advised then this will be good enough unless the bank knows that she has not.

   (iii) The solicitor should explain why the bank wants the wife to have a solicitor and that this will prevent her from later claiming that her husband pushed her into the agreement or that she did not understand it. As a core minimum the solicitor should make sure that the wife understands: the nature of the documents and their legal effect; the seriousness of the risks involved; that she has a choice not to go ahead; and that she definitely does want to go ahead. All of this should be explained at a face-to-face meeting without the husband being present and the solicitor should get any information he needs from the bank.

   (iv) Except in glaringly obvious cases of the wife being grievously wronged, the solicitor should not refuse to act for the wife because he considers the agreement to be contrary to her best interests.

   (v)   The solicitor can also act for the bank or the husband, as long as this does not give rise to a conflict of duty or interests.

(vi) Once the bank has been put on enquiry, and is looking for protection from the fact that the wife has been advised by a solicitor, the bank should take the following steps. First, write to the wife telling her to choose a solicitor to act for her and that once she has been legally advised she will not be able to dispute the validity of what she has agreed. She should be told that the solicitor may be the one acting for her husband but that she has the right to choose another. The bank should not proceed until it has received an appropriate response directly from the wife. Second, if the bank does not want to explain the husband's financial affairs directly to the wife, it should make sure that the wife's solicitor has all the financial information to make such an explanation. Third, if the bank suspects that the wife has been misled by the husband or is not entering the transaction of her own free will, it must tell the wife's solicitor why it believes this to be the case. Fourth, the bank should get written confirmation from the wife's solicitor that the previous three matters have been complied with. If the solicitor confirms to the bank that the wife has had explained to her the risks she was running in respect of previous transactions, the bank will be regarded as having discharged its duty regarding these previous transactions.

(3) In future, banks will be put on enquiry every time the relationship between the person providing surety and the debtor is not commercial. The bank must make sure that the guarantor understands the risks of providing surety. If the bank does not do this, it will be deemed to have notice of any claim the guarantor may have that the transaction was entered into on account of undue influence or misrepresentation by the debtor.

COMMENT Although the judgment talked in terms of husband and wife, it was made plain that it could equally apply to father and daughter, between cohabitees or to any other type of relationship.

In the following case the Privy Council considered both duress and undue influence.

■ *R* v *Attorney General for England and Wales* [2003] UKPC 22

R, the appellant, was a former member of the 22 SAS Regiment. He was a member of Bravo Two Zero patrol which had been dropped behind enemy lines during the 1991 Gulf War. Of this patrol three died, one escaped to Syria and four, including R, were captured and tortured. Both the member who escaped and one of the members who had been captured wrote books about the patrol. This angered other members of the patrol and members of the SAS generally, who did not consider the books accurate. It was thought that action should be taken to prevent the future publication of such books. All members of the SAS were balloted on this point and of the 73% who replied 96.8% were in favour of a binding contract to prevent further disclosure. Later all members of the SAS were told that if they did not sign a confidentiality agreement they would be returned to unit, which was generally a punishment for a disciplinary offence or ordered on the grounds of unsuitability for the SAS. In October 1996 R was told to sign the confidentiality agreement or he would be returned to his unit. He asked if he could seek legal representation and was told that he could not. R signed because it was the only way he could stay in the SAS. The contract was straightforward and easy to understand. Two weeks later R decided to leave the Army and he was discharged in April 1997. He went home to New Zealand and in 1998 decided to write his own version of the Bravo Two Zero patrol. The publishers sent a copy of the manuscript to the Ministry of Defence. The Attorney General applied for an injunction to prevent publication and to claim damages and an account of profits. R argued that the agreement he signed was obtained by duress or undue influence, that it was an unconscionable bargain, not supported by consideration and that it was against public policy. The Court of Appeal found that the contract which R had signed was valid and that R was in breach of it. It did not order an injunction preventing publication, but it did order an account of profits and damages. R appealed to the Privy Council.

Held. The Privy Council upheld the Court of Appeal decision. The threat of an unlawful act would generally make a contract voidable for duress. Where, as here, the threatened act was lawful, the contract might yet be voidable for duress, but only if the threat could not be justified. Here the MOD had good reasons for imposing the ban and could regard anyone who would not agree to it as being unsuitable for the SAS. Therefore, the contract was not voidable for duress. (If R had not had a choice, but had been ordered to sign, their Lordships indicated that the outcome might well have been different.) As regards undue influence, and following *Etridge (No.2)* [1998] 4 All ER 705, the burden of proving that consent was gained by unacceptable means fell on the party alleging this. It was accepted that the Army as an institution, and R's commanding officer as an individual, were able to exercise undue influence over him. But the real question was whether the nature of the transaction was such that it could be inferred that agreement to it had been obtained by an unfair exploitation of that relationship. Their Lordships did not think that the agreement had been so obtained. R's not being able to gain legal advice did not affect the fairness of the transaction. There had been a need to keep matters confidential, R understood the agreement and all a solicitor could have advised him to do was to think about things before signing. He could have made that decision without legal advice.

COMMENT (i) The argument that the agreement was an unconscionable bargain was dismissed in one sentence.

(ii) The Army's consideration was their forbearance from sending him back to his unit, which conferred a practical benefit upon R.

(iii) Lord Scott of Foscote dissented and argued that the contract should have been voidable for undue influence. He thought that the relationship between R and his senior officers meant that undue influence should have been presumed. As no evidence had been introduced to rebut the presumption, and as legal advice had not been available, the contract should have been voidable for undue influence even though none of the senior officers had behaved improperly.

Test your understanding

1 Historically, in what circumstances would the common law hold a contract voidable for duress?

2 In what circumstances will the common law now hold a contract voidable on account of economic duress?

3 What must a party prove in order to establish actual undue influence? What will be the effect on the contract if this is proved?

4 In what types of relationships is undue influence automatically presumed? What is the effect of this presumption?

5 In what circumstances will undue influence be presumed if the relationship is not one where it is automatically presumed?

Answers

1 Historically, the common law held a contract voidable for duress only if the contract was entered into as a consequence of physical violence or the threat of it.

2 A contract can be voidable for economic duress if it was entered into as a consequence of commercial pressure which coerced the other party's will so as to vitiate consent. Generally, a threat to commit a lawful act cannot amount to economic duress.

3 Equity will hold a contract voidable on the grounds of actual undue influence without the need to prove a special relationship between the parties. The party claiming to have been unduly influenced must prove that undue influence was in fact exerted.

4 In certain types of relationships undue influence is automatically presumed. Contracts made between parties in such relationships will be voidable at the option of the influenced party unless the other party can prove that there was no undue influence. The relationships are solicitor and client, doctor and patient, parent and child, guardian and ward, trustee and beneficiary, and religious advisor and disciple. The victim will need to prove that the contract was manifestly to his disadvantage.

5 In relationships other than those where undue influence is automatically presumed, it may still be presumed if the influenced party proves that the relationship was such that he placed great trust and confidence in the other party. It must also be proved that the contract entered into could not easily be explained by the relationship between the parties.

6.4 · Illegal and void contracts

A contract may be illegal either at common law or because a statute makes it illegal. The illegality may relate to the nature of the contract itself, or as to the way in which it is performed. If a contract is illegal then it will generally be unenforceable. Certain types of contracts, while not illegal, are void because they contravene public policy.

6.4.1 Contracts illegal at common law

The following types of contracts are illegal at common law:

6.4.1.1 Contracts tending to promote corruption in public life

An example is provided by *Parkinson* v *College of Ambulance Ltd* [1925] 2 KB 1. The claimant was promised that he would receive a knighthood if he made a donation to a charity. He made the donation but sued for its return when he did not get the knighthood. His action failed because the contract was illegal.

6.4.1.2 Contracts tending to impede the administration of justice

A contract to make sure that a person is not prosecuted would be illegal and void. However, a contract not to pursue a civil action is perfectly valid. (See settling out of court in Chapter 2 at 2.4.)

6.4.1.3 Contracts to trade with enemy nations

In times of war certain nations become enemy nations. A contract to trade with a person voluntarily living in an enemy nation is generally void.

6.4.1.4 Contract to commit a tort, fraud or crime

A strange example is provided by *Everett* v *Williams* (1725) noted in [1899] 1 QB 826. One highwayman tried to sue another on an agreement to rob a stagecoach. The highwayman failed in this action. (Both the claimant and the defendant were hanged and the solicitors were fined £50 for bringing the case!)

6.4.1.5 Contracts tending to promote sexual immorality

An example is provided by *Pearce* v *Brooks* (1866) LR 1 Ex 213, where a prostitute hired a carriage which the owner knew was to be used for immoral purposes. The prostitute refused to pay for the hire of the carriage but the owner was not allowed to recover the agreed payments.

6.4.1.6 Contracts to defraud the Revenue

If a contract is made to defraud the Revenue then the whole contract is void and a court will not enforce any of its terms.

■ *Miller v Karlinski* (1945) 62 TLR 85 (Court of Appeal)

The claimant was employed under an oral contract. He was paid a salary of £10 a week and it was further agreed that the amount of tax which he paid on this salary should be paid to him as 'travelling expenses'. The claimant sued for ten weeks of unpaid wages and also claimed expenses of £21. Of these expenses £4 were genuine travelling expenses, the remaining £17 represented the amount of tax which would have been payable on his wages.

Held. The whole agreement was contrary to public policy and the court would therefore enforce no part of it.

COMMENT Du Parcq LJ, who gave the only judgment, said that it made no difference whether or not the parties were ignorant that what they were doing was illegal.

6.4.2 Contracts which contravene public policy

Three types of contract are void as contravening public policy. Of the three types, contracts in restraint of trade are far and away the most important. The other two are as follows.

6.4.2.1 Contracts damaging to marriage

Contracts agreeing that one will never marry, and marriage brokage contracts, are void rather than illegal. A marriage brokage contract is one where a third party procures a marriage in return for a consideration.

6.4.2.2 Contracts to oust the jurisdiction of the courts

These contracts are void, rather than illegal. See *Baker* v *Jones* in Chapter 4 at 4.1.1.1.

6.4.3 Contracts in restraint of trade

It is generally desirable that people should carry on their trade, business or profession without hindrance. Therefore, any contract in restraint of trade is void at common law unless it can be proved to be reasonable between the parties to the contract and reasonable as regards the public interest. The categories of agreements which can be in restraint of trade are not closed, but three particular types of agreement are relatively common.

6.4.3.1 Restraints when a business is sold

It is quite common that the vendor of a business agrees with the purchaser that he will not carry on a competing business after the sale has taken place. Such an agreement will be valid if it is reasonable but will be void if it is unreasonable. Two competing areas of public policy are evident. First, it is public policy that people should work and so in general such agreements should be void. Second, no one is going to buy a business if the vendor would be free to open a competing business next door, so a restraint of trade clause can be valid if it was reasonable. In deciding whether or not the agreed restraint was reasonable the main factors to be considered are the length of time for which the agreement is to run, the geographical area in which the restraint applies, and the types of activity which the contract prohibited.

■ *Nordenfelt v The Maxim Nordenfelt Guns and Ammunition Company Ltd* [1894] AC 535 (House of Lords)

The defendant had been a manufacturer of military guns and ammunition and had owned patents relating to the business. He sold the patents and the business to the claimants and made a restraint of trade agreement. The agreement was to last for 25 years and prohibited the defendant from trading in or manufacturing guns, gun mountings or carriages, gunpowder, explosives or ammunition. It also prohibited the defendant from working in any business likely to compete with that of the claimant. The defendant later agreed to work for another manufacturer of guns and ammunition and the claimant sought an injunction to prevent this.

Held. The restraint agreeing not to manufacture guns etc was valid because it was reasonable. It was not wider than was necessary to protect the claimant company and nor was it detrimental to the interests of the country. The agreement not to work for any business competing with the claimant company was too wide. It was unreasonable and therefore void.

COMMENT It might seem unreasonable to agree not to manufacture guns etc for such a long period, but a business such as this had very few customers (the Governments of a few wealthy countries).

6.4.3.2 Restraints in a contract of employment

A restraint which prevents an ex-employee from working for competitors will be valid only if it was necessary to protect trade secrets, trade connections or confidential information. Such a restraint will not be upheld merely to prevent the ex-employee from exercising the skills which he learnt in the course of his past employment.

■ *Fitch* v *Dewes* [1921] 2 AC 158 (House of Lords)

The claimant, a solicitor practising at Tamworth, employed the defendant from 1899 to 1914. The defendant worked his way up from junior clerk, to articled clerk to managing clerk. When made managing clerk, on a three year contract, the defendant agreed that he would never 'be engaged or manage or concerned in the office, profession or business of a solicitor, within a radius of seven miles of the Town Hall of Tamworth'. After the termination of his employment the defendant, in 1919, deliberately breached this agreement to test its validity.

Held. Even though the agreement was to run for an unlimited period of time it was reasonable. It was not against the public interest and was reasonably necessary to protect the commercial interests of the claimant.

6.4.3.3 Solus agreements

A solus agreement is one by which a person agrees to buy from, or be supplied by, only one supplier. Retailers of petrol commonly make such agreements with the large oil companies. In the leading case, *Esso Petroleum Co Ltd* v *Harper's Garage (Stourport) Ltd* [1968] AC 269, the claimant, who owned two garages, made a solus agreement with Esso in respect of both garages. In return for a price discount the two garages were to buy only Esso's petrol. As regards the first garage the agreement was to run for four years and five months, as regards the second garage the agreement was to run for 21 years. The House of Lords held that the agreement regarding the first garage was valid because it was reasonable. The agreement regarding the second garage was unreasonable and so it was void.

6.4.3.4 Other situations

There is no closed list of situations in which a contract can be void because it is in restraint of trade. The following case shows that if parties of very unequal bargaining power make a very one-sided agreement, whereby one of them agrees to provide his services exclusively to the other, the contract may well be void.

■ *Schroeder Music Publishing Co Ltd* v *MacAuley* [1974] 1 WLR 1308 (House of Lords)

A 21-year-old unknown songwriter made a contract with a music publishing company on the company's standard terms. The songwriter was to work exclusively for the company for the period of the agreement. The songwriter gave the company the copyright in all of his songs, his remuneration being royalties on the songs published. The agreement was to last for five years but if the total royalties exceeded £5 000 the agreement was automatically extended for another five years. The publisher could end the agreement at any time by giving one month's notice. The songwriter had no right to terminate the agreement. The publishers could assign their rights under the agreement, the songwriter could not do this without the company's agreement. The songwriter sought an application that the agreement was void.

Held. The agreement was unduly restrictive and therefore void. The House of Lords took into account the excessive length of time for which the agreement was to run, the fact that the company could assign their rights, and the fact that the company did not have to publish any of the songwriter's songs and might thus sterilise his talent.

6.4.3.5 The effect of a contract being held to be void

The general rule is that if a contract is void as in restraint of trade a court will not allow either side to sue on it. However, it may be that the whole contract is not void and that the void part can be severed from the remainder of the contract. If severance is allowed then the rest of the contract will be valid and will stand. If severance is not possible then the whole contract is void. Severance will not be allowed where this would alter the whole nature of the contract. Nor will it be allowed if it requires the courts to rewrite the contract. A 'blue pencil' test applies so that severance is only allowed if the offending clauses of the contract could be isolated and clearly crossed out with a blue pencil, leaving behind a valid contract.

The following two cases demonstrate how this test works.

■ *Goldsoll v Goldman* [1915] 1 Ch 292 (Court of Appeal)

The claimant and the defendant both carried on businesses selling imitation jewellery. The two businesses were situated very close to each other in London. The defendant sold his business to the claimant and agreed that for two years he would not sell real or imitation jewellery in London, the UK, France, Russia or Spain or within 25 miles of Berlin or Vienna. The defendant breached this agreement and the claimant sought an injunction.

Held. The agreement, in its entirety, covered too wide an area and was therefore unreasonable. However, the unreasonable part could be severed from the rest of the agreement. Once this had been done the agreement not to deal in imitation jewellery in the UK, which was reasonable and necessary for the protection of the claimant's business, could stand.

■ *Attwood v Lamont* [1920] 3 KB 571 (Court of Appeal)

The claimant was a draper, tailor and general outfitter in Kidderminster. He employed the defendant in the tailoring department of the business. The defendant agreed never to compete as a tailor, dressmaker, general draper, milliner, hatter, haberdasher, gentlemen's, ladies' or children's outfitter within a ten mile radius of Kidderminster. This agreement was contained in one covenant (clause) of the contract.

Held. The agreement was wider than necessary and therefore void as unreasonable. The unreasonable part of the contract could not be severed from the reasonable part without altering the whole nature of the agreement. Severance was not therefore allowed and the whole agreement was void.

COMMENT (i) The difference between the two cases is that in *Goldsoll v Goldman* the covenant in restraint of trade was written in such a way that it could be made reasonable, without altering the whole nature of the agreement or the intended effect of it. The way that the covenant was written in *Attwood* meant that severance would not be possible without altering the whole nature of the agreement. The claimant intended the covenant to protect his whole business, not just the tailoring department. When the unreasonable parts of the contract are contained in distinct covenants severance is much more likely.

Younger LJ: 'The doctrine of severance has not, I think, gone further than to make it permissible in a case where the covenant is not really a single covenant but is in effect a combination of several distinct covenants. In that case and where severance can be carried out without the addition or alteration of a word, it is permissible. But in that case only.'

(ii) A majority of the Court of Appeal held that even if severance had been allowed, so as to restrict the covenant to the tailoring business it would still have been void as in restraint of trade.

6.4.4 Contracts made illegal by statute

Many types of contracts are expressly or impliedly made illegal by a statute. There are so many of these, relating to so many different matters, that it is not appropriate to list them in this book. It is worth noting that gaming contracts, while not illegal, are void and unenforceable. A gaming contract is one under which it is agreed that one of the parties shall pay a sum of money to the other, but which of the parties is to pay is dependent upon the outcome of some uncertain event. In order to be a gaming contract both parties must stand to win or to lose. Money paid as a result of a gaming contract is not recoverable. Contracts of insurance are not gaming contracts as the insured has an interest in the non-occurrence of the event insured against.

6.5 · Competition law

It is generally accepted that competition amongst businesses produces better results than monopoly. Free competition leads to lower prices, better goods and services and more choice for consumers as producers are forced to work with ever greater efficiency to maintain their position. Consequently, a body of competition law has been created. This body of law aims to protect consumers and businesses and to ensure that no one producer can take advantage of its dominant position in the market place. Small producers are given some protection from their most powerful competitors and mergers may be forbidden. In the UK there are three main sources of competition law; Articles 81–82 of the EC Treaty, the Competition Act 1998 and the Enterprise Act 2002. It is not possible in a book of this nature to examine these matters in any depth, but it is possible to give an outline explanation of their effect and the interface between the three sources of competition law.

6.5.1 Articles 81–82 of the EC Treaty

Article 81 renders void all agreements between undertakings, decisions by associations of undertakings and concerted practices which may affect trade between Member States and which have as their object or effect the prevention, restriction or distortion of competition within the EC. The word 'undertaking' is not defined by the Treaty but includes any entity engaged in economic activity, regardless of its legal status. There is no requirement that the undertaking should seek to make a profit and so members' clubs and cooperatives can fit within the definition, as of course do companies, partnerships, limited liability partnerships and sole traders. Associations of undertakings means trade associations. Concerted practices exist where there is evidence of collusion, in the absence of being able to point to an actual agreement.

Article 81(1) provides some examples of the types of activity caught by this provision, listing agreements etc which:

'(a) directly or indirectly fix purchase or selling prices or any other trading conditions;
(b) limit or control production, markets, technical development, or investment;
(c) share markets or sources of supply;
(d) apply dissimilar conditions to equivalent transactions with other trading parties, thereby placing them at a competitive disadvantage;
(e) make the conclusion of contracts subject to the acceptance by other parties of supplementary obligations which, by their nature or according to commercial usage, have no connection with the subject of such contracts.'

It is important to remember that the above lists examples of the type of 'behaviour' that contravenes Article 81 and is not intended to be exhaustive.

Article 81(2) provides that any agreement or decision prohibited under Article 81(1) is automatically void.

Article 81(3) provides that the provisions of Article 81 are inapplicable if the 'agreement' meets specified criteria, namely:

'– any agreement or category of agreements between undertakings;
– any decision or category of decisions by associations and undertakings;
– any concerted practice or category of concerted practices
which contributes to improving the production or distribution of goods or to promoting technical economic progress, while allowing consumers a fair share of the resulting benefit, and which does not:
(a) impose on the undertakings concerned restrictions which are not indispensable to the attainment of these objectives;
(b) afford such undertakings the possibility of eliminating competition in respect of a substantial part of the products in question.'

Prior to the Modernisation Regulation (Regulation 1/2003), which came into effect on 1 May 2004, the European Commission had sole power to grant an exemption under Article 81(3).

The Modernisation Regulation completely changes the procedural rules underlying Article 81, whilst at the same time transferring the power to deal with 'run of the mill' cases to the Member States (i.e. away from the Commission).

Before 1 May 2004 it was possible to apply to the Commission, prior to any agreement being entered into, for individual exemption under Article 81(3). This is no longer possible.

Instead, the undertakings will proceed on the basis that the 'agreement' falls outside Article 81 until being challenged by the national competition authority (NCA).

In the UK the NCA is the Office of Fair Trading (together with the Courts).

Once challenged by the NCA, the burden falls upon the undertaking concerned to argue convincingly that the 'agreement' satisfies the Article 81(3) criteria.

In addition to the Article 81(3) exemption, the Commission has drafted a significant number of Block Exemptions that allow undertakings to enter into very specific agreements which meet requisite criteria.

Detailed consideration of the Block Exemptions falls outside the scope of this text. By way of very general summary, the Block Exemption allow undertakings to enter into certain agreements providing the agreement does not contain 'hardcore' (i.e. absolutely prohibited) terms (e.g. price fixing, partitioning of territory etc.).

It is crucial, therefore, to scrutinise any proposed agreement between undertakings in order to be completely sure that either a Block Exemption will apply, or, in the event of being challenged by the NCA, that the agreement is covered by the Article 81(3) exemption.

An example of the effect of Article 81 can be seen in *ICI v Commission (Dyestuffs)* [1972] ECR 619. Leading producers of aniline dye introduced identical price increases at identical times for the three years 1964, 1965 and 1967. The Commission found that the businesses had colluded amongst themselves so that the prices were increased at the same time. Customers therefore had no choice but to pay the increased prices. The businesses were 'substituting co-operation for the risks of competition'.

Article 81 does not apply to: agreements between undertakings which form one single economic entity; agreements which have no appreciable effect on competition; or agreements which have no appreciable effect on trade between Member States.

Whereas Article 81 is concerned with 'agreements' between undertakings (etc.) that may distort competition, Article 82 aims to prevent dominant undertakings from acting unilaterally in an abusive way.

Article 82 provides that:

> 'Any abuse by one or more undertakings of a dominant position within the common market or in a substantial part of it shall be prohibited as incompatible with the common market in so far as it may affect trade between Member States. Such abuse may, in particular, consist in:
> (a) directly or indirectly imposing unfair purchase or selling prices or unfair trading conditions;
> (b) limiting production, markets, or technical development to the prejudice of consumers;
> (c) applying dissimilar conditions to equivalent transactions with other trading parties, thereby placing them at a competitive disadvantage;
> (d) making the conclusion of contracts subject to acceptance by the other parties of supplementary obligations which, by their nature or according to commercial usage, have no connection with the subject of such contracts.'

In *United Brands Co v Commission* [1978] ECR 207 the ECJ said that the term a dominant position in Article 82 'relates to a position of economic strength enjoyed by an undertaking which enables it to prevent effective competition being maintained on the relevant market by affording it the power to behave to an appreciable extent independently of its competitors, customers and ultimately of its consumers'. Article 82 does not define exactly what is meant by 'abuse' and conduct can be abusive even if it is not within the particular examples set out in paragraphs (a)–(d).

United Brands Co v Commission gives an example of the effect of Article 82. United Brands, an American undertaking, was dominant with respect to production, distribution and retailing of bananas within the EC. They were found to be in breach of Article 82 as a result of abusing their dominant position on a number of counts, including refusal to supply to an individual wholesaler and operating discriminatory pricing between customers.

It is crucial to recognise that an undertaking will not breach Article 82 simply by being dominant in a particular product market. It is only where an undertaking abuses its dominant position (i.e., takes advantage of the fact) that it will be in breach of Article 82.

6.5.1.1 Enforcement

Article 6 of the Modernising Regulation gives NCAs the power to enforce Articles 81 and 82.

The Modernisation Regulation also sets out fines that can be imposed by NCAs for both procedural (i.e. failing to supply information when requested) and substantive contraventions of Articles 81 and 82.

Procedural infringements now carry a potential fine up to 1% of the previous years' turnover. Much harsher fines will be imposed for substantive breaches (i.e. where undertakings, etc. act in a way that contravenes the anti-competitive rules contained in Articles 81 or 82). Fines for substantive breaches can amount to up to 10% of the undertaking's turnover in the previous year.

6.5.2 The Competition Act 1998

The Competition Act 1998 is comprised of four parts. Part 1 is divided into five chapters. Chapter I contains prohibitions which are similar to Article 81 of the EC Treaty. Chapter II contains prohibitions which are similar to Article 82. However, the provisions of the Competition Act apply to practices affecting competition within the UK, rather than within the EC.

Section 2(1) sets out the Chapter I prohibition:

'Subject to subsection 3, agreements between undertakings, decisions by associations of undertakings or concerted practices which –
(a) may affect trade within the UK, and
(b) have as their object or effect the prevention, restriction or distortion of competition within the UK, are prohibited unless they are exempt in accordance with the provisions of this Part.'

Section 2(3) provides that s.2(1) applies only if the agreement, decision or practice is, or is intended to be, implemented in the UK. Section 2(2) sets out examples of practices which would infringe s.2(1) and these examples are identical to those set out in Article 81(1). They are not exhaustive. If an agreement or decision does infringe s.2(1), it is rendered void and illegal. It follows that a party who has made a payment under such an agreement may not be able to recover it. However, severance, considered earlier in this chapter at 6.4.3, may be allowed.

The Office of Fair Trading (OFT) has issued Guidelines on the Chapter I prohibitions and these make it plain that s.2(1) will apply only where the impact on competition is appreciable. The Guidelines also indicate that, generally, an agreement will not have an appreciable effect if the relevant undertakings' combined share of the relevant market does not exceed 25%.

Certain types of agreements are exempt from s.2(1), generally because they are already covered by some other statute. In addition, s.9 sets out block exemptions which are virtually identical to those found in the criteria for Article 81(3).

Section 18(1) sets out the Chapter II prohibition. It provides:

'Subject to subsection 19, any conduct on the part of one or more undertakings which amounts to the abuse of a dominant position in a market is prohibited if it may affect trade within the UK.'

Section 18(2) sets out specific examples of such abuse and is identical to Article 82. Section 18(3) provides that dominant position means a dominant position within the UK; and 'the UK' means the UK or any part of it. So a local undertaking not represented elsewhere in the country could infringe s.18(1). The Act does not specifically say so, but it seems that any agreement which infringes s.18(1) will be void. Section 19 exempts merger situations and certain other technical situations.

The Competition Act gives wide enforcement powers to the OFT, who can conduct inquiries and investigations. The OFT can also authorise officers of the OFT to enter premises without a warrant. Those who do not comply with investigations can commit criminal offences. The OFT can order that infringements cease and impose penalties.

6.5.3 The Enterprise Act 2002

The Enterprise Act 2002 does not replace the Competition Act 1998 but rather it complements it. The Act has 11 parts.

Part 1 abolishes the position of Director General of Fair Trading, transferring his duties to the Office of Fair Trading (OFT). Previously, the OFT had not existed as a legal entity in its own right but had given administrative support to the Director General. The OFT tries to promote good consumer practice and to make the public aware of how competition may benefit consumers. It also gives advice to Ministers and investigates a market which it does not think is working well for consumers. It has a board consisting of a chairman and at least four other members.

Part 2 sets up a new Competition Appeal Tribunal (CAT).

Part 3 puts in place a new framework for controlling UK mergers and acquisitions. Decisions on whether mergers need to be controlled have been taken away from the Secretary of State and are to be taken by the OFT or the Competition Commission (CC). Furthermore, mergers will be prohibited on the basis that they would cause a substantial lessening of competition, rather than on the previous basis that they were contrary to the public interest. The OFT has a duty to investigate if a company targeted for merger has a UK turnover of over £70m. It also has a duty to investigate if the merged companies would between them supply at least 25% of either goods or services of a particular description in the UK or in a substantial part of the UK. If the OFT considers that a merger may result in a substantial lessening of competition it must either refer the matter to the CC or get appropriate assurances from the companies which propose to merge. But the OFT does not have to refer if the market is not important enough to justify a reference or if the obvious benefits to consumers would outweigh the adverse effect on competition. If the CC considers that there will be a substantial lessening of competition it can either prohibit the merger, impose remedies or seek assurances. Special rules apply to newspaper and water company mergers. The CAT has the right to review decisions on mergers taken by the OFT, the CC or the Secretary of State if such a review is applied for.

Part 4 allows the CC to investigate markets where it appears that competition is being harmed by the structure of the market or the conduct of suppliers or customers. Either the OFT or the regulators of industries which were previously nationalised, such as the Rail Regulator, can refer a market to the CC for investigation. The OFT can do this on the grounds that one or more features of the market prevents, restricts or distorts competition in relation to the supply or acquisition of goods or services in the UK or a part of the UK. Ministers have a similar power. If the CC finds that competition is being prevented, restricted or distorted it can take remedies to rectify the situation. An appeal can be made to the CAT, asking it to review a decision of the OFT, the CC or the Secretary of State.

Part 6 creates a new cartel offence. Section 188 of the Enterprise Act provides that an individual is guilty of an offence if he or she dishonestly agrees with one or more other persons that undertakings will engage in one or more of the following prohibited cartel activities: price-fixing; limitation of supply or production; market-sharing; or bid-rigging. The offence is committed by the mere fact of agreement, there is no need that the agreement should be implemented. However, the offence applies only to horizontal agreements, that is to say to agreements between individuals at the same level in the supply chain. It does not apply to vertical agreements, that is to say to agreements between individuals at different levels of the supply chain. There is a requirement for dishonesty but there is no requirement that the agreement be actually implemented. On conviction on indictment, offenders can be sentenced to five years' imprisonment and an unlimited fine. The OFT has the power to grant a 'no-action letter' to give immunity to prosecution to individuals who admit participation in the criminal offence. Such a letter will be granted to individuals who provide the OFT with all information which they have about the cartel if they maintain cooperation throughout the investigation, did not coerce another undertaking to take part in the cartel and refrain from participating in the cartel. If these conditions are subsequently breached, the no action letter can be revoked. Further offences can be committed by: unreasonably failing to comply with a requirement to answer questions or provide information or documents (maximum sentence six months); making false or misleading statements (maximum sentence two years); and destroying, concealing or falsifying documents which are relevant to an investigation (five years' imprisonment). As regards all of these offences the offender can be fined instead of, or as well as, imprisoned.

Part 7 gives the OFT the power to ask the High Court to make a Competition Disqualification Order. Such an order would be granted, and would disqualify an individual from being a director of a company, if the court was satisfied that his conduct as an individual makes him unfit to be concerned in the management of a company. Such conduct might have arisen in connection with the cartel offence, or infringements of Articles 81 or 82, or Chapter I or Chapter II of the Competition Act prohibitions.

Part 8 allows designated consumer bodies to make 'super complaints' about market features which relate to markets as a whole.

Part 9 sets out new rules on the enforcement of certain consumer regulations. (See Chapter 22 at 22.6.)

Part 10 changes insolvency law. (See Chapter 19 at 19.1.4.5.)

Part 11 deals with several technical matters.

Test your understanding

1 What types of contract are illegal at common law?

2 What types of contract are void at common law?

3 In what circumstances will contracts in restraint of trade be valid?

4 What is meant by severance?

5 What is the effect of Articles 81 and 82 of the EC Treaty?

6 What is the effect of the Chapter I and Chapter II prohibitions in the Competition Act 1998?

7 On what basis can mergers be prohibited under the Enterprise Act 2002?

8 On what basis can the OFT refer a market to the CC for investigation?

9 How is the cartel offence in s.188 of the Enterprise Act committed?

Answers

1 The following contracts are illegal at common law: contracts tending to promote corruption in public life; contracts tending to impede the administration of justice; contracts to trade with enemy nations; contracts to commit a tort, fraud or crime; contracts tending to promote sexual immorality; contracts to defraud the Revenue.

2 Contracts damaging to the institution of marriage, to oust the jurisdiction of the courts or in restraint of trade are void at common law.

3 A contract in restraint of trade will be void unless it can be proved to be reasonable as between the parties and as regards the public interest.

4 Where severance is allowed the unreasonable part of a contract in restraint of trade can be severed from the reasonable part, leaving the reasonable part to stand. Severance will only be permitted if the unreasonable parts of the contract could be crossed out with a blue pencil, leaving the reasonable parts unaffected.

5   Article 81 renders void all agreements between undertakings, decisions by associations of undertakings and concerted practices which may affect trade between Member States which have as their object or effect the restriction or distortion of competition within the EC. Article 82 tries to prevent dominant undertakings from acting unilaterally in an abusive way.

6   The Competition Act 1998 Chapter I prohibition prohibits agreements between undertakings, decisions by associations of undertakings or concerted practices which may affect trade within the UK, and which have as their object or effect the prevention, restriction or distortion of competition within the UK. The Chapter II prohibition prohibits any conduct on the part of one or more undertakings which amounts to the abuse of a dominant position in a market if it may affect trade within the UK.

7   Mergers can be prohibited on the basis that they would cause a substantial lessening of competition.

8   The OFT can refer a market to the CC for investigation on the grounds that one or more features of the market prevents, restricts or distorts competition in relation to the supply or acquisition of goods or services in the UK or a part of the UK.

9   Section 188 of the Enterprise Act provides that an individual is guilty of an offence if he or she dishonestly agrees with one or more other persons that undertakings will engage in one or more of the following prohibited cartel activities: price-fixing; limitation of supply or production; market-sharing; or bid-rigging.

Key points

■ A voidable contract can be avoided (called off) by one of the parties within a reasonable time of making the contract.

■ A void contract is a nullity and confers no legal rights on either party.

Misrepresentation

■ An actionable misrepresentation is an untrue statement of fact made by a party to a contract which induced the other party to make the contract.

■ Silence is not generally capable of amounting to an actionable misrepresentation. It can however do so if there has been a change of circumstances, if the contract is of the utmost good faith, if the parties were in a fiduciary relationship or if the silence made a statement misleading.

■ A fraudulent misrepresentation is one made knowing that it was false, or without belief in its truth or recklessly careless whether it was true or false.

■ A non-fraudulent misrepresentation will be a negligent misrepresentation unless its maker can prove that he did believe that the representation was true, with reasonable grounds for such a belief, up until the time of the making of the contract. If this can be proved the misrepresentation will be wholly innocent.

■ A fraudulent misrepresentation gives a right to rescind the contract. Damages will be assessed on the tort of deceit basis and will cover any consequential losses, whether foreseeable or not.

■ Rescission is available for negligent or wholly innocent misrepresentation. However, under s.2(2) of the Misrepresentation Act 1967 a court may award damages in lieu of rescission where it would be equitable to do so. Such damages are calculated on a breach of warranty basis.

■ Damages for negligent misrepresentation can be claimed under s.2(1) of the Misrepresentation Act 1967. Such damages are calculated on the tort of deceit basis.

■ Damages are not available for wholly innocent misrepresentation, unless a court awards them in lieu of rescission under s.2(2) of the Misrepresentation Act 1967. Such awards of damages are very rare.

■ The right to rescind can be lost if the contract is affirmed, if it is impossible to restore the parties to their pre-contract positions or if a third party in good faith has acquired rights in the subject matter of the contract.

■ A contract may be affirmed by mere lapse of time. As regards a fraudulent misrepresentation time starts to run from the time when the fraud was discovered. As regards non-fraudulent misrepresentation time starts to run from the date of the contract.

Mistake

■ The parties make a common mistake when they both make the same mistake. A common mistake as to the existence of the subject matter, or as to the ownership of the subject matter, can render the contract void.

■ The parties make a mutual mistake when they are at cross purposes so that there is no real agreement. Such a mistake will render the contract void if the reasonable man could not infer that the view of one or other of the parties was what was objectively intended.

■ A unilateral mistake as to the identity of the other contracting party can make the contract void if the contract was in writing and the parties did not meet face to face. However, the mistake must have been as to the identity of the other contracting party rather than as to his attributes, and the mistake must have been material.

■ A unilateral mistake as to the terms of the contract will render the contract void only if the person not mistaken could not reasonably have supposed that the other party intended to agree to the terms in question.

■ A party who has signed a document while under a complete misapprehension as to its effect may be able to escape liability on the grounds of *non est factum*. This plea is not open to a party who is careless in signing the document.

Duress and undue influence

■ A contract may be voidable for economic duress if there was commercial pressure which coerced the victim's will so as to vitiate consent.

■ In order for economic duress to arise there must generally have been a threat to perform an unlawful act.

■ A contract or gift can be set aside if it was made as a result of undue influence.

■ In certain relationships undue influence is automatically presumed. These relationships are those of solicitor and client, doctor and patient, parent and child, guardian and ward, trustee and beneficiary, and religious advisor and disciple. Where the parties in such a relationship make a contract which cannot readily be explained by their relationship the contract will be set aside unless the dominant party can prove that there was no undue influence.

■ In relationships other than those where undue influence is automatically presumed, it may still be presumed if the victim can prove the existence of a relationship in which he placed great trust and confidence in the other party and can also prove that the contract cannot readily be explained by their relationship.

Void and illegal contracts

■ The following contracts are illegal at common law: contracts tending to promote corruption in public life; contracts tending to impede the administration of justice; contracts to trade with enemy nations; contracts to commit a tort, fraud or crime; contracts tending to promote sexual immorality; contracts to defraud the Revenue.

■ Three types of contracts are void at common law: contracts damaging to the institution of marriage; to oust the jurisdiction of the courts; or in restraint of trade.

■ A contract in restraint of trade will be void unless it can be proved to be reasonable.

■ If a contract contains unreasonable restraint of trade clauses the whole contract will be void unless the offending clauses could be severed with a blue pencil, leaving the unaffected clauses to stand.

Competition law

- Article 81 renders void all agreements between undertakings, decisions by associations of undertakings and concerted practices which may affect trade between Member States which have as their object or effect the prevention, restriction or distortion of competition within the EC.

- Article 82 prevents dominant undertakings from acting in an abusive way.

- The Competition Act 1998 Chapter I prohibits agreements between undertakings, decisions by associations of undertakings or concerted practices which may affect trade within the UK, and which have as their object or effect the prevention, restriction or distortion of competition within the UK.

- The Chapter II prohibition prohibits any conduct on the part of one or more undertakings which amounts to the abuse of a dominant position in a market if it may affect trade within the UK.

- The Enterprise Act 2002 abolished the office of Director General of Fair Trading, his duties passing to the Office of Fair Trading.

- Under the Enterprise Act mergers will be prohibited if they would cause a substantial lessening of competition.

- The OFT has a duty to investigate if a company targeted for merger has a UK turnover of over £70m. It also has a duty to investigate if the merged companies would between them supply at least 25% of either goods or services of a particular description in the UK or in a substantial part of the UK.

- The Competition Commission can investigate markets where it appears that competition is being harmed by the structure of the market or the conduct of suppliers or customers.

- Section 188 of the Enterprise Act provides that an individual is guilty of an offence if he or she dishonestly agrees with one or more other persons that undertakings will engage in one or more of the following prohibited cartel activities: price-fixing; limitation of supply or production; market-sharing; or bid-rigging.

- The High Court can make a Competition Disqualification Order, disqualifying an individual from being a director of a company, if it was satisfied that his conduct as an individual makes him unfit to be concerned in the management of a company. Such conduct might have arisen in connection with the cartel offence, or infringements of Articles 81 or 82, or the Chapter I or Chapter II Competition Act prohibitions.

Summary questions

1   A supermarket advertises in the press that, 'In independent tests carried out by WhatVac magazine, our own make of XR3 vacuum cleaner outperformed all the big name brands.' Alan was about to buy a Hover vacuum cleaner from a different retailer, but when his friend showed him the supermarket's advertisement he changed his mind and bought an XR3. Alan made no mention of the advertisement when buying the XR3. The vacuum cleaner does not work at all well, and Alan has now discovered that the WhatVac Magazine tests rated the XR3 vacuum cleaners very poorly as the worst on the market. Has there been an actionable misrepresentation? If an actionable misrepresentation has been made what remedies would be available to Alan?

2   Belinda bought a vase from an antique shop for £500 because the owner of the shop said that the vase was a fine early Victorian antique. Five years later, when Belinda tried to sell the vase, an expert told her that the vase was very modern and that the owner of the antique shop must have known this and must also have known that it was practically worthless. Advise Belinda of any remedies available to her.

3   Charles bought a garage because the vendor said that the garage had a turnover of £120 000 p.a. After the first month Charles' turnover is only £3 000. The written contract made no mention of turnover.

a Is the statement about turnover a term of the contract?

b Has an actionable misrepresentation been made?

c What remedies would be available to Charles?

c In practical terms, what would you advise Charles to do?

4 Dinah bought a painting from a dealer. The dealer said that the painting was worth £700, and Dinah paid £650 for it. Dinah' s aunt was sure the painting was extremely valuable. An auction house confirmed this and the following week, with a good deal of publicity, the painting was sold for £1m. The antique dealer saw the publicity and recognised the picture as the one he had sold to Dinah. Advise the dealer of any rights he might have against Dinah.

5 A rogue, by pretending to be a clergyman, induces Edward to take a stolen cheque for his car. Shortly after gaining possession of the car the rogue sells it to Edwina, an innocent third party who pays a reasonable price for the car.

a Will the contract between Edward and the rogue be void for mistake?

b Did the rogue make an actionable misrepresentation to Edward?

c Will Edward get the car back from Edwina?

6 George is a retired bank manager. Fay has agreed to buy George' s boat, so that she can sail to the Channel Islands. How would the contract be affected if, unknown to both parties:

a The boat did not belong to George?

b The boat was completely unseaworthy?

c The boat had been destroyed by fire five minutes before the contract was made?

7 Harriett buys a painting from a junk shop for £100. What would the effect on the contract be if:

a Harriett discovered that the painting was utterly worthless?

b The shop owner had untruthfully said that the painting was by the minor Edwardian artist, René Dulux and therefore worth at least £100? (In fact the painting is worthless.)

8 Jim signs a document, believing that it is a contract to buy a new computer system. In fact the computer salesman has tricked Jim into signing a bill of exchange. Jim was in a hurry so he did not read the document. A bank validly takes the bill of exchange for value. The bank now intend to sue Jim on the bill of exchange.

a On what grounds might Jim argue that the signed document is not binding upon him?

b Will the bank be able to hold Jim liable on the bill of exchange?

Multiple choice questions

1 In *Hands* v *Simpson, Fawcett & Co Ltd* (1928) 44 TLR 295 the facts of the case were as follows.
The claimant was employed as a commercial traveller and had to use a car in his work. He was convicted of dangerous driving and banned from driving for three months. His employers dismissed him. The fact that the claimant had been banned was not enough to justify a dismissal, because a substitute could have been used for three months. The employers claimed that the claimant's not having revealed that he had been imprisoned for drunken driving when he took the job amounted to a misrepresentation and that this misrepresentation justified the dismissal. The claimant argued that as the employers had never asked about previous convictions, he had no duty to reveal them.
Which one of the following was the decision of the court?

a The claimant had not made a misrepresentation because he had no duty to disclose his convictions.

b The claimant had made a misrepresentation because there was a fiduciary relationship between the employers and the claimant.

c The claimant had made a misrepresentation because he must have known that the employers would never have given him the job if they had known of his convictions.

d The claimant had made a misrepresentation because his subsequent conviction amounted to a change of circumstances, as in *With* v *O'Flanagan*.

2 In *Brown* v *Raphael* [1958] 2 All ER 79 (Court of Appeal) the facts of the case were as follows.

A buyer bought a trust fund at an auction because the auction particulars stated that the seller did not believe that the fund was subject to estate duty. After buying the fund, the buyer discovered that it was subject to estate duty. The buyer could not easily have discovered this before the sale was made, but the seller should have known it all along. The buyer claimed that the seller's statement, although only an opinion, implied facts which justified the opinion. In particular he claimed that one of these facts (that the seller had reasonable grounds for believing his opinion to be true) amounted to a misrepresentation.

Which of the following was the decision of the court?

a There had been no actionable misrepresentation because the seller's statement was just an opinion.

b The seller's statement was an actionable misrepresentation because it implied facts which would justify the seller's opinion.

c That the fund was not subject to estate duty was a term of the contract because the seller had more knowledge than the buyer.

d The contract would be void for mistake as both parties proceeded on a mistaken assumption about the quality of what was being sold.

3 On Monday Bob sells his car to a rogue, who calls at his house. The rogue pays with a stolen cheque. Bob only takes the cheque because the rogue produces false identification. On Tuesday the rogue sells the car to Charles, an innocent third party who pays a reasonable price for the car. On Wednesday Bob's bank inform him that the rogue's cheque has bounced, and Bob immediately contacts the local police and the AA. Which one of the following statements is true?

a Bob will get the car back from Charles. As the rogue's misrepresentation was fraudulent, time will not start to run against Bob until he discovered the fraud.

b Bob will be too late to avoid for misrepresentation and will have no remedy for mistake.

c Bob will be too late to avoid for misrepresentation, but the contract will be void for mistake as to the person.

d The contract will be void for *non est factum*.

4 David, an expert collector of antique clocks, sees an old clock in a dealer's showroom. The dealer assures him that the clock is early eighteenth century, made by Toblerone the Swiss artist, and worth £13 000. David says that he has been looking for a Toblerone clock for some time, but before buying it he would like to check the dealer's valuation. An independent expert assures David that such a price would be fair for a genuine Toblerone clock. David buys the clock under a written contract which makes no mention of the clock's maker or of its value. Three years later when he comes to resell it David discovers that, unknown to the dealer who sold it to him, the clock is a fake worth about £2 000. Which one of the following is true?

a The dealer will be liable for breach of contract because his statement about the clock was a term.

b The dealer made an innocent misrepresentation and so David can rescind the contract.

c The dealer made an innocent misrepresentation but David will be too late to avoid the contract. Furthermore, there will be no remedy for mistake.

d As David relied on his own expert, the dealer made no misrepresentation. Furthermore, there will be no remedy for mistake.

5 Which one of the following statements is not true?

a Generally, a common mistake as to quality will not make a contract void.

b A unilateral mistake as to the person can make a contract void if the parties did not meet face to face and the mistake was as to the identity of the other party and not merely as to his attributes.

c A unilateral mistake as to the quality of what is being bought will make the contract void if the other contracting party knew at the time of the contract that the mistake was being made.

d A person who signs a document under a complete misapprehension as to its effect, and who was not careless in signing, will not be bound by the contract, on the grounds of *non est factum*.

6 Which one of the following statements is not true?

   a If a party to a contract can establish that he made it only as a consequence of the threat of physical violence the contract will be void for duress.

   b A contract will be voidable for economic duress if it was made as a consequence of unlawful pressure which coerced one party's will so as to vitiate his consent.

   c A contract between solicitor and client is one where undue influence is presumed.

   d The relationship between husband and wife is not one where undue influence is automatically presumed.

7 Which one of the following statements is not true?

   a A contract which involves the evasion of tax is a contract to defraud the Revenue and cannot be sued upon by either party.

   b Contracts in restraint of trade will be void unless they can be proved to be reasonable.

   c A restraint of trade agreement will not be upheld merely to prevent an ex-employee from exercising the skills which he learnt in the course of his employment.

   d If it can be easily done, a court will rewrite a contract to sever the parts which were in restraint of trade. Once this has been done, the rest of the contract will stand.

Task 6

A friend of yours who is a keen collector of antiques has several times bought 'antiques' which turned out to be fakes. He has also on occasion sold antiques in return for stolen cheques. Your friend has asked you to write a report, briefly explaining:

a The nature of an actionable misrepresentation and the remedies available to a person to whom a misrepresentation has been made.

b The circumstances in which a contract can be void for mistake.

c The circumstances in which a contract can be voidable for duress, economic duress or undue influence.

d The types of contracts which can be void or illegal at common law.

Chapter 7

DISCHARGE OF LIABILITY · REMEDIES FOR BREACH OF CONTRACT

Introduction

The first half of this chapter considers the different ways in which a party's contractual liability can be discharged. Once a party's liability is discharged it will cease to exist. The second half of the chapter considers the remedies for breach of contract and the time limits within which these remedies must be claimed.

7.1 · Discharge of liability

When a party's contractual liability is discharged it ceases to exist. A party's liability can be discharged by performance of the contract, by agreement, by frustration or by the other party's breach of contract. Each of these methods needs to be considered in some detail.

7.1.1 Discharge by performance of the contract

Once both of the parties to a contract have completely performed all of their contractual obligations, the contract will be discharged and neither party will have any remaining liability under the contract. However, if one of the parties does not completely perform his contractual obligations then he will have broken a term of the contract and the other party will be entitled to claim damages. In addition to claiming damages, the injured party may also be able to treat the contract as repudiated, in which case his own obligation to perform the contract will be discharged. In Chapter 5 we saw that the injured party will be able to treat his further contractual obligation as discharged if the term which was broken can be classified as a condition, rather than as a warranty, and that whether a term is a condition or a warranty is a matter of construction of the contract. In Chapter 5 we also saw that a term might be classified as an innominate term, in which case the injured party's liability will be discharged only if the breach of the term deprived him of substantially the whole benefit of the contract.

In unilateral contracts terms are not evaluated as conditions, warranties or innominate terms. When an offer of a unilateral contract is made the promise given is dependent on the complete performance of the act requested. If a person is promised £100 if he walks to York, he will not be entitled to any payment if he walks to within one mile of York. The promisor set out what needed to be done in order to create the contract. If it is not done then no contract is created.

In contracts of sale of goods the seller will generally be entitled to treat the contract as repudiated if the buyer breaches one of the terms implied by the Sale of Goods Act 1979. (See for example *Arcos Ltd* v *E. A. Ronaasen & Son* [1933] AC 470 and *Re Moore & Co Ltd and Landauer & Co Ltd* [1921] 2 KB 519 in Chapter 8 at 8.2.3.) However, in Chapter 8 at 8.4.4 we shall see that s.15A of the Sale of Goods Act 1979 provides that a buyer who does not deal as a consumer will only be able to treat breach of a statutory implied term as a breach of warranty, rather than as breach of a condition, if the breach is so slight that it would be unreasonable for the buyer to reject the goods. The statutory terms implied into sales of goods and other contracts, and the remedies available for their breach, are examined in the following chapter. Here we are concerned with general contract principles, that is to say situations which are not governed by a statutory provision.

Where a bilateral contract imposes on a party an obligation to do one particular thing, the general rule is that the obligation to do that thing is entire, unless the parties have agreed otherwise. If an obligation is entire then it must be completely performed or the other party will be entitled to refuse to perform his side of the contract. Put another way, it is a condition precedent of the other party performing his side of the contract that the entire obligation is completely performed. An example can be seen in the following case.

■ *Cutter v Powell* (1756) 6 TR 320

Cutter agreed to be a ship's mate on a voyage from Jamaica to Liverpool for a fee of 30 guineas. The ship's master had given Cutter a note setting out the terms of the contract. The note said, 'Ten days after the ship "Governor Parry", myself master, arrives at Liverpool, I promise to pay Mr. T. Cutter the sum of thirty guineas, provided he proceeds, continues and does his duty as second mate in the said ship from hence to the port of Liverpool.' The voyage from Jamaica to Liverpool would generally have taken about eight weeks and a second mate would generally have been paid about £1 a week. After seven weeks of the journey Cutter died. Cutter's widow sued for a *quantum meruit* payment, that is to say for an amount which made payment for the work he had performed.

Held. The widow was not entitled to any payment. It was a condition precedent of Cutter receiving any payment that he reached Liverpool. His obligation to do this was entire. As it had not been fully performed, the promise given in exchange for it did not have to be performed.

In *Cutter* v *Powell* the widow claimed to be entitled to a payment on a *quantum meruit* basis. When such a payment is ordered a party who has partly performed his contract is entitled to a payment, the amount he deserves, for work performed. The court rejected the widow's claim. Whether or not such a party who has not completely performed is entitled to such a payment depends upon the interpretation of the terms of the contract. The court did not think that Cutter should be paid for part performance of the contract. The high rate of pay indicated that it had been agreed that he should be paid 30 guineas if he did work all the way to Liverpool, but nothing if he did not.

7.1.1.1 Divisible or severable contracts

If a contract was intended to be divisible or severable then it will consist of a number of separate obligations rather than of one entire obligation. A party who performs only some of these obligations will be entitled to payment for the obligations performed but will be liable in damages in respect of the obligations not performed. If the contract is intended to be entire, consisting of only one obligation, then the intention is that this obligation must be performed or no payment will be due.

Where the terms of a contract to supply goods provide that the goods should be paid for at a certain price per pound or per ton, this is an indication that the parties regarded the contract as severable.

■ *Ritchie v Atkinson* (1808) 10 East 295

The master of a ship contracted to carry a complete cargo of hemp and iron from St Petersburg to London. The freight was £5 per ton for the hemp and 5 shillings per ton for the iron. The ship only carried part of the cargo. *Held*. Delivery of the complete cargo was not a condition precedent of payment of the freight. The ship's master was paid for the cargo which he did carry, but had to pay damages for the cargo which he did not carry.

A contractual obligation to carry goods to a particular destination is likely to be entire. For example, in *Vierboom* v *Chapman* (1844) 13 M & W 230 a contract was made to carry a cargo of rice from Jakarta to Rotterdam. The ship only carried the rice as far as Mauritius. The ship owner was not entitled to claim any of the freight.

Even if a contractual obligation is regarded as entire, a party who has very nearly performed in full may be said to have **substantially performed** and may therefore be entitled to payment of the contract price. (Less an amount by way of damages in respect of the part of the obligation which was not performed.) When a contract is substantially performed the breach of the entire obligation is, in effect, treated as breach of warranty.

■ *Hoenig v Isaacs* [1952] 2 All ER 176 (Court of Appeal)

The claimant agreed to furnish and decorate the defendant's flat for £750, 'net cash as the work proceeds, and balance on completion'. £400 was paid but the defendant refused to pay the balance of the contract price, alleging faulty design and bad workmanship. The Official Referee found that there were defects in the claimant's work. A wardrobe door needed replacing, a bookshelf which was too short would have to be replaced, and this replacement would require alterations to a bookcase. The Referee found that these defects would have cost £56 to rectify. He found that the claimant had substantially performed and was therefore entitled to the balance of the contract price, less £56. An appeal was made to the Court of Appeal.

Held. The Referee's decision was upheld. The claimant had substantially performed the contract.

COMMENT (i) Somervell LJ regarded the question as to whether or not substantial performance had been rendered as a matter of fact. He thought that the case was near the borderline and said that if the Referee had decided the case the other way the Court of Appeal would not have interfered with this finding.
(ii) Somervell also made it plain that 'each case turns on the construction of the contract'. He thought that if, in *Cutter* v *Powell*, Cutter had reached Liverpool but had failed on some occasion in his duty as a ship's mate he would have been entitled to the contract price less an amount in damages.

In the following case the claimant was not regarded as having substantially performed.

■ *Bolton v Mahadeva* [1972] 2 All ER 132 (Court of Appeal)

The claimant agreed to install central heating in the defendant's flat for a lump sum payment of £560. The work was performed in such a way that the gas flue was defective and fumes therefore made the rooms uncomfortable. In addition, the system was inefficient in that it did not distribute heat evenly around the flat. These defects would have cost £174 to rectify.

Held. The claimant had not substantially performed and was not therefore entitled to any of the contract price.

In a contract of employment the fact that wages are to be paid weekly or monthly suggests that the contract is divisible.

7.1.1.2 Acceptance of partial performance of an entire obligation

Below at 7.1.2 we shall see that the parties to a contract are free to make a new contract, thereby discharging the obligations which arose under the first contract. Therefore if the parties make a second contract under which one party agrees to accept partial performance of an entire contractual obligation, the party who has partially performed will be entitled to payment for work done on a *quantum meruit* basis. The Sale of Goods Act 1979 s.30(1) gives a statutory example: 'Where the seller delivers to the buyer a quantity of goods less than he contracted to sell, the buyer may reject them, but if the buyer accepts the goods so delivered he must pay for them at the contract rate.'

The acceptance of partial performance may be express or implied but either way it must have been made as a matter of genuine choice.

■ *Sumpter v Hedges* [1898] 1 QB 673 (Court of Appeal)

The claimant agreed to build two houses and stables on the defendant's land for the sum of £565. After doing work to the value of £333 the claimant said that he had run out of money and could not carry on. The judge found that he had abandoned the contract. The defendant finished the buildings himself, using some of the materials which the claimant had left on the site. The trial judge gave the claimant judgment for the value of the materials used but would allow him nothing for the value of the work which he had done. The claimant appealed to the Court of Appeal.

Held. The claimant was not entitled to any payment for work done. Chitty LJ said, 'There is no evidence from which the inference can be drawn that he [the defendant] entered into a fresh contract to pay for the work done by the plaintiff'.

7.1.1.3 Prevention of performance

If one of the parties prevents the other from performing his contractual obligations then the party prevented may sue for work done on a *quantum meruit*. In *Planché* v *Colburn* (1831) 5 C & P 58, for example, the claimant had been commissioned by the defendant to write a book. The book was on costumes and armour, part of a series called the Juvenile Library, and the claimant was to be paid £100 on completion. The defendant cancelled the series when the claimant's book was partly written. The claimant was entitled to a *quantum meruit* payment of £50 for the work he had done.

7.1.1.4 Tender of performance

A party who tenders performance of a contract offers to perform it in accordance with its terms. If a tender of goods is refused by the buyer the seller is discharged from contractual liability. For example, in *Startup* v *MacDonald* (1843) 6 Man & G 593 the claimant contracted to deliver ten tons of oil 'within the last 14 days in March'. He tendered performance at 8.30 on Saturday 31 March. The defendant refused to accept the oil on account of the lateness of the hour, although the oil could have been examined, weighed and received before midnight. The claimant was awarded damages for non-acceptance and was discharged from further obligation to perform the contract. Although the principle of this case holds good, the case might today be differently decided on its facts. Section 29(5) SGA 1979 now provides that, 'Demand or delivery of tender may be treated as ineffectual unless made at a reasonable hour; and what is a reasonable hour is a question of fact'. A modern court might well hold that 8.30 on a Saturday night is not a reasonable hour to deliver ten tons of oil.

If money is tendered, but not accepted by the seller, the buyer is not discharged from the obligation to pay the price. However, if the buyer pays the money into court this will be a good defence if he is sued by the seller for the price. Bank notes are legal tender for any amount, but coins are only legal tender up to an amount specified for each type of coin. Strictly speaking, payment of the price should be in cash unless the parties have agreed otherwise. In practice cheques are usually accepted, although a payment by cheque is only a good tender if the seller does not object. Once the cheque is honoured and the money transferred to the seller's account this is regarded as payment in cash. If the cheque is dishonoured the recipient can sue either on the cheque or on the original contract.

7.1.1.5 Time of performance

In Chapter 10 we shall see that in contracts of sale of goods the time of delivery may be fixed by the express or implied terms of the contract. We shall also see that the time of delivery of the goods is a condition whereas the time of payment for the goods is a warranty. Both of these rules are subject to a contrary intention having been expressed by the parties.

In contracts other than sales of goods, time is generally not of the essence unless the parties have expressly agreed that it should be, or the nature of the contract or the surrounding circumstances indicate that it should be. If there is an unreasonable delay in performance, the party who has been subjected to this can make time of the essence by giving reasonable notice.

7.1.2 **Discharge by agreement**

Once a contract has been made the parties who made it are free to vary the agreement or to discharge each other from their contractual obligations. However, a discharge or variation will only be effective if there is 'accord and satisfaction' amounting to the creation of a new contract.

Accord means agreement. This is obviously essential. One of the parties cannot unilaterally say that he is varying the agreement or discharging his own obligations. Both parties must agree.

Satisfaction means consideration. Just as consideration was an essential element when the contract was being formed, it is also essential when the contract is being called off. This is because the agreement to call the contract off must amount to a second contract. If the agreement to call the contract off is contained in a deed then there is no need for any additional consideration.

An example demonstrates the possibilities.

■ Example

Let us assume that a contract is made whereby A is to decorate B's office for £2 000. There are five possibilities to be considered.

(i) Both parties agree to call the contract off before A has started work.
Here the contract is discharged. There is agreement, and there is consideration. (Both parties provide consideration by giving back the rights they gained when the contract was made. A lets B off with his obligation to pay the money. B lets A off with his obligation to perform the work.)

(ii) A begins the work but does not want to finish the job. A says that he is not bothered about getting paid for the work he has done, and B agrees to release him from the contract.
Again the contract is discharged. (A lets B off with the obligation to pay the money. B lets A off with the obligation to finish the job.)

If B had agreed to pay A for the work done, then the contract would still have been discharged. (A lets B off with paying the rest of the money, B lets A off with finishing the job.)

(iii) A completes the work but agrees that B need not pay him.
The contract is not discharged. There is accord, but no satisfaction. (B has given A no consideration in return for being released from his obligation to pay the money.)

(iv) A completes the work and agrees to take B's car instead of the £2 000.
The contract is discharged. There is accord and satisfaction. Nor will the court be concerned with whether or not B's car was worth £2 000. (Consideration must be sufficient but does not need to be adequate, see Chapter 4 at 4.2.2.)

(v) A completes the work but agrees that B need only pay £1 500, instead of the £2 000 originally agreed.
The contract is not discharged. There is agreement but no satisfaction. *Foakes* v *Beer* approved the rule in *Pinnel's Case*, which held that a lesser sum of money cannot be satisfaction for a greater sum owed. (Subject to promissory estoppel. See Chapter 4 at 4.2.3.1.)

The contract itself may provide that it becomes discharged after a certain time, or upon the happening of a certain event. If the time expires or the event occurs the contract is discharged without the need for accord and satisfaction. For example, a contract of hire will usually be for a fixed time and a contract of employment may stipulate the amount of notice which must be given in order to terminate the contract. (There are however statutory minimum periods of notice. See Chapter 20 at 20.3.1.)

Just as contracts can be made orally or in writing, so they can generally be discharged without the need for any formalities. A contract made in writing or by a deed can be rescinded or varied by oral agreement. However, a contract which is required by statute to be in writing, although it can be rescinded by oral agreement, cannot be varied by oral agreement. (Except under the doctrine of promissory estoppel.)

7.1.2.1 Waiver

We have seen that the parties may discharge their contractual rights by accord and satisfaction. However, if one of the parties waives his rights and is not given anything in return for doing this then there is no accord and satisfaction as no consideration was provided in return for the waiver.

Let us consider an example where X is to build a garage for Y for £6 000. The contract stipulates that the work is to be completed by 1 November. If Y tells X that it will be all right to finish the job by 1 December he has waived his right to have the job finished by 1 November. What is the legal effect of this?

First, the party who granted the waiver cannot claim that the other party has breached the contract by doing an act allowed for by the waiver.

■ *Levey* v *Goldberg* [1922] 1 KB 688

The claimants claimed damages from the defendant for not accepting cloth which he had agreed to buy. Delivery was due to be completed by 20 August 1920. During August and September 1920 the defendant asked the claimants if they would extend the time for delivery. The claimants agreed. Later the defendant refused to accept delivery of the goods on the grounds that the delivery had not been made within the contract time.

Held. The claimants were entitled to damages for non acceptance of the goods. The defendant had waived his right to delivery by 20 August.

Second, promissory estoppel may prevent the party who granted the waiver from insisting upon his strict legal rights. We examined promissory estoppel in Chapter 4 at 4.2.3.1 and saw that a party who leads the other party to believe that he is not going to insist on his strict legal rights, intending that the other party will act upon this belief, cannot later insist on his strict legal rights if it would be inequitable for him to do so.

Third, a party who has waived his right to insist upon delivery of goods on time, can reintroduce the right to delivery within a reasonable time by giving notice. (See *Charles Rickards* v *Oppenheim* in Chapter 10 at 10.1.1.3.)

Test your understanding

1 Can a party treat his further obligation to perform a contract as discharged on account of a breach of (i) a condition, (ii) a warranty, (iii) an innominate term?

2 What is the effect of a contractual obligation being entire?

3 How will a court decide whether or not a contractual obligation was entire? What is a divisible or severable contract?

4 What exceptions are there to the general rules as regards entire contractual obligations?

5 What is the effect of tendering delivery of goods?

6 What is the effect of tendering the price?

7 What are the two requirements for a contract to be discharged by accord and satisfaction?

Answers

1 A breach of condition will allow the injured party to treat his further contractual obligations as discharged, whereas a breach of warranty will not. A breach of an innominate term will allow the injured party to treat his further contractual obligations as discharged only if the breach deprived the injured party of substantially the whole benefit of the contract.

2 If a contractual obligation is held to be entire, then the general rule is that it is a condition precedent of the other party's performance of the contract that the entire obligation be fully performed.

3 A contractual obligation will be entire if the construction of the contract indicates that this is what the parties to the contract intended. If the contract was intended to be divisible or severable then it will consist of a number of separate obligations rather than of one entire obligation. Where the contract is divisible or severable a party who performs some of

the obligations will be entitled to payment for the obligations performed but will be liable in damages for the obligations not performed.

4   Failure to perform an entire obligation will not discharge the other party from performing his own contractual obligations in three circumstances: where partial performance was genuinely accepted by the other contracting party; where the other party prevented performance of the entire obligation; or where the contract was substantially performed.

5   Tendering delivery of goods discharges the seller from further liability under the contract. If the tender is not accepted the seller will be entitled to damages for non acceptance.

6   Tendering the price does not discharge the buyer from liability to pay it. However, if the buyer pays the money into court this acts as a defence to being sued on the contract.

7   A contract can be discharged or varied by accord and satisfaction. Accord means that both parties must agree to the discharge or variation. Satisfaction means that both parties must give some consideration in return for their liabilities being discharged or varied.

7.1.3 Discharge by frustration

If the contract which the parties make subsequently becomes illegal or impossible to perform, or becomes radically different from what the parties contemplated when they made it, then the contract may be frustrated. If a contract is frustrated the parties are discharged from further performance of it. However, frustration is a doctrine of last resort. The courts will only reach the conclusion that a contract is frustrated if they cannot help but do so. It is also worth emphasising that frustration only applies where circumstances change so that performance of the contract **becomes** illegal, impossible or radically different from what was contemplated when the contract was made. If the parties make an agreement which is illegal at the outset then the contract will be void. (See Chapter 6 at 6.4.) If one of the parties agrees to something which is plainly impossible then the agreement is void because one cannot give as consideration a plainly impossible act. If, unknown to the parties, the circumstances at the time of formation of the contract were radically different from what they both believed them to be then the contract might or might not be void for common mistake, a subject considered in Chapter 6 at 6.2.1.

There is some dispute as to the theoretical basis of frustration. It may be that a contract is frustrated because the court implies a term to that effect, or it may be that the court regards it as unjust to hold the parties to their original obligations in the light of the changed circumstances. In *Great Peace Shipping Ltd* v *Tsavliris Salvage International Ltd* [2002] EWCA Civ 1407 Lord Phillips MR was dismissive of the implied term theory, saying that 'the theory of the implied term is as unrealistic when considering common mistake as when considering frustration'.

7.1.3.1 Circumstances in which a contract will be frustrated

It is possible that a contract can be frustrated on the following grounds: the subject matter of the contract has ceased to exist before the contract is performed; a person who has undertaken to perform the contract personally has become unavailable; an event central to the contract has not occurred; the contract cannot be performed in the manner specified; and the contract becomes illegal to perform. These matters are considered in turn.

The subject matter of the contract ceases to exist

If the subject matter of the contract did exist when the contract was made, but ceases to exist before the contract was performed, then the contract may be frustrated. In *Taylor* v *Caldwell* (1863) 3 B & S 826, for example, the defendant agreed to let the claimant have the use of a music hall for certain specified days, so that concerts could be performed there. The contract made no stipulation as to what should happen if the music hall should be destroyed by fire. The music hall was accidentally burnt down before the specified days came around. The contract was held to be frustrated and consequently the defendant was not in breach of contract.

Section 7 of the Sale of Goods Act 1979 makes a statutory rule which applies to an agreement to sell specific goods where the goods have ceased to exist before the risk has passed to the buyer. It provides that, 'Where there is an agreement to sell specific goods and subsequently the goods, without any fault on the part of the seller or buyer, perish before the risk passes to the buyer, the agreement is avoided.' The effect of this section is examined in Chapter 9 at 9.1.1.1. It should be noted here that when s.7 applies, the contract is not frustrated for the purposes of the Law Reform (Frustrated Contracts) Act 1943.

Unavailability of a person who had undertaken to perform personally

If the terms of the contract were such that a person undertook to perform obligations personally, the contract may become frustrated if that person is incapable of performing the contract. If the person has died, or become permanently incapable then the contract will be frustrated. If the unavailability is only for a very short time then the contract will almost certainly not be frustrated.

■ *Condor* v *The Barron Knights Ltd* [1966] 1 WLR 87

In December 1962 the claimant, then aged 16, became a drummer with the defendant band. The contract was to last for five years and required the claimant to perform seven nights a week, sometimes giving two performances in one night. In January 1963 the claimant collapsed and was detained in a mental hospital for a few days. On his release doctors ordered him to work no more than four nights a week, saying that if he did he would suffer a more severe breakdown. The claimant claimed to be fit to work seven nights a week but the band refused to accept that he was capable of this. They dismissed him because it was not practical for the claimant to rehearse and drum for four nights a week while a replacement rehearsed and drummed for three nights a week. The claimant sued for damages for wrongful dismissal.

Held. The claimant was not entitled to damages. The contract had become frustrated because it had become impossible for the claimant to perform the terms of the contract.

Non-occurrence of an event central to the contract

If the parties make the contract on the understanding that an event which is central to the contract will happen, the contract may become frustrated if that event does not happen. However, this will only be the case if the non-occurrence of the event was the fault of neither party and if the fact that it did not occur made the contract radically different from what the parties contemplated when they made the contract. The following two cases show the extent to which the contract must have become radically different.

■ *Krell* v *Henry* [1903] 2 KB 740 (Court of Appeal)

The defendant made a written contract, agreeing to pay the claimant £75 for the hire of a flat on Pall Mall on the days of 26 and 27 June 1902. A £25 deposit was paid. Neither the contract nor the parties mentioned the purpose of hiring the flat, but both parties knew that it was hired for these days because the coronation of Edward VII was due to take place and the coronation processions were due to pass down Pall Mall on 26 and 27 June. The coronation was cancelled because the king was ill. The claimant sued for the remainder of the contract price, £50.

Held. The contract was frustrated. It was necessary to infer from the circumstances that the whole purpose of the contract was that the defendant might view the coronation processions. When this became impossible the contract was frustrated.

■ *Herne Bay Steamboat Co* v *Hutton* [1903] 2 KB 683 (Court of Appeal)

The defendant agreed to hire the claimants' steamship, Cynthia, on 28 June to take paying passengers from Herne Bay 'for the purpose of viewing the naval review and for a day's cruise round the fleet; also on 29 June for similar purposes: price £250, payable £50 down, balance before ship leaves Herne Bay'. The £50 down was paid but it was then announced that the naval review was cancelled on account of the king's illness. The claimants telegrammed the defendants saying that they were still willing to perform the contract. The claimants received no reply and so used the Cynthia on the contract dates to make a profit. They then sued for the balance of the contract price. The defendants claimed that the contrast was frustrated.

Held. The contract was not frustrated. The venture was at the defendant's risk and the happening of the naval review was not the sole basis of the contract. It would have still been possible for the defendant to have used the Cynthia to take passengers for a day's cruise around the fleet.

Contract cannot be performed in manner specified

If the contract specifies that it must be performed in a certain manner then it will become frustrated if it is not possible to perform the contract in the manner specified.

■ *Nickoll and Knight* v *Ashton, Eldridge & Co* [1901] 2 KB 126 (Court of Appeal)

Cotton-seed was to be shipped from Egypt to London. The contract specified that the goods should be shipped on the steamship Orlando. The Orlando was severely damaged by a peril of the sea and could not be repaired in time to ship the cotton-seed within the contract period. The damage to the ship was not the fault of either of the parties.

Held. The contract was frustrated. The court implied a condition that if the Orlando should cease to exist as a ship for the purpose of shipping the cargo the contract should be treated as at an end.

COMMENT   The contract was frustrated only because the Orlando was named as the ship which should carry the cargo. It would not have been frustrated if the shipowner had merely contemplated that this particular ship would be used.

However, a contract will not be frustrated merely because the cost of performing it has significantly increased.

■ *Tsakiroglou & Co Ltd* v *Noblee Thorl GmbH* [1962] AC 93 (House of Lords)

Under a written contract made on 4 October 1956 sellers agreed to ship Sudanese peanuts to Hamburg during November or December 1956. On 2 November the Suez Canal was blocked and closed to shipping, and was not re-opened for several months. The peanuts could still have been shipped to Hamburg within the contract period but this would have involved a journey around the Cape of Good Hope. Such a journey would have been four times as long as the journey through the Suez Canal and the freight for such a journey would have been double. The shippers did not perform the contract, claiming that it was frustrated. The longer time at sea would not have damaged the peanuts.

Held. The contract was not frustrated. The court could not imply a term that the cargo should be carried via the Suez Canal. Carrying the cargo via the Cape of Good Hope was a change in the method of performing the contract but it was not such a fundamental change that the sellers could claim that the contract was frustrated.

■ *Davis Contractors Ltd* v *Fareham UDC* [1956] 2 All ER 145 (House of Lords)

In March 1946 the claimants agreed to build 78 houses for the defendants in eight months. Owing to a shortage of skilled labour the contract took 22 months to perform. The claimants were paid the contract price but they claimed to be paid more on account of the contract having been frustrated.

Held. The contract was not frustrated.

Lord Radcliffe: '… it is not hardship or inconvenience or material loss itself which calls the principle of frustration into play. There must be as well such a change in the significance of the obligation that the thing undertaken would, if performed, be a different thing from that contracted for.'

COMMENT In this case Lord Radcliffe criticised the implied term theory of frustration as artificial. He went on to say: 'So perhaps it would be simpler to say at the outset that frustration occurs whenever the law recognises that without default of either party a contractual obligation has become incapable of being performed because the circumstances in which performance is called for would render it a thing radically different from that which was undertaken by the contract ... It was not this that I promised to do.'

Supervening illegality

If a contract becomes illegal to perform then it will be frustrated. An example can be seen in *Fibrosa Spolka Akcyjna* v *Fairbairn Lawson Combe Barbour Ltd* [1943] AC 32. In July 1939 an English company agreed to supply machinery to a Polish company. In September 1939 Germany occupied Poland. The contract was frustrated because it is illegal to trade with an enemy occupied country.

7.1.3.2 Limits on frustration

Even if a contract does become impossible to perform, illegal to perform or fundamentally different from what the parties contemplated, it will nevertheless not be frustrated in certain circumstances.

Fault of either party

If the 'frustrating' event is the fault of either party, the party at fault cannot claim that the contract is frustrated. Whether the 'frustrating' event was caused deliberately or negligently, self-induced frustration is no frustration.

■ *Maritime National Fish Ltd* v *Ocean Trawlers Ltd* [1935] AC 524 (Privy Council)

The claimants owned a steam trawler, the St Cuthbert, which was fitted with a type of fishing net known as an otter trawl. The St Cuthbert was chartered out to the defendants, it being a term that the trawler could only be used in the fishing industry. In 1932 the charterparty was renewed for one year. Both parties knew that it would be illegal for a trawler fitted with an otter trawl to leave a Canadian port if it had not first obtained a licence from a Canadian Minister. The defendants had four other boats fitted with otter trawls and applied for five licences. They were granted only three licences and had freedom to assign these to whichever boats they pleased. The defendants assigned the licences to three of their own boats. When sued for the contract price, they claimed that their contract with the claimants was frustrated.

Held. The contract was not frustrated. The absence of a licence had been caused by the defendants' own actions and could not therefore be a frustrating event.

Force majeure clauses

If the parties to the contract foresee the 'frustrating' event and make provision for it in their contract, the clause doing this is known as a '*force majeure*' clause. Such clauses will generally be given effect so that the contract will not be frustrated and the parties' rights and obligations will be those specified in the contract. However, a *force majeure* clause will only prevent frustration if this was its intention (rather than to exclude one of the parties from liability for breach) and if the frustrating event which subsequently occurred would have been within the contemplation of the parties as within the *force majeure* clause.

■ *Jackson* v *The Union Marine Insurance Co Ltd* (1874) LR 10 CP 125

The claimant's ship was chartered to proceed with all possible despatch 'dangers and accidents of navigation excepted' from Liverpool to Newport and from there to take iron rails to San Francisco. The claimant took out insurance on the chartered freight. On 2 January the ship set out from Liverpool, but on 3 January it ran aground. The ship was not both freed and repaired until the end of August. On 15 February the charterers had engaged a different ship to take the rails to San Francisco. The claimant sued the insurance company for the lost freight. The insurance company denied liability, arguing that the claimant should have sued on the charterparty, in which case he would not have suffered a loss of the freight. The jury found that the time necessary to get the ship ready again put an end, in a commercial sense, to the common speculation which the claimant and the charterer had entered into.

Held. The claimant could claim on his insurance. The charterparty was frustrated, despite the *force majeure* clause. The charterers had therefore been entitled to hire a different ship and refuse to pay the freight to the claimant. Literally interpreted, the delay was within the *force majeure* clause. But the clause had never been designed to cater for such a long delay.

Frustrating event foreseen by one of the parties

If only one of the parties either foresaw, or ought to have foreseen, the frustrating event then that party cannot claim that the contract was frustrated.

■ *Walton Harvey Ltd* v *Walker & Homfrays Ltd* [1931] 1 Ch 274

A hotel owner made two contracts under which an advertising agency was to be entitled to put electronically illuminated advertisements on the roof of his hotel. Before the contract was due to expire the local authority compulsorily purchased the hotel and demolished it. The advertising agents claimed damages for breach of contract. The hotel owner argued that the contract was frustrated.

Held. The hotel owners were liable on the contract. They could not claim that the compulsory purchase and demolition of the hotel was a frustrating event because at the time of the contract they knew that this might happen and the advertising agency did not.

If both of the parties foresee the frustrating event then it seems likely that the contract can be frustrated.

If one of the parties gives an absolute undertaking that an act will be performed then that party cannot claim that the contract is frustrated.

■ *Peter Cassidy Seed Co Ltd* v *Osuustukkuk-Auppa Ltd* [1957] 1 WLR 273

Sellers in Finland agreed to sell an English company a large quantity of ants' eggs, 'Delivery: prompt, as soon as export licence granted'. The sellers had admitted that it was their responsibility to apply for an export licence and had assured the buyers that this would be a 'pure formality'. In fact, the Finnish authorities refused to grant the sellers an export licence.

Held. The contract was not frustrated and the sellers were liable in damages. On the true construction of the contract the sellers had warranted that they would get an export licence, rather than warranted that they would use all due diligence to try to get a licence.

Leases

It seems likely that a lease cannot be frustrated. A lease is more than a contract as it creates an interest in land.

7.1.3.3 The effect of frustration

If a contract is frustrated the common law holds that it comes to an end as soon as the frustrating event occurs. In addition, the Law Reform (Frustrated Contracts) Act 1943 makes the following provisions:

(a) All money still owing under the contract ceases to be due (s.1(2)).
(b) Money already paid under the contract is recoverable. However, the court does have a discretion to allow a party to keep some money paid or payable if he has incurred expenses in performing the contract. The court will do this if it considers it just to do so, having regard to the circumstances of the case. The amount given to cover expenses cannot exceed the amount paid or payable at the time of the frustrating event (s.1(2)).

(c) Whether or not any money was paid or payable at the time of the frustrating event, a party who had already received a valuable benefit under the contract (other than the payment of money) can be ordered by the court to pay whatever amount is fair to compensate for this. This amount should be the amount which the court considers just, having regard to the circumstances of the case, but cannot exceed the value of the benefit received (s.1(3)).

An example might make the effect of the Act clearer. Let us assume that Firm X has agreed to supply Firm Y with 1 000 imitation rifles. The contract price was £50 000, half payable in advance. After 200 of the rifles have been made and delivered, the Government outlaws the sale of such rifles. The contract will have become frustrated on the grounds that it has become illegal to perform. Applying the Act:

(a) Firm Y will cease to owe the amount unpaid, £25 000.
(b) Firm Y will be entitled to a refund of the £25 000 already paid. However, Firm X might be able to keep some of the money to cover expenses already incurred. (Such matters as administration, rifles which have been part produced, etc.) The court has a wide discretion in allowing such expenses and it is never possible to predict accurately what sum a court might allow.
(c) Firm X may receive an amount to compensate for the valuable benefit received, the 200 rifles already delivered. If the payment was on a proportional basis, it would amount to one fifth of the total price, £10 000. (However, the amount payable is at the court's discretion.)

Finally, it should be noted that the provisions of the Act will not apply if the parties make their own provisions for the effects of frustration (s.2(3)). So if, in the example above, the contract had stated that in the event of frustration the loss should lie where it fell, then this is what would happen.

The Act does not apply to charterparties, contracts of insurance or to contracts to which s.7 of the Sale of Goods Act 1979 applies.

7.1.4 Discharge by acceptance of breach

When considering discharge by performance we saw that if one of the parties breaches a condition, rather than a warranty, the injured party may elect to treat the contract as discharged and that if an entire obligation is not completely performed then the consideration promised in return for it need not be performed. We also saw that breach of an innominate term will allow the injured party to treat the contract as repudiated only if the injured party was deprived of substantially the whole benefit of the contract.

Furthermore, if one of the parties repudiates the contract, that is to say shows an intention not to be bound by the contract, then the other party may accept this repudiation and treat his own obligations as discharged. Where the repudiation occurs before the time for performance of the contract has become due this is known as an anticipatory breach. However, it is not only by committing an anticipatory breach that a party can show an intention to repudiate the contract. Such an intention can also be shown during performance of the contract.

7.1.4.1 Anticipatory breach

If one of the parties, before the time of performance becomes due, expressly or impliedly lets the other party know that he does not intend to perform the contract then this is an anticipatory breach. The party faced with the anticipatory breach has two options. He can either accept the breach and treat the contract as repudiated (as well as having a right to sue for damages) or can wait until the time when the contract should be performed. If the contract is then not performed he can sue for actual breach of contract.

■ *Hochster* v *De La Tour* (1853) 2 E & B 678

On 12 April 1852 the defendant contracted to employ the claimant as a courier for a three month period, beginning on 1 June. On 11 May the defendant informed the claimant that he had changed his mind and no longer required the claimant's services. The claimant sued for damages on 22 May. The defendants argued that there could be no breach before 1 June.

Held. An anticipatory breach had been committed on 11 May, and this entitled the claimant to sue before 1 June.

COMMENT   The injured party has a duty to mitigate his loss (take all reasonable steps to reduce it). This duty arises as soon as the anticipatory breach is accepted as terminating the contract. In this case the claimant managed to mitigate by getting an equally good position which started on 4 July. The fact of the claimant accepting this position reduced the amount of his damages because it reduced his actual loss. However, if it could be shown that he had refused the new position his damages would have been reduced anyway on the grounds that he should have mitigated his loss.

■ *Frost* v *Knight* (1872) LR 7 Exch 111

The defendant promised the claimant that he would marry her as soon as his father died. While his father was still alive, the defendant announced that he would not be marrying the claimant and he married someone else. While the defendant's father was still alive, the claimant sued for breach of contract (breach of promise to marry).

Held. An anticipatory breach of contract had been committed and so the claimant was immediately entitled to sue.

In both of these cases there was a repudiation of the contract because the anticipatory breach showed beyond reasonable doubt that the party committing the breach did not intend to be bound by the contract. If the party committing the anticipatory breach does not show an absolute refusal to perform the contract there will not have been a repudiation of the contract.

A party who treats the contract as repudiated on account of an anticipatory breach which did not show an absolute intention not to be bound by the contract will himself be in anticipatory breach. Let us assume, for example, that X has contracted to service Y's photocopiers for a fee of £400. X lets Y know that he might not be able to fully perform the contract on time. If this anticipatory breach shows an absolute intention not to be bound by the contract, Y can treat the contract as repudiated. (He can therefore refuse to pay the contract price and claim damages.) If X's anticipatory breach does not show an absolute intention not to be bound by the contract, then if Y treats the contract as repudiated Y will himself be in breach of contract. (X will therefore be entitled to refuse to perform the contract and be entitled to damages.)

The damages for an anticipatory breach will be the same as they would have been for an actual breach. However, if it can be proved that the party claiming anticipatory breach would not himself have been able to perform the contract then no damages will be available.

If one of the parties shows an intention to repudiate the contract then the other party has the option to accept this and treat the contract as repudiated. However, the contract is not repudiated until the innocent party clearly and unequivocally indicates that he accepts the repudiation. In *Howard* v *Pickford Tool Co* [1951] 1 KB 417 Lord Asquith LJ said: 'An unaccepted repudiation is a thing writ in water and of no value to anybody; it affords no legal rights of any sort or kind.'

If the repudiation is not accepted then the repudiating party may yet perform the contract. However, there is always the risk that some outside event might frustrate the contract.

■ *Avery* v *Bowden* (1856) 5 E & B 714

The defendant agreed to supply the claimant's ship with a cargo at Odessa within 45 days. The claimant's ship arrived in Odessa. The defendant repeatedly told the claimant that he would not be able to supply the cargo and advised the claimant to sail away. The claimant did not do this but stayed in Odessa, hoping that the defendant would after all be able to supply a cargo. Before the 45 days had expired the Crimean War broke out.

Held. The contract had become frustrated because Odessa had become an enemy port and it would be illegal to load there. The claimant had therefore lost the right to sue for breach. If the claimant had accepted the anticipatory breach and sailed away then he would have been entitled to damages for breach of contract.

In the following case the anticipatory breach was not accepted, and the injured party continued to perform the contract. The case was unusual in that the injured party could do this without the co-operation of the party who committed the anticipatory breach.

■ *White and Carter (Councils)* v *MacGregor* [1962] 2 WLR 713 (House of Lords)

The claimants were advertising agents who agreed to advertise the defendant's garage for a three year period. On the same day that the contract was made the defendants wrote to the claimants asking them to cancel the contract. The claimants did not accept this anticipatory breach but began to advertise the defendants' business as agreed. One of the terms of the contract said that if any of the instalments which the defendants were required to pay became four weeks overdue, then the claimants could sue for the whole contract price. The defendants refused to pay any of the instalments. The claimants advertised the defendants' garage as agreed for the whole three year period and then sued for the whole contract price.

Held. The claimants were entitled to perform the contract and sue for the whole contract price. They were not bound to accept the repudiation and sue for damages.

COMMENT (i) Where a party accepts an anticipatory breach he will not be able to claim for a loss which he should have mitigated. (As we saw when considering *Hochster* v *De La Tour*.) Where the party does not accept the anticipatory breach, as in this case, he can claim even for losses which could have been mitigated. (Mitigation is explained below at 7.2.2.3.)

(ii) Lord Reid thought that a party who has no legitimate interest in performing the contract, other than claiming damages, ought not to be allowed to saddle the other party with a burden with no benefit to himself. Subsequent cases have limited the decision of this case in this way.

(iii) The contract was unusual in that it could be performed without the cooperation of the other party. The decision will not apply in cases where such cooperation is required.

7.1.5 Discharge under a statutory right

Once a contract has been concluded then the common law approach is that both sides are bound by it. However, several statutes give consumers the right to cancel concluded contracts. The Consumer Credit Act 1974 gives such a right, in circumstances which are considered in Chapter 14 at 14.1.4. The Timeshare Act 1992 gives consumers who have entered into a timeshare agreement a 14 day period in which to cancel the contract.

The Consumer Protection (Cancellation of Contracts Concluded Away From Business Premises) Regulations 1987 give a consumer a right to cancel a contract which was made during an unsolicited visit by a trader to a consumer's home or place of work. The contract might have been to supply either goods or services. The contract is unenforceable by the trader unless, at the time of the contract, the consumer is given written notice of the right to cancel the contract within 7 days. The consumer must also be given a statutory cancellation form. If the consumer does serve written notice to cancel then any goods supplied to the consumer must be returned to the trader. Any sum of money paid by the consumer is repayable and any sum owed ceases to be due.

The Consumer Protection (Distance Selling) Regulations 2000 seek to protect consumers who buy goods or services from a supplier by means of a 'distance contract'. Significant obligations are imposed on suppliers, who must supply the consumer with information about the goods or services sold. The Regulations also give the consumer a 7 day cooling-off period.

A 'distance contract' is defined as 'any contract concerning goods or services concluded between a supplier and a consumer under an organised distance sales or service provision run by the supplier who, for the purposes of the contract, makes exclusive use of one or more means of distance communication up to and including the moment at which the contract is concluded'. It can be seen that the Regulations only protect consumers dealing with suppliers who operate an organised distance sales or service provision. The Regulations would therefore not apply to a one-off supply of goods or services which was made in response to a request from a customer. However, if several such customers were supplied the seller would then probably be regarded as operating an organised provision. Consumers are only protected, whether buying goods or services, if the supplier makes exclusive use of one or more means of distance communication up to and including the moment at which the contract is concluded. If the consumer visits the supplier's showroom, or if a door-to-door salesman visits the consumer, the Regulations will not apply.

Regulation 3 defines 'means of distance communication' as any means which, without the simultaneous presence of the supplier and the consumer, may be used for the conclusion of a contract between those parties. So a contract is made by means of distance communication if it is made without the seller and the supplier being in each other's physical presence. Schedule 1 to the Regulations gives an indicative list of 13 means of distance communication which includes letter, press advertising with order form, catalogue, telephone, radio, television, computer, email, fax and television shopping. Home deliveries by regular roundsmen (such as milkmen) and contracts to provide accommodation, transport, catering and leisure, are excluded from the main provisions of the Regulations.

Regulation 8(2)(b) requires that the supplier provides information about how the right to cancel can be exercised. Unless a term of the contract requires the consumer to do so, a consumer who cancels the contracts under the Regulations will not have to return the goods to the supplier. If a term does require the consumer to return the goods, Reg. 8(2)(b) requires that the consumer is notified of this and who would be responsible for the cost of returning the goods.

It is possible for the consumer to agree that a service may be begun before the end of the cooling-off period and that the consumer will not be able to cancel once performance of the service has begun. If this is the case, Reg. 8(3) requires the supplier to inform the consumer, in writing or other durable medium, that the consumer will not be able to cancel such a contract once the performance of the services has begun with the consumer's agreement.

If a consumer serves a notice of cancellation then the contract will be treated as if it had never been made (Reg. 10(2)). Notice of cancellation must be made in writing or in some other durable medium available and accessible to the supplier. However expressed, it must indicate an intention to cancel the contract (Reg. 10(3)). Regulation 10(4) provides that a notice of cancellation is to be treated as having been properly given if it is left at the supplier's address, posted to the supplier, sent by fax or sent by email. Regulation 10(5) provides that in the case of a company the notice of cancellation can be left at the address of the company or sent to the company secretary or company clerk. In the case of a partnership the notice can be left with or sent to a partner or a person having control or management of the partnership business.

In contracts for the supply of goods the cancellation period begins with the day on which the contract is concluded. The time when the cooling-off period ends varies, depending upon whether Reg.8 was or was not complied with. If Reg. 8 was complied with the cancellation period ends after 7 working days have expired, beginning with the day after the day on which the consumer receives the goods (Reg. 11(2)). If Reg. 8 is never complied with then an additional 3 months are added to the cooling-off period (Reg. 11(4)). If Reg. 8 is complied with late, but within 3 months of the day on which the consumer received the goods, the time period expires after 7 working days, beginning with the day after the day on which the consumer receives the information.

If the contract is to supply services the time periods are the same except that the cooling-off period begins to reduce on the day after the day on which the contract was concluded.

There are in Regulation 13 important exceptions to the right to cancel. First, there is no right to cancel in a contract to supply a service where the supplier complied with Reg. 8(3) by informing the consumer before the conclusion of the contract that the consumer would not be able to cancel once the performance of the contract had begun with his agreement. Second, there is no right to cancel if the price of the goods or services supplied is dependent upon fluctuations in the financial market which cannot be controlled by the supplier (for example, if the contract was to supply Krugerrands). Third, there is no right to cancel if the goods were made to the consumer's specifications or are clearly personalised or were goods which by reason of their nature cannot be returned or are liable to deteriorate or expire rapidly. Fourth, a consumer will not be able to cancel a contract to buy audio or video recordings or computer software once he has broken the seal on the goods. Fifth, contract for the supply of newspapers or magazines or for gaming, lottery or betting services cannot be cancelled.

If the contract is cancelled the supplier must return any money paid by the consumer within 30 days. Any security provided by the consumer shall be treated as if it had never taken effect.

A supplier can make a charge in respect of returned goods only if the goods were the goods ordered (not substituted goods) and a term of the contract provided that the consumer must return any goods supplied if he cancels the contract under Reg. 10. The charge can then be made only if the consumer does not return the goods or returns the goods at the expense of the supplier. Any such charge made must not exceed the costs of recovering any goods supplied under the contract (Reg. 14(5)). The supplier's right to make a charge does not apply where any express or implied term of the contract gives the consumer a right to reject. Nor does it apply if any term requiring the consumer to return any goods supplied if he cancels the contract is an 'unfair term' within the meaning of the Unfair Terms in Consumer Contracts Regulations 1999.

If the consumer does cancel a contract any related credit agreement is automatically cancelled (Reg. 15(1).)

Regulation 17(2) imposes duties on a consumer who cancels the contract under Reg. 10. The consumer must retain possession of the goods and take reasonable care of them. A consumer who cancels also has a duty to restore the goods to the supplier (Reg. 17(3)). Restoration does not involve returning the goods to the supplier, but rather making them available for collection by the supplier. The consumer has no duty to deliver the goods except at his own premises. Even then a request to do so must have been made in writing, or some other durable medium accessible to the consumer, and have been given to the consumer either before, or at the time when, the goods are collected from the premises (Reg. 17(4)). When the consumer delivers the goods to the supplier, or sends the goods back to the supplier at his own expense, he is discharged from any obligation to retain possession of the goods or to restore them to the supplier. The consumer's duties to retain possession of the goods and take reasonable care of them lasts for 21 days, beginning with the day on which notice of cancellation was given. However, if within the 21-day period the consumer receives a request to deliver the goods at his own premises, which is in writing or some other durable medium, and unreasonably either refuses or fails to comply with it, the duties to retain possession of the goods and take reasonable care of them continue until the consumer does deliver the goods (at his own premises or elsewhere) or does, at his own expense, send them back to the supplier.

The Regulations do not provide that if the consumer cancels the contract he must return the goods to the supplier. However, as we have seen, a term of the contract may provide that the consumer must do this. If there is such a term a consumer who cancels must retain the goods and take reasonable care of them for a 6 month period. If the supplier makes a written request for the return of the goods this time period is extended until the consumer does send the goods back.

If the consumer traded in goods in part exchange then these goods must be returned to the consumer upon cancellation of the contract in a condition substantially as good as they were when they were delivered to the supplier. If this is not done the supplier must pay a sum equal to the part-exchange allowance (Reg. 18(2)). Upon paying such a sum the supplier becomes the owner of the part-exchanged goods.

Unless the parties agree otherwise, the supplier must perform the contract within 30 days, beginning with the day after the day the consumer sent his order to the supplier (Reg. 19(1)). If the goods or services are unavailable the supplier must inform the consumer and reimburse any sum paid (Reg. 19(2)). The contract is then treated as never having been made, except for any rights or remedies for non-performance which the consumer might have.

It is not possible to contract out of the provisions of the Regulations.

Test your understanding

1 In what circumstances can a contract be frustrated?

2 What is the effect of the 'frustrating' event being the fault of one of the parties?

3 What is a *force majeure* clause? Are such clauses given legal effect?

4 Can a contract be frustrated if one of the parties foresaw the frustrating event?

5 How does the Law Reform (Frustrated Contracts) Act 1943 apportion loss in cases of frustration?

6 How does an anticipatory breach of contract arise?

7 What options are open to a party faced with a repudiatory anticipatory breach?

Answers

1 A contract can be frustrated if, after the contract has been created but before it has been performed, any of the following matters occur: the subject matter of the contract ceases to exist; a person who was to perform personally has become unavailable; an event which was central to the contract has not occurred; the contract cannot be performed in the manner agreed in the contract; or the contract has become illegal to perform.

2 If the frustrating event is the fault of one of the parties, that party cannot claim that the contract was frustrated.

3 A *force majeure* clause is a clause in the contract which provides what should happen if the 'frustrating' event occurs. Such clauses are given legal effect.

4 If only one of the parties foresaw, or should have foreseen, the frustrating event then that party cannot claim that the contract was frustrated.

5 The Law Reform (Frustrated Contracts) Act 1943 provides that when a contract is frustrated: money owing ceases to be due; money paid is recoverable, although the court has a power to allow some money paid or payable to be retained to cover expenses; a party who has received a valuable benefit may be ordered to pay a just amount to compensate for this.

6 An anticipatory breach occurs when a party expressly or impliedly indicates an unwillingness to perform the contract before the time for performance has become due.

7 A party faced with a repudiatory anticipatory breach can treat the contract as discharged and sue for damages. Alternatively, he may affirm the contract and sue for damages when an actual breach occurs. If the contract can still be performed without the cooperation of the party committing the anticipatory breach, the injured party may be able to perform the contract and then sue for the contract price.

7.2 · Remedies for breach of contract

Whenever a contract is breached, one or more remedies will be available to the injured party.

7.2.1 Refusal to further perform the contract

Earlier in this chapter we considered discharge by breach and discharge by performance. We saw that the innocent party will be able to treat his obligations as discharged, and therefore be entitled to refuse to perform the contract further, in the following circumstances: if the other party repudiates the contract; or if a non-repudiatory breach amounts to breach of condition rather than to breach of warranty; or if a non-repudiatory breach amounts to breach of an innominate term which deprived of substantially the whole intended benefit of the contract.

As well as treating his further obligations as discharged, the injured party may also be entitled to claim damages. However, when assessing these damages account will be taken of any benefit which the injured party has received.

7.2.1.1 Rescission distinguished

It should be remembered that treating the contract as repudiated on account of a breach of contract by the other party is not the same as rescinding a contract for misrepresentation, duress or undue influence. Rescission, an equitable remedy considered in Chapter 6 at 6.1.3, is not a remedy for breach of contract. Unfortunately, some confusion has been caused over the years because at times both writers and judges have used the word rescission to mean treating a contract as repudiated on account of breach of contract.

When we considered misrepresentation we saw that rescission will only be allowed if the parties can be restored to their pre-contract positions. This is because the contract is regarded as having never existed. This requirement is not present when a contract is treated as repudiated for breach. In that case it is further performance of the contract which is discharged. Therefore the fact that the party treating the contract as repudiated cannot restore the parties to their pre-contract positions will not prevent him from treating the contract as repudiated.

7.2.2 **Damages**

Any breach of contract will entitle the injured party to damages. However, if the injured party has suffered no real loss these damages will be nominal only and costs may not be recoverable. The primary purpose of contract damages is to put the injured party in the financial position he would have been in if the contract had been properly performed. Two steps are necessary to achieve this. First, it must be asked whether or not the loss is too remote for damages in respect of it to be recoverable at all. Then, if the loss is not too remote, damages must be quantified.

7.2.2.1 **Remoteness of damage**

The injured party cannot claim damages for every loss which was caused by the breach of contract. Damages can only be recovered for losses which were caused by the breach of contract and which fit within one of the two rules in *Hadley* v *Baxendale* (1854) 9 Exch 341.

Rule 1 states that damages are recoverable for a loss which arose naturally from the breach, according to the usual course of things. Rule 2 states that damages are recoverable for a loss which may reasonably be supposed to have been in the contemplation of both parties, as the probable result of breach, at the time when they made the contract. The following case shows how the two rules work.

■ *Victoria Laundry* v *Newman Industries* [1949] 1 All ER 997 (Court of Appeal)

The defendants agreed to sell a second-hand boiler to the claimants, a company of launderers and dyers. At the time of the contract the defendants knew that the claimants wanted the boiler for immediate use. The defendants breached the contract by delivering the boiler twenty weeks late. The claimants claimed £16 a week, representing the increased ordinary profit which they could have made with the boiler which the defendants were to supply. They also claimed £262 a week, representing the value of an exceptionally lucrative contract to dye army uniforms. The unavailability of the new boiler had caused the claimants to lose this contract.

Held. The loss of £16 was recoverable within the first rule in *Hadley* v *Baxendale*. The loss of £262 was neither within the first nor the second rule and was therefore not recoverable.

COMMENT (i) If the claimants had told the defendants about the lucrative dyeing contract, and that the boiler which the defendants were to supply would be needed in time or the dyeing contract would be lost, then the £262 a week would have been recoverable under the second rule.

(ii) The Court of Appeal held that a defendant who breached a contract would be liable for losses which were reasonably foreseeable. Asquith LJ delivered the judgment of the court and used the expressions a 'serious possibility', or a 'real danger' or 'on the cards' to indicate the degree of foreseeability required. These expressions were criticised by Lord Reid in the case which follows.

■ *Koufos* v *C. Czarnikow Ltd, The Heron II* [1967] 1 AC 350 (House of Lords)

The defendants contracted to deliver 3 000 tons of sugar to Basrah by 22 November 1960. The ship did not arrive until 2 December. During the ten days by which the delivery was late the market price of sugar had fallen from

£32 10s per ton to £31 2s 9d per ton. The buyers claimed the difference in price, £4 183. The sellers knew that the buyers were sugar merchants, and also knew that there was a sugar market in Basrah. They did not know that the sellers had intended to resell the sugar as soon as they got it.

Held. The buyers were entitled to the £4 183 under the first rule in *Hadley* v *Baxendale*.

COMMENT Lord Reid thought the loss should be recoverable because it was 'not unlikely' or 'quite likely' to occur. He thought such a test was preferable to one of reasonable foreseeability, which is the test for remoteness of damage in tort. The contract test is whether the loss could reasonably have been contemplated, not whether it could reasonably have been foreseen.

Lord Reid: 'It appears to me that in the ordinary use of language there is a wide gulf between saying that some event is not unlikely or quite likely to happen and saying merely that it is a serious possibility, a real danger or on the cards. Suppose one takes a well-shuffled pack of cards, it is quite likely or not unlikely that the top card will prove to be a diamond: the odds are only 3 to 1 against. But most people would not say that it is quite likely to be the nine of diamonds for the odds are then 51 to 1 against. On the other hand I think that most people would say that there is a serious possibility or a real danger of its being turned up first and of course it is on the cards.'

7.2.2.2 Quantification of damages

The purpose of contract damages is to put the injured party, as regards foreseeable losses, in the financial position which he would have been in if the contract had not been breached. Contract damages are not designed to penalise the party in breach and should not put the injured party in a better financial position than he would have been in if the contract had been properly performed. Therefore, a party who has suffered no loss as a result of the breach of contract will ordinarily not be entitled to more than nominal damages.

Loss of the bargain

Where the seller commits a breach of contract by failing to deliver goods, the Sale of Goods Act 1979 lays down statutory rules in assessing the buyer's damages. These rules are examined in Chapter 10 at 10.4.1. Where the buyer in a contract of sale of goods refuses to accept and pay for the goods or refuses to take delivery of them the seller will be entitled to damages. Again, statutory rules are set out in the Sale of Goods Act 1979. These rules are examined in Chapter 10 at 10.3.2.2. These statutory rules reflect common law principles that a party faced with a breach of contract should be compensated for the loss of the bargain he had made.

If the breach of contract consisted of improperly performing a contract other than a sale of goods then the loss of the bargain damages will usually be the cost of rectifying the defect and an amount to compensate for other foreseeable consequential losses. However, this will not be the case where it would be unreasonable to assess damages in this way.

■ *Ruxley Electronics and Construction Ltd* v *Forsyth* [1995] 3 All ER 268 (House of Lords)

The defendant agreed that the claimants should build a swimming pool in his garden for a price of £70 178. The contract expressly stated that the maximum depth of the pool should be 7 feet 6 inches. When the work was completed the defendant discovered that the maximum depth was only 6 feet 9 inches, and that at a point where people were likely to dive in it was only 6 feet. The defendant paid various amounts but the balance due still amounted to £39 000. The claimants sued for this balance and the defendant counterclaimed for breach of contract. The trial judge awarded the defendant damages of £2 500 for loss of amenity. Despite the fact that the shortfall in depth did not decrease the value of the swimming pool, the Court of Appeal nevertheless awarded the defendant £21 560 damages. This figure was based on the cost of making good the breach of contract by re-digging the swimming pool. The claimants appealed to the House of Lords.

Held. The defendant's damages should not be the cost of re-digging the swimming pool to make it conform to the contract specifications. It would be unreasonable for the defendant to insist on this and out of all proportion to the benefit which he would obtain. The defendant was therefore only entitled to damages for the difference in value between the pool as it was and the pool as it ought to have been. However, even where there had been no diminished value modest damages could be awarded for loss of expectation of performance, loss of a pleasurable amenity or failure to satisfy a personal preference. The trial judge's award of £2 500 was restored.

As well as damages generally being available for the cost of remedying a defect, they would also be available for other foreseeable consequential losses. Let us assume that Y Ltd is a small bakery and that X contracts to service the bakery's oven, knowing that it is the bakery's only oven. If X's service is badly performed and renders the oven useless then Y Ltd will be able to claim damages not only for the cost of remedying the defect but also for profits lost until the oven could be repaired or replaced. An example of this sort of situation was seen in *Victoria Laundry v Newman Industries*, where the £16 per week ordinary business profit was claimable from the date when the boiler should have been supplied until the date when it was actually supplied.

Where a loss suffered by the injured party would be subject to taxation (for example, lost earnings) the amount of damages should be the amount which the injured party would have received after tax had been paid. This is a logical consequence of contract damages being designed to put the injured party in the position he would have been in if the contract had been performed.

Damages paid by the injured party

It commonly happens that a business buyer who is supplied with defective goods finds himself in breach of contract when such goods are sold on. Damages paid to the second buyer will be recoverable by the first buyer if the selling on was within one of the two rules in *Hadley v Baxendale*.

■ *Pinnock Bros v Lewis & Peat Ltd* [1923] 1 KB 690

The defendants sold copra cake, which was to be used as cattle food, to the claimant. The claimant resold the cake to B, who resold it to C, who resold it to farmers, who used it for feeding cattle. The cake was poisonous to cattle. The claimant sought damages from the defendants.

Held. The claimant was entitled to recover damages to cover the damages and costs he had himself had to pay out, because it was within the contemplation of the parties that such a loss would arise.

Damages which are difficult to quantify

The fact that damages are hard to quantify will not prevent an award of damages.

■ *Chaplin v Hicks* [1911] 2 KB 786 (Court of Appeal)

The defendants had advertised a beauty contest in their newspaper. There were 6 000 entrants and these were whittled down to 50, one of whom was the claimant. There were to be twelve winners, and their prizes were that they would be employed as actresses for three years. The first four winners were to be paid £5 a week, the next four £4 a week and the last four £3 a week. The defendants breached the contract by not allowing the claimant the chance to become one of the winners. The other 49 women did proceed and twelve were selected as winners. The jury awarded the claimant £100 damages and an appeal was made to the Court of Appeal.

Held. The claimant was entitled to damages for loss of opportunity to win one of the prizes and the jury's award was allowed to stand.

Damages for injured feelings and disappointment

As a general rule damages are not recoverable for loss of enjoyment, although they are clearly recoverable for physical injury or physical or mental illness.

However, in exceptional cases damages are recoverable for loss of enjoyment, particularly where the object of the contract was to provide the claimant with enjoyment and relaxation. In *Jarvis v Swan Tours Ltd* [1973] 1 QB 233 (Court of Appeal), for example, the claimant was awarded damages for disappointment and distress caused by a skiing holiday being particularly disastrous. In *Watts* v *Morrow* [1991] 4 All ER 97 Bingham LJ said that damages were not generally available for distress, frustration, anxiety, displeasure, tension or aggravation. However, he recognised two exceptions. First, where the very object of the contract was to provide pleasure, relaxation, peace of mind or freedom from molestation and the contract did not succeed in achieving that. (A contract to survey a house for a prospective purchaser was not an example of such a contract.) Second, damages could be recovered for physical inconvenience and discomfort caused by a breach of contract and also for mental suffering which was directly related to that physical inconvenience or discomfort. These views were approved by the House of Lords in the following case.

■ *Farley* v *Skinner* [2001] UKHL 49 (House of Lords)

A surveyor was employed by a potential house purchaser to survey a house and particularly to find out if there were any problems with noise from aircraft. The surveyor breached the contract by stating that there was no problem with aircraft noise. In fact there was, as aircraft were 'stacked' above the house before coming in to land. This noise materially affected the use and enjoyment of the house, particularly at weekends. Relying on the survey, the potential purchaser bought the house. The county court judge thought that the noise did not affect the value of the house but nevertheless awarded damages of £10 000. The Court of Appeal overturned this award. Applying *Watts* v *Morrow*, it thought that the very object of the contract was not to provide pleasure and that the noise did not amount to physical inconvenience. An appeal was made to the House of Lords.

Held. The judge's award of £10 000 was restored. The case came within the first category set out in *Watts* v *Morrow*. The contract was not one designed principally to provide pleasure, relaxation or peace of mind but it was enough that a major object of the contract was to do this.

COMMENT   Lords Scott and Steyn also thought that damages could be recovered under the second category set out in *Watts* v *Morrow*. Stressing that it can be very difficult to decide when inconvenience is 'physical', Lord Scott thought that the distinction should be based on the cause of the inconvenience, not on a distinction between different types of inconvenience. He said: 'If the cause is no more than disappointment that the contractual obligation has been broken, damages are not recoverable even if the disappointment has led to a complete mental breakdown. But if the cause of the inconvenience or discomfort is a sensory (sight, touch, hearing, smell etc) experience, damages can, subject to the remoteness rule, be recovered.'

Damages for losses caused to third parties

This subject was considered under the heading privity of contract in Chapter 4 at 4.2.2.2.

Damages for expenses incurred in reliance on the contract

Instead of claiming damages to compensate for the lost bargain, the injured party may instead claim damages for expenditure wasted in reliance on the contract.

■ *Anglia Television Ltd* v *Reed* [1972] 1 QB 60

Robert Reed, a well-known actor, agreed to play the lead part in a television play which the claimants were producing. Shortly after making the contract the defendant repudiated it. The claimants, who could not get a substitute at short notice, accepted the repudiation. The claimants claimed all of their wasted expenditure, which amounted to £2 750. The defendant argued that they should only get the amount of expenditure wasted after the contract had been concluded, £854.

Held. The claimants could choose to claim their wasted expenditure instead of their lost profits. Furthermore, they could recover £2 750 because when the contract was made this was the amount which would reasonably be in the parties' contemplation as the amount wasted if the contract were broken.

COMMENT Although the injured party may generally elect to claim either on the basis of the loss of the bargain or on the basis of wasted expenditure, this is not always the case. The court may force the injured party to claim on the loss of the bargain basis where he has made a bad bargain and where the circumstances show that the wasted expenditure would not have been recovered anyway (*C & P Haulage* v *Middleton* [1983] 3 All ER 94).

7.2.2.3 Mitigation of loss

A party faced with a breach of contract will not be able to claim for losses which could have been mitigated by taking reasonable steps. Whether or not a loss would have been avoided by the taking of reasonable steps is a question of fact, depending upon the circumstances of the case.

■ *Brace* v *Calder* [1895] 2 QB 253 (Court of Appeal)

On 23 December 1892 a partnership of four partners appointed the claimant their office manager for a two year period at £300 a month. In May 1893 the partnership was dissolved when two of the partners retired. The two remaining partners carried on business in the firm's name and the claimant did not find out that the original partnership had been dissolved until the end of July 1893. The dissolution was a breach of the claimant's contract of employment and, technically, meant that he had been wrongfully dismissed. When the claimant did find out about the dissolution the two remaining partners agreed to honour the contract he had made. The claimant sued for breach of contract.

Held. A breach of contract had occurred, but the claimant should have mitigated his loss by accepting the offer of alternative employment. He was therefore only entitled to nominal damages from the original partners.

Earlier in this chapter we examined *White and Carter (Councils)* v *MacGregor* and saw that a party faced with an anticipatory breach, who chooses to keep the contract alive, and who can perform the contract without the assistance of the other party, can claim damages even in respect of losses which could have been mitigated.

7.2.2.4 Agreed damages

Generally, the damages for breach of contract will be unliquidated, meaning that they will be fixed by the court rather than by the parties. Sometimes, however, a term of the contract provides exactly what the damages should be in the event of breach. These agreed damages may be one of two things; liquidated damages or penalties.

Liquidated damages

Liquidated damages are a **genuine pre-estimate of the loss** and will be applied no matter what the actual loss.

Penalties

Penalties are not a genuine pre-estimate of the loss, but are designed to warn a party against breaking his contract. The courts will ignore penalty clauses completely and calculate damages in the usual way.

An example will show how penalties and liquidated damages operate.

■ Example

Let us assume that a builder agrees to build a new shop, and that a term of the contract provides that if the shop is not ready on time the builder will pay £1 000 damages for every week that completion is late.

If the court considered that this sum of £1 000 a week was what the parties genuinely thought the loss to the shop owner would be, when the contract was made, then the term would be liquidated damages and the builder would have to pay at the rate of £1 000 a week no matter what the actual loss which the shop suffered. (The £1 000 a week would have been a 'genuine pre-estimate of the loss'.)

If the court considered that the figure of £1 000 a week was not what the parties thought the loss would be, but was designed to warn the builder against breaking the contract, then the term would be a penalty and would be ignored. Damages would then be calculated in the usual way.

In *Dunlop Pneumatic Tyre Co Ltd v New Garage Ltd* [1915] AC 79 (House of Lords) Lord Dunedin laid down five rules for distinguishing penalties and liquidated damages:

(1) If the stipulated damages are greater than could conceivably flow from the breach then the clause providing for such damages will be a penalty.
(2) 'It is no obstacle to the sum stipulated being a genuine pre-estimate of damage, that the consequences of breach are such as to make precise pre-estimation almost an impossibility. On the contrary, that is just the situation where it is probable that pre-estimated damage was the true bargain between the parties.'
(3) The clause will be presumed to be a penalty if it makes the same sum payable as damages for several different breaches which are likely to cause different amounts of loss.
(4) If the breach of contract consists solely of not paying a fixed sum of money, and the clause provides that in the event of breach a greater sum shall be payable as damages, this will invariably be a penalty.
(5) Calling the clause a 'penalty' or 'liquidated damages' is relevant in deciding its status but is not decisive.

A clause which is intended only to limit one party's potential losses, rather than to warn a party against breaking the contract, will not be a penalty even if the amount specified is not a genuine pre-estimate of the loss.

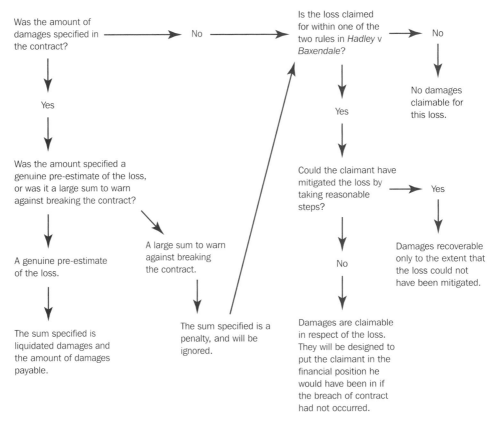

Figure 7.1   An outline of the availability of damages for a loss caused by a breach of contract

■ *Cellulose Acetate Silk Co v Widnes Foundry* [1933] AC 20 (House of Lords)

The claimants agreed to deliver and erect an acetone recovery plant by a certain date. A 'penalty' clause said that they would pay £20 per week damages for every week they were in default. The claimants were thirty weeks late in performing the contract. When the claimants sued for the contract price the defendants counterclaimed for £5 850 which was the full cost to them of the delay.

Held. The clause agreeing to pay £20 per week was a liquidated damages clause even though it was less than the genuine pre-estimate of the loss. The clause was only intended to limit the claimants' liability. £600 was therefore all that the defendants were entitled to counterclaim.

7.2.2.5 Interest

A court is allowed to order the payment of interest on all claims for judgment or damages. The interest is payable from the date when the claim arose. In addition, the parties may expressly or impliedly agree to pay interest at a certain rate.

Figure 7.1 shows an outline of the law relating to damages for breach of contract.

Test your understanding

1 What are the two rules in *Hadley* v *Baxendale*? What is their significance?

2 Can damages be claimed for expenditure wasted in reliance on contract?

3 What is meant by mitigation of loss?

4 What is the difference between penalties and liquidated damages? In what way is the difference significant?

Answers

1 The two rules in *Hadley* v *Baxendale* are used to assess whether or not a loss caused by a breach of contract is too remote for damages to be claimed in respect of it. The first rule is that damages can be claimed in respect of a loss if the loss arose naturally from the breach according to the usual course of things. The second rule is that damages can be claimed in respect of a loss if both of the parties would have contemplated that the loss would be the probable result of breach, at the time when they made the contract.

2 Damages for wasted expenditure can generally be claimed as an alternative to damages for loss of the bargain.

3 The injured party will not be able to claim damages in respect of losses which could have been mitigated by taking reasonable steps.

4 When the parties specify in the contract itself the amount of damages payable in the event of breach this amount may be either a penalty or liquidated damages. If the amount is a genuine pre-estimate of the loss it will be regarded as liquidated damages and applied no matter what the actual loss. If the amount specified is a large sum designed to warn the other party against breaching the contract it will be ignored as a penalty and damages will be assessed in the usual way.

7.2.3 An action for an agreed sum

A person who brings an action for an amount agreed in the contract, perhaps for the price in a contract of sale of goods, is not suing for damages. For example, if X agrees to buy Y's car for £3 500 but then refuses to pay the price Y might bring an action for the price. Because such a claim would not be for damages the rules on remoteness, quantification and mitigation of damages would not be relevant. The seller's action for the price in a contract of sale of goods is examined in Chapter 10 at 10.3.2.

Earlier in this chapter, when considering discharge of obligations by performance, we saw that the general rule is that a party will only be able to sue for the contract price when he had completely discharged his own obligations. We also saw that there are several exceptions to this general rule.

7.2.4 Specific performance

As we have seen, the usual remedy for a breach of contract is an award of damages. However, in certain circumstances such an award does not adequately achieve justice. Equity therefore developed the remedies of specific performance and injunction to cater for these situations.

Specific performance is a court order requiring a person to perform his contract. If the party disobeys this order he will be in contempt of court. For example, if A agrees to sell a painting to B but then refuses to hand it over, a decree of specific performance would order A to hand the painting over. If A still refused to do so he would be in contempt of court and would be liable to a fine or imprisonment.

The courts are somewhat reluctant to order specific performance, and there are many circumstances in which it will not be ordered.

First, specific performance will not be ordered where damages would be an adequate remedy, unless the court considers specific performance the more appropriate remedy. Therefore it will not normally be ordered where a seller refuses to deliver mass-produced goods, because generally the buyer will be able to use his damages to buy similar goods elsewhere.

However, if a seller refuses to deliver unique goods then damages will not be an adequate remedy. If a person agreed to sell a painting by Picasso, for example, and then went back on his contract it is quite likely that specific performance would be ordered. Damages would not adequately compensate the buyer because he would not be able to use the damages to buy a similar painting.

All plots of land are regarded as unique and if a seller of land refuses to go through with the sale specific performance will generally be ordered. The Courts of Equity thought it only fair that if specific performance could be ordered in favour of one party then, as a general principle, it should also be available to the other party. Therefore if a buyer of land refuses to complete, specific performance will generally be ordered against him.

A second limitation on the awarding of specific performance is that, being an equitable remedy, it will not be ordered in favour of a party who has behaved unfairly. An ancient equitable maxim expressed this by saying '*He who comes to Equity must come with clean hands*'. In the following case the claimant did not have 'clean hands' and so equity would not help him.

■ *Falcke v Gray* (1859) ER 4 Drewry 651

A landlady let a room to the claimant, an antique dealer. It was agreed that when the six month lease had expired the dealer could buy a pair of china vases from the landlady for £20 each. The dealer told the landlady that he thought this a fair price. Shortly afterwards the landlady began to have her doubts. She asked another dealer for a valuation. This dealer offered £200 for the vases. The landlady accepted this offer and the second dealer took the vases away. The claimant claimed specific performance against the landlady and that the second dealer should be ordered to hand the vases over to him.

Held. Although this was not a contract where damages would be an adequate remedy, specific performance was not granted because the claimant had behaved inequitably. The parties were not on an equal footing and the claimant knew that the price he had agreed to pay was grossly inadequate.

However, a party will not be protected against specific performance merely because he has made a bad deal. As long as the other party has behaved fairly specific performance can be ordered, as the following case demonstrates.

■ *Mountford v Scott* [1975] 1 All ER 198 (Court of Appeal)

In December 1971 the defendant sold an option for £1. The option gave the claimant the right to buy the defendant's house for £10 000, if he so wished, at any time within the next six months. The claimant had taken options on three other houses because he was considering developing the land on which the four houses stood. In January 1972 the defendant tried to call the option off. In March the claimant exercised the option. The defendant refused to vacate the house, saying that with the £10 000 he could not find another suitable house. The claimant sued for specific performance.

Held. Specific performance was granted.

Russell LJ: 'If the owner of a house contracts with his eyes open … it cannot in my eyes be right to deny specific performance to the purchaser because the vendor then finds it difficult to find a house to buy that suits him and his family …'

COMMENT (i) It was suggested that £1 was insufficient consideration for the granting of the option. This was rejected as 'a startling proposition' by Russell LJ.

(ii) The bargain was not in any way unconscionable. At the time of the contract the house was not worth more than £10 000. The defendant had in fact successfully held out for £1 000 more than his neighbours.

Equitable remedies are only awarded at the court's discretion. There are many circumstances in which the courts use their discretion and refuse to order specific performance. For example, a court will not order specific performance where to do so would cause undue hardship to the defendant. Similarly, specific performance will not be ordered for on-going contracts which would require constant supervision because of the rule that '*Equity does nothing in vain*'. Specific performance will not therefore be ordered in contracts of employment. To order specific performance of employment contracts would be in vain, because the court would find it impossible to check that the employer and employee were fulfilling their respective duties. Nor will specific performance be awarded in favour of or against a minor.

It should be noted that despite this an employer can be ordered to reinstate an unfairly dismissed employee under the Employment Rights Act 1996 s.112. This is not specific performance, it is merely a statutory provision. If the employer refuses to obey the order he will not be in contempt of court but will have to pay greater compensation. (See Chapter 20 at 20.4.4.2.)

7.2.5 Injunction

An injunction is a court order requiring a person to do or not to do a certain thing. A person who refuses to obey an injunction will be in contempt of court. The granting of an injunction, to prevent an action which would deliberately cause a breach of contract, is an equitable remedy for breach of contract. It is, however, not ordered where damages would be an adequate remedy.

It is possible that an injunction which would amount to specific performance will be ordered in a contract to supply generic goods. In *Sky Petroleum* v *VIP Petroleum* [1974] 1 All ER 954 the defendants had a ten year contract to supply the claimants with petrol. During an oil crisis oil became exceedingly difficult to get. The defendants threatened to terminate the agreement, claiming a breach of contract by the claimants. The court granted the claimants an injunction which prevented the defendants from withholding supplies of petrol, even though in effect this amounted to specific performance of the contract.

Specific performance of a personal service contract will not be ordered, as we have seen. In the following case the claimant applied for an injunction to prevent a breach of a personal service contract.

■ *Lumley* v *Wagner* (1853) 1 De GM & G 604

The defendant agreed to sing at the claimant's theatres twice a week for three months, and not to perform elsewhere during this period. She decided to break the contract and sing elsewhere.

Held. An injunction was granted, ordering her not to perform elsewhere until the three months were up.

However, an injunction will not be granted if its effect would amount to an order of specific performance of a personal service contract.

■ *Page One Records Ltd* v *Britton* [1968] 1 WLR 157

A pop group, the Troggs, made a written agreement with the claimant in 1967. The agreement provided that the claimant should be the group's manager for a five year period, and that the group would not appoint anyone else as manager. Shortly afterwards the Troggs wanted to replace the claimant as their manager. The claimant could not have asked for specific performance because this will not be ordered in personal service contracts. Instead the claimant asked for an injunction to prevent the Troggs from employing anyone else as their manager.

Held. This injunction could not be granted. It would amount to specific performance. The Troggs definitely needed a manager. If they could not employ anyone else they would be compelled to employ the claimant or to disband. Stamp J, 'Indeed, it is the claimant's own case that the Troggs are simple persons, of no business experience, and could not survive without the services of a manager.'

However, there is no reason why an injunction should not be granted if it merely persuades, rather than compels, a person to honour a contract of employment.

■ *Warner Bros Pictures Inc* v *Nelson* [1936] 1 KB 209

The defendant, better known as the actress Bette Davis, made a two year contract with the claimants. Under this contract, which was made in the USA, she agreed to act for the claimants and not to act for anyone else. The defendant came to the UK with the intention of appearing in a film not made by the claimants. The claimants sought an injunction to prevent her from doing this.

Held. The injunction was granted. It did not compel the defendant to act for the claimants because she could earn a living performing other jobs. It was however very likely to persuade her to act for the claimants as this paid far more than any other types of work she was likely to obtain.

The injunctions which we have so far considered have been prohibitory injunctions, that is to say that they have been sought to prevent a person from breaching the terms of a contract. A mandatory injunction orders a person to commit some positive act to prevent a further breach of contract. Such an injunction is very rarely granted as a remedy for breach of contract.

7.2.5.1 Freezing injunction (formerly known as *Mareva injunction*)

A person who knows that an injunction against himself is about to be sought might attempt to pre-empt the effect of this by moving assets out of the jurisdiction of the English courts. A freezing injunction prevents specified assets from being moved out of the court's jurisdiction. It is an interlocutory injunction, meaning that it can only be ordered once court proceedings have commenced, and that it is not the final outcome of the dispute in question. The injunction was first used in *Mareva Compania Naviera SA* v *International Bulk Carriers SA* [1975] 2 Lloyd's Rep 509 and its use is now provided for by Supreme Court Act 1981 s.37(3).

The party seeking the injunction will normally do so without the other party being present. The court has a discretion as to whether or not to grant the injunction and will try to balance the interests of the parties. The claimant will have to prove not only that he is likely to win the case, but also that the defendant has assets which may well be moved out of the jurisdiction. The claimant must specify over precisely which assets the injunction is being sought, and may be asked to provide an indemnity against the injunction turning out not to have been justified.

7.2.5.2 Search order (formerly known as *Anton Pillar order*)

This injunction allows the claimant to inspect, photocopy or take away documents belonging to another party. It is sought without the other party being present and it must be necessary to prevent the other party from destroying or removing the documents. Because of the drastic nature of the injunction it is only ordered in very exceptional circumstances. The injunction was first used in the case immediately below, but is now granted by virtue of Supreme Court Act 1981 s.33.

■ *Anton Pillar KG* v *Manufacturing Processes Ltd* [1976] 1 All ER 779 (Court of Appeal)

The defendants were an English company who acted as agents for the claimants, a German company who manufactured frequency converters for computers. The claimants claimed that the defendants were passing on confidential information about their products to other German companies. The claimants applied for an interim injunction to prevent the defendants from infringing their copyrights and disclosing confidential information. They wanted permission to enter the defendants' premises to inspect all such documents and to allow the claimants' solicitor to have custody of them.

Held. An injunction was granted, allowing the claimants' solicitor to enter the defendants' premises and to remove the confidential material. This was allowed only because the claimants seemed to have a very strong case, because the actual or potential damage to the claimants was very serious, and because there was clear evidence that the defendants possessed vital material which they might destroy or dispose of so as to defeat the doing of justice.

In enforcing rights granted under a search order the claimants must act carefully and with full respect for the defendants' rights.

7.2.6 Rectification

Rectification is an equitable remedy which allows a written document to be corrected if it does not accurately reflect the terms of an oral contract which the parties subsequently decided to reduce to writing. It is not a remedy for breach of contract.

Rectification will only be ordered if the following conditions are satisfied: the parties did reach a definite oral agreement as to the terms of the contract; this agreement did not change up until the time when the contract was written down; and what was written down did not accurately record what had been agreed. An example of rectification can be seen in *Craddock Brothers Ltd* v *Hunt* [1923] 2 Ch 136. In that case there was a verbal agreement for the sale of land. When this agreement was reduced into writing there was a mutual mistake so that the written agreement did not accurately reflect what the parties had agreed. The mistake was embodied in a deed of conveyance, but the Court of Appeal ordered that the conveyance be rectified to reflect the true intentions of the parties.

7.2.7 *Quantum meruit*

A party to a contract may occasionally claim for payment on a *quantum meruit*. Such a claim will be for work done, paying the amount that is deserved. A *quantum meruit* can only be claimed in the following circumstances: if the other party prevented completion of the contract (see *Planché* v *Colburn* above at 7.1.1.3); or if work has been done and accepted under a void or partially performed contract; or if the contract did not expressly provide what the remuneration should be. If it were not for the possibility of a claim on a *quantum meruit* one of the parties to the contract might become unjustly enriched.

7.2.7.1 Restitution

Restitution is not a remedy for breach of contract, but allows a party to recover money which has been paid. In relation to the law of contract, restitution can arise in two circumstances. First, where there has been a total failure of consideration (see *Rowland* v *Divall* [1923] 2 KB 500 in Chapter 8 at 8.2.1). Second, where money was paid under a common mistake as to fact which avoided the contract (see *Scott* v *Coulson* in the previous chapter at 6.2.2.1).

Restitution, in the form of accounting for profits made while acting in breach of contract, also arose in the following case.

■ *Attorney General* v *Blake (Jonathan Cape Ltd, third party)* [2001] 1 AC 268 (House of Lords)

In 1961 a spy, George Blake, was sentenced to 41 years' imprisonment. He escaped from prison in 1966 and went to live in Moscow. In 1990 he published his autobiography, in which he described his life as a spy. This was a breach of contract because when he joined the secret services he had signed an agreement that he would never reveal anything about this work. The case was brought because Blake's British publishers had £90 000 which they intended to pay to Blake.

Held. Blake had to account to the Government, the other contracting party, for the profits he had made by doing the very thing he had contracted not to do. Such a remedy would arise only in very exceptional circumstances and only where the claimant had a legitimate interest in preventing the defendant's profit-making activity and of depriving him of his profit.

COMMENT (i) Lord Hobhouse dissented, believing that the court had sacrificed general contract principles in their desire to prevent Blake from benefiting from his deplorable criminal behaviour. (ii) In the somewhat similar case of *R* v *Attorney General for England and Wales* [2003] UKPC 22, set out in detail in Chapter 6 at 6.3.2.2, the Privy Council upheld an order for an account of profits.

7.2.8 Time limits on remedies

A person sued on a contract may be able to plead the Limitation Act 1980 as a defence.

A simple contract, that is to say one not made by a deed, cannot be sued upon after six years have expired from the date when the right to sue arose (Limitation Act 1980 s.5). It should be noted that this is not necessarily six years from the making of the contract. It is six years from the breach. If the claim is for personal injuries then the time limit is reduced to three years after the time when the right to sue arose or from the date when the injured person knew of the injury, but the court has a discretion to extend this period. Section 8(1) of the Act provides that a contract made by deed cannot be sued upon when more than twelve years have expired from the time when the right to sue arose.

Where a party is suffering from a legal disability the time limits do not run until the disability has been removed. They do not therefore run against minors until they reach the age of 18 and do not run against mentally disordered persons until they cease to be mentally disordered. Where a party is the victim of fraud the time limits will not start to run until the fraud is discovered or ought to have been discovered.

Where the claim is for a debt or is otherwise a liquidated claim, then the time limits will begin again if a person acknowledges the debt in writing. (There is no need for an agreement to pay it.) It also begins again with every payment made in respect of the debt. Where the amount claimed is unliquidated, and therefore cannot be quantified in figures, acknowledgement of it or a payment will not cause the time limits to start again.

The statutory time limits do not apply to equitable remedies, but these are lost much more quickly through 'laches' or unreasonable delay in pursuing them.

Test your understanding

1 Is an action for an agreed sum the same as an action for damages?

2 What is a claim on a *quantum meruit*? In what circumstances can such a claim be made?

3 What is specific performance?

4 What is an injunction?

Answers

1 An action for an agreed sum is not the same as an action for damages. It is an action in debt. Hence the rules on remoteness, quantification and mitigation of damage do not apply.

2 A claim on a *quantum meruit* is a claim for reasonable remuneration for work performed. Such a claim can be made: if the other party prevented completion of the contract; or if work has been done and accepted under a void or partially performed contract; or where the contract does not expressly provide what the remuneration should be.

3 Specific performance is a discretionary equitable remedy ordering a party to actually do what he agreed in the contract that he would do. Failure to comply with the order will be contempt of court.

4 An injunction is a court order requiring a person to do or not to do a certain act. It can be used to prevent a party from breaking the terms of his contract.

Key points

Discharge of liability by performance

■ A party will be entitled to treat his further obligation to perform the contract as discharged if the other party breached a condition rather than a warranty, or if the other party breached an innominate term in such a way that this breach deprived of substantially the whole benefit of the contract.

■ The general rule is that if a contract consists of one entire obligation then that obligation must be completely performed or the other party will have no obligation to perform the contract.

■ If a contract is divisible or severable then it will consist of several obligations. If only some of the obligations are performed this will not necessarily discharge the other party from performing the contract. However, damages will have to be paid as regards the parts of the contract which were not performed.

■ A party can receive payment for an entire obligation which was not completely performed if the other contracting party genuinely accepted the partial performance, or if the obligation was substantially performed or if the other party prevented complete performance.

■ A seller who properly tenders the delivery of goods discharges himself from further obligation and can sue for damages for non-acceptance if the tender is not accepted.

■ A buyer who tenders the price cannot be sued on the contract if he pays the sum tendered into court.

Discharge of liability by agreement

■ A contract can be discharged or varied by accord and satisfaction (agreement and consideration). The accord and satisfaction must amount to a new contract.

■ A party who waives a strict legal right will not later be able to claim breach of contract on account of the right waived not being adhered to. However, the right waived may be reintroduced by reasonable notice.

Frustration

■ A contract can be frustrated if after the contract has been created, but before it has been performed, any of the following circumstances arise: the subject matter of the contract ceases to exist; a person who was to perform personally has become unavailable; an event which was central to the contract has not occurred; the contract cannot be performed in the manner agreed in the contract; or the contract has become illegal to perform.

■ Frustration cannot be claimed by a party if the 'frustrating' event was his own fault, or if he was the only party who foresaw the event or should have foreseen it.

■ A *force majeure* clause spells out what should happen if an event which would ordinarily frustrate a contract arises. Such clauses are given legal effect.

■ The Law Reform (Frustrated Contracts) Act 1943 provides that when a contract is frustrated the following provisions apply: money owing ceases to be due; money paid is recoverable, although the court has a power to allow some money paid or payable to be retained to cover expenses; a party who has received a valuable benefit may be ordered to pay a just amount to compensate for this.

Discharge by breach

■ An anticipatory breach occurs when, before the time when performance of the contract was due, one of the parties lets the other know that he does not intend to be bound by the contract.

■ A party faced with an anticipatory breach may sue at once for breach of contract or keep the contract alive. If the contract is kept alive but not performed as agreed an actual breach of contract will then have occurred.

Damages

- Contract damages are designed to put the injured party in the financial position which he would have been in if the contract had been properly performed.

- Damages will not be awarded to compensate for losses which were too remote from the breach.

- A loss arising from a breach of contract will be too remote unless it it within one of the two rules in *Hadley* v *Baxendale*. The first rule is that damages can be claimed for a loss if the loss arose naturally from the breach according to the usual course of things. The second rule is that damages can be claimed for a loss if both of the parties would have contemplated that the loss would be the probable result of breach, at the time when they made the contract.

- Losses cannot be claimed in respect of a loss which could have been mitigated by the taking of reasonable steps.

- If damages agreed in the contract were a genuine pre-estimate of loss they will be classified as liquidated damages and the amount specified will be the amount recoverable no matter what the actual loss. If the sum set out is a large sum designed to warn the other party against breaking the contract it will be a penalty clause. Such a clause will be ignored and damages will be calculated as if the clause had not existed.

Other remedies

- An action for an agreed sum is an action in debt. Therefore the rules on remoteness, quantification and mitigation of damage do not need to be considered.

- A party claiming on a *quantum meruit* claims for reasonable remuneration for work performed. Such a claim can be made if: the other party prevented completion of the contract; or if work has been done and accepted under a void or partially performed contract; or where the contract does not expressly provide what the remuneration should be.

- Specific performance is a discretionary equitable remedy. When specific performance is granted a party is ordered to perform his contract. Failure to comply will put the party in contempt of court.

- An injunction can be granted to prevent a person from breaking the terms of his contract. The remedy is equitable and discretionary.

- A simple contract cannot be sued upon more than six years after the right to sue arose. If personal injuries are claimed these must generally be claimed within three years of the injuries arising. If the contract is made by deed the claim must be brought within 12 years of the right to sue arising.

- The Limitation Act does not apply to the remedies of specific performance or injunction. These equitable remedies are lost if there is an unreasonable delay in pursuing them.

Summary questions

1   Arthur agrees to sell his car to Brian for £5000. Thinking that he has won the pools, Arthur delivers the car and tells Brian that he will accept a compact disc instead of the money. Brian happily gives Arthur the disc. Arthur has now discovered that he has not won the pools. Advise Arthur as to whether or not:

   i   He can he give the disc back and insist on receiving the £5000?
   ii He could insist that Brian pays the remainder of the money if Arthur had promised to take £5 (rather than the compact disc) in full settlement of the debt.

2   Firm X has two contracts, one to supply pipes to Iran and the other to supply pipes to Iraq. During the Gulf war Britain declares war on Iraq and outlaws the export of goods to that country. It is still possible to supply the pipes to Iran but it means taking a much longer route. Advise Firm X as to whether or not either of these contracts would be frustrated.

3   In the *Davis Contractors* case Lord Radcliffe said: 'So, perhaps it would be simpler to say at the outset that frustration occurs whenever the law recognises that, without default of either party, a contractual obligation has become incapable of being performed because the circumstances in which performance is called for would render it a thing radically different from that which was undertaken by the contract.'

It can be useful to examine other cases in the light of this statement, asking whether the contractual obligation was incapable of being performed because the circumstances in which performance is called for would render it radically different from what was agreed in the contract.

For example, in *Krell* v *Henry* to have had the use of the room on a day when the procession did not take place would have been a radically different thing than what was envisaged when the contract was made.

Analyse the following cases in this way. In which of the cases would the circumstances have changed matters so that performance of the contract would be radically different from what was agreed in the contract?

a *Herne Bay Steamboat Co* v *Hutton* (the day's cruise around the fleet).

b *Davis Contractors* v *Fareham UDC* (building the 78 houses in eight months).

c *Tsakiroglou* v *Noblee Thorl* (carrying the peanuts from Sudan to Germany).

Does the use of Lord Radcliffe's test in each case provide the same result as the actual decision of the court?

4   How would *Taylor* v *Caldwell* have been decided if:

a The defendant had deliberately burnt down his own music hall?

b The defendant's own negligence had caused a fire which destroyed the music hall?

5   How would *Maritime National Fish Ltd* v *Ocean Trawlers Ltd* have been decided if the Canadian Government had issued no licences to the defendants?

6   A taxi driver orders a new car, asking the garage to adapt the car for use as a taxi. The taxi was to be delivered the following week, but due to a shortage of labour, the garage cannot deliver on time. As soon as he had made the contract, the taxi driver sold his old taxi and went on holiday for a week. On his return the taxi driver loses business until he can acquire another taxi. The stress of this causes him to suffer a nervous breakdown and he consequently spends several thousand pounds on alternative medicines. Advise the taxi driver of the amount of damages he is likely to be able to recover from the garage.

7   On Grand National day a customer hires a car to take him to Aintree. The car does not turn up. Could the customer claim damages for having missed a day at the races?

Multiple choice questions

1   A builder agreed to build a house for £50 000. The builder completed all of the work. However, he failed to glaze the windows properly, with the result that the glass is likely to fall out of the windows in a moderate to strong wind. The builder found that he had no time to replace the glass, because he had started another job at the other end of the country. The owner of the house could not move into the house until the glass was replaced, so he hired a glazier to reglaze the windows, at a cost of £500.

Which one of the following statements is likely to reflect the legal position?

a The builder will not be entitled to any payment as he did not fully perform his contract.

b The builder substantially performed and therefore will be entitled to £49 500.

c The contract was frustrated and the builder will receive an amount calculated by reference to the Law Reform (Frustrated Contracts) Act 1943.

d The builder will be entitled to the full contract price. The owner, by employing the glazier to finish the job, impliedly accepted the work the builder had done.

2   Alice decides to have her house decorated and makes a contract under which Jackie is to do the work. The contract price is £1 500, which is to be payable on completion of the work. Shortly after the contract is made Alice decides that she would rather not have the work done. Jackie has plenty of work on and agrees that Alice can pull out of the contract if she pays £50 for materials which Jackie had bought especially for this job. Alice agrees to this. The following day Jackie loses a big contract to work elsewhere. Jackie now wants to hold Alice to the original agreement.

Which one of the following statements is true?

  a The original contract is discharged. Alice will therefore have to pay the £50 for materials but no more.
  b Jackie's obligation to do the work is discharged. Alice is completely discharged from any obligation to pay any money.
  c Jackie has discharged her obligations by being willing to do the work. She can therefore insist on full payment of the £1 500.
  d Jackie can insist that the contract goes ahead. She will be entitled to full payment, but only if she decorates Alice's house as originally agreed.

3 Cilla books a room in the Granchester Hilton for the first week in August, paying her bill in advance. The price of a room in the Hilton varies throughout the year, depending on the tourist trade. The Granchester Festival takes place in the first week in August. During the first week in August the rooms in the Granchester Hilton are 10% more expensive than in other summertime weeks. Because of a protest by local residents, the Granchester Festival is cancelled. Hearing of the Festival's cancellation, Cilla phones the Hilton to say that she no longer wishes to have the room for the week and that she wants a return of her money. The Hilton refuse to return any of the money. No mention of the Granchester Festival was made when Cilla booked the room, but as it happened the whole purpose of Cilla's holiday was to attend the Festival.
      Which one of the following statements is true?

  a Cilla will not be entitled to any refund.
  b Cilla will be entitled to a full refund. The contract has become frustrated because it has become radically different.
  c Cilla will be entitled to a full refund. The contract has become frustrated because it has become impossible to perform.
  d The hotel has committed an anticipatory breach of contract. Cilla will be able to reclaim her money and perhaps also claim damages.

4 X Ltd orders 10 000 widgets from Y Ltd. The price is £10 000 and £5 000 is paid in advance. After Y Ltd have manufactured 5 000 widgets, and delivered 1 000 of them to X Ltd, the Government outlaws the manufacture and sale of widgets.
  Which one of the following statements is true?

  a The contract is frustrated. The loss will lie where it falls. Y Ltd will therefore keep the £5 000 already paid, but be entitled to no more. X Ltd can keep the widgets already delivered.
  b The contract is not frustrated because it was not X Ltd's fault that the production and sale of widgets became illegal.
  c The contract is frustrated. The £5 000 paid to Y Ltd is returnable and the £5 000 owed is no longer due. However, X Ltd will have to return the widgets already delivered.
  d The contract is frustrated. The £5 000 paid to Y Ltd is returnable and the £5 000 owed is no longer due. In addition, Y Ltd may be awarded expenses and X Ltd may have to pay an amount which is fair in respect to compensate for the benefit of the widgets already delivered.

5 Which one of the following statements is not true?
  a Damages in respect of a loss arising from a breach of contract can be recovered if the loss arose naturally from the breach.
  b Damages in respect of a loss arising from a breach of contract can be recovered if the loss would have been contemplated by both of the parties when they made the contract.
  c A party cannot recover damages for a loss arising from a breach of contract if he could have avoided the loss by taking reasonable steps.
  d A party can recover damages for a loss caused by a breach of contract as long as he can definitely prove that the loss would not have arisen if the contract had been properly performed.

6 A roofer agrees to put a new roof on a shop by 1 December for a price of £3 000. The shop owner explains that in December last year the shop made a profit of £300 per day. The roofer assures the shop owner that the job can be done on time. As the parties agree that the shop owner is likely to lose £300 a day for every day on which the shop cannot be opened, a term of the contract states that in the event of the roofer not performing the contract on time he will pay £300 damages for every day that he is late. The job turns out to be more difficult than the roofer had envisaged. The roofer does his best but cannot finish the job until 6 December. The shopkeeper admits that trade in the area has been well down on last year as a new supermarket has opened nearby. The profits made by neighbouring small shops indicate that this year the shop would only have made £150 profit per day.

Which one of the following statements is likely to reflect the true legal position?

a The contract is frustrated and the roofer is absolved from all liability. As the shop has received a valuable benefit worth £3 000, it will have to pay for this.

b The roofer will be entitled to the contract price, but will have to compensate the shop for the actual loss suffered. The roofer will therefore have to pay £150 per day damages.

c The roofer will be entitled to the contract price but will have to pay £300 damages per day, even though the shop did not suffer such a loss.

d The roofer will not be entitled to any payment. He did not perform his contractual obligations in accordance with the terms of the contract.

7 Which of the following contracts might be specifically enforceable?

i Arthur has agreed to sell his house to Bill, but no longer wishes to sell.

ii Charles has agreed to buy Duncan's house, but no longer wishes to buy it.

iii Edward has agreed to buy a new Ford Ka from a garage, but the garage is now refusing to go ahead with the contract.

iv Georgina has agreed to buy from Harold a painting by Rembrandt. Harold later changed his mind and refused to hand the painting over.

v Luciano Pavadomingo has agreed to perform a concert at Julian's theatre. Luciano has a better engagement elsewhere and therefore does not intend to perform his contract with Julian.

vi A confused World War I veteran has agreed to sell his unique medal collection to a dealer for a quarter of its real value.

a All of the agreements.

b i, iii, v and vi only.

c i, ii and iv only.

d i, ii, iv and v only.

Task 7

Last year your company, Amcafe, made a contract to buy 10 000 tons of coffee beans from a coffee wholesaler. Due to a terrible frost in South America, there is now a world shortage of coffee. The wholesaler has managed to get only 10 000 tons of coffee beans, rather than the 50 000 tons he was expecting. The price of coffee beans has increased fourfold. The wholesaler intends to sell the 10 000 tons of beans to a new customer at the current higher price.

Your employer has asked you to draft a preliminary report, indicating:

1 Whether Amcafe will be able to force the wholesaler to deliver the 10 000 tons of beans, as agreed in the contract.

2 Whether Amcafe will be able to prevent the wholesaler from selling the beans to the new customer.

3 If Amcafe do not get the beans they will have to close their factory and will also be in breach of several contracts to supply supermarkets. Assuming that they do not get the beans, and that this is a breach of contract, would they be able to claim damages against the wholesaler in respect of:

a The cost of closing their factory?

b The damages which they themselves will have to pay to the supermarkets?

c Profits they would lose by not making and selling coffee?

d Health care required by the managing director, who had a heart attack when he heard that the contract had been breached?

Chapter 8

TERMS IMPLIED BY STATUTE

Introduction

The original Sale of Goods Act was passed in 1893, and for many years it was the only statute conferring protection on those who bought goods or services. This protection was given by implying terms into the contract between buyer and seller. The 1893 Act was re-enacted and consolidated as the Sale of Goods Act 1979, the Act which is currently in force. The implied terms have been slightly modified over the years but those to be found in the 1979 Act are still very similar to the terms implied by the 1893 Act. In this chapter references to 'the Act' are references to the Sale of Goods Act 1979.

Two other statutes now imply terms in favour of those who acquire goods. We consider the terms implied by the Sale of Goods Act before the terms implied by the other two statutes for two reasons. First, the Sale of Goods Act is the oldest and most established of the statutes. Second, the other statutes modelled themselves on the Sale of Goods Act and so the case law which has refined the meaning of the Sale of Goods Act implied terms is applicable to the other statutes. Although the 1893 Sale of Goods Act was the original Act setting out implied terms, it is important to realise that the substance of the original Sale of Goods Act was not the creation of Parliament. The 1893 Act was merely a codifying statute which put all of the judge-made law into one comprehensible piece of legislation. As we shall see, in recent times this has caused difficulty with some of the words used.

8.1 · The Sale of Goods Act 1979

8.1.1 The definition of a contract of sale of goods

If a contract can be classified as a contract of sale of goods then it is the Sale of Goods Act (SGA) 1979 which implies the relevant terms into the contract in question. Our first task is therefore to examine the definition of a contract of sale of goods. This definition is to be found in SGA 1979 s.2(1), which states:

> 'A contract of sale of goods is a contract by which the seller transfers or agrees to transfer the property in goods to the buyer for a money consideration, called the price.'

There are then three requirements which must be satisfied before a contract can be classified as a contract of sale of goods. First, the buyer's obligation under the contract must be to pay a money consideration called the price. Second, the subject matter of the contract must be goods. Third, the seller's obligation under the contract must be transferring or agreeing to transfer the property in the goods to the buyer. Each of these three matters needs to be considered in turn.

8.1.1.1 A money consideration, called the price

In order for a transaction to be classified as a contract of sale of goods the buyer's consideration must consist of money. It does not matter whether the buyer pays the price in cash, or by cheque or by credit card. But a free gift, where the buyer pays no money, cannot be a sale. As well as excluding gifts, the requirement that the buyer's consideration be money rules out several types of contracts, such as contracts of barter or contracts where the buyer's consideration consists of performing some action.

It can be difficult to say whether or not a contract of part-exchange coupled with a payment of money is a sale of goods. In *Aldridge* v *Johnson* (1857) 7 El & Bl 885 the claimant gave the defendant 32 bullocks and £23 cash in return for 100 quarters of barley. The Court of Queen's Bench held that the parties intended this to be two contracts of sale of goods as the parties had valued the barley and the bullocks in monetary terms. The court was helped in reaching this conclusion because the contract stated that the barley was valued at £215 and the bullocks at £192. If the goods had not been given a price in this way then the contract would not have been a sale of goods but a contract of barter.

8.1.1.2 Sale and agreement to sell

Where the contract takes effect to immediately pass ownership to the buyer this is called a sale. Where the contract takes effect so that ownership is passed at some future time or when some condition is fulfilled this is called an agreement to sell. The time at which ownership passes from seller to buyer is considered in Chapter 9 at 9.1. Both sales and agreements to sell are covered by the provisions of SGA 1979. However, as we shall see, some very few sections apply only to sales and not to agreements to sell.

8.1.1.3 The meaning of goods

Section 61(1) of the Act defines goods as 'all personal chattels other than things in action'.

A **personal chattel** is a physical thing which can be **touched** and **moved**, for example a bicycle, a bed or a book.

A **thing in action** is a right which can only be enforced by suing (bringing a legal action). A guarantee, for example, is a thing in action. A guarantee may be written on a piece of paper but the paper is not the property. The property is the right which the guarantee gives and, ultimately, that right can only be enforced by suing the person who gave it. (See legal concepts of property in Chapter 23 at 23.1.)

Contracts to sell land or an interest in land are not included as goods, but s.61(1) tells us that emblements, which are annual crops cultivated by human labour, are included. Section 61(1) also includes as goods things attached to or forming part of the land if they are to be severed before sale or under the contract of sale.

Contracts to supply a service are not governed by the Sale of Goods Act 1979. A person who sells a service agrees to perform some action and does not 'agree to transfer the property in goods to the buyer', as required by s.2(1)'s definition. A contract of work and materials is not a sale of goods. For example, if a sculptor agrees to make a sculpture for a fixed price this is a contract of work and materials. If a sculptor sold a finished sculpture this would be a sale of goods. In making this distinction a court will try to ascertain the substance of the contract.

Goods can be existing or future. Existing goods are either owned or possessed by the seller at the time of the contract of sale. Future goods are to be manufactured or acquired by the seller after the contract of sale. There can also be a sale of goods when it is not certain that the seller will be able to acquire the goods. When future goods are sold this is, technically, an agreement to sell rather than a sale. The important point is that the agreement is governed by the Act.

8.1.1.4 Transfer of the property in goods to the buyer

When the Sale of Goods Act 1979 talks of transferring the property in goods it means that the seller must transfer the ownership of the goods. So a contract will only be a sale of goods if the seller has transferred or agreed to transfer the ownership of the goods to the buyer. This requirement rules out contracts to hire or to lease, where possession of the goods is transferred but ownership is not. Nor is a contract of hire-purchase a sale of goods. Under a contract of hire-purchase the hirer has an option to buy the goods at the end of the period of hire, but has no obligation to buy. Therefore, until the hirer exercises the option to buy, it cannot be said that the seller has transferred or agreed to transfer the property in the goods to the buyer (*Helby* v *Mathews* [1895] AC 471).

Test your understanding

1 What is the definition of a contract of sale of goods?

2 How are goods defined by the SGA 1979?

3 Which of the following contracts could be classified as contracts of sale of goods?

    a Having the windows of a house cleaned in return for £6 cash.

    b A purchase of the patent on a new invention for £12 000.

    c A purchase of a new car, paid for with a cheque for £14 000.

    d A purchase of a trolley of groceries, paid for with a credit card.

    e A 'free chicken' to customers who spend £20 in a supermarket.

    f A house bought for £95 000.

    g The sale by a farmer of 100 tons of potatoes for £6 000. The potatoes have not been grown yet, but the delivery date is fixed at 30 June next year.

    h A purchase of the copyright in a song for £100 cash.

    i A pen is bought in a shop for £19.99 cash.

    j A bicycle is exchanged for a personal stereo. Neither item is given a price.

    k A landscape painting is commissioned at a price of £200.

    l A ticket to the cinema is bought for £6 cash.

    m A television is hire-purchased over three years, at £20 a month.

    n 1 000 shares in a company are purchased for £2 000.

Answers

1 A contract of sale of goods is a contract by which the seller transfers or agrees to transfer the property in goods to the buyer for a money consideration, called the price.

2 Goods are defined as all personal chattels other than things in action. A thing in action is a right which can only be enforced by suing. A personal chattel is a physical object which can be touched and moved.

3 **a** Not a contract of sale of goods. A contract for the supply of a service.

    b Not a contract of sale of goods. A patent is a thing in action.

    c A contract of sale of goods.

    d A contract of sale of goods.

    e Not a contract of sale of goods. The customer's consideration is not money, but rather the act of purchasing the £20 worth of groceries.

    f Not a contract of sale of goods. A contract to sell land.

    g An agreement to sell future goods. The agreement is governed by the 1979 Act.

    h Not a contract of sale of goods. The sale of copyright is the sale of a thing in action.

    i A contract of sale of goods.

    j Not a contract of sale of goods. A contract of barter.

    k Not a contract of sale of goods. A contract for work and materials.

    l Not a contract of sale of goods. The ticket is a thing in action.

    m Not a contract of sale of goods. A contract of hire-purchase.

    n Not a contract of sale of goods. A share is a thing in action.

8.2 · The terms implied by the Sale of Goods Act 1979

Sections 12–15 of the Sale of Goods Act 1979 imply terms which favour the buyer into contracts of sale of goods. These terms do not need to be mentioned by the buyer or the seller, as the Act will automatically imply them. However, the terms as to satisfactory quality and fitness for the buyer's purpose are implied only into sales which are made in the course of a business.

- **Section 12(1)** implies a condition that the **seller has the right to sell the goods.**
- **Section 12(2)** implies warranties that the goods are **free from encumbrances** and that the buyer will enjoy **quiet possession** of the goods.
- **Section 13(1)** implies a condition that where goods are sold by description they will **correspond with the description.**
- **Section 14(2)** implies a condition that goods sold in the course of a business are of **satisfactory quality.**
- **Section 14(3)** implies a condition that goods sold in the course of a business are **fit for the buyer's purpose.**
- **Section 15(2)** implies two conditions when goods are sold by sample. First it is implied that the **bulk will match the sample in quality.** Second it is implied that the goods will be **free from defects** which would make their quality unsatisfactory if these defects would not be apparent on a reasonable examination of the sample.

These implied terms are important, and each one must be examined closely. It should also be realised that a new part of the SGA, Part 5A, gives significant new remedies to consumer buyers where the goods do not conform to the contract of sale (see Chapter 10 at 10.4.6).

8.2.1 The right to sell (s.12(1))

Section 12(1) of the Act provides that:

> 'There is an implied [condition] on the part of the seller that in the case of a sale he has a right to sell the goods, and in the case of an agreement to sell that he will have such a right at the time when the property is to pass.'

This term is the most fundamental of the implied terms. We have seen that the seller's obligation under a contract of sale is to transfer, or agree to transfer, the ownership of the goods to the buyer. A seller who does not have the right to sell the goods will not be able to transfer ownership to the buyer.

Section 12(3) prevents the application of s.12(1) where there appears from the contract, or is to be inferred from the circumstances, an intention that the seller should transfer only such title as he or a third person may have.

Section 12(5A) states that the term set out in s.12(1) is a **condition**, and in Chapter 5 we saw that if a condition is breached the injured party can treat the contract as repudiated and claim damages. A buyer who treats a contract as repudiated is entitled to a refund of the purchase price. As breach of s.12(1) is seen as a total failure of consideration, a buyer can claim back all of the purchase price even if he has enjoyed the use of the goods for some time, and even if the goods cannot be returned to the seller.

■ *Rowland v Divall* [1923] 2 KB 500 (Court of Appeal)

A thief stole a car from its owner and sold the car to the defendant. The claimant, a motor dealer, bought the car from the defendant for £334. The claimant painted the car and displayed it in his showroom for two months before selling it to a customer, Colonel Railsdon, for £400. Two months after this sale the police discovered that the car had been stolen. The police took the car from Colonel Railsdon and returned it to its original owner. Colonel Railsdon went back to the claimant, who returned the £400 he had paid. The claimant then sued the defendant for the return of the £334 which he had paid, arguing that there had been a total failure of consideration.

Held. The claimant was entitled to all of his money back, as there had been a total failure of consideration. Section 12(1) says that the seller must have the right to sell, and when the defendant sold the car to the claimant he did not have this right because he did not own the car. The thief never owned the car and therefore could not pass ownership to the defendant, who could not pass ownership to the claimant, etc. None of the parties except the original owner ever had the right to sell the car.

Atkin LJ: 'It seems to me that in this case there has been a total failure of consideration, that is to say that the buyer has not got any part of that for which he paid the purchase price. He paid the money in order that he might get the property, and he has not got it. It is true that the seller delivered to him the de facto [actual] possession, but the seller had not got the right to possession and consequently could not give it to the buyer. Therefore the buyer, during the time that he had the car in his actual possession had no right to it, and was at all times liable to the true owner for its conversion.'

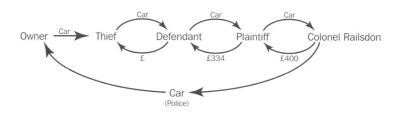

Figure 8.1

In *Rowland* v *Divall* the claimant and his customer between them had the use of the car for about four months. The case has been criticised on the grounds that in effect they got these four months' use for nothing. It has been argued that the defendant should get an allowance to cover the use of the car which the claimant had. The Law Commission examined this problem in 1987 and decided that as the defendant never had the right to sell in the first place he therefore had no right to an allowance for use of the car by the claimant or the claimant's customer. To change the law would have meant changing the law of conversion and this would have been very difficult. (The tort of conversion is examined briefly in Chapter 13 at 13.6.)

When a thief steals a car which is then sold along a chain of innocent buyers the loser will generally be the person who bought from the thief, as in *Rowland* v *Divall*. Of course this person could successfully sue the thief, but in practical terms this would be a waste of money as it is most unlikely that the thief could be found and would have the money to pay.

However, if any of the sellers in the chain has become insolvent then the person who bought from the insolvent seller will be the one with no practical remedy.

For example, let us assume that a thief steals a car from its owner and then sells the car to A, who sells it to B, who sells it to C, who sells it to D. As can be seen from Figure 8.2, A is likely to be the loser.

But now let us further assume that B has become insolvent. D can recover from C, but C cannot recover from B. Nor can C leapfrog B and sue A – there is no contract between the two of them.

The goods will always be returned to the owner because he has owned them all along. Others might have had possession of the goods, and believed that they owned them, but ownership remained throughout with the person from whom the thief stole the goods.

It is not only on account of the seller of goods not owning them that s.12(1) can be breached. In *Niblett Ltd* v *Confectioners' Materials Co Ltd* [1921] 3 KB 387 (Court of Appeal), 3 000 tins of condensed milk were sold. 1 000 of the tins were labelled 'Nissly Brand'. Nestlés warned the buyers of the milk that the word 'Nissly' was too similar to their trademark [Nestlé], and that if they attempted to sell the milk they would be prevented from doing so by an injunction. The buyers accepted that this was the legal position, and that they would be unable to resell the milk without removing the labels. They therefore sued the sellers for damages on the grounds that the sellers had breached

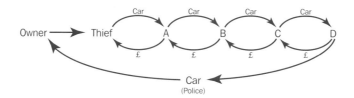

Figure 8.2

s.12(1). The Court of Appeal held that s.12(1) had been breached. The sellers did own the milk when they sold it, but they had no right to sell the milk because they could have been restrained by an injunction from doing so.

8.2.2 Implied warranties about title (s.12(2))

Section 12(2) implies two terms about title. Section 12(5A) makes it plain that these terms are warranties, so if they are breached the buyer will not be entitled to treat the contract as repudiated but will be entitled to damages.

Section 12(2)(a) implies a term that the goods are free from any charge or encumbrance which is not disclosed or known to the buyer before the contract is made.

Section 12(2)(b) implies a warranty that the buyer will enjoy quiet possession of the goods, except as regards rights of others which were disclosed or known by the buyer before the contract.

The first of these terms means that the seller warrants that at the time when ownership of the goods is to pass to the buyer nobody else has any ownership rights regarding the goods. The second warranty is an ongoing assurance that no one will interfere with the buyer's right to possess the goods. An example of breach of s.12(2)(b) can be seen in *Microbeads AG v Vinhurst Road Markings* [1975] 1 WLR 218. The sellers sold road marking machines. Unknown to the buyers or sellers a third party was applying for a patent which would affect these machines. The patent was granted and became effective shortly after the contract was made. The third party then brought an action against the buyers for breach of patent. The buyers sued the sellers for breach of s.12(1) and s.12(2). It was held that s.12(1) had not been breached because the buyers had the right to sell the machines at the time of the sale. However, s.12(2)(b) had been breached because the buyers could not continue to enjoy quiet possession of the machines.

Section 12(3) allows a seller to make a contract to transfer only such ownership as he or another person may have. For example, a seller who does not know if he owns certain goods (perhaps because of an ongoing legal dispute about the ownership of the goods) can contract to sell only such ownership as he may have. When a seller takes advantage of s.12(3) the terms implied by ss.12(1) and 12(2) do not apply. However two warranties, contained in sections 12(4) and 12(5), require the seller to disclose to the buyer all charges and encumbrances which the seller knows about and to warrant that the buyer's quiet possession will not be disturbed.

Test your understanding

1 What term is implied by SGA s.12(1)?

2 What terms are implied by SGA s.12(2)?

3 Read s.12(1) of the Sale of Goods Act 1979 on page 235. Does it provide that the seller must **have** the right to sell the goods or does it say that the seller must **think** that he has the right to sell the goods?

4 A grain merchant agrees to sell 1 000 tons of grain to a buyer, delivery to be made next November. The merchant intends to buy the grain from a Canadian exporter, but as yet this contract has not been made and so the merchant does not yet own the grain. Does this mean that the merchant breaches s.12(1)?

5 In *Rowland v Divall*, Lord Atkin stated that the seller did deliver de facto [actual] possession of the car. Why then was the buyer entitled to all of his money back?

6 A thief steals a consignment of batteries and, after the batteries have passed through a succession of buyers, a shopkeeper buys them in good faith. The shopkeeper sells the batteries to a customer who uses them until their power is exhausted.

   a Did the customer ever have ownership of the batteries?

   b Did the customer ever have de facto [actual] possession of them?

   c Did the customer ever have legal possession?

   d Ought the customer be able to claim all of his money back from the shop?

Answers

1 Section 12(1) implies a condition on the part of the seller that in the case of a sale he has a right to sell the goods, and in the case of an agreement to sell he will have such a right at the time when the property is to pass.

2 Section 12(2) implies warranties as to quiet possession and freedom from encumbrances.

3 Section 12(1) says that it is a condition that the seller must have the right to sell the goods. In *Rowland v Divall* the defendant thought that he had the right to sell, but this was no defence.

4 There is no breach of s.12(1). This is an agreement to sell in the future, and s.12(1) only requires that the seller will have the right to sell at the time when the property is to pass.

5 Because although the buyer had actual possession he never had what he paid for; the right to legal possession and ownership of the car.

6 **a** Ownership remained throughout with the person from whom the thief stole the batteries.

    b The customer did have actual possession of the batteries.

    c The customer never had legal possession, as per Lord Atkin in *Rowland v Divall* (1923).

    d The customer will be able to claim all of his money back from the shop. This involves an element of unjust enrichment, but the Law Commission Report 160 saw no way around this problem.

8.2.3 Correspondence with description (s.13(1))

Section 13(1) of the Act provides that:

> 'Where there is a contract for the sale of goods by description, there is an implied [term] that the goods will correspond with the description.'

The starting point with this section must be to consider the circumstances in which goods are sold **by description**. If the goods are not sold by description then s.13 will not help the buyer. As we shall see, the fact that there has been some description of the goods does not necessarily mean that they have been sold by description.

First we need to distinguish unascertained, future and specific goods. Specific goods are identified and agreed upon at the time of the contract, whereas unascertained goods are not. As we saw earlier in this chapter, future goods had yet to be manufactured or acquired by the seller at the time of the contract. Unascertained and future goods are always sold by description, otherwise the parties could not identify what was being sold. Furthermore, in contracts for the sale of unascertained future goods all descriptive words are likely to be part of the description by which the goods were sold. In *Reardon Smith Line v Hansen Tangen* [1976] 1 WLR 989 Lord Wilberforce indicated that in other contracts of sale of goods the sale will only be 'by description' if the descriptive words are a substantial part of the identity of what is being bought, a matter which will depend upon the intentions of the parties.

As regards specific goods, the mere fact of the seller describing specific goods to the buyer does not necessarily mean that the goods are sold by description, even if the descriptive words were identifying what was being bought. It is also necessary that the buyer relies on the description and that the description is an essential term of the contract.

■ *Harlingdon & Leinster Enterprises Ltd* v *Christopher Hull Fine Art Ltd* [1991] 1 QB 564

The sellers sold two oil paintings for £6 000, saying that the paintings were by Gabriele Munter (1877–1962), a German expressionist painter. Both the sellers and the buyers were London art dealers. The buyers were specialists in German expressionistic painting, the sellers were not. In 1980 auction particulars had attributed the paintings to Munter. The sellers had also taken the paintings to Christies who had shown an interest in them. The sellers phoned the buyers, knowing that they were specialists in German expressionist art, and asked if they might be interested in the paintings. The buyers sent round an employee to view the paintings, and the employee was told that the sellers knew nothing about the paintings and nothing about Munter. It later came to light that the paintings were a fake and were worth under £100. The buyers rejected the paintings under s.13(1).

Held. The buyers could not reject the paintings under s.13(1). The sellers had clearly made a description, but the buyers had not relied on this description when deciding to buy the paintings. The description was not an essential term of the contract and so the sale was not made by description.

Section 13(2) envisages that a sale might be made by sample as well as a sale by description and states that if this is the case then not only must the bulk of the goods correspond with the sample, but the goods must also correspond with the description. In *Nichol* v *Godts* [1854] 10 Exch 191 oil was bought by sample, the oil being described as 'foreign refined rape oil'. The bulk of the oil did correspond with the sample, but neither the bulk nor the sample matched the description as the oil was in fact a mixture of rape and hemp oil. It was held that the buyer could reject the oil, a conclusion which would nowadays be reached by applying s.13(2).

Section 13(3) states that a sale of goods is not prevented from being a sale by description by reason only that, being exposed for sale or hire, they are selected by the buyer. So the mere fact that a shopper in a supermarket has selected the goods which are to be bought will not automatically prevent the sale from being by description.

Descriptions which do not come within s.13 may still be terms of the contract. However, they might be innominate terms or warranties rather than conditions. (The difference between conditions, warranties and innominate terms is explained in Chapter 5 at 5.4.) The true significance of s.13 is that it allows the buyer to treat the contract as repudiated without having to prove that the breach has deprived him of substantially the whole benefit of the contract. Descriptions which do not amount to a term at all may be actionable misrepresentations if they were untrue statements of fact which induced the buyer to make the contract. (See Chapter 6 at 6.1.)

Having decided that a sale is made by description we then need to consider how closely the goods must correspond with the description. The old cases suggest that the required degree of correspondence is very high. Only if the description could be regarded as a trifle would s.13 not have been breached. (*De minimis non curat lex* – the law is not concerned with trifles.)

■ *Arcos Ltd* v *E. A. Ronaasen & Son* [1933] AC 470 (House of Lords)

The sellers contracted to sell a quantity of wooden staves. The staves, which were to be shipped to England, were to be of Russian wood and the sellers knew that the buyers intended to use them to make cement barrels. The contract described the length and breadth of the staves and allowed for some deviation in these matters. However, there was no allowance for deviation in the thickness of the staves, the contract describing the staves as half an inch thick. When the staves were delivered the buyers discovered that 6.4% were half an inch thick, 75.3% were between half an inch and nine sixteenths, and 18.3% were over nine sixteenths. None of the staves was over five eighths of an inch thick. The buyers rejected all of the staves, even though they were of merchantable (now satisfactory) quality and perfectly fit for making barrels.

Held. The buyers could reject all of the staves, as they did not correspond with the description by which they had been sold.

Lord Atkin: 'It was contended that in all commercial contracts … there must always be some margin … I cannot agree. If the written contract specifies conditions of weight, measurement and the like, these conditions must be complied with. A ton does not mean about a ton, or a yard about a yard. Still less when you descend to minute measurements does 1/2 inch mean about 1/2 inch. If the seller wants a margin he must and in my experience does stipulate for it. Of course by recognised trade usage particular figures may be given a different meaning, as in a baker's dozen …

If a condition is not performed the buyer has a right to reject … No doubt, in business, men often find it unnecessary or inexpedient to insist on their strict legal rights. In a normal market if they get something substantially like the specified goods they may take them with or without grumbling and claim for an allowance. But in a falling market I find that buyers are often as eager to insist on their legal rights as courts of law are ready to maintain them.'

■ *Re Moore & Co Ltd and Landauer & Co Ltd* [1921] 2 KB 519 (Court of Appeal)

The sellers, who were in Australia, sold a consignment of 3 100 tins of peaches which were to be sent to the buyers in London. The buyers rejected the consignment because the peaches had been described in the contract as packed 30 tins to a case, whereas in fact about half of the tins were packed 24 to a case instead of 30. The correct number of tins was delivered. The market value of the goods would have been the same whether they were packed 24 or 30 tins to the case.

Held. The buyers could reject all of the tins, as they did not correspond with the description by which they had been sold.

In both of these cases the buyer was a commercial buyer rather than a consumer. In holding that s.13 had been breached, and that the two buyers could therefore treat the contract as repudiated, the courts were influenced by two factors. First, commercial buyers do not include descriptions in their contracts if they do not consider them important. Second, a commercial buyer might well have sold the goods under the same description, and the easiest way to nip this ongoing problem in the bud is to hold that the first seller has breached s.13.

These two cases also demonstrate that s.13 is not concerned with the quality of the goods. In *Arcos v Ronaasen* there was nothing wrong with the quality of the staves, in *Re Moore & Co Ltd and Landauer & Co Ltd* there was nothing wrong with the quality of the tins of peaches.

It might be thought unfair that such a slight breach as occurred in each of the above two cases should be classified as a condition of the contract and therefore entitle the buyer to treat the contract as repudiated. The House of Lords considered this matter in *Reardon Smith Line v Hansen Tangen* [1976] 1 WLR 989 and suggested that some of the old decisions on s.13 might be ready for a fresh examination. However, since that case was heard the remedies available for breach of the term implied by s.13(1) have been changed. Since the amendments made by the Sale and Supply of Goods Act 1994, s.15A of the Sale of Goods Act 1979 has altered the status of s.13(1) so that it is no longer always a condition. The term remains a condition where the buyer deals as a consumer. But if the buyer does not deal as a consumer the term is not a condition where the breach of it is so slight that it would be unreasonable for the buyer to reject the goods. So if *Re Moore & Co Ltd and Landauer & Co Ltd* were to arise today the buyer would not be able to treat the contract as repudiated and reject the goods, even if s.13(1) had been breached. The buyer would of course be able to claim damages for breach of warranty.

Test your understanding

1 What term is implied by SGA s.13(1)?

2 Are unascertained future goods always sold by description?

3 In what circumstances are specific goods sold by description?

4 Mary is an antique dealer who specialises in old billiard cues and billiard accessories. She visits a local snooker hall, explaining her expertise and what she is looking for. The manager of the snooker hall shows Mary a cue and tells her that it is an excellent ash cue which is probably 50 years old. Mary asks how he knows this to be true. The manager says that he does not know much about cues, but he bought it from a customer who said it was ash and 50 years old. Mary examines the cue carefully and then buys it for £100. Mary later discovers that the cue is made of maple and relatively modern. Has s.13(1) been breached?

5 If a supermarket shopper does buy goods which are sold by description, s.13(1) will imply a term that the goods must correspond with the description. What remedies would be available to the shopper if s.13(1) was breached? Assuming that the supermarket bought the goods under the same description as that under which it sold the goods, and that s.13(1) had again been breached, would the same remedies always be available to the supermarket?

Answers

1 SGA s.13(1) implies a term that where there is a contract for the sale of goods by description, then the goods will correspond with the description.

2 Unascertained future goods are always sold by description.

3 Specific goods are sold by description where the description was an essential term of the contract on which the buyer relied, and where the descriptive words are a substantial part of the identity of what is being bought.

4 Section 13(1) has not been breached. The description given by the manager was not an essential term of the contract on which Mary relied, as per *Harlingdon & Leinster Enterprises Ltd* v *Christopher Hull Fine Art Ltd*.

5 Section 13(1) is always regarded as a condition in consumer sales. Therefore the shopper would be entitled to treat the contract as repudiated and/or claim damages. The supermarket, although not dealing as a consumer, would generally be entitled to the same remedies, for breach of condition. However, if the breach was so slight as to make rejection of the goods unreasonable, the supermarket would only be able to claim damages and would not be entitled to treat the contract as repudiated.

8.2.4 Satisfactory quality (s.14(2))

Section 14(2) provides that:

> 'Where the seller sells goods in the course of a business, there is an implied [condition] that the goods supplied under the contract are of satisfactory quality.'

This is the most significant of the statutory implied terms, but it is important to begin by considering the circumstances in which the term will not be implied.

First, the term as to satisfactory quality will not be implied unless the seller sells the goods in the course of a business. Section 61(5) SGA, the Act's definition section, tells us that business includes professions and the activities of public departments and local or public authorities. But is everything which a business sells sold in the course of a business? Until recently this matter was in some doubt, but the following case has now provided an authoritative answer.

■ *Stevenson v Rogers* [1999] 1 All ER 613 (Court of Appeal)

The defendant, who had been in business as a fisherman for 20 years, sold a fishing boat to the claimant. The boat was not being used as part of the defendant's stock in trade at the time of the sale. Subsequently the claimant argued that the boat was not of merchantable quality (the case having arisen before the requirement of merchantable quality was changed to a requirement of satisfactory quality). The trial judge ruled that s.14(2) SGA 1979 did not apply because the boat was not sold in the course of the defendant's business. An appeal was made to the Court of Appeal.

Held. The boat was sold in the course of the defendant's business. Consequently, s.14(2) implied a term that the boat was of merchantable quality. For the purposes of s.14(2) SGA 1979 the words 'in the course of a business' should be taken at face value. Any sale made in the course of a business is within s.14(2), without the need to prove any degree of regularity of such sales. Therefore sporadic sales which are no more than incidental to the seller's business are included. By contrast, purely private sales which are outside the confines of the business carried on by the seller are not within s.14(2).

If an agent, acting in the course of a business, makes a sale of goods on behalf of a principal then the principal will be liable if the goods are not of satisfactory quality and fit for the buyer's purpose. However, if the buyer is aware that the principal is not selling the goods in the course of a business, or if reasonable steps have been taken to bring this to the buyer's attention, then neither the term as to satisfactory quality nor as to fitness for the buyer's purpose is implied.

The seller's liability under s.14(2) is strict. It is immaterial whether or not it is the seller's fault that the goods are not of satisfactory quality. Often, as in the case of a retailer selling pre-packaged goods, a seller in breach of s.14(2) will have had no opportunity to discover the defect which renders the goods unsatisfactory. In such cases the seller in breach of the implied term can in turn sue the person from whom the goods were ordered. If goods are manufactured in such a way that their quality is defective, and later sold down the line to a succession of buyers who do not examine the goods or have the defect specifically pointed out to them, then every person who sells the goods in the course of a business can be sued under s.14(2).

Section 14(2C) lists two circumstances in which the term as to satisfactory quality will not be implied. First, there is no requirement of satisfactory quality as regards defects which are **specifically** drawn to the buyer's attention before the contract is made. This is the case even if the cost of repairing these defects turns out to be considerably greater than the buyer envisaged.

■ *Bartlett* v *Sidney Marcus Ltd* [1965] 1 WLR 1013 (Court of Appeal)

The sellers, who were motor dealers, sold a second-hand Jaguar. A sales executive employed by the sellers had told the buyer that the clutch was defective and that he thought this would be a minor repair, costing £2 or £3. The buyer traded in his old car and agreed to pay £550 cash. The buyer had chosen this option rather than pay £575 and letting the sellers repair the clutch. Two weeks later the buyer arranged for his own garage to repair the clutch. The total cost of this repair came to slightly over £84. The buyer claimed damages for breach of s.14(2).

Held. B could not claim damages under s.14(2). The defect in the clutch had been drawn to B's attention, and could not therefore render the car of unmerchantable (now unsatisfactory) quality.

Second, s.14(2C) provides that if the buyer examines the goods before the contract is made there is no requirement of satisfactory quality as regards defects which the examination ought to reveal. However, it is important to note that the buyer has no obligation to examine the goods. If the buyer chooses not to examine the goods before the contract is made then even highly apparent defects will render the goods of unsatisfactory quality.

The requirement of satisfactory quality extends not only to the goods bought but also to any other things supplied under the contract. In *Geddling* v *Marsh* [1920] 1 KB 668 the claimant bought a bottle of mineral water. Although the mineral water was sold, the bottle itself was not, as it remained throughout the property of the manufacturer of the mineral water. (Customers were expected to return the empty bottles to the shop and to reclaim a deposit.) The bottle exploded and injured the claimant, who was able to recover damages under s.14(2) even though the bottle itself was not sold. The bottle was supplied under the contract.

The requirement that the goods be of satisfactory quality (rather than merchantable quality) is fairly recent, having been added to the 1979 Act by the Sale and Supply of Goods Act 1994. Section 14(2A) SGA 1979 provides the definition of satisfactory quality:

'For the purposes of this Act, goods are of satisfactory quality if they meet the standard that a reasonable person would regard as satisfactory, taking account of any description of the goods, the price (if relevant) and all the other relevant circumstances'.

It can be seen that goods will be of satisfactory quality if they meet an objective standard, that which a reasonable person would regard as satisfactory. Although the description, the price (if relevant) and all the other relevant circumstances have to be taken into account, it is important to notice that the word description here is much more general than the meaning of the word under s.13. Here there is no need for the sale to be made by description. Any description of the goods will be taken into account in deciding whether the goods meet the standard which a reasonable person would regard as satisfactory. Section 14(2B) amplifies the meaning of the quality of goods, listing five aspects of quality to be taken into account in appropriate cases:

'For the purposes of this Act, the quality of goods includes their state and condition and the following (among others) are in appropriate cases aspects of the quality of goods —
(a) fitness for all the purposes for which goods of the kind in question are commonly supplied,

(b) appearance and finish,
(c) freedom from minor defects,
(d) safety, and
(e) durability.'

It is important to note that these five matters listed are not hard and fast requirements, the absence of which will mean that goods are not of satisfactory quality. They are only aspects of the quality of goods in appropriate cases. In a consumer sale of a new product all of the aspects are likely to be appropriate.

Sections 14(2A) and 14(2B) were enacted to give effect to the proposals set out by the Law Commission Report 160, 'Sale and Supply of Goods' (1987). The requirement of satisfactory quality replaced a requirement that goods sold in the course of a business should be of merchantable quality. Merchantable quality was defined by s.14(6) of the Act in the following way:

> 'Goods ... are of merchantable quality ... if they are as fit for the purpose or purposes for which goods of that kind are commonly bought as it is reasonable to expect having regard to any description applied to them, the price (if relevant) and all the other relevant circumstances.'

The Law Commission found the term merchantable quality gave rise to various problems. First, the courts interpreted it in different ways, as we shall shortly see. Second, the word 'merchantable' suggested contracts between merchants and was therefore not suitable for consumer sales. Third, the definition concentrated too heavily on the goods' fitness for their purpose and did not consider sufficiently their other characteristics. Fourth, the definition did not specify that the goods should be reasonably durable, although the case law would indicate that if they were not reasonably durable then they were not merchantable. The Law Commission accepted that it was not possible to have a single formula defining the quality required of goods sold in the course of a business. The possible circumstances in which goods might be sold in the course of a business are so varied that no single formula could possibly define the required quality in every case. Feeling that it would be wrong to apply a qualitative adjective such as 'good' (because sometimes the buyer and seller did not expect the quality of the goods to be good) the Commission considered several neutral adjectives, before settling for 'satisfactory'. It was suggested that the standard should be assessed by reference to that expected by the reasonable person, rather than that expected by a reasonable buyer, because the Commission thought that standards would drop if that test of a reasonable buyer was applied. Sellers might argue that goods of a certain type often had minor defects and that such defects would not therefore amount to a breach of contract as a reasonable buyer would be expecting them.

The views of the Law Commission on the aspects of the quality of the goods in appropriate cases are also worth considering. The Commission envisaged that all or any of the aspects might be taken into account in any particular case. Other factors might also be relevant, but the five aspects listed were commonly found to be important aspects of the quality of goods. The first aspect, fitness for all the purposes for which goods of the kind in question are commonly supplied, applies unless there is an indication to the contrary. The second and third aspects, appearance and finish and freedom from minor defects, were considered particularly appropriate to new goods and particularly to new consumer goods. As regards new consumer goods, even very minor blemishes would mean that the implied term as to quality was breached, unless the blemishes were so trifling as to be quite negligible and not breaches of contract at all. The fourth aspect, safety, was considered to be an important aspect of the quality of many consumer goods such as electrical appliances and cars. It was recognised that inherently unsafe goods which required safety precautions to be taken might not be of satisfactory quality if appropriate warnings were not given. The fifth requirement, durability, is that the goods should last for a reasonable time. The Commission did not think it possible to lay down a certain time (a week, a month or a year) for which all goods should last, as goods are so varied in their nature. The Commission considered that the requirement of durability should bite at the time of supply. At that time, the goods should be reasonably durable. If the goods subsequently break down this will be strong evidence that they were not reasonably durable at the time of supply.

However, it will not be conclusive proof. All the evidence will need to be examined, particularly the way in which the goods were treated after the time of supply.

As yet, there has been little significant case law on the meaning of satisfactory quality. In assessing the meaning of satisfactory quality, we can consider some of the cases on the meaning of merchantable quality and speculate as to whether the outcome of those cases would now be the same. When doing this it must be borne in mind that when the test was one of merchantable quality there was no s.14(2B) and no equivalent section.

In deciding whether or not goods were of merchantable quality the courts, in recent years, tended to adopt two different tests, the acceptability test and the usability test. The acceptability test regarded goods as merchantable if their condition was such that a reasonable buyer would still have bought the goods at the same price, and without any special terms, if he had known of the actual condition of the goods, including any defects, when making the purchase. The usability test regarded the goods as merchantable if a reasonable buyer could have used the goods for any of the purposes for which goods of that contract description were commonly used. The acceptability test, which tends to be more favourable to the buyer, was used more in consumer cases whereas the usability test was used more in commercial cases. The following four cases show how the two tests were applied by the courts.

■ *Aswan Engineering Establishment Co* v *Lupdine Ltd* [1987] 1 All ER 135 (Court of Appeal)

The claimants bought a large consignment of liquid waterproofing compound from the first defendants. The compound, which was for shipment to Kuwait, was contained in heavy duty plastic pails. These pails were stored inside containers. When they arrived in Kuwait the containers were left outside in the sun in temperatures of up to 70 degrees centigrade. The pails could only have tolerated these temperatures if they had been packed into the containers in a certain way. As they were not stacked in this way the pails melted and the compound was lost. Similar pails had been exported to other countries without any mishap. The claimants sued the first defendants, claiming that the pails made the compound unmerchantable. In turn, the first defendants claimed against the second defendants, the manufacturers from whom they had bought. The second defendants knew the pails were to be exported to Kuwait. The contract between first and second defendants described the pails as 'heavy duty pails suitable for export'. The first defendants went into liquidation. The claimants carried the case on against the second defendants (in negligence, alleging that the second defendants owed them a duty of care).

Held. Applying the usability test, the pails were of merchantable quality.

COMMENT (i) It might seem that this case would now be differently decided in the light of s.14(2B)(a). The Law Commission report made it plain that it considered that s.14(2B)(a) changed the principle set out in this case, that goods did not necessarily need to be fit for all their normal purposes. However, it seems unlikely that the case would now be differently decided. Leaving the goods out in the Kuwaiti sun, stacked in the way in which they were stacked, could not be regarded as a common purpose for the goods. A reasonable person would probably regard the pails as satisfactory.

(ii) If the buyer wants to use the goods for a particular purpose he should make this purpose known to the seller and ask for an assurance that the goods are fit for that particular purpose. If it turns out that the goods are not fit for that particular purpose the buyer can rely on the term implied by s.14(3).

■ *Sumner Permain & Co* v *Webb & Co* [1922] 1 KB 55 (Court of Appeal)

The buyer bought a large quantity of tonic water, intending to export it to Argentina. The Argentinian authorities refused to let the tonic water into the country because it contained salicylic acid. Other countries would not have been concerned about the presence of salicylic acid, which is an ingredient of aspirin. However, Argentinian law did not allow the acid to be present in drinks. The buyer rejected the tonic water claiming that it was not of merchantable quality. The buyer had bought the tonic water under its trade name, telling the seller that it was for export to Argentina. The seller did not know that Argentinian law prohibited the sale of drinks containing salicylic acid.

Held. Applying the usability test, the Court of Appeal held that the tonic water was of merchantable quality. The tonic water could have been used for just about any purpose other than the one for which the buyer intended to use it.

COMMENT (i) It seems likely that the tonic water would nowadays be regarded as being of satisfactory quality. There was nothing wrong with it. None of the factors set out in s.14(2B) seem to be of any relevance. Looking at the definition of satisfactory quality set out in s.14(2A), it would seem that a reasonable person would regard the tonic water as satisfactory.

(ii) The buyer was unable to succeed in a claim under s.14(3) because he ordered the goods using their trade name.

■ *Shine* v *General Guarantee Corporation Ltd* [1988] 1 All ER 911

A motorist bought a second-hand specialist sports car and found that the car gave him few problems. However, he later discovered that the car had been involved in a crash and totally submerged in water. The motorist claimed to be able to reject the car under s.14(2).

Held. The car was not of merchantable quality. Bush J applied the acceptability test and said that no member of the public who was aware of the car's history 'would touch [it] with a barge pole unless they could get it at a substantially reduced price to reflect the risk they were taking'.

COMMENT It would seem quite plain that the car would not now be of satisfactory quality. The definition set out in s.14(2A) would not be satisfied – a reasonable person would not regard the quality as satisfactory. Section 14(2B) factors (a), (c), (d) and (e) would all seem to be appropriate aspects of the quality of the car. Perhaps in the light of the new law cases such as this will no longer be defended in court.

In the following case there seems no doubt that the new requirement of satisfactory quality would result in a different outcome.

■ *Millars of Falkirk Ltd* v *Turpie* 1976 SLT 66

The claimant bought a new Ford Granada car from a dealer, trading in a Zodiac in part exchange. The Granada's power steering system leaked oil onto the claimant's garage floor. The defendants collected the car, repaired the leak and redelivered the car. However, the steering system again leaked oil onto the claimant's garage floor. This defect, which was obvious, should have been sorted out by the mere tightening of a nut and could certainly have been sorted out by installing a new power steering unit. Installing a new unit would have been quick and easy and would have cost under £25. The defendants wanted to effect this repair, but the claimant claimed to reject the car under s.14(2).

Held. The car was of merchantable quality, and so the buyer could not reject it under s.14(2). The defect was easy to cure and it was unlikely that the car could be driven for long enough to create danger. In addition, such minor defects are relatively common in new cars.

COMMENT The Law Commission thought that this case would now be differently decided. A reasonable person would not regard the car as satisfactory. Section 14(2B) factors (a), (b), (c) and (d) would all seem to be aspects of the quality which would point to this conclusion.

As we have seen, there is as yet little significant case law on the meaning of satisfactory quality. However, the following cases have given us some insight.

In *Jewson Ltd v Kelly* [2003] EWCA Civ 1030, which is considered below in relation to s.14(3), the Court of Appeal held that boilers supplied to a property developer were of satisfactory quality because there was nothing inherently wrong with the boilers. The property developer had claimed that they were not of satisfactory quality because they happened not to work well in the flats in which he had installed them. There had been discussions about the boilers' suitability between the property developer and the sellers but the developer did not rely upon the skill and judgment of the sellers as to whether the boilers were suitable for the flats in question. Clarke LJ held that in these circumstances it would be 'a startling result' if the sellers were in breach of s.14(2) when they were not in breach of s.14(3). Sedley LJ said: 'Section 14(2) is directed principally to the sale of substandard goods. This means that the court's principal concern is to look at their intrinsic quality, using the tests indicated in subsection (2A)(2B) and (2C). Of these, it can be seen that the tests postulated in paragraphs (a) and (d) of subsection (2B), and perhaps others too, may well require regard to be had to extrinsic factors. These will typically have to do with the predictable use of the goods. But the issue is still their quality: neither these provisions nor the residual category of "all the other relevant circumstances" at the end of subsection (2A) make it legitimate, as a general rule, to introduce factors peculiar to the purposes of the particular buyer. It is section 14(3) which is concerned with these.' He also said that the reasonable person in s.14(2A) was a reasonable person 'equipped with the buyer's personal agenda'. He then went on to use a soft toy as an example. The safety and durability of such a toy would ordinarily be evaluated in relation to how a toddler might handle it. If it harmed the toddler when it got into his mouth s.14(2) might well have been breached. But if it was given to a dog, and harmed the dog's mouth, the claim would have to be brought under s.14(3) or fail. (Unless the toy was bought in a pet shop, in which case this would be a relevant circumstance for the purposes of s.14(2A).)

A Scottish case, *Thain v Anniesland Trade Centre* 1997 SLT 102 Sh Ct considered whether a second-hand car which soon developed a major fault could be rejected on the grounds that it was not of satisfactory quality. The car was a five- or six-year-old Renault 19, which had done 80 000 miles. To buy such a car new would have cost about £11 000. The claimant had bought the car from a dealer for £2 995, declining to take out a three month warranty. Some two weeks after the car was purchased a differential bearing in the automatic gearbox began to make a noise. This noise became worse as the claimant continued to use the car and it soon became apparent that the gearbox would need to be replaced. This would have been uneconomic in a car of this age. The sheriff principal held that the action failed. The problem with the gearbox was one which had to be expected and one which could happen at any time, as the claimant should have been aware. The car had been examined by several knowledgeable drivers before it had been purchased, and they had found nothing wrong with it. At the time of sale the car had met the standard which a reasonable person would regard as satisfactory because there had been no noise from the gearbox, and it could reasonably be inferred that there was no defect present. As it was well known that the gearbox on a car such as this could fail at any time, the reasonable person would accept that the risk of its failing, and the need for an expensive repair, could arise at any time. It was a matter of luck when this would happen. The claimant had been unlucky. But in all the circumstances of the case durability was not a quality that a reasonable person would have demanded of this particular car. If the car had been new, one could reasonably have expected to use it for at least the guarantee period without an important component or system failing.

In *Clegg v Andersson* [2003] 2 Lloyd's Rep 32 Lady Justice Hale stated that a customer buying a high priced quality product 'may be entitled to expect that it is free from even minor defects, in other words perfect or nearly so.' (This case is considered in detail, in relation to s.35 of the Act, in Chapter 10 at 10.4.3.)

8.2.4.1 Public statements on the specific characteristics of the goods

In March 2002, SGA 1979 was amended by the Sale and Supply of Goods to Consumers Regulations 2002 and ss.14(2D), (2E) and (2F) were inserted. Section 14(2D) provides that where the buyer deals as a consumer, the relevant circumstances in s.14(2A) include any public statements on the specific characteristics of the goods made about them by the seller, the producer or his representatives, particularly in advertising or labelling. (Producer means the manufacturer of the goods, or the person who imported them into the EC or a person who put his own name, trade mark or other distinctive mark on the goods.) However, s.14(2E) provides that a public statement is not by virtue of s.14(2D) to be considered a relevant circumstance if the seller can show one of three things. First, that at the time of the contract the seller was not, and could not reasonably have been, aware of the statement. Second, that the statement had been withdrawn in public or corrected in public before the contract was made. Third, that the decision to buy the goods could not have been influenced by the statement. Section 14(2F) provides that ss.14(2D) and 14(2E) do not prevent any public statement from being a relevant circumstance for the purposes of s.14(2A) if the statement could have been a relevant circumstance regardless of ss.14(2D) and 14(2E). For the circumstances in which a buyer deals as a consumer, the SGA adopts the test set out in 5.12(1) UCTA 1977 (see 8.5 below).

A breach of s.14(2) will always be regarded as a breach of condition where the buyer deals as a consumer. Where the buyer does not deal as a consumer breach will be a breach of condition unless the breach is so slight that it would be unreasonable for the buyer to reject the goods. In such cases breach of s.14(2) will be regarded as breach of warranty, entitling the buyer to damages but not to reject the goods. (Section 15A.)

8.2.5 Fitness for purpose (s.14(3))

Section 14(3) of the Act provides that:

> 'Where the seller sells goods in the course of a business and the buyer, expressly or by implication, makes known ... to the seller ... any particular purpose for which the goods are being bought, there is an implied [condition] that the goods supplied under the contract are reasonably fit for that purpose, whether or not that is a purpose for which such goods are commonly supplied, except where the circumstances show that the buyer does not rely, or that it is unreasonable for him to rely, on the skill or judgment of the seller.'

Before we examine the liability which this term imposes on the seller, we should be aware of the four circumstances in which the term will not be implied.

First, like s.14(2), the term will not be implied unless the seller sells the goods in the course of a business. Second, the term will not be implied unless the buyer expressly or impliedly makes known to the seller, the particular purpose for which the goods are being bought. Third, the term will not be implied where the buyer does not rely on the skill and judgment of the seller. Fourth, the term will not be implied where it is unreasonable for the buyer to rely on the skill and judgment of the seller.

The buyer does not need to indicate expressly the particular purpose for which the goods are being bought, or make plain that he is relying on the seller's skill and judgment. Both of these matters can be implied. When consumers buy goods which they put to their usual purpose it will be implied that they had made known the purpose for which the goods were being bought, and that they relied on the seller's skill and judgment to supply goods which are fit for that usual purpose. However, s.14(3) does not require the goods to be fit for an unusual purpose which the buyer did not make known to the seller.

■ *Grant v Australian Knitting Mills Ltd* [1936] AC 85 (Privy Council)

While in the defendant's shop, Dr Grant selected and bought a pair of long woollen underpants. The underpants had been badly manufactured in that a chemical had not been rinsed out properly. The presence of this chemical caused Dr Grant to suffer dermatitis which hospitalised him for several months.

Held. The terms as to merchantable (now satisfactory) quality and fitness for purpose had both been breached.

Lord Wright: '[Section 14(3) SGA 1979] entitles the buyer to the benefit of an implied condition that the goods are reasonably fit for the purpose for which the goods are supplied, but only if that purpose is made known to the seller "so as to show that the buyer relies on the seller's skill and judgment". It is clear that the reliance must be brought home to the mind of the seller, expressly or by implication. The reliance will seldom be express: it will usually arise by implication from the circumstances: thus to take a case like the one in question, of a purchase from a retailer, the reliance will in general be inferred from the fact that a buyer goes to the shop in the confidence that the tradesman has selected his stock with care and skill.'

The buyer's purpose is often made known by the circumstances of the case. In *Manchester Liners Ltd v Rea Ltd* [1922] 2 AC 74 (House of Lords), for example, the seller was a coal merchant in Liverpool, who regularly supplied coal as fuel for steamships. The buyers contracted to buy 500 tons of South Wales coal to be used as fuel on the *Manchester Importer*, a steamship on the Manchester Ship Canal. The coal supplied was as described, but was unfit for use on this type of steamship. As a consequence the ship had to return to port after it had set off. The coal merchant was held liable under what is now s.14(3) of the Sale of Goods Act because the circumstances showed that the buyers had relied on the seller's skill and judgment to supply a type of coal which was fit for the buyer's purpose when placing the order. However, s.14(3) will not protect a buyer who fails to make known, either expressly or impliedly, the particular purpose for which the goods are bought. In *Griffiths* v *Peter Conway Ltd* [1939] 1 All ER 685 (Court of Appeal) the buyer bought a Harris tweed coat, which was specially made for her by the seller. Shortly after beginning to wear the coat, the buyer contracted dermatitis. The buyer had abnormally sensitive skin, but had not made this fact known to the seller. The coat would not have caused anyone with normal skin to contract dermatitis. The Court of Appeal held that the sellers were not in breach of either s.14(2) or s.14(3).

It is also possible that the buyer makes a partial reliance on the skill and judgment of the seller.

■ *Ashington Piggeries Ltd* v *Christopher Hill Ltd* [1971] 1 All ER 847 (House of Lords)

The buyers, who were manufacturers of animal feedstuffs, were asked to make food for mink, according to a certain formula. As this formula included herring meal, the buyers agreed to buy herring meal from the sellers. The sellers knew that the herring meal was going to be used to feed mink, but had never previously made mink food. The meal was contaminated with a chemical (DMNA) which reacted with the meal so that it became poisonous. The meal would have been poisonous to all animals, but it was only fatally poisonous to mink. At the time the state of scientific and technical knowledge was such that this contamination of the foodstuff could not have been suspected.

Held. Section 14(3) had been breached. The buyers had made a partial reliance on the seller's skill and judgment. The buyers might have supplied the formula, but still relied on the seller's skill and judgment to use wholesome materials.

■ *Jewson Ltd v Kelly* [2003] EWCA Civ 1030

Jewsons of Bideford, builders' merchants, sold 12 boilers to a property developer, Kelly, who was converting a former convent school building into 13 self-contained flats. Kelly wanted each flat to have a separate boiler. Having decided that oil, gas and solid fuel were all unsuitable, he realised that he had to go for electric boilers. One of the flats, however, already had an oil burning boiler so he needed only 12 more boilers. Kelly described his needs to an employee of Jewsons', who said that he would look into the problem of finding suitable boilers. The employee later told Kelly that he had been in touch with a boiler manufacturer, Amptec, and that their boilers seemed ideal. Kelly knew that the employee was only passing on what he had been told by Amptec. A meeting was held at the premises to be converted. At the meeting were Kelly, his electrician, his plumber, an employee from Jewsons and an employee from Amptec. Kelly was given a leaflet extolling the virtues of Amptec's boilers. In reliance upon what he was told at this meeting, Kelly bought the boilers from Jewsons. However, when they were installed the boilers gave very low SAP readings. (These readings are the Government's way of giving home energy ratings to individual residences.) The readings were low in respect of the flats because electricity is an expensive way of heating a residence and because the flats were poorly insulated. These low ratings caused some purchasers of the flats to be put off, as the readings meant that they could not get mortgages to buy the flats. The trial judge found that Jewsons were in breach of s.14(3) of the Act. Jewsons appealed to the Court of Appeal.

Held. Section 14(3) was not breached. Kelly did make known to the seller the purpose for which the boilers were being bought. The boilers were not fit for that purpose as they increased the risk of a delayed sale of the flats. It would be up to the sellers to show that the buyer did not rely on their skill and judgment or, that if he did, it was unreasonable for him to have done so. However, Kelly did not rely on the skill and judgment of the sellers that the boilers would be suitable for the particular flats in question. The effect of the boilers on the flats' SAP ratings was within the expertise of Kelly and his advisers, it was not within the expertise of Jewsons or Amptec.

COMMENT Clarke LJ said that the case provided an example of the principle stated by Lord Steyn in *Slater* v *Fleming Ltd* [1997] AC 471 at 486: 'After all, if the buyer's purpose is insufficiently

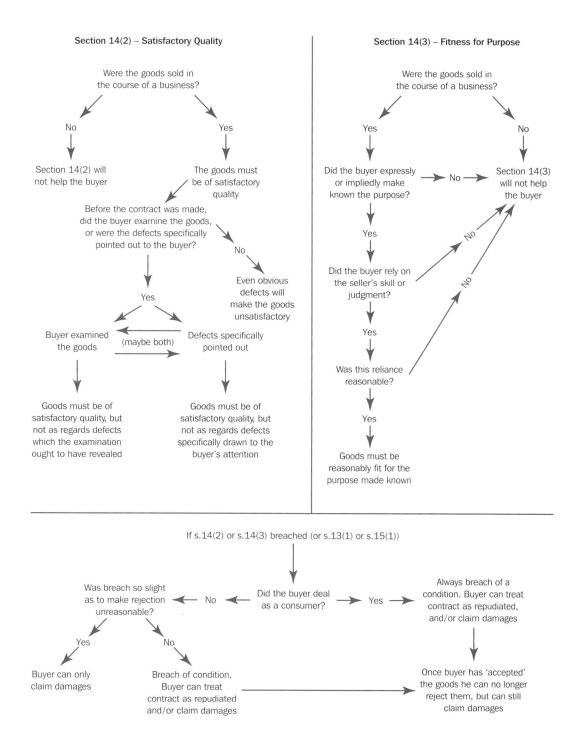

Figure 8.3   An overview of ss.14(2) and 14(3) SGA 1979

communicated, the buyer cannot reasonably rely on the seller's skill and judgment to ensure that the goods answer that purpose.'

In *Grant* v *Australian Knitting Mills Ltd* we saw that the goods sold were neither of satisfactory quality nor fit for the buyer's purpose. The seller was therefore in breach of both s.14(2) and s.14(3). Where unsatisfactory goods are bought and used for their usual purpose it will commonly be the case that the seller will be in breach of both of the implied terms. However, it is important to notice the different circumstances in which the terms are implied. Section 14(2) does not require any reliance on the seller's skill and judgment. However, it does not apply where the buyer examined the goods and ought to have noticed the defect or where the defect was specifically pointed out to the buyer. Section 14(3) does require reliance on the seller's skill and judgment, although this can be implied from the circumstances, and it does require that this reliance is reasonable. Section 14(3) can help a buyer as regards defects which were specifically pointed out, or which the buyer ought to have noticed while examining the goods. This would be unusual, but would be the case if the buyer relied on assurances from the seller that the defect pointed out or discovered would not affect the fitness of the goods for the buyer's purpose.

The following case shows that even when highly defective goods are bought for their usual purpose it is not necessarily true that both s.14(2) and s.14(3) have been breached.

■ *Wren* v *Holt* [1903] 1 KB 610

A customer bought beer from a pub. The beer made the customer ill because it was contaminated with arsenic. The seller's pub was a tied house, selling only Holden's beer. The customer knew this and had sought the pub out because he particularly liked Holden's beer.

Held. The beer was plainly not of merchantable (now satisfactory) quality and so s.14(2) had been breached. However, s.14(3) had not been breached. The customer had not relied on the the seller's skill and judgment to supply goods which were fit for his purpose in that he knew that the pub only sold the one type of beer.

When the term as to fitness for purpose is implied the standard required of the goods is that they must be fit for the particular purpose which the buyer expressly or impliedly made known to the seller. The seller's liability is strict and if an unusual purpose was made known by the buyer the standard required can be well in excess of the standard of satisfactory quality. Let us suppose for example that a consumer buys an ordinary road bicycle from a shop, having been assured by the seller that the bicycle is fit for off road use. When used on a country path one of the bicycle's wheels buckles. The seller will be in breach of s.14(3) even if the bicycle was of satisfactory quality and perfectly fit for use on roads.

Section 15A applies to a breach of s.14(3) so that the breach is always regarded as a condition, unless the buyer dealt otherwise than as a consumer and the breach was so slight as to make rejection of the goods unreasonable.

Test your understanding

1 To what extent will the term as to satisfactory quality be implied into the following contracts?

   a Adam, a postman, sells his car to Brian, a builder.

   b Adam buys a second-hand car from a garage for £8 000 after giving the exterior of the car a thorough visual examination. The car's brakes are totally unsafe (because the car's brake cylinders are worn out) and the car is very rusty underneath. Adam did not notice the rust and did not give the car a test drive as he was not insured to drive it at the time.

   c Charlene buys a new motorbike from a garage. The garage point out that the bike's fuel tank is slightly damaged and £50 is knocked off the price to take account of this. The repair to the fuel tank costs £150, three times as much as Charlene had anticipated that it would.

d David buys a new bicycle from a shop. The seller explains that some of the bicycles have been damaged in transit and so 10% is knocked off the price 'to take account of any defects'. David does not examine the bicycle before the contract is made. The bicycle's gears will not work as they have been knocked out of shape.

2 What term is implied by SGA s.14(3)?

3 Generally second-hand cars are more expensive to buy from a garage than they are to buy privately. Why might a customer who knows little about cars be better off buying from a garage?

4 David, who knows little about cars, feels that he will get a better price from a garage if he appears to have some mechanical expertise. Before buying a car he therefore kicks the tyres, looks underneath the chassis, and examines the engine. Why might these be unwise moves?

Answers

1 a The term as to satisfactory quality will not be implied at all, as the sale was not made in the course of a business.

   b If, as seems highly likely, the examination by Adam should have revealed the rust, then the fact of the car being rusty will not make the quality of the car unsatisfactory. Adam's examination of the car ought to have revealed this defect. The car will be unsatisfactory on account of the brakes being so poor. It is not the case that Adam's examination ought to have revealed this defect.

   c The damage to the fuel tank will not cause the bike to be of unsatisfactory quality. The defect was specifically pointed out to Charlene.

   d The bicycle would not be of satisfactory quality, as the gears would not work. No defect was specifically pointed out to David.

2 Section 14(3) provides that where the seller sells goods in the course of a business and the buyer, expressly or by implication, makes known … to the seller … any particular purpose for which the goods are being bought, there is an implied [term] that the goods supplied under the contract are reasonably fit for that purpose, whether or not that is a purpose for which such goods are commonly supplied, except where the circumstances show that the buyer does not rely, or that it is unreasonable for him to rely, on the skill or judgment of the seller.

3 Those who purchase privately will not be protected by either s.14(2) or s.14(3) SGA, whereas those who purchase from a garage will be protected by both implied terms.

4 David might be unwise to behave in this way because the protection conferred by s.14(2) will be lost as regards defects which the examination ought to have revealed. Furthermore, it is possible that the examination might indicate that David did not reasonably rely on the seller's skill and judgment that the car was fit for any particular purpose. This might happen if defects were particularly apparent and the seller gave no assurances about these defects.

8.3 · Sale by sample (s.15(2))

Section 15(2) SGA gives the following definition of a sale by sample:

'A contract of sale is a contract for sale by sample where there is an express or implied term to that effect.'

Where there is an express term stating that the sale is by sample then this is straightforward enough. A sale will impliedly be by sample where all of the circumstances would suggest that this is what the parties intended. In *Drummond* v *Van Ingen* (1887) 12 App Cas 284 Lord MacNaghten described the purpose of a sample. 'The office [function] of a sample is to present to the eye the real meaning and intention of the parties with regard to the subject matter of the contract which, owing to the imperfection of language, it may be difficult or impossible to express in words. The sample speaks for itself.' However, it is important to remember that not everything shown to the buyer in advance of the contract will be a sample. The parties must intend the contract to be a sale by sample.

Section 15(2) implies two terms into contracts of sale by sample:

'In the case of a contract for sale by sample there is an implied [condition] –
(a) that the bulk will correspond with the sample in quality; …
(c) that the goods will be free from any defect, making their quality unsatisfactory, which would not be apparent on reasonable examination of the sample.'

These terms are implied into all sales by sample, whether made in the course of a business or not. Section 15(2)(a)'s requirement that the bulk should correspond with the sample in quality is similar to the requirement of s.13 that when goods are sold by description they should correspond with the description. In effect the sample is the description. As we saw earlier in this chapter, it is possible that goods are sold by sample and by description, in which case they must correspond with both the sample and the description.

We have already seen that where goods are sold in the course of a business then they will have to be of satisfactory quality and that the buyer will have no obligation to examine the goods before the contract is made. Goods sold by sample will have to be of satisfactory quality, but s.15(2)(c) imposes on the buyer an obligation to examine the sample. If the bulk of the goods are of unsatisfactory quality, and if this defect could have been discovered by making a reasonable examination of the sample, then the buyer will have no remedy on the grounds of unsatisfactory quality. If the defect could not have been discovered by making a reasonable examination of the sample then s.15(2)(c) will have been breached.

■ *Godley* v *Perry* [1960] 1 All ER 36

A small newsagent who also sold toys, sold a catapult to a boy aged six for 6d. The boy was using the catapult in the normal way when it snapped and caused him to lose his left eye. The newsagent had bought several catapults from a wholesaler with whom he had dealt previously. The sale between the newsagent and the wholesaler had been a sale by sample. The newsagent's wife had tested a sample catapult, by pulling the elastic back and had then ordered two dozen. The testing of the sample had not revealed the defect which was in all of the catapults. The defect could only have been discovered by snapping a catapult or testing it to destruction. The newsagent was sued by the injured boy and himself claimed against the wholesaler.

Held. The wholesaler was liable to the newsagent for breach of s.15(2)(c). The defect which made the bulk of the catapults unsatisfactory was not apparent on a reasonable examination of the sample.

Section 15A applies to the terms implied into a contract for sale by sample. So if either of the two terms implied by s.15 are breached then this will be a breach of condition, unless the buyer did not deal as a consumer and the breach was so slight as to make rejection of the goods unreasonable.

Test your understanding

1 Which of the following sales are likely to be sales by sample?

   a A grain merchant buys 100 tons of wheat which is lying in another merchant's store.

   b A shopper examines a square metre of carpet in a shop and then orders 16 square metres of this type of carpet.

   c After test driving a demonstration model, a motorist buys a new car.

   d A shop agrees to stock a new type of pen.

   e A householder orders a three piece suite which he saw described in a magazine advertisement.

2 What two terms are implied into a sale by sample?

3 In *Godley* v *Perry* the boy sued the shopkeeper and won. Under which section(s) would the boy have sued?

Answers

1 a This is quite likely to be a sale by sample. It seems highly likely that the buyer would have insisted on examining a sample before making the purchase. Alternatively, or in addition, it might be a sale by description.

   b This would be a sale by sample.

   c This is not a sale by sample as there is no bulk and no sample. It is a sale by model. There is no SGA term requiring correspondence with the model, but there would be a common law term to this effect.

   d This could well be a sale by sample. When selling to retailers salesmen often bring samples of new products. (As was the case in *Godley* v *Perry*.) If the retailer examined such a sample and then placed the order in reliance on the examination the sale would be by sample.

   e This would be a sale by description rather than a sale by sample.

2 The two implied terms are that the bulk will correspond with the sample in quality; and that the goods will be free from any defect, making their quality unsatisfactory, which would not be apparent on reasonable examination of the sample.

3 The boy would sue the shop under s.14(2) and (3) SGA. The catapult was plainly not of satisfactory quality. Nor was it fit for the boy's purpose. (As this purpose was the usual purpose, it would have impliedly been made known to the shop-keeper.) Both s.14(2) and (3) would therefore have been breached.

8.3.1 Additional rights of buyer in consumer cases

When there is a breach of ss.13–15 of the Act and the buyer deals as a consumer then Part 5A of the Act, ss.48A–F, gives additional remedies. These remedies which arise when the goods do not conform to the contract, are considered in detail in Chapter 10 at 10.4.6.

8.4 · Implied terms in contracts other than sales of goods

As we have seen, the terms implied by the Sale of Goods Act have given excellent protection to buyers of goods since 1893. However, the Act has never applied to contracts which do not fit within the definition of a contract of sale of goods. In the 1970s Parliament passed several statutes which extended the Sale of Goods Act implied terms into other types of contract.

8.4.1 Terms implied into contracts of hire-purchase

The Supply of Goods (Implied Terms) Act (SGITA) 1973 extended the statutory implied terms into contracts of **hire-purchase**. The terms are virtually identical in effect to the terms implied by ss.12–15 of the Sale of Goods Act, and are contained in the following sections.

- **Section 8(1)(a) – The right to sell** (When the property is to pass)
- **Section 8(1)(b) – Quiet possession and freedom from encumbrances**
- **Section 9(1) – Correspondence with description**
- **Section 10(2) – Satisfactory quality** (Where goods hired in the course of a business)
- **Section 10(3) – Fitness for buyer's purpose** (Where goods hired in the course of a business)
- **Section 11(1) – Correspondence with sample**

As the terms implied are so similar to the SGA implied terms we do not need to examine them in any detail. Case law on the Sale of Goods Act will be applicable to the terms implied by SGITA 1973. Although SGITA 1973 s.8(1)(a) does not imply a term that the bailor owns the goods at the commencement of the hire-purchase contract, such a term is implied at common law. It is well settled that if this term is breached the bailor is entitled to a full refund of all payments made and to claim damages for additional expenses incurred.

A contract of hire-purchase is one whereby a person (the bailee) agrees to hire goods for a fixed period, and is given an option to purchase the goods for a nominal sum at the end of that period. Let us look, for example, at Mrs Smith who takes a car on hire-purchase from a garage. The car would have cost £7000 to buy, but Mrs Smith takes it on hire-purchase for three years at £340 a month. Until the final payment is made Mrs Smith is merely hiring the car. If she continues to hire the car for the full three year period her final instalment will contain a nominal purchase price and she will have bought the car. The nature of a contract of hire-purchase is examined in more detail in Chapter 14 at 14.2.2. Here we are concerned with the statutory terms implied into such contracts.

When we consider the Consumer Credit Act 1974, we shall see that it gives many other rights to hire-purchasers. But it is ss.8–11 SGITA 1973 which imply terms as to title, correspondence with description, quality and correspondence with sample. Section 10 SGITA 1973, which implies the terms as to satisfactory quality and fitness for purpose, applies only if the owner of the goods makes the hire-purchase agreement in the course of a business. The other sections apply to all contracts of hire-purchase. In almost all hire-purchase agreements the owner of the goods will make the agreement in the course of a business. Earlier in this chapter, at 8.2.4.1 we saw that the recently introduced SGA 1979 ss.14(2D)–(2F) set out the circumstances in which public statements made about the specific characteristics of the goods can be relevant circumstances for the purposes of determining whether the goods meet the standard which a reasonable person would regard as satisfactory. These sections are reproduced in relation to contracts of hire-purchase as SGITA 1973 ss.10(2D)–10(2F).

8.4.2 Terms implied into contracts for the transfer of property in goods and contracts of hire

Part 1 of the Supply of Goods and Services Act 1982 implies terms into contracts for the **transfer of property in goods**, and into contracts for the **hire of goods**. The terms are contained in the following sections.

Contracts for the transfer of property in goods

- Section 2(1) – **The right to transfer the property**
- Section 2(2) – **Quiet possession and freedom from encumbrances**
- Section 3(2) – **Correspondence with description**
- Section 4(2) – **Satisfactory quality** (Where the property is transferred in the course of business)
- Section 4(5) – **Fitness for buyer's purpose** (Where the property is transferred in the course of business)
- Section 5(2) – **Correspondence with sample**

Contracts of hire

- Section 7(1) – **The right to hire**
- Section 7(2) – **Quiet possession and freedom from encumbrances**
- Section 8(2) – **Correspondence with description**
- Section 9(2) – **Satisfactory quality** (Where goods are supplied in course of business)
- Section 9(5) – **Fitness for buyer's purpose** (Where goods are supplied in course of business)
- Section 10(2) – **Correspondence with sample**

A contract for the transfer of property in goods includes any contract which involves ownership of the goods passing, unless such a contract is a sale of goods, a hire-purchase agreement, or is made by redeeming trading stamps. The types of contracts which are excluded do not need SGSA 1982 to imply the terms as other pre-existing statutes already do this. A contract to have central heating put in a house would be a contract for the transfer of property in goods and the terms implied by SGSA 1982 ss.2–5 would therefore be implied into it. The contract would also be a contract for the supply of a service, and so s.13(1) SGSA (which is explained below at 8.4.3) would also imply a term that the service was carried out using reasonable care and skill. If goods supplied to a consumer do not conform to the contract then SGSA ss.11M–S give important new remedies to the consumer (see Chapter 10 at 10.4.6).

A contract of hire is not a contract to transfer the property in goods as the customer never acquires ownership of the goods hired, but only temporary possession. The Sale of Goods Act does not therefore apply to contracts of hire and so ss.7–10 SGSA 1982 are needed to cater for contracts of hire. Earlier in this chapter, at 8.2.4.1 we saw that the recently introduced SGA 1979 ss.14(2D)–(F) set out the circumstances in which public statements made about the specific characteristics of the goods can be relevant circumstances for the purposes of determining whether the goods meet the standard which a reasonable person would regard as satisfactory. These sections are reproduced as ss.4(2B)–4(2D) SGSA (in relation to contracts for the transfer of property in goods) and ss.9(2B)–9(2D) SGSA (in relation to contracts of hire).

Figure 8.4 shows which sections of which statutes imply the terms into the various types of contracts under which the ownership or possession of goods are passed.

Type of contract / Term implied	Sale of goods	Hire-purchase	Transfer of the property in goods	Hire
Right to sell	SGA 1979 s.12(1)	SGITA 1973 s.8(1)(a)	SGSA 1982 s.2(1)	SGSA 1982 s.7(1)
Quiet possession and freedom from encumbrances	SGA 1979 s.12(2)	SGITA 1973 s.8(1)(b)	SGSA 1982 s.2(2)	SGSA 1982 s.7(2)
Correspondence with description	SGA 1979 s.13(1)	SGITA 1973 s.9(1)	SGSA 1982 s.3(2)	SGSA 1982 s.8(2)
Satisfactory quality in business sales	SGA 1979 s.14(2)	SGITA 1973 s.10(2)	SGSA 1982 s.4(2)	SGSA 1982 s.9(2)
Fitness for purpose in business sales	SGA 1979 s.14(3)	SGITA 1973 s.10(3)	SGSA 1982 s.4(5)	SGSA 1982 s.9(5)
Correspondence with sample	SGA 1979 s.15(2)	SGITA 1973 s.11(1)	SGSA 1982 s.5(2)	SGSA 1982 s.10(2)

Figure 8.4   **The terms implied by SGA 1979, SGITA 1973 and SGSA 1982**

8.4.3 Terms implied into contracts for the supply of a service

All of the terms which we have so far considered are implied only into contracts under which the ownership or possession of **goods** is transferred. Part II of the Supply of Goods and Services Act 1982 codified the common law to imply three terms into contracts for the supply of a service. These terms are implied by the following sections:

- **Section 13(1) – Implies a term that the supplier should exercise reasonable care and skill** (Where supplier is acting in the course of a business)
- **Section 14(1) – Implies a term about time of performance** (Where supplier is acting in the course of a business)
- **Section 15(1) – Implies a term about consideration**

As there are no such equivalent terms implied by the Sale of Goods Act, we need to consider the effect of these three terms in some detail.

8.4.3.1 Reasonable care and skill (s.13)

Section 13 of the Supply of Goods and Services Act 1982 provides that:

> 'In a contract for the supply of a service where the supplier is acting in the course of a business, there is an implied term that the supplier will carry out the service with reasonable care and skill.'

This term is implied only where the supplier of the service is acting in the course of a business. It might therefore be thought that the term is similar in effect to the SGA implied terms as to satisfactory quality and fitness for purpose. However, the term as to carrying out the service with reasonable care and skill is very different in that it implies a tort standard of reasonable care rather than the strict liability standard of satisfactory quality. In *Greaves & Co Contractors Ltd* v *Baynham, Meickle & Partners* [1975] 3 All ER 99 Lord Denning MR contrasted the different standards required of a surgeon agreeing to provide a service and a dentist agreeing to sell goods, 'The surgeon does not warrant that he will cure the patient. Nor does the solicitor warrant that he will win the case. But, when a dentist agrees to make a set of false teeth for a patient, there is an implied warranty that they will fit his gums.'

The standard required of a person providing a service in the course of a business was considered in the following case. Although the case pre-dates the Supply of Goods and Services Act 1982, that Act codified the law and so the case is still relevant in determining the standard required.

■ *Bolam v Friern Hospital Management Committee* [1957] 2 All ER 118

The claimant was suffering from a mental illness. On the advice of a consultant he attended the defendant hospital for electro-convulsive therapy. He signed a consent form which did not warn him that this treatment involved a 1 in 10 000 risk of fractures. The claimant suffered fractures while undergoing the treatment. The risk of fractures could have been greatly reduced by the use of relaxant drugs. At the time there were two prevailing bodies of medical opinion about the use of relaxant drugs and manual control while undergoing the treatment. One body of opinion, which had subsequently become accepted as correct, was that relaxant drugs should be used unless there was a reason why they would be considered inappropriate. The alternative view was that relaxant drugs might discourage mentally ill patients from undergoing the treatment. The claimant argued that the defendants had been negligent in administering the treatment without either relaxant drugs or manual control and in not warning him of the risks of the treatment.

Held. The hospital had not been negligent. A doctor who acts in accordance with the opinion of skilled medical men is not negligent merely because there are other skilled medical men who take a contrary view.

However, in *Bolitho v City & Hackney Health Authority* [1998] AC 232 the House of Lords held that the mere fact that some distinguished experts would agree with the actions taken by a defendant doctor would not necessarily mean that the defendant doctor had not been negligent. (See Chapter 12 at 12.2.2.)

It may of course be the case that the supplier of the service does guarantee that the service will have the desired effect. If this is the case then breach of this express term will result in strict contractual liability. In *Thake and another v Maurice* [1986] 1 All ER 497 a surgeon carried out a vasectomy which did not have the desired effect. The surgeon had performed the operation successfully, but the effect of a very few vasectomies can be reversed naturally. The doctor was not liable to the patient, although he would have been if he had expressly and clearly guaranteed that the operation would be successful.

The yardstick by which those who supply services is measured is that of reasonable care and skill. However, this is an objective assessment. It is no defence to a person who has only recently begun to supply a service that he is not quite up to scratch yet. In *Nettleship v Weston* [1971] 2 QB 691 a learner driver crashed the car and this injured the person who was teaching her to drive. The Court of Appeal held that the duty of care which the driver owed to passengers and the public was the same objective and impersonal standard as every other driver owed, even though she was a learner.

This term implied by s.13 is an innominate term rather than a condition or a warranty. The customer will therefore only be entitled to treat the contract as repudiated if the breach of the term deprived him of substantially the whole benefit of the contract. (Innominate terms were considered in Chapter 5 at 5.4.2.) If a service is supplied other than in the course of a business s.13 will not apply. However, the common law would imply a term that the service be supplied using reasonable care and skill, as was demonstrated by *Nettleship v Weston*. The degree of care and skill expected would be that of a competent amateur rather than that of a competent tradesperson.

Contracts can be classified as contracts for the supply of a service even though the possession or ownership of goods is also to be transferred. So a contract to buy tyres from a garage, where the garage is to fit the tyres, would be a contract of sale of goods as well as a contract for the supply of a service. Sections 13–15 of SGSA 1982 would imply terms into the contract, but so would ss.13–15 of SGA 1979. If the tyres were not of satisfactory quality the buyer would sue under SGA s.14(2). If the tyres were not fitted properly the buyer would sue under s.13(1) SGSA 1982. If a contract was made to service a car then this would be a contract to provide services. If the car owner was injured as a result of the service being negligently performed he would sue under SGSA s.13. If he was injured because a spare part fitted as part of the service was not of satisfactory quality he would sue under SGSA s.4(2).

8.4.3.2 Time of performance (s.14(1))

Section 14(1) of the Supply of Goods and Services Act 1982 provides that:

> 'Where, under a contract for the supply of a service by a supplier acting in the course of a business, the time for the service to be carried out is not fixed by the contract, left to be fixed in a manner agreed by the contract or determined by the course of dealing between the parties, there is an implied term that the supplier will carry out the service within a reasonable time.'

Again this term is implied only into contracts for the supply of a service where the supplier is acting in the course of a business. It is important to note that the term will only be implied where the time for the service to be carried out is not fixed by the contract, left to be fixed in a manner agreed by the contract or determined by a course of dealing between the parties. Section 14(2) tells us that what is a reasonable time is a question of fact.

8.4.3.3 Reasonable price (s.15(1))

Section 15(1) SGSA 1982 provides that:

> 'Where, under a contract for the supply of a service, the consideration for the service is not determined by the contract, left to be determined in a manner agreed by the contract or determined by the course of dealing between the parties, there is an implied term that the party contracting with the supplier will pay a reasonable charge.'

Unlike the other two terms implied into contracts to supply a service, this term is implied whether the supplier is acting in the course of a business or not. The term is not implied where the consideration for the service has been determined by the contract, or left to be determined in a manner agreed by the contract, or has been determined by a course of dealing between the parties. Difficulties can arise when a customer is given a price in advance but it is not made clear whether this is definitely the contract price. A quotation is regarded as a definite price at which the contract will be performed, whereas an estimate is only an indication of what the price is likely to be. When s.15(1) takes effect, s.15(2) tells us that what is a reasonable charge is a question of fact.

8.4.4 The status of the statutory implied terms

The terms as to the right to sell goods contained in SGA 1979 s.12(1), and the equivalent terms contained in SGITA 1973 s.8(1)(a) and SGSA 1982 ss.2(1) and 7(1) are conditions. Breach of these terms will always give the buyer the right to treat the contract as repudiated and reclaim all of the price because if the seller or owner does not have the right to sell or hire the goods this amounts to a total failure of consideration.

The terms as to freedom from encumbrances and quiet possession are classified by the various statutes as warranties. Breach of these terms will therefore entitle the buyer or hirer to damages but will not give the right to treat the contract as repudiated.

Section 15A SGA 1979 deals with the status of the SGA terms as to correspondence with description, satisfactory quality, fitness for purpose and correspondence with sample. It tells us that although these terms are conditions, a buyer who does not deal as a consumer will only be able to treat breach of them as a breach of warranty if the breach is so slight that it would be unreasonable for the buyer to reject the goods. This is the case unless a contrary intention appears in the contract or can be implied from it. The section does not state that a buyer who deals as a consumer will always be able to reject the goods for breach of the implied terms, but it does imply this.

So when the implied terms in SGA 1979 ss.13–15 are breached the buyer is always given a right to reject the goods unless: (i) the buyer does not deal as a consumer; and (ii) the breach is so slight that it would be unreasonable for the buyer to reject; and (iii) the contract has not expressly or impliedly given the buyer a right to reject even as regards a breach which is so slight that it would be unreasonable for him to reject. However, s.11(4) SGA 1979 provides that where a buyer has accepted goods, or part of them, he can only treat a breach of condition by the seller as a breach of warranty. The ways in which goods are accepted are rather technical and are dealt with in Chapter 10 at 10.4.3.

Terms which are the direct equivalent of SGA 1979 s.15A are contained in the SGITA 1973 s.11A and SGSA 1982 ss.5A and 10A.

The term implied by s.13 SGSA 1982 is not classified by the Act as either a condition or a warranty and is therefore an innominate term. The buyer can therefore treat the contract as repudiated only if the breach substantially deprives of the whole intended benefit of the contract.

Test your understanding

1 By which section of which statute are the following terms implied? If the term is implied only where the seller/hirer is acting in the course of a business indicate that this is so.

   a Satisfactory quality in contracts of hire?

   b The right to sell in contracts for the transfer of property in goods?

   c Correspondence with description in sales of goods?

   d That reasonable care and skill will be used when a service is supplied?

   e Fitness for the buyer's purpose in contracts of hire-purchase?

2 Are the following statutory implied terms conditions, warranties or innominate terms? What is the significance of the distinction?

   a The implied term as to satisfactory quality in contracts of hire-purchase.

   b The implied terms as to freedom from encumbrances and quiet possession in contracts of sale of goods.

   c The implied term that reasonable care and skill will be used in the supply of a business service.

Answers

1 a SGSA 1982 s.9(2). (Only if the owner of the goods is acting in the course of a business.)
   b SGSA 1982 s.2(1).
   c SGA 1979 s.13(1).
   d SGSA 1982 s.13. (Only if the supplier of the service is acting in the course of a business.)
   e SGITA 1973 s.10(3).

2 a A condition.
   b Warranties.
   c An innominate term.
   Breach of warranty will entitle the buyer/hirer to damages but not to treat the contract as repudiated. Breach of a statutory condition as to correspondence with description, satisfactory quality, fitness for purpose or correspondence with sample will entitle the buyer/hirer to damages and to treat the contract as repudiated unless the buyer was not a consumer, and the breach was so slight as to make rejection of the goods unreasonable, and no term gave the right to reject the goods for such a breach. Breach of an innominate term will entitle the injured party to treat the contract as repudiated only if the breach deprived of substantially the whole benefit of the contract. Damages for breach will always be available.

8.5 · Exclusion of the statutory implied terms

We saw in Chapter 5 that an exclusion clause is a contractual term which tries to limit or exclude liability. Until relatively recently exclusion clauses could take away a customer's statutory rights, and this severely limited the effect of the terms implied by the Sale of Goods Act. We saw an example of this in *L'Estrange* v *Graucob* [1934] 2 KB 394. It might be remembered that in that case a café owner who bought a cigarette vending machine signed a sales agreement without reading it. The sales agreement said, in regrettably small print, that the café owner gave up all of her statutory rights. The machine did not work properly and was not therefore fit for the buyer's purpose. Even so, there was nothing the café owner could do. She had unwittingly agreed that the implied terms as to merchantable (now satisfactory) quality and fitness for purpose should be excluded from the contract which she was making.

In Chapter 5 at 5.6 we considered the Unfair Contract Terms Act 1977 in some detail. We saw that UCTA specifically mentions the terms implied by ss.12–15 of the Sale of Goods Act, and that subsequent legislation has extended the protection conferred by UCTA to cover the terms implied by SGITA 1973 and SGSA 1982. It is worth repeating this protection, in outline, here.

In the context of excluding the statutory implied terms under which the ownership or possession of goods is to pass, the Unfair Contract Terms Act makes a distinction between a person who 'deals as a consumer' and one who does not.

This distinction is vitally important here because ss.6 and 7 UCTA provide that:

(a) When the buyer deals as a consumer the terms as to correspondence with description, satisfactory quality, fitness for purpose or correspondence with sample cannot be excluded or restricted by any contract term.
(b) When the buyer does not deal as a consumer these terms can be excluded or restricted, but only by a term which satisfies the Act's requirement of reasonableness.

Section 6 UCTA 1977 deals with exclusion of the terms implied by the Sale of Goods Act 1979 and the Supply of Goods (Implied Terms) Act 1973. Section 7 UCTA 1977 deals with exclusion of the terms implied by the Supply of Goods and Services Act 1982.

It will be remembered that s.12(1) UCTA provides that a person deals as a consumer if:

(a) he neither makes the contract in the course of a business nor holds himself out as doing so; and
(b) the other party does make the contract in the course of a business; and
(c) (which applies only in cases where the potential consumer is a company rather than an individual) the goods supplied under the contract are of a type ordinarily supplied for private use or consumption.

For example, when a customer buys a television from a shop for his own personal use the customer deals as a consumer. He is not in the business of buying televisions, whereas the shop is in the business of selling televisions. When the shop orders a new consignment of televisions from the manufacturer the shop does not deal as a consumer because the shop is buying the televisions in the course of business. In Chapter 5 we saw that in *R & B Customs Brokers Ltd* v *United Dominions Trust Ltd* [1988] 1 All ER 847 the Court of Appeal held that a company can in some circumstances buy as a consumer.

However, this will bring in the requirement in UCTA s.12(1)(c) that the goods are of a type ordinarily supplied for private use or consumption (such as a television). Section 12(2)(b) provides that companies who buy goods at auction or by competitive tender are never to be regarded as consumers. Section 12(2)(a) provides that individuals who buy goods at public auctions are not to be regarded as consumers if the goods were second-hand and the individuals had the opportunity of attending the auction in person. When a person claims to deal as a consumer the burden of proof is on the other party to show that he does not deal as a consumer.

Sections 6 and 7 UCTA provide that as regards a person who is not dealing as a consumer the terms implied by the various statutes are excludable only to the extent that the term excluding liability satisfies the Act's requirement of reasonableness. Schedule 2 to the Unfair Contract Terms Act describes the factors which a court will consider in assessing whether or not the exclusion clause was reasonable. It might be remembered that these factors are:

(a) The relative strength of the parties' bargaining position, which will include whether or not the customer could find another supplier.
(b) Whether the customer was given any inducement to agree to the term, or could have agreed a similar contract with another person without having to agree to a similar term.
(c) Whether the customer knew or ought reasonably to have known of the existence and extent of the term.
(d) Where the term excludes liability unless some condition is complied with, whether or not it was reasonably practicable to comply with that condition.
(e) Whether the goods were manufactured, altered or adapted to the special order of the customer.

It should also be remembered that the Unfair Terms in Consumer Contracts Regulations 1999, considered in Chapter 5 at 5.7, might provide additional protection as regards terms made between a supplier and a consumer if these terms were not individually negotiated.

Sections 6 and 7 UCTA provide that the implied terms as to title cannot be excluded by any contract term. If the supplier does not have title to what he supplies under the contract then there has been a total failure of consideration, and no term can protect against this.

UCTA applies to the term implied by s.13 SGSA (that a service supplied in the course of a business will be supplied using reasonable care and skill), in a rather different way. Sections 6 and 7 UCTA do not apply to the term implied by s.13 SGSA. However, s.2 UCTA will apply. In Chapter 5 we saw that s.2(1) UCTA provides that a person cannot by reference to any contract term exclude or restrict liability for death or personal injury caused by negligence. Section 2(2) UCTA allows a term to exclude or restrict liability for other loss or damage caused by negligence in so far as the term satisfies the requirement of reasonableness. A supplier in breach of s.13 SGSA 1982 will have been negligent for the purposes of UCTA.

Test your understanding

1 How does s.12(1) UCTA 1977 define dealing as a consumer?

2 To what extent will UCTA 1977 allow a term to exclude liability for breach of the following statutory implied terms?

 a Section 9(2) SGSA 1982 is breached when a car hire business hires a car which is not of satisfactory quality to Jemima, a doctor.

 b Section 14(2) and 14(3) SGA 1979 are breached when bicycles sold to a shop by the manufacturer prove not to be of satisfactory quality or fit for the buyer's purpose.

 c Section 13 SGSA 1982 is breached when a plumber repairs a burst water pipe in a negligent manner, so that it soon begins to leak.

Answers

1 s.12(1) UCTA provides that a person deals as a consumer if: (a) he neither makes the contract in the course of a business nor holds himself out as doing so; and (b) the other party does make the contract in the course of a business; and (c) (which applies only in cases where the potential consumer is a company rather than an individual) the goods supplied under the contract are of a type ordinarily supplied for private use or consumption.

2 a As Jemima deals as a consumer, s.7 UCTA 1977 provides that liability for breach of s.9(2) SGSA 1982 cannot be excluded by any contract term.

 b As the shop owner did not deal as a consumer, s.6 UCTA 1977 provides that liability for breach of the terms implied by s.14(2) and (3) SGA 1979 can be excluded only in so far as the term excluding liability satisfies UCTA's requirement of reasonableness.

c   If the failure to supply the service using reasonable care and skill caused death or personal injury to any person then s.2(1) UCTA 1977 provides that no term can exclude liability for this. If the failure to supply the service using reasonable care and skill caused other loss or damage, s.2(2) UCTA 1977 provides that liability for this can be excluded to the extent that the term which excludes liability satisfies UCTA's requirement of reasonableness.

Key points

Terms implied by the Sale of Goods Act 1979

- The Sale of Goods Act 1979 implies terms only into contracts of sale of goods.

- A contract of sale of goods is a contract by which the seller transfers or agrees to transfer the property in goods to the buyer for a money consideration, called the price.

- Section 12(1) implies a condition that the seller has the right to sell the goods. If this term is breached the buyer will be entitled to a full refund of the price even if he has had the use of the goods for some time.

- Section 12(2) implies warranties that the goods are free from encumbrances and that the buyer will enjoy quiet possession of the goods.

- Section 13(1) implies a condition that goods will correspond with any description by which they were sold.

- Unascertained future goods are always sold by description. In other contracts of sale of goods the sale will only be 'by description' if the descriptive words are a substantial part of the identity of what is being bought and if the description is an essential term of the contract.

- Section 14(2) implies a condition that goods sold in the course of a business are of satisfactory quality.

- The seller's liability under s.14(2) is strict. However, there is no requirement of satisfactory quality as regards defects which are specifically drawn to the buyer's attention before the contract is made.

- If the buyer examines the goods before the contract is made, which he has no obligation to do, there is no requirement of satisfactory quality as regards defects which the examination ought to have revealed.

- Goods are of satisfactory quality if they meet the standard which a reasonable person would regard as satisfactory, taking account of any description of the goods, the price (if relevant) and all the other relevant circumstances.

- If the buyer deals as a consumer, public statements about the specific characteristics of the goods can be a relevant circumstance for deciding whether or not the goods meet the standard which a reasonable person would regard as satisfactory.

- In appropriate cases the following matters, among others, are aspects of the quality of goods: (a) fitness for all the purposes for which goods of the kind in question are commonly supplied; (b) appearance and finish; (c) freedom from minor defects; (d) safety; and (e) durability.

- Section 14(3) implies a condition that goods sold in the course of a business will be fit for the buyer's purpose.

- The term implied by s.14(3) will not be implied unless the buyer expressly or impliedly makes known to the seller, the particular purpose for which the goods are being bought. Nor will it be implied where the buyer does not rely on the skill and judgment of the seller. Nor where it is unreasonable for the buyer to rely on the skill and judgment of the seller.

- Section 15(2) implies two conditions when goods are sold by sample. First, it is implied that the bulk of the goods will match the sample in quality. Second, it is implied that the goods will be free from defects which would make their quality unsatisfactory if these defects would not be apparent on a reasonable examination of the sample.

Terms implied by other statutes

- Terms which are virtually identical to those implied by SGA 1979 are implied by SGITA 1973 into contracts of hire-purchase, and by SGSA 1982 into both contracts for the transfer of property in goods and into contracts of hire.

- Section 13 SGSA 1982 provides that in a contract for the supply of a service where the supplier is acting in the course of a business, there is an implied term that the supplier will carry out the service with reasonable care and skill. This term imposes a tort standard of reasonable care rather than the strict liability standard of satisfactory quality.

- Where no time is fixed for the provision of a service which is to be supplied in the course of a business, s.14(1) SGSA 1982 implies a term that the supplier will carry out the service within a reasonable time.

- Where the consideration is not fixed in a contract for the supply of a service, s.15(1) SGSA implies a term that the price will be a reasonable price.

Exclusion of the statutory implied terms

- The statutory terms as to the right to sell/hire/transfer the property cannot be excluded by any contract term.

- Where the customer deals as a consumer liability for breach of the statutory implied terms as to correspondence with description, satisfactory quality, fitness for purpose and correspondence with sample cannot be excluded by any contract term. Where the customer does not deal as a consumer liability for breach of these terms can only be excluded in so far as the term which excludes liability satisfies the UCTA 1977 requirement of reasonableness.

- A supplier in breach of s.13 SGSA 1982 will, for the purposes of UCTA 1977, be regarded as having been negligent. Section 2(1) UCTA provides that a person cannot by reference to any contract term exclude or restrict liability for death or personal injury caused by negligence. Section 2(2) UCTA allows a term to exclude or restrict liability for other loss or damage caused by negligence in so far as the term satisfies UCTA's requirement of reasonableness.

Summary questions

1   Naseem who has begun to work as a market trader, bought several items from Rashid, a market trader who is retiring. Naseem has experienced several problems with the items bought. These problems might be summarised as follows.

    a   The van which Rashid sold for £2 000 has proved to be totally unroadworthy. Rashid said that the van had a steering problem and 10% was knocked off the price to take account of this. When Naseem took the van to the garage he was told that the steering would cost £500 to put right and that to fix the brakes, the clutch and the bodywork would cost another £500, which is more than the van would be worth.

    b   A tarpaulin which Naseem bought has been seized by the police because, unknown to Rashid, it was one of a consignment stolen from the manufacturer. Naseem has been using the tarpaulin for several months.

    c   Naseem bought Rashid's stock, including a box of digital watches. Several customers have returned these watches claiming that they do not work. Rashid says that he never had any such problems, and that as the watches are still in the manufacturer's packing this cannot be his fault.

Advise Naseem of any rights he might have against Rashid under the Sale of Goods Act 1979.

2 If the case of *Millars of Falkirk Ltd* v *Turpie* were to arise today, what remedies would be available to the solicitor who bought the car from the garage? What remedies would be available to the garage against the manufacturer? (You should assume that the garage bought the car direct from the manufacturer and that the defect was present when the car was sold to the garage.)

3 In *Godley* v *Perry* there was a chain of buyers, as follows.

Manufacturer → importer → wholesaler 1 → wholesaler 2 → shopkeeper → boy

a Who was the eventual loser likely to be?
b How would the bankruptcy of wholesaler 1 have affected the position?

4 Gerald, a teacher, buys a car at a car auction. The car was put into the auction by Acme Finance Ltd. At the auction a prominently displayed notice states that all cars are to be sold without any guarantee, and that the terms implied by ss.13–15 are expressly excluded. The notice also says that bidders should satisfy themselves as to the quality of any cars before making a bid. The auctioneer reads this notice out before the sale starts. Gerald paid £2 000 for a four-year-old Ford Granada. The car's brakes are very poor, the bodywork is badly corroded and the engine is virtually worn out. Advise Gerald of his legal position.

5 Mrs Smith buys a new computer as a wedding present for her niece. When she gets the computer home she notices that the mouse has been damaged and cannot be used. She returns the computer to the shop who say that they can easily supply another mouse immediately and that the computer is otherwise perfect.

a Can Mrs Smith reject the goods and demand her money back?
b Could the shop reject the computer and return it to the manufacturer from whom they bought it?

6 A motorist buys a new car from a garage but the car has a serious defect in the steering system. No mention of the steering was made when the contract was formed. Which section(s) of which statute gives the motorist a remedy?

7 How would your answer to question 6 be different if

a The motorist had hired the car?
b The motorist had bought the car from his friend, an accountant who is employed by the city council?

8 Hugh decides to have his garden landscaped. Gardener and Son agree to do the job for £1 200. Soon after he starts work, Mr Gardener arrives at Hugh's house with a load of Tarmac. He says that this is left over from another job and that the original contract could easily be extended to include Tarmacking Hugh's small driveway. Hugh is pleased to agree to this, although no price is mentioned. The landscaping work turned out to be unsatisfactory. The lawn has not been levelled, as Hugh was assured that it would be, and the grass on the lawn is of very poor quality. Gardener and Son are demanding that Hugh pay the full price, and have also submitted a bill of another £2 050 for Tarmacking the drive. Hugh had thought that the additional cost for Tarmacking might be about £50.
Advise Hugh of his statutory rights.

9 In the following contracts which of the buyers would be regarded as dealing as a consumer, as defined by the Unfair Contract Terms Act 1977?

a A motor dealer orders a dozen new cars from Ford.
b A manufacturing company buys a new car for one of its salesmen.
c A salesman fills his company car with petrol at a filling station.
d A lady who has inherited an extremely valuable painting sells it to a gallery.
e A postman sells his old television to his neighbour.
f An amateur DIY enthusiast orders a reinforced steel joist from a builder's merchant.

Multiple choice questions

1   A firm of builders hire a JCB digging machine from a hire company for a three week period. The builders asked the hire company whether the machine supplied would be capable of digging through rock. The hire company assured the builders that the machine was suitable and so the builders made the contract. The digger is a small model which is unable to dig through rock, but is perfectly adequate for smaller jobs. The builders have to hire a more powerful machine from another company. Under which one of the following will the builders have a remedy against the hire company?

   a   Sections 13(1) and 14(3) of the Sale of Goods Act 1979.

   b   Sections 13(1) and 14(2) of the Sale of Goods Act 1979.

   c   Sections 8(2) and 9(5) of the Supply of Goods and Services Act 1982.

   d   Sections 9(1) and 10(3) of the Supply of Goods (Implied Terms) Act 1973.

2   For many years a fish and chip shop has bought potatoes from a local farmer. The quality of the potatoes was never formally described, but the potatoes supplied were always large enough to be cut into chips. The latest consignment consisted of small potatoes, which cannot be turned into chips. Which one of the following statements is true?

   a   The chip shop has no remedy.

   b   The chip shop can reject the potatoes under s.14(2) of the Sale of Goods Act 1979.

   c   The chip shop can reject the potatoes under s.14(3) of the Sale of Goods Act 1979.

   d   The chip shop can reject the potatoes under s.15(2) of the Sale of Goods Act 1979.

3   A farmer buys a large quantity of seed potatoes from a local seed merchant. The merchant tells the farmer that the potatoes in question are for export to Egypt because they do not grow well in English conditions. The farmer says that his farmland is most untypical and will grow any sort of potatoes. The farmer, as usual, signs an invoice which says that the seed merchant cannot be responsible for any defect in goods supplied. The potatoes do not grow at all well and the farmer consequently loses a great deal of money. The potatoes would have grown well enough in Egypt. Which one of the following statements is true?

   a   The seed merchant will have incurred no liability.

   b   The seed merchant will be liable under s.14(2) and (3) of the Sale of Goods Act. This liability cannot be excluded or restricted by any contract term.

   c   The seed merchant will be liable under s.14(2) and (3) of the Sale of Goods Act unless the exclusion clause satisfied UCTA 1977's requirement of reasonableness.

   d   The seed merchant will be liable under s.13(1) of the Sale of Goods Act unless the exclusion clause satisfied UCTA 1977's requirement of reasonableness.

4   Buildo Ltd, a firm of builders, hire a JCB digging machine from Hire Co Ltd. Buildo's manager signs a contract, without reading it, which contains a clause, 'All terms expressed or implied by statute or otherwise are hereby expressly excluded'. The JCB will not excavate due to a mechanical fault. Hire Co refuse to repair it, exchange it for another machine or return Buildo's money. Which of the following is true?

   a   Buildo will win under s.14(2) and (3) of the Sale of Goods Act, unless the exclusion clause satisfied UCTA 1977's requirement of reasonableness.

   b   Buildo will win under s.9(2) and (5) of the Supply of Goods and Services Act, unless the exclusion clause satisfied UCTA 1977's requirement of reasonableness.

   c   Hire Co Ltd will be liable under s.14(2) and (3) of the Sale of Goods Act. This liability cannot be excluded or restricted by any contract term.

   d   Hire Co Ltd will be liable under under s.9(2) and (5) of the Supply of Goods and Services Act. This liability cannot be excluded or restricted by any contract term.

5   Anjana, the managing director of Anjana Enterprises Ltd, hires a professional magician for the staff Christmas party. The magician arrives very drunk and is unable to perform any tricks. Which one of the following will provide a remedy?

a Sections 9(2) and (3) of the Supply of Goods and Services Act 1982.

b Section 4(2) and (5) of the Supply of Goods and Services Act 1982.

c Section 10(2) and (3) of the Supply of Goods (Implied Terms) Act 1973.

d Section 13 of the Supply of Goods and Services Act 1982.

6 Geraldine bought a pair of shoes at half price in the January sale. Above the till was a sign which clearly stated, 'No refunds on sale goods'. The shop assistant pointed the sign out to Geraldine when the sale was made. Within a week the heel fell off one of the shoes. Which one of the following statements is true?

a Geraldine has no remedy.

b Geraldine can get her money back unless the exclusion clause satisfied UCTA 1977's requirement of reasonableness.

c Geraldine can get her money back because the sign cannot exclude or restrict liability to her for breach of ss.13–15 of the Sale of Goods Act 1979.

d Geraldine cannot get her money back but is entitled to exchange the shoes for another pair.

7 Arthur bought a bicycle from Bill's shop. The bicycle frame was defective and snapped in half, injuring Arthur. At Arthur's request Bill had ordered the bicycle from Charles' wholesale company, which in turn had bought it from the manufacturer. Which of the following is true?

a Section 14(2) of the Sale of Goods Act will protect only Arthur.

b Section 14(2) of the Sale of Goods Act will impose liability on Bill, Charles' company and the manufacturer.

c Bill will not be able to sue Charles under the Sale of Goods Act. It was his business to know about bicycles and he should have spotted the fault.

d Bill will be liable under s.13 of the Supply of Goods and Services Act because he should have serviced the bicycle before selling it.

Task 8

You work for a firm which installs double-glazing in houses. Your firm buys most of its materials, but occasionally hires machinery. Your employer has asked you to write a report, briefly indicating.

a What statutory protection is given to your firm when it buys materials from suppliers.

b What statutory protection is given to customers for whom your firm works.

c The extent to which liability for breach of the statutory implied terms can be excluded by the contract under which goods and services are provided.

d To what extent the Unfair Contract Terms Act 1977 and the Unfair Terms in Consumer Contracts Regulations 1999 adequately protect consumers.

Chapter 9

SALE OF GOODS – THE PASSING OF OWNERSHIP

Introduction

When goods are sold the seller contracts to pass ownership of the goods to the buyer. The Sale of Goods Act 1979 lays down detailed rules which determine exactly when ownership of the goods is to pass. In the first part of this chapter we examine these rules and the circumstances in which the 1979 Act can cause a contract of sale of goods to be frustrated or void for mistake.

A reservation of title clause allows a seller to retain ownership of goods which have been sold until the buyer pays the full price. The Sale of Goods Act 1979 allows reservation of title clauses to be effective, but the precise extent to which they can be effective is a matter of some complexity. The middle section of this chapter examines the statutory rules on reservation of title and the way in which the courts have applied these rules.

This chapter concludes by considering the extent to which it is possible for a person who does not own goods to pass ownership of those goods to someone else. The general rule is that a non-owner of goods cannot pass ownership to someone else. However, we shall see that the Sale of Goods Act 1979 lays down several important exceptions to this rule.

9.1 · The passing of the property and the risk

The purpose of a contract of sale of goods is to pass the property in the goods (ownership of the goods) to the buyer in return for payment of the price. There are several circumstances in which it can be important to know exactly when the property passes. It might be thought that the property would pass either upon delivery of the goods or upon payment of the price. As we shall see, the property does not generally pass at either of these times.

A dispute over whether or not the property has passed from the seller to the buyer will usually arise if either of the parties has become insolvent, or if the goods have become damaged, lost or destroyed. However, it can also be important to know whether or not the property has passed because generally the seller only has a right to sue for the price once the property has passed.

First, let us consider the position where the seller of the goods, having made the contract of sale, becomes insolvent. If the seller becomes insolvent before the property in the goods passes to the buyer, then the buyer will not own the goods and will not therefore be entitled to claim possession of the goods from the seller's liquidator. If the buyer already has possession of the goods then the liquidator will be entitled to reclaim the goods from the buyer. This is the case even if the buyer has paid for the goods, although the buyer will be able to bring a claim as an unsecured creditor for the return of money he has paid. However, if the property does pass to the buyer before the seller becomes insolvent then the buyer will be entitled to claim the goods from the seller's liquidator or to retain the goods if they have already been delivered. The buyer owns the goods and is therefore entitled to possession of them. (The buyer will of course have to pay for the goods if payment has not already been made.) As the seller's insolvency necessarily means that all those to whom the seller owes money are not going to be paid in full, if they are paid at all, a buyer would obviously be in a far better position claiming ownership of the goods bought rather than claiming damages for breach of contract as an unsecured creditor.

Next, we consider the position where the buyer has become insolvent after the contract of sale was made. If the buyer has already paid the full price then there will be no problem. The buyer (or his liquidator) will either have received possession of the goods if they have already been delivered or will be entitled to demand possession from the seller if they have not. But if the full price has not been paid then the seller will want to know whether or not the property in the goods had passed at the time of the insolvency. If the property had passed, then the seller might only be able to make a claim as an unsecured creditor. (However, if the unpaid seller exercises one of his real remedies (see Chapter 10 at 10.3.1) he can resell the goods to a second buyer and pass a good title to that second buyer.) If the property in the goods had not passed, the seller could reclaim the goods if they have been delivered or refuse to deliver them if they have not. A seller who did this would of course have to refund to the buyer's liquidator any part of the price already paid.

Finally, we consider the position where the goods have become lost, damaged or destroyed after the contract of sale was made. Generally, as we shall see below at 9.1.4, the risk of damage to or deterioration of the goods passes at the same time as the property. Therefore if the goods were damaged etc. before the property had passed to the buyer, the seller would have to bear this loss as the goods belonged to him at the time of the damage. If the damage meant that the goods were of unsatisfactory quality then the buyer would be entitled to refuse to accept and pay for the goods. If the goods were specific the seller would be in breach of contract, if the goods were unascertained the seller could deliver other goods matching the contract description. If the goods were damaged after the property had passed to the buyer then the loss would fall on the buyer, as the buyer would have been the owner of the goods at the time when the damage occurred.

It is possible that the buyer and seller agree that the risk of the goods being lost, damaged or destroyed should not pass with the property in the goods. If this is expressly or impliedly agreed then the party who has accepted the risk will bear the loss when the goods are damaged etc. However, this is not the usual position. Unless there is an express or implied agreement to the contrary, the risk passes at the same time as the property in the goods.

Sections 16–20 SGA 1979 lay down rules as to when the property in the goods is to pass. These rules make a distinction between specific goods and unascertained goods. Specific goods are defined by s.61 as goods which are identified and agreed on at the time a contract of sale is made. The Act does not define unascertained goods, but any goods which are not specific are unascertained. Future goods, that is goods which have yet to be acquired or manufactured by the seller, are always regarded as unascertained in this context. This is the case even if the buyer and seller identify the particular goods which the seller is to acquire and sell.

Test your understanding

1 What is meant by the passing of the property in the goods?

2 What is meant by the risk?

3 How are specific goods defined?

4 What is the definition of unascertained goods?

5 What is the meaning of future goods? Are future goods regarded as specific or unascertained?

6 Are the following contracts sales of specific or unascertained goods?

   a Arthur, who has owned a bicycle for six years, agrees to sell it to Bill.

   b Arthur telephones Charles' shop and orders a new Raleigh Super Tourer Mark 2 bicycle. Charles has several such bicycles in stock.

   c Charles knows that David is thinking of selling his antique penny-farthing bicycle, which is in Charles' shop to be repaired. Charles agrees with Edward that if he can buy the bicycle from David he will then sell it to Edward. (Consider both the sale from David to Charles and the sale from Charles to Edward.)

Answers

1 The passing of the property in the goods means the passing of the ownership of the goods.

2 In this context, the risk means the risk of the goods becoming lost, damaged or destroyed.

3 Specific goods are defined as goods which are identified and agreed on at the time a contract of sale is made.

4 Unascertained goods are not defined by the Act, but would include all goods which are not specific.

5 Future goods are goods which have yet to be acquired or manufactured by the seller. In this context future goods are always regarded as unascertained goods.

6 (a) Specific goods. (b) Unascertained goods. (c) The sale from David to Charles would be a sale of specific goods. The sale by Charles to Edward would be a sale of future goods and therefore of unascertained goods.

9.1.1 Specific goods

Section 17 of the Sale of Goods Act 1979 provides that the property in specific goods passes when the parties to the contract intend it to pass, and this intention can either be a term of the contract or can be inferred from the conduct of the parties and the circumstances of the case. (In this Chapter all references to 'the Act' are references to the Sale of Goods Act 1979 unless it is made clear that they are not.)

If the parties' intentions cannot be found, then s.18 Rule 1 will apply. It provides that:

> 'Where there is an unconditional contract for the sale of specific goods in a deliverable state the property in the goods passes to the buyer when the contract is made, and it is immaterial whether the time of payment or the time of delivery, or both, be postponed.'

Before considering the meaning of s.18 Rule 1 it is essential to understand that this Rule is to be applied only if s.17 does not apply. All the five Rules in s.18 are subservient to s.17. Section 18 itself makes this quite clear. Before setting out any of its five Rules, s.18 begins, 'Unless a different intention appears, the following are rules for ascertaining the intention of the parties as to the time at which the property in the goods is to pass to the buyer …' As a practical matter it can be very difficult to say whether or not the parties have sufficiently shown an intention for s.17 to apply.

In order for Rule 1 to apply the contract must be unconditional, meaning that the passing of the property must not have been made subject to any condition. The goods must also be in a deliverable state, which means that the seller must have no more obligation to do anything to the goods as goods.

■ *Underwood Ltd* v *Burgh Castle Sand and Cement Syndicate* [1922] 1 KB 343 (Court of Appeal)

On 20 February 1920 the claimants agreed to sell a horizontal condensing engine to the defendants, to be delivered 'free on rail'. The engine weighed 30 tons. It was bolted to a concrete floor and had become embedded in the floor by its own weight. The machine had to be taken from the floor and dismantled before it could be delivered free on rail. The unfastening would take two days, the dismantling about two weeks. The machine was damaged while it was being loaded onto the railway wagon.

Held. Section 18 Rule 1 did not apply because at the time of the contract the machine was not in a deliverable state. As the parties had agreed that the machine was to be delivered free on rail they had shown an intention that the property was not to pass until the machine was loaded onto the train. If no intention had been shown the contract would have been governed by s.18 Rule 2 (see immediately below) and the property would not have passed as the buyer had not been informed that the goods were in a deliverable state.

COMMENT In this case Bankes LJ explained that a full-size billiard (snooker) table could be in a deliverable state despite its size and that the need to pack goods would not prevent them from being in a deliverable state. He said that in order for an item to be in a deliverable state 'it must have everything done to it that the sellers had to do to it as an article'.

Rule 2 applies where the contract is for the sale of specific goods which the seller has to put into a deliverable state:

> 'Where there is a contract for the sale of specific goods and the seller is bound to do something to the goods for the purpose of putting them into a deliverable state, the property does not pass until the thing is done and the buyer has notice that it has been done.'

Rule 2 would have been applied in *Underwood Ltd* v *Burgh*, if the parties had not shown an intention as to when the property was to pass. If Rule 2 had been applied the property in the goods would not have already passed at the time of the damage as the goods would not at that time have been put into a deliverable state. Even if the goods had been put into a deliverable state the property would not have passed until the buyer had received notice of this.

Rule 3 applies to contracts for the sale of specific goods which the seller must weigh, measure, test, etc to find the price:

> 'Where there is a contract for the sale of specific goods in a deliverable state but the seller is bound to weigh, measure, test, or do some other act or thing with reference to the goods for the purpose of ascertaining the price, the property does not pass until the act or thing is done and the buyer has notice that it has been done.'

This Rule is of limited effect. It only applies where the seller is the person doing the weighing etc and it only applies where this is being done in order to ascertain the price. When the Rule does apply the property passes only when the buyer has notice that the weighing etc has been done.

Rule 4 applies when goods are delivered to the buyer on approval or sale or return or other similar terms:

> 'When goods are delivered to the buyer on approval or on sale or return or other similar terms the property in the goods passes to the buyer —
> (a) when he signifies his approval or acceptance to the seller or does any other act adopting the transaction;
> (b) if he does not signify his approval or acceptance to the seller but retains the goods without giving notice of rejection, then, if a time has been fixed for the return of the goods, on the expiration of that time, and, if no time has been fixed, on the expiration of a reasonable time.'

Goods are delivered on approval when the buyer has the choice as to whether or not to approve the contract. Goods are delivered on sale or return when the buyer has the option to return the goods to the seller if he cannot himself sell them. In either of these circumstances, or if the goods are sold on similar terms, Rule 4 sets out four circumstances in which the property will pass. First, the property will pass when the buyer signifies his approval. Second, when the buyer does an act adopting the transaction. (Any act which would prevent the buyer from returning the goods to the seller, such as selling the goods on, will be regarded as an act adopting the transaction.) Third, if the contract fixes a time by which the goods must be returned to the seller then the property will pass if the goods are not returned by this time. Fourth, if there is no such time limit then the property will pass once the buyer has retained the goods for more than a reasonable time.

9.1.1.1 Mistake and frustration

In Chapter 6 we examined the circumstances in which the common law will render a contract frustrated or void for mistake. Sections 6 and 7 SGA 1979 make two further rules which apply only to contracts for the sale of specific goods.

Section 6 states that:

> 'Where there is a contract for the sale of specific goods, and the goods without the knowledge of the seller have perished at the time when a contract is made, the contract is void.'

Not only is this section restricted to contracts for the sale of specific goods, it is also necessary that the goods must have perished at the time of the contract and that the seller was not aware of this when the contract was made. If the seller was aware that the goods had perished then he cannot take advantage of s.6 and will be liable for breach of contract. Section 6 only applies where the goods have perished. Goods which have been stolen will be regarded as having perished. The following case considered whether goods which had become damaged could be regarded as having perished. When s.6 makes a contract void, the seller will not be in breach of contract for failure to deliver the goods. The buyer need not pay the price and can recover any amount of the price which has already been paid.

■ *Asfar & Co Ltd v Blundell* [1896] 1 QB 123 (Court of Appeal)

Dates which were on board a ship were sold. The ship sunk on the river Thames, but later it was raised. Although the dates still looked like dates, and although they were still worth a good deal for the purposes of distilling into spirit, the dates were covered in sewage and had begun to ferment. The dates were clearly no longer of merchantable (now satisfactory) quality but they were of some value as they could be distilled into spirit.

Held. For insurance purposes, the cargo could be regarded as a total loss.

COMMENT There is no direct authority on the meaning of perish under ss.6 and 7 SGA. It would seem that if the dates could be regarded as a total loss for insurance purposes then they would surely have perished for the purposes of ss.6 and 7.

Section 7 deals with the frustration of an agreement to sell specific goods:

> 'Where there is an agreement to sell specific goods and subsequently the goods, without any fault on the part of the seller or buyer, perish before the risk passes to the buyer, the agreement is avoided.'

Here the specific goods which have been agreed to be sold must perish after the agreement to sell has been made but before the risk has passed to the buyer. It is possible to separate risk and the passing of the property, as we shall see below at 9.1.4. When the parties have not agreed to separate the passing of the property and the passing of the risk s.7 can only apply to contracts governed by s.18 Rules 2 and 3, it cannot apply to contracts governed by Rules 1 or 4. If Rule 1 operates there will be no time gap between the agreement to sell and the passing of the risk. Under Rule 4 there is no agreement to sell until the buyer signifies his approval or otherwise causes the property in the goods to pass. If s.7 is to frustrate the contract, the perishing of the goods must not be the fault of either party.

When s.7 applies the contract is avoided. The seller will have no obligation to deliver the goods. The buyer will have no obligation to pay the price and will be able to recover any part of the price already paid. Other losses will lie where they fall. The Law Reform (Frustrated Contracts) Act 1943, which we considered in Chapter 7 at 7.1.3.3, does not apply where s.7 SGA does apply. The courts will not therefore be empowered to apportion the loss between buyer and seller.

Test your understanding

1 What rule does s.17 make about the passing of the property in specific goods?

2 When considering the time at which the property in specific goods passes, does s.17 take precedence over s.18, or does s.18 take precedence over s.17?

3 In *Tarling v Baxter* [1827] 6 B & C 360 a haystack was sold. Before the price had been paid, and before the contract allowed the haystack to be moved, the haystack was accidentally destroyed by fire. The parties did not show an intention as to when the property or the risk was to pass. Applying SGA 1979 to the facts of this case, what would the outcome now be?

4 What is the test for deciding whether or not specific goods are in a deliverable state, for the purposes of s.18 SGA 1979?

5 Specific goods which the seller has yet to put into a deliverable state are sold. At what time will the property pass to the buyer?

Answers

1 Section 17 provides that the property in specific goods passes when the parties to the contract intend it to pass, and this intention can either be a term of the contract or can be inferred from the conduct of the parties and the circumstances of the case.

2 Section 17 takes precedence over s.18. The Rules in s.18 are to apply only if the parties have not expressly or impliedly shown an intention as to when the property is to pass.

3 The property in the haystack would have passed to the buyer when the contract was made. Risk would also have passed at this time. The buyer would therefore be obliged to pay the full price for what he received – ownership of the haystack. (This case was codified by the 1893 Act, and so the outcome was the same in 1827.)

4 Goods are in a deliverable state, for the purpose of s.18, when the seller has no more obligation to do anything to the goods as an article.

5 The property will pass to the buyer at such time as the parties expressly or impliedly agreed (s.17). Assuming no agreement, the property will pass when the goods are put into a deliverable state and the buyer has notice of this (s.18 Rule 2).

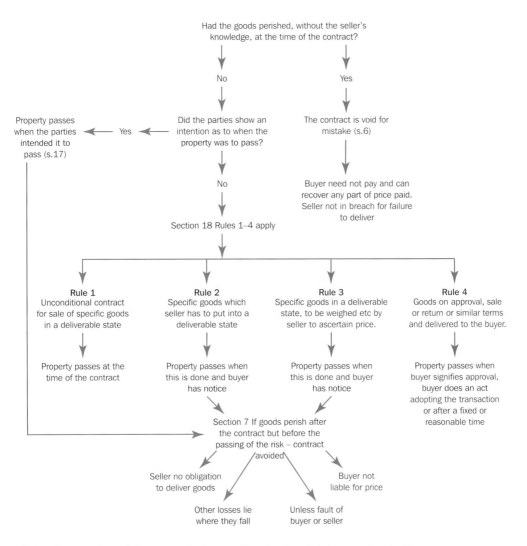

Figure 9.1   The passing of the property in specific goods mistake and frustration

9.1.2 Unascertained goods

Several sections of SGA 1979 apply to the passing of the property in unascertained goods. These sections are hierarchical and must be applied in the correct order. The starting point is s.16, which states that:

> '[Subject to section 20A below] Where there is a contract for the sale of unascertained goods no property in the goods is transferred to the buyer unless and until the goods are ascertained.'

The goods will become ascertained when they are identified in accordance with the agreement after the contract of sale has been made. Until this has happened the property in unascertained goods cannot pass to the buyer. (Subject to s.20A, which only applies in very limited circumstances and which it is convenient to ignore until the usual rules have been explained.) Once the goods have become ascertained, s.17 will pass the property to the buyer at such time as is indicated by the terms of the contract, the conduct of the parties or the circumstances of the case.

If s.17 does not help, s.18 Rule 5(1) provides as follows:

> 'Where there is a contract for the sale of unascertained or future goods by description, and goods of that description and in a deliverable state are unconditionally appropriated to the contract, either by the seller with the assent of the buyer or by the buyer with the assent of the seller, the property in the goods then passes to the buyer; and the assent may be express or implied, and may be given either before or after the appropriation is made.'

In order for the property in the goods to pass under Rule 5, several conditions must be fulfilled. First, the goods in question must match the contract description. Second, the goods must be in a deliverable state. Third, the goods must be unconditionally appropriated to the contract. Fourth, the unconditional appropriation must be made either by the seller with the assent of the buyer or by the buyer with the assent of the seller. (However, the assent to the appropriation is easily inferred. When a buyer makes a contract for goods to be delivered to him it will be inferred that he assented to the seller unconditionally appropriating the goods to the contract.)

Pearson J in *Carlos Federspiel & Co SA v Charles Twigg & Co Ltd* [1957] 1 Lloyd's Rep 240 explained what is meant by appropriating the goods to the contract: 'To constitute an appropriation of the goods to the contract, the parties must have had, or be reasonably supposed to have had, an intention to attach the contract irrevocably to those goods, so that those goods and no others are the subject of the sale and become the property of the buyer.'

So merely sorting out goods which match the contract description, or separating such goods from other goods, or even attaching the buyer's name to such goods is not enough. The intention must be to attach the goods irrevocably to the contract so that they become the property of the buyer. The seller will generally be taken to have done this at the point when it becomes out of his control to change his mind and use the goods for some other purpose. When considering the passing of the property in unascertained goods it is important to remember that you do not change s.18 Rules once the goods become ascertained. If the contract was for the sale of unascertained goods then ss.16, 17 and 18 Rule 5 will determine when the property passes. Rules 1–4 will be of no relevance. Unascertained goods may become ascertained, but they never become specific.

Section 18 mentions two special circumstances in which goods will be regarded as having been unconditionally appropriated to the contract. Section 18 Rule 5(2) states that where the seller in pursuance of the contract delivers goods to the buyer or to a carrier or other bailee for the purpose of transmission to the buyer, and does not reserve the right of disposal, he is to be taken to have unconditionally appropriated the goods to the contract. Section 18 Rule 5(3) provides that where a specified quantity of unascertained goods in a deliverable state forming part of a bulk has been sold to a particular buyer then if the bulk is reduced to that quantity (or to less than that quantity) the remaining goods are to be taken as having been unconditionally appropriated to the contract. The buyer must, at this stage, be the only buyer to whom goods are due out of the bulk. The bulk must have been identified either in the contract or by subsequent agreement between the parties. So if Buyer A agreed to buy 600 tons of wheat, out of a cargo of 1 000 tons aboard a certain ship, and the seller delivered 400 tons to a different buyer, the 600 tons remaining would be regarded as having been unconditionally appropriated to Buyer A's contract by exhaustion under s.18 Rule 5(3).

The following case provides an example of a dispute as to whether or not the property in unascertained goods which had deteriorated had passed at the time of the deterioration.

■ *Healy v Howlett and Sons* [1917] 1 KB 337

The claimants, who were fish exporters in Ireland, agreed to sell 20 boxes of mackerel to the defendant, a fish merchant in London. The claimants sent 190 boxes of mackerel to their agents at Holyhead. The fish were consigned to the claimants' own order, but the claimants sent a telegram instructing their agents at Holyhead to deliver 20 boxes to the defendant, 20 boxes to C and 150 boxes to D. The train on which the 190 boxes were carried to Dublin was delayed and consequently a boat to Holyhead was missed. At Holyhead the agents picked out and earmarked 20 boxes for the defendant, 20 for C and 150 for D. The mackerel were not of merchantable (now satisfactory) quality when they reached the defendant. The defendant refused to accept the goods and the claimants sued for the price. The claimants argued that when the goods had been sent to the agents in Holyhead, along with the instructions, the goods had been unconditionally appropriated.

Held. There was no appropriation of the goods to the defendant until the agents at Holyhead earmarked and picked out the 20 boxes which were to be delivered to the defendant. (By this time the fish had already become unmerchantable.) The defendant was therefore entitled to reject the goods because at the time when the property and the risk passed to him the goods were unmerchantable.

9.1.3 Undivided shares in goods forming part of a bulk

Sections 20A and 20B were introduced into the Sale of Goods Act 1979 by the Sale of Goods (Amendment) Act 1995. Section 20A allows a person who has bought a specified quantity of unascertained goods which form part of a bulk to become an owner in common of the bulk even though his share of the bulk has not been ascertained. The following conditions must be satisfied:

(1) A specified quantity of unascertained goods which form part of a bulk must have been bought.
(2) These goods must form part of a bulk which is identified in the contract or by subsequent agreement between the parties. It is not enough that the seller happens to have a bulk of goods out of which the specified quantity might be delivered.
(3) The buyer must have paid the price for some or all of the goods which are the subject of the contract and which form part of the bulk.

The buyer does not become owner of his share of the goods. He becomes a co-owner of the bulk. Only when goods are unconditionally appropriated to the buyer will he become owner of those goods.

A 'bulk' is defined by s.61 SGA 1979 in the following way:

'a mass or collection of goods of the same kind which —
(a) is contained in a defined space or area; and
(b) is such that any goods in the bulk are interchangeable with any other goods therein of the same number and quantity.'

Where these conditions are met, property in an undivided share in the bulk is transferred to the buyer and the buyer becomes an owner in common of the bulk. The buyer's share of the bulk will be such share as the quantity of goods paid for and due to the buyer out of the bulk bears to the quantity of goods in the bulk at that time.

Let us suppose for example, that B examines 100 bicycles in S's warehouse and agrees to buy 30 of these bicycles. B pays the price in advance. Upon payment B becomes a 3/10 co-owner of the bulk of 100 bicycles. B is therefore immediately protected against the prospect of S becoming insolvent.

However, if all of the bicycles were to be accidentally damaged B might have to take his share of the loss, depending upon whether or not the risk had passed to him.

Now let us assume that S sells 1 000 tons of wheat, from an identified bulk, to three buyers who pay the full price in advance. A buys 400 tons, B buys 300 tons and C buys 300 tons. A, B and C own the wheat in common, A having 2/5 ownership, while B and C have 3/10 ownership. If it transpired that the identified wheat amounted to only 500 tons rather than 1 000 tons then s.20A(4) would apply and the proportions owned by the three buyers would remain the same, so that A could claim 200 tons while B and C could each claim 150 tons. The three buyers could sue the seller for non-delivery of the shortfall. Section 20A(3) seems to suggest that if the goods are partially destroyed then the loss should first fall on the seller, unless there has been an agreement to the contrary.

It does this by stating that the undivided share of a buyer in a bulk at any time shall be such share as the quantity of goods paid for and due to the buyer out of the bulk bears to the quantity of goods in the bulk at that time. So if X had bought 300 tons of potatoes from a specified bulk of 1 000 tons and paid in advance, while Y had similarly bought and paid for 200 tons, the seller would still have 500 tons unsold. X would be a 3/10 owner of the 1 000 ton bulk, Y would be a 2/5 owner and the seller would be a 1/2 owner. If 500 tons were damaged there would be 500 tons left. Applying s.20A(3), X would be 3/5 owner of this remaining bulk, while Y would be a 2/5 owner. Therefore, the loss of the other 500 tons would have fallen on the seller. If 950 tons were destroyed X and Y would have their shares reduced proportionately, so that X would be a 3/5 owner of the remaining 50 tons while Y would be a 2/5 owner. Whether or not they could sue the seller for non-delivery of the remaining goods due under their contracts would depend upon whether the risk had passed to them at the time of destruction.

Section 20B(1) provides that a person who has become an owner in common by virtue of s.20A is deemed to have consented to any delivery of the goods out of the bulk to any other owner in common of the bulk, being goods which are *due to him under his contract*. So let us assume that A has bought and paid for 40 computers out of a specified bulk of 100 computers while B has bought 50 of these computers and paid 20% of the price. (A is therefore a 4/10 owner of the bulk and B is 1/10 owner.) A is deemed to consent to B removing 50 computers from the bulk, even though B has only a 1/10 ownership of the bulk. This is because s.20B(1) specifies that a co-owner under s.20A consents to any other co-owner removing goods 'due to him under his contract' and not just to goods representing his co-ownership. When B removed the 50 computers, 50 would remain and A would become a 4/5 owner of this remaining bulk. If B had bought 60 computers and removed 60 then A would become complete owner of the remaining 40 computers. When B removed the 60, the property in the remaining 40 would have passed to A by virtue of s.18 Rule 5(3).

Sections 20A and 20B do not specify when the risk should pass to a co-owner. As we have seen, s.20A(3) implies that if the seller is still a co-owner of the bulk then the risk of damage to goods forming the bulk first falls on the seller. This aside, it might be thought that s.20(1) would apply, placing a share of the risk on the buyer in proportion to his share of the bulk. Against this must be weighed s.20B(3)(c), which states that nothing under s.20A shall affect the rights of any buyer under his contract. This suggests that even if the whole bulk is destroyed a buyer who has become a co-owner under s.20A can still sue the seller for non-delivery.

The parties may contract out of ss.20A and 20B and provide that property in an undivided share of a bulk of goods shall pass to B at some time after payment.

Section 19 allows the seller to retain ownership of specific goods, or of goods which have subsequently been appropriated to the contract, until the payment of the price or until some other condition has been fulfilled. A seller can reserve title to the goods even though they may have been delivered to the buyer. This matter is explored in more detail below at 9.2.

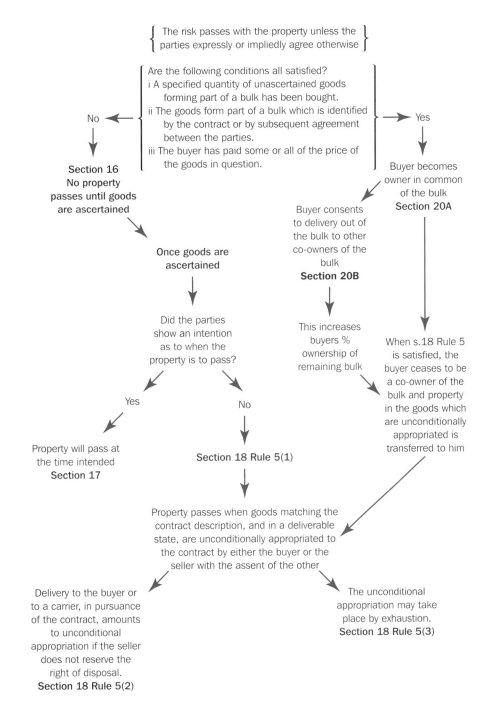

Figure 9.2   The passing of the property in unascertained goods

9.1.4 The passing of the risk

If the risk has passed to the buyer at the time when the goods are damaged or suffer from deterioration then the buyer will need to pay the full price of the goods. This is the case even if the goods are destroyed. Furthermore, the fact of the goods having been damaged etc will not give the buyer a right to sue the seller for non-delivery or for damages for breach of s.14(2). If the risk is with the seller at the time of deterioration etc then the position depends upon whether the goods were specific or unascertained. If the goods were specific the seller will not be able to perform the contract unless the goods can be repaired. If the goods were unascertained the seller can perform the contract by delivering replacement goods. The party with whom the risk lies ought to insure the goods.

Section 20 lays down the general rule on the passing of the risk:

'Unless otherwise agreed, the goods remain at the seller's risk until the property in them is transferred to the buyer, but when the property in them is transferred to the buyer the goods are at the buyer's risk whether delivery has been made or not.'

So although the risk will generally pass at the same time as the property in the goods, the parties may expressly or impliedly agree that this is not to be the case. For example in international sales of goods made on CIF terms the property and the risk do not pass at the same time. (International sales are examined in Chapter 10 at 10.5.) The following case provides an example of an implied agreement that the risk should not pass at the same time as the property.

■ *Sterns Ltd v Vickers Ltd* [1922] All ER 126 (Court of Appeal)

The sellers sold 120 000 gallons of white spirit, which was part of a larger consignment of spirit lying in a tank at a storage company. The storage company was to select the spirit to be delivered. The buyers took a delivery order from the storage company and this would have entitled them to demand delivery of the spirit. The buyers sold the spirit on to sub-buyers. As the delivery order was indorsed to the sub-buyers they could have demanded immediate delivery. However, the sub-buyers did not take delivery of the spirit for several months. When the sub-buyers did take delivery of the spirit they found that it had deteriorated in quality. The buyers sued the sellers for breach of warranty.

Held. The property in the goods had not passed to the buyers as the sale was of unascertained goods. (No equivalent to what is now s.20A of the 1979 Act was in force at the time and so the buyers did not become co-owners of the bulk.) However, the risk passed to the buyer at the time they took the delivery order as the sellers then no longer had any control over the spirit and had done everything they had undertaken to do. The buyers therefore could not sue for breach of warranty.

The risk is not concerned with damage to the goods which is caused by the fault of either of the parties, but only with accidental damage or destruction. Section 20(2) provides that where the delivery of the goods is delayed through the fault of either the buyer or the seller the goods are at the risk of the party at fault as regards any loss which would not have occurred but for such fault.

Section 20(3) states that: 'Nothing in this section affects the duties or liabilities of either seller or buyer as a bailee or custodier of the goods of the other party.'

A bailee consents to take possession of goods which he does not own. The main duties of a bailee are to take reasonable care of the goods and to be ready to deliver them to the owner if asked to do so. Bailment is common and often arises informally. For example, when a seller sells specific goods in a deliverable state then, unless there has been an agreement to the contrary, both risk and the property will pass to the buyer immediately. So if the seller retains possession of the goods for any time then he will become a bailee of the goods and s.20(3) will place on him a duty to look after the goods. If the seller does not take reasonable care of the goods then the buyer will be able to sue the seller for breach of a duty of a bailee. Sometimes the buyer will be a bailee of the seller's goods. For example, when s.18 Rule 4 operates the buyer will be a bailee of the seller's goods until the property passes. If the buyer fails to take reasonable care of the goods the seller will be able to sue him for breaching a duty of a bailee.

9.1.4.1 Passing of risk in consumer sales

Section 20(4) provides that in a case where the buyer deals as a consumer, sub-ss.20(1)–(3) must be ignored and the goods remain at the seller's risk until they are delivered to the consumer. Section 32(1) has also been amended by s.32(4), which provides that where the buyer deals as a consumer the general rule that delivery to the carrier is delivery to the buyer (see Chapter 10 at 10.1.1.1) is changed. Instead, s.32(4) specifically states that where the buyer deals as a consumer delivery of the goods to a carrier is not delivery to the buyer. So if, for example, a consumer ordered a book which was to be posted to him by the seller, the book would remain at the seller's risk until the book was delivered to the consumer, that is to say delivered to his home.

Test your understanding

1 Is it possible for the property in unascertained goods to pass to the buyer before the goods have become ascertained?

2 How do unascertained goods become ascertained?

3 If the parties show an intention as to when the property in unascertained goods is to pass, what will the effect of this be?

4 Assuming that s.18 Rule 5 applies, at what time will it operate so as to pass the property in unascertained goods to the buyer?

5 What three conditions must be satisfied for s.20A to operate so as to make a buyer of unascertained goods forming a bulk the owner in common of the bulk?

6 What is meant by the risk in this context?

7 In what circumstances will the risk not pass with the property in the goods?

8 What is a bailee? What are the two main duties of a bailee?

Answers

1 Subject to s.20A, it is not possible for the property in unascertained goods to pass to the buyer before the goods have become ascertained.

2 Unascertained goods will become ascertained when they are identified in accordance with the agreement after the contract of sale has been made.

3 As long as the goods have become ascertained, the intention shown will dictate when the property in the goods passes (s.17). However, if the goods have not become ascertained then, subject to s.20A, no property can pass to the buyer.

4 Where s.18 Rule 5 applies, it will pass the property in the goods when goods which match the contract description and which are in a deliverable state are unconditionally appropriated to the contract, either by the seller with the assent of the buyer or by the buyer with the assent of the seller.

5 The three conditions are that: (i) A specified quantity of unascertained goods must have been bought. (ii) These goods must form part of a bulk which is identified in the contract or by subsequent agreement between the parties. (iii) The buyer must have paid the price for some or all of the goods which are the subject of the contract and which form part of the bulk.

6 In this context the risk means the risk of the goods becoming lost, damaged or destroyed.

7 Risk will usually pass with the property in the goods, but not if the parties have expressly or impliedly agreed that it should not (s.20).

8 A bailee is a person who has possession of property which he does not own. The two main duties of a bailee are to take reasonable care of the goods and to deliver them to the owner if asked to do so.

9.2 · Reservation of title clauses

When goods are sold in a commercial context, particularly when large quantities of manufactured goods are sold, it is often the case that the seller reserves title to the goods. This means that the seller lets the buyer have possession of the goods, but the terms of the contract stipulate that the property in the goods is not to pass to the buyer until the full price of the goods has been paid. Reservation of title clauses will be particularly useful where the buyer has become insolvent. If the property in the goods has not passed to the buyer then the seller, as owner, will be able to reclaim the goods from the buyer's liquidator. Without a reservation of title clause the seller would be restricted to making a claim as an unsecured creditor. See Chapter 19 at 19.1.3.

Section 19(1) SGA plainly allows for reservation of title clauses:

'Where there is a contract for the sale of specific goods or where goods are subsequently appropriated to the contract, the seller may, by the terms of the contract or appropriation, reserve the right of disposal of the goods until certain conditions are fulfilled; and in such a case, notwithstanding the delivery of the goods to the buyer ... the property in the goods does not pass to the buyer until the conditions imposed by the seller are fulfilled.'

The following case provides an example of an effective reservation of title clause.

■ *Clough Mill Ltd* v *Geoffrey Martin* [1985] 1 WLR 111 (Court of Appeal)

The claimant company entered into four contracts to sell yarn to a company which manufactured fabric. Each of the contracts contained a reservation of title clause which provided as follows: the claimants retained ownership of the yarn until they received full payment for all the yarn supplied under the particular contract in question; if payment became overdue the claimants could enter the buyers' premises to reclaim the yarn; if insolvency proceedings were commenced against the buyers payment should become due immediately; and that if the yarn was incorporated into other goods the claimants should own these other goods unless the buyers had sold the goods on to a bona fide purchaser. The defendant was appointed the buyers' liquidator. The claimants wrote to the defendant saying that they wished to collect unused yarn and that the buyers should stop being allowed to continue to use the yarn sold in their manufacturing process. The defendant did not pay the purchase price or prevent the buyers from continuing to use the yarn in their manufacturing process. The claimants, who had been refused permission to enter the buyers' premises, sued the defendant for conversion of the yarn.

Held. The claimants were entitled to reclaim the unused yarn, as the property in this yarn never passed to the buyer. (The Court of Appeal stated *obiter* that ownership of the manufactured product would depend upon the intentions of the parties. It would generally be taken that they intended the product to belong to the buyer. Any clause which provided that the seller owned the manufactured product would give the seller a windfall profit and involve assets being transferred to him and would therefore be void as an unregistered charge.)

Although there is no doubt that reservation of title clauses can be effective, there are a variety of situations where they are not effective or where their effect is not clear.

9.2.1 All moneys clauses

A simple reservation of title clause provides that the title in the goods sold is not to pass until those particular goods have been paid for. An all moneys clause states that the title is not to pass until all sums owing to the seller, whether under the contract in question or under previous contracts, have been paid. If such clauses are effective they can mean that the buyer will never own any of the goods which he has bought from the seller. For example, let us suppose that a motor manufacturer supplies a car dealer with new cars every six weeks under a contract containing an all moneys reservation of title clause. The car dealer pays for each delivery of cars two months after delivery and so never completely settled his debts to the manufacturer. If the clause is effective the dealer will not own any of the cars he has ever bought from the manufacturer. (As we shall see at 9.2.2, this would not generally affect customers who bought cars from the dealer.)

We shall see that where the buyer is a company an all moneys clause might be ineffective as an unregistered company charge. A company which issues a charge over property gives that property as security for a loan, while retaining possession of the property. On dissolution of the company those creditors who have taken a charge over assets are entitled to sell the assets mortgaged to ensure payment of their loans ahead of the unsecured creditors. (Although a certain amount of the money raised may be top-sliced for payment to the unsecured creditors if the floating charge was created after 15 September 2003. See Chapter 19 at 19.1.3.) In *Re Bond Worth Ltd* [1980] Ch 228 Slade J, when considering a retention of title clause, said: 'any contract which, by way of security for payment of a debt, creates an interest in property defeasible [capable of being made void] on payment of such debt, must necessarily be regarded as creating a charge'. However, a charge must be registered with the Registrar of Companies, or it will have no effect (under s.395 of the Companies Act 1985). (Charges are examined in detail in Chapter 18 at 18.8.)

In *Clough Mill Ltd* v *Geoffrey Martin* it was held that if the seller retains 'equitable and beneficial ownership' in the goods sold a charge is created. The logic was that if legal ownership was not retained then the buyer must have acquired this, and any security the seller had over the goods must therefore have been transferred back to the seller by the buyer, thus creating a charge. However, in a Scottish case *Armour* v *Thyssen Edelstahlwerke AG* [1990] 3 All ER 481 the House of Lords held that an all moneys clause did not create a charge and that the clause was therefore valid. The logic was that if the clause was effective then it prevented any property from ever passing to the buyer. As the buyer never owned the property it could not issue a charge in respect of it.

If the seller does reclaim goods sold under a previous contract it seems likely that the buyer can reclaim the price paid under that previous contract on the basis that there has been a total failure of consideration.

9.2.2 The position where the buyer resells the goods

If the buyer of the goods which are the subject of a reservation of title clause resells the goods to a second buyer who takes delivery of the goods, the property in the goods will pass to the second buyer as long as the second buyer did not know of the reservation of title clause when making the contract and as long as he acted in good faith. (Section 25 SGA 1979, considered below at 9.3.5.)

Often the original seller knows that the buyer intends to resell the goods and so the reservation of title clause may stipulate that the seller is entitled to the proceeds of sale. In the following case such a claim was successful.

■ *Aluminium Industrie Vaasen BV* v *Romalpa Aluminium Ltd* [1976] 2 All ER 552 (Court of Appeal)

The claimants, a Dutch company which manufactured aluminium foil, sold foil to the defendants, an English company. Clause 13 of the terms and conditions on which the foil was sold contained a complex retention of title clause which provided that: ownership of the foil would only pass to the defendants when they had paid all money owing to the claimants; until the date of payment the defendants could be required to store the foil in such a way that it was clearly the claimants' property; if the foil was mixed with other materials to produce new goods, the ownership of the new goods was to be transferred to the claimants as surety for the full payment of the price; until the full payment of the price the defendants were to hold the mixed goods for the claimants as fiduciary owner of them; the defendants could sell mixed goods but if the full price had not been paid to the claimants the defendants were to assign to the claimants the benefit of any claim against sub-purchasers. The defendants got into financial difficulties and a receiver was appointed. At this time the defendants owed the claimants £122 000. The receiver certified that he was holding £35 151 which represented the proceeds of sale of unmixed aluminium foil supplied by the claimants and sold on to sub-purchasers. The claimants claimed this money.

Held. As it was the intention of the parties that the defendants should have the power to sell unmixed foil, and that they should account for the proceeds of such a sale until all the money owed to the claimants had been paid, terms were implied to give effect to these intentions. The claimants could trace the proceeds of sale of the unmixed foil because the defendants, as between themselves and the claimants, sold the foil in their fiduciary capacity as agents and bailees of the claimants. (If the goods are traced they are followed and the proceeds of sale taken when the fiduciary sells the goods.) As between the defendants and the sub-purchasers the defendants sold the foil as principals, on their own account.

Although the claim to the proceeds of sale was successful in the *Romalpa* case, this outcome has not been reached in any subsequent case. In *Romalpa* the Court of Appeal did not even consider the possibility that a charge had been created and that such a charge would be void for non-registration. The court's decision that the defendants resold the foil in a fiduciary capacity also causes considerable difficulty. If this were the case then all of the proceeds of sale should have been paid into the separate bank account and even the profit made on the resale of the aluminium should have been the property of the claimants. The parties clearly did not contemplate this happening and so it is very hard to see how such a term could be implied. Furthermore, in the *Romalpa* case the defendants conceded that they were bailees of the goods. In fact it is highly likely that they were not bailees as a bailee has a duty to redeliver the goods, something the parties did not contemplate. Subsequent courts have avoided following the decision on this ground. If the reservation of title clause only allows the seller to reclaim the proceeds of sale to the extent that he is owed the price of the goods by the buyer, it will be void as an unregistered charge.

In *Pfeiffer GmbH* v *Arbuthnot Factors* [1988] 1 WLR 150 it was held that where the terms of a contract allowed the buyer to resell the goods in the normal course of his business before paying the seller for them, it would normally be implied that the buyer did so on his own account rather than as a fiduciary who would have to account to the seller for the proceeds. However, if the buyer did sell the goods on as a fiduciary of the original seller then the parties would have intended that the seller was only entitled to what he was owed, rather than the whole proceeds of sale. The retention of title clause would not therefore have retained complete ownership in the goods sold, but only have created an interest by way of security for the amount owed. It would therefore be void as an unregistered charge.

9.2.3 Claims to goods manufactured out of the goods sold

Where the goods sold are to be used in a manufacturing process a reservation of title clause often states that the seller should be entitled to any goods manufactured out of the original goods sold. It may be possible for the seller to reclaim the goods sold if they are still recognisable, despite the manufacturing process, and if they could easily be detached from other goods used in the process and returned to their original state. However, once the goods have become altered beyond this point then the right to reclaim the goods will be lost.

■ *Borden (UK) Ltd* v *Scottish Timber Products Ltd* [1981] Ch 25 (Court of Appeal)

The claimants supplied resin to the defendants. The resin was to be used in the creation of chipboard and it was clearly contemplated that it would be used in this way before it had been paid for. Once the resin had been mixed with other materials it could not physically be recovered. A reservation of title clause stipulated that the property in the resin was to pass to the defendants only when all goods supplied under the contract had been paid for in full. A receiver was appointed and the claimants argued that they were entitled to claim the chipboard and the proceeds of sale of chipboard which had been manufactured using the resin.

Held. The resin had ceased to exist once it was manufactured into chipboard and so the claimants could not trace it into the chipboard. They could not therefore claim either the chipboard or the proceeds of sale.

■ *Re Peachdart Ltd* [1983] 3 All ER 204

The claimants supplied a company with leather, which the company was to use to manufacture into handbags. A reservation of title clause provided that: the claimants retained ownership of the leather until they were paid in full; that until they were paid the claimants owned any products made from the leather until these were sold by the company; and that when products made from the leather were sold by the company the claimants were entitled to trace the proceeds of sale of the handbags. The company got into financial difficulties and a receiver was appointed. It was conceded that the claimants had the right to leather which remained unmanufactured. However, the claimants also claimed the proceeds of sale of handbags and ownership of partly manufactured handbags.

Held. The parties intended that once the leather was manufactured into handbags it was no longer the exclusive property of the claimants. If the claimants did have any rights over the handbags or the proceeds of sale this must have been given to them by the company. Therefore any such rights would be by way of a charge and void as the charge had not been registered.

The law on reservation of title clauses is not particularly clear. All of the decisions result from a consideration of the complex facts of each case. The courts have tended to solve the difficulties presented by the case in front of them rather than to lay down any definite policy.

Test your understanding

1 What is meant by a reservation of title clause?
2 If a reservation of title clause is in fact a company charge how might this cause problems for the seller of the goods?
3 Susan sells goods to Brian. The contract of sale states that Susan is reserving title to the goods until the full price has been paid. Brian takes possession of the goods and sells them to Belinda, who did not know about Susan's reservation of title clause. Can Susan recover the goods from Belinda?

Answers

1 A reservation of title clause reserves the title in goods sold until the price is paid. If the clause is effective, the seller therefore owns the goods until such time as the buyer pays the price.
2 A company charge which has not been registered with the Registrar of Companies is void under s.395 of the Companies Act 1985.
3 Belinda will be able to keep the goods as long as she acted in good faith and in ignorance of the reservation of title clause. Brian would have passed title to Belinda under s.25 SGA as a buyer in possession of the goods.

9.3 · Sale by a person who is not the owner

It is almost always the case that a person who does not own goods cannot pass ownership to anyone else unless he sells the goods as the agent of the owner. This rule, which is often expressed in the Latin maxim *nemo dat quod non habet* (nobody gives what they do not have), is contained in s.21 SGA 1979, which provides as follows:

'Subject to this Act, where goods are sold by a person who is not their owner, and who does not sell them under the authority or with the consent of the owner, the buyer acquires no better title to the goods than the seller had, unless the owner of the goods is by his conduct precluded from denying the seller's authority to sell.'

So the general position is that if a seller of goods does not own the goods a person who buys from the seller will not own the goods either. The true owner of the goods will be able to reclaim the goods from the person who bought the goods and sue the seller or the buyer for the conversion of the goods. This is true not only where the goods were stolen by the person who later sells them, but also where the owner is tricked or defrauded into parting with possession. Although it was not the point at issue in the case, we saw an example of the *nemo dat* rule in *Rowland* v *Divall* in Chapter 8. The thief did not own the car which he sold. Therefore, none of the three subsequent buyers acquired ownership. All three of these buyers could have been liable in conversion to the true owner, who was entitled to reclaim the car.

Despite the logic of this rule there are six exceptions to it, which we now examine in turn. All of these exceptions can only apply in favour of a person who acquires the goods in good faith, without notice that the seller does not have the right to sell. Good faith is a subjective matter, as is made clear by s.61(3) of the Sale of Goods Act 1979: 'A thing is deemed to be done in good faith within the meaning of this Act when it is in fact done honestly, whether it is done negligently or not.' In this context notice means actual notice, not constructive notice. The final exception which we consider is contained in the Hire Purchase Act 1964, rather than in the Sale of Goods Act, but again whether or not the person in favour of whom the exception operates is in good faith is a subjective matter.

As regards ownership of the goods the law takes an all or nothing approach. The loss is never apportioned between the innocent parties.

9.3.1 Agency

Agency is an obvious exception to the *nemo dat* rule. When an agent sells the principal's goods the whole point of the contract is that the agent (who does not own the goods) passes ownership to the purchaser.

Section 21(1) impliedly recognises agency with the words 'and who does not sell them under the authority or with the consent of the owner'.

When the agency is disclosed the third party will know that the agent is acting as an agent and will know that he is creating a legal relationship with the principal rather than with the agent. But even where the agency is undisclosed, so that the third party thinks he is contracting with the agent rather than with the principal, s.21(1) recognises that the agent passes a good title to the principal's goods to the third party. (Undisclosed agency is considered in some detail in Chapter 11 at 11.3.)

9.3.1.1 Mercantile agents

Section 2(1) of the Factors Act 1889 provides that a mercantile agent can pass ownership of goods to a third party, even if the mercantile agent did not have the authority of the owner to do this. Ownership can be passed if the mercantile agent sells the goods, or pledges them as security or makes any other disposition of the goods. Section 21(2) SGA recognises this by saying that nothing in SGA affects the provisions of the Factors Acts.

Section 1 of the Factors Act 1889 defines a mercantile agent as an agent 'having in the customary course of his business as such agent authority either to sell goods or to consign goods for the purpose of sale, or to buy goods, or to raise money on the security of goods'.

Note the requirements to this exception to the *nemo dat* principle:

(a) The agent must be a mercantile agent, that is to say a professional agent who is in business to sell or deal with other people's goods.
(b) The agent must either be in possession of the goods or of documents of title at the time when the goods are sold or disposed of. A bill of lading is a document of title but a car log book is not.
(c) This possession must have been gained with the consent of the owner, even if this consent was obtained by means of deception.
(d) Possession must have been acquired by the mercantile agent for some purpose connected with his business as a mercantile agent. So if the mercantile agent had possession so that he could repair the goods this would not be enough. Possession must be granted for the purpose of sale, or receiving offers, or display or something of that kind.
(e) The sale or disposition of the goods must have been made in the ordinary course of business as a mercantile agent. (During business hours, from a proper place of business and not in such a way as to make the third party think that there was anything wrong.) Also, an agreement to sell will not be within s.2(1) of the Factors Act. For the difference between a sale and an agreement to sell see Chapter 8 at 8.1.1.2.
(f) The person taking the goods must have done so in good faith, without notice of the agent's lack of authority and it is up to him to prove this.

■ **Example**

Customers have for some time been in the habit of leaving jewellery at a jeweller's shop so that the jeweller could sell the jewellery. The jeweller is therefore a mercantile agent. Oswald left his diamond ring at the jeweller's shop, asking the jeweller to try to get offers for the ring. Oswald tells the jeweller that he must not sell the ring without express permission to do so. If the jeweller sold the ring to a customer who bought it in good faith then s.2(1) of the Factors Act 1889 would pass ownership to that customer. Oswald could not reclaim the ring but could sue the jeweller for damages.

In *Folkes* v *King* [1923] 1 KB 282 a mercantile agent gained possession of a car by deception. The owner had given the car to the mercantile agent but had expressly instructed him not to sell it for less than £575. The mercantile agent immediately sold the car to A, who bought it in good faith, for £340. The car passed to several other buyers before passing to K. The owner sued K to recover the car but could not do so. A good title had passed to A under s.2(1) of the Factors Act, and this title had passed through the other buyers to K.

If a mercantile agent sells a car without the registration book then generally this will not be a sale in the ordinary course of business of a mercantile agent and so title will not be passed to the purchaser. Furthermore, the owner of the car must have consented to the mercantile agent's possession of the registration book. In *Pearson* v *Rose and Young Ltd* [1951] 2 All ER 1027 a mercantile agent received possession of a car with the consent of the owner. The mercantile agent also tricked the owner into handing over the registration book, claiming that he wanted to have a look at it. Then when the owner was distracted by a trick the mercantile agent kept hold of the registration book and the same day sold the car with the registration book. The purchaser of the car did not receive good title. The owner had consented to the mercantile agent having possession of the car, but had not consented to him having possession of the registration book.

When all of the conditions are met, the title passed by a mercantile agent is the title of the principal who gave possession of the goods to the agent. This may seem somewhat hard on the principal, but the principal must have consented to the mercantile agent having possession of the goods or the documents of title to the goods. If ownership is given without the consent of the principal, the principal can sue the mercantile agent for damages. If the principal who entrusted the goods to the mercantile agent has no title to the goods, then the mercantile agent will not be able to pass any better title to anyone else.

When a mercantile agent sells goods with the consent of the owner then he will pass good title under general agency principles.

9.3.2 Estoppel

A person who is estopped from denying that someone else is the owner of goods is prevented from denying it. The Sale of Goods Act does not expressly mention estoppel as an exception to the *nemo dat* principle, but s.21 impliedly recognises estoppel with the words 'unless the owner of the goods is by his conduct precluded [prevented] from denying the seller's authority to sell'.

So if the owner of goods makes a representation to a third party that a seller of goods has the right to sell the goods, either as agent or owner, the owner will be estopped (prevented) from denying the truth of the representation later. The following case provides an example of this.

■ *Eastern Distributors Ltd* v *Goldring* [1957] 2 All ER 525 (Court of Appeal)

M wanted to take a car from C, a motor dealer, on hire-purchase but did not have enough money to pay the deposit. As part of a complex fraud to finance the deal, M authorised C to sell his (M's) van to a finance company, the claimants. The finance company was then to pass the van to M on hire-purchase terms and the proceeds of the sale of the van were to pay the deposits on the hire-purchase of both the van and the car. C only had authority to sell the van if he went along with the whole scheme. M signed blank hire-purchase documents and left them with C to complete. The forms stated that C was the absolute owner of the van. C sold the van to the claimants, the finance company, as if it were his own even though the proposal to take the car on hire-purchase did not go through. The claimants then took M's proposal to take the van on hire-purchase at face value and sent M a copy of the agreement. Upon finding out that the deal to take the car on hire-purchase was not going ahead, M told C that the whole deal was off. M then sold the van to the defendant, Goldring, who bought it in good faith and with no knowledge that it did not belong to M. M did not pay the hire-purchase instalments and so the claimants claimed the van or its value from Goldring.

Held. The claimants were entitled to recover the van. C had no actual authority to sell the van. However, M was estopped from denying that C had authority to sell it. M's title to the van therefore passed to the claimants and so M had no title to pass when he sold the van to the defendant.

In order for the estoppel to arise the owner of the goods must make a representation to the third party. Mere negligent behaviour by the owner will not be enough to amount to a representation unless the owner owes the third party a duty of care. Lord MacNaghten in *Farquharson Bros and Co v C. King & Co* [1902] AC 325 gave the following example (at 336): 'If a person leaves a watch or a ring on a seat in the park or on a table at a cafe and it ultimately gets into the hands of a bona fide purchaser, it is no answer to the true owner to say that it was his carelessness and nothing else that enabled the finder to pass it off as his own.' As regards mere economic loss a duty of care will only be owed in very exceptional circumstances.

Generally, only the person who represented that the seller had the right to sell the goods is estopped from denying that the seller had this right. If the person making this representation had good title to the goods, then the third party who buys the goods on the strength of it will acquire complete title. But if the person who made the representation did not have title to the goods then no title will be passed.

9.3.3 Sale under a voidable title

In Chapter 6 we saw that a seller who is induced to make a contract by a misrepresentation has the right to rescind the contract. A contract which is capable of being rescinded is said to be voidable (capable of being made void). So a person who makes a misrepresentation when buying goods does not acquire a complete title to the goods, but only a voidable title. (One which can be avoided by the seller within a reasonable time, as explained in Chapter 6 at 6.1.3.) We also saw that duress might make a contract voidable.

Section 23 SGA provides that: 'When the seller of goods has a voidable title to them, but his title has not been avoided at the time of the sale, the buyer acquires a good title to the goods, provided he buys them in good faith and without notice of the seller's defect of title.'

So if a person with only a voidable title to goods sells the goods *before* the contract was avoided then a new buyer who acts in good faith will get complete ownership of the goods. This is an exception to the *nemo dat* principle because a seller with only a voidable title is giving more than he has got; he is giving a complete title. (And, of course, the seller's voidable title would become worthless once the contract was avoided.) If the seller with only the voidable title resells the goods *after* the contract has been avoided then the third party acting in good faith will acquire no title at all. Once the contract was avoided the seller's voidable title had been extinguished and the seller no longer had any title to pass on.

Two cases, both considered in Chapter 6, demonstrate the way in which s.23 works. In *Lewis v Averay* [1971] 3 All ER 907 a rogue bought a car with a bad cheque, pretending to be Richard Greene, the television actor. As this was a fraudulent misrepresentation, the rogue therefore had only a voidable title to the car. In the long run this voidable title would have been worth very little to him as the owner would surely have avoided the contract as soon as he discovered that the cheque was worthless. Before the owner discovered this, the rogue sold the car to the defendant, who bought the car in good faith. The Court of Appeal held that the defendant had a complete title to the car as he had bought it before the owner avoided the contract with the rogue.

In *Car and Universal Finance Co Ltd* v *Caldwell* [1964] 1 All ER 290 another rogue bought a car with a bad cheque. As this was again a fraudulent misrepresentation, it again made the contract voidable. The rogue sold the car to a company called Motobella, but before he did this the owner of the car informed the police and the AA that the car had been stolen. Motobella did not buy the car in good faith but three days after acquiring the car they sold it to a buyer in good faith. After passing through the hands of several purchasers the car ended up with the claimants, who had bought it in good faith. The Court of Appeal held that the contract had been avoided by informing the police and the relevant authorities. So the original owner did get the car back and the innocent third party was left with nothing but the worthless right to sue the rogue. (Although the Court of Appeal decided that telling the police and the AA was enough to avoid the contract in the circumstances where the rogue had behaved fraudulently and was subsequently impossible to contact, it left open the question whether or not such actions would have been enough to avoid in the case of a non-fraudulent misrepresentation.)

It is possible that a rogue who acquired possession of a car under a voidable contract which has been avoided might nevertheless pass title as a buyer in possession of the goods. (See *Newtons of Wembley Ltd* v *Williams* [1964] 3 All ER 532 below at 9.3.5.) If this is the case then the effect of *Car and Universal Finance* will be of limited practical importance.

9.3.4 **Sale by a seller in possession after a sale**

Section 24, a very lengthy section of the Sale of Goods Act, provides that if a seller sells goods to one buyer, but keeps possession of the goods or of documents of title to the goods, and then sells or disposes of the same goods to a second buyer, who takes delivery of the goods or the documents of title, then the second buyer will get ownership of the goods. Section 8 of the Factors Act 1889 is virtually identical to s.24 SGA.

This is an exception to the *nemo dat* rule in circumstances in which the first buyer would have got ownership of the goods before the sale to the second buyer. (As we saw earlier in this chapter this would generally be the case where the contract was for the sale of specific goods in a deliverable state. Applying s.18 Rule 1 ownership would pass to the first buyer as soon as the contract was made.) When s.24 takes effect the first buyer can of course sue the seller for damages in conversion or for breach of contract.

■ **Example**

A shop has a grand piano in its New Year Sale. X makes a contract to buy the piano and pays the full price. As we saw earlier in this chapter, this means that X is now owner of the piano, by virtue of SGA s.18 Rule 1. By mistake, another shop assistant later sells the same piano to Y, who takes it away. Y will get title to the piano. X can sue the shop for damages.

The rule set out in s.24 seems to be based on convenience. In the above example either X or Y will get ownership of the piano and the other will be left with the right to sue the shop for damages. X and Y have behaved identically, and justice does not favour either one of them more than the other. It is more convenient to let Y keep the piano, as he already has possession of it, than to say that X has ownership of the piano.

The title passed is only the title of the seller in possession. If at the outset the seller in possession did not have complete title to the goods then complete title will not be passed to either the first or the second buyer.

The following New South Wales case shows the operation of the seller in possession exception in a commercial context.

■ *Pacific Motor Auctions Pty Ltd* v *Motor Credits (Hire Finance) Ltd* [1965] AC 867 (Privy Council)

M Ltd, a company dealing in cars had an arrangement with a finance company called Motor Credits Ltd. Under the agreement M bought cars and then sold them to Motor Credits for 90% of the price which they had paid. M then sold the cars as the agents of Motor Credits. (The purpose of this arrangement was to allow M to have money available for future trading.) The cars were never physically transferred to Motor Credits, but were continuously in the possession of M. Knowing that M was in financial difficulty, Motor Credits revoked M's agency to sell the cars. Despite this, M sold 29 cars to Pacific Motors which Pacific Motors took away. Pacific Motors were ignorant of the fact that these cars had previously been sold to Motor Credits and acted in good faith.

Held. Pacific Motors became the owners of the cars under s.28 of the Sale of Goods Act 1923 of New South Wales (which is identical to s.24 SGA 1979).

9.3.5 Sale by a buyer in possession

Section 25(1) applies where a person who has bought or agreed to buy goods obtains the goods, or documents of title to the goods, with the seller's consent. If such a buyer in possession delivers the goods or the documents of title to a third party acting in good faith as part of a contract of sale or other disposition of the goods, the title which the buyer in possession had is passed to the third party as if the buyer in possession had been a mercantile agent acting on behalf of the owner. Section 9 of the Factors Act 1889 is virtually identical to s.25(1) SGA except that it allows the buyer in possession to pass the goods on under an agreement to sell.

■ Example

S owns goods and sells them to B, who has not yet paid the price. Under the terms of the contract ownership of the goods is not to pass to B until the full price has been paid. If B gets possession of the goods and sells them to C (who does not know that ownership has not yet passed to B) then C will own the goods as soon as they are delivered to him.

Section 25(1) will not apply if 'the first buyer' took the goods on hire-purchase, or on sale or return. In neither of these cases will the first buyer have bought or agreed to buy the goods. Section 25(2) provides that s.25(1) does not apply where the first buyer has taken the goods on a conditional sale agreement, payable by instalments, which is regulated by the Consumer Credit Act 1974. (A conditional sale agreement is virtually identical to a hire-purchase agreement except that the buyer is committed at the outset to paying all of the instalments. Property in the goods will not pass to the buyer until this has been done. Such an agreement is likely to be governed by the Consumer Credit Act if the total *credit* supplied is under £25 000.) (See Chapter 14 at 14.2.3.)

There is considerable uncertainty about the circumstances in which s.25 will apply. In one of the leading cases, *Newtons of Wembley Ltd* v *Williams* [1964] 3 All ER 532 the Court of Appeal decided that s.25 would only apply in cases where the buyer in possession resold the goods in the manner in which a mercantile agent would have sold them. (The requirements for a person to be acting as a mercantile agent were set out above at 9.3.1.1.) In *Newtons of Wembley Ltd* v *Williams* a rogue bought a car with a bad cheque. The owner of the car successfully avoided the contract before the rogue resold the car. The rogue could not therefore pass good title under s.23 of the Act. The rogue then resold the car at a streetside market. The Court of Appeal held that the rogue did pass a good title to the purchaser under s.25, but only because the rogue had sold the car in the way in which he would have sold it if he had been a mercantile agent. (In business hours, from business premises, etc.) This requirement that the buyer in possession should act as a notional mercantile agent would seem to make the effect of s.25 very limited.

Section 25 will only operate to pass the title which the person who sold to the buyer in possession had. If that person did not own the goods, perhaps because he had bought them from a thief, then ownership will not be passed to the buyer in possession or to the third party buying from the buyer in possession. In *National Employers Mutual General Insurance Association Ltd* v *Jones* [1988] 2 WLR 952 a thief stole a van and sold it to A. The van passed through several more hands before being acquired by Jones, who bought it in good faith. The original owner sued Jones for the return of the van. Jones claimed to be the owner of the van under s.25. The House of Lords held that Jones was not the owner. Section 25 operates to pass good title as if the buyer in possession was a mercantile agent. We saw above at 9.3.1.1 that a mercantile agent only passes the title of the person who entrusted him with possession of the goods. Neither the thief nor any of the subsequent purchasers had a good title to the van. In *Car and Universal Finance Co Ltd* v *Caldwell* the claimants could not claim to have title to the car as a buyer in possession because the person who bought from the rogue, Motobella, did not act in good faith and did not therefore acquire title as a buyer in possession. It followed that no later buyer in the chain could claim title as a buyer in possession.

In *Re Highway Foods Ltd* [1995] BCLC 209 the owner of goods sold them to X under a retention of title clause. X sold the goods to Y, again under a retention of title clause. As the goods were resold under a retention of title clause this was an agreement to sell by the buyer in possession. We saw earlier that s.9 of the Factors Act is wider than s.25 SGA in that it encompasses an agreement to sell by the buyer in possession. Nevertheless, it was held that no title was passed. This was because both s.9 Factors Act and s.25 SGA state that the effect of the buyer in possession fulfilling the statutory requirements is as if the buyer in possession were a mercantile agent in possession of the goods with the consent of the owner. Adopting a similar line of reasoning to that in *Newtons of Wembley Ltd* v *Williams*, it was held that because a mercantile agent could not pass title by making an agreement to sell nor could a buyer in possession. Both of these cases took the line that the buyer in possession exception to the *nemo dat* rule can apply only to make the buyer in possession a notional mercantile agent.

9.3.6 Motor vehicles on hire-purchase

A person who takes goods on hire-purchase does not own the goods until all of the hire-purchase instalments have been paid. It follows that if such a person sells the goods before all of the instalments have been paid the buyer of the goods will not own them. Ownership will remain with the finance company who let the goods out on hire-purchase.

The Hire Purchase Act (HPA) 1964 Part III makes an exception where a motor vehicle on hire-purchase is sold to a private purchaser who takes it in good faith, without notice of the hire-purchase agreement. In such circumstances the title of the creditor (the finance company) will pass to the third party. The exception also applies where the goods are the subject of a conditional sale agreement. It applies only to motor vehicles. Section 29(1)(a)(iii) defines a motor vehicle as 'a mechanically propelled vehicle intended or adapted for use on roads to which the public has access'.

■ Example

A takes a car on hire-purchase. (A does not therefore own the car.) A sells the car to B, a dealer in cars. B sells the car to C, a private purchaser who takes it without knowing about the hire-purchase agreement. C will own the car, even though A and B did not. (If A had sold the car directly to C, then again C would own the car.)

Note the requirements:

(a) The Act only applies in favour of the first private purchaser, that is to say a purchaser who is not in business as a motor dealer or a finance company. If such a private purchaser gains a good title under HPA 1964 then he becomes the owner of the motorised vehicle and can pass ownership on to subsequent buyers.

(b) The first private purchaser must act in good faith and in ignorance of the hire-purchase agreement. If the first private purchaser acts otherwise than in good faith then no subsequent purchaser, private or otherwise, is protected.

(c) The protection only applies to motor vehicles on hire-purchase. It does not apply to other goods on hire-purchase. A motor vehicle is defined by s.29(1) of the Hire Purchase Act 1964 as 'a mechanically propelled vehicle adapted or intended for use on roads to which the public has access'.

(d) To be protected, the third party must either agree to buy the motor vehicle or must agree to take it on hire-purchase.

The title passed under the Act is only the title which the creditor had. If the creditor had no title then no title can be passed.

9.3.7 Special powers of sale

Section 21(2) of the Act states that:

'Nothing in this Act affects —
(a) the provisions of the Factors Acts …
(b) the validity of any contract of sale under any special common law or statutory power of sale or under the order of a court of competent jurisdiction.'

This section allows for a variety of situations in which it is recognised that a non-owner has the right to sell goods. Examples would include pawnbrokers selling unredeemed pledges, repairers selling unclaimed goods, and bailiffs selling goods seized under writs or warrants of execution.

9.3.8 Market overt

This exception to the *nemo dat* rule, which used to be contained in s.22 SGA 1979, was abolished by the Sale of Goods (Amendment) Act 1994 with effect from 3 January 1995. The exception can still apply as regards goods sold before that date. This was the only exception to the *nemo dat* rule which allowed a thief to pass a good title. It allowed a seller of goods to pass a good title if the goods were sold at an established market, according to the normal usage of the market, between the hours of sunrise and sunset, to a buyer who acted in good faith and without notice that the seller had a defective title to the goods. The exception also applied if goods were sold in the city of London.

Test your understanding

1 What is meant by the maxim *nemo dat quod non habet*?

2 What is a mercantile agent?

3 In what circumstances can a mercantile agent pass title to another person's goods without that person's consent?

4 In what circumstances will s.21 SGA regard a person as estopped?

5 What provision does s.23 make regarding a seller who has a voidable title to goods?

6 In what circumstances can a seller in possession after a sale pass a good title to goods?

7 In what circumstances does s.25 allow a buyer in possession to pass title to goods?

8 What exception to the *nemo dat* rule is set out in the Hire Purchase Act 1964?

Answers

1 The maxim means that a person who is not the owner of goods cannot pass ownership to another person, unless he does so as the agent of the owner.

2 A mercantile agent is an agent who has in the customary course of his business as such an agent authority to sell goods, to buy goods or to raise money on the security of goods.

3 If a mercantile agent has possession of goods, or of documents of title to goods, with the consent of the owner, for a purpose connected with his business as a mercantile agent, a sale or other disposition by the mercantile agent made in the ordinary course of business as a mercantile agent can pass title to the goods to a third party acting in good faith and without notice of the mercantile agent's lack of authority.

4 Section 21 SGA provides that an owner of goods who makes a representation to a third party that a seller of goods has the right to sell the goods will be estopped (prevented) from later denying the truth of the representation.

5 Section 23 provides that where a seller of goods has a voidable title to the goods, and this title has not been avoided at the time of the sale, a buyer who buys the goods in good faith and without notice of the seller's defect of title will acquire a good title to the goods.

6 Section 24 provides that if a seller (a seller in possession) sells goods to one person, but retains possession of the goods, and then sells or disposes of the same goods to a second person who takes delivery of the goods or of documents of title to the goods, the second buyer acquires title to the goods even if title had already passed to the first buyer.

7 Section 25 allows a person who has bought or agreed to buy goods (a buyer in possession) to pass title to the goods to a third party, as if the buyer in possession were acting as a mercantile agent on behalf of the owner of the goods. The buyer in possession must have obtained the goods, or documents of title to the goods, with the owner's consent. The third party must act in good faith and the goods, or documents of title, must be delivered to the third party under a contract of sale or other disposition of the goods.

8 The Hire Purchase Act 1964 Part III provides that a private purchaser acting in good faith who agrees to buy a motor vehicle which is the subject of a hire-purchase agreement, or who agrees to take the motor vehicle on hire-purchase, while acting in ignorance of the hire-purchase agreement, acquires title to the motor vehicle.

Key points

The passing of the property and the risk

- Once the property in goods sold passes to the buyer he will own the goods. Until the property passes the buyer will not own the goods.

- The property in specific goods passes when the parties to the contract intend it to pass, and this intention can either be a term of the contract or can be inferred from the conduct of the parties and the circumstances of the case (s.17).

- The Rules in s.18 apply only if the parties have not shown an intention as to when the property is to pass.

- Section 18 Rule 1 provides that where there is an unconditional contract for the sale of specific goods in a deliverable state the property in the goods passes to the buyer when the contract is made.

- Section 18 Rule 2 provides that where there is a contract for the sale of specific goods and the seller is bound to do something to the goods for the purpose of putting them into a deliverable state, the property does not pass until the thing is done and the buyer has notice that it has been done.

- Where there is a contract for the sale of specific goods, and the goods without the knowledge of the seller have perished at the time when a contract is made, the contract is void (s.6).

- Where there is an agreement to sell specific goods and subsequently the goods, without any fault on the part of the seller or buyer, perish before the risk passes to the buyer, the agreement is avoided (s.7).

- Subject to s.20A, where there is a contract for the sale of unascertained goods no property in the goods is transferred to the buyer unless and until the goods are ascertained (s.16).

- Section 18 Rule 5 provides that where there is a contract for the sale of unascertained or future goods by description, and goods of that description and in a deliverable state are unconditionally appropriated to the contract, either by the seller with the assent of the buyer or by the buyer with the assent of the seller, the property in the goods then passes to the buyer; and the assent may be express or implied, and may be given either before or after the appropriation is made.

- Section 20A makes it possible for a person who has bought a specified quantity of unascertained goods which form part of a bulk to become an owner in common of the bulk even though his share of the bulk has not been ascertained.

- Unless otherwise agreed, the goods remain at the seller's risk until the property in them is transferred to the buyer, but when the property in them is transferred to the buyer the goods are at the buyer's risk whether delivery has been made or not (s.20).

Reservation of title

- When goods are sold subject to a reservation of title clause the seller lets the buyer have possession of the goods, but the terms of the contract stipulate that the property in the goods is not to pass to the buyer until the full price of the goods has been paid.

- An all moneys clause states that the title is not to pass until all sums owing to the creditor, whether under the contract in question or under previous contracts, have been paid. When the buyer is a company, it is unclear whether such clauses are void as unregistered company charges.

- If the buyer of the goods which are the subject of a reservation of title clause resells the goods to a second buyer who takes delivery of the goods, the property in the goods will pass to the second buyer as long as the second buyer did not know of the reservation of title clause when making the contract and acted in good faith. It is possible, but very unlikely, that a reservation of title clause may entitle the original seller to the proceeds of sale.

Sale by a non-owner

- Subject to certain exceptions, a person who is not the owner of goods cannot pass ownership to anyone else. This rule is known by the Latin maxim *nemo dat quod non habet*.

- In certain circumstances a mercantile agent can pass ownership of goods to a third party, even if the mercantile agent did not have the authority of the owner to do this.

- If the owner of goods makes a representation to a third party that a seller of goods has the right to sell the goods, either as agent or owner, the owner can be prevented from denying the truth of the representation later.

- When the seller of goods has a voidable title to them, but his title has not been avoided at the time of the sale, the buyer acquires a good title to the goods, provided he buys them in good faith and without notice of the seller's defect of title (s.23).

- If a seller sells goods to one buyer, but keeps possession of the goods or of documents of title to the goods, and then sells or disposes of the same goods to a second buyer, who takes delivery of the goods or the documents of title, then the second buyer will get ownership of the goods (s.24).

- A person who has bought or agreed to buy goods can pass ownership of those goods to a sub-buyer, even if he had not himself acquired ownership. The goods, or documents of title to them, must be delivered to the sub-buyer as part of a contract of sale or other disposition of the goods (s.25).

- Where a motor vehicle on hire-purchase is sold to a private purchaser who takes it in good faith, without notice of the hire-purchase agreement, the title of the creditor (the finance company) can pass to the private purchaser (Hire Purchase Act 1964 Part III).

Summary questions

1 S Ltd sell goods to B Ltd for £1 000. B Ltd pays £400 in advance. The parties do not agree to separate the property from the risk. Why would it be important to know whether or not the property had passed if:

a S Ltd had become insolvent after the contract had been made?

b B Ltd had become insolvent after the contract had been made?

c The goods had become accidentally damaged, to the extent of making them of unsatisfactory quality, after the contract had been made?

2 Adam, a builder visits a wood yard and makes contracts to buy the following goods. A large industrial planing machine which is attached to the ground, an extremely heavy slab of slate which is lying in the wood yard and a heap of '3 by 2' timber. The timber is sold at 20p a foot and the seller is to measure it to see how many feet there are so that the price can be calculated. That night, before any of the goods have been paid for or taken away, the wood yard is burnt down by a fire caused by a stray firework and all of the goods are destroyed. Advise Adam of his legal position.

3 Belinda makes leather belts and bags which she sells to shops. Belinda leaves 20 bags at Cedric's shop on a sale or return basis. In what four ways might the property in the bags pass to Cedric?

4 David phones Edward's house and contracts to buy Edward's bench saw, which is embedded in the floor of Edward's workshop. No mention is made of the passing of the property or the risk.

a At what time would the property in the saw pass to David?

b What would be the legal position if, unknown to either party the saw had been destroyed by fire one hour before the contract was made?

c What would be the legal position if the saw was destroyed by fire one hour after the contract was made?

5 Look again at the facts of *Tarling* v *Baxter*, set out at p. 270 the 'Test your understanding' questions in this chapter. What would the legal position have been if it had been the seller's fault that the haystack was burnt down?

6 S Co Ltd, a company which sold china and pottery by mail order has gone into liquidation. Brian had ordered and paid for ten china plates depicting England's World Cup winning rugby squad. At the time of the order S Co Ltd had 200 cases of these plates. Billy had ordered two dozen Coronation tea cups and saucers. Unknown to Billy, S Co Ltd happened to have just two dozen such cups and saucers in their warehouse, but more would probably have been obtained by S Co Ltd fairly shortly. Bert had asked if S Co Ltd had any reject Coronation plates. S Co's manager had told Bert that there was a consignment of 50 such plates sitting in the warehouse, that this consignment had been bought at auction and that this was a one-off chance to buy as much of the consignment as Bert liked. Bert agreed to buy ten of these plates. All of the buyers paid the full price for the goods which they ordered. At the time of liquidation S Co Ltd had packed the orders for the three buyers and attached the buyer's names to the orders. Advise the three buyers of their legal positions.

7 S sold 100 gearboxes to B Co Ltd, a car manufacturer. B Co Ltd have now gone into liquidation. The contract of sale stated that S retained equitable and beneficial ownership of the gearboxes until B Co Ltd paid the price of the goods and also paid any other moneys owing to S. Over the years many such contracts had been made between the two parties and B Co Ltd had never entirely cleared its debts to S. The contract also stated that if B Co Ltd sold the gearboxes on to another buyer the gearboxes still remained the property of S and could be recovered from the sub-buyer; that if the gearboxes were sold while in finished cars S would own the cars until the cars were sold by B Co Ltd; and that if B Co Ltd sold the cars S would be entitled to the proceeds of sale. Ten of the gearboxes sold are lying in B Co Ltd's warehouse and can be identified. Fifty of the gearboxes have been fitted as components of finished cars which are waiting to be sold by B Co Ltd. Twenty of the gearboxes have been sold on to sub-buyers. These last 20 could be identified and have not been altered or mixed with other goods. Advise S of the likely effect of his reservation of title clause.

8 Work out who will own the goods in the following examples.

i A has agreed that B can borrow his bicycle while A goes on a month's holiday. Without permission or authority, B sells the bicycle to C, who believes that B is the owner of the bicycle. A did not know B well and made no attempt to check whether or not he was honest.

ii D buys a car from a garage, paying with a bad cheque. The following day the garage owner discovers that the cheque has bounced and tells the police and the AA to look out for the car. One week later D sold the car to E, an innocent purchaser who paid a reasonable price for the car.

  iii F has taken a car on hire-purchase from a finance company. F sells the car to G, a dealer in cars who does not know that the car is the subject of a hire-purchase agreement. G sells the car to H, another dealer in cars. I, a carpenter, buys the car from H in good faith and then sells it on to J.

  iv An art dealer who often sells paintings on behalf of clients is asked to renovate a painting by K, so that K can sell it at auction. L visits the art dealer's shop while the art dealer is having his lunch and the art dealer's shop assistant, M, sells the painting to L.

  v N visits an art dealer's shop and examines a painting for some considerable time. Later N phones the shop and makes a definite agreement to buy the painting for £2 000. The dealer is to deliver the painting to N's house the following day. Later, by mistake, a shop assistant sells the same painting to O, who takes it away.

  vi P buys a machine from Q for £4 000. Ownership is not to pass to P until the full price has been paid. P takes possession of the machine and, without Q's permission or knowledge, sells the machine to R. P has now become insolvent.

Multiple choice questions

1 On Thursday Alice, a dealer in fine art, visited Belinda's shop where she agreed to buy a large vase for £400. Alice gives Belinda a cheque for £400 and Belinda agrees to deliver the vase to Alice's house the following day. Later on Thursday Belinda takes the vase to her van, but she accidentally drops it and the vase is destroyed. Which one of the following is true.

  a No property passed to Alice and so she will not have to pay the price.

  b The property in the vase did pass to Alice. However, Belinda broke a duty of a bailee and will therefore be liable for destroying Alice's property.

  c The property in the vase would have passed at the time of the contract. However, the risk would have stayed with Belinda and so she would have to bear the loss.

  d The property in the vase would not have passed to Alice because the vase would not have been in a deliverable state until Belinda took it to her van.

2 Cedric agrees to buy 1 000 tons of Canadian wheat from David Ltd. David Ltd happens to have 5 000 tons of such wheat in his warehouse, although Cedric is not aware of this. Cedric pays the price immediately. Before the wheat is delivered David Ltd goes into liquidation. Which one of the following is true?

  a As the contract was for the sale of unascertained goods no property can have passed to Cedric. Cedric can only claim as an unsecured creditor of David Ltd.

  b Under s.20A SGA 1979, Cedric will have become a 1/5 owner of the 5 000 tons in David Ltd's warehouse. Cedric will therefore be able to claim his 1 000 tons from David Ltd's liquidator.

  c The contract would have become frustrated when David Ltd became insolvent. Under s.7 SGA 1979 Cedric would therefore be able to claim back the money which he paid.

  d If at the time of liquidation David Ltd had delivered 4 000 of the 5 000 tons of wheat in the warehouse to other buyers, Cedric's 1 000 tons would have become ascertained and would have become unconditionally appropriated to the contract by virtue of s.18 Rule 5(3). Cedric would therefore own the 1 000 tons remaining.

3 On Monday a private college agrees to buy all of a school's old whiteboards, which are attached to the walls of the school. On Tuesday the school detaches the whiteboards from the walls. On Wednesday the school phones the college to say that the whiteboards have been detached and that the college can pick them up during school hours. On Thursday the college collects the whiteboards from the school. The parties did not expressly or impliedly indicate when ownership was to pass. On which day will ownership of the whiteboards have passed to the college?

  a On Monday.

  b On Tuesday.

  c On Wednesday.

  d On Thursday.

4 Consider the following statements:

i The only circumstance in which any property in unascertained goods can pass from seller to buyer is by the operation of SGA s.20A.

ii Section 20A will operate to pass the property in the goods to the buyer whenever the buyer agrees to buy a specified quantity of an unidentified bulk.

iii Section 20A can only operate to pass the property in the goods to the buyer if the bulk of goods is identified either by the contract or by subsequent agreement between the parties.

iv Section 20A will operate in favour of a buyer who has agreed to pay some or all of the price.

v Section 20B provides that a person who becomes an owner in common of the bulk by virtue of s.20A is deemed to have consented to a delivery out of the bulk to any other owner in common of the bulk.

Which one of the following statements is correct?

a All of the above statements are true.

b (i), (iii) and (v) only are true.

c (i), (ii), (iv) and (v) only are true.

d (ii), (iii), (iv) and (v) only are true.

5 Which **one** of the following statements is **not** true?

a If a charge on company assets is not registered with the Registrar of Companies it will be invalid.

b Once goods which are the subject of a retention of title clause have been manufactured into other goods, so that they have lost their identity, then the seller's right to reclaim the goods sold will be lost.

c Goods may be sold subject to a reservation of title clause. But once the buyer takes delivery of the goods the seller's title will always be extinguished.

d A retention of title clause will be ineffective against a sub-buyer who buys the goods in good faith and who takes delivery of the goods.

6 On Friday Alice advertises her car for sale in the evening newspaper. A rogue, pretending to be Paul Gascoigne the ex-international footballer, persuades Alice to part with the car in exchange for a stolen cheque. Alice later wonders whether she should have taken the cheque. On Monday she presents the cheque to her bank and asks for quick clearance. The bank ring Alice to tell her that the cheque was stolen. Alice contacts the police and the large motoring organisations to report the deception and to ask them to keep a look out for the car. The police trace the car to Mr Smith, who bought it from the rogue at a second-hand car dealership which the rogue used to operate before he fled.
Which **one** of the following statements is **not** true?

a The rogue only had a voidable title to the car, but as long as Mr Smith bought the car in good faith before Alice told the police and the motoring organisations Mr Smith will get a complete title to the car under s.23 SGA 1979.

b The rogue only had a voidable title to the car. If Alice had avoided the contract before the rogue sold the car to Mr Smith then s.23 will not operate so as to pass a good title to Mr Smith.

c Regardless of s.23 of the Act, Mr Smith might have gained ownership of the car as the rogue could possibly have passed title under s.25 as a buyer in possession after a sale.

d Regardless of s.23 of the Act, Mr Smith might have gained ownership of the car as the rogue could possibly have passed title under s.24 as a seller in possession after a sale.

7 Mr Bibliophile discovers an antique book in his attic. Knowing that his local book dealer often sells goods on behalf of customers, he takes the book to his shop to find out the value of the book. The dealer tells Mr Bibliophile that the book is worth at least £2 000 and, if the prints are originals, could be worth much more. Mr Bibliophile agrees to pay the dealer 5% of the selling price if he finds out the value of the book and places it in a suitable auction. It is agreed that the dealer is not to sell the book without express permission from Mr Bibliophile. The dealer says that he will need to take the book to London to show it to an expert. While in his local pub the dealer gets drunk and sells the book to a wealthy collector. Which **one** of the following statements is true?

a The wealthy collector will own the book because the dealer was a buyer in possession after a sale.

   b The wealthy collector will own the book because the dealer was a seller in possession after a sale.

   c The wealthy collector will own the book because the dealer sold it as a mercantile agent.

   d Mr Bibliophile will still own the book and will be able to sue the wealthy collector for its return.

8 A rogue takes a car, a car radio and a trailer on hire-purchase from three different suppliers. The rogue sells all three items to Fred, who does not suspect that the rogue does not own the goods and who knows nothing of the hire-purchase agreements.

Which **one** of the following statements is true?

   a As the rogue owned none of the goods, Fred cannot own any of them either.

   b The rogue had a voidable title to the goods, and so Fred will have a complete title as long as he bought the goods before the various hirers discover the rogue's fraud and avoided the various contracts.

   c Fred will have a complete title to all of the goods.

   d Fred will have a complete title to the car, but no title to the radio or the trailer.

Task 9

A market trader friend of yours has recently bought several car battery chargers which, unbeknown to him, had been stolen six months ago. The police took the battery chargers from your friend and returned them to the owner. Your friend also bought tyre pumps from a company which went into liquidation before the pumps were delivered. So far none of the price of the pumps which your friend paid has been refunded by the company's liquidator. Your friend has asked you to write a report dealing with the following matters. In order that the report should be easy to understand you should include examples which relate to the business of a market trader wherever possible.

1 At what time does ownership of goods which have been bought pass to the buyer? What is the significance of ownership passing?

2 In what circumstances will a contract for the sale of specific goods become frustrated or void for mistake? What will be the effect of the contract becoming frustrated or void for mistake?

3 To what extent is it possible to sell goods but to retain ownership of them until the full price is paid?

4 Outline the circumstances in which a person who is not the owner of goods can nevertheless pass ownership to someone else.

Chapter 10

SALE OF GOODS – DUTIES OF THE PARTIES · REMEDIES · INTERNATIONAL SALES

Introduction

The Sale of Goods Act 1979 imposes duties on both the buyer and the seller of goods. It also sets out statutory remedies for breach of these duties. We begin this chapter by considering the seller's duty to deliver the goods. We then consider the three duties of the buyer: to pay the price, to accept the goods and to take delivery of the goods. Having considered the duties of the buyer and the seller, we examine the statutory remedies available for breach of these duties.

We conclude this chapter by examining international sales of goods. We begin by considering the legal effect of a bill of lading, a document which is central to international sales. We then consider the nature of two particular types of international sales, contracts made 'fob' (free on board) and 'cif' (cost insurance and freight).

10.1 · Duties of the seller

Section 27 of the SGA 1979 states that:

'It is the duty of the seller to deliver the goods, and of the buyer to accept and pay for them in accordance with the terms of the contract of sale.'

It can be seen from this that whereas the seller has only the one duty, the duty to deliver the goods, s.27 imposes two duties on the buyer, to accept the goods and to pay for them. The buyer has an additional duty to take delivery of the goods when requested to do so (s.37(1)).

The seller's duty to deliver the goods and the buyer's duty to pay for them are said by s.28 to be 'concurrent conditions', unless otherwise agreed. This does not mean that delivery and payment must necessarily take place simultaneously but rather that, unless otherwise agreed, the seller must be ready and willing to deliver the goods and the buyer must be ready and willing to pay for them. If the seller shows that he is not ready and willing to deliver, then the buyer can sue for damages without having actually paid the price, as long as he can show that he was ready and willing to pay. If the buyer shows that he is not ready and willing to pay the price, then the seller can sue for damages without having actually delivered the goods, as long as he can show that he was ready and willing to deliver. In many business contracts the rule in s.28 is varied as credit is given to the buyer. In most retail contracts payment of the price and delivery of the goods do take place at the same time.

10.1.1 The seller's duty to deliver

Section 27 states that the seller must deliver the goods 'in accordance with the terms of the contract'. If the contract was for the sale of specific goods, then the buyer must deliver the goods specified. If the contract was for the sale of unascertained goods, then the seller must deliver goods which match the contract description.

If the seller should fail to deliver as required the buyer can sue for damages for non-delivery and refuse to pay the price. If any part of the price has already been paid this can be recovered.

Section 61 defines delivery as 'voluntary transfer of possession from one person to another'. This does not necessarily mean that the seller must physically bring the goods to the buyer. Depending on the terms of the contract, it may mean only that the seller allows the buyer to come and collect the goods. It should be remembered that delivery concerns the transfer of possession of the goods, not the transfer of ownership.

10.1.1.1 Ways of effecting delivery

Delivery will usually take the form of physical delivery of the goods. However delivery can also be achieved by:

(a) Delivering the means to control the goods. (For example, giving the buyer the keys to a car or the keys to a warehouse where the goods are stored.)

(b) Getting a third party who holds the goods, such as a warehouseman, to acknowledge (attorn) that he now holds the goods for the buyer rather than for the seller.

(c) Delivering a document of title, such as a bill of lading, to the buyer. (In the previous chapter we saw that a car registration book is not a document of title. The legal status of a bill of lading is explained below at 10.5.1.)

(d) A buyer who has possession of the goods as a bailee retaining possession of the goods. For example, in hire-purchase contracts such a notional delivery will usually take place when the buyer pays the final instalment.

(e) Delivering the goods to a carrier. This is regarded as delivery to the buyer if the seller is authorised or required by the contract to send the goods to the buyer, as long as the carrier is not the seller's employee or agent (s.32(1)). The seller must make a reasonable contract with the carrier (s.32(2)). If the seller fails to make a reasonable contract the buyer may decline to treat delivery to the carrier as delivery to himself, or may hold the seller responsible in damages (s.32(2)). However, where the buyer deals as a consumer s.32(4) provides that s.32(1) and (2) must be ignored. If in pursuance of a contract of sale the seller is authorised or required to send the goods to a buyer who deals as a consumer, delivery of the goods to a carrier is not delivery of the goods to the buyer. (As we saw in the previous chapter, s.20(4) also provides that where the buyer deals as a consumer the goods remain at the seller's risk until they are delivered to the consumer.)

10.1.1.2 The place of delivery

Section 29 deals with the place of delivery:

(1) Whether it is for the buyer to take possession of the goods or for the seller to send them to the buyer is a question depending in each case on the contract, express or implied, between the parties.

(2) Apart from any such contract, express or implied, the place of delivery is the seller's place of business if he has one, and if not, his residence; except that, if the contract is for the sale of specific goods, which to the knowledge of the parties when the contract is made are in some other place, then that place is the place of delivery.

If the express or implied terms of the contract stipulate that the seller is to take the goods to the buyer or that the buyer is to go and pick the goods up from the seller then the place of delivery is agreed by the parties. If there is no such agreement then as regards unascertained goods the place of delivery is the seller's place of business or, if he has not got a place of business, his home. The place of delivery will also be the seller's place of business or his home as regards specific goods the whereabouts of which are not known to both parties. But when the contract is for the sale of specific goods which both parties know to be at some other place then that place is the place of delivery.

So unless the parties have shown a contrary intention it is up to the buyer to go and collect the goods. The seller fulfils the duty to deliver by making the goods available to the buyer. Very often the parties do show a contrary intention. The contract might stipulate, for example, that the goods are to be delivered to the buyer's house or place of business.

10.1.1.3 Time of delivery

If no time of delivery is fixed by the contract then delivery must be made within a reasonable time (s.29(3)). A tender of delivery must be made at a reasonable time of day and what amounts to a reasonable time of day is a question of fact (s.29(5)). A seller makes a tender of delivery by showing a willingness and readiness to deliver.

Any late delivery of the goods will amount to a breach of contract and so the buyer will always be entitled to damages for breach of warranty. In many cases however the buyer will want to go further and treat the contract as repudiated, as well as or instead of claiming damages. Whether or not the buyer will have this right will depend upon whether or not the term which the seller has broken by delivering late can be classified as a condition of the contract. Section 10(2) makes it plain that no general rule can be laid down by stating that whether or not the time of delivery is of the essence (a condition of the contract) depends upon the intentions of the parties. Case law has established that in commercial contracts any time of delivery fixed by the contract is presumed to be of the essence, and that this presumption is particularly strong where the goods are to be carried by sea.

■ *Bowes v Shand* (1877) 2 App Cas 455 (House of Lords)

A cargo of rice was sold on terms that the rice was to be shipped on board the Rajah of Cochin during the months of March or April 1874. Seven eighths of the rice was loaded on board in February 1874. The buyer refused to accept the rice as it had not been shipped at the correct time.

Held. The buyer was entitled to reject the cargo. Even though the early shipment did not affect the value of the rice, a condition had been broken.

If late delivery does amount to breach of condition the buyer may waive his right to treat the contract as breached if his conduct leads the seller to believe that he intends to carry on with the contract. Once the right to repudiate has been waived the buyer can only reintroduce it by giving the seller reasonable notice of his intention to do so.

■ *Charles Rickards v Oppenheim* [1950] 1 All ER 420 (Court of Appeal)

The claimants agreed to supply the defendant with a specialist car. The car was to be finished within seven months and a term of the contract stated that time was to be of the essence. The car was not completed on time but the defendant waived the original stipulation as to time by continuing to press for delivery on later dates. Three months after the original delivery date the defendant was told that the car would be ready within two weeks. The defendant then gave written notice that if it was not ready within one month he would refuse to take delivery of it. The car was not completed for another 15 weeks, at which time the defendant refused to take delivery of it.

Held. The defendant was entitled to refuse to take delivery. Having waived the initial stipulation that time was of the essence, the defendant had re-introduced it by giving reasonable notice.

If no time is initially fixed for delivery, so that delivery within a reasonable time is implied, this implied term is not initially a condition. However, the buyer can make the term a condition by giving the seller reasonable notice of his intention to do so. Even if the buyer does not do this the mere fact that more than a reasonable time has elapsed will entitle the buyer to treat the contract as repudiated.

■ *McDougall* v *Aeromarine of Emsworth Ltd* [1958] 3 All ER 431

The defendants contracted to build a yacht for the claimant, the yacht to comply with the claimant's specifications. The defendants agreed to try to finish the yacht by 1 May 1957, but this delivery date could not be guaranteed. The defendant paid the first instalment of the price in November 1956. The yacht was presented for a trial run on 3 June 1957. However, the yacht was not fit for its purpose. Negotiations took place between the claimant and the defendants, but by the beginning of September 1957 the yacht was still four or five weeks away from being ready for delivery. Four-fifths of the 1957 yachting season was by now over. The claimant therefore terminated the contract and demanded the repayment of his first instalment.

Held. The contract obliged the defendants to deliver the yacht within a reasonable time after 1 May 1957. This time had expired by September 1957. Applying s.10 SGA, the obligation as to time of delivery was a condition of the contract. The claimant was therefore entitled to repudiate the contract and get his money back.

10.1.1.4 Delivery of wrong quantity

Where the seller delivers to the buyer a quantity of goods which is less than the quantity he contracted to sell, the buyer may reject the goods, but if the buyer accepts the goods delivered he must pay for them at the contract rate (s.30(1)). So if, for example, a buyer of coal ordered ten tons of coal at a price of £1 000 and the seller delivered only nine tons the buyer could either reject the lot or pay £900 for the nine tons delivered. If the buyer rejected the lot, he could recover any of the price paid and make a claim for damages for non-delivery. If he accepted the nine tons he could recover part of the price and claim damages for non-delivery of the shortfall.

Where the seller delivers to the buyer a quantity of goods larger than he contracted to sell, the buyer may accept the quantity of goods which should have been delivered and reject the rest, or he may reject the whole (s.30(2)). Alternatively, the buyer may accept the whole of the goods delivered and pay for them at the contract rate (s.30(3)). So if in the above example the seller delivered 11 tons of coal, the buyer could either keep ten tons and pay £1 000, or reject the lot, or keep the lot and pay £1 100.

The rules in s.30 are subject to any usage of trade, special agreement or course of dealing between the parties (s.30(5)). They are also subject to the rule *de minimis lex non curat* – the law is not concerned with trifles. So if the extra quantity delivered amounted to a trifle then the seller will not have breached the contract.

■ *Shipton Anderson & Co* v *Weil Bros* [1912] 1 KB 574

A cargo of wheat was sold. The cargo was to weigh 10% more or less than 4 500 tons. The maximum quantity would therefore have been 4 950 tons. The sellers delivered 55 lb more than 4 950 tons. The buyers rejected the cargo on the grounds that the quantity delivered was in excess of the contract quantity. The sellers did not demand any extra payment for the extra 55 lb, which would have been worth about four shillings (20p).

Held. The excess delivered was a trifle and so the sellers had not breached the contract.

Section 30(2A), an amendment introduced by the Sale and Supply of Goods Act 1994, provides that a buyer who does not deal as a consumer cannot reject the goods on account of delivery of the wrong quantity if the seller can show that the shortfall or excess is so slight as to make rejection unreasonable. The rights of consumer buyers are not affected by this amendment. Consumers will be entitled to reject for delivery of the wrong quantity, subject to the *de minimis* rule.

10.1.1.5 Delivery by instalments

Unless otherwise agreed, a buyer of goods is not bound to accept delivery of them by instalments (s.31(1)). When the contract does allow for delivery by instalments problems can arise when the delivery of one or more instalments amounts to a breach of condition by the seller. Is the buyer entitled to terminate the whole contract, or is he only entitled to reject the defective instalment?

If the instalment contract can be regarded as entire, that is to say as one indivisible obligation, then a breach of condition as regards any of the instalments will entitle the buyer to treat the whole contract as repudiated. The buyer will therefore be entitled to return instalments already delivered and demand all of his money back.

If the contract is not entire, then s.31(2) will apply. It states that:

> 'Where there is a contract for the sale of goods to be delivered by stated instalments, which are to be separately paid for, and the seller makes defective deliveries in respect of one or more instalments, or the buyer neglects or refuses to take delivery of or pay for one or more instalments, it is a question in each case depending on the terms of the contract and the circumstances of the case whether the breach of contract is a repudiation of the whole contract or whether it is a severable breach giving rise to a claim for compensation but not a right to treat the whole contract as repudiated.'

Section 31(2) tells us that when considering whether the breach of a severable instalment contract amounts to a repudiation of the whole contract regard must be had to the terms of the contract and the circumstances of the case. That regard should be had to the terms of the contract is obvious enough; if the parties agree to a solution the courts will apply it. The following cases show that when the courts look to the circumstances of the case the two most important circumstances to be considered are: (i) the ratio of the breach to the contract as a whole; and (ii) the likelihood of the breach being repeated.

■ *Maple Flock Co Ltd* v *Universal Furniture Products (Wembley) Ltd* [1934] 1 KB 148 (Court of Appeal)

100 tons of rag flock (waste wool) were sold. The flock was to be delivered in three loads a week, each load weighing one and a half tons and each to be separately paid for. The contract contained a written guarantee that the flock would conform to Government standards, which permitted 30 parts of chlorine to 100 000 parts flock. It was a criminal offence to use flock containing more chlorine than this. The sixteenth load delivered contained 250 parts chlorine. The defendants did not realise this until two further loads had been delivered. On discovering that the sixteenth load was defective the defendants claimed to treat the contract as repudiated.

Held. The claimants' breach of contract did not amount to a repudiation of the whole contract. The breach affected only a small ratio of the contract and was unlikely to be repeated.

By contrast, in *Robert A. Munro & Co Ltd* v *Meyer* [1930] 2 KB 312 the buyers were entitled to treat the whole contract as repudiated. The contract was for the sale of 1 500 tons of bone and meal by instalments. The first 651 tons delivered had been adulterated with cocoa husks and this amounted to a repudiation of the whole contract by the sellers. The buyers were not therefore obliged to take future instalments and were entitled to damages in respect of the deliveries already received. They could have refused to accept these deliveries if they had discovered the defect in time to do so.

10.1.1.6 The importance of delivery

Delivery is concerned with possession of the goods rather than with ownership. It is however important because once delivery has been made or tendered:

(i) the buyer must accept the goods or face the prospect of paying damages for non-acceptance;

(ii) the seller can demand payment (although it is possible that he may not be able to sue for the price);

(iii) it will no longer be possible for an unpaid seller to have a lien over the goods. (The unpaid seller's lien is considered below at 10.3.1.)

If the seller breaches the duty to deliver the buyer will be able to sue for damages for non-delivery. The buyer may also have a right to treat the contract as repudiated or to bring an action for specific performance. (The buyer's remedies are considered later in this chapter at 10.4.)

Test your understanding

1 A buyer of goods has indicated to the seller that he is not ready and willing to pay for the goods. Must the seller deliver the goods in accordance with the contract before he can sue for damages for non-acceptance?

2 If the contract does not contain a term fixing the place of delivery, where will this place be as regards

    a Unascertained goods?

    b Specific goods, the whereabouts of which are not known to both of the parties?

    c Specific goods, the whereabouts of which are known to both of the parties?

3 What is the significance of the time of delivery being of the essence in a contract of sale of goods? How will a court decide whether or not time was of the essence?

4 What options are open to the buyer if;

    a the seller delivers too large a quantity of goods?

    b the seller delivers too small a quantity?

5 In a severable instalment contract, a buyer wishes to terminate the whole contract on account of a breach of condition as regards one instalment. How will it be decided whether or not the buyer can do this?

Answers

1 The seller would not have to actually deliver the goods. He could sue for damages for non-acceptance as long as he could show that he had been ready and willing to deliver the goods. Section 28 makes it plain that the duty of the seller to deliver the goods and of the buyer to pay for them are concurrent conditions.

2 (a) and (b) the place of delivery is the seller's place of business or, if he has not got a place of business, his home (s.29(2)). (c) The place of delivery will be the place where both of the parties know the goods to be (s.29(2)).

3 If time of delivery is of the essence then the time of delivery is a condition. Consequently the buyer can treat the contract as repudiated, and/or claim damages, if the goods are delivered late. If time was not of the essence then the buyer will only be able to claim damages. Whether or not time is of the essence depends upon the intentions of the parties (s.10(2)).

4 (a) If the seller delivers too large a quantity of goods then the buyer may accept the correct quantity of goods and reject the rest, or he may reject the whole (s.30(2)). Or the buyer may accept the whole of the goods delivered and pay for them at the contract rate (s.30(3)). (b) If the seller delivers too small a quantity then the buyer may reject the goods, or accept the goods delivered and pay for them at the contract rate (s.30(1)).

5 The buyer will be able to treat the whole contract as repudiated only if the breach by the seller amounted to a repudiation of the whole contract. It is a question in each case depending on the terms of the contract and the circumstances of the case whether the breach of contract is a repudiation of the whole contract or whether it is a severable breach giving rise to a claim for compensation but not a right to treat the whole contract as repudiated (s.31(2)).

10.2 · Duties of the buyer

The buyer has three duties; to pay the price, to accept the goods, and to take delivery of the goods.

10.2.1 The duty to pay the price

Unless otherwise agreed, payment of the price and delivery of the goods are concurrent conditions. As we have seen, this means that the seller must be ready to give possession of the goods to the buyer in exchange for the price, and the buyer must be ready and willing to pay the price in exchange for possession of the goods (s. 28). If one of the parties shows an unwillingness to perform the contract then the other party is entitled to withhold performance. Late payment of the price, unlike late delivery of the goods, amounts only to a breach of warranty unless a different intention appears from the terms of the contract (s.10(1)).

Section 8 explains how the price is to be fixed:

'(1) The price in a contract of sale may be fixed by the contract, or may be left to be fixed in a manner agreed by the contract, or may be determined by the course of dealing between the parties.

(2) When the price is not determined as mentioned in subsection (1) above the buyer must pay a reasonable price.

(3) What is a reasonable price is a question of fact dependent on the circumstances of each particular case.'

To illustrate the effect of s.8, let us assume that Firm A orders goods from Firm B. It would usually be the case that the price would be expressly agreed in the contract. However, the contract might instead specify the manner in which the price is to be fixed. It might, for instance, state that the price will be fixed by an independent third party. If the contract neither fixed the price nor agreed the manner of fixing it, the court would look at previous dealings between Firm A and Firm B. If it discovered that the same price was always paid for goods of the type sold then, in the absence of any indication to the contrary, this would be taken to be the price. If none of the above methods helped, Firm A would have to pay a reasonable price, which would depend upon the circumstances of the particular case. If the parties agree that they will themselves fix the price at some future date then there will be no concluded contract. (See *May and Butcher Ltd* v *R*, Summary Question 10 in Chapter 3.)

10.2.2 The duty to accept the goods

The word 'accept' is not used here in its everyday sense of taking possession of the goods. Rather it means that the buyer must not wrongfully reject the goods. If the buyer does wrongfully reject the goods then this will constitute a repudiatory breach. The seller will therefore be entitled to terminate the contract and to sue the buyer for damages for non-acceptance.

10.2.3 The duty to take delivery of the goods

The buyer has a duty to take delivery of the goods. Where the seller is ready and willing to deliver the goods, and requests the buyer to take delivery, and the buyer does not within a reasonable time after such request take delivery of the goods, he is liable to the seller for any loss occasioned by his neglect or refusal to take delivery, and also for a reasonable charge for the care and custody of the goods (s.37(1)).

10.3 · Remedies of the seller

Whenever the buyer breaches the contract the seller will be entitled to a remedy. The remedies available to the seller can be classified as real remedies or personal remedies. Real remedies are taken against the goods, personal remedies are taken against the buyer.

10.3.1 Real remedies of the unpaid seller

The real remedies against the goods are only available to an unpaid seller. Section 38 defines a seller as an unpaid seller –

(a) when the whole of the price has not been paid or tendered;
(b) when a bill of exchange or other negotiable instrument has been received as conditional payment, and the condition on which it was received has not been fulfilled by reason of dishonour of the instrument or otherwise.

Section 38(a) allows a seller to be classed as an unpaid seller even if the buyer has been granted credit. Where the buyer pays by cheque, s.38(b) makes the seller an unpaid seller if the buyer's cheque is dishonoured.

There are three real remedies which the unpaid seller might have: a lien on the goods; the right to stop them in transit; or the right to resell them. These remedies are available even though the property in the goods has already passed to the buyer.

10.3.1.1 Lien

Section 41(1) explains the seller's right to a lien:

'(1)Subject to this Act, the unpaid seller of goods who is in possession of them is entitled to retain possession of them until payment or tender of the price in the following cases:—
  (a) where the goods have been sold without any stipulation as to credit;
  (b) where the goods have been sold on credit but the term of credit has expired;
  (c) where the buyer becomes insolvent.'

■ Example

Farmer A visits farmer B's farm and agrees to buy a second-hand tractor for £3 000. There is no mention of credit and the parties do not discuss when the property or the risk are to pass. As the tractor is specific goods in a deliverable state, the property in the goods would pass to farmer A upon the making of the contract (s.18 Rule 1). However, farmer B would be entitled to keep possession of the tractor until the full £3 000 had been paid or tendered. If farmer A gave farmer B a cheque farmer B would still be entitled to exercise his right of lien. Offering a cheque as payment does not amount to a tender of the price, the exact sum of money in cash would have to be offered.

A seller who exercises his right of lien and retains possession of the goods does not thereby terminate the contract (s.48(1)). If the price is later paid by the buyer, or by the buyer's liquidator, then the seller will have to hand possession of the goods to the buyer. The right to a lien is excluded when the seller has granted credit to the buyer, unless the credit has expired. A lien is most likely to be useful where goods have been sold to a buyer without granting any credit and the buyer has become insolvent before paying the full price of the goods.

Section 43 sets out three ways in which an unpaid seller will lose the lien:

'(a) when he delivers the goods to a carrier or other bailee or custodier for the purpose of transmission to the buyer without reserving the right of disposal of the goods;
  (b) when the buyer or his agent lawfully obtains possession of the goods;
  (c) by waiver of the lien or right of retention.'

Section 43 makes it clear that retention of possession by the seller is the key to the lien.

10.3.1.2 Stoppage in transit

Once the seller has delivered the goods to a carrier nor other bailee for transmission to the buyer he has waived his lien by giving up possession of the goods. However, if the buyer is insolvent, the seller can stop the goods while they are still in transit. The carrier must then redeliver the goods as directed by the seller and the seller must pay the expenses of this (s.46(4)). If the seller does not stop the goods while they are in transit the buyer's trustee in bankruptcy or liquidator will regard the goods as just another asset, to be applied in paying off all the creditors. The exercise of stoppage in transit does not of itself terminate the contract (s.48(1)). The trustee in bankruptcy or liquidator may choose to tender the price and enforce the contract.

An actual physical stopping of the goods is not necessary. The seller merely needs to give the carrier notice that he is exercising his right. However, once the goods have been delivered to the buyer the seller will be too late. The carrier must be a common carrier and not the agent of either the buyer or the seller. (If the carrier is the seller's agent, the seller can exercise the right of lien; if the carrier is the buyer's agent, the right of stoppage in transit will be ended when the carrier receives the goods.)

■ Example

S Ltd has sold 100 garden tables to B Ltd. S has delivered the tables to a common carrier for delivery to B Ltd. The property in the goods has therefore passed to B Ltd. S Ltd hears on the local news that B Ltd has become insolvent. S Ltd contacts the carrier to give notice that they are effecting stoppage in transit. The carrier must redeliver the goods to S Ltd, who must pay the costs of this redelivery. B Ltd's liquidator could still choose to pay for the goods as the contract of sale is not terminated.

Stoppage in transit was a more potent right in the last century when delivery of goods was a much slower process.

Neither the unpaid seller's lien nor the right of stoppage in transit are affected by any sale or other disposition of the goods which the buyer may have made, unless the seller has assented to it (s.47(1)). However, if the buyer is given a document of title, and if he transfers this to a third party acting in good faith and for valuable consideration, then the unpaid seller's rights of lien and stoppage in transit are lost or can only be exercised subject to the rights of the transferee (s.47(2)). Where an unpaid seller who has exercised his right of lien or retention or stoppage in transit resells the goods, the second buyer acquires good title to them against the original buyer (s.48(2)).

The unpaid seller's lien and right to stop the goods in transit apply where the property in the goods has already passed to the buyer. Where the property in the goods has not passed to the buyer the unpaid seller has (in addition to his other remedies) a right of withholding delivery similar to and coextensive with his rights of lien or retention and stoppage in transit where the property has passed to the buyer (s.39(2)).

10.3.1.3 The right to resell the goods

The purpose of a contract of sale of goods is to pass ownership of the goods from the seller to the buyer. Once ownership has passed the seller therefore has no right to resell the goods to anyone else because the goods are no longer his. You should notice that here we are talking about the right to resell, not the power to do so. Section 24 SGA (considered in the previous chapter at 9.3.4) would give a seller in possession the power to pass ownership to a second buyer. However, this would generally amount to a breach of the contract made with the original buyer. When the seller has a right of resale he commits no breach of contract by exercising it and can recover damages from the original buyer. Section 48(2) and (3) give the seller a right to resell the goods to a second buyer in three circumstances:

(a) Where the goods are of a perishable nature and the buyer does not pay or tender the price within a reasonable time.
(b) Where the unpaid seller gives the buyer notice of an intention to resell the goods and the buyer does not pay or tender the price within a reasonable time.
(c) Where the contract expressly allows for a right of resale.

An unpaid seller would also have a right to resell where the first buyer repudiates the contract, that is to say where the buyer expressly or impliedly makes known to the seller that he no longer regards himself as bound by the contract.

If the seller exercises his right of resale this terminates the contract with the original buyer. As long as the resale was justified, the seller can sue the original buyer for damages if he has to resell at a lower price. He can keep any extra profit if he resells at a higher price. The seller will of course not be able to sue for the price and will have to refund any part of the price already paid. The insolvency of the buyer is not enough to give the unpaid seller the right to resell, as the liquidator has the option of paying the price and enforcing the contract.

10.3.2 Personal remedies of the seller

The seller has two personal remedies against the buyer: to sue for the price, or to sue for damages for non-acceptance.

10.3.2.1 An action for the price

Section 49 stipulates that the seller can only sue for the price if the property in the goods has passed to the buyer or if the contract fixed a definite date for payment.

■ *Colley* v *Overseas Exporters Ltd* [1921] 3 KB 302

A quantity of unascertained leather goods were sold on fob terms. (Fob is explained below at 10.5.2.) The buyer had a duty to nominate an effective ship on to which the goods could be loaded. The buyer breached the contract because, despite five attempts, he could not secure an effective ship. The goods were left lying on the docks. The sellers sued for the contract price.

Held. The sellers could not sue for the price because the contract did not fix a definite date for payment and the property in the goods had not passed to the buyer. (In an fob contract the property in the goods passes to the buyer when the goods are passed over the ship's rail.)

COMMENT At first sight this seems particularly harsh on the seller. However, the seller would be able to claim damages for non-acceptance (see immediately below).

If the seller sues for the price then questions of mitigation or remoteness of damage will not arise. The seller will be suing for a debt, not suing for damages. (See Chapter 7 at 7.2.3.)

10.3.2.2 Damages for non-acceptance

If the buyer has refused to accept and pay for the goods the seller will be able to sue for damages for non-acceptance. This remedy is available whether the property in the goods has passed to the buyer or not. A seller who has the right to sue for the price might elect to sue for damages for non-acceptance instead.
  Section 50 states that:

'(1) Where the buyer wrongfully neglects or refuses to accept and pay for the goods, the seller may maintain an action against him for damages for non-acceptance.
(2) The measure of damages is the estimated loss directly and naturally resulting in the ordinary course of events, from the buyer's breach of contract.
(3) Where there is an available market for the goods in question the measure of damages is *prima facie* to be ascertained by the difference between the contract price and the market or current price at the time or times when the goods ought to have been accepted or (if no time was fixed for acceptance) at the time of the refusal to accept.'

Section 50(2) reiterates the first Rule in *Hadley* v *Baxendale* (which we considered in Chapter 7 at 7.2.2.1). It would cater for the seller recovering any foreseeable losses caused by the buyer's breach, such as profit which the seller would have made on the sale. The second Rule in *Hadley* v *Baxendale* is not mentioned by the Act but it would be applied under the common law. Where there is an available market for the goods s.50(3) explains how the courts will assess the loss directly and naturally flowing from the breach. There will be an available market if the goods were not unique, if a different buyer of the goods could be found, and if the price of the goods could be fixed by the prevailing conditions of supply and demand. There is no available market for second-hand cars as they are regarded as unique.
  Where there is such an available market the *prima facie* measure of damages will be the difference between the contract price and the price at the time when the goods ought to have been accepted or, if the time for acceptance was not fixed, at the time when the buyer refused to accept. If the market price of the goods has risen or remained the same, then the seller ought to mitigate his loss by reselling the goods to another buyer. If the seller does not do this then he will not be entitled to damages for loss of profit on the sale. If the market price of the goods has fallen, then generally the seller's lost profit will be calculated as the contract price minus the market price at the time when the goods ought to have been accepted.

■ **Example**

On 1 April A sells a ton of wheat to B at a price of £1 000, delivery to be made on 20 April. On 20 April B refuses to accept the wheat. If on 20 April the market price of a ton of this type of wheat was £1 200 then the seller will not be entitled to damages for any loss of profit. He could have mitigated his loss by selling the wheat to another buyer. If on 20 April the price of wheat was £800 then *prima facie* the seller's damages for loss of profit will be £200. If on 20 April the price of wheat was £1 000 then the seller will not be entitled to any damages for loss of profit.

It should be noticed that the seller does not have to sell in the available market. He can, instead, take a gamble and hold on to the goods, hoping that the market price will rise. However, the damages will still be assessed by reference to the market price at the time when the goods ought to have been accepted, even if the seller does not try to resell the goods in the market.

Section 54 states that:

'Nothing in this Act affects the right of the buyer or seller to recover interest or special damage in any case where by law interest or special damage may be recoverable, or to recover money paid where the consideration for the payment has failed.'

This section preserves the common law rules on damages and allows the seller to claim for other expenses reasonably incurred if they can reasonably be supposed to have been in the contemplation of the parties at the time of the contract. These might include matters such as the cost of reselling the goods, or of storing them or insuring them.

10.3.2.3 Damages for refusing to take delivery

If the buyer accepts the goods late then damages for refusing to take delivery can be recovered under s.37, which states that:

'(1) When the seller is ready and willing to deliver the goods, and requests the buyer to take delivery, and the buyer does not within a reasonable time after such request take delivery of the goods, he is liable to the seller for any loss occasioned by his neglect or refusal to take delivery, and also for a reasonable charge for the care and custody of the goods.

(2) Nothing in this section affects the rights of the seller where the neglect or refusal of the buyer to take delivery amounts to a repudiation of the contract.'

These damages are not designed to compensate for loss of bargain, but only for delay in taking delivery. Although s.37(1) mentions a reasonable charge for care and custody of the goods, other expenses, such as extra insurance, or the costs involved in attempting to deliver, might also be recoverable. Sellers suing for damages for non-acceptance would include the losses mentioned in s.37(1) as part of their claim for damages under s.50.

10.3.2.4 The seller's right to terminate the contract

If the buyer has repudiated the contract the seller may accept the repudiation and treat the contract as terminated. The seller will then have no further obligation to perform the contract and may sue for the price or for damages. Whether or not the buyer's behaviour can be taken as repudiating the contract will be decided upon general contract principles.

Test your understanding

1 By what methods can the price of goods in a contract of sale be fixed?

2 What is the definition of an unpaid seller?

3 What three remedies are available only to an unpaid seller?

4 In what two circumstances does a seller of goods have a right to sue for the price?

5 As far as the market rule in s.50(3) is concerned, what is the meaning of an available market for the goods? Where there is such an available market how will the courts assess the loss directly and naturally flowing from the breach?

Answers

1 The price of the goods can be fixed by the contract, or by a manner agreed by the contract, or may be determined by a course of dealing between the parties (s.8(1)). If the price is not fixed in any of these ways then the buyer must pay a reasonable price (s.8(2)). What amounts to a reasonable price is a question of fact dependent on the circumstances of each particular case (s.8(3)).

2 An unpaid seller is a seller to whom the whole of the price has not been paid or tendered, or a seller who has taken a negotiable instrument as conditional payment and the condition on which this was taken has not been fulfilled (s.38(1)).

3 The three remedies available only to an unpaid seller are: the unpaid seller's lien; stoppage in transit and the right of resale.

4 The seller can only sue for the price if the property in the goods has passed to the buyer or if the contract fixed a definite date for payment (s.49).

5 There will be an available market if the goods were not unique, if a different buyer of the goods could be found, and if the price of the goods could be fixed by the prevailing conditions of supply and demand. Where there is such an available market the court will *prima facie* assess the loss directly and naturally flowing from the breach as the difference between the contract price and the price at the time when the goods ought to have been accepted or, if the time for acceptance was not fixed, at the time when the buyer refused to accept (s.50(3)).

10.4 · Remedies of the buyer

Any breach of contract by the seller will entitle the buyer to damages. These damages will be available either for non-delivery of the goods, or for late delivery or for breach of warranty. Where the seller has breached a condition, or where the breach of an innominate term has deprived the buyer of substantially the whole benefit of the contract, the buyer will also be entitled to treat the contract as repudiated and reject the goods. The buyer will lose the right to reject the goods once the goods have been accepted, although the right to damages will remain.

10.4.1 The buyer's right to damages

Section 51(1) gives the buyer the right to sue for damages for **non-delivery** where the seller wrongfully neglects or refuses to deliver the goods. This right would also be available if the seller breached a condition and the buyer treated the contract as repudiated. The measure of damages is the estimated loss directly and naturally resulting in the ordinary course of events from the seller's breach of contract (s.51(2)).

Section 51(3) states that where there is an available market for the goods in question the measure of damages is *prima facie* to be ascertained by the difference between the contract price and the market price of the goods at the time or times when they ought to have been delivered or (if no time was fixed) at the time of the refusal to deliver. This 'market price' rule is the inverse of s.50(3). The principles set out in s.51 are very similar to the principles in s.50. In addition special damages might be available under s.54.

■ **Example**

On 1 September S agrees to sell a ton of wheat to B for £10 000. The date of delivery is fixed as 20 September but S does not deliver on that date. If there was an available market for the goods in question, then under s.51(3) B's right to damages would *prima facie* be as follows: (a) if the market price of this type of wheat was £9 500 on 20 September then B will be entitled to no damages; (b) if the market price had gone up to £11 000 then *prima facie* B will be entitled to damages of £1 000; (c) if the market price had remained at £10 000 B will be entitled to no damages. Whatever B's entitlement under s.51, special damages which were in the seller's contemplation at the time of the contract, such as additional transport costs, might be recoverable under s.54. Where the market rule did not apply then under s.51(2) B would be entitled to claim damages for foreseeable losses or losses which can reasonably be supposed to have been contemplated by S at the time of the contract, on ordinary contract principles. These damages might be in respect of profit lost by B, or the expenses of finding another seller of wheat.

Section 53 deals with damages where there has been **a breach of warranty,** or where the **buyer elects (or is compelled) to treat a breach of condition as a breach of warranty.** In these circumstances the buyer cannot reject the goods, but can either sue the seller for damages for breach of warranty or can deduct damages which would be payable for breach of warranty from the price the seller is to be paid (s.53(1)). The measure of damages is to be calculated under *Hadley* v *Baxendale* Rule 1 (s.53(2)). In the case of a breach of warranty of quality the buyer's loss is *prima facie* the difference between the value of the goods in the state they were in and the value which they would have had if the warranty had not been breached (s.53(3)).

In the following case the Court of Appeal did not apply the *prima facie* rule set out in s.53(3).

■ *Bence Graphics International Ltd* v *Fasson UK Ltd* [1997] 1 All ER 979 (Court of Appeal)

The defendants supplied cast vinyl film to the value of £564 328 to the claimants. This film was used by the claimants to manufacture decals, the purpose of which was to identify bulk containers in the shipping industry. A term of the contract provided that the film should remain in good legible condition for at least five years. In fact the film degraded prematurely and many of the decals became illegible. As a consequence the claimants were unable to sell on about £22 000 worth of film. Although the claimants received several complaints from customers, very few actual claims were made against the claimants. When the claimants sued for breach of warranty the defendants admitted liability. Applying s.53(3) the judge awarded damages of £564 328, plus interest as the amount of damages. He regarded this as the amount which the parties would have thought would have been recoverable for breach of warranty when the contract was made.

Held. Where goods containing a latent defect were sold, and the defect only became apparent after the goods were converted in a manner contemplated by both parties and then sold on, the measure of damages should be the actual loss suffered by the buyer under or arising from a breach of contract for onward sales. In these circumstances the *prima facie* rule was displaced. At the time of making the contract the parties were aware of facts which indicated to both of them that the loss would not be that set out in the *prima facie* rule in s.53(3). The parties would have contemplated the measure of damages as the claimants' liability to the ultimate user. The defendants knew that the claimants sold the film on and therefore knew that a breach of warranty would result in the claimants having to pay damages.

The Sale of Goods Act makes no special rules on damages when the goods are delivered late and the buyer accepts them. Damages for **late delivery** will therefore be assessed on ordinary contract principles. If time is of the essence and the buyer chooses to treat the late delivery as a breach of condition then damages will be available for non-delivery and quantified under s.51.

10.4.2 The right to reject the goods

The buyer will have the right to reject the goods in four circumstances. First, if the seller has breached a condition of the contract or delivered the wrong quantity of goods. Second, if the seller has breached an innominate term and this breach has deprived the buyer of substantially the whole benefit of the contract. Third, if the express or implied terms of the contract conferred upon the buyer a right to reject. Fourth, if the seller has repudiated the contract.

The buyer can reject the goods after they have been delivered and after ownership of the goods has passed to him, as long as he has not accepted the goods. When the buyer rightfully refuses to accept the goods he does not have to return them physically to the seller, it is enough that he lets the seller know that he is refusing to accept them (s.36). Having rightfully rejected the goods, the buyer can sue for damages for non-delivery. The buyer can also refuse to pay the price and recover any amount of the price which has already been paid.

If the buyer wrongfully rejects then the seller can treat the contract as repudiated. The seller will then be able to treat the contract as discharged and sue for damages for non-acceptance.

A buyer faced with a breach of condition does not have to reject the goods. The buyer may elect to treat the breach of condition as a breach of warranty and sue for damages instead (s.11(2)).

10.4.3 Acceptance of the goods

Acceptance of the goods by the buyer is highly significant because once goods sold under a non-severable contract have been accepted a breach of condition by the seller can only be treated by the buyer as a breach of warranty. The buyer will therefore be able to claim damages for the breach of warranty but will not be able to reject the goods and treat the contract as repudiated (s.11(4)).

Under s.35 a buyer is deemed to have accepted the goods when:

(a) he intimates to the seller that he has accepted them (s.35(1)(a));
(b) when the goods have been delivered to him and he does any act in relation to them which is inconsistent with the ownership of the seller (s.35(1)(b));
(c) when after the lapse of a reasonable time the buyer retains the goods without intimating to the seller that he is rejecting them (s.35(4)).

The buyer would intimate to the seller that he is accepting the goods by letting the seller know that the goods have been accepted or by giving the seller the impression that they have been accepted. Where goods are delivered to the buyer and he has not previously examined them, the buyer will not be deemed to have accepted the goods by intimating acceptance to the seller unless he has had a reasonable opportunity to examine the goods to see whether they are in conformity with the contract (s.35(2)). If the buyer is a consumer he cannot lose this right conferred by s.35(2) (s.35(3)).

A buyer will be deemed to have accepted goods delivered to him when in relation to the goods he does an act which is inconsistent with the seller's continuing ownership. Such an act might take the form of selling the goods on, or using them or asking for them to be repaired. (Although s.35(6), which was added by the Sale and Supply of Goods Act 1994, tells us that neither asking the seller to repair the goods nor delivering the goods to a sub-buyer are necessarily to be taken as acceptance of the goods.) However, a buyer will not be deemed to have accepted the goods in this way unless he has had a reasonable opportunity to examine the goods to see whether they are in conformity with the contract (s.35(2)). A consumer buyer cannot lose this right (s.35(3)).

A buyer who retains the goods for more than a reasonable time, whether a consumer buyer or not, can be deemed to have accepted the goods even though he has not had a chance to examine the goods to see whether they are in conformity with the contract. However, whether or not the buyer has had a reasonable opportunity of examining the goods to see whether they are in conformity with the contract is material in deciding what amounts to a reasonable time (s.35(5)). A term of the contract which fixed a date for rejection would be held to be effective, as long as it was not an exclusion clause. If it was an exclusion clause then it could be effective against a non-consumer buyer as long as it satisfied the UCTA 1977 requirement of reasonableness, but could not be effective against a consumer buyer.

The meaning of s.35 was considered in the following two cases.

■ *Truk (UK) Ltd* v *Tokmakidis GmbH* [2000] 1 Lloyd's Rep 543

The claimants, an English company, contracted to supply and fit towing and lifting equipment to a chassis supplied by the defendants, a German company. This was a sale of goods. The essence of the contract was the delivery and sale of the lifting and towing equipment, which would allow broken down HGV vehicles to be recovered. The claimants delivered the vehicle on 14 June 1996. However, the contract was breached in that the vehicle did not comply with certain guidelines specified in the contract. The defendants had bought the goods for resale. The contract envisaged that the resale of the vehicle might take more than 6 months, in that it provided that the price should be paid six months after delivery or on resale, whichever was sooner. The claimants had not intimated that they were rejecting until they discovered, in December 1996, that the vehicle did not comply with the contract specifications. (A potential buyer had pointed this out.) The parties then entered into negotiations which lasted until July 1997, when the defendants rejected the goods and refused to accept redelivery of a repaired vehicle.

Held. A reasonable time in which to intimate rejection had not passed. When goods are sold for resale, defects in the goods are often only discovered when the sub-buyer examines the goods. Therefore, a reasonable time in which to intimate rejection of the goods would usually be the time which it would be expected would be needed to resell the goods plus an additional period in which the sub-purchaser might inspect them and try them out. (If the vehicle had not been for resale, a month or two might have been a reasonable time on these facts, although discussions about remedying defects might have extended this period.) In July 1997 the defendants were still entitled to reject because they had done nothing to affirm the contract. Nor were they deemed to have accepted the goods by failing to reject them within a reasonable time. They had reserved their position while they were discovering what was wrong and negotiating, and they were allowed a reasonable time for that.

■ *Clegg* v *Andersson* [2003] 2 Lloyd's Rep 32

In December 1999 Clegg agreed to buy a new Malo 42 yacht from Andersson for £236 000. The shoal draught keel was to be in accordance with Malo's specification. Malo delivered the yacht to Andersson on 25 July 2000 and he delivered the yacht to Clegg on 12 August 2000. At the time of delivery Andersson told Clegg that the yacht's keel was considerably heavier than the weight prescribed by Malo's specification. This extra weight caused the yacht to sit low in the water. Having taken the yacht on an eight-day cruise to Falmouth and Alderney, Clegg told Andersson that he liked the yacht and the way it sailed. Later Clegg complained about the extra weight, which gave the yacht too much stability, a matter which affected sailing performance and the rig loads. Andersson wrote to Clegg saying that Malo would reduce the weight of the keel. Clegg asked to delay this work until after the Southampton boat show, adding that he wanted time to discuss the problem with his legal advisors and others. After considerable correspondence between Andersson and Clegg, about the overweight keel, its consequences and possible remedies, Clegg rejected the yacht on 6 March 2001. The trial judge found that there was no breach of s.14(2) SGA and that even if there had been Clegg would be deemed to have accepted the yacht, and therefore lost the right to reject in all three ways set out in s.35 SGA. An appeal was made to the Court of Appeal.

Held. (i) The yacht was not of satisfactory quality. The reasonable person would not regard it as satisfactory because its overweight keel affected its safety and would need considerable remedial work.
(ii) Clegg had not intimated his acceptance of the yacht under s.35(1)(a). First, Clegg's statement of late August 2000 that he liked the yacht was counter-balanced by his requests for further information. Nor did a letter of 13 January 2001, informing Andersson that Clegg intended to move the yacht to Portugal or Gibraltar in early May intimate acceptance. The letter did not indicate that this would be done if the results of the testing of the yacht were unsatisfactory. Finally, leaving personal possessions on the yacht could not intimate acceptance in the light of the outstanding request for further information.
(iii) Clegg had not accepted the yacht under s.35(1)(b). Property in the yacht had passed to Clegg and he had done nothing which would be inconsistent with the ownership of the seller. (The reversionary interest of the seller should the yacht be rejected.) Insuring the yacht would not affect Anderson's reversionary interest. Furthermore, the loan agreement under which Clegg borrowed the money to buy the yacht required him to insure it. Nor did an attempt to insure the yacht amount to an inconsistent act, because the attempt was made before the yacht was delivered and the loan agreement required insurance.
(iv) Clegg had not accepted the yacht under s.35(4) by keeping it for more than a reasonable time without intimating his rejection of it. Section 59 SGA provides that what is a reasonable time is a question of fact. Section 35(5) provides that whether or not the buyer has had a reasonable time to inspect the goods is only one of the questions to be answered in deciding whether there has been acceptance under s.35(4) and that s.35(6) shows that time taken by Clegg requesting or agreeing to repairs, and for carrying them out, should not to be counted. As Clegg had not received all the information about modification or repair until 15 February 2001, only three weeks had elapsed before he rejected on 6 March 2001 and this did not exceed a reasonable time for the purposes of s.35(4).

Prior to amendments to the Sale of Goods Act made in 1994, a buyer who accepted part of the goods could not reject any of the goods. (This was not the case where the contract was severable or where the buyer was rejecting on account of the seller having delivered too large a quantity.) Section 35A now deals with the position where the seller commits a breach of contract by delivering goods which are not in conformity with the contract. If this breach only affects some of the goods but would give the buyer the right to reject all of the goods, the buyer can either:

(i) reject all of the goods,
(ii) accept the goods which do conform to the contract and reject those which do not, or
(iii) accept all of the goods which do conform to the contract as well as some of those which do not.

What the buyer cannot do is reject some of the goods which are unaffected by the breach once other unaffected goods have been accepted. If the breach affects all of the goods the buyer can reject all of the goods or reject some while accepting others.

However, this right of partial rejection will not apply where the goods form one commercial unit as s.35(7) provides that:

'Where the contract is for the sale of goods making one or more commercial units, a buyer accepting any goods included in a unit is deemed to have accepted all the goods making the unit; and in this subsection 'commercial unit' means a unit division of which would materially impair the value of the goods or the character of the unit.'

The Law Commission, at whose suggestion the subsection was included, gave as examples of a commercial unit, a pair of shoes, a set of encyclopedias, or a component in a car. So a buyer who had bought a set of encyclopedias, and who had accepted the first volume, would be deemed to have accepted the later volumes, even if their pages were blank. Although this acceptance would prevent the buyer from rejecting the later volumes it would not of course prevent him for suing for damages for breach of warranty.

Earlier in this chapter we saw that if an instalment contract was severable a buyer could in certain circumstances reject later instalments even if he had already accepted some earlier instalments. Prior to the amendments made by the Sale and Supply of Goods Act 1994, a buyer who accepted one instalment of an indivisible contract could not reject later deliveries even for breach of condition. Now, unless the contract is for the sale of a commercial unit, even a buyer under an indivisible contract can have the right to reject later instalments despite having accepted earlier ones.

10.4.4 Rejection in other supply contracts

The rules on acceptance of the goods which we have just considered apply only to contracts which can be classified as contracts of sale of goods. Where the contract is one of hire, hire-purchase or for the transfer of the property in goods then the provisions of the SGA 1979 will not apply. In these contracts the right to treat the contract as repudiated will be lost once the contract has been affirmed. (However, in *Jones* v *Callagher* [2004] EWCA Civ 10 the Court of Appeal applied s.35 SGA 1979 to a breach of ss.3&4 SGSA 1982.) There are no statutory rules on the meaning of affirmation. General common law principles regard affirmation as a matter of choice so that a person only affirms a contract when, knowing of the breach, his conduct indicates that he intends to go on with the contract. When a customer in a contract other than a sale of goods does rightfully treat the contract as repudiated there is no automatic right to regain all money paid. The customer will only be entitled to a full refund of the price if there has been a total failure of consideration. (See *Yeoman Credit Ltd* v *Waragowski* in Chapter 14 at 14.1.9.6.)

10.4.5 Specific performance

Where the seller is in breach of an obligation to deliver specific or ascertained goods, s.52 allows the court to order specific performance of the contract. However, the court will only order this if it thinks fit to do so. In Chapter 7 at 7.2.4 we examined the circumstances in which specific performance will not be ordered.

10.4.6 Lack of conformity with the contract

In March 2002 the SGA 1979 was amended by the Sale and Supply of Goods to Consumers Regulations 2002 to introduce Part 5A of the Act, ss.48A–F. Before examining the details of these sections, it is very important to note that the rights which they confer are **additional** to any other rights which the Act might confer. The new Part 5A does not therefore diminish any existing rights gained under ss.12–15 of the Act.

Section 48A sets out the two requirements for Part 5A to apply. First, the buyer must deal as a consumer. Second, the goods must not conform to the contract of sale at the time of delivery.

10.4.6.1 Dealing as a consumer

Section 61(5A) of the Act refers us to Part 1 of the Unfair Contract Terms Act 1977 to find the meaning of dealing as a consumer. In Chapter 5 at 5.6.1 we saw that s.12(1) UCTA 1977 provides that a person deals as a consumer if: (a) he neither makes the contract in the course of a business nor holds himself out as doing so; and (b) the other party does make the contract in the course of a business. We also saw that if a company (rather than an individual) is to be regarded as dealing as a consumer the goods passing under or in pursuance of the contract must be of a type ordinarily supplied for private use or consumption.

10.4.6.2 Lack of conformity with the contract

Section 48F provides that the goods do not conform to a contract of sale if there is, in relation to the goods, a breach of an express term of the contract or a term implied by ss.13–15 of the Act. Section 48A(3) provides that goods which do not conform to the contract at any time within the period of six months starting with the date on which the goods were delivered to the buyer must be taken not to have conformed at that date. So when there is a lack of conformity within six months of the date of delivery there is a presumption that they did not conform at the date of delivery. However, s.48A(4) provides that this presumption can be rebutted in two circumstances: (a) if it is established that the goods did conform to the contract at the date of delivery; or (b) if the presumption is incompatible with the nature of the goods or the nature of the lack of conformity.

10.4.6.3 The hierarchy of rights

Having established that the buyer dealt as a consumer and that the goods did not conform to the contract, ss.48A–48F set out a hierarchy of rights.

Repair or replacement of the goods

Section 48B(1) provides that the buyer may require the seller to repair or replace the goods. If the buyer does request either of these remedies then s.48B(2) provides that the seller must: (a) repair or replace the goods within a reasonable time but without causing significant inconvenience to the buyer; and (b) bear any necessary costs incurred in so doing (including in particular the cost of labour, materials or postage). Repair is defined by s.61(1) as meaning bringing the goods into conformity with the contract.

However, the right to repair or replacement is not absolute. Section 48B(3) provides that the buyer must not require the seller to repair or replace the goods in three circumstances: (a) if this would be impossible; (b) if this would be disproportionate in relation to the other of those remedies (that is to say, if repair was requested and this would be disproportionate to replacement, and vice versa); (c) if it would be disproportionate in comparison with either of the lower level remedies, reduction in the purchase price or rescission. Section 48B(4) tells us that one remedy is disproportionate in comparison to another if it imposes costs on the seller which, in comparison to the costs imposed by the other remedy, are unreasonable, taking into account: (a) the value which the goods would have if they conformed to the contract of sale; (b) the significance of the lack of conformity: and (c) whether the other remedy could be effected without significant inconvenience to the buyer. Section 48B(5) provides that any question as to what is a reasonable time or as to what is significant inconvenience is to be determined by reference to: (a) the nature of the goods; and (b) the purpose for which the goods were acquired.

Section 48D provides that if the buyer requires the seller to repair or replace the goods he must give the seller a reasonable time in which to do this before rejecting the goods and terminating the contract for breach of condition. So if the lack of conformity was caused by a breach of s.14(2), a buyer who has requested repair or replacement can no longer reject the goods under s.14(2) until the seller has been given a reasonable time in which to repair or replace the goods as requested. Nor can a buyer who has requested repair or replacement request the other of these two remedies (repair or replacement) until the seller has had a reasonable time in which to effect the remedy requested.

Reduction of the price or rescission of the contract

Section 48C(1) sets out the secondary remedies of the buyer: (a) requiring the seller to reduce the purchase price of the goods in question by an appropriate amount; and (b) rescinding the contract with regard to those goods. However, s.48C(2) provides that these secondary remedies are available in only two circumstances: (a) that the buyer can require neither repair nor replacement because the remedies are either impossible or disproportionate in relation to one of the secondary remedies; or (b) the buyer has required the seller to repair or replace the goods, but the seller is in breach of the s.48B(2)(a) requirement to do so within a reasonable time and without significant inconvenience to the buyer.

In Chapter 6 at 6.1.3 we examined the meaning of rescission in relation to misrepresentation, and the ways in which the right to rescind can be lost. It should be stressed that rescission has a different, statutory, meaning here and that the right to rescind will not be lost in the ways explained at 6.1.3.1. The meaning of rescission in ss.48A–48F is much closer to treating the contract as repudiated for breach of condition. However, s.48C(3) provides a very significant difference. It provides that if the buyer rescinds under s.48C(1)(b) any reimbursement to him may be reduced to take account of the use he has had of the goods since they were delivered to him. There is no such concept when a contract is treated as repudiated for breach of condition or breach of an innominate term. However, as we saw at 10.4.3, where a condition is breached in a contract of sale, s.11(4) will apply to prevent a buyer who has accepted the goods from rejecting the goods and treating the contract as terminated. Section 11(4) will not apply to ss.48A–48F because lack of conformity with the contract is not a condition. Indeed, the main use of Part 5A may be to allow a consumer to rescind the contract even after he would have been deemed to have accepted the goods.

10.4.6.4 Powers of the court

Section 48E sets out additional powers of the court where proceedings have been brought under ss.48A–48F. Section 48E(2) allows, if the buyer applies for it, specific performance of the seller's obligation to repair or replace as requested under s.48B. Section 48E(4) applies if the buyer applies for any of the four remedies set out in ss.48B and 48C but the court decides that another ss.48B or 48C remedy is more appropriate. The court may then award the other remedy instead. Section 48E(6) allows the court to grant any ss.48B or 48C remedy unconditionally or on such terms and conditions as to damages, payment of the price or otherwise as it thinks just.

10.4.6.5 Likely effect of Part 5A of the Act

The effect of Part 5A is likely to be limited. First, as we have seen, the rights which it confers are additional rights in consumer cases. These rights will not apply in non-consumer cases. Furthermore, the existing rights to terminate the contract and reject the goods for breach of condition will remain a consumer's strongest remedies where a breach of ss.13–15 of the Act has occurred. Even if a consumer buyer is prevented from rejecting the goods because the goods have been accepted the right to damages will remain. The Part 5A remedies might be most useful where a consumer wants to reject the goods but can no longer do so for breach of a condition on account of having accepted the goods. Part 5A might provide a backdoor means of rejecting the goods. However, it does not seem easy for a consumer to get to rescission under s.48C, as this is a secondary remedy. Furthermore, even if rescission is allowed under s.48C the reimbursement of the price to the buyer will take account of any use he has had of the goods. Perhaps courts will, in some cases, award an equal amount of damages put rescission under ss.48A–48F on a par with rejecting the goods for breach of condition. (Although, of course, damages can be awarded in addition to rejection for breach of a condition.)

Part 5A is also likely to cause difficulties in that it raises many uncertainties. When the buyer rescinds under s.48C, how will the extent to which the reimbursement should be reduced be decided? If the buyer and seller cannot agree then more cases are likely to be taken to court. Similar difficulties are likely to arise in relation to the other secondary remedy, reduction of the purchase price. By how much will the price be reduced? The answer given by s.48C(1)(a) is by 'an appropriate amount'. But how is this to be calculated?

■ Example

The way in which Part 5A might work can be demonstrated by considering the case of *Shine* v *General Guarantee Corporation Ltd* [1988] 1All ER 911, which is set out in Chapter 8 at 8.2.4. On the actual facts of *Shine*, Part 5A would be of no interest to the buyer as he gained the remedy he wanted, termination of the contract and rejection of the car, under s.14(2). Let us now change the facts slightly, and assume that the buyer had had the car re-sprayed before discovering that it had been submerged in water and trying to reject it.

Section 14(2) has been breached and the car was not of satisfactory quality. Section 11(4) would prevent rejection for breach of condition if the buyer had accepted the car. The buyer would have been deemed to have accepted the car under s.35(1)(b). Damages would still be available to the buyer but he would no longer be able to reject. The buyer was a consumer and the car did not conform to the contract because s.14(2) was breached. Therefore, s.48A(1) and (2) would allow the buyer the primary s.48B(1) remedies of repair and replacement. However, neither of these remedies is possible. (The car could not be replaced as it was specific goods. Repair would have to remove the lack of conformity, which would not be possible as the lack of conformity was caused by the car having been submerged in water.) Therefore, s.48C(2)(a) would allow the buyer to choose between reduction of the purchase price and rescission. Reduction of the price would put him in no better position than would damages for breach of s.14(2), to which he remains entitled. The buyer could choose to rescind under s.48C(1)(b). The purchase price might be reduced to take account of any use of the car which he had had (s.48C(3)). However, the court could award the buyer damages under s.48E(6).

10.4.6.6 Conformity with the contract in contracts other than sales of goods

The Supply of Goods and Services Act 1982 has been amended to include rules which are virtually identical to those contained in ss.48A–48F of the SGA 1979. However, these amendments do not apply to contracts of hire, but only to contracts for the transfer of property in goods. (For the different ways in which the SGSA 1982 classifies these contracts, see Chapter 8 at 8.4.) The new rules are contained in SGSA 1982 ss.11M–11S. Section 11S sets out the two circumstances in which goods do not conform to a contract for the supply or transfer of property in goods. The first is that there has been a breach of an express term or of one of the statutory implied terms as to correspondence with description, satisfactory quality, fitness for purpose or correspondence with sample. (These statutory implied terms are contained in ss.3–5 of the SGSA, see Chapter 8 at 8.4.2.) The second circumstance is that installation of the goods forms part of the contract for the transfer of goods, and the goods were installed in breach of s.13 SGSA or in breach of any term implied by any rule of law as to the manner in which the installation is carried out. (Section 13 SGSA is considered in Chapter 8 at 8.4.3.1.)

We saw above that in a sale of goods the new rules on conformity with the contract are most likely to be useful when a consumer buyer cannot reject the goods for breach of condition because he has accepted the goods. In a contract for the transfer of property in goods it is probably affirmation, rather than acceptance, which would prevent rejection for breach of condition. (See above at 10.4.4.) The new rules on lack of conformity are therefore most likely to be useful once the consumer has affirmed the contract.

10.4.7 Auction sales

Section 57 of the Sale of Goods Act lays down the following rules about auction sales.

'(1) Where goods are put up for sale by auction in lots, each lot is *prima facie* deemed to be the subject of a separate contract of sale.
(2) A sale by auction is complete when the auctioneer announces its completion by the fall of the hammer, or in other customary manner, and until the announcement is made any bidder may retract his bid.
(3) A sale by auction may be notified to be subject to a reserve or upset price, and a right to bid may also be reserved expressly by or on behalf of the seller.
(4) Where a sale by auction is not notified to be subject to a right to bid by or on behalf of the seller, it is not lawful for the seller to bid himself or to employ any person to bid at the sale, or for the auctioneer knowingly to take any bid from the seller or any such person.
(5) A sale contravening (4) above may be treated as fraudulent by the buyer.
(6) Where, in respect of a sale by auction, a right to bid is expressly reserved (but not otherwise) the seller or any one person on his behalf may bid at the auction.'

As the property in the lot passes to the buyer at the fall of the hammer, it will then be too late for the auctioneer later to insist on conditions to be fulfilled before the buyer becomes the owner of the lot.

■ *Dennant and Skinner v Collom* [1948] 2 All ER 29

A rogue bought several cars at an auction. After the sale the auctioneer allowed the rogue to take the cars away in return for a cheque. The auctioneer only did this because the rogue gave him a certificate which said that the property in the vehicles would not pass until the cheque was cleared. The rogue's cheque was dishonoured. The rogue sold one of the cars to a third party who sold it to the defendant. The auctioneer sued to get the car back.

Held. The auctioneer failed. The purchaser gained the property in the car at the fall of the hammer.

An auctioneer is, of course, an agent and as such he warrants his authority to sell the goods and that he does not know of any defects in the principal's title. (The agent's liability for breach of warranty of authority is considered in Chapter 11 at 11.3.1.) The auctioneer also undertakes to give possession of the goods in exchange for the price and that this possession will not be disturbed by either himself or the principal.

Where an auctioneer sells specific goods, without disclosing the name of the principal, he does not warrant that the principal owns the goods.

■ *Benton v Campbell, Parker & Co Ltd* [1925] 2 KB 410

The defendants sold cars at auction. The claimant bought a car which had been put into the auction by S Co. The defendants did not reveal the name of S Co. The claimant paid the price to the defendants and after deducting their commission the defendants paid S Co for the car. It later transpired that S Co had not owned the car at the time of the auction as they had taken it on hire-purchase from B. B saw the car being driven by T, to whom the claimant had sold it, and claimed it back. The claimant refunded to T the price he had paid for the car and then sued the defendants for the price he had paid.

Held. The claimant did not succeed as he knew that the defendant was an auctioneer and that the sale was of specific goods. The defendant did not therefore warrant that the principal owned the goods.

The auctioneer has a right to sue the purchaser for the price, even if the purchaser has paid the principal directly. He also has a lien over the proceeds of sale to safeguard his commission and other charges.

The auction particulars, or notices, may contain exclusion clauses. These clauses can be overridden by the auctioneer making an oral warranty. Exclusion clauses would also be subject to the Unfair Contract Terms Act 1977. In Chapter 8 we saw that a person who buys goods at an auction or by competitive tender is not in any circumstances to be regarded as dealing as a consumer for the purposes of the UCTA (UCTA s.12(2)).

The Auction (Bidding Agreements) Act 1969 makes it an offence for a dealer to give any person any consideration in return for not bidding at an auction. Both the dealer and the person who took the consideration can be banned from attending auctions for up to three years. The seller of the goods can avoid the contract and if it is not possible to reclaim the goods may recover any loss he has suffered (the difference between the sale price and the true price) from any party to the prohibited agreement.

Test your understanding

1 How will the buyer's damages for non-delivery by the seller be assessed (a) where there is no available market for the goods, and (b) where there is an available market for the goods?

2 How are damages for breach of warranty of quality of the goods to be assessed?

3 In what four circumstances will the buyer have a right to reject the goods?

4 What is the significance of the buyer having accepted the goods?

5 In what three ways can the buyer be deemed to have accepted the goods?

6 At an auction sale at what time does the property in the goods pass to the buyer?

Answers

1 (a) Where there is no available market for the goods the buyer's damages will be quantified as the estimated loss directly and naturally resulting in the ordinary course of events from the seller's breach of contract (s.51(2)). (b) Where there is an available market for the goods the measure of damages is *prima facie* to be ascertained by the difference between the contract price and the market price of the goods at the time or times when they ought to have been delivered or (if no time was fixed) at the time of the refusal to deliver (s.51(3)).

2 In the case of a breach of warranty of quality the buyer's loss is *prima facie* the difference between the value of the goods in the state they were in and the value which they would have had if the warranty had not been breached (s.53(3)).

3 The buyer will have the right to reject the goods if the seller has breached a condition of the contract; if the seller has breached an innominate term and this breach has deprived the buyer of substantially the whole benefit of the contract; if the express or implied terms of the contract conferred upon the buyer a right to reject; or if the seller has repudiated the contract.

4 Once the buyer has accepted the goods he will no longer be able to reject, even for breach of condition. The buyer will still be entitled to sue for damages.

5 The buyer can be deemed to have accepted the goods when he intimates to the seller that he has accepted them; when the goods have been delivered to him and he does any act in relation to them which is inconsistent with the ownership of the seller; or when after the lapse of a reasonable time the buyer retains the goods without intimating to the seller that he is rejecting them.

6 The property in the goods passes to the buyer at the fall of the hammer.

10.5 · International sales

International sales of goods are usually made on special terms. The two most important sets of terms are fob (free on board) and cif (cost insurance and freight). An outline meaning of these special terms is set out below, but before we examine them we need to understand the legal significance of a bill of lading.

10.5.1 The bill of lading

A bill of lading is a document issued to a shipper of goods by the shipowner which states that certain goods have been delivered on board ship. It is signed by or on behalf of the shipowner and sets out the terms on which the goods are to be carried. Generally, a mate's receipt is issued when the goods are first loaded on board. The mate's receipt will note the condition of the goods loaded on board and these details will then be transferred to a bill of lading, which will be issued to the shipper when the ship leaves port.

A bill of lading has legal significance in three different ways. It is evidence of the contract of carriage, it is a receipt for the goods shipped and it is a document of title. Each of these matters needs to be considered in outline.

Although a bill of lading sets out the terms of the contract of carriage it is not the contract itself. The contract of carriage will be made when the ship is booked, and the bill of lading is not issued until the goods have been loaded on board. The bill of lading usually contains the terms of the contract of carriage and so, between the shipper of the goods and the shipowner, the bill of lading is very strong evidence of the contract of carriage. Once the bill of lading is transferred by the shipper to a third party, the third party will take over the contract of carriage and the bill of lading. The bill of lading then becomes conclusive evidence of the contract of carriage.

The bill of lading is a receipt for the goods shipped. If the bill is a **clean bill** it will state that the correct quantity of goods are shipped in apparent good order and condition. If the bill is '**claused**' or '**dirty**' it will specify the ways in which the goods did not appear to be in apparent good order or condition. It might for example state that some packages were broken or waterlogged. By issuing a clean bill of lading the shipper is not guaranteeing that the goods conform to the contract, but merely saying that the goods loaded on board outwardly appear to conform to the contract.

The Hague-Visby Rules, which govern most international sales of carriage by sea involving the UK, require a clean bill of lading to show four things: the 'leading marks' by which the goods can be identified; the quantity of goods shipped; the apparent order and condition of the goods; and the date on which the goods were shipped. If, upon arrival, the holder of the bill finds that the goods do not outwardly conform to the contract then the shipowner will be liable for issuing a clean bill of lading. If the goods do outwardly conform to the contract, but are found to have some defect which was not outwardly apparent, the shipowner will have no liability in respect of this defect. Between the shipper and the shipowner the bill of lading is only *prima facie* evidence of the quantity and apparent condition of the goods. Once the bill has been transferred to a third party it becomes conclusive evidence of these matters. The third party will take over the rights under the contract of carriage by virtue of s.2 of the Carriage of Goods by Sea Act 1992.

A bill of lading is said to be a document of title. This does not mean that the holder of the bill definitely has ownership of the goods to which the bill relates. It does mean that the holder has constructive possession of the goods and that the shipowner will acknowledge that the goods are now held on behalf of the holder of the bill. Mustill LJ in *Enichem Anic SpA* v *Ampelos Shipping Co Ltd, the Delfini* [1990] 1 Lloyd's Rep 252 said 'It [the bill of lading] is a symbol of constructive possession of the goods which (unlike many such symbols) can transfer constructive possession by endorsement and transfer: it is a transferable "key to the warehouse". The holder of the bill will therefore be entitled to take the goods from the ship and the shipowner should only allow the holder of the bill to do this. Very commonly the property in the goods passes to the buyer along with the bill of lading as this is what the parties intended. If the bill of lading is negotiable the buyer can transfer it to a third party. However, a bill of lading is not a negotiable instrument and so the description of a bill of lading as negotiable does not mean that a subsequent holder can have a better title than the person from whom he took the bill.

10.5.2 **Fob (free on board) contracts**

Where a contract is made on fob terms, the seller contracts to deliver the goods free on board a ship nominated by the buyer. Although such contracts are generally international sales this is not always the case. Under an fob contract it is the duty of the buyer to nominate an effective ship, and traditionally it is also the buyer's duty to make the contract of carriage with the shipowner. If the buyer wants the goods to be insured whilst they are being shipped then it is up to the buyer to arrange insurance. It is the seller's duty to deliver the goods on board ship by passing them over the ship's rail and also to pay the loading charges. Once the goods have been put on board the ship, delivery of the goods is completed. The port identified in an fob contract is the port at which the goods are to be loaded.

It is not always the case that it is the buyer's duty to make the contract of carriage. In *Pyrene & Co Ltd* v *Scindia Steam Navigation Co Ltd* [1954] 2 All ER 158 Devlin J identified three types of fob contracts. Under Devlin's 'classic' fob contract the seller makes the contract of carriage, booking a ship nominated by the buyer. When the seller delivers the goods on board the ship he is given a bill of lading by the shipowner and he forwards this to the buyer. The bill of lading will give the buyer constructive possession of the goods. Under Devlin's 'fob with additional services' the seller again makes the contract of carriage, booking a ship nominated by the buyer, and possibly arranges insurance. The seller has the bill of lading made out in his own name. This indicates a presumption that the property in the goods is not to pass to the buyer upon shipment of the goods (s.19(2) SGA). If the carriage costs increase the buyer must pay the extra amount. In Devlin's third category, 'strict fob', the buyer makes the contract of carriage. The seller puts the goods on board and gets a mate's receipt for them. The seller sends the mate's receipt to the buyer who uses it to get a bill of lading.

When the seller does make the contract of carriage s.32(2) SGA requires him to make a reasonable contract, having regard to the nature of the goods and the circumstances of the case. If, for example, the goods were of a type which would be needed to be kept at a certain temperature, the seller would have to make a contract which ensured that the shipowner would keep the goods at this temperature.

Unless the parties agree otherwise it is the buyer's duty to nominate an effective ship, that is to say a ship which is both physically capable of carrying the goods and ready and willing to do so. The nominated ship must arrive in time to allow the seller to load the goods on board within the contract period. This duty is a condition and so if an effective ship is not nominated in time the seller can treat the contract as repudiated. The buyer can nominate an alternative ship as long as this is done in time. Once the nominated ship arrives at the port, it is the seller's duty to load the goods on board within the shipment period. Failure to load on time will be a breach of condition entitling the buyer to treat the contract as repudiated.

■ Example

Goods are sold on strict fob terms Hull, September shipment. The parties have therefore agreed that: the buyer is to make the contract of carriage; the port named, Hull, is the port where the goods are to be loaded; the buyer must nominate an effective ship which will arrive at Hull in time for the seller to load the goods before the end of September; the seller must load the goods on board before the end of September. As the buyer made the contract of carriage, the seller takes a mate's receipt for the goods once they are loaded on board. The seller will probably send the mate's receipt to the buyer, who will then have a duty to pay the price of the goods. The buyer will use the mate's receipt to obtain a bill of lading, which will give the buyer the right to take possession of the goods at the port of arrival.

When the goods are not loaded within the shipment period disputes commonly arise as to whose fault this was.

■ *Bunge & Co Ltd v Tradax England Ltd* [1975] 2 Lloyd's Rep 235

One thousand tons of barley were sold on fob terms. The buyers nominated a ship in due time but the ship was delayed and so they nominated another ship. Delivery of the goods was to be made between the 1 and 20 January

1973, both dates inclusive. The second ship nominated was expected to be ready to load on Friday 19 January. The sellers protested that this would not give them time to load all of the goods within the shipment period, which ended at midnight on Saturday 20 January. The ship arrived at 1500 hours on Friday 19 January and only 110 tons could be loaded that day as the normal working hours ended at 1700 hours. The buyers agreed to pay overtime rates so that the barley could be loaded on Saturday 20 January but it rained all day and nothing more was loaded.

Held. The sellers had an obligation to begin loading as soon as the ship arrived but they had no obligation to continue loading after the expiry of the shipment time. Both the obligation to deliver and the obligation to accept delivery were strictly confined to the contract time. The buyers had no right to demand shipment outside this time.

When the contract is governed by English law then the SGA 1979 will apply. In an international contract almost any description of the goods is likely to be regarded as a condition. The goods will of course have to be of satisfactory quality if they are sold in the course of a business. In an international sale it is not, as it is in a domestic sale of goods, at the time of delivery that the goods must be of satisfactory quality. The goods must remain satisfactory until they arrive at the port of destination and are disposed of.

■ *Mash & Murrell Ltd* v *Joseph I Emanuel Ltd* [1961] 1 All ER 485 (Court of Appeal)

The defendants sold the claimants 2 000 bags of spring crop potatoes. The potatoes had been exported from Cyprus and were due to be delivered to Liverpool. The defendants knew that the claimants would sell the potatoes on for human consumption. Upon arrival the potatoes were not of merchantable (now satisfactory) quality.

Diplock J held that in an international sale the goods must remain of merchantable quality until a reasonable time has elapsed for their disposal at the port of arrival.

COMMENT This was not an fob contract. However, the principle of the case applies to fob contracts so that the seller must put the goods on board ship in such a state that they will remain of satisfactory quality until a reasonable time after their arrival. The Court of Appeal approved Diplock's judgment. However, the case was reversed on its facts. The Court of Appeal found that the potatoes were loaded in good condition but that they had deteriorated because of excessive heat and poor ventilation on the voyage. The buyer therefore did not succeed against the seller although he would have been able to succeed against the shipowner.

The SGA rules on the passing of the property and the risk, which we examined in the previous chapter, will apply to fob contracts. Subject to s.20A, no property can pass until the goods are ascertained. We saw that once goods have become ascertained the property in them will pass when the parties intend it to pass under s.17, but that if the parties do not express an intention then the five rules of presumed intention contained in s.18 will determine when the property in the goods is to pass. When a contract is made on fob terms the s.18 rules of presumed intention are not needed. If the parties have not expressly indicated otherwise, it is taken that they intend the property in the goods to pass when the goods pass over the ship's rail. However, if the seller has the bill of lading made out in his own name, rather than in the buyer's name, then it is presumed that the seller is reserving title to the goods until the price has been paid (s.19(2) SGA). Under s.20 SGA the risk will pass at the same time as the property in the goods. However, in fob contracts risk passes when the goods go over the ship's rail even in circumstances where the property did not pass as this is taken to be the intention of the parties.

10.5.3 Cif (cost insurance and freight) contracts

Under a cif contract it is the seller's duty to make the shipping contract, insure the goods and pay the freight. Having done this the seller must then deliver to the buyer three documents: the bill of lading, a policy of insurance and an invoice for the goods. The buyer must accept and pay for these documents if they are in order, even if the goods have been lost or damaged. The named port is the port of destination, not the port of loading. A cif contract is always an international sale.

■ Example

One thousand tons of wheat are sold cif New York. The seller makes the shipping contract and pays all the costs of this. Once the goods are loaded the seller will be given a bill of lading. The seller insures the goods, acquiring a policy of insurance. The seller sends the bill of lading, the policy of insurance and an invoice for the goods to the buyer. The buyer must accept the three documents and pay for them, if they are in order. Once the goods arrive in New York the bill of lading will entitle the buyer to gain possession of them.

If the shipping documents are not in order, then the buyer has no duty to accept them and can treat the contract as repudiated. The bill of lading must therefore be clean and must show the date on which the goods were shipped. A policy of insurance rather than a certificate of insurance must be delivered. Even if the buyer knows that the goods have been lost before their arrival, there is no right to refuse to accept and pay for the documents.

■ *Manbre Sacharine Co Ltd v Corn Products Co Ltd* [1919] 1 KB 198

The claimants claimed damages for failure to deliver goods. The defendants had made two cif contracts to sell starch and syrup. The price included war risk insurance. One of the ships carrying the goods was sunk by a German submarine and some of the goods were not delivered. Both parties knew of the ship's loss at the time when the seller presented the documents. The buyer refused to take the documents.

Held. The buyers were in breach of contract by not taking the documents and paying the price. The seller's obligation was to deliver the documents rather than the goods. All the buyers could call for was the delivery of the documents.

Although this case seems particularly hard on the buyer, it should not ordinarily cause any inconvenience. The goods have been insured by the seller, and the buyer takes over the policy of insurance and the contract of carriage. If the goods are damaged or lost due to the negligence of the shipowner, then the buyer will sue the shipowner on the contract of carriage. If the goods are lost or damaged in some other way then the buyer will claim on the policy of insurance.

The buyer's right to reject the documents if they are not in order, is quite distinct from his right to reject the goods if they do not conform to the contract. The shipowner who issues a bill of lading will merely be stating that the goods which were loaded on board outwardly appeared to conform to the contract. The shipowner would therefore indicate, for example, that the right number of boxes were delivered and that the boxes were labelled and not damaged. If the buyer later discovers that the goods shipped are not of satisfactory quality, or do not match the contract description, the shipowner will have no liability for this unless the breach was outwardly apparent. However, the buyer will be able to treat the contract as repudiated and reject the goods, even though the property in the goods may have passed to the buyer when he discovers the seller's breach.

In a cif contract the property in ascertained goods will pass when the parties intend that it should under s.17 SGA 1979. The parties might well express an intention. However, if they do not then the property will pass when the shipping documents are delivered to the buyer and the price is paid. Property in unascertained goods cannot pass, subject to s.20A SGA 1979, until the goods are ascertained (SGA 1979 s.16). No matter when the property in the goods passes, the risk passes to the buyer as soon as the goods are delivered on board ship. This is because from that time the buyer has taken over the contract of carriage and the rights under the policy of insurance. Cif buyers commonly buy goods which are afloat, having already begun their journey. When this happens the risk passes to the buyer retrospectively from the time of loading. As the rights under the contract of carriage and the policy of insurance also pass retrospectively this should not cause the buyer any problems.

The property in the goods is likely to have passed to the buyer by the time that he gets physical possession of the goods and the right to examine them. However, if a condition relating to the description or the quality of the goods has been breached the buyer can still reject the goods, even if he appears to have accepted them. (The buyer will commonly have done an act inconsistent with the seller's continuing ownership, by pledging the documents with a bank to raise money to finance the purchase of the goods, and therefore seem to be deemed to have accepted the goods. See above at 10.4.3.) However, the property passed to the buyer only conditionally on the goods conforming to the contract. If the goods do not conform to the contract then the buyer can reject the goods and pass the property back to the seller (*Kwei Tek Chao* v *British Traders and Shippers Ltd* [1954] 2 QB 459).

Test your understanding

1 To what extent can a bill of lading be taken as representing the contract of carriage?

2 What is meant by the bill of lading being a document of title?

3 What is meant by (a) A clean bill of lading? (b) A claused bill of lading?

4 What are the duties of the buyer and the seller under an fob contract?

5 What are the duties of the buyer and the seller under a cif contract?

Answers

1 The bill of lading is only evidence of the contract of carriage, rather than being the contract of carriage itself. However, as between the shipowner and a third party to whom the bill of lading has been transferred, the bill becomes conclusive evidence of the contract of carriage.

2 As a document of title, the bill transfers constructive possession of the goods to the holder of the bill.

3 (a) A clean bill of lading will certify that the goods were shipped in apparent good order and condition. (b) A claused bill will specify in what way the goods shipped were not in apparent good order and condition.

4 The seller has the duties to put the goods on board ship and pay the loading charges. The buyer has the duties to nominate an effective ship and pay the shipping costs. It is generally also the buyer's duty to make the contract of carriage.

5 The seller has the duties to present to the buyer a clean bill of lading, a policy of insurance and an invoice for the goods. The buyer must take these documents and pay for them if they are in order. If the goods do not conform to the contract the buyer will be able to reject the goods. However, the buyer must accept the three documents and pay for them even if he knows that the goods have been lost or damaged.

Key points

Duties of the parties

- The seller has a duty to deliver the goods. The buyer has duties to accept and pay for the goods and to take delivery of them.

- Unless otherwise agreed, the seller's duty to deliver the goods and the buyer's duty to pay for them are concurrent conditions. This means that the seller must be ready and willing to deliver and in return the buyer must be ready and willing to pay.

- Delivery is concerned with the transfer of possession of the goods, not with the transfer of ownership. It can be achieved in various ways and does not necessarily mean the seller taking or sending the goods to the buyer.

- Unless otherwise agreed the place of delivery is the seller's place of business or, if he has not got a place of business, his home. However if the contract is for the sale of specific goods which both of the parties know to be in some other place that place is the place of delivery.

- A term fixing the time of delivery may be either a condition or a warranty, depending upon the intentions of the parties. In commercial contracts it is presumed that the parties intended such a term to be a condition.

- If too small a quantity of goods is delivered the buyer can either reject the lot or accept the goods delivered and pay at the contract rate.

- If too large a quantity of goods is delivered the buyer can either reject the lot, or accept the correct quantity and reject the excess, or accept the lot and pay for the excess at the contract rate.

- In a severable instalment contract, whether a breach of condition by the seller as regards one or more instalments amounts to a repudiation of the whole contract will depend upon the terms of the contract and the circumstances of the case. The two most important circumstances will be the ratio of the breach to the contract as a whole and the likelihood of the breach being repeated.

Remedies of the seller

- An unpaid seller is a seller to whom the whole of the purchase price has not been paid or tendered.

- An unpaid seller may have three real remedies (remedies which can be taken against the goods rather than against the buyer); a lien, stoppage in transit and the right of resale.

- The lien gives the unpaid seller the right to retain possession of the goods even though the property in the goods has passed to the buyer.

- Stoppage in transit allows the seller to reclaim the goods from a carrier who is not the agent of the buyer up until the time when the goods are delivered to the buyer.

- The right of resale allows the seller, in certain circumstances, to sell the goods to a different buyer without being in breach of the contract made with the original buyer.

- The seller may sue for the price only if the contract fixed a definite date for payment or if the property in the goods had passed to the buyer.

- If the buyer refuses to accept and pay for the goods the seller can sue for damages for non-acceptance. The measure of damages will be the estimated loss directly and naturally resulting, in the ordinary course of events, from the buyer's breach of contract.

- Where there is an available market for the goods in question the measure of the seller's damages for non-acceptance is *prima facie* to be ascertained by the difference between the contract price and the market or current price at the time or times when the goods ought to have been accepted or (if no time was fixed for acceptance) at the time of the refusal to accept.

- The seller will have a right to terminate the contract if the buyer has repudiated the contract.

The buyer's remedies

- The buyer will have the right to sue for damages for non-delivery where the seller wrongfully neglects or refuses to deliver the goods.

- The measure of the buyer's damages is the estimated loss directly and naturally resulting in the ordinary course of events from the seller's breach of contract. Where there is an available market for the goods this loss will generally be ascertained by using the market rule.

- The buyer may also claim damages to compensate for breach of warranty or for late delivery.

- Once the buyer has accepted the goods then rejection of the goods will no longer be possible. However, the right to sue for damages will remain.

- The buyer can be deemed to have accepted the goods: (a) when he intimates to the seller that he has accepted them; (b) when he does an act which is inconsistent with the seller's continuing ownership; or (c) where he retains the goods for more than a reasonable time without letting the seller know that he is rejecting them.

- At a sale by auction the property in each lot passes at the fall of the hammer.

International sales

- A bill of lading is evidence of the contract of carriage, a receipt for the goods shipped and a document of title.

- A clean bill of lading indicates that the goods shipped outwardly appeared to be in good order and condition.

- Under an fob contract the seller's duty is to pass the goods over the ship's rail within the shipment period. The buyer must nominate a ship which will arrive in time for the seller to do this.

- Unless otherwise agreed, the property in ascertained goods, and the risk, will pass to the buyer under an fob contract when the goods pass over the ship's rail.

- Under a cif contract the seller must deliver to the buyer a clean bill of lading, a policy of insurance and an invoice for the goods. The buyer must accept and pay for these documents if they are in order.

- Unless otherwise agreed, the property in ascertained goods sold on cif terms will pass to the buyer when the buyer accepts the documents and pays for them. The risk will pass to the buyer from the time when the goods were loaded on board ship.

- Even though the property may have passed to the buyer under a cif contract, he can still reject the goods (although not the documents) if he discovers that the goods do not conform to the contract.

Summary questions

1 In November Ken ordered a new customised surfboard from HiSurf Ltd, who manufacture surfboards. Ken paid a 20% deposit. The contract stated that the board was to be ready by 1 April and that Ken would take delivery of the board and pay for it within one week of this date. The surfboard was not ready by 1 April, but Ken was told that it would be ready within two weeks. Ken agreed to this. On 15 April Ken was told that the board was still not ready but would be within one more week. Ken begrudgingly agreed to wait for another week. When told, on 22 April, that the board was still not ready Ken said that if it was not ready within one more week then he would refuse to take it and buy a surfboard elsewhere. On 22 April Ken was told that although the board was not finished it would be within two days. Advise Ken as to whether or not he can refuse to be bound by the contract and claim the return of his deposit.

2 Jane entered into a contract under which she agreed to buy 600 boxes of candles from Candle Co Ltd. The candles are to be delivered to Jane's shop in 12 instalments of 50 each. Each instalment is to be comprised of 25 white candles and 25 gold candles. The first three instalments present no problem. The candles delivered in the fourth instalment cannot be lit as their wicks have not been sufficiently trimmed. Jane receives complaints from several customers. She contacts Candle Co who assure her that the problem will not recur as it was caused by a technical problem which has since been fixed. The fourth instalment contains only 20 white and 20 gold candles. Jane finds that demand for candles has fallen away. Can she reject the fourth instalment? Can she terminate the whole contract?

3 In July Bill ordered 100 tons of corn from Sid Suppliers Ltd. A contract was signed and the corn was to be delivered on 1 August. The day after signing the contract Bill explained that he had changed his mind and intended to buy corn from elsewhere. Sid Suppliers Ltd had ordered the corn from a Canadian exporter but are likely to have little trouble in selling it to a different customer. Advise Sid Suppliers Ltd of their legal position. How would your answer be different if Bill had ordered a second-hand combine harvester, and not the corn, for delivery on 1 August and had made it plain that he would refuse to be bound by the contract?

4 Six months ago Arthur's business sold a new car to David for £9 995, which was paid in full. Yesterday David had the car towed back to Arthur's garage, claiming that he was rejecting it and wanted a return of the pur-

chase price. The car had only travelled 2 250 miles but its engine had then seized up because the oil had leaked from the engine due to an oil seal leaking. This problem was caused by negligence when the car was manufactured. Arthur offers to repair the car under the manufacturer's warranty. David refuses to accept this and says that he wants all of his money back. Advise David of his legal position.

5   Pelham Products Ltd, which manufacture garden furniture, have contracted to sell 200 garden tables to Sunny Garden Centres Ltd. None of the price was paid, although no mention of credit was made. After handing over the garden chairs to a carrier, who was to transport them to Sunny Garden Centres Ltd, the manager of Pelham Products hears that Sunny Garden Centres Ltd have gone into liquidation. Pelham Products Ltd could easily find another buyer for the chairs. Advise them of their legal position.

6   Exporters Ltd buy 1 000 tons of barley from Grain Supply Ltd, fob Lowestoft. Under the contract Exporters Ltd have a duty to nominate the ship. Delivery of the goods is to be made in March. Exporters Ltd nominate a ship, the Hulk, which arrives on Thursday 26 March. The barley is loaded on board the Hulk on Friday 27 March. On Saturday 28 March the barley is infested by a swarm of locusts. Advise Exporters Ltd of their legal position.

8   Importers Ltd bought 1 000 tons of wheat, cif London, from Exporters Ltd. After they have made the contract Importers Ltd discover that the wheat is not of satisfactory quality. Exporters Ltd present to Importers Ltd a clean bill of lading, an invoice for the wheat and a policy of insurance covering the wheat. Advise Importers Ltd of their legal position.

Multiple choice questions

1   Bill examines an ex-demonstration model television at Super Stores Ltd. Bill buys the television, paying the full price cash. No mention of delivery is made, although Bill is asked to give his name and address. Bill lives within one mile of the store. Bill does not take the television with him when he leaves the store.
    Consider the following statements.

    i   It is up to Bill to collect the television from Super Stores Ltd, who will have to make it available for collection.
    ii   Super Stores Ltd will have to deliver the television to Bill's house. Bill will have to ensure that someone is in to take delivery.
    iii Until delivery is made Super Stores Ltd will have a lien over the television.
    iv   As the times of delivery and payment are concurrent conditions, Super Stores Ltd are in breach of contract as they did not deliver the television at the same time as payment was made.

    Which of the statements are true?

    a   (i) and (iii) only.
    b   (ii) and (iii) only.
    c   (ii) and (iv) only.
    d   (i) only.

2   S Ltd sells to B 1 000 tons of wheat. The wheat is unascertained goods. The parties do not expressly or impliedly agree upon a place of delivery.
    Consider the following statements.

    i   The place of delivery will be S Ltd's place of business.
    ii   Once S Ltd has separated 1 000 tons of wheat to be used to perform the contract, and told B where that wheat is, the place of delivery will be the place where both of the parties know the wheat to be.
    iii If S Ltd deliver too much wheat, B can accept the correct quantity, accept the lot and pay for the excess at the contract rate or reject the lot.
    iv   Delivery of the goods to a carrier would amount to delivery of the goods to B if S Ltd were authorised or required by the contract to send the goods to B.

    Which of the following statements are true?

    a   (i), (iii) and (iv) only.

    b   (ii), (iii) and (iv) only.

    c   (ii) and (iii) only.

    d   All of the statements.

3   Which **one** of the statements is true?

    a   If the seller breaches the contract and the buyer consequently rightfully rejects the goods, the buyer can bring an action against the seller for non-delivery.

    b   The seller can always sue for the contract price once the goods have been delivered to the buyer.

    c   If there is an available market for the goods, then the seller's damages for non-acceptance will be calculated according to the market rule, but only if the seller actually sells the goods in the available market.

    d   A seller will not be able to sue for the price unless he can show that he has mitigated his loss.

4   Which **one** of the following statements is **not** true?

    a   A buyer who rightfully refuses to accept the goods does not need to physically return the goods to the seller, but only to let the seller know that he is rejecting them.

    b   Once the buyer has accepted, or has been deemed to have accepted, the goods then he will not be able to reject them, even for breach of condition.

    c   A buyer, whether a consumer buyer or not, can be deemed to have accepted the goods if he retains the goods for more than a reasonable time. This is the case even if he has not had a reasonable opportunity to examine the goods.

    d   If a buyer sells the goods on to a sub-buyer this will amount to performing an act which is inconsistent with the seller's continuing ownership. Therefore the buyer will always be deemed to have accepted the goods.

5   Which **one** of the following statements is true?

    a   The issue of a clean bill of lading amounts to a representation by the shipowner that the goods shipped conform to the contract absolutely when shipped.

    b   A buyer of goods sold on cif terms must accept and pay for the documents even if he knows that the goods themselves have been destroyed.

    c   As between the shipper and the shipowner, the bill of lading is conclusive evidence of the contract of carriage.

    d   As the bill of lading is a document of title, the holder of the bill will always own the goods to which the bill relates.

6   Which **one** of the following statements is **not** true?

    a   In an fob contract the named port is the port of loading, whereas in a cif contract the named port is the port of arrival.

    b   If a seller of goods on fob terms has the bill of lading made out in his own name then it is presumed that he is reserving title to the goods until payment of the price.

    c   If goods which are already afloat are bought on cif terms, the property in the goods will usually pass to the buyer when the documents are taken and paid for. However, the risk will pass as from the time when the contract was made.

    d   Under a cif contract the property in the goods will usually pass to the buyer when the documents are taken and paid for. However, the risk will pass upon shipment of the goods.

Task 10

As a consequence of a supplier not delivering components on time your employer has had to find alternative supplies of these components at a higher price. Your employer has asked you to write a report, briefly dealing with the following matters.

    a   To explain the duties of the buyer and the seller under a contract of sale of goods.

    b   To explain the remedies available to a buyer or seller when a contract of sale of goods has been breached.

    c   The meaning of the terms fob and cif in international contracts of sale.

Chapter 11

AGENCY

Introduction

We begin this chapter by considering the nature of agency and the ways in which agency can be created. We shall see that when an agent makes a contract on behalf of a principal three parties are involved: the agent, the principal and the third party with whom the agent makes the contract. We examine in turn the rights and duties of these three parties, and then conclude the chapter by considering the ways in which agency can be terminated.

11.1 · The concept of agency

An agent has the power to alter the legal position of another person, known as the principal. Generally, an agent will have the power to make contracts on the principal's behalf, and this is the particular aspect of agency on which we concentrate. If an agent with the necessary authority makes a contract on the principal's behalf then the principal will be bound by the contract.

Auctioneers provide an easily understood example of agency. When an auctioneer sells a Lot it is not his own property which he is selling but the property of his principal, the person who put the goods into the auction. If X instructs an auctioneer to auction a painting, and the painting is knocked down to a third party for £100, then the contract of sale takes effect between X (the principal) and the third party. However, the contract was actually formed by the agent, the auctioneer and the third party.

No economy could function effectively without agency. If every person wishing to enter into a contract had to make the contract personally then the business world would come to a standstill. Boards of Directors act as agents of their companies. Partners act as agents of the firm and of their fellow partners for the purpose of the business of the partnership. These types of agency are recognised by most people, but few people realise how common agency is. Shop assistants, for example, are agents. The goods which they sell belong not to themselves but to the shop owners who employ them. Strangely, many people who call themselves agents are not in fact agents in the legal sense. Retailers of motor vehicles, for example, commonly call themselves sole agent of a particular manufacturer in a particular locality. However, these retailers are not agents in the legal sense. They do not sell the cars on behalf of the manufacturer, rather they buy the cars from the manufacturers and sell them on their own behalf. They might be more accurately described as sole distributors rather than as sole agents. Some agents act for more than one principal, and thereby offer customers a wide choice of services or products. Others provide a specialist service which their principals would find hard to provide themselves.

Agents are usually employed to buy or to sell. Commonly they also have the power to dispose of the principal's property or to receive property on the principal's behalf. For example, shop assistants have the power to receive payment for goods sold on the principal's behalf. If a dishonest shop assistant pockets money paid by a customer, rather than putting it into the till, this is not the concern of the customer. Having paid the price in good faith to the shop assistant, the customer is regarded as having paid the price to the shop owner.

11.2 · Creation of agency

An agent can only act to alter the principal's legal position if he has authority to do so. There are several ways in which an agent may acquire this authority. As many legal disputes are concerned with whether or not an agent had the power to alter a principal's legal position, we need to examine each method by which authority might be acquired in some detail.

11.2.1 Express actual authority

Actual authority, whether express or implied, arises from an agreement between principal and agent. An agent has express actual authority when the principal and agent agree in words that the agent will have authority to act for the principal. The agreement may be made orally or in writing and will usually be a contract, although this is not necessary. An agent who agrees to act for no reward is known as a gratuitous agent. An agreement to act gratuitously will not amount to a contract as the agent is given no consideration for his services.

11.2.2 Implied actual authority

An agent has implied actual authority to act for the principal where the principal and agent agree, otherwise than in words, that the agent should have such authority. Implied actual authority arises from the principal and agent's relationship to each other or from their conduct. It is often an extension of express actual authority, but in the following case the agent's actual authority was entirely implied.

■ *Hely-Hutchinson v Brayhead Ltd* [1968] 1 QB 549 (Court of Appeal)

The directors of a company allowed the company chairman to act as if he was the managing director of the company. In fact the chairman had never been appointed managing director and so had no express authority to bind the company. The chairman made a contract with a third party on the company's behalf.

Held. The chairman had implied actual authority to bind the company and so the company was bound by the contract which the chairman had made. The company, by its conduct, had impliedly agreed with the chairman that he should have the same authority as if he had actually been appointed managing director.

COMMENT   In this case Lord Denning MR explained the difference between express actual authority and implied actual authority in the following way: '… actual authority may be express or implied. It is *express* when it is given by express words, such as when a board of directors pass a resolution which authorises two of their number to sign cheques. It is *implied* when it is inferred from the conduct of the parties and the circumstances of the case, such as when the board of directors appoint one of their number to be managing director. They thereby impliedly authorise him to do all such things as fall within the usual scope of that office.'

The whole of an agent's actual authority can be entirely implied. More commonly, implied authority can add to an agent's express authority, extending it beyond the powers expressly conferred. The courts can imply terms into contracts (as we saw in Chapter 5 at 5.3) on the grounds that it is necessary to do so to make the contract work as the parties intended, or on the grounds of custom. Contracts of agency are no different in this respect. An agent's authority is often implied on the grounds that the actions which the agent took are customarily taken on the principal's behalf. For example, a solicitor who has been given express authority to sue also has implied authority to abandon the action and reach a settlement. However, the implied actual authority of an agent can never contradict a limitation on authority which has been expressly agreed. In *Waugh* v *HB Clifford and Sons Ltd* [1982] 2 WLR 679 a firm of builders who had negligently built houses employed a firm of solicitors to defend proceedings brought against them. The solicitors suggested a compromise to the builders, but the builders ordered the solicitors not to compromise on this basis. The solicitors ignored these instructions and did compromise. The Court of Appeal recognised that generally solicitors employed to defend proceedings would have implied actual authority to enter into a compromise. This could not be the case, however, when they had been expressly ordered not to do this. Terms implied by the court on the basis that they were obviously what the parties intended can always be excluded by an express term.

11.2.3 Apparent (or ostensible) authority

We have seen that actual authority, whether express or implied, arises from an agreement between principal and agent. Apparent authority is quite different. It arises not from any agreement between principal and agent, but on account of the principal having made a representation to a third party that the agent has the authority to act on his behalf. If a principal's words or actions give the impression that he has consented to a person acting as his agent, then the principal may be estopped (prevented) from denying this once the third party has acted upon the representation. Generally the third party acts upon the representation by entering into a contract.

Three requirements are necessary to give rise to such an estoppel:

  (i) there must have been a representation that the person was an agent;
 (ii) this representation must have been made by the principal or by someone on his behalf;
(iii) the third party must have relied on the representation.

In *Freeman & Lockyer* v *Buckhurst Park Properties Ltd* [1964] 2 QB 480 the directors of a company allowed one director, Kapoor, to act as if he had been appointed managing director of the company. Kapoor engaged a firm of architects to act on the company's behalf. The company later refused to pay the architects, arguing that Kapoor was not managing director and had no power to make contracts on the company's behalf. The Court of Appeal held that the company were bound by the contract. They had given the impression that Kapoor had the power to bind the company and so the company was liable on the contract to the architects who had relied on this representation by making the contract.

This case is somewhat similar to *Hely-Hutchinson* v *Brayhead Ltd*. In that case the chairman was held to have implied actual authority to bind the company. In *Freeman & Lockyer* Kapoor was held to have apparent authority to do so. The two types of authority often overlap, as Lord Denning MR explained in *Hely-Hutchinson* v *Brayhead Ltd*:

> 'Ostensible or apparent authority is the authority of an agent as it *appears* to others. It often coincides with actual authority. Thus, when the board appoint one of their number to be managing director, they invest him not only with implied authority, but also with ostensible authority to do all such things as fall within the usual scope of that office. Other people who see him acting as managing director are entitled to assume that he has the usual authority of a managing director. But sometimes ostensible authority exceeds actual authority. For instance, when the board appoint the managing director, they may expressly limit his authority by saying he is not to order goods worth more than £500 without the sanction of the board. In that case his *actual* authority is subject to the £500 limitation, but his *ostensible* authority includes all the usual authority of a managing director. The company is bound by his ostensible authority in his dealings with those who do not know of the limitation. He may himself do the "holding out". Thus, if he orders goods worth £1 000 and signs himself "Managing Director, for and on behalf of the company", the company is bound to the other party who does not know of the £500 limitation ...'

Lord Denning recognised that in *Hely-Hutchinson* v *Brayhead Ltd* the chairman who was allowed to act as if he had been appointed managing director had apparent authority as well as implied actual authority.

The principal will be bound to the third party whether the agent had either actual or apparent authority. However, if an agent acts with apparent authority, but without actual authority, the principal cannot sue the third party on the contract, unless he ratifies the contract. (The principal has represented to the third party that the agent has authority, but the third party has made no representation to the principal.) However, the principal would be able to counterclaim and raise appropriate defences if sued on the contract by the third party. As regards the rights between principal and agent it also matters whether or not the agent had actual authority. If the agent had actual authority to do what he did then the agent will not become liable to the principal for so doing. Furthermore, if the agent has a contractual right to payment for his services then he will have a right to be paid for executing his actual authority. On the other hand an agent without actual authority, but with apparent authority, can be liable to the principal for acting in contravention of his instructions. In *Waugh* v *HB Clifford and Sons Ltd* we saw that the solicitors did not have implied actual authority to make the compromise on behalf of the builders. They did, however, have apparent authority to do so. Therefore, although the builders were bound by the compromise which the solicitors had made, the solicitors would have been liable to the builders for acting without actual authority. An agent without actual authority can also become liable to a third party for breach of warranty of authority, as explained below at 11.3.1.

The representation which gives rise to apparent authority must be made by the principal and not by the agent. Where the principal is a company the board of directors will almost invariably be given actual authority to exercise all the powers of the company by the company's articles of association. Using this actual authority the board can confer actual authority on others, such as salesmen. Furthermore, if the board of directors appoint a person to a certain position within the company then they may confer actual or apparent authority on that person to do certain things. In deciding whether or not a person within a company had apparent authority to do a certain act the courts will consider what representation the company has made to a third party, either by appointing the person to the position in question or otherwise. If the third party knows that the agent does not have authority to do a certain thing, or should have known this, then the agent cannot have apparent authority to do that thing because the third party cannot be said to have relied upon the representation (*Overbrooke Estates* v *Glencombe Properties Ltd* [1974] 1 WLR 1335). In *First Energy (UK) Ltd* v *Hungarian International Bank Ltd* [1993] 2 Lloyd's Rep 194 the Court of Appeal had to decide whether or not the defendant bank was bound by an offer to provide credit to the claimants. The claimants had dealt with one Jamison, the senior manager of the Manchester branch of the bank. Jamison had made it plain that he himself did not have authority to grant the credit facilities. Later Jamison informed the claimants that the credit facility had been approved by the bank's head office, although no such approval had in fact been given. It was held that the bank was bound by the offer to provide the credit. Jamison would not have had apparent authority to grant the credit himself, as the claimants knew that he did not have such authority. However, Jamison did have authority to communicate decisions of the bank. By appointing Jamison to a senior position the defendants had represented to those with whom he dealt that he had such authority.

It will almost always be the case that the representation which gives rise to apparent authority will be made before the third party makes the contract. However, the following case shows that it is possible for the representation to be made after the contract has been concluded.

■ *Spiro* v *Lintern* [1973] 1 WLR 1002 (Court of Appeal)

The defendant owned a house and asked his wife to find a buyer. Through a firm of estate agents the defendant's wife found a buyer, the claimant, who made an unconditional offer to buy the house for £25 000. A written contract was drawn up and signed by the claimant and by the estate agent acting on instructions from the defendant's wife. However, the defendant had not authorised his wife to make a binding contract and so she had no authority to do so or to enable the estate agents to do so. The defendant was advised by his solicitor that the sale was probably binding upon him. Later the claimant sent an architect to the house and some days later the claimant visited the house and was introduced to the defendant as the new owner. The defendant did not dispute this in any way. The defendant then allowed a builder to work on the house on behalf of the claimant. The defendant then went abroad, instructing his wife to complete the sale to the claimant. Instead the defendant's wife sold the house to a third party for £30 000. The claimant sued for specific performance.

Held. The claimant was granted specific performance. By failing to correct the claimant's belief that the defendant was under an obligation to sell the house, the defendant represented that such an obligation did in fact exist.

11.2.4 Agency by operation of law

It is possible that an **agency of necessity** will be implied in circumstances where one person acts to safeguard the property of another. This will only be the case if the following requirements are satisfied:

(i)   The agent must have been in control of the principal's property.
(ii) It must have been impossible for the agent to obtain the principal's instructions.
(iii) There must have been a real emergency which made it necessary for the agent to act as he did.
(iv) The agent must have acted in good faith as regards all parties.

Such agency of necessity is usually found in maritime emergencies. Established cases have given the captains of ships the power to sell cargoes which were perishing and to borrow money on the shipowner's behalf.

Occasionally, agencies of necessity can be found on dry land, but only if the four conditions are satisfied. In *Springer* v *Great Western Railway* [1921] 1 KB 257 carriers of tomatoes which had been imported from Jersey were delayed first by bad weather and then by a dock strike. The tomatoes were rapidly going bad and so the carriers took the decision to sell them locally. The carriers were liable to the owners of the tomatoes for doing this, even though the court was sure that the owners would have consented to it. No agency of necessity arose because the carriers could have communicated with the owners and asked them if this is what they wanted them to do.

Agency can also arise by cohabitation. A person cohabiting with another may have authority to pledge that other's credit to buy necessary goods and services.

Agency is occasionally imposed by statute. In Chapter 14, for example, we shall see that a person who conducts negotiations on behalf of a creditor can in certain circumstances be deemed to do so as the agent of the creditor, by virtue of s.56(2) of the Consumer Credit Act 1974.

11.2.5 Usual authority

The following, difficult, case does not easily fit within any of the established ways in which agency can be created, but nevertheless it was held that an agency did exist.

■ *Watteau* v *Fenwick* [1893] 1 QB 346

A pub owner (the principal) let a manager (the agent) run a pub. The owner authorised the manager to buy only bottled drinks and expressly forbade him to buy tobacco on credit. Acting against these instructions, the manager bought cigars on credit. The tobacco salesman had no idea that the manager was an agent. He thought that the manager owned the pub because the manager had previously owned the pub and his name was still painted above the door. When the manager could not pay for the cigars the seller sued the owner claiming that the owner was liable on the contract.

Held. The owner was liable on the contract.

COMMENT The manager had no express or implied actual authority to buy the cigars. (On the contrary, he had been forbidden to do this.) Nor did the manager have apparent authority because the principal never represented to the third party that the manager did have such authority. (The third party did not believe the manager to be an agent, and did not therefore even know of the principal's existence.) The case is perhaps best explained by saying that the manager had usual authority. The owner of the pub did make the manager an agent and so the agent was clothed with all the authority which one would usually expect an agent of this type to have. There is considerable doubt about the correctness of this case, but until it has been overruled it will operate as a precedent.

There is considerable uncertainty about the way in which the term usual authority should be used. It can not only be used to describe the situation in *Watteau* v *Fenwick*, but can also be used to describe a particular type of either implied actual authority or apparent authority. Implied actual authority may give an agent the power to do whatever is usual in the context of his trade, profession or position in order to execute his actual authority. Some writers call this usual authority. An agent who is appointed to a position in which he would usually have authority to do a certain act can have apparent authority to do that act, even if the principal has forbidden him to do it, and some writers call this authority usual authority. The terminology is used in a very confusing way and whenever the term usual authority is used it is best to make clear the sense in which it is used.

11.2.6 Agency by ratification

Agency by ratification occurs when an agent acts for a principal either without any authority at all, or in excess of the authority which he does have. If the principal ratifies the contract (later agrees to adopt it), either expressly or impliedly, then he retrospectively confers actual authority on the agent. The principal and third party will therefore become contractually bound to each other and the agent will not be liable to the third party on the contract or for breach of warranty of authority. (Breach of warranty of authority is explained below at 11.3.1.) The agent will not be liable to the principal for having exceeded his authority and may have a claim against the principal for reasonable remuneration or an indemnity. The principal has no obligation to ratify and may choose not to do so.

■ Example

X sees a bargain which he is sure that Y would want to buy. X therefore buys the bargain on Y's behalf, even though Y has given X no authority to do this. Y is not bound by the contract as he gave X no authority to buy the goods and has made no representation that X has such authority. But if Y later ratifies the contract then he will retrospectively give X actual authority. This will mean that there is now a good contract between Y and the seller of the goods and that X will be absolved from liability on the contract.

It might be thought that ratification would be as simple as the example given. However, five conditions must be satisfied for the ratification to be effective, and these are set out below.

(1) *The agent must have purported to act as an agent*

The principal cannot ratify the contract unless the agent expressly made the contract as an agent. Only the principal who was either named or capable of being ascertained can sue. An undisclosed principal cannot ratify.

■ *Keighley Maxted & Co* v *Durant* [1901] AC 240 (House of Lords)

An agent was authorised to buy wheat on behalf of a partnership at a certain price. He bought wheat at a greater price, by telegram, intending it to be for the partnership. He did not tell the corn merchant that he was buying the wheat for the partnership, but this was always his intention. The partnership ratified the contract the following day. Later the partnership refused to accept delivery of the wheat.

Held. The ratification was not effective because the agent had not made it plain that he was acting as an agent when he bought the wheat. Therefore, the partnership was not bound by the contract.

Similarly, in *Watteau* v *Fenwick* the owner of the hotel could not have ratified the contract which the manager made. (However, if he were sued by the tobacco salesman the hotel owner would be able to counterclaim for the price and raise any appropriate defences.)

(2) The principal must have had full capacity to make the contract both when the agent made the contract and when it was ratified

■ *Kelner* v *Baxter* (1866) LR 2 CP 174

A, B and C were intending to form a company. Before the company was formed, they bought £900 worth of wine on behalf of the company. The company was formed as planned and the wine was consumed. The company went into liquidation before paying for the wine. The supplier sued A, B and C, who argued that as the company had ratified the contract they were no longer liable on it.

Held. The ratification was not effective because the company did not have the capacity to make the contract when the agents made it. (Because the company had not yet been formed it had no capacity.)

COMMENT This case illustrates a general rule on the need for the principal to have capacity. In *Kelner* v *Baxter* A, B and C were personally liable on the contract because they intended to contract personally. However, as regards companies, s.36C(1) of the Companies Act 1985 must now be considered. This makes the promoters of a company personally liable on pre-incorporation contracts made on the company's behalf unless there has been an agreement to the contrary between the supplier and the promoters. (See Chapter 16 at 16.5.)

(3) At the time of ratification the principal must either have known all of the material facts or intended to ratify no matter what they were

The principal can adopt an action which another person fraudulently claimed to be making on his behalf. However, the ratification will only be effective if, at the time of the ratification, either:

(i) the principal knew of all the material facts and made an unequivocal adoption of the actions; or

(ii) the circumstances showed a clear inference that the principal was adopting the actions of the purported agent whatever the nature of the actions (*Marsh* v *Joseph* [1897] 1 Ch 213)

(4) A void contract cannot be ratified

(5) Ratification must take place within a reasonable time, and will not be allowed where third parties have acquired property rights which would be adversely affected by ratification

11.2.6.1 Effect of ratification

If a contact is successfully ratified then it is effective as if the agent had had actual authority at the time the contract was made.

■ *Bolton Partners* v *Lambert* (1889) 41 ChD 295 (Court of Appeal)

On 8 December 1886 the defendant wrote to the managing director of a company, offering to buy the company. On 13 December a works committee decided to accept the offer, although it did not have the authority to do this. The managing director wrote to the defendant that the Board of Directors of the company had accepted the offer. On 13 January the defendant said that he was revoking his offer. On 17 January the Board of Directors issued a writ claiming specific performance of the agreement and on 28 January the Board ratified the acceptance made by the managing director.

Held. As soon as the Board of Directors ratified the contract it became effective from 13 December. The defendant could not therefore revoke his offer on 13 January.

Although the rule in *Bolton Partners* v *Lambert* seems somewhat unfair to the third party, it is modified by the requirement that ratification must take place within a reasonable time, and will not be allowed where third parties have acquired property rights which would be adversely affected by ratification. Nor does the rule apply where the third party knew that the agent's authority was limited or that the contract would have to be ratified.

The principal will generally ratify by informing the third party that he is doing so. However, ratification can be implied from the principal's conduct and even silence or inactivity can amount to ratification in some circumstances. What is important is that the principal unequivocally shows that he is adopting the agent's actions.

Test your understanding

1 Alice puts goods into Belinda's auction. Celia asks Denise to go to the auction and Bid for Lot 1. Denise is the highest bidder and buys Lot 1 on behalf of Celia. Identify the two principals and the two agents.

2 What is the difference between express actual authority and implied actual authority?

3 How does apparent authority differ from actual authority?

4 Why in *Watteau* v *Fenwick* did the manager not have (a) Actual authority? (b) Apparent authority?

5 How can agency by ratification arise?

Answers

1 Belinda, the auctioneer is Alice's agent. Denise is Celia's agent.

2 Both express and actual authority arise by agreement between principal and agent. Express actual authority arises where the principal and agent agree in words that the agent shall have the authority. Implied actual authority arises where this is agreed otherwise than in words.

3 Apparent authority arises when a principal represents to a third party that someone is his agent. Once the third party has acted on the representation the principal will be estopped from denying its truth. Actual authority does not arise on account of a representation to a third party, but by agreement between principal and agent.

4 (a) The manager did not have actual authority because the hotel owner had not agreed with the manager that the manager had authority to buy tobacco on credit. (b) The manager did not have apparent authority because the hotel owner had not made a representation to the third party that the manager was his agent.

5 Agency by ratification can arise when a principal agrees to adopt a transaction conducted on his behalf by an agent who had no authority to bind the principal. Retrospective actual authority is conferred.

11.3 · Liability on contracts made by agents

The rights of a third party to sue on a contract made by an agent differ, depending upon whether the agency was disclosed or undisclosed. Agency is disclosed when the agent indicates that he is acting as an agent, whether or not the principal for whom he is acting is actually identified.

If an agent makes a contract for a disclosed principal then generally the agent incurs no liability on the contract. By disclosing that he was acting for a principal, the agent will be taken to have shown the third party that he did not intend to become personally liable on the contract. If the circumstances show otherwise, however, the agent can incur personal liability.

If the principal was undisclosed (i.e. the agent did not reveal that he was acting for a principal) then the agent will be liable to the third party on the contract. If the agent had actual authority to make the contract the principal will also be liable to the third party on the contract. Where such joint liability arises, the third party can choose to sue either the agent or the principal. However, having made an unequivocal election to hold one or other liable on the contract, the third party will not be able to change his mind. If the agent did not have actual authority to make the contract then the principal will not be liable on the contract. Nor can the principal ratify the contract because ratification is only permissible where the agent purported to act as an agent.

There are three situations where an undisclosed principal cannot sue on the contract, even if the agent did have actual authority to make the contract. These situations are:

(i) that a term of the contract excluded agency;
(ii) that the third party would have refused to contract with the undisclosed principal;
(iii) that the third party made the contract with the agent because he particularly wanted to contract with the agent personally.

■ *Said v Butt* [1920] 3 KB 497

The claimant, a theatre critic, wanted to attend the first night of a play at a certain theatre. He knew that the theatre owners would refuse to supply him with a ticket, as he had made serious unfounded allegations against members of the theatre. He therefore asked his friend to buy him a ticket, but not to state who the ticket was for. The defendant, the managing director of the theatre, refused to let the claimant use the ticket to gain entry to the theatre. The claimant sued the defendant for maliciously procuring the theatre owners to breach a contract.

Held. The defendant was not liable as there was no contract between the claimant and the theatre owners. The identity of the claimant was a material element in the formation of the contract.

COMMENT This case provides an example of a case where the third party would have refused to have contracted with the undisclosed principal. McCardie J said that in this case the personal element was 'strikingly present' as the reviews of a play's first night could make or break the play. If the ticket had said that it was not transferable, as many nowadays do, then a term of the contract would have excluded agency. In *Shogun Finance Ltd v Hudson (FC)* [2003] UKHL 62 Lord Millett (at para.88) indicated that the evidence showed that the ticket was not transferable and so an undisclosed principal could not intervene on a contract intended to be made with the agent personally.

■ *Dyster v Randall* [1926] Ch 932

The claimant wanted to buy two plots of land from the defendants. The claimant used to work for the defendants but had been dismissed by them. He knew that the defendants profoundly distrusted him and would not sell him the land. The claimant therefore asked one Crossley to buy the land for him, asking Crossley not to reveal for whom he was acting. Crossley bought the land as requested. When the defendants discovered that Crossley had been acting for the claimant they refused to be bound by the contract. The claimant sued for specific performance.

Held. The claimant was granted specific performance. There was no personal element strikingly present and so there was no reason why an undisclosed principal should not buy the land on behalf of the claimant.

Greer v *Downs Supply Co* [1927] 2 KB 28 provides an example of undisclosed agency not being allowed because the third party particularly wanted to contract with the agent personally. The agent owed the third party £17. The third party contracted to buy timber from the agent for £29, it being a term of the contract that the third party could set the £17 off against the price. The agent had dishonestly told the third party that he was not selling the wood on behalf of an undisclosed principal, but in fact he was. The Court of Appeal held that the undisclosed principal could not sue on the contract. The third party had particularly wanted to contract with the agent so that he could deduct the £17 from the price of £29.

Whether or not the principal is liable on the contract will depend upon whether or not the agent had any type of authority to act for the principal. (As explained above at 11.2.) If the third party is sued on the contract by an undisclosed principal, he will be able to take advantage of defences which he would have had against the agent.

In *Siu Yin Kwan* v *Eastern Insurance Co* [1994] 1 All ER 213 Lord Lloyd of Berwick summarised the law as regards undisclosed principals as follows:

(1) An undisclosed principal may sue and be sued on a contract made by an agent on his behalf, acting within the scope of his actual authority.
(2) In entering into the contract the agent must intend to act on the principal's behalf.

(3) The agent of an undisclosed principal may also sue and be sued on the contract.

(4) Any defence which the third party may have against the agent is available against his principal.

(5) The terms of the contract may, expressly or by implication, exclude the principal's right to sue, and his liability to be sued. The contract itself, or the circumstances surrounding the contract, may show that the agent is the true and only principal.

11.3.1 Breach of warranty of authority

We have seen that an agent will generally incur no liability on a contract made for a disclosed principal. However, if an agent makes a representation to a third party, warranting that he has authority to act for a principal when he does not in fact have such authority, and if the third party acts on this representation to his detriment, then the agent will be liable to the third party for breach of this warranty of authority. Usually, the third party will act upon the warranty by making the contract with the principal. The agent can also become liable for breach of warranty of authority where he exceeds the authority which he does have. Liability for breach of warranty of authority is independent of liability on the contract made on the principal's behalf, and can arise even if the agent could not have known that his authority had been revoked.

■ *Yonge v Toynbee* [1910] 1 KB 215 (Court of Appeal)

A client (the principal) instructed a solicitor (the agent) to defend a case. The client became certifiably insane and this automatically terminated the solicitor's authority to act for him. The solicitor did not know that the client had become insane and continued to act for him.

Held. As soon as the client was certified insane the solicitor lost his authority to act for the client. All proceedings taken after this date were therefore struck out, and the solicitor had to pay all the other party's costs which were incurred after this date.

If the principal ratifies the agent's actions then the agent will not be liable for breach of warranty of authority. Nor will the agent be liable for breach of warranty of authority if the third party knew, or should have known, that the agent did not have the authority warranted. Damages for breach of warranty of authority are calculated by reference to the two rules in *Hadley* v *Baxendale*. These damages are designed to put the third party in the position which he would have been if the warranty had not been breached. This does not make the agent liable on the contract between third party and principal.

An example of damages for breach of warranty of authority is provided by *Simons* v *Patchett* [1857] 7 E & B 568. A bought a ship from T claiming to have authority from P (Rostron & Co.). In fact A had exceeded his limited authority in doing this. The contract price was £6 000. P refused to be bound by the contract. T therefore sold the ship to another buyer, X, for £5 500. This was the best price T could get, and was a fair price at the time. T sued A for breach of warranty of authority. It was held that A had to pay £500 damages. If the agent's warranty of authority had not been broken, T would either have received the full price of £6 000 from P, or would have been able to sue P for breach of contract. If sued for breach of contract, P would (under *Hadley* v *Baxendale*) have had to pay damages of £500. Either way, A's breach of warranty of authority had cost T £500, representing the difference between the £6 000 originally agreed and the £5 500 actually received. P was, therefore, entitled to £500 damages from A.

The following case shows that the claimant can recover damages greater than the normal measure for breach of warranty of authority as long as the damages claimed are within *Hadley* v *Baxendale*.

■ *Habton Farms (an unlimited company) v Nimmo and another* [2003] EWCA Civ 68 (Court of Appeal)

In October 1998 the defendant purported to buy a racehorse from the claimant, on behalf of one Williamson, for £70 000. The defendant warranted that he had authority to do this as Williamson's agent. The purchase was subject to the horse being inspected by a vet and X-rays being approved. The defendant later told the claimant that the vet's inspection and the X-rays were satisfactory and arranged for the horse to be collected on 2 or 3 November. On one of these dates the claimant was told that Williamson would not buy the horse. The claimant was not told that defendant had no actual or apparent authority to act for Williamson. The claimant continued to ask for the price and refrained from selling the horse to anyone else. At the end of November the horse contracted peritonitis, from which it died on 2 December. The claimant then discovered that the defendant had no authority to act for Williamson and sued for damages for breach of warranty of authority. The judge ordered the defendant to pay damages of £70 000. An appeal was made to the Court of Appeal.

Held. The Court of Appeal dismissed the appeal. The defendant had warranted his authority to act for Williamson both when he made the contract and when he indicated that the vet's inspection and the X-rays were satisfactory. If this warranty had been true the claimant would have received the purchase price of £70 000. The ordinary measure of damages for breach of warranty of authority was the difference between the contract price and the market price at the relevant time (here 2 or 3 December). However, the warranty of authority had caused the claimant not to sell the horse to anyone else and to try to enforce the contract of sale. This meant that it was inappropriate to deduct the market price from the contract price and so the defendant was liable to pay £70 000 damages.

An agent acting with only apparent authority can be liable for breach of warranty of authority. However, as the principal is liable on the contract made the third party is usually likely to have suffered no loss as a consequence of the breach and therefore be entitled to no damages.

In *Halbot* v *Lens* [1901] 1 Ch 344 it was established that an agent will not be liable for breach of warranty of authority if he specifically denies having authority, or if the third party did not rely on the existence of his authority.

Test your understanding

1 In what circumstances is agency undisclosed?

2 Where agency is disclosed: (a) In what circumstances will the principal be liable on the contract? (b) What liability might the agent have towards the third party?

3 Where agency is undisclosed, what is the liability on the contract to the third party of (a) The principal? (b) The agent?

4 In what circumstances can the undisclosed principal not sue on the contract?

Answers

1 Agency is undisclosed where the agent does not reveal that he is acting as an agent. Agency is disclosed where the agent reveals that he is acting as an agent.

2 (a) Where the agency is disclosed then the principal will be liable on the contract only if the agent had some type of authority to act for the principal. (b) The agent will have no liability on the contract, unless the circumstances show that he intended to be personally liable on it. However, the agent might be liable to the third party for breach of warranty of authority. This liability would arise if the agent warranted that he had authority which he did not have, and if reliance on this warranty caused a loss to the third party.

3 (a) The principal will be liable on the contract as long as the agent acted within the scope of his actual authority. (b) The agent will be liable on the contract, whether or not the principal is also liable on it.

4 An undisclosed principal cannot sue on the contract: (a) Where a term of the contract excluded agency; (b) where the third party would have refused to contract with the undisclosed principal; (c) where the third party made the contract with the agent because he particularly wanted to contract with the agent personally.

11.4 · Duties of the agent

Agents owe several duties to their principals. These duties arise either from the agreement made between principal and agent, whether a contract or not, or from the fiduciary nature of agency. The fiduciary duties are imposed by the law because the nature of agency is such that a principal has to place great trust and confidence in the agent.

11.4.1 To obey instructions

An agent with actual authority will have agreed to act for the principal. If this agreement amounts to a contract, as will generally be the case, then the agent can be liable for failure to perform the contract. Furthermore, an agent must obey lawful instructions, even if he thinks he is helping the principal by not doing so. For example, in *Bertram Armstrong and Co v Godfrey* (1830) 1 Kn 381 an agent was ordered to sell shares as soon as they reached a certain price. The shares did reach the appropriate price, but the agent did not sell because he thought they would go higher. In fact the price of the shares fell. The agent was held liable, and had to pay damages for not obeying his instructions.

11.4.2 Care and skill

An agent must exercise care and skill when performing his duties. The precise degree of care and skill required will depend upon several factors, including any expertise which the agent has expressly or impliedly claimed to have. For example, if a professional person such as a solicitor is employed as an agent he should show the degree of care and skill which one could reasonably expect from a solicitor. Where the agency is to provide a service in the course of a business s.13 SGSA 1982 requires that the agent provides the service using reasonable care and skill. Where the agent was not acting in the course of a business the common law would impose a similar duty to that imposed by s.13 SGSA. If there is no contract between principal and agent the duty to use reasonable care and skill will arise in tort.

■ *Chaudry v Prabhakar* [1988] 3 All ER 718 (Court of Appeal)

The claimant, who had recently passed her driving test and knew nothing about cars, asked a friend, the first defendant, to find her a suitable second-hand car. The defendant was not a mechanic but had some knowledge of cars. The claimant stipulated that she did not want any car which had been in an accident. The first defendant found a car being sold by the second defendant, a car sprayer and panel beater. The first defendant noticed that the bonnet had been crumpled and straightened but thought the car was in good condition. He therefore recommended that the claimant buy the car, which she did at a price of £4500. Some months later the claimant discovered that the car had been in a very bad accident, that it had been badly repaired and that it was quite unroadworthy. The judge found the second defendant liable for breach of the 1979 Sale of Goods Act implied term that the car was of merchantable (now satisfactory) quality and the first defendant liable for breach of his duty to take reasonable care. The first defendant appealed.

Held. The first defendant was liable. A gratuitous agent owes a duty to show the degree of care and skill which could be expected of him in all the circumstances. This standard is assessed objectively.

COMMENT   In this case counsel for the first defendant conceded that a duty of care was owed. May LJ indicated that he thought that this concession should not have been made and that it was inappropriate to impose a duty of care when a person gratuitously did a favour for a friend in a social context. If the concession had not been made then the first defendant might well not have been liable.

11.4.3 Personal performance

Generally, the agent must perform personally and must not delegate his authority. This is sometimes expressed by the Latin maxim, *delegare non potest delegare* (a delegate must not sub delegate).

There are four exceptions to this rule. An agent is allowed to delegate his duties in the following circumstances:

(i) If the principal expressly authorises delegation.
(ii) If the agent can imply a power to delegate from the circumstances.

(iii) If the delegation is of an act requiring no care and skill.

(iv) If the delegation became necessary due to unforeseen circumstances.

In *John McCann & Co v Pow* [1975] 1 All ER 129 (Court of Appeal) it was held that an estate agent who had been given the task of selling a house, and who described himself in his advertisements as 'sole agent', could not delegate the task. Therefore, the agent's claim to commission, on the basis that he had delegated to a different estate agent who actually sold the property, failed.

11.4.4 Fiduciary duties

As agency is a fiduciary relationship, having its origins in equity, fiduciary duties are placed upon the agent. Although we consider four fiduciary duties it is important to realise that these duties often overlap, so that a breach of one involves a breach of another. The fiduciary duties are as follows:

11.4.4.1 To avoid any conflict of interest

An agent must avoid a conflict between his own interests and those of his principal. For example, an agent who is employed to sell the principal's property cannot buy it himself unless he makes full disclosure of this to the principal. Similarly, an agent employed by the principal to buy cannot perform the contract by selling his own property to the principal without full disclosure. So in *Armstrong* v *Jackson* [1917] 2 KB 822 a stockbroker who had been asked to buy 600 shares in a certain company had a conflict of interest when he sold the principal 600 shares which he himself owned in the company. The agent had been a promoter of the company in question and pretended that he had bought the shares in the open market. Some years later the principal discovered what had happened and the court set the agreement aside. McCardie J said: 'It matters not that the agent sells at the market price, or that he acts without intent to defraud ... The prohibition of the law is absolute. It will not allow an agent to place himself in a situation which, under ordinary circumstances, would tempt a man to do that which is not the best for his principal.'

11.4.4.2 Not to make a secret profit

The agent must not make any profit other than that which has been agreed with the principal. In the following case Lord Denning MR identified that such a profit might arise from the agent's use of the principal's property, from the use of his position of authority, or from information or knowledge which he had acquired in the course of his agency.

■ *Boardman v Phipps* [1967] 2 AC 46 (House of Lords)

The defendant acted as a solicitor to a trust. The trust owned shares in a certain company and the solicitor advised the trust to buy more of these shares. Despite being repeatedly advised to buy more shares, the trust did not do so. The solicitor himself bought shares in the company. This meant that the solicitor and the trust between them controlled the company and it enabled both the solicitor and the trust to make large profits. The trust sued the solicitor, claiming the profits he had made.

Held. The solicitor had to account to the trust for the profit he had made and hold these profits on constructive trust for the trust. The solicitor had used knowledge which he had acquired in the course of his agency to make the profit.

COMMENT (i) Although this case seems rather unfair to the solicitor he was awarded very generous payment, on a *quantum meruit* basis, for the work he had done on the company's behalf. The case illustrates that the fiduciary duties are enforced even where their breach causes no loss to the principal. (ii) Lord Denning explained the rule that an agent must not make a secret profit in the following way: 'It is quite clear that if an agent uses *property*, with which he has been entrusted by his principal, so as to make a profit for himself out of it, without his principal's consent, then he is accountable for it to his principal ... So, also, if he uses a *position of authority*, to which he has been appointed by his principal, so as to gain money by means of it for himself, then also he is accountable to his principal for it ... Likewise with *information or knowledge* which he has been employed by his principal to collect or discover, *or which he has otherwise acquired*, for the use of this principal, then again if he turns it to his own use, so as to make a profit by means of it for himself, he is accountable ... for such information or knowledge is the property of the principal, just as much as an invention is.'

11.4.4.3 **Not to take a bribe**

In this context a bribe does not necessarily indicate corruption. In *Anangel Atlas Compania Naviera SA v Ishikawajima-Harima Heavy Industries Co Ltd* [1990] 1 Lloyd's Rep 167 Leggatt J gave the following definition: 'a bribe consists in a commission or other inducement, which is given by a third party to an agent as such, and which is secret from his principal'. For example, if a firm's buyer is given inducements to favour a particular supplier a court will almost certainly regard this as a bribe. Much of 'corporate hospitality' and the giving of 'free samples' to people who buy on behalf of others is potentially a bribe.

If an agent does take a bribe the principal has the following remedies: dismiss the agent and recover commission or salary paid to the agent; recover the bribe from either the agent or the person who paid it, or alternatively regard the bribe as held on trust for the principal; as an alternative to recovering the bribe, sue the agent or the person who paid the bribe for losses sustained as a result of the bribe; rescind the contract made with the third party.

11.4.4.4 **The duty to account**

This duty requires that the agent keeps his own property separate from the principal's property. If the agent mixes the two up, the principal will be entitled to all of the property unless the agent can clearly show what property belonged to him. The agent will also be obliged to keep a record of his dealings on the principal's behalf, which the principal can ask to inspect. The principal might have a right to inspect records held on computer. In *Yasuda Ltd v Orion Underwriting Ltd* [1995] QB 174 the claimants were entitled by an express clause of the contract to inspect 'all necessary books accounts records and other documentation'. It was held that this clearly included all computer material. If the defendants could not reasonably quickly separate material on the computer which did not relate to the claimants' business then they would have to allow the claimants access to all material which included reference to the claimants' business.

11.4.5 **Additional duties of commercial agents**

The Commercial Agents (Council Directive) Regulations 1993 Reg.2(1) define a commercial agent as:

> 'a self-employed intermediary who has continuing authority to negotiate the sale or purchase of goods on behalf of another person (the "principal"), or to negotiate and conclude the sale or purchase of goods on behalf of and in the name of that principal.'

This definition is considered more fully below at 11.6.2.

Regulation 3(1) imposes on a commercial agent the duties to look after the interest of the principal, to act dutifully, and to act in good faith. These duties seem similar to a combination of the common law fiduciary duties and duty to obey instructions. Regulation 3(2) amplifies the three duties somewhat by stating:

In particular, a commercial agent must:

(a) make proper efforts to negotiate and, where appropriate, conclude the transactions he is instructed to take care of;

(b) communicate to his principal all the necessary information available to him;

(c) comply with reasonable instructions given by the principal.

Regulation 5(1) provides that the parties cannot contract out of these duties.

11.5 · The rights of the agent

An agent may have any of the following rights: a right to an indemnity for expenses incurred, a right to the remuneration agreed in the contract, a right to a lien over the principal's goods. We examine the three rights in turn.

11.5.1 Indemnity

Unless the contract which created the agency provides otherwise, an agent will be entitled to an indemnity from his principal for liability incurred or money spent in the performance of the agency. This means that the principal must repay any expenses which the agent has properly incurred. For example, in *Rhodes v Fielder, Jones and Harrison* (1919) 89 LJ KB 15 a country solicitor had to indemnify a firm of London solicitors who had paid barrister's fees on behalf of the country solicitor. The country solicitor had asked the London firm to engage a barrister to act for them, but had later instructed the London firm not to pay the barrister's fees. The London firm had paid the barrister's fees because, although they had no legal duty to do so, they had a very strong moral duty to do so.

The right to an indemnity can be lost if the agent exceeds his duty or acts negligently.

11.5.2 Remuneration

The agent's contract with the principal may expressly provide that the agent should be paid and may fix the amount of remuneration. Many professional agents offer to act only on their standard terms and conditions, leaving their principals with a take it or leave it choice.

If there is no agreement as to remuneration then the agent must rely on an implied term in order to get paid. Such a term will be implied on the same basis as any other term implied by the courts. (The factors which the court will consider were examined in Chapter 5 at 5.3.) Section 15 SGSA 1982 states that where under a contract for the supply of a service the consideration for the supply of a service is not determined by the contract, left to be determined by a manner agreed by the contract or determined by the course of dealing between the parties, there is an implied term that the party contracting with the supplier will pay a reasonable charge. Where an express term deals with the amount of remuneration the agent will not be able to argue that an implied term entitles him to more, and nor will s.15 SGSA apply.

■ *Re Richmond Gate Property Co Ltd* [1965] 1 WLR 335

The articles of association of a company set out the remuneration of the managing director. The relevant article provided that the managing director should receive 'such remuneration (whether by way of salary, commission or participation in profits, or partly in one way and partly in another) as the directors may determine'. The company went into liquidation nine months after incorporation. The managing director had been paid nothing during this time and claimed £400.

Held. The managing director was not entitled to any payment. An express term of the contract determined what he should be paid. An implied term could not contradict this and nor could more be paid on a *quantum meruit.*

Even if the contract does provide that the agent should be paid, it is often difficult to decide whether or not he has done enough to be entitled to the payment.

■ *Luxor (Eastbourne) Ltd* v *Cooper* [1941] AC 108 (House of Lords)

Estate agents were offered £10 000 commission for selling two cinemas, the commission to be paid on completion. The estate agents found buyers for the cinemas, but the cinema owners changed their minds and refused to sell. The estate agents asked for an implied term that the cinema owners would not refuse to complete the sale to a suitable buyer.

Held. No such term could be implied. The commission was so huge that the contract was in the nature of a gamble. If the whole deal went through the estate agents would get their commission. But if anything went wrong, they would not.

Lord Russell: 'I can find no safe ground on which to base the introduction of any such implied term. Implied terms, as we all know, can only be justified under the compulsion of some necessity. No such compulsion or necessity exists in the case under consideration ... The chances are largely in favour of the deal going through, if a purchaser is introduced. The agent takes the risk in the hope of a substantial remuneration for comparatively small exertion.'

Some estate agents nowadays ensure that the contract with the customer provides that if a buyer is found, the agents will be paid whether the seller proceeds with the sale or not.

11.5.3 Lien

A lien is a right to hold onto goods until a claim is satisfied. An agent to whom the principal owes money may have a lien over the principal's goods. The lien of an agent is a particular lien and so it can only allow the agent to retain possession of goods until debts which relate to those particular goods, or to related transactions, are satisfied. (A general lien gives the right to hold onto any of the debtor's goods until a debt is satisfied.) A lien can only arise if the agent has possession of the goods. Furthermore, the lien must not be excluded by the contract. For example, a salesman who has not been paid by his employer might have a lien over the goods he was employed to sell until he does get paid. An agent may lose a lien by waiving it. (By voluntarily parting with possession of the goods or otherwise indicating that he intends to abandon the lien.)

To exercise the lien, the agent must have lawfully come into possession of the goods in his capacity as an agent. The lien only gives a right to possession of the goods over which it is exercised. It does not give a right to sell or dispose of the goods.

11.6 · Termination of agency

An agent acts for a principal on account of having the principal's authority to do so. (Although an agent can make a principal liable on account of having apparent authority.) Apart from some exceptional circumstances which make an agency irrevocable, the principal can withdraw the agent's authority at any time. However, unless third parties are informed of this, the agent might still be able to bind the principal on account of having apparent authority. For example, in *Trueman and others* v *Loder* (1840) 11 Ad & El 589 it was well known that an agent in London represented a principal in St Petersburg and that the agent conducted no business on his own account. The principal withdrew the agent's authority, but the agent went on to buy tallow from a third party who believed that the agent was, as usual, acting on behalf of the principal. It was held that the principal was bound by the contract as the agent still had apparent authority to act for the principal. To make sure that such apparent authority does not continue, the principal should inform third parties to whom it has been represented that the agent has authority that the authority has been terminated.

If the principal does withdraw the agent's authority then this might or might not be a breach of contract, depending upon what was agreed between principal and agent. Similarly, an agent who terminates the agreement early may be liable for breach of contract. If the parties agree to end the agency there can be no question of breach of contract. Specific performance will not be ordered to compel a party to continue to act as agent, as it will not be ordered to enforce personal service contracts. (See Chapter 7 at 7.2.4.) Nor will an injunction be ordered if it would, in effect, amount to specific performance of an agency contract. So in *Warren* v *Mendy* [1989] 3 All ER 103 a professional boxer who had agreed to employ the claimant as his manager, and not to employ any other manager, for a three year period could not be restrained by injunction from employing another manager before the end of the period.

A fixed term agency ends when the term is up. If the agency is for an indeterminate term either party can end it by giving a reasonable amount of notice of his intention to do so, subject to minimum requirements where the Commercial Agents Regulations apply. If the principal unilaterally ends a contract of agency under which the agent was an employee there may be a claim for unfair dismissal (see Chapter 20 at 20.4) or for damages for breach of contract.

11.6.1 Termination by operation of law

Agency is terminated automatically in the following ways:

(i) By frustration. (This will occur for the usual reasons: that performance of the contract becomes impossible, illegal or radically different.)
(ii) By the death of either party.
(iii) By the insanity of either party.
(iv) By the bankruptcy of the principal.
(v) By bankruptcy of the agent if this would render him unfit to perform his duties.

If either principal or agent terminates the agency in breach of contract, damages will be assessed on normal contract principles under the two rules in *Hadley* v *Baxendale*.

11.6.2 Termination under the Commercial Agents (Council Directive) Regulations 1993

11.6.2.1 Definition of a commercial agent

Earlier in this chapter we saw that the Commercial Agents (Council Directive) Regulations 1993 Reg.2(1) define a commercial agent as:

'a self-employed intermediary who has continuing authority to negotiate the sale or purchase of goods on behalf of another person (the "principal"), or to negotiate and conclude the sale or purchase of goods on behalf of and in the name of that principal.'

Now we examine this definition in more detail before going on to consider the rights which may accrue to a commercial agent when the agency is terminated.

First, it should be noted that the commercial agent must buy or sell goods rather than services. It is also necessary that the commercial agent is self-employed, rather than an employee. Limited companies have been held to be commercial agents.

A commercial agent must be paid (Reg.2(2)(a)) but does not need to be paid on commission. (However, if the agent is not paid on commission several of the regulations, which deal with commission, do not apply.)

Earlier in this chapter, at 11.1, we saw that some retailers call themselves agents when in fact they are not. The example given was of motor retailers calling themselves sole agents of manufacturers in a certain area, when in fact these retailers bought from the manufacturers and sold on their own behalf, rather than selling on behalf of the manufacturers. Such retailers would clearly not be commercial agents as the definition in Reg.2(1) requires a commercial agent to sell 'on behalf' of the principal.

Having given the definition of a commercial agent, Reg.2(1) goes on to specifically exclude company officers acting on behalf of their companies, partners acting on behalf of their firms and insolvency practitioners.

Regulations 2(3) and (4) provide that the Regulations do not apply to persons whose activities as commercial agent are to be considered 'secondary'. The Schedule to the Regulations attempts to clarify the meaning of this. Case law seems to have established that the Schedule requires that 'secondary' should be seen in the context of the duties which the agent performs for the principal, rather than in the context of what other activities the agent carries out on his own behalf.

11.6.2.2 Minimum notice periods

Regulation 16 provides that the Regulations do not apply if the agency agreement is justifiably immediately terminated on account of one of the parties having failed to carry out all or part of his obligations under the contract, or where exceptional circumstances apply.

Where the agency agreement is for an indefinite period, Reg.15 sets out minimum notice periods, as follows. In the first year of the agency contract the minimum period is one month. In the second year it is two months, After two years it is three months. The parties cannot agree to shorter notice periods. They can agree to longer periods, as long as the notice to be observed by the principal is not less than that to be observed by the agent. Unless the parties agree otherwise, the notice period must end at the end of a calendar month.

If the agency agreement was for a fixed period but it continues to be performed by both sides after the notice has expired, Reg.14 provides that it is deemed to have been converted into an agreement for an indefinite period. The notice periods set out in Reg.15 will then apply and, in calculating the required notice, the earlier fixed notice period is taken into account.

11.6.2.3 Compensation and indemnity payments

Regulations 17 and 18 entitle the commercial agent to indemnity or compensation on termination of the agency contract. Furthermore, Reg.19 provides that these two regulations cannot be contracted out of to the detriment of the agent. However, the agent will lose the rights to indemnity or compensation if he does not inform the principal, within one year of termination of the agency contract, that he intends pursuing his entitlement (Reg.17(8)).

Indemnity and compensation are not the same things, and the agent is entitled to be compensated rather than indemnified, unless the agency contract provides otherwise (Reg.17(2)). So compensation is the usual remedy and we consider it before considering indemnity.

Compensation

Regulation 17(6) provides that the commercial agent shall be entitled to compensation for the damage he suffers as a result of the termination of his relations with the principal. The agent must therefore have suffered a loss but there is no requirement that this should be the principal's fault.

Regulation 17(7) then states that such damage to the agent shall be deemed to occur particularly when the termination takes place in either or both of two circumstances. First, circumstances which deprive the commercial agent of the commission which proper performance of the agency contract would have procured for him whilst providing his principal with substantial benefits linked to the activities of the commercial agent. Second, circumstances which have not enabled the commercial agent to recoup the costs and expenses that he had incurred in the agency contract on the advice of his principal.

Indemnity

The two requirements for an indemnity are: (a) that the agent has brought the principal new customers or has significantly increased the volume of business with existing customers and the principal continues to derive substantial benefits from the business with such customers; and (b) the payment of the indemnity is equitable, having regard to all of the circumstances and, in particular, the commission lost by the commercial agent on the business transacted with such customers (Reg.17(3)).

Regulation 17(4) provides that the amount of the indemnity cannot be more than a figure equivalent to an indemnity for one year, calculated by reference to the agent's actual pay over the previous five years or, if the agent has not worked for five years, such time as he has worked.

The grant of an indemnity does not prevent the agent from seeking common law damages (Reg.17(5)).

Loss of indemnity and compensation

Regulation 18 sets out three circumstances in which neither indemnity nor compensation are payable, as follows.

(a) Where the principal has justifiably terminated the contract on account of the agent's breach of contract.
(b) Where the agent has himself terminated the contract. (Unless this was justified by circumstances attributable to the principal, or unless the agent had become so old, ill or infirm that he could not reasonably be required to carry on with his activities.)
(c) Where the commercial agent, with the agreement of the principal has assigned his rights to a third party.

11.6.2.4 Other duties of the principal

If the agent's remuneration is not fixed, Reg.6(1) provides that the agent should receive the remuneration which a commercial agent selling the type of goods sold, in the place where they are sold, would customarily receive. If there is no such customary practice he should be paid a reasonable amount.

Regulation 4(2) imposes two duties on the principal. First, the principal must provide the commercial agent with the necessary documentation relating to the goods concerned. Second, he must obtain for the commercial agent the information necessary for the performance of the agency contract, and in particular notify the agent within a reasonable time if he anticipates that the volume of commercial transactions will be significantly lower than that which the commercial agent could normally have expected.

Regulation 4(3) requires the principal to inform his commercial agent, within a reasonable time, of any acceptance, refusal or non-execution of a commercial transaction which the commercial agent procured for him. The duties set out in Reg.4 cannot be excluded by agreement between the parties.

Test your understanding

1 What non-fiduciary duties are imposed on an agent?

2 What fiduciary duties are imposed on an agent? Why are these fiduciary duties imposed?

3 What rights against the principal might an agent have?

4 Once a principal has withdrawn an agent's authority, is it possible for the agent to continue to make contracts which bind the principal?

5 In what ways may agency be terminated by operation of law?

Answers

1 The non-fiduciary duties imposed on an agent are: to obey instructions, to use an appropriate amount of care and skill, and to perform personally.

2 The fiduciary duties imposed on an agent are: to avoid a conflict of interest, not to make a secret profit, not to take a bribe and to account to the principal. These duties are imposed because the very nature of agency causes the principal to place great trust and confidence in the agent.

3 An agent might have the right to an indemnity to cover expenses necessarily incurred in performing the agency. An express or implied term of the contract between principal and agent might entitle an agent to remuneration. An agent might have a particular lien over the principal's goods until some claim has been satisfied.

4 An agent whose authority has been withdrawn could continue to have apparent authority to bind the principal to third parties who do not know that the authority has been withdrawn.

5 Agency may be terminated by operation of law by: frustration, the death of either party, the insanity of either party, the bankruptcy of the principal or by the bankruptcy of the agent if this would render him unfit to perform his duties.

Key points

- An agent has the power to alter the legal position of his principal. Most agents do this by making contracts on the principal's behalf.

Creation of authority

- An agent has actual authority when the principal and agent agree that he should have such authority. If this agreement is made in words the authority is express actual authority. If the agreement is made otherwise than in words, the authority is implied actual authority.

- An agent has apparent or ostensible authority when a third party acts upon a representation made by the principal that the agent had authority to act on the principal's behalf. Once the third party has acted upon the representation the principal will be estopped from denying it.

- Agency may arise by operation of law. In an emergency there may be an agency of necessity, and various statutes impose agency.

- Agency by ratification arises where a principal later agrees to adopt a transaction entered into on his behalf by an agent who did not have the necessary authority. Once the contract has been ratified it takes effect as if the agent had had actual authority from the outset.

Liability on contracts made by agents

- Agency is disclosed when the agent indicates that he is acting as an agent, whether or not the principal for whom he is acting is actually identified.

- If an agent makes a contract for a disclosed principal then generally the agent incurs no liability on the contract.

- If an agent makes a contract for an undisclosed principal then the agent will be liable to the third party on the contract.

- A principal will be bound by an agent's actions on his behalf only if the agent had some type of authority to act for the principal.

- Where both agent and principal are liable on the contract the third party may sue either agent or principal. However, once an unequivocal election has been made to hold either agent or principal liable on the contract the third party will not be able to change his mind.

- An undisclosed principal can sue on a contract made on his behalf as long as the agent acted within his actual authority. However, the undisclosed principal will not be able to sue on the contract: where a term of the contract excluded agency; where the third party would have refused to contract with the undisclosed principal; where the third party made the contract with the agent because he particularly wanted to contract with the agent personally.

- An agent can be liable for breach of warranty of authority if he warrants to a third party that he possessed authority which he does not in fact possess. The third party's damages will be calculated on general contract principles under *Hadley* v *Baxendale*, being designed to put the third party in the position which he would have been in if the warranty had not been breached.

Rights and duties of the agent

- Agents have non-fiduciary duties to obey the principal's instructions, to use an appropriate amount of care and skill and to perform their duties personally.

- Agents also have fiduciary duties to avoid a conflict of interest with the principal, to avoid making a secret profit, not to take bribes and to account to the principal.

- The Commercial Agents (Council Directive) Regulations 1993 impose additional duties on self-employed commercial agents as follows: to look after the interests of the principal, to act dutifully, and to act in good faith.

- Unless the contract provides otherwise, an agent will be entitled to an indemnity to cover expenses necessarily incurred in the execution of the agency.

- The express or implied terms of the contract between principal and agent will govern the amount of remuneration to which the agent is entitled.

- The agent may have a particular lien over the principal's goods until some claim is satisfied.

Termination of agency

- Unless the agency is irrevocable, the principal can withdraw authority from the agent at any time. This might amount to breach of a contract with the agent.

- Even if the principal has withdrawn the agent's authority, the agent may still have apparent authority to bind the principal.

- Agency will be terminated automatically by: frustration; death of either party; insanity of either party; bankruptcy of the principal; or bankruptcy of the agent if this would render him unfit to perform his duties.

- Upon termination of the agency self-employed commercial agents may be entitled to an indemnity or to compensation under the Commercial Agents (Council Directive) Regulations 1993.

Summary questions

1 Peter runs and owns a shop which sells second-hand hi-fi equipment. When Peter booked his two weeks annual holiday, he arranged that his friend Alec should run the shop while he was away. Alec is told that he can sell any equipment in stock, as long as he gets at least 75% of the price displayed on it. He is told that under no circumstances should he buy any equipment.

While Peter is away Alec sells an amplifier to Keith for 70% of the price shown on it. Keith thinks that Alec owns the business. Louise, who regularly does business with Peter, buys a stereo system for 60% of the price shown on it. She knows that Peter usually insists on at least 80% of the price shown, even as regards a trade buyer such as herself. Alec buys a stereo system from Harry because he is sure that it is such a bargain that Peter would want it. On his return, Peter discovers that the stereo system bought from Harry is in very bad condition and worth nothing like the price which Alec paid.

Advise Peter as to whether or not he will be bound by the contracts which Alec made.

2 Hangpaper Ltd is a company which buys and sells wallpaper and decorating materials. Hangpaper Ltd's articles of association allow for the appointment of a managing director, but none had ever been appointed. Adrian, a director of Hangpaper Ltd, has for the past three years been allowed by the other directors to act as if he had been appointed managing director. Without the authority of his fellow directors, Adrian buys a large consignment of wallpaper paste from Glueit and Co. When the paste ordered is delivered, it is found to be of a type which is

unsuitable for Hangpaper's purposes. Hangpaper Ltd phone Glueit to say that Adrian had no authority to buy the paste. Glueit insist that the contract must stand as they believed that, as managing director, Adrian would have had authority. Advise Hangpaper Ltd as to whether or not they will be bound by the contract with Glueit and Co, and of any rights they might have or might acquire against either Adrian or Glueit and Co.

3   Anthony has been given actual authority by Pedro to buy up to 1000 gallons of spirit, as long as the price does not exceed £20 a gallon. The type of spirit in question has become hard to obtain and Anthony can only manage to buy it from Toby at £24 a gallon. Anthony buys the spirit from Toby, saying that he is acting as Pedro's agent and has authority to make the purchase. Toby has heard of Pedro but has never had any dealings with him. However, Anthony's intention at the time of the contract was to buy the spirit for himself so that he could use it in an industrial process. Anthony then finds that he will not need the spirit as he had thought that he would. When Pedro finds out that the spirit was purchased at the higher price he tells Anthony that he will pay the higher price. Now Pedro has found out about Anthony's dishonesty and is refusing to take delivery of the spirit from Toby. Advise the parties of their legal positions.

4   Anita works for Pamela as a buyer of second-hand cars. Anita has been expressly forbidden to buy any cars for more than £1000 each, but she can buy several cars for less than this price as long as she does not spend more than £15000 in any one month. Acting in contravention of her instructions, Anita buys a car from Tina for £1750.

   a   Explain the circumstances in which this contract could be ratified by Pamela and how such a ratification would be made.

   b   If there is an effective ratification of the contract, how would this affect the rights of Pamela against Anita and Tina?

5   Phil and Ted are antique dealers who used to be good friends but have fallen out to the extent that they absolutely refuse to have any dealings with each other. Phil employs an agent, Alphonse, to buy antiques. Alphonse buys at auctions, antique fairs and from other dealers. Alphonse also deals in antiques on his own account. Alphonse has had several business dealings with Ted. Phil asked Alphonse to try and sell a silver salver and to keep his eyes out for any old barometers. He gave Alphonse authority to sell the silver salver for a price of at least £4000 and to pay up to £2000 for a good Victorian barometer. Alphonse finds that Ted has a good Victorian barometer for sale and buys it for £1500. Alphonse also manages to sell Phil's silver salver to Ted for £5000, being slightly surprised to get such a good price. Alphonse does not know that Phil and Ted refuse to have any dealings with each other. He does not think it worth mentioning to Ted that he is buying and selling the barometer and the silver salver for Phil. When Phil asks Ted for delivery of the barometer, Ted says that he would never have sold it if he had known that Alphonse was buying on behalf of Phil and that he is therefore refusing to be bound by the contract. Phil claims that Ted will have to deliver and to pay the £5000 for the silver salver. Ted refuses to be bound by this contract either, saying that he would never have bought the silver salver if he had known that it was Phil's and that he only bought it from Alphonse because Alphonse owed him £3000 and this seemed to be the best way of getting the money. Advise Phil and Ted of their rights and obligations in respect of the two contracts.

6   Alfred is employed by Polish Co Ltd as a buyer of materials at a salary of £26000 p.a. Alfred's job requires him to visit various manufacturers of solvents and to buy solvents which can be used in the manufacture of polish. Recently Alfred placed a large order with Madeit Ltd, a company with which Polish Co Ltd had not previously dealt. The solvent delivered by Madeit is slightly more expensive than that delivered by the previous supplier, but Alfred insists that it is definitely of higher quality. Alfred also switched a regular order to SolvCo Ltd, a small company with which Polish Co Ltd had not previously dealt. The solvent delivered by SolvCo Ltd is slightly cheaper than that delivered by the previous supplier. It appears to be of exactly the same quality. The managing director of Polish Co Ltd was watching the FA Cup Final on television when he noticed Alfred sitting in the crowd. The managing director has now discovered that Alfred went to the the Cup Final by courtesy of corporate hospitality supplied by Madeit Ltd. The managing director has also discovered that Alfred has a significant shareholding in SolvCo Ltd, and that the solvent supplied by Madeit is of no higher quality than that previously supplied.

   Advise Polish Co Ltd of any rights which they may have against either Alfred, Madeit Ltd or SolvCo Ltd.

Multiple choice questions

1 Mr Phillips asks an auctioneer to auction his old computers. The auctioneer says that the computers might fetch between £5000 and £9000. Mr Phillips says that he wants a reserve of £5000 on the computers and that he will be pleased to get £7500. The auctioneer is to get a commission of 10% of the selling price. The computers do not attract a bid of £5000 and are not therefore sold at the auction. After the auction is finished, a dealer agrees to pay £5000 for the computers and the auctioneer sells at this price. Mr Phillips has sold goods through this auctioneer previously and on several occasions his goods have been sold after the auction for the reserve price. Mr Phillips never objected to this, and always paid the auctioneer's commission, but he never expressly agreed to it either. Which **one** of the following statements is true?

    a The auctioneer had no authority to sell other than at the auction. Mr Phillips can therefore claim damages from the auctioneer and get the computers back from the dealer.

    b The auctioneer originally had no authority to sell other than at the auction. However, the auctioneer ratified the contract by selling later. The auctioneer will therefore be entitled to keep his commission and Mr Phillips will have no remedy.

    c The auctioneer had implied actual authority to sell the computers. Mr Phillips will be bound by the contract with the third party and will have to pay the auctioneer's commission.

    d The auctioneer would have had usual authority to sell the computers, as in *Watteau v Fenwick*. Therefore, Mr Phillips will be bound by the contract with the third party and will have to pay the auctioneer's commission.

2 Which **one** of the following statements is **not** true?

    a Both express actual authority and implied actual authority arise by virtue of an agreement between principal and agent.

    b Apparent authority arises where the agent makes a representation to a third party that he (the agent) has authority to act for the principal.

    c When a principal effectively ratifies a contract, the contract takes effect from the time when the agent made it, not from the time of the ratification.

    d Apparent authority can arise on account of a representation made after the agent has made the contract with the third party.

3 Andrew visits a car showroom and buys a second-hand car for £4000. Andrew intends to purchase the car on behalf of Peter. Consider the following statements.

    i If Andrew claimed that he was acting for Peter, when the contract was made, then the contract will always take effect between Peter and the owner of the car showroom.

    ii If Andrew claimed that he was acting for Peter, when the contract was made, then the contract will take effect between Peter and the owners of the car showroom only if Andrew had prior actual authority to act for Peter, or if Andrew had apparent authority, or if Peter ratified the contract.

    iii If Andrew did not disclose that he was acting for Peter, then Peter will not be bound by the contract unless he ratifies it. If Peter does ratify the contract he will be bound by it.

    iv If Andrew did not disclose that he was acting for Peter then Peter will be bound by the contract as long as Andrew had actual authority to act for Peter and intended to act for him.

Which **two** of the following statements are **not** true?

    a i and iii only.

    b ii and iv only.

    c i and iv only.

    d ii and iii only.

4 Boy Billy, a struggling musical artiste, appoints Frank King as his agent for a five year period. Due to Frank King's efforts Boy Billy becomes very successful, earning over £1m in the first year. It was agreed that King should take 40% of any earnings over £25000 p.a. Two years into the agreement Boy Billy wishes to get rid of King as his agent as he feels that he can negotiate a better deal with another agent. Which **one** of the following statements is true?

   a Boy Billy can terminate the agency. Frank King has made a great deal of money from the agency and must accept the risk of the agency being ended, as in *Luxor (Eastbourne) Ltd* v *Cooper*.

   b Under no circumstances can Boy Billy terminate the agency before the end of the five-year period.

   c Boy Billy can terminate the agency but will be committing a breach of contract. He will have to pay damages to Frank, these damages being calculated under the rules in *Hadley* v *Baxendale*.

   d Boy Billy can terminate the agency but Frank will be entitled to an indemnity or to compensation under the Commercial Agents (Council Directive) Regulations 1993.

5 Which **one** of the following statements is **not** true?

   a A gratuitous agent can be liable for failure to use an appropriate amount of care and skill.

   b An agent must obey the principal's instructions even though he thinks it would be more beneficial to the principal not to do so.

   c Any payment made to the agent by the third party with whom the agent was contracting will constitute a bribe if it was kept secret from the principal.

   d If the contract between principal and agent fixes the agent's remuneration, but contrary to the expectation of both parties this remuneration is very low, then the agent can be paid more under an implied term of the contract.

6 Which **one** of the following statements **is** true?

   a Bankruptcy of either the principal or the agent will automatically end the agency.

   b If no other agent could be found, a decree of specific performance could be ordered, requiring an agent to continue as agent until the end of the agreed agency period.

   c Unless the agency is irrevocable the principal can withdraw the agent's authority at any time.

   d An agent will never have the power to bind the principal once the principal has revoked the agent's authority.

Task 11

Read the following case study and then write a brief report, answering the questions which follow.

Each summer Arthur is employed by Peter to sell saddles and riding equipment at horse shows and fairs. Peter makes the saddles by hand, and in the winter months Arthur helps out in the workshop.

Peter pays all of the expenses of sale. He books a stand at the horse shows and pays all the travelling expenses, including putting Arthur up at bed and breakfast accommodation while he is away.

For the past two years Arthur has taken his unemployed son along to the horse shows. Peter has heard about this from customers. He suspects that the son does a good deal of Arthur's selling for him, and is sure that Arthur and his son sleep in the van. Arthur never mentions that his son goes with him. Peter does not mind reimbursing Arthur for his fictitious payment on accommodation as this is a tax free expense, and he just regards it as part of Arthur's wages.

Last month things went badly wrong. Peter had spent a lot of time in the winter making a new design of saddle. He asked Arthur to show it around to customers, but definitely not to sell it. While Arthur was away at the pub, his son sold the saddle to Harvey Jones, a leading show jumper. When Peter heard what had happened he travelled to the horse show, but Harvey Jones absolutely refused to return the saddle, saying that he had paid for it and was keeping it.

Peter also noticed that Arthur was selling his own leather work on the stall. Arthur's son had spent the winter making this and it was displayed more prominently than Peter's wares. Peter told Arthur's son that Arthur was sacked and would not receive any more wages or expenses at all. Arthur responded by driving away Peter's van and all of Peter's unsold goods.

Arthur refuses to return anything to Peter, who is not only refusing to pay future wages and expenses, but claiming back all sums paid to Arthur that summer.

1 Is Arthur Peter's agent?

2 Does Arthur have authority to get his son to perform some of his duties? If so, what type of duties?

3 Does Harvey Jones own the newly designed saddle, or must he return it to Peter?
4 When Arthur sells his own leather goods on Peter's stall does he break a duty to Peter? If so, which one(s)? What remedies would Peter have?
5 On what basis might Arthur possibly have a right to take the van and the unsold goods?
6 What do you think the outcome of this dispute would be?

Chapter 12

THE LAW OF TORTS 1

Introduction

This is the first of two chapters on the law of torts. In this chapter we begin by comparing tortious liability with contractual liability, noticing several differences between the two. The tort of negligence is by far the most important tort and we consider this tort in some detail. Liability arising under the Occupier's Liability Acts 1957 and 1984 and liability arising under the Consumer Protection Act 1987 are also considered, but in somewhat less detail.

In the following chapter we consider the torts of nuisance, trespass and defamation. We also consider the circumstances in which employers can be vicariously liable for torts committed by their employees.

12.1 · Nature of tortious liability

It is notoriously difficult to define a tort, but a possible definition would be that a tort is a civil wrong other than a breach of contract. This definition makes it plain that civil liability can arise in two ways; either on account of a breach of contract or on account of a tort having been committed. Before considering individual torts, we need to examine the fundamental differences between contractual and tortious liability.

In earlier chapters we have seen that contractual liability is voluntarily assumed, and that it is assumed in return for the benefits promised by the other contracting party. For example, if Company A makes a contract to buy a computer system from a retailer, Company B, then both the decision to buy and the decision to sell will have been freely made. Both sides will have chosen to make the bargain and to give some consideration to the other. The liabilities assumed under the contract will have been given in exchange for the rights gained under the contract.

Liability in tort is not undertaken voluntarily. It is imposed by the courts on the basis that certain types of behaviour warrants the imposition of tortious liability. If a person injures another by such behaviour the injured person may bring a legal action in order to gain compensation. If, for example, a driver injures a pedestrian by driving badly then the injured pedestrian will be able to bring an action against the driver. The driver has no choice about whether or not to accept such liability, the courts will impose it. Nor will the driver have received any benefit in return for accepting the liability. It will have arisen not as a result of a bargain, but as a consequence of a tort (the tort of negligence) having been committed.

Another difference between the two types of liability is that liability in contract is generally strict, whereas liability in tort is based on fault. In Chapter 8, at 8.2.4, we considered the nature of the contractual term that goods sold in the course of a business should be of satisfactory quality. As we saw, retailers are liable for breach of this term even if they could not possibly have known that the goods which they sold were not of satisfactory quality. But in almost all circumstances a person will only incur tortious liability if his conduct does not match up to an objective, reasonable standard.

To extend the earlier examples, once Company B has made the contract to supply the new computer system to Company A, it will have to do so or face the legal consequences. It will be no excuse for Company B to show that it was unable to deliver on time because vital components became more expensive, or to argue that although the computer was not of satisfactory quality they could not possibly have known this as the computer was sold in unopened packaging. But the driver who injured the pedestrian will only be liable if it can be shown that he drove badly and failed to take reasonable care. If it cannot be shown that the driver drove badly then he will not be liable, no matter how severe the pedestrian's injuries.

Both the breaking of a contract and the commission of a tort give rise to liability in damages. However, the purpose of contract damages is not the same as the purpose of tort damages. Both of course are designed to compensate. But contract damages achieve this by putting the injured party in the position he would have been in if the contract had been performed. Tort damages achieve it by putting the injured party in the position he would have been in if the tort had never been committed.

To once again extend the earlier example, if the computer system which Company B agreed to sell to Company A was delivered one month late, then Company A would be entitled to damages. Subject to the test of foreseeability laid down in *Hadley* v *Baxendale*, these damages would be assessed by reference to the amount it had cost Company A that the computer system was not delivered on time. Such damages might include an amount for business lost as a result of the computers not being available, or for the cost of employing extra workers who were needed to do the work which the computers were meant to do. (Contract damages are examined in Chapter 7 at 7.2.2.)

As long as a pedestrian run over by a driver could establish that his injuries were caused by the driver having committed the tort of negligence, he too would be awarded damages. The purpose of these damages would be to put him in the position he would have been in if he had not been run over, subject to the loss being of a type which was a foreseeable consequence of the tort. He might be awarded an amount for pain and suffering, for lost wages and perhaps for damage to his clothes. These losses would be recoverable because if the tort had not been committed, none of the losses would have arisen.

Often a person affected by a tort which continues to be committed seeks an injunction rather than damages. If the injunction is granted, the person committing the tort will be restrained from continuing to do so, on pain of a fine or imprisonment. As we saw in Chapter 7 at 7.2.5, injunctions can also be ordered to prevent a person from breaking a contract. Such injunctions are, however, very rarely granted.

In this book several chapters have been devoted to the law of contract and the particular rules which apply to contracts of sale of goods. Contractual rights and obligations have always been the heart of any book on Business Law. But the law of tort is becoming increasingly important in a business context. The English courts are showing a willingness to extend tortious liability to an ever increasing number of situations. Even if the parties have a contractual relationship with each other, this will not necessarily prevent one of the parties from suing the other in tort if this would produce a better remedy. In *Henderson and others* v *Merret Syndicates Ltd* [1994] 3 All ER 506 the House of Lords held that an existing contractual relationship would only preclude the possibility of an action in tort where the contract so provided.

12.2 · Negligence

Negligence is the most important tort, covering an enormous number of situations. To a certain extent, negligence fills the gaps left by the more strictly defined torts.

In order to establish the tort of negligence the claimant must prove three things:

(a) that the defendant owed him a duty of care;
(b) that the defendant breached this duty; and
(c) that a reasonably foreseeable type of damage was caused by the breach.

We need to examine each of these three matters in turn. However, it is important to realise that the three matters often overlap. As we shall see when considering the cases, the courts do not always regard them as separate matters to be established one after the other. But in understanding the tort of negligence this is the easiest approach to take.

12.2.1 That the defendant owed the claimant a duty of care

The case which follows created the modern law of negligence. As we shall see, it concerned the liability of a manufacturer to an eventual user of his product. However, the language used by the House of Lords judges was so broad that it became possible to extend the tort of negligence to other situations in which one person had not taken sufficient care to see that another avoided injury.

■ *Donoghue* v *Stevenson* [1932] AC 562 (House of Lords)

The claimant and her friend visited a café in Glasgow. The claimant's friend ordered a 'ginger beer float' for the claimant. This consisted of ice-cream in a glass, along with a bottle of ginger beer to pour over the top of it. The ginger beer arrived in an opaque stone bottle. Having poured some of the ginger beer over the ice cream, the claimant ate some of the ginger beer float. The claimant's friend poured the remainder of the ginger beer into her own glass. A nauseating substance, which might have been a decomposed snail, fell out of the bottle. The claimant became ill. She might have been poisoned by the ginger beer, or made ill by the sight of the foreign body, or made ill by a combination of poisoning and the sight of the foreign body. The claimant sued the manufacturer of the ginger beer, Stevenson, arguing that he owed a duty of care to her. Stevenson argued that there was no case to answer, even if all the facts alleged by the claimant were true. This issue was appealed all the way to the House of Lords.

Held. (By a majority of 3 to 2) Manufacturers owe a duty of care to see that the ultimate users of their products are not injured by these products.

Lord Atkin: 'You must take reasonable care to avoid acts and omissions which you can reasonably foresee would be likely to injure your neighbour. Who, then, in law is my neighbour? The answer seems to be – persons who are so closely and directly affected by my act that I ought reasonably to have them in contemplation as being so affected when I am directing my mind to the acts or omissions which are called in question.'

COMMENT (i) If the claimant had herself ordered the ginger beer she would have sued the café rather than the manufacturer. Liability would have been strict, being contractual. There would nowadays be a statutory requirement that the ginger beer should be of satisfactory quality, and a contractual claim would proceed on the basis that this term had been breached.
(ii) If the case were to arise today, on precisely the facts alleged by the claimant, the possible effect of the Contracts (Rights of Third Parties) Act 1999, which is set out in Chapter 4 at 4.2.2.2, would also have to be considered.
(iii) As the claimant's injury was caused by the ginger beer not being safe the manufacturer could nowadays be made liable, without the need to prove fault, under the Consumer Protection Act Part 1. This Act is considered at 12.4.
(iv) The claimant never took the case to trial.

Donoghue v *Stevenson* was particularly important, not only because it established that manufacturers could owe a duty of care to the eventual users of their products, but also because it demonstrated that the tort of negligence could be expanded to cover new situations to which it had never previously been applied.

Lord Atkin's neighbour speech was obviously *obiter dicta*, rather than the *ratio decidendi* of the case, as it was a far wider statement of law than was needed to deal with the facts of the case. (For the meaning of *ratio decidendi* and *obiter dicta* see Chapter 1 at 1.3.2.2.) However, the courts have subsequently tended to treat the statement as *ratio decidendi*, so that claimants who can show that their relationship with the defendant satisfied the 'neighbour test' are presumed to have shown that the defendant owed them a duty of care in the particular circumstances of the case.

In certain types of situations case law has established that a duty of care will be owed. For example, it is now established that duties are owed by repairers to their customers, by parents to children, by professional persons to their clients and of course by manufacturers to their customers. When a new situation arises the courts tend to develop the law of negligence incrementally and by analogy with earlier precedents. The court will consider the relationship between the parties, the type of risk involved and whether or not it would be in the public interest to find that a duty of care existed. In *Caparo Industries plc* v *Dickman* [1990] 1 All ER 568 (House of Lords), the facts of which are set out in Chapter 17 at 17.3.3, Lord Roskill said: 'I agree with your Lordships that it now has to be accepted that there is no simple formula or touchstone to which recourse can be had in order to provide in every case a ready answer to the questions whether, given certain facts, the law will or will not impose liability for negligence or in cases where such liability can be shown to exist, determine the extent of that liability.' Lord Roskill went on to say that he thought it infinitely preferable that there should be a return to the traditional categorisation of cases pointing to the existence and scope of any duty of care, rather than a duty being imposed by recourse to wide generalisations which leave their practical application matters of difficulty and uncertainty. The other Law Lords expressed much the same opinion and cases decided since *Caparo* have tended to adopt the incremental approach to deciding whether or not a duty of care is owed. Under this approach new categories of negligence will be created incrementally and by analogy with established categories. This incremental approach is adopted more in cases of pure economic loss and psychiatric injury than in cases of physical injury, damage to property and consequential economic loss.

It is now established that the mere fact that harm is foreseeable is not enough to give rise to a duty of care. Rather, it might be regarded as the first necessary step. A second step is 'proximity of relationship' between the claimant and the defendant. This proximity can be present only if it was foreseeable that harm would be caused to the claimant, but often it goes further than mere foreseeability. What amounts to the necessary proximity will depend upon the facts of the case. For example, if a driver runs over a pedestrian, causing physical injury, then the necessary proximity is established merely because the injury was foreseeable. But if a second claimant suffered nervous shock as a result of seeing the accident, whether there was the necessary proximity would depend upon matters such as how far from the accident the second claimant was and also how close the relationship between the first and second claimants was. The third and final step is that it must be just and reasonable to impose a duty of care. Ultimately, this will depend upon whether the court thinks that it needs to protect the claimant by imposing liability. Where the claimant has suffered physical injury, the courts are much more likely to find it just and reasonable to impose a duty than where the defendant has suffered only economic loss or nervous shock. Although these three steps sound logical enough, it must be said that in many cases they are hard to find as separate concepts. As Lord Oliver said in *Caparo Industries plc* v *Dickman* [1990] 1 All ER 568 at 633:

> 'Indeed it is difficult to resist a conclusion that what have been treated as three separate requirements are, at least in most cases, in fact merely facets of the same thing, for in some cases the degree of foreseeability is such that it is from that alone that the requisite proximity can be deduced, whilst in others the absence of that essential relationship can most rationally be attributed simply to the court's view that it would not be fair and reasonable to hold the defendant responsible. "Proximity" is, no doubt, a convenient expression so long as it is realised that it is no more than a label which embraces not a definable concept but merely a description of circumstances from which, pragmatically, the courts conclude that a duty of care exists.'

Although Lord Atkin's neighbour speech referred to omissions as well as to acts, it is a general principal of English law that a person is not to be made liable for mere failure to act. This is the case even where it is apparent that failure to act will result in another person suffering injury. However, omissions can give rise to a duty of care where the defendant has undertaken to do something which he later fails to do or where he has led someone else to believe that he has done something which he has not in fact done. The ownership or occupation of land might also create a duty to do something for the benefit of those coming onto the land or for the benefit of neighbours. Also, once it is established that a duty is owed, for example that a driver owes a duty to a pedestrian, it would not matter that the duty was breached by a failure to act, such as not applying the brakes.

In certain circumstances the Congenital Disabilities (Civil Liability) Act 1976 allows a child who is born disabled as a result of an occurrence before his or her birth to sue the person who caused the occurrence. The Act therefore creates a statutory duty of care in favour of an unborn child.

12.2.2 Breaching the duty

Merely owing a duty of care is not enough to give rise to liability for the tort of negligence. Every time a person drives across a town he owes a duty of care to many people. He is not liable to be sued by any of these people unless he injures them by breaching the duty of care which he owes them.

A duty of care will be breached if the defendant does not take the care which a reasonable person would have taken in all the circumstances of the case. This is an **objective** standard. It is no defence that the defendant was doing his incompetent best. For example, In *Nettleship* v *Weston* [1971] 2 QB 691 the Court of Appeal held that the duty of care which a learner driver owed to passengers and the public was the same objective and impersonal standard as every other driver owed. (Notice the contrast with criminal law here. The *mens rea* of most serious crimes require an intention to do the act which a statute or the common law made illegal. See Chapter 22 at 22.1.)

A higher standard of care is expected of professional people and those who claim to have some special competence. Professional people must show the degree of care which a reasonably competent person in that profession would show, and failure to show this standard will amount to breach of duty. In Chapter 8 at 8.4.3.1 we considered *Bolam* v *Friern Hospital Management Committee* [1957] 1 WLR 582. In that case McNair J said: 'Where you get a situation which involves the use of some special skill or competence … the test is the standard of the ordinary skilled man exercising and professing to have that special skill.'

In *Bolam* the Court of Appeal held that a doctor who acts in accordance with the opinion of skilled medical professionals will not be negligent merely because other skilled medical professionals would have taken a contrary view. However, in *Bolitho* v *City & Hackney Health Authority* [1998] AC 232 the House of Lords held that the mere fact that some distinguished experts would agree with the actions taken by a defendant doctor would not necessarily mean that the defendant doctor had not been negligent. It would be very likely to mean this, but it was still up to the court to decide, in the light of all the circumstances, whether or not the defendant doctor had acted reasonably. The court had to be satisfied that the expert opinion upon which the defendant relied had a logical basis and in particular that those holding the opinion had directed their minds, where appropriate, to the question of comparative risks and benefits and, having done so, had reached a defensible conclusion. It would be possible that in rare cases the expert opinion could not stand up to logical analysis. In such cases the court could hold that the opinion did not provide the benchmark by which the doctor's conduct should be assessed.

In deciding whether or not a duty of care was breached, the state of scientific and technical knowledge which prevailed at the time may be an important consideration.

■ *Roe* v *Minister of Health* [1954] 2 All ER 131 (Court of Appeal)

In 1947 two claimants underwent operations in hospital for relatively minor complaints. Each of the claimants was given a spinal injection of Nupercaine, which was administered by a specialist anaesthetist. The Nupercaine had been contained in glass ampoules which were stored in a solution of phenol. After the operations both claimants were paralysed from the waist downwards. This paralysis was caused by phenol having seeped through invisible cracks in the glass ampoules. The cracks had developed when the container moving the ampoules was moved, but nobody had become aware of the cracks. The anaesthetist had examined the ampoules for cracks prior to administering the injection. Nobody had been aware that there might be a crack which an ordinary visual inspection would not reveal.

Held. The defendant was not liable because in 1947 competent anaesthetists generally did not appreciate that glass ampoules of Nupercaine stored in phenol could become contaminated through invisible cracks. Neither the anaesthetist nor any member of the hospital staff had been negligent.

Of course a hospital would have been liable if a similar accident had occurred after this fact had become known. But, as Denning LJ said, the court, 'must not look at the 1947 accident with 1954 spectacles'.

In deciding whether or not a duty has been breached the following four factors are likely to be of considerable importance:

(a) the likelihood of harm being caused to the claimant;
(b) the potential seriousness of injury which was likely to be caused;
(c) the cost of making sure that injury was not caused; and
(d) the usefulness of the objective which the defendant's actions were trying to achieve.

The first two factors tend to be weighed against the second two. If it is highly likely that injury would be caused to the claimant then this is an indication that the duty of care was breached. This is especially true in cases in which the injury is likely to be serious. However, if the defendant was trying to achieve some particularly valuable objective, or if the cost of making sure that no injury was caused was exceptionally high, then these are indications that the duty was not breached. The following three cases show these considerations being given weight by the courts. However, it would be wrong to think that they form an exhaustive check list. Rather it would be true to say that an overall appreciation of all the relevant cases would tend to indicate that the four matters specified are, consciously or subconsciously, weighed against each other by the courts.

■ *Bolton* v *Stone* [1951] AC 850 (House of Lords)

The claimant was standing in the road outside her house when she was hit by a cricket ball. A game of cricket was in progress at the Cheetham Cricket Club and a batsman had hit the ball for six, striking it right out of the Club's grounds. Cricket had been played on these grounds since 1864 and the nearby houses had been built long after this date. It was most unusual for a ball to be hit out of the ground. The evidence suggested that this had happened about six times in the previous 28 years. The ball which hit the claimant had travelled over 100 yards, clearing a fence which was 78 yards from the pitch and 17 feet higher than the pitch. The claimant sued the committee and members of the Cheetham Cricket Club in both negligence and nuisance.

Held. The duty of care was not breached and so the claim did not succeed.

COMMENT In this case the cost of making sure that no injury occurred was enormous (erecting a much higher fence around the relevant part of the ground) and so the defendants did not breach the duty by continuing to play cricket on the ground. It was also most unlikely that anyone would be injured, although it was foreseeable to some extent because balls had previously been hit out of the ground and people did walk up and down the road. The usefulness of playing cricket was not much of a factor in this case. However, it was accepted that people need to take recreation and that cricket is a traditional type of English recreation.

■ *Paris* v *Stepney Borough Council* [1951] 1 All ER 42 (House of Lords)

The claimant, a fitter who had the use of only one eye, was told by his employers to hammer and grind the underneath of a vehicle. He was not given protective goggles and lost the use of his good eye when this was pierced by a shard of metal which flew off when he was hammering a bolt in order to remove it.

Held. The duty of care owed by the employers was breached. The likelihood of harm and the potential seriousness of damage were very considerable, especially as the employers knew that the claimant had the use of only one eye. The cost of making sure that the accident did not happen, by providing goggles, was minimal.

The usefulness of the defendant's actions tends to be an important factor in cases where the defendant acted in an emergency.

■ *Watt* v *Hertfordshire CC* [1954] 2 All ER 268 (Court of Appeal)

A fire station received a call that a woman was trapped under a heavy vehicle about 250 yards away from the station. The officer in charge of the station set off immediately, ordering that a lorry should be loaded with a large jack for lifting heavy weights and that this lorry should follow as soon as possible. The jack, which weighed two or three hundredweight and had four small wheels, was loaded onto the back of the lorry. The jack could not be lashed down so the men in the back of the lorry were meant to hold it steady. When the lorry driver suddenly applied the brakes one of the firemen travelling with the jack was severely injured. If the standard procedures had been followed another fire station would have been contacted to provide a safe means of carrying the jack. This would have caused a delay of at least ten minutes.

Held. The fire authorities had not breached the duty of care which they owed to the injured fireman. The risk to the firemen had to be balanced against the end to be achieved.

Denning LJ: 'If this accident had happened in a commercial enterprise without any emergency, there could be no doubt that the [fireman] would succeed. But the commercial end to make profit is very different from the human end to save life and limb. The saving of life and limb justifies the taking of considerable risk.'

12.2.3 The burden of proof

As a claim in negligence is a civil action, the burden of proof is generally upon the claimant to prove the case. However, the Civil Evidence Act 1995 s.11 provides that a defendant who has been convicted of a crime can be taken in civil proceedings to have committed that crime unless he can prove that he did not. In such cases the burden of proof is therefore reversed.

A difficulty which claimants often face is that, although the evidence seems to suggest that the defendant did breach a duty of care, the claimant cannot prove exactly how the injury was caused or who caused it. In such cases the claimant might be able to claim that 'the thing speaks for itself' (formerly known by the Latin maxim *res ipsa loquitur*). If the claimant can claim that the thing speaks for itself the defendant will be taken to have breached the duty of care unless he can show that he did not in fact breach it.

When the claimant is able to say that 'the thing speaks for itself' the burden of proof is, in effect, reversed and put upon the defendant. However, this will only happen if the following three conditions are satisfied:

(a) the defendant must have been in exclusive control of the thing or the situation which caused the damage;
(b) the accident must be of a kind which would not normally happen without negligence on the part of some person; and
(c) the precise cause of the accident must not be capable of being ascertained by the court.

An example can be seen in *Ward* v *Tesco Stores* [1976] All ER 219, in which a shopper in a supermarket slipped on yoghourt on the supermarket floor. The customer did not know how long the yoghourt had been there. Tesco would only have been liable if the yoghourt had been there for an unreasonable time and there was no evidence as to how long it had been there. By a majority the Court of Appeal found for the claimant, even though Tesco showed that they normally swept the floor five or six times a day.

Megaw LJ said:

'It is for the [claimant] to show that there occurred an event which is unusual and which, in the absence of explanation, is more consistent with fault on the part of the defendants than on the absence of fault ... When the [claimant] has established that, the defendants can still escape from liability ... if they could show that the accident must have happened, or even on balance of probability would have been likely to have happened, irrespective of the existence of a proper and adequate system, in relation to the circumstances, to provide for the safety of customers.'

12.2.4 That a reasonably foreseeable type of damage was caused by the breach of duty

A claimant can only recover damages if he can prove that he suffered a loss and that the defendant's breach of duty caused this loss. Furthermore, he must prove that the loss in question was of a type which would reasonably foreseeably follow from the defendant's breach.

A defendant who has suffered no loss cannot claim. But even where the defendant's negligence has caused a loss to the claimant the courts may choose not to regard this loss as damage. Recently, for example, the courts have had to consider whether an unwanted pregnancy could amount to damage. In *McFarlane and another* v *Tayside Health Board* [1999] 4 All ER 961 a man who had had a vasectomy, and been told that it was successful, impregnated his wife. The couple already had four children and wanted no more but chose not to terminate the pregnancy. The House of Lords held that where a healthy child was born as a result of medical negligence damages could not be recovered for the cost of rearing the child. It was not fair, just or reasonable to impose liability for such economic loss on the negligent doctor and his employer. Damages were allowed for the pain and distress suffered during pregnancy and birth, and for financial losses which were associated with the pregnancy. In *Parkinson* v *St James and Seacroft University Hospital NHS Trust* [2001] EWCA Civ 530 a mother of four children was sterilised. However, the operation was negligently performed and she gave birth to a fifth child. During the pregnancy the mother was warned that the child might be disabled. The mother chose not to terminate the pregnancy and the child was disabled, in that he had behavioural problems which might have been caused by Autistic Spectrum Disorder. It was accepted that the disability was not caused by negligence. The Court of Appeal held that damages were recoverable for the costs of providing for special needs and care which were attributable to the child's disability. However, damages could not be recovered for the child's ordinary upbringing. It was fair, just and reasonable to award damages for the additional costs involved in bringing up a significantly disabled child. But it was not fair, just and reasonable to award damages which went further than such costs.

In *Rees* v *Darlington Memorial Hospital NHS Trust* [2003] 4 All ER 987 the House of Lords considered the case of a claimant who suffered from a severe visual disability. She wanted to be sterilised because she thought that, on account of her disability, she could not properly bring up any children she might have. The sterilisation operation was negligently performed and she gave birth to a healthy son. The surgeon who performed the operation knew why the claimant wanted to be sterilised. The House of Lords followed *McFarlane* and held that the cost of bringing up the child could not be recovered. Nor could there be recovery of any extra costs of bringing up the child which were attributable to the claimant's disability. However, by a majority of 4 to 3, the claimant was rewarded £15 000 in recognition that a wrong had been done. The majority held that such an award was not compensatory and should be made in all such cases to mark the injury and loss. It would be added to any compensatory award made in respect of the pain, inconvenience and expense of pregnancy and childbirth.

12.2.4.1 Causation

The claimant can only recover damages in respect of a loss which he can prove was caused by the defendant's breach of duty. This is a factual matter, which is generally assessed on a 'but for' test; that is to say but for the defendant having breached the duty, the claimant would not have suffered the injury in respect of which he is claiming.

If therefore, the claimant would have suffered exactly the same loss even if the defendant had not breached his duty the defendant will not be liable in respect of that loss. For example, in *Barnett* v *Chelsea Hospital* [1969] 1 All ER 428 a doctor at a hospital negligently failed to diagnose a patient who had been admitted with vomiting as having been poisoned with arsenic. The patient was turned away and died. However, as the patient would have died anyway, regardless of whether he had been admitted to the hospital or not, the hospital was not liable for his death.

Where several people cause the loss in circumstances such that the loss would have occurred on account of the actions of any one of them, common sense is applied and the 'but for' test does not exonerate all of the causers of the loss from liability. Rather, they will all be liable on a proportional basis.

The claimant must prove that the defendant's breach caused the loss for which he is claiming. To do this he will need to show that there was a chain of causation between breach of a duty of care and the loss which the claimant suffered. This chain must not be broken by a new act intervening (formerly known as *novus actus interveniens*). Actions taken by third parties may break the chain of causation, but they will generally not do so if was foreseeable that such actions might be taken.

■ *The Oropesa* [1943] 1 All ER 211 (Court of Appeal)

The Oropesa collided with another ship, the Manchester Regiment. Both ships were negligently navigated and both were badly damaged. The Manchester Regiment had a crew of 74, 50 of whom travelled to the safety of the Oropesa in a lifeboat. More than an hour later the captain of the Manchester Regiment, with the remaining 24 crew, decided to travel in a lifeboat to the Oropesa to discuss a salvage claim. The Oropesa was by this time more than a mile away. The captain of the Manchester Regiment was persuaded to row to the Oropesa by the fact that his ship was a dead weight in the water and the seas were becoming increasingly rough. The lifeboat capsized in the heavy sea. The claimants' son was one of nine crew who were drowned. The other 15 crew members were saved by the Oropesa.

Held. The owners of the Oropesa were liable to the claimants in respect of the death of their son. The actions of the captain of the Manchester Regiment did not break the chain of causation because they were reasonable under the circumstances.

Unreasonable actions will usually break the chain. This is particularly true if the action was both unreasonable and unforeseeable. So if one of the first lifeboat's crew had drowned after deciding to swim to the Oropesa then the chain would have been broken and the owners of the Oropesa would not have been liable for his death.

We shall see that a claimant has a duty to mitigate the loss caused by the breach of duty. If the claimant takes action which attempts to mitigate loss then it is likely that this will not cause the chain of causation to be broken. Nor will reflex actions break the chain of causation. In *Carmarthenshire CC v Lewis* [1955] AC 549 the House of Lords held that a primary school was liable for the death of a lorry driver who had killed himself when swerving to avoid a four-year-old boy whom the school had negligently allowed to get on to the road.

12.2.4.2 Multiple causes

Difficulties arise where the claimant's loss was caused not only by the defendant's negligence but also by other causes as well.

■ *McGhee v National Coal Board* [1972] 3 All ER 1008 (House of Lords)

The claimant's employers asked him to clean out brick kilns. No washing facilities were provided even though the work was hot and dirty and exposed the claimant to clouds of brick dust. The claimant used to ride his bicycle home while caked with sweat and grime. The claimant soon developed dermatitis. This was caused by working in the kiln, but the risk of dermatitis was materially increased by the claimant cycling home without washing. The Court of Session held that the employers were in breach of duty by not providing washing facilities. However, the claimant failed in his action because it could not be shown that this breach of duty caused the dermatitis. There was no positive evidence that he would not have contracted dermatitis anyway, even if proper washing facilities had been provided. The claimant appealed to the House of Lords.

Held. The claimant won. A defendant was liable to a claimant if his breach of duty had caused, or had materially contributed to, the claimant's injury. This was the case even if there were other factors which contributed to the injury. If the court found that the defendant's breach of duty had materially increased the risk of injury this amounted to a finding that the breach had materially contributed to the injury (unless the defendant could positively prove the contrary).

In *Hotson* v *East Berkshire Health Authority* [1987] AC 750 the defendant's negligence had a 25% chance of having caused the claimant's injury. The House of Lords held that to prove causation on a balance of probabilities what was required was at least a 51% probability that the negligence caused the injury. Consequently, the claim failed.

In *Wilsher* v *Essex Area Health Authority* [1988] AC 1074 the House of Lords considered the case of a prematurely born baby who was negligently given too much oxygen whilst in hospital. The baby developed retrolental fibroplasia which eventually caused him to go blind. Although retrolenta fibroplasia can be caused by being given too much oxygen, there were in this case five other possible causes. The trial judge held that the burden of proof was shifted so that the hospital had to prove that it was not their breach of duty which caused retrolental fibroplasia. The House of Lords rejected this approach and insisted that it was up to the claimant to prove that the hospital's negligence was a material cause of the injury. (A retrial was ordered so that the medical evidence could be assessed in the light of this ruling.)

Recently, the House of Lords considered multiple causation again, in the following case.

■ *Fairchild* v *Glenhaven Funeral Services Ltd* [2002] 3 All ER 305 (House of Lords)

The case was brought by several claimants who had contracted mesothelioma, a type of lung cancer which is invariably fatal. Mesothelioma is caused by inhaling a single strand of asbestos dust. It is not caused by cumulative exposure and once it has been contracted further exposure will not make it worse. The claimants had been employed at different times, and at different places, by various employers who had negligently exposed them to the risk of inhaling asbestos dust. However, none of the claimants could prove, on a balance of probabilities, that they had inhaled the strand of asbestos dust while working for any particular employer. Furthermore, some of the employers could not be sued as they had ceased to carry on business. Applying the 'but for' test, the Court of Appeal held that the claimants could not succeed against employers who were still in business.

Held. The claimants could succeed, and recover full damages, against any of the employers who had been negligent. (The employer who had to pay the damages could gain a contribution from the other employers.) To apply the 'but for' test would yield unfair results. In special circumstances the 'but-for' test could be departed from and a lesser degree of causal connection would then be sufficient. This lesser degree would be that the defendant's breach of duty had materially contributed to causing the claimant's injury by materially increasing his risk of contracting the disease. All the employers who had negligently exposed the claimants to the risk made a material contribution to the claimants contracting the disease. Any injustice which might be caused to the employers by this approach was heavily outweighed by the injustice which would be caused to the claimants if this approach were not taken.

COMMENT (i) The principle set out in this case seems to apply: (a) where there is a causal agent such as fabric dust or asbestos; and (b) where it is scientifically impossible to identify whether it was the defendant's breach which led to the exposure to the agent which actually caused the injury in the 'but for' sense.

(ii) In *Fairchild* the *McGhee* principle was approved, so materially increasing the risk is to be regarded as materially contributing to the risk. *Wilsher* was not overruled but approved on its own facts. *Wilsher* differs from *McGhee* in that in *Wilsher* there were several different ways in which the injury could have arisen whereas in *McGhee* there was only one, exposure to brick dust.

12.2.4.3 Remoteness of damage

The damage suffered by the claimant must be a **type of damage** which was reasonably foreseeable, otherwise it will be regarded as too remote. However, the extent of the damage does not need to be foreseeable, nor does the precise way in which it arose.

■ *The Wagon Mound* [1961] AC 388 (Privy Council)

The defendant's negligence caused a large quantity of furnace oil to spill into the bay of Sydney harbour. The oil spread on the water to the claimant's wharf, some 600 feet away. The claimants stopped welding on their wharf until they were assured by the wharf manager that it was safe to continue. When they resumed welding a spark from a welding torch ignited a piece of cotton waste which was floating in the water. The cotton ignited the oil and considerable damage was caused to the claimant's wharf. The defendants did not know that furnace oil could be ignited when floating on water and could not reasonably have been expected to know this.

Held. The defendants were not liable for the fire, even though they had been negligent in spilling the oil on the water. The test on remoteness of damage is whether the damage in question is of a type which was reasonably foreseeable. In this case a fire was not a reasonably foreseeable type of damage and so the defendants were not liable for any fire damage. If a claim for general fouling by oil had been made it would have been successful as this was a foreseeable type of damage.

COMMENT (i) This case overturned the decision set out in *Re Polemis* [1921] 3 KB 560. In that case the Court of Appeal had held that the test was whether or not the claimant's loss was a direct consequence of the defendant's tort. The defendant would be liable if the loss was a direct consequence, even if the loss was not a foreseeable type of damage.

(ii) This is an interesting example of a decision of the Judicial Committee of the Privy Council being taken to overrule a long-standing decision of the Court of Appeal. (See the hierarchy of the courts in Chapter 1 at 1.3.2.1.)

In the following case the House of Lords held that the complete series of events which caused the injury does not need to be foreseeable.

■ *Hughes v Lord Advocate* [1963] 1 All ER 705 (House of Lords)

Workmen had dug a hole in the road. They left it unattended with a tent on top of it and paraffin lamps around about it. Two young boys took a lamp into the manhole. When one of them dropped the lamp an explosion was caused. This injured one of the boys. An injury by burning was foreseeable but an injury by explosion was not. The explosion had been caused by the paraffin vaporising, an unusual occurrence.

Held. The claimant could recover. The distinction between burning and explosion was too fine a distinction to mean that the danger was not of a reasonably foreseeable type. It was not necessary that the whole series of events satisfied the foreseeability test.

COMMENT (i) In this case the *Wagon Mound* was not considered by the House of Lords.

(ii) The Law Lords strongly made the point that each case must depend upon its own particular facts.

In *Doughty* v *Turner Manufacturing Co* [1964] 1 All ER 98 the Court of Appeal took the *Wagon Mound* approach rather than the approach taken in *Hughes* v *Lord Advocate*. A workman dislodged an asbestos cover into a furnace of very hot liquid sodium cyanide. Some minutes later the presence of the asbestos in the liquid caused an explosion in which the workman was severely injured. The workman, however, could not recover damages against his employers. A splash of molten metal was foreseeable but an explosion was not. Diplock LJ said that in the light of the *Wagon Mound*, the decision in *Re Polemis* was no longer the law. He also stated that the House of Lords in *Hughes* v *Lord Advocate* treated the *Wagon Mound* as correctly stating the law, but distinguished the case on its facts.

Once it has become established that a particular type of damage was a foreseeable consequence of the defendant's breach the defendant will be liable for all damage of that type, no matter what the extent of this.

The 'egg shell skull' rule is concerned with the extent of the injury caused, in circumstances in which a certain amount of injury was inevitable. The defendant must take his victim as he finds him. So if a certain amount of damage of a particular type was inevitable, the defendant will be liable for all damage of this type caused to a particularly sensitive claimant. For example, in *Smith* v *Leech Brain* [1962] 2 QB 405 a worker had the task of removing galvanised objects from a tank of molten metal. As a consequence of the defendant's negligence, the worker was injured when a drop of molten metal splashed onto his lip. The worker was particularly susceptible to cancer and consequently the burn became malignant and caused him to die of cancer. Those who were not particularly susceptible would not have suffered cancer as a consequence of the burn. Nevertheless, the defendants were liable for the cancer.

12.2.4.4 Nervous shock

A claimant who suffers psychiatric injury as a result of negligence may well be able to claim damages for this. However, damages will not be claimable in respect of sorrow, grief or anxiety. Many of the older cases classify psychiatric injury caused by a tort as 'nervous shock'. Partly because psychiatric injuries are much more easily feigned than physical injuries the courts have adopted a cautious approach to awarding damages for nervous shock. *Hambrook* v *Stokes* [1964] 1 WLR 1314 was one of the first cases in which damages for nervous shock were awarded and that case held that in order to claim in respect of such damages the claimant must have witnessed something at first hand. It was not enough for the claimant to have been told of an horrific event by a third party.

As regards most of the cases in which a claim for nervous shock has been successfully made, the nervous shock has been caused by the sight of injury to a close relative. The following case provides a fairly typical example.

■ *Hinz* v *Berry* [1970] 2 QB 40 (Court of Appeal)

The claimant, her husband, and their eight children and foster children, had a day out in their Dormobile van. When they stopped at a lay-by the claimant and one of the children crossed the road to pick bluebells. The defendant's car crashed into the van, where the husband was making tea. The claimant turned around and saw the accident. The husband died some hours later and several of the children were injured. The accident changed the claimant from a happy, robust woman who loved children to a person who suffered lengthy morbid depression.

Held. The claimant was entitled to damages in respect of the recognisable psychiatric illness which witnessing the accident had caused. However, damages were not available for grief and sorrow, for worry about the children, for financial strain and stress, or for problems caused by adjusting to her changed circumstances.

More recently, the courts have extended the possibility of a claim for nervous shock to rescuers who suffered Post Traumatic Stress Disorder at the sight of the injuries of those whom they were rescuing. The courts have also allowed the possibility of a claim to workers who suffered nervous shock when they thought that their work mates were about to be killed or severely injured (*Dooley* v *Cammell Laird & Co Ltd* [1951] 1 Lloyd's Rep 271). In general, bystanders who witness an accident to others who are not work mates, or to whom they are not particularly close emotionally, will not be able to claim for nervous shock. However, if the event is sufficiently horrific, even a mere bystander might recover damages.

■ *Alcock* v *Chief Constable of South Yorkshire Police* [1991] 4 All ER 907

95 people died, and many more were severely injured, as a consequence of the defendant's negligent policing of a football match. The disaster was seen by the claimants, who were all relatives or friends of those involved. Some claimants saw the events from the other side of the stadium, others saw them on television or heard them described on the radio. All of the claimants suffered psychiatric illness and claimed in respect of this against the defendant.

Held. A claim for psychiatric illness caused by witnessing injury to others could only be successful if the relationship between the claimant and those injured was sufficiently proximate. It is not possible to make a closed list of relationships, such as husband and wife or parent and child, which will be regarded as sufficiently proximate. The necessary proximity would be based on ties of love and affection and the closeness of this would require careful scrutiny in every case. It is also necessary that the claimant prove closeness to the accident or its aftermath in terms of both time and space. Those who saw the accident on television could not be regarded as having been within sight and hearing of it and so their claims failed. Two claimants who were inside the football ground failed in their claim because they were not in a sufficiently proximate relationship to the victims of the disaster.

If the defendant's breach would not have caused a reasonably robust person to suffer any injury then the egg shell skull rule will not help a claimant who is particularly prone to nervous shock. If, however, the defendant's breach would have caused a reasonably robust claimant to suffer nervous shock then a claimant who suffers greater nervous shock will have a greater claim. As Lane J put it in *Malcolm v Broadhurst* [1970] 3 All ER 608: 'The defendant must take [the claimant] as he finds her and there is no difference in principle between the egg-shell skull and the egg-shell personality.'

Damages will not be awarded for trauma suffered immediately before death by a claimant who is killed by the defendant's breach of duty. It is also the case that the nervous shock must be caused by witnessing a sudden horrific event and not by witnessing a gradual process, such as death from a wasting disease.

12.2.4.5 Pure economic loss

In Chapter 7 we saw that a claim for economic loss is often the basis of a claim for damages for breach of contract. Tort damages are concerned with compensation in respect of injury to the person and damage to property. Damages may also be recoverable in respect of economic loss which is a direct consequence of physical injury or damage to the claimant's own property. (For example, lost earnings if a claimant is injured and unable to work.)

An example of such claimable economic loss can be seen in *British Celanese v A H Hunt (capacitors) Ltd* [1969] 1 WLR 959. The defendants negligently caused the claimant's factory to suffer a loss of power by allowing foil strips to blow onto a power line. This caused damage to the claimant's machines. The Court of Appeal held that the resulting economic loss of not being able to use the machines was fully recoverable. *Spartan Steel and Alloys Ltd v Martin & Co (Contractors) Ltd* [1973] QB 27 provides a contrast. Here the defendant's power shovel negligently cut a cable belonging to the utility company. This caused the defendant's factory to be without electricity for 14 hours. Damages could be recovered for the reduction in value of metal which had to be removed from a furnace and for the profit which would have been made on that particular 'melt' of metal. However, the Court of Appeal did not award damages for four other lost 'melts' which would have been produced but for the power cut. This loss was economic loss which did not flow directly from the claimant's own physical loss. However, damages in respect of pure economic loss have generally not been recoverable. In *Weller v Foot and Mouth Research Institute* [1966] 1 QB 569, for example, a firm of auctioneers were not able to claim damages in respect of lost profits caused by the defendants negligently allowing foot and mouth disease to escape from their laboratory. The ensuing outbreak caused the claimants to be prevented from holding auctions but the defendants owed them no duty in respect of their lost profits. This principle is necessary to limit the number of persons who might have a claim. If the auctioneers had been able to claim in respect of their economic loss then a similar claim could have been made by a large number of other businesses, such as pubs and cafés, which had also been caused economic loss. It may, however, be possible for the claimant to succeed in an action for damages for pure economic loss if he can bring himself within one of several exceptions to the general rule. These exceptions would include liability for negligent misstatement, which is considered below at 12.3.

12.2.5 Damages

If the defendant's negligence destroys or damages the claimant's property or goods, the measure of damages will ordinarily be the cost of restoration of the goods. This cost will generally be assessed by reference to the market value. A claim might also be made for loss of the use of the goods if replacement goods could not easily be obtained. Such a claim could take account of profit lost on account of the goods not being available.

Claims in respect of damages for personal injuries might be made in respect of pecuniary losses or non-pecuniary losses. Damages in respect of pain and suffering are awarded, and so are damages for loss of amenity, that is to say loss of the ability to enjoy life. Loss of earnings and the costs of health care are also recoverable. Damages are not subject to tax, and so when a claim for loss of earnings is made the claimant is only to be compensated in respect of the amount of earnings he would have received after tax had been deducted. The fact that the claimant has taken out insurance will not reduce his damages.

If the claimant is killed then damages will necessarily not include some heads of damage which are recoverable in cases of personal injury. First, funeral expenses are payable. No claim for the personal injuries of the deceased will be claimable unless there was a significant period of time between the injury and the death. Section 1A of the Fatal Accidents Act 1976 allows bereaved spouses and the parents of a deceased minor to make a statutory claim of £10 000. Dependants of the deceased may also be able to claim damages in respect of lost earnings of the deceased, but only if they can show that the deceased was supporting them.

As tort damages are compensatory in nature, aggravated and exemplary damages are not awarded.

A claimant is expected to take reasonable steps to mitigate his loss. Damages will not be recoverable in respect of losses which the claimant brought upon himself by his own careless actions after the tort had been committed by the defendant. If a reasonable attempt to mitigate in fact increases the loss to the claimant, he will be able to claim in respect of this increased loss.

12.2.6 Defences to negligence

12.2.6.1 Contributory negligence

Contributory negligence is not a complete defence, but reduces the damages payable to the claimant. In extreme cases individual damages for personal injuries can run to several million pounds, and any percentage reduction can amount to a good deal of money.

The Law Reform (Contributory Negligence) Act 1945 s.1 provides that:

'Where any person suffers damage as the result partly of his own fault and partly of the fault of any other person or persons, a claim in respect of that damage shall not be defeated by reason of the fault of the person suffering the damage, but the damages recoverable in respect thereof shall be reduced to such extent as the court thinks just and equitable having regard to the claimant's share in responsibility for the damage.'

Capps v Miller [1989] 2 All ER 333 provides an example of how this works. A motorcyclist suffered head injuries when the defendant negligently crashed into him. The motorcyclist was wearing a safety helmet, but had not fastened the strap properly. He suffered head injuries as a result of the crash and these were increased by his helmet coming off. The Court of Appeal reduced his damages by 10% as it considered this reduction to be just and equitable having regard to the claimant's share in responsibility for his injuries.

In order for the Act to apply, the claimant must have been to some extent responsible for his injuries. It is not necessary that he must have been responsible to some extent for the accident itself. (In *Capps v Miller*, for example, he was not.) The Act is not limited to damages for personal injuries but also covers claims for damage to property.

It is possible for a claimant who is more than 50% to blame for his own injuries to succeed in a claim for negligence, as the following case shows.

■ *Green v Bannister* [2003] EWCA Civ 1819 (Court of Appeal)

The defendant reversed along a road. It was dark but the road was lit by a single sodium lamp. The defendant looked over her right shoulder to make sure that she did not reverse into parked cars. After reversing for about 35 yards the defendant ran over the claimant, who was lying in the road in a drunken stupor. The trial judge found that the defendant had not been negligent merely on account of having been reversing down the road, but that she had been negligent in not looking in her mirror or over her left shoulder. The judge also apportioned blame 60% to the claimant and 40% to the defendant. The defendant appealed against both of these findings.

Held. Both findings were upheld by the Court of Appeal. If the defendant had looked over her left shoulder and in her mirror she would probably have seen the claimant lying in the road. Her not having done these things was negligent and caused the accident. The apportionment of liability made by the trial judge was correct and so the claimant was entitled to damages for his injuries, subject to a reduction of 60%.

12.2.6.2 *Volenti non fit injuria*

Literally translated, *volenti non fit injuria* means 'to one who volunteers, no harm is done'. *Volenti* can act as a complete defence. There are two elements to the rule. First, that the claimant knows of the risk. Second, that he consents to accept the risk.

The consent which gives rise to the defence may be express or implied. The following case shows an example of implied consent.

■ *Morris* v *Murray* [1990] 3 All ER 801 (Court of Appeal)

The claimant met his friend at a pub where they had a few drinks. After several more drinks the friend suggested that they go for a joy ride in the friend's light aircraft. Conditions were poor and flying at the aerodrome had been suspended. The plane did manage to get into the air briefly but then crashed. The claimant was badly injured, the friend was killed. An autopsy showed that the deceased friend was three times over the drink-driving alcohol limit. The claimant sued the deceased friend's estate.

Held. The claimant was defeated by *volenti non fit injuria*. By his actions the claimant had implicitly waived his right to damages.

Volenti can also provide a complete defence where the claimant has agreed not to sue, or where the defendant has excluded liability by means of a contractual term or a notice. However, as we saw in Chapter 5 at 5.6.1, the Unfair Contract Terms Act 1977 s.2(1) would not allow a business to exclude liability for death or personal injury caused by negligence by reference to any contract term or notice. We also saw that s.2(2) of the 1977 Act would not allow a business to exclude liability for other types of loss or damage caused by negligence unless the term or notice so doing satisfied the Act's requirement of reasonableness. It would also be the case that the defendant would have had to have taken reasonable steps to bring the term or notice to the attention of the claimant before the claimant could be said to have agreed to it.

In employment cases the consent of the employee is not easily proved, as employees often have very little true choice about whether or not to agree to conditions imposed or suggested by the employer. However, it is possible for the defence to be successfully invoked by the employer. (See *ICI Ltd* v *Shatwell* [1965] AC 656 in Chapter 21 at 21.5.7.4.) Also, the Road Traffic Act 1988 s.149 provides that *volenti* is not available as a defence if a passenger in a car sues a driver who should be compulsorily insured.

A claimant who is making an effort to effect a rescue will not be defeated by *volenti*. So in *Haynes* v *Harwood* [1935] 1 KB 146 (Court of Appeal) a policeman who suffered injury when he stopped a runaway horse which was pulling a van was able to claim for his injuries. The policeman had been on duty inside a police station when he saw the horses coming down the street. At the time the police station had contained a large number of people, including children.

12.2.6.3 Illegality

A claimant who is injured whilst committing an illegal act with the defendant may be debarred from making a claim against him. However, the outcome will depend upon the seriousness of the illegal act, and the degree of connection with the harm which the claimant suffers.

■ *Ashton* v *Turner* [1981] QB 137

Three young men committed a burglary after an evening drinking together. They tried to escape in a car driven by the defendant. The defendant crashed the car and the claimant was severely injured.

Held. The defendant did not owe a duty of care to the claimant. As a matter of policy the law will not in certain circumstances allow a perpetrator of a crime to bring an action against a fellow perpetrator in respect of actions done in the course of committing the crime. (*Volenti non fit injuria* would also have prevented the claimant from succeeding.)

Test your understanding

1 What are the three main differences between contractual and tortious liability?

2 What three things will the claimant need to prove in order to succeed in an action for negligence?

3 In what circumstances will a breach of duty owed by a defendant to a claimant have been breached?

4 What four factors have emerged from the case law as being of significance when deciding whether or not a defendant breached a duty of care?

5 What is the effect of the 'but for' test, which can be used to assess whether or not the defendant's breach of duty caused the claimant's loss?

6 To what extent does the injury suffered by the claimant have to have been a foreseeable consequence of the defendant's breach of duty?

7 In what circumstances can damages for psychiatric injury caused by witnessing an accident to a loved one be claimed?

8 Can damages be claimed for pure economic loss caused by the defendant's negligence?

9 What is meant by contributory negligence?

10 What is meant by *volenti non fit injuria*?

Answers

1 Contractual liability is voluntarily undertaken, tortious liability is imposed by the courts; contractual liability is generally strict, tortious liability is generally based on fault; contract damages are designed to put the party in the position he would have been in if the contract had been properly performed, tort damages are designed to put the injured party in the position he would have been in if the tort had never been committed.

2 In order to establish that the tort of negligence has been committed the claimant will need to prove that the defendant owed him a duty of care, that the defendant breached that duty and that a foreseeable type of injury was caused by this breach.

3 A duty of care owed by a defendant to a claimant will have been breached if the defendant did not take the care which a reasonable person would have taken in all the circumstances of the case.

4 The four factors which are likely to be of particular significance in deciding whether or not a duty of care was breached are: the likelihood of harm being caused to the claimant; the potential seriousness of injury; the cost of making sure that injury was not caused; and the usefulness of the objectives which the defendant was trying to achieve.

5 The 'but for' test asks whether the claimant would have suffered the same damage but for the defendant's actions. If the claimant would have suffered the same loss anyway, damages can generally not be recovered in respect of the loss.

6 The claimant will only be able to succeed in respect of loss or damage of a type which was a reasonably foreseeable consequence of the defendant's breach of duty.

7 Damages in respect of psychiatric injury can only be claimed if there is a sufficient proximity based on ties of love and affection between the claimant and the injured loved one. The claimant would also have to be sufficiently close in terms of time and space. The death or injury of the loved one must be caused by a sudden horrific event.

8 Damages cannot be claimed for pure economic loss. Damages can however be claimed for financial loss which was a direct consequence of a foreseeable type of damage to goods or a foreseeable type of physical injury.

9 Contributory negligence on the claimant's part entitles the court to reduce the claimant's damages to the extent which the court considers just and equitable, having regard to the claimant's share in responsibility for the damage which he has suffered.

10 *Volenti non fit injuria* is a complete defence. It allows the defendant to escape liability where the claimant voluntarily consented to running the risk which injured him or where the claimant agreed that liability should be excluded.

12.3 · Negligent misstatement

Negligent misstatement is not a tort in its own right, but is merely an aspect of the tort of negligence. However, it is convenient to consider liability for negligent misstatements separately from general liability for negligence.

Liability for negligent misstatements was first imposed by the House of Lords in the following case.

■ *Hedley Byrne & Co Ltd* v *Heller and Partners Ltd* [1963] 2 All ER 575 (House of Lords)

A bank asked the defendants, who were merchant bankers, about the financial position of E Ltd, one of their customers. The bank asked in confidence, and without responsibility on the defendants' part, whether E Ltd were sound as regards an advertising contract worth between £8 000 and £9 000. A few months later the bank made a similar request, this time asking whether E Ltd were trustworthy in the way of business to the amount of £100 000 a year. The defendants replied, in a letter headed 'For your private use and without responsibility on the part of the bank or its officials', that E Ltd were respectably constituted and considered good for their normal business engagements. This information was passed on to the claimants, advertising agents, who placed advertising orders on E Ltd's behalf. These deals were made in such a way that the claimants made themselves personally liable on them. E Ltd went into liquidation without paying the claimants some £17 000 owing in respect of the advertisements placed. The claimants sued the defendants for this money, claiming that the defendants had been negligent by giving a misleading indication as to E Ltd's creditworthiness.

Held. The defendants were not liable because their disclaimer that the advice was given without responsibility prevented a duty of care from arising. However, but for the disclaimer a duty of care might have arisen. Such a duty of care arises where there is a special relationship between the parties, on account of the very close proximity between them.

Since this case was decided it has been recognised that a duty of care could be owed in respect of negligent misstatements, even as regards pure economic loss. Mere foreseeability of loss would not be enough to give rise to liability. Liability can only arise where a special relationship exists between the parties. In order for such a special relationship to arise the defendant must be a person on whom the claimant can reasonably and foreseeably expect to be able to place reliance. The special relationship can possibly arise even where the relationship is purely gratuitous. (See *Chaudry* v *Prabhakar* [1988] 3 All ER 718 (Court of Appeal) which is set out in Chapter 11 at 11.4.2.) A special relationship will only arise where the defendant gives a response to an inquiry made by the claimant, it will not arise where advice is volunteered.

In *Caparo Industries plc* v *Dickman* [1990] 1 All ER 568, the House of Lords held that a very proximate relationship must exist between claimant and defendant before liability in negligent misstatement will arise. The claimants were shareholders in a company who had relied upon the audited accounts of the company when deciding to make a take-over bid for the company. After the take-over had been successfully completed the claimants discovered that the company accounts, which had been audited by the defendants, showed a pre-tax profit of £1.2m, whereas they should have shown a loss of £0.4m. The House of Lords held that the defendants owed no duty of care to the claimants as their relationship was not sufficiently proximate. The auditors owed a duty of care to the company and to the shareholders of the company as a body, but not to individual shareholders or to members of the public. The Law Lords also emphasised that the tort of negligence should be developed incrementally, and not by means of one broad general principle.

In Chapter 6, at 6.1.2, we saw that a person to whom an actionable negligent misrepresentation has been made can sue rescind the contract or under s.2(1) of the Misrepresentation Act 1967, and that a remedy might be more easily gained rescind the contract or under the 1967 Act than under negligent misstatement. In addition, it is worth noticing that the Financial Services Act 1986 can make promoters of companies liable for misstatements when shares, debentures or securities are issued. In Chapter 20 at 20.2.4.7 the case *Spring* v *Guardian Assurance plc* [1994] 3 All ER 129 is set out. The case shows that an employer who carelessly or inaccurately prepares a reference for an employee can be liable for negligent misstatement.

12.4 · The Consumer Protection Act 1987 Part I

The Consumer Protection Act 1987 is divided into three parts. Part I imposes civil liability, allowing a claimant who is injured by an unsafe product to sue the manufacturer of the product (and possibly others) without having to prove the tort of negligence. Part II imposes criminal liability on producers of unsafe products and is considered at 22.4. Section 41(1) of the Act provides that a civil action for breach of a statutory duty can be brought by a person affected by a breach of the Part II safety regulations. Civil actions for breach of statutory duty are considered in Chapter 13 at 13.9. Part III of the Act imposes criminal liability in respect of misleading price indications, and is considered in Chapter 22 at 22.3. Liability under Part I of the Act is strict. This means that, in the absence of one of the defences listed in the Act, injured consumers will be entitled to damages if they show that they were injured by a product which was less safe than could reasonably be expected. The defences available are, as we shall see, narrow and specific.

12.4.1 Who may sue?

The Act gives the right to sue to any person who is injured by a product, the safety of which was 'not such as persons generally are entitled to expect'.

For over a hundred years the Sale of Goods Act required that goods sold by a business were of merchantable quality. As we have seen, this requirement has been replaced by a requirement that the goods must be of satisfactory quality. They must also be fit for the buyer's purpose and must correspond with any description by which they were sold. If a buyer of goods is injured because goods sold by a business were not of satisfactory quality the Sale of Goods Act 1979 will provide the buyer with a remedy against the seller. But privity of contract restricts the remedies offered by the Sale of Goods Act to the buyer of the goods. (Subject to the Contracts (Rights of Third Parties) Act 1999, the effect of which is considered in Chapter 4 at 4.2.2.2.) The Consumer Protection Act now gives a similarly high level of protection to anyone injured by the goods. Claims such as the one in *Donoghue* v *Stevenson*, which are made against a manufacturer by a person injured by one of the manufacturer's products, would now be more easily established under the Consumer Protection Act Part I rather than in the tort of negligence.

12.4.2 Who is liable?

The Act places liability on the 'producer' of the product. Sections 1 and 2 of the Act define the producer as including:

(a) The manufacturer of the product.
(b) The extractor of raw materials.

(c) Those who subject game or agricultural produce to an industrial process.
(d) 'Own branders' who add their label to products which they did not produce.
(e) Anyone who imports the product into the European Union.

Anyone involved in the chain of supply can also be liable if he does not, upon request, name a party who would be primarily liable (s.2(3)). If more than one of these people are liable they are jointly and severally liable. Each person is therefore liable for the full amount of the damage suffered. The retailer of the product is not liable unless he is an own-brander. An own-brander uses distinguishing marks to hold himself out as the producer of the product. Most supermarkets, for example, have their own brands of foods such as baked beans. (Retailers are of course liable to the purchasers of any defective goods under the Sale of Goods Act 1979.) A third party might also be able to sue on the contract if the contract expressly provided that he could or if a term of the contract which he is seeking to enforce purported to confer a benefit upon him. (See the Contracts (Rights of Third Parties) Act 1999 at 4.2.2.2.)

12.4.3 Defective products

Section 3 of the Act says that products can be regarded as defective if their safety is not such as persons are generally entitled to expect, and that safety embraces not only risks of death or personal injury, but also the risk of damage to property. Products include any goods or electricity, and also include a product which is comprised in another product, whether by virtue of being a component part or raw material or otherwise. So a car is a product, the car tyres are a product and the rubber from which the tyres are manufactured is a product.

The court will consider all the circumstances when deciding whether or not this objective standard has been breached. Section 3(2) mentions a number of factors to be considered, including:

(a) The way in which the product was marketed.
(b) Instructions and warnings issued with the product.
(c) What might reasonably be expected to be done with or in relation to the product.
(d) The time at which the product was supplied by its producer to another.

This last factor is designed to give some protection to manufacturers producing new products. These are not to be considered unsafe just because later products were safer. (This is linked to the controversial 'development risks' defence, which is considered below.) Warnings may not only make an unsafe product safe, if they are inappropriate they might also make a safe product unsafe. Advertisements and their context might also affect the safety or otherwise of a product.

The burden of proof is on the consumer to prove that the product was defective (unsafe).

The Court of Appeal considered the meaning of a defective product in the following case.

■ *Abouzaid v Mothercare (UK) Ltd 2000* WL 1918530 (Court of Appeal)

A 12-year-old boy was injured while fitting a child's sleeping bag to a pushchair. The sleeping bag, which was manufactured by the defendants, was designed to be attached to pushchairs by elasticated straps. A metal buckle attached to one of the straps was to be used to attach the elasticated straps to each other. While trying to attach the straps the boy let go of one of them. This caused the metal buckle to hit him in the eye, severely damaging his retina.

Held. The product was defective. It was designed in such a way that an accident such as this could happen. There was no need for the straps to be elasticated and instructions could have warned of the dangers. The risk of injury to the eye, and the seriousness of such injuries, meant that the safety of the product was not such as persons generally are entitled to expect.

12.4.4 Damage suffered

Section 5 allows a claimant to claim for death or any personal injury caused by the unsafety of the goods. Damage to property is only claimable if it causes an individual to suffer a loss of more than £275. The loss may be made up of damage to several items.

Damage to the product in question is not recoverable. Nor is damage to other products supplied with the product in question. So if a car battery caught fire and destroyed both the car and the battery the Act would provide no remedy for either loss. (However, the purchaser of the car could gain a remedy against the vendor of the car, under s.14(2) of the Sale of Goods Act 1979, as long as the vendor sold the car in the course of a business.)

■ Example

Mr and Mrs Smith are bought a microwave oven as a wedding present. The microwave is defective and this causes it to catch fire and burn Mr Smith's hand. The kitchen work surface is damaged and the microwave itself is destroyed. Under the Act, damages could be claimed for the injury to Mr Smith and for all of the damage to the work surface as long as this amounted to more than £275. Damage to the microwave itself could not be claimed under this Act. (The buyer of the microwave could claim back the price of the microwave under the Sale of Goods Act 1979 s.14(2), as the microwave was not of satisfactory quality.)

Compensation for injury, death and damage to goods must be claimed within three years of the loss becoming apparent. In addition, there is an absolute time limit of ten years after the date when the product was supplied. This means that a person injured by a product more than ten years after buying it will have no remedy.

Contributory negligence on the part of the claimant can reduce the damages. So if in the above example the court considered that Mr Smith was 25% to blame for his injuries, perhaps because his injuries worsened on account of his not seeking medical help, then his damages would be reduced by 25%.

Section 5(3) excludes liability for loss or damage to business property. At the time of the loss or damage, the property must be 'of a description of property ordinarily intended for private use, occupation or consumption; and intended by the person suffering the loss or damage mainly for his own use, occupation or consumption.'

12.4.5 Defences

Liability is strict and this means that the claimant does not need to prove fault. Nor can liability be excluded by any contract term, notice or other provision. There are however certain defences available. These defences are as follows:

(a) That the defect was caused by complying with EC or UK legislation.
(b) That the product was not supplied or manufactured in the course of a business. For example, a person who made jam as a hobby would not be liable under this Act if the jam poisoned a person who consumed it.
(c) That the defect in the product did not exist when the product was supplied by the defendant to another.
(d) A supplier of a component will have a defence if the defect constitutes a defect in the ultimate product, and was wholly due to the faulty design of the ultimate product or to compliance with instructions given by the producer of the ultimate product.
(e) The development risks defence gives a defence to a producer if he can show that when he produced the product the state of scientific and technical knowledge was 'not such that a producer of products of the same description as the product in question might be expected to have discovered it'.

This is a controversial defence. It would have meant that the victims of the drug Thalidomide would not have had a remedy because when the drug was created scientists were not aware of its danger. (For the same reason the drug manufacturers would not have been liable in negligence.) The Government included the development risk defence because it thought that not to do so would make the manufacture of drugs and certain other products so hazardous as to be economically impractical.

Ultimately, the balance to be struck between the interests of drug manufacturers and drug users is a matter of politics. However, the wording of the Directive which gave rise to the Act is wider in respect of this defence than the wording of the Act. The Directive requires the defendant to prove that 'the state of scientific and technical knowledge at the time when he put the product into circulation was not such as to enable the existence of the defect to be discovered'. This wording concentrates on not only whether the state of scientific and technical knowledge was such that the producer of the product could have discovered the defect, but whether it was such that anybody could have discovered it. (For the circumstances in which an incorrectly implemented Directive can be relied upon see Chapter 1 at 1.4.2.4.)

The development risks defence was raised in *Abouzaid* v *Mothercare (UK) Ltd*. The defendants argued that they could rely on the defence because there was no record of a similar accident having occurred before, and there was no research which showed that the elasticated straps could cause injury. The Court of Appeal rejected these arguments because they did not show that the defect was not discoverable at the time when the product was manufactured.

The Act does not replace the common law but supplements it.

12.5 · The Occupier's Liability Acts 1957 and 1984

Occupiers of premises owe a duty of care to all lawful visitors, and a separate duty of care to trespassers. The Occupier's Liability Act 1957 sets out the duty owed both to lawful visitors, and trespassers. Almost all businesses must occupy some premises, and so almost all are potentially liable.

Section 1(2) of the 1957 Act provides that the common law definition of an occupier should apply when considering liability under the Act. The common law also provides the definition of an occupier for the purposes of the 1984 Act. The common law shows us that the person who has control over the premises is the occupier and this might include an independent contractor, such as a builder. In the leading case, *Wheat* v *Lacon* [1966] AC 552 (House of Lords), Lord Denning stated that any person with any degree of control over the state of the premises would be an occupier. It is obvious from this that there might be more than one occupier. Section 1(3) of the 1957 Act makes it plain that liability can be imposed not only on the occupier of premises, but also on the occupier of any fixed or moveable structure, including any vessel, vehicle or aircraft. This is a wide area of liability and ladders, for example, have been held to be a moveable structure within the meaning of the Act. However, the Acts are to be used only for problems arising from structures and not for activities that happen to take place in or on these. As regards these activities, *Fairchild* v *Glenhaven Funeral Services Ltd* indicated that the common law of negligence is more appropriate.

12.5.1 Lawful visitors

Any person who comes on to premises with either express or implied permission of the occupier will be a lawful visitor. Express permission is simply a question of fact. Whether implied permission has been granted is more problematic. It is a matter which must be proved on a balance of probabilities by the person claiming to be a lawful visitor. The fact that the defendant tolerates persons to be on his premises does not necessarily mean that he has granted them implied permission to be there, although it could have this effect.

Even when a person is invited onto premises he is not necessarily invited onto the whole of the premises and is not invited to abuse the part of the premises to which he is invited. A person who wrongfully uses premises on to which he has been invited becomes a trespasser. It is possible, where there are several occupiers, that a person on the premises might be a lawful visitor as regards some occupiers and a trespasser as regards others. People who enter the premises as of right, such as the postman, will be lawful visitors whether invited onto the premises or not.

Section 2(2) of the Occupier's Liability Act (OLA) 1957 defines the common duty of care which is owed to all lawful visitors.

> 'The common duty of care is a duty to take such care as in all the circumstances of the case is reasonable to see that the visitor will be reasonably safe in using the premises for the purposes for which he is invited or permitted by the occupier to be there.'

As the duty is to provide such care as is reasonable, different occupiers might find themselves liable to provide different standards of care. In ascertaining whether or not an occupier has satisfied the common duty of care a court will consider all the circumstances of the case, including the likelihood of injury, the type of danger and the steps which would need to be taken to prevent injury.

Section 2(3) of the 1957 Act provides that an occupier must be prepared for children to be less careful than adults. It also provides that an occupier may expect that a person, in the exercise of his trade or profession, will appreciate and guard against any special risks ordinarily incident to the trade or profession, so far as the occupier leaves him free to do so.

Section 2(4)(a) deals with warnings provided by the occupier. Whilst the section recognises that warnings may mean that the occupier has discharged his common duty of care, it also provides that a warning is not to be treated without more as absolving the occupier from liability. It will only have this effect if in all the circumstances it was enough to enable the visitor to be reasonably safe.

Section 2(4)(b) provides that an occupier who has properly entrusted work to an independent contractor should not necessarily be liable for damage caused to a visitor by the faulty execution of that work. The occupier should not be liable if he acted reasonably in entrusting the work to the contractor, and if he had taken such steps as he reasonably ought to have done to satisfy himself that the contractor was competent and that the work had been properly done.

Mere warning notices will not be subject to the Unfair Contract Terms Act 1977, but notices which attempt to exclude or restrict liability will. We have already examined the UCTA 1977 in Chapter 5 at 5.6. There we saw that the Act only applies to business liability, which can include liability arising from the occupation of business premises. Section 2(1) and (2) of the 1977 Act will prevent the restriction of liability for negligence. As we have seen, s.2(1) UCTA 1977 does not allow any contract term or notice to exclude liability for death or personal injury caused by negligence. We have also seen that s.2(2) UCTA 1977 does allow liability for damage other than death or personal injury caused by negligence to be excluded, but only by a term or notice which satisfies the 1977 Act's requirement of reasonableness. Subject to the provisions of UCTA 1977, a non-contractual notice can be enough to exclude or restrict liability. This is made plain by the final two words of s.2(1) OLA 1957 which states that: 'An occupier of premises owes the same duty, the "common duty of care", to all his visitors, except in so far as he is free to and does extend, restrict, modify or exclude his duty to any visitor or visitors by agreement or otherwise.'

Damages can be claimed in respect of personal injury, or damage to property or financial loss, but only if the loss was of a type which was reasonably foreseeable. *Volenti non fit injuria* is a defence. However the defence must be considered in the light of s.2(3) UCTA 1977, which states: 'Where a contract term or notice purports to exclude or restrict liability for negligence a person's agreement to or awareness of it is not of itself to be taken as indicating his voluntary acceptance of any risk.'

Contributory negligence may be raised as a defence in the same way as it may be raised as a defence to the tort of negligence.

12.5.2 **Non-visitors**

Any person who enters the premises other than as a lawful visitor will do so as a non-visitor. Trespassers are the most common type of non-visitor. Frequently, such trespassers will be children, and the courts have recognised that even trespassers need considerable protection from inherently dangerous things such as live railway lines. In *British Railways Board* v *Herrington* [1972] AC 877 the House of Lords held that the general common law duty towards trespassers was not to deliberately or recklessly harm them. However, it also held that where the occupier knew that the condition of his land or the activities of the trespasser meant that the trespasser was likely to be injured, the duty of 'common humanity' required the occupier to ensure that the trespasser avoided the danger. The Railways Board was held liable to young children who were electrocuted by a live railway line. The children had gained entry through a broken down fence and the Railways Board had been warned that children were in the habit of trespassing through the fence and playing near the live line.

The Occupier's Liability Act 1984 has replaced the common law duty owed to trespassers.

Section 1(3) of the 1984 Act states that a person owes a duty of care to a person other than a lawful visitor if:

(a) he is aware of the danger or has reasonable grounds to believe that it exists;
(b) he knows or has reasonable grounds to believe that the other is in the vicinity of the danger concerned, or that he may come into the vicinity of the danger … and
(c) the risk is one against which, in all the circumstances of the case, he may reasonably be expected to offer the other some protection.

Section 1(4) of the 1984 Act states that: 'Where, by virtue of this section, an occupier of premises owes a duty to another in respect of such a risk, the duty is to take such care as is reasonable in all the circumstances of the case to see that he does not suffer injury on the premises by reason of the danger concerned.'

Volenti non fit injuria can provide a defence. Section 1(6) of the 1984 Act provides that: 'No duty is owed by virtue of this section to any person in respect of risks willingly accepted as his by that person (the question whether a risk was accepted to be decided on the same principles as in other cases in which one person owes a duty of care to another).'

Section 1(5) deals with the effect of warnings: 'Any duty owed by virtue of this section in respect of a risk may, in an appropriate case, be discharged by taking such steps as are reasonable in all the circumstances of the case to give warning of the danger concerned or to discourage persons from incurring the risk.'

The Unfair Contract Terms Act 1977 does not apply to the duty created by OLA 1984. Section 1 of the 1977 Act states that, as far as the 1977 Act is concerned, 'negligence' means: (a) the breach of any obligation, arising under the express or implied terms of a contract, to take reasonable care or exercise reasonable skill in the performance of the contract; or (b) breach of any common law duty to take reasonable care or exercise reasonable skill (but not any stricter duty); or (c) breach of the common duty of care imposed by the Occupier's Liability Act 1957.

Liability under OLA 1984 is limited to personal injury. Section 1(8) of the 1984 Act states that: 'Where a person owes a duty by virtue of this section, he does not, by reason of any breach of that duty, incur any liability in respect of any loss or damage to property.'

12.6 · Time limits

Earlier in this chapter we saw that when a claim is brought under the Consumer Protection Act Part I compensation for injury, death and damage to goods must be claimed within three years of the loss becoming apparent. We also saw that there is an absolute time limit of ten years from the date when the product was supplied.

As regards common law actions, s.2 of the Limitation Act 1980 provides that an action in tort, other than an action for personal injuries, must be brought within six years of the date when the right to sue accrued. As regards latent damage, s.14A provides an alternative period of three years from the date when the claimant knew the following: that the damage was serious enough to justify proceedings; that it was capable of being attributed to the defendant's negligence; and the identity of the defendant. Latent damage is damage which does not become apparent for some time after it was caused. There is a longstop period of 15 years from the act or omission which is alleged to have caused the claimant's damage, after which no action can be brought (s.14B Limitation Act 1980).

In the case of a claim for personal injuries the limitation period is three years either from the date on which the right of action accrued or from the date on which the claimant had knowledge of his injury (s.11 Limitation Act 1980). A person is regarded as having knowledge of his injury when he knows that the injury was significant; that it was capable of being attributed to the defendant's negligence, nuisance or breach of duty; and the identity of the defendant (s.14 Limitation Act 1980). If personal representatives claim on behalf of a deceased person the claim must be brought within three years of the date of the death or three years from the date on which they had knowledge (ss.11(5) and 12 Limitation Act 1980). In exceptional cases, s.33 allows the court to override the limits on bringing claims in respect of personal injuries or death if it would be equitable to do so.

Time does not run against minors (persons under 18) until they become 18. Nor does time run against a person who is suffering from a mental disorder, within the meaning of the Mental Health Act 1983, to the extent of being incapable of managing and administering his property and affairs. Where a claim is based upon the defendant's fraud, such as a claim under the tort of deceit, time does not run against the claimant until he discovered the fraud or could with reasonable diligence have done so (s.32(1)(a) Limitation Act 1980). Similarly, time does not run if the defendant has deliberately concealed the claimant's right of action (s.32(1)(b)).

Section 36(1) of the Limitation Act provides that the usual limitation periods do not apply where the claimant is seeking an equitable remedy, such as an injunction. Such remedies will be defeated by the equitable doctrine of laches or acquiescence. The court has a wide power to allow or refuse a claim for an equitable remedy and it is not possible to state a maximum time period within which such a remedy must be claimed.

Test your understanding

1 In what circumstances can a defendant be liable for negligent misstatements?

2 What is the main effect of the Consumer Protection Act 1987 Part I?

3 As regards what type of damage can a claim be made under the 1987 Act?

4 Who is an occupier of premises for the purposes of the Occupier's Liability Acts 1957 and 1984?

5 What duty does an occupier of premises owe to a lawful visitor?

6 What duty does an occupier of premises owe to a trespasser?

Answers

1 Liability for negligent misstatements can only be incurred where there is a special relationship between the defendant and the claimant. A special relationship will only arise where the defendant gives a response to an inquiry made by the claimant, it will not arise where advice is volunteered. In order for the special relationship to arise there must be a very proximate relationship between the claimant and the defendant. Appropriately worded disclaimers of responsibility might mean that a duty of care does not arise.

2 The Consumer Protection Act 1987 Part I allows a person injured by an unsafe product to sue the manufacturers, extractors of raw materials, own branders and importers into the EC (and possibly others in the chain of supply), who can be liable even if they were not at fault.

3 Under the 1987 Act a claim can be made for death or personal injury. A claim can also be made for damage to property as long as the property was not business property and as long as the damage to property amounted to more than £275.

4 An occupier of premises is a person who has any degree of control over the state of the premises.

5 Section 2(2) of the Occupier's Liability Act 1957 provides that an occupier has a duty to take such care as in all the circumstances of the case is reasonable to see that the visitor will be reasonably safe in using the premises for the purposes for which he is invited or permitted by the occupier to be there.

6 Section 1(4) of the Occupier's Liability Act 1984 provides that an occupier of premises has a duty to take such care as is reasonable in all the circumstances of the case to see that a trespasser does not suffer injury on the premises by reason of a danger of which the occupier is aware. The duty only arises if the occupier knows or has reasonable grounds to believe that the trespasser is in the vicinity of the danger concerned and the risk is one in respect of which he might reasonably be expected to offer some protection.

Key points

The nature of tortious liability

■ Tortious liability is imposed by the courts and is generally based on fault. Tort damages are designed to put the claimant in the position in which he would have been if the tort had never been committed.

Negligence

■ In order to establish that the tort of negligence has been committed the claimant will need to prove three matters: that the defendant owed him a duty of care; that the defendant breached this duty; and that the claimant suffered a foreseeable type of damage caused as a consequence of this breach.

■ A duty of care will have been breached if the defendant does not take the care which a reasonable person would have taken in all the circumstances.

■ In an action for negligence the claimant can only succeed in respect of a type of damage which was a foreseeable consequence of the defendant's breach. The extent of the damage does not need to be foreseeable.

■ The claimant will only succeed if there is an unbroken chain of causation between the defendant's breach of duty and the damage suffered by the claimant.

■ Claims in respect of psychiatric injury, often known as 'nervous shock', have been restricted by the courts.

■ A claimant will not be awarded damages in respect of pure economic loss.

■ The Law Reform (Contributory Negligence) Act 1945 allows the court to reduce the claimant's damages to the extent that it considers this just and equitable, having regard to the claimant's responsibility for the damage which he suffered.

■ A claimant who, expressly or impliedly, voluntarily consents to running a risk may be defeated by *volenti non fit injuria*.

Negligent misstatement

■ A negligent misstatement can give rise to liability in negligence if there is a sufficiently proximate special relationship between the claimant and the defendant.

■ A suitably worded disclaimer can prevent a duty of care in respect of negligent misstatements from arising.

■ Liability for negligent misstatement can arise in respect of economic loss.

The Consumer Protection Act 1987 Part I

■ The Consumer Protection Act 1987 Part I allows a person injured by an unsafe product to sue the manufacturer of the product, the extractor of raw materials, the person who imported the product into the EC, processors of the product, own-branders or, possibly, others in the chain of supply. A claim can only be made in respect of death or personal injury, or in respect of damage to non-business property which amounted to more than £275.

■ The Act does provide limited defences. However, liability is strict and is not therefore based on fault.

Occupier's liability

■ An occupier of premises has a degree of control over the state of the premises.

■ An occupier of premises owes the common duty of care to visitors, under the Occupier's Liability Act 1957, to take such care as in all the circumstances of the case is reasonable to see that they are reasonably safe in using the premises for the purposes for which they are invited or permitted by the occupier to be there.

■ Under the Occupier's Liability Act 1984, occupiers of premises owe a duty to trespassers if they are aware of a danger or have reasonable grounds to believe it exists, and know or have reasonable grounds to believe that the trespasser is or might come into the vicinity of the danger. The duty of care is to take such care as is reasonable in all the circumstances of the case to see that the trespasser does not suffer injury on the premises by reason of the danger concerned.

Summary questions

1 In *Haley* v *London Electricity Board* [1965] 3 All ER 185 (House of Lords) the facts of the case were as follows. Electricity Board workers dug a 60 foot trench in the pavement and left warning signs at both ends of the trench. They also placed a long-handled hammer across one end of the trench and picks and shovels across the other. One end of the hammer lay on the pavement, the other was hooked on to some railings. These precautions would have been quite sufficient for ordinarily sighted people. But the claimant, who was blind, tripped over the hammer and banged his head on the pavement. The claimant often walked along the pavement in question. As a result of this accident he became almost totally deaf and was forced to retire early from his job. The claimant was not himself negligent, his white stick passed over the hammer. He sued the Electricity Board for the tort of negligence. Government figures showed that at the time of the case about 1 in 500 people were blind.

   a Do you think that the defendants owed a duty of care to the claimant?
   b Assuming that a duty of care was owed to the claimant, do you think that the defendants breached the duty?
   c If a duty was owed and was broken, would the type of damage suffered by the claimant have been sufficiently foreseeable for the claimant to be awarded damages in respect of it?
   d Assuming that a duty was owed, that it was broken and that the type of injury suffered was sufficiently foreseeable, would any defence be available to the Electricity Board?

2 In the school holidays Martha took her two young children, Bill and Jack, to a play-day run by the local authority. After dropping the children off Martha picked up her friend Jill as the two of them intended to go shopping. As Martha's car drove past the play event a large explosion occurred. This was caused because a local authority employee negligently allowed gas to escape from a large container. Martha and Jill rushed towards the scene but were prevented from getting closer than 100 yards by the police who swiftly cordoned off the area. Bill and Jack were both badly burnt in the explosion and died before they reached hospital. Martha, who had always been a cheerful person suffered Post Traumatic Stress Disorder as a consequence of seeing the accident. She also suffered debilitating grief and sorrow. As a consequence she was unable to continue in her job as a teacher. Jill had a long history of nervous disorders. She suffered severed depression which left her

unable to go to work or look after her family. Martha's mother, Mary, watched the local television news and suffered extreme anxiety when she saw the accident. She had not been warned by anyone that the accident had occurred. Since suffering this attack of anxiety, Mary has become agoraphobic and unable to leave her house. Advise the local authority of any liability they might have in respect of Martha, Jill and Mary's problems.

3   John buys a second-hand electric lawn mower from his neighbour. The lawn mower was bought by the neighbour from SupaStores Unlimited one year ago. SupaStores Unlimited bought it from a wholesaler, who bought it from the manufacturer, Supamowers Ltd. The lawn mower catches fire when John is using it. John is badly burnt and so are his clothes. The lawn mower itself is destroyed and John's garden shed, containing all of his tools, is burnt down. Advise John of any claim which he might have against SupaStores Unlimited or Supamowers Ltd. How would your answer be different if John had himself bought the lawn mower from SupaStores Unlimited?

4   Cedric hosts a party at his house to celebrate his 40th birthday. Cedric is a keen amateur inventor. He absent-mindedly leaves his soldering iron turned on in a bedroom when he answers the door to the first guest. Later in the evening one of the newly arrived guests, Cecilia, is told by Cedric to leave her coat upstairs in the bedroom. The light bulb in the bedroom expires as Cecilia switches it on and so the bedroom is in darkness. Cecilia does not see the soldering iron and her hand is badly burnt when it comes into contact with it. Jimmy, who was not invited to the party decides to try and get in via an unlocked window at the rear of the house. The room into which Jimmy gains entry is locked, so Jimmy cannot get into the party. Jimmy turns on the light in this room but is severely electrocuted as Cedric was in the process of rewiring this room and had forgotten to isolate the supply of electricity to it. Advise Cedric of any liability he might have towards either Cecilia or Jimmy.

Multiple choice questions

1   Consider the following statements. Apart from the first one, the statements apply to the tort of negligence.
   i   Liability in contract is generally strict, whereas liability in tort is generally based on fault.
   ii A duty of care will be breached if the defendant did not take the care which a reasonable person would have taken in all the circumstances.
   iii If the defendant caused the claimant's injury while trying to achieve some particularly useful objective, this makes it less likely that a duty of care owed was breached.
   iv If it can be shown that the claimant would have suffered the loss in respect of which he is claiming even if the defendant had not breached a duty of care owed, then generally the defendant will not be liable for the claimant's loss.
   v   Neither reflex actions, nor reasonable attempts to mitigate loss, will generally break the chain of causation which must link the defendant's breach of duty and the claimant's loss.

   Which of the above statements are true?

   a All of the statements.
   b (i), (iii) and (v) only.
   c (i), (ii) and (iv) only.
   d (ii), (iv) and (v) only.

2   Which one of the following statements is not true?

   a The 'egg-shell skull' rule means that a claimant can claim in respect of a loss which was not a foreseeable type of loss if he was particularly susceptible to such losses.
   b A claim for psychiatric injury caused by witnessing injury to others can only be successful if the relationship between the claimant and the injured person was sufficiently proximate.
   c In an action for negligence, damages can be recovered in respect of economic loss which was a direct consequence of a foreseeable type of physical injury or a foreseeable type of damage to property.
   d If a claimant's reasonable attempt to mitigate loss in fact increases his loss, the claimant will be able to recover damages for the increased loss.

3 Which one of the following statements is not true?

   a *Volenti non fit injuria* can be a complete defence. Contributory negligence can reduce the amount of damages to which the claimant is entitled.

   b A claimant's damages can only be reduced on account of contributory negligence if the claimant had some responsibility for the breach of duty which caused his injuries.

   c A claimant will not be defeated by *volenti non fit injuria* if he is injured while making a reasonable attempt to effect a rescue.

   d In certain circumstances the law will, as a matter of public policy, prevent a perpetrator of a crime from suing a fellow perpetrator in respect of actions done while committing the crime.

4 Which one of the following statements is not true?

   a Liability for negligent misstatements is a branch of the tort of negligence, rather than a tort in its own right.

   b Liability for negligent misstatements can only arise where there is a special relationship between the parties.

   c A suitably worded disclaimer can prevent liability for negligent misstatements from arising.

   d A person who acts entirely gratuitously, and who is not even in business on his own account, cannot become personally liable on account of a negligent misstatement.

5 Consider the following statements, which are made in relation to the Consumer Protection Act 1987 Part I.

   i Liability under the Act is strict. A manufacturer of a product can therefore become liable under the Act even if he has not been negligent.

   ii Liability under the Act can arise in respect of any product the quality of which is not such as persons are generally entitled to expect.

   iii A claim for damages under the Act can be made in respect of either personal injury or damage to property, but in either case only if the claim is for more than £275.

   iv A claim in respect of damage to business property cannot be made under the Act.

   v Contributory negligence on the part of the claimant can reduce the damages to which he is entitled under the Act.

Which of the above statements are true?

   a All of the statements.

   b (i), (iv) and (v) only.

   c (ii), (iii) and (iv) only.

   d (i), (iii) and (v) only.

6 Which one of the following statements is not true?

   a Any person with any degree of control over the state of the premises can be an occupier, for the purposes of the Occupier's Liability Acts 1957 and 1984.

   b An occupier who has entrusted work to an independent contractor cannot become liable for damage caused to a visitor by the faulty execution of that work.

   c The Unfair Contract Terms Act 1977 does not apply to the duty of care created by the Occupier's Liability Act 1984.

   d Subject to the effect of the Unfair Contract Terms Act 1977, even a non-contractual notice can be enough to restrict or exclude liability of the common duty of care owed by occupiers to lawful visitors to their premises.

Task 12

A group of American students who are visiting your University, wish to know how the different English torts can be committed. Using a local business as an example, write a report giving details of the following:

   a The meaning of owing a duty of care and breach of duty in the tort of negligence.

   b The extent to which damage caused by a breach of a duty of care must be foreseeable in order to be recoverable.

   c The extent to which a person can become liable for negligent misstatements.

   d The outline effect of the Consumer Protection Act 1987 Part I.

   e The extent to which an occupier of land owes a duty of care to lawful visitors and to trespassers.

Chapter 13

THE LAW OF TORTS 2

Introduction

In the previous chapter we considered the tort of negligence, the Consumer Protection Act 1987 and the Occupier's Liability Acts 1957 and 1984. In this chapter we consider the torts of nuisance, strict liability, trespass and defamation, as well as several minor torts. We also consider the circumstances in which employers can be made vicariously liable for the torts of their employees.

13.1 · Private nuisance

A private nuisance is an indirect unlawful interference with another person's land or his use or enjoyment of his land. For example, if a manufacturing company makes persistent unreasonable noise in a residential area this would be a private nuisance. There is nothing unlawful in the company manufacturing goods. What makes it unlawful, and therefore a private nuisance, is that it unreasonably prevents others from enjoying the use of their property.

As private nuisance is an interference with the use and enjoyment of land, only the owner or occupier of land, with a recognised legal or equitable interest in the property, can sue. The House of Lords confirmed this in *Hunter* v *Canary Wharf Ltd* [1997] AC 655, holding that a person who merely occupied the premises as a home, without a recognised legal or equitable interest, could not sue. However, this ruling may have to be changed in the light of the Human Rights Act 1998. In Chapter 1, at 1.5.1. we said that s.6(1) of the 1998 Act makes it unlawful for a court to act in a way which is inconsistent with a Convention right. We also saw that Article 8(1) gives all citizens the right to respect for their private and family life and their home. This probably means that anyone who occupies a house as their home will now also be able to claim.

A direct interference with a person's land, such as dumping rubbish onto it, would amount to the tort of trespass to land. Indirect interferences, such as noise, are nuisance. However nuisance is by no means limited to noise. Vibrations, noxious fumes, encroaching roots from trees and even the use of premises as a sex shop have all been held to amount to a private nuisance.

A claimant can only bring an action if he suffers some damage. This need not necessarily involve physical injury or damage to property, it can also include the damage suffered by not being able to enjoy using the land.

■ *Leeman* v *Montagu* [1936] 2 All ER 1677

The claimant bought a house in a residential area which bordered on open countryside. The defendant, a poultry breeder, kept a flock of 750 cockerels in an orchard about 100 yards from the claimant's house. These cockerels crowed from 2 am to 7 am. The claimant and his wife had to sleep with cotton wool in their ears and with the windows shut. Even when adopting these measures it was very difficult to sleep. The claimant asked the court for an injunction to prevent the defendant from keeping the cockerels on his land. The defendant claimed that he could not rearrange his farm so as to move the cockerels further from the claimant's house, although there was some expert evidence that this could be done without much difficulty.

Held. The defendant had committed a nuisance and so the injunction was granted. However, the injunction was suspended for one month to give the defendant a chance to reduce the noise.

The law attempts to strike a balance between the different interests of people trying to enjoy the use of their land. Furthermore, to amount to nuisance the interference must be substantial. All users of land must make a certain amount of noise etc. The question is whether this unreasonably prevents neighbours from enjoying the use of their land. What is reasonable will depend upon the area in which the alleged nuisance was committed. In *Sturges* v *Bridgman* (1879) 11 Ch D 852 Thesiger LJ famously said: 'What would be a nuisance in Belgrave Square would not necessarily be so in Bermondsey.'

Noisy manufacturing operations have to be carried on somewhere. If they are carried on in an industrial estate the noise (as well as the smell, vibrations etc.) are unlikely to constitute a nuisance. Similarly, if the defendant in *Leeman* v *Montagu* had kept his cockerels in a completely rural area, the noise they made would not have constituted a nuisance. The frequency with which the interference is caused is also relevant. If a manufacturer conducted a noisy cleaning process once a year this would be more likely to be reasonable than if he conducted it every day.

Claimants who suffer damage only because they are abnormally sensitive are not protected. The interference must be such that it would prevent an ordinary person from using and enjoying his property. In *Robinson* v *Kilvert* (1889) 41 Ch D 88 (Court of Appeal) Lopes LJ said: 'a man who carries on an exceptionally delicate trade cannot complain because it is injured by his neighbour doing something lawful on his property, if it is something which would not injure anything but an exceptionally delicate trade'.

The motive of the defendant may be relevant. If a defendant causes the interference maliciously then this is much more likely to be a nuisance.

■ *Christie* v *Davey* [1893] 1 Ch 316

Much to the defendant's annoyance, the claimant, his next door neighbour, gave music lessons and held musical parties. The music lessons were held for about 17 hours a week and besides the lessons there was often singing and practising on the violin and the piano. Practice on the cello often continued until 11 pm. The defendant's house was semi-detached from the claimant's. The defendant retaliated by blowing whistles, shrieking, shouting, banging trays and hammering whenever there was music played in the claimant's house. This noise often imitated what was being played in the claimant's house. The defendant said that he made the noises solely for his own musical entertainment. The claimant asked the court to grant an injunction to prevent the defendant from continuing to make the malicious noises.

Held. The defendant's actions amounted to a nuisance because they were done maliciously. Therefore, an injunction was granted restraining the defendant from making sounds or noises designed to vex or annoy the claimant.

The tort of private nuisance was recently considered by the House of Lords in the following case.

■ *Cambridge Water Co* v *Eastern Counties Leather* [1994] 1 All ER 53 (House of Lords)

Cambridge Water Co (CWC) claimed damages in respect of the contamination of water available for extraction from their borehole. This contamination was caused by Eastern Counties Leather (ECL) using a solvent while tanning leather about 1.3 miles away from the borehole. The solvent seeped through the ground and was carried by water into the borehole. ECL had carried on business for over a hundred years and generally ran the business well. The particular solvent had been in common use in the tanning of leather since the early 1950s. The solvent had found its way into the borehole as a consequence of regular small spillages. It was not foreseeable by a reasonable supervisor that these spillages would pollute a borehole. Although water from the borehole could not be used as drinking water because it was 'unwholesome' under EC Regulations, it was not in fact injurious to health.

Held. ECL were not liable in either private nuisance or under the rule in *Rylands* v *Fletcher* (which is considered later in this chapter at 13.3).

In the above case, Lord Goff, who gave the only speech, said that the fact that the defendant had taken all reasonable care would not necessarily exonerate him from liability. However, he also said that the defendant would only be liable in nuisance for damage of a type which he could reasonably foresee. This makes liability strict but not absolute.

13.1.1 Remedies

13.1.1.1 Damages

Damages for private nuisance are designed to compensate only for diminution in the value of the land or diminution of the benefits of using and enjoying the land. These damages can cater for lost business. As we have seen, damages will only be awarded in respect of a type of loss which is foreseeable. In *Cambridge Water Co Ltd* v *Eastern Counties Leather plc* the House of Lords held that the *Wagon Mound* test of reasonable foreseeability applied, so that the type of damage in respect of which a claim was made must have been a reasonably foreseeable type of damage. However, if the type of damage was reasonably foreseeable then even a defendant who had taken all reasonable care could be liable. In *Loftus-Brigham and another* v *Ealing London Borough Council* [2003] EWCA Civ 1490 the Court of Appeal held that the rules relating to causation were the same in nuisance and negligence.

13.1.1.2 Injunction

In addition to, or as an alternative to, seeking damages the claimant may seek an injunction to restrain the defendant from continuing to commit the nuisance. As an injunction is a discretionary equitable remedy, it may be refused by the courts even if a nuisance is being committed. It is often the case than an injunction is suspended, to give the defendant a chance to stop committing the nuisance. We saw an example of this in *Leeman* v *Montagu*.

13.1.1.3 Abatement

This is a self-help remedy whereby the victim removes the nuisance himself. It is generally only allowed if it does not involve entering onto the defendant's land. An example is provided by *Lemmon* v *Webb* [1895] AC 1, in which the Court of Appeal held that an owner of land was entitled to trim overhanging branches of mature trees on his neighbour's land, as long as he did not trespass on the neighbour's land and as long as he only trimmed the branches to the extent that they were overhanging his own land. In *Burton* v *Winters* [1993] 3 All ER 631 the Court of Appeal held that the right of abatement could only arise where legal proceedings were inappropriate or where it was necessary to take urgent action.

13.1.2 Defences

13.1.2.1 Statutory authority

If a statute merely permits something to be done, it is presumed that the statute does not absolve a person from liability in private nuisance for doing the thing which the statute permitted. If the statute authorises the act which is alleged to be a nuisance then the statute must be interpreted to see whether liability in nuisance can still arise.

■ *Allen v Gulf Oil Refining Ltd* [1981] 1 All ER 353 (House of Lords)

The Gulf Refining Act 1965 gave Gulf Oil the right to compulsorily purchase land and build an oil refinery on it. The preamble to the Act stated that: 'it is essential that further facilities for the importation of crude oil and petroleum products and for their refinement should be made available'. The statute also conferred powers to compulsorily purchase land. Once the refinery was running a nearby resident said that its noise, smell and vibrations amounted to a nuisance.

Held. The preamble indicated that Parliament had intended that the refinery should be built and had not merely allowed for such a refinery to be built. The statute also expressly or impliedly gave a right to operate the refinery once it was built. Therefore, Gulf Oil were entitled to the defence of statutory authority.

13.1.2.2 Prescription

If a person has committed a nuisance continuously for 20 years, prescription might give him a right to continue committing the nuisance as an easement without redress. (An easement is a property right allowing the land of another person to be used or restricted in some way.) It is not enough that the defendant has been committing the act complained of continuously for 20 years. It must also have amounted to a nuisance for 20 years. It must also have been done without force, openly and without permission.

Sturges v *Bridgman* (1879) 11 ChD 852 (Court of Appeal)

A confectionery manufacturer occupied premises next door to a doctor. For more than 20 years the confectioner had operated heavy pestles and mortars which were noisy and caused vibrations. This did not bother the doctor until he built a consulting room which adjoined the room where the pestles and mortars were used. The doctor then applied for an injunction to stop the use of the pestles and mortars.

Held. The noise and vibration were a nuisance and the injunction was granted. Prescription was not available as a defence because although the noise had been committed for 20 years, the nuisance had not.

13.1.2.3 Consent of the claimant (*volenti non fit injuria*)

Consent of the claimant is a defence to private nuisance. In *Leakey* v *National Trust* [1980] 1 All ER 17 Megaw LJ said: 'While it is no defence to a claim in nuisance that the [claimant] has "come to the nuisance", it would have been a properly pleadable defence ... that the [claimants], knowing of the danger to their property, by word or deed, had shown their willingness to accept that danger.'

So if the claimant consents to the commission of the nuisance then this will give the defendant a complete defence. However, the claimant does not consent merely by occupying or buying land with the knowledge that a nuisance is being committed.

13.2 · Public nuisance

Public nuisance is any nuisance which materially affects the reasonable comfort and convenience of life of a class of Her Majesty's subjects. To commit such a nuisance is a crime. It will also give rise to liability in tort to an individual who has suffered particular damage, that is to say damage of a higher degree than that generally suffered by the class. Physical injury and loss of trade will suffice, but the loss must be more than mere inconvenience. The local council has the power to seek an injunction to prevent a public nuisance under s.221 of the Local Government Act 1971. Individuals have the power to apply for an injunction to prevent a public nuisance, bringing an action in the name of the Attorney General.

Obstructing the highway is perhaps the most common type of public nuisance. Other, more unusual, examples where a public nuisance has been held to have been committed include: permitting travellers to camp near a residential neighbourhood; making many obscene phone calls to a number of women in a particular area; and quarrying to an extent which caused personal discomfort and dust.

A claimant does not need any property interest in order to bring a claim for public nuisance. Nor need the public nuisance arise from the defendant's use of his land. Prescription is a defence to public nuisance. A claim for public nuisance can be for pure economic loss. The defences of contributory negligence and *volenti non fit injuria* are both available.

13.3 · Strict liability (the rule in *Rylands* v *Fletcher*)

Rylands v *Fletcher* is best understood as a special branch of private nuisance. The basis of the tort was explained by Blackburn J in the case itself, which is set out below.

Rylands v *Fletcher* (1866) LR 1 Ex 265 (House of Lords)

The defendant, Mr Rylands, wanted to improve the water supply to his mill. One Lord Wilton agreed that a reservoir could be built on his land. Reputable engineers, acting as independent contractors, were taken on to build the reservoir. The engineers came across disused mine shafts which they failed to seal properly. As a consequence water from the reservoir flooded the claimant's coal mine. The engineers had failed to take reasonable care but the defendant had not.

Held. The defendant was liable for the flooding even though he was not vicariously liable and had not been negligent.

Blackburn J: 'We think that the true rule of law is, that the person who for his own purposes brings on his lands and collects and keeps there anything likely to do mischief if it escapes, must keep it at his peril, and, if he does not do so, is prima facie answerable for all the damage which is the natural consequence of its escape.'

13.3.1 Requirements of the tort

The defendant must bring something on to his land or deliberately let it accumulate there

The tort would not apply as regards things, such as rainfall or weeds, which are on the land without any action on the defendant's part. In *Transco plc* v *Stockport Metropolitan Borough Council* [2003] UKHL 61 considered below, Lord Walker said that the gradual and invisible saturation of the adjacent ground by a water pipe which was not known to be burst could not be described as an accumulation made by human design and so the conditions for strict liability had not been fulfilled. He contrasted the behaviour of Mr Rylands, who had planned, constructed and started to fill his reservoir.

The bringing of the thing onto the land, or the allowing it to accumulate there, must be a non-natural use of the land

In *Transco plc* v *Stockport Metropolitan Borough Council* Lord Bingham said: 'I think it clear that ordinary user is a preferable test to natural user, making it clear that the rule in *Rylands* v *Fletcher* is engaged only where the defendant's use is shown to be extraordinary and unusual.' He rejected a test of reasonable user because a user could be quite out of the ordinary but not unreasonable: 'The question is whether the defendant has done something which he recognises, or ought to recognise, as being quite out of the ordinary in the place and time when he does it.' Lord Hoffmann said: 'A useful guide in deciding whether the risk has been created by a "non-natural" user of land is therefore to ask whether the damage which eventuated was something against which the occupier could reasonably be expected to have insured himself.'

The thing must be likely to do mischief if it escapes

Water, petrol, gas, fumes and explosives have all been held to be hazardous things, which are likely to do mischief if they escape. In *Transco plc* v *Stockport Metropolitan Borough Council* Lord Bingham thought that the mischief test should not be easily satisfied. 'It must be showed that the defendant has done something which he recognised, or judged by the standards appropriate at the relevant place and time, he ought reasonably to have recognised, as giving rise to an exceptionally high risk of danger or mischief if there should be an escape, however unlikely an escape may have been thought to be.'

The thing must escape and cause damage

For example, in *Read* v *J Lyons & Co* [1947] AC 146 (House of Lords) a factory inspector killed by an explosion at a war-time munitions factory did not succeed in an action under *Rylands* v *Fletcher*. The dangerous munitions exploded, but they did not escape from the defendant's premises.

Earlier in this chapter we considered *Cambridge Water Co Ltd* v *Eastern Counties Leather plc* [1994] 1 All ER 53. In this case the House of Lords decided that, as regards *Rylands* v *Fletcher*, the appropriate test on foreseeability is the *Wagon Mound No. 1* test: i.e. was the damage which subsequently occurred of a type and extent which was reasonably foreseeable? If it was not, then damages cannot be claimed in respect of the damage. However, if the type of damage caused was foreseeable then the defendant can be liable for this even if he acted without fault. The case also went some way to classifying *Rylands* v *Fletcher* liability as type of nuisance, rather than as a tort in its own right. In *Transco plc* v *Stockport Metropolitan Borough Council* [2003] UKHL 61 Lord Hoffmann said that the defendant could be liable even if he could not reasonably have foreseen that there would be an escape but that he should be liable only for foreseeable consequences of that escape.

In *Transco plc* v *Stockport Metropolitan Borough Council* the House of Lords thoroughly reviewed the rule in *Rylands* v *Fletcher* and held that it did exist as a tort in its own right. Lord Bingham, who gave the leading judgment, categorised it as a sub-species of nuisance. (Lord Hobhouse as an 'aspect' of the law of private nuisance.) Lord Bingham also said that the claim cannot include a claim for death or personal injury because such a claim does not relate to any right in or enjoyment of land.

The case arose because a local authority was piping a supply of water from a mains supply to a block of flats which it owned when the pipe burst. The local authority had not been negligent. The burst in the pipe was not immediately detectable and this caused a great deal of water to escape so that an embankment became flooded and collapsed. This meant that a gas pipe belonging to the claimant became unsupported, and a claim was made for the cost of carrying out remedial work. The claim under *Rylands* v *Fletcher* failed because the local authority had not brought onto its land something likely to do mischief if it escaped, they were making an ordinary user of the land and they had never accumulated any water. Lord Hoffmann noted that counsel in the case could not find a single case since the second world war in which anyone had succeeded under the rule. Lord Scott said that the essential element of escape was also absent. The water 'began its "escape" on the council's property, accumulated on the council's property and eventually damaged the embankment, also the council's property. It is in respect of damage to the embankment that Transco seek damages'.

The rules on who can sue are the same as those for private nuisance. This should mean that as well as those with an interest in the land, anyone who occupies a house as a home will probably be able to claim, now that the Human Rights Act 1998 is in force. Damages for personal injuries may be recovered only by an occupier of land.

13.3.2 Defences

There are defences to the tort created by *Rylands* v *Fletcher*. However, as we have seen, the defendant can be liable without having been negligent although the type of damage caused must have been foreseeable.

The defences are:

(a) That the claimant consented to the defendant bringing the dangerous thing onto his land, or that it was the claimant's fault that the thing escaped.

(b) That the escape was caused by an act of God (i.e. such an extraordinary event that it could not possibly be foreseen and provided against).

(c) That the escape was caused by the act of a stranger. The stranger must not be an employee of, or an independent contractor working for, the defendant.

(d) Statutory authority.

(e) Contributory negligence.

13.4 · Trespass to land

Any unauthorised direct interference with another person's land will amount to trespass to land. This is the case whether the interference was intentional or negligent. The tort can be committed not only by persons entering another's land, but also by depositing things onto it. If, for example, a business deposits rubbish onto someone else's land this will be a direct invasion of the land and will therefore amount to trespass to land.

Trespass can be committed underneath the ground or in the airspace above the land. Without the defence given by statutory authority, aeroplanes would commit trespass when they flew above a person's land and mining companies would commit a trespass when they mined underneath it.

Trespass is actionable without proof of damage. However, unless some damage has been caused the amount of damages will be nominal. An injunction could be gained to prevent repeated trespass from continuing. The landowner may use reasonable force to eject a trespasser, but not once the trespasser has secured occupation of the land. Section 61 of the Criminal Justice and Public Order Act 1994 allows the police to remove squatters from land in certain circumstances.

Statutory authority and permission to enter the land are both defences to trespass to land.

The distinctions between trespass to land, private nuisance and *Rylands* v *Fletcher* are somewhat arbitrary. To summarise, to be liable under *Rylands* v *Fletcher* a dangerous thing brought on to the land, or allowed to accumulate there, must **escape** from the land. Private nuisance is an **indirect** interference with another's use and enjoyment of his land. Trespass to land is a **direct** invasion of another person's land.

13.5 · Trespass to the person

There are three forms of trespass to the person.

Battery is the direct infliction of unlawful force on another person, without that person's consent. The force must be inflicted intentionally. So if a night club bouncer unlawfully punched a customer this would amount to battery.

Assault occurs when a person is directly and reasonably made to feel frightened that he is about to be immediately battered. This must be done intentionally. For example, it would be an assault for a security guard to point a loaded gun at a person, making the person believe that he was about to be shot. An assault can be committed by words alone. On the other hand, words may prevent an assault from having been committed. For example, in *Tuberville* v *Savage* (1669) 1 Mod Rep 3 the defendant put his hand on his sword in a way that might well have constituted assault. However, as he said, 'If it were not Assize time I would not take such words from you,' no assault was committed.

False imprisonment consists of wrongfully depriving another person of his personal liberty, either intentionally or negligently. It is not necessary that the claimant is locked up. If a shop prevents a customer from leaving the premises, in the mistaken belief that the customer has been shoplifting, this would amount to false imprisonment. In *Thompson* v *Metropolitan Police Commissioner* [1998] QB 498 the Court of Appeal indicated that, as a rough guide, the first hour of false imprisonment might give rise to damages of £500, the first 24 hours might give rise to £3 000 and that the amount payable for subsequent days should reduce progressively.

Assault and battery are also crimes; false imprisonment is not. These torts are of little significance in a business context.

13.6 · Trespass to goods

A person commits **conversion**, a form of trespass to goods, if he intentionally deals with goods in a way which is inconsistent with the right of another to possess those goods. Usually the person suing will be the owner of the goods. A person whose goods are damaged or destroyed can sue the perpetrator for conversion.

A person can be liable for conversion even though he has acted innocently. He must intend to deal with the goods, but does not need to know that this is denying another the lawful right to possession of the goods. For example, if a thief steals a car and sells it to an innocent purchaser, this innocent purchaser will be liable in conversion even though he did not know that the car was stolen. He will therefore have to return the car to its owner and might also be liable in damages. In Chapter 8 at 8.2.1 we considered the case of *Rowland* v *Divall* and saw that Lord Atkin explained that a person innocently coming into possession of a stolen car would be liable in conversion to its true owner.

Section 2(2) of the Torts (Interference with Goods) Act 1977 provides that a bailee is to be regarded as having committed conversion in respect of loss or damage to goods which he has allowed to happen in breach of his duty to his bailor. As we saw in Chapter 9 at 9.1.4, a bailee consents to take possession of goods which he does not own. So a person who borrows a book from a library is a bailee. If such a person allows the book to be damaged he will be liable to the library in conversion.

Conversion may be committed in various other ways, such as destroying or damaging goods, wrongfully using goods, wrongfully taking possession of them, wrongfully disposing of them or wrongfully refusing to surrender them to the person entitled to possession of them. In *Vine* v *Waltham Forest London Borough Council* [2000] 1 WLR 2383 the Court of Appeal held that wheel-clamping a car amounted to trespass to goods unless it could be proved that the owner of the car had consented to the risk of the car being clamped or willingly assumed that risk. The person doing the clamping would be liable to the owner of the car unless he could show that the owner both saw and understood a notice warning that the car might be clamped. This was the case even where the car was committing an act of trespass to land. In the case the recorder had found that the owner of the car had not seen the signs warning that cars might be clamped because the signs were not particularly well displayed and the car owner had been in a very distressed condition at the time. The Court of Appeal found that if notices were displayed where they were bound to be seen the normal inference would be that they had been seen. The claimant had had to pay £105 for the release of her car and a £3.68 administration fee for the use of her credit card. She was awarded damages of £108.68 plus interest, and £5 in respect of the loss of use of her car. However, she was not awarded the exemplary damages she had claimed.

Damages are available for conversion, generally being the market value of the goods or, if the goods are returned, the loss caused to the claimant by not having had possession of the goods. It is also possible that a restitutionary claim can be made in respect of the advantage which the defendant gained by his possession of the goods. Consequential losses are also recoverable.

Section 3 of the Torts (Interference with Goods) Act 1977 allows the court to make an order for delivery of the goods to the person entitled to possession, either instead of or in addition to the payment of damages.

Test your understanding

1 What is the tort of private nuisance?

2 As regards private nuisance, to what extent does the defendant have to have been negligent and to what extent does the damage caused have to have been foreseeable?

3 What remedies are available in respect of private nuisance?

4 What is the tort of public nuisance?

5 What is the tort of strict liability, as set out in *Rylands* v *Fletcher*?

6 What is trespass to land?

7 What are the three forms of trespass to the person and how might they be defined?

8 What is the tort of conversion?

Answers

1   A private nuisance is an indirect unlawful interference with another person's land or his use or enjoyment of his land.

2   The tort can be committed even if the defendant does not act negligently, but an action can only be brought in respect of a type of damage which was a foreseeable consequence of the nuisance.

3   Damages or an injunction will be the usual remedies. Abatement of the nuisance is a possibility.

4   Public nuisance is very hard to define. It has, however, been defined as any nuisance which materially affects the reasonable comfort and convenience of life of a class of Her Majesty's subjects.

5   The tort of strict liability is committed by allowing a dangerous thing, which has deliberately been brought on to the defendant's land or allowed to settle there, to escape. The defendant can be liable for damage caused by this escape even if he has not been negligent. However, damages can only be recovered in respect of losses which are a foreseeable type of consequence.

6   Trespass to land is an unauthorised, direct interference with another person's land.

7   The three forms of trespass to the person are: battery, the direct and intentional infliction of unlawful force on another person; assault, directly and reasonably making another feel frightened that he is about to be immediately battered; and false imprisonment, wrongfully depriving another person of his personal liberty.

8   The tort of conversion is committed by intentionally dealing with goods in a way which is inconsistent with the right of another to possess those goods. It is not necessary that the defendant should know that another has the right to possess the goods.

13.7 · Defamation

Defamation occurs when the defendant publishes a statement which either lowers the claimant in the estimation of right-thinking people generally or causes the claimant to be shunned and avoided.

If the publication is in some permanent form, such as writing, the defamation will be libel. If the publication has no permanent form, as in the case of mere spoken words, the defamation will be slander. In *Monson* v *Tussauds Ltd* [1894] 1 QB 671 at 692 Lopes LJ said: 'Libels are generally in writing or printing, but this is not necessary; the defamatory matter may be conveyed in some other permanent form. For instance, a statue, a caricature, an effigy, chalk marks on a wall, signs or pictures may constitute a libel.'

Statements of opinion can amount to defamation. Both trading companies and living people can be defamed. A statement which does not directly cause people to think less of the claimant can be defamatory if reasonable people would infer something against the claimant. Sometimes the claimant can establish that the statement, although not defamatory to most reasonable people, was defamatory to those with special knowledge. When the claimant pleads this type of special knowledge this is known as innuendo. The drawback to pleading innuendo is that the damages are likely to be reduced because the claimant has been defamed only as regards people who understood the innuendo.

In defamation cases in which there is a jury, the judge first decides whether or not the defendant's statement is capable of being defamatory and the jury then decide whether or not it actually is defamatory. However, many cases are tried without a jury as this substantially reduces costs. In defamation proceedings Legal Aid is not available to either defendant or claimant.

The defendant does not need to intend to defame or even know that his statement is defamatory. Although the claimant does not need to be mentioned in the statement, words can be defamatory only if they are understood to be published about the claimant. A statement cannot be defamatory unless it was published. However, in this context publishing merely means making the statement known to one person other than the claimant. This could be done, for example, by dictating a letter to a typist. As regards the creator of the statement, liability is strict and neither a worthy motive nor a belief that the statement was true are relevant.

Libel is the more serious form of defamation and is always actionable without proof of actual damage (actionable *per se*). Slander is generally not actionable unless actual damage can be proved.

However, slander is actionable *per se* in the following circumstances: where it clearly and unambiguously imputes that the claimant has committed an imprisonable crime; if it disparages (damages the reputation of) the claimant in any office, profession, calling, trade or business held by the claimant at the time of publication; if it imputes that the claimant is currently suffering from a contagious disease to which a stigma is attached; or if it imputes that a woman is not chaste or has committed adultery. The last two of these exceptions are in modern times of much reduced significance. Where it is necessary to prove actual damage the *Wagon Mound* test on remoteness of damage applies. Therefore, the claimant can claim only for a type of loss which was a reasonably foreseeable consequence of the defendant's act.

13.7.1 Defences

13.7.1.1 Consent of the claimant

A claimant who consented to the publication, expressly or impliedly, cannot sue for defamation.

13.7.1.2 Justification

It is a complete defence for the defendant to prove that the statement was true. This is the case even if the statement was made maliciously.

13.7.1.3 Innocent publication

Section 1 of the Defamation Act 1996 provides a defence to a distributor, who was not the author, editor or publisher of the defamatory statement, if he took reasonable care in relation to its publication and did not have reason to believe that his actions caused or contributed to the publication of the defamatory matter. For the purposes of s.1 of the Act, organisations which sell access to the Internet are not 'publishers' of material posted on the Internet by their customers.

Godfrey v Demon Internet Ltd [2001] QB 201

The defendants, Internet service providers, received and stored on their news server an article which defamed the claimant. The defendants did not know who had posted the article. The claimants told the defendants that the article was defamatory and asked them to remove it. The defendants did not remove the article and so it remained on the Internet until it automatically expired ten days later. When sued for libel, the defendants relied on s.1 of the Defamation Act 1996.

Held. The defence was not available because once the defendants had been informed of the defamatory material, and had chosen not to remove it, they could no longer claim that they had taken all reasonable care in relation to the publication. Nor could they claim that their actions did not cause or contribute to the defamatory matter.

So once it has been pointed out to an Internet service provider that material which they publish is defamatory, they will have to remove the material immediately in order to escape liability.

13.7.1.4 Offer of amends

Sections 2–4 of the Defamation Act 1996 allow a defendant who did not know, and had no reason to believe, that his statement referred to the claimant and defamed him to offer to make amends. There are four requirements:

(a) the offer must be in writing;
(b) it must correct and apologise for the original statement;
(c) it must offer to publish the correction and apology; and
(d) it must also offer to compensate the claimant and pay his legal expenses.

If the claimant accepts the offer of amends then no action can later be brought in respect of the defamatory statement. If the claimant does not accept the defendant can raise the offer of amends as a defence.

13.7.1.5 Absolute privilege

Absolute privilege allows for statements made in certain contexts to be immune from liability for defamation. The contexts are: Parliamentary proceedings; communications between high ranking civil servants; statements made in court cases; fair and accurate reports of court proceedings; and some solicitor–client communications.

13.7.1.6 Qualified privilege

Qualified privilege is not an absolute defence but it can be a defence as long as the statement was not published with malice. The defence applies where the defendant has a duty or an interest to pass on information about the claimant to a third party and the third party has a duty or an interest to receive the information. An example would be passing information to the police to help detect a crime.

13.7.1.7 Fair comment

A person who acted without malice can have a defence of fair comment when commenting on matters of public interest. The comment must be based on true facts, must be fair and made without malice.

13.7.2 Remedies

13.7.2.1 Damages

Damages for defamation are designed to compensate the claimant for loss of reputation. It follows that a defendant who already had a poor reputation is unlikely to receive as much in damages as a person who had a good reputation. In cases heard before a jury it is the jury which sets the level of damages and this has led to some very high awards being made. (However, the Court of Appeal has the power to reduce any award to the amount which seems proper.) The way in which the statement was published and the extent of the publication will be relevant factors in quantifying damages.

13.7.2.2 Injunction

A defendant may seek an injunction to prevent further publication of a defamatory statement.

13.8 · Vicarious liability

A person who is vicariously liable takes the blame for the fault of someone else. The concept is an ancient one. In the Middle Ages if a royal schoolboy misbehaved, his 'whipping boy' was punished.

These days vicarious liability is placed on employers. They are vicariously liable for employees who commit torts during the course of their employment. So if an employee, while performing his work, injures another person then both the employee and his employer will be liable. The employee will be personally liable and the employer will be vicariously liable.

The injured person is likely to sue the employer rather than the employee. (The employer ought to be insured, and should therefore have the assets to pay any damages awarded.)

Vicarious liability will only arise if two conditions are satisfied:

(a) the relationship between the worker and the person for whom the work was done was that of employer and employee; and

(b) the employee committed the tort during the course of his employment.

The distinction between employees and independent contractors is essentially a matter of employment law and is considered in Chapter 20 at 20.1. Here, therefore, we need only consider the circumstances in which an employee can be taken to have been acting in the course of his employment. One point which is not considered in Chapter 20 is which of the employers will be vicariously liable when one employer 'lends' an employee to another employer. In *Mersey Docks & Harbour Board* v *Coggins and Griffiths (Liverpool) Ltd* [1946] 2 All ER 345 the House of Lords held that there is a strong presumption that the lending employer will retain liability. This presumption can be displaced if it can be shown that the employer to whom the employee was lent did in fact have sufficient control of the employee.

13.8.1 When is an employee acting in the course of his employment?

Employers are only liable for the torts of their employees if these torts were committed in the course of the employee's employment. If a bus driver, for example, crashes a bus while at work, the bus company will be liable to people who are injured. If the same driver crashes his own car while driving to the supermarket the bus company will not be liable.

In many cases, as with the bus driver in the example above, it is easy to tell whether or not an employee is acting in the course of his employment. In other cases it is not so easy, and over the years the courts have developed the following rules.

An employee will be acting in the course of his employment when he is doing what he is expressly or impliedly authorised to do

Poland v *John Parr and Sons* [1927] 1 KB 236 (Court of Appeal)

A carter who was employed by the defendants was on his way home for his dinner at midday. He was walking close behind a wagon carrying five tons of bagged sugar which was being driven by one of his employers. A boy was walking beside the wagon and had one of his hands on a bag of sugar. The carter thought that the boy was stealing sugar and hit him on the back of his neck. The boy fell beneath the wheel of the wagon and his foot was injured.

Held. The employer was vicariously liable. The employee had implied authorisation to take reasonable actions to protect the employer's property.

If an employee is authorised to do an act properly then the employer will be liable if the employee performs the act negligently

This is obviously the case. If all employees performed their duties properly then it would be most unusual for cases of vicarious liability ever to arise. It is when employees perform their duties negligently that accidents happen.

Century Insurance Co v *Northern Ireland Road Traffic Board* [1942] AC 509 (House of Lords)

The driver of a petrol tanker, while emptying his tanker, lit a cigarette and threw away the match. The match set fire to material on the ground and the fire spread to a manhole into which the petrol was being emptied. The owner of the garage used a fire extinguisher to try to put the fire out. The delivery driver drove the tanker out into the street, without turning off the stop-cock. The fire ran along the trail of petrol until it reached the tanker, which exploded causing damage to the garage owner's car and neighbouring houses.

Held. The employer was liable. The driver was employed to empty his tanker and that was what he was doing, badly, when he caused the explosion.

If an employee commits the tort while doing some act which is designed to help the employer then the employer will be liable

Kay v ITW Ltd [1967] 3 All ER 22 (Court of Appeal)

O, a general assistant in the defendant's warehouse, was authorised to drive trucks and small vans. O was driving a fork lift truck when he found that he could not get into a warehouse because the entrance was blocked by a five ton diesel lorry. This lorry did not belong to the defendants, O's employers. The lorry driver was in the back of the lorry with the claimant, stacking cases. O climbed into the lorry and started the engine so that he could move it and get into the warehouse. O did not appreciate that the lorry had been parked in reverse gear. He did not warn the driver or the claimant of what he did. The lorry jerked backwards and the claimant was injured.

Held. The employers were liable for O's actions. O had been moving the lorry so that he could get the fork lift truck into the warehouse, an act which was clearly within the scope of his employment. He was therefore acting within the scope of his employment when reversing the lorry because his conduct was not so gross and extreme as to take him outside the scope of his employment.

If the employee does something entirely for his own benefit

If the employee does something which is entirely for his own benefit he may be said to be 'on a frolic of his own', in which case the employer will not be liable. (See, however, *Lister v Hesley Hall* [2001] UKHL 22 at 13.8.3 below.)

Hilton v Thomas Burton (Rhodes) Ltd [1961] 1 WLR 705

The deceased and H were employed demolition contractors. They were driven in the employer's van to their place of work, arriving at 7.30 am and leaving at 5.30 pm. Any of the men were allowed to use the van for purposes such as going to get refreshment while at work. On the day of the accident seven men were working about 30 miles from the employer's place of business. At 12.20 the deceased, H and a third man went to a pub for about an hour. At 3.30 the same three men decided to go to a cafe some seven miles distant for tea. As they got near the cafe the three realised that they would not have time to go in because they had to pick up the other workers to return to the employer's premises. On the return journey the deceased was killed, the accident being caused by H's negligent driving. The deceased's widow claimed against the employer.

Held. The employer was not liable because at the time of the accident H was not doing anything which he was employed to do. The men were on a frolic of their own.

13.8.2 Liability for prohibited acts

If the employer prohibits the employee from performing certain acts then generally he will not be liable if the employee ignores the prohibition. But if the employer's prohibition is only as to the manner of performing an authorised act then he will remain liable. Two cases illustrate this distinction. In *Rose v Plenty* [1976] 1 WLR 141 (Court of Appeal) a milk roundsman used a 13-year-old boy to help him on his milk round. The employers had expressly prohibited roundsmen from using young people to help them. The boy was injured as a consequence of the roundsman's negligence and brought an action against the employer. The Court of Appeal held that the employer was liable to the boy. The prohibition was only as to the manner in which the roundsman should deliver the milk and collect the bottles. In *Iqbal v London Transport Executive* [1973] KIR 329 a bus conductor who had been prohibited from driving buses ignored the prohibition and negligently caused an accident while driving a bus. The employers were not liable because the conductor was not authorised to drive buses at all.

If a prohibition as to the manner of performing authorised duties could be used to escape vicarious liability then all transport firms could avoid easily liability for accidents caused by their drivers. They would merely need frequently to order the drivers to obey the highway code at all times.

Several cases have considered the position where drivers are ordered by their employers not to give lifts to people. If the driver does give a lift to a passenger, who is injured when the driver negligently causes a crash, can the passenger sue the employer? In *Conway* v *George Wimpey & Co Ltd* [1951] 2 KB 266 the defendants employed drivers to give their own employees a lift to work and ordered the drivers not to carry any other employer's workers. The defendants were not liable when their drivers ignored this order because the prohibition was not as to the manner of what they were doing but as to the scope. The drivers were doing something (giving a lift to the workers of other employers) which they had been forbidden to do. However, as we have seen, in *Rose* v *Plenty* the employers of a milk roundsman were liable when, in contravention of his instructions, the roundsman gave a lift on his milk float to a boy who helped deliver the milk. The Court of Appeal held that the prohibition was only as to the way in which the roundsman should deliver the milk. It must be said that it is hard to find a great deal of difference between these cases. Perhaps the difference is that in *Rose* v *Plenty* the driver's act of giving a lift to the boy was for a purpose which helped the employer whereas in *Conway* v *George Wimpey & Co Ltd* the giving of the lift did not help the employer at all.

13.8.3 Overtly criminal acts

For most of the last century it was thought that an employer would not be vicariously liable for serious criminal acts committed by an employee. In *Warren* v *Henlys Ltd* [1948] 1 All ER 935, for example, a petrol pump attendant battered a customer whom he thought was trying to drive away without paying and the employer was not vicariously liable. This was because the act was one of personal vengeance rather than one done within the course of the employment.

The House of Lords considered this matter recently in *Lister* v *Hesley Hall* [2001] 1 AC 215 where a warden at a boarding school for children with emotional and behavioural difficulties sexually abused some of the children while they were in his care. The Court of Appeal found that the employer was not liable because the warden's acts could not be regarded as an unauthorised way of doing what he was authorised to do. The House of Lords rejected this and found the employer liable. The abuse of the boys had been inextricably interwoven with the task the warden was employed to do and was so closely connected with what the warden was employed to do that it was fair and just to hold the employers vicariously liable. It was also relevant that the employers should have realised that the risk of sexual abuse by wardens was inherent in the nature of their business. The employer would not have been liable if the abuse had been committed by an employee, such as a gardener, whose work merely gave him the opportunity to be on the premises.

Until recently liability for the fraud of an employee would fall on the employer only if all aspects of the fraud occurred within the course of the employment. So in *Lloyd* v *Grace, Smith & Co* [1912] AC 716 a firm of solicitors were held vicariously liable for the act of their managing clerk who, while conducting a conveyancing transaction, fraudulently induced a customer to sign documents in such a way that she transferred her property to the clerk. By contrast, in *Credit Lyonnaise Bank Nederland NV* v *Export Credits Guarantee Department* [1999] 1 All ER 929 a fraud was committed partly by an employee and partly by a third party. The employee had committed some aspects of the fraud whilst he was at work and other aspects while he was not. The House of Lords refused to hold the employer vicariously liable because not all of the acts which amounted to the tort occurred during the course of the employee's employment. However, in *Dubai Aluminium Co Ltd* v *Salaam and others* [2002] UKHL 48 the House of Lords indicated that this approach was incorrect. Lord Nicholls said that when deciding whether or not an act was done in the ordinary course of an employee's employment the relevant question was not simply whether the employee was authorised by the employer to do the act he did: 'Perhaps the best general answer is that the wrongful conduct must be so closely connected with acts the ... employee was authorised to do that, for the purpose of liability of the ... employer to third parties, the wrongful conduct *may fairly and properly be regarded* as done by the [employee] while acting in the ordinary course of the [employer's] business.'

The question whether or not this actually happened is a question of law, not fact, to be decided with regard to all of the circumstances of the case and previous decisions. Lord Nicholls thought it wrong to say that an employer could not be liable unless all of the acts or omissions which made the employee personally liable took place within the course of his employment. He thought that 'vicarious liability is not imposed unless all the acts or omissions which *are necessary* to make the employee personally liable took place within the course of his employment'. If this were the case, it would not matter that other acts which would have made the employee personally liable were done while acting outside the ordinary course of his employment.

13.8.4 Defences

Both *volenti non fit injuria* and contributory negligence will be available to an employer who is sued on the grounds of vicarious liability. An employer may also be able to claim a contribution to indemnify him for his loss from the employee who caused the accident, under the Civil Liability (Contribution) Act 1978. In practice, such claims are rare.

13.8.5 Liability for independent contractors

In general, a person who uses the services of an independent contractor will not be liable for any torts committed by the contractor. However, liability can arise if the 'employer' authorises the contractor to commit the tort or if the tort is one which can be committed without negligence. We saw an example of such liability earlier in this chapter in the case of *Rylands* v *Fletcher* (1866) LR 3 HL 330. As regards torts where negligence does need to be proved, the 'employer' of an independent contractor will not be liable unless he is himself negligent, for example by appointing an obviously incompetent contractor, or unless the duty delegated was a kind of duty where responsibility cannot be delegated. Statute creates several non-delegable duties which are generally rather technical.

13.9 · The tort of breach of statutory duty

In some cases a statute may impose duties without mentioning sanctions or while mentioning only criminal sanctions. In such a situation a person who has suffered harm as a result of the breach of duty will try to sue in tort. He could either sue in negligence or for the tort of breach of statutory duty. To show the latter he must show that Parliament intended liability in tort to ensue, despite its not having mentioned such liability in the statute.

The principles here are based on a series of presumptions. First, it is essential that the legislation in question imposes an obligation upon the defendant. Second, if the statute provides for some special remedy then it is taken that this excludes the possibility of other tortious remedies. Third, the claimant must show that he was within a class which was intended to benefit from the statute. It is also necessary that the statute indicates that Parliament intended to give a right to sue if the statute was breached.

In the previous chapter, at 12.4, we saw that s.41(1) of the Consumer Protection Act 1987 expressly allows an action for breach of the criminal regulations set out in Part II of that Act. In the absence of such express provisions the courts are not generally inclined to award a civil remedy on the strength of a statute which creates criminal liability. However, they have done so in relation to numerous criminal or regulatory statutes which do not expressly allow for a civil action on the basis that this is justified as a matter of construction of the statutes in question. Contributory negligence is available as a defence.

13.10 · Economic torts

It may be tortious intentionally to harm the business interest of another by an unlawful act. Several 'economic torts' exist to protect business interests. These torts could take the form of interfering with a subsisting contract, intimidation, conspiracy, interference with trade by unlawful means or passing-off. Passing-off is considered in Chapter 15 at 15.4.1.3. Here we need to consider briefly the other economic torts.

13.10.1 Interfering with a subsisting contract

If X intentionally persuades Y to breach his contract with Z, to the detriment of Z, then Z will have an action against X. Liability will arise only if X knows of the existence of the contract between Y and Z and either knows that he is interfering with Z's contractual rights or is reckless as to whether or not he is doing so. Generally, X would commit the tort by persuading Y to breach the contract. However, the tort could also be committed by X entering into a contract with Y in the knowledge that this contract makes Y's performance of his contract with Z impossible. No right of action would arise if X merely persuaded Y not to enter into a contract with Z. Nor would there be a right of action if X's actions merely made a contract between Y and Z less valuable to Z. Z will only be able to bring an action in respect of damage suffered as a result of the interference.

13.10.2 Intimidation

The tort of intimidation might be three-party intimidation or two-party intimidation. If X intimidates Y and intentionally causes him to act to Z's detriment then this is three-party intimidation and Z can have a right of action against X. If X intimidated Y into acting to his own detriment this would be two-party intimidation. Intimidation must involve the threat to do some unlawful act and the threat must be coercive in effect.

13.10.3 Conspiracy

Conspiracy is committed when two or more persons agree to do something with the intention of harming the claimant's business interests. If what the defendants agreed to do was unlawful then they will be liable for harm so caused even if their primary intention was to benefit themselves. If the defendants conspired to harm the claimant by lawful means then the defence of justification will be available if their main aim was to advance their own legitimate interests.

13.10.4 Interference with trade by unlawful means

It can be a tort to inflict harm on the trade or business of another by unlawful means in such a way that the situation is not covered by one of the other economic torts. It seems likely that the tort can protect only identifiable legal rights.

The economic torts are often concerned with the effects of strikes and other activities of trade unions. The law relating to these torts is not particularly clear and it is beyond the scope of this book to examine the torts in any detail.

Test your understanding

1 How is defamation committed?

2 What is the difference between libel and slander?

3 What is meant by vicarious liability of employers?

4 What are the four 'economic torts'?

Answers

1 Defamation is committed by publishing a statement which lowers the claimant in the estimation of right-thinking people generally or causes the claimant to be shunned and avoided.

2 Libel is committed when the defamatory statement is published in some permanent form, slander when it is published in a non-permanent form.

3 Employers are vicariously liable for the torts of their employees which are committed during the course of their employment. This means that although the employee committed the tort the employer can be sued.

4 The four 'economic torts' are: interfering with a subsisting contract, intimidation, conspiracy and interference with trade by unlawful means.

Key points

Nuisance

■ A private nuisance is an indirect interference with another person's use and enjoyment of his land.

■ Only a person with a legal or equitable interest in land can sue in private nuisance.

■ Damages for private nuisance are designed to compensate for the reduction in the value of the land or the dimunition of the benefits of using and enjoying the land.

■ A public nuisance is a nuisance which materially affects the comfort and convenience of a class of Her Majesty's subjects. Public nuisance is also a crime.

Rylands v *Fletcher*

■ A person who brings on to his land, or allows to accumulate there, something which is likely to do harm if it escapes is liable without negligence if the thing does escape and does cause harm. However, damages can only be claimed in respect of a type of loss which was a foreseeable consequence.

Trespass to land

■ Trespass to land is a direct unauthorised interference with another person's land.

Trespass to the person

■ There are three forms of trespass to the person. **Battery** is the direct infliction of unlawful force on another person. **Assault** is directly making another person reasonably fear that he is about to be immediately battered. **False imprisonment** is wrongfully depriving another person of his personal liberty.

Trespass to goods

■ Conversion is committed by intentionally dealing with goods in a way which is inconsistent with the right of another to possess those goods. It can be committed innocently, in that the defendant can be liable even if he did not know of the other's right to possess the goods.

Defamation

■ Defamation is committed by publishing a statement which lowers the claimant in the estimation of right-thinking people generally or which causes the claimant to be shunned and avoided.

■ If the publication is in a permanent form the defamation will be libel, if in a non-permanent form it will be slander. Libel is actionable without proof of damage.

Vicarious liability

■ An employer will be vicariously liable for the torts of employees which are committed during the course of the employment.

■ An employer can be vicariously liable for prohibited acts if the prohibition was as to the way in which the act should be performed rather than as to the scope of the act itself.

■ It is possible for an employer to be vicariously liable for an overtly criminal act of an employee.

■ Generally, a person who uses the services of an independent contractor will not be vicariously liable for torts committed by the contractor while performing the services.

Breach of statutory duty

■ It is possible, if certain conditions are fulfilled, to bring a civil claim on the grounds that breach of a statute caused loss.

Economic torts

■ The torts of interfering with a subsisting contract, intimidation, conspiracy and interference with trade by unlawful means are known as economic torts.

Summary questions

1   The Smalltown Sports Centre was taken over by new owners two years ago. The new owners have considerably expanded the Centre's activities and the Centre now has three times the number of members it used to have. The Centre's car park is not sufficiently large to cater for all the cars of the new members and so they park around the local streets (where parking is permitted). For the past 12 months the Centre has run a monthly football competition which has proved remarkably popular. Generally, about 16 teams take part in these competitions which run from midday until 11 p.m. on a Saturday. Local residents have complained about the noise of these competitions, as several of the teams bring large numbers of rowdy supporters. The buses of these teams have often parked in such a way that they cut off vehicular access to a small group of shops. One of these shops, a small builders' merchant, claims that their trade is well down on days when football competitions are held as customers cannot drive into their car park and the builders' merchants delivery vans have been prevented from making deliveries. Advise the owners of the Sports Centre as to any liability they might have in respect of these facts.

2   Dirty Ltd manufacture pesticides. Six months ago Clean Ltd, a manufacturer of wholefood products, moved to premises adjacent to those of Dirty Ltd. Clean Ltd have encountered the following two problems. First, a barrel containing a toxic chemical rolled downhill from the premises of Dirty Ltd onto the premises of Clean Ltd. The chemical has contaminated a consignment of wholemeal flour. Dirty Ltd claim that they were not negligent in allowing the chemical to escape from their premises, as the accident was caused by a squirrel eating through a cable which secured the barrel in place. Second, Clean Ltd claim that fumes from Dirty Ltd's furnace are being blown towards the warehouse in which they store their raw materials and that if their customers discovered this they might not buy their products. Dirty Ltd reply that they have been emitting the same fumes for 30 years and that any contamination would be so slight as to be incapable of being detected, even by chemical analysis. Advise Clean Ltd of any rights which they might have in respect of these facts.

3   Jim works as a security guard for X Ltd. One night, whilst guarding X Ltd's premises, Jim comes across an intruder. The intruder says that he has accidentally walked on to the premises and offers to leave. Jim is convinced that the intruder is the person who stole X Ltd's safe three months ago. Jim threatens to attack the intruder with a crowbar if he tries to leave. This frightens the intruder who runs away. Jim rugby tackles the intruder and punches him several times. Jim then locks him in a store room while the police are summoned.

When the police arrive, an hour later, it is established that the intruder had been acting innocently throughout. The intruder has suffered a broken nose and his clothes are ripped. What torts might Jim have committed? (You should explain the essential requirements of these torts.) Will Jim's employer be vicariously liable for any torts committed?

4 At the Christmas Dinner of Office Ltd Jan is asked to give a speech celebrating the career of the managing director, Keith, who is retiring. Halfway through the speech Jan breaks into speaking Dutch, a language which the managing director speaks fluently, and says that any success which the managing director has enjoyed has been achieved by personal meanness and by spying on the activities of competing firms. Later that day Keith posts an article on the Internet which says that Jan is incapable of telling the truth and that this condition has been brought about because he is suffering from AIDS. Jan's friend, Lenny, tells Jan about this article. Jan contacted the Internet service provider on whose news server this article had appeared and the provider immediately removed the article. Advise the parties of any torts which might have been committed in respect of the above facts.

5 Mick is employed by Noreen, a business adviser, as an office administrator. Noreen has told Mick that he must never give advice to clients, and in particular must not advise clients on the suitability of investments as he is not qualified to do this. In contravention of this instruction, Mick advises Oliver to invest heavily in Z plc. Oliver immediately does so but loses a great deal of money as a consequence because, as was well known in financial circles, Z Ltd had suddenly been faced with difficulties which looked bound to lead to its liquidation. Mick also cheated Parveen out of her life savings by getting her to sign her house over to Mick as security for a loan. Parveen was at first reluctant to do this but did so after Mick took her to the pub, where an accomplice of Mick's lied to her. Satisfied with what she had heard Parveen returned to Noreen's premises and signed her house over to Mick. Mick, who would have had had authority to take Parveen's house as security for a loan made by Noreen, has now disappeared. Advise Oliver and Parveen of any rights which they might have against Noreen.

Multiple Choice Questions

1 Which one of the following statements is not true?
  a A direct invasion of land would be trespass to land rather than nuisance.
  b The fact that a defendant has taken all reasonable care will not necessarily protect him from liability for private nuisance.
  c A person who takes possession of property knowing that a nuisance is being committed there cannot bring an action in respect of continuation of that nuisance.
  d A nuisance can only be a public nuisance if it affects the comfort and convenience of life of a class of Her Majesty's subjects.

2 Which one of the following statements is not true?
  a A person who has taken all reasonable care can be liable in private nuisance as long as a reasonably foreseeable type of damage is caused.
  b A person affected by private nuisance may always take steps to abate the nuisance, as long as this does not involve the commission of a tort or breaking the criminal law.
  c A person who has committed a private nuisance continuously for 20 years may gain the right to continue committing the nuisance in the future.
  d A claimant in private nuisance must have some interest in land but a claimant in public nuisance need not have an interest in land.

3 Which one of the following statements is not true?
  a A defendant can be liable under the rule in *Rylands* v *Fletcher* only if he brings a thing onto his land or allows it to accumulate there.

b A defendant can be liable under the rule in *Rylands* v *Fletcher* only if the thing brought onto the land escapes and causes damage.

c A defendant cannot be liable under the rule in *Rylands* v *Fletcher* if he acted without fault.

d Trespass to land could be committed by depositing rubbish onto another's land.

4 Which one of the following statements is not true?

a A person can be assaulted without being touched or in any way physically molested.

b A person can be falsely imprisoned without being locked up.

c Wheel-clamping a car could amount to the tort of conversion.

d A person who innocently bought stolen goods would not commit conversion.

5 Which one of the following statements is not true?

a Defamation can be committed only if a defamatory statement is published commercially.

b Libel is actionable without proof of actual damage.

c A claimant who has consented to the publication of a defamatory statement cannot sue in respect of it.

d A person sued for defamation can have a defence if he acted without malice when commenting on matters of public interest.

6 Which one of the following statements is not true?

a An employer can be vicariously liable for the tort of an employee even if the employee was acting in a way in which he had been forbidden to act.

b A employer cannot be liable for an overtly criminal act committed by an employee.

c An employer cannot be vicariously liable unless all the acts or omissions which made the employee personally liable took place within the course of his employment.

d Generally, a person using the services of an independent contractor will not be liable for torts committed by the contractor while performing those services.

7 Which one of the following statements is not true?

a It is possible that a statute which imposes liability, without mentioning sanctions, can be relied upon to bring a civil claim.

b If two or more people agree to do something to harm the business interests of another then they can be liable for the tort of conspiracy.

c A person who persuades another not to make a contract with a third party can be liable to the third party.

d A person who intimidates another into acting to the detriment of a third party can be liable to the third party.

Task 13

A group of American students, who are visiting your University, wish to know how the different English torts can be committed. Using a local business as an example, write a report giving details of the following

a The meaning of owing a duty of care and breach of duty in the tort of negligence.

b The extent to which damage caused by a breach of a duty of care must be foreseeable in order to be recoverable.

c The extent to which a person can become liable for negligent misstatements.

d The outline effect of the Consumer Protection Act 1987 Part 1.

e The essentials of the torts of private nuisance, public nuisance and strict liability as imposed by the rule in *Rylands* v *Fletcher*.

f The extent to which an occupier of land owes a duty of care to lawful visitors and to trespassers.

g The essence of the tort of conversion.

h The circumstances in which an employer can be vicariously liable for torts committed by his employees.

Chapter 14

CREDIT TRANSACTIONS

Introduction

Businesses very commonly arrange credit when supplying goods or services. The Consumer Credit Act 1974 applies to the vast majority of credit transactions and most of this chapter is concerned with setting out the main provisions of this Act. Towards the end of the chapter the more common types of credit transactions are described and analysed.

14.1 · The Consumer Credit Act 1974

The Consumer Credit Act received the Royal Assent in 1974 but due to its technicality and wide aims, it did not become fully implemented until 1985. The Act is extraordinarily lengthy and yet it only provides a framework of the law, leaving the details to be filled in by delegated legislation. As well as regulating the civil law on credit the Act creates 35 criminal offences relating to the provision of credit. Despite its name, the Act is not restricted to protecting consumers. It can also help those who are provided with credit in the course of a business.

Section 189(1), the definition section, defines over 100 words and phrases used in the Act. Most of these definitions are only relevant to certain sections of the Act. However, certain key definitions must be mastered before the Act can be understood.

14.1.1 The key definitions contained in the Act

The key definitions which the Act uses are complex. The most important definition is that of a regulated agreement but, as we shall see, this definition requires us to understand the definitions of three other types of agreements. If the main provisions of the Act are to be understood, the definitions of different types of credit and different types of credit agreements must also be understood. Despite the difficulty involved, mastery of these key definitions is essential to understanding the Act.

1.4.1.1.1 Regulated agreements

In general, the Consumer Credit Act only exercises direct control over agreements which can be classified as regulated agreements. (The rules on extortionate credit bargains are an exception. They apply whether the agreement is regulated or not.)

Section 189(1) gives the following definition:

> '"regulated agreement" means a consumer credit agreement, or consumer hire agreement, other than an exempt agreement, and "regulated" and "unregulated" shall be construed accordingly.'

Before this definition can have any real meaning, we need to define consumer credit agreements, consumer hire agreements and exempt agreements.

14.1.1.2 Consumer credit agreements

Section 8(2) defines a consumer credit agreement as 'a personal credit agreement by which the creditor provides the debtor with credit not exceeding [£25 000]'.

Section 8(1) defines a 'personal credit agreement' as 'an agreement between an individual (the "debtor") and any other person (the "creditor") by which the creditor provides the debtor with credit of any amount'.

In this context an individual is either a living person or a partnership. Companies cannot be individuals. The creditor can either be a company, a partnership or a living person and does not need to be in business. However, if the credit is not supplied in the course of a business the agreement may be a non-commercial agreement. If this is the case then, as we shall see, certain sections of the Act will not apply to it.

Personal credit agreements are consumer credit agreements only if the credit provided is not more than £25 000. This figure relates solely to credit provided. It would not include any deposit or any interest on the credit. For example, if a farmer takes a combine harvester on hire purchase for £35 000, putting down a deposit of £5 000 and paying a total of £5 000 interest the agreement is still a consumer credit agreement. The credit provided to the farmer is £25 000. Credit is defined by s.9(1) as including 'a cash loan and any other form of financial accommodation'. However, to be within the Act the deferment of payment must have been contractual and so some consideration must have been given in return for it.

In the following landmark case the House of Lords considered whether a form of short-term car hire, which was available to motorists whose cars had been damaged by the fault of another, was a consumer credit agreement.

■ *Dimond v Lovell* [2000] 2 All ER 897 (House of Lords)

Mr Lovell ran into Mrs Dimond's car. Although Mrs Dimond's car was damaged, it could still be driven. Mrs Dimond's husband arranged for a garage to repair the car. Mrs Dimond's insurance broker advised her to hire a car from 1st Automotive Ltd until the repairs were completed. 1st Automotive specialised in hiring cars to accident victims. It would collect the money later from the insurers of the negligent car owner. The owner of the damaged car would be under no liability at any time, as the car hire company would not pursue them for money, even if they failed to collect from the insurance company. The charges were quite high, at £30 a day. The hire agreement could not last for more than 28 days. Mr Lovell's insurers, CIS, accepted that the accident was Mr Lovell's fault but refused to pay the hire car charges. They argued that as the agreement for the hire of the car was a regulated agreement under the Consumer Credit Act, it was unenforceable because the Act's requirements relating to the entry into regulated agreements had not been complied with. Section 65(1) of the Act provides that an improperly executed regulated agreement is enforceable against the debtor or hirer on an order of the court only. (See below at 14.1.3.6.) Such a court order had not been made. The agreement was not a consumer hire agreement because under the terms of the contract of hire it was not capable of running for more than 28 days. (See the definition of a consumer hire agreement in s.15, set out immediately below this case.) The issue for the House of Lords was then whether or not the agreement was a consumer credit agreement. This involved deciding whether or not the agreement was a personal credit agreement, as defined by s.8(1). Examining this definition and the definition of credit set out in s.9(1), the question to be asked was whether 1st Automotive supplied Mrs Dimond with credit. The standard form contract of hire made references to the 'credit allowed', a 'credit facility', and allowing the hirer 'credit'.

Held. The agreement was a 'personal credit agreement', and therefore a consumer credit agreement and therefore a regulated agreement. As it had not been entered into in the manner required by the Act it was unenforceable. Mrs Dimond had been given credit because she had been given the hire of the car and if there had been no credit she would have been required to pay for it during the contract of hire or at the end of that contract.

COMMENT (i) 1st Automotive could have made the agreement an exempt agreement by requiring that fewer than four payments should be made by the hirer of the car within a 12-month period beginning with the date of the agreement. (See exempt agreements below.)

(ii) For the reasons why the agreement was improperly executed, see below at 14.1.3.

(iii) Mrs Dimond appeared to be unjustly enriched. She did not have to pay for the hired car. If such a payment had been made it would have been paid out of the money recovered from CIS, and this would have been Mrs Dimond's money. However, statute had said that improperly executed agreements were to be unenforceable and in the face of such plain words a common law theory against unjust enrichment could not prevent the agreement from being unenforceable.

(iv) Lord Hobhouse of Woodborough made the point that the fact that payment under a contract has been deferred will not necessarily mean that credit has been granted. In commercial contracts payment might be deferred for reasons other than providing credit, for example as security for the performance of some other obligation by the creditor.

(v) The proceedings were brought by 1st Automotive Ltd, in Mrs Dimond's name.

14.1.1.3 Consumer hire agreements

Section 15 provides us with the following definition:

'(1) A consumer hire agreement is an agreement made by a person with an individual (the "hirer") for the bailment … of goods to the hirer, being an agreement which –
   (a) is not a hire-purchase agreement, and
   (b) is capable of subsisting for more than three months, and
   (c) does not require the hirer to make payments exceeding [£25 000].
(2) A consumer hire agreement is a regulated agreement if it is not an exempt agreement.'

To qualify as a consumer hire agreement the agreement must be **capable** of running for more than three months. However, there is no minimum time for which the agreement must actually run. The hirer might end up paying more than £25 000 and yet the agreement still qualify as a consumer hire agreement. However, if the hirer is **required** to pay more than £25 000 the agreement cannot be a consumer hire agreement. An exempt agreement can be a consumer hire agreement, but it cannot be a regulated agreement. Hire-purchase agreements are not consumer hire agreements because they are consumer credit agreements.

14.1.1.4 Exempt agreements

An exempt agreement will not be a regulated agreement. Exempt agreements are defined by the very lengthy s.16 of the Act and by delegated legislation. We can summarise the combined effect of s.16 and the delegated legislation by saying that the following types of agreements would be exempt agreements.

(a) Mortgages given on land, provided that they are given by a local authority or by a non-profit making organisation, such as a building society or by one of the major High Street banks.

(b) Debtor–creditor agreements where the rate of interest is either lower than 13% or lower than 1% above the base rate of the London Clearing Banks and the credit is offered to only a limited class of individuals, such as employees, and not to the public generally.

(c) Fixed-sum debtor–creditor–supplier agreements, other than a conditional sale or hire-purchase agreements, where the number of payments within 12 months of the date of the agreement does not exceed four, where these payments are required to be made within a 12-month period from the date of the agreement.

(d) Purchases made on a credit card which require the debtor to settle the account in full with one payment within a certain time. A purchase with an American Express credit card would therefore be exempt as this is the way that American Express cards operate. However, a purchase made with an Access card or a Barclaycard would not be an exempt agreement because the holders of Access cards and Barclaycards do not have an obligation to settle the account with one payment within a given period.

Figure 14.1 might be helpful in understanding the undoubted complexity of the definition of a regulated agreement.

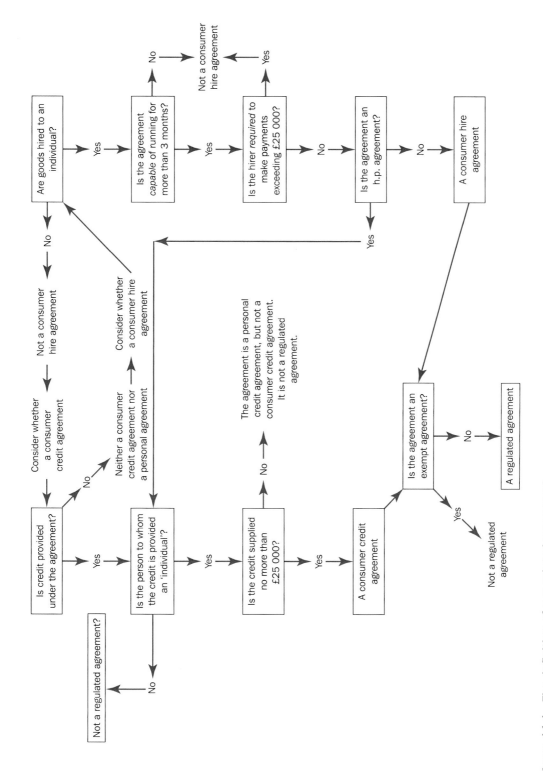

Figure 14.1 The definition of a regulated agreement

14.1.1.5 Running-account credit and fixed-sum credit

Fixed-sum credit differs from running-account credit in that the amount of credit is either fixed at the beginning of the agreement or can be calculated by reference to the agreement. A bank loan of £1000 would be a fixed sum credit agreement. A fixed-sum credit agreement will be discharged once the credit has been repaid.

Running-account credit is provided under a master agreement which is made at the outset. This master agreement allows for separate contracts to be made under it. Running-account credit can continue indefinitely. A credit limit will be agreed, but as the contracts are separate the rate of interest cannot be determined in advance. The debtor will make payments periodically, which will be deducted from the amount of credit outstanding. A bank credit card, such as an Access card or a Barclaycard, provides running-account credit. All credit other than running-account credit is fixed-sum credit.

A fixed-sum credit agreement will be regulated if the credit fixed is less than £25000. A running-account credit agreement will be regulated if the credit limit is fixed at £25000 or less. The fact that a term of a running-account credit agreement allows the maximum credit to exceed £25000 will not prevent the agreement from being a regulated agreement if the agreement only allows for this to happen temporarily (s.10(2)). Where there is no credit limit, or where the credit limit is over £25000, a running-account credit agreement will still be a regulated agreement if:

(a) it is not possible for the debtor to draw an amount exceeding £25000 at any one time; or
(b) the rate of interest goes up, or some other condition favourable to the creditor comes into operation, on account of the credit balance having exceeded a figure of £25000 or less; or
(c) at the time the agreement is made it is probable that the amount of credit will not at any time exceed £25000.

(Section 10(3).)

14.1.1.6 Restricted-use credit and unrestricted-use credit

Credit is restricted-use where it is transferred directly from the creditor to the supplier of the goods or services being acquired by the debtor. The credit is also restricted-use if the creditor and the legal supplier of the goods or services are the same person. For example, in *Dimond* v *Lovell* 1st Automotive Services Ltd provided Mrs Dimond with both the hired car and the credit. Contracts of hire-purchase, conditional sale agreements and credit card transactions are examples of restricted-use credit. If the money is actually received by the debtor personally the credit is not restricted use. This is so even if the credit has been granted for some definite purpose and even if the debtor would be in breach of contract if he did not use it for this particular purpose (s.11(3)).

14.1.1.7 Debtor–creditor–supplier agreements and debtor-creditor agreements

When there is no connection between the creditor and the person who supplies the goods or services to the debtor then there is no reason why the Consumer Credit Act should interfere with the contract between the supplier and the debtor. Where there is a connection then the contract of supply is influenced to some extent by the provision of credit and therefore comes within the ambit of the Act. What used to be known as a connected loan is now known as a debtor–creditor–supplier agreement, meaning that either the creditor is the legal supplier of the goods or services, or the creditor has an existing or contemplated future business connection with the supplier. A debtor–creditor agreement is any agreement other than a debtor–creditor–supplier agreement.

Section 12 defines three types of debtor–creditor–supplier agreements. The first definition, set out in s.12(a), covers agreements where the creditor and the supplier are the same person. Examples would be a contract of hire-purchase where the goods are taken directly from the finance company, credit sales, conditional sales and store 'charge cards' under which retailers themselves provide the credit.

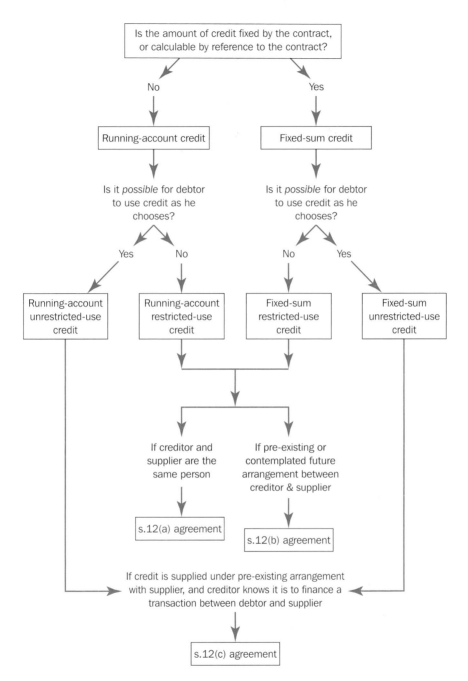

Figure 14.2   Types of regulated agreements

Section 12(b) and (c) embrace loans to the debtor (or payments to the supplier at the debtor's request) made under a pre-existing arrangement, or in contemplation of future arrangements, between the creditor and the supplier. Here there are of course three parties: the debtor, the creditor, and the supplier with whom the creditor has or will have a connection. The main difference between the two is that s.12(b) applies to restricted use agreements, whereas s.12(c) applies to unrestricted-use agreements. Payment for goods with a credit card would be an example of a s.12(b) debtor–creditor–supplier agreement. Examples of s.12(c) debtor–creditor–supplier agreements are uncommon. One example would be the case where a debtor actually receives a loan from a finance company to purchase from a supplier, the finance company having a pre-existing arrangement with the supplier and knowing that the loan is to finance a transaction with the supplier. Generally, though, in this type of situation the finance company would hand the money direct to the supplier, making the credit restricted-use and therefore within s.12(b).

14.1.1.8 Non-commercial and small agreements

A non-commercial agreement is defined by s.189 as 'a consumer credit agreement or consumer hire agreement not made by the creditor or owner in the course of a business carried on by him'. The definition does not specify that the business carried on by the creditor or owner must be a consumer credit business. However, in *Hare* v *Schurek* [1993] CCLR 47 the Court of Appeal held that only consumer credit or consumer hire businesses were included in the definition.

A 'small agreement' is either a regulated consumer credit agreement for credit not exceeding £50, other than a hire-purchase or conditional sale agreement, or a regulated consumer hire agreement which does not require the hirer to make payments exceeding £50. The agreement must be either unsecured or secured only by a guarantee or an indemnity (s.17(1)). Non-commercial and small agreements are exempt from certain of the Act's provisions, occupying a half-way house between regulated and exempt agreements. If the same parties make two or more small agreements, where it appears probable that their intention in doing so was to avoid the provisions of the Act, then the small agreements are regarded as regulated agreements other than small agreements (s.173(b)).

14.1.1.9 Linked transactions

Linked transactions can be taken into account when calculating the total charge for credit. They are also important in respect of the debtor's right to cancel or terminate an agreement. Section 19 of the Act provides a very complex definition. The section could be summarised by saying that a linked transaction is one entered into by the debtor or by a relative of the debtor in relation to an actual or prospective regulated agreement, known as the principal agreement, if any one of the three following conditions is fulfilled:

(a) the transaction is entered into in compliance with a term of the principal agreement, or
(b) the principal agreement is a debtor–creditor–supplier agreement and the transaction is financed, or to be financed, by the principal agreement, or
(c) either the creditor, or the owner or the negotiator initiates the transaction by suggesting it to the debtor or hirer, who enters into it for a purpose related to the principal agreement.

A linked transaction entered into before the making of the principal agreement has no effect until such time (if any) as the agreement is made (s.19(3)).

Test your understanding

1 What is the definition of a regulated agreement?
2 Why is it necessary to know whether or not an agreement is a regulated agreement?
3 What is the difference between running-account credit and fixed-sum credit?
4 What is the difference between restricted-use and unrestricted-use credit?
5 What is the difference between a debtor–creditor–supplier agreement and a debtor–creditor agreement?
6 What are non-commercial agreements and small agreements?

Answers

1 A regulated agreement is a consumer credit agreement, or consumer hire agreement, other than an exempt agreement.
2 The definition of a regulated agreement is significant because most of the Act's provisions apply only to regulated agreements.

3   Running-account credit is given under a master agreement which allows for separate credit agreements to be made under it. Fixed-sum credit fixes the amount of credit in the agreement or allows the amount of credit to be calculated by reference to the agreement.

4   Restricted-use credit is transferred directly from the creditor to the supplier of the goods or services being acquired by the debtor, or is provided by the supplier. Any credit actually received by the debtor is unrestricted-use credit.

5   Under a debtor–creditor–supplier agreement the creditor is either the legal supplier of the goods or services or has an existing or future contemplated connection with the legal supplier. Any agreement other than a debtor–creditor–supplier agreement is a debtor–creditor agreement.

6   A non-commercial agreement is one made by the creditor or owner otherwise than in the course of a business carried on by him. A small agreement is one where the credit extended is less than £50 or one where the hirer does not need to make payments exceeding £50.

14.1.2 Advertising, canvassing and licensing

14.1.2.1 Form and content of advertisements

The Consumer Credit (Advertisement) Regulations 1989 create three categories of advertisements: simple credit advertisements, intermediate credit advertisements and full credit advertisements. Different rules apply to each category, but it is beyond the scope of this book to examine the regulations in any detail. Where an advertisement in any of the three categories states that a charge on a debtor's home is or may be required, the advertisement must state: 'YOUR HOME IS AT RISK IF YOU DO NOT KEEP UP REPAYMENTS ON A MORTGAGE OR OTHER LOAN SECURED ON IT.' The APR, the Annual Percentage Rate of interest, must be given special prominence in all three types of advertisements. The APR is important because it is calculated according to statutory formulae and debtors can therefore regard it as providing a true reflection of the rate of interest payable. Calculating the APR is often complex and can most easily be achieved by reference to consumer credit tables published by HMSO.

14.1.2.2 Criminal offences relating to advertisements

If there is no cash price for goods supplied on credit then it is not possible to ascertain whether or not a stated rate of credit is true. Consequently, s.45 makes it an offence for an advertiser to indicate that he is willing to provide credit under a restricted-use credit agreement relating to goods or services to be supplied by any person if at the time when the advertisement is published that person is not holding himself out as prepared to sell the goods or services for cash. This offence relates to most advertisements but some mail order firms are exempted.

Section 46 makes it an offence for an advertiser of credit to convey information which is false or misleading in a material respect. Information stating or implying an intention on the advertiser's part is false if he has not got that intention.

If a person offering to provide credit commits an offence under ss.44–46, then publishers, devisers and procurers of the advertisement are guilty of a like offence (s.47). A person charged with an offence under ss.44–46 could rely on the general defence set out in s.168. The person charged would have to prove that he exercised all due diligence and took all reasonable precautions to prevent the commission of the offence. It would also be necessary for him to prove that his act or omission was due to a mistake, or to reliance on information supplied to him, or to an act or omission by another person, or to an accident or some other cause beyond his control. An additional defence is available to publishers, devisers of advertisements and those who procure advertisements if they published the advertisement in the course of a business and did not know and had no reason to suspect that it would be contrary to the provisions of the Act (s.47).

The fact that an advertising regulation has been breached does not affect the validity of any agreement entered into by a consumer (s.170(1)). Nor does it rule out the possibility of an action by the debtor for misrepresentation or breach of contract.

14.1.2.3 Canvassing

Canvassing of regulated agreements off trade premises is defined by s.48 as the soliciting of an individual to enter into a regulated agreement by making oral representations during a visit by the canvasser to a place other than the place of business of the creditor, owner, a supplier, the canvasser or the consumer. However, if the oral representations were made in response to a request made on a previous occasion they will not amount to canvassing.

Section 49(1) makes it an offence to canvass debtor–creditor agreements off trade premises. Section 49(2) makes it an offence to solicit entry into a debtor–creditor agreement during a visit requested by the debtor on a previous occasion unless the request by the debtor was in writing and signed. It is not an offence to canvass a debtor–creditor–supplier agreement, or a consumer hire agreement. However, a debtor would be able to get out of such an agreement under the 'cooling-off period' (considered below at 14.1.4).

The commission of either of the s.49 offences does not affect the validity of an agreement which was canvassed or solicited (s.170(1)).

Section 50 makes it an offence to send circulars offering any form of credit or the hire of goods to minors. Breach of the section does not automatically render an agreement which the minor subsequently enters into unenforceable (s.170(1)).

14.1.2.4 Licensing

The Act lays down comprehensive rules on the licensing of businesses which provide consumer credit or consumer hire and ancillary businesses. The Office of Fair Trading administers the system. It is a criminal offence for a person to carry on a business which requires a licence if no licence has been obtained. Regulated credit agreements made by an unlicensed business will generally be unenforceable against the debtor.

14.1.3 Entry into credit or hire agreements

14.1.3.1 Antecedent negotiations

Antecedent negotiations, which are defined by s.56, can be important in two ways. First, the negotiations may be deemed to have been conducted as the agent of a creditor. This statutory agency is considered below at 14.1.5. Second, antecedent negotiations are important in the context of cancellable agreements (considered below at 14.1.4).

Section 56(1) defines antecedent negotiations as:

'any negotiations with the debtor or hirer –
(a) conducted by the creditor or owner in relation to the making of any regulated agreement, or
(b) conducted by a credit-broker in relation to goods sold or proposed to be sold by the credit-broker to the creditor before forming the subject-matter of a debtor–creditor–supplier agreement within section 12(a), or
(c) conducted by the supplier in relation to a transaction financed or proposed to be financed by a debtor–creditor–supplier agreement within section 12(b) or (c), and "negotiator" means the person by whom negotiations are so conducted with the debtor or hirer.'

Section 56(1)(a), which has significance only in relation to cancellable agreements, is relatively straightforward. The only two parties involved are the creditor (or owner) and the debtor, and the only requirement is that the agreement is a regulated agreement.

A credit broker is defined as a person who introduces individuals desiring to obtain credit to those who carry on a consumer credit or a consumer hire business (ss.189(1) and 145(2)). Section 56(1)(b) includes as antecedent negotiations any negotiations conducted by a credit broker where the credit broker sells or proposes to sell the goods to the creditor, so that the goods can become the subject of a debtor–creditor–supplier agreement within s.12(a). A debtor–creditor–supplier agreement is within s.12(a) where the creditor and the supplier are the same person. An example of such an agreement would be a hire-purchase contract where the debtor, having conducted negotiations with the dealer (the credit broker), takes the goods from a finance company introduced by the dealer.

Section 56(1)(c) makes negotiations antecedent negotiations where the supplier makes the negotiations and where the transaction is to be financed by a debtor–creditor–supplier agreement within s.12(b) or (c). Section 12(b) and (c) encompass loans to the debtor (or payments to the supplier at the debtor's request) made under a pre-existing arrangement, or in contemplation of future arrangements, between the creditor and the supplier. There are three parties involved, the debtor, the creditor, and the supplier with whom the creditor has or will have a connection. Section 12(b) applies to restricted-use agreements, whereas s.12(c) applies to unrestricted-use agreements. An example of s.56(1)(c) negotiations would be a shopkeeper describing goods which the customer then brought with a Barclaycard.

Antecedent negotiations are taken to begin when the negotiator and the debtor or hirer first enter into communication (including communication by advertisement) and include any representations made by the negotiator to the debtor or hirer and other dealings between them (s.56(4)).

14.1.3.2 Withdrawal from prospective agreements

At common law a person can withdraw from a prospective agreement at any time before the contract has been concluded. In the case of a prospective regulated agreement, this common law right is extended by s.57, which provides that if a party does withdraw from a prospective regulated agreement not only is that agreement cancelled, but so are any linked transactions or any other things done in anticipation of the making of the agreement (s.57(1)). A written or oral withdrawal notice indicating an intention to withdraw, however expressed, may be given to the creditor or owner at any time before the agreement is concluded (s.57(2)). A credit-broker or supplier who acted as a negotiator, or any other person who negotiated the agreement in the course of a business is deemed to be the agent of the creditor or owner for the purposes of receiving the notice (s.57(3)). The rights conferred by s.57 apply to all agreements, whether cancellable agreements or not (s.57(4)).

14.1.3.3 Making the agreement

The Consumer Credit (Agreements) Regulations 1983 set out in great detail the information which must be contained in relevant documents, the precise form of statements on debtors' rights which must be included and the precise forms of signature boxes which must be included in the various agreements. It is beyond the scope of this book to consider these requirements. Section 61(1) provides that a regulated agreement is not properly executed unless a document containing all the prescribed terms and conforming to regulations made under s.60(1) is signed by the debtor or hirer and by or on behalf of the creditor or owner. The document must embody all the terms of the agreement, other than implied terms, and all the terms must be readily legible.

14.1.3.4 Duty to supply copies of agreements

An agreement is executed when both of the parties have signed it. When only one of the parties has signed the agreement it is unexecuted.

If an unexecuted document is presented personally to the debtor or hirer for signature he must there and then be given a copy of the agreement and of any document referred to in it (s.62(1)). Later, within seven days of the making of the agreement the creditor or owner must send a copy of the executed agreement, and of any other document referred to in it, to the debtor or hirer (s.63(2)). The agreement will be made once the debtor or hirer has notice that the creditor or owner has signed it. However, if this notice is sent by post then the postal rule will apply to make it effective from the date of posting.

Section 62(2) deals with the situation where the unexecuted document is sent to the debtor, and it has not yet been signed by the creditor. It requires that a copy of the agreement and of any document referred to in it, must also be sent at the same time. Again the agreement will be made once the debtor or hirer has notice that the creditor or owner has signed it, and again s.63(2) will require that within seven days of the making of the agreement the creditor or owner must send a copy of the executed agreement, and of any other document referred to in it, to the debtor or hirer.

If the creditor has already signed a document which is presented personally to the debtor for signature then the debtor or hirer must there and then be given a copy of the executed agreement and any documents referred to in it (s.63(1)). There is no need to send another copy later (s.63(2)(a)). If the document was sent to the debtor or hirer for signature, having already been signed by the creditor, then a copy of the unexecuted agreement and of any document referred to in it must be sent to the debtor or hirer at the same time (s.62(2)). Again, there is no need to send another copy later.

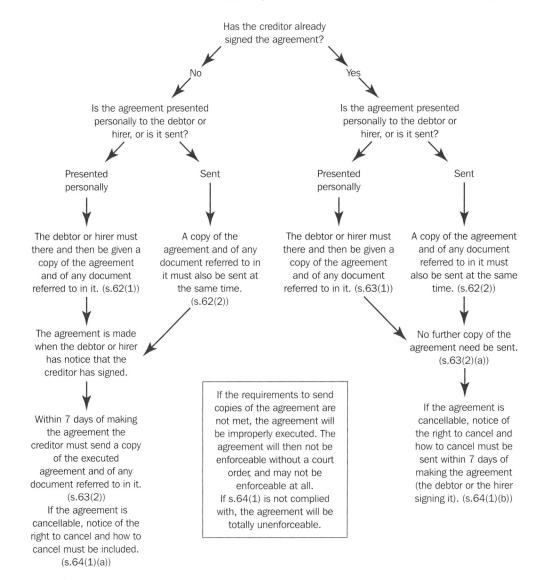

Figure 14.3   Duty to send copies of regulated agreements and cancellation rights

If any of these requirements as to sending copies of agreements are not met then a regulated agreement is not properly executed (ss.62(3) and 63(5)). This can be a serious consequence as an improperly executed agreement is not enforceable without a court order, and may not be enforceable at all.

Sections 62 and 63 are designed to ensure that a debtor knows the terms of the agreement, and is aware of the right to revoke the agreement and the right to cancel the agreement.

14.1.3.5 Duty to give notice of cancellation rights

In the case of a cancellable agreement (see 14.1.4), a notice in the prescribed form indicating the right of the debtor or hirer to cancel the agreement, how and when that right is exercisable, and the name and address of a person to whom notice of cancellation must be given must be included in every copy which is required to be given or sent to the debtor or hirer under ss.62 or 63 (s.64(1)(a)). Such a notice must also be sent by post to the debtor or hirer within seven days of making a cancellable agreement in cases where there is no need to send further copies of the agreement itself (s.64(1)(b)). If s.64(1) is not complied with then the agreement is not enforceable even by court order (s.127(4)(b)). The rules relating to copies of agreements and to notice of cancellation rights do not apply to non-commercial agreements, overdrafts on current accounts, small debtor–creditor–supplier agreements for restricted-use credit or certain payments arising on or connected with a person's death.

14.1.3.6 The consequences of improper execution

An improperly executed regulated agreement can only be enforced against the debtor or hirer by order of the court (s.65(1)). In an application to enforce an improperly executed agreement the court shall dismiss the application if, and only if, it considers it just to do so, having regard to (i) prejudice caused to any person by the contravention in question, and the degree of culpability for it, and (ii) the powers conferred on the court to discharge or reduce any sum payable by the debtor, and its power to impose conditions and vary agreements (s.127(1)).

Earlier we saw in *Dimond* v *Lovell* that the car hire agreement entered into by Mrs Dimond was improperly executed, and therefore unenforceable, even though this meant that Mrs Dimond was unjustly enriched. The House of Lords considered that the document was improperly executed (there was no real argument against this point of view) because the requirements of s.61(1) had not been complied with. A document containing all the prescribed terms and conforming to regulations made under s.60(1) had not been signed by both parties. One of these terms (under regulations made by the Secretary of State) would have been 'a term stating the amount of the credit, which may be expressed as the total cash price of the … services'.

In the following circumstances an agreement cannot be enforced at all, not even by order of the court:

(a) If the debtor or hirer has not signed the agreement, or a document containing all of the prescribed terms (s.127(3)).
(b) The document which the debtor or hirer did sign did not contain all of the prescribed terms (s.127(3)).
(c) If, in the case of a cancellable agreement, the provisions of ss.62 and 63 were not complied with and the creditor or owner did not give a copy of the executed agreement, and of any other document referred to in it, to the debtor or hirer before the commencement of the proceedings in which the order is sought. If the debtor is given a copy late, but before the commencement of proceedings, the cooling-off period will begin at the time when the copy was received (s.127(4)(a)).
(d) If s.64(1) was not complied with. So if the debtor was not sent notice of cancellation rights in a copy, under ss.62 and 63, or was not sent a separate notice of cancellation rights when such a notice was required, then the relevant notice cannot be sent late and the agreement is totally unenforceable (s.127(4)(b)).

■ *Wilson v First County Trust Ltd* [2003] UKHL 40 (House of Lords)

The debtor had taken a loan from a pawnbroker and pledged her car as security for the loan. Section 60(1) CCA 1974 was breached because the agreement which both parties signed did not include a 'term stating the amount of the credit', as required by Schedule 6 para 2 to the Consumer Credit (Agreements) Regulations 1983. (The signed document stated that the amount of credit was £5 000. This did not include a £250 document fee. In the county court it was held that the amount of credit had been correctly stated at £5 000. The Court of Appeal reversed this decision and held that the amount of credit which should have been stated was £5 250.) This omission had not caused any prejudice to the debtor. Section 127(3) CCA 1974 provided that the agreement was totally unenforceable because s.60(1) had not been complied with and no document containing all the prescribed terms had been signed by both parties. The debtor would not therefore have to repay the loan and the pawnbroker could not enforce the security. As a public authority, a court is bound to avoid acting in a way which is incompatible with the European Convention on Human Rights (see Chapter 1 at 1.5). The Court of Appeal therefore declared that to exclude a judicial remedy by virtue of s.127(3) CCA 1974 was incompatible with the defendant's rights under Articles 6 and 1 of the First Protocol to the Convention. The Secretary of State for Trade and Industry made an appeal to the House of Lords.

Held (i) The court had no jurisdiction to make a declaration of incompatibility because Parliament had not intended that the HRA 1998 should operate retrospectively to alter the rights and obligations of parties to an agreement made before the HRA came into force on 2 October 2000.

(ii) Section 127(3) CCA 1974 was not incompatible with Art. 6 of the ECHR (see Chapter 1 at 1.5.2). Article 6 of the Convention did not create civil rights but rather guaranteed the right to have a claim about a civil right heard by an independent court or tribunal. Section 127(3) CCA 1974 rendered some improperly executed agreements unenforceable, but it did not prevent anyone from going to court to find out whether an agreement was enforceable. So s.127(3) was not incompatible with Article 6 of the Convention.

(iii) Article 1 of the First Protocol to the Convention (see Chapter 1 at 1.5.2) gave a right to peaceful enjoyment of possessions and in this context 'possessions' included contractual rights. However, since the agreement between debtor and creditor was unenforceable all along there never were any contractual rights to which Article 1 might apply. For policy reasons (the protection of debtors) Parliament had decided that it was appropriate to render some improperly executed agreements completely unenforceable, even if this meant the unjust enrichment of a debtor at the expense of a creditor acting in good faith. Section 127(3) was a proportionate way to achieve this policy and so it was not incompatible with Article 1 of the First Protocol.

14.1.4 Cancellable agreements

A regulated agreement may be cancelled by the debtor or hirer if the antecedent negotiations included oral representations made when in the presence of the debtor or hirer by an individual acting on behalf of the negotiator unless:

(a) the agreement is secured on land, or a bridging loan to purchase land or a restricted-use credit agreement to finance the purchase of land; or
(b) the unexecuted agreement is signed by the debtor or hirer at the business premises of either the creditor or hirer, or a linked party or the negotiator. (It is where the debtor signed, rather than where the negotiations took place, that is important here.)

Negotiations will not be made in the presence of the debtor or hirer if they are made entirely by telephone.

14.1.4.1 The cooling-off period

Section 68 states that if a debtor or hirer wishes to cancel a cancellable agreement he must serve notice of cancellation between his signing of the unexecuted agreement and:

(a) the end of the fifth day following the day on which he received a copy under s.63(2) or statutory notice of cancellation rights under s.64(1)(b), or

(b) if s.64(1)(b) does not apply (because of regulations made by the Office of Fair Trading under s.64(4)) the end of the fourteenth day following the day on which he signed the unexecuted agreement.

Earlier in this chapter we saw that s.63(2) imposes a duty to send a copy of the executed agreement to the debtor or hirer within seven days of making the agreement when the debtor or hirer's signature did not make the agreement an executed agreement because the creditor had yet to sign it. If the agreement was a cancellable agreement this copy of the agreement would have to contain notice of cancellation rights. We also saw that where the agreement is a cancellable agreement, and where s.63(2) does not apply, notice of cancellation rights must be sent to the debtor or hirer within seven days (s.64(1)(b)). Where the copy or notice is sent late then the cooling-off period does not begin until it is received.

The notice can be served on (a) the creditor or owner, (b) the person specified in the notice under s.64(1), or (c) the agent of the owner or creditor, or a person who carried on antecedent negotiations on behalf of the creditor or owner in the course of a business carried on by him (s.69(1)). Whoever the notice is served upon, it must be in writing (s.189(1)). It can be expressed in any way as long as it indicates an intention to withdraw from the agreement (s.69(1)).

Whether or not it is actually received by him, a notice of cancellation sent by post to a person shall be deemed to be served on him at the time of posting (s.69(7)).

An agreement which is cancelled shall be treated as an agreement which was never entered into (s.69(4)).

14.1.4.2 The effect of cancellation

Once a regulated agreement, or any linked agreement, is cancelled the effect of this is as follows:

(a) Any sum paid by the debtor or hirer, or by his relative, under or in contemplation of the agreement or transaction, including any item in the total charge for credit, becomes repayable (s.70(1)(a)).

(b) Any sum payable by the creditor or hirer or by his relative, including any item in the total charge for credit, ceases to be due. This includes any item on the total charge for credit which would have been payable had the agreement not been cancelled (s.70(1)(b)).

(c) In the case of a debtor–creditor–supplier agreement falling within s.12(b), any sum paid on the debtor's behalf by the creditor to the supplier becomes repayable to the creditor (s.70(1)(c)).

(d) If, under the terms of the cancelled agreement or transaction, the debtor or hirer or his relative is in possession of any goods, he shall have a lien over them for any sum repayable to him under s.70(1) in respect of that agreement or transaction, or any other linked transaction (s.70(2)).

(e) A sum repayable under s.70(1) is repayable by the person to whom it was originally paid. However, in the case of a debtor–creditor–supplier agreement falling within s.12(b) the creditor and the supplier are jointly and severally liable to repay the sum (s.70(3)).

(f) Linked agreements are also cancelled (s.69(1)).

(g) If the total charge for credit included a fee or commission charged by a credit-broker, the credit-broker can retain £5, but must return any excess (s.70(6)).

(h) When a regulated agreement is cancelled, other than a debtor–creditor–supplier agreement for restricted-use credit, the agreement shall continue in force so far as it relates to repayment of credit and payment of interest (s.71(1)). (Where the agreement was a debtor–creditor–supplier agreement for restricted-use credit then the debtor would never have received any money. Obviously in such a case therefore would not have to repay anything to the creditor.) However, if the debtor repays all or some of the credit either before the expiry of one month following service of the notice of cancellation, or before the date on which the first instalment is due, no interest is payable on the amount repaid (s.71(2)). If the whole of a credit repayable by instalments is not repaid before the first instalment, the debtor only has to repay the amount outstanding on receipt of a request in writing in the prescribed form, signed by the creditor or on his behalf, stating the amounts of the remaining instalments, but excluding any sum other than principal and interest (s.71(3)).

(i)   Any person who possesses goods acquired under a cancelled agreement has a duty to restore the goods to the other party, and meanwhile to retain possession of the goods and to take reasonable care of them (s.72(4)). The possessor of goods does not have to return them but only to make them available for collection. The duty to take reasonable care of the goods ends after 21 days unless a written request for their return is received within that period (s.72(8)). Section 72 does not apply to perishable goods, goods which by their nature are for consumption and which have been consumed, goods supplied to meet an emergency, or goods which before cancellation have become incorporated into land or into some thing not comprised in the agreement (s.72(9)).

(j)   If the debtor or hirer gave goods in part exchange then these must be returned to him in substantially the same condition as that in which they were taken within ten days of cancellation, or the debtor or hirer can recover from the negotiator the amount of the part-exchange allowance given (s.73(2)). In the case of a debtor–creditor–supplier agreement within s.12(b) the creditor and the negotiator are under a joint and several liability to pay this sum (s.73(3)). Until the debtor or hirer receives part-exchanged goods, or the amount allowed in part-exchange, he will have a lien on the goods supplied under the cancelled agreement (s.73(5)). This will enable the debtor or hirer to keep possession of the goods until he has received all that he is due.

(k)   Any term in any agreement which attempts to evade the provisions protecting the debtor or hirer is void (s.173(1)).

Test your understanding

1   If an unexecuted agreement is presented personally to a debtor or hirer, what is the position as regards the duty to supply copies of the agreement?

2   What is the position as regards copies of the agreement where an unexecuted agreement is sent to the debtor or hirer for signature?

3   What is the position as regards copies of the agreement where an agreement which has already been signed by the creditor is presented personally to the debtor or hirer for signature?

4   What is the position as regards copies of the agreement where an agreement which has already been signed by the creditor is sent to the debtor or hirer for signature?

5   What is the effect of the debtor or hirer not being given his cancellation rights as required by s.64?

Answers

1   If an unexecuted document is presented personally to the debtor or hirer for signature he must there and then be given a copy of the agreement and of any document referred to in it (s.62(1)). Within seven days of the making of the agreement the creditor or owner must send a copy of the executed agreement, and of any other document referred to in it, to the debtor or hirer (s.63(2)). If the agreement is cancellable notice of the right to cancel and how to cancel must be included in the copy of the regulated agreement (s.64(1)(a)).

2   If an unexecuted agreement is sent to the debtor or hirer for signature, a copy of the agreement and of any document referred to in it must also be sent (s.62(2)). Within seven days of the making of the agreement the creditor or owner must send a copy of the executed agreement, and of any other document referred to in it, to the debtor or hirer (s.63(2)). If the agreement is cancellable notice of the right to cancel and how to cancel must be included in the copy of the regulated agreement (s.64(1)(a)).

3   If the creditor has already signed a document which is presented personally to the debtor for signature then the debtor or hirer must there and then be given a copy of the executed agreement and any documents referred to in it (s.63(1)). There is no need to send another copy later (s.63(2)(a)). However, s.64(1)(b) requires that if the agreement is a cancellable agreement the debtor or hirer must be sent notice of the right to cancel and how to cancel within seven days of making the agreement.

4   Where the creditor has already signed a document which is sent to the debtor for signature then a copy of the unexecuted document and of any document referred to in it must also be sent at the same time (s.62(2)). There is no need to send

another copy later (s.63(2)(a)). However, s.64(1)(b) requires that if the agreement is a cancellable agreement the debtor or hirer must be sent notice of the right to cancel and how to cancel within seven days of making the agreement.

5   If the debtor or hirer is not given his cancellation rights, as required by s.64, the agreement is totally unenforceable.

14.1.5 Liability of creditor for breaches by supplier

Often a debtor entering into a credit deal does not have any contact with the creditor. Section 56(2) helps the debtor by providing that in two and three party debtor–creditor–supplier agreements a person who conducts negotiations on behalf of the creditor is deemed to do so as the agent of the creditor. Section 75(1) provides that in debtor–creditor–supplier agreements where the creditor is not also the supplier of the goods the creditor assumes joint and several liability for breaches of contract or misrepresentations made by the supplier. Both s.56(2) and s.75(1) can provide the debtor with important rights against the creditor.

14.1.5.1 Antecedent negotiations made as agent of creditor

In Chapter 11 we examined the nature of agency and saw that an agent has the power to alter the legal position of his principal. Section 56(2) of the Consumer Credit Act makes a credit-broker or supplier the agent of a creditor in certain circumstances.

Earlier in this chapter we examined s.56(1), which defines antecedent negotiations. Section 56(2) states that:

'Negotiations with the debtor in a case falling within subsection (1)(b) or (c) shall be deemed to be conducted by the negotiator in the capacity of agent of the creditor as well as in his actual capacity.'

So this statutory agency only arises as a consequence of antecedent negotiations which were made within s.56(1)(b) and (c), not within antecedent negotiations made within s.56(1)(a). When examining the definition of antecedent negotiations we saw that s.56(1)(a) deals with the situation where the negotiations are made by the creditor or owner. Obviously there is no need for s.56(2) in these situations.

Negotiations conducted by a credit-broker with a debtor are antecedent negotiations within s.56(1)(b) where they relate to goods sold or proposed to be sold by the credit-broker to the creditor before forming the subject matter of a debtor–creditor–supplier agreement within s.12(a). That is to say, debtor–creditor–supplier agreements where the creditor and legal supplier are the same person. A common example arises when a dealer in goods sells the goods to a finance company which then arranges a contract of hire-purchase or conditional sale with a debtor, who was introduced to the finance company by the dealer.

Negotiations would be antecedent negotiations within s.56(1)(c) if they were conducted with the debtor by the supplier in relation to a transaction financed or proposed to be financed by a debtor–creditor–supplier agreement within s.12(b) or (c). Common examples of this would be a supplier accepting payment for goods by a credit card issued by a third party, or a dealer in goods selling the goods to a debtor for cash which the debtor had taken on loan from a finance company introduced by the dealer. A supplier accepting payment by debit card would not be included, whether or not the customer's account was in credit (s.187(3)(b)).

Section 56(2) only applies to regulated agreements, because the types of debtor–creditor–supplier agreements set out in s.12(a), (b) and (c) are defined as being regulated agreements. Section 56(2) does not apply to consumer hire agreements, even if they are regulated agreements. Nor does it apply to debtor-credit agreements, even if a credit-broker conducted negotiations for the creditor. (Because the credit-broker would be the agent of the creditor at common law.) It is important to remember that in order for s.56(2) to apply there must be existing or contemplated connection between negotiator and creditor or the supplier and the creditor must be the same person.

Liability arising under s.56(2) is additional to any personal liability of the credit-broker or supplier.

Any agreement which purports to avoid the statutory agency created by s.56(2) is void (s.56(3)). Section 56(2) will only create a statutory agency as regards antecedent negotiations which either relate to the goods sold or proposed to be sold by the credit-broker, or which relate to the transaction financed or to be financed by a s.12(b) or (c) debtor–creditor–supplier agreement.

The effect of the statutory agency is that the creditor is liable for any misrepresentations made by the negotiator, the creditor is liable for breach of contract if the negotiator's statements become terms of the agreement, money paid to the negotiator will be regarded as paid to the creditor, and notice given to the negotiator will be regarded as having been given to the creditor.

14.1.5.2 Liability of creditor for breaches by supplier

Where the creditor and the legal supplier are not the same person s.75 provides that a debtor who has a claim for breach of contract or misrepresentation against the supplier has a like claim against the creditor. (It does not apply in cases of hire-purchase where the creditor and the legal supplier are the same person.)

Section 75(1) states that:

'If the debtor under a debtor–creditor–supplier agreement falling within section 12(b) or (c) has, in relation to a transaction financed by the agreement, any claim against the supplier in respect of a misrepresentation or breach of contract, he shall have a like claim against the creditor, who, with the supplier, shall accordingly be jointly and severally liable to the debtor.'

Between them s.12(b) and (c) encompass debtor–creditor–supplier agreements where the supplier and the creditor are not the same person, but have an existing or contemplated future connection.

Section 75(3) limits the effect of s.75(1) slightly:

'Subsection (1) does not apply to a claim –
(a) under a non-commercial agreement, or
(b) so far as the claim relates to any single item to which the supplier has attached a price not exceeding [£100] or more than [£30 000].'

Points to note about s.75(1):

(a) In order for the section to apply the creditor and supplier must be different persons. So where a finance company supplies goods on hire-purchase it will not apply. (This is unlikely to matter much to the debtor. First, s.56(2) of the Consumer Credit Act will help the debtor if the dealer made antecedent negotiations. Second, the Supply of Goods (Implied Terms) Act 1973 will impose liability directly on the finance company if it breaches a term as to correspondence with description.) (See Chapter 8 at 8.4.1.)
(b) The section only applies to regulated agreements. (Because the debtor–creditor–supplier agreements which fall within s.12(b) and (c) are defined as being regulated agreements.)
(c) Section 75 only makes the creditor liable for the misrepresentations and breaches of contract of the supplier if the supplier would himself have been liable. If an effective exclusion clause prevents the supplier from incurring liability for misrepresentation or breach of contract, then no liability will be incurred by the creditor under s.75.
(d) The creditor and supplier are made jointly and severally liable, so the debtor can sue the supplier or the creditor or both. Gaining judgment against one does not prevent an action from being taken against the other. (Civil Liability (Contribution) Act 1978 s.3.)
(e) In order for liability to arise under s.75 the transaction as regards which the debtor is claiming must be the same transaction as is financed by the debtor–creditor–supplier agreement.
(f) Section 75 does not apply to non-commercial agreements.
(g) Section 75 will apply where goods are bought with a credit card, but not where goods are bought with a debit card or with a cheque guarantee card.

(h) Section 75 only applies to claims which are in respect of a single item to which the supplier has attached a price of between £100 and £30 000. If several items costing less than £100 are bought under the same debtor–creditor–supplier agreement s.75 will not apply, even if the total price of all the items is well over £100.

(i) The fact that the debtor, in entering into the transaction, exceeded the credit limit or otherwise contravened any term of the agreement will not prevent the application of s.75 (s.75(4)).

(j) The creditor's liability under s.75 is not restricted to the amount of credit given. For example, let us assume that goods costing £10 000 are bought from a supplier. The purchaser pays £9 500 cash and £500 with an Access credit card. Before delivery of the goods the supplier goes into liquidation. The creditor is liable to refund the full £10 000. The creditor could also incur heavy damages if the goods had been delivered, but had proved defective and had caused serious injury to the debtor. The creditor would be liable to pay contract damages to compensate for the injury.

(k) It is not possible to contract out of s.75's provisions (s.173(1)).

(l) It is the credit agreement which needs to be a regulated agreement, not the contract of supply. The contract of supply could be hire, conditional sale, credit sale or cash sale. However, the creditor and supplier must be separate people.

(m) A creditor who becomes liable under s.75 may have a right of indemnity against the supplier. This indemnity could cover costs reasonably incurred in defending proceedings brought by the debtor. It is possible for the creditor and supplier to contract out of this indemnity.

14.1.6 Credit-tokens and credit-token agreements

The Act does not use the term 'credit card' but makes rules about credit tokens. Section 14(1) defines a credit token:

> 'A credit token is a card, check, voucher, coupon, stamp, form, booklet or other document or thing given to an individual by a person carrying on a consumer credit business, who undertakes –
> (a) that on the production of it (whether or not some other action is also required) he will supply cash, goods and services (or any of them) on credit, or
> (b) that where, on the production of it to a third party (whether or not any other action is also required), the third party supplies cash, goods and services (or any of them), he will pay the third party for them (whether or not deducting any discount or commission), in return for payment to him by the individual.'

A credit-token agreement is a regulated agreement for the provision of credit in connection with the use of a credit token (s.14(2)).

Some cards which are generally known as credit cards fit within this definition and their use will therefore give rise to a credit-token agreement. However this is not true of all such cards.

(a) **Credit cards,** such as Access cards and Barclaycards are credit tokens because in return for payment by the debtor the bank agrees to pay third parties for cash, goods or services supplied. As the agreement under which the credit is provided in connection with the credit token is a regulated agreement, it is therefore a credit-token agreement.

(b) **Bank cash cards** are not normally credit tokens, as they do not provide credit nor do they guarantee payment by the bank to a third party. However, if a bank cash card allows the holder to go overdrawn, then it will be a credit token by virtue of s.14(4).

(c) **Cheque guarantee cards** are not credit tokens. These cards do not involve the bank providing the holder with credit or paying for goods or services supplied. The bank merely guarantees that the holder's cheque will be honoured.

(d) **American Express cards** are credit tokens. In return for payment by the card holder, the bank agrees to pay third parties for cash, goods or services supplied. However, the agreement under which the card is supplied is not a regulated agreement as it is an exempt agreement. (This is because the account must be settled by the making of a single payment at the end of each month, as explained at 14.1.1.4 above.) Therefore the agreement is not a credit-token agreement.

(e) **Store cards** are credit tokens. On production of such a card, goods or services are provided on credit. The agreement under which the credit is provided in connection with such a card is a regulated agreement, and is therefore a credit-token agreement.

(f) **Debit cards**, such as Visa cards, are credit tokens because they can be used to pay third parties for goods and services, Visa paying the third party in return for payment by the card holder. However, the agreement under which a debit card is supplied is not a credit-token agreement, as no credit is provided in connection with the credit token.

14.1.6.1 Prohibition of unsolicited credit tokens

It is an offence to supply a credit token to a person who has not asked for it in a signed document (s.51). Where the credit-token agreement is a small debtor–creditor–supplier agreement there must still be a request, but it does not need to be in a signed document (s.51(2)). No offence is committed when previously accepted credit tokens are renewed or replaced, nor if the credit token is supplied under a credit-token agreement previously made (s.51(3)).

If s.51 is breached, the agreement will be improperly executed. The effect of this was considered above at 14.1.3.

14.1.6.2 Sections 56 and 75 as they relate to credit tokens

The use of a credit token to acquire goods or services constitutes a three party debtor–creditor–supplier agreement. Consequently, the issuer of the credit token can be jointly and severally liable with the supplier of the goods or services under s.75(1) of the Act. Section 56(2) might also make a negotiator the agent of the creditor. Negotiations with the debtor which were conducted by the supplier in relation to a transaction financed or proposed to be financed by a debtor–creditor–supplier agreement are within s.56(1)(c). The use of credit cards at approved outlets would be within this definition.

Where a debtor buys goods by using an American Express card American Express would not be liable under s.56(2) or under s.75(1), as the agreement under which the card was supplied would be an exempt agreement. If the goods had been bought by the use of an Access card Access could become liable under either s.56(2) or s.75(1). If a debtor took money from a cash machine, thereby going overdrawn, so as to be able to buy goods, the bank would not be liable under s.56(2) as there is no connection between the bank and the retailer. Nor would the bank be liable under s.75(1), as there would be no debtor–creditor–supplier agreement within s.12(b) or (c). Payment for goods or services with a debit card would not bring either s.56(2) or s.75(1) into play, whether or not the customer's account was overdrawn.

14.1.6.3 Duty on issue of new credit tokens

Section 85(1) provides that:

> 'Whenever, in connection with a credit-token agreement, a credit token (other than the first) is given by the creditor to the debtor, the creditor shall give the debtor a copy of the executed agreement (if any) and of any other document referred to in it.'

Failure to comply with this means that the creditor cannot enforce the agreement while the default continues, and that he commits an offence if the default continues for more than one month (s.85(2)). However, s.85 does not apply to small agreements (s.85(3)).

Section 85 does not apply to the first credit token as the rules in ss.60–66 apply.

14.1.6.4 Liability for misuse of credit facilities

Section 83(1) provides that:

> 'The debtor under a regulated consumer credit agreement shall not be liable to the creditor for any loss arising from the use of the credit facility by another person not acting, or to be treated as acting, as the debtor's agent.'

Section 83(1) does not apply to a non-commercial agreement, or to any loss in so far as it arises from misuse of an instrument to which s.4 of the Cheques Act 1957 applies (s.83(2)). It is not possible for any term of the agreement to exclude the protection conferred by s.83(1) (s.173(1)).

Section 83(1) does not prevent the debtor under a credit-token agreement from being made liable to the extent of £50 (or the credit limit if it is lower) for loss to the creditor arising from use of the credit token by other persons during a period beginning when the credit token ceases to be in the possession of any authorised person and ending when the credit token is once more in the possession of an authorised person (s.84(1)). Section 83(1) does not prevent the debtor under a credit-token agreement from being made liable to any extent for loss to the creditor from use of the credit token by a person who acquired possession of it with the owner's consent (s.84(2)). Both s.84(1) and (2) do not apply to the use of the credit token after the creditor has been given oral or written notice that it has been lost or stolen, or that it is for any other reason liable to misuse (s.84(3)). The oral notice is treated as not taking effect unless it is confirmed in writing within seven days (s.84(5)).

It is important to realise that when considering ss.83 and 84 we have again been considering 'loss to the creditor'. The section will only protect the debtor to the extent that his account is taken into deficit or taken further into deficit. It does not require the creditor to indemnify the debtor for loss suffered by the misuse of a credit token.

However, the Banking Code, a voluntary code to which all of the major banks and building societies subscribe when dealing with 'personal customers', offers protection when a 'card' is misused. This is the case even if the customer's account is not taken into debit. A personal customer is one who has an account which is not held as a business, club, society, executor or trustee. The Code defines a card as any plastic card which a customer may use to pay for goods or services or to withdraw cash. It includes debit, credit, cheque guarantee and charge cards. Section 12.9 of the Code provides that a personal customer who acts fraudulently will be responsible for all losses on their account. The customer may also be liable for all losses for his acting without reasonable care (for example, by not keeping a PIN secret).

If the bank or building society cannot show that the customer has acted fraudulently or without reasonable care, the customer's liability is limited by s.12(10) in three ways.

First, if the card is used before the customer tells the bank that it has been lost or stolen, or that someone else knows the PIN, the customer's loss is limited to £50. (Once the customer has told the bank that the card has been lost or stolen, or that someone else knows the PIN, he will suffer no loss if the card is subsequently misused.) Second, if the card details are used without the card holder's permission in a transaction where the customer does not need to be present, the customer will not have to pay anything. Third, if the card is misused before the customer receives it the customer will not have to pay anything.

In Chapter 7 at 7.1.5 we considered the effect of the Consumer Protection (Distance Selling) Regulations 2000. Regulation 21(1) allows a consumer to cancel a payment where fraudulent use has been made of his payment card in connection with a distance contract by another person not acting, or to be treated as acting, as his agent. We saw that the Regulations define a 'consumer' as a natural person who is acting for purposes which are outside his business and a 'distance contract' is one concluded making exclusive use of distance communications. Regulation 21(6) says that a 'payment card' includes credit cards, charge cards, debit cards and store cards. If the consumer alleges that any use made of the payment card was not authorised by him it is for the card issuer to prove that the use was so authorised (Reg.21(3)).

When a consumer cancels a payment, Reg.21(2) provides that the card issuer must recredit the consumer's account with all sums taken from the account by fraudulent use of the payment card.

Regulation 21 does not apply to an agreement to which CCA 1974 s.83(1) applies (because there is no need for Reg.21 to apply). CCA 1974 s.84(1) and (2) do not apply where a card which is a credit token is used in connection with a distance contract (because Reg.21 applies instead).

So if a card is fraudulently used in connection with a distance contract a consumer card holder will suffer no loss. As regard non-distance contracts, if the card was lost or stolen, the card holder's loss is limited to £50 if the card holder is a personal customer within the Banking Code. Any card holder who acts fraudulently will be liable for all losses thereby incurred.

Examples:

1. A thief steals a debit card and uses it in a shop to obtain goods to the value of £1 000. If this reduced the card holder's credit from £1 900 to £900 then ss.83 and 84 CCA 1974 would have no application as no loss would have been caused to the creditor (the card issuer). However, if the card holder was a personal customer then the card issuer would have to recredit the account with £950 as s.12(10) of the Banking Code would limit the customer's loss to £50.

2. A thief steals a credit card and uses it in a shop to obtain goods worth £500. This increases the card holder's debit from £100 to £600. Section 84(1) would limit the card holder's liability to £50. If the card holder had informed the card issuer of the theft before the thief used the card then the card holder would not be liable for any of the £500 loss.

3. A debtor gives his credit card to a friend for safe-keeping. The friend steals the card and uses it in several shops to order £900 of goods. This increases the card holder's debit from £600 to £1 500. The debtor telephones the creditor (card issuer) to explain what has happened and the creditor asks for written confirmation, which is sent. At the time of the phone call the thief had increased the card holder's debit from £600 to £900. By the time the letter of confirmation arrived the debit had increased to the full £1 500. Under ss.83(1) and 84(1) the debtor is liable only for the £300 increase in debit. The oral notice that the card had been stolen prevented further liability from arising. However, if the card holder was a 'personal customer' s.12(10) of the Banking Code would limit the card holder's liability to £50, unless the card issuer could prove that the customer had acted fraudulently or without reasonable care.

4. If in example (3) the card had been misused entirely in connection with distance contracts then as long as the card holder was a 'consumer' within the Consumer Protection (Distance Selling) Regulations 2000, and as long as the card issuer could not prove that the use of the card was authorised, the consumer could cancel all payments made.

5. A thief steals a consumer's debit card and uses it to order goods over the internet. This reduces the card holder's balance from £480 to £150. Regulation 21(1) of the Consumer Protection (Distance Selling) Regulations 2000 would allow the card holder to cancel the payment made with the card. If the card had been a credit card and the thief's actions had taken the card holder's debit from £100 to £430, s.84(1) and (2) CCA 1974 would not apply and Reg.21(1) Consumer Protection (Distance Selling) Regulations 2000 would still allow the customer to cancel the payment.

Test your understanding

1 How can s.56(2) help a debtor?

2 How can s.75(1) help a debtor?

3 What is a credit token?

4 What is a credit token agreement?

5 How is a debtor protected against misuse of a stolen credit token?

Answers

1 Section 56(2) can help a debtor because it provides that in two and three party debtor–creditor–supplier agreements a person who conducts negotiations on behalf of the creditor is deemed to do so as the agent of the creditor.

2 Section 75(1) can help a debtor because it provides that in debtor–creditor–supplier agreements where the creditor is not also the supplier of the goods the creditor assumes joint and several liability for breaches of contract or misrepresentations made by the supplier.

3 A credit token is a card etc. provided by a person carrying on a consumer credit business who undertakes that on production of it he will supply cash, goods or services on credit or that on production of it to a third party he will pay the third party for cash, goods or services in return for payment to him by the individual.

4 A credit-token agreement is a regulated agreement for the provision of credit in connection with the use of a credit token.

5 A debtor whose credit token is stolen is not liable to the creditor for losses over £50 arising from unauthorised misuse of the credit card.

14.1.7 Enforcement of the agreement

14.1.7.1 Duty to give notice before taking certain action

Where the debtor has not breached the agreement, s.76(1) prohibits the creditor from enforcing a term of a regulated agreement in three ways without giving seven days' notice of his intention to do so. The three ways are to:

(a) demand earlier payment of any sum, or
(b) recover possession of any goods or land, or
(c) treat any right conferred on the debtor or hirer by the agreement as terminated, restricted or deferred.

Section 76(1) will only apply where the agreement is for a fixed time, although either party might be able to terminate it before that time has expired (s.76(2)(a)).

Where a regulated agreement is for a fixed time which is specified in the agreement, the creditor or owner is not entitled to end the agreement early unless seven days' notice of the termination is given to the debtor or hirer (s.98). This section does not prevent a creditor from treating the right to draw on any credit as restricted or deferred or from taking such steps as may be necessary to make the restriction or deferment effective (s.98(1)).

It might be thought odd that the creditor can terminate the agreement or demand early payment even though the debtor is not in breach of the agreement. However, many agreements give the creditor such rights if the debtor becomes unemployed or bankrupt or changes his address.

14.1.7.2 The duty to give information

Sections 77–79 require the creditor or owner to give either copies of agreements or statements of account to the debtor or hirer, who must pay 50p for each agreement requested. The copy of the agreement or the statement of account must then be provided within 12 working days of its being requested in writing or the creditor cannot enforce the agreement while the default continues, and if the default continues for more than one month he commits a criminal offence.

Where, under a regulated agreement other than a non-commercial agreement, a debtor or hirer is required to keep goods under his possession or control then upon receiving a written request from the creditor or owner the debtor or hirer must tell the creditor or owner where the goods are within seven working days (s.80(1)). If the debtor or hirer fails to comply with s.80(1), and the default continues for 14 days, he commits a criminal offence (s.80(2)).

14.1.7.3 Appropriation of payments

If a debtor or hirer is liable to make payments to the same person under two or more regulated agreements, and sends less than the total sums due, he can allocate the payments towards one or more of the agreements as he sees fit (s.81(1)). If the debtor makes no such appropriation then the sum sent is allocated between the various agreements in proportion to the amount due under each (s.81(2)).

The right to appropriate payments can be important when the creditor is attempting to repossess goods. (See Repossession of the goods below at 14.1.9.8.)

14.1.7.4 Death of debtor or hirer

If the agreement is fully secured, s.86(1) prevents the creditor or owner from doing the following things on the death of the debtor or hirer:

(a) terminating the agreement; or
(b) demanding earlier payment of any sum; or
(c) recovering possession of any goods or land; or
(d) treating any right conferred on the debtor or hirer by the agreement as terminated, restricted or deferred; or
(e) enforcing any security.

If the agreement was only partly secured at the time of the death then the creditor or hirer cannot do any of the five things without a court order.

14.1.7.5 Need for default notices

Section 87 requires the creditor or owner to serve a default notice on a debtor or hirer who is in breach of a regulated agreement before doing any of the following:

(a) terminating the agreement; or
(b) demanding earlier payment of any sum; or
(c) recovering possession of any goods or land; or
(d) treating any right conferred on the debtor or hirer by the agreement as terminated, restricted or deferred; or
(e) enforcing any security.

The default notice must be in the form prescribed by the Consumer Credit (Enforcement, Default and Termination) Regulations 1983. Section 88(1) requires a default notice to specify:

(a) the nature of the alleged breach;
(b) if the breach is capable of remedy, what action is required to remedy it and the date before which that action is to be taken; and
(c) if the breach is not capable of remedy, the sum (if any) required to be paid as compensation for the breach, and the date before which it is to be paid.

If a date is specified it must be at least seven days after the date of service of the default notice. The creditor or owner cannot take any action before the seven days have expired (s.88(2)). The debtor or hirer can take the action required before the date specified, in which case the breach shall be treated as not having occurred (s.89). A default notice is not needed to prevent the debtor from having any further credit (s.87(2)). Nor is a default notice necessary where a creditor or owner is suing for arrears, as this is not demanding early payment of any sum. Where a debtor is in breach of a regulated consumer credit agreement, the rate of interest is not to be increased on default (s.93).

14.1.7.6 Protection orders

On application to the court by a creditor or owner under a regulated agreement, the court may make such order as it thinks fit for protecting any property belonging to the creditor or owner from damage or depreciation pending court proceedings. Such an order can restrict or prohibit the use of the property or give directions as to its custody (s.131).

14.1.7.7 Extortionate credit bargains

If the court finds a credit bargain extortionate it may reopen the credit agreement so as to do justice between the parties (s.137(1)). This provision applies to any agreement, regulated or not, where a creditor supplies credit of any amount to a debtor.

An extortionate credit bargain is defined by s.138(1) as one under which the debtor has to make payments which are grossly exorbitant, or which otherwise grossly contravene ordinary principles of fair dealing. In determining whether or not a credit agreement is extortionate sub-s.(2)–(4) of s.138 require regard to be had to the following matters:

(a) the prevailing interest rates at the time when the agreement was made;
(b) the debtor's age, experience, business capacity and state of health;
(c) the degree to which the debtor was under financial pressure when making the agreement, and the nature of that pressure;
(d) the degree of risk to the creditor, having regard to the value of any security provided;
(e) the creditor's relationship with the debtor;
(f) whether or not a colourable (plausible) cash price was quoted for any goods or services included in the bargain.
(g) any other relevant consideration.

Section 139 gives the court very wide powers to alter an extortionate credit agreement. The court might alter the rate of interest, or set aside obligations imposed on the debtor and can order the creditor to repay sums already received.

■ *A. Ketley Ltd* v *Scott and another* [1981] ICR 241

The claimant company lent £20000 to the defendant and his wife, to enable them to buy a house. The amount of money to be borrowed had gone up from £18000, on the day that the loan was made, because the defendant (a businessman) could not borrow as much as he had expected from his bank. The defendant did not reveal to the claimants that the bank had been given a legal charge over the property or that the property had been valued at less than the price he was paying for it. In the presence of solicitors acting for both sides, the defendant signed an agreement that the loan was to be for three months, at an interest rate of 48% per annum. When the loan was not repaid the claimant company gained repossession of the property and arrears. In deciding what sum the defendant ought to pay the court had to decide whether or not the bargain was extortionate, within the meaning of the Consumer Credit Act 1974.

Held. The rate of interest was not extortionate. Even if it had been extortionate it would not have been just and equitable to reopen the bargain, bearing in mind the deceitful behaviour of the defendant.

14.1.8 Termination by the debtor or hirer

14.1.8.1 Early payment by debtor

The debtor under a regulated consumer credit agreement is entitled to discharge the debt at any time by giving the creditor notice in writing and by repaying the whole debt (s.94(1)). If the debtor does this he will be entitled to a rebate of charges for credit (s.95(1)). Where the debtor terminates a hire-purchase or conditional sale agreement there is no right to a rebate as ss.99 and 100 deal with the debtor's liability. (The effect of ss.99 and 100 is considered immediately below.) Nor is there any right to a rebate where the debtor terminates a hire agreement. (The effect of a consumer terminating a consumer hire agreement early is considered below.)

Where for any reason a debt under a regulated consumer credit agreement is discharged early, the debtor is also discharged from any liability under a linked transaction, other than a debt which has already become payable (s.96(1)).

The Consumer Credit (Settlement Information) Regulations 1983 require the creditor, within 12 working days of receiving a written request to do so from a debtor under a regulated consumer credit agreement, to give the debtor a statement showing how much is needed to pay off the debt and how this amount was calculated. Although the provisions relating to early settlement cannot be contracted out of to the detriment of the debtor, an agreement can give the debtor additional rights.

14.1.8.2 Termination by the debtor of hire-purchase and conditional sale agreements

Section 99(1) provides that:

> 'At any time before the final payment by the debtor under a regulated hire-purchase or regulated conditional sale agreement falls due, the debtor shall be entitled to terminate the agreement by giving notice to any person entitled or authorised to receive the sums payable under the agreement.'

If the debtor does choose to terminate under s.99(1) this does not affect any liability which has already accrued under the agreement, so arrears continue to be due (s.99(2)). If the debtor has been served with notice (under s.76(1) or s.87) of the activation of an accelerated payments clause the right to terminate under s.99(1) will be lost when the final payment falls due. This would be the time when the notice expired. (Accelerated payments clauses are considered below at 14.1.9.)

This right to terminate will not apply where the debtor is deemed to have repudiated the agreement. (See *Yeoman Credit Ltd* v *Waragowski* below at 14.1.9.6.)

When a debtor terminates a hire-purchase or conditional sale agreement early, the financial position is calculated as follows. First, arrears are payable (s.99(2)). Second, unless the agreement provided that a lower sum be payable or that no sum be payable, the debtor can be required to bring payments made up to half of the total price (s.100(1)). Third, if the debtor has failed to take reasonable care of the goods, the amount payable should be increased to compensate the creditor for this (s.100(4)).

■ Example

Dudley made an agreement to buy a television under a regulated conditional sale agreement. He paid a deposit of £100 and then committed himself to paying £20 a month for 24 months. At the time of cancellation, four months after making the agreement, he was two monthly payments in arrears. The goods have been kept in good condition. Ownership of the goods will never pass to Dudley and the creditor may repossess the television as the conditional sale agreement has been terminated. First, Dudley must pay the arrears of £40. Even when the arrears had been paid, Dudley would only have paid £100 deposit, £40 in monthly payments, and £40 arrears, making a total of £180. Dudley could be required to pay an additional amount of £110 to bring the payments up to £290, half of the total payments of £580. So in total Dudley would need to pay £150 (£40 arrears and the additional £110). As the goods were kept in good condition no compensation will be added.

Where the debtor gives goods in part-exchange, then the allowance given on the part-exchanged goods is counted as a payment made. Section 100(3) allows the court to reduce the amount payable under s.100(1) to the actual loss suffered by the creditor as a result of the debtor's early termination. A debtor who terminates a hire-purchase or conditional sale agreement must of course return the goods to the creditor.

14.1.8.3 Right to terminate regulated consumer hire agreement

Section 101 allows a consumer who is locked into a long term hire agreement to terminate the agreement early, whatever the length of the agreement. Notice must be given to any person entitled or authorised to receive the sums payable under the agreement, but the notice cannot expire earlier than eighteen months after the making of the agreement. Termination does not affect any liability under the agreement which has already accrued before the termination. The hirer must either give three months' notice, or the shortest interval between payments, whichever is the shorter period of time. (Subject to the rule that the notice cannot expire earlier than eighteen months after making the agreement.) There is no right to terminate early under s.101 if the hirer has to make total payments exceeding

£1 500 a year, or if the goods are bailed to the hirer for business purposes, or if the hirer chooses goods which the owner subsequently acquires from another person at the hirer's request. Nor can s.101 apply where the hirer is a company, because in such circumstances the agreement would not be a regulated agreement. It is not possible to contract out of s.101, so any additional payments or penalties will be void.

14.1.9 Remedies of the creditor

If a debtor breaches a credit agreement the creditor might possibly have four rights as follows: to bring an action for arrears, to terminate the contract, to bring an action for damages or to bring an action to repossess the goods. We need to consider each of these matters in turn.

14.1.9.1 An action for arrears

A creditor has a common law right to sue a debtor for arrears which have accrued. However, four of the Act's provisions might be relevant. First, as we have seen, s.93 provides that the rate of interest payable on arrears should not be higher than the interest rate specified in the total charge for credit. Second, the court may make a time order under s.129. (The effect of this is explained immediately below.) Third, as we saw above, the creditor must give the debtor notice (under either s.76(1) or s.87(1)) before demanding early payment of any sum. Fourth, the court has the power to re-open an extortionate credit bargain. (This power was considered above at 14.1.7.)

14.1.9.2 Time orders

A court may make a time order under s.129 in certain circumstances, including those where the creditor has brought an action to enforce a regulated agreement, or any security, or recover possession of any goods or land to which a regulated agreement relates. The time order would make sums due under a regulated agreement payable by instalments at intervals which the court would set, having regard to the means of the debtor or hirer and any surety given. Generally, a time order only relates to sums actually owed. However, in the case of hire-purchase and conditional sale agreements it can also apply to sums which would become payable if the agreement remained in force (s.130(2)).

14.1.9.3 Termination of the agreement

At common law a creditor will be entitled to terminate a credit agreement if the terms of the agreement allowed him to do so, or if the breach by the creditor was such that it amounted to a repudiation of the contract. The Act does not prevent the creditor from terminating the agreement. However, the provisions of ss.87–89 and s.98 (considered above at 14.1.7) would have to be observed.

14.1.9.4 Accelerated payment clauses

Many credit agreements which are repayable by instalments contain a term stating that all future instalments become payable immediately if the debtor defaults. Such a term is known as an accelerated payment clause. These clauses are particularly useful to the creditor where the debtor's breach does not amount to a repudiation of the contract or where goods which might be repossessed have become worth much less than the value of future instalments.

Accelerated payment clauses are valid as long as they do not amount to penalties. (See Chapter 7 at 7.2.2.4.) However, an accelerated payment clause in a regulated agreement cannot be activated unless a default notice is served under s.87 or, where the debtor is not in default, notice is given under s.76(1). The debtor could then apply to the court for a time order under s.129. (See above at 14.1.9.2.) If granted, the time order would set the intervals at which the instalments should be paid and, in effect, defeat the accelerated payment clause. The Unfair Terms in Consumer Contracts Regulations 1999 might provide additional protection. (See Chapter 5 at 5.7.)

14.1.9.5 Damages

If a hire-purchase or conditional sale agreement is breached by the debtor then the creditor can sue for damages. (Breach of a loan or credit sale will consist of not repaying the instalments and the creditor can sue to recover payment of the unpaid instalments plus interest. This would be an action for an agreed sum rather than an action for damages. See Chapter 7 at 7.2.3.)

Under the common law the damages will be assessed, under the rule in *Hadley* v *Baxendale*, to put the creditor in the position which he would have been in if the contract had been performed as agreed. (See *Yeoman Credit Ltd* v *Waragowski* [1961] 3 AllER 145 below.) If the breach consists of early termination of a hire-purchase or conditional sale agreement by the debtor then the damages will be calculated according to s.100(1), as explained above at 14.1.8.

The measure of damages differs depending upon whether the debtor repudiated the agreement or whether the creditor terminated on account of a breach by the debtor which did not amount to a repudiation.

14.1.9.6 Damages where the debtor repudiated the agreement

The following case represented the position before the Act came into force.

■ *Yeoman Credit Ltd* v *Waragowski* [1961] 1 WLR 1124 (Court of Appeal)

The claimants made a hire-purchase agreement with the defendant in respect of a second-hand van. The agreement required the defendant to pay £72 down and to make 36 monthly instalments of £10 0s 9d. The sale price of the van was £360, but the total price including interest and charges was £434 7s 0d. The defendant did not pay any of the monthly instalments. Six months into the agreement the claimants terminated the agreement and repossessed the van. The claimants sold the van for £205 and then sued for arrears of £60 4s 6d and damages.

Held. The claimants were entitled to damages for breach of contract as well as arrears of £60 4s 6d. The damages were assessed as the difference between the amount of money which the claimants had actually received and the amount which they would have received if the defendant had continued with the agreement for the full three years. The damages were therefore £97 2s 6d. (£434 7s 0d – (£72 + £205 + £60 4s 6d))

COMMENT It is not certain whether the debtor's right to escape paying the whole of the agreed price (under ss.99 and 100) would now have to be taken into account. If it would, damages should be based on the maximum amount which might be recovered under s.100(1) less any payments actually made.

If the agreement was a regulated agreement then upon payment of the amount due, the debtor would be entitled to a rebate of charges for credit for early settlement under s.95.

14.1.9.7 Termination by creditor where debtor does not repudiate

If the creditor terminates when the debtor has breached the contract but has not repudiated, then it is the creditor who is bringing it to an end, rather than the debtor. Consequently the creditor will only be entitled to claim arrears and interest plus any amount to compensate for the defendant having failed to take reasonable care of the goods. There will be no damages for the loss of the bargain.

In *Financings Ltd* v *Baldock* [1963] 2 QB 104 (Court of Appeal) a debtor took a truck on hire-purchase, paying a deposit and agreeing to pay monthly instalments for two years. The defendant missed making the first two payments. The creditor used a term of the agreement to repossess the truck and then sold it. It was held that the debtor's behaviour did not amount to repudiation of the contract. A term of the agreement stated that if the debtor defaulted and the creditor repossessed the debtor would pay as damages an amount equal to two-thirds of total payments as compensation for depreciation of the goods. This term was void as a penalty and the debtor was ordered to pay the two instalments in arrears + 10% interest up to the date of judgment. (In Chapter 7 at 7.2.2.4 we saw that where the damages are fixed in advance this will amount either to liquidated damages or to a penalty. If the amount fixed is a 'genuine pre-estimate of the loss' then it will be liquidated damages and the amount fixed will be the amount of damages payable. If the amount fixed is not a genuine pre-estimate of the loss then it will be a penalty, which the courts will ignore. Damages will then be calculated according to ordinary common law principles.)

In *Lombard North Central* v *Butterworth* [1987] 1 All ER 267 (Court of Appeal) a term in a hire contract stated that prompt payment of all instalments was of the essence of the contract. The defendant made several late payments, which would not ordinarily have amounted to a repudiation of the contract. However, the term making prompt payment of the essence was a condition of the contract. Therefore the creditor could terminate the contract and recover damages for the loss of the whole bargain. It is now common for hire-purchase and conditional sale agreements to include a term that prompt payment of all instalments is of the essence.

14.1.9.8 Repossession of the goods

A creditor may terminate a hire-purchase or conditional sale agreement, and repossess the goods, if the debtor does not make all of the payments. However, the Act protects a debtor in three ways, as without this protection a debtor who had made substantial payments before defaulting could suddenly lose all rights when the creditor 'snatched-back' the goods.

First, the creditor will not be able to repossess goods without giving notice and observing the provisions of ss.76, 87–89 and 98. Second, the creditor or owner is not entitled to enter premises to retake possession of the goods without a court order, unless the debtor agrees to this (s.92(1)). Most important though, the goods may become protected goods as explained by s.90(1):

'At any time when –
(a) the debtor is in breach of a regulated hire-purchase or a regulated conditional sale agreement relating to goods, and
(b) the debtor has paid to the creditor one-third or more of the total price of the goods and
(c) the property in the goods remains in the creditor,

the creditor is not entitled to recover possession of the goods from the debtor except on an order of the court.'

If an installation charge is included in the total price for the goods, the amount which the debtor must have paid is the whole of the installation charge and a third of the remainder of the total price (s.90(2)).

Section 90(1) shall not apply, or shall cease to apply, to an agreement if the debtor has terminated, or terminates, the agreement (s.90(5)).

The consequences of the creditor breaching s.90 are severe, as s.91 makes plain:

'If goods are recovered by the creditor in breach of s.90 –
(a) the regulated agreement, if not previously terminated, shall terminate, and
(b) the debtor shall be released from all liability under the agreement, and shall be entitled to recover from the creditor all sums paid by the debtor under the agreement.'

■ Examples

a Dave takes a motorbike on hire-purchase from Bikes Ltd. Dave pays a deposit of £1 000 and commits himself to paying £100 a month for 36 months. After ten monthly payments Dave defaults on his next payment. Bikes Ltd immediately repossess the motorbike. If Bikes Ltd repossessed the motorbike without a court order then they would be in breach of s.90. Section 91 would therefore terminate the agreement, and entitle Dave to recover all sums paid under the agreement. As the agreement would be terminated, Bikes Ltd would be entitled to possession of the motorbike. Dave, however, would be entitled to the return of the £1 000 deposit and the ten instalments of £100 already paid.

b If after ten monthly payments Dave had written to say that he no longer wanted the motorbike he would appear to have terminated the agreement under s.99. Therefore, applying s.90(5), s.90(1) would not apply. As owners of the motorbike, Bikes Ltd would have the right to repossess it. Dave would not be able to recover money already paid. Dave would, under s.100(1) have to make his payments up to half the total price. As Dave has paid £2 000 and the total price was £4600, he would have to pay a further £300. However, if the court was satisfied that Bikes Ltd's loss was less than £300 then Dave would not have to pay this extra £300 (s.100(3)).

Although it is possible for the debtor to consent to the repossession of protected goods, if a term of the contract states that the debtor gives such consent then the term will be void under s.173(1). The creditor can repossess the goods which have been abandoned, as this is not recovery of goods from the debtor.

14.1.9.9 Provisions protecting hirers of goods

Section 132 gives financial relief to a hirer of goods under a regulated consumer hire agreement where the owner takes the goods back without taking court action. The hirer can apply for a court order that:

(a) the whole or part of any sum paid by the hirer to the owner in respect of the goods shall be repaid, and

(b) the obligation to pay the whole or part of any sum owed by the hirer to the owner in respect of the goods shall cease.

The court will only grant the order if it appears just to do so, having regard to the extent of the enjoyment of the goods by the hirer.

14.1.9.10 The court's powers in hire-purchase and conditional sale agreements

Section 133 applies to regulated hire-purchase and conditional sale agreements, enabling the court to make a return order or a transfer order when the creditor sues to recover goods or when there is an application for an enforcement order or a time order. A return order requires that goods to which the agreement relates are returned to the creditor. A transfer order allows for the transfer to the debtor of the creditor's title to some of the goods to which the agreement relates, while the remainder of the goods are returned to the creditor.

Section 135 gives the court the power to impose conditions in any regulated agreement. Section 136 gives the court the power to amend or vary any agreement when it makes an order under the Act. If the debtor contravenes a return order or a transfer order it can be revoked by the court (s.133(6)).

Test your understanding

1 What is the debtor's right to appropriate payments to a creditor? In what circumstances might appropriation of payments help a debtor?

2 What power does a court have in relation to an extortionate credit agreement?

3 What rights of early payment does a debtor have?

4 What payments must be made by a debtor who terminates a hire-purchase or conditional sale agreement?

5 How are the creditor's damages for loss of the bargain affected if a debtor's breach of a hire-purchase agreement does or does not amount to a repudiation of the agreement?

Answers

1 If a debtor or hirer is liable to make payments to the same person under two or more regulated agreements, and sends less than the total sums due, he can allocate the payments towards one or more of the agreements as he sees fit (s.81(1)). Appropriation of payments to a particular transaction might protect the debtor against the creditor snatching back the goods, by making the goods protected goods, on account of the debtor having paid more than one third of the total price.

2 If the court finds a credit bargain extortionate it may reopen the credit agreement so as to do justice between the parties (s.137(1)).

3 The debtor under a regulated consumer credit agreement is entitled to discharge the debt at any time by giving the creditor notice in writing and by repaying the whole debt (s.94(1)).

4 If a debtor terminates a regulated hire-purchase or conditional sale agreement early, arrears must be paid. The debtor

may also be required to bring payments made (including arrears) up to half of the total price. If the debtor has failed to take reasonable care of the goods, the amount payable should be increased to compensate the creditor for this.

5 If a debtor repudiates a hire-purchase agreement the creditor will be able to sue for arrears and for damages for the whole loss of the bargain. If the creditor terminates a hire-purchase agreement on account of a breach by the debtor which did not amount to a repudiation the creditor will be entitled to arrears (plus interest) but not to damages for the loss of the bargain.

14.2 · Types of credit transactions

Credit is an underlying fact of commercial and consumer business. It is not usual for commercial organisations to pay cash, or to pay in advance, when making a business deal. Whenever payment for goods or services is deferred some sort of credit will have been provided. There are many different ways of providing credit, and the principal methods are now considered in outline.

14.2.1 Loans

A loan is the most fundamental form of credit. If a loan is made a creditor lends money to a debtor so that the debtor can buy goods or services. The debtor agrees to repay the money, with interest, over a period of time.

The creditor is often not connected with the transaction he is financing. A bank, for example, may lend money to enable a business to buy new machinery. If the bank has no existing or contemplated future connection with the supplier, the contract between the business and the supplier of the machinery is nothing to do with the bank. The bank merely lends the money. As we saw earlier in this chapter at 14.1, this would be a debtor–creditor agreement. If the bank did have an existing or contemplated future connection with the supplier the agreement would be a debtor–creditor–supplier agreement.

Creditors are, however, likely to want **security** for the money they lend. If the debtor is a company the creditor will probably register a **charge** over the company's assets. The effects of this are considered in detail in Chapter 18 at 18.8. Essentially, a charge is a mortgage over some of the company's property. The company is free to continue to use the property but not to pass ownership to anyone else or do anything which would reduce its value. If the company does not repay the debt as agreed, the bank can order the sale of the assets over which it has a charge and take what it is owed. To preserve the rights granted, a chargeholder should register the charge with the Registrar of Companies.

If the debtor is a partnership or a sole trader the creditor may take a **mortgage** of property. The property mortgaged does not need to be business property, it might well be the house of the sole trader or of one of the partners. If the loan is not repaid the creditor will be able to repossess the property. (Sell it and take the amount still owed.)

Alternatively the creditor may be willing to accept a **third party guarantee** of the loan. The guarantor would then be liable to repay the loan if the debtor defaulted. For example, in *Lloyds Bank* v *Bundy* which is set out in Chapter 6 at 6.3.2 the father guaranteed the loans made to his son's business, promising that he would repay the loans if his son failed to do so. Such guarantees are effective as long as they are evidenced in writing and as long as they were not made as a consequence of duress or undue influence.

Security for a loan is not always necessary. Sometimes a bank will allow an **overdraft** without requiring security. An overdraft is a form of loan whereby customers can overdraw their bank accounts (take more money out of the account than has been deposited into it) on the understanding that money will be deposited later. There will be a limit above which the customer may not overdraw.

The rate of interest on an overdraft is usually higher than on a bank loan. However, the customer can clear his overdraft as soon as he wishes, and if the account is overdrawn for only a short time he might not pay much interest. Large overdrafts are a risky way for a small business to borrow money as the bank can insist that they be repaid at any time.

Figure 14.4   Triangular transactions

14.2.2 Hire-purchase

Under a hire-purchase agreement a debtor hires goods for a fixed period, and has an option to buy the goods for a nominal sum at the end of that period. Payment for the hire of the goods is usually made by regular instalments. As there is no agreement to carry on with the agreement and pay all of the instalments there is no agreement to sell and the Sale of Goods Act 1979 will not apply until the final payment is made, at which time the agreement becomes a contract of sale.

This can be demonstrated by considering the case of *Yeoman Credit Ltd* v *Waragowski*, the facts of which are set out above at 14.1.9. The defendant paid a deposit and this was to be followed by the payment of 36 monthly instalments. If the agreement had run its full course then the defendant would have acquired ownership of the van upon making the final payment. Up until the time of the final payment the defendant would have been hiring the van which would have remained the property of the finance company. The defendant would not have made a commitment to continue with the agreement for the full 36 months. (The consequences of not continuing with the agreement until it had run its course were considered above at 14.1.8–9.)

Usually a finance company, rather than the dealer in the goods, makes the hire-purchase agreement with the debtor. Many debtors under hire-purchase agreements are not aware of this. If the finance is provided by a third party, the hire-purchase agreement takes the form of a triangular transaction as shown in Figure 14.4.

(1)   The dealer sells the goods to the finance company.
(2)   The finance company makes the hire-purchase agreement with the customer.
(3)   There may be a collateral contract between the dealer and the customer. (The meaning of this is considered shortly.)

When the agreement is a regulated agreement within the Consumer Credit Act 1974 s.56(2) will provide the debtor with a remedy against the finance company if the dealer makes a misrepresentation, or a statement which becomes a term of the credit agreement, when conducting antecedent negotiations. (See above at 14.1.5.) In *Branwhite* v *Worcester Works Finance Ltd* [1969] 1 AC 552 the House of Lords held that the dealer is not normally the agent of the finance company at common law. However, when the agreement is unregulated a court might be willing to find a **collateral contract** between the dealer and the customer. If no such collateral contract could be found then the dealer would not have any contractual liability to a debtor who made a triangular transaction. The dealer might, however, be liable for fraud or negligent misstatement but these types of liability are hard to establish.

The following case, decided before the Consumer Credit Act was enacted, shows an example of a collateral contract in a triangular transaction.

■ *Andrews v Hopkinson* [1957] 1 QB 229

The claimant visited a motor dealer to look at second-hand cars. He took a vehicle on hire-purchase, through a finance company, because the dealer told him 'It's a good little bus. I would stake my life on it. You will have no trouble with it.' In fact the vehicle had defective steering. This caused an accident in which the claimant was badly injured.

Held. The dealer was liable on the collateral contract which he made with the claimant. This collateral contract was created when the claimant agreed to take the vehicle on hire-purchase (thus benefiting the defendant) and the defendant promised that it was 'a good little bus' (thus benefiting the claimant).

To some extent collateral contracts are a fiction, invented by the court to do justice in a particular case. However, they can be useful when no other remedy is available. Since the Consumer Credit Act came into force the court will only need to find a collateral contract if the hire-purchase agreement is not regulated by the Act. (For example where the customer is a company, or the credit is over £25 000.)

The Supply of Goods (Implied Terms) Act 1973 ss.8–11 imply into hire-purchase contracts terms very similar to those which ss.12–15 SGA imply into contracts for the sale of goods. (See Chapter 8 at 8.4.1.)

Figure 14.5   Collateral contracts in triangular transactions

14.2.3 Conditional sales

A conditional sale agreement is a sale of goods in which ownership of the goods stays with the seller until all of the price has been paid. The buyer usually takes immediate possession of the goods and commits himself to making full payment, often by instalments.

For example, a garage might make a conditional sale of a delivery van to a butcher. The terms of the contract might provide that the butcher is to pay for the van in 36 monthly instalments. The butcher will take immediate possession of the van, but the van will remain the property of the garage until all the instalments have been paid.

Where the payment is to be made in regular instalments a conditional sale agreement appears very similar indeed to a hire-purchase agreement. The difference is that under a hire-purchase agreement the buyer does not commit himself to completing the payments, whereas under a conditional sale agreement he does. An important consequence of this is that the Sale of Goods Act applies **immediately** in the case of a conditional sale, as there is an agreement to sell. The Sale of Goods Act will not apply to hire-purchase until the sale is actually made with payment of the final instalment. (However, in Chapter 9 at 9.3.5 we saw that s.25 SGA does not apply where the first buyer has taken the goods on a conditional sale agreement, payable by instalments, which is regulated by the Consumer Credit Act 1974.) Conditional sale agreements often involve a finance company in a triangular transaction. A regulated conditional sale agreement is classified by the Consumer Credit Act as a debtor–creditor–supplier agreement for restricted use credit within s.12(a).

14.2.4 Credit sales

Under a credit sale ownership of the goods passes to the buyer immediately, either upon the making of the contract or upon the delivery of the goods, and the seller extends credit to the buyer.

For example, a mail order catalogue firm might sell a coat to a customer under a credit sale. The coat becomes the customer's property as soon as goods matching the contract description are unconditionally appropriated to the contract by the seller with the assent of the buyer. (This will generally be when the coat is posted to the customer, see Chapter 9 at 9.1.2.) The mail order firm gives the customer credit, and the customer is obliged to pay the price of the coat under the credit terms specified in the contract.

Credit sales are commonly used where the goods supplied have a low second-hand value, there being no point in the seller retaining ownership if the goods are worth very little. The Sale of Goods Act applies to credit sales. If a finance company finances a credit sale then there may well be a triangular transaction, the debtor buying the goods from the finance company rather than from the dealer. A regulated credit sale is classified by the Consumer Credit Act as a debtor–creditor–supplier agreement for restricted use credit within s.12(a).

14.2.5 Hire and rental agreements

A person who rents goods to another gives possession of the goods in return for regular payments. He does not agree to sell the goods. Hire is very similar, but is usually for a longer period.

The Sale of Goods Act does not apply to hire agreements, but the Supply of Goods and Services Act ss.7–10 imply terms very similar to those implied by SGA ss.12–15. (See Chapter 8 at 8.4.2.) As we saw at 14.1.1, a consumer hire agreement (within the definition given by s.15 of the Consumer Credit Act 1974) will be regulated consumer credit agreement as long as it is not an exempt agreement.

14.2.6 Pawn

Goods are pawned when possession of them is given to a lender as security for a loan. When the debtor repays the loan he is given the goods back. If the debtor does not repay, the creditor can sell the goods. A pawn differs from a mortgage in that the debtor does not retain possession of the security. Easily transportable goods of high value are suitable to pledge, often to a pawnbroker.

For example, a person who wanted to borrow £100 might pledge a camera worth £1 000 to a pawnbroker. As long as the debtor repays the £100 with interest within a certain time the pawnbroker will return the camera. If the debtor does not repay the debt then eventually the pawnbroker will be able to sell the camera and take what he is owed from the proceeds.

Neither the Sale of Goods Act nor the Supply of Goods and Services Act apply to pawns, but the Consumer Credit Act does as long as the credit is under £25 000.

1.4.2.7 Payment by credit card

When a supplier accepts payment by credit card, the customer/cardholder signs the voucher and this entitles the supplier to a payment which fully discharges the customer's liability for the price of the goods or services. The credit card company will pay the price to the supplier, deducting commission. The supplier knows that when the cardholder/customer signs the voucher he renders himself liable to the credit card company to pay the price of the goods or services. Both the supplier and the cardholder would previously have made contracts with the credit card company. The supplier accepts the payment by credit card in substitution of payment in cash, i.e. as an unconditional discharge of the price. (*Re Charge Card Services Ltd* [1989] Ch 497.) Payment by credit card is classified by the Consumer Credit Act 1974 as a debtor–creditor–supplier agreement for restricted use credit within s.12(b).

14.2.8 Trade credit

Trade credit arises when payment for goods or services is informally deferred. Immediate payment for goods is not the norm in commercial life. Just as the newsagent delivers newspapers before he is paid for them, so businesses informally accept deferred payment for goods and services which they supply. For policy reasons this type of informal credit is largely unregulated by the Consumer Credit Act.

14.3 · Interest on trade debts

Businesses which supply goods or services on credit to others might insist that a term is included in the contract making interest payable on the money owed. However, many suppliers are reluctant to do this for fear of losing future contracts with the person to whom credit is provided.

The Late Payment of Commercial Debts (Interest) Act 1998 now gives all businesses a statutory right, by way of an implied term, to claim interest on late payment of commercial debts for the supply of goods or services. Such a claim can be made against another business or a public sector body. A debt is a commercial debt for the supply of goods and services if both the supplier and the purchaser are acting in the course of business.

Interest becomes payable under the Act from the day after the relevant date for the debt. This date can be fixed in various ways. It can be the date for payment which the supplier and purchaser agreed, or can be fixed by trade custom or a course of dealing between the parties. If the relevant date is not fixed in one of these ways it is set at 30 days after the supplier performed his obligations under the contract, or at 30 days after the purchaser is given notice of the debt, whichever is the later. So payment would generally become due 30 days after goods or an invoice were delivered. However, there is no need for the notice of the debt to be written and it could be given in person or over the telephone.

The rate of interest is currently set at 8% above the base rate. The interest on the debt can be claimed for as a separate claim from the principal debt and can be assigned to a third party, such as a debt collector.

The effect of the Act cannot be avoided by means of a contractual term unless there is a 'substantial' remedy available for the late payment of the debt. A remedy is not regarded as substantial if it is insufficient for compensating the supplier, or if it would not be fair to allow the remedy to oust or vary the statutory interest payable under the Act. In deciding whether or not a remedy is substantial the court will consider all the circumstances at the time when the debt was agreed. It is only possible for a contractual term to postpone the time at which a debt is created to the extent that the term satisfies the UCTA 1977 requirement of reasonableness. (The UCTA requirement of reasonableness is examined in Chapter 5 at 5.6.1.)

It has been widely reported in the media that the Act has not yet made a significant impact. There is nothing wrong with the drafting of the Act, but it seems that most businesses are reluctant to use it for fear of offending their customers.

In addition to court fees, a successful creditor can claim reasonable compensation for the cost of collecting the debt. The Late Payments of Commercial Debts Regulations 2002 fix this compensation at £40 if the debt was under £1 000, £70 if the debt was at least £1 000 but under £10 000 and £100 if the debt was £10 000 or more.

The late payment interest rate is calculated by adding the current statutory rate to the Bank of England base rate. At the time of writing the current statutory rate is 8% and the Bank of England base rate is 3.75%. The late payment interest rate is therefore currently 11.75%.

■ Example

Five months ago Company A ordered goods to the value of £1 000 from Company B. The relevant date for payment was not fixed. The goods were delivered, along with an invoice, 130 days ago. A commercial debt of £1 000 has been payable for 100 days since the relevant date for the debt. The daily interest rate is calculated as:

$$\frac{£1\,000 \times 11.75\%}{365} = 0.32\text{p per day}$$

Therefore, £32.00 interest is already owed and the interest will increase by 0.32p per day until the debt is paid.

Any part payment made will first be set off against interest owed and then against the original debt.

The 2002 Regulations allow established representative bodies to apply for injunctions to prevent the use of written standard terms which try to oust or vary the right to statutory interest. The representative bodies must represent either a particular business sector or small and medium sized businesses in general.

Test your understanding

1 What is a hire-purchase agreement?

2 In what way is a conditional sale agreement different from a hire-purchase agreement?

Answers

1 A hire-purchase agreement is an agreement under which a debtor hires goods for a fixed period, and has an option to buy the goods for a nominal sum at the end of that period. The debtor has no obligation to continue with the agreement for the whole of the fixed period.

2 Under a conditional sale a buyer agrees to buy goods but the ownership of the goods is not to pass to the buyer until all of the price has been paid. Usually the price is to be paid by instalments, in which case a conditional sale agreement is very similar to hire-purchase. However, under a conditional sale agreement there is an agreement to sell from the outset and the buyer agrees to make all of the payments. Under a hire-purchase contract the debtor has no obligation to continue paying instalments until the end of the agreement.

Key points

Regulated agreements and other definitions

■ A regulated agreement is a consumer credit agreement, or consumer hire agreement, other than an exempt agreement.

■ The definition of a regulated agreement is significant because most of the Act's provisions apply only to regulated agreements.

■ Running-account credit is given under a master agreement which allows for separate credit agreements to be made under it. Fixed-sum credit fixes the amount of credit in the agreement or allows the amount of credit to be calculated by reference to the agreement.

■ Restricted-use credit is transferred directly from the creditor to the supplier of the goods or services being acquired by the debtor, or is provided by the supplier. Any credit actually received by the debtor is unrestricted-use credit.

■ Under a debtor–creditor–supplier agreement the creditor is either the legal supplier of the goods or services or has an existing or future contemplated connection with the legal supplier. Any agreement other than a debtor–creditor–supplier agreement is a debtor–creditor agreement.

■ A non-commercial agreement is one made by the creditor or owner otherwise than in the course of a business carried on by him. A small agreement is one where the credit extended is less than £50 or one where the hirer does not need to make payments exceeding £50.

Cancellation and copies of regulated agreements

■ If the rules concerning the supply of copies of credit agreements are not complied with the agreements are only enforceable by court order and may be unenforceable.

■ If the debtor or hirer is not given notice of cancellation rights, as required by s.64, the agreement will be totally unenforceable.

Statutory liability of creditor

■ Section 56(2) provides that in two and three party debtor–creditor–supplier agreements a person who conducts negotiations on behalf of the creditor is deemed to do so as the agent of the creditor.

■ Section 75(1) provides that in debtor–creditor–supplier agreements where the creditor is not also the supplier of the goods the creditor assumes joint and several liability for breaches of contract or misrepresentations made by the supplier.

Credit tokens

■ A credit token is a card etc. provided by a person carrying on a consumer credit business who undertakes that on production of it he will supply cash, goods or services on credit or that on production of it to a third party he will pay the third party for cash, goods or services in return for payment to him by the individual.

■ A credit-token agreement is a regulated agreement for the provision of credit in connection with the use of a credit token.

■ A debtor whose credit token is stolen is not liable to the creditor for loss of more than £50 arising from unauthorised misuse of the credit card.

■ If a consumer's card is misused in connection with a distance contract the card holder will suffer no loss.

Enforcement and termination of the agreement

■ If a debtor or hirer is liable to make payments to the same person under two or more regulated agreements, and sends less than the total sums due, he can allocate the payments towards one or more of the agreements as he sees fit (s.81(1)).

■ If the court finds a credit bargain extortionate it may reopen the credit agreement so as to do justice between the parties (s.137(1)).

■ The debtor under a regulated consumer credit agreement is entitled to discharge the debt at any time by giving the creditor notice in writing and by repaying the whole debt (s.94(1)).

■ If a debtor terminates a regulated hire-purchase or conditional sale agreement early, arrears must be paid. The debtor may also be required to bring payments made (including arrears) up to half of the total price. If the debtor has failed to take reasonable care of the goods, the amount payable should be increased to compensate the creditor for this.

■ If a debtor repudiates a hire-purchase agreement the creditor will be able to sue for arrears and for damages for loss of the bargain.

■ If the creditor terminates a hire-purchase agreement on account of a breach by the debtor which did not amount to a repudiation, the creditor will be entitled to arrears (plus interest) but not to damages for the loss of the bargain.

■ A hire-purchase agreement is an agreement under which a debtor hires goods for a fixed period, and has an option to buy the goods for a nominal sum at the end of that period. The debtor has no obligation to continue with the agreement for the whole of the fixed period.

■ Under a conditional sale a buyer agrees to buy goods but the ownership of the goods is not to pass to the buyer until all of the price has been paid. There is an agreement to sell from the outset and the buyer agrees to make all of the payments.

Summary questions

1 Are the following agreements regulated agreements within the meaning given by the Consumer Credit Act 1974? If not, why not?

   a Acme Ltd buys a new van on conditional sale from Ace Finance Ltd. Acme is to make 24 monthly payments of £600. The total interest to be paid, at a rate of 15%, is £2 500.

   b Bill, a self-employed carpenter, hires a van for one year. Bill agrees to pay £200 a month in hire charges.

   c Charlene borrows £2 000 from the bank at which she works so that she can go on an expensive holiday. The loan is to be repaid over 12 months at an APR of 6%, a rate available only to the bank's employees.

   d David, a postman, sells his car to Edward, a plumber. Edward agrees to pay £200 a month for 12 months. This figure includes interest at an APR of 15%.

   e Felicity takes a car on hire-purchase from Ace Finance Ltd. The agreement provides for 24 monthly payments of £200. The APR is 24%.

   f Gerald, a partner in a firm of builders, takes a JCB digger on hire-purchase from Ace Finance Ltd, on behalf of the firm. Gerald pays a deposit of £3 000. 36 instalments of £1 000 are to be paid. The APR is 14%, and the total interest payable if the agreement runs its course will be £7 500.

2 Jim goes to an electrical retailer to buy a new stereo system. A salesman explains which system he considers the best buy and Jim is persuaded to take such a system under a regulated hire-purchase agreement. Jim signs an unexecuted copy of the agreement while in the shop. What copies, if any, must be sent to Jim? What cancellation rights, if any, does Jim have?

3 Jim went to a local garage because he was thinking of buying a car. A salesman explained which car he thought would best suit Jim's needs. The next day Jim phoned the garage to say that he was thinking of buying the recommended car. The garage sent Jim a copy of an unexecuted regulated conditional sale agreement. Jim signs this and sends it back. What copies or notices must Jim be supplied with? Is there a cooling-off period?

4 Tony visits Ace Computers Ltd's shop where a salesman persuades him that a particular model of computer will be perfect for his needs. As Tony cannot afford to pay cash, the salesman arranges a hire-purchase agreement under which Tony takes the recommended computer from Acme Finance Ltd. Tony soon discovers that the computer is totally unsuitable for his needs. Ace Computers Ltd has gone into liquidation. Advise Tony of any way in which the Consumer Credit Act 1974 might help him.

5 Mary bought a new bed from Sleepy Stores Ltd, paying the price with her Access card. Before the bed was delivered, Sleepy Stores Ltd went into liquidation. Advise Mary of any way in which the Consumer Credit Act 1974 might help her.

6 Delia takes a new cooker on hire-purchase from Acme Finance Ltd, paying a £50 deposit. The agreement is to run for 36 months and ownership of the cooker is to pass to Delia when she has paid 36 monthly instalments of £50. Delia pays the first ten instalments but she defaults on the eleventh payment. Motors Ltd repossess the cooker immediately, without a court order. Explain Mary's legal position. How would your answer be different if after paying ten monthly instalments Mary had written to Acme Finance Ltd saying that she could not make any more payments?

7 In the transactions described below, company A has agreed to supply machinery to company B. The seven transactions described provide one example of each of the following types of credit: trade credit; a loan; hire-purchase; a conditional sale; a contract of hire; a credit sale; and an overdraft. Match the transactions to the various types of credit. You might, for example, think that (a) was an example of a hire-purchase.

   a Company B takes possession of the machinery, but ownership is not to pass to company B until they have paid all 36 instalments of the price. At the outset company B commits itself to making all 36 payments.

   b Company B takes possession of the machinery, but ownership is not to pass to company B until they have paid all 36 instalments of the price. Company B does not commit itself to making all 36 payments.

   c Along with the machinery, company A sends an invoice which requests payment in full within 28 days.

d Company B has agreed to pay £1 000 a month for the use of the machinery until it has filled an order. After that the machinery will be returned to company A.

e Company B's bank has agreed that company B can pay for the machinery by writing a cheque for £10 000. The company bank balance stands at £2 300.

f Company B's bank has credited the company account with £10 000 so that the machinery can be bought. Company B are to repay this money by paying £560 a month for two years.

g Company B takes immediate possession of the machinery and gets immediate ownership of it. The contract of sale says that the price is to be paid by 12 monthly instalments of £1 000 each.

Multiple choice questions

1 Peter, a self-employed builder, agrees to buy a new van on conditional sale for £17 500. Peter is allowed £1 000 for his old van and pays £2 000 cash. Peter is to pay for the van by making 36 monthly instalments and the total interest payable is £4 500. For the purposes of the Consumer Credit Act 1974, how much credit has been extended to Peter?

a £10 000.

b £13 000.

c £14 500.

d £17 500.

2 Mary bought a new bed and a bedside lamp from a large department store. The bed cost £650 and the lamp £22. Mary paid for both items with her credit card. Before the goods were delivered the department store went into liquidation. Which **one** of the following statements is true?

a Mary will have no remedy, other than to claim against the department store as an unsecured creditor.

b As Mary had paid for the goods she would have a charge over them and would therefore be entitled to delivery of them.

c The credit card company will have to recredit Mary's account with both the price of the bed and of the lamp.

d The credit card company will have to recredit Mary's account with the price of the bed. It will not have to recredit the account with the price of the lamp.

3 Which **one** of the following statements is true?

a A credit agreement with an APR of 130% is automatically void.

b A credit agreement can be a debtor–creditor–supplier agreement even if there are only two parties involved – the creditor (who is also the legal supplier of the goods or services) and the debtor.

c All credit agreements where the credit is less than £25 000 will be regulated agreements, for the purposes of the Consumer Credit Act.

d The Consumer Credit Act protects only consumers, that is to say people who take the credit other than in the course of a business.

4 Gerald is a policeman. Gerald's debit card is stolen from his wallet. Before Gerald notices the theft, the thief uses the card to order goods over the Internet. This reduces Gerald's credit balance from £1 200 to £950. Gerald then phones the bank to tell them of the theft. The bank ask for written confirmation which Gerald sends the following day. Just before the letter was posted the thief reduced Gerald's bank balance to £700 by using the card to buy goods in a shop. By the time the letter arrived Gerald's balance had been reduced by the thief to £500 as the thief had used the card to buy more goods over the Internet. Which one of the following statements is true?

a The bank will have no liability to recredit Gerald's account with any of the stolen money.

b The bank will have to recredit Gerald's account with £250.

c The bank will have to recredit Gerald's account with £450.

d The bank will have to recredit Gerald's account with £700.

5 MacNavvy Ltd need a new steamroller in order to complete a lucrative contract. MacNavvy have not got enough money to pay the full price outright. Steamrollers Ltd deliver a new steamroller to MacNavvy. The contract states that MacNavvy are to have immediate possession of the steamroller and that they commit themselves to paying for it in 24 equal instalments. Ownership of the steamroller is not to pass until MacNavvy have paid all of the instalments. Is this contract an example of:

a Hire-purchase?

b Conditional sale?

c Credit sale?

d Trade credit?

6 John visits a car dealer's showroom and selects a new car. A triangular transaction is entered into and John takes the car on hire-purchase from the finance company. Which **one** of the following statements reflects the legal position?

a John owns the car. He has committed himself to paying all of the instalments due under the hire-purchase agreement. If John fails to pay all of these instalments then the finance company will be able to repossess the car.

b John owns the car. He has not committed himself to paying all of the instalments due under the hire-purchase agreement. However, if John fails to pay all of these instalments then the finance company will be able to repossess the car.

c The finance company own the car. John has not committed himself to paying all of the instalments due under the hire-purchase agreement. However, if John fails to pay the instalments then the finance company will be entitled to take possession of the car from him.

d The dealer owns the car. John has not committed himself to paying all of the instalments due under the hire-purchase agreement. However, if John fails to pay the instalments then the dealer will be entitled to take possession of the car from him.

Task 14

MacThomson Roadworks is a partnership repairs roads and drives. The partners decide that they would like to buy a new steamroller, but the firm does not have the money to make such a purchase.

Write a report for the partners, indicating:

a The various ways in which the steamroller might be acquired without paying the full price immediately.

b The main provisions of the Consumer Credit Act 1974.

Chapter 15

PARTNERSHIP

Introduction

This is the first of five chapters which examine the law relating to companies, partnerships and limited liability partnerships. A person who trades on his own account does so as a sole trader. When two or more people go into business together, with the intention of making a profit for themselves, they must either do so as a company, a partnership or a limited liability partnership. The law relating to companies is examined in the following four chapters. In this chapter we examine the law relating to partnerships.

It has recently become possible to trade as a limited liability partnership. The law relating to such partnerships is examined in Chapter 19. In this chapter we examine the law relating to ordinary partnerships. In Chapter 19 we also consider the relative merits of trading as a company, a partnership, a limited liability partnership or a sole trader. Once the law relating to the different types of business organisations has been understood, the relative merits of each are more readily appreciated.

In recent years it has become increasingly easy to run a company, as the formalities with which companies must comply have been considerably reduced. To some extent this has made trading as a partnership a less attractive option. However, over half a million businesses continue to trade as partnerships.

More than a hundred years ago the Partnership Act 1890 codified the common law relating to partnership. The 1890 Act is generally easy to understand and has remained the foundation of the law. Section 4 of the Act provides that people who have entered into a partnership with one another are known as a firm and throughout this chapter the word firm is used to mean a partnership.

15.1 · The nature of partnership

Partnership is a contractual relationship. The partners make a contract with each other and, as regards their relationship with each other, partners are generally free to agree whatever terms they wish. In the absence of agreement to the contrary, s.24 sets out nine terms which are implied into the contract which the partners make. As we shall see, these terms are generally expressly excluded by a formal partnership agreement.

In addition to the s.24 implied terms, ss.28–30 of the Act set out three fiduciary duties which partners owe to each other. These duties have their origins in equity and are aspects of the wider fiduciary duties which partners owe to each other. Although the fiduciary duties cannot be contracted out of, it can be a defence to breach of a fiduciary duty to show that the other partners consented to the breach.

The liability of partners to those outside the firm is based on the law of agency. The partners have wide authority to bind the firm. This authority might be actual, apparent or usual. (As we saw in Chapter 11 at 11.2, actual authority would be created by agreement between the principal and agent, apparent authority would be created by a representation made by the principal to the third party with whom the agent contracted, and usual authority would exist on account of the agent occupying a certain role or position.) These types of authority often overlap. It can be important to distinguish between them because actual authority can only arise by agreement between the partners, whereas apparent and usual authority arises regardless of agreement that it should arise, and can give a partner authority to do an act which he has been forbidden to do.

In Chapter 19 at 19.2 we shall see that it is possible to register a partnership at Companies House as a Limited Liability Partnership. Such firms have a legal existence of their own, as companies do. However, an ordinary partnership, a firm, has no legal existence of its own. Partnership is a relationship not a legal entity. Partnership property is owned not by the partnership itself, but is held by the partners on trust for each other.

15.2 · The definition of a partnership

The Partnership Act 1890 s.1(1) gives the following definition: 'Partnership is the relation which subsists between persons carrying on a business in common with a view of profit.' Although this definition is short, it is a matter of some complexity. It is most easily understood if broken down into its constituent parts.

Before analysing the definition, it is important to realise that, for several reasons, the question as to whether or not a partnership exists can be a matter of considerable significance. Perhaps the most important of these reasons is that if a partnership does exist the actions of an individual partner can make all of the partners liable to outsiders. Another important reason is that if a partnership exists an individual partner will have rights against the other partners, such as the right to share profits or the right to have the other partners share the losses. The Inland Revenue will also take an interest in whether or not a business constitutes a partnership. A person who operates as a partner will be taxed accordingly.

15.2.1 Partnership is the relation which subsists between persons

This opening phrase of the definition is important because it shows that partnership is merely a relationship. A partnership is not a separate legal identity (as a company and limited liability partnership are) with a legal existence of its own. It follows from this that a partnership cannot, as an entity separate from the partners, employ staff or own property. (As we shall see below, at 15.6, it is convenient to talk of partnership property. However, this property is not owned by the partnership, but owned by the partners who hold it on trust for each other.) When in Chapter 19 at 19.2 we examine Limited Liability Partnerships (LLPs) we shall see that LLPs do have a separate legal identity of their own. However, LLPs can be created only by registration with Companies House and are, as yet, quite uncommon. Throughout this chapter when reference to a partnership is made it is reference to an ordinary partnership and not to an LLP.

The relationship which constitutes a partnership is based on a contract, as the following statement of Jessel MR in *Pooley* v *Driver* (1876) 5 ChD 458 makes clear:

> 'But it [partnership] is a contract of some kind undoubtedly – a contract, like all contracts, involving the mutual consent of the parties: and it is undoubtedly a contract for the purpose of carrying on a commercial business – that is, a business bringing profit, and dividing the profit in some shape or other between the partners. That certainly partnership is.'

Although a partnership is a contract of some kind, it is important to realise that what must be agreed in the contract is that the partners should carry on a business together with a view of making a profit. Whether or not a partnership exists is not a matter of asking whether or not the parties agreed with each other that they should be in partnership. We shall see below at 15.3 that there is no need for the partners to agree that they are in partnership with each other, and that people can be partners even without realising that they are.

By stating that a partnership is the relation which subsists between persons, s.1(1) of the Act also makes it plain that a person who trades solely on his own account, a sole trader, cannot be a partnership. As we shall see in Chapter 17, it is possible for a person trading without others to form a registered company in which he is the sole shareholder and sole director, and to trade through the company. (However, a different person will be needed to act as company secretary.)

As a company is regarded by the law as a legal person, it is possible for a company to be a member of a partnership. Companies can go into partnership with each other, or they can go into partnership with a natural person. A company which does become a partner will be liable for the firm's debts in the same way as any other partner. However, if the company is limited its shareholders cannot become personally liable for company debts incurred as a consequence of the company being a partner. Although a company can go into partnership with other people, s.1(2) of the Act provides that a company cannot itself be a partnership.

15.2.2 Carrying on a business

Section 45 of the Partnership Act defines 'business' as including 'every trade, occupation or profession'. However, some professions, such as the Bar, have rules which prevent their members from operating as partnerships. Other professions might prevent partnership with unqualified persons. Solicitors, for example, are not allowed to go into partnership with persons who are not themselves either solicitors or registered as foreign lawyers.

Although a partnership can only exist if a business is carried on, this does not necessarily prevent persons engaging in a one-off commercial enterprise from being in partnership. In *Mann v D'Arcy and others* [1968] 2 All ER 172 a partner in a firm of produce merchants made a one-off agreement with the claimant, whereby the firm and the claimant were to make a single purchase of 350 tons of potatoes to sell at a profit. It was held that this did create a partnership between the firm of produce merchants and the claimant, but only as regards this one deal.

We have seen that s.1(2) of the Act provides that a registered company cannot itself be a partnership, although it could be a member of a partnership. In the following case the Court of Appeal had to decide whether the promoters of a company were in partnership with each other.

■ *Keith Spicer Ltd v Mansell* [1970] 1 All ER 462 (Court of Appeal)

The defendant and B agreed to go into business together. They intended to form a limited company, which was to run the defendant's restaurant. Before the company was formed B ordered goods from the claimants. These goods were intended to be used by the company. The defendant and B also opened a bank account in the name of the proposed company, but without the word 'Limited'. The claimant was not paid for the goods which B ordered. He sued the defendant for the price, alleging that B and the defendant were in partnership.

Held. B and the defendant were not in partnership and so the claimant's claim failed. B and the defendant were not carrying on a business in common with a view of profit, they were merely working together to form a company. They did not intend to carry on a partnership prior to incorporation.

In the following case the House of Lords had to consider whether persons intending to trade as a partnership could be partners before the business actually began to trade.

■ *Khan v Mia* [2000] 1 WLR 2123 (House of Lords)

The two claimants and the three defendants proposed to open a restaurant. One of the parties was to be the restaurant manager, two were to be chefs and the other two were to provide capital. The proposed manager took a lease on suitable premises and he and one of the chefs opened a bank account, describing themselves as 'partners' in a business which was to be created at the beginning of December 1993. Furniture, laundry services and equipment were purchased and the business was advertised in the local press. The freehold of the restaurant premises was bought at auction but completion did not take place until January 1994. There were then delays in the building work and in one party finding capital and this caused the parties' relationship to break down. The relationship between the parties was ended by a solicitor's letter in January. In order to sort out the rights of the parties it became necessary to know whether or not a partnership had ever existed. The trial judge found that there had been a partnership, the Court of Appeal reversed this ruling and an appeal was made to the House of Lords.

Held. The parties had been in partnership. There was no rule of law that parties could not become partners until trading actually began. People who agreed to carry on a business as a joint venture became partners when they embarked on the agreed activity and made contracts on behalf of the joint venture. The purchasing of the freehold, and the purchasing of the goods and the services were all part of the joint venture which the parties had undertaken with a view of profit and so they formed part of the business which the parties had been carrying on as partners.

COMMENT (i) It would not be enough that the parties had merely agreed to become partners in the future. According to Lord Millett, who gave the leading judgment, it depended upon whether they had 'actually transacted any business of the joint venture'.

(ii) Lord Millett made it plain that whether or not parties who proposed to enter into a business venture had actually entered into it would be a question of fact for the trial judge. The House of Lords heard this case to refute the Court of Appeal's finding that there was a rule of law that parties to a joint venture cannot become partners until trading actually begins.

15.2.3 In common

A person will not become a partner in a firm merely on account of working for the firm. In order to become a partner a person must carry on a business in common with the other partners. The following case gives an indication as to what is required.

■ *Saywell* v *Pope* (1979) 53 TC 40

Since 1960 Mr P and Mr S had been partners in a firm which repaired and sold agricultural machinery. When the firm was created there was no written partnership agreement. Mrs P and Mrs S were employed by the firm and were paid small salaries. A partnership agreement was drawn up in 1975, on an accountant's advice. The agreement said that the four parties had gone into partnership on 6 April 1973, and the accounts credited the wives with a share of the profits from April 1973. Neither of the wives ever drew any profits from the firm. The wives contributed no capital to the business.

The wives ould not write cheques or draw upon the firm's bank account, but they were warned of the risk of becoming partners. Neither the firm's bank, its creditors or its customers were told that the wives had become partners. The Revenue decided that the wives were not partners in the tax years from 1973 to 1975, and an appeal against this decision was made to the High Court.

Held. The wives were not partners during the relevant tax years as they did nothing in their capacities as partners during those years. The written agreement could not operate retrospectively to make the wives partners. The decision as to whether or not the wives were partners at any particular time could only be made by examining all the facts of the case.

An employee of a business will not become a partner merely on account of receiving a share of the business profits. Something more is required, namely that the business is carried on together (that is to say carried on in common). Similarly, a person who supplies goods or services to a business will not be in partnership with the business merely because payment is taken in the form of a share of the profits. In *Strathearn Gordon Associates Ltd* v *Commissioners of Customs and Excise* [1985] VATTR 79 a limited company, SGA Ltd, acted as a management consultant for several companies involved in property developments. SGA Ltd did not charge a flat fee, but agreed to take a share of the various companies' profits as payment. The VAT tribunal unanimously decided that SGA Ltd was not in partnership with the seven companies. SGA Ltd were not carrying on a business in common with the seven companies. The taking of a share of the profits was merely a way of SGA Ltd getting paid for services provided to the companies.

15.2.4 With a view of profit

It is not necessary that a profit must be made before a partnership can exist. Many of the cases concerned with whether or not a partnership exists arise precisely because the business did not make a profit. What is required is that the partners should intend to make a profit. It is this requirement of an intention to make a profit which distinguishes partnerships from unincorporated associations, such as members' clubs. The members of an unincorporated association might talk of having made a profit or a loss, but what is really meant is that they have run a surplus or gone into debt. A distinguishing feature of a partnership is that the partners must have intended that the firm should make a profit which could be shared by the partners. Unincorporated associations are not set up with this purpose. They are set up with other purposes, such as to provide recreational facilities for their members.

■ *Pitreavie Golf Club* v *Penman* 1934 SLT 247

The Pitreavie Golf Club was an unincorporated association, set up for the purposes of playing golf. A person who was owed money by the club's council of members had not been paid, and wanted to make the club bankrupt. Under Scots law this would only have been possible if the club was either a partnership or a company. As the club was clearly not a company, it was argued that it was a partnership.

Held. The club was not a partnership. The club's motivation was to allow its members to play golf, not to make a profit to be shared amongst the members.

15.3 · Specific indications as to whether or not a partnership exists

Whether or not a partnership exists will always depend upon whether or not the definition of partnership which is set out in s.1(1) of the Act has been fulfilled. However, s.2 of the Act lays down rules which can help determine whether or not a partnership exists. It is important to remember that these rules are no more than indications.

15.3.1 Joint or common ownership of property

Section 2(1): 'Joint tenancy, tenancy in common, joint property, common property, or part ownership does not of itself create a partnership as to anything so held or owned, whether the tenants or owners do or do not share any profits made by the use thereof.'

 This section was considered in the following case.

■ *Davis* v *Davis* [1894] 1 Ch 393

Under his will, a testator left property to his two sons, as tenants in common. At the time of inheriting the property, which was comprised of a business and three houses, the sons were not in partnership. The sons carried on the business and both usually took £3 a week from it. Whenever one son took more than this, the other took an identical amount. One of the three houses was rented out, and the rent was used to enlarge workshops attached to the other two houses.

Held. The sons were in partnership as regards the business because their conduct suggested partnership. The fact of drawing out identical sums of money inferred that they had agreed to share the profits. They were not in partnership as regards the three houses, as their conduct did not show anything to overturn the presumption contained in s.2(1). Consequently the workshops did not become partnership property.

15.3.2 Sharing of gross returns

Section 2(2): 'The sharing of gross returns does not of itself create a partnership, whether the persons sharing such returns have or have not a joint or common right or interest in any property from which or from the use of which the returns are derived.'

Gross returns might today be referred to more commonly as gross takings. They would consist of all the money which the firm took in. Gross profits are quite different, consisting of any surplus which remained after all liabilities had been discharged.

■ *Cox* v *Coulson* [1916] 2 KB 177 (Court of Appeal)

The defendant, who leased and managed a theatre, agreed to stage a play with the manager of a touring theatrical company. The defendant was to provide the use of the theatre and the lighting. The manager of the theatrical company was to provide the actors and the scenery. The defendant was to get 60% of the gross takings, the manager of the touring theatre company was to get 40%. During a performance of the play an actor had to shoot a gun which should have been loaded with a blank. Somehow the gun contained a live bullet. When the gun was fired the claimant, a member of the audience, was hit in the wrist and suffered a severe injury. The claimant claimed damages from the defendant on the grounds that the defendant was in partnership with the manager of the touring company.

Held. There was no partnership and so the defendant was not liable. There was nothing in the behaviour of the two managers to contradict the presumption in s.2(2). Neither of them was the agent of the other, and it would have been possible for one of them to have made a profit while the other made a loss.

15.3.3 The receipt of a share of the profits

Section 2(3) begins by stating that: 'The receipt by a person of a share of the profits of a business is *prima facie* evidence that he is a partner in the business, but the receipt of such a share, or of a payment contingent on or varying with the profits of a business, does not of itself make him a partner in the business; ...' The subsection goes on to list situations, examined below, in which there is a presumption against a person who receives a share of the profits being a partner. In the absence of evidence to the contrary, though, a person who receives a share of the profits will be a partner. If there is other evidence, it must be considered.

The five situations listed in s.2(3), where it is presumed that a person is not a partner merely on account of receiving a share of the profits, are as follows:

(i) Where a share of the profits is taken as the payment of a debt, whether taken by instalments or not;
(ii) Where a share of the profits is taken as a salary;
(iii) Where a widow or a child of a deceased partner receives a share of the profits by way of an annuity;
(iv) Where a written contract makes the interest on a loan vary according to the profits of the business;
(v) Where a share of the profits is taken as payment for the goodwill of a business.

The following case demonstrates the working of this last exception.

■ *Pratt* v *Strick* [1932] 17 TC 459

One doctor sold his practice and the goodwill to another doctor. Part of the price was paid. The selling doctor agreed to remain at the practice for three months to introduce the new doctor to his patients and to help him generally. For these three months the profits of the business were split equally. The Revenue argued that for these three months the two doctors were in partnership. An appeal was made against this decision.

Held. The doctors were never in partnership. The practice was sold and after this the selling doctor agreed to help the other in return for payment.

It should be remembered that s.2(3) only provides that a receipt of a share of the profits is *prima facie* evidence that a person is a partner. It does not provide conclusive evidence of this, even as regards situations other than the five listed by s.2(3). Shortly after the Act was passed, North J in *Davis* v

Davis said: 'by sect.2, sub-sect 3, of the Act, the receipt by a person of a share of the profits of a business is *prima facie* evidence that he is a partner in it, and, if the matter stops there, it is evidence upon which the Court must act. But, if there are other circumstances to be considered, they ought to be considered fairly together – taking all the circumstances together, not attaching undue weight to any of them but drawing an inference from the whole.' In fact there must always be other evidence to be considered. Otherwise the agreement would have consisted solely of an agreement to share profits.

Test your understanding

1 What is the definition of a partnership?

2 Does a partnership have a separate legal identity of its own?

3 Can people be in partnership without having agreed with each other that they should be?

4 Can a company be a partner? Can a company be a partnership?

5 Can a partnership exist if no profit was ever made?

6 What is the essential difference between a partnership and an unincorporated association (such as a members' club)?

7 If a person takes a share of the profits of a business does this automatically make him a partner?

Answers

1 Section 1(1) of the Partnership Act 1890 defines a partnership as 'the relation which subsists between persons carrying on a business in common with a view of profit'.

2 A partnership does not have a legal identity of its own. A partnership is only a relationship between the partners. (Limited Liability Partnerships are different and do have a separate legal identity of their own.)

3 People can be in partnership with each other without having agreed that they should be. They must however make a contract with each other, agreeing to carry on a business together with the intention of making a profit.

4 A company can be a partner in a firm. A company cannot be a partnership.

5 A partnership can exist even though no profit was ever made. However, a partnership can only exist if the partners intended to make a profit for themselves.

6 An unincorporated association differs from a partnership in that its members do not have the intention of making a profit which they will share amongst themselves.

7 The receipt by a person of a share of the profits of a business is only *prima facie* evidence that he is a partner. The Partnership Act lists five situations where it is presumed that a person receiving a share of the profits is not a partner. Even in other situations the decision as to whether or not a person receiving a share of the profits is a partner must be based on all of the evidence to see if what was agreed fits within s.1(1)'s definition of a partnership.

15.4 · The partnership agreement

Although there is no need to have a formal partnership agreement, the vast majority of partnerships do draw such an agreement up. However, before examining the terms which are likely to be found in such agreements, we should remember that a partnership can be created informally and that people can be partners without realising that this is the case.

Earlier in this chapter, at 15.2.1, we saw that partnership is based upon a contractual agreement. Therefore a partnership is only created if all of the requirements of a contract are fulfilled. There must be an offer, an acceptance, an intention to create legal relations and consideration. The contract must not be void for mistake or illegality, and it might be rendered voidable by misrepresentation, duress or undue influence. The contract might become frustrated if it subsequently becomes impossible to perform, or illegal to perform, or if it can be performed only in a manner which is radically different from what the parties contemplated when they made it.

Where the terms of the agreement are not expressed by the partners they might either be implied by the Partnership Act or implied as a matter of general construction of contracts. (The circumstances in which terms will be implied into a contract were considered in Chapter 5 at 5.3.)

15.4.1 Formal partnership agreements

Formal partnership agreements are often known as articles of partnership. Such agreements are commonly set out as a deed, although there is no requirement that they should be. There are 13 or so matters which would be dealt with by almost any formal partnership agreement. We therefore make a brief consideration of these 13 'universal' articles.

15.4.1.1 The parties to the agreement

The agreement should clearly set out who is a partner and who is not. However, as we saw in *Saywell v Pope*, the final decision as to whether or not a person is a partner can only be made in the light of all of the evidence. It should also be realised that the fact that a person is not included in the agreement as a partner will not prevent him from being liable as a partner if he is, with his knowledge, held out as a partner to third parties. (Liability by holding out is considered below at 15.8.3.)

15.4.1.2 The nature of the business

There are three principal reasons why it is important to clearly set out the nature of the partnership business. First, s.5 of the Act makes partners agents of the firm and of their fellow partners for the purposes of the firm's business, but not for other purposes. Second, s.30 imposes a fiduciary duty preventing partners from carrying on a business which competes with the business of the firm or is of the same nature as the business of the firm. (It is however a defence to breach of this duty that the other partners consented to the competition.) Third, having been defined, the nature of the partnership business can only be varied by the consent of all of the partners (s.24(8)). However, this consent can be inferred from the partners' behaviour (s.19).

15.4.1.3 The name of the firm

The name of the firm should be clearly identified. Partners commonly choose to be known by their collective surnames, although they can in general choose to be known by any other name. There is no need to register the firm's name. There is a register of company names and LLP names but there is no central registry of partnership names. However, three factors should be borne in mind when choosing a name. First, the name must comply with the requirements of the Business Names Act 1985. Second, the name must not be designed to deceive the public by causing confusion with another business. Third, s.34 of the Companies Act 1985 makes it a criminal offence for a partnership to use the word 'limited' or 'Ltd' in its name.

Business Names Act 1985

This Act applies to partnerships if they carry on business in a name other than the surnames of all the partners. The Act will not apply if the partners merely add their forenames or initials to their surnames. However, the use of any other name, even the use of their surnames and '& Co', will mean that the name used must comply with the provisions of the Act.

Section 2 makes it a criminal offence to use certain names unless the written approval of the Secretary of State for Trade and Industry is granted. Section 2(1)(a) prohibits the use of names which would suggest a connection with Government or with any local authority. Section 2(1)(b) prevents the inclusion of words or expressions contained in the Companies and Business Names Regulations 1981, as amended. About 100 or so words are specified, including authority, charity, chartered, dental, English, European, institute, Irish, nursing, police, Royal, Scottish, society and Welsh. The

Secretary of State can grant permission for such names to be used after a request has been made to the relevant body specified in the Regulations. For example, to use the word 'dental' the applicant would first need to write to the relevant body, the General Dental Council, and then send a copy of the letter and the written response to the Secretary of State who could then grant permission.

Section 4 states that a notice containing the names of each partner, and an address at which they can be served with documents, must be prominently displayed at any business premises to which the customers or suppliers have access. Further, partnerships with 20 or fewer members must include the names of each partner, and an address at which they can be served with documents, on all business letters, written orders for goods or services, invoices and receipts. Partnerships with more than 20 partners do not have to include the names of all partners on all these business documents, but have to keep a list of all the partners' names and addresses at the firm's principal place of business, along with a statement on the firm's stationery saying where this document is kept and at what times it is available for inspection. The list must be available for inspection during office hours. Failure to comply with the requirements of s.4 is a criminal offence.

Section 5 states that a party who breaches s.4 may not be able to enforce contracts made while s.4 was being breached. However, this will only be the case if the defendant can show that he could not pursue a claim against the firm because of the breach of s.4 or can show that he has suffered financial loss in connection with the contract by reason of the firm's breach of s.4.

Confusion with other businesses

As long as the provisions of the Business Names Act are complied with, and as long as the intention is not to deceive the public, partners can trade under any name they like. However, if a name is likely to cause confusion with another business, or to deceive the public, an action for the tort of passing-off might be brought. If successful such an action could result in an injunction preventing the further use of the name or in the payment of damages. James LJ put the position as follows in *Levy* v *Walker* (1879) 10 ChD 436: 'It should never be forgotten in these cases that the sole right to restrain anybody from using any name that he likes in the course of any business he chooses to carry on is a right in the nature of a trade mark, that is to say, a man has a right to say "You must not use a name, whether fictitious or real, you must not use a description, whether true or not, which is intended to represent, or calculated to represent, to the world that your business is my business, and so, by a fraudulent misstatement, deprive me of the profits of the business which would otherwise come to me."'

The following case provides a clear example of passing-off.

■ *Croft* v *Day* (1843) 7 Beav 84

A well-established firm had for a long time carried on business selling lampblack as Day and Martin at 97 High Holborn. (Lampblack could be used to give a black finish to shoes or metal.) A certain Mr Day, having obtained permission from one Martin to use his name, set up in the same trade at 90 High Holborn. This new outfit sold lampblack, in bottles which resembled those of the old firm, under the name Day and Martin 90 High Holborn.

Held. An injunction was granted preventing the new firm from trading under the name Day and Martin. The intention of the new firm was to deceive the public.

The tort of passing-off is not limited to the use of the name or trade mark of a business. In *Cadbury Schweppes Ltd* v *Pub Squash Co Ltd* [1981] 1 WLR 193 the Privy Council held that passing-off was wide enough to encompass other descriptive materials, such as slogans or visual images associated with the claimant's product by means of an advertising campaign. However, it is still required that the public must be deceived or misled into thinking that the defendant's product was the claimant's product. As long as the public is not deceived in this way, the tort of passing-off will not prevent one business from taking advantage of an advertising campaign conducted by another business.

15.4.1.4 Dates of commencement and dissolution

A formal partnership agreement will almost always state the date on which the partnership is to commence. However, as we saw in *Saywell* v *Pope*, this is not conclusive evidence as to whether or not the partnership did in fact commence on that date. The date at which a partnership commenced is a matter of fact, which will be determined by examining all of the evidence. However, the fact that a partnership agreement states a date of commencement is likely to be very strong evidence of a partnership having existed from that date.

A formal partnership agreement might or might not give a date on which the partnership is to end. If such a date is specified then the partnership can only be ended in advance of that date by one of the matters specified in the Partnership Act or by a court order. (These matters are examined below at 15.9.2 and 15.9.3.) So if a date for dissolution is fixed no single partner will be able to dissolve the firm by giving notice before that date.

If no date for dissolution is fixed, the partnership is known as a partnership at will, and any one of the partners can dissolve the firm by giving notice. Section 26(1) provides that: 'Where no fixed term has been agreed upon for the duration of the partnership, any partner may determine the partnership at any time on giving notice of his intention so to do to all the other partners.' This section is not as straightforward as it might appear, and has to be considered in conjunction with s.32(c), which states: 'Subject to any agreement between the partners a partnership is dissolved … if entered into for an undefined time, by any partner giving notice to the other or others of his intention to dissolve the partnership.' The effect of these two provisions was considered in the following case.

■ *Moss* v *Elphick* [1910] 1 KB 846 (Court of Appeal)

In 1907 the claimant and the defendant made a written agreement to be partners in a tobacconist's business in Brighton. Clause 4 of the agreement stated that 'This agreement shall be terminated by mutual agreement only.' In 1909 one of the partners gave the other a fortnight's notice in writing to dissolve the partnership. The other partner argued that this could not be done as the termination had not been mutually agreed.

Held. The partnership could not be ended by the one partner giving notice. Section 32(c) did not apply because it begins with the words, 'Subject to any agreement between the partners …' Clause 4 was such an agreement. Section 26(1) did not apply either. It is to apply only where no fixed term has been agreed for the duration of the partnership. This was interpreted as meaning in cases where the partnership agreement was silent as to the duration of the partnership. Fletcher Moulton LJ explained that the parties had made an agreement for the duration of the joint lives of the parties, unless they both agreed otherwise. He regarded this as for a fixed (i.e. defined) term. He did not think that s.26(1) was intended to interfere with freedom of contract.

The partners do not have to end the partnership upon expiry of a fixed term. Section 27 provides that if all the partners carry the firm on then, unless they agree to the contrary, it is presumed that they carry on under the terms of the agreement which has expired.

15.4.1.5 The capital of the firm and of the individual partners

Section 24(1) provides that 'All the partners are entitled to share equally in the capital and the profits of the business, and must contribute equally towards the losses, whether of capital or otherwise sustained by the firm.'

This presumption that partners will contribute capital equally, and be entitled to equal repayment of capital on dissolution, is very commonly varied. In many partnerships one partner provides the capital while the others provide business skills. The repayment of capital on dissolution is examined below at 15.9.6, where we shall see that the provisions of the Act apply unless there has been a contrary agreement. For the sake of certainty, the partnership agreement should clearly spell out the intentions of the parties.

Section 24(4) provides that, 'A partner is not entitled, before the ascertainment of profits, to interest on the capital subscribed by him.' This implied term is commonly varied so that partners are paid interest on their capital, as if capital contributed were a loan to the firm.

Partnership property is an important concept which is examined below at 15.6. Here it is enough to say that as well as dealing with capital contributions the agreement should make it plain whether property which is used by the firm is partnership property or remains the property of the individual partners.

15.4.1.6 The salary and profit entitlement of the partners

Very commonly, partners do not share equally in the profits of the firm. We have already seen that s.24(1) rules that profits and losses are to be shared equally unless the partners agree otherwise. Obviously, the partnership agreement is the most appropriate place for unequal share in profits to be spelled out. Sometimes the partnership agreement provides for the payment of a notional salary to a partner. This no more than a way of distributing the profits amongst the partners and does not make the recipient an employee.

15.4.1.7 The management of the business

Section 24(5) states that 'Every partner may take part in the management of the partnership business.' As all of s.24 applies only if no contrary agreement is expressly or impliedly made, it is possible to have a dormant or sleeping partner who has no right to manage the business. Such a partner will normally take advantage of the Limited Partnership Act 1907, which is examined below at 15.10.

The partnership agreement should set out the duties of the various partners, how majority decisions should be taken, and whether or not some partners are excluded from the right to do certain things. It is commonly the case that partners do not have equal voting or management rights. If a partner is excluded from the management of the firm without having agreed to this, the courts will regard this as a reason to dissolve the firm.

15.4.1.8 Banking arrangements and the right to draw cheques

The partnership agreement should name the firm's bank and specify whether or not individual partners have the right to draw cheques on the partnership account. It is commonly agreed that the signatures of two partners are required on cheques to the value of more than a specified amount. The bank will not be bound by the partnership agreement but has a duty to obey the mandate given by the customer. Therefore if the provisions of the partnership agreement are reproduced in the mandate given to the bank, the bank will not be entitled to debit the firm's account if the provisions of the partnership agreement are not observed.

15.4.1.9 The firm's accounts

The agreement will generally arrange for accounts to be drawn up on certain dates. By reference to these accounts the partners will know how they stand as regards each other, and the firm will know how it stands as regards outsiders.

15.4.1.10 Admission and expulsion of partners

The agreement should set out the grounds on which a partner can be expelled from the partnership. It is also sensible to set out the circumstances in which new partners can be admitted. If there is no express or implied agreement to the contrary, a new partner can only be admitted by the consent of all of the existing partners (s.24(7)). Very often partnership agreements do agree otherwise, so that a new partner can be admitted without the consent of all the existing partners.

15.4.1.11 Death or retirement of partners

Section 33(1) provides that the death of a partner dissolves the firm unless the partners agree otherwise. It would be usual in a commercial firm for the partnership agreement to state that the firm should be carried on after the death of a partner, and to provide a right for a partner to retire from the firm after giving a stated period of notice. (Technically, the firm would still have been dissolved. Section 33(1) deals with whether the firm should continue or be wound up.) In addition, it is important to set out the financial arrangements to be applied when a partner dies or retires. The partnership agreement might also contain a restraint of trade clause preventing a partner from competing with the firm after retirement. In Chapter 6 at 6.4.3 we examined the circumstances in which such a clause will be valid.

15.4.1.12 Valuation of the goodwill

The goodwill is considered below at 15.9.5. The agreements should set out how the goodwill should be valued and the entitlement, in respect of the goodwill, of partners who die or retire.

15.4.1.13 Arbitration

One of the most important provisions of a partnership agreement is that disputes should be referred to arbitration. If there is no such provision then disputes between partners could become the subject of litigation. The publicity which this might generate could be very damaging to the firm, and perhaps to the future prospects of the partners as individuals.

In addition to these 13 'universal articles', the following points should also be considered.

15.4.1.14 Variation of partnership agreement

Having been made, a partnership agreement can be altered by the consent of all of the partners, but this consent can be inferred from a course of dealing (s.19). Lord Eldon gave an example of how this might happen in *Const v Harris* (1824) 37 ER 1191: 'If in a common partnership, the parties agree that no one of them shall draw or accept a bill of exchange in his own name, without the concurrence of all the others, yet, if they afterwards slide into a habit of permitting one of them to draw or accept bills, without the concurrence of the others, this Court will hold that they have varied the terms of the original agreement in that respect.'

Simple partnership agreement

This partnership agreement is made on *(date)*...............................

between *(name 1)*...........................of *(address*

(1)...

and *(name 2)*.................................. of *(address*

(2)...

and *(name 3)*..................................of *(address*

(3)...

It is agreed as follows:

(1) The partners shall carry on business in partnership as *(nature of business)*

....

under the firm name of *(partnership name)*...

of *(partnership address)*...

....

(2) The partnership will commence on the date of this agreement and shall continue in existence for five years.

(3) The partnership capital shall be contributed by the partners in equal shares and the partners shall be entitled to the profits arising from the partnership in equal shares.

(4) The bankers of the firm shall be

(name).. of

(address)...

....

Cheques drawn in the name of the firm must be signed by all of the partners.

(5) Each partner shall devote his or her whole time to the business of the partnership.

(6) Each partner shall be entitled to *(number)*...................................weeks' holiday each year.

(7) None of the partners shall without the consent of the other: engage in any business other than partnership business; or employ or dismiss any partnership employee.

(8) Each partner shall be entitled to draw *(amount)*................as salary from the partnership bank account each month.

(9) All matters relating to the management of the affairs of the partnership shall be decided by votes taken at a meeting of the partners. At such meetings each partner shall be entitled to one vote and resolutions shall be passed by a simple majority vote.

(10) The accounts of the firm shall be made up on the close of business on the 4th of April each year.

(11) No majority of the partners shall be entitled to expel any partner. New partners may only be admitted with the consent of all existing partners.

(12) If any disputes should arise as to the meaning of this partnership deed, or as to the rights and liabilities of the partners under it, such disputes shall be referred to an arbitrator to be appointed by the President of the Chartered Institute of Arbitrators. The decision of the arbitrator shall be binding on all of the partners.

Signed as a deed by (name 1).............................in the presence of (witness)

....

Signed as a deed by (name 2).............................in the presence of (witness)

....

Signed as a deed by (name 3).............................in the presence of (witness)

....

A very simple model partnership agreement is set out above. Such an agreement could be adapted to suit the requirements of a very small firm starting up in business. More complicated partnership deeds can run to several thousand words. They cover the same matters as the simple deed in very much more detail. In addition, they might contain articles dealing with matters such as leasing premises, payment of private debts, negative covenants, banking arrangements, provisions for retiring partners, options to purchase the share of outgoing partners, income tax and retirement annuities.

15.4.1.15 Numbers of partners

Until recently most firms were not allowed to have more than twenty partners. This prohibition has now been lifted so that there is no upper limit on the number of members any firm may have.

15.4.1.16 Capacity of partners

It is possible for a minor (a person under 18 years of age) to become a partner. However, the partnership agreement is voidable, at the minor's option, until he reaches the age of 18 and for a reasonable time thereafter. If the minor does avoid the agreement it will no longer bind him and he will not be liable for debts incurred by the firm. If the minor does not avoid the agreement within a reasonable time of becoming 18 he will be bound by future debts of the firm, but not by debts incurred whilst he was a minor. So whether the minor avoids the agreement or not, he cannot be made liable for partnership debts incurred while he was a minor. However, adult partners are entitled to insist that the partnership assets, including capital contributed by a minor partner, shall be applied in payment of the liabilities of the partnership. Furthermore, the adult partners can insist that any losses suffered by the firm are settled before the minor receives any profit.

A mentally disordered partner can set aside a partnership agreement if he can prove that at the time of making the agreement he was of unsound mind so as not to understand what he was doing, and that the other partners were aware of this.

Test your understanding

1 Can people be in partnership if they do not make a formal partnership agreement?

2 What are the 13 'universal' matters which all formal partnership agreements are likely to deal with?

3 In what circumstances will the Business Names Act 1985 apply to a partnership?

4 What are the main provisions of the Business Names Act 1985, as they apply to partnerships?

5 What is a passing-off action?

6 In what circumstances can a partner terminate the partnership by giving notice?

7 How can a formal partnership agreement be varied?

8 Can minors (persons under 18 years of age) become partners?

Answers

1 People can become partners without making any formal agreement. They will be partners if they carry on a business in common with the intention of making a profit.

2 The 13 'universal' articles deal with: the parties to the agreement; the nature of the business; the name of the firm; the dates of commencement and dissolution; the capital of the firm and of the individual partners; the salary and profit entitlement of the partners; the management of the firm; the banking arrangements; the firm's accounts; admission and expulsion of partners; death and retirement of partners; valuation of the goodwill; and reference of disputes to arbitration.

3 The Business Names Act 1985 will apply to a partnership if the partners carry on business in a name other than the surnames of all of the partners. The addition of the partners' forenames or initials will not mean that the Act applies to the firm.

4 The Business Names Act makes it a criminal offence to use certain words in the firm's name and to use other specified words without gaining permission from the Secretary of State. It also requires that the names of all the partners, and an address at which they can be served with documents, be clearly displayed at the firm's place of business and on the firm's business documents.

5 A passing-off action can be brought to prevent a firm from using a name which is likely to cause confusion with another business, or to deceive the public, so as to divert trade from that other business.

6 A partner can only terminate a partnership by giving notice if the partnership is a partnership at will. A partnership at will arises when the partners have not themselves agreed a fixed term for the duration of the partnership.

7 A formal partnership agreement can be varied by the agreement of all the partners. This agreement does not need to be express and can arise from the partners' course of dealing.

8 Minors can become partners, but cannot become liable for debts of the firm which were incurred while they were minors.

15.5 · Partners' relationship with each other

As we have already seen, the partners make a contract with each other and the Partnership Act implies certain terms into this contract. We therefore need to examine these terms and the extent to which partners can exclude the terms by express or implied agreement. In addition, partners owe each other fiduciary duties which arise independently of any contractual agreement. These fiduciary duties are examined at 15.7.

15.5.1 The terms implied by the Partnership Act 1890

Section 24 implies nine terms. When considering the clauses which should be contained in a formal partnership agreement, we examined three of these: the right to share equally in capital and profits (s.24(1)); the right to take part in the management of the business (s.24(5)); and that a new partner can only be admitted by unanimous consent of existing partners (s.24(7)). Before examining the other terms implied by s.24 it is worth reiterating that all of the terms contained in s.24 are implied only if the partners do not make any express or implied agreement to the contrary. For this reason they are often referred to as default provisions.

15.5.1.1 The right to an indemnity

Section 24(2) provides that:

> 'The firm must indemnify every partner in respect of payments made and personal liabilities incurred by him –
> (a) In the ordinary and proper conduct of the business of the firm; or,
> (b) In or about anything necessarily done for the preservation of the business or property of the firm.'

A right to an indemnity gives a right to be reimbursed for expenses properly incurred. In Chapter 11 at 11.5.1 we examined an agent's right of indemnity. This section merely summarises those common law rules.

15.5.1.2 Advances given to the firm

When considering the articles of partnership, we saw that s.24(4) provides that a partner is not entitled to interest on capital which he subscribes to the firm. If nothing is agreed to the contrary, a partner is entitled to interest at 5% per annum on a loan (an advance) made to the firm. Section 24(3) provides: 'A partner making, for the purpose of the partnership, any actual payment or advance beyond the amount of capital which he has agreed to subscribe, is entitled to interest at the rate of five per cent per annum from the date of the payment or advance.' Many partnership agreements specify a rate of interest other than 5% per annum.

15.5.1.3 Right to a salary

Section 24(6): 'No partner shall be entitled to remuneration for acting in the partnership business.' First, it should be realised that when a partner is paid a salary this is really just a way of apportioning the profits of the firm. Second, we should realise that in very many cases profits are apportioned by the payment of a salary to a partner.

It is also worth noting that 'salaried partners' in large firms may or may not in fact have the full rights and obligations of partners, depending upon all the facts of the case, and may be held to be merely employees, especially for taxation purposes. Whether a partner or not, a salaried partner will have the liability of a partner to outsiders to whom has been held out to be a partner. (Liability by holding out is considered below at 15.8.3.)

15.5.1.4 Introduction of new partners

When considering the articles of partnership we set out s.24(7), which states that no partner can be admitted as a partner without the consent of all existing partners. We also saw that such consent is commonly given in the partnership agreement. The following case shows that the consent given can be very wide.

■ *Byrne v Reid* (1902) 87 LTR 507 (Court of Appeal)

The claimant had contributed most of the capital to a firm of five partners, and was entitled to three quarters of the profits. Article 29 of the partnership agreement provided that the claimant could introduce any of his sons, or other person whom he considered fit, as a partner as long as the person was over 21 years old. Any such partner introduced could take over all or part of the claimant's profit entitlement. The claimant introduced his son, to take one twelfth of the firm's profits. The other partners refused to consent to this.

Held. The other partners could not refuse to admit the claimant's son as a partner. Section 24(7) was to apply only if there was no agreement to the contrary. In this case there clearly was such an agreement.

15.5.1.5 Resolving differences

Section 24(8) deals with resolving differences, but makes a distinction between differences on ordinary matters and changes made in the nature of the partnership business: 'Any difference arising as to ordinary matters connected with the partnership business may be decided by a majority of the partners, but no change may be made in the nature of the partnership business without the consent of all existing partners.'

The Act provides no help in resolving whether a matter is an ordinary matter or a change in the nature of the partnership business. The essential difference is that an ordinary matter is concerned with the day-to-day running of the business whereas a change in the nature of the business would be the equivalent of a company changing its objects clause. (The objects clause, examined in Chapter 17 at 17.1.8, sets out the purposes for which a company is set up.)

15.5.1.6 The partnership books

Section 24(9) provides: 'The partnership books are to be kept at the place of business of the partnership (or the principal place, if there is more than one), and every partner may, when he thinks fit, have access to and inspect and copy any of them.'

The partners will want access to the partnership books so that they can understand the financial position of the firm. A partner who suspects that he is being unfairly treated will need to inspect the books to find out if his suspicions are well founded. An agent may be needed to assess the books, and the right to inspect the books can be delegated to an agent as long as the agent is not a person to whom the other partners might reasonably object.

15.5.1.7 The right to expel a partner

This right is contained in s.25, which states that 'No majority of partners can expel any partner unless a power to do so has been conferred by express agreement between the partners.' It is significant that this section was not incorporated into s.24. All the provisions of s.24 can be excluded by implied agreement between the partners. The rule preventing the majority from expelling a partner can only be contradicted by express agreement between all of the partners.

Even when acting under an express agreement which enables them to expel a partner, the partners doing the expelling must observe the rules of natural justice and act in good faith. They must also act strictly within the terms of the partnership agreement.

If a partner is wrongly expelled he may sue for reinstatement as well as for contract damages.

15.6 · Partnership property

Partnership property belongs to all of the partners as partners. This is achieved by the partners holding it in trust for each other. If the property consists of land then there can be a maximum of four trustees. As partnership property belongs to all of the partners, no partner can claim complete ownership of any specific item of it. Upon dissolution, however, a partner may become sole owner of certain items of partnership property.

Partnership property must be distinguished from property belonging to the individual partners for three main reasons. First, if the property increases in value this increase will belong to the firm rather than to any individual partner. Second, partnership property should be used exclusively for the purposes of the partnership, as defined by the partnership agreement. Third, on dissolution creditors are first paid out of partnership property.

Section 20(1) sets out three ways in which property can become partnership property. It can either be originally brought into the partnership, or property acquired on behalf of the firm, or property acquired for the purposes of and in the course of the partnership business.

Section 21 provides that, unless the contrary intention appears, property bought with money belonging to the firm is deemed to have been bought on account of the firm (that is to say, bought as partnership property).

It is always a question of fact whether any particular property is partnership property. An express agreement that property is to be partnership property will be conclusive. In the absence of an express agreement property will be partnership property if there is an implied agreement to that effect.

■ *Miles* v *Clarke* [1953] 1 All ER 779

A and B went into partnership as photographers. A had a lease of the premises from which the business operated but had no skill as a photographer. B was a successful freelance photographer and he introduced his considerable business connections. All that was agreed was that profits should be shared equally and that B should be able to draw £125 a month on account of his share of the profits. After flourishing for some time, the business was wound up when the partners fell out. A dispute arose as to what property, if any, had become partnership property.

Held. The consumable stock in trade of the business should be treated as partnership property, even though it was bought by A. All the other property (the lease, equipment and personal goodwill) should be treated as the property of the partner who brought it in. As the partners had made no express agreement, the court would only imply a term that property was partnership property if this was necessary on the grounds of business efficacy.

COMMENT The implying of a term on the grounds of business efficacy is examined in Chapter 5 at 5.3.2.

In the following case the Court of Appeal considered s.20.

■ *Don King Productions Inc* v *Warren* [1999] 2 All ER 218 (Court of Appeal)

The leading American boxing promoter, K, went into partnership with the leading British boxing promoter, W, to promote boxing in Europe. W assigned to the firm all the benefits and burdens of all of his management agreements with boxers. In fact, these agreements were incapable of being assigned because they were for personal services and some of them had express terms forbidding assignment. A second agreement required all agreements relating to the business of the firm to be held for the benefit of the firm absolutely. Later W made a multi-fight agreement for his own benefit. K insisted that W had no right to do this and ended the partnership.

Held. W had breached the partnership agreement by entering into the multi-fight agreement for his own benefit. Even property which was not assignable could be partnership property within s.20. The agreements indicated that each partner held the entire benefit of any management agreement made with a European boxer on trust for the firm, from the time of the first agreement. These benefits continued to be held on trust after the dissolution of the firm right up until the time when the firm was wound up. Even such agreements entered into after dissolution but before the winding up of the firm were held on trust for the firm, as long as they were renewing contracts with boxers who had previously had a contract with W during the partnership.

COMMENT The implying of a term on the grounds of business efficacy is examined in Chapter 5 at 5.3.2.

15.7 · Partners' fiduciary duties to each other

Partners owe each other fiduciary duties out of which they cannot contract. Three of these duties are set out in ss.28–30 of the Act. These three duties often overlap and are not meant to be exhaustive, merely being part of the wider equitable duties which partners owe to each other. As these duties are equitable, they are fluid in nature. Although the partners cannot contract out of their fiduciary duties, it is a defence to a breach of fiduciary duty that the breach was consented to by the other partners. Nor is there any reason why such consent should not be contained in the articles of partnership. (In *Bentley* v *Craven*, set out below, the partnership agreement allowed one partner who acted as the firm's buyer to buy on his own account. As consent had been given, the other partners would not have been able to claim that the partner's buying on his own account had breached a fiduciary duty.) We now need to look at the three duties set out in the Partnership Act.

15.7.1 Duty to render accounts

Section 28 states that: 'Partners are bound to render true accounts and full information of all things affecting the partnership to any partner or his legal representatives.'

This is a strict, positive duty. It reflects the fact that partnership is a relationship of the utmost good faith.

■ *Law* v *Law* [1905] 1 Ch 140

Four sons were in partnership with their father as manufacturers of woollen clothes in Halifax. After the father died the four sons carried on the business. There was no formal partnership agreement and the sons had equal shares in the business. Two of the sons died, both in turn leaving their share of the business to their remaining brothers in equal shares. The two surviving brothers, W and J carried the firm on, each having an equal share in the partnership. W lived in London and ceased to take an active part in the firm's management. W was paid £600 a month but never asked for any account. J agreed to buy W out for £21 000. After this agreement was made, W discovered that there were partnership assets which J had never revealed to him. The money was to be paid in two instalments. Four days after receiving the second instalment, W commenced legal action to have the agreement set aside.

Held. The agreement to buy W's share was voidable, at W's option.

Cozens-Hardy LJ: 'Now it is clear that, in a transaction between co-partners for the sale by one to the other of a share in the partnership business, there is a duty resting upon the purchaser who knows, and is aware that he knows, more about the partnership accounts than the vendor, to put the vendor in possession of all material facts with reference to the partnership assets, and not to conceal what he alone knows; and that, unless such information has been furnished, the sale is voidable and may be set aside.'

COMMENT On the facts of the case W had lost the right to avoid the contract as he had elected not to insist on his right to full disclosure of the firm's assets. He had done this by taking the money while knowing that full disclosure had not been made.

■ *Hogar Estates Ltd* v *Shebron Holdings Ltd* (1980) 101 DLR (3d) 509 (High Court of Ontario)

H and S were in partnership to develop a piece of land. It was agreed that the partnership should be ended by S buying H's share. S, who suggested this, told H that the authorities had refused to give planning permission to develop the land. This was true when S said it, but S knew that it had become untrue by the time the dissolution agreement was made.

Held. The agreement to dissolve the firm could be set aside, even though there was no misrepresentation and no proof of dishonesty. S had breached his fiduciary duty to disclose the true state of affairs to H.

15.7.2 Accounting for profits

Section 29(1) states that: 'Every partner must account to the firm for any benefit derived by him without the consent of the other partners from any transaction concerning the partnership, or from any use by him of the partnership property name or business connection.'

■ *Bentley* v *Craven* [1853] 18 Beav 75

C and three others were in partnership as sugar refiners in Southampton. C was the firm's buyer. C was very skilled at buying sugar and he was authorised by the other partners to carry on his own business as an independent dealer in sugar. On several occasions C bought a consignment of sugar very cheaply and sold it to the firm at the going wholesale rate.

Held. C could not retain the profit which he made from these transactions. The profit had to be handed over to the firm. C had used a partnership asset, his position in the firm, to make the profit from the deals.

The strictness of the duty imposed by s.29 can be demonstrated by *Pathirana* v *Pathirana* [1967] 1 AC 233 (Privy Council). Two brothers, R and A, carried on a partnership running a service station owned by Caltex. They fell out and A gave R three months' notice to dissolve the firm. R informed Caltex that the firm was dissolved and asked Caltex to transfer the service station to his sole management. Caltex did this and R carried on the business as before without accounting to A for his share of the capital and profits. The Privy Council held that under s.29 A was entitled to a share of the profits which R made. Until the notice dissolving the partnership took effect the new agreement, which enabled the firm to build up a profitable business, was treated as a partnership asset. R was also entitled to a share of the profits made since the dissolution of the firm under s.29 because A had used R's share of the capital and profits without accounting for them.

Generally, no fiduciary duty will be broken if information gained in the capacity of a partner is used for purposes wholly outside of, and not competing with, the partnership. In *Aas* v *Benham* [1891] 2 Ch 244 (Court of Appeal), for example, a partner in a firm of shipbrokers helped to form a company, the purpose of which was to build ships. The partner used information gained as a partner and occasionally used the firm's notepaper. He was paid a fee for setting up the company and was also made a director of it. The Court of Appeal held that because the business of the company was beyond the scope of the business of the partnership, the partner did not have to account for benefits received in connection with the new company.

However, in the light of two House of Lords cases, the authority of *Aas* v *Benham* is in some doubt. Lord Hodgson, when delivering the leading judgment in *Boardman* v *Phipps* (the facts of which are set out in Chapter 11 at 11.4.4) indicated that he was not confident that the decision in *Aas* v *Benham* was correct. The House of Lords decision in *Regal (Hastings) Ltd* v *Gulliver* [1942] 1 All ER 378 also appears to conflict with the decision in *Aas* v *Benham*. (The facts of *Regal* are set out in Chapter 17 at 17.1.9.)

Doubts as to the correctness of *Aas* v *Benham* look better founded in the light of the following recent Court of Appeal decision.

■ *John Taylors v Masons and Wilsons* [2001] EWCA Civ 2106 (Court of Appeal)

A partnership at will had five partners. The firm were in business as livestock auctioneers. On 4 December 1998 two partners (A and B) gave notice to dissolve the firm with effect from 31 December. The other three partners (C, D and E) carried the firm on. The firm had used premises licensed by the local council since 1947. A ten-year licence was due to expire on 31 December 1998. On 4 December A and B wrote to the local council asking that the licence on the premises be granted to them. C, D and E protested to the council, which wanted to remain neutral. However, C, D and E were not ready to take over the premises on 1 January 1999 so the council granted a provisional licence to A and B, who had formed a new firm. Aware that a dispute had arisen, the local council invited tenders for a new licence. There were three applications; one from A and B; one from the C, D and E; and one from a third party. In their application A and B stressed their wealth of experience and their long association with the market. Their tender was successful. C, D and E made a claim for breach of fiduciary duty and under s.29 of the Act.

Held. The opportunity to renew the licence or to get a new licence was a partnership asset. The relationship between the original firm and the local council was a 'business connection', within the meaning of s.29. The goodwill of the original firm, its general business connections, were partnership property. The duty to account can cover assets which were acquired after dissolution but before the winding up was completed. So, under s.29, A and B were accountable for the benefit of the goodwill which they had taken for themselves and for profits and benefits derived from any use of the original partnership's assets. This would include profits made under the provisional and the 1999 licences. Both A and B had also breached the very strict general fiduciary duty imposed on all trustees. The provisional licence and the 1999 licence were obtained whilst there was a conflict of interest, or a possible conflict of interest, between A and B and the original firm. Liability for breach of fiduciary duty was not based on bad faith, but merely on account of a trustee having made a profit from his trust.

In *Don King Productions Inc* v *Warren* (see above at 15.6) the Court of Appeal similarly held that a partner's general fiduciary duty continued after dissolution until the firm was wound up. On the facts of the case, which were set out above, W was in breach of his fiduciary duty to his partner. He should not have taken out the multi-fight agreement for his own benefit when he knew that the firm could have benefited from having it until the firm was wound up. Nor should he have renewed any boxer's contract after dissolution but before the firm was wound up. To do so was an obvious conflict of interest. Furthermore, the multi-fight agreement and the renewed contracts were obtained by reason of W's fiduciary position or by reason of an opportunity or knowledge resulting from such a position.

15.7.3 Competing with the firm

Section 30 provides: 'If a partner, without the consent of the other partners, carries on any business of the same nature as and competing with that of the firm, he must account for and pay over to the firm all profits made by him in that business.'

There is a considerable overlap between this section and s.29. However, their effect is not the same. Under s.30 a partner can be liable merely by competing with the firm, whether or not he used the firm's assets. Under s.29 the partner is liable for using the firm's assets, whether or not he is also competing with the firm.

■ *Trimble* v *Goldberg* (1906) 95 LTR 163 (Privy Council)

G, T and B were in partnership together. The three agreed to buy property belonging to one Hollard, this consisting of land and 5 500 shares in a company, Sigma Syndicate. T bought the property on behalf of the firm, but he also took an option to buy other property belonging to Sigma Syndicate. T invited B to share in this deal. When G found out about it, a year later, he sued for a share of the profits.

Held. B and T did not need to share the profits with G. The purchase of the option was not within the scope of the partnership's business. It was not competing with the firm or the carrying on of a rival business. Nor did T gain the information upon which he acted in his capacity as a partner in the firm.

Test your understanding

1 Can partners contract out of the nine terms implied by s.24 of the Partnership Act 1890?

2 Can a majority of partners expel a partner?

3 To what extent does a partner own partnership property?

4 In what ways does property become partnership property?

5 What three fiduciary duties, which partners owe to each other, are specified in the Partnership Act? Are these three duties an exhaustive description of partners' fiduciary duties to each other? Can the duties be contracted out of?

Answers

1 All of the terms implied by s.24 are to apply only if the partners do not expressly or impliedly agree to exclude them. Plainly, the partners can contract out of them.

2 A majority of partners can only expel a partner if a power to do so has been conferred by express agreement between all of the partners.

3 Partnership property is held on trust by the partners for the benefit of each other. Prior to dissolution a partner does not personally own any particular item of partnership property.

4 Property will be partnership property if the partners have expressly or impliedly agreed that it should be. Section 20(1) provides that property can become partnership property either if it was originally brought into the partnership; or if the property was acquired on behalf of the firm; or if the property was acquired for the purposes of and in the course of the partnership business. Section 21 provides that unless a contrary intention appears, property bought with money belonging to the firm is also deemed to be partnership property.

5 The three fiduciary duties specified by the Act are: to render accounts; to account for profits; and not to compete with the firm. These duties are not intended to be exhaustive. The fiduciary duties cannot be contracted out of, but it is a defence to breach of a fiduciary duty that the act complained of was consented to.

15.8 · Partners' relationship with outsiders

Partners are agents of the firm and of their fellow partners for the purpose of the business of the partnership. They may also incur liability for torts which were committed in the ordinary course of the firm's business, or which the other partners authorised them to commit. In addition, a person who is not a partner can be liable as if he were a partner on account of his having allowed himself to be held out (represented) as a partner. These important matters need to be examined in some detail.

15.8.1 Partners as agents

Section 5 of the Act states that:

'Every partner is an agent of the firm and his other partners for the purpose of the business of the partnership; and the acts of every partner who does any act for carrying on in the usual way business of the kind carried on by the firm of which he is a member bind the firm and his partners, unless the partner so acting has in fact no authority to act for the firm in the particular matter, and the person with whom he is dealing either knows that he has no authority, or does not know or believe him to be a partner.'

In Chapter 11 we studied the different types of authority which an agent might have to bind his principal. We saw that if an agent does have actual authority to bind his principal then the principal will be liable on the contract which the agent made. (If you have not read, or have forgotten, Chapter 11 it might pay to have a look at the Key Points at the end of Chapter 11.) Section 5 is merely reflecting common law principles as the following analysis shows.

If a partner (A) makes a contract with a third party (T), with the express or implied agreement of his fellow partners (B and C) then A will have actual authority and consequently B and C will be bound by the contract.

If A did not have actual authority to enter into a contract which he has made, B and C will nevertheless be liable on the contract if A had apparent authority to make it. This apparent authority would have arisen on account of B and C having made a representation to T, that A had authority to make the contract, and on account of T having acted upon the representation by making the contract.

If A has no actual authority or apparent authority to make the contract, we need to consider whether or not A had what might be called 'usual authority' to make it. The lack of actual authority is likely to have arisen because it has been agreed between the partners (generally in the articles of partnership) that A should not have authority to make certain types of contract on behalf of the firm. We then need to consider whether or not the contract made by A was done in relation to the activities of the partnership business, and 'for carrying on in the usual way business of the kind carried on by the firm'. If not, then B and C will not be liable on the contract in the absence of actual or apparent authority.

Now we consider the position where A makes a contract 'for carrying on in the usual way business of the kind carried on by the firm', but where A has been forbidden by B and C from making such a contract on behalf of the firm. Section 5 tells us that B and C will nevertheless be bound by the contract which A made unless either T did not know or believe A to be a partner in the firm, or unless T knew that A had no authority from B and C to make such a contract. (In Chapter 11 at 11.2.5 we considered the meaning of an agent's 'usual authority' and saw that the term could be used in several different senses and that it is always best to make clear the sense in which it is being used, if the sense is not apparent from the context.)

It is important to remember that s.5 only makes a partner the agent of the firm and his fellow partners as regards 'any act for carrying on in the usual way business of the kind carried on by the firm of which he is a member'. The meaning of this was considered in the following two cases.

■ *Mercantile Credit Co* v *Garrod* [1962] 3 All ER 1103

P and G were partners in a firm, the main business of which was repairing cars and letting lock-up garages. G was a sleeping partner and therefore took no part in the management of the firm. The partnership agreement prohibited the buying and selling of cars. Without G's knowledge, P contracted to sell a car to a finance company. P did not own this car and so his act was a clear breach of contract. The finance company wanted to make G liable on the contract. The finance company had previously made several similar contracts with P, each time believing that they were dealing with the partnership. The finance company did not know of the prohibitions in the partnership agreement.

Held. G was bound by the contract by virtue of s.5. Making the contract was the doing of an 'act for carrying on in the usual way business of the kind carried on by the firm'.

■ *JJ Coughlan Ltd* v *Ruparelia and others* [2003] EWCA Civ 1057 (Court of Appeal)

The claimant company had £1m cash which it wanted to invest. As part of an incredible scheme the firm was induced to pay $500 000 to a solicitor, R, who was acting for some fraudsters. R and the fraudsters were present at meetings at which the claimant company was fraudulently induced to part with the money and R was a party to the fraud. R was in partnership with one other solicitor, T. In return for the $500 000 the claimants were meant to receive a risk free annualised return of 6 000%. A contract made by the claimants with both R and the fraudsters guaranteed that the $500 000 would be returned if the claimants did not receive $2.5m from a bank within one month. The $500 000 was paid into R's solicitor's account. There was in fact no intention ever to return this money. The claimants sued for breach of contract and in the tort of deceit. The claim in tort arose because R guaranteed the claimants that their funds were protected and that there was no risk to their money. It was claimed that R's firm would be liable on the contract under s.5 of the Partnership Act and for the tort of deceit under s.10.

Held. There is no difference between the words the 'ordinary course of the business' in s.10 Partnership Act 1890 and the words 'the usual way of business of the kind carried on' in s.5. The key question was whether R's acts were the kind or class of acts that are carried out by solicitors in the ordinary course of their business. In answering this, the starting point was to consider whether the general description of the act falls within the scope of the ordinary course of business of solicitors. This requirement has to be satisfied. So a solicitor selling double-glazing would not bind his partners under s.5 or make the firm vicariously liable under s.10. The solicitor's motive, or the fact that he was acting honestly or dishonestly, was not relevant. Then it would be necessary to look at the substance of the transaction to see whether, viewed fairly and properly, it is the kind of transaction which forms part of the ordinary business of a solicitor. This would require the details of the transaction to be examined, including its nature and characteristics, and the court should not be too ready to find the ordinary business requirement unsatisfied. In this case the firm was not liable under s.5. The scheme proposed by R and the confidence tricksters gave a risk free annual return of 6 000%. There was nothing normal about the transaction. The scheme was preposterous and what R did in connection with it could not objectively be viewed as being within the ordinary course of a solicitor's business. Nor was there liability under s.10 (see below at 15.8.2) for the same reasons. The nature of the incredible scheme was so far from what R was authorised to do that it could not be regarded as having been done in the ordinary course of his business as a solicitor. Therefore, R's firm could not be liable under s.5 or s.10.

COMMENT (i) Dyson LJ, who gave the only significant judgment, said the fact that the R made a number of false statements to the claimants is not something which it is in the ordinary course of a solicitor's business to do. But if the scheme had been otherwise unremarkable the defendant firm could not have escaped liability. But engaging in a preposterous investment scheme of this kind, which was not at all a normal transaction, was not, viewed objectively, part of a solicitor's business. Therefore R's acts were not carried out in the ordinary course of business of the defendant firm.

(ii) The important question is how the facts reasonably appeared to the third party, not what was actually going on. As Lord Glidewell said in *United Bank of Kuwait* v *Hammoud* [1988] 1 WLR 105, the test was: 'On the facts represented to the [third party] would a reasonably careful and competent person [such as the third party] have concluded that there was an underlying transaction of a kind which was part of the usual business of a solicitor?' In answering this question both the nature of the act and the way in which it was carried out would to be considered in turn.

15.8.1.1 Trading and non-trading firms

There has been much case law on whether a particular act is carried on 'in the usual way' of the firm's business. These decisions have tended to recognise that partners in all firms have usual authority to do certain types of acts, and that partners in trading firms have usual authority to do additional types of acts. A trading firm is one which necessarily buys and sells goods.

In all firms an individual partner has usual authority to do the following: buy goods for the partnership to use; sell any goods belonging to the firm; employ and dismiss employees on the firm's behalf; receive payments on the firm's behalf, and by so doing release the payer from further obligation; employ an agent to act for the firm; employ a solicitor to take legal action on the firm's behalf; sign or endorse cheques in the firm's name.

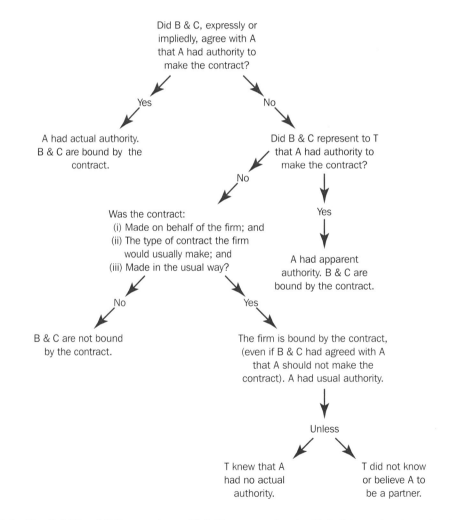

Figure 15.1 The liability of fellow partners (B & C) on a contract which A (a partner) made with T

In a trading firm an individual partner will have additional usual authority to: borrow money on the firm's behalf; give the firm's goods as security for a loan; accept and issue all types of negotiable instruments on behalf of the firm.

In neither trading nor non-trading firms will a partner have usual authority to execute deeds in the firm's name; or give guarantees in the firm's name; or submit a dispute to arbitration.

Although a partner, whether in a trading firm or a non-trading firm, would not normally have usual authority to execute a deed on the firm's behalf, the firm will be bound by a deed executed by one partner if the other partners gave that partner actual or apparent authority to execute the deed.

Section 7 of the Act is concerned with contracts which were not made in the ordinary course of the firm's business. It states that:

> 'Where one partner pledges the credit of the firm for a purpose apparently not connected with the firm's ordinary course of business, the firm is not bound, unless he is in fact specially authorised by the other partners; but this section does not affect any personal liability incurred by an individual partner.'

A partner will pledge the firm's credit if he orders goods or services in the firm's name and indicates to the supplier that the firm will pay the price. If the partner has been authorised to do this by his fellow partners then he has actual authority and obviously the firm and fellow partners are liable to pay the price to the supplier. Section 7 seems to suggest that if the partner has no actual authority then the fellow partners will not be bound to pay the price to the supplier. However, under common law principles the fellow partners would be liable if they had represented to the supplier that the partner had authority, and had thereby given him apparent authority. The partner making the contract will be personally liable on it whether or not the firm and the fellow partners are also liable.

It is possible to sue the firm in the firm name. If judgment is gained against the firm all of the partners become liable to pay the debt if the firm does not have enough assets to pay it. A partner who pays will be entitled to a contribution from his fellow partners. The contribution made by each partner will generally be equal, although the court can order unequal contribution where it considers this just and equitable. Partners also have the right to sue in the firm name. The fact that a firm can sue and be sued in the firm name does not indicate that the firm has a separate legal existence of its own. The rule is merely one of convenience.

15.8.2 Liability for a partner's torts and other wrongful acts

Section 10 provides that:

> 'Where, by any wrongful act or omission of any partner acting in the ordinary course of the business of the firm, or with the authority of his co-partners, loss or injury is caused to any person not being a partner in the firm, or any penalty is incurred, the firm is liable therefore to the same extent as the partner so acting or omitting to act.'

This section is somewhat similar to s.5, except that it deals with liability in tort rather than with liability in contract. In effect it states that fellow partners will be vicariously liable for the torts of an individual partner if the individual partner had actual, apparent or usual authority to commit the act which gave rise to the tortious liability.

In *Blyth* v *Fladgate* [1891] 1 Ch 337, for example, a partner in a firm of solicitors made a loan on behalf of a client, the loan being secured by a mortgage on a house. The solicitor was negligent in that he did not check that the house was worth at least as much as the loan. The client lost money as a consequence and all of the partners were held vicariously liable because the solicitor had committed the tort while doing an act which was in the usual course of the firm's business. In *Arbuckle* v *Taylor* (1815) 3 Dow 160 a partner in a firm thought that an outsider had stolen from the firm. He brought a private prosecution which failed. The outsider then sued the firm for the torts of malicious prosecution and false imprisonment. The other partners were not liable for these torts because the act which gave rise to the tort (bringing criminal proceedings against an outsider) was not an act which was within the usual course of the firm's business.

Section 10 will not apply where the tort of one partner injures another partner. Obviously the partner who committed the tort will be personally liable. Although the position is unclear, it seems likely that the other partners will not incur liability under the common law.

In *Dubai Aluminium Co Ltd* v *Salaam and others* [2002] UKHL 48, the House of Lords recently considered the scope of s.10 in detail. The case concerned the liability of fellow partners for a solicitor who had acted dishonestly. The errant solicitor had set up sham contracts under which the claimant company had been defrauded out of $50m. Although the solicitor had knowingly assisted in the fraud, he had benefited only by earning relatively modest fees for the work he did. His co-partners were innocent of any dishonesty. The Court of Appeal had held that the co-partners were not vicariously liable for the errant partner because it was not in the ordinary course of the business of a solicitor's firm to plan, draft and sign sham contracts. The House of Lords reversed this judgment and held the co-partners liable. The following points can be taken from the judgment.

(1) Lord Nicholls held that the dishonest solicitor did not commit a common law tort, such as deceit or negligence, but that did not prevent him from having committed a 'wrongful act or omission' within the meaning of s.10 of the Partnership Act. When deciding whether or not an act was done in the ordinary course of a firm's business the relevant question was not simply whether the partner was authorised by his co-partners to do the act he did. This would ignore the policy behind vicarious liability of partners – that being in partnership carries the risk of liability for the wrongful acts of the agents who carry the business on. 'Perhaps the best general answer is that the wrongful conduct must be so closely connected with acts the partner or employee was authorised to do that, for the purpose of liability of the firm or the employer to third parties, the wrongful conduct *may fairly and properly be regarded* as done by the partner while acting in the ordinary course of the firm's business.' The question whether or not this actually happened is a question of law, not fact, to be decided with regard to all of the circumstances of the case and previous decisions. Applying this test to the facts, the firm was liable for the errant solicitor because his acts in drawing up the sham contracts were so closely connected with acts which he was authorised to do that they could fairly and properly be regarded as done by him while acting in the ordinary course of the firm's business. He drew up the sham contracts while 'acting in his capacity as a partner' because he was acting on behalf of the firm, not on behalf of himself or a third party. He was trying to promote the firm's business.

(2) The errant solicitor committed some of the acts which made him personally liable while acting as a director of the fraudulent companies. He did not therefore commit all such acts while acting within the course of his employment as a partner. Lord Nicholls said that this did not prevent his co-partners from being vicariously liable because the solicitor had committed enough acts to make himself personally liable while acting within the course of his employment.

(3) Lord Hobhouse thought that on the facts the errant partner had committed the tort of deceit in the course of the partnership business and so the other partners were plainly vicariously liable under s.10 of the Partnership Act.

(4) Lord Millett said that s.10 of the Partnership Act was not restricted to common law torts. The section is concerned with fault based liability but this could arise under the common law, a statute or an equitable wrong. He also said that whether or not a partner was acting 'in the ordinary course of the business of the firm' was a question of fact, once it had been legally established that the act in question was legally capable of being performed in this way. (He was the only one of the Lords who saw the question as one of fact.) He saw vicarious liability as a loss distribution device. A partner or employer ought to be liable for all the torts which could fairly be regarded as reasonably incidental risks to the type of business carried on.

(5) Lord Millett also cleared up confusion about the meaning of ss.9, 11 and 13 of the Act. Section 9 is not concerned with the firm's liability but with the individual liability of each partner. It makes each partner jointly liable with the other partners for any debts and obligations of the firm which were incurred while he was a partner. Section 11 makes the firm liable to account for money which was properly received by the firm but which one of the partners later misappropriated. Section 13 deals with the situation where a partner who is also a trustee misuses trust money. All of the partners are made liable to restore the money. Neither s.11 nor s.13 is concerned with vicarious liability, as it would not be in the ordinary course of the firm's business to misappropriate money in the ways which the sections envisage. But this does not prevent the firm from being liable to account for the money misused.

In *JJ Coughlan Ltd* v *Ruparelia and others* (see above at 15.8.1) there was no liability under s.10 of the Partnership Act. In reaching this conclusion regarding s.10, Lord Dyson who gave the only significant judgment of the Court of Appeal, relied on the extract from Lord Nicholls' speech from *Dubai Aluminium Co Ltd* v *Salaam* which is set out in (1) above.

15.8.3 Liability by holding out

A person holds himself out as being a partner if he represents himself as being a partner or allows himself to be so represented. Any person who holds himself out as being a partner will become liable as if he really was a partner, as regards a third party who gave credit to the firm as a consequence of the holding out. This provision is set out in s.14(1) of the Act, and is a form of estoppel. The person represented as a partner will be estopped from denying that he is a partner as regards a third party who has given credit to the firm as a consequence of the representation. The representation can be made by words or conduct. An example of holding out can be seen in *D & H Bunny Ltd* v *Atkins* [1961] VLR 31, where the credit manager of a company let N have goods on credit because A and N told him that they had decided to go into partnership together. A was liable for the price of the goods, even though no partnership was ever formed.

A person cannot become liable in tort as a consequence of s.14(1). The section is concerned only with those outsiders who gave credit to the firm. The representation does not need to be made directly to the outsider who consequently gave credit to the firm. If A represents to B that he (A) is a partner in a firm and B tells C, who relies on the representation, A can be liable to C. However, what is required is that at some stage the person made liable either represents himself to be a partner or knowingly allows himself to be represented as a partner.

■ *Tower Cabinet Co Ltd* v *Ingram* [1949] 1 All ER 1033

The claimant, Tower Cabinet Company Ltd, sued a firm for six suites of furniture sold and delivered. Having gained judgment, the claimant sought to enforce this against a retired partner, Ingram. Upon retiring, Ingram had informed persons with whom the firm had previously dealt that he had retired. However, he did not advertise the fact of his retirement in the *London Gazette*. The remaining partner, now in business on his own, had ordered the goods from the claimant on partnership notepaper which indicated that Ingram was a partner. Ingram did not know that this had been done.

Held. Ingram was not liable to the claimants. He had neither represented himself as a partner or knowingly allowed himself to be represented as a partner.

Lynskey J: 'Before the company can succeed in making Mr Ingram liable under this section [section 14(1)], they have to satisfy the court that Mr Ingram, by words spoken or written or by conduct, represented himself as a partner. There is no evidence of that. Alternatively, they must prove that he knowingly suffered himself to be represented as a partner ... it is impossible to say that Mr Ingram knowingly suffered himself to be so represented.'

Section 14(2) provides that the continued use of the firm's name after a partner's death does not automatically make the deceased partner's estate liable for any partnership debts incurred after his death.

15.8.3.1 Admissions and representations by partners

An admission or representation made by any partner concerning the partnership affairs, and in the ordinary course of its business, is evidence against the firm. However, this is only the case where the admission or representation was made with actual, apparent or usual authority (s.15).

Section 16 states that if an outsider gives a partner notice of a matter relating to the firm's affairs this is regarded as notice to the firm. There are, however, two exceptions. Notice to a dormant or sleeping partner would not be notice to the firm. And notice of a fraud would not be notice to the firm if the notice was given to the very partner who was committing the fraud.

15.8.3.2 Liability of incoming and outgoing partners

Section 17 provides that a partner coming into a firm is not liable for the pre-existing debts of the firm. It also provides that a partner retiring from a firm remains liable for debts which were incurred before his retirement. A retiring partner can only be discharged from existing liabilities if a contract to that effect is made between himself, the newly constituted members of the firm and the creditors. Such a contract is known as a novation. It can either be made expressly or it can be inferred from a course of dealing between the creditors and the firm as newly constituted. Such a novation can be inferred from conduct fairly easily, but it is not enough that a creditor adopts the newly constituted firm as a debtor.

Section 36(1) provides that an outsider dealing with the firm after a change in the firm's constitution is entitled to regard all apparent members of the old firm as still being members of the firm until he has notice of the change. Apparent authority will continue as regards outsiders who had previously dealt with the firm until they are given actual notice of the change. As regards those who had not previously dealt with the firm a notice in the *London Gazette* is sufficient notice (s.36(2)).

A retiring partner will generally be liable for debts incurred before his retirement. A partner who has retired is not liable for debts incurred after his retirement if the person dealing with the firm did not know that he was a partner. Nor is the estate of a dead or bankrupt partner liable for debts incurred after the death or bankruptcy if the person dealing with the firm had not known the deceased to be a partner (s.36(3)).

15.8.3.3 Guarantees of the firm given by outsiders

If an outsider gives a guarantee to a firm, or guarantees a third party that he will pay the firm's debts, either guarantee will normally be revoked if a partner leaves or joins the firm. This provision is set out in s.18 and is to apply unless there is any agreement to the contrary.

15.9 · Dissolution and winding up

When a partnership is dissolved it comes to an end. Often this can be little more than a technicality. A firm is dissolved each time there is a change in the membership, although in a commercial firm the remaining partners are likely to carry on in very much the same way as before. Where the firm is dissolved and not carried on much as before there will be a winding up. This will involve the firm's assets being realised, creditors being paid off and any remaining surplus being divided amongst the partners. A partnership can be dissolved either by the partners themselves, or under one of the provisions of the Partnership Act 1890.

15.9.1 Dissolution by the partners

Earlier in this chapter, at 15.2.1, we saw that partnership arises on account of a contract having been made by the partners. The general common law of contract might allow one or more of the partners to terminate this contract. For example, all of the partners might make a new contract, agreeing to end the partnership, or a formal partnership agreement might set out the circumstances on which the partnership can be ended. In addition, a partner can rescind the contract if he made it in consequence of a misrepresentation, and a partner may apply to the court to terminate the contract if the other partners commit a repudiatory breach of contract.

At 15.4.1 we saw that s.25 provides that no majority of the partners can expel any partner unless a power to do this has been conferred by express agreement between the partners. If a partner is expelled then the firm is dissolved. Although this might be little more than a technicality in a large firm, if there were only two partners the expulsion would lead to a winding up of the firm.

15.9.2 Dissolution under a provision of the Act

The Partnership Act lays down that a partnership is dissolved in the following circumstances.

(1) If the partnership was entered into for a fixed term or for a single purpose, it is dissolved by the expiry of that term or the termination of that purpose. (The common law would regard the contract as discharged by performance.)
(2) The firm is dissolved by the death or bankruptcy of a partner, unless the partners have agreed otherwise. Although the partners can agree that the firm should not be wound up upon the death or bankruptcy of a partner, the firm would technically be dissolved anyway. However, if the remaining partners carried on this might be of little practical importance.
(3) A firm may be dissolved, at the option of the partners, if a partner assigns his share of the partnership assets to a creditor so as to satisfy a private debt. This may happen involuntarily, in that a creditor who has gained judgment against a partner in a matter not connected with the partnership can be granted a charging order against the partner's interest in partnership property, up to the amount of the debt. A creditor who does become an assignee of a partner's share in the partnership assets gains no rights to manage the firm.
(4) Section 34 states that in every case a firm is automatically dissolved on the happening of an event which makes it unlawful for the business of the firm to be carried on or for the the members of the firm to carry on the business in partnership.

15.9.3 Dissolution by court order

Section 35 gives a partner the right to apply to the court for dissolution on five grounds, as follows:

(1) That a partner has become permanently incapable of performing his part of the partnership contract.
(2) That the court considers, having regard to the nature of the business, that a partner has been guilty of such conduct as is calculated to prejudicially affect the carrying on of the business.
(3) That a partner wilfully or persistently breaches the partnership agreement, or otherwise conducts himself in matters relating to the partnership business in such a way that it is not reasonably practicable for the other partners to carry on in business with him.
(4) That the business of the partnership can only be carried on at a loss.
(5) That the court considers it just and equitable that the partnership should be dissolved.

It is also possible for a court to dissolve a partnership under the Mental Health Act 1983. A court will do this if it is satisfied that a partner is, by reason of mental disorder, incapable of managing his property or affairs.

15.9.4 Winding up

After the dissolution of a partnership the authority of each partner to bind the firm, and the other rights and obligations of the partners, may continue despite the dissolution. However, this authority continues only to the extent that this may be necessary in order to wind up the affairs of the partnership, and to complete transactions begun but unfinished at the time of the dissolution (s.38). In *Re Bourne* [1906] 2 Ch 427, for example, a partnership of two was dissolved when one of the partners died. The surviving partner mortgaged partnership land in order to get an overdraft to temporarily carry the business on. It was held that this act was validly done as it was done in order to wind up the affairs of the firm. The executors of the deceased partner were therefore bound by the mortgage.

After dissolution the firm is not bound by the acts of a bankrupt partner. In addition, any partner can apply to the court to have a receiver appointed. If the court does appoint a receiver the continuing authority of partners to bind the firm will cease. Partners do not need to appoint a receiver to wind a firm up. Partners can themselves generally wind the firm up in a shorter time, more cheaply and with less publicity. A court order may also take away a partner's continuing authority to bind the firm.

15.9.5 Realisation of the firm's assets

On dissolution any of the partners is entitled to have the partnership property applied in payment of the debts and liabilities of the firm (s.39). We saw earlier, at 15.6, that this was one of the most important reasons to identify partnership property in the partnership agreement.

15.9.5.1 The goodwill

The goodwill of the firm may be one of the firm's most valuable assets. Accountants might define the goodwill as the excess of the market value of a business over the value of its individual assets. Various legal definitions have been put forward.

In *Trego* v *Hunt* [1896] AC 7 Lord MacNachten defined goodwill as 'the whole advantage, whatever it may be, of the reputation and connection of the firm, which may have been built up by years of honest work or gained by lavish expenditure of money'.

In *Hill* v *Fearis* [1905] 1 Ch 466 Warrington J said that the goodwill was 'the advantage, whatever it may be, which a person gets by continuing to carry on, and being entitled to represent to the outside world that he is carrying on, a business which has been carried on for some time previously'.

Once the goodwill has been sold for the benefit of all of the partners, those partners will not be able to use the firm's name or solicit its customers. There is no reason why they should not otherwise carry on a rival business, unless a valid restraint of trade clause forbids this. Lord MacNachten, in *Trego* v *Hunt* explained the position in this way:

> 'A person who has sold the goodwill of his business is under no obligation to retire altogether from the field. Trade he undoubtedly may, and in the very same line of business. If he has not bound himself by special stipulation … he is free to set up business wherever he chooses. But, then, how far may he go? He may do everything that a stranger to the business, in ordinary course, would be in a position to do. He may set up where he will. He may push his wares as much as he pleases. He may thus interfere with the custom of his neighbour as a stranger and outsider might do; but he must not, I think, avail himself of his special knowledge of the old customers to regain, without consideration, that which he has parted with for value. He must not make his approaches from the vantage ground of his former position. He may not sell the custom and steal away the customers.'

15.9.6 Distribution of the firm's assets

Once the firm's assets have been sold, a set of realisation accounts will be produced. Then the position will depend upon whether or not the firm was solvent and whether or not there were any losses.

15.9.6.1 **Losses where the firm is solvent**

If the firm is solvent, that is to say where it has enough money to pay all of its debts, then outsiders are guaranteed to receive all that the firm owes them. However, even where the firm is solvent it may have made a loss. For example, if A, B and C went into partnership, each contributing £10 000 capital the firm might only have £20 000 of capital left once the assets have been realised. The firm is solvent, but there has been a loss of £10 000 capital.

First, it is important to realise that the partners may themselves have agreed how this loss should be borne. If they have made such an agreement this will apply. If there is no agreement between the partners on this matter, s.44 spells out how the assets should be distributed.

Section 44(a) provides that 'Losses, including losses and deficiencies of capital, shall be paid first out of profits, next out of capital, and lastly, if necessary, by the partners individually in the proportion in which they were entitled to share profits.'

It is perhaps best to illustrate this by way of an example. Let us assume that firm X, Y, Z has three partners who are to share profits equally. X contributed £15 000 capital, Y £10 000 and Z £5 000. The total capital was therefore £30 000. If, after realisation of the assets, there is only £24 000 capital left the firm will have suffered a loss of capital of £6 000. Each partner would have to contribute to this loss equally and pay £2 000.

Consequently, X would receive a net £13 000 (£15 000 capital originally contributed minus £2 000); Y would receive £8 000 (£10 000 capital originally contributed minus £2 000); Z would receive £3 000 (£5 000 capital originally contributed minus £2 000).

If the partners had agreed that each loss would be borne according to capital contributions then the position would have been different. The £24 000 of capital remaining is equal to 80% of the original capital. Each partner would therefore be entitled to 80% of his original capital contribution. X would therefore be entitled to £12 000, Y to £8 000 and Z to £4 000.

15.9.6.2 **Applying the firm's assets**

When producing the final accounts the partnership must discharge its various obligations. Section 44(b) tells us that these obligations must be discharged in the following order.

- First, outsiders are paid what they are owed in full.
- Second, each partner is paid rateably what he is owed in respect of loans made to the firm.
- Third, each partner is paid rateably the capital he contributed to the firm.
- Finally any residue is divided amongst the partners in the proportion in which they were entitled to share profits.

If there is not enough money to discharge each class of obligation, then any deficiency is treated as a loss and s.44(a) will apply unless there has been an agreement to the contrary.

- Example

Let us assume that in firm PQR there were three partners, who were to share profits equally. The realisation accounts show that the firm has assets of £100 000. £8 000 is owed to the Inland Revenue. P loaned the firm £10 000. P also contributed £10 000 capital and Q contributed £6 000 capital. First the Revenue is paid the £8 000 which it is owed. Then P is paid the £10 000 which he loaned to the firm. Then P is repaid his £10 000 capital and Q is repaid his £6 000 capital. The remaining £66 000 is divided amongst the three partners equally, as they were to share profits equally.

Consequently, the Revenue receives £8 000, P receives £42 000, Q receives £28 000 and R receives £22 000.

If there had only been £25 000 of assets remaining, the position would have been as follows. First, the Revenue would receive full payment of the £8 000 they were owed. Then P would have received full payment of his £10 000 loan. The fact that there was only £7 000 remaining would mean that there was a shortfall of £9 000 in capital. This loss would be borne equally by the three partners under s.44(a). Each partner would therefore have to contribute £3 000 towards this. P would therefore receive an additional £7 000 (capital contribution of £10 000 minus £3 000). Q would receive £3 000 (capital contribution of £6 000 minus £3 000). R would have to make a further contribution of £3 000.

The rule in *Garner* v *Murray* [1904]1 Ch 57 applies where the loss in capital is attributable to the insolvency of one or more of the partners. In such a case the solvent partners are not liable to make good the insolvent partner's contribution to capital. First the solvent partners contribute to lost capital according to their profit-sharing ratio (but they only contribute their own share). Second, the solvent partners share whatever capital is accumulated in the ratio of their original capital contributions.

■ **Example**

Let us assume that firm DEF had three partners who were to share profits equally. D contributed £6 000 capital, E contributed £3 000 and F contributed £1 000. There was therefore a total capital contribution of £10 000. When the firm is wound up F has become insolvent and there has been a capital loss of £6 000. D and E must pay towards the lost capital. However, they only pay their own share, in accordance with their profit-sharing ratio. They both therefore pay one third, £2 000, as both were entitled to one third of the firm's profits. After these payments have been made the capital is up to £8 000. D and E share this in the ratio of their capital contributions, that is to say in the ratio 2 : 1. D therefore receives £5 333, suffering a capital loss of £667. E receives £2 667, suffering a capital loss of £333.

The rule in *Garner* v *Murray* does not to apply where there is an agreement to the contrary and does not affect outside creditors in any way.

15.9.6.3 The position where the firm is insolvent

The firm will be insolvent if it does not have enough assets to pay its debts. In such a situation it may well be that one or more of the partners remain solvent. All of the solvent partners will be jointly liable to pay creditors whose debts have not been fully satisfied. Section 44(a) of the Act will require the solvent partners to repay the firm's debts in the proportion in which they were going to share profits, unless there has been an agreement to the contrary.

An insolvent firm can be compulsorily wound up as an unregistered company under the Insolvency Act 1986. Either a partner or a creditor may petition the court for such a winding up. (The winding up of companies is considered in Chapter 19 at 19.1.) It is possible for an insolvent partnership to come to a voluntary agreement with creditors. As long as the correct procedure is followed, such an arrangement will even bind creditors who did not agree to it. If bankruptcy proceedings are also brought against one or more of the partners these will be heard by the same court at the same time.

15.10 · Limited partners

It is possible for one or more of the partners to have limited liability for the firm's debts under the Limited Partnerships Act 1907. However, the Act requires that there must always be at least one general partner who has unlimited liability.

Every limited partnership must be registered with the Registrar of Companies. All of the partners must sign a statement, giving the following information:

(a) The firm name.
(b) The general nature of the business.
(c) The principal place of business.
(d) The full name of each of the partners.
(e) The date of commencement and the length of time for which the business is entered into.

(f) A statement that the partnership is limited, and the description of every limited partner.

(g) The sum contributed by every limited partner, and whether paid in cash or otherwise.

Limited partners contribute a certain amount of capital and are not liable beyond this amount. However, limited partners are not allowed to take part in the management of the business and are not agents of the firm. A limited partner who does take part in management will lose his limited liability.

The Limited Partnerships Act has not been much of a success. There are few firms which have both general and limited partners. Limited Liability Partnerships, where all of the partners have limited liability are considered in Chapter 19.

Test your understanding

1 To what extent does s.5 of the Partnership Act make a partner who acts without actual or apparent authority an agent of the firm and fellow partners?

2 In what circumstances will fellow partners be liable for the torts of an individual partner?

3 How can a person become liable by holding out?

4 Is an incoming partner liable for debts of the firm which have previously arisen?

5 How can a retiring partner cease to be liable for debts which arose prior to his retirement?

6 On what four grounds may a partnership be dissolved under a provision of the Partnership Act 1890?

7 On what five grounds can a partnership be dissolved by court order?

8 How are losses of a solvent partnership to be borne?

9 In what order are the assets of a solvent firm distributed?

10 Can one partner have limited liability for the firm's debts? Can all of the partners have limited liability?

Answers

1 Partners are agents of their firms and of their fellow partners if: (i) the act done was done as a partner; (ii) the act was the type of act which would ordinarily be done by a partner in the firm; and (iii) the act was done in the way in which it ordinarily would be done. However, there is no liability if the outsider either knows that the partner has no authority to do the act, or does not know or believe him to be a partner.

2 All of the partners will be liable for the torts of an individual partner if the tort was committed while the partner was doing an act which he had actual, apparent or usual authority to do.

3 A person who represents himself as a partner, or who knowingly allows himself to be represented as a partner, will become liable as if he was a partner to anyone who relied on the representation to give credit to the firm.

4 A partner coming into the firm is not liable for debts which had previously arisen.

5 A retiring partner can be discharged from liability by a novation (a contract to that effect) between himself, the firm as newly constituted and the creditors.

6 A firm can be dissolved under a provision of the Act if: (i) a fixed term has expired or a single purpose been achieved; (ii) a partner has died or become bankrupt; (iii) a partner has assigned his share of the partnership assets to a creditor in order to satisfy a private debt; (iv) an event has happened which makes it unlawful to carry on the business of the firm.

7 Any partner can apply for a court order to dissolve the partnership on the following grounds: (i) a partner has become permanently incapable of performing his role in the partnership; (ii) a partner has been guilty of conduct which prejudicially affects the carrying on of the business; (iii) a partner has wilfully or persistently breached the partnership agreement or acted in such a way that it is not reasonably practicable for the other partners to carry on in partnership with him; (iv) the business can only be carried on at a loss; (v) the court considers it just and equitable to wind the firm up.

8 In the absence of agreement to the contrary, the partners are to bear the losses in the same ratio as they were to share the profits.

9 First outsiders are paid, then loans from partners are repaid, then capital contributions of partners are repaid. Any remaining assets are shared by the partners in the ratio in which they were to share profits.

10 Individual partners can have limited liability for the firm's debts if they register as limited partners under the Limited Partnerships Act 1907. The Act requires that at least one general partner must have unlimited liability. If a business is registered as a Limited Liability Partnership, under the Limited Liability Partnerships Act 2000, then all of the members can have limited liability for the firm's debts. However, an LLP is quite different to a partnership.

Key points

Definition and nature of a partnership

- Partnership is the relation which subsists between persons carrying on a business in common with a view of profit.

- A partnership, unlike a company, has no separate legal identity of its own. It is merely a relationship between the partners. (Limited Liability Partnerships, which can only be created by registration with Companies House, do have a legal identity of their own.)

- A partnership can be created only if the partners intended to make a profit to share amongst themselves. It is not necessary that any such profit actually was made.

- Being a joint owner of property, or sharing the gross takings of a business, do not necessarily create a partnership.

- Taking a share of the net profits of a business is *prima facie* evidence of being a partner. However, this will not be the case if the other circumstances indicate that there was no partnership.

The partnership agreement

- Although there is no need for partners to have a formal partnership agreement, most firms do have such an agreement.

- The Business Names Act 1985 applies to partnerships if they carry on business in a name other than the surnames of all of the partners. The Act makes it a criminal offence to use certain words in the firm's name, or to use specified words without having gained permission from a relevant body and the Secretary of State. It also requires that the names of all of the partners, and an address at which documents can be served on them, must be displayed on the firm's documents and at the firm's main place of business.

- A passing off action may prevent the use of a name which is likely to cause confusion with another business, or likely to deceive the public, so as to divert trade from the other business.

- A partnership agreement can be varied by the consent of all of the partners, and this consent can be inferred from the partners' course of dealing.

- Minors can become partners but cannot be made liable for partnership debts incurred while they were minors.

Partners' relationship with each other

- Section 24 of the Partnership Act implies nine terms which govern the partners' relationship with each other. These terms are implied only if the partners do not expressly or impliedly agree that they should not be.

- A majority of partners cannot expel a partner unless all of the partners have made an express agreement allowing for expulsion.

- Partnership property is held on trust by the partners for each other.

- Property will be partnership property if the partners have expressly or impliedly agreed that it should be. The Partnership Act s.20(1) provides that partnership property consists of property originally brought into the partnership, or property acquired on behalf of the firm, or property acquired for and in the course of the firm's business. Section 21 provides that unless a contrary intention appears, property bought with money belonging to the firm is also deemed to be partnership property.

- Partners owe each other fiduciary duties. Three fiduciary duties are mentioned in the Act. These duties, which are not exhaustive, are: to render accounts, to account for profits and not to compete with the firm. It is a defence to breach of fiduciary duty that the other partners consented to the act complained of.

Partners' relationship with outsiders

- Partners can be agents of the firm even where they have no actual or apparent authority. This agency would arise as regards an act which was done as a partner if the act was the type of act which would ordinarily be done by a partner in the firm, and the act was done in the way in which it ordinarily would be done. However, there is no liability if the outsider either knows that the partner had no authority to do the act, or did not know or believe him to be a partner.

- All of the partners will be liable for the torts of an individual partner if the tort was committed while the partner was doing an act which he had actual, apparent or usual authority to do.

- A person who is not a partner can be made liable as if he was a partner if he represented himself as a partner, or if he knowingly allowed himself to be represented as a partner. The liability only arises in respect of a person who gave credit to the firm on the strength of the representation.

Dissolution of the firm

- A partnership can be dissolved by the partners themselves, or under a provision of the Partnership Act, or by a court order.

- Where the firm is solvent, losses are paid by the partners in the same ratio as profits would have been shared, unless there was an agreement to the contrary.

- Where the firm is solvent, the partnership assets are distributed in the following order: first outsiders are paid, then partners are repaid loans made to the firm, then partners are repaid their capital contributions. Any surplus is divided amongst the partners in the proportion in which they were entitled to share profits.

- An individual partner can register under the Limited Partnerships Act 1907 and thereby acquire limited liability for the firm's debts. However the 1907 Act requires that at least one general partner should have unlimited liability. A limited partner will lose his protection under the 1907 Act if he takes any part in the firm's management.

Summary questions

1   What must partners agree with each other in order for a partnership to be formed? What matters are specified by the Partnership Act 1890 as indicating that a partnership either does or does not exist?

2   Amanda, Beryl and Claire intend to go into partnership together as fashion designers as soon as they graduate from university. Amanda is to work full-time in the business and is to be entitled to 40% of the profits. Beryl, who is to work only one day a week, and who is to contribute all of the firm's capital of £5000, is to be entitled to 40% of the firm's profits. Claire is to work two and a half days a week and be entitled to 20% of the firm's profits. Claire has applied for a job as a stewardess on an ocean-going liner, as it has always been her ambition to follow such a career. She has been told that she has little chance of getting the job but that she will be interviewed for the job two months after her graduation. If Claire is given the job she intends to take it up two weeks after the interview. Beryl is to buy materials for the firm. She might occasionally need to write a cheque for up to £1000 if she is offered a bargain. It is not envisaged that Amanda and Claire would write cheques for more than £50. If the venture is a success one year from commencement, the partners intend to

take professional advice and to have a detailed partnership deed drawn up on their behalf. However, they do not want to incur any unnecessary costs at the outset and intend to make their own partnership agreement.

Examine the model partnership agreement set out on pp. 448–450 and indicate how the agreement might be amended so that it would become suitable for the proposed firm.

3 X, Y and Z have gone into partnership. Their partnership agreement said that the firm could only be terminated by the partners themselves if two of the three partners agree to this. Would this agreement be given legal effect, or could one of the partners terminate the partnership by giving notice?

4 In a firm of doctors there is some dispute as to whether or not the premises from which the firm operates is partnership property.

  a What is the significance of the premises either being or not being partnership property?

  b How does property become partnership property?

5 **a** The partnership deed of a firm of builders says that goods can only be bought on the firm's behalf if all of the partners agree to the purchase. One of the partners in the firm orders a new pneumatic drill, without the knowledge or permission of his fellow partners, saying that it is for the firm. Advise the other partners as to whether or not they will be bound by the contract.

  b Would your advice differ if one of the other partners had told the supplier of the drill that the partner who ordered the drill had no authority to order such goods on behalf of the partnership?

  c Would the firm of builders be bound if one of the partners, without authority, ordered a new snooker table for the partnership?

6 **a** As part of his everyday work, a partner in a firm of medical practitioners performs a minor operation to remove a skin cancer on a patient's nose. The operation is performed negligently, and this causes the patient to become permanently disfigured. Advise the other partners as to whether or not the partners as a whole could incur liability for the negligence of the doctor who performed the operation.

  b Advise a partner in a firm of doctors as to the circumstances in which the partnership might be liable for a partner in the firm who caused injury to a patient while negligently removing one of the patient's wisdom teeth.

7 In a firm of six partners, five partners want the partnership agreement to be changed and one partner does not. In what circumstances could the partnership agreement be changed by the majority? Can a partnership agreement ever be changed without the partners expressly agreeing that it should be?

8 A firm had three partners, G, H and I. The three partners were to share profits equally. G contributed £25 000 capital, H contributed £14 000 and I contributed £11 000. On dissolution, after all outside creditors have been paid, only £20 000 of capital remains. How would this loss be borne by the partners?

9 Explain the circumstances in which it might be possible for:

  a One of the partners in a firm to have limited liability for the firm's debts;

  b All of the partners in a firm to have limited liability for the firm's debts.

Multiple choice questions

1 A partner in a firm of general medical practitioners orders a new carpet for the surgery. The two other partners are furious about this because they ordered a new carpet, from a different shop, two days earlier. Which **one** of the following statements is true?

  a The firm is liable on the contract under s.5.

  b The firm is not liable on the contract, but the partner who ordered the carpet is, under s.7.

  c The firm is not liable on the contract under s.5 or s.7 because only one partner, without the authority of the others, made the contract.

  d The firm is liable on the contract under s.10.

2   A partner in a firm of solicitors orders a very expensive telescope, saying that it is for the partnership. His fellow partners did not authorise him to make the contract, or make any representation that he had authority to make it, and are refusing to be bound by it. Which **one** of the following statements is true?

   a   The firm is liable on the contract under s.5.

   b   The firm is liable on the contract under s.7.

   c   The firm is not liable on the contract under s.5 or s.7, but the partner who made the order is personally liable.

   d   The firm is liable on the contract under s.10.

3   A partner in a firm of builders, while drunk, drives a van through a customer's greenhouse. Which **two** of the following statements are true?

   a   The firm is liable if the partner was driving the van in the ordinary course of the firm's business when he drove through the greenhouse.

   b   If the van in question belonged to the firm, the firm will be liable even if the partner was not driving the van in the ordinary course of the firm's business when he had the accident.

   c   The firm is not liable under any circumstances. It would never be within the ordinary course of the firm's business to drive vans through greenhouses.

   d   Even if the partner had not been driving the van in the ordinary course of the firm's business, the other partners would be liable if they had egged him on to see how close to the greenhouse he could drive.

4   A, B and C are in partnership. No agreement has been made as to how profits or capital are to be shared. At the outset A contributed £10 000 capital, B £5 000 and C £1 000. B also loaned £1 000 to the firm. (When the answers refer to dissolution it should be assumed that the firm is solvent and has enough assets to pay all of its debts.) Which **one** of the following is true?

   a   Profits should be shared equally and (on dissolution) so should capital.

   b   Profits should be shared equally and the partners should be paid interest on the capital advanced.

   c   Profits and capital should be shared in the proportion to which capital was contributed.

   d   Profits should be shared equally, but (on dissolution) capital should be shared unequally.

5   D, a partner in DEF Wholesale Fruit and Vegetables, impulsively makes the following contracts in the firm's name. E and F make no representations to any of the suppliers. By which of the contracts would his partners be bound?

   i   He takes out an unnecessary bank loan on the firm's behalf.

   ii   He orders a new computer game for F's son's 21st birthday.

   iii   He orders a top of the range computer to help with the firm's accounts.

   iv   He orders a new, and unnecessary delivery van.

   v   He orders a ton of ripe bananas.

   a   By all of the contracts.

   b   By i, iii, iv and v only.

   c   By i, iv and v only.

   d   By i, ii and v only.

6   Consider the following statements.

   i   A company can be a partner in a firm, although it cannot itself be a partnership.

   ii   A person who is entitled to a share of the profits of a business venture will inevitably be in partnership with others who are entitled to a share of the profits.

   iii   No partnership agreement can contradict the nine terms implied by s.24 of the Partnership Act 1890.

   iv   Minors can become partners, but cannot be made liable for the firm's debts if these arose before the minor became 18 years old.

   v   If, in contravention of specific instructions given by all of his fellow partners, a partner makes a contract with a third party, that contract cannot be binding on any partner except the one who made it.

   vi   A person who allows himself to be represented as a partner can become liable as if he really was a partner to a third party who gave the firm credit on the strength of the representation.

Which of the above statements were true?

a i, iv and vi only.

b i, ii, v and vi only.

c ii, iii, iv and v only.

d i, v and vi only.

7   H, a partner in a firm of property developers is sent to Scotland to bid for a smallholding. All of his expenses are paid by the firm. H bids as high as he was authorised, but does not secure the smallholding. After the auction, a farmer who is desperate for cash offers to sell his Land-Rover to H personally at a very low price. H goes to a local bank and withdraws the cash from his personal account. The following week H sells the Land-Rover at a good profit. Which **one** of the following is true?

a H will not have to share the profit made with his fellow partners.

b H will have to share the profit under s.28.

c H will have to share the profit under s.29.

d H will have to share the profit under s.30.

8   Consider the following statements.

i   Individual partners may register as limited partners under the Limited Partnerships Act 1907, but the number of limited partners must not outnumber the number of general partners.

ii Partners registered as limited partners under the Limited Partnerships Act 1907 may not take part in the management of the firm.

iii Limited partners are agents of the firm for contracts made in the ordinary course of the firm's business.

iv A Limited Liability Partnership can be set up, but only by registration with Companies House.

v   The members of Limited Liability Partnerships all have limited liability for the firm's debts.

Which of the above statements are true?

a i, ii and iii only.

b i, ii and iv only.

c ii, iv and v only.

d ii and iv only.

Task 15

Three friends of yours are considering going into business together to run a garage. Using a firm of builders as an example, write a report indicating:

a The extent to which one partner can be liable for goods ordered by another partner.

b The extent to which a partner can be liable for another partner's torts.

c The duties which partners owe to each other.

d The extent to which an individual partner can limit his potential liability.

e In what order, and by whom, the assets of a solvent firm will be applied in settling the firm's debts.

Chapter 16

THE NATURE OF A COMPANY AND FORMATION OF A COMPANY

Introduction

There are over 1.5 million registered companies in the UK. The law regards each of these as a legal person, with its own legal rights and obligations. However, it is quite obvious that a company is not a human being, and that it does not have human attributes such as eyesight or the ability to walk. We therefore begin by examining the nature of a company and assessing the essential characteristics which companies possess. We also outline the different types of companies and consider the various ways in which companies can be classified.

Almost all companies were created by registration with the Registrar of Companies. A registered company comes into existence when the Registrar, satisfied that a promoter has supplied all the required information, issues the company's certificate of incorporation. We examine the steps which a promoter of a company must take in order to gain a certificate of incorporation, and the liability of promoters on contracts made before the certificate is issued.

The company name is important because it is the means of identifying the company. At the end of this chapter we consider the limitations on the names which a company may choose and the rules which require companies to display their names.

16.1 · The nature of a company

When most people think of a company they think of a vast public company, with many thousands of employees. But many more companies are very small, often owned and run by just one person, and often having a share capital of less than £100. All companies, no matter what their size, have certain characteristics in common. To some extent these characteristics are interconnected, but they are easier to understand if considered individually.

16.1.1 The company is a separate legal entity

The most important consequence of incorporation is that a company is regarded as being a legal person in its own right. This means that a company has a legal identity of its own, which is quite separate from the legal identity of its owners. It follows that if a wrong is done to a company it is the company, and not those who own the company's shares, who have the right to sue. Conversely, a person who is injured by a company will have the right to sue the company, but will not have the right to sue the company's shareholders or its officers. This well-established principle that a company is a legal person in its own right was laid down by the House of Lords in the following case.

■ *Salomon v Salomon and Co Ltd* [1897] AC 22 (House of Lords)

For several years Salomon had carried on a business as a boot repairer and manufacturer. He formed a limited company and sold his business to the company for slightly over £39 000. The company paid the purchase price by issuing Salomon with 20 000 £1 shares, by regarding him as having loaned the company £10 000, by paying off the existing debts of the business at the time of incorporation and by making up the balance in cash. Salomon's wife and five children each took one £1 share. Salomon took all of the company's assets as security for the £10 000 loan which he had made to the company. Unsecured creditors later loaned the company further substantial sums of money. Shortly after the company was incorporated it got into financial difficulty and was wound up. When the company's assets were realised there was not enough money to repay all of the £10 000 loan which Salomon had made to the company. Creditors who have been given security for their loan are entitled to be repaid before unsecured creditors. Salomon therefore claimed all of the money which was realised. The company liquidator claimed that Salomon should personally pay all of the company's debts, in the same way as he would have been liable to pay all of the business debts if he had carried on his business as a sole trader.

Held. The company had been formed properly and without any fraud. Although Salomon owned all but six of the issued shares he was one person and the company was another. Salomon therefore had no more obligation to pay the company's debts than he had to pay his next-door neighbour's debts.

COMMENT When the High Court heard the case Salomon was held liable for the company's debts, on the grounds that the company had acted as Salomon's agent. In the Court of Appeal Salomon was held liable on the grounds that the company had run the business as a trustee for Salomon. Both of these arguments were rejected by the House of Lords.
Lord MacNachten said:

> 'The company is at law a different person altogether from the subscribers to the memorandum [the people who take the first shares]; and, though it may be that after incorporation the business is precisely the same as it was before, and the same persons are managers, and the same hands receive the profits, the company is not in law the agent of the subscribers or trustee for them. Nor are the subscribers as members liable, in any shape or form, except to the extent and in the manner provided by the Act.'

Salomon's case is regarded as one of the most important in English law, mainly because of the protection which it offers to the shareholders and the officers of companies. However, the decision that a company has a legal identity of its own has many other consequences, as the following two cases show.

■ *Macaura* v *Northern Assurance Ltd* [1925] AC 619 (House of Lords)

Macaura owned a timber estate. He sold all of the timber in the estate to a company in return for fully paid up shares in the company. Macaura and his nominees were the only shareholders in the company. (They could also have been described as the only members. The members of the company are the shareholders.) The company owed money to Macaura, but not to anyone else. After the company was formed Macaura insured the timber in his own name with several insurance companies. Most of the timber was destroyed in a fire and Macaura claimed on his insurance policies.

Held. Macaura could not claim on the insurance policies because he had no insurable interest in the timber. (A person has an insurable interest only if he is likely to suffer some monetary loss or be subject to a claim made by another person who has suffered a loss. A person without an insurable interest cannot enforce a contract of insurance.) Macaura had no insurable interest in the timber because he did not own the timber or own any part of it. Macaura might have owned the vast majority of the company's shares, and the company might have owed Macaura a great deal of money, but this did not escape the fact that it was the company, not Macaura, which owned the timber. The company had an insurable interest in the timber, but Macaura did not.

■ *Tunstall* v *Steigmann* [1962] 2 All ER 417 (Court of Appeal)

Mrs Steigmann ran a pork butcher's shop and leased the shop next door to Mrs Tunstall. Mrs Steigmann wanted to end the lease. Under the Landlord and Tenant Act 1954 Mrs Steigmann could order Mrs Tunstall to leave only if she intended to occupy the building herself, to carry on a business there. Mrs Steigmann did intend to occupy the shop herself to carry on her butchery business. But before the case came to court she turned her business into a company. Mrs Steigmann claimed that as she owned all but two of the shares in the company it was still herself that wanted to take over the premises.

Held. Mrs Steigmann was not entitled to end the lease. It was not Mrs Steigmann who wanted to occupy and run a business from the leased shop. It was Mrs Steigmann's company which wanted to do this.

Willmer LJ: 'There is no escape from the fact that a company is a legal entity entirely separate from its corporators – see *Salomon* v *Salomon and Co*. Here the landlord and her company are entirely separate entities. This is no matter of form; it is a matter of substance and reality. Each can sue and be sued in his own right; indeed, there is nothing to prevent the one suing the other. Even the holder of 100% of the shares in a company does not by such holding become so identified with the company that he or she can be said to carry on the business of the company.'

Although a company is regarded as a legal person, it does not have human characteristics. For example, a company does not enjoy human rights, such as the right to vote at elections and does not feel human emotions. In *Firsteel Products Ltd* v *Anaco Ltd* (1994) Times, 21 November, Owen J decided that a company could not sue for 'stress and aggravation', which it claimed to have suffered as a result of a breach of contract: 'This [claim] alleges that "generally the defendant has been put to a considerable amount of inconvenience, stress and difficulty ..." The defendant is a limited company, in respect of which the language used is inappropriate.' Similarly, in *Richmond London Borough Council* v *Pinn and Wheeler Ltd* [1989] RTR 354 the Divisional Court held that a company cannot drive a lorry. Pill J said: 'The act of driving a lorry is a physical act which can be performed only by natural persons.'

16.1.2 Limited liability

In *Salomon*'s case we saw that Salomon was not personally liable for the debts of the company. The vast majority of companies are registered as limited companies, as was Salomon and Co Ltd. (Below at 16.3.2 we shall see that some very few companies are unlimited, and that the shareholders in such companies do not have limited liability in respect of the company's debts.) When people buy shares in a limited company the only commitment which they make is that they agree with the company that they will pay the price of the shares. Generally, these days, the full price is paid immediately but this is not necessarily the case. For example, when the public utilities were privatised investors were often required to pay half of the share price when subscribing for their shares and remained liable for the other half. If one of these privatised companies had gone into liquidation before shareholders had paid their second instalment the shareholders would have been liable to pay the amount outstanding to the company liquidator. None of the companies did go into immediate liquidation. The shareholders therefore became liable to pay the amount outstanding on their shares to the company when payment became due under the terms of the contract which they made with the company. If the shares were transferred to another person before their full price had been paid to the company, the person taking the shares would have taken over liability to pay the rest of the price. None of the shareholders would have assumed liability to pay the debts of the company.

It must of course be emphasised that although a shareholder in a limited company will have limited liability, the company itself will not. If a company has debts it must pay them, even if this means selling all of its assets and going into liquidation. In Chapter 19 we examine the respective advantages and disadvantages of trading as a company, a partnership or a limited liability partnership. For many business owners limited liability is the main advantage attached to trading as a company.

16.1.3 Perpetual succession

A three-quarters majority of the members of a company can decide to liquidate it at any time. If they do liquidate the company it will cease to exist. However, companies can continue in existence indefinitely, and therefore it is said that they have perpetual succession.

Shareholders, of course, must die. But even if all the shareholders in a company die, their shares will be inherited by others and the company will continue in existence. The Hudson's Bay Company is the oldest corporation in the world, having been in existence since 2 May 1670. Generations of its share-holders have died, but the company still exists.

As we saw in Chapter 15, the death of a partner always ends the partnership. The partners may have agreed that in the event of the death of a partner the remaining partners will carry the firm on. Even so, technically at least, the death of a partner will dissolve the firm.

16.1.4 Ownership of property

A company can own property, and this property will continue to be owned by the company regardless of who owns the shares in the company (as was demonstrated in *Macaura v Northern Assurance Ltd*). This can be important when a company is trying to borrow money, because the company can give its own property, both present and future assets, as security for a loan. This matter is considered in more detail in Chapter 18.

16.1.5 Contractual capacity

A company has the power to make contracts and can sue and be sued on these contracts. This power must obviously be delegated to human agents, and it is the company directors, or persons who have been authorised by the directors, who actually go through the process of forming the contracts. But the important point is that it is the company itself which assumes the rights and liabilities which the contract creates. As well as being able to make contracts, companies can also sue and be sued in tort.

16.1.6 Criminal liability

As a general principle, a defendant can only be convicted of a crime if it can be proved that he committed a guilty act (*actus reus*) while having a guilty mind (*mens rea*). (The nature of a crime is analysed in Chapter 22 at 22.1.) At first sight it would seem that companies cannot commit crimes because they have not got minds of their own. The point was made as long ago as 1768, when Lord Blackstone said: 'A corporation cannot commit treason, or felony, or other crime, in its corporate capacity; though its members may in their distinct individual capacities.'

However, these days the courts can find companies guilty of crimes if they are prepared to regard the controllers of the company as the minds of the company. In *Tesco Supermarkets v Nattrass* [1971] 2 All ER 127 (House of Lords) Lord Reid said 'A living person has a mind which can have knowledge or intention or be negligent and he has hands to carry out his intention. A corporation has none of these; it must act through living persons, though not always one or the same person. Then the person who acts is not speaking or acting for the company. He is acting as the company and his mind which directs his acts is the mind of the company ... If it is a guilty mind then that guilt is the guilt of the company. It must be a question of law whether, once the facts have been ascertained, a person in doing particular things is to be regarded as the company or merely as the company's servant or agent.'

In 1994 a company called OLL Ltd, and its managing director, were both found guilty of manslaughter after four sixth form students died as a result of grossly inadequate safety measures while on a canoe trip across Lyme Bay. The *mens rea* of the managing director was attributed to the company. The managing director was sentenced to three years' imprisonment, reduced on appeal to two years, the company was fined £60 000, which represented all of its assets. This case was the first one in which a company had been convicted of manslaughter. Such convictions are very difficult to secure and new statutory regulation of corporate manslaughter is proposed by the government.

A large number of statutes, such as the Health and Safety at Work etc. Act 1974 and the Trade Descriptions Act 1968, specifically impose liability on both companies and company officers.

16.2 · The corporate veil

We have seen that a company has a legal identity of its own. A natural consequence of this is that only the company itself can be liable in respect of a wrong done by the company. The owners of the company will normally be free of any liability. They are said to be protected by the 'veil of incorporation'. This metaphor regards the company's artificial legal personality as a veil, which separates the company and the members of the company.

As we have already seen, this idea is very well established. But there are circumstances in which a court or a statute will lift the corporate veil so that the members of the company are not protected by the company's artificial legal personality.

There is no rigid list of circumstances in which a court will lift the corporate veil. They have, however, done so in the following circumstances.

16.2.1 Where the company was formed for a fraudulent purpose

■ *Gilford Motor Co Ltd* v *Horne* [1933] Ch 935 (Court of Appeal)

Mr Horne was employed as managing director of GMC Ltd. In his contract of employment Horne agreed that after leaving GMC he would not solicit its customers. When his contract was terminated Horne did begin to solicit GMC's customers. He knew that GMC would not allow him to get away with this, so he formed a company, the sole purpose of which was to employ him while he continued to solicit the customers. Horne's defence, when sued by GMC, was that his promise in his contract of employment was binding only on himself, not on the new company.

Held. An injunction was granted preventing either Horne or the company from soliciting GMC's customers.

Hanworth MR: 'I am quite satisfied that this company was formed as a device, a stratagem, in order to mask the effective carrying on of a business of Mr E. B. Horne. The purpose of it was to try to enable him, under what is a cloak or a sham, to engage in business … in respect of which he had a fear that the plaintiffs might intervene and object.'

In *Creasey* v *Breachwood Motors Ltd* (1992) BCC 638 the manager of a company, Breachwood Motors Ltd, was dismissed and wanted to bring a claim of wrongful dismissal against the company. To avoid liability, the controllers of the company transferred all the assets of the company to another company which they controlled, Breachwood Welwyn Ltd, and then had Breachwood Motors Ltd struck off the register of companies. It was held that the manager could pursue his claim directly against Breachwood Welwyn Ltd. In the following case this decision was held to be wrong by the Court of Appeal.

■ *Ord and another* v *Belhaven Pubs* (1998) BCC 607 (Court of Appeal)

The claimants took a 20-year lease from the defendant company in 1989. In 1991 the claimants sued, alleging misrepresentation and breach of warranty. In 1997 the action was still continuing and the claimants asked to substitute the defendant's holding company for the defendant company as the defendant company no longer had substantial assets owing to restructuring of the group of companies between 1992 and 1995.

Held. The holding company could not be substituted for the defendant company as the defendant company was not a mere façade for the holding company. No facts had been concealed, all the transactions had been overt and no fraud had been alleged. The companies had operated as trading companies without any sham or ulterior motive. To make the holding company liable would be at odds with the decision of *Salomon* v *Salomon & Co Ltd*. The claimants could not bring themselves within any principle which would allow the corporate veil to be pierced.

COMMENT Hobhouse LJ, giving the only judgment of the Court of Appeal, said: 'But it seems to me inescapable that the case in *Creasey* v *Breachwood* as it appears to the court cannot be sustained. It represents a wrong adoption of the principle of piercing the corporate veil and an issue of the power … to substitute one party for the other following death or succession. Therefore in my judgment the case of *Creasey* v *Breachwood* should no longer be treated as authoritative.' He did not accept that there had been asset stripping in *Creasey*. If in *Creasey* there had been impropriety in the restructuring of the group then s.423 of the Insolvency Act 1986 (examined in Chapter 19 at 19.1.4.3) could have provided a remedy.

16.2.2 If the company can be characterised as an enemy in time of war

A country at war with another country is likely to restrict the activities of citizens of the other country, who may be regarded as enemy aliens. If a company is owned by enemy aliens then the court may lift the veil and regard the company as having an enemy character.

■ *Daimler Ltd v Continental Tyre and Rubber Co Ltd* [1916] 2 AC 307 (House of Lords)

The Continental Tyre Co was registered in England. It was owed money by Daimler and sued to recover the debt. Daimler argued that as all but one of the £25 000 shares in the Continental Tyre Co were owned by German residents the company should not be allowed to sue on the debt when Britain was at war with Germany.

Held. The company could not sue on the debt. The company had assumed an enemy character and therefore anyone trading with it would be trading with the enemy.

COMMENT The action was brought by the company secretary, who lived in England and had become registered as a British subject. It was dismissed by the House of Lords because the company secretary did not have authority to issue the writ which commenced the proceedings. However, the point that the company could be regarded as having enemy characteristics was clearly made by four of the eight Law Lords who heard the case. Two of the Law Lords thought that it could not be characterised in this way.

16.2.3 Groups of companies regarded as one

Commonly one company, known as a holding company, owns a majority or all of the voting shares in another company, known as a subsidiary company. As a general principle, the veil of incorporation will hang between the two companies. In exceptional circumstances a court may lift the veil either on the grounds of agency or on the grounds of economic reality. In the following case the veil was lifted in this way.

■ *DHN Foods Ltd v London Borough of Tower Hamlets* [1976] 3 All ER 462 (Court of Appeal)

DHN ran a business which imported and distributed groceries through two subsidiary companies, both of which it wholly owned. One of these subsidiaries, Bronze, had only one asset, the premises from which DHN carried on business. The second subsidiary owned the vehicles which DHN used, but like Bronze it carried on no operations of its own. The local authority compulsorily purchased the premises owned by Bronze. DHN claimed damages for disturbance of their business. The local authority argued that the matter was nothing to do with DHN.

Held. The group of companies could be treated as one economic enterprise, because they were virtually a partnership with the three companies as partners. Consequently DHN was entitled to damages.

COMMENT This decision has been much criticised. In *Woolfson v Strathclyde Regional Council* 1978 SLT 159 the House of Lords came to a different conclusion on very similar facts. The distinction between the two cases was that in DHN the holding company completely owned the subsidiary, which had the same directors.

The decision in *DHN Foods Ltd* must now be regarded as a quirk. The courts have in recent years shown a marked reluctance to lift the corporate veil so as to regard holding companies and their subsidiaries as one economic enterprise.

■ *Adams v Cape Industries plc* [1991] 1 All ER 929 (Court of Appeal)

The defendants were two associated English companies which owned South African companies and an American company. The South African companies mined asbestos and the American company marketed the asbestos in the

United States. The American company was successfully sued by 250 claimants who had been injured by asbestos marketed in the USA by the American company. Having gained judgment in the United States, the claimants sought to enforce these judgments in the UK against the two defendants. (The American company had gone into liquidation.) This claim depended upon the defendant companies having been present in the United States when proceedings were commenced. The judge held that the presence of the defendants' subsidiary American company could not be regarded as the presence of the defendant companies themselves.

Held. The corporate veil could not be lifted. The presence of the subsidiary could not be treated as the presence of the defendant companies. There was no reason why the defendant companies should not use their corporate structure to ensure that liabilities fell on subsidiary companies rather than on themselves. The defendants and the subsidiary company could not be treated as one economic unit even though the subsidiary was set up as a façade to enable the defendants to sell asbestos in the United States while reducing their appearance of being involved in such sales.

COMMENT The circumstances in which the veil will be pierced on the grounds that companies are one economic unit were regarded by the Court of Appeal as extremely limited indeed.

16.2.4 Treating a company as a partnership in order to wind it up

In *Ebrahimi* v *Westbourne Galleries* [1972] 2 All ER 492 the House of Lords wound up a small company on the just and equitable ground by treating it as if it were a partnership. The business had originally been a partnership and was founded on a personal relationship. (The circumstances in which a partnership can be wound up by a court order were examined in Chapter 15 at 15.9.3.)

16.2.5 Other situations where the veil may be lifted

It is often said that the courts have the power to lift the veil in other situations if they think that this is the best way to do justice in the case. It might be more accurate to state that the exact circumstances in which the veil can be lifted cannot be precisely defined. In recent times the courts have shown a reluctance to lift the veil except in specified circumstances.

Various statutory provisions may lift the veil. Section 24 of the Companies Act 1985 requires all companies other than private limited companies to have at least two members. (In this chapter, and the other chapters on company law, the Companies Act 1985 will be referred to as the Act.) If the number of members falls to only one, the sole member can become liable for the company's debts which arose more than six months after the membership of the company was reduced to one. This provision can be avoided by having a single share transferred to a person who holds it as a nominee. (The nominee would agree to do nothing, other than hold the share in his own name, except as directed by the person on whose behalf he was holding it.)

Other statutes also look behind incorporation. For example, the Income and Corporation Taxes Act 1988 will not allow a company to escape UK tax by registering itself abroad, if the management and control of the company is exercised within the UK. In addition, s.214 of the Insolvency Act allows a court to make directors liable for wrongful trading, a matter considered in Chapter 19 at 19.1.4.1. This liability arises only in respect of the liquidation of insolvent companies where directors have continued to run the company when they knew, or should have known, that there was no reasonable prospect of avoiding insolvency. Directors cannot become liable for wrongful trading unless they have been negligent, but if they have been negligent they can become liable to make such contribution to the company's assets as the court thinks proper. We shall see in this chapter, at 16.3.1, that the directors of public companies can become liable on transactions made by the company while the share capital requirements set out in s.117 have not been complied with. At 16.6.3 we shall see that s.349(4) can make a company officer liable if he signs, on behalf of the company, a cheque or order for goods which does not set out the company name. This liability only arises if the company does not itself pay. Strictly speaking, these matters are not a lifting of the corporate veil because when the veil is lifted it is the members who become liable. In many cases, however, the directors will also be members of the company.

1 Is it true to state that a company has a separate legal identity of its own, or is this merely a matter of convenience?

2 What is meant by limited liability in the context of limited companies?

3 What is meant by perpetual succession?

4 Can a company itself own property and make contracts?

5 Can a company commit a crime which requires a *mens rea*?

6 What is meant by the corporate veil? In what circumstances can the veil be lifted?

Answers

1 It is true to state that a company has a separate legal identity of its own.

2 The concept of limited liability means that the members of a limited company do not become liable to pay the debts of the company. The company itself does not have limited liability.

3 Perpetual succession, a consequence of a company being a legal person in its own right, means that a company can continue in existence indefinitely, even though its shareholders and officers either leave the company or die.

4 As a company is a legal person, it can both own property and make contracts.

5 A company can be guilty of a crime which requires a *mens rea* if a person who is sufficiently senior to be regarded as the mind of the company acts on the company's behalf with the necessary *mens rea*. The *mens rea* of the person who can be regarded as the mind of the company is attributable to the company.

6 The corporate veil is an image used to demonstrate that the company cannot be regarded in law as its members: a veil separates them. The veil can be lifted in a variety of situations, including: if the company was formed for a fraudulent purpose; if the company can be characterised as an enemy in time of war; in exceptional circumstances groups of companies may be regarded as one; small companies which are like partnerships may be wound up as partnerships; various statutory provisions may look behind incorporation.

16.3 · Classification of companies

Companies can be classified in several different ways, but from a business perspective only the following classifications are useful.

16.3.1 Public companies and private companies

When a company is registered it must state in its memorandum of association whether it is to be registered as a public company or a private company. Public companies can offer shares and debentures for sale to the public and these shares can be listed on the London Stock Market. There is no requirement that shares should be listed. In fact, only the securities of some 2000 public companies are listed as it is a requirement of the Listing Rules that a class of listed shares must have a minimum value and only the largest public companies can comply with this requirement. The securities of many more public companies are bought and sold on the Alternative Investment Market, where there is no requirement as to the minimum value of the class of shares in question. The articles of private companies usually restrict the sale of the companies' shares. The most common restrictions are either that the shares must first be offered to other members of the company, or that the shares can only be sold to persons of whom the directors approve. Whatever the articles of association might say, it is a criminal offence to offer shares or debentures in a private company to members of the public (Financial Services Act 1986 s.170).

Public companies cannot be unlimited companies whereas private companies can. Private companies do not have a lower limit on the amount of contributed capital. A public company must have an allotted share capital of £50 000 (that is to say, at least £50 000 of shares must have been allotted to members) and a quarter of the value of each share must have been paid up before the company is allowed to conduct any business or borrow any money. The company must therefore have £12 500 contributed capital and a right to call a further £37 500. Section 117 of the Act prevents the issue of a certificate to commence business until a director or the company secretary has sent a form to the Registrar of Companies, stating that the allotted share capital is at least £50 000. If such a certificate is not obtained within one year of incorporation then an application can be made for a compulsory winding up of the company. Furthermore, s.117(8) provides that if a company enters into a transaction in contravention of s.117, and fails to comply with its obligations arising under the transaction within 21 days of being called upon to do so, the directors of the company are jointly and severally liable to the other contracting party in respect of any loss or damage caused by the company's failure to comply with the obligations in question. Payment for shares allotted by a public company must either be in cash or the assets given as payment must be valued. This valuation must be done by a person qualified to act as an auditor of the company, or by someone appointed by a person qualified to act as an auditor of the company.

The names of public companies must end with the words 'public limited company' or its abbreviation, 'plc'. The name of a private limited company must end with the word 'limited' or its abbreviation, 'Ltd'.

Public companies must have at least two members and at least two directors. The company will also need a company secretary, who must be suitably qualified. By suitably qualified it is meant that he must be a lawyer or an accountant, or have been the secretary of a public company for at least three of the previous five years. A private company can be formed with only one member, who can also be the sole director. A different person will need to act as the company secretary, but this person does not need to hold any qualifications.

Private companies have, in the past decade or so, become increasingly de-regulated. It is now possible for the members of a private company to elect to dispense with the need to have an Annual General Meeting, and to pass written resolutions without the need to actually hold a meeting. (These matters are dealt with in Chapter 18.) Public companies must hold an Annual General Meeting at least once each calendar year and cannot pass resolutions other than at company meetings.

There are other minor differences between public and private companies, but Table 16.1 shows the major differences.

Although public companies, such as Marks and Spencer and ICI, make up only about 1% of all companies they tend to be very much larger than most private companies. The assets of the 1% of companies which are public would far outweigh the assets of the 99% of companies which are private.

It is possible for a public company to re-register as a private one and vice versa. If this is successfully done then a new certificate of incorporation will be issued. Section 53 allows a public company to re-register as a private company by passing a special resolution. (A special resolution would only be passed if three quarters of company members who vote on the resolution vote in favour.) The special resolution must alter the company's memorandum so that it no longer states that the company is to be a public company. It must also make such alterations to the articles and the memorandum as the circumstances require. Section 54 allows shareholders who hold at least 5% of the nominal value of the plc's issued share capital or any class of share capital, or any 50 members of the plc, to apply for a court order cancelling the special resolution as long as they did not vote in favour of it. The application must be made within 28 days, and the court can either confirm the resolution, or cancel it. A plc cannot register as an unlimited company. A plc wishing to become an unlimited company would need first to re-register as a private limited company and then re-register as an unlimited company.

Table 16.1 Differences between public and private companies

Public companies	Private companies
Must have at least two members	Need have only one member
Name must end with the words 'Public Limited Company' or 'plc'	Name must end with 'Limited' or 'Ltd' (unless the company is unlimited)
Must have £50 000 allotted share capital, one quarter of which must be paid up	No limit on share capital
Shares can be listed on stock exchange (no requirement that they should be listed).	Shares cannot be listed on stock exchange, or advertised for sale
Must have at least two directors	Need have only one director
Shares allotted by the company must be paid for in cash (or qualified auditor must value assets given as payment)	Shares can be given away by the company
Company secretary must be suitably qualified	Company secretary needs no qualifications
Must hold AGM every calendar year	Can elect to dispense with AGM
Cannot pass written or elective resolutions	Can pass written or elective resolutions

Section 43 also allows a private company to re-register as a public company. This is the way in which most plcs are created – a small private company grows to the point where the shareholders decide to turn it into a plc. Again, a special resolution proposing the change will need to be passed. This special resolution must alter the company's memorandum and articles to bring them into line with the Act's requirements in respect of a public company. Again, a new certificate of incorporation will be issued. It will therefore only be possible for a private company to re-register as a plc if the requirements as to authorised and paid-up share capital which apply to the formation of a plc have been complied with. A director or the company secretary must send to the Registrar the following:

(a) an application to be re-registered as a public company, along with a £20 fee;
(b) a printed copy of the memorandum and articles as altered in pursuance of the resolution to become a public company;
(c) a copy of a written statement by the company's auditors that in their opinion the amount of the company's net assets are not less than the aggregate of its called-up share capital and undistributable reserves; and
(d) a statutory declaration by a director or the company secretary that the special resolution has been passed and that there has been no change in the company's financial position which has meant that the statement made by the auditors has become untrue.

If the Registrar is satisfied he issues the company with a certificate of incorporation stating that the company is a public company.

16.3.2 Limited and unlimited companies

16.3.2.1 Unlimited companies

Fewer than half of 1% of companies are registered as unlimited companies. These companies do have a legal personality distinct from that of the company members, but the members have agreed with the company that they will have unlimited liability for the debts of the company. This liability only arises if the company is wound up, it is not direct liability to creditors of the company. But if the company, on winding up, has insufficient assets to pay all of its debts the members of an unlimited company will have unlimited liability to supply the company with money so that it can pay its debts. If the company has a share capital, the liability of members to contribute to the debts of the company, and to the costs of winding up, is in proportion to the nominal value of the shares held. If there is no share capital then the members are obliged to contribute equally. If one member is unable to pay his share, the other members assume liability to pay it.

The names of unlimited companies must not contain the words 'limited' or 'Ltd'. Public companies may not register as unlimited companies.

Unlimited companies enjoy some advantages over limited companies. For example, their accounts need not be published or delivered to the Registrar of Companies, and it is possible to repay capital to members without a court's permission. However, these advantages have become increasingly insignificant as companies have become de-regulated. The advantages are generally considered to be far outweighed by the unlimited liability of the members, and very few unlimited companies are nowadays created. Throughout this book reference to a company should be taken as reference to a limited company.

16.3.2.2 Limited companies

Limited companies can themselves be classified into two types.

(a) Companies limited by shares

The vast majority of companies are limited by shares. As we have seen, this means that in the event of liquidation a member's liability is limited to paying off any amount unpaid on his shares. Each share must be for a fixed amount, known as the 'nominal' value or the 'par' value. A person who takes a share from a company agrees to pay the nominal value of the share to the company. In addition, the shareholder may agree with the company that he will pay an additional amount, known as a premium.

The total amount of the shares which a company may issue must be stated in the Memorandum of Association, which has to be registered with the Registrar of Companies when the company is formed. This amount is known as the 'authorised' share capital, the 'nominal' capital or the 'registered' capital. The memorandum must also state the total number of shares issued and the nominal value of each. For example, Acme Ltd might be registered as a company with an authorised share capital of £100, made up of 100 shares with a nominal value of £1 each. It should be borne in mind that this sum might well not reflect the value of the shares.

Often shares are in fact worth more than their nominal value and sometimes those taking shares agree with the company that they will pay an additional amount on each share, known as a share premium. When a share is sold at a premium, the company can enforce the contract it has made with a member and insist that any amount owing, as regards either the nominal value of issued shares or the share premium, must be paid. However, if the company goes into liquidation only the amount owing on the nominal value of the issued shares must be paid. The share premium is a matter between the company and the members.

■ Example

Acme Ltd has an authorised share capital of £100. There are 100 shares, each having a nominal value of £1. X took 50 shares when subscribing to the memorandum. Y was later issued with the other 50 shares, and agreed to pay a premium of £5 per share. Both members have only paid 20p per share so far. Acme Ltd can call upon X to pay the 80p per share which he has not yet paid and call upon Y to pay the £5.80 per share which he has not yet paid. If the company went into liquidation before X and Y had paid more than 20p per share, the liquidator could only require each member to pay the remaining 80p of each share's nominal value.

Each subscriber to the memorandum must take at least one share, and the memorandum must show how many shares each subscriber has taken. These subscribers are the original members of the company. We have already seen that a public company must have at least £50000 authorised share capital, but that there is no such requirement for a private company.

When shares are transferred by one member to another, the new holder of the shares takes over the rights and obligations attaching to the shares.

(b) Companies limited by guarantee

The liability of members of companies limited by guarantee is limited to paying an amount which they have agreed to contribute in payment of the company's debts in the event of the company being wound up. This amount is usually small, typically £5, and is spelt out in the Memorandum of Association. It may also be included in the Articles of Association. A company limited by guarantee has no right to ask for the amount guaranteed while the company is a going concern. If the amount guaranteed by those who are members at the time of liquidation is insufficient to pay the debts of the company, the liquidator can ask those who have ceased to be members within one year to pay the amount they guaranteed. However, these ex-members can only be asked to contribute in so far as this is necessary to cover liabilities which arose while they were members.

Before the Companies Act 1980 a company could be limited by shares and by guarantee, in which case the members were liable to pay both the amount guaranteed and the amount unpaid on their shares. Some such companies, formed before 1980, continue to exist and are known as hybrid companies. However, nowadays a newly formed company must either be registered as limited by shares or be limited by guarantee.

Most companies limited by guarantee are educational or charitable. Guarantee companies are not a suitable medium for trading companies. Public limited companies have never been allowed to be limited by guarantee. They must be limited by shares.

16.3.3 Method of creation

Companies can be created by registration under the Companies Acts, by statute, or by Royal Charter.

16.3.3.1 By registration under the Companies Acts

Almost all companies currently in existence were created by registration under the Companies Acts. Registration is quick and cheap, and it is generally understood that when people speak of a company this is the type of company which they mean. The process of registration is considered below at 16.4.

16.3.3.2 By statute

When most of the public utilities (such as the gas, electricity and water boards) were set up they needed special powers to enable them to compulsorily purchase land, and to prevent competition. These powers could only be granted by Parliament and so the companies were created by various statutes. When the utilities were nationalised, by other Acts of Parliament, they became corporations.

Many of these utilities have now been privatised. In effect, this means that other statutes have changed their status so that they became registered public limited companies.

16.3.3.3 By Royal Charter

A company can be created by Royal Charter. The Hudson's Bay Company was given its Royal Charter by King Charles II. Unless created a very long time ago such companies will not be trading companies. It is far easier to register under the Companies Act than to gain a Royal Charter.

If an institution is granted a Royal Charter this is usually seen as conferring a special prestige. The BBC, Oxford and Cambridge Universities, the Law Society and the Institute of Chartered Accountants were all created by Royal Charter.

16.3.3.4 Corporations sole

Certain types of office or position are regarded as having a legal personality of their own and are known as corporations sole because only one person could hold that office at any particular time. Bishops, for example, are regarded as corporations sole. Other types of corporation are known as corporations aggregate. The Public Trustee, a civil service position, is a corporation sole. This is convenient as the corporation can become the legal holder of the land with which the Public Trustee has to deal. It was similarly convenient, historically, for bishops to be capable of holding the legal title to church land. Single member companies, which are considered immediately below, are not regarded as corporations sole.

16.3.3.5 Single member companies

As a general rule, all companies must have at least two members. However, since 1992 it has been possible for a private company to be registered with only one member. New private companies can be created with only one subscriber to the memorandum, or an existing private company can allow its membership to fall to one. If the membership of an existing private company falls to one then s.352A requires that a statement that this has happened be entered into the company's register of members, along with the date on which the company became a company with only one member. Conversely, if the membership of a single member company increases then a statement that this has happened must be entered into the company's register of members, along with the date when this happened. Public companies must have at least two members.

As regards single member companies, s.370A states that a meeting of a single member company will be quorate if one member is present in person or by proxy. This is the case even if the articles of association say otherwise.

The member of a single member company can make decisions by written resolution, considered in Chapter 18 at 18.4.4.

Single member companies are likely to elect to do away with the need to hold an Annual General Meeting and the need to lay accounts before a general meeting. (Elective resolutions are considered in Chapter 18 at 18.4.3.) If a single member company makes a contract with the single member, no formalities are required as long as the contract is made in the ordinary course of business. However, in other circumstances s.322B requires the terms of the contract to be set out in a written memorandum, or recorded in the minutes of the first board meeting held after the contract was made.

16.3.4 Small, medium-sized and large companies

Companies which can be classified as either small or medium-sized can submit abbreviated accounts to the Registrar of Companies, although full accounts will still have to be delivered to the members. (This matter is examined in the following chapter at 17.6.2.) In addition, certain small companies are exempt from having to have their accounts audited (see 17.3.1).

Section 247 defines both small and medium-sized companies. A company is regarded as a small company if it meets two out of the following three requirements:

  (i)   The company's annual turnover is £5.6m or less.
  (ii) The total assets of the company are £2.8m or less.
  (iii) The company has 50 or fewer employees.

A company is regarded as a medium-size company if it meets two of the three following requirements:

  (i)   The company's annual turnover is £22.8m or less.
  (ii) The total assets of the company are £11.4m or less.
  (iii) The company has 250 or fewer employees.

Test your understanding

  1 What are the main differences between public companies and private companies?

  2 Is an unlimited company regarded by the law as having a legal personality of its own?

  3 What is a share premium?

4 What is the liability of the members of a company which is limited by guarantee?

5 Almost all companies are created by registration under the Companies Acts. In what other ways is it possible for a company to be created?

6 What is a corporation sole?

Answers

1 Public companies can advertise their shares for sale and their shares may be quoted on the London Stock Exchange; public companies need at least two members and at least two directors, private companies need have only one shareholder and one director; public companies must have at least £50 000 authorised share capital, one quarter of which must be paid up; public companies must have 'public limited company' or 'plc' as the end of their names, private companies must have 'limited' or 'Ltd', unless they are unlimited; public companies cannot be unlimited; public companies cannot pass written resolutions or elect to dispense with the holding of an AGM; the company secretary of a public company must be suitably qualified.

2 An unlimited company is regarded as having a legal personality of its own. However, the members of the company have agreed with the company that they will have unlimited liability to pay the debts of the company in the event of the company being wound up.

3 A share premium is an additional amount, over and above the nominal value of a share, which a person taking the share from a company agrees that he will pay for the share. A member of a company who has agreed to pay a share premium can be called upon by the company to pay that premium. However, on liquidation the creditors cannot insist that a share premium is paid. (They can insist that any unpaid amount of the nominal share value be paid.)

4 The members of a company limited by guarantee agree with the company that on liquidation they will contribute the amount which they have guaranteed, towards payment of the company's debts and the costs of winding up. Usually this amount is small.

5 Companies can also be created by Royal Charter or by statute.

6 A corporation sole is an office or position which can only be held by one person at a time, and which is regarded as having a legal personality of its own.

16.4 · Formation of registered companies

A registered company is formed by promoters, who must register certain documents with the Registrar of Companies. If the Registrar is satisfied with the documents he will issue a certificate of incorporation, and the company will then exist as a corporate body.

The documents which must be sent to the Registrar are:

(1) The company's memorandum of association.
(2) The company's articles of association.
(3) A statement giving the names of the company's first directors and of the company secretary. (Companies House issue a form, Form 10, on which this information must be set out.)
(4) A statement that all the statutory requirements of registration have been complied with. (Again, Companies House issue a form on which this statement must be made, Form 12.)

If the company is to be registered in either England or Wales it will be governed by the law of England and Wales and the documents must be sent to the Registrar of Companies in Cardiff. If the company is to be registered in Scotland it will be governed by Scots law and the documents must be sent to the Registrar of Companies in Edinburgh. A fee for registration, currently £20, is payable.

The Registrar must issue a certificate of incorporation if satisfied that all the requirements have been complied with. The certificate will show the company's registered number. The Registrar will also advertise the fact of the company's incorporation in the *London Gazette*.

The Registrar can refuse to register a company if it is not being formed for a lawful purpose. It is not the case that a purpose must involve the commission of a criminal offence or a tort to be regarded as unlawful. For example, it is not a criminal offence to trade as a prostitute but in *R* v *Registrar of*

Companies, ex parte Attorney General [1991] BCLC 476 it was held that the Registrar did not have to register a company set up to engage in prostitution. If the Registrar refuses to register a company then this decision can be challenged by judicial review. (Judicial review is examined in Chapter 2 at 2.6.1.)

16.4.1 The memorandum of association

A company's constitution is contained in its memorandum and articles of association. The memorandum sets out the structure of the company. Those who do business with a company have constructive notice of the company's memorandum. This notice arises because the memorandum of a company is a registered document which is available for inspection.

Section 2 of the Companies Act 1985 states that the memorandum of a company limited by shares must contain five obligatory clauses.

16.4.1.1 The company name (Clause 1)

This clause states the name of the company. If the company is a private limited company then its name must end with the word 'limited' or the abbreviation 'Ltd'. If the company is a public company then the name must end with the words 'public limited company' or the abbreviation 'plc'. If the company is registered in Wales the Welsh equivalents of these words and abbreviations may be used instead. Thus a public company with a registered office in Wales may end the company name with 'cwmni cyfyngedig cyhoeddus' or the abbreviation 'c.c.c.' instead of with 'public limited company'. A private limited company registered in Wales may end the company name with 'cyfyngedig' or the abbreviation 'cyf.' instead of with 'limited'. These specified words and abbreviations must only be used at the end of the name. The name of the company can be altered by a special resolution. (The restrictions on what name can be chosen are examined below at 16.6.)

16.4.1.2 The registered office (Clause 2)

This clause must state whether the company's registered office is in England and Wales, Wales or Scotland. The address does not need to be given here. However the address will have to be declared in Form 10. It is not possible for a company to change its jurisdiction except by a private Act of Parliament. A company can change its address within its jurisdiction by giving notice in the prescribed form to the Registrar of Companies. The Registrar will publish notice of the altered address in the *Gazette*. The address of a company's registered office is particularly important because a person can serve a document on the company by leaving it at, or sending it by post to, the registered office (s.725(1) 1985 Act).

16.4.1.3 The objects (Clause 3)

The objects clause states the purposes for which the company is being formed and sets out the contractual capacity of the company. (That is to say it sets out the contracts which the company can validly make.) At common law any contract which a company makes is *ultra vires* and therefore void if in making the contract the company acts in excess of its contractual capacity, as defined by the objects clause. For this reason most companies tend to have extremely long objects clauses, often running to several pages. Such clauses are no longer necessary as a company can register its objects as to carry on business as a general commercial company. The problems caused by the *ultra vires* rule, and the extent to which these problems have been resolved, are considered more fully in Chapter 17 at 17.1.8.

Section 4 allows a company's objects clause to be altered by special resolution. Shareholders who did not vote in favour of the resolution can submit an objection to the court, but only if they hold 15% of the company's issued share capital or 15% of any class of share capital. The objection must be made within 21 days of the special resolution being adopted (s.5 1985 Act). The court then has the power to forbid the alteration or to confirm it wholly or in part and on such terms and conditions as it thinks fit. The court may also order that the company purchase the shares of any member and that the company's share capital be reduced accordingly.

16.4.1.4 Limited liability (Clause 4)

If the liability of the members is to be limited then this clause must state that this is the case. If all of the company members consent, a private limited company may be re-registered as an unlimited company. A change from being an unlimited company to being either a private limited company or a public company can be achieved by special resolution.

16.4.1.5 Share capital (Clause 5)

The company must state the amount of share capital with which it is to be registered and the way in which this capital is to be divided into shares. For example, a company might state that it has a share capital of £100, divided into 100 shares of £1 each.

The amount of share capital declared in clause 5 is known as the authorised share capital, or the nominal capital or the registered capital. The authorised share capital is the maximum number of shares, of a stated value, which the company is authorised to issue. Not all of this authorised capital needs to be issued as shares. The authorised share capital of a company does not reflect the value of the company's assets. If the company is to be limited by guarantee then an equivalent clause must set out the amount which members agree to contribute in the event of the company being wound up.

The authorised share capital can only be altered if the company's articles of association allow for this. In the model set of articles set out in Table A article 32 allows the capital clause of the company's memorandum to be altered by an ordinary resolution of the members.

16.4.1.6 Additional clauses

As well as the five compulsory clauses there may be additional clauses. If an additional clause is stated to be unalterable then it cannot be altered by the members. If some special procedure for alteration is set out then alteration is only possible by following this procedure. If no special procedure is laid down, and the clause is not stated to be unalterable, an additional clause in the memorandum can be altered by special resolution, subject to an objection by those holding 15% of the company's issued share capital or any class of share capital.

The memorandum must also have an association and subscription clause. Those who sign the association clause indicate that they wish to be formed into a company and that they agree to take shares in the company. The subscription clause indicates how many shares each subscriber is taking. The subscribers must indicate their names and addresses and their signatures must be witnessed. Since 1992 it has been possible to have single member private companies. Such a company might have a share capital of £1, made up of a single £1 share. If the company is to be registered as a public company then there must be at least two subscribers to the memorandum. The signatures of the subscribers must be witnessed by another person (see Table 16.2).

16.4.2 The articles of association

The articles of association are the internal rules of the company. They bind the members and the company as if signed and sealed by each member. (The legal effect of the articles and the memorandum is examined in detail in Chapter 18 at 18.5.)

If a company does not register its own articles a model set of articles will be used. These model articles are contained in Table A of the Companies Regulations 1985 (SI 1985 No. 805).

Table 16.2   Table B SI 1985 No 805

A PRIVATE COMPANY LIMITED BY SHARES

<u>MEMORANDUM OF ASSOCIATION</u>

1   The company's name is 'The South Wales Motor Transport Company cyfyngedig'.

2   The company's registered office is situated in Wales.

3   The company's objects are the carriage of passengers and goods in motor vehicles between such places as the company may from time to time determine and the doing of all such other things as are incidental or conducive to the attainment of that object.

4   The liability of the members is limited.

5   The company's share capital is £50,000 divided into 50,000 shares of £1 each.

We, the subscribers to this memorandum of association, wish to be formed into a company pursuant to this memorandum; and we agree to take the number of shares shown opposite our respective names.

Names and Addresses of Subscribers		Number of shares taken by each Subscriber
1. Thomas Jones, 138 Mountfield Street, Tredegar		1
2. Mary Evans, 19 Merthyr Road, Aberystwyth		1
	Total shares taken	2

Dated   20 ■■.
Witness to the above signatures,
Anne Brown, 'Woodlands', Fieldside Road, Bryn Mawr

Table A articles can be used by either public or private companies, but are not suitable for all companies. For example, Regulation 94 prevents directors from voting at board meetings on anything in which they have a personal interest. This Regulation might be quite unsuitable for one-person companies or other small private limited companies.

The articles of most companies will at least use Table A as a basis for their own articles. If Table A is adopted in its entirety then this can be stated in the memorandum of association and there is no need to print separate articles to be sent to the Registrar. Perhaps too many companies adopt the whole of Table A, on account of the convenience of doing this.

16.4.2.1 Contents of Table A

Table A runs to 118 lengthy articles, dealing with the following matters.

Article 1	Interpretation of the articles
Articles 2–5	Share capital
Articles 6–7	Share certificates
Articles 8–11	Lien
Articles 12–22	Calls on shares and forfeitures
Articles 23–28	Transfer of shares
Articles 29–31	Transmission of shares
Articles 32–34	Alteration of share capital
Article 35	Purchase of own shares
Articles 36–37	General meetings

Articles 38–39	Notice of general meetings
Articles 40–53	Proceedings at general meetings
Articles 54–63	Votes of members
Article 64	Number of directors
Articles 65–69	Alternate directors
Articles 70–71	Powers of directors
Article 72	Delegation of directors' powers
Articles 73–80	Appointment and retirement of directors
Article 81	Disqualification and removal of directors
Articles 82–83	Remuneration and expenses of directors
Articles 84–86	Directors' appointment and interests
Articles 87–98	Directors' gratuities and pensions
Article 99	The secretary
Article 100	Minutes
Article 101	The company seal
Articles 102–108	Dividends
Article 109	Accounts
Article 110	Capitalisation of profits
Articles 111–116	Notices
Article 117	Winding up
Article 118	Indemnity

Table 16.3   Table A Regulations 23–28

TRANSFER OF SHARES

23. The instrument of transfer of a share may be in any usual form or in any other form which the directors may approve and shall be executed by or on behalf of the transferee.

24. The directors may refuse to register the transfer of a share which is not fully paid to a person of whom they do not approve and they may refuse to register the transfer of a share on which the company has a lien. They may also refuse to register a transfer unless—

(a) it is lodged at the office or at such other place as the directors may appoint and is accompanied by the certificate for the shares to which it relates and such other evidence as the directors may reasonably require to show the right of the transferor to make the transfer;

(b) it is in respect of only one class of shares; and

(c) it is in favour of not more than four transferees.

25. If the directors refuse to register a transfer of a share, they shall within two months after the date on which the transfer was lodged with the company send to the transferee notice of the refusal.

26. The registration of transfers of shares or of transfers of any class of shares may be suspended at such times and for such periods (not exceeding thirty days in any year) as the directors may determine.

27. No fee shall be charged for the registration of any instrument of transfer or other document relating to or affecting the title to any share.

28. The company shall be entitled to retain any instrument of transfer which is registered, but any instrument of transfer which the directors refuse to register shall be returned to the person lodging it when notice of the refusal is given.

There is little point in reproducing all of these articles as many of them deal with technical matters. Table A is written in legal language. An idea of the tone of Table A can be seen from the extract (Table 16.3), which reproduces Regulations 23–28.

The articles of association must be printed, signed by all the subscribers to the memorandum and by a witness to these signatures, and be sent to the Registrar of Companies. The articles can be altered by special resolution. A clause which stipulates that the articles are unalterable or need a majority vote in excess of 75% of the members to alter them is void (s.9(1) 1985 Act). However, a provision in a company's articles will be invalid to the extent that it conflicts with the company's memorandum of association. Section 17(2)(b) provides that a provision contained in the memorandum, which could have been contained in the articles instead of the memorandum, will be unalterable if the memorandum itself provides that it should be unalterable.

16.4.3 Forms 10 and 12

As well as the memorandum and articles of association, the promoters must also send a statement giving the names of the company's first directors and of the company secretary, and a statement that all the statutory requirements of registration have been complied with. Companies House issue standard forms, Forms 10 and 12, on which this information can easily be supplied.

Form 10 requires the full name of the company to be stated, along with the proposed address of the registered office. The names, previous names and addresses of the company secretary and directors must be given. The directors must also state their dates of birth, business occupations and other directorships. The secretary and directors must sign their consent personally. An agent can sign on behalf of the subscribers to the memorandum. Form 12 is merely a declaration that all the necessary requirements of the Companies Act have been complied with.

The promoters of a company stand in a fiduciary position to the company and must therefore not make any unauthorised profit from their positions. The promoters of a company need no special qualifications. It is possible for the promoter to be the only shareholder and the only director. However, it should be noticed that although the promoters of the company can complete all of Form 10, Form 12 requires that the signature of the promoter is attested by a qualified person. This means that the promoter of the proposed company must sign Form 12 in the presence of a solicitor, a Justice of the Peace, or a Commissioner for Oaths, who must also sign to say that he has witnessed the signature. Along with the four documents the promoters must send a cheque for £20, payable to Companies House.

16.4.4 Off the shelf companies

An alternative to the promoters themselves forming a company is for them to buy an 'off the shelf' company. Some businesses form companies in large numbers, in the hope that customers will wish to buy the companies. Those who form such companies register themselves as the company's first director and company secretary and take one share. Then, when a customer wishes to buy an off the shelf company, the share is transferred to whoever the customer nominates, and the original director and secretary resign and, having first procured the appointment of a new director and secretary, notify Companies House that they have resigned. The risk involved in this can be substantial, in that a company's articles must be suitable for that particular company. Many businesses, in too much of a hurry to become incorporated, adopt unsuitable articles, either by buying an off the shelf company or by adopting Table A without considering its effect. Of course, it is always possible to alter these articles by a special resolution. But all too often the members are in too much of a hurry to set the company up to realise the importance of ensuring that the articles suit their needs.

Test your understanding

1 What documents must a promoter send to the Registrar of Companies in order to form a company?

2 What is the significance of a certificate of incorporation being issued?

3 What obligatory clauses must the memorandum of association contain?

4 What is the purpose of a company's articles of association? What are Table A articles of association?

Answers

1 The Registrar will incorporate a company if he receives a £20 fee and (i) the company's memorandum of association; (ii) the company's articles of association; (iii) a statement giving the names of the company's first directors and of the company secretary; and (iv) a statement that all the statutory requirements of registration have been complied with.

2 Once a certificate of incorporation is issued the company comes into existence.

3 The memorandum of association must contain five clauses which state: (i) the name of the company; (ii) the jurisdiction of the registered office; (iii) the objects of the company; (iv) that the members of the company is limited (if it is); and the amount of share capital and how it is divided into shares. Every subscriber to the memorandum must sign it, indicating how many shares he has taken, and that the subscribers wish to be formed into a company. These signatures must be witnessed.

4 A company's articles of association act as the internal rules of the company. Table A articles are a model set of articles contained in a statutory instrument. Table A articles are frequently adopted as the articles of a newly formed company.

16.5 · Contracts made before the company is formed

A company does not come into existence until the Registrar of Companies issues its certificate of incorporation. It follows that until the certificate is issued the company has no capacity to make contracts.

However, the promoters might want to make contracts on the company's behalf in advance of incorporation. For example if a shop intended to begin trading, as a company, on 1 September then the promoters would need to buy stock in advance of that date.

It might be thought that the easiest way to do this would be for the promoters to make the contract personally, and for the company to ratify the contract as soon as the company is formed. (A person ratifies a contract if he agrees to be bound by it after it has been made (see Chapter 11 at 11.2.6).) Such a ratification would not be effective, as *Kelner* v *Baxter* (1866) LR 2 CP 174, already considered in Chapter 11, shows. It might be remembered that in that case promoters of a company ordered wine on the company's behalf before the company was formed. The company was successfully formed, the company ratified the contract and the wine was consumed. The company went into liquidation before paying for the wine. The promoters were personally liable to pay for the wine, but only because the wording of their contract with the supplier would have suggested to the reasonable man that they should be liable. The ratification by the company was ineffective.

If the promoters in *Kelner* v *Baxter* had worded the contract in such a way that the reasonable man would not have thought that they should be personally liable on the contract then they would not have been personally liable, and the supplier of the wine would never have been paid.

Such a situation is now covered by s.36C(1) of the 1985 Act, which provides:

> 'A contract which purports to be made by or on behalf of a company at a time when the company has not been formed has effect, subject to any agreement to the contrary, as one made with the person purporting to act for the company or as agent for it, and he is personally liable on the contract accordingly.'

Section 36C(1) says that the person purporting to act on behalf of the company can be personally liable on the contract made on the company's behalf but does not state that this person can also enforce the contract on the company's behalf. However, the section does state that the contract 'has effect' as one made with such a person. In *Braymist Ltd* v *Wise Finance Co Ltd* [2002] EWCA Civ 127 it was held that the section also entitles the person who made the contract on behalf of the company to enforce the contract against the other contracting party.

The Contracts (Rights of Third Parties) Act 1999, considered in Chapter 4 at 4.2.2.2, can allow companies to enforce contracts which were made before the company was formed. However, the promoter who made the contract would also be liable on the contract, along with the company.

The easiest ways to get around the problem of pre-incorporation contracts would seem to be either to wait until the company is formed before getting the company to make the contract, or to make the contract as agent for an off the shelf company which, being in existence at the time of the contract, could ratify it later.

It will be noticed this section applies 'subject to any agreement to the contrary'. It is therefore possible for the promoters to disclaim personal liability when they make the contract on the company's behalf. However, it would be inadvisable for the other contracting party to deal with the promoters on this basis. In effect they would be making contracts which could be enforced against them but which they themselves might not be able to enforce.

Promoters who are personally liable on contracts made on the company's behalf can later escape personal liability by novation. This would be achieved by the company, after it is formed, making a second contract with the supplier on the same terms as the pre-incorporation contract. The supplier agrees in this contract that the promoters cease to be liable on the pre-incorporation contract in return for the company assuming liability. The novation will only be effective if the supplier and the company agree to it.

16.6 · The company name

Earlier in this chapter we saw that the promoters must include the company's proposed name in the memorandum of association. The name of a company is important because it is the means by which the company, a legal person, can be identified. We also saw the circumstances in which the name must end 'public limited company', 'limited' or their abbreviations. The word 'Company' is not often included in the names of companies. Strangely, the word appears in the names of partnerships more frequently than in the names of companies. Although, in general, a company is free to choose any name it pleases there are some restrictions on the choice of name.

16.6.1 Prohibited names

Sections 25 and 26 prohibit the use of certain names, as follows:

(i) The words 'limited' or 'unlimited' or 'public limited company', or their Welsh equivalents, can only be used at the end of the name.

(ii) The Registrar will refuse to register a name which is identical to the name of another company already on the register. (It is therefore essential to check whether the proposed name has already been registered. This can be done quickly and easily by phoning Companies House or by accessing the Companies House web site.) Nor will a name be registered if it is identical except for: (i) the inclusion of the word 'The' at the beginning of the name; (ii) the way the letters which spell out the name are differently punctuated or differently divided into words; or (iii) the use of the words 'company', 'limited', unlimited or 'public limited company' at the end of the name.

(iii) The Registrar will refuse to register a name the use of which would, in the opinion of the Secretary of State, constitute a criminal offence or be offensive.

(iv) Regulations made by the Secretary of State prohibit the use of certain words which suggest a connection with the Government or with local authorities. The Registrar can register such a name but permission from an appropriate body may be required. The Company and Business Names Regulations 1981, as amended, also include a list of words and expressions which can only be used if the Secretary of State gives permission, after a request has been made to the relevant body specified in the Regulations.

Under s.28 the Secretary of State can order a company to change its name. Such an order can be made within 12 months of registration if the company name is too similar to one which is already on the register, or should have been on the register. If misleading information was given at the time of registration the Registrar can order the company to change its name within five years of registration.

If the name gives such a misleading indication of the nature of the company's activities that harm is likely to be caused to the public the Registrar can order a change of name at any time (s.32).

The Insolvency Act 1986 s.216 makes it a criminal offence for a person who was a director or a shadow director of an insolvent company within 12 months of the company's liquidation to be a director of a company using the name of the insolvent company or of a company using a name which is so similar as to suggest a connection with the insolvent company. It is also prohibited for the ex-director to take part in the promotion, formation or management of a new company using the same or a similar name. The prohibition lasts for five years from the date of insolvency. A person in breach of s.216 not only commits a criminal offence of strict liability for which he could be fined or imprisoned, but can also become personally responsible for all the debts of the new company. This liability is joint and several with that of the company and any other person who could become liable under s.216. A person who is involved in the management of the new company under the instructions of a director or shadow director who could be liable under s.216 becomes jointly and severally liable for the new company's debts along with the company and any other person who is liable.

Miscellaneous other statutes prohibit the inappropriate use of names which would indicate matters such as a connection with charitable organisations or that the company is a bank or a building society.

16.6.2 Passing-off

If a company registers a name which is too similar to the name of an established business, an action for the tort of passing-off might be brought by the established business to prevent the company from trading under its registered name. If such a passing-off action is brought the court will grant an injunction to prevent use of that name. However, a passing-off action will only be successful if the use is likely to divert customers away from the established business or cause confusion between the two businesses. (*Croft* v *Day* (1843) 7 Beav 84, an example of a partnership bringing a successful passing-off action, was considered in the previous chapter at 15.4.1.3.)

A passing-off action may be brought whether the name was deliberately made similar or was done so accidentally. But the fact that it was done deliberately is likely to influence the court's decision against the new name.

■ *Ewing* v *Buttercup Margarine Co Ltd* [1917] 2 Ch 1 (Court of Appeal)

The claimant carried on an unincorporated business under the name Buttercup Dairy Company. The business was substantial, with 150 shops, and sold margarine, tea and similar products. The business was carried on mainly in Scotland, but also in the North of England. The defendant company was registered under the name the Buttercup Margarine Company Limited. It intended to manufacture and sell margarine, but in the South of England. The claimant brought a passing-off action. The defendants argued that there would be no confusion between the two businesses as they were wholesalers and the claimant was a retailer and because they only intended to carry on business in and around London. There was nothing in the defendants' memorandum of association to prevent them from retailing margarine.

Held. The claimant's action was successful. The defendant company was prohibited from continuing to trade under its registered name. The public might have thought that there was a connection between the two businesses.

Cozens-Hardy MR: 'In my opinion it is a perfectly plain and clear case, not very near the line, but well over the line … I can see no principle which withholds us from preventing injury to the plaintiff in his business as a trader by a confusion which will lead people to conclude that the defendants are really connected in some way with the plaintiff or are carrying on a branch of the plaintiff's business.'

16.6.3 Publication of name and address

All companies must publish their names legibly and conspicuously:

(1) Outside the registered office and all places of business (s.348(1)).
(2) On all letters, invoices, notices, cheques, orders for goods and receipts (s.349).
(3) On the company seal, if it has a seal (s.350).

If the company does not publish its name as required then every one of its officers is liable to be fined. Section 351(1) provides that company letters and orders for goods must also show the company number, the address of the registered office and the place (i.e England and Wales, Wales or Scotland) where the company is registered. Furthermore, an officer of the company who signs company letters or cheques on behalf of the company which do not publish the company name will be personally liable to any creditor who relies on the document and loses money as a result of the company not honouring its obligation (s.349(4)). This liability will also be imposed if the company name is incorrectly stated.

For example, in *Penrose v Martyr* (1858) El Bl & El 499, a company secretary accepted a cheque on the company's behalf and was held personally liable because the word 'Limited' was omitted from the company name.

16.6.3.1 Change of name

Either a public or a private company may change its name by special resolution. A private company may alternatively change its name by written resolution.

The same prohibitions will apply to a change of name as applied to the use of a name on formation of a company. The Registrar has the same powers to refuse to register the changed name.

16.6.3.2 Business names

Sometimes companies trade under a name other than their registered corporate name. A company which does trade under another name will have to comply with the Business Names Act 1985. The Act will apply if the company carries on business in any name other than its exact registered name, except that it may add to that name that it is carrying on business as a successor to a former owner of that business. The effects of this Act were considered in Chapter 15, at 15.4.1.3, as the Act applies more often to partnerships than to companies.

Even if the company does trade under another name it must continue to print its proper corporate name on all business documents, as explained above.

16.7 · The Registrar of Companies

The Registrar of Companies is an official of the Department of Trade and Industry and is the head of an agency known as Companies House. The Registrar has many other duties besides registering newly formed companies. The main duties of the Registrar are:

(a) To issue a certificate of incorporation when a company is first registered. This is conclusive evidence that the company has been formed and, if appropriate, that it is limited.
(b) To issue a certificate of incorporation on change of company name. (Although a new certificate is issued the company remains the same legal person and its registered number remains the same.)
(c) To keep a list of the names of all UK registered companies, Limited Partnerships and Limited Liability Partnerships. This list is published on microfiche.
(d) To issue certificates of re-registration when a private company changes to a public one, or vice versa, or from unlimited to limited, or vice versa.

(e) To receive the annual return and the annual financial statements of companies.

(f) To register and keep safe the documents which statutes require him to hold.

(g) To issue certificates which register mortgages and charges.

(h) To strike companies off the register when they are dissolved.

(i) To allow any member of the public to see the file of a particular company.

(j) To register special and extraordinary resolutions.

(k) To publish in the *London Gazette* the fact of receipt of various documents.

Test your understanding

1 Once formed, can a company ratify a contract made on the company's behalf before the company was incorporated?

2 Will a promoter of a company be personally liable on a pre-incorporation contract which he made on the company's behalf?

3 In what circumstances will the Registrar refuse to register a company under the name proposed?

4 What is meant by a passing-off action?

5 In what places and documents must the name of a company be publicised?

6 What are the main duties of the Registrar of Companies?

Answers

1 A company cannot ratify a contract which was made before the company was formed.

2 Under s.36C(1) a promoter will be personally liable on a pre-incorporation contract made on the company's behalf unless there is an agreement to the contrary.

3 The Registrar will refuse to register a name if it would constitute a criminal offence or be offensive, if it is identical to a name already on the register, or if the name is prohibited by regulations made by the Secretary of State. The Registrar can also refuse to register a company if it is not being formed for a lawful purpose.

4 A passing-off action is an action in tort to prevent a business from trading under a name which is too similar to the name of an existing business. If trading under the new company name would be likely to divert customers away from the existing business, or cause confusion between the two businesses, an injunction can be granted to prevent this.

5 The company name must be published, clearly and conspicuously: (i) outside all places of business; (ii) on all letters, invoices, notices, cheques, order forms and receipts; (iii) on the company seal, if the company has a seal.

6 The Registrar issues certificates of incorporation and of re-registration; keeps a list of the names of registered companies; keeps basic information on all registered companies; and strikes companies off the register of companies when they are wound up.

Key points

The nature and characteristics of a company

■ A company is a legal person.

■ Members of limited companies are not liable to pay the companies' debts.

■ A company can continue in existence indefinitely. It can also own property.

■ A company can make contracts in its own name.

■ A company can be guilty of a crime. If the crime requires *mens rea*, the *mens rea* of a person senior enough to be regarded as the mind of the company can be attributed to the company.

■ The corporate veil is said to separate a company and its members. The veil can be lifted in a variety of situations, including: if the company was formed for a fraudulent purpose; if the company can be characterised as an enemy in time of war; in exceptional circumstances groups of companies may be regarded as one; small companies which are like partnerships may be wound up as partnerships; in line with various statutory provisions.

Classification of companies

- The shares of public companies can be listed on the London Stock Exchange. The shares and debentures of private companies cannot be offered to the public.

- Public companies must have an authorised share capital of at least £50 000 and at least one quarter of this must be paid up. There is no minimum amount of share capital for private companies.

- When an unlimited company is wound up its members have unlimited liability to pay the company's debts.

- The liability of members of a company limited by shares is limited to paying any amount of the nominal value of the shares which has not yet been paid. The company can require the members to pay this amount before winding up or a liquidator can insist that they pay it upon a winding up.

- The liability of members of a company limited by guarantee is to contribute the amount which they have guaranteed. This amount only becomes payable if it is needed to pay the company's debts when the company is wound up.

- It is possible for companies to be created by statute or Royal Charter, but almost all companies were created by registration under the Companies Acts.

Formation of registered companies

- A registered company is formed by registration with the Registrar of Companies.

- The Registrar will register a company upon receiving a memorandum of association; articles of association; a statement giving the names of the company's first directors and of the company secretary; a statement that all the statutory requirements of registration have been complied with; and a £20 fee.

- The memorandum of association must contain five obligatory clauses, setting out: (i) the name of the company; (ii) the jurisdiction of the registered office; (iii) the objects of the company; (iv) that the members of the company is limited (if it is); and the amount of share capital and how it is divided into shares. Every subscriber to the memorandum must sign it, indicating how many shares he has taken, and indicating that the subscribers wish to be formed into a company. The signatures must be witnessed.

- The articles of association set out the internal rules of the company. A company may adopt the model set of articles contained in Table A as its articles.

Liability on contracts made before the company is formed

- A company cannot validly ratify a contract which was made before the company was formed.

- A promoter who makes a contract on behalf of a company which has not been formed will be personally liable on the contract, unless there is an agreement to the contrary.

- The Registrar will not register a company under a name which is identical to the name of a company already on the register, or under a name which the Secretary of State would consider would constitute a criminal offence. Certain words may only be used in a company name if permission is gained from the Secretary of State.

■ A passing-off action is an action in tort to prevent a company from trading under a name which is too similar to the name of an existing business.

■ The Registrar of Companies is an official of the Department of Trade and Industry, who heads a government agency known as Companies House.

Summary questions

1 Explain the main differences between public and private companies.

2 Y Co Ltd allotted 100 shares to Arthur. The shares had a nominal value of £1 each and Arthur agreed to pay a premium of £4 per share. Arthur has only paid Y Co Ltd 30p per share.

   a What liability does Arthur have to Y Co Ltd in respect of the shares?

   b If the company became insolvent before Arthur had paid any more money, how much would Arthur have to contribute towards the company's debts?

3 Explain what is meant by the corporate veil and the circumstances in which the veil can be lifted.

4 In which of the documents sent to the Registrar of Companies will the following information be found?

   a The address of the company's registered office.

   b The company's capacity to make contracts.

   c The rules on the transfer of shares.

   d The name and address of the company secretary.

   e A declaration that all of the necessary formalities have been complied with.

   f The previous names of the directors.

   g The company's authorised share capital.

5 X Co Ltd was incorporated in 1993 with X as the sole member and sole director. X's husband, a teacher, is the company secretary. X Co Ltd has been extremely successful and now operates a successful dot.com business. X has decided that she would like to turn X Co Ltd into a public company. Outline the changes which will need to be made before the Registrar of Companies will re-register the company as a public company.

6 Your firm has been approached to refurbish a restaurant on behalf of a company which is soon to be incorporated. The contract is lucrative and you know that the promoter who approached you to make the contract is financially sound. The promoter does not want to remain personally liable on the contract. Can the contract be made in such a way that the promoter is not personally liable on it? Assuming that the promoter is personally liable on the contract, can he ensure that this liability should cease once the company comes into existence?

Multiple choice questions

1 A business is registered under the name Acme Trading Ltd. Which one of the following must the business be?

   a A public limited company.

   b A partnership.

   c A private limited company.

   d Either a private limited company or a private unlimited company.

2 David owns 100 shares in a private limited company which has debts which amount to 50 times its assets. The company has no prospect of paying the debts. David has paid half the nominal price of his shares. Which one of the following statements is true?

   a As the company is limited it need not pay its debts.

   b Limited liability will mean that David has to pay nothing towards the company's debts.

   c The amount of the company's debts must be paid by all shareholders in proportion to their shareholding.

   d David must pay the other half of the nominal price of his shares. Beyond that he need pay no more.

3   Consider the following statements.

   i   A public company need have only two members.
   ii   A public company cannot be unlimited.
   iii   A public company's shares must be quoted on the stock exchange.
   iv   A public company must have at least £50 000 of allotted, fully paid up, capital.
   v   A private company will need to pass an ordinary resolution in order to convert to a public company.

   Which of the above statements are true?

   a   (i) and (ii) only.
   b   (i), (iii) and (iv) only.
   c   (ii) and (iv) only.
   d   All of the statements.

4   Which one of the following is not a legal person?

   a   A small family company.
   b   A public limited company.
   c   The BBC.
   d   A partnership of chartered accountants.

5   Consider the following statements.

   i   A private company will continue in existence indefinitely unless it is liquidated.
   ii   The members of an unlimited company have unlimited liability to contribute money to the company if the company, acting in good faith, asks them to do this.
   iii   The members of a company limited by guarantee can at any time be asked by the company to contribute the amount guaranteed.
   iv   It is no longer possible for a company to be created by Royal Charter. However, some companies created in this way still exist.
   v   A corporation sole is any company with only one member.

   Which of the above statements are true?

   a   (i), (ii) and (iv) only.
   b   (ii), (iii) and (v) only.
   c   (iii), (iv) and (v) only.
   d   (i) only.

6   When a company is first registered, which of the following pieces of information need not be provided to the Registrar of Companies?

   a   The type of business which the company may carry on.
   b   The number and nominal value of the shares which the company is authorised to issue.
   c   The names and addresses of the directors.
   d   The value of the company's assets.

7   Consider the following statements.

   i   A company's articles of association bind all the members of the company as if they had all signed them.
   ii   Upon registration a public or private company which does not wish to register its own individual articles can elect to adopt a model set of articles, known as Table A.
   iii   A company's articles of association can always be altered by special resolution, even if the articles themselves say that they are unalterable.
   iv   If a clause in a memorandum of association is additional to the five compulsory clauses and is stated to be unalterable, the members of the company will have no power to alter the clause.
   v   The Registrar can refuse to register a company on the grounds that it is being formed for an unlawful purpose, even if that purpose does not amount to the commission of a criminal offence.

   Which of the above statements are true?

   a   (i), (ii) and (iv) only.

b (ii), (iii) and (v) only.

c (iii), (iv) and (v) only.

d All of the statements.

8 Which one of the following statements is not true?

a A promoter of a company will be liable on a pre-incorporation contract made on the company's behalf, unless there is an agreement to the contrary.

b If a company named Acme Company Limited is already registered, the Registrar will refuse to register a company under the name The Acme Company Limited.

c A passing-off action will only be successful if the claimant can show an intention to deceive the public.

d Either a public or a private company may change its name by special resolution.

Task 16

A friend of yours, currently running his car repair business as a sole trader, wants to form a company. Draft a report explaining the following matters.

a The steps which must be taken in order for a company to be formed.

b The nature and essential content of a company's articles and memorandum of association.

c The extent to which a shareholder can be liable for the debts of a company.

d The restrictions on the choice of name with which a company may be registered.

Chapter 17

THE MANAGEMENT OF A COMPANY

Introduction

The first half of this chapter examines the law relating to those who manage companies, the directors. We look at the rules relating to the appointment and removal of directors, the circumstances in which persons can be disqualified from being a director, the register of directors which a company must keep, the remuneration of directors, the powers and duties of directors and the capacity of directors to make contracts on behalf of the companies in which they hold office.

As well as having at least one director, every company must also have a company secretary. We consider the way in which a company secretary is appointed, the duties of the secretary and the qualifications which must be held by the secretaries of public companies.

The auditors of a company are neither the managers nor the employees of the company. However, every company, other than a small private company or a dormant company, will need to have the annual accounts audited and will therefore need to have an auditor. We look at the ways in which auditors are appointed and can be dismissed, their qualifications and their duties.

In the final part of this chapter we consider the registers and documents which a company must keep and make available for inspection, and the accounts which must be laid before the members of the company and filed with the Registrar of Companies.

17.1 · Directors

We have seen that every company is regarded by the law as a legal person in its own right. However, it is obvious that companies can only function through the actions of living people. The task of managing a company is therefore entrusted to the directors, who act as agents of the company. Ultimately, control of a company lies with the shareholders. They have the power to appoint and remove the directors or to alter the company's articles to take away some of the directors' powers. But while the directors hold office it is they, and not the shareholders, who run a company. Section 741(1) provides that the use of the term 'director' in the Act includes any person occupying the position of director, whether he calls himself a director or not. This section was needed because sometimes those who act as directors of a company call themselves managers, governors or some other title.

As a company will need to have directors, it is not possible to register a company without specifying who the first directors should be. Generally, there is no requirement that the directors of a company should also be shareholders, although they very commonly are.

In Chapter 16 we saw that a public company cannot be incorporated with fewer than two directors, and must at all times have at least two directors in office. A private company is not required by statute to have more than one director. However, the articles of association of many private companies require that there be at least two directors. For example, article 64 of Table A states that the company must have at least two directors unless the members by ordinary resolution determine otherwise. It also states that there is no maximum number of directors.

Executive directors devote substantially the whole of their working time to performing their duties and derive most of their income from their connection with the company. They are usually employees of the company. Non-executive directors do not devote their whole time to performing their duties. They are generally paid a small fee for their services and so they do not generally derive most of their income from the company. There is no requirement that directors should be human beings, and companies may be appointed as directors of other companies.

17.1.1 Appointment of directors

In Chapter 16 we saw that the promoters of a company must send a statement to the Registrar of Companies, giving the names and addresses of the company's first directors and the first company secretary. All of the subscribers to the memorandum must sign this statement, and the directors so appointed must also sign it to show that they agree to their appointment. Upon registration of the company the persons named as directors will become the first directors of the company.

A company's articles of association will almost always set out how subsequent directors are to be appointed. New directors may need to be appointed either to increase the number of directors or to fill a vacancy created by the retirement of a director. If the articles do not deal with the matter, directors will be appointed by ordinary resolution of the members. (An ordinary resolution is passed by a simple majority of company members who vote at a company meeting.) Article 78 of Table A gives the members of the company the power to appoint a director by ordinary resolution and the articles of most companies would contain a similar article. There is no reason why a private company should not appoint a director by means of the written resolution procedure, instead of by ordinary resolution. (The written resolution procedure is examined in Chapter 18 at 18.4.4. It allows the members of a private company to pass a resolution, without the need to hold a meeting, by way of all of the members signing the resolution.) Article 79 of Table A allows the directors to appoint a director. A person can only be appointed as a director if he consents to being appointed, and the appointment must be exercised for the benefit of the company as a whole.

As regards public companies, s.292(1) disallows the appointment of two or more directors by a single resolution, unless there has been a unanimous vote at the meeting to allow such a resolution. If this section is contravened the appointment of the directors is void, even if no one voted against the resolution at the time (s.292(2)).

The dates of birth of the first directors will have been included in the statement of directors delivered to the Registrar of Companies, and the dates of birth of directors currently holding office can be found in the register of directors which every company must keep. Unless the articles provide otherwise, there is no minimum age for directors. Nor is there any maximum age for directors in private companies. However, the directors of public companies, and their subsidiaries, must be under 70 years of age at appointment, unless the articles provide otherwise (s.293). However, the members of a public company can appoint a person over 70 by ordinary resolution if special notice of the resolution, which states the age of the proposed director, is given (s.293(5)).

17.1.2 Retirement and removal of directors

A director may give notice of his resignation of office at any time, and the company is obliged to accept such a resignation. The articles of association may also set out circumstances in which a director is deemed to have resigned. Table A article 81, for example, states that a director shall automatically be deemed to have resigned in the following circumstances: if the law or the Companies Act 1985 requires this; if he has become bankrupt, or of unsound mind; if he resigns by giving notice to the company; or if he has been absent from board meetings for more than six months without the permission of the other directors. The articles may also provide that directors shall retire by rotation.

(Table A articles 73 and 74 provide for one third of the directors, those who have held office for the longest, to retire by rotation at the company's annual general meeting. The retiring directors can offer themselves for re-election and can be automatically re-elected if no one else stands to fill the vacancy.)

No matter what a company's articles might say, and no matter what might have been agreed between the director and the company, s.303(1) provides that a director can always be removed by an ordinary resolution of which the company has been given special notice (28 days). If a company receives special notice of a resolution to remove a director, s.379 requires that the members are given at least 21 days' notice of both the resolution and the meeting at which it will be proposed. Even if he is not a member of the company, the director whose dismissal is proposed has a right to speak at the meeting (s.304). Section 304 also allows the director to make written representations, of a reasonable length, to the members. If the company receives these representations in time, it must send them out to members along with notice of the meeting. If the representations are not received in time, the director has the right to require them to be read out at the meeting. As the director whose dismissal is proposed has a right to speak at the general meeting, the written resolution procedure may not be used to dismiss a director under s.303.

Although s.303 always allows a director to be dismissed by ordinary resolution, the shares of the director whose removal is proposed might have enhanced voting power. In some companies these enhanced voting rights might make removal of a director against his will an impossibility.

■ *Bushell* v *Faith* [1970] AC 1099 (House of Lords)

The 300 shares in a company were owned equally by a brother and two sisters. The brother and one of the sisters were the only directors. The articles provided that in any resolution to remove a director that director's shares should carry three votes per share. The two sisters wanted to remove their brother as a director. At a general meeting the sisters voted for removal, the brother voted against. The sisters claimed that the resolution had been passed by 200–100. The brother claimed that it had been defeated by 200–300.

Held. The article giving the enhanced voting rights was perfectly valid. Therefore the resolution to remove the brother from the board had been defeated by 200 votes to 300.

COMMENT (i) There is no reason why a member's votes should not carry 1 000 or a 1 000 000 votes per share in a vote to remove that person as a director. However, those with three-quarters of the voting shares might change the articles to remove these weighted voting rights. Section 9(1) of the Act would not allow an article which gave a person a veto over a change in the articles to be effective. It states that the articles of a company can always be altered by special resolution. (But in *Bushell* v *Faith* the Court of Appeal recognised that an article might give some shares weighted voting rights on any resolution to change the article which gave weighted voting rights to a director whose removal was proposed.) However, a provision in the memorandum which could have been in the articles, and which was stated by the memorandum to be unalterable, could not be altered by the members (s.17(2)(b)). (ii) If the resolution had proposed the removal of one of the sisters, as well as the removal of the brother, then it would seem that the sister whose removal was proposed would have had enhanced voting rights. The resolution could therefore have been passed, thus removing both the brother and the sister, and the sister who was removed could later have been reappointed.

Another obstacle to the removal of a director might be that the directors would not include the resolution proposing the director's removal on the agenda of the annual general meeting. Section 376 allows members representing 5% of the voting rights, or 100 members holding shares on which at least £10 000 in total has been fully paid up, to compel the directors to put a resolution on the agenda of the next AGM. (The requirements of s.376 are considered in Chapter 18 at 18.3.1.) In *Pedley* v *Inland Waterways Association Ltd* [1977] 1 All ER 209 Slade J held that a member or members who did not satisfy the requirements of s.376 could not compel the directors to put a resolution to remove a director on the agenda of the annual general meeting, even if they gave notice of the resolution to the company in the proper way. A shareholder who can muster the support of 10% of the paid-up voting shares can requisition the directors, under s.368, to hold an extraordinary general meeting to consider the objects specified in the requisition, and would not therefore have to wait for the annual general meeting to ensure that a resolution proposing the removal of a director is put to the members. (The requirements of s.368 are examined in Chapter 18 at 18.3.2.)

When a director is removed under s.303(1), a replacement director cannot be voted in at the same meeting unless special notice of the resolution proposing the appointment has been given (s.303(2)).

Directors can be removed otherwise than under s.303 if the articles allow this. In a private company the articles might provide that the director whose removal is proposed had no right to speak at the meeting, or that special notice of a resolution to dismiss a director was not needed, or that removal could be achieved by written resolution. The articles of many companies provide that a director can be removed if all the other directors request this in writing. When the articles do allow other ways to dismiss a director, the members may choose whether to remove the director under s.303 or under the other power. However, if they elect to use s.303 they must comply with all the necessary formalities.

When a director is removed from office this might amount to breach of contract by the company. If the director is an employee of the company there might be a claim for unfair or wrongful dismissal. Section 303(5) provides that nothing in s.303 is to be taken as depriving a person removed under s.303 of compensation or damages payable in respect of the termination of his appointment as director.

Section 293(3) provides that a director of a public company is deemed to have retired at the first annual general meeting after he became 70 years old. However, a director deemed to retire by virtue of s.293(3) could be reappointed if the conditions described above at 17.1.1 are fulfilled.

17.1.3 Disqualification of directors

There are no special qualifications needed to hold office as a director. Even a person who has held office in several companies which have gone into liquidation is free to become the director, or even the sole director, of another company. However, in certain circumstances a person will be disqualified from directing or managing a company. A person who is disqualified automatically ceases to hold office as a director.

Section 11 of the Company Directors Disqualification Act (CDDA) 1986 makes it a criminal offence of strict liability for an undischarged bankrupt to be concerned in the management of a company, without permission from the court which made the bankruptcy order. This applies not only to directors, but to those who act as directors without calling themselves directors.

A separate matter is that a person may be made the subject of a disqualification order, in which case he may not take part in the management of a company, or promote a company, or act as an insolvency practitioner. Both individuals and companies may be the subject of a disqualification order. Not only is it a criminal offence to ignore such an order, but a person who does ignore it can be made personally liable for all debts and liabilities incurred while acting in contravention.

A disqualification order may be made under CDDA 1986 on the following grounds:

(i) Conviction of an indictable offence in connection with promotion, formation, management, or liquidation of a company, or with the receivership or management of a company's property. Although the offence must be indictable, disqualification under s.2 is still possible if the offence was in fact tried in the magistrates' court (CDDA 1986 s.2).

(ii) Persistent default in sending annual returns, accounts or other documents which have to be filed with the Registrar of Companies. Three convictions within five years is conclusive evidence of persistent default (CDDA 1986 s.3).

(iii) If an officer or receiver of a company which is in liquidation has been guilty of fraud in relation to the company, or has been in breach of his duty as a company officer, or has committed an offence of knowingly being a party to fraudulent trading. (A criminal conviction for this is not necessary.) (CDDA 1986 s.4.)

(iv) Conviction in the magistrates' court, of an offence only triable summarily, of failing to provide the Registrar of Companies with information required to be provided. However, it must also be shown that this is the third conviction for doing this within the past five years (CDDA 1986 s.5).

(v) If a person acting as a director or shadow director of a company which has become insolvent, has engaged in conduct which makes him unfit to be concerned with the management of a company (CDDA 1986 s.6).

(vi) If the Trade Secretary concludes from an inspector's report that the person's conduct makes him unfit to be concerned in the management of a company, or that a disqualification order should be made in the public interest (CDDA 1986 s.8).

(vii) If the person has been held by a court to be responsible to contribute to the assets of a liquidated company on the grounds of fraudulent or wrongful trading which are considered below at 19.1.4 (CDDA 1986 s.10).

Orders made on the ground of (ii) above, may not be for longer than five years. Nor may an order on the grounds of (i) and (iv), if made by a magistrates' court. As regards the other grounds the maximum period is 15 years, and if the order is made on ground (v) it may not be for less than two years.

A register of disqualification orders is kept at Companies House and members of the public may inspect this free of charge.

17.1.4 **The register of directors**

Section 288(1) of the Act requires every company to keep a register of directors and secretaries at its registered office. This register must give the same information about directors as must be given when the company is first registered. That is to say, their full names, residential addresses, previous names, dates of birth, nationalities, details of any other directorships held in the previous five years and business occupations.

Members of the company are entitled to inspect this register free of charge. Non-members are entitled to inspect it upon payment of a small fee (s.288(3)). If the register is not open to inspection, the company and its officers may be fined (s.288(4)) and the court may order immediate inspection to be allowed (s.288(5)). If a person is responsible for refusing to allow the register to be inspected, a court must have regard to this when considering if such a person is unfit to be concerned in the management of a company (CDDA 1986 s.9).

Section 288(2) provides that if there is a change in the directors of a company, or in the particulars contained in the register of directors, the Registrar of Companies must be informed within 14 days. The Registrar will publicise the change in the *Gazette* (s.711(1)(c)), and until this has happened the company cannot rely on the change of directors (s.42(1)(c)). This does not mean that a person cannot act as a director until his appointment is notified. But it does mean that a person is held out as a director until notification of his having left office is published in the *Gazette*. (The meaning of holding out was considered in Chapter 15 at 15.8.3.)

When a company is listed on the Stock Exchange, the Listing Rules require that the register also gives the following information about each director: details of management experience; unspent convictions; details of personal insolvencies or of insolvencies of companies in which they acted as an executive director; details of public criticism by statutory authorities; and whether they have ever been disqualified as a director.

Companies do not have to state the names of directors on business letters. However, if the name of any director is stated on such a letter then s.305 requires that the name of all directors and shadow directors must be stated.

17.1.5 **The board of directors**

When the directors act collectively they act as the board of directors. Meetings of the board of directors are known as board meetings and, unless the articles provide otherwise, any director may call a board meeting. A reasonable amount of notice of a board meeting must be given to all of the directors whose whereabouts are known, but there is no need to give notice of matters which may be raised and voted upon. As well as raising matters to be voted upon during the board meeting itself, directors can make informal decisions, without the need for a meeting, if all of the directors agree to this.

One of a director's duties is to attend board meetings, and directors have a right to attend board meetings, and to vote at them. Directors entitled to vote at a board meeting will count towards the quorum of the meeting. Table A article 89 allows the directors to fix the quorum for a board meeting, but states that if it is not fixed by them it shall be two. A private company with only one director should state in the articles that the quorum shall be one. If a meeting is inquorate any decisions taken at such a meeting will be invalid. Where not all of the directors attend the board meeting, decisions taken at the meeting will nevertheless be valid as long as the meeting was properly convened and was quorate.

The articles of a company may allow any director to appoint an **alternate director** to carry out his duties while he is absent. Companies House must be informed both when such an alternate director is appointed and removed. An alternate director may have all the powers of a director and may count towards a quorum at a board meeting. However, an alternate director will not count towards a quorum if the person who appointed him is also present at the meeting. All the company law requirements which apply to directors also apply to alternate directors.

A board resolution is not passed unless more directors vote in favour than vote against. However, many articles include an article similar to article 88 of Table A, which allows the chairman of the board of directors to have the casting vote where the votes of the directors are equally split. Article 88 allows the directors to elect a chairman, whose election must be noted in the minutes, and also to remove him from office. A company's articles might also give weighted voting rights, so that some directors have more votes than others. Articles very commonly provide that a director should not vote on a matter in which he has a personal interest. (Article 94 of Table A provides an example.) Article 95 of Table A provides that a director who is prevented from voting under article 94 may not count towards the quorum.

Section 382(1) requires that minutes of board meetings be kept, although the failure to keep minutes does not render invalid decisions taken. Once the minutes are signed by the chairman they are *prima facie* evidence of the proceedings at the board meeting (s.382(2)).

A company's articles may allow the directors to delegate any of their powers to a committee as long as the purpose behind this is not to exclude a particular director from participation in board meetings.

A company's articles may allow for the existence of a **managing director** and may allow the managing director to exercise powers of the directors without the need to consult the board of directors. Article 84 of Table A, for example, allows for the appointment of a managing director by the directors. The members of a company with Table A articles would not therefore be allowed to themselves appoint the managing director. The members would, however, be entitled to remove the managing director from office as a director, under s.303(1). This might of course amount to breach of contract.

If a company gives the impression that a person has the necessary authority to make a transaction then the company will be bound by such a transaction, whether or not the person who made it really did have such authority. This is known as **holding out**. The company is said to have held out that the person had authority and is therefore estopped from denying this. In Chapter 11, at 11.2.3, we saw that three requirements are necessary to give rise to such an estoppel:

(i) there must have been a representation that the person was an agent;
(ii) this representation must have been made by the principal or by someone on the principal's behalf;
(iii) the third party must have relied on the representation.

A person who has not validly been appointed managing director may be held out to be managing director, as the following case shows.

■ *Freeman & Lockyer* v *Buckhurst Park Properties Ltd* [1964] 2 QB 480 (Court of Appeal)

A company was formed to buy and resell an estate. The directors had the power to appoint a managing director but they never did so. One of the directors, K, acted as if he had been appointed managing director. K made a contract asking a firm of architects to do work on behalf of the company. The other directors knew that K acted as if he had been appointed managing director and also knew that he had made the contract to employ the architects. When the architects sued the company for their fees the company argued that K had no authority to employ architects and therefore the contract was not binding on the company.

Held. A managing director would usually have authority to employ architects. The company had given the impression that K was managing director. Therefore, as regards persons dealing with the company in good faith, K had the authority to bind the company as if he really was managing director. The company had held him out to have such powers to bind the company, so as regards persons to whom this representation had been made he did have such powers.

Test your understanding

1 Can a shareholder in a company also be a director of that company? Can one company be a director of another company?

2 After formation of a company, how are a company's subsequent directors appointed?

3 How may a director be removed from office?

4 Is it possible to give shares weighted voting rights on a resolution to remove a director?

5 Why can the written resolution procedure not be used to dismiss a director under s.303(1)?

6 Are directors required to hold any special qualifications? Are any persons prohibited from holding office as directors?

7 What is meant by the board of directors?

Answers

1 There is no requirement that a director should be a shareholder in the company but there is no reason why a director should not be a shareholder. One company can act as the director of another company.

2 A company's directors are appointed according to the rules set out in the company's articles of association. If no article deals with the matter, the directors are appointed by an ordinary resolution of the members.

3 A director may resign from his office at any time. The articles of the company may set out other ways in which a director can be removed. No matter what the articles say, s.303(1) allows the members of the company to remove a director by an ordinary resolution of which special notice has been given.

4 It is possible for some of the shares to carry weighted voting rights, as happened in *Bushell* v *Faith*.

5 A written resolution cannot be used to dismiss a director under s.303(1) because that section allows the director the right to address the members at the meeting which considers the resolution proposing to dismiss him.

6 No special qualifications are needed by directors. Undischarged bankrupts may not hold office as directors without the permission of the court which heard the bankruptcy proceedings. Persons disqualified under CDDA 1986 may not hold office as directors.

7 Directors are known as the board of directors when they act collectively.

17.1.6 Remuneration of directors

Directors will only be entitled to be paid fees for their services if the constitution of the company provides for payment. Payments to directors do not depend upon the company having made a profit. As directors stand in a fiduciary position to the company, they are not permitted to make a profit which has not been expressly provided for.

The articles of most companies provide that directors should be paid for their services as directors. Article 82 of Table A, for example, provides that:

'The directors shall be entitled to such remuneration as the company may by ordinary resolution determine and, unless the resolution provides otherwise, the remuneration shall be deemed to accrue from day to day.'

So if a company has Table A as its articles, a director will not be entitled to any fees for their services except as determined by ordinary resolution of the members. If the members of a company governed by Table A do not resolve to pay the directors anything, then they will not be entitled to any fees.

In Chapter 11 at 11.5.2 we considered *Re Richmond Gate Property Co Ltd* [1965] 1 WLR 335. In that case the company's articles provided that the managing director should receive 'such remuneration (whether by way of salary, commission or participation in profits, or partly in one way and partly in another) as the directors may determine'. At the time of the company liquidation the directors had not determined to pay the managing director anything, even though he had put in a considerable amount of work in the performance of his role as managing director. It was held that the managing director could not be entitled to anything on a *quantum meruit*. No term allowing a *quantum meruit* could be implied. There was an express term dealing with the managing director's remuneration and no implied term of a contract can contradict an express term. Directors are exempted from s.13 SGSA 1982, which requires those that carry out a service in the course of a business to carry it out with reasonable care and skill, by statutory instrument (SI 1982 No. 1771).

If a person acting as a director has no contract with the company then he can be paid for his services on a *quantum meruit*.

■ *Craven-Ellis* v *Canons Ltd* [1936] 2 All ER 1066

The claimant was appointed as managing director of a company and had a contract which entitled him to remuneration. The articles required the claimant to gain qualifying shares within two months of his appointment as managing director. The claimant never acquired such shares and so after two months the claimant was not a director and had no contract with the company. Nevertheless the claimant did considerable work for the company and claimed to be entitled to be paid on a *quantum meruit* for this work.

Held. The claimant was entitled to be paid on a *quantum meruit* because he had worked for the company without a binding contract.

The articles of a company may allow for other payments to be made to directors. Article 83 of Table A, for example, allows directors to be paid an indemnity for expenses incurred in the execution of their duties. Article 84 allows the directors to either employ any director on such terms as they think fit, or make such payment as they see fit to a director in respect of duties which exceed his ordinary duties as a director. The board of directors of a company governed by Table A can therefore employ individual directors on the company's behalf on whatever salary they think fit. The director so employed could not vote on his own appointment, but could count towards a quorum of the meeting where the appointment was proposed. The directors should however limit payments to directors to what the company can afford.

Neither directors nor the managing director are automatically regarded as employees of the company. If directors are employees of the company then obviously they will have a contract of employment and if this is breached they may be entitled to remedies for either wrongful or unfair dismissal. However, the mere fact that a person acts as a director does not necessarily mean that that person has any contract with the company. Being a director has traditionally been regarded as 'holding office' rather than as being an employee. A director who does have a contract to supply his services, but who does not supply them as an employee, will supply his services as an independent contractor. It is not permissible for a company to pay a director free of tax (s.311).

Any voluntary payment to a director in respect of the director's loss of office must be approved by the company. Section 312 of the 1985 Act provides that:

> 'It is not lawful for a company to make to a director of the company any payment by way of compensation for loss of office, or as consideration for or in connection with his retirement from office, without particulars of the proposed payment (including its amount) being disclosed to members of the company and the proposal being approved by the company.'

The members' approval could either be by ordinary or written resolution.

If this section is breached the directors hold the payment made in trust for the company. Section 312 does not apply to a payment which is *bona fide* made by way of damages for breach of contract or by way of pension for past services. It only applies to payments which the company was under no legal obligation to make.

A company's accounts do not need to show exactly how much each director was paid. However, they do need to show the aggregate amount paid to the directors, whether paid as salary, fees or as other benefits. If the aggregate amount is over £200 000, the amount paid to the highest director must be shown, as well as the amount of his accrued retirement benefits. A note in the annual accounts must also show any amount paid to directors in respect of loss of office.

If a director is employed under a contract of employment, the terms of the contract must be made available for inspection by the members (s.318). If the company is listed, the Stock Exchange Listing Rules additionally requires the company to make the terms of the contract available at its registered office, for inspection by any person. In addition, the Listing Rules require that the terms of the contract must be available for inspection at the place where the annual meeting is held, for 15 minutes before the meeting.

17.1.7 Directors' powers

The powers of the directors will be contained in the company's articles of association. The balance of power between the members and the directors therefore varies from company to company. In many companies the members and the directors are the same people.

Article 70 of Table A provides that:

> 'Subject to the provisions of the Act, the memorandum and the articles and to any directions given by special resolution, the business of the company shall be managed by the directors who may exercise all the powers of the company ...'

So under Table A the directors are given very wide powers to manage the company, and most companies' articles will contain a provision similar to Table A article 70. However, it is possible that the articles will give the directors very much less power, stipulating that a variety of decisions must be made by resolutions of the members. The power conferred on the directors by article 70 is subject to the provisions of the Act, the memorandum and the articles. The Act provides that many powers can only be exercised by a special or extraordinary resolution of the members. In this and the previous chapter we have already seen that a special resolution is needed to change the company name, to re-register from a public company to a private one and vice versa, to change the company's articles of association and to change the objects of the company. In this chapter we have already seen that the Act provides that compensation paid to directors for loss of office must be approved by an ordinary or written resolution. We have also seen that the Act provides that directors can be removed from office by an ordinary resolution. Later in this chapter we shall see that the auditor is appointed by ordinary resolution of the members. In the following two chapters we shall see that the Act provides that a special resolution is needed to reduce the company's share capital, to approve the giving of financial assistance to a private company to buy its own shares, to give authority for an off-market purchase by a company of its own shares, and to resolve that the company is voluntarily wound up. Table A allows the members by ordinary resolution to determine the rights which attach to new issues of shares.

As long as the directors stay within the powers conferred by the articles, they need not obey resolutions passed by the members. However, if Table A articles are adopted the directors must obey directions which they have been given by special resolution. The members of the company own the company's shares but the directors control the company.

■ *Automatic Self-Cleansing Filter Syndicate Co Ltd* v *Cuninghame* [1906] 2 Ch 34 (Court of Appeal)

The objects of a company gave the company the power to sell the company, or any part of it, to any other company which had similar objects. Article 96 of the company stated that 'The management of the business and the control of the company shall be vested in the directors, who ... may exercise all such powers and do all such acts and things as may be exercised or done by the company ...' This article went on to state that the directors would not be able to do an act which was in contravention of an extraordinary resolution passed by the members. At a general meeting an ordinary resolution was passed, ordering the directors to sell the company's assets to another company which had been recently formed with the purpose of acquiring these assets. The directors did not think that it would be in the best interests of the company to do this, and so they refused to do it.

Held. The directors were within their rights. Whether or not to sell was a question for them and not for the shareholders.

Other articles may confer other, more specific, powers on the directors. We have already seen an example of this in article 84 of Table A, which gives the directors the power to appoint a managing director.

However, it must be remembered that a majority of the shareholders have very considerable powers. Subject to a *Bushell* v *Faith* clause in the articles, the members can always vote directors out of office. Furthermore, if three-quarters of the shareholders decide to do so, they can pass a special resolution to change the articles. Section 9(1) of the Act provides that, subject to the provisions of the Act or the conditions contained in the memorandum, any attempt to take this power to change the articles away from the company is void. (But in *Bushell* v *Faith* it was recognised that an article might give some shares weighted voting rights on any resolution to change the articles.) If the majority shareholders could change the articles they could either alter the powers of the directors or remove any *Bushell* v *Faith* clause. But these changes would only apply in the future. The articles cannot be changed retrospectively.

Although the directors have the power to manage the company there are numerous powers which can only be exercised by means of the members of the company passing a resolution. These powers, such as the power to alter the articles or objects, are set out in Chapter 18 at 18.4. In Chapter 18 we shall also see that members of the company may petition the court on the grounds of unfair prejudice. If a court is satisfied that there has been unfair prejudice it may make any order which it sees fit, and this would obviously include rendering ineffective any power exercised by the directors.

We have seen that article 70 of Table A confers general management powers on the directors and this would include the power to sue in the company name.

The members of a company can ratify acts committed by company agents in excess of their actual authority. If this is done the authority which was lacking is supplied retrospectively and the act in question is adopted as an act of the company. An ordinary resolution is needed, unless the act was outside the company's objects, in which case a special resolution is needed. This special resolution would confer retrospective actual authority on the agent, but a separate special resolution would be needed to prevent the agent from incurring personal liability. However, neither a special nor an ordinary resolution could validate an act which amounted to a breach of a director's fiduciary duties.

17.1.8 Directors as agents

The directors are not the agents of the company members, but are the agents of the company. However, the directors are only agents of the company to the extent that they have some type of authority to act for the company. We have already seen that generally a company's articles of association will give the board of directors actual authority to exercise all the powers of the company. In two circumstances though an act done by a director or by the board of directors might be done outside this actual authority.

First, the act might be done in an irregular way. Second, the act might be one which the company's constitution did not allow to be done at all.

In order to understand this area of law, it is necessary to consider the ways in which a director, or a board of directors, acquire authority to act as agents of the company. Actual authority will be conferred by agreement between the director, or the board of directors, and the company. This is the type of authority possessed by the vast majority of the directors who act on behalf of a company. The company's constitution sets out the powers of the directors and the directors agree that they shall be able to exercise these powers, thereby acquiring actual authority to do so. If a director or the board of directors, with actual authority, make a contract on a company's behalf then the company will be bound by the contract.

Alternatively, a person without actual authority to act on the company's behalf might have apparent authority by having been held out by the company as having authority to do the act in question, as we saw in *Freeman & Lockyer* v *Buckhurst Park Properties Ltd*. Having held the person out as having the authority, the company will be estopped from denying the representation which it has made as regards a third party who has acted on the strength of the representation.

A company may also ratify an act done on its behalf by a person having no actual or apparent authority. If such a ratification is effective, retrospective actual authority is conferred and so the company is bound by the act.

A person who represents that he has authority to act for a company when he does not in fact have any authority can be liable to a person relying on this representation for breach of warranty of authority. However, breach of warranty of authority cannot make the company itself liable. Only the person claiming to act for the company, and not the company itself, warranted that he had authority to act for the company.

A director will only be able to act on the company's behalf for the purposes of pursuing acts which are within the company's objects clause. (We saw in Chapter 16 that the memorandum of association must include an objects clause, which sets out the objects for which the company was formed.) If a director acts for a purpose outside the company's objects clause the contract is said to be *ultra vires*. If this contract causes loss to the company the director who made the contract is personally liable to reimburse the company for the money lost. The members can excuse the director from making this payment, but as we have seen a special resolution is needed to do this and this must be in addition to a special resolution ratifying the *ultra vires* transaction.

Prior to the UK's entry into the EU, an *ultra vires* contract entered into was automatically void and could not therefore be enforced by the party who made the contract with the company.

For example, in *Ashbury Railway Carriage and Iron Co Ltd* v *Riche* (1875) LR 7 HL 653 the House of Lords held that a company was not liable on a contract it had made to finance one Riche to build a railway line. After Riche had begun work and incurred expenses the company repudiated the contract. Riche was left without any remedy as the contract was made outside the company's objects clause, which allowed the company to build railway carriages and railway machinery, but not to build a railway line. As the contract was *ultra vires*, the company could not have enforced the contract, or the members of the company have ratified the contract. The *ultra vires* rule may seem strange, but it was felt necessary to protect shareholders. They invested money in the company to pursue the purposes set out in the objects clause. They did not invest their money to be used for other purposes. The House of Lords also regarded the rule as protecting creditors. Creditors who contracted with the company were deemed to have read the company's constitution and the contents of this would be a factor in their deciding whether or not to extend credit to the company. In fact very few creditors did read the constitution and the rule usually worked very much against creditors, as the facts of the case demonstrated.

Section 35(1) of the 1985 Act was retrospectively put into that Act by the Companies Act 1989. It states:

> 'The validity of an act done by a company shall not be called into question on the ground of lack of capacity by reason of anything in the company's memorandum.'

A company's objects clause is necessarily in its memorandum, as we saw in the previous chapter. Section 35 therefore means that when the act done on the company's behalf was done by a person who had actual authority to act for the company then the *ultra vires* rule cannot be used by anyone to call that act into question. The act in question does not need to be a contract, it could be a gift. So if the facts of *Ashbury Railway Carriage and Iron Co Ltd* v *Riche* were to arise today, then those who contracted with the company would be protected by s.35(1) and could sue on their contract with the company.

However, s.322A provides that an *ultra vires* transaction entered into by the company with the directors of the company, or the directors of a holding company, is voidable by the company despite s.35(1). The members can ratify these voidable transactions by ordinary or special resolution or otherwise as the case may require (s.322A(5)).

When a director, or the board of directors, acts irregularly, that is to say acts outside their actual authority, then it is arguable that s.35(1) should have no application because the act in question was not done by the company. Section 35A(1) of the 1985 Act provides:

> 'In favour of a person dealing with a company in good faith, the power of the board of directors to bind the company, or authorise others to do so, shall be deemed to be free of any limitation under the company's constitution ...'

For the purposes of this section, the company's constitution includes its memorandum and articles, as well as resolutions of the company and agreements between the company and its members.

Section 35B provides that:

> 'A party to a transaction with a company is not bound to enquire as to whether it is permitted by the company's memorandum or as to any limitation on the powers of the board of directors to bind the company or authorise others to do so.'

Sections 35A and 35B therefore protect a third party dealing with the company in good faith if either (i) the board of directors made the contract to bind the company, or (ii) the contract was made by others authorised by the board of directors. Even if the board, or the person authorised by the board, acted irregularly in making the contract, the contract will nevertheless be binding upon the company. If the contract was made neither by the board of directors nor by a person authorised by the board the section will not apply. Whether or not the company will be bound will then depend upon general agency principles, in particular whether or not the person making the contract was held out by the company as having authority to make it.

Section 35A(2) allows a person dealing with a company to be in good faith, for the purposes of s.35A(1), even if he knows that the act done is beyond the powers of the directors under the company's constitution. It also provides that a person shall be deemed to have acted in good faith unless the contrary is proved.

The following case demonstrates the effect of s.35A(1) as it applies to an act done by the board of directors.

■ *TCB Ltd* v *Gray* [1986] 1 All ER 587

A company issued a debenture to a bank in respect of a loan made by the bank. A solicitor signed the debenture, as agent for one of the directors, having been given power to do this by a power of attorney. Issuing the debenture would have been within the power of the board of directors. One of the company's articles required that debentures should be signed by a director. The company later claimed that the debenture was invalid as it had not been properly entered into.

Held. The debenture was valid under s.35A. The section protected the bank not only against lack of authority but also against improper procedure having been followed.

COMMENT Section 35A had not been passed at the time of the case. However, s.9(1) of the European Communities Act 1972 had the same effect.

Any member who knows that an *ultra vires* contract is about to be entered into can ask the court to order the company not to enter into the transaction (s.35(2)). The members cannot however do this if they have ratified the *ultra vires* act by a special resolution. However, if the company has already made a contract to do an *ultra vires* act the court cannot restrain the company from doing what it has agreed to do, because of s.35(1). Nor can the members ask for an injunction if they have ratified the *ultra vires* act by special or written resolution.

Finally, it should be noticed that directors who enter into an *ultra vires* contract will be liable to the company for losses which the transaction caused. Section 35(3) allows the directors to be relieved from such liability by a special resolution of the members. However, it is made plain by s.35(3) that a resolution ratifying the *ultra vires* action would not be enough. The resolution absolving the directors from liability would need to be separately agreed.

17.1.9 Directors' duties

17.1.9.1 Fiduciary duties

A director stands in a fiduciary position to the company, and is therefore in a position of great trust. The implications of this are contained in the classic quotation of Lord Cranworth in *Aberdeen Railway Co v Blaikie Bros* (1854) 1 Macq 461.

'The Directors are a body to whom is delegated the duty of managing the general affairs of the Company … Such agents have duties … of a fiduciary nature … And it is a rule of universal application, that no one, having such duties to discharge, shall be allowed to enter into engagements in which he has, or can have, a personal interest conflicting, or which possibly may conflict, with the interests of those whom he is bound to protect.'

There are two separate aspects of the fiduciary duty owed by directors:

(1) The directors must exercise their powers *bona fide* for the benefit of the company as a whole.
(2) There must be no conflict between the directors' interests and the interests of the company.

These duties are imposed on directors by equity, to ensure that the directors protect those on whose behalf they act. The first duty is a subjective one, as the following case shows.

■ *Rolled Steel Products (Holdings) Ltd* v *British Steel Corporation* [1985] 3 All ER 52 (Court of Appeal)

S, a director of Rolled Steel, owned 51% of the shares in the company. S was also a director of Scottish Steel in which he owned all the issued shares. Scottish Steel owed money to BSC and S personally guaranteed the loan. When BSC wanted additional security, S caused Rolled Steel to give this guarantee, even though doing so was of no benefit to Rolled Steel. Both Scottish Steel and Rolled Steel went into liquidation.

Held. Although the guarantee given by Rolled Steel was not *ultra vires*, BSC could not claim on the loan. S and BSC both knew that the contract was of no benefit to Rolled Steel, and that it had therefore been given for an improper purpose.

In *Regentcrest plc* v *Cohen* [2001] 2 BCLC 80 Parker J (at 105) said:

'The question is not whether, viewed objectively by the court, the particular act or omission which is challenged was in fact in the interests of the company; still less is the question whether the court, had it been in the position of the director at the relevant time, might have acted differently. Rather, the question is whether the director honestly believed that his act or omission was in the interests of the company. The issue is as to the director's state of mind.'

Parker J went on to say that the more detrimental to the company the act or omission turned out to be, the harder the director would find it to satisfy this objective test.

Whether or not there has been conflict between the directors' interests and that of the company is an objective test.

■ *Regal (Hastings) Ltd* v *Gulliver* [1942] 1 All ER 378 (House of Lords)

Regal Ltd owned a cinema. It wanted to acquire two more cinemas so that it could sell all three as a going concern. A subsidiary company was formed to make the purchase. The sellers of the cinemas would not go ahead with the deal unless the subsidiary company had at least £5 000 paid up share capital. Regal could only provide £2 000 of the money which the subsidiary needed. The directors of Regal therefore personally subscribed for a further 3 000 £1 shares in the subsidiary. At the conclusion of the whole business the shares in the subsidiary were sold for £3.80 each. Both Regal and its directors had therefore made a handsome profit.

Held. The directors had to account to Regal for the profit they had made. It was only because they were directors of Regal that they gained the opportunity to make the profit.

COMMENT As the directors had not been fraudulent, they would not have had to hand over the profit if their acts had been ratified by a general meeting of the company.

Boardman v *Phipps* [1967] 2 AC 46 (set out in Chapter 11 at 11.4.4.2) had similar facts, except that in that case the profit was made by a solicitor advising a trust. Lord Denning MR said:

'It is quite clear that if an agent uses *property*, with which he has been entrusted by his principal, so as to make a profit for himself out of it, without his principal's consent, then he is accountable for it to his principal … So, also, if he uses a *position of authority*, to which he has been appointed by his principal, so as to gain money by means of it for himself, then also he is accountable to his principal for it … Likewise with *information or knowledge* which he has been employed by his principal to collect or discover, *or which he has otherwise acquired*, for the use of this principal, then again if he turns it to his own use, so as to make a profit by means of it for himself, he is accountable … for such information or knowledge is the property of the principal, just as much as an invention is.'

As the fiduciary duties are owed to the company as a whole, that is to the members collectively, and not to the members individually, it is only the company which can enforce the fiduciary duties or sue directors for breach of them. Neither individual members of the company nor the directors can enforce the duties. Although a director does not have to devote his whole time to carrying out his duties as a director, he must at all times ensure that a fiduciary duty is not breached.

A contract which does benefit a director, in breach of his fiduciary duties, is voidable at the company's option, but only if the other party to the contract either knew or should have known that the director acted in breach of a fiduciary duty. The company may also require the director in breach to account for any money or benefit received. (There is no need to prove that the director behaved dishonestly.) The directors in breach may alternatively be regarded as holding any profits made in constructive trust for the company, so that if the profit increased in value this increase will belong to the company. The remedies are all equitable and will not be granted where it would be inequitable to grant them. In the following case the Court of Appeal recently considered the fiduciary duty of a director, the remedies for breach of such a duty and the time limits within which the remedies might be obtained.

■ *JJ Harrison (Properties) Ltd v Harrison* [2001] EWCA Civ 1467 (Court of Appeal)

Since 1975 the defendant had been the chairman and managing director of a company which developed agricultural and residential land. His three sisters were also directors but took little interest in the company. In 1983 the company applied for planning permission to develop a three acre plot. Permission was refused because the land was in agricultural use. The tenant who farmed the land which included this plot gave up the lease. In July 1985 the company's general manager asked a valuer to value the three acre plot, but expressly telling him to ignore any development potential. The buildings on the plot were dilapidated and the valuer gave a valuation of £8 400. In September 1985 the defendant drew up a contract under which he was to buy the plot from the company for £8 400. A further planning permission application was refused in January 1986. On 5 February 1986 an amended application for planning permission was put in, taking account of the local authority's objections to the previous one. This application was put in by architects acting in the company name. On 10 February the company resolved to sell the plot to the defendant, who did not vote on the resolution because he had an interest in it. The sisters voted in favour of the resolution but did not know about the two latest applications for planning permission or that the architects were confident that planning permission would be granted. On 3 April planning permission was granted. The plot was sold in two lots. The first lot fetched £110 300 in December 1988. The second lot fetched £122 500 in April 1992. The defendant resigned as director in March 1996. The other directors knew that the defendant had made a profit on the land but did not realise that he had done anything wrong until a new motorway was to be built in 1997. This caused all the old documents relating to the land to be looked at and only then did the other directors realise what had happened between the valuation in July 1985 and the granting of planning permission.

Held. (1) The directors of a company had to exercise their powers for the purposes, and in the interests, of the company. This meant that the directors owed fiduciary duties to the company in respect of those powers. Breach of such duties would be treated as breach of trust.
(2) A director who disposed of the company's property in breach of his fiduciary duties was in breach of trust and was a constructive trustee.
(3) On appointment, a director assumed the duties of a trustee in relation to the company's property. If that property was conveyed to him he was a trustee of it, this duty arising out of his duties as a director before the property was conveyed to him.
(4) The defendant had been in breach of his fiduciary duties by failing to see that the land was sold for its full value. The land should not have been sold at all until the company had received and considered advice as to what it was worth with planning permission having been granted. On this basis it was impossible to reach any conclusion other than that the defendant was a constructive trustee of the land.
(5) Section 21(3) of the Limitation Act 1980 provided that the right to recover trust property in respect of any breach of trust was six years. But here the action was not to recover trust property in possession of the trustee. Here the action was to recover trust property, or the proceeds of trust property, which the trustee had previously received and converted to his use. In such a case s.21(1)(b) of the Limitation Act provided that s.21(3) did not apply.
(6) The equitable defence of laches did not prevent the company from succeeding because the defendant had committed a serious breach of trust and the other directors could not challenge this until they found out what had happened in 1997.
(7) The defendant had to account for the value of the land when the first plot was sold in December 1988.

Article 85 of Table A contemplates that a director might make a contract with the company but that he must disclose any material interest which he has in the contract to the directors. No special formalities are required. Section 317 of the Act requires a director who has any interest in a contract which he makes with the company to declare that interest at a meeting of the directors. In *Neptune (Vehicle Washing Equipment) Ltd v Fitzgerald* [1996] Ch 274 it was held that the sole director of a company making a contract with the company in which he has a personal interest must hold a board meeting and formally declare his interest in the contract or it will be voidable by the company. The sole director had authorised payment to himself of £100 892 which he claimed he was owed under an earlier contract. A resolution to this effect was passed in the presence of the company secretary. The minutes of the meeting did not show that a declaration of the director's interest had been made as required by s.317. After the company was sold the contract was avoided and the money had to be repaid.

It should also be noticed that s.320 of the Companies Act 1985 makes it illegal for a company to enter into a substantial property transaction with a director unless the transaction is first approved by a resolution of the company in general meeting.

17.1.9.2 Non-fiduciary duties

The directors have other duties besides the fiduciary ones.

Care and skill

Directors owe a duty of care and skill to the company, the general standard expected being that of a reasonable man looking after his own affairs. Romer J in *Re City Equitable Fire Insurance Co Ltd* [1925] Ch 407 outlined three propositions which could be extracted from the general case law on the matter. First, directors need only show the amount of care and skill which could be expected from someone with their own personal levels of knowledge and experience. Second, a director is not expected to give continuous attention to the company's affairs. (His duties arise at board meetings, which he ought to attend whenever he can reasonably do so.) Third, a director is entitled to trust that an official to whom duties have been delegated is exercising those duties properly. (However, in *Re Barings plc (No. 3)* [2000] 1 WLR 634, a case on the disqualification of directors who had failed to supervise the activities of a rogue derivatives trader in Singapore, it was made clear that delegates must be properly monitored and it is not enough for directors simply to trust a delegate merely because he is a responsible person.)

In *Re D'Jan of London Ltd* [1944] 1 BCLC 561 Hoffmann LJ said that the common law standard expected of the director is that of a reasonably diligent person who has both the general knowledge, skill and experience which could be objectively expected of such a director and the skill, knowledge and experience which the director in question actually has. This dual objective/subjective standard is set out in s.214 of the Insolvency Act 1986, which deals with liability for wrongful trading. (See Chapter 19 at 19.1.4.1.) The statement made was similar to one which Hoffmann LJ had made in *Norman* v *Theodore Goddard* [1991] BCLC 1028 when he was a High Court judge. Neither statement was the *ratio decidendi* of the case in question and therefore neither creates a binding precedent. Although the two statements made by Hoffmann LJ have been criticised, it seems likely that the dual objective/subjective standard does apply in relation to the standard of care and skill expected of a director.

Although a director does not need to have special qualifications, if he does have any special qualifications then he must show the degree of care and skill which could be expected of a person possessing those qualifications. Unless a director makes a contract requiring him to perform certain actions, he will only be liable for failures to act.

Duties to employees

Section 309 provides that the directors should have regard to the interests of the company's employees as well as to the interests of the members. This duty is owed to the company and not to the employees. This appears to be little more than a statement of intention, and if there is any conflict between the interests of the company and the interests of the employees the directors must put the company's interests first.

Creditors

At common law the directors of an insolvent company must have regard to the interests of the company's creditors and can become liable to the creditors for failure to safeguard their interests. If a company becomes insolvent insolvency procedures allow the assets of the company to be controlled by the creditors rather than by the directors. The liquidator will be able to prohibit the directors from acting in certain ways. If the directors ignore these instructions they can become personally liable.

17.1.9.3 Effects of breach of duty

A director will not be liable to the company for the act of his co-directors if he did not know of the act and should not have suspected it. This is because the other directors are neither his employees nor his agents. However, if a director became aware of serious breaches of duty by fellow directors then he could be liable in negligence if he failed to inform the members or take control of the company's assets. If more than one director is liable for a breach they are jointly and severally liable. Any of the directors in breach can therefore be sued for the whole amount, but will be able to claim a contribution from the other directors liable.

Even if the directors do exceed their powers or use them irregularly or negligently, the shareholders may still ratify their acts at a general meeting, as long as the directors did not act fraudulently, illegally or in bad faith.

■ *Bamford* v *Bamford* [1970] Ch 212 (Court of Appeal)

The company was in danger of being taken over. To avoid this the directors issued an extra 500 000 shares to a business which distributed the company's products. This might have been contrary to the articles. (This point was never decided.) The shareholders approved the issue of the shares by passing an ordinary resolution at a general meeting.

Held. Even if the directors had irregularly exercised their powers, the ratification by the shareholders made the contract a good one, and absolved the directors from all liability.

Harman LJ: 'Directors can, by making a full and frank disclosure and calling together the general body of the shareholders, obtain … forgiveness of their sins; and … everything will go on as if it had been done right from the beginning. I cannot believe that this is not a commonplace of company law. It is done every day. Of course, if the majority of the general meeting will not forgive and approve, the directors must pay for it.'

Section 727 allows the court to grant relief to a director in breach of his duty if the director 'acted honestly and reasonably and ought fairly to be excused'. An example of this section can be seen in the following case, which applied a section of the 1948 Act which had a similar effect.

■ *Re Duomatic Ltd* [1969] 1 All ER 161

A company had 100 £1 ordinary shares and 80 000 £1 redeemable non-voting preference shares. The three original directors, E, H and T owned all of the ordinary shares. E and T wanted to remove H from the board of directors because they had become critical of the way he performed his duties. They could have voted to remove him from office, but instead paid him £4 000 to leave the company because he had threatened to sue the company if dismissed. This payment was not shown in the company's accounts. After ceasing to be a director H transferred all of his shares to E. Later E transferred some of his shares to W, C and K, who were all officers of a finance company which had provided finance to the company. W also became a director. The articles allowed the directors to be paid a salary if a resolution was passed authorising a salary, but no such resolution had ever been passed. Instead the directors drew money out of the company as they needed it and at the end of the year the amount drawn out was entered into the accounts as 'directors' salaries'. When the company went into liquidation the liquidator sought repayment of several sums paid, as follows.

(i)   £10 161 and £5 510 taken out by E and H respectively, at a time when they were the only ordinary shareholders. They had approved these payments as directors, but had not passed a resolution authorising them.

(ii) £9 000 paid to E at a later time, when he was the majority shareholder. There had been no resolution approving the payment, but this was an oversight as past procedures were still being followed and E had not acted unreasonably.

(iii) £4 000 which H had received as compensation for loss of office. The payment was *ultra vires* and had not been disclosed to the preference shareholders. E and T had not acted reasonably, in that they did not take professional advice.

Held (i)   These payments should not be disturbed. The assent of E and T was as binding as a resolution in a general meeting.

(ii) E was entitled to retain this payment.

(iii) E and T were jointly and severally liable to repay the £4 000 which H had received. As they had acted unreasonably in not taking professional advice, they ought not reasonably to be excused. (H was also required to hold the £4 000 received on constructive trust for the company.)

Test your understanding

1 Are directors automatically entitled to be paid for their services? Can the directors fix their own salaries?

2 What powers do directors have to manage the company?

3 Can an act done by a company be invalidated on the grounds that it was *ultra vires*?

4 If the board of directors act irregularly in making a contract, can the person with whom the contract was made nevertheless sue on the contract?

5 What are the two aspects of the fiduciary duties which directors owe to the company?

6 What level of care and skill is generally required of a director?

7 Can a director who has breached his duties to the company be absolved from personal liability?

Answers

1 Directors can only be paid fees for their services if the company's constitution allows for such payments. Most articles (Table A article 84, for example), allow the directors to employ individual directors on such terms as they see fit in respect of duties which exceed their ordinary duties as directors. The board of directors of such companies can therefore fix the salaries of individual directors as regards these duties. Article 84 of Table A provides that a director whose employment is proposed cannot vote on the appointment.

2 The powers of the directors will be set out in the company's articles of association and therefore differ from company to company. Generally, the directors are given very wide powers to manage the company's affairs.

3 Section 35(1) provides that an act done by a company cannot be invalidated on the grounds that it was *ultra vires*.

4 Despite the irregular way in which the contract was made, the outsider who made the contract can always sue on the contract unless it can be proved that he acted in bad faith. The outsider is not to be regarded as having been in bad faith merely because he knew that the contract in question was beyond the powers of the company as set out in the company's constitution.

5 The two aspects of the directors' fiduciary duties are that they should exercise their powers *bona fide* for the benefit of the company as a whole, and there must be no conflict of interest between the directors' interests and the interest of the company.

6 The general standard of care and skill required of a director is that of a reasonable man looking after his own affairs. If the director is qualified in some way, it is the standard expected of a reasonable person holding the qualifications in question.

7 Directors can be excused from liability for breach of duty either by an ordinary resolution of the members or under s.727, which allows a court to grant relief to a director if he acted honestly and reasonably and ought fairly to be excused.

17.2 · The company secretary

Section 283(1) of the Act requires every company to have a company secretary. Section 283(2) provides that the secretary may also be a director, but may not be the sole director. One company can be the company secretary of another company, but not if the two companies both have the same person as their sole director (s.283(4)(a)). The articles of a company usually provide that the company secretary is appointed, and can be removed, by the directors. (Article 99 of Table A provides this.) The articles will also usually provide that the directors fix the secretary's conditions of employment and the length of time for which he is to hold office. The secretary is regarded as an employee of the company for the purposes of preferential payments of debts on liquidation, and is also an officer of the company.

In Chapter 16 we saw that when a company is formed a statement giving details of the first company secretary must be sent to the Registrar of Companies, and that the first secretary must sign the form to indicate that he consents to being appointed. The statement must also be signed by all of the subscribers to the memorandum.

The secretary's duties are to look after the administration of the company. This would include keeping the company register up to date, sending information to the Registrar of Companies, arranging meetings, sending notice of meetings and resolutions to members, employing office staff and keeping up to date with legislation which affects the company. The secretary owes the company fiduciary duties which are similar to the fiduciary duties owed by the directors. A few of the secretary's duties, such as the duty to submit the annual return, are imposed by statute, in this case by s.363.

Although concerned in the management of the company's business, the secretary is not a manager of the company and is not concerned in carrying on the business of the company. The company secretary has a limited power to bind the company, but only as regards the type of administrative contracts which a company secretary could be expected to make. He cannot borrow money on the company's behalf, nor sue on the company's behalf, without authority.

■ *Panorama Developments (Guildford) Ltd* v *Fidelis Furnishing Fabrics Ltd* [1971] 3 All ER 16 (Court of Appeal)

B was the secretary of a well-respected company. He used the company's notepaper to order cars from the claimants, a car-hire company. B falsely stated that the cars were needed by the company for business purposes, such as meeting customers at airports. Before supplying the cars the claimants asked for references about the company, which B provided. In the hire agreements, B was stated to be the hirer, and he was described as 'company secretary'. In fact B used the cars for his own purposes. The company knew nothing about the car hire transactions and when the claimants sent in a bill they refused to pay it.

Held. The company was liable. B, as company secretary, had apparent authority to hire the cars on behalf of the company.

Lord Denning MR: 'A company secretary ... is no longer a mere clerk. He regularly makes representations on behalf of the company and enters into contracts on its behalf which come within the day to day running of the company's business. So much so that he may be regarded as held out as having the authority to do such things on behalf of the company. He is certainly entitled to sign contracts connected with the administrative side of the company's affairs, such as employing staff, and ordering cars, and so forth.'

Section 286 of the Act requires the directors to ensure that the secretary of a public company is a suitably qualified person. This means either that he must hold professionally recognised qualifications (as an accountant, or a UK qualified lawyer, or a public company secretary for three of the past five years) or must have been in post as the secretary or assistant secretary of the company in question since December 1980. In addition, the directors may appoint a person who appears to them to be capable of discharging the duties and functions of a company secretary, by virtue of holding or having held any other position, or being a member of any other body.

17.2.1 Register of secretaries

As we saw earlier, s.288(1) requires that every company must keep a register of its directors and secretaries at its registered office. The register must give the same details of the company secretary as were required in the form sent to the Registrar on incorporation of the company. That is to say, full name, previous names and home address. If the company secretary is changed, s.288(2) requires that notification must be sent to the Registrar within 14 days, along with signed consent by the new secretary appointed. If the details on the register change, s.288(2) requires that the Registrar is informed within 14 days. Members can inspect the register of directors and secretaries free of charge, non-members can be charged a small fee (s.288(3)). If the register is not open to inspection, the company and its officers may be fined (s.288(4)) and the court may order immediate inspection to be allowed (s.288(5)).

17.3 · The auditor

Except as regards very small companies, companies will generally need to employ an accountant to prepare the accounts which must be given to members of the company and submitted to Companies House. The accountant will be appointed by the directors of the company. The auditor is not the company accountant, but a different accountant who keeps an eye on the company's accounts and accounting procedures. The auditor is appointed by the members of the company and reports to the members.

17.3.1 The need to have an auditor

Certain small companies are exempt from having to have their accounts audited, by virtue of s.249A. Dormant companies can pass a special resolution to exempt themselves from having to appoint an auditor, by virtue of s.250. These two exemptions apart, all companies must have an auditor (s.384(1)).

In Chapter 16, at 16.3.4, we examined the definition of a small company given by s.247. Section 249A exempts a small company from having to have its accounts audited if its annual turnover is not more than £5.6 million and its total assets are not worth more than £2.8 million. However, even if a small company does elect not to appoint an auditor, shareholders holding at least 10% of the nominal value of the company's shares, or any class of shares, can require the company to have the accounts audited. The members who wanted an auditor to be appointed would have to deposit written notice of this at the company's registered office at least one month before the end of the company's financial year (s.249B(2)).

Section 250(3) provides that a company is dormant in a period during which no significant accounting transaction occurs.

The auditor is neither a manager nor an employee of the company. Unlike the directors and the secretary, the auditor is an independent contractor.

17.3.2 Appointment and leaving office

Officers and employees of the company are prohibited from being appointed as the company auditor or as the auditor of a parent or subsidiary company on the grounds of lack of independence. The business partners and employees of officers and employees of the company are also banned (Companies Act 1989 s.27(1)). However, members of the company can be appointed as the auditor if they are suitably qualified. With a few minor exceptions, a person can only be appointed as an auditor if he is a chartered or certified accountant. Partnerships can be appointed as auditors if the firm is controlled by qualified persons or if the individual responsible for the firm's audit work is suitably qualified. A company can be appointed as an auditor as long as qualified persons control the company and its board of directors. A register of persons qualified to act as auditors is kept and it is an offence for a person to describe himself as a registered auditor if his name does not appear on this register.

Section 385(3) provides that the first auditor of a public company is appointed by the directors and holds office until the first general meeting at which the accounts are considered. Section 385(2) provides that subsequent auditors are appointed by the members at each general meeting at which the accounts are considered. If a person other than a retiring auditor is proposed as auditor, special notice of the resolution which makes the proposal must be given. The auditors appointed at the meeting then hold office until the next such meeting. The same rules apply to private companies except that a small company is exempt from having to appoint an auditor, and any private company may elect to dispense with the obligation to appoint an auditor annually by virtue of s.386(1). If a private company does elect not to appoint an auditor annually, s.386(2) provides that the existing auditors are deemed to be reappointed. They will therefore remain as the company's auditors until they resign or until the company decides to appoint a different auditor. (Elective resolutions are considered in Chapter 18 at 18.4.3.)

An auditor can be removed from office at any time (s.391). This can be achieved by an ordinary resolution of which special notice has been given (s.391A(1)). (We have already seen that special notice requires that the company is given 28 days' notice of the resolution.) The auditor must be given a copy of the resolution, and has the right to compel the company to circulate written representations of reasonable length to all the members entitled to vote at the meeting. If these representations are received too late by the company to be issued in time, the auditor can require them to be read out at the meeting. In addition, the auditor has a right to speak to the meeting. The written resolution procedure cannot therefore be used to dismiss an auditor. If an auditor is removed the Registrar must be informed within 14 days.

When a private company has elected to dispense with the annual appointment of auditors, s.393(1) provides that any member may submit a written notice to the registered office proposing that the current auditor should leave office. The directors must then hold a general meeting of the company within 28 days to consider a resolution to remove the auditor from office (s.393(2)). If the company does not do this the member who submitted the notice can convene a meeting and charge the company reasonable expenses incurred (s.393(4)–(6)). A member is entitled to submit only one such notice in any financial year (s.393(1)).

An auditor can resign by delivering written notice of the fact to the company's registered office (s.392). To be effective, the resignation notice must either contain a statement that there are no circumstances connected with the resignation which ought to be brought to the attention of the members of the company or the creditors, or it must state what those circumstances are (s.394(1)). If the auditor's notice does state that there are circumstances which should be brought to the attention of the members or the creditors, the company must send copies to all the members and debenture holders (s.394(3)). A copy of the auditor's notice of resignation must be sent to the Registrar of Companies within 14 days of its being deposited at the company's registered office (s.392(3)). In addition, the auditor may require the directors to call an extraordinary general meeting of the company. At the meeting the explanation given by the auditor for his resignation must be considered. The auditor has a right to speak at such a meeting.

The 1989 Act has extended these rules which only used to apply when an auditor resigned. Now they have been extended to all situations where an auditor leaves office. So they now also apply when an auditor is not reappointed or where he is removed from office.

17.3.3 Remuneration and duties

Section 390A(1) provides that the remuneration which the auditor is to receive must either be fixed by the members at a general meeting, or it must be fixed in such a way as the members in a general meeting determine. In practice it is usually fixed by the directors, because the members usually determine that the directors should fix it. A note in the accounts must indicate how much the auditors are paid, as well as expenses and benefits.

The auditor has two duties, to audit the accounts and to report to the members regarding the accounts. Auditing of the accounts involves carrying out a series of checks and tests to see that they are fair and accurate. The second duty means that the auditor must certify that in his opinion the books give a true and fair reflection of the company's financial position and have been properly prepared in accordance with the Companies Act 1985. The report is not made to the members directly, but can be delivered to the company secretary. It must, however, be available for inspection by any member. If the directors' report (see below at 17.6.2) seems at odds with the annual accounts this must be stated in the auditor's report.

Section 389A(1) of the Act states:

> 'The auditors of a company have a right of access at all times to the company's books, accounts and vouchers, and are entitled to require from the company's officers such information and explanations as they think necessary for the performance of their duties as auditors.'

It is a criminal offence for any company officer to knowingly or recklessly give false, deceptive or misleading information to an auditor (s.389A(2)). Subsidiary companies are required to submit information which the auditors of the parent company may require to carry out their duties as auditors. (s.389(3)). Section 390(1) gives auditors the right to attend company meetings and be given notice of them. Section 390(2) gives them a right to receive written resolutions.

Lopes LJ described the care and skill required of an auditor in *Re Kingston Cotton Mill Co (No. 2)* [1896] 2 Ch 279 (Court of Appeal). 'An auditor is not bound to be a detective, or, as was said, to approach his work with suspicion or with a foregone conclusion that there is something wrong. He is a watch-dog, but not a bloodhound. He is justified in believing tried servants of the company in whom confidence is placed by the company. He is entitled to assume that they are honest, and to rely upon their representations, provided he takes reasonable care. If there is anything calculated to excite suspicion he should probe it to the bottom; but in the absence of anything of that kind he is only bound to be reasonably cautious and careful.'

The auditor does not guarantee that he will discover all fraud. In *Fomento (Sterling Area) Ltd* v *Selsdon Fountain Pen Co Ltd* [1958] 1 All ER 11 Lord Denning asked 'What is the proper function of an auditor?' and gave the following explanation.

> 'It is said that he is bound only to verify the sum, the arithmetical conclusion, by reference to the books and all necessary vouching material and oral explanations … I think this is too narrow a view. An auditor is not to be confined to the mechanics of checking vouchers and making arithmetical computations. He is not to be written off as a professional "adder-upper and subtractor". His vital task is to take care to see that errors are not made, be they errors of computation, or errors of omission or commission, or downright untruths. To perform this task properly he must come to it with an inquiring mind – not suspicious of dishonesty, I agree – but suspecting that someone may have made a mistake somewhere and that a check must be made to ensure that there has been none.'

The auditor owes his duty of care and skill to the company and to the membership as a whole. However, the duty is not owed to members of the public nor to individual members of the company.

■ *Caparo Industries plc* v *Dickman* [1990] 1 All ER 568 (House of Lords)

The claimants owned shares in F plc. After receiving the audited accounts of F plc the claimants bought more shares in the company and later made a successful take-over bid for the company. Later they sued the auditors of F plc because the accounts had shown a pre-tax profit of £1.2m and the claimants alleged that it should have shown a loss of £0.4m. The claimants alleged that the auditors had owed them a duty of care, which they had breached.

Held. The auditors owed no duty of care to the claimants. The following points were made.

(i) Whether or not a duty of care exists depends upon foreseeability of damage, proximity of relationship and the reasonableness of imposing a duty.

(ii) When a statement was put into more or less general circulation, and the maker had no reason to anticipate that a stranger might rely on it, there was no relationship of proximity between the maker and the person relying on it. This would not be the case if the maker of the statement knew that it would be communicated to the person relying on it specifically in connection with any particular transaction which he was considering entering into.

(iii) The auditors of a company owe no duty to members of the public who relied on the accounts to buy shares in the company. Nor do they owe a duty to individual members of the company who wish to buy more shares in the company.

COMMENT Even where a duty of care is owed by the auditors it must be shown that the breach of this duty caused the loss in respect of which damages are claimed. In *JEB Fasteners Ltd* v *Marks, Bloom & Co* [1983] 1 All ER 583 the claimants took over a company after having seen audited accounts which showed an inflated figure for profit. The claimants had no remedy against the auditors, even if a duty of care was owed to them by the auditors, because their real motive in taking over the company was to acquire the services of two directors who worked for the company. They would have taken the company over to acquire the services of these two even if they had not been misled by the accounts, and therefore the auditors' breach of duty did not cause the loss.

Auditors should be familiar with the company's constitution, but have no duty to ensure that the company is well run.

Auditors can be liable to the company either for breach of contract or in negligence if they breached a duty of care owed to the company. An auditor who follows accounting standards and guidelines is most unlikely to be in breach of a duty of care. Auditors can be relieved from liability for breach of duty in the same way that directors can, that is to say by a resolution of the company or under s.727 of the Act. (Relief of directors was considered earlier in this chapter at 17.1.9.)

Test your understanding

1 What is the role of a company secretary?

2 Can a company secretary make contracts which bind the company?

3 Do company secretaries need to hold special qualifications?

4 What is the role of the company auditor? Must all companies have an auditor?

5 Who appoints the auditor?

6 What rules apply when an auditor leaves office?

Answers

1 The company secretary looks after the administration of the company.

2 A company secretary has apparent authority to make contracts which are concerned with the day to day administration of the company.

3 Secretaries of private companies need have no special qualifications. Secretaries of public companies must be suitably qualified.

4 The auditor audits the company accounts and reports to the members that these give a true and fair reflection of the company's position and have been properly prepared. All companies except for dormant companies and some small companies will need to have an auditor.

5 The first auditor is appointed by the directors of the company. Subsequent auditors are appointed by the members at the general meting at which the accounts are considered.

6 An auditor leaving office can compel the directors to hold an extraordinary general meeting of the company at which the auditor has a right to speak. In addition, the auditor must either make a statement that there are no circumstances connected with the resignation which ought to be brought to the attention of the members, or must state what these circumstances are. Copies of this statement must be sent to all members and debenture holders.

17.4 · Company registers

A company is obliged to keep certain registers and documents at its registered office. Most of these registers can be inspected by members of the public, although some can only be inspected by company members.

17.4.1 Registers held at the registered office

The following registers and documents must be kept at the registered office of a company, and can be inspected by a member of the public.

(i) The register of directors and secretaries. (Described above at 17.1.4 and 17.2.1.)

(ii) The register of members. Section 352 of the Act requires every company to hold a register of members, giving their names and addresses, the dates on which they became or ceased to be a member, the number of shares held and the amount paid up on each share. Details of a person's membership must be left on the register for 20 years after the membership has ceased. If the company has more than 50 members the company must also keep an up to date index of the members. This index can be a part of the register of members. During office hours any member has the right to inspect the register of members free of charge, others are also entitled to inspect it but may be charged a small fee. A member also has the right to require the company to supply a copy of the register, or any part of it, within ten days, although a fee may be charged for this. Instead of being kept at the registered office, the register of members may be kept at the business premises of a business which makes the register up for the company. The register of members of companies which are registered in England and Wales must be kept in this jurisdiction. If the register of members is not kept at the company's registered office, the Registrar must be notified of where it is kept. A company officer who does not allow inspection of the register, or who refuses to send a copy to a member who has requested one, is guilty of an offence. The court can order the company to allow inspection or to send a copy.

(iii) The register of directors' interests. Section 325 of the Act requires the company to keep a register of any interest which the directors, or their immediate family, have in the company's shares or debentures. The register must show the price paid for shares and any share options which the directors might hold. It is available for inspection in the same way as the register of members. The register must be kept at the registered office or at the place where the register of members is kept. Members can inspect the register free of charge, non-members can be charged a small fee. A copy can be obtained from the company by any person if a fee is paid. The register must be available for inspection at every annual general meeting of the company.

(iv) Section 407 requires that every company keep a register of charges at its registered office. (Charges are explained in Chapter 18 at 18.8.) Section 406 requires that copies of all documents creating a charge are held for inspection at the registered office. The register of charges is therefore a summary giving brief details of each charge. (The property charged, the amount of the charge and the person entitled to it.) Members and creditors can inspect this register free of charge, others may be charged up to 5p. Failure to comply with these requirements mean that the company officers can be fined, but does not make the charge invalid in any way. However, charges must also be registered with the Registrar and if they are not registered with him then they are void against any liquidator or creditor of the company.

(v) A copy of every contract under which a public company bought its own shares must be held at the registered office for ten years after the contract was performed or should have been performed. Any person may inspect this free of charge (s.169(4) and (5)).

(vi) A company does not need to hold a register of debenture holders. However, if such a register is kept, it must be kept at the registered office or the place of business of a business which makes up the company's registers (s.190(3)). Debenture holders and company members may inspect this free of charge, others may be charged a small fee. A copy can be obtained from the company on payment of a fee.

(vii) A public company must keep a register of people who control more than 3 per cent of the voting rights of its shares at the same place as the register of directors' interests is kept (s.211). There is no fee for inspection of this register, but a fee may be charged if a copy is obtained from the company. Any report of an investigation of a public company's interests in shares must also be kept and be made available for inspection in the same way.

Only members of the company have the right to inspect the following documents:

(i) A copy of every contract under which a private company buys its own shares. A copy of the contract must be kept at the registered office for ten years after the purchase (s.169(4) and (5)).

(ii) A copy of the contract of service of every director or shadow director, either with the company or with one of its subsidiaries (s.318). Where the contract is not in writing a written memorandum of its terms must be kept available for inspection. The contract, or written memorandum, must be kept at a place where the register of members must be kept. The Registrar must be told where the contract or written memorandum are kept. There is no fee for inspection.

(iii) The minutes of any general meeting must be kept at the registered office (s.383(1)). There is no fee for inspection. The company can be required to send a copy to a member who pays a small fee.

(iv) The records of written resolutions of a private company which were agreed as if they were resolutions at a general meeting must be kept at the registered office (s.382A).There is no fee for inspection. The company can be required to send a copy to a member who pays a small fee.

The accounting records of a company must be held at the registered office or such other place as the directors may determine (s.222(1)). The members have no right to inspect these, but they must be kept open at all times for inspection by company officers. (The accounting records are examined below at 17.6.1.)

17.5 · The annual return

Section 363 requires every company to submit an annual return to Companies House. This gives basic information about the company on a particular date, its return date, every year. A company which fails to submit an annual return within 28 days of the return date commits a criminal offence. A company officer who cannot prove that he took all reasonable steps to prevent the commission of the offence is similarly guilty. Persistent failure to supply an annual return can lead to a director being disqualified. Once the annual return becomes 14 days overdue, a member or creditor of the company can apply to the court for an order that an annual return be submitted by the company. The company will have to bear the costs of this application.

Section 364 requires that the following information must be given in the annual return.

(i) The address of the registered office.

(ii) Whether the company is public or private; whether it is limited by shares, limited by guarantee or unlimited; its principal business activities; and whether it is exempted from using the word limited in its name.

(iii) The name and address of the company secretary.

(iv) The names and addresses of the directors and shadow directors; their nationalities; dates of birth; usual business occupations; and details of other directorships held within the past five years.

(v) Notice of any elective resolutions which have been made to dispense with the requirement to hold an annual general meeting or to lay accounts before the members at a general meeting of the company.

(vi) The number and nominal value of the company's issued shares.

(vii) The names and addresses of every member, showing the number and class of shares which he holds, and the names and addresses of every person who has ceased to be a member since the last annual return.

(viii) If either the register of members or the register of debenture holders is not kept at the company's registered office, the address of the place where these registers are kept.

A £15 annual fee is charged for registration of the annual return. The Registrar operates a shuttle system. This involves sending the company the information contained in the previous year's annual return and asking that changes are notified, or that the company indicates that no changes have been made. The return must be signed by a director or the company secretary. The annual return can be inspected at Companies House without this fact being revealed to the company. If Companies House is visited there is a charge of £5 to inspect the microfiche and then of 10p per photocopy. Companies House will post a company's annual return for a fee of £9 and fax it for a fee of £12.

17.6 · Accounts and accounting records

Companies are under a duty to keep accounting records, and to prepare annual accounts.

17.6.1 Accounting records

Section 221 of the Act requires every company to keep accounting records for inspection by the officers of the company. These are not the same as the accounts, but are the documents which enable the accounts to be prepared. (Ledger, order forms, cash books, receipts etc.) They must show with reasonable accuracy the financial position of the company at any particular moment. They should be sufficiently detailed to enable the directors to ensure that any balance sheet or profit and loss account prepared gives a true and fair view of the company's affairs. The accounting records must have day to day entries of all money spent or received, with details of the transactions, and a record of assets and liabilities. If the company sells goods then:

(i) all sales other than retail sales must be recorded, showing details of buyers and sellers sufficient to identify them; and

(ii) the records must include statements of stock held at the end of the financial year and statements of stocktaking to back these records up.

A public company must hold such records for six years, a private company for three years. Officers in default of the requirement to keep accounting records can be imprisoned for up to two years and/or fined. Members of the company do not have a right to inspect the accounting records, unless they are given such a right by the articles of association or by the directors. (Article 109 of Table A allows the members to inspect the accounting records if they pass an ordinary resolution to this effect.) The auditors do have a right to inspect the accounting records. Accounting records can be, and often are, kept on computer.

17.6.2 The annual accounts

A company's accounts consist of a balance sheet, a profit and loss account, the directors' report and the auditor's report. The auditor's report has already been considered above, at 17.3.

Every company will have an accounting reference period. For a newly formed company this date is the last date of the month arising one year after the company was incorporated. For example, if X Ltd was incorporated on 4 November 2004, its first accounting reference date would be 30 November 2005. The accounting reference date will remain the same each successive year, although the directors have a general discretion to move it up to seven days forward or backwards. The period from one accounting reference date to the next makes up the company's financial year and its accounting reference period. A company may resolve to shorten or extend this period as permitted by s.225.

Section 234 requires the directors to prepare a directors' report for each financial year. This should contain a fair view of the development of the company's business and of the company's position at the end of the financial year. If the directors are recommending a dividend this must be stated in the report. The directors' report is therefore of considerable interest to shareholders. Either the company secretary or any director may sign the directors' report, but it must be approved by the board of directors.

The profit and loss account shows the income and expenses of the company over the financial year. If the income exceeds the expenditure the company will have made a profit, if it is less than the expenditure the company will have made a loss. Capital profits, which arise when the company sells a fixed asset such as land, are also generally included as an exceptional item.

The balance sheet shows the assets and liabilities of the company.

Section 241(1) requires that the directors lay the annual accounts before a general meeting of the members, except in the case of private companies which have elected to dispense with this requirement. A copy of the annual accounts must be sent to every member of the company and this requirement cannot be dispensed with. The annual accounts must also be registered with the Registrar. Public companies have seven months from their accounting reference date in which to do this, private companies have ten months.

The directors can be convicted of a criminal offence if the annual accounts are not laid before the members at a general meeting and filed with the Registrar. If the accounts are filed late a private company can be fined on a scale sliding from £100 to £1 000. The scale for public companies slides from £500 to £5 000.

The annual accounts must be approved by the board of directors and at least one director must sign the balance sheet.

17.6.2.1 Abbreviated accounts

Small and medium-sized companies can submit abbreviated accounts to the Registrar, although full accounts will still have to be delivered to the members. (For the definition of small and medium-sized companies see Chapter 16 at 16.3.4.) The abbreviated accounts submitted by a small company can register an abbreviated balance sheet instead of filing a directors' report and profit and loss account. Outsiders examining these abbreviated accounts would not be able to see how much the directors were paid, or the amount paid to the auditors, or the amount of the dividend recommended. In addition, certain items can be left out of small company accounts which are laid before members or sent to members. However, these accounts for the members are still much more detailed than the abbreviated accounts which can be filed with the Registrar. The members of a private company can elect to dispense with the requirement that the accounts are laid before the company in general meeting (s.252). However, s.253 gives any member or the auditor the right to require that a general meeting is held for the purpose of laying the accounts before the company. This is achieved by depositing written notice at the company's registered office. If the directors do not convene a meeting within 21 days of receiving such a notice the person who deposited it may convene a meeting himself and claim the expenses of doing so from the company.

Medium-sized companies can file 'modified' accounts. These are full accounts except that the following can be omitted from the profit and loss account: turnover, the cost of sales information and the division of turnover and profit into different markets. Unmodified accounts will still need to be sent to the members. They will also need to be laid before the members in a general meeting unless the medium-sized company, as a private company, has elected to dispense with this requirement.

Test your understanding

1 What registers and documents must be held at the registered office and made available for inspection by members of the public?

2 What registers and documents must be held at the registered office and made available for inspection only by company members?

3 What is the annual return?

4 What four documents comprise the company's accounts which must be filed with the Registrar?

Answers

1 The following documents and registers must be held at the registered office and made available for inspection by members of the public: the register of directors and secretaries; the register of members; the register of directors' interests; the register of charges; a copy of every contract under which a public company bought its own shares; the register of debenture holders, if the company has such a register; and a register of the interests in shares of a public company.

2 The following documents and registers must be held at the registered office and made available for inspection by members of the company: a copy of every contract under which a private company bought its own shares; a copy of the service contract of every director or shadow director; the minutes of general meetings; and the records of written resolutions which were agreed as if they were resolutions at a company meeting.

3 The annual return must be completed once a year, on the return date, and sent to the Registrar. It gives basic information about the company.

4 The accounts which a company must file consist of the balance sheet, a profit and loss account, the directors' report and the auditor's report.

Key points

Directors

- The directors of a company manage the company.

- A company's articles of association will almost always set out how directors are to be appointed. If the articles do not do this, directors can be appointed by an ordinary resolution of the members.

- A company's articles usually set out how a director can be removed from office. Such provisions are effective. No matter what the articles say, a director can be removed by an ordinary resolution of which special notice has been given (s.303(1)).

- On a resolution to remove a director, the shares of the director whose removal is proposed might carry enhanced voting rights.

- Undischarged bankrupts may not take part in the management of a company without the court's permission. Persons may be disqualified from acting as directors under the CDDA 1986.

- A register of directors and secretaries must contain personal details of all of a company's directors and be kept up to date. The Registrar must be informed of changes within 14 days.

- When directors act collectively they act as the board of directors.

- A company's articles might allow for a managing director to be appointed and for the managing director to exercise the powers of the directors.

- Directors have no automatic right to be paid a fee for their services. The board of directors usually have the power to employ individual directors to perform duties which exceed their ordinary duties and to pay such salary as they consider fit.

- The articles will set out the powers of the directors. Usually the board of directors is given very wide powers to manage the company.

- Directors will be agents of the company if they have some type of authority to act for the company.

- An outsider acting in good faith is entitled to assume that the board of directors, or persons appointed by the board, have the power to bind the company.

- Directors owe fiduciary duties to the company. These require them to exercise their powers *bona fide* for the benefit of the company as a whole, and not to have a conflict between their own interests and those of the company.
- Directors owe a duty of care and skill to the company. The general standard expected is that of a reasonable man looking after his own affairs.

Company secretary and auditors

- All companies must have a company secretary, who cannot also be the sole director.
- The secretary is concerned with the day to day running of the company.
- The secretary of a private company needs no special qualifications. The secretary of a public company must be suitably qualified.
- All companies except certain small companies and dormant companies must have an auditor.
- The auditor audits the accounts and reports on these to the members of the company.
- The first auditor is appointed by the directors, subsequent auditors are appointed by the members at the meeting at which the accounts are considered.
- Special rules apply when an auditor leaves office.

Company registers and accounts

- A company must keep certain registers at its registered office. These registers can be inspected free of charge by company members and by outsiders who pay a small fee.
- Every year a company must send an annual return to the Registrar of Companies. This gives basic information about the company and can be inspected by an outsider without the company being aware of this.
- A company must keep accounting records which record the day to day financial transactions of the company.
- A company's accounts consist of a directors' report, an auditor's report, a profit and loss account and a balance sheet.
- Company accounts must be filed with the Registrar and given to members of the company.
- Small companies may file with the Registrar abbreviated accounts, medium-sized companies may file modified accounts.
- A private company may elect to dispense with the requirement that the accounts must be laid before the company at general meeting. However, the company members are entitled to receive full accounts.

Summary questions

1. Jane Smith owns all the shares in a company. She wants to leave her shares to three of her five children, in equal shares. Jane wants all three children to be directors and she wants to ensure that they can all remain directors for as long as they want.
   Advise Jane as to whether:

   a It will be possible for her to ensure that the three children each have the right to remain as directors.

   b Whether she could make all five children directors and ensure that no four could remove the other one against his wishes.

2. David is the managing director of Goliath Ltd. There are three other directors, but David has always made whatever decisions he considered necessary and then informed the others at board meetings. Goliath's articles used to provide that the managing director could make any contracts up to the value of £20 000.

Recently the articles were changed so that contracts worth more than £5 000 had to be authorised by the full board.

Yesterday David saw what seemed like a good business opportunity for the company. He therefore ordered goods worth £17 000 on the company's behalf. The supplier of the goods did not know that Goliath's articles limited David's authority to make contracts over the value of £5 000. The other directors are convinced that the £17 000 contract is a bad one and are refusing to honour it. Advise the supplier as to whether the company can refuse to honour the contract.

3   Acme Ltd is a medium-sized construction company. The company secretary, without the knowledge of the directors, ordered a new car, a new computer and six pneumatic drills on the company's behalf. None of these items was paid for. The company secretary has subsequently sold the items ordered and disappeared with the money. Advise the company as to whether or not it will have to pay the suppliers of the various items.

4   Arthur, who is neither a shareholder, creditor nor company officer of X Co Ltd, wants to find information about X Co Ltd. Will Arthur be able to find the information detailed below? If so, where will it be found? Will Arthur have to make any payment for access to the information?

   a   The number and nominal value of X Ltd's issued shares.
   b   Whether or not James held shares in X Ltd four years ago.
   c   Whether the directors of X Ltd have any interest in X Ltd's debentures.
   d   Whether or not there are any charges over X Ltd's property.
   e   The service contracts of the directors of X Ltd.
   f   The day-to-day expenditure of X Ltd.
   g   Whether X Ltd has passed a resolution electing to dispense with holding an AGM.

5   Some of the shareholders of Y Co plc think that the auditor has not performed his duties properly. These shareholders bought additional shares in the company as a result of last year's accounts, which mistakenly stated that the company made a profit when in fact it made a large loss. The directors of the company have faith in the auditors and do not want them to be removed from office. The company has passed an elective resolution to dispense with the annual appointment of auditors. Explain any procedure by which the auditors could be removed from office, and the extent to which the auditors could be liable if the accounts were misleading in the way in which the shareholders allege that they were.

6   The directors of Y Ltd, a haulage company, used surplus assets to buy Chinese pottery as an investment. This transaction was not *ultra vires* and the directors acted on the recommendation of an investment expert, who persuaded them that the purchase of the pottery was a wise investment. In fact the pottery was worthless, and consequently the company has lost a great deal of money. Will the company have any remedy against the directors? Assuming that the directors are liable for the loss, are there any ways in which they can be exempted from liability? If the purchase of the pottery had been *ultra vires*, could the shareholders subsequently absolve the directors from liability?

Multiple choice questions

1   Which **one** of the following statements is true?

   a   No matter what the articles of a company might say, the members of a company can always dismiss a director if they pass an ordinary resolution to do so of which special notice has been given.
   b   No matter what the articles of a company might say, the members of a company can always dismiss a director, by passing an extraordinary resolution to do so of which special notice has been given.
   c   Directors of a company cannot be dismissed against their will except by a resolution of the company members.
   d   In a private limited company a director can always be dismissed by a unanimous written resolution of the members.

2   Which **one** of the following statements is **not** true?

   a   When a resolution to remove a director is voted upon, the articles might validly provide that the shares of any director whose removal is proposed carry weighted voting rights.

b At the AGM of a small company with a nominal capital of £1 000, the directors of a company do not have to put forward a resolution to remove a director unless holders of at least 5% of the voting shares ask them to do so.

c When a director is removed under s.303, a replacement director cannot be voted in at the same meeting unless special notice of the resolution proposing the appointment has been given.

d Shareholders holding 5% of the paid up voting shares can compel the directors to hold an EGM and could compel the directors to put forward a resolution to dismiss a director.

3 Which **one** of the following statements is true?

a Directors are always entitled to a salary, and in addition may award themselves such payments as they think fit.

b Directors are always entitled to a salary, and in addition the shareholders may award such payments as they think fit.

c Directors are always entitled to a salary, but may not receive any extra payment from the company.

d Directors have no entitlement to a salary.

4 Which **two** of the following statements are true?

a All directors whose whereabouts are known must be given 21 days' notice of a board meeting and of motions to be proposed at the meeting.

b If a company holds a person out as having authority to make a contract on the company's behalf then the company will be bound by that contract whether the person held out had actual authority or not.

c All companies must have a managing director, who may exercise the same power as the board of directors.

d Table A article 89 allows the directors to fix the quorum for a board meeting, but states that if it is not fixed by them it shall be two.

5 Which of the following statements are true?

i All new company secretaries must be 'suitably qualified'.

ii Company secretaries can make contracts concerned with the administration of the company which bind the company.

iii The company secretary is appointed and can be removed by the directors.

iv In a single member company, but only in a single-member company, the only director can also be the company secretary.

a ii and iii only.

b ii and iv only.

c ii, iii and iv only.

d i, ii, iii and iv.

6 Which of the following statements are true?

i An auditor owes a duty of care and skill to the company and to the membership as a whole, but not to individual members.

ii All companies other than dormant companies must have their accounts audited every financial year.

iii A limited company can never be appointed the auditor of another company.

iv When an auditor leaves office he must attach a statement saying that there are no circumstances which ought to be brought to the attention of the members or creditors, or must state what those circumstances are.

a i, ii, iii and iv.

b i, iii and iv only.

c i, ii and iv only.

d i and iv only.

7 Which of the following statements are **not** true?

i Auditors are appointed annually by the directors.

ii Auditors draw up the company's accounts and must state that these give a true and fair reflection of the company's financial position.

iii All single member companies are exempted from the requirement to appoint an auditor.

iv A member of a company cannot be the auditor of that company.

   a i and iii only.

   b ii and iv only.

   c i and iv only

   d i, ii, iii and iv.

8 Which **one** of the following statements is **not** true?

   a Every company must keep a register of members, which must show the number of shares held by each member and the amount paid up on each share.

   b The minutes of any general meeting of a company must be kept at the registered office. Members can inspect these minutes free of charge. Other persons can inspect but must pay a small charge.

   c A company has no need to keep a register of debenture holders. If it does keep such a register debenture holders and members may inspect it free of charge.

   d Every company must have a register of members, but this does not always need to be kept at the company's registered office.

9 Which **one** of the following statements is **not** true?

   a Members of a company always have the right to inspect the company's accounting records unless the articles of association say otherwise.

   b A company's annual return can be inspected at Companies House without the company knowing this.

   c Small companies can file abbreviated accounts with the Registrar, medium-sized companies can file modified accounts.

   d Any private company can pass an elective resolution to dispense with laying accounts before the members of the company in general meeting.

Task 17

A friend of yours has been offered the chance to buy shares in a small private limited company. Your friend has asked you to write a report, giving details of the following matters.

a The powers of the directors of the company.

b The ways in which directors are appointed and can be removed from office.

c The duties which directors owe to the company.

d The roles of the company secretary and the auditor of the company.

Chapter 18

SHAREHOLDERS · RESOLUTIONS · MAINTENANCE OF CAPITAL · MINORITY PROTECTION · DEBENTURES

Introduction

We begin this chapter by examining the definition of a shareholder and the nature of shares. We then consider different classes of shares, and the way in which shares can be issued and paid for.

In Chapter 17 we saw that the shareholders delegate the power to manage a company to the directors. In this chapter we see that the shareholders can pass resolutions at meetings of the company, and that the ability to pass such resolutions gives the shareholders a lasting and very real power. We examine the relevant procedures by which the different types of resolutions can be passed, the purposes which they can achieve, and the requirements as to registration and minuting which must be fulfilled.

A company's articles of association have legal effect both between the company and its shareholders and between every shareholder and every other shareholder. We examine the legal effect of the articles of association and the way in which a company's articles can be changed.

Companies gain a certain amount of capital when they issue shares. Creditors of the company are entitled to expect that this capital is not given back to the members of the company. In recognition of this, companies are generally prevented from returning capital to shareholders. However, this rule has certain exceptions, and we therefore examine both the rule and the various exceptions to it.

Members of the company with a minority shareholding can find themselves in a very vulnerable position. The majority shareholders may abuse their power to the detriment of the minority or to the detriment of the company. The general rule is that the minority shareholders cannot sue on the company's behalf or question the internal management of the company. However, minority shareholders can be protected by the court if the majority commit a fraud on the minority. We examine the nature of this common law remedy. We also examine the statutory protection which gives a member the right to petition the court on the grounds of unfair prejudice or to petition that the company be wound up.

Finally, in this chapter we examine a company's loan capital. A security given by a company is known as a debenture. Such a debenture may be secured by a fixed or floating charge on the company's assets. We examine these two types of charge and the ways in which a floating charge can crystallise to become a fixed charge.

18.1 · Shareholders

The shareholders of a company limited by shares are known as the members of the company. As we have seen, the shareholders do not manage the company – that task is delegated to the directors. However, the members of a company have considerable powers, despite the delegation of the powers of management to the directors. The members are given these powers because they have invested money in the company and they hope to profit from the company. While the company exists, the profit to the members might come in the form of a dividend paid on their shares or from their investment increasing in value. A much larger profit might come to them if a solvent company is liquidated.

Upon liquidation the surplus assets of the company will be divided amongst some or all of the members.

Section 22 of the Act defines a company member:

'(i) The subscribers of a company's memorandum are deemed to have agreed to become members of the company, and on its registration shall be entered as such in its register of members.
(ii) Every other person who agrees to become a member of a company, and whose name is registered on its register of members, is a member of the company.'

So s.22(1) provides that the company's first members consist of those who sign the memorandum, a matter we examined in Chapter 16. Section 22(2) provides that subsequent members must not only have their names entered on the register of members, but they must also agree to this. This agreement does not need to amount to a contract.

Section 361 provides that the register of members is *prima facie* evidence of any matters which are directed or authorised by the 1985 Act to be inserted in it. In the previous chapter we saw that the register would have to include the names and addresses of members, the dates on which they became or ceased to be a member, the number of shares held and the amount paid up on each share. The register is therefore *prima facie* evidence of all of these matters.

Section 359 allows the register of members to be rectified if anyone's name has either been entered in, or has been omitted from, the register without sufficient cause, or if there is a delay in entering that a person has ceased to be a member. Either the aggrieved person, or any member of the company, or the company itself may apply to the court to have the register rectified. The court has a discretionary power to rectify the register and to order the company to pay damages to an aggrieved party.

18.2 · The nature of shares

A share is a thing (or chose) in action. That is to say it is a form of property which does not have a physical existence of its own, but rather confers certain rights upon the holder. These rights can, ultimately, only be enforced by taking legal action, hence the name a thing in action. (Legal concepts of property are explained in Chapter 23 at 23.1.) The Companies Acts have never defined a share, but the following well-recognised definition was given by Farwell J in *Borland's Trustees* v *Steel Brothers & Co Ltd* [1901] 1 Ch 279:

'A share is the interest of a shareholder in the company measured by a sum of money, for the purpose of liability in the first place, and of interest in the second. A share is an interest measured by a sum of money and made up of various rights.'

This definition mentions both liability and rights. The liability of a person taking shares in a limited company is to contribute the amount of capital which he agreed with the company that he would contribute. Generally this amount is paid when the share is issued. If it is not paid upon issue of the share the company can ask that it be paid at any time. Beyond this, the shareholders cannot be forced to contribute more capital or to pay the debts of a limited company. If the company is liquidated the liquidator can insist that members pay any amount of the nominal value of their shares which has not yet been paid. The money is used to satisfy the company's debts and liabilities. The liquidator cannot insist that a shareholder pays any amount of a share premium which has not been paid. (See the example in Chapter 16 at 16.3.2.2.)

Becoming a shareholder will confer several rights, and the articles may provide for different classes of shares, with different rights attaching to the various classes. Members do not have an automatic right to a dividend. A dividend cannot exceed the recommendation made by the directors. Nor can a dividend be paid if the company has insufficient distributable profit out of which to pay it. Some, if not all, of the company's shares will carry the right to vote at company meetings. If no dividend is paid these voting shareholders might replace the directors with other directors who they see as more capable of making a profit or more willing to declare a dividend. As shares are measured by a sum of money, those who contribute the most capital acquire the most shares. Assuming that a company has only one class of shares, a member with a greater number of shares has more influence in the company, and more of a right to receive any dividends declared, than a member with fewer shares.

18.2.1 Nominal capital and shares issued at a premium

As regards companies having a share capital, s.2(5) of the Act requires every share to have a nominal value. This value represents the amount which the member and the company have agreed should be paid in return for the share, and it is not possible for them to agree that less should in fact be paid. As we have seen, a shareholder can, however, agree to pay more for the share, the extra payment being a share premium. The nominal capital is also called the authorised share capital.

The **paid-up** share capital of a company is the amount of the nominal share capital which has been actually paid by the members. Share premiums do not count towards this paid-up share capital. The **called-up** share capital consists of the paid-up share capital and additional amounts which have become due to be paid towards the nominal value by the members.

Section 130(1) requires that amounts received by a company by way of share premium must be paid into **a share premium account**. This requirement exists to prevent the amount paid by way of premium from being distributed as dividends. Although an amount paid by way of share premium is not part of the authorised share capital of the company, it must be treated as capital and the balance held in a share premium account must be shown in the balance sheet. Section 130(2) does allow the company to apply the share premium account in paying up unissued shares which are to be allotted to members as fully paid bonus shares. It also allows the company to apply the share premium account in writing off the company's preliminary expenses, or the expenses of, or the commission paid or discount allowed on, any issue of shares or debentures of the company. The share premium account may also be used to provide the premium payable on redemption of the company's debentures.

18.2.2 Classes of shares

The articles of a company may provide that there shall be different classes of shares, with different rights attaching to the various classes. Table A article 2, for example, provides that: 'Subject to the provisions of the Act and without prejudice to any rights attached to any existing shares, any share may be issued with such rights or restrictions as the company may by ordinary resolution determine.'

Special classes of shares might carry more votes per share than other classes, or might carry the only right to vote, or might effectively have a veto over any proposed change to the company's constitution.

Generally, those who have acquired shares by contributing towards the company's nominal capital will gain the following rights: the right to vote at company meetings, the right to a dividend if one is declared, the right to have their capital returned if the company is solvent when wound up and the right to a share of the company's surplus assets, if any, when the company is wound up.

Although the Act does not use the term, members with these rights are called ordinary members and own ordinary shares.

If a dividend is payable, the size of a dividend to which any member is entitled normally depends upon the nominal value of shares held. However, many articles, such as Table A article 104, make the amount of dividend to be paid dependent upon the number of paid-up shares held.

When a company has only one class of shares the rights of the members are usually set out in the articles of association. If a new class of shares is created this could be achieved either by altering the

articles to cater for such a class or by contractual agreement between the company and those taking the new shares. The rights of a class of shareholders can also be contained in the memorandum.

Since 1980 companies have been required to register with the Registrar the various rights attaching to different classes of shares if they are not contained in the memorandum or articles.

18.2.2.1 Preference shares

Often a company issues two types of shares, ordinary shares and preference shares. The articles and memorandum will define the precise rights attaching to preference shares, and obviously these rights will vary from company to company. If the members and the company do not expressly agree with a class of shareholders what their rights should be, then all shares will carry equal rights. Generally, it will be agreed that the rights of preference shares will be as follows.

Preference shares are usually paid a rate of interest per annum as a dividend. For example, the articles might stipulate that preference shares carry a dividend of 7% per annum. If preference shares are not paid a dividend in one year they usually carry a cumulative right to a dividend the following year. This means that the preference share dividend which was not paid in the previous year must be paid before any dividend is paid on ordinary shares. (However, preference shareholders, like ordinary shareholders, have no automatic right to be paid a dividend every year.)

Preference shares will carry the same voting rights as other shares in the absence of agreement to the contrary. (However, articles commonly provide that preference shares do not carry a vote, except when their dividend is in arrears or when the motion to be voted upon proposes to alter their special rights.)

On dissolution the preference shareholders usually have the right to have their shares repaid in full before the ordinary shares are repaid at all. If this is the case then the preference shares do not have the right to share in the company's surplus assets.

If, after winding up, there is a surplus of assets this will be divided among the shareholders. Whether or not the preference shareholders are entitled to participate in this division will depend upon the provisions of the articles.

Non-voting shares may be issued by a company. These shares would have no right to vote at company meetings but would have a right to a dividend if one is declared and a right to share in the surplus assets on dissolution of the company.

18.2.2.2 Becoming a shareholder of a company with a share capital

A person might acquire shares either directly from the company (by buying them or through an employees' share scheme), or from an existing member who transfers the shares, or by transmission by operation of law (for example, where shares are inherited).

We saw in Chapter 16 that the authorised share capital must be stated in the memorandum of association, and that this represents the maximum number of shares which the company is allowed to issue. Shares are **issued** when members take them from the company. They are **allotted** when a person acquires an unconditional right to be included in the company's register of members in respect of those shares (s.738(1)).

Section 2(7) of the Act prevents a company from altering the memorandum, except as expressly provided in the Act. Section 121 allows the capital clause in a company's memorandum to be altered in only five ways, and then only if the articles authorise the alteration. These five ways allow the company to:

(a) increase its share capital by new shares of such amount as it thinks expedient;
(b) consolidate and divide all or any of its share capital into shares of larger amount than its existing shares;
(c) convert any or all of its paid-up shares into stock, and re-convert that stock into paid-up shares of any denomination;

(d) sub-divide its shares, or any of them, into shares of smaller amount than is fixed by the memorandum (but this is subject to the final exception);

(e) cancel shares which, at the date of the passing of the resolution to cancel them, have not been taken or agreed to be taken by any person, and diminish the amount of the company's share capital by the amount of the shares so cancelled.

These alterations can be achieved by an ordinary resolution or, in the case of a private company, by a written resolution. The Registrar must be informed of any resolution to increase the authorised share capital within 15 days. When shares are cancelled the Registrar must be informed of the resolution within one month. Either way, the company's memorandum will have been altered and so the Registrar must also be sent a copy of the altered memorandum, and he will publish notice of receiving this in the *Gazette*.

When shares are allotted, the contract of allotment between the company and the allottee (the person to whom the shares are to be allotted) must state: the amount of capital which is going to be contributed; when it is to be contributed; in what way it is going to be contributed; the time when the allottee will have an unconditional right to the shares; and the rights which attach to each share.

The articles will set out how the terms on which a company allots shares will be decided. Section 80(1) provides that a company may not allot shares unless it is authorised to do so by the company in general meeting (an ordinary resolution) or by the company's articles. (This does not apply when shares are allotted to the subscribers to the memorandum or issued under an employee share scheme.) As regards public companies, the directors cannot be given authority to allot shares for more than five years at a time. Private companies can give the directors longer periods of authority, but only if there has been an elective resolution (which would require a unanimous vote) to this effect (s.80A).

An authority to allot shares must specify the maximum number of shares which may be allotted, and the date on which the authority is to expire (unless it was granted for an indefinite period by elective resolution). The authority to allot shares can always be revoked or varied by an ordinary resolution, even if this involves changing the articles. (A change in the articles usually requires a special resolution.) When an authority to allot shares is renewed all of the same rules as applied to the initial authority similarly apply.

The Registrar must be sent a copy of any resolution which gives authority to allot shares, or of any resolution which varies, revokes or renews such authority, within 15 days. As regards public companies, the Registrar will publish receipt of such notice in the *Gazette*.

If the authority gives the power to alter rights attaching to different classes of shares, three-quarters of the members of that class must approve the variation (s.125(3)). This approval can be given in writing by three-quarters of the members of the class or by extraordinary general meeting of the class. Section 127(2) allows holders of at least 15% of the issued shares of the class in question to apply to the court to have the alteration cancelled, as long as they did not consent to the alteration or vote in favour of the resolution for the alteration.

Once shares are allotted, details must be sent to the Registrar within one month.

18.2.2.3 Pre-emption rights

Shareholders with pre-emption rights are offered the first chance to buy new shares. Section 89 of the Act provides that equity shares may not be allotted to new company members for cash unless they are first offered to existing members, in proportion to their existing shareholding, on terms which are equally favourable. (An equity share is one on which the right to receive dividend payments or the right to share in the company's assets on dissolution is not limited to a specified amount. It would not therefore include typical preference shares.) A private company can exclude this right in its articles or memorandum (s.91). Public companies can exclude pre-emption rights for up to five years at a time by a provision of the articles or by special resolution (s.95). Directors who contravene s.89 are not guilty of a criminal offence but become civilly liable to shareholders who should have been offered new shares.

The rules on pre-emption rights do not apply when shares are allotted under an employees' share scheme. The company's annual accounts must disclose any allotment of shares, giving details of the class of shares allotted, the number of shares allotted, their total nominal value and the amount of capital contributed. Within two months of allotment of shares the company must issue a share certificate.

18.2.2.4 Payment for shares

Generally, payment for shares may be in money or money's worth and so payment does not have to be in cash. Often shares in a different company or fixed assets are given in return for shares. Generally, the court will not query the valuation of the consideration received in exchange for the shares. However, shares in public companies can only be sold for cash or for an asset which has been independently valued as being worth at least as much as the amount credited as having been paid up. This valuation must be made by a person qualified as an auditor or by someone appointed by a qualified auditor.

Either a public or a private company which allots shares otherwise than for cash must, in addition to the details of allotment mentioned above, also send to the Registrar a copy of the contract of allotment within one month. In addition, public companies have to send a copy of the valuation report and the Registrar will publish notice of having received this in the *Gazette*.

A public company may not accept promises to perform work or services in return for issuing shares (s.99(2)). If this section is breached the allottee is regarded as not having paid the amount credited for the shares and remains liable to pay the price and interest at the rate of 5% per annum. The allottee's promise remains enforceable by the company. Company officers who knowingly or wilfully breach s.99 commit an offence. Past services, for which full payment has not yet been made, can be given as consideration for the allotment of shares in a public company, but only if they are valued as worth the amount credited as having been paid.

Section 113 allows a court to excuse a person from liability for having breached the rules on allotment of shares, if it considers that to do so would be just and equitable.

18.2.2.5 Section 117 certificates

Section 117(1) provides that a newly incorporated public company may not begin trading or borrow money until it has received a s.117 certificate (also called a certificate to commence business or a trading certificate). The Registrar will issue such a certificate only if satisfied that the company's allotted share capital is not less than the authorised minimum (s.117(2)). This means that the company must have allotted shares with a nominal value of at least £50 000 and that each share has been paid up to at least one quarter of the nominal share value and any premium. Shares allotted under employees' share schemes will not count unless one quarter of the nominal value has been paid up.

A director or the secretary must complete and sign Form 117 in order to get a certificate. The Form states that at least £50 000 of nominal share capital has been allotted and indicates how much of this has been paid up. It must also state the amount of preliminary expenses, including the amounts to be paid to promoters and the benefits received in return, and who is going to pay the preliminary expenses. If Form 117 is correctly completed the Registrar must notify receipt of it in the *Gazette* and must issue the certificate.

If a public company does conduct business before receiving a certificate, an offence is committed by any company officer who knowingly or wilfully authorised the transaction. The transaction itself is not automatically void. However, the directors will become jointly and severally liable on it if the company does not honour it within 21 days of being asked to do so.

A public company can be compulsorily wound up if it does not receive a s.117 certificate within one year of incorporation.

18.2.2.6 Re-registration as a public company

A private company can re-register as a public company and commence business without a s.117 certificate. The members will need to pass a special resolution to register as a public company. On the day on which the resolution is passed the company must have allotted at least £50 000 nominal share capital. A quarter of the nominal value of each share and any share premium must have been paid up, and all the requirements regarding allotted capital in a public company must have been complied with. A balance sheet, prepared no more than seven months before the application, must be sent to the Registrar along with the application. An auditor's written statement must say that in their opinion the net assets of the company were not less than the total of called up share capital and undistributable reserves. If any shares were issued other than for cash, after the preparation of the balance sheet but before the re-registration, then the rules pertaining to the valuation of assets received in return for shares in a public company apply.

The directors must issue a statement that all the requirements relating to capital have been complied with, and that the value of the assets of the company have not fallen since the balance sheet to less than the total of called up share capital and undistributable reserves. When a private company re-registers as a public company it does not need to get a s.117 certificate.

Test your understanding

1 How does a person become a member of a company?

2 What type of property is a share?

3 What is a company's share premium account?

4 Is it possible for a company to have different classes of shares?

5 What rights usually attach to preference shares?

6 In what three ways may a person acquire shares?

7 What are pre-emption rights?

8 What is a s.117 certificate?

Answers

1 A person becomes a member of a company either by subscribing to the company's memorandum and on registration being entered on the register of members, or by agreeing to become a member and his name being registered on the register of members.

2 A share is a thing in action.

3 A share premium account is an account into which share premiums are paid. Rules governing such an account require the company to treat the money in the account as capital, and therefore prevent its distribution as dividends.

4 The articles of a company may allow for different classes of shares, with different rights attaching to the various classes.

5 Generally, it is agreed that preference shares carry a cumulative right to a dividend expressed as a rate of interest per annum, and the right to be paid ahead of the ordinary shareholders on dissolution of the company. Preference shares might or might not have the same voting rights as the ordinary shares.

6 A person may acquire shares from the company, by a transfer from an existing member, or by transmission by operation of law.

7 Pre-emption rights give existing shareholders the right to have new shares offered to them in proportion to their existing shareholdings before they are allotted for cash to new members.

8 A s.117 certificate must be issued by the Registrar before a public company can commence trading or borrow money. The certificate will only be issued if the Registrar is satisfied that the company has allotted shares with a nominal value of at least £50 000, and that a quarter of the nominal value of each share and any share premium has been paid up.

18.3 · Company meetings

The members of the company delegate to the directors the task of managing the company. However, the members have the power to take certain decisions themselves and these decisions are usually taken at a meeting of the company. Some decisions can be taken by ordinary resolution, others require a special or extraordinary resolution.

Members entitled to vote at a meeting must be given proper notice of the meeting, and there must be a quorum (minimum number of members present) before a meeting can be properly convened.

18.3.1 The annual general meeting (AGM)

Section 366 requires that every company should hold an annual general meeting once every calendar year. There is no need to hold an AGM in the calendar year of incorporation as long as one is held within 18 months of incorporation. No more than 15 months may elapse between the date of one AGM of the company and the next.

If these requirements are not complied with any member can apply to the Secretary of State to call a general meeting (s.367).

Section 366A gives the members of a private company the right to elect to dispense with the holding of AGMs. This would be achieved by **all** of the company members agreeing to the elective resolution. The agreement would be effective for the year in question and for subsequent years. However, any member of the company may apply for an AGM to be held in any calendar year by giving notice to the company at least three months before the end of that year (s.366A(3)).

The AGM presents the members with their most important opportunity to question the way in which the company is run and to use their votes in their own best interests. The usual business of such a meeting would include the following: directors would lay the accounts before the members; auditors would be reappointed or new auditors appointed; the directors' report would include the amount of dividend which the directors are recommending; and directors might retire by rotation if the articles provide for this.

Section 376 allows members to requisition the company to put forward a resolution at the AGM, but only if the members doing so hold at least 5% of the voting rights entitled to vote at the meeting or if they represent at least 100 members of the company who between them have paid up at least £10 000 share capital. In addition, the company can be required to circulate a statement of not more than 1 000 words concerning the matter to be put forward in the resolution. This advantage is limited to some extent by the fact that those who submit the requisition will have to pay the costs involved unless the company resolves otherwise. The members submitting the requisition must deposit it at the company's registered office at least six weeks before the AGM. They are also required to put down a deposit to cover the likely cost.

If the articles of the company do not set out the business of the AGM (Table A does not) the notice convening the meeting would have to set out details of the business to be conducted.

18.3.2 Extraordinary general meeting (EGM)

Any general meeting of the members which is not an AGM is an EGM. Table A allows the directors to call an EGM. However, the directors cannot call an EGM for their own purposes but must exercise the power as fiduciaries for the benefit of the company. The directors of a public company are compelled by s.142 to call an EGM if half of the company's capital has been lost. The meeting must be called within 28 days, and actually be held within 56 days, of a director becoming aware of the loss. The purpose of the meeting is to consider whether any, and if so what, steps should be taken to deal with the situation.

Section 368 gives the members of the company the power to call an EGM. They do this by depositing a requisition at the company's registered office. This requisition demands that the directors convene an EGM within 21 days to consider the objects specified in the requisition. The power conferred by s.368 can only be exercised by members who hold at least 10% of the company's paid-up share capital with voting rights. Each of the members putting in the requisition must sign it. If the requisition is properly submitted the members must be given notice of an EGM to be held within 28 days of the notice. If the directors do not convene a meeting the members submitting the requisition can do this themselves and the company must pay reasonable expenses incurred in doing so.

At the meeting called in response to the requisition, those requisitioning the meeting have a right to have business put on the agenda, and so do the directors. However, other members have no such right.

18.3.3 Meetings ordered by the court

Section 371 gives the court the power to order meetings in any manner it sees fit where it is impracticable for a meeting to be called. The court will do this on the application of a director or a member who is entitled to vote at a company meeting. The court might make such an order if, for example, members with a minority shareholding were needed to make a quorum and they stayed away from meetings so that they could not be dismissed as directors. The court is also given the power to order meetings for other specific purposes.

18.3.4 Notice of meetings

Table A articles 38 and 111 require that written notice of meetings should be given to company members, to persons entitled to a share in consequence of the death or bankruptcy of a member, to the directors and to the auditors. Section 390(1) gives the auditors a statutory right to be given notice of general meetings to be held during their term of office.

Section 369(1) lays down minimum periods of notice. A company's articles may specify that more notice should be given. The minimum statutory period is 21 days' written notice for an AGM and 14 days' written notice for an EGM. If a special resolution is to be proposed at an EGM s.378(2) requires that 21 days' notice of the meeting, specifying the intention to propose the resolution as a special resolution, must be given. (If an extraordinary resolution is to be proposed at an EGM, the usual 14 days' notice of the meeting and the resolution must be given.) If any member is not given the proper amount of notice then all proceedings of the meeting are invalid. (This is not the case if members who were not given notice actually attend the meeting and agree to treat the meeting as a meeting.) In *Young* v *Ladies' Imperial Club Ltd* [1920] 2 KB 523, for example, a club held a meeting and expelled a member of the club. One member of the committee was not given notice of the meeting because she had previously informed the chairman that she would not be able to attend. The Court of Appeal held that the expulsion was invalid because a member had not been given notice of the meeting. Table A article 39 provides that the accidental omission to give notice shall not invalidate the proceedings at that meeting and nor should non-receipt of the notice.

If a special, extraordinary or elective resolution is proposed, the notice of the meeting must set out the exact wording of the resolution. Table A article 38 also requires that the notice of the meeting specifies the time and place of the meeting and the general nature of the business to be transacted.

Shorter notice of the AGM may be given if all of the members entitled to vote agree to this (s.369(3)). As regards other meetings of public companies (EGMs), shorter notice is permissible if at least 95% of the members entitled to attend the meeting and vote agree to this (s.378(3)). By elective resolution the members of a private company may agree to shorter notice of an EGM if 90% of members entitled to attend and vote agree to this.

Special notice is required of the following resolutions:

(i) To dismiss a director under s.303(1).
(ii) To appoint a director to replace a director dismissed under s.303(1).
(iii) To dismiss an auditor, or to replace an auditor other than a retiring auditor.

Special notice requires that the company is given notice of intention to propose the resolution 28 days before the meeting at which the resolution is to be proposed. The company must give the members 21 days' notice of the resolution and of the meeting at which it is to be proposed.

18.3.5 Proxies and quorum of meetings

A proxy is a person entitled to attend a company meeting and to vote on behalf of a company member. Section 372 provides that any member of a company entitled to attend and vote at a company meeting is entitled to appoint another person (whether a member or not) as his proxy to attend and vote instead of him. It also provides that in the case of a private company a proxy appointed to attend and vote instead of a member also has the same right as the member to speak at the meeting.

Unless the articles provide otherwise, a proxy is not entitled to vote on a show of hands but only on a poll. (Table A does not provide otherwise.) Any provision in the articles preventing a proxy from demanding a poll is void. A member of a private company may only appoint more than one proxy if the articles allow for this. (Table A article 59 provides that a member may appoint more than one proxy to vote at the same meeting.) Anything in a company's articles which requires an instrument appointing a proxy to be received by the company or any other person more than 48 hours before the meeting is void. Corporate members of companies have the right to appoint a proxy.

A company meeting is not properly convened unless a quorum (minimum number) of members attend. Only persons entitled to vote at the meeting can count towards the quorum. If the articles do not provide otherwise then only the members present in person, and not proxies, count towards the quorum and the quorum is set at two persons (s.370). However, Table A article 40 allows proxies to count towards the quorum.

Section 370A provides that in single member companies the quorum is one person, either a member or a proxy, despite anything to the contrary in the articles. The quorum may also be set at one person as regards other companies if the court orders a company meeting to be held.

18.3.5.1 Chairman

Generally, a company's articles will provide that there should be a chairman who supervises the conduct of general meetings. The chairman decide matters of procedure. He must act fairly and in good faith, taking into account all of the members' interests and the interest of the company. He cannot stop the meeting because he does not like the way it is going.

18.4 · Resolutions

Members of companies take decisions by passing resolutions, which may be ordinary, special, extra-ordinary or elective. In private companies any of these types of resolution may be passed by the written resolution procedure (which is explained below at 18.4.4).

18.4.1 Ordinary resolutions

An ordinary resolution is passed if more members vote in favour of it than vote against it. Only the votes of members present and voting, or the votes of proxies, count. So a majority of all members entitled to vote is not required.

Decisions can be taken by ordinary resolution unless either the company constitution or the Act require a special or extraordinary resolution. Under s.303(1) a director can always be dismissed from office by an ordinary resolution of which special notice has been given. Members can excuse directors from liability for breach of duty by ordinary resolution, as long as the directors did not act outside the objects clause or act fraudulently, illegally or in bad faith. The auditors are appointed and removed by ordinary resolution.

18.4.2 Special and extraordinary resolutions

Both special and extraordinary resolutions need to be passed by three-quarters of the votes of members either present and voting or voting by proxy. The difference between the two is that notice of a special resolution must be given at least 21 days before the meeting at which the resolution is to be proposed, even if it is to be proposed at an EGM, whereas only 14 days' notice of an extraordinary resolution to be proposed at an EGM is needed. If an extraordinary resolution is to be proposed at the AGM, 21 days' notice of the meeting and the resolution must be given. The notice of a special, extraordinary or elective resolution must contain the entire substance of the resolution, although minor grammatical errors will not invalidate it. Amendment of the substance of the resolution will not be allowed at the meeting.

A special resolution is required in order to:

(a) Change the company's objects (s.4);
(b) Alter the articles of the company (s.9(1));
(c) Alter the company name (s.28(1));
(d) Ratify actions of the directors which were outside the objects clause; and relieve the directors from any liability for having acted outside the objects clause (s.35(3));
(e) Re-register a company from private to public (s.43(1)), from unlimited to private limited (s.51(1)), or from public to private (s.53(1));
(f) To reduce the company's share capital in accordance with a provision in the articles (s.135(1));
(g) To approve a payment out of capital to redeem or purchase the company's own shares (s.173);
(h) To authorise the terms on which a company makes an off-market purchase of its own shares, or to vary revoke or renew any such authority (s.164);
(i) To exempt a dormant company from having to have its accounts audited (s.250);
(j) To petition for compulsory liquidation of the company (Insolvency Act 1986 s.122(1)).

Extraordinary resolutions are very rarely required. However, they can be required at a class meeting of shareholders to vary the rights of classes of shares. They can also be required to initiate a creditors' voluntary winding up where the company is insolvent and, in a members' voluntary winding up, to enable the liquidator to settle debts owed by the company.

18.4.3 Elective resolutions

The members of a private company may pass an elective resolution to achieve the following:

(a) Dispense with the laying of accounts before a general meeting (s.252);
(b) Dispense with holding AGMs (s.366A);
(c) Dispense with the annual appointment of auditors (s.386);
(d) Give directors the power to allot shares for more than a five-year period (s.80A);
(e) Reduce the majority required to approve short notice of an EGM from 95% to 90% (s.369(4)).

Elective resolutions must be agreed to in writing by all the members of the company. Otherwise elective resolutions can be passed at company meetings, but **all** of the members entitled to vote must vote in favour, in person or by proxy. At least 21 days' notice of an elective resolution must be given to members, but this requirement can be dispensed with if all the members entitled to vote agree. The notice must state that an elective resolution is to be proposed and set out the terms of the resolution. Despite having to be unanimous, elective resolutions can later be undone by ordinary resolution. Section 379A(3) provides that the company may revoke an elective resolution by passing an ordinary resolution to that effect.

18.4.3.1 Voting

Generally, every member has one vote and voting is taken on a show of hands. However, it would be unusual for a company not to allow a poll to be demanded. Section 373(1)(a) renders a provision in the articles void in so far as it excludes the right to demand a poll at a general meeting on any question other than the election of the chairman of the meeting or the adjournment of the meeting. Often articles provide that a specified number of members may demand a poll. Section 373(1)(b) renders void any provision which requires more persons to demand a poll than either (a) five members entitled to vote at the meeting, or (b) members representing 10% of the voting rights, or (c) members representing more than 10% of the paid-up capital conferring a right to vote. It also provides that on such a poll the members' voting power would be in proportion to the number of voting shares held. Table A article 57 does not allow a member to vote unless his shares are paid up. As we have seen, members who do not attend the meeting personally can appoint proxies to go in their place. Table A article 50 provides that if there is equality of voting the chairman should have the casting vote, in addition to any other vote he may have.

18.4.3.2 Registration of resolutions

Minutes of all proceedings at a general meeting must be kept. Once signed by the chairman, the minutes are *prima facie* evidence of the proceedings of the meeting. A record of written resolutions of private companies which were passed as if a resolution at a company meeting must also be similarly kept. Members of the company must be entitled to inspect the minutes of a general meeting at the registered office free of charge. Members are entitled to be sent a copy of the minutes within seven days on payment of a fee which the company may prescribe.

Section 382B provides that where the only member in a single member company takes a decision which may be taken by the company in general meeting, and which has effect as if agreed by the company in general meeting, then the member must give the company a written notice of the decision. This does not apply if the meeting was taken by written resolution. Failure by the member to comply with this provision does not invalidate the decision but does make him liable to a fine.

Section 380(4) provides that the following types of resolutions must be registered with the Registrar within 15 days of being passed, and a copy must be attached to any copy of the articles issued subsequently to the passing of the resolution, unless the articles have been reprinted including amendments effected by extraordinary resolution.

(a) Special resolutions.
(b) Extraordinary resolutions.
(c) Elective resolutions.
(d) Resolutions which revoke elective resolutions.
(e) Resolutions which were passed by a unanimous resolution of the company and which would have needed to have been passed as special or extraordinary resolutions.
(f) Resolutions which give the directors authority to allot shares, or which vary renew or revoke such an authority.
(g) Resolutions which allow a company to purchase its own shares, or which vary renew or revoke such a power.
(h) Resolutions to voluntarily wind the company up under the Insolvency Act 1986.
(i) Resolutions which increase the authorised share capital.

18.4.4 Written resolutions

If all of the members of a company who have a right to attend and vote at a general meeting agree to a decision which a general meeting of the company could agree to, then the assent they have given is as binding as a resolution passed at a general meeting would be. However, this right is subject to any prohibitions contained in the Act or the general law.

Section 381A allows the members of a private company, or a class of any members, to pass a written resolution. To achieve this **all** of the members who would have been entitled to attend a meeting of the company and vote must sign the resolution. Such a written resolution could be used to pass any type of resolution, ordinary, special, extraordinary or elective, but could not be used to dismiss a director under s.303(1) or to dismiss an auditor. (Because the director or auditor in question has a right to address the meeting at which the resolution is proposed.) A written resolution can be passed without the need to hold a meeting or to give notice. A written resolution can be passed by a private company notwithstanding any provisions of the articles or the memorandum. Single member companies may use the written resolution procedure.

Members of a class can also pass written resolutions in the same way. A written resolution is passed when the last member entitled to vote signs it. If the company has auditors, they must be informed of the written resolution at the time when it is proposed, or the directors and the secretary will commit an offence. The resolution will not however be invalidated. Written resolutions must be recorded by the company in the same way as the minutes of a general meeting.

Test your understanding

1 Must all companies hold an AGM every year?

2 Can company members ensure that a resolution is proposed at the AGM?

3 What is an EGM?

4 Can the members of a company call an EGM?

5 What are the minimum statutory notice periods which must be given of AGMs and EGMs?

6 What is a proxy?

7 What is meant by a quorum?

8 What percentage of members' votes is required to pass an ordinary resolution? What percentage is required to pass a special or extraordinary resolution?

9 What is an elective resolution?

10 What is a written resolution?

11 Must resolutions be registered with the Registrar?

Answers

1 With the exception of private companies which have passed an elective resolution to dispense with the holding of AGMs, all companies must hold an AGM every calendar year. An AGM need not be held in the year of incorporation, as long as one is held within 18 months of incorporation.

2 Members cannot ensure that a resolution is proposed at the AGM unless they satisfy the requirements of s.376 of the Act. Members do satisfy the requirement of s.376 only if they hold 5% of the voting shares or represent at least 100 members who between them have paid up at least £10 000 share capital. They may then serve notice of a resolution upon the company, who must give notice of the resolution to members and include it on the agenda of the AGM.

3 Any general meeting of the company members other than an AGM is an EGM.

4 The articles of most companies allow the directors to call an EGM. Section 368 gives members who hold at least 10% of the company's paid-up share capital with voting rights a right to compel the directors to call an EGM by depositing a requisition at the company's registered office.

5 The minimum statutory periods of notice are: 21 days' written notice of an AGM; 14 days' written notice of an EGM; 21 days' written notice of an EGM if a special resolution is to be proposed.

6 A proxy is a person entitled to attend and vote at a company meeting on behalf of a company member who has appointed him.

7 A quorum is a minimum number of members who must be present before a company meeting can validly be commenced. If the articles do not provide otherwise, two persons will constitute a quorum. In single member companies one person constitutes a quorum notwithstanding any provision to the contrary in the articles.

8 An ordinary resolution is passed by a simple majority of members' votes cast at the meeting. A special or extraordinary resolution is passed if at least 75% of the votes cast are in favour.

9 An elective resolution can only be passed by a private company and only if all of the company members vote in favour of it. By elective resolution the company may resolve to dispense with laying accounts before a company meeting, dispense with holding AGMs, dispense with the annual appointment of auditors, give directors the power to allot shares for more than a five year period or reduce the majority required to approve the holding of a company meeting on short notice.

10 A written resolution can be passed by a private company if all of the members of the company sign the resolution. There is therefore no need to hold a meeting to pass the resolution.

11 Ordinary resolutions do not usually need to be registered with the Registrar, but s.380(4) requires certain ordinary resolutions to be registered. Special, extraordinary and elective resolutions do need to be registered. Unanimous resolutions which could only have been passed by special or extraordinary resolution must also be registered. Minutes of all proceedings at company meetings must be kept.

18.5 · The legal effect of the articles and memorandum

Section 14 of the Act provides that:

> 'Subject to the provisions of this Act, the memorandum and articles, when registered, bind the company and its members to the same extent as if they respectively had been signed and sealed by each member, and contained covenants on the part of each member to observe all the provisions of the memorandum and the articles.'

The opening phrase of s.14 makes it plain that provisions of the memorandum or articles will have no effect if they are inconsistent with the provisions of the Act. That said, the articles have legal effect to make a contract between each shareholder and the company and between every shareholder and every other shareholder.

18.5.1 The articles as a contract between the company and the members

The company can insist that the members stick to the provisions of the articles.

■ *Hickman* v *Kent or Romney Marsh Sheep-Breeders' Association* [1915] 1 Ch 881

The Sheep-Breeders' Association was registered as a non-profit making company. One of the Association's articles provided that any dispute between the Association and a member should be referred to arbitration. The claimant sued the Association in respect of various matters. The Association argued that the court case should be stayed because there was a binding contract to take disputes to arbitration. (Whenever parties have made a valid contract to refer a dispute to arbitration, the court will suspend any proceedings, known as staying the proceedings, on the basis that the dispute should have been taken to arbitration rather than to the court. See Chapter 2 at 2.4.1.)

Held. The proceedings were stayed. The articles form a contract between a company and its members in respect of their ordinary rights as members.

Equally, the members can insist that the company stick to the provisions of the articles. In *Wood* v *Odessa Waterworks Co* (1889) 42 ChD 636, for example, the company's articles gave the company the power to declare a dividend 'to be paid' to the members. An ordinary resolution was passed to the effect that no dividend should be paid, but that instead members should be given interest-paying debentures. It was held that 'to be paid' meant paid in cash. As the resolution was therefore inconsistent with the articles, a member was granted an injunction to prevent the resolution from being given effect. Another example can be seen in the following case.

■ *Pender v Lushington* (1877) 6 ChD 70

The articles of a company provided that every ten shares commanded one vote, as long as the shareholder had possessed the shares for the three months before the meeting, but that no member should be entitled to more than 100 votes. Shareholders who held more than 1000 shares transferred some of these to Pender and other nominees so that the shares could use their full voting power. The chairman of the company, Lushington, refused to accept the votes of Pender and the nominees, even though their names had been on the register of members as owners of the shares for over three months.

Held. The shares had been properly transferred and so Pender and the other shareholding nominees had a contractual right to have the votes of their shares accepted. Pender was therefore granted an injunction restraining the directors from refusing to count their votes.

It is important to realise that members are only bound to the company in their capacity as members, and that the company is only bound to members in their capacity as members. An example of a member trying to rely on the articles otherwise than in his capacity as a member can be seen in *Beattie v E and F Beattie Ltd* [1938] 3 All ER 214. In that case the defendant, a director who was also a member of the company, was sued by the company for the return of money which had been improperly paid to him as a director. An article similar to that in *Hickman v Kent or Romney Marsh Sheep-Breeders' Association* said that disputes between a member and the company should be referred to arbitration. The defendant was not able to rely on this article. He was not attempting to rely on the articles as a contract in his capacity as a member of the company but in his capacity as a director. Lord Greene MR said: 'the contractual force given to the articles of association by [s.14] is limited to such provisions of the articles as apply to the relationship of the members in their capacity as members.' It follows from this that the articles cannot create a contract between the company and persons who are not members of it.

18.5.2 The articles as a contract between the members

Section 14 tells us that the articles create a contract between the members and other members. However, this is only true in relation to matters concerning membership of the company.

■ *Rayfield v Hands* [1960] Ch 1

Article 11 of the company of which the claimant was a member provided that if any member intended to transfer shares in the company he should inform the directors who 'will take the said shares equally between them at a fair price'. The claimant informed the directors that he intended to transfer the shares and they refused to buy them, arguing that the articles imposed no such liability upon them.

Held. The directors were bound by Article 11 and therefore had to take the shares at a fair price. Article 11 was concerned with the relationship between the claimant as a member and the defendants as members of the company.

The articles and the memorandum do not make any contract with outsiders. However, outsiders may make a contract in which they expressly or impliedly include the provisions of the articles or the memorandum.

18.5.3 Alteration of the articles

Section 9(1) of the Act provides that:

'Subject to the provisions of this Act and to the conditions contained in the memorandum, a company may by special resolution alter its articles.'

Although s.9(1) states that a special resolution is required, an agreement by all of the members to alter the articles will be valid even if it was not agreed as a special resolution or at a company meeting. If the alteration varies the rights attaching to different classes of shares then a dissentient minority of 15% of the holders of a class of shares may apply to the court to have the alteration declared invalid. (See below at 18.5.3.1.)

Section 80(1), as we saw earlier in this chapter, provides that a company may not allot shares unless it is authorised to do so by an ordinary resolution or by the company's articles. If the authority is given by ordinary resolution, and is contrary to a provision in the articles, the articles will then be regarded as having been altered even though no special resolution has been passed.

If something cannot be done by a company unless the articles authorise it, then a special resolution authorising the thing will not be effective because the articles will not be impliedly changed. In some cases this has defeated a special resolution to reduce capital because the articles did not authorise the company to reduce capital. But if the resolution states that it is doing the thing 'notwithstanding anything in the articles' then the thing will be validly done.

Any change in the articles must be notified to the Registrar within 15 days of the alteration having been made (s.380). The company must send not only the resolution which altered the articles but also the articles in their altered state (s.18(2)). If this is not done both the company and any officer who knowingly or wilfully authorised or permitted the default will be guilty of an offence. They can be fined and are liable to a daily default fine if they continue to fail to send the articles in their altered state (s.18(3)). The Registrar must notify the *Gazette* of the receipt of any document which makes or evidences an alteration of a company's articles.

Section 16 provides that a member is not bound by any alteration of the articles which requires him to take or subscribe for more shares, or become more liable to contribute to the company's share capital or otherwise pay money to the company unless the member has expressly agreed to this in writing. Neither the memorandum nor the articles can exclude the effect of this section.

In Chapter 17 we saw that s.9 prevents articles from stating that they are unalterable. We also saw that it is possible that some shares might have specially weighted rights when voting on a special resolution and that these weighted rights might apply in a resolution to change the articles. If a provision which could have been put in the articles is put in the memorandum and is stated to be unalterable then the provision cannot be altered (s.17(2)). It is therefore possible to make articles unalterable by putting them in the memorandum and stating that they are unalterable. The memorandum takes precedence over the articles so that anything in the articles which conflicts with the memorandum is invalid.

An alteration of the articles must not include an illegal article or deprive members of rights given to them by the court.

When the members do alter the articles they must exercise this power *bona fide* for the benefit of the members of the company as a whole, that is to say for the benefit of the company in its capacity as a separate legal person.

■ *Greenhalgh v Arderne Cinemas Ltd* [1951] 2 All ER 1120 (Court of Appeal)

The claimant had a minority shareholding in a company. One of the articles provided that shares should not be transferred to non-members if a member was willing to buy the shares at a fair value. Majority shareholders wanted to sell shares to an outsider at 6 shillings a share. An EGM was called to alter the article already described so that shares could be sold to an outsider without first being offered to a member, if an ordinary resolution was passed to this effect. This special resolution was passed and then an ordinary resolution was subsequently passed, authorising the sale of 500 shares to the outsider. The claimant claimed that the special resolution was invalid because the interests of the minority shareholders had been sacrificed to the interests of the majority.

Held. The special resolution had been validly passed.

COMMENT The court is considering, objectively, the position of a hypothetical member of the company. Such a member might well benefit from having the right to sell his shares to outsiders. However, the decision did rather ignore the reality of the situation at the time of the case. The shareholders were very firmly fixed into two camps. At the time of the decision, the minority did appear to be harmed because they could not pass an ordinary resolution, and were therefore still obliged to sell their shares to the majority. The majority could pass ordinary resolutions and therefore sell their shares without first offering them to the minority.

Members of a company have no automatic right to be given copies of the articles and the memorandum. However, upon payment of 5p the company must send a copy of the articles or memorandum to any member who requests that he be sent a copy. If such a request is refused both the company and its officers commit an offence.

18.5.3.1 Variation of class rights

If a company has different classes of shares, any definition of the rights attaching to a class of shares will generally be found in the articles rather than in the memorandum. If the rights are contained in the memorandum and the memorandum sets out the procedure by which such rights can be changed, or refers to a procedure set out in the articles, then the articles can only be changed by following that procedure. If the rights are set out in the memorandum and there is no procedure for variation in the memorandum, or referred to in the articles by the memorandum, then the rights can only be varied by the members if all the members of the company agree to the variation (s.125(5)). It would also be possible to alter the articles if the court sanctioned the agreement under s.425.

If the rights are set out otherwise in the memorandum, and the articles set out the procedure for variation, then that procedure must be followed. If no procedure is specified in the articles, a variation of class rights can be made only if three-quarters of the holders of the nominal value of the issued shares of the class in question agree to the variation. This consent might be given by the written consent of three-quarters of the members of the class in question or by an extraordinary resolution passed at a separate meeting of members of the class in question (s.125(2)). If the variation of class rights involves a variation of the articles then a special resolution of company members would be needed to approve the variation.

However an alteration of class rights is achieved, s.127(2) allows the holders of not less than 15% of the issued shares of the class in question to apply to the court to have the variation cancelled. However, they can only do this if they did not vote in favour of the alteration. If such an application is made the variation has no effect unless and until it is confirmed by the court. The court may refuse to allow the variation if it is satisfied that it is unfairly prejudicial to the holders of the class concerned.

18.6 · Maintenance of capital

The shareholders contribute, or agree to become liable to contribute, the nominal share capital of the company. The company's creditors must accept the risk that the capital will be lost as a result of the company carrying on its business. However, they do not expect the capital to be returned to the members. Companies are therefore prohibited in general from returning capital to their members. Dividends can only be paid out of distributable profits.

The remuneration of directors does not depend on a profit having been made, and the amount paid to directors does not have to be reasonable. But if a payment to a director is in fact a repayment of capital contributed by the director then the amount paid must be returned to the company.

18.6.1 Reduction of capital

A reduction in a company's capital is illegal unless it is authorised by statute. The term reduction in capital means that either the company's issued or authorised share capital is reduced. However, the cancelling of unissued shares is not regarded as a reduction in capital because it does not reduce the amount of capital available to the company in any way.

A company may carry out a reduction of capital under s.135(1), but only if its articles permit this. A special resolution must be passed and the reduction must be approved by the court. Section 135(1) allows for a reduction of capital made in any way, and s.135(2) states that this includes reducing or extinguishing liability on share capital not fully paid up, cancelling paid-up share capital which is lost or unrepresented by available assets, or paying off any share capital which is in excess of the company's wants. The company may then alter its memorandum, in so far as this is necessary, by reducing the amount of the share capital and its shares. The main reasons for wanting to reduce share capital would be either to reflect the fact that the value of the company's assets had decreased, or to completely extinguish the interests of some members, or to replace share capital with debt capital.

How the reduction in capital is carried out is up to the members of the company, but the reduction must comply with ss.135–141 of the Act. If all the members of a class of equity shareholders are not treated equally, then either all members of the class must agree to the reduction, or the court must sanction it. It is quite common not to treat all the members of a class equally. For example, all members of a class are not treated equally when the shares of some members in a class are bought by the company but the shares of other members in the class are not.

A company's articles may adopt the s.135 procedure to reduce capital. If this is the case then nothing in the articles or the memorandum can restrict the company's power to follow the procedure.

No reduction in capital can be carried out unless it is confirmed by the court, which will ensure that creditors' interests are protected and that the correct procedure is followed. The court will also ensure that the reduction is fair to all existing shareholders. Anyone opposing the reduction must show that it is not fair on account of all shareholders of the same type not being treated equally. This will not be possible if those treated in a different manner have agreed to this.

If the reduction in capital consists of repaying capital to the members, or reducing the amount which members are liable to pay, then the interests of creditors will be safeguarded by ss.136–137. A list of all the company's creditors will be drawn up and the court cannot agree to the reduction until either every creditor on the list has either positively consented to the reduction or had his debt repaid, or the court is satisfied that the company has made adequate provision to ensure that the creditor will be paid.

Public companies may not reduce the nominal value of their allotted share capital below £50 000. If a public company loses more than half of its called-up share capital s.142 requires the directors to call an EGM within 28 days of becoming aware of this. The meeting considers what needs to be done to deal with the problem and must be held within 56 days of the directors becoming aware of the problem. If the EGM is not convened as required, every director who knowingly and wilfully authorises the failure to convene the meeting, or permits the failure to continue after the meeting should have been convened, commits an offence.

When a company has different classes of shares, the rights of one class might be varied on a reduction of capital under a provision in the memorandum or articles. This is only possible if, in addition to any other procedure which needs to be followed, three-quarters of the members of that class approve the variation. The consent of the three-quarters of the members of the class can either be written or it can be by extraordinary resolution of a class meeting.

18.6.1.1 Redeemable shares

Redeemable shares are issued by the company on the understanding that they will be bought back by the company on a certain date. The holders of redeemable shares are therefore temporary members of the company. A company may issue redeemable shares as long as its articles permit this. The purchase back of these shares will not contradict the general rule that a company must not acquire its own shares. When the shares are redeemed they must be cancelled. A company may only issue redeemable shares if there will at all times be some members holding shares other than redeemable shares.

18.6.2 Dividends

The members of a company expect to be paid a return on the capital which they invest in the company. This return might come either by sharing in the surplus assets when the company is wound up, or by way of dividend. Dividends must be paid out of profit, or the payment of them would amount to a reduction of capital.

There is no requirement that a company must distribute profit as dividends. It might consider it more prudent to retain the profit for expansion of the company. A dividend only becomes payable if the company declares a dividend. Table A article 102 provides that the members declare a dividend at a general meeting, but that no dividend can exceed the amount recommended by the directors. (This recommendation is made in the directors' report.) The members may reject the directors' recommendation to declare a dividend, or may declare a dividend smaller than that recommended by the directors. If the directors refused to recommend a dividend in line with the wishes of the members the members might begin steps to remove the directors under s.303(1), in order to replace them with directors who would recommend the dividend. Dividends must be paid in cash unless the articles provide otherwise.

The rule against payment of dividends out of capital is designed to protect the creditors of the company, but the creditors do not have any power to prevent a proposed dividend out of the company's capital. Sections 263–281 set out the rules on the payment of dividends and other distributions of the company's assets to its members. However, these sections do not apply to a company's purchase of its own shares or to the issue of bonus shares.

Section 263(3) states that:

> 'A company's profits available for distribution are its accumulated, realised profits, so far as not previously utilised by distribution or capitalisation, less its accumulated, realised losses, so far as not previously written off in a reduction or reorganisation of capital duly made.'

A company's realised profits will be the amount by which income produced by the sale of assets exceeds expenses. (Unrealised profits arise when the assets held by the company increase in value.) A realised loss occurs when expenses exceed the income produced by asset sales.

A dividend is not payable unless the profits made in one year also clear any losses made in previous years. If a dividend is declared but not paid then the member entitled to the dividend has a time limit of 12 years to sue on the debt.

If an illegal distribution is made then the directors who recommended the dividend are liable to repay it to the company. Any of the directors can be sued for the whole amount but, having paid, would then be entitled to a contribution from the other directors. The members receiving the dividend are not obliged to return it, unless they knew or had reasonable grounds to believe that it was paid in contravention of the Act.

18.6.3 Purchase of own shares

Section 143(1) of the Act sets out a general prohibition against a company purchasing its own shares, but such a purchase is permitted by s.162(1) as long as the company's articles permit it. (Article 35 of Table A permits this.) The members of the company must approve the terms on which the shares are purchased. Shares cannot be purchased by the company unless they are fully paid up. It follows that a company must buy the shares from members to whom they have been issued, they cannot purchase unissued shares. After the purchase of the shares some shares other than redeemable shares must still be held by some members. If the shares are purchased on a recognised stock market this is known as a market purchase. (Obviously, it is only public companies which are listed on the London Stock Exchange, or admitted to dealings on some other recognised UK investment exchange, which can purchase their own shares in this way.) If the shares are bought in any other way then this is known as an off-market purchase.

As long as the company's articles permit for the purchase of its own shares, authority for a market purchase may be given by ordinary resolution of the members. The resolution must state the maximum number of shares which can be purchased, and the maximum and minimum prices which can be paid. The authority given cannot last for longer than 18 months. However, authority to make a market purchase may be renewed, revoked or varied by another ordinary resolution. A copy of the resolution which gives the authority must be registered with the Registrar within 15 days of its being passed. While the authority still exists, a copy must also be attached to every copy of the articles or the memorandum issued by the company. Once the shares have been purchased they must be cancelled.

An off-market purchase can be made by either a public or a private company, but only if the company's articles permit this. In addition, the terms of the contract to purchase the shares must be approved by the members of the company in advance of the purchase. The members need to give authority to make the purchase by special resolution. The authority may not be for longer than 18 months if the company is a public company. The votes attaching to the shares which are to be bought are not allowed to vote on the special resolution. If the member whose shares are being bought holds other shares which are not being bought he may vote with these other shares in a poll, but may not vote at all on a show of hands. If a written resolution is used to give authority, the resolution is passed without the signature of the member whose shares are being bought. Regardless of what the articles might say, any member is entitled to demand a poll if the resolution is proposed at a general meeting. If the resolution is put forward at a general meeting, then a copy of the proposed contract must be available at the meeting, and must have been available for inspection at the company's registered office for 15 days before the meeting. If the resolution is to be adopted by written resolution then every member must be sent a copy of the proposed terms when the resolution is sent for signature. The authority to make an off-market purchase may be renewed, varied or revoked by another special resolution.

Once a company has purchased its own shares the Registrar must be informed within 28 days. A private company must state the number of shares purchased and their nominal value. A public company must also state the amount paid for the shares. In their annual report the directors must state the number of shares purchased, their nominal value, the price paid, the reason for the purchase and how large a percentage of the paid-up capital of the company the shares purchased represented. For ten years after the purchase the company must keep a copy of the contract to purchase the shares at its registered office. In a private company this is available for inspection only to members. In a public company it is available for inspection to the public. All shares purchased must be cancelled.

18.6.4 Financial assistance to buy shares

Section 151(1) makes it *prima facie* unlawful for a company to give financial assistance, direct or indirect, for the acquisition of its own shares or the shares of a holding company, whether before or after or at the same time as the shares are acquired. This prohibition applies whether the shares are being bought from an existing member or whether they are unissued shares. Section 151(2) makes it *prima facie* unlawful to reduce or discharge liability incurred as a consequence of taking shares in a company. As the prohibitions apply to direct or indirect financial assistance, they would include the company guaranteeing a loan which was taken out by a person buying the company's shares. Gifts, guarantees or indemnities, or the giving of a loan or any other transactions which reduce the company's assets to a material extent, are all treated as financial assistance.

If a company acts in breach of s.151, it is liable to a fine, and every officer of it who is in default is liable to imprisonment, or a fine, or both. In addition, the directors will incur civil liability for breach of duty and other persons involved in the financial assistance may be liable to the company if they knowingly received company property or knowingly took part in the illegal transaction. Any guarantee or security given in connection with prohibited financial assistance is void. Loans made in the ordinary course of a money-lending business will not be included and nor will money provided in good faith for the purchase of the company's shares under an employee share scheme.

Section 153(3) provides that the prohibition in s.151 does not extend to the following matters: lawfully distributing dividends; distributions made on the winding-up of the company; the allotment of bonus shares; a reduction of capital confirmed by the court under s.127; a properly conducted redemption; or a purchase of shares or certain specified arrangements involving creditors of the company.

Section 153(1) does allow financial assistance for the purpose of acquiring shares in the company or in a holding company. But only if the company's principal purpose in giving the assistance is not to give it for the purpose of such acquisition, or the giving of the assistance for that purpose is but an incidental part of some larger purpose of the company. The assistance must also be given in good faith in the interest of the company. It can be difficult to prove that the requirements of s.153(1) have been satisfied, and the fact that the company benefited from the financial assistance will not necessarily be enough. Often financial assistance is given to facilitate a management buy-out of the company.

Section 155 creates a second exception in the case of private companies. A private company is allowed to give financial assistance to buy its shares, or reduce liabilities incurred in acquiring the shares, in two circumstances. First, if the assistance does not reduce the net assets of the company; or, second, if the assistance is provided out of profits which could have been used to pay a dividend. Although a gift would reduce the assets of the company, a loan would not. (The amount given as the loan would be balanced in the accounts by the fact that the borrower owed the amount of the loan to the company.) Financial assistance can only be given under s.155 if the members agree to it by special resolution. The directors will also need to make a statutory declaration in the prescribed form. Section 157(2) allows the holders of 10% of the nominal value of the company's issued shares, or any class of it, to make an application to the court to cancel the resolution.

The statutory declaration must set out the nature of the financial assistance given, the nature of the business of the company and to whom the assistance was given. It must also state that after the assistance has been given the directors have formed the opinion that there will be no grounds on which the company is unable to pay its debts. An auditor's report must be attached, saying that the auditors have enquired into the state of the company and that they have not seen anything which makes the directors' declaration unreasonable in all of the circumstances.

Within 15 days the Registrar must be given a copy of the special resolution, the directors' declaration and the auditor's report. Holders of 10% of the company's nominal issued share capital may apply to the court, within 28 days, to cancel the resolution. The court has the power to cancel it, vary it or order that the shares of the dissenters be bought. The financial assistance must not be actually provided until four weeks after the passing of the resolution which proposed it, unless the resolution was passed unanimously. It must not be made more than eight weeks after the directors make the statutory declaration.

18.6.5 Insider dealing

In order to maintain confidence in Stock Exchanges it is necessary that all those who might deal on the Exchanges have the same information available to them. Those who have special information about a company are prohibited from using this information to deal in the company's securities.

Section 52(1) of the Criminal Justice Act (CJA) 1993 provides that an individual who has information as an insider is guilty of insider dealing if he **deals in securities** that are price-affected securities in relation to the information. The acquisition or disposal which the dealing involves must occur on a regulated stock market, or the person dealing must either be a professional intermediary (a stockbroker) or rely on a professional intermediary. Securities are defined widely to include shares, debentures, options and futures.

Section 52(a) CJA 1993 creates a second offence, whereby an individual who has information as an insider is also guilty of insider dealing if he **encourages another person to deal in price-affected securities** in relation to the information, knowing or having reasonable cause to believe that this would cause insider dealing to take place.

Section 52(b) CJA 1993 creates the third offence of **disclosing the information to another person,** otherwise than in the proper performance of the functions of his employment, office or profession.

Inside information means information which:

(a) relates to particular securities;
(b) is specific or precise;
(c) has not been made public; and
(d) if it were made public would be likely to have a significant effect on the price of the securities. (CJA 1993 s.56(1).)

A person has information as an insider if, and only if, he knows that it is inside information and he knows that he has it from an inside source (CJA 1993 s.57(1)). A person has information as an inside source if, and only if, he has it as a consequence of being a director, employee or shareholder of an issuer of securities, or directly or indirectly has the information from such a person, or has access to the information by virtue of his employment, office or profession (CJA 1993 s.57(2)).

Section 53(1) CJA 1993 provides a defendant with a defence to the main offence of dealing in securities if he shows:

(a) that he did not at that time expect the dealing to result in a profit attributable to the fact that the information in question was price-sensitive information in relation to the securities; or
(b) that at the time he believed on reasonable grounds that the information had been disclosed widely enough to ensure that none of those taking part in the dealing would be prejudiced by having the information; or
(c) that he would have done what he did even if he had not had the information.

Very similar defences are provided by s.53(2) and (3) to the other two crimes of encouraging others to deal and disclosing information.

Those convicted can be fined and imprisoned for up to seven years.

The Listing Rules of the London Stock Exchange attempt to reduce insider dealing by requiring that listed companies publish all price-sensitive information as quickly as possible. Companies which breach the Listing Rules can have their listing suspended and thereby lose a valuable method of raising capital.

Test your understanding

1 Between whom, if anyone, do a company's articles create a contract?
2 Can a company's articles provide that they are unchangeable?
3 What are the three main requirements of s.135, which allows a company to reduce its capital?
4 Can a company's capital be reduced by the payment of a dividend?
5 Can the members of a company governed by Table A articles increase the dividend which the directors recommend?

6 What is the difference between a market purchase of a company's own shares and an off-market purchase?

7 What are the three offences of insider dealing?

Answers

1 The articles create a contract between the company and the members, in their capacity as members. They also create a contract between each member and every other member, in their capacity as members. They do not create a contract between the company and outsiders.

2 Section 9 of the Act prevents the articles of a company from making the articles unchangeable. Any provision to this effect would be void.

3 The three main provisions of s.135 are that the articles must permit the reduction, a special resolution must authorise the reduction and the court must approve it.

4 A company cannot reduce its capital by paying a dividend. Dividends must be paid out of profits.

5 The members of a company governed by Table A cannot increase the dividend recommended by the directors. They can reduce the dividend or declare that no dividend should be paid.

6 A market purchase of a company's own shares is made on a recognised stock market and can therefore only be made by a public company which is listed or a member of a UK recognised investment exchange. An off-market purchase is one made in any other way.

7 The three offences relating to insider dealing are: using inside information to deal in price-affected securities; encouraging others to do this; or disclosing inside information.

18.7 · Protection of minority shareholders

A member of a company who owns the majority of the company's voting shares can ensure that an ordinary resolution is passed. A member with 75% of the shares can ensure that extraordinary or special resolutions are passed. Similarly, members who between them can muster over 50% or 75% have the power to see that the various types of resolution are passed.

These percentages can be vitally important when a person is considering whether or not to invest in a company. Let us look at an example. If A invites B to form a company with him, and suggests that B take 49% of the one class of ordinary shares, while A takes 51%, then their investment in the company is almost equal. However, their control of the company is far from equal, and B should be very wary about accepting such a proposition. B's holding of 49% of the voting shares would give him no power to block or pass an ordinary resolution, but would at least give some degree of 'negative control', in that he could block a special or extraordinary resolution. If B was offered only 25% of the shares he would in effect have no control of the company at all.

If two shareholders each own 50% of a company's shares then they will both have negative control of the company. Neither member will be able to force through any resolution without the consent of the other. This might sound an ideal way to run a company owned by two people, and while the shareholders are in harmony with each other it probably is. But if complete deadlock is reached then the court may well wind the company up (if either party so requests) on the ground that to do so would be just and equitable. This happened in *Re Yenidje Tobacco Co Ltd* [1916] 2 Ch 426 (Court of Appeal), where the court wound up a profitable company because the two shareholder/directors, Mr Weinberg and Mr Rothman, had reached complete deadlock and only communicated with each other through notes passed via the company secretary. Cozens-Hardy MR said: 'Certainly, having regard to the fact that there are only two directors who will not speak to each other, and no business which deserves the name of business in the affairs of the company can be carried on, I think the company should not be allowed to continue.'

If complete deadlock is reached, a minority shareholder is of course in a far worse position than a 50% shareholder. (One can imagine how Weinberg would have felt if he had owned 49% of the shares to Rothman's 51%.) We have seen that directors can be removed under s.303(1) by an ordinary resolution of which special notice is given. Assuming that there is no *Bushell* v *Faith* clause in the articles, a majority shareholder can exclude the minority shareholders from management of the company and from appointing the managers.

18.7.1 The rule in *Foss* v *Harbottle*

The position of minority shareholders is not improved by the rule in *Foss* v *Harbottle* (1843) 2 Hare 461. This rule provides that if a wrong is done to a company then only the company has the right to sue in respect of that wrong, and that the court will not interfere with the internal management of a company while the company is acting within its powers. The rule in *Foss* v *Harbottle* is a logical extension of *Salomon* v *Salomon & Co Ltd*, which established that a company is a legal person in its own right. It follows that if a company is wronged then it alone has the power to sue in respect of that wrong.

The main benefit of the rule in *Foss* v *Harbottle* is that it prevents the huge number of legal actions which would inevitably arise if any member of a company had the power to sue on the company's behalf. The rule also upholds a general principle of company law – that if the members of a company are in disagreement they should resolve this at a general meeting of the company. If the rule in *Foss* v *Harbottle* did not exist the courts would constantly be asked to judge whether or not companies were adopting sound business policies.

However, the rule in *Foss* v *Harbottle* causes obvious problems when the shareholders who control the company defraud the minority shareholders or distribute all of the company's profits as salary at the expense of paying any dividends. If there were no exceptions to the rule the minority would be powerless. The courts will therefore intervene, despite the rule, in four circumstances: if the personal rights of a member are infringed; if the company proposes to enter into an *ultra vires* transaction; if the act confirmed by the majority required a special or extraordinary resolution; or if there has been a fraud on the minority. The last of these exceptions is the most significant.

18.7.2 The personal rights of a member have been infringed

In this chapter we have already seen an example of a court holding that a member's personal rights had been infringed in *Pender* v *Lushington* at 18.5.1. It might be remembered that the company chairman refused to accept the votes of Pender's shares, as the articles required him to do, and the court held that this was a breach of Pender's rights as a member. However, this is not a true exception to the rule in *Foss* v *Harbottle*. A member whose rights have been infringed will have a contractual right to sue on account of the articles forming a contract between himself and the company and between himself and the other members. Such an action does not allege any wrong done to the company.

18.7.3 Actions which are *ultra vires*

In Chapter 17 at 17.1.8 we saw that any member of a company has the right to prevent the company from entering into an *ultra vires* transaction, but that if the transaction has already been concluded a member has no power to undo it. We also saw that the members will not have the power to prevent the company entering into an *ultra vires* transaction if the transaction has been approved by special resolution.

18.7.4 The act confirmed by the majority required a special or extraordinary resolution

The rule in *Foss* v *Harbottle* does not allow a majority of shareholders sufficient to pass an ordinary resolution to approve a transaction which required approval by a special or extraordinary resolution or by some other special majority vote.

18.7.5 Fraud on the minority

Fraud on the minority is not precisely defined, covering a wide range of underhand behaviour. Several of the cases, such as the two which follow, involve the company being defrauded.

■ *Cook* v *Deeks* [1916] 1 AC 554 (Privy Council)

Cook was one of four directors in a construction company. The company had often done profitable business with the Canadian Pacific Railway Company and had built up a good relationship with this company. When a new contract with the Canadian Pacific Railway Company had finished being negotiated, the other three directors made the contract in their own names rather than in the company name. The three directors (who owned 75% of the shares) then passed a resolution that the company had no interest in the new contract. Cook claimed that the resolution was ineffective and that the benefit of the contract should go to the company.

Held. The resolution was ineffective and the company was entitled to the benefit of the contract.

■ *Menier* v *Hooper's Telegraph Works* (1874) LR 9 Ch App 350 (Court of Appeal)

E. Limited (E) had allotted 5 325 ordinary shares, 3 000 of these being allotted to H. Limited (H). E had won a concession from the Portuguese government to lay a transatlantic cable from Portugal to Brazil. H were to manufacture the cable. H then found that they could make more money by laying the cable for another company, and H managed to persuade the Portuguese government to transfer the cable-laying concession to this other company. To prevent E from suing, H used its 3 000 shares to wind E up. The claimant, a minority shareholder, brought an action on behalf of himself and the other minority shareholders.

Held. The claimant was entitled to bring the action. H had committed a fraud on the minority and had to account to E for the profits made.

When a wrong is done to a company, a shareholder who is allowed to sue despite the rule in *Foss* v *Harbottle* is said to have a right to bring a derivative action. He is bringing an action for the company's benefit, or to enforce a right of the company, and joins the company as a defendant because those who control the company will not allow the company to act as a claimant. (The member's right to sue derives from the right to sue which the company has not exercised.) If the action is successful a remedy is given to the company rather than to the claimant. A representative action is brought when the member suing represents other shareholders who have the same interest in the proceedings. Any judgment gained is enforceable by the other shareholders and is binding upon them.

A fraud on the minority does not necessarily mean defrauding the company. It may be that only the minority are defrauded, as the following two cases show.

■ *Alexander* v *Automatic Telephone Co* [1900] 2 Ch 56 (Court of Appeal)

All the subscribers to a company paid 6d. The five directors, who owned 75% of the shares, passed a resolution that all shareholders who were not directors should pay a further 2s 6d. Two of these directors (who had voted for the resolution) brought a representative action, claiming that this amounted to fraud on the minority.

Held. The directors' actions did amount to fraud on the minority, and they too were compelled to pay the 2s 6d per share.

■ *Clemens* v *Clemens Bros Ltd* [1976] 2 All ER 268

The claimant held 45% of the issued share capital of a company and her aunt held 55%. The company operated in the building trade and was very successful. The articles provided that if either shareholder wished to sell her shares, the other had the right to buy them. The claimant therefore had negative control of the company and if she outlived her aunt would eventually have total control. The aunt and four non-shareholders were directors. The five directors proposed to issue a large number of new shares to themselves and to a special employees' trust. The effect of this would be that the claimant's holding would fall to below 25%. The aunt used her shares to pass the resolution. In the three years prior to the resolution the directors' total emoluments exceeded the company's pre-tax profit. The claimant brought an action against the company and her aunt, asking for the resolution to be set aside.

Held. The resolution was set aside. It was a fraud on the minority, its real purpose being to deprive the claimant of her control of the company. The aunt was bound by equitable considerations which could prevent her from exercising her control of the company in certain ways.

A claim for fraud on the minority will not be possible where the act complained of is merely negligent, rather than fraudulent, and where no personal benefit is conferred on those who control the company and commit the act.

■ *Pavlides* v *Jensen* [1956] 2 All ER 518

A minority shareholder in a company brought an action against the directors, alleging that they had sold a mine for far less than it was worth, and that this therefore amounted to fraud on the minority. The directors were not shareholders in the company, but the majority of the shares were held by another company and the directors were also directors of this company. The directors did have the power to sell the mine and there was no suggestion that they had been fraudulent or dishonest. However the directors had committed an error of judgment, and they had been negligent in selling the mine at the price at which they had sold it. The sale of the mine was not put to a general meeting of members.

Held. The claimant's action failed. The directors had not been fraudulent and the act in question was one which could have been approved by a majority of shareholders. As the directors had been negligent, but not fraudulent, the majority shareholders could pass an ordinary resolution absolving them from liability.

Daniels v *Daniels* [1978] 2 All ER 89 distinguished this case because on its facts the negligent act resulted in a profit being made by one of the directors. The two directors of the company, a husband and wife who were also the majority shareholders, had caused the company to sell land to one of them for very much less than it was worth. Templeman J allowed the minority shareholders to bring an action against the two directors and the company, even though fraud was not proved. He said: 'If minority shareholders can sue if there is a fraud, I see no reason why they cannot sue where the action of the majority and the directors, though without fraud, confers some benefit on those directors and majority shareholders themselves ... To put up with foolish directors is one thing; to put up with directors who are so foolish that they make a profit of £115 000 odd at the expense of the company is something entirely different.' In *Prudential Assurance Co Ltd* v *Newman Industries (No 2)* [1981] Ch 257 Vinelott J reviewed the case law and found that a derivative action could be brought even though fraud is not actually proved.

18.7.6 **Statutory protection of the minority**

Those with a minority shareholding in a company are given various statutory rights. We have already seen that s.368 allows those holding 10% of the voting shares to convene an EGM; that those holding 5% can ensure that a resolution is put on the agenda of the AGM; that s.5 allows the holders of 15% of the issued shares to object to an alteration of the objects clause; that s.127 allows 15% of the holders of a class of shares whose rights are to be varied to apply for a cancellation of the variation; that s.54 allows 5% of the holders of a public company's nominal issued share capital to apply for the cancellation of a resolution to convert to a private company; that s.157 allows the holders of 10% of the company's issued share capital, or any class of it, to object where the company is giving financial assistance to buy its own shares; and that s.176 allows any member to apply for cancellation of a resolution whereby the company is to buy its own shares from capital, as long as the member in question did not approve or vote in favour of the resolution. In addition, those who hold 10% of a company's issued share capital can ask for an inspection by the DTI, a matter considered below at 18.7.7.

18.7.6.1 Unfair prejudice under ss.459–461 of the Companies Act 1985

Any company member, or the personal representative of a deceased member, may petition the court on the grounds that the affairs of the company are being, or have been, or will be, conducted in a manner which is unfairly prejudicial to the members generally or to particular members. (The right of a personal representative is important because after the death of a member directors sometimes refuse to register either the personal representative or the beneficiary as a shareholder. If they are not registered they cannot vote at company meetings, although they would still have a right to dividends declared.) If the court agrees that the conduct is unfairly prejudicial it can:

(a) Order the company to behave in a certain way in the future.
(b) Prevent the company from doing certain acts.
(c) Order the company to sue for a wrong done to it.
(d) Order some members of the company, or the company itself, to buy the shares of other members at a fair price.
(e) Make any order which it sees fit.

■ *Re HR Harmer Ltd* [1958] 3 All ER 689 (Court of Appeal)

Harmer had a successful business dealing in postage stamps. In 1947 he formed a company to take the business over. His two sons were, like him, life directors. Harmer retained voting control of the company although his sons held most of the shares. When Harmer was 88 his sons asked the court for relief on the grounds that he completely ignored their wishes, running the company as if he still owned all of it. He had made bad business decisions, employed private detectives to watch the staff and countermanded resolutions passed by the board.

Held. The court ordered that Harmer should be made president of the company for life (without any special powers) and be paid a salary. They also ordered him not to interfere in the company's business otherwise than in accordance with the valid decisions of the board of directors.

In *Re Saul D. Harrison and Sons Ltd* [1995] 1 BCLC 14 (Court of Appeal) it was held that the conduct complained of must be both prejudicial and unfair. Hoffmann LJ stated that, 'the very minimum to make out a case of unfairness is that the powers of management have been used for an unlawful purpose or the articles otherwise infringed'. This may not be the case, however, in companies which are quasi-partnerships. (A quasi-partnership company would be a small company where the members, often members of the same family, have a mutual understanding that they should all remain directors and continue to manage the company much as if it were a partnership. Often such companies evolve from partnerships.)

In *O'Neill* v *Phillips* [1999] 1 WLR 1092 Lord Hoffmann gave the only judgment of the House of Lords and considered unfair prejudice in considerable detail. He made the following points.

(1) Although fairness was the criterion on which relief under s.459 might be granted, and although the court has a wide power to do whatever it considers just and equitable, the concept must be applied rationally and upon judicial principles.
(2) In deciding what is fair the context and background will be extremely important.
(3) Generally, members will be bound by the articles as these were the terms on which they agreed that the company's affairs should be conducted. However, equitable principles might make it unfair to rely strictly on the articles in a way which equity would regard as contrary to good faith.
(4) The way in which equitable principles are applied is reasonably well settled. These should not be abandoned in favour of some uncertain notion of fairness. Unfair prejudice petitions are often very expensive. If lawyers cannot advise clients of their chances of success this will operate to the detriment of their clients.
(5) Conduct can be unfair under s.459 even if it would not be sufficient to wind the company up.

(6) In deciding whether conduct is unfair, it should be asked whether the exercise of the power complained of is contrary to what the parties agreed, either by words or conduct.

(7) In quasi-partnership companies what was agreed will usually be found in the understandings between the members when they entered into association. Promises exchanged in quasi-partnership companies should be binding as a matter of equity even if they are not binding as a matter of law.

(8) Breaching a promise or undertaking is not the only ground on which unfair prejudice may be founded. An analogy could be made with frustration of a contract. (See Chapter 7 at 7.1.3.) The majority might use their powers in a way which the minority can reasonably say that they did not agree to. This might allow winding up of the company or it might afford a remedy for unfair prejudice.

(9) The majority must not use their powers, in breach of equitable principles, to defeat the 'legitimate expectation' of other members. For example, if members have entered the company in the understanding that they have all put in capital and will all manage the company, a member would have a 'legitimate expectation' that this agreement would be honoured or that he would be able to withdraw from the company on reasonable terms. An expectation will not be a 'legitimate expectation' merely because the minority shareholder reasonably and legitimately thought it likely to happen. In fairness or equity the minority shareholder must have a right to expect it to happen.

(10) There would be no unfair prejudice if the majority offered to buy the minority's shares at a reasonable price. This price should not be at a discount on account of the shareholding being a minority shareholding, it should amount to the value of the equivalent proportion of the share capital. (In special circumstances a discounted valuation might be appropriate.) An independent expert should usually make this valuation. Both sides should have access to all company information which would affect the value of the shares.

(11) The majority shareholders should be given a reasonable time in which to make the offer to buy out the minority.

In *Exeter City AFC Ltd* v *Football Conference Ltd* (2004) Times, 12 February Judge Weeks QC held that the statutory right to apply for relief under s.459 was inalienable and could not be removed or diminished by a contract term or otherwise.

18.7.6.2 Petition for winding-up under the Insolvency Act 1986

A court can wind a company up under ss.122–124 of the Insolvency Act 1986 on the grounds that it is just and equitable to do so. Even a single shareholder can petition the court to do this. Whether or not it is just and equitable to wind a company up is a question of fact in every case and will depend upon the circumstances of the case.

In *Loch* v *John Blackwood Ltd* [1924] AC 783 (Privy Council) a profitable company was wound up because the managing director omitted to hold general meetings, or to submit accounts, or to recommend a dividend. His object was to keep the other shareholders in ignorance of the company's position and to acquire their shares at an under value.

In the following case a quasi-partnership company was wound up as if it had been a partnership.

■ *Ebrahimi* v *Westbourne Galleries* [1972] 2 WLR 1289 (House of Lords)

Since 1945 E and N had been equal partners in a firm dealing in rugs and carpets. In 1958 they formed a company. The company took the business over. E and N were the first directors, although N's son soon became a third director. The company did not pay any dividends, but the profits were used as directors' remuneration. N and his son held a majority of votes at general meetings and removed E as a director of the company. E applied for the other directors to buy his shares or for the company to be wound up under what is now s.122 Insolvency Act 1986.

Held. The company should be wound up. The corporate veil was lifted and the company was treated as a partnership and wound up on the grounds that it would be just and equitable to do so.

COMMENT (i) It is not clear how the court's decision in this case has been affected by the introduction of the unfair prejudice remedy under s.459. It might be the case that s.459 provides the more appropriate remedy, even as regards quasi-partnership companies. A just and equitable winding up will not be ordered if there is a more appropriate remedy.
(ii) The Court of Appeal had refused to order a winding-up.
(iii) The case might have been differently decided if N and his son had offered to buy E's shares.

The winding up of a company on the grounds that it is just and equitable to do so is considered in slightly more detail in Chapter 19 at 19.1.1.2.

18.7.7 Company investigations

Officers of the Department of Trade and Industry have the power to inspect a company's documents. No publicity attaches to this. The Secretary of State also has the power to appoint inspectors (usually a senior accountant and a senior barrister) to investigate a company's affairs. This is a serious matter as the fact that inspectors have been appointed is publicly announced and the report produced is usually published.

Inspectors appointed to inspect a company's documents can inspect any form of information. Any person in possession of the documents who cannot claim privilege may be required to produce them, and this would include the company's bank being required to hand over details of the company bank account. Copies of any documents can be made and any company officer, past or present, can be asked to explain them. If the documents requested cannot be produced, the person required to produce them can be asked to state where they are. It is a criminal offence to knowingly or recklessly give any false explanation. It is not possible to refuse on the grounds of not wanting to give incriminating evidence against oneself, and any response can be used in evidence against its maker. It is an offence not to comply with an order to produce documents and a search warrant may be obtained to find documents. Destroying, mutilating or falsifying documents relating to the company's affairs is an offence. There is however a defence that the accused did not intend to conceal the company's affairs or defeat the law.

When inspectors are appointed by the Secretary of State, their function is to investigate the company's affairs and to inquire into them. It is not however a judicial role. The investigation is carried on in private but the inspectors produce a report which will usually be published. The company may itself request the investigation, as may the holders of at least 10% the company's issued share capital or any 200 shareholders. Those requesting the investigation may be required to pay for it and they must provide the Secretary of State with evidence showing that an investigation is required. The Secretary of State may himself decide that a company should be investigated on account of fraud or the company's members not being given all the evidence to which they are entitled. Investigations may be as to ownership or control of the company, directors' share dealings or insider dealing. An investigation may be extended to include inspecting a holding company or subsidiary company.

The Secretary of State may petition for the company to be wound up under the Insolvency Act 1986 on the grounds that this would be just and equitable. He may also sue in the company's name, apply for a disqualification order or make a petition under s.459 to relieve unfair prejudice. If any person is convicted of an offence he may have to pay the expenses of the investigation to the extent which the court orders.

18.8 · Loan capital

It is possible that the members of the company will contribute all the capital which the company needs. However, most companies also borrow money, either as a loan or by buying goods on credit. A trading company has an implied power to borrow money for purposes which are incidental to the company's business. Generally, an express power to borrow can also be found in the memorandum. A non-trading company will only be allowed to borrow if it has an express power to do so in the memorandum. Either an express or implied power to borrow carries with it a similar power to give security for the loan.

The articles usually provide that the board of directors shall exercise any power to borrow which the company has. However, any director might have actual authority to borrow or might be held out to have authority. If borrowing money is *ultra vires* then the effect of ss.35 and 35A would have to be considered. (See Chapter 17 at 17.1.8.) Although outsiders who lend money will not be affected by the company's lack of capacity to make the loan, the directors who authorise the loan might be personally liable if loss is caused to the company.

Providers of credit are likely to want security for the money they are owed. If the security is given by the company, rather than by the directors or shareholders, it is known as a debenture. Section 744 of the Act defines a debenture as including debenture stock, bonds and other securities of a company, whether constituting a charge on the company's assets or not. Debenture stocks raise money from a large number of lenders. Each of the lenders is invited to take a holding of a specified value in a large loan made to the company. There must be a trust deed which sets out the terms of the loan and which operates to protect the lenders. Public companies may also offer debentures to the public in a series. Generally, there is an express provision that all the debentures in the series rank equally, that is to say that none of them become payable before any others. If this is the case then any action brought by a debenture holder is regarded as a representative action brought on behalf of all the holders in the series. A bond is a bearer security of a nominal value which the company issues for cash, which is to be repaid on a certain date. Until that date the bond pays interest.

A company may purchase its own debentures and there is nothing to prevent debentures from being issued at a discount. Private companies are not allowed to offer debentures to the public. Debentures usually have a redemption date, on which the company is bound to repay the debenture. However, some debentures are perpetual. Debenture holders are not members of the company, they are creditors of it. There is nothing to prevent the interest on debentures from being paid out of capital if there is insufficient profit from which to pay it.

The person lending money to a company will want his debenture to be backed up by security. This is commonly provided by a personal guarantee made by a director or shareholder. The company itself can give security by granting a charge over some or all of the company's assets. If the debt is not repaid the lender will be able to sell the charged assets and take what is owed. Companies can give two types of charges; fixed charges and floating charges.

18.8.1 Fixed charges

A company can provide security for a loan by granting a fixed charge on certain assets. In effect this means then it mortgages those assets to the creditor (the debenture holder). Consequently, the company will not be able to dispose of, or change the nature of, the property charged without the permission of the debenture holder.

For example, A Co Ltd wants to borrow £120 000 from the bank. The bank lends the money but takes a fixed charge on the company's factory. As long as the company is repaying the loan as agreed it will retain possession of the factory and can use it in the ordinary way. The company cannot however sell the factory without the bank's permission. Furthermore, if the company fails to repay the debt the bank can sell the factory and deduct what it is owed from the proceeds of sale.

All charges must be registered with the company and with the Registrar of Companies, within 21 days after the date of its creation (s.395(1)). If a charge is not registered it will be invalid, although the debenture holder will still be able to sue as an unsecured creditor. If a fixed charge is properly created and properly registered its holder will take priority over any subsequent claims to the property charged. If, however, a fixed charge is stated to rank behind an existing floating charge, then it will not only rank behind that floating charge but also behind preferential creditors (*Re Portbase Clothing Ltd* [1993] 3 All ER 829).

Following the Privy Council decision in *Agnew* v *Commissioner of Inland Revenue (Re Brumarck Investments Ltd)* [2001] UKPC 28, a fixed charge cannot exist over book debts unless the debenture holder controls the realisation of the debts and requires them to be paid into a bank account which the company cannot access without the debenture holder's consent. In most cases this would be quite impractical, in which case what is stated to be a fixed charge over book debts will be regarded as a floating charge.

18.8.2 Floating charges

A company may grant more than one fixed charge on any particular asset.

Let us assume that a few years ago B Co Ltd borrowed £40 000 from the bank and granted a fixed charge over the company factory, currently worth £200 000. If the company now wanted to borrow a further £20 000 from a different creditor then that creditor would be quite happy to register a second fixed charge on the company factory. If the company does not repay its debts then the factory could be sold by the creditors. The bank would always be entitled to its £40 000 first because it was the first charge registered. But the sale of the factory would easily realise enough to repay the second charge holder.

If, however, there were no assets on which a fixed charge could be secured the creditor might be prepared to accept a floating charge. This means that the creditor would take a class of, or all of, the company's property, both present and future assets, as an equitable security. In *Re Yorkshire Woolcombers' Association Ltd* [1903] 2 Ch 284 Romer LJ said that a floating charge had the three following characteristics:

  (i) it is a charge on a class of assets of a company, both present and future;
 (ii) that class is one which, in the ordinary course of the company's business, would be changing from time to time; and
(iii) it is contemplated that, until some future step is taken by or on behalf of the chargeholder, the company may carry on business in the ordinary way as far as concerns the particular class of assets charged.

In *Buchler and another* v *Talbot and another* [2004] UKHL 9 Lord Nicholls described floating charges in the following way:

> 'They are a means whereby a financier, typically a bank, provides a company with money on the security of the company's assets which continue to be used and turned over in the ordinary course of business until, when certain events happen, the charge "crystallises" into a fixed charge on the assets then within its scope. Notable among crystalising events are the appointment of receivers by the charge holder or the company being wound up.'

A floating charge does not attach to any particular items of property until it crystallises, because it is recognised that the class of assets charged will change from time to time in the ordinary course of the company's business. It is also recognised that a floating charge does not prevent the company from selling the assets over which it is granted. It is particularly useful then when a company has a good deal of money tied up in raw materials, stock in trade or book debts.

In *Buchler* v *Talbot* Lord Nicholls explained the usefulness of floating charges in the following way:

'Over the years floating charges have played an invaluable role in the development of business. They bridge a gap between businessmen and financiers. Businessmen need money but may have insufficient fixed assets to offer as security. Financiers have money but want security for any loans they make. They wish to rank ahead of the company's unsecured creditors if the business does not prosper. They wish to minimise their risks by having a charge over whatever assets a company may acquire in the course of carrying on its trade. Floating charges have provided a legal mechanism by which in these circumstances capital and business enterprise can be harnessed. Typically, a floating charge extends to substantially all the assets of a company. On its face this gives a charge holder a high degree of control over the assets and fortunes of a company.'

A third party who acquires property which is the subject of a floating charge from the company takes it free of the charge. A fixed charge created on property which is already the subject of a floating charge will take precedence over the floating charge. (This is not the case if the floating charge has crystallised, because upon crystallisation it will have become a fixed charge on the assets charged.)

■ Example

Let us assume that C Co Ltd, which manufactures televisions, has already granted a fixed charge over all those assets, such as its factory and its company cars, which it does not need to sell. Let us further assume that the company has a warehouse stocked with televisions ready for sale, that it is owed money by various creditors and that it has a large stock of materials with which it makes the televisions. None of these remaining assets could be the subject of a fixed charge without crippling the company's activities. The company would not be able to sell the televisions already manufactured, or work the raw materials into televisions, without the permission of the fixed chargeholder. If such permission was granted the chargeholders would then lose their security.

But the finished televisions, the money owed and the raw materials are worth a great deal. A creditor might well therefore take a floating charge over these assets, secure in the knowledge that if the company did not repay him he could recoup his loan by calling in the charge, selling the assets charged, and deducting what he was owed from the proceeds.

The contract which created the floating charge would state that the company would only use the assets charged in its normal course of business, and that the company would not grant a fixed charge over any such assets.

If more than one floating charge is issued, the charges take priority in the order in which they were created. However, this is not the case if an earlier floating charge provides that the company may create a later floating charge to take priority over it. It would seem unlikely that many floating charges would provide this. A floating charge does not provide the cast-iron security of a fixed charge. It is up to the creditor to ensure that it provides adequate security for the loan. Like a fixed charge, a floating charge must be registered with the Registrar of Companies.

In Chapter 19, at 19.1.4.4, we shall see that in some circumstances floating charges created within two years of a company's insolvency can be invalid to the extent that the company did not receive a new benefit in consideration of creating the charge.

18.8.2.1 Rules applying to floating charges created on or after 15 September 2003

The Enterprise Act 2002 came into force on 15 September 2003. In respect of floating charges created on or after this date, the holder of the charge, a 'qualifying holder', does not have the power to appoint an administrative receiver of the company. Instead the chargeholder can appoint an administrator. Such an administrator will try to rescue the company as a going concern. Furthermore, a proportion of the assets which are subject to a qualifying floating charge may be 'top-sliced' or earmarked for distribution to unsecured creditors. The holders of fixed charges and holders of floating charges created before September 2003 still have the power to appoint an administrative receiver. In addition, none of the assets secured by such floating charge will be earmarked for distribution to the unsecured creditors. The effect of a company going into administration and the role of an administrative receiver are considered in Chapter 19 at 19.1.4.5. The top-slicing of assets for distribution to the unsecured creditors is considered in Chapter 19 at 19.1.3.

18.8.3 Crystallisation

A company can continue to sell assets over which a floating charge has been granted up until the time of 'crystallisation'. So in the example just considered, C Co Ltd could still sell the finished televisions even though they were the subject of a floating charge. But when crystallisation occurs the floating charge will become a fixed charge attaching to the assets of the company charged at that time. This, of course, will mean that the company is no longer free to dispose of the assets.

Crystallisation occurs automatically:

(a) When a receiver is appointed.
(b) When the company goes into liquidation.
(c) When the company ceases to carry on business.
(d) On the occurrence of an event which the contract stipulated would lead to automatic crystallisation. (The contract would have been made when the charge was created. It might, for example, state that if the company created another charge over the same class of assets then the first charge should crystallise. Or that it should crystallise if the assets charged are not kept in good repair, or if the stock of assets charged is run down below a certain level.)

Crystallisation may also occur when the debenture holder gives notice that he is converting the floating charge into a fixed charge. (This can only be done if the contract which created the charge allows for it.) If the assets which were the subject of the charge are sold after crystallisation then the chargeholder can recover them from the party to whom they were sold.

18.8.4 Registration of charges

Companies must register charges with the Registrar of Companies within 21 days of the creation of the charge. This registration is necessary so that others who might wish to do business with the company can see what charges exist over the company's property. Although registration confers notice that a charge exists, it does not amount to notice of the charge's terms and conditions. Any person may inspect the register of charges kept by the Registrar. It is possible for any person to register the charge with the Registrar and in practice the lender often registers the charge. If a charge is not registered within 21 days then both the company and any company officer who knowingly or wilfully authorised or permitted the failure to register it are guilty of an offence.

If a charge is not registered it is invalid against a liquidator or any person taking a subsequent charge. In addition the money lent becomes immediately repayable. Chargeholders are allowed to register charges themselves and claim the cost from the company. The details which must be registered set out: the name and number of the company; the date and description of the instrument which creates the charge; the name and addresses of the persons taking the charge; and brief details of the property charged.

The company must also keep a copy of the documents which created the charge, as well as a register of all the charges affecting its property. This register gives brief details of each charge. (The property charged, the amount of the charge and the person entitled to it.) Members and creditors can inspect this register free of charge, others may be charged up to 5p. If a charge is not entered on the company's register of charges the directors and secretary may be fined, but the charge will not be rendered invalid.

18.8.5 **Priority of charges**

As regards properly registered charges, the order of priority is as follows.

(i) A fixed charge has immediate effect from the moment it was created. It ranks higher than existing floating charges unless the floating charge expressly prohibits the creation of another charge over the same property and the person taking the later fixed charge knew that this was the case. (Registration is not enough on its own to amount to actual notice of the prohibition.)

(ii) Floating charges only attach to property from the moment of crystallisation.

(iii) Floating charges generally rank amongst themselves in order of priority of creation. This is not the case where the debenture securing the first floating charge provides that a later floating charge may have priority.

Preferential creditors (see Chapter 19 at 19.1.3), take priority over floating charges but not over fixed charges. A valid retention of title clause, even though not registered as a charge, can take effect in priority to a floating charge (see Chapter 9 at 9.2). A company cannot give a fixed charge over property which it has taken subject to an effective retention of title clause. The company does not own the property to which the clause relates, and cannot therefore grant a fixed charge over it.

Test your understanding

1 What are the two main aspects of the rule in *Foss* v *Harbottle*?

2 In what three ways can a member with a minority shareholding bring a common law action despite the rule?

3 What two statutory remedies are available to a minority member of a company?

4 What is the difference between a fixed and a floating charge?

5 What is meant by crystallisation of a floating charge?

Answers

1 The rule in *Foss* v *Harbottle* is to the effect that only the company can sue for a wrong done to the company and the court will not interfere with the internal management of a company acting within its powers.

2 The rule does not prevent a minority shareholder from bringing an action which alleges that his personal rights have been infringed, or which prevents the company from entering into an *ultra vires* contract, or which alleges fraud on the minority.

3 A member can claim unfair prejudice under ss.459–461 of the 1985 Act, or may petition for the winding up of the company under ss.122–124 of the Insolvency Act 1986.

4 A fixed charge is a mortgage over specific assets belonging to the company. The company may not therefore dispose of those assets once the charge has been created. A floating charge gives a lender security over a class of assets, but does not prevent the company from dealing with those assets in the course of its business.

5 When a floating charge crystallises it becomes a fixed charge on the assets charged.

Key points

Shares

■ A person becomes a member of a company either by subscribing to the memorandum and being entered in the register of members, or by agreeing to become a member and having his name entered in the register of members.

■ A share is a thing in action, conferring certain rights on its holder.

■ A company's articles may allow the company to have different classes of shares, with different rights attaching to the various classes.

- Preference shares usually have a cumulative right to a dividend which is expressed as a rate of interest per annum. They also usually have a right to be paid in full on dissolution of the company before ordinary shareholders are paid anything. They may or may not carry the same voting rights as the ordinary shares.

- A person acquires shares in a company by acquiring them from the company, or from an existing member or by transmission by operation of law.

- A public company will not be able to begin trading or borrow money until it has been issued with a s.117 certificate. Such a certificate will only be issued if the company has allotted at least £50 000 nominal share capital, at least a quarter of the nominal value of each share being paid up.

Meetings and resolutions

- Except in the case of private companies which have elected to dispense with holding AGMs, a company must hold an AGM every calendar year.

- Members with at least 5% of the voting rights entitled to vote at the meeting can requisition the company to put forward a resolution at the AGM.

- Members holding at least 10% of a company's paid-up share capital with voting rights can requisition the directors to call an EGM. Otherwise it is the directors who choose to call an EGM.

- A minimum of 21 days' notice of an AGM must be given to company members. The minimum period of notice of an EGM is 14 days, unless a special resolution is to be proposed. (In which case 21 days' notice is required.)

- A proxy is a person empowered by a company member to attend a meeting and vote on behalf of that member.

- A company meeting can only commence if it is quorate. Unless the articles provide otherwise the quorum will be two members, although in a single member company the sole member constitutes a quorum.

- An ordinary resolution is passed by a simple majority of company members who vote on the resolution.

- Special and extraordinary resolutions are only passed if 75% of the votes cast are in favour.

- Ordinary resolutions do not need to be registered with the Registrar, but special, extraordinary and elective resolutions do.

- The members of a private company may pass elective resolutions: to dispense with laying accounts before a general meeting; to dispense with holding AGMs; to dispense with the annual appointment of auditors; to give directors the power to allot shares for more than a five-year period; and to reduce the majority needed to approve short notice of an EGM to 90%.

- Private companies can pass written resolutions by all of the company members signing the resolution.

Legal effect of the articles and memorandum

- A company's articles form a contract between the company and every member and between every member and every other member. However, this is only true to the extent that the members are acting in their capacity as members.

- Subject to the 1985 Act and the memorandum, a company may always alter its articles by special resolution.

- A company can reduce its capital by following the procedure set out in s.135 of the Act. The articles must allow for the reduction, a special resolution must authorise it and court must approve it.

- Dividends are payable out of profits. They must not be paid out of capital.

■ Public companies may make a market purchase of their own shares or an off-market purchase. Private companies can make an off-market purchase.

■ The three offences relating to insider dealing are:
(a) dealing in price-affected securities in relation to inside information;
(b) encouraging others to do this;
(c) disclosing the information to others.

Minority protection

■ The rule in *Foss* v *Harbottle* provides that only a company can sue in respect of a wrong done to that company and that the court will not interfere with the internal management of a company acting within its powers.

■ Despite the rule, a member of a company can sue if his personal rights are infringed, or to prevent the company from entering into an *ultra vires* transaction, or if there has been a fraud on the minority.

■ The 1985 Act allows any member to sue for unfair prejudice. The Insolvency Act 1986 allows any member to petition for the winding up of the company on the grounds that it would be just and equitable to do so.

Fixed and floating charges

■ A fixed charge is a mortgage over specific assets of the company, and therefore prevents the company from disposing of the assets charged.

■ A floating charge is a security given over a class of assets. It does not prevent the company from disposing of those assets in the ordinary course of its business.

■ Once a floating charge crystallises it become a fixed charge on the specific assets of the class of property charged.

Summary questions

1 Compare the rights which usually attach to ordinary shares to those which usually attach to preference shares. Are preference shares more similar to ordinary shares than they are to debentures?

2 Len and his sister Elaine each own 27.5% of the shares in a company which has adopted Table A articles. The company has passed an elective resolution to dispense with annual general meetings. Their brother David owns 45% of the shares and is the sole director. The company made a reasonable profit this year. Len and Elaine believe that this profit should be paid as a dividend. David refuses to recommend a dividend, insisting that the profits should be invested in the company. Advise Len and Elaine as to any powers they might have to force the payment of a dividend.

3 Acme Ltd has five shareholders, Alice, Bertha, Carol, Dinah and Elizabeth, all of whom own 20% of the shares in a private company which has adopted Table A articles. All of the shares are fully paid up. Alice and Bertha are the only two directors. Carol is the company secretary. Carol wants to see the articles altered so that shareholders can sell their shares only to the company. Dinah, who is much older than the others, is very much opposed to this. Alice, Bertha and Elizabeth are open to persuasion on the matter.

a Explain what support Carol will need in order to achieve the change.

b Assuming that the necessary support will be gained, explain how much notice of the meeting at which the resolutions making the changes are proposed must be given, and how the voting will take place.

c Explain any formalities which would have to be complied with if the articles were changed in the way which Carol would like them to be changed.

4 Elizabeth wants to call an EGM of Acme Ltd to propose a resolution to dismiss Alice as a director. Both Alice and Bertha are opposed to this. Advise Elizabeth as to:

a Any means by which she can insist that an EGM is called.

b Any means by which she can ensure that a resolution proposing Alice's dismissal is put to the members.

c The support which she will need to dismiss Alice as a director. (Assuming that a meeting is held and that the resolution is proposed.)

5 Ace Ltd has three directors, A, B and C. Each of the directors own 25% of the company's share capital. D owns the other 25%. The directors have discovered that D has been operating a business which competes with Ace Ltd. They therefore want to change the articles to include an article as follows. 'Any shareholder who carries on a business competing with that of the company may be required by the directors to sell his shares to the directors at a fair price.'
Explain the steps which would need to be taken for the articles to be changed. Explain also whether D would have any right to object to the change.

6 For several years John and Jack were the sole partners in a successful building firm. Ten years ago they formed a limited company. John and Jack were the only two directors. The company had an authorised share capital of 100 £1 ordinary shares, and Jack and John each took 50 of these. Two years ago Jack's son, Alan, was appointed a director of the company and Jack and John each transferred ten shares to Alan.
Last year John discovered that the company had sold building materials to another company in which Jack and Alan are the only shareholders. John brought this matter up at a board meeting. Since this time Alan and Jack have passed two ordinary resolutions. The first removed John as a director. The second ratified the sale of the building materials.
Advise John of any rights which he might have.

7 The firm in which you work is considering lending a large sum of money to Acme Ltd. Acme Ltd is proposing to give a charge over some of its assets as security for the loan. Your employer has asked you to draft a report, dealing briefly with the following matters.

a The nature of a fixed charge.

b The nature of a floating charge.

c The meaning of crystallisation of a floating charge.

d The measures which should be taken to ensure that Acme's assets are not already the subject of an existing charge.

e The steps which should be taken to ensure that the charge granted by Acme Ltd gives adequate security for the loan.

Multiple choice questions

1 Which **one** of the following statements is **not** true?

a A company which converts from being a private company to a public company cannot begin trading until a s.117 certificate has been issued.

b A public company may not accept promises to work or perform services in return for issuing shares.

c If preference shares have a right to have their capital repaid ahead of ordinary shareholders, on dissolution of the company, they do not have a right to share in the surplus assets after dissolution.

d Preference shares will carry a right to vote in the absence of agreement to the contrary.

2 Acme Ltd held its last AGM on 10 October 2003. Assuming that the company has not elected to dispense with next year's AGM, what is the latest date on which it could be held?

a 10 October 2004.

b 31 December 2004.

c 10 January 2005.

d 10 October 2005.

3   Which of the following statements are true?

    i   A written resolution, signed by all the members of a company, cannot be undone by a later resolution which is not unanimous.

    ii   A public company cannot use the written resolution procedure.

    iii   A private company can only use the written resolution procedure if all the members who would be entitled to vote on the resolution at a meeting sign the resolution.

    iv   A written resolution cannot be used to effect a matter which would ordinarily require a special or extraordinary resolution.

    a   i, ii and iv only.

    b   i and iv only.

    c   ii, iii and iv only.

    d   ii and iii only.

4   Which **one** of the following statements is **not** true?

    a   A company's articles create a contract between the company and a member, in his capacity as a member.

    b   A company's articles cannot provide that the articles are unalterable.

    c   If the rights attaching to a class of shares are altered, a dissentient minority of at least 15% of the holders of the shares in question can apply to the court to have the alteration cancelled, as long as they did not vote in favour of the alteration.

    d   It is never lawful for a company to deliberately reduce its own capital.

5   Which **one** of the following statements is **not** true?

    a   Authority for a market purchase of a company's own shares must be given by ordinary resolution of the members.

    b   Authority for an off-market purchase of a company's own shares must be given by special resolution of the members.

    c   Authority to make an off-market purchase of shares can be renewed, varied or revoked by ordinary resolution.

    d   Neither a market nor an off-market purchase of a company's own shares is allowed unless the company's articles permit it, and the shares purchased must be cancelled.

6   Which **one** of the following statements is true?

    a   A person can only be guilty of insider dealing if he deals in price-affected securities.

    b   Information can only be inside information, for the purposes of insider dealing, if it is specific or precise.

    c   Information which a person receives indirectly cannot be inside information, for the purposes of insider dealing.

    d   It is a defence to a charge of insider dealing that no profit resulted from the dealing.

7   Which **one** of the following statements is **not** true?

    a   Negligence cannot generally amount to a fraud on the minority, but a minority shareholder may sue if the negligence conferred a benefit on those who controlled the company and committed the negligent act.

    b   Once inspectors have been appointed by the Secretary of State, it is a criminal offence, to which there is no defence, to destroy company documents.

    c   The personal representative of a deceased company member can bring an action alleging unfair prejudice under s.459 of the Act.

    d   Any shareholder may petition the court to wind a company up, under s.122 Insolvency Act 1986, no matter how small the size of his shareholding.

8   Which **one** of the following statements is **not** true?

    a   If a fixed charge is granted over an asset then the company will not be able to dispose of that asset, even in the ordinary course of its business.

b If a floating charge is granted over a class of a company assets, then even assets subsequently acquired by the company would be charged if they were within the class of assets charged.

c When a floating charge crystallises, it will become a fixed charge attaching to the assets charged at the time of crystallisation.

d As soon as an asset becomes the subject of a fixed or floating charge, a third party who acquires the asset will always do so subject to the rights of the chargeholder.

Task 18

A friend of yours has for many years carried on an unincorporated business as a carpet fitter. Your friend is considering forming a limited company in conjunction with three other carpet fitters. He has asked you to draw up a report, explaining briefly the following matters.

a The nature of shares and the difference between ordinary and preference shares.

b How company resolutions are passed, and the matters for which resolutions are required.

c The legal effect of a company memorandum and articles of association.

d What is meant by the rule in *Foss* v *Harbottle*, and the way in which the courts and statutes protect minority shareholders.

e The extent to which a company charge provides a creditor with security, and the steps which should be taken by both the company and the creditor when a charge is issued.

Chapter 19

WINDING UP OF COMPANIES · LIMITED LIABILITY PARTNERSHIPS · BENEFITS OF TRADING AS A COMPANY, PARTNERSHIP OR LIMITED LIABILITY PARTNERSHIP

Introduction

There are seven grounds upon which a court can order the compulsory winding up of a company, if petitioned to do so. Alternatively, the members of the company may resolve to wind the company up voluntarily. Such a voluntary winding up could either be a members' voluntary winding up or a creditors' voluntary winding up. We begin this chapter by considering these different processes by which a company can be wound up, and then set out the order in which creditors of liquidated companies are paid. We conclude our study of company liquidation with an outline of certain types of liability which can arise as a consequence of insolvency.

Having completed our study of company law, we then consider the law relating to limited liability partnerships. We consider the nature of LLPs, how they are formed, how members join and leave, the members' relationship with each other, minority protection and winding up.

Having considered the law relating to LLPs, we will then be in a position to consider the advantages and disadvantages of trading as a company, an LLP or a partnership, while referring to matters of law previously covered.

Although the preferred trading medium will depend upon the nature and circumstances of any particular business, it is possible to discern certain advantages and disadvantages of trading either as a company, an LLP or as a partnership.

19.1 · Winding up of companies

We have already seen that companies have a legal personality of their own. We have also seen that a company's personality is artificially created, by the process of registration with the Registrar of Companies. The legal personality of a company ceases to exist in an artificial way, when the company is liquidated or wound up. (Liquidation and winding up mean the same thing; that the company ceases to exist as a commercial entity. After liquidation the company is dissolved and it then ceases to exist as a legal entity.) A company liquidation may be brought about by one of two legal processes. Either the court may order a compulsory liquidation of a company, or the members of the company may resolve to voluntarily wind the company up. If the members resolve to wind up a company which is not solvent the liquidation is known as a creditors' voluntary winding up.

19.1.1 Liquidation by court order

Section 122(1) of the Insolvency Act 1986 lists seven grounds for compulsory liquidation of a company. These grounds are that:

(a) The company has by special resolution resolved that the company be wound up by the court.
(b) The company is a public company which has not been issued with a s.117 certificate and more than a year has passed since the company was registered.
(c) The company is an old public company which had not re-registered as a public or private company by March 1982.
(d) The company does not commence its business within a year of its incorporation or suspends its business for a whole year.
(e) The number of members in a public company falls below two.
(f) The company is unable to pay its debts.
(g) The court is of the opinion that it is just and equitable that the company should be wound up.

The first five of these grounds are essentially straightforward matters of fact. The final two need to be considered in a little detail.

19.1.1.1 The company cannot pay its debts

Either the company itself, the directors, a shareholder or a creditor of the company may petition the court to wind a company up on the grounds that the company cannot pay its debts. In practice such a petition is likely to be made by a creditor.

Section 123(1) of the Insolvency Act states that a company is deemed unable to pay its debts if:

(a) A creditor to whom the company owes more than £750 has served a written demand for payment on the company, by leaving it at the company's registered office, and, three weeks later, the company has neither paid nor given the creditor a security which he finds acceptable; or
(b) Execution issued on a court judgment in favour of a creditor of the company is returned un-satisfied in whole or in part; or
(c) It is proved to the satisfaction of the court that the company is unable to pay its debts as they fall due. Section 123(2) states that a company is deemed unable to pay its debts if it is proved to the satisfaction of the court that the value of the company's assets is less than the amount of its liabilities. In making this assessment the court also considers possible liabilities which may arise in the future.

The court does not have to wind the company up, even if it is satisfied that the company cannot pay its debts. If, however, the court does order a winding up then a liquidator is appointed. The liquidator will collect assets owing to the company, sell the assets off, and then distribute the proceeds amongst the creditors according to the specified order. If any surplus did happen to be generated it would be distributed amongst the company members. As regards all matters relating to the winding up of a company, s.195 of the Insolvency Act gives the court the power to call a meeting of creditors and contributories, if it thinks fit, for the purpose of ascertaining their wishes. (Contributories are liable to contribute to the company's assets when the company is wound up.) Regard is had to the value of each of the creditor's debts and the number of votes conferred on each contributory. If the company is insolvent then only the views of the creditors are considered.

19.1.1.2 The court is of the opinion that it is just and equitable to wind the company up

We shall see that a company may initiate a voluntary winding up by passing a special or an extraordinary resolution that the company should be wound up. Also, as we have seen, the company may pass a special resolution that the company be compulsorily wound up by the court. In order for a special or extraordinary resolution to be passed, three-quarters of the votes cast would have to be in favour of the resolution. A petition to wind the company up on the ground that it would be just and equitable to do so can be used by members with insufficient votes to ensure that a special resolution is passed. Even a single member of a company may petition the court to wind the company up on this ground. The petition might alternatively be presented by the company, by the directors, or by a creditor.

In considering whether it would be just and equitable to wind a company up the court has enormous discretion. Whether or not it is just and equitable to wind the company up is a question of fact, each case depending upon its own circumstances. It is, however, a serious matter to wind up a company which is trading successfully and the courts are reluctant to take such a step. The person petitioning the court for the winding up must have some tangible interest in this happening. A member whose shares are all fully paid up could not have such an interest unless there would be surplus assets available for distribution among the members after the dissolution. As long as the petitioner is acting reasonably, the court can order the winding up even though other remedies (such as relief under s.459 of the 1985 Act) are available to the petitioner. Over the years the courts have wound companies up on the following grounds, amongst others.

(a) That the substratum of the company has failed

The substratum of a company will be regarded as having failed if the main object for which the company was formed fails for some reason. A company's main object is usually to be found in the first clause of its objects clause, or in the first few clauses if these are closely related. If there is a main object, which indicates a distinct purpose which is the foundation of the company, other clauses which are unrelated may be regarded as ancillary to the main purpose. If that main purpose cannot be achieved, the substratum of the company may have failed.

■ *Re German Date Coffee Co* (1882) 20 ChD 169 (Court of Appeal)

The company's objects clause had eight articles. The first of these was to acquire a patent on an invention to turn dates into a coffee substitute. The next five articles all concerned exploitation of the patented invention. The seventh article was to acquire patents on similar inventions. The eighth article was more general, allowing importing and exporting of food generally and buying or leasing the means to do this. The founders of the company were sure that they would be granted the necessary patent. In fact the patent was not granted to them.

Held. It was just and equitable to wind the company up as the company substratum had failed.

These days a company's substratum is much less likely to fail. The objects clauses of most companies tend to be very broad indeed, perhaps in recognition that the company might change its line of business. As Lord Greene put it, in *Re Kitson and Co Ltd* [1946] 1 All ER 435: '... a business is a thing which changes. It grows or it contracts. It changes; it disposes of the whole of its plant; it moves its factory; it entirely changes its range of products, and so forth. It is more like an organic thing.'

It is also now possible, as we saw in Chapter 16, that a company can register its objects as to carry on business as a general company. If this is done then the substratum cannot disappear. In *Cotman* v *Brougham* [1918] AC 514 the House of Lords accepted that a statement in the objects clause to the effect that each sub-clause in the objects should be construed as a separate object, independent of the other clauses, was valid as far as the *ultra vires* rule was concerned. However, such a clause might not prevent the company substratum from having failed. Lord Parker said 'The question whether or not a company can be wound up for failure of substratum is a question of equity between a company and its shareholders. The question whether or not a transaction is *ultra vires* is a question of law between the company and a third party.'

(b) Where there is deadlock in the management of a small company

A court may consider it just and equitable to wind a small company up if the management of the company has reached deadlock and is unable to make decisions. An example of such a winding up is *Re Yenidje Tobacco Co Ltd* [1916] 2 Ch 426. In that case Cozens Hardy MR said: 'In those circumstances, supposing it had been a private partnership, an ordinary partnership between two people having equal shares, and there being no other provisions to terminate it, what would have been the position? ... All that is necessary is to satisfy the Court that it is impossible for the partners to place the confidence in each other which each has a right to expect, and that such impossibility has not been caused by the person seeking to take advantage of it ... I think that in a case like this we are bound to say that circumstances which would justify the winding up of a partnership between these two ... are circumstances which should induce the Court to exercise its jurisdiction under the just and equitable clause and to wind up the company.'

If the company is a quasi-partnership then it may be just and equitable to wind the company up where one faction excludes another faction from any management of the company. An example was seen in the previous chapter in *Ebrahimi* v *Westbourne Galleries* [1972] 2 All ER 492.

(c) Where there is a justifiable lack of confidence in the management

In order to justify a winding up on this ground the lack of confidence held by the petitioner must be due to a lack of probity (integrity) in the conduct of the company's affairs. This lack of probity must relate to business matters, rather than to personal matters, and must amount to more than merely being outvoted.

In the previous chapter we saw an example of lack of probity in the management of the company's affairs which was sufficient to justify winding up in *Loch* v *John Blackwood* [1924] AC 783. In that case Lord Shaw said: 'The lack of confidence must spring not from dissatisfaction at being outvoted on the business affairs or on what is called the domestic policy of the company. On the other hand, wherever the lack of confidence is rested on a lack of probity in the conduct of the company's affairs, then the former is justified by the latter, and it is under the statute just and equitable that the company should be wound up.'

(d) Where the company was formed for a fraudulent purpose

If a company is formed for an entirely fraudulent purpose then it will be just and equitable to wind the company up.

■ *Re Thomas Edward Brinsmead and Sons* [1897] 1 Ch 45 (Court of Appeal)

John Brinsmead and Sons were a well-known firm of piano manufacturers. Three of their former employees, all named Brinsmead, formed the company in question, intending to pass their pianos off as having been produced by the well established firm. An injunction was granted, preventing the company from the passing off, but the public had already subscribed for a large number of shares in the company.

Held. It was just and equitable to wind the company up as this would enable members of the public to get their money back.

19.1.1.3 The petition

Section 124(1) of the Insolvency Act states that a petition for the court to wind the company up may be presented to the court by any of the following:

(a) The company itself.
(b) The directors of the company.
(c) Any creditor of the company (including prospective creditors).
(d) Any contributory (person who might have to contribute when the company is liquidated). Current shareholders are regarded as contributories, even if their shares are fully paid up.

(e) The Secretary of State for Trade and Industry, but only if the reason for the winding up is that the company is a public company which has failed to be issued with a s.117 certificate within one year of its incorporation.

(f) The Official Receiver, if the court is satisfied that a voluntary winding up cannot be continued with due regard to the interests of the creditors or contributories.

Although any of these petitioners may petition the court, in practice it is likely to be a creditor or a contributory who does so. The court may or may not make a winding up order. It may also order the Official Receiver to take over the company's affairs immediately. The court is likely to do this if it considers that the directors might try to dissipate the company's assets.

19.1.1.4 Winding up order

The court does not have to order the company to be wound up, even if a creditor does present a petition showing that he is owed more than £750. If other creditors think that their best chance of being paid lies in allowing the company to continue trading then the court may allow this. Usually, the court will only allow this if the creditors who want to allow the company to continue trading are owed the majority of the money which the company owes. Ultimately, however, the decision is for the court which has a discretion to order the winding up or not.

If the court does order the company to be wound up, the liquidation is deemed to have taken effect from the date when the petition to wind the company up was presented to the court. The Official Receiver becomes the liquidator until another is appointed.

After a winding up order has been made the following rules apply:

(a) Any disposition of the company's property, and any transfer of shares, or alteration of the status of the company members, made after the commencement of the winding up is void, unless authorised by the court (Insolvency Act s.127).

(b) All actions in debt against the company are stopped. If any of the company's assets are seized to satisfy a debt such a seizure will be void (Insolvency Act ss.128 and 130).

(c) The directors' powers cease and are taken over by the liquidator.

(d) The company's employees are dismissed, although the liquidator can re-employ them until the winding up is completed.

(e) Floating charges crystallise.

(f) The business may still be carried on by the liquidator, but only to try to effect the most beneficial realisation of the company's assets.

The liquidator's powers to re-employ the workers and carry on the business are useful in a variety of circumstances, such as where the company has a stock of relatively worthless raw materials which could quickly be manufactured into products of some value.

When a winding up order is made a copy is sent to the Registrar of Companies. He publishes notice of having received the order in the *London Gazette*.

Once the court has made a winding up order, s.131 of the Insolvency Act allows the Official Receiver to require that a statement of the company's affairs is made. The statement would give particulars of the company's assets, debts and liabilities, the names and addresses of the company's creditors, the securities held by the respective creditors, the dates on which the securities were given and such further information as the Official Receiver might require. The statement can be required of past and present company officers, of the promoters if the company was formed within the previous year, and of employees who the Official Receiver thinks might be able to give the information. If another company is an officer of the company which is wound up, those who are similarly connected with the other company can be required to make the statement.

Section 132 of the Insolvency Act provides that where a winding up order is made by the court it is the duty of the Official Receiver to investigate: (a) the causes of failure if the company has failed; and (b) the promotion, formation, business, dealings and affairs of the company generally, and to make such report (if any) to the court as he sees fit. In any proceedings such a report is *prima facie* evidence of the facts stated in it.

Where the court orders a company to be wound up s.133 of the Insolvency Act gives the Official Receiver the power to conduct a public examination of past and present officers of the company or of a person who has taken part in the promotion, formation or management of the company. The examination is as to that person's role in the promotion, formation or management of the company or as to the conduct of its business and affairs, or his conduct or dealings in relation to the company.

19.1.2 Voluntary liquidation

There are two types of voluntary liquidations; members' voluntary liquidations and creditors' voluntary liquidations. A company will need to pass a resolution to initiate either type of voluntary winding up, and notice of this resolution must be published in the *Gazette* within 14 days of its being passed.

19.1.2.1 Members' voluntary liquidation

Companies are often wound up when they are solvent. The shareholders might decide that they would rather end the company and share out its assets than continue to own it. A company which can pay its debts can be liquidated by a members' voluntary winding up if the members pass a special resolution that it should be. (A special resolution will be passed if 75% of members at a company meeting vote in favour of it.) In a members' voluntary winding up the liquidator is appointed by the company in general meeting.

Section 89 of the Insolvency Act says that to effect a members' voluntary winding up the directors (or a majority of them if there are more than two) must make a declaration of solvency within the five weeks before the date on which the resolution to wind the company up is passed.

This declaration of solvency will state that the directors have made a full enquiry into the company's affairs and that, having done so, they have formed the opinion that the company will be able to pay its debts in full, together with interest, within a period specified in the statement (which must not exceed 12 months from the commencement of the winding up). The directors must also attach a statement of liabilities and assets to the declaration, at the latest practicable date before the making of the declaration. The declaration must be delivered to the Registrar of Companies within 15 days of the passing of the resolution to wind the company up, as must a copy of the resolution itself. If any director makes the statement without reasonable grounds he will commit a criminal offence and be liable to a fine and imprisonment. Section 95 of the Insolvency Act provides that where the liquidator is of the opinion that the company will be unable to pay its debts in full (together with interest at the official rate) within the period stated in the directors' declaration of solvency he shall summon a meeting of creditors within 28 days of forming that opinion. The effect of this is to cause the winding up to proceed as a creditors' voluntary winding up.

As soon as a members' voluntary winding up is completed the liquidator has to make up an account of the winding up, showing how it has been conducted and how the company's property has been disposed of. He must then call a general meeting of the company to lay the account before the meeting and to give an explanation of it.

19.1.2.2 Creditors' voluntary liquidation

This is the method by which the members voluntarily wind a company up when the directors are unable to make a declaration of solvency. The company must pass an extraordinary resolution to wind the company up and then, within 14 days, they must call a meeting of creditors. An extraordinary resolution, like a special resolution, needs the vote of 75% of members voting at a company meeting. The difference between the two is the amount of notice of the resolution which needs to be given. A special resolution needs 21 days' notice, an extraordinary resolution can be called with a shorter period of notice. An extraordinary resolution is more appropriate for a creditors' voluntary liquidation because, as the company cannot pay its debts, delay should be kept to a minimum. A copy of the resolution must be sent to the Registrar of Companies within 15 days.

In addition to calling a meeting of creditors the company must post notice of the meeting to all creditors at least seven days before the meeting is to be held. Notice of the meeting must also be advertised in the *Gazette* and at least once in two newspapers circulating in the locality in which the company's principal place of business is situated.

The creditors have the choice of who the liquidator should be and fix his renumeration. If they wish to do so, they can approve one nominated by the members of the company at the meeting at which the resolution to wind the company up was proposed.

At their meeting the creditors can appoint a committee of inspection. This will contain no more than five members. This committee does not have all the powers of the liquidator but can make recommendations, such as to pay a particular class of creditors in full. The liquidator can then act on these recommendations without calling a full meeting of all the creditors.

The directors have to lay a statement of affairs before the creditors. This statement of affairs contains the same information as that which can be required by the Official Receiver under s.131 of the Insolvency Act.

As soon as the company's affairs are fully wound up, the liquidator is required to make up an account of the winding up. This shows how the winding up has been conducted and how the company's property has been disposed of. The liquidator must also call a meeting of the members and the creditors to lay the account before the meeting and to give an explanation of it.

19.1.2.3 Consequences of a voluntary winding up

From the time when the resolution to wind the company up is passed, a voluntary winding up has the following consequences:

(1) The company must cease trading immediately, except in so far as may be required for a beneficial winding up.
(2) Shares cannot be transferred without the liquidator's consent, and any alteration in the status of the members is void.
(3) If the company is insolvent its employees are automatically dismissed, although the liquidator has the power to re-employ them.
(4) The directors' powers cease to exist as soon as a liquidator is appointed or nominated, except in so far as the liquidation committee (or, if there is no such committee, the creditors) sanction their continuance. Before that time the directors may take such actions as are necessary to protect the company's assets and to dispose of perishable goods.

19.1.2.4 The liquidator

Only a person who is a qualified insolvency practitioner may act as a company liquidator. The liquidator's function is to collect the assets of the company and to distribute the value of these to the company's creditors and members, according to the statutory order for payment. In order to achieve these ends, a liquidator is given the following powers by ss.165–167 of the Insolvency Act.

(1) To pay any class of creditors in full.
(2) To enter into compromises or arrangements with creditors of the company.
(3) To enter into compromises as regards debts owed to the company, and claims of the company.

(4) To defend or bring any action or other legal proceedings in the name of, and on behalf of, the company.
(5) To carry on the business of the company so far as may be necessary for its beneficial winding up.
(6) To sell any of the company's property by public auction or by private contract.
(7) To do all acts in the name of and on behalf of the company, including executing deeds, receipts and other documents, using the company seal where necessary.
(8) To draw and indorse cheques and other bills of exchange in the name of, and on behalf of, the company.
(9) To raise money by giving the company's assets as security.
(10) To appoint an agent to do business which the liquidator is himself unable to do.
(11) To do all such things as may be necessary for winding up the company's affairs and distributing its assets.

In a voluntary winding up the first three of these powers may only be exercised by the liquidator if they are sanctioned: (a) in the case of a members' voluntary winding up, by an extraordinary resolution of the company; or (b) in the case of a creditors' voluntary winding up, with the sanction of the court or the liquidation committee or (if there is no liquidation committee) a meeting of the company's creditors. The other powers may be exercised without sanction in either type of voluntary winding up. In a winding up by the court the first five powers may only be exercised with the sanction of the court or the liquidation committee. The sixth to eleventh powers may be exercised without any sanction.

Section 178 of the Insolvency Act gives the liquidator the power to disclaim onerous property. This means that he can release the company from any obligation under an unprofitable contract and disclaim any company property which is unsaleable or which might give rise to a liability to pay money or incur other expenses. A person who incurs loss as a consequence can claim against the company as an unsecured creditor.

19.1.3 Distribution of the company's assets

The order in which the company's assets are distributed is the same whether the winding up is compulsory or voluntary. However, there are now two regimes in place: those which are subject to the amendments made by the Enterprise Act 2002 and those which are not. As regards both of these regimes the order in which assets are distributed has been significantly altered by the House of Lords decision in *Buchler and another v Talbot and another* [2004] UKHL 9. This decision unanimously overruled *Re Barleycorn Enterprises Ltd* [1970] Ch 465 to hold that when a company is wound up the general costs and expenses of winding up cannot be paid out of assets comprised in a crystallised floating charge in priority to the claims of the charge holder. However, the costs and expenses of realising the floating charge are to be recouped by an administrative receiver in priority to the claims of the charge holder.

When a company is wound up a creditor with a fixed charge will have the right to sell the assets over which he has the charge. The proceeds of the sale will go to the charge holder rather than into the pool of assets, but only to the extent that this is necessary to pay the charge holder what he is owed. Any excess money which is realised goes into the pool of assets. Charges were dealt with in some detail in Chapter 18 at 18.8. We saw that a person with a fixed charge lends money to the company and takes a charge (a mortgage) over specific company assets. If the loan is not repaid the charge holder is entitled to sell those assets and take what he is owed, but only what he is owed, from the proceeds. If the sale of the assets does not yield enough money to pay his debt in full, the holder of a fixed charge can take the amount which is generated and then claim for the rest as an unsecured creditor.

After the holders of fixed charges have called them in, the Insolvency Act sets out the order in which payment must be made. If some or all of the company's assets are subject to a floating charge, the order differs depending upon whether the charge was created before or after 15 September 2003. The order of priority is of significance only where there are insufficient assets to pay all of the creditors in full. In such cases the company has usually granted a floating charge over all of its assets which are not the subject of a fixed charge. If the floating charge was created before 15 September 2003 the charge holder still has the power to appoint an administrative receiver and the charge is not subject to 'top slicing' (see below at 19.1.3.1). As regards insolvencies occurring in the next few years, it is likely that the majority of floating charges will have been created before 15 September 2003.

In *Buchler* v *Talbot* the House of Lords made it clear that when the floating charge holder appoints a receiver to realise the charged assets and the company then goes into liquidation, there will then be two funds available for distribution. First, the fund comprising the assets which were subject to the floating charge, this fund being dealt with by the receiver. Second the fund comprising the other, 'free', assets, this fund being dealt with by the liquidator. If the assets which were subject to the floating charge realise enough money to pay the floating charge holders (and those above them) in full, any surplus will become part of the free assets.

As regards companies where a floating charge was created before 15 September 2003 the order of payment is as follows.

(a) Payments from the assets subject to a floating charge
    (i)   The costs of preserving and realising these assets.
    (ii) The receiver's remuneration and expenses.
    (iii) The preferential creditors at the date when the company went into receivership. (The types of creditors who are preferential are listed below at 19.1.3.2.)
    (iv) The amount owed to the floating charge holder (including interest).
    (v)   The company.

(b) Payments from the company's free assets
    (i)   The costs of preserving and realising these assets.
    (ii)   The liquidator's remuneration and the costs and expenses of winding up.
    (iii) The preferential creditors at the time of winding up.
    (iv)   The holder of a floating charge (who has not yet been fully paid) can recover any amount which was paid to the preferential creditors out of assets subject to the floating charge.
    (v)   The unsecured creditors.
    (vi)   Sums due to members but not yet paid. For example, dividends declared but not yet paid.
    (vii) The members of the company, as set out in the memorandum and articles of association.

As regards companies where a floating charge was created on or after 15 September 2003 the order of payment is as follows.

(a) Payments from the assets subject to a floating charge
    (i)   The costs of preserving and realising these assets.
    (ii)   The receiver's remuneration and expenses.
    (iii) The preferential creditors at the date when the company went into receivership.
    (iv)   Top-sliced assets for distribution to the unsecured creditors (see below at 19.1.3.1).
    (v)   The amount owed to the floating charge holder (including interest).
    (vi)   The company.

(b) Payments from the company's free assets
    (i)   The costs of preserving and realising these assets.
    (ii)   The liquidator's remuneration and the costs and expenses of winding up.
    (iii) The preferential creditors at the date of winding up.
    (iv)   The charge holder (who has not yet been fully paid) can recover any amount which was paid to the preferential creditors out of assets subject to the floating charge.

   (v) The unsecured creditors.

  (vi) Sums due to members but not yet paid. For example, dividends declared but not yet paid.

 (vii) The members of the company, as set out in the memorandum and articles of association.

As regards floating charges created on or after 15 September 2003, floating charge holders will lose the right to appoint an administrative receiver but will have the power to appoint an administrator. The administrator will generally realise the floating charge. There will still be two funds and the charge holder will have no liability for the general costs of winding up.

It may be that the costs of preserving and realising the assets comprised in a floating charge are incurred by the liquidator, rather than by an administrative receiver. If this is the case, the liquidator may take the costs and expenses of preserving and realising the charged assets ahead of the charge holder. However, the general costs of winding up cannot be taken out of the funds generated by the charged assets. These costs can be paid only out of the free assets. The charge holder will have no liability for the general costs of winding up. So if no receiver is appointed and the liquidator both realises the floating charge and winds the company up, the order of priority is as follows.

(i)   The costs of preserving and realising the assets which are subject to the floating charge.

(ii)   The preferential creditors to the extent that these cannot be paid out of the free assets.

(iii)   Top sliced fund for unsecured creditors (but only charges created after 15 September 2003 are subject to such top slicing).

(iv)   The amount owing to the floating charge holder (including interest).

(v)   Liquidation expenses other than the costs of preserving and realising charged assets (These expenses can be paid only out of free assets. If the charged assets realised more than enough to pay the floating charge holder what he was owed, any surplus becomes part of the free assets).

(vi)   The unsecured creditors (who can be paid only out of free assets).

(vii) Sums due to members but not yet paid. For example, dividends declared but not yet paid.

(viii) The members of the company as set out in the memorandum and articles of association.

In Chapter 9, at 9.2, we considered reservation of title clauses and the circumstances in which they can be effective. It should be borne in mind that goods with which the liquidated company has been supplied will not belong to the company, and will not therefore be available for distribution to the creditors and members, if the goods were supplied subject to a valid reservation of title clause. It should also be borne in mind that goods which the company is hiring or which it has taken on hire-purchase will not belong to the company.

When the winding up process is completed the company can be dissolved.

19.1.3.1 Top slicing

As regards floating charges created on or after 15 September 2003 top slicing applies. This means that the liquidator must set aside a certain percentage of the assets which would otherwise be payable to floating charge holders so that this amount can be paid to the unsecured creditors. It might typically take between three and five years until floating charges created after 15 September 2003 enter the insolvency procedure and so top slicing is unlikely to apply immediately in many cases. The amount which must be set aside for the unsecured creditors is 50% if the company's net property (after the payment of the costs of realising the company's assets and the preferential creditors) does not exceed £10 000 in value. If the company's net property exceeds £10 000 then the amount to be set aside is 50% of the first £10 000, then 20% of the remainder, the fund having a ceiling of £600 000. However, if the value of the company's net property (after the payment of those ranking in priority to floating charges) is less than £10 000 the liquidator does not have to distribute the funds to the unsecured creditors if he considers that this would be disproportionate to the costs of doing so.

■ Example

After the costs of realising the company's assets, paying the receiver's expenses and paying the preferential creditors, a company has net assets of £1 010 000. The only floating charge secures a debt of £2m. If the charge was created before 15 September 2003, all of the £1 010 000 will be used to pay the debt secured by the charge. The charge holder will then be regarded as an unsecured creditor as regards the £990 000 which was not paid. If the charge was created on or after 15 September 2003, £205 000 will be ring-fenced for the unsecured creditors (50% of £10 000 = £5 000 + 20% of £1m = £200 000, making a total of £205 000). The remaining £805 000 will go to the charge holder. As regards the £1 195 000 which he was not paid, the charge holder will be regarded as an unsecured creditor.

19.1.3.2 Preferential creditors

The Enterprise Act 2002 abolished Crown preference (that is to say it has removed debts payable to the Government from the list of preferential creditors) and the preferential creditors are now as follows:

- *Contributions to occupational pension schemes.* Up to four months' wages to employees (up to a maximum of £800) earned prior to the relevant date. (This is either the date of the winding up order, or special resolution in the case of a voluntary winding up, or the date of appointment of a receiver.)
- *Any amount of holiday pay accrued before the relevant date.*
- *Loans made by a third party for the purpose of enabling wages and holiday pay (as specified above), to be paid* and which were used for this purpose.
- *Any loan used specifically to pay the employee's wages.*
- *Levies on coal and steel production* arising under the European Coal and Steel Community Treaty.

These preferential debts rank equally among themselves. If there are sufficient assets, all of the preferential debts must be repaid before other creditors are paid anything. If there are not sufficient assets to pay all the preferential debts in full, then each of the preferential creditors are paid the same proportion of their claim, for example 10p or 50p in the pound.

   Floating charge holders seem to have most to gain from the abolition of Crown preference because after the preferential creditors they are next in line to be paid. As regards floating charges created before 15 September 2003, floating charges rank after the preferential creditors and are not subject to the 'top slicing' which was introduced by the Enterprise Act 2002.

19.1.4 Liability arising from insolvency

In general, a liquidator will not be able to claim assets which do not belong to the company or which are not owed to the company. However, there are certain exceptions to this principle. These exceptions are set out in outline here. It should be noted that these powers can only be exercised by a liquidator or someone acting on behalf of a liquidator. Company officers pursuing insolvency litigation are often severely disadvantaged on account of not having sufficient funds to bring an action.

19.1.4.1 Wrongful trading

Section 214 of the Insolvency Act allows a liquidator to apply to the court to declare that a person who is, or has been, a director should be liable to make such contribution to the company's assets as the court thinks proper. The court may declare a person liable to make a contribution if:

(a) the company has gone into liquidation; and
(b) at some time before the commencement of the winding up of the company, that person knew or ought to have concluded that there was no reasonable prospect that the company would avoid going into insolvent liquidation; and
(c) that person was a director or shadow director of the company at that time.

However, a person shall not be liable for wrongful trading if the court is satisfied that he took every step which he ought to have taken to minimise the potential loss to the company's creditors. The standard expected of the director, both as regards the offence and the defence, is that of a reasonably diligent person who has both the general knowledge, skill and experience which could be objectively expected of such a director and the skill, knowledge and experience which the director in question actually has. An incompetent director will therefore be judged on the standards of a competent one, and a highly competent director will be judged on his own standard. So the director will be judged by whichever standard leads to the higher expectations. The type of company concerned and the functions being carried out by the directors will be relevant considerations in assessing whether or not a director is liable for wrongful trading. A director who can see the inevitability of insolvent liquidation would be well advised to seek advice from a qualified insolvency practitioner before doing anything which could be construed as wrongful trading.

19.1.4.2 Fraudulent trading and misfeasance

Section 213 of the Insolvency Act 1986 provides that if in the course of the winding up of a company it appears than any business of the company has been carried on with the intention of defrauding the creditors of the company, or any other creditors, or for any fraudulent purpose, the court may declare that any persons who were knowingly parties to the fraudulent carrying on of the business are liable to make such contributions to the company's assets as the court thinks proper. In addition, a disqualification order could be made under s.10 of the Company Directors Disqualification Act 1986. In order to be liable under s.213 a person must have deliberately been dishonest by the standards of ordinary business people. It is only the liquidator who can apply to the court for a declaration of fraudulent trading. A separate criminal offence of fraudulent trading is set out by s.458 of the Companies Act 1985. Although both s.458 and s.213 refer to carrying on the business with intent to defraud, the provisions of both sections can be invoked even if there was only one fraudulent transaction defrauding one creditor.

Section 212 of the Insolvency Act 1986 allows the court to examine any person who is or has been an officer of the company, or any other person who has been involved in the promotion, formation or management of the company, in misfeasance proceedings. Such an examination takes place on the application of the Official Receiver, or the liquidator, or any creditor or contributory. Contributories may openly apply to the court with the court's permission, but do not need to benefit from any order the court may make on the application. Misfeasance will have taken place if the officer etc has misapplied or retained, or become accountable for, any money or other property of the company. It will also have taken place if the officer etc has been guilty of any misfeasance or breach of any fiduciary or other duty in relation to the company. The court can compel the officer etc. (a) to repay, restore or account for the property or any part of it, with interest at such rates as the court thinks just, or (b) to contribute such sum to the company's assets by way of compensation in respect of the misfeasance or breach of duty as the court thinks just. Liquidators and administrators can also be made liable in misfeasance proceedings. Misfeasance proceedings are important in practice and might be brought to get back from the directors dividends which were paid out of capital.

19.1.4.3 Transactions at undervalue and preferences

Section 238 of the Insolvency Act provides that where the company has gone into liquidation, the liquidator may apply to the court for an order if the company has at a relevant time entered into a transaction with any person at an undervalue. The court has the power to make such order as it thinks fit for restoring the position to what it would have been if the company had not entered into that transaction. A company enters into a transaction at an undervalue with a person if (a) the company makes a gift to that person or (b) enters into a transaction with that person for a consideration which, in money or money's worth, is significantly less than the value of the consideration provided by the company. However, the court will not make the order if satisfied that (a) the company which entered into the transaction did so in good faith and for the purpose of carrying on its business, and (b) that at the time it did so there were reasonable grounds for believing that the transaction would benefit the company. The section is therefore intended to prevent the defrauding of creditors and members by giving away the company's assets, or selling them too cheaply, prior to liquidation.

Section 239 of the Insolvency Act allows the court, upon an application by a liquidator, to make an order where the company has given preference to any person at a relevant time. If satisfied that this has happened the court can make such an order as it sees fit for restoring the position to what it would have been if the company had not given that preference. A company gives a preference to a person if (a) that person is one of the company's creditors or a surety or guarantor for any of the company's debts or other liabilities, and (b) the company does anything, or allows anything to be done, which has the effect of putting that person into a position which, in the event of the company going into insolvent liquidation, will be better than the position he would have been in if the thing had not been done. Although the court will not make the order unless the company which gave the preference was influenced in deciding to give it to put the person to whom it was given into a better position on the company's insolvent liquidation, if the preference is given to a person connected with the company at the time the preference was given it is presumed to have been influenced in deciding to give it for this purpose. A connected person does not include a person whose only connection is that he is an employee of the company. It does include directors and shadow directors, as well as their husbands and wives, their business partners, their employers or their employees.

For the purposes of both ss.238 and 239, the 'relevant time' is defined by s.240 as:

(a) In the case of a transaction at an undervalue or of a preference which is given to a person connected with the company, the time is two years prior to the onset of insolvency.
(b) For preferences in favour of non-connected persons the time period is six months.

As regards both (a) and (b) it is also a requirement that at the time of entering into the transaction or giving the preference the company was unable to pay its debts, or became unable to do so as a consequence of the transaction or the preference.

Section 423 of the Insolvency Act also confers on the court the power to set aside transactions to defraud creditors by entering into transactions at an undervalue. These powers are not dependent on the company becoming insolvent. A victim of such a transaction may apply to the court, which may make such order as it sees fit to (a) restore the position to what it would have been if the transaction had not been entered into, and (b) protect the interests of persons who are victims of the transaction. A transaction will be regarded as to defraud creditors if the court is satisfied that the person who entered into the transaction did so (a) to put assets beyond the reach of a person who is making, or may at some time make, a claim against him, or (b) to otherwise prejudice the interests of such a person in relation to the claim which he is making or may make. There is no time limit attached to s.423.

19.1.4.4 Invalidity of floating charges

Section 245 of the Insolvency Act renders a floating charge invalid if it was given to a connected person within two years of the commencement of winding up proceedings, whether the company was solvent at the time the charge was created or not. As regards an unconnected person, his charge will be invalid if it was created within 12 months of the commencement of winding up proceedings unless the company was solvent after the creation of the charge. However, in neither case will the charge be invalid to the extent that the company did receive money, or services or goods, or the reduction of a debt, in consideration of the creation of the charge.

This section prevents a company from benefiting an existing creditor by granting him a charge over a previously unsecured debt. The company can still issue valid floating charges to the extent that it receives new funds or assets in return for doing so.

19.1.4.5 Administration and administrative receivership

Administration

Administration is a concept which was introduced by the Insolvency Act 1986. It is a measure short of receivership under which the administrator attempts to rescue an ailing company. So administration may well not lead to the winding-up of the company. In recent years several professional football clubs have gone into administration but have escaped liquidation.

An administrator must be a qualified insolvency practitioner and can be appointed by court order, after an application by the directors, or by a creditor of the company. The Enterprise Act 2002 has also created a new out of court mode of appointment of administrators. Such an appointment can be made by either the holder of a qualifying floating charge, or by the company, or by the directors of the company. (As regards floating charges created on or after September 2003, the charge holder can no longer appoint a receiver.) The administrator must perform his functions in the interests of the company's creditors as a whole and has three hierarchical objects. First, to rescue the company as a going concern (the primary purpose). Second, to achieve a better result for the company's creditors than would be achieved if the company was wound up. Third, to realise (sell) property to make a distribution to one or more secured or preferential creditors.

A court will appoint an administrator only if it is satisfied that the company cannot pay its debts or that the administration order is likely to achieve the primary purpose. A floating charge holder can appoint an administrator, but only if his charge or charges relate to substantially the whole of the company's property. (Thus making him a 'qualifying' floating charge holder.) The company or the directors can appoint an administrator, but not if an administrative receiver has been appointed or a petition for winding up has been presented. Also, if qualifying floating charge holders object the court will generally allow them to appoint the administrator.

An important feature of administration is that it applies a moratorium. The Enterprise Act 2002 inserts a new interim moratorium which comes into force on the date of either the application to the court or, in the case of an out of court appointment, the date of the presentation of the notice to appoint an administrator. The interim moratorium gives more limited protection to the company than does the full moratorium which is in date from the date of the administrator's appointment. During the period of the interim moratorium it is still possible for a winding up petition to be presented to the court and a pre-15 September 2003 floating charge holder can apply to the company to appoint an administrative receiver.

Once a company is in administration any petition to wind the company up will either be dismissed or suspended until the period of administration is over. An administrative receiver who has already been appointed is dismissed. No steps can be taken to enforce any security without the consent of the administrator or the permission of the court. All business documents (invoices, orders for goods or services and business letters) issued by or on behalf of the company must state the name of the administrator and that he is managing the company's affairs. All creditors must be informed that the administrator has been appointed.

As soon as is reasonably practicable after his appointment the administrator must require an officer or employee of the company to give him a statement of the company's affairs. (If the company had been formed within the previous year a promoter can be required to give the statement.) The statement must be in a prescribed form and state and give details of the company's creditors and the company's property, debts and liabilities. A person requested to submit a statement of affairs has 11 days in which to do so. The administrator then sets out his proposals for achieving the purpose of the administration and sends details to the registrar of companies, and all of the company's creditors and members. This must be done as soon as is reasonably practicable and within eight weeks of the company entering administration.

All creditors are invited to a creditors' meeting to consider the administrator's proposals. The creditors can approve the proposals with or without modification. Then the administrator might amend the proposals and resubmit them to the creditors who once more might approve them with or without modification. If the creditors do not approve the proposals the court may replace the administrator or make any other order which it sees fit. There may be a further creditors' meeting if the court orders one or if creditors holding at least 10% of the company's debt demand one. A creditors' committee may be formed. This committee can demand that the administrator attend a meeting to give information on the way he is performing his role.

The administrator may do anything necessary or expedient for the management of the affairs, business and property of the company, including removing or appointing directors. He takes control of all the property to which he thinks the company is entitled and may pay off creditors. He can sell off property which is subject to a floating charge but the charge holder gets the same priority in respect of any property then acquired. (In effect this reverses the crystallisation of the charge.) By court order he can sell off property subject to a fixed charge. But only if the charge holder is given towards payment of his debt the net proceeds of sale and any other sum which the court thinks would bring the amount up to the market value of the charged property.

A creditor or member can apply to the court challenging the administrator's conduct. The court then has power to make any order which it considers appropriate. An administrator's appointment ends automatically one year after his appointment but can be extended by a further six months. However, this requires the consent of all secured creditors and the consent of creditors holding at least 50% of the company's unsecured debts. However, unsecured creditors who do not respond to an invitation to give consent are disregarded.

Administrative receivership

As long as their charges were registered before 15 September 2003, one or more floating charge holders can appoint a receiver to realise the company's property so that the secured debt can be paid. If the charge(s) relate to all or substantially all of the company's assets the receiver is called an administrative receiver. These charge holders can instead appoint an administrator and, as we have seen, holders of floating charges created after 15 September 2003 cannot appoint an administrative receiver but will have to appoint an administrator. The right to appoint an administrative receiver will have been contained in the contract which created the charge. Although administrative receivership is an insolvency procedure, it is not a liquidation procedure. Generally, receivers can be appointed without a court order.

As soon as a receiver is appointed he, and not the directors, has the power to deal with the property which is subject to the floating charge. (Generally, this will be all of the company's property which is not subject to a fixed charge.) An administrative receiver is an agent of the company and his task is to see that the secured creditors get paid. As soon as this is done he will be finished with the company. The floating charge holders will only be paid after the costs of realising the charge and the payment of creditors who were preferential at the date of the receivership. The floating charge holder will not have to contribute to the general liquidation expenses if the company goes into liquidation. The work of an administrative receiver often causes a company to go into liquidation because once all or most of the company's assets have been sold off to satisfy the secured creditors there is often not much left.

Test your understanding

1   Can a company be voluntarily wound up by the members?

2   In what circumstances will a company be deemed unable to pay its debts, thereby justifying the court in ordering the company to be wound up?

3   State four grounds on which a court has decided that it is just and equitable to wind a company up.

4 What are the main differences between a members' voluntary liquidation and a creditors' voluntary liquidation?

5 In what order are the creditors of an insolvent company paid?

6 What purposes does an administrator of a company try to achieve? What purpose does an administrative receiver try to achieve?

Answers

1 A company can be voluntarily wound up by the members, or compulsorily wound up by order of the court.

2 A company is deemed unable to pay its debts if: (a) a creditor who has properly demanded payment of more than £750 has not been paid within three weeks; (b) execution of a court's judgment against the company in favour of a creditor is returned unsatisfied; or (c) it is proved to the satisfaction of the court that the company is unable to pay its debts as they fall due.

3 The courts have wound companies up on the grounds that this is just and equitable for the following reasons: (a) the substratum of the company has failed; (b) there is deadlock in the management of a company; (c) there is a justifiable lack of confidence in the management of a company; (d) the company was formed for a fraudulent purpose. There is no closed list of grounds on which a court might consider it just and equitable to wind a company up.

4 A members' voluntary liquidation is initiated by a special resolution. The directors must file a declaration of solvency and the members appoint the liquidator. A creditors' voluntary liquidation is initiated by an extraordinary resolution of the members. The directors do not have to file a declaration of solvency and the creditors appoint the liquidator.

5 First, the costs of realising assets subject to a floating charge are paid. Then the preferential creditors; then (if appropriate) a top-sliced fund goes to the unsecured creditors; then holders of floating charges are paid what they are owed; then the general costs of liquidation are paid; then unsecured creditors are paid; finally, any surplus is distributed to members of the company.

6. An administrator of a company tries primarily to rescue the company as a going concern, secondarily to achieve a better result for the company's creditors than would be achieved by a winding up, thirdly to realise property to distribute to secured or preferential creditors. An administrative receiver realises company property to pay the debts of the floating charge holder who appointed him.

19.2 · Limited liability partnership

19.2.1 The nature of limited liability partnerships

Since April 2000 it has been possible for two or more persons to trade as a limited liability partnership (LLP). It is important at the outset to realise that an LLP is not an ordinary partnership which has limited liability. Nor is an LLP the same as, or even similar to, a limited partnership registered under the Limited Partnership Act 1907. Indeed, as corporate entities, LLPs have more in common with limited companies than with ordinary or limited partnerships.

Like shareholders in a company, participants in an LLP are known as members and not as partners. It is possible for companies to be members of an LLP, just as it is possible for companies to be members of an ordinary partnership. An LLP can engage in any kind of business. Although an LLP is closer to a limited company than to an ordinary partnership, an LLP does share some of the features of an ordinary partnership. One significant similarity is that the profits of an LLP are not subject to corporation tax. The members of an LLP are taxed on profits in the same way as partners in an ordinary partnership. The members of an LLP will therefore be liable to pay income tax on profits received.

The Limited Liability Partnerships Act 2000 (the 2000 Act) created a framework of the law applicable to LLPs, leaving the details to be filled by secondary legislation. The Limited Liability Partnerships Regulations 2001 (the 2001 Regulations) have begun this process. The general approach of the 2001 Regulations has been to apply to LLPs provisions of the Companies Act 1985, the Company Directors Disqualification Act 1986 and the Insolvency Act 1986. Many of these provisions have been modified slightly so that they do not apply in exactly the same way as they apply to companies. Other provisions do apply exactly as they apply to companies. It is because so much company law applies to LLPs, slightly modified or not, that we consider the law relating to LLPs after we have considered the law relating to companies.

Section 1(5) of the 2000 Act provides that, unless the Act provides otherwise, the law relating to partnerships does not apply to an LLP. However, some sections of the Act are obviously based on the Partnership Act 1890. As the law relating to LLPs is an amalgam of company law and partnership law, it would be very difficult to understand it unless one first had an understanding of the law relating to companies and ordinary partnerships.

19.2.2 Formation of an LLP

An LLP is created by registration with the Registrar of Companies. Once the Registrar has registered an LLP and issued a certificate of incorporation a new corporate body, with a legal personality of its own, is created.

Section 2(1) of the 2000 Act sets out three requirements for incorporation. First, s.2(1)(a) requires that two or more persons associated for carrying on a lawful business with a view to profit must have subscribed their names to an incorporation document. Second, s.2(1)(b) requires that this document, or a copy of it, is delivered to the registrar of companies. Third, s.2(1)(c) requires that a statement that the requirements of s.2(1)(a) have been complied with is also delivered to the registrar. This statement must be made by one of the subscribers to the incorporation document or by a solicitor who was engaged in the formation of the LLP. These requirements make it plain that there must be at least two members, there cannot be a single member LLP. Schedule 2 to the 2001 Regulations applies s.24 of the Companies Act 1985 to LLPs. So if an LLP carries on business with only one member for more than six months the single member becomes liable for debts incurred while he was the only member. It should also be noticed that although the business of an LLP must be carried on with a view to profit there is no requirement that every member should be intended to share in this profit.

Section 2(2) requires the incorporation document to be in a form approved by the registrar and to state five matters: the name of the LLP; whether the registered office is in England and Wales, in Wales or in Scotland; the actual address of the registered office; the names and addresses of all the members on incorporation; and a statement of who the designated members (see below) are or a statement that all members of the LLP, at any time, are to be designated members. (It is possible to apply to the Secretary of State for a Confidentiality Order so that the names and addresses of the members are not publicly registered.) Form LLP2, which is available from the registrar of companies, is the official form which serves as both the incorporation document and the written statement.

It is apparent that the incorporation document closely resembles a company's memorandum of association. (See Chapter 16 at 16.4.1.) However, it should be noticed that there is no equivalent of an objects clause and so questions of *ultra vires* will not arise. When the registration requirements have been satisfied, the Registrar will then issue the LLP with a number and a certificate of incorporation and publish the fact of incorporation in the London Gazette.

Section 9 of the 2000 Act provides that when a person becomes or ceases to become a member or a designated member the registrar must be informed within 14 days. If a member changes his name or address the registrar must be informed within 28 days.

19.2.3 The LLP name

Part 1 of Schedule 1 to the 2000 Act deals with the names of LLPs. It provides that the name of an LLP must end with 'limited liability partnership', 'llp' or 'LLP'. If the registered office is in Wales the Welsh equivalents, 'partneriaeth atebolrwydd cyfyngedig', 'pac' or 'PAC' can be used instead. An

LLP must not use the words set out above otherwise than at the end of its name. A name which is identical to that of a registered company or a registered LLP cannot be used. Nor can a name be used if it would constitute a criminal offence or, in the opinion of the Secretary of State, be offensive, indicate a connection with the Government or a local authority or be a name for which a company would need approval. These rules, and the rules relating to a **change of name**, and the circumstances in which the **name must be displayed**, are identical to the rules relating to companies, which were examined in Chapter 16 at 16.6.

19.2.4 Members and designated members

Section 4(1) of the 2000 Act provides that on incorporation an LLP's members are the person who subscribed to the incorporation document (unless they have died or, in the case of companies, been dissolved). Section 4(2) provides that any other person may become a member by agreement with all existing members. (Regulation 7(5) of the 2001 Regulations provides that, subject to the terms of any LLP agreement, all existing members must agree to the introduction of a new member.) Section 4(3) of the Act provides that a person may cease to be a member either by agreement with the other members or by giving reasonable notice to the other members. It also makes it plain that a member who has died or, in the case of a company, been dissolved will cease to be a member. Section 4(4) of the Act provides that a member of an LLP should not be regarded as an employee of the LLP unless he would be regarded as an employee of the partnership if the LLP were a partnership. Members of LLPs are therefore self-employed.

Section 8(1) of the 2000 Act deals with the identification of designated members, stating that they may be stated to be designated members in the incorporation document or may become or cease to become designated members by agreement with the other members of the LLP. Section 8(2) provides that where there would otherwise be no designated member, or only one designated member, then every member of the LLP is a designated member. In addition, s.8(3) allows the incorporation document to state that all members of the LLP from time to time are designated members. Section 8(4) provides that an LLP may give notice to the registrar that a person is a designated member, or that all the members of the LLP are designated members, and that this shall have effect as if stated in the incorporation document. Such a notice has to be signed by a designated member. A person who ceases to be a member of an LLP ceases to be a designated member.

Designated members have certain specific duties such as signing the LLP's accounts and delivering them to the registrar, giving the registrar notice that an LLP has changed its name, giving the registrar notice of who the designated members are and signing the annual return form. If company legislation which is applicable to LLPs imposes duties on directors or officers of the company, it is presumed that these duties fall on all members of an LLP unless legislation has allocated the particular duty to designated members.

The rules on approval and removal of auditors, on filing an annual return and on filing of accounts are essentially the same as those which apply to limited companies. These matters were considered in Chapter 17 at 17.3, 17.5 and 17.6.

In Chapter 18, at 18.7.7, we considered the circumstances in which the DTI can investigate a company's affairs. These rules apply also to LLPs, in a somewhat modified way. Such an investigation can arise if a court orders it or if at least 20% of the members demand it.

19.2.5 Members as agents

An LLP will be bound by a contract if the contract was made by an agent who had authority to make it. So, like a company, an LLP can confer actual authority to make contracts on employees, such as shop assistants and salesmen, or on non-employees. Section 6(1) of the 2000 Act provides that every member of the LLP is an agent of the LLP. But s.6(2) then limits this by stating that an LLP is not bound by anything done by a member in dealing with a person if: (a) the member in fact has no authority to act for the LLP by doing that thing; and (b) the person knows that he has no authority or does not know or believe him to be a member of the LLP. The rules set out in these two subsections seem very similar to the rules set out in s.5 of the Partnership Act 1890, which was examined in detail in Chapter 15 at 15.8.1. Whilst the law applicable to s.5 of the Partnership Act 1890 would generally apply to s.6 of the 2000 Act, we should note several points of difference. First, in the case of an LLP the principal is the LLP itself, whereas in the case of an ordinary partnership each of the partners is the principal and is therefore bound by the contract. Second, s.6(1) does not have the s.5 Partnership Act requirement that the partner's act should be done 'for carrying on in the usual way business of the kind carried on by the firm of which he is a member'. Third, in relation to the limitation in s.6(2) it is arguably the case that the requirement that every member of an LLP should be registered on a register which can be inspected by any person means that it might be difficult for a third party to argue that he did not know that the contracting member was a member of the LLP.

Section 6(3) provides that a person dealing with an LLP can still regard a former member of an LLP as a member unless: (a) he has been given notice that the former member has ceased to be a member; or (b) notice that the former member has ceased to be a member has been delivered to the registrar. These rules on the apparent authority of a former member are similar to the rules applying to former partners in a partnership. However, it seems a little surprising that a third party is regarded as having notice when this is delivered to the registrar, rather than when the registrar alters the register.

Section 36C of the Companies Act 1985 applies to LLPs, so a person making a pre-incorporation contract on behalf of an LLP will be liable on it (see Chapter 16 at 16.5). If the contract is properly drafted the LLP, once formed, will be able to enforce the contract under the Contract (Rights of Third Parties) Act (C(RTP)A) 1999. Section 6(2A) C(RTP)A 1999 provides that neither an incorporation document of an LLP, nor any LLP agreement, can confer rights on a third party to **enforce** a term.

Section 5(2) of the 2000 Act provides that an agreement made before the incorporation of an LLP, between the subscribers to the incorporation document, may impose obligations on the LLP to take effect at any time after its incorporation.

19.2.6 Liability in tort

Section 4(4) of the 2000 Act provides that an LLP will be vicariously liable to outsiders for a wrongful act or omission of a member committed either during the course of the business of the LLP or with the authority of the LLP. This is a partial application of s.10 of the Partnership Act 1890, which was considered in Chapter 15 at 15.8.2. However, it should be noticed that under s.4(4) of the Act it is the LLP, rather than the other members, which becomes liable.

The decision of the House of Lords in *Dubai Aluminium Co Ltd* v *Salaam and others* [2002] 3 WLR 1913, considered at 15.8.2, would seem to be a starting point for the vicarious liability of LLPs. However, s 4(4) differs from s.10 of the Partnership Act 1890 in that it requires the tort to be committed in the course of business of the LLP, rather than in the ordinary course of business. It therefore seems likely that this will make the liability of an LLP wider than the liability of partners under s.10 of the Partnership Act.

19.2.7 Members' relationship with each other

Section 5(1) of the 2000 Act provides that the mutual rights and duties of the members of an LLP as between each other, and as between the members and the LLP, shall be governed by agreement between the members or by agreement between the LLP and the members. In the absence of such agreement the default provisions set out in Reg.7 of the 2001 Regulations apply. Section 5 therefore deals with two different sets of duties. First, the duties which every member owes to every other member. Second, the duties which every member owes to the LLP. Section 5 also makes it plain that a statute, such as the Insolvency Act 1986, may override any agreement made.

When acting as agents of the LLP, members will owe a fiduciary duty to the LLP. This fiduciary duty applies to all agents, including of course partners dealing on behalf of their fellow partners and directors dealing on behalf of a company. It is not clear whether members of an LLP will owe a general fiduciary duty to other members. Partners do owe a fiduciary duty to other partners but directors do not generally owe a fiduciary duty to individual shareholders. It seems likely that members of an LLP will not owe a fiduciary duty to other members, as an LLP is a corporate body rather than a relationship between its members. However, there is nothing to prevent the LLP agreement imposing fiduciary duties. Also, the default provision set out in Reg.7(8), see immediately below, imposes a fiduciary duty which a member will owe to other members (unless the members have agreed otherwise).

19.2.8 **The default provisions**

Like s.24 of the Partnership Act 1890, Reg.7 of the 2001 Regulations set out default provisions which are to apply unless the general law or any LLP agreement provides otherwise. The ten default provisions are as follows.

- Regulation 7(1) – All members are entitled to share equally in the capital and profits of the LLP. (Regulation 7(1) does not refer to losses because such losses will be borne by the LLP rather than by the members.)
- Regulation 7(2) – The LLP must indemnify each member in respect of payments made and liabilities incurred in the ordinary and proper conduct of the business of the LLP or for the preservation of the LLP or its property.
- Regulation 7(3) – Every member may take part in the management of the LLP.
- Regulation 7(4) – No member is entitled to remuneration for acting in the business or management of the LLP.
- Regulation 7(5) – No new member may be introduced, nor may a member voluntarily assign an interest in an LLP, without the consent of all existing members.
- Regulation 7(6) – Differences arising as to ordinary matters may be resolved by a majority vote, but no change may be made in the nature of the business of the LLP without the consent of all of the members.
- Regulation 7(7) – Every member shall have access to the books and records of the LLP and may inspect and make copies of them.
- Regulation 7(8) – Every member shall render true accounts and full information of all things affecting the LLP to any other member or his legal representative.
- Regulation 7(9) – If a member, without the consent of the LLP, carries on any business of the same nature as and competing with the LLP, he must account for and pay over to the LLP all profits made by him in that business.
- Regulation 7(10) – Every member must account to the LLP for any benefit derived by him without the consent of the LLP from any transaction concerning the LLP, or for any use by him of the property of the LLP, name or business connection.

The first seven of these default provisions are modelled very closely on s.24 of the Partnership Act 1890. The last three are modelled on ss.28–30 of the Partnership Act. We examined s.24 in Chapter 15 at 15.5.1 and we examined ss.28–30 in Chapter 15 at 15.7.

Regulation 8 mirrors s.25 of the Partnership Act by providing that no majority can expel any member unless a power to do so has been conferred by express agreement between the members. (This suggests that the matters set out in the Reg. 7 default provisions can be altered by express or implied agreement.) If a member is expelled then, at the very least, this power will have to be exercised bona fide for the benefit of the LLP. It is not clear whether in exercising such a power the majority would owe fiduciary duties to the expelled member.

19.2.9 Ceasing to be a member

Section 7 of the 2000 Act deals with the position where a member has ceased to be a member, died, become bankrupt or assigned all or part of his share in the LLP to another person. It provides that neither the member, nor his trustee in bankruptcy, nor his personal representatives, nor the person to whom the share was assigned may interfere in the management or business affairs of the LLP. However, this does not affect any right to receive an amount from the LLP which arose on the member ceasing to be a member, becoming bankrupt etc.

As we have seen, s.4(3) of the 2000 Act allows a member to leave an LLP by agreement with the other members by giving the other members reasonable notice. In Chapter 15 at 15.4.1.4 we saw that only in the case of a partnership at will can a partner give notice to dissolve the firm. If the firm is not a partnership at will no partner has the right to leave by giving notice. So the idea that a member of an LLP can leave by giving reasonable notice is a key difference. Another key difference is that an LLP will not be dissolved when a member leaves. The member who leaves will not therefore have any right to a share of the LLP's assets, unless an agreement has given him such rights. So unless the minority protection provisions which apply in company law are applicable also to LLPs a member of an LLP who wanted to leave might effectively find himself unable to do so.

As we have already seen, s.9 requires that the registrar is informed within 14 days of a member ceasing to be a member. We have also seen that s.6(3) allows the former member's apparent authority to make contracts to continue until the registrar is notified that he has ceased to be a member.

19.2.10 Minority protection

If a member of an LLP is expelled from the LLP, or is being treated unfairly by a majority of members, or wants to leave the LLP with an appropriate share of the assets having been denied him, the law on minority protection becomes relevant.

As an LLP is a corporate body it would seem that the rule in *Foss v Harbottle* would apply. This rule, set out in Chapter 18 at 18.7.1, holds that if a wrong is done to a company then only the company has the right to sue in respect of that wrong. However, as we saw in Chapter 18 minority shareholders may be given various forms of protection. To what extent do these forms of protection apply to members of an LLP?

First, it seems likely that the common law would give a member the right to bring a derivative action where the behaviour of the majority amounted to a fraud on the minority (see Chapter 18 at 18.7.5).

Second, a member may be able to petition the court for a winding-up order, under s.122 of the Insolvency Act 1986, on the grounds that this is just and equitable. As we saw earlier, default Reg.7(3) gives every member a right to manage the LLP. Such a default term could of course be changed by agreement but it would seem unlikely that an agreement would exclude the right of any member to take part in management. A member who was expelled might be able to argue that this breached his right to take part in the management of the LLP and that this would therefore justify a winding up on the just and equitable ground. Winding up under s.122 of the Insolvency Act was examined in Chapter 18 at 18.7.6.

Third, the provisions of s.459 Companies Act 1985 regarding unfair prejudice apply to LLPs. However, s.459(1A) provides that: 'The members of a limited liability partnership may by unanimous agreement exclude the right contained in subsection 459(1) for such period as shall be agreed. The agreement referred to in this subsection shall be recorded in writing.' This potential exclusion of the right to petition the court on the grounds of unfair prejudice seems, at first sight, very significant. However, since the exclusion has to be unanimous and in writing it seems probable that it would only apply where the members had agreed some alternative method of dealing with minority protection. Section 459 was examined in Chapter 18 at 18.7.6.

A member who wants to leave an LLP, but who has been denied an appropriate share of the assets, might gain relief from any of the matters set out above. However, none of these matters provides an easy remedy. Appropriate drafting of the incorporation agreement therefore seems particularly essential when dealing with a leaving member's right to a share of the LLP assets.

19.2.11 Loan capital

As we have seen in the previous five chapters, partnerships cannot issue floating charges but companies can. The company regime on fixed and floating charges applies to LLPs (see Chapter 18 at 18.8).

19.2.12 Winding up

The Insolvency Act 1986 applies to LLPs in the same way that it applies to companies. Reference should therefore be made to the early part of this chapter, where company winding up was considered.

19.2.13 Members' liability to contribute to the LLP's assets

An LLP is a corporate body and so, as a general principle, it alone will be liable for its debts. If an LLP becomes insolvent the members will lose money which they have invested in the LLP but will not have to pay its debts. However, there are circumstances in which members may have to contribute towards an LLP's debts.

Earlier in this chapter, at 19.1.4.1 and 19.1.4.2 we examined a director's liability for wrongful trading and fraudulent trading under ss.213 and 214 of the Insolvency Act 1986. Both of these sections apply equally to members of an LLP and can make them liable to contribute to the assets when an LLP is wound up. Members can also be made liable by ss.74 and 214A of the Insolvency Act. These two sections do not apply to companies.

Section 74 of the Insolvency Act provides that:

> 'When a limited liability partnership is wound up every present and past member of the limited liability partnership who has agreed with the other members or with the limited liability partnership that he will, in circumstances which have arisen, be liable to contribute to the assets of the limited liability partnership in the event that the limited liability partnership goes into liquidation is liable, to the extent that he has agreed, to contribute to its assets to any amount sufficient for payment of its debts and liabilities, and for the expenses of the winding up, and for the adjustment of the rights of the contributories amongst themselves.'

It is therefore envisaged that members of an LLP might agree to assume limited liability for the company's debts in the same way that members of a company limited by guarantee might assume limited liability. There are several points to note about s.74. First, a member can only become liable if he has agreed to assume liability. Such an agreement might be with the other members or with the LLP. Second, the liability arises only if the LLP goes into liquidation. Third, the member is liable only to the extent which he has agreed. Fourth, the liability arises only to the extent necessary to pay the LLP's debts, the winding up expenses and to adjust the rights of other members who have agreed to contribute. Fifth, a past member can be liable only if the obligation arising from such an agreement survived his ceasing to be a member of the LLP.

Section 214A of the Insolvency Act 1986 applies to a member of an LLP who, within two years of the commencement of winding up, withdrew LLP property while having reasonable grounds for believing either that the LLP could not pay its debts or would have been unable to pay its debts once the property had been withdrawn. The property withdrawn might be a share of profits, salary, interest on a loan, repayment of a loan or in any other form. On an application by the liquidator the court can order that the member pay such a contribution to the LLP's assets as the court thinks proper. However, this amount must not be more than the amount of the property withdrawn over the two year period. The court will make the order only if the member knew or ought to have known, at the time of the relevant withdrawal, that the LLP had no reasonable prospect of avoiding going into insolvent liquidation. When deciding what the member knew or ought to have known that the LLP could not avoid insolvent liquidation, the standards of general knowledge, skill and experience are those which the member actually had **and** those which could reasonably be expected of a person carrying out the functions which the member carried out. Like the test for s.124 then, the test is both objective and subjective. However, this dual standard is not stated to apply when considering whether the member knew that the company could not pay its debts. Section 124A applies to shadow members as well as to members. However, since the section requires the member to know both that the LLP could not pay its debts nor avoid insolvent liquidation, it would seem that it may not be applied much in practice. As we saw at 19.1.4.1, wrongful trading requires a knowledge that the LLP had no reasonable prospect of avoiding insolvent liquidation, but it does not require knowledge that the LLP was unable to pay its debts.

19.2.14 Disqualification of members

Regulation 4(2) applies the Company Directors Disqualification Act 1986 to both members and shadow members of LLPs. (The CDDA 1986 was considered in Chapter 17 at 17.1.3.) Regulation 4 states that references to a company in the CDDA 1986 shall include references to an LLP and references to a director or shadow director shall include reference to a member or a shadow member. Therefore, it seems that a person disqualified from being either a director of a company or a member of an LLP will be disqualified from being a director of any company or a member of any LLP. A person who acts as an LLP member in defiance of a disqualification order commits a criminal offence and can be liable without limit for the LLP's debts.

Test your understanding

1 How is an LLP formed?

2 An LLP incorporation document closely resembles a company's memorandum of association. However, there is no equivalent of an objects clause. What is the significance of this?

3 With what words must the name of an LLP end?

4 How many designated members must an LLP have? What is the significance of being a designated member of an LLP?

5 Is a member of an LLP an agent of the LLP?

6 Is an LLP vicariously liable for the torts of a member of the LLP?

7 How are the rights and duties of one member of an LLP to another member fixed?

8 Is an LLP dissolved when a member leaves?

9 What protection is afforded to a minority member of an LLP?

10 In general, will a member of an LLP be liable to pay the debts of the LLP?

Answers

1 An LLP is formed by registration with the registrar of companies. Two or more persons associated for carrying on a lawful business must subscribe to a registration document and send it to the registrar.

2 As there is no objects clause, questions of *ultra vires* will not arise.

3 The name of an LLP must end with the words 'limited liability partnership' or 'llp' or 'LLP' (or their Welsh equivalents).

4 Every LLP must have at least two designated members, who have certain specified duties such as signing the LLP's accounts and delivering them to the registrar.

5   Every member of an LLP is an agent of the LLP. However, an LLP is not bound by anything done by a member in dealing with a person if: (a) the member in fact has no authority to act for the LLP by doing that thing; and (b) the person knows that he has no authority or does not know or believe him to be a member of the LLP.

6   An LLP will be vicariously liable to outsiders for the tort of a member if the tort was committed either during the course of the business of the LLP or with the authority of the LLP.

7   The rights and duties of the members between themselves are fixed by agreement. However, in the absence of agreement ten default provisions apply.

8   An LLP is not dissolved when a member leaves.

9   A member of an LLP can petition the court for a just and equitable winding up under s.122 of the Insolvency Act 1986. A member can also claim unfair prejudice under s.459 of the Companies Act 1985, unless the right to do so has been excluded by unanimous written agreement. It seems likely that a member can bring a derivative action where the behaviour of the majority amounts to a fraud on the minority.

10 In general, members will not have to pay the debts of an LLP.

19.3 · Choice of legal status

People who intend to go into business together must choose what sort of business organisation they wish to form. Often they might have very clear views. They might be quite sure that they want to trade either as a company, as an LLP or as a partnership. In many other cases, however, the choice may not be so clear cut.

When a business is being set up there are often many matters requiring urgent attention. Perhaps staff must be employed, money borrowed or premises leased. It is easy to regard the decision as to the choice of legal status as less pressing. However, the choice of business status is a very important one. Prospective business people should consider the advantages and disadvantages of trading as a company, a partnership or an LLP in some detail. Even after the initial decision has been made, attention should be given as to whether or not it would be wise to change in the light of changing circumstances, such as rates of taxation.

Most of the matters which follow have been examined in greater detail in previous chapters. Here we are reconsidering such matters solely from the perspective of whether or not they make a company, an LLP or a partnership the most advantageous medium in which to trade.

19.3.1 Limited liability

In Chapter 15 we saw that partners are personally liable, without limit, for the acts of themselves and their fellow partners which were committed in the ordinary course of the firm's business. Cases such as *Mercantile Credit Co v Garrod* [1962] 3 All ER 1103 and *Blyth v Fladgate* [1891] 1 Ch 337 indicated what a risk this can be. Although an active partner can limit this liability by agreeing a limit on liability with his fellow partners, and informing the third party with whom the firm deals of this limitation, this rarely happens in practice. The partnership agreement may set out how losses are to be borne between the partners, but all partners are jointly and severally liable to outsiders for the firm's debts. If any of the partners are unable to pay their shares then the other partners assume unlimited liability to do so. In Chapter 16 we saw that a company is a legal entity in its own right, and that the members of a limited company have limited liability for the debts of the company. This is, perhaps, the principal advantage of trading as a company rather than as a partnership and it is an advantage also enjoyed by those who trade as an LLP.

However, the extent to which limited liability is a true advantage depends very much upon the circumstances of each individual business. If the business is to engage in a highly speculative line, and can find people willing to provide credit, then limited liability may indeed be a very real advantage. But, as we have seen, the corporate veil can be pierced in certain circumstances, and directors or LLP members who commit wrongful or fraudulent trading can be compelled to contribute towards the company's assets on dissolution. It is also true that many creditors, especially commercial lenders such as banks, are perfectly well aware of a shareholder's limited liability and will not therefore extend any credit to a small limited company or a small LLP unless the loan is personally guaranteed by the company directors or the members.

In business it is not usual to pay for goods and services in advance. If suppliers are eager to do business they will probably accept deferred payment. But suppliers who are aware of the limited liability of shareholders or LLP members might also be unwilling to supply goods or services without first getting personal guarantees. On the other hand, suppliers dealing with a partnership need not have any worries about getting paid as long as they know that some or all of the partners are financially sound.

Many small businesses do not borrow money. Instead, the owners of the business themselves contribute all the capital which the company needs. If such a business should fail, limited liability is not going to prevent the capital which they contributed from being lost.

Despite the matters outlined above, limited liability can be a real advantage to a member of a company or an LLP, especially where the member has considerable personal wealth. Those who spurn the advantage of limited liability should consider the following words of James LJ in *Re Agriculturist Cattle Insurance Co, Baird's Case* (1870) LR 5 Ch App 725.

'Ordinary partnerships are by the law assumed to be based on the mutual trust and confidence of each partner in the skill, knowledge and integrity of every other partner. As between the partners and the outside world (whatever may be their private arrangements between themselves), each partner is the unlimited agent of every other in every matter connected with the partnership business ... A partner who may not have a farthing of capital left may take money or assets of the partnership to the value of millions, may bind the partnership by contracts to any amount ... and may even – as has been shewn in many painful instances in this court – involve his innocent partners in unlimited amounts for frauds which he has carefully concealed from them.'

19.3.2 The right to manage

The rights of partners to manage the affairs of the partnership are usually set out in the partnership agreement. In Chapter 15 we saw that partners may be excluded from certain rights of management, but that if a partner is excluded from management without having agreed that he should be then this is a reason for the court to dissolve the firm. The position regarding members on an LLP is essentially the same.

Shareholders, no matter how large their percentage holding, do not have a right to manage a company. The right to manage is vested in the Board of Directors, who are elected by a simple majority of the shareholders voting at a general meeting. A shareholder, or a group of shareholders, with over 50% of the voting shares has the power to change the directors. But until that power is exercised the directors in place have the right to manage the company's affairs.

A shareholder with less than 50% of the voting shares can be outvoted on a resolution to appoint or remove a director. Therefore minority shareholders are in the unfortunate position of having no right to manage the company's affairs, and no power to change this situation. A person going into business with one other person might therefore be very unwilling to form a company unless he was to own 50% of the shares. Similar problems arise when there are several other shareholders. A minority shareholder can find himself in a very precarious position if the other shareholders have a closer relationship with each other than they have with him.

In Chapter 17 we saw that a *Bushell v Faith* clause in the articles can give some protection to a director with less than 50% of the company's shares. In that case a director with only 33% of the company's shares could remain in office indefinitely because the articles said that in any vote to remove a director the shares belonging to the director whose removal was proposed should carry three votes per share. However, even this protection will not apply if the shareholders who wish to remove the directors can muster 75% of the votes. By passing a special resolution, the shareholders with 75% of the votes could alter the articles to remove the *Bushell* v *Faith* clause. (However another article might prevent this, by giving special weightings to some shares so that the holder of these shares could prevent any removal of the *Bushell* v *Faith* clause.)

In small companies the members of the company are often all directors. Often they receive a return by way of director's remuneration rather than as dividends. A member who is removed as a director might therefore not only lose the right to manage the company but might also be financially disadvantaged as well. There is some safeguard in that a court might make an order on the grounds of unfair prejudice or wind the company up in such a situation. (As we saw in the previous chapter in *Ebrahimi* v *Westbourne Galleries* [1972] and in Lord Hoffmann's speech in *O'Neill* v *Phillips*.) However, such a winding up is not readily ordered, and the costs of petitioning the court might well be more than the net assets of many small companies.

In most partnerships and LLPs the partnership or LLP agreement will set out how the profits are to be divided. (If no agreement deals with the matter then the profits will be divided equally.) Once an agreement has been made it can only be altered by unanimous consent of the partners or LLP members, unless the agreement provides otherwise. Therefore a partner or LLP member who negotiates an acceptable share of the profits upon joining the firm cannot later be deprived of this share. Nor can a partner or LLP member be dismissed unless there has been an express agreement providing for the dismissal. However, even if there is no express agreement, a partner or LLP member can be dismissed in effect if the other partners dissolve the business and then trade as a new firm or LLP. Upon dissolution the partner or LLP member would be able to share in the assets of the dissolved firm, and the firm's goodwill might well be a very significant asset.

19.3.3 Withdrawal from the business

Partnerships are either entered into for a fixed period of time or they are partnerships at will. (See Chapter 15 at 15.4.1) Any partner can withdraw from a partnership at will by giving notice. If a partner does withdraw by giving notice the firm will then be dissolved, and each partner will recover his share of the assets. If a partnership is for a fixed term a partner wishing to withdraw must wait until the end of that term. Even so, an end is in sight.

It is possible for a partner to assign his share in the firm before the end of the term (unless the partnership deed prevents this). The assignee will receive the share of the profits to which the partner would have been entitled, but will have no right to manage the partnership's affairs. This lack of the right to manage might considerably reduce the value of the share which is assigned.

LLPs will not be dissolved merely because one of the members leaves. As a corporate body, the LLP will continue to exist. Furthermore, members of an LLP have the right to leave the LLP by agreement with the other members or by giving reasonable notice. However, as we have seen, a member leaving an LLP will not have a right to any share of the LLP's asseets unless an agreement has given him such rights. Ordinarily, there should be such an agreement. But if there is not a member might find it impractical to leave an LLP.

Members of companies may or may not have a right to transfer their shares to whoever they wish. It all depends on the articles, which might well say that the Board of Directors can refuse to register a transfer to persons of whom they disapprove. The articles of many private companies give the directors the power to refuse to register any transfer of shares at their absolute discretion, without giving reasons for their refusal. Although this right has to be exercised *bona fide* for the benefit of the company, if no reasons for the refusal are given it is very difficult to mount a legal challenge to the decision of the directors. So the members of many small companies, no matter how much they dislike the way the company is being run, have no right to transfer their shares. If unfair prejudice was proved the court might order that their shares be purchased at a fair value. But, as we have seen, unfair prejudice is difficult and expensive to prove.

Shareholders who are worried about this happening might do well to insist that they will not buy the shares unless the articles do allow them to be freely transferred. Whether or not the other members would agree to include such an article might well depend on how badly they wanted the particular shareholder's investment. There would also be the problem that the holders of 75% of the voting shares could pass a special resolution to alter the articles.

19.3.4 Borrowing power

If sole traders want to borrow money then they will need to provide security for the loan. There are several ways in which they might do this, but generally they will either need to find a guarantor (who agrees to repay the loan if the trader defaults) or they will need to mortgage their own property. Because of the current high level of business failures banks are demanding very solid security for any money advanced.

Partners are in the same position as sole traders, except that since there are more of them they might well find it easier to find guarantors, or might have more property to mortgage. Creditors who are to be repaid out of partnership profits should make it very clear that they do not intend that this should make them partners.

Members of a company or an LLP can raise money in the same way as partners or sole traders. But companies and LLPs also have additional options.

First, companies can sell shares to people who wish to invest in the company but who have no desire to manage it. Shares in a private limited company cannot be offered to the general public but, subject to the articles, they can be offered to individuals.

An investor who is convinced that the company will be a commercial success might be more than willing to pay for shares. Some small companies achieve spectacular success and eventually change into PLCs with enormous assets. If an investor had contributed capital into such a company when it was first formed for, say, 10% of the shares he would have made an outstandingly good bargain. The converse of course is that very many small companies go to the wall, in which case the shares become worthless.

Second, companies and LLPs can raise capital by giving a floating charge over their assets. We saw in Chapter 18, at 18.8.2, that a floating charge gives a class or all of the company's assets as security for a loan, while still maintaining the right to use and dispose of those assets. (Assets of the class which are acquired in the future become subject to the charge.) However, many lenders take a particularly jaundiced view of the value of a company's or an LLP's assets. They value them on the basis that everything which could possibly reduce their value will in fact do so. This can make it difficult for companies or LLPs without substantial assets to raise much money by issuing floating charges. Partnership property cannot belong to the partnership because a partnership has no separate legal existence of its own. It therefore belongs to the partners jointly (see Chapter 15 at 15.6). A partnership is not allowed to offer a floating charge over partnership property. The partners can of course mortgage the property, but this will limit the use of the property.

19.3.5 Ease of formation

A business which wants to trade immediately will have to do so as a partnership rather than as a company or an LLP.

A partnership can be created without any formalities. As soon as two people carry on a business in common with a view of profit they will be a partnership, whether they realise this or not.

It is however quite likely that partners will want to have a deed of partnership drawn up by a lawyer. If this is the case, then this is bound to involve some expense and delay. Indeed, the expense of this can be considerably greater than the expense of buying an 'off-the-shelf' company.

Both companies and LLPs are formed by registration, which involves sending documents to the Registrar of Companies and waiting for him to register the company. However it is possible to buy an 'off-the-shelf' company, that is to say a company which has been formed with the sole purpose of selling it to people who wish to own a company but who do not want to bother with forming one themselves. If the purchasers of the off-the-shelf company wanted to change the articles or the memorandum they would still have to wait for the Registrar to register the alterations. An off-the-shelf company generally costs between £75 and £125.

It is not at all difficult to create a company or an LLP. A fee of £20 is charged to register a company and £95 to register an LLP. The business will usually be registered within one week. If a fee of £80 is paid, a company will be registered within 24 hours. As regards both the purchase of an off-the-shelf company and the formation of a company it is important to get appropriate articles of association and an appropriate memorandum. Advice from an expert in the field, which is bound to incur cost, is recommended. The same considerations apply when drawing up an LLP agreement. It would also be advisable for those entering a partnership to have an expert draw up a partnership agreement. However, there is the advantage that in the absence of any agreement the Partnership Act provides a framework which is much more suitable to a very small business than Table A articles. (Which are all too often adopted in their entirety, without any regard to their suitability, by those in a hurry to register a company.) LLPs also have a statutory framework of default provisions.

19.3.6 Formalities

Partners do not need to adhere to any formalities. There is no need for them to hold meetings.

A company must have at least one meeting a year, its Annual General Meeting, unless all the members agree to dispense with the meeting. Notice of meetings and of resolutions to be proposed must be given to members, and minutes of meetings must be kept. An annual return must be sent to the Registrar of Companies along with a fee, which is currently £15. LLPs do not have to hold an AGM, but do submit an annual return.

The recent trend is to de-regulate companies. The formalities with which they must comply have been greatly reduced in recent years. As a consequence, the advantage which partnerships enjoy by virtue of not having to comply with any formalities is nowadays less marked. Companies House issue excellent leaflets, written in very plain English, which set out the steps which company officers must take. Most people who are competent to run any kind of successful business ought to be able to follow these directions without seeking professional advice.

If a company wishes to engage in a new type of business then it may be necessary to alter the objects clause to avoid the problem of *ultra vires*. (Considered in Chapter 17 at 17.1.8.) Partnerships and LLPs do not have any such problem.

Small companies and small LLPs will be exempt from having to have their accounts audited if their annual turnover is not more than £1m and their total assets are not worth more than £1.4m. However, if a company or an LLP is not entitled to take advantage of this exemption then two accountants will be needed each year, one to draw up the accounts and the other to audit them. A partnership has no duty to have its accounts audited. However, partnerships will need to produce accounts which are sufficient to satisfy the Inland Revenue.

19.3.7 Publicity

The affairs of a partnership are completely private. Like anyone else, the partners will of course need to declare their earnings to the Inland Revenue. Beyond this there is no need to reveal details of the firm to anyone.

The affairs of companies and LLPs are much more public. Any member of the public will be able to inspect the annual return, the registered accounts, registers held by the Registrar, and most of the registers which the company is required to keep at its registered office.

The accounts are likely to represent the publicly available information which the company members and directors and LLP members would least like to reveal. However, small companies and small LLPs can deliver abbreviated accounts. These accounts would not reveal the remuneration of the directors or LLP members or the amount of dividend recommended. Nor would they need to include a profit and loss account. An abbreviated balance sheet can be delivered instead. These abbreviated accounts would therefore give only very limited information to outsiders and competitors.

A company or an LLP is regarded as small if it meets two out of the following three requirements:

  (i) Its annual turnover is £5.6m or less.
 (ii) Its total assets are £2.8m or less.
(iii) It has 50 or fewer employees.

Medium-sized companies and LLPs can deliver modified accounts, which conceal information about the breakdown of profit, loss and turnover. A company or LLP is regarded as medium-sized if it meets two of the three following requirements:

  (i) Its annual turnover is £22.8m or less.
 (ii) Its total assets are £11.4m or less.
(iii) It has 250 or fewer employees.

As can be seen these qualifications are fairly generous. A business which was too large to start trading as a small company or a small LLP might not wish to trade as a partnership. Unlimited companies do not need to deliver any accounts to the Registrar.

19.3.8 Tax position

Individuals and companies are not taxed in the same way. Individuals pay Income Tax and National Insurance, companies pay Corporation Tax.

For tax purposes partners, LLP members and sole traders are all treated as individuals, and Income Tax is payable on all of the profits which they make. Even profits which are left in the business are taxed.

However, individuals are given personal allowances for Income Tax purposes. In the tax year April 2004 to April 2005 the single person's allowance is currently £4 745. This means that on the first £4 745 which a single person earns he pays no Income Tax.

Once an individual exceeds his allowance he pays tax at varying rates. The single person pays 10% on the first £2 020 in excess of his allowance, 22% on the next £29 380 and then 40% on anything above this.

National Insurance contributions must also be paid. The self-employed pay a flat rate of £2.05 a week, as long as profit exceeds £4 215. A further 8% is payable on profits between £4 745 and £31 720.

It is therefore possible that a self-employed person with substantial other earnings could be paying a tax rate of 48% on some of his business profits.

Companies too are taxed on profits made, in the form of Corporation Tax. Profits of under £10 000 are taxed at 0%. Profits over £50 000 are taxed at 19%. Profits between £10 000 and £50 000 are taxed on a sliding scale rising from 0% to 19%. On profits over £50 000 Corporation Tax rises by degrees until companies pay the full rate of 30% on profits over £1.5m.

Money left in the company is taxed at these rates as Corporation Tax. The owners of the company can withdraw money by paying themselves director's salaries. Corporation Tax would not be paid on such money withdrawn. (Removing the money from the company would reduce the company's profit.) However, self-employed people who wish to trade as a company should bear in mind that if a person arranges to be paid income by a company then they will be an employee of the company. The company will need to pay the employer's National Insurance contribution (12.8%) and the employee's contribution (11%). This combined rate of 23.8% is well in excess of the rate paid by the self-employed. In addition, Income Tax must be paid by the person receiving the income.

Companies do not receive personal allowances. However, it can be seen that the rates of Corporation Tax can be considerably lower than the rates of tax paid by individuals.

It would therefore seem advantageous for many business people to form a company. They could then pay themselves what they needed to live on as a salary, and leave the rest in the company to grow. However, this is complicated by Capital Gains Tax, which is payable when a person sells assets which have grown in value since he acquired them. If money is left in the company then the value of the company, and therefore the value of the shares, will grow. Ultimately, the owners must sell their shares in order to take the money.

Capital Gains Tax, which is payable at 10%, 20%, or 40% (depending on the individual's income tax bracket), could mean that money left in the company is taxed twice. (First it is taxed as company profit. When the shares are sold it is taxed as a capital gain.) Some relief is provided in that individuals are given an annual Capital Gains allowance of £8 200 a year.

Capital Gains Tax liability can be very much reduced by taper relief. The regulations governing this relief are very complicated, but they mean that the Capital Gains Tax payable on assets which have been held by the company for two or more years can be reduced to 25% of what it otherwise would be. Such a rate of tax is considerably below the combined rates of Income Tax and National Insurance. However, using this method of reducing tax has several disadvantages. First, it means dissolving the company to realise the capital gain. Second, it means that the profits generated by the company cannot be touched until the company is dissolved. Third, it means that as no National Insurance is paid the benefits of having paid National Insurance cannot be claimed.

Before the 2004 Budget there were definite tax advantages attached to trading as a company, and taking money in the form of a dividend, rather than trading as a self-employed person. The Chancellor of the Exchequer became so concerned about this that a new minimum rate of Corporation tax of 19% became payable on dividends paid. (This new rate is not payable on profits retained by the company.) The effect of this new rate of tax is that if profits of under £50000 are paid to basic rate taxpayers then the total tax payable is 19%. If these profits are paid to higher rate taxpayers, or to the extent that they take taxpayers into the higher rate, they are taxed at 44%. (As we have seen the rate of Corporation Tax on profits over £50000 rises on a sliding scale from 19% until it reaches the full rate of 30%.) In the light of these changes, many companies which were formed to reduce tax have been dissolved. The extra administration involved in running a company do not justify the very marginal tax benefits.

19.3.9 Perpetual succession

Companies continue in existence until they are wound up. The death of a shareholder, or even the death of all the shareholders, will not end the company. In the same way, LLPs stay in existence until they are wound up.

By contrast, the death of a partner will end the partnership. However, the partnership deed might well provide that the surviving partners should carry the business on. (In which case they must pay an appropriate amount to the estate of the deceased partner.) If the surviving partners do carry the business on, then the dissolution of the partnership will only amount to a technical dissolution.

19.3.10 Sole traders

By definition a sole trader is in business on his own. However, sole traders should consider the benefits of forming a company. Now that it is possible to have a company with a single shareholder, who can also be the only director, a sole trader can incorporate his business and, in effect, still be in business on his own. The company will need to have a different person to act as company secretary, but in small companies the duties of company secretary need not amount to very much. Generally, a sole trader's spouse or other relative will be able to perform the necessary obligations. However, the decision in *Neptune (Vehicle Washing Equipment) Ltd* v *Fitzgerald* [1996] Ch 274, which is set out at 17.1.9, shows that a sole director/member must recognise that he is no longer a sole trader and must adhere to certain formalities and procedures.

In this chapter we have considered whether groups of people forming a business should trade as companies or partnerships. Sole traders should consider the same advantages and disadvantages of incorporation.

Key points

Winding up and insolvency

- A court can order the winding up of a company on seven grounds, if petitioned to do so. The two most important grounds are that the company cannot pay its debts or that the court considers it just and equitable to wind the company up.

- The petition may be presented to the court by the company itself, the directors, a creditor of the company or a member of the company. In limited circumstances the Secretary of State for Trade and Industry or the Official Receiver may present the petition.

- If a winding up order is made by the court the company cannot dispose of its property without a court order; actions in debt against the company are stopped; the directors' powers are taken over by the liquidator; floating charges crystallise; and the company's employees are dismissed. The liquidator may re-employ the employees and also carry on the company business, but only in order to effect the most beneficial winding up.

- A members' voluntarily liquidation is initiated by a special resolution of the company. The directors must be able to file a declaration of solvency. The members appoint the liquidator.

- A creditors' voluntary liquidation is initiated by an extraordinary resolution. The directors do not file a declaration of solvency. The creditors appoint the liquidator.

- As from the time when the resolution to wind up is passed, the company must cease trading except as may be required for a beneficial winding up; shares cannot be transferred without the liquidator's consent; the company employees are dismissed. The directors' powers are limited and cease when the liquidator is appointed.

- After liquidation the various classes of creditors are paid. Each class is paid in full before the lower-ranking classes are paid at all. (However, as regards floating charges created on or after 15 September 2003, some of the company's assets may be earmarked for distribution to the unsecured creditors.) If there are insufficient assets to pay a class in full, each member of the class is paid the same percentage of what he is owed.

- First, the costs of realising assets subject to a floating charge are paid. Then the preferential creditors; then (if appropriate) a top sliced fund goes to the unsecured creditors; then holders of floating charges are paid what they are owed; then the general costs of liquidation are paid; then unsecured creditors are paid; finally, any surplus is distributed to members of the company.

- A director or shadow director can be liable for wrongful trading if he knew that the company could not avoid going into insolvent liquidation, and he did not take all reasonable steps to minimise the potential loss to the company's creditors.

- After a company has gone into liquidation the liquidator may apply for a court order to avoid transactions entered into at an undervalue or preferences given to creditors.

- A floating charge will be invalid, to the extent that the company did not receive value in return for creating it, if it was created within 12 months of winding up proceedings, unless the company was solvent after creating the charge.

- A floating charge created in favour of a connected person within two years of the commencement of winding up proceedings will be invalid, to the extent that the company did not receive value in return for creating it, whether or not the company was solvent at the time the charge was created.

- When a company is in administration the administrator has three hierarchical objectives. First, to rescue the company as a going concern (the primary purpose). Second, to achieve a better result for the company's creditors than would be achieved if the company was wound up. Third, to sell property to pay to the company's secured or preferential creditors.

- Whilst it is in administration, a petition to wind a company up will be dismissed or suspended.

- Floating charge holders whose charges were created before 15 September 2003 can appoint an administrative receiver. (If created after this date they can only appoint an administrator.) An administrative receiver realises the charged property so that the floating charge holders can be paid. An administrator also has the power to do this, but it is not his primary purpose.

LLPs

- Two or more people can trade together as an LLP.

- An LLP is a corporate body which is created by registration with the registrar of companies.

- The members of an LLP must carry on a lawful business with a view to profit.

- The name of an LLP must end with the words 'limited liability partnership' or 'llp' or 'LLP' (or their Welsh equivalents). Other than this, the rules relating to the names of LLPs are identical to the rules relating to the names of companies.

- Every LLP must have at least two designated members. These designated members have certain specified duties, such as signing the LLP's accounts.

- Every member of an LLP is the agent of the LLP and can therefore make contracts which will bind the LLP.

- The relationship between one member of an LLP and another member, and between members and the LLP itself, is governed by agreement between the members. In the absence of such agreement, ten default provisions apply.

- No majority of members can expel any member unless a power to do so has been conferred by express agreement between the members.

- A member of an LLP can leave by agreement with the other members or by giving the other members reasonable notice. An LLP will not be dissolved when a member leaves.

- A member may be able to petition the court for a winding up order, under s.122 of the Insolvency Act 1986, on the grounds that this is just and equitable.

- The provisions of s.459 Companies Act 1985 apply to LLPs, unless the members unanimously agree in writing that they should not.

- LLPs can issue fixed and floating charges in the same way as companies.

- In general, members of an LLP will not have any liability to pay the debts of the LLP.

- Members of an LLP can be liable to pay the debts of an LLP if they have agreed with the other members or with the LLP that they will. They can also be liable for wrongful trading or fraudulent trading, as directors of companies can.

- Members of an LLP can be liable to make a contribution to the debts of the LLP if they withdrew LLP property within two years of the LLP's insolvency, while having reasonable grounds for believing that the LLP would not be able to pay its debts and should have known that the LLP could not avoid insolvent liquidation.

- LLP members can be disqualified from becoming LLP members or company directors.

Choice of legal status

■ The members of limited companies, and of LLPs, have limited liability for the debts of the business. Members of ordinary partnerships enjoy no such limited liability.

■ All partners and all LLP members generally have a right to manage the firm or the LLP. The board of directors act as the managers of a company.

■ Depending upon the articles, it can be difficult to withdraw from a company.

■ Companies and LLPs can borrow by giving a floating charge over the company's assets. Companies, but not LLPs, can also raise money by selling shares to investors who do not want to manage the business.

■ Companies are taxed differently from partners, LLP members and sole traders.

Summary questions

1   Benjamin, a building contractor, is owed £2 000 by Acme Ltd. When Benjamin phoned asking for payment Acme acknowledged the debt and sent him a cheque. Unfortunately the cheque was dishonoured. A month later, after several promises to pay, Acme sent another cheque. This too was dishonoured. Benjamin discovers that Acme owes money to several other traders. Last week the managing director of Acme wrote to Benjamin, explaining that the Government was due to pay the company £30 000 in 12 weeks' time. The letter promised that as soon as the money was received all of the company's debts would be paid with interest. Advise Benjamin as to:

   a   The steps he should take if he wants to see the company wound up.
   b   Whether or not the court would have to order liquidation.

2   On 1 November 2003, following a petition from a creditor, the court ordered that Ace Ltd be wound up. The day before the court order was made the managing director sold the company car in order to pay his own salary. Ace Ltd's work force are due to finish a large Government contract on the 5 November. This contract will bring in £20 000. This is not enough money to clear Ace's debts, but it will be a big help. In August the managing director's wife was granted a floating charge to secure a loan of £5 000 which she had made to the company three years earlier. At the same time the company also sold the company's business premises to the managing director's wife for about half of its market value.
Advise the creditors as to:

   a   Whether the sale of the company car is valid.
   b   Whether Ace Ltd's workers are still employed.
   c   Whether Ace Ltd's business can be carried on in order to finish the Government contract.
   d   Who would have the power to make decisions about re-employing the workers and finishing the contract?
   e   The legal position as regards the floating charge and the sale of the company's business premises.

3   BrokeCo Ltd was wound up on 2 June 2004. The company has various creditors as follows.

   a   Arthur is owed £10 000 in respect of goods supplied to BrokeCo and subsequently sold on by BrokeCo.
   b   Seven employees are each owed four weeks' pay (total £1 000 per employee) and £200 accrued holiday pay.
   c   The Revenue is owed last month's PAYE bill of £4 000.
   d   Billy has a floating charge over all of the company's assets, registered four years ago, to secure a debt which currently stands at £5 000.
   e   The members of the company have not been paid the dividend declared in the previous year (total dividend is £600).

   In what order will these creditors be paid? How much will each creditor be paid if, after the costs of winding up, the assets raised by the sale of the company's assets, and available for distribution to creditors and members, amounts to: (a) £10 000; (b) £20 000; (c) £30 000?

4 Three years ago Sarah finished a college course in Health and Beauty Therapy. After a year working in a Salon she spent three months in the United States. On a trip to California Sarah was extremely impressed by some of the alternative beauty treatments available there.

Sarah now wants to market some of the Californian ideas in England, and is worried that if she waits too long others will beat her to it.

Sarah's grandfather, Stanley, has recently retired from the Board of a multinational company. He has a variety of interests but, seeing Sarah as a 'chip off the old block', he is prepared to invest in her proposed business and help her in the running of it.

Sarah is very fond of her grandfather but thinks that he is too cautious, not realising that in the modern age opportunities must be seized immediately, before it becomes too late. Stanley is very proud of Sarah but feels that, expert though she might be in the field of Beauty Therapy, she has a great deal to learn as far as business goes.

Stanley has agreed to invest £25 000 in the business and put in three or four hours work a week. Sarah is putting in her savings of £3 000 and will devote all of her time to the business.

a Do you think that Stanley would prefer that the business was a company, an LLP or a partnership?

b Which do you think Sarah would prefer?

c As an objective outsider, which type of business organisation do you think they should become?

5 In what ways is an LLP more similar to a limited company than to an ordinary partnership?

6 Steve, Trevor and Ursula are members of an LLP which offers financial advice to small businesses. At the outset each member contributed £30 000 capital to the business. Trevor and Ursula are the designated members. Last year, without any authority from his fellow members, Steve made a contract with a local authority, on behalf of the LLP, to offer financial advice to members of the public for £1 an hour. (Steve thought that this would lead to a good deal of profitable business.) Trevor and Ursula do not regard the LLP as bound by this contract. Steve now wishes to leave the LLP. Trevor and Ursula are happy to see Steve leave, but are not prepared to allow him to take any capital with him. Advise the parties of their legal postions.

Multiple choice questions

1 In which **one** of the following circumstances would the company be regarded as unable to pay its debts, under s.123 of the Insolvency Act?

a The company has owed Arthur £300 for six months. It has refused to pay, despite Arthur having left a written request for payment left at the company's registered office three months ago.

b The company has owed Bill £2 000 for two weeks. It has refused to pay, despite Bill having left a written request for payment at the company's registered office two weeks ago.

c The company owes Charlene £1 000. It has refused to pay, despite Charlene having left a written request for payment at the company's registered office four weeks ago.

d The company owes Derek £4 000. He has phoned once a week, for the past six weeks, demanding payment. Each time the company agreed to pay immediately, but as yet it has not paid.

2 Which one of the following is unable to petition the court to compulsorily wind up a company which is not defunct?

a The Registrar of Companies.

b A member of the company whose shares are fully paid up.

c The company itself.

d The directors of the company.

3 Caput Ltd has gone into liquidation. The assets have been realised and have generated £20 000. Of this amount £6 000 came from the sale of the company car over which Charlene had a fixed charge. The following debts and liabilities exist:

   i Caput owes Charlene £5 000 (secured by the fixed charge).

   ii The three directors are each owed £2 000 a month salary for the past three months.

   iii Suppliers of components are owed £20 000.

   iv Dividends amounting to £8 000 are owed to shareholders. These dividends were declared three months ago, but have not yet been paid.

   v £5 000 is owed to David, a director of Caput, who loaned the money to the company so that the work force could be paid last month's wages (each worker was owed and paid £750).

   vi Three months' VAT, amounting to £1 000, is owed to the Revenue.

   vii Costs of winding up, which amount to £1 500.

Which of the creditors will receive payment in full, and which will receive part payment of their debts?

   a The Revenue, Charlene, David and the costs of winding up would be paid in full. The supplier of the components and the directors would receive part payment.

   b The Revenue, Charlene, the directors, David and the costs of winding up would be paid in full. All the other creditors would receive part payment.

   c David and the costs of winding up would be paid in full. Charlene, the directors, and the suppliers of the components would receive part payment.

   d The Revenue, David and the costs of winding up would be paid in full. All the other creditors would receive part payment.

4 Jade and Rachel are in partnership as interior designers, sharing profits equally. Jade also owns all of the shares in a Mail Order company. Which **one** of the following statements is **not** true?

   a Jade and Rachel will be liable to pay Income Tax on profits which they leave in the business.

   b If Jade's company pays her a salary, then Jade will have to pay Income Tax on this money. In addition, both Jade and the company will have to pay National Insurance contributions on the salary paid.

   c If the assets of the company increase in value then Jade must pay Income Tax on this increase in value.

   d If the company makes a profit then the company will have to pay Corporation Tax on this profit. In addition, Jade may become liable to pay Capital Gains Tax when she sells her shares in the company and realises the profit.

5 Consider the following statements. Which of the statements are true?

   i As an LLP is a corporate body, it is possible to have a single member LLP.

   ii Every LLP must have at least two designated members.

   iii Every member of an LLP is the agent of the LLP.

   iv Neither an incorporation document, nor an LLP agreement, can confer rights on a third party to enforce a term of the document or agreement.

   v An agreement made before the incorporation of an LLP, between the subscribers to the incorporation document, can impose obligations on the LLP to take effect at any time after its incorporation.

   a All of the statements.

   b All of the statements except i.

   c All of the statements except iv.

   d Only statements ii and iii.

   e None of the statements.

6 Consider the following statements. Which **one** of the statements is **not** true?

   a When acting as agents of an LLP the members will owe a fiduciary duty to the LLP.

   b Unless the members have agreed to the contrary, no member of an LLP is entitled to any remuneration for acting in the business or management of the LLP.

   c No majority can expel any member unless a power to do so has been conferred by express agreement between the members.

   d If a member of an LLP assigns his share of the LLP to an assignee, the assignee has the right to take part in the management of the LLP, unless there has been an agreement to the contrary.

   e The right contained in s.459(1) of the Companies Act 1985 apply to LLPs, unless the members of the LLP have unanimously agreed in writing to exclude the right.

Task 19

Three friends of yours, who work as builders, are owed money by several companies for which they have worked. One of these companies has now been wound up. Your friends have asked you to draft a report, briefly dealing with the following matters.

a Explain the grounds upon which a company may be compulsorily wound up, and the persons entitled to petition for such a winding up.

b How company members can voluntarily wind the company up.

c The order in which creditors of liquidated companies are paid by the liquidator.

d How the law attempts to ensure that creditors of insolvent companies are not defrauded.

e The main advantages and disadvantages which attach to trading as a company, an LLP or partnership.

Chapter 20

EMPLOYMENT 1 · DUTIES OF EMPLOYER AND EMPLOYEE · DISMISSAL · REDUNDANCY

Introduction

The law relating to employment is derived both from the common law and from legislation. As the relationship between employer and employee is contractual, the general principles of the law of contract underpin the employment relationship and must constantly be borne in mind. Thus a contract of employment is formed by offer and acceptance, the terms of the contract can be express or implied, the contract can be discharged by agreement or frustration, and an employee who is dismissed in breach of contract can sue for contract damages.

Despite the essentially contractual nature of the employment relationship, in recent years employment law has become increasingly regulated by statute and statutory instrument. Much of this legislation was passed to give effect to EC Directives and so the subject has a strong EC element. Some aspects of employment law are governed by Codes of Practice. Although these Codes are not legally binding, they are admissible as evidence.

We begin this chapter by identifying the courts and tribunals which hear employment cases, and considering the extent to which decisions of these courts are binding precedents. We then distinguish employees from independent contractors. Although independent contractors provide services for those who hire them, they do not do so as employees. Consequently, they do not gain certain rights such as the right to compensation if unfairly dismissed or made redundant. After examining how employees can be identified, we consider the terms which are implied by the courts into contracts of employment. We end this chapter by considering two major rights afforded to employees – the right to compensation if unfairly dismissed and the right to a redundancy payment if made redundant. In the following chapter we examine discrimination in employment, health and safety at work and miscellaneous aspects of employee protection.

Courts and tribunals

Before beginning our study of employment law it is necessary to understand the role of the two tribunals which have jurisdiction to hear employment cases and appeals. Almost all claims relating to employment begin in an employment tribunal (previously known as industrial tribunals). In such a tribunal a lawyer who has been qualified for at least seven years sits as chairman, along with two lay members. These lay members generally represent the two 'sides' of industry, one having been nominated by an employer's association whilst the other was nominated by a trade union. Some claims, such as those for breach of a contract, are generally heard by the chairman alone. An employment tribunal has the power to hear any claim based on an employment statute. It also has the power to hear any common law case for breach of a contract of employment, or for breach of most other contracts connected with employment, where the damages claimed are not more than £25 000. The decision of the tribunal is by a majority. It is possible, although very unusual, for the two lay members to outvote the chairman. Legal aid is not available for a case heard by an employment tribunal. It is not essential to have legal representation and the proceedings are relatively informal. A claim must generally be brought within three months of the effective date of termination of the contract of employment or, if there is no such date, within three months of the last day on which the employee worked. If the claim is for personal injury then it is heard by the ordinary civil courts, rather than by the employment tribunal.

Appeals from an employment tribunal are heard by the Employment Appeal Tribunal (the EAT). This is a wholly appellate court, no cases begin here. (When damages in excess of £25 000 are claimed for breach of a contract of employment the case begins in the ordinary civil courts.) The president of the EAT will either be a High Court judge or a Court of Appeal judge. The president usually sits with either two or four lay members, but sometimes sits alone. Appeals from cases which were heard by the chairman alone in the employment tribunal are generally heard by the president of the EAT sitting alone. Legal aid is available for appeals heard by the EAT, subject to the usual financial limitations. The Court of Appeal hears appeals from the Employment Appeal Tribunal, but permission to make the appeal must be given by either the EAT or the Court of Appeal. An appeal can be made from the Court of Appeal to the House of Lords, if either the Court of Appeal or the House of Lords grants permission. The decisions of an employment tribunal are not binding upon any other courts.

The decisions of the Employment Appeal Tribunal are binding upon employment tribunals, but not upon later sittings of the Employment Appeal Tribunal. They are therefore similar in status to decisions of the High Court. The binding force of decisions of the Court of Appeal and House of Lords was considered in Chapter 1 at 1.3.2.1.

Much of employment law has an element of EC law, which is supreme over national law (see Chapter 1 at 1.4.4). Any national court may refer a case which involves a matter of EC law to the European Court of Justice (the ECJ). The ECJ gives an opinion and the case then returns to the UK court for this opinion to be applied to the facts of the case. In addition, a member state can be taken to the European Court for failure to live up to its EC obligations by either the European Commission or a different Member State.

The ECJ does not use a system of precedent, so its own decisions are not binding upon future sittings of the ECJ. However, the decisions of the ECJ are binding upon all of the UK courts, whether the decision in question concerned a UK case or a case from a different Member State. In Chapter 1 at 1.4.3.1 we examined the way in which a case could be sufficiently concerned with EC law for it to be referred to the ECJ. All of the ways which we set out are relevant in employment law. Many cases are referred to the ECJ to give an opinion on an article of a treaty, particularly upon Article 141 of the Treaty of Rome which provides that men and women should receive equal pay for doing equal work. Many more cases concern UK legislation which was passed in order to give effect to a Directive of the EC. Although UK legislation gives effect to Article 141 of the Treaty of Rome, the ECJ retains the power to give an opinion as to the interpretation of the Article. Similarly, the ECJ has the power to give opinions on the interpretation of directives even after the UK has implemented these by legislation.

Codes of practice

Although not sources of law, several codes of practice may be used in evidence in an employment case. These Codes do not have legal force, but failure to observe them will weigh heavily against an employer's argument that he behaved reasonably. Codes have been drawn up by ACAS, the Commission for Racial Equality, the Secretary of State for Employment, the Equal Opportunities Commission and the Health and Safety Commission.

ACAS conciliation

Before a case is heard by an employment tribunal a conciliation officer from the Advisory and Conciliation Service (ACAS) will try to get the parties to reach an agreement without taking the case further. This procedure has a high success rate and most cases are settled at this stage. If they make an agreement to settle, both employer and employee are bound by it. Matters revealed to the ACAS officer cannot be admitted in evidence without the permission of the party who communicated them. Agreements by which an employee opts out of his statutory rights which were reached otherwise than through ACAS conciliation are only binding upon the employee if they were in writing and the employee received independent legal advice. If conciliation is not reached either party may apply to the employment tribunal for a pre-hearing assessment. This assessment considers the likely outcome of proceedings and can warn an employee with a frivolous or vexatious complaint that costs may be awarded against them.

ACAS has several functions other than conciliation in individual cases. It can give advice to employers, workers or trade unions on matters likely to affect industrial relations. This advice can be given when requested, or ACAS can give it without having been requested to do so. ACAS has a similar role to conciliate when a trade dispute arises. ACAS issues Codes of Practice, as already mentioned. It can in some circumstances refer a trade dispute to arbitration, after all other procedures have been exhausted. ACAS also conducts enquiries into industrial relations. These enquiries may either be of a general nature or they may be into industrial relations within one industry or one undertaking.

20.1 · Employees contrasted with independent contractors

People employed under a contract of employment, or a 'contract of service' as such a contract is commonly known, are employees. People who contract to provide services for another otherwise than under a contract of employment are known as independent contractors.

The distinction between employees and independent contractors is an important one for several reasons. First, various terms which are implied into contracts of employment are not implied into contracts under which services are supplied by independent contractors. Second, employers can be vicariously liable for torts committed by employees during the course of their employment, but are not generally liable for the torts of independent contractors who provide a service for them. (Vicarious liability is examined in Chapter 13 at 13.8.) Third, many statutes confer employment protection rights only upon employees. (As we examine the various statutes, we shall see that those which outlaw discrimination also confer protection on independent contractors who personally provide a service.)

Over the years the courts have evolved several tests to distinguish employees and independent contractors. One of the first tests, the control test, held that employees could not only be told what to do but they could also be told how to do it. Independent contractors could be told what purposes to achieve, but it was up to the contractors to use whatever method they thought fit to achieve these purposes. This test did not work particularly well with some skilled employees and so further tests evolved.

In *Stevenson, Jordan and Harrison Ltd* v *MacDonald and Evans* [1952] 1 TLR Denning LJ put forward an integration test.

> 'One feature which seems to run through the cases is that, under a contract of service [contract of employment], a man is employed as a part of the business and his work is done as an integral part of the business; whereas under a contract for services [contract made by an independent contractor] his work, although done for the business, is not integrated into it but only accessory to it.'

This test worked better than the control test for some skilled employees, such as surgeons. Their employers do not control the way surgeons act when operating upon patients, although they can insist that certain procedures are followed. However, the work of surgeons is done as an integral part of the hospitals in which they work. The work of a roofer, paid £500 to fix the hospital roof, is not done as an integral part of the hospital's business but is only accessory to it. Denning LJ made the point more simply when he said that employees were 'part and parcel of the organisation', whereas independent contractors were not.

Neither the control test nor the integration test seemed to produce entirely satisfactory results, and in *Ready Mixed Concrete (South East) Ltd* v *MPNI* [1968] 2 QB 497 Mackenna J formulated the economic reality test, which held that a worker would be an employee only if three conditions are satisfied. First, the worker must agree to provide his own work and skill in return for a wage or other payment. Second, the worker must agree, expressly or impliedly, that he will be under the control of the person paying for his work. Third, the rest of the terms of the contract must be consistent with a contract of employment. (This would include matters such as who paid the worker's tax, what type of National Insurance contributions were paid and who provided equipment.)

In *Lee Ting Sang* v *Chung Chi-Keung* [1990] IRLR 236 the Privy Council held that there is no single test for deciding whether or not a person is working as an employee or as an independent contractor. The fundamental question being, 'Is the person who has engaged himself to perform these services performing them as a person in business on his own account?' This test was first formulated by Cooke J in *Market Investigations* v *Minister of Social Security* [1969] 2 QB 173 and in *Lee* v *Chung* the Privy Council strongly approved Cooke J's reasoning as to how to answer the question. Cooke J said:

> 'No exhaustive list has been compiled and perhaps no exhaustive list can be compiled of the considerations which are relevant in determining that question, nor can strict rules be laid down as to the relative weight which the various considerations should carry in particular cases. The most that can be said is that control will no doubt always have to be considered, although it can no longer be regarded as the sole determining factor; and that factors which may be of importance are such matters as whether the man performing the services provides his own equipment, whether he hires his own helpers, what degree of financial risk he takes, what degree of responsibility for investment and management he has, and whether and how far he has an opportunity of profiting from sound management in the performance of his task.'

In *Lee* v *Chung* the Privy Council also stated that the question as to whether or not a person provided services as an employee was a question of fact. (In exceptional cases where the relationship depended solely upon the true construction of a written document it might be a question of law.) As it was a question of fact it was a matter to be decided by the trial court. An appellate court would only interfere with the finding of the trial court if it took 'a view of the facts which could not reasonably be entertained'. (In the case, the Privy Council concluded that the trial court had made such an error and reversed the decision of the trial court.) In *Hall* v *Lorimer* [1994] IRLR 171 the Court of Appeal warned against the use of 'mechanical tests', indicating that each case should be decided on its own particular facts.

Difficult questions arise in respect of agency workers and casual workers. The circumstances in which such workers will be employees are far from being settled, but one important factor is the 'mutuality of obligation' test. If the employer has no duty to provide work, and the worker has no duty to accept work, then it is likely that there will be no contract of employment while the workers are not actually at work. In the following case the House of Lords had to consider whether or not the relationship between casual workers and National Power, for whom they worked as guides, was regulated by a contract of employment when the workers were not working. Making it plain that they were not considering whether or not the workers were employees when actually working as guides, the House of Lords held that the guides were not governed by a contract of employment when they were not working.

■ *Carmichael* v *National Power* [1999] 4 All ER 897 (House of Lords)

Mrs L and Mrs C worked as casual guides at a power station. By 1995 they worked up to 25 hours a week and were paid a flat rate for hours worked. When they first worked for National Power in 1990 they worked about 3.75 hours a week. Mrs L and Mrs C claimed to be employees working under a contract of employment and therefore to be entitled to written particulars of the terms of their employment. (See below at 20.2.1.1.) Mrs L and Mrs C claimed that an exchange of correspondence between the parties created a contract of employment. Some of this correspondence referred to guides as being employed. When accepting the work both women signed a pre-typed letter which said, 'I am pleased to accept your offer of employment as a Station Guide on a casual as required basis.' They were both trained, and both worked when they were available and chose to work. When they did work they were on the payroll for PAYE purposes. The employment tribunal held that when the women were not working as guides they had no contractual relationship of any kind. The tribunal held that their claim 'founders on the rock of absence of mutuality', that is to say failed because they had no obligations towards National Power, who had no obligations to them.

Held. There was no contract between the claimants and the defendants. The defendants had no obligation to provide work and the claimants had no duty to accept it. The true intention of the parties was that there should be no contractual relationship. This outcome could be deduced from the following matters: the documents exchanged between the parties did not set out when, how and with what frequency work would be offered; there were no provisions relating to notice or termination; the guides were not part of the full-time employees' sickness, holiday or pension schemes; the usual grievance and disciplinary procedures did not apply; Mrs C had not been available for work on 17 occasions and Mrs L had not been available on eight occasions, and no question of disciplining them had arisen; when taking the job Mrs C had said that the part time/casual arrangement would suit her circumstances ideally. Taking all this into account, the employment tribunal had correctly concluded that the case 'founders on the rock of absence of mutuality'. All the circumstances indicated that the parties did not intend there to be a contractual relationship while the women were not actually working as guides.

The status of agency workers has continued to cause difficulty.

■ *Johnson Underwood Ltd* v *Montgomery* [2001] EWCA Civ 318

The claimant was registered with the defendants' employment agency. The defendants sent the claimant to a local firm where she worked as a telephonist for two and a half years. The defendants paid the claimant's wages. The local firm asked the defendants to get rid of the claimant as they were dissatisfied with her. The defendants therefore withdrew the claimant from the local firm and sent her to work for a different firm. The claimant refused to accept this and sued both the defendants and the firm where she had worked for unfair dismissal.

Held. Neither of the claims succeeded. The claimant was clearly not an employee of the firm where she had worked. Nor was she an employee of the defendants because the defendants had no control over her work.

COMMENT The Court of Appeal thought that perhaps the claimant was neither an employee nor an independent contractor but had a special type of contract somewhere between the two. The logical consequence of this case would seem to be that if the claimant had injured somebody whilst working for the local firm she, and she alone, would have been liable. As she would have been highly unlikely to have thought of herself as a self-employed she would also have been highly unlikely to have carried insurance against such a risk.

■ *Dacas* v *Brook Street Bureau (UK) Ltd* [2004] EWCA Civ 217 (Court of Appeal)

Mrs Dacas was registered with the defendants' employment agency and they sent her to a Wandsworth Council residential care home, where she worked as a cleaner for six years. Wandsworth Council exercised day-to-day control over the claimant but the defendants also exercised considerable control in that they paid her wages, deducting tax and National Insurance Contributions, and could discipline her and could terminate her contract. However, the claimant's contract with the defendants clearly stated that she was not employed by them.

Held. The claimant was not employed by the defendants because they had no obligation to provide her with work and she had no obligation to accept work. The defendants paid the claimant but did not control her day-to-day activities. Such control was exercised by the local authority.

COMMENT The Court of Appeal thought that the tribunals should have considered whether or not there was an implied contract of service between the claimant and Wandsworth Council. This question was not relevant in the case only because Wandsworth Council were not a party to the proceedings. However, in future cases tribunals should consider whether or not such an implied contract existed between agency workers and the clients to whom there were sent.

The fact that the parties describe the worker as self-employed will not be conclusive if the facts of the case indicate otherwise. The following two cases indicate the matters which must be considered.

■ *Ferguson* v *John Dawson & Partners (Contractors) Ltd* [1976] 3 All ER 817 (Court of Appeal)

The claimant was employed as a casual building worker on the defendants' building site under an oral contract. He was told that there were no cards as the labourers were 'purely working as a lump labour force'. The claimant was paid an hourly rate. No tax or national insurance was deducted from the labourers' pay. The foreman told the labourers what to do and the defendants provided their tools. The claimant was injured while working. He claimed compensation against the defendants under the Construction (Working Place) Regulations 1966. In order to succeed under the Regulations it was essential that the claimant was employed by the defendants. As part of their defence, the defendants argued that the claimant was not employed under a contract of employment.

Held. Even if the parties' true intention was that the claimant was not an employee, this was only a relevant factor rather than a conclusive factor. Regard had to be had to the arrangement as a whole and in particular to the rights and obligations of the parties. The terms of the contract indicated that the claimant was an employee.

■ *Massey* v *Crown Life Insurance Co* [1978] ICR 590 (Court of Appeal)

From 1971 to 1973 the claimant worked as a branch manager of an office of the defendant insurance company and was treated as an employee. The claimant also had an agency agreement with the company and in 1973, at his own request, he entered into an agreement whereby he continued to perform the same services as previously, but as self-employed for tax purposes. This agreement was made in the claimant's registered business name. When the agreement was terminated by the company in 1975 the claimant claimed compensation for unfair dismissal. This claim could only succeed if the claimant was an employee.

Held. Although the parties cannot alter the true nature of their relationship by putting a name on it, the 1973 agreement was genuinely intended by the parties to make the claimant an independent contractor rather than an employee. He was therefore an independent contractor and accordingly he could not claim compensation for unfair dismissal.

COMMENT There were significant differences between this case and *Ferguson*'s case, which was distinguished. The two cases do not necessarily conflict with each other. The important differences were as follows: Massey asked for the change, Ferguson had little choice but to accept it; Massey was a skilled worker, Ferguson was not; the courts are more ready to find employment in cases where a claim for personal injury depends upon such a finding, rather than in cases concerning tax or unfair dismissal.

In the light of the above cases, it must be said that the decision as to whether or not a worker is an employee or an independent contractor can be very difficult. The law is still evolving, particularly as employment practices change. It seems likely that many cases involving 'teleworkers', who provide a service from their homes, will soon be before the courts.

Test your understanding

1 To what extent do decisions of an employment tribunal and the Employment Appeal Tribunal create binding precedents?

2 In what circumstances can questions of employment law be referred to the European Court of Justice. To what extent are decisions of the ECJ binding upon other courts?

3 What is the role of ACAS?

4 Is there any exhaustive list of matters which can determine whether or not a worker is an employee or an independent contractor? Why is the distinction important?

5 Is the question as to whether a worker is an employee or an independent contractor one of law or fact? Why should this matter?

Answers

1 The decisions of employment tribunals are not binding upon any other courts. The decisions of the Employment Appeal Tribunal are binding upon employment tribunals, but not upon later sittings of the Employment Appeal Tribunal.

2 Any UK court can refer a case to the ECJ if the case involves a matter of European law. Member States of the EC can also be taken to the European Court by other Member States of the European Community. The decisions of the ECJ are binding upon all UK courts.

3 ACAS attempts conciliation before a case is taken to an employment tribunal. It also advises employers, workers and trade unions on matters likely to affect industrial relations, attempts to settle trade disputes, conducts enquiries into industrial relations, has the power to refer disputes to arbitration and issues Codes of Practice.

4 There is no exhaustive list of matters which can determine whether or not a worker is an employee or an independent contractor. A wide variety of factors needs to be considered in every case. The distinction between employees and independent contractors is important because terms which are implied into contracts of employment are not implied into contracts with independent contractors, because employers can be vicariously liable for the torts of their employees and because many employment rights are afforded only to employees.

5 The question as to whether a worker is an employee or an independent contractor is generally a question of fact. Consequently, an appellate court will only overturn the decision of the trial court if that court took a view of the facts which could not reasonably be entertained. An appellate court overturns a decision of law made by an inferior court whenever it considers that the decision was wrong.

20.2 · The terms of the contract of employment

Section 230(2) of the Employment Rights Act (ERA) 1996 restates the common law position that a contract of employment may be made expressly or impliedly, and that there is no need for such a contract to be in writing. Generally a contract of employment, like other contracts, will contain both express and implied terms. If any of these terms are breached a remedy will be available for breach of contract.

20.2.1 Express terms

In general, the parties are free to agree whatever express terms they wish. However, several statutes which we study in this and the following chapter confer rights upon employees out of which they may not contract. In addition, s.2(1) of the Unfair Contract Terms Act 1977 renders ineffective any term which seeks to exclude the employer's liability for death or personal injury caused by negligence.

It is obviously desirable that the employer and employee should agree as many express terms as possible when the contract is formed, and that the meaning of these terms should be clear and unambiguous.

20.2.1.1 Written particulars

Section 1 ERA 1996 requires an employer to give an employee a written statement of particulars of the employment. This statement must be given not later than two months after the commencement of the employment. The statement, which can be given in instalments, must contain particulars of the following matters:

(a) The names of the employer and the employee.
(b) The date on which the employment began.
(c) The date on which the employee's continuous employment began and whether any previous employment is to count as continuous employment. (Continuous employment is an important factor in connection with redundancy and unfair dismissal, and is examined later in this chapter at 20.4.1.2.)

(d) The scale and rate of remuneration and the way in which this is calculated.
(e) The intervals at which remuneration is paid (weekly, monthly etc.).
(f) Any terms and conditions relating to hours of work, including any terms and conditions relating to normal working hours.
(g) Any terms and conditions relating to: holiday entitlement and holiday pay; incapacity for work due to sickness and injury, including any provisions for sick pay; pensions and pension schemes.
(h) The length of notice needed to terminate the employment.
(i) The title of the employee's job or a brief description of the work for which he is employed.
(j) If the employment is not intended to be permanent, the period for which it is expected to continue or, if it is for a fixed term, the date on which the term is to end.
(k) Either the place of work or, where the employee is required or permitted to work at various places, an indication of that and of the address of the employer.
(l) Any collective agreements which affect the terms and conditions of the employment.
(m) Where the employee is required to work outside the UK for a period of more than one month, the period for which he is to work outside the UK, the currency in which he is to be paid in while working outside the UK, and any additional remuneration or benefits to be paid or provided by reason of his being required to work outside the UK.

Section 3 ERA 1996 requires that the statement issued under s.1 shall include a note specifying any disciplinary rules applicable to the employee, or referring the employee to the provisions of a document specifying such rules. The document in question must be reasonably accessible to the employee. The note must specify the persons to whom the employee can apply if dissatisfied with any disciplinary decisions relating to him, and the person to whom the employee can apply for the purpose of seeking redress of any grievance relating to his employment. It must also set out the manner in which such an application should be made. However, there is no need to provide these details of disciplinary and grievance procedures if on the date when the employment began the relevant number of employees was fewer than 20.

The employer may refer the employer to other documents, in respect of sick pay and pension schemes, as long as these are reasonably accessible to the employee.

The written particulars which must be provided do not constitute the contract of employment. Unless the employee accepts the offer of employment by signing an agreement which contains all of the written particulars, the contract will have been formed before the employee sees the particulars. However, the written particulars are very strong evidence of the terms of the contract of employment and in the absence of strong conflicting evidence that they were not the terms of the contract a tribunal is likely to conclude that they were. In *Systems Floors* v *Daniel* [1981] IRLR 475 Browne-Wilkinson J, sitting as President of the EAT, said, 'It seems to us, therefore, that in general the status of the statutory statement is this. It provides very strong *prima facie* evidence of what were the terms of the contract between the parties, but does not constitute a written contract between the parties. Nor are the statements of the terms finally conclusive: at most, they place a heavy burden on the employer to show that the actual terms of the contract are different from those which he has set out in the statutory statement.'

If the employer does not provide a statement of written particulars, or provides an incomplete statement, an employee can apply to an employment tribunal to decide upon the matters which should have been included. Under s.38 the Employment Rights Act (ERA) 2002, the tribunal will make a minimum award of two weeks' pay and a maximum award of four weeks' pay to an employee bringing a case of discrimination, unfair dismissal or redundancy if the employee had not, at the start of proceedings, been given his statement of employment particulars. For these purposes the week's pay is capped at the limit of £270 which applies when calculating a basic award for unfair dismissal. (See below at 20.4.4.2.) If the matters specified in the written particulars change, the employer must give the employee a written statement containing particulars of the change within one month.

20.2.1.2 Itemised pay statements

Section 8 ERA 1996 gives an employee the right to be given by his employer, at or before the time at which any payment of wages or salary is made to him, a written itemised pay statement. This must contain particulars of:

(a) the gross amount of the wages or salary;
(b) the amount of any deductions from that gross amount, and the purposes for which they are made;
(c) the net amount of wages and salary payable; and
(d) where different parts of the net amount are paid in different ways, the amount and method of payment of each part-payment.

The total amount of fixed deductions must always be stated. However, rather than give a detailed breakdown of the particulars of these every time wages are paid, the employer may give a detailed breakdown annually.

Where an employee fails to give an employee an itemised pay statement, or where there is a dispute as to the contents of such a statement, the employee can apply to an employment tribunal to determine what matters ought to have been included in an itemised pay statement. Where the employer has made deductions from pay without notifying the employee, the tribunal has the power to award the employee the amount of deductions not notified in the previous 13 weeks.

If an employer has an occupational pension scheme then the Occupational Pension Schemes (Disclosure of Information) Regulations 1986 require that details of the scheme are given to members. The Working Time Regulations 1998 state that if an employer requires holidays to be taken on specified dates, or not to be taken on specified dates, then at least four weeks' notice of these dates must be given to employees.

20.2.2 Collective agreements as terms

A collective agreement is defined by s.178 of the Trade Union and Labour Relations (Consolidation) Act 1992 as an agreement or arrangement made by or on behalf of one or more trade unions and one or more employers or employers' associations, and relating to one or more of the following:

(a) terms and conditions of employment, or the physical conditions in which any workers are required to work;
(b) engagement or non-engagement;
(c) allocation of work or the duties of employment between workers or groups of workers;
(d) matters of discipline;
(e) a worker's membership or non-membership of a trade union;
(f) facilities for officials of trade unions; and
(g) machinery for negotiation or consultation, and other procedures, relating to any of the above matters.

Many industries, especially the old-fashioned heavy industries, operate with collective agreements. Collective agreements, or part of them, may be incorporated into a contract by express agreement between the parties to the contract. This is the case whether or not the employee is a member of the union which made the collective agreement. For example if, before agreeing to take a job, an employee was told that the employment was subject to the terms of a collective agreement, then this will be an express term of the contract and the agreement will be binding upon the employee, whether he is in the relevant trade union or not. The written particulars required by s.1 ERA 1996 may also expressly incorporate the terms of a collective agreement into the contract of employment. If not expressly agreed as a term of the contract, the terms of a collective agreement will only be incorporated into the contract if that is what the employer and employee intended.

The terms of collective agreements may be impliedly incorporated into the contracts of members of the union who negotiated the agreement. However, the union member must have had specific knowledge of the collective agreement, and must have shown in some way that he accepted it. This will not be possible if the employee did not know of the existence or content of the agreement. The terms of a collective agreement will not be impliedly incorporated into the contract of an employee who is not a union member.

Once part of the contract of employment, terms incorporated as part of a collective agreement may only be altered by express agreement by the parties to the contract of employment or under a right to alter contained in the contract of employment. If the trade union unilaterally negotiates a change, they do not do so as agents of the individual employees.

20.2.3 Implied obligations of the employee

At common law, several terms are implied into a contract of employment. As we saw in Chapter 5 at 5.3.2, the courts can imply a term into a contract, as a matter of law, on the basis that the term is generally implied into contracts of the type in question. When examining the terms which are implied into a contract of employment we first consider the terms which impose obligations on the employee, then those which impose obligations on the employer.

20.2.3.1 Duty of mutual respect

Both the employer and the employee owe each other a duty of mutual respect. In *Donovan v Invicta Airways Ltd* [1970] 1 Lloyd's Rep 486 the Court of Appeal held that an airline pilot was entitled to treat his contract of employment as repudiated when he was asked to fly in breach of regulations and was subsequently treated discourteously by his employers. The Court of Appeal held that the correct question to ask was whether the defendants' conduct was such as to make the continuance of the relationship of employer and employee impossible.

20.2.3.2 Duty of faithful service

The employment relationship is one of trust and confidence, and therefore an employee owes a duty to faithfully serve the employer. There have been decisions which indicate that this duty would prevent the employee from competing with the business of the employer whilst the employment continued. In *Hivac Ltd v Park Royal Scientific Instruments Co* [1946] 1 All ER 350 the Court of Appeal granted an injunction preventing employees from working for a competitor of their employer. However, a contractual term might allow such work to be done and there is no reason why an employee should not do work for someone other than a competitor of his employer, as long as doing so does not affect the way in which the employee performs his work.

In *Nottingham University v Fishel* (2000) Times, 31 March Elias J held that an employee's duty not to pursue his own interests at the expense of the employer's interests arose only where there was a definite contractual obligation for the employee to act only in the interests of his employer. The employment relationship was not a typical fiduciary relationship such as that between directors and their companies. As a general proposition a contract of employment did not require an employee to place the employer's interests above his own. It could, however, do so if there was a contractual term to this effect.

The duty of faithful service might be breached in a great number of other ways. In the past the courts have held that the duty was breached by such matters as the employee deliberately obstructing the employer's business, being persistently late, or deliberately falsifying the clocking-in card of a fellow employee. In *Secretary of State for Employment* v *ASLEF* [1972] 2 All ER 853 Roskill LJ thought that it was clear that a 'work to rule' by railwaymen, which was designed to disrupt the rail service, involved a breach of the positive obligation of faithful service owed by employee to employer.

20.2.3.3 Duty to obey lawful and reasonable orders

An employee is required to obey orders which are lawful and reasonable, but has no obligation to obey orders which are unlawful or unreasonable. The difficulty then is in deciding what amounts to a lawful and reasonable order. There is an abundance of case law on the matter. Each case depends upon its own facts. The express terms of the contract and all the circumstances of the case must be taken into consideration.

If an employee is dismissed for refusing to obey an order, the manner and tone of the refusal may be of relevance in considering whether the dismissal amounted to wrongful dismissal.

■ *Pepper v Webb* [1969] 2 All ER 216

A head gardener, who lived in a cottage in the employer's grounds, was required to work from 8 am until noon on Saturdays. He began to fall out with his employer. Between 9 am and 10 am on Saturday the gardener was asked to put some plants in the ground because otherwise they would die. The gardener replied, 'I am leaving at 12 o'clock; you can do what you like about them. If you don't like it you can give me notice.' Shortly before noon further appeals to the gardener to put the plants in, and not to be so awkward, were made. The employer pointed out that it would only take about half an hour to put the plants in. The gardener replied, 'I couldn't care less about your bloody greenhouse and your sodding garden.' The gardener was dismissed immediately, without notice or wages in lieu.

Held. The gardener's action for wrongful dismissal failed. The gardener had repudiated his contract by his refusal to obey the lawful and reasonable order to put the plants in, by his statement that he could not care less about the garden and by his insolence towards the employer.

COMMENT This case arose before the statutory remedy of unfair dismissal became available. Even if the gardener had had the necessary continuous employment to qualify for unfair dismissal, any such claim would have failed on the grounds that the dismissal was fair on the grounds of the employee's conduct.

It is possible for an employee to be fairly dismissed for refusing to obey an order which was outside the requirements of his contract of employment. In *Robinson* v *Flitwick Frames Ltd* [1975] IRLR 261 a general maintenance fitter refused to work overtime when requested to do so by the management. The overtime became necessary for a two month period and all the employees on the claimant's section agreed that it was necessary. However, on the evening of the meeting which decided this, the claimant made it clear that he would not work after 5 o'clock. The claim for unfair dismissal failed. The variation in working time which the management proposed was reasonable and had been accepted by all the other workers. The claimant had behaved unreasonably in refusing to obey the order and could not give a satisfactory explanation as to why he had refused. (When we study unfair dismissal, below at 20.4, we shall see that a dismissal is unfair unless it is made for one of four specified reasons, or unless it was made, as this dismissal was, for some other substantial reason of a kind such as to justify the dismissal of an employee holding the position which the employee held.)

Several cases have been concerned with whether or not the employee can be required to work elsewhere. In *United Kingdom Atomic Energy Authority* v *Claydon* [1976] IRLR 6, for example, the EAT had to consider whether an employee of the Atomic Energy Authority in Orfordness could be transferred against his will to the atomic energy site at Aldermaston. A construction of his contract of employment indicated that he could be transferred, and so he could. If the construction of the contract had not indicated this then he could not have been transferred.

Even if an employee can be required to work at a different place of employment, refusal to work at the other place may not always mean that a dismissal is fair, for the purposes of unfair dismissal. In *Wilson v IDR Construction Ltd* [1975] IRLR 260, for example, a bricklayer was unfairly dismissed for failure to work at another site even though the employer had the right to send him to this site. The bricklayer did not want to go because his wife was ill, the trouble having arisen since he last worked away from home, and because his car was in for repairs and an MOT. The bricklayer refused to ring the office to discuss the move. A general manager came to the site to see the bricklayer and, after a slightly rancorous conversation, the bricklayer was dismissed without notice or wages in lieu. The EAT thought that if the bricklayer had been given a proper chance to explain his reasons for not wanting to travel he would probably not have been unfairly dismissed. On the facts the EAT held that the bricklayer's dismissal was unfair, although his damages were reduced by 25% because he contributed to the dismissal.

20.2.3.4 Duty to use reasonable care and skill

An employee agrees to perform his duties using reasonable care and skill. The higher the level of skill which the employee professes to have, the higher the standard expected. Employees who are professionally qualified will be expected to show the care and skill which could reasonably be expected of a member of that profession. Breach of the duty to use reasonable care and skill may give rise to a claim in damages and may also justify dismissal.

The damages claimed for breach of the duty to use reasonable care and skill may be substantial. For example, in *Janata Bank v Ahmed* [1981] IRLR 457 the Court of Appeal held that a bank manager who had cost the bank £34 640 by negligence was liable to pay damages to compensate for this loss. An employee who negligently loses the employer's property may also be in breach of the implied duty to use reasonable care and skill.

20.2.3.5 Duty not to accept bribes

In some areas of employment it is well recognised that employees may accept tips. However, an employee should not accept a bribe or secret commission. The mere fact of having received such a payment gives rise to an irrebuttable presumption that it influenced the employee's behaviour in favour of the donor. The employer may recover the amount of the payment from the employee and in many cases the payment will justify the employee's dismissal.

In *Boston Deep Sea Fishing and Ice Co v Ansell* (1888) 39 ChD 339, for example, the managing director of a company ordered two new vessels for the company. The shipbuilder paid the managing director a secret commission. The managing director also placed orders with two companies in which he held shares, and received bonuses from these companies. The Court of Appeal held that the managing director could be dismissed and that he also had to repay the money received, with interest.

20.2.3.6 Duty not to reveal confidential information

An employee is under a duty not to reveal confidential information about the employer's business, except where there is a legal duty to do so.

The Public Interest Disclosure Act 1998 protects employees, generally known as 'whistleblowers' who make a 'protected disclosure' of information. A worker protected by the Act cannot suffer a detriment in consequence of the disclosure, nor be dismissed or made redundant. As a dismissal in breach of the Act will be automatically unfair, even workers with less than one year's continuous employment and those over 65 are protected against unfair dismissal. A disclosure is a protected disclosure if, in the reasonable belief of the worker making the disclosure, it tends to show one or more of the following:

(a) that a criminal offence has been committed, is being committed or is likely to be committed;
(b) that a person has failed, is failing or is likely to fail to comply with any legal obligation to which he is subject;

(c) that a miscarriage of justice has occurred, is occurring or is likely to occur;

(d) that the health and safety of an individual has been, is being or is likely to be endangered;

(e) that the environment has been, is being or is likely to be damaged; or

(f) that information tending to show any of the above matters has been, or is likely to be concealed.

20.2.3.7 Patents, inventions and copyright

The extent to which patents, inventions and copyrights which were created by the employee belong to the employer is considered in Chapter 23.

20.2.3.8 Duty of disclosure

Although an employee does not have a duty to disclose his own shortcomings, unless asked about them by the employer, he does have a duty to disclose the shortcomings of his subordinates.

■ *Sybrom Corporation* v *Rochem Ltd* [1983] 2 All ER 707 (Court of Appeal)

The employee was a manager working for the defendant company, and was the overseer of the company's European operations. The employee took early retirement and received a lump sum of £13 200. Other sums were held in trust for him by the company. After paying the £13 200 the company discovered that the employee and his subordinates had committed a massive fraud on the company. The company claimed to be entitled to the £13 200 already paid and also to have no duty to hold the other money on trust for the employee. The employee argued that he had no duty to disclose the fraud and that he was therefore entitled to the pension payment as previously agreed.

Held. The employee had no duty to disclose his own misconduct. However he had breached a duty to disclose the breaches of duty of his subordinates, even if disclosing this would have meant revealing his own breaches of duty. The employee's breach of this duty would have entitled the employer to dismiss the employee summarily and, under the rules of the pension scheme, refuse to make any pension payment. If the employers had known this they could validly have refused to pay under the pension scheme rules. They therefore made the payment under a mistake as to fact which was induced by the employee's breach of duty. The money paid was recoverable and the sums held in trust reverted to the employer.

20.2.4 Implied obligations of the employer

20.2.4.1 Duty of mutual respect

This duty has become increasingly important as the relationship of employer and employee has moved away from the master/servant relationship of Victorian times. The courts have held the duty breached on various grounds, including: failure to provide a grievance procedure, in breach of a statutory obligation to do so; requiring a doctor who was coming back to work after suspension to undergo psychiatric tests when there was no evidence of psychiatric illness; berating an inexperienced employee, in front of his work mates, for incompetence; falsely accusing an employee of theft; and refusing to give one employee a pay rise when all of the other employees were given a rise.

20.2.4.2 Duty to provide work

An employer generally does not have a duty to provide work for an employee, as long as the employee is paid. Asquith J in *Collier* v *Sunday Referee Publishing Ltd* [1940] 2 KB 647 said: 'It is true that a contract of employment does not necessarily, or perhaps normally, oblige the master to provide the servant with work. Provided I pay my cook her wages regularly she cannot complain if I choose to take any or all of my meals out.' However, in some circumstances there is a duty to provide work. The most notable of these circumstances are as follows: where the work is needed for the employee to maintain his reputation or skill; where the failure to provide work leads to the employee earning less money, as for example where the employee is on piecework; and where the failure to provide work can be taken as a repudiation of the contract of employment.

20.2.4.3 Duty to pay wages

Unless the contract of employment expressly or impliedly provides otherwise, the employer has a duty to pay wages to the employee whether work is provided or not. In *Devonald* v *Rosser & Sons* [1906] 2 KB 728, for example, a pieceworker who was given one month's notice during which no work was provided, was entitled to a payment based on his average monthly earnings. In some circumstances where the lack of work is for a reason beyond the employer's control, there might not be a duty to pay wages.

Wages must be paid in money but not necessarily in cash. The employer must not make any deductions from wages unless the deduction is required to be made by a statutory provision, or a relevant provision of the worker's contract, or unless the worker has previously signified in writing his agreement or consent to the making of the deduction (ERA 1996 s.13(1)). Section 13(1) does not apply to deductions made for over-payment of wages or expenses, or for having taken part in a strike action.

20.2.4.4 Duty of confidentiality

Earlier we saw that employees owe a duty of confidentiality to their employers. The employer owes a similar duty to the employee. In *Dalgleish* v *Lothian and Borders Police Board* [1992] SLT 721 Lord Cameron of Lochbroom, sitting in the Court of Session, held that an employer asked to provide the names and addresses of employees to the local council, so that they could detect those who had not paid the community charge, was contractually bound not to disclose information held in personal files without the consent of the employees concerned.

20.2.4.5 Duty to indemnify the employee

An employer will be under a duty to indemnify an employee for expenses and costs reasonably incurred in the performance of his employment. In *Re Famatina Development Corporation Ltd* [1914] 2 Ch 271, for example, the claimant was employed under a written contract to go to Argentina and report on some mines which the employer was considering buying. The claimant sent a report saying that the managing director of the company which employed him had committed serious fraud. The claimant was sued for libel. The libel action failed, but the claimant was unable to recover a large part of his costs. The Court of Appeal held that as the report was written in pursuance of the claimant's duties as an agent, and written without malice, he was entitled to an indemnity and reimbursement from the employer.

20.2.4.6 Duty to insure

Employers are required by the Employers' Liability (Compulsory Insurance) Act 1969 to take out insurance for the benefit of employees who are working within the UK.

20.2.4.7 Duty to provide references

An employer does not have a duty to provide a reference for an employee. There are two reasons why an employer might be loath to provide a reference. First, the employer may be sued for defamation if the reference is defamatory. Second, the employer may be liable for negligent misstatement if the reference is so careless or inaccurate that this involves breaching a duty of care owed to the employee. (Negligent misstatement is examined in Chapter 12 at 12.3.)

■ *Spring* v *Guardian Assurance plc* [1994] 3 All ER 129 (House of Lords)

The claimant was employed as sales director and office manager of C Ltd, the second defendants, who were agents for the sale of life assurance policies. C Ltd were taken over by G plc, the first defendants, and the claimant was dismissed. The claimant wanted to work selling the policies of another company. That company was obliged by Lautro rules to to get a reference from the previous employer. The previous employer was required by Lautro rules to provide a reference which made 'full and frank disclosure of all matters which are believed to be true'.

G plc provided a very bad reference, which said that the claimant kept the best business for himself, had little integrity, could not be regarded as honest and had mis-sold a policy to make a large commission for himself at the client's expense. Having failed to gain employment with two other members of Lautro, the claimant sued claiming breach of an implied contractual term that the defendants would prepare any reference in regard to him using reasonable care and skill and would provide a reference which was full, frank and truthful. He also sued in negligence, alleging breach of a duty of care.

Held. An employer's duty to take reasonable care and skill in preparing a reference in respect of an employee could, in appropriate circumstances, arise from an implied term of the contract of employment. The employer would therefore have to exercise due care and skill in preparing the reference. However, the duty arising under the implied term did not add anything to the duty arising in negligence.

COMMENT The claimant won the case on the grounds of the defendant's negligence. The employer owed a duty of care to the employee in respect of the preparation of the reference. Having breached this duty, the employer was liable in damages for economic loss suffered by the employee as a consequence. The employer had a duty to avoid negligently making untrue statements or expressing unfounded opinions, even if these were honestly believed to be true or were reasonably held. The duty arose because economic loss, in the form of failure to obtain employment, was clearly foreseeable if a careless reference was given and because there was an obvious proximity of relationship between employer and employee.

Sometimes an employer gives a bad employee an unrealistically good reference to get rid of him. It is possible that such a reference will give the new employer the right to sue for deceit or negligent mis-statement if he relied upon the reference to his detriment. However, the employer writing the reference can protect himself against such liability by means of a disclaimer.

The duty to ensure the employee's safety is considered in Chapter 21.

20.2.5 Terms implied by custom and practice

It is possible for a term to be incorporated into a contract of employment by custom and practice. In order for this to happen, the term must be notorious, certain and reasonable. For example, in *Sagar v Ridehalgh & Son Ltd* [1931] Ch 310 a local custom entitled a Lancashire mill owner to deduct wages from a weaver who had spoiled three yards of cloth by defective workmanship. The mill had deducted money in similar circumstances for many years, as had most mills in Lancashire. The importance of terms implied by custom and practice has declined considerably and in modern times the incorporation of terms in this way is of little significance.

20.2.6 Works rule books

An employer's works rule book, or list of rules, may be contractually agreed as being part of the contract of employment. If this is the case then the rules can only be altered by agreement between the parties. If the rules are unilaterally imposed by the employer, rather than being agreed as contractually binding by employer and employee, then failure to observe the rules may be a breach of the duty to obey instructions, and the rules may be unilaterally altered by the employer. However, rules unilaterally imposed would not be able to alter the terms of the contract previously agreed. In the following case the claimant argued that new anti-smoking rules breached her contract of employment.

■ *Dryden* v *Greater Glasgow Health Board* [1992] IRLR 469

Ms Dryden worked as a nursing auxiliary in the theatre section of a Glasgow infirmary. Her job did not allow her to leave the premises during the day. She smoked 30 cigarettes a day, but until 1991 certain areas on the premises were available for smoking. Then the hospital introduced a no smoking policy. Employees were sent letters giving notice of the change and offered advice and counselling. Ms Dryden resigned and claimed to have been constructively dismissed.

Held. The introduction of the no-smoking policy did not breach Ms Dryden's contract of employment. There was no express or implied term in her contract that smoking would continue to be permitted. Where a new rule was introduced for a legitimate purpose, the fact that the rule works harshly against some employees is not enough to justify an inference that the employer has acted in such a way as to breach the contract with the employee.

Generally, job descriptions are likely to be drawn up unilaterally by the employer. The employee will have a duty to perform the duties set out. The employer will be able to change the job description unilaterally, as long as this does not amount to a breach of contract.

The difficulties in determining the legal effect of rule books is demonstrated by *Secretary of State for Employment* v *ASLEF*, considered earlier in this chapter. The railwaymen who 'worked to rule', that is to say strictly according to their rule book were held to be in breach of contract. Lord Denning clearly said that these particular rules were not the terms of the railwaymen's contracts of employment, but merely instructions on how they should do their work. In addition, there was an implied term that the rules would be interpreted reasonably.

20.2.7 Disciplinary and grievance procedures

The Employment Act 2002, in Part 2 of Schedule 2, sets out a standard grievance procedure and a modified grievance procedure. If the employer or employee fail to comply with these procedures then any award for unfair dismissal will be increased or reduced by between 10% and 50%. The procedures are considered below at 20.4.3.4.

If the contract of employment sets out additional disciplinary or grievance procedures then failure to follow these procedures will amount to a breach of contract. For example, in *Gunton* v *London Borough of Richmond upon Thames* [1980] 3 All ER 577 the Court of Appeal held that where a contract of employment incorporated regulations which set out a disciplinary procedure, that procedure had to be followed before the employee could be dismissed on a disciplinary matter. The employee's contract provided that he could be dismissed with one month's notice, and the employee was so dismissed on a disciplinary matter. However, if the disciplinary procedure had been followed this would have taken much longer than one month to implement. The employee was awarded damages to cater for the extra time it would have taken to go through the disciplinary procedure set out and then to be given one month's notice.

Where a grievance procedure exists an employee should make use of the procedure rather than immediately taking a case to an employment tribunal.

The written particulars which must be supplied under s.1 ERA 1996 provide that they should include a note setting out grievance procedures.

20.2.8 Variation of terms of the contract

As we saw in Chapter 7 at 7.1.2, a contract cannot be unilaterally varied by one of the parties, but both parties may agree to a variation as long as they both provide some consideration to each other. These general contract principles apply equally to contracts of employment. However, it is clear that employees cannot expect that the conditions of employment will remain unaltered for the whole period of employment, no matter how long that might be.

If the employer unilaterally alters the terms of a contract of employment (other than for a reason which is objectively necessary) and the employee does not accept the variation, then this will amount to a repudiation of the contract and the employee may justifiably regard the contract as terminated. If the employee continues to work without protest this will generally be taken as acceptance of the unilateral change. Whether or not an employee has accepted a unilateral variation of the contract by the employer is a question of fact, to be determined from all the circumstances of the case. In *Marriott* v *Oxford and District Co-operative Society Ltd* [1969] 3 All ER 1126 a foreman was offered a job as a supervisor, at a reduced wage, because there was insufficient work for a foreman. The foreman protested about this and tried to find work elsewhere. He received a letter saying that his wages would be reduced by about £1 a week, and again he protested. After three or four weeks of receiving the reduced wage he left to take another job. The Court of Appeal held that the letter terminated his contract unless the foreman chose to accept the terms which it proposed. Even though the foreman continued to work for three or four weeks the circumstances indicated that he did not accept the variation. He was therefore entitled to regard himself as dismissed and claim a redundancy payment.

Not only is reducing wages a variation of the contract, but so is a demotion or insisting that an employee performs duties which are outside the contract of employment.

If a repudiation is not accepted by an employee who continues in the employment, the damages are assessed to compensate for the entire period of breach, not merely for the period of notice to which the employee would have been entitled. In *Rigby* v *Ferodo Ltd* [1987] IRLR 516 the employer unilaterally reduced the employee's wages by £30 a week. The employee did not accept this. The contract could have been terminated by 12 weeks' notice. The claimant continued to work at the lower rate, without accepting the alteration, and then sued for breach of contract. The House of Lords held that he was entitled to the lost wages for the whole of the period of the breach.

An employee who continues to work under protest at a unilateral variation can be regarded as having been dismissed for the purposes of unfair dismissal. (See *Alcan Extrusions* v *Yates*, below at 20.4.2.1.) An express term of the contract may allow for variation of some of the terms. If the employee consistently works in a manner which is inconsistent with the express terms for a considerable time, then an implied variation can be inferred. When a trade union negotiates a collective agreement which changes the terms of an individual's contract of employment, the change is only effective if it is agreed by the employee individually or if he was collectively represented when the change was agreed. It will not therefore be binding on workers who are not members of the union which negotiated the agreement, unless they expressly agree to it or unless a term of their contracts allowed the terms to be varied by a new collective agreement.

The employer can insist on change if necessary. If the employee refuses to accept such change then the employer should give notice to terminate the employment. This will amount to a dismissal for the purposes of unfair dismissal. However, the dismissal might or might not be regarded as unfair.

Test your understanding

1 Within what period must an employee be given written particulars of the employment? Are these written particulars the contract of employment itself?

2 What are collective agreements? To what extent are such agreements terms of individual contracts of employment?

3 What duties are impliedly imposed on employees?

4 What duties are impliedly imposed on employers?

5 To what extent are works rule books contractually binding? Can the rules be changed unilaterally by the employer?

6 What is the effect of an employer failing to observe agreed disciplinary and grievance procedures?

7 What is the effect of the employer unilaterally altering the terms of the contract of employment?

Answers

1 An employee must be given written particulars of the contract of employment not later than two months after the commencement of the employment. The written particulars are not the contract of employment itself, unless expressly agreed as such, but are very strong evidence of the terms of the contract.

2 Collective agreements are agreements negotiated between employers and trade unions which set out terms and conditions of employment. They can become terms of an individual contract of employment if expressly agreed as terms of the

contract by an individual employee. They can impliedly become the terms of the contracts of union members who knew of the terms and accepted them.

3   The following duties are impliedly imposed on employees: the duty of mutual respect; the duty to give faithful service; the duty to obey lawful and reasonable orders; the duty to use reasonable care and skill; the duty not to accept bribes; the duty not to disclose confidential information; and the duty to disclose the shortcomings of subordinates.

4   The following duties are impliedly imposed on employers: the duty of mutual respect; the duty to pay wages; the duty of confidentiality; the duty to indemnify the employee; the duty to take out insurance for the benefit of the employee; and the duty to ensure the employee's safety. There is generally no duty to provide references or to provide the employee with work.

5   The parties may agree that a works rule book is incorporated as part of the contract of employment. If a works rule book is agreed as part of the contract of employment it can only be altered by agreement. An employer may unilaterally impose duties by means of a works rule book as long as the duties do not alter the terms of the employment previously agreed. Rules unilaterally imposed can be altered unilaterally by the employer as long as this does not amount to a breach of contract.

6   If the employer does not follow agreed disciplinary and grievance procedures this will be a breach of contract. The breach may entitle the employee to claim constructive dismissal. If the employer does not comply with the statutory grievance procedure set out in Part 2 of Schedule 2 to the Employment Act 2002 then any award for unfair dismissal will be increased by between 10% and 50%.

7   If the employer unilaterally alters the terms of the contract of employment, the employee may accept this in which case the contract will be varied by mutual agreement. If the employee does not accept the variation the employee may regard the contract as terminated on the grounds of the employer's repudiation of it.

20.3 · Termination of employment

Where a contract of employment is terminated it is possible that the employee might have a remedy for either wrongful or unfair dismissal. Unfair dismissal is a statutory remedy which is considered below at 20.4. Wrongful dismissal is the common law remedy of an employee to sue for contract damages on account of his contract of employment having been breached.

Generally a dismissed employee would rather sue for the statutory remedy of unfair dismissal rather than for wrongful dismissal. However, it is sometimes advantageous to sue for wrongful dismissal. This might either be because the damages for wrongful dismissal would be higher than the compensation for unfair dismissal or because the employee is unable to sue for unfair dismissal. It would be unusual for an employee's damages for wrongful dismissal to be higher than the compensation available for unfair dismissal. However, in the case of very highly paid employees who are entitled to long periods of notice, or who are working under a fixed term contract, the damages for wrongful dismissal could well be higher. As we saw in Chapter 7, the purpose of contract damages is to put the injured party in the financial position he would have been in if the breach of contract had not occurred. Certain categories of employees are precluded from claiming unfair dismissal, as we shall see below at 20.4.1. These employees, such as those who have less than one year's continuous employment, might nevertheless be able to bring a claim for wrongful dismissal. Many contracts are terminated by the employer giving notice and this would preclude a claim for wrongful dismissal, although not a claim for unfair dismissal.

A contract of employment may be terminated in several ways. One or other of the parties might give notice to terminate the contract, or both of the parties might agree to end the contract. The employee might complete the task for which he was employed, or might work for the whole of the time period specified in the contract. The contract might become frustrated. The employer might dismiss the employee without notice or might repudiate the contract, thereby entitling the employee to regard the contract as terminated. First, we examine each of these methods by which a contract may be terminated. Then we consider whether or not the termination could give rise to a claim for wrongful or unfair dismissal.

20.3.1 Termination by notice

An employment contract can be terminated by either the employer or the employee giving notice. Section 86 ERA 1996 lays down minimum periods of notice which the employer must give in order to terminate the contract. As these statutory notice periods are minimum periods, more notice will be required if there is a term of the contract to this effect. A greater period may also be required by the common law requirement of an employer to give a reasonable period of notice where there is no term as to the period required. The notice which is reasonable will depend upon all the circumstances of the case.

The minimum notice periods set out by s.86 are as follows.

If the employee has been continuously employed for between one month and two years, the minimum period of notice is one week. After the employee has been continuously employed for two years or more the minimum period becomes one week's notice for every year of continuous employment between two and 12 years. If the continuous employment has lasted for more than twelve years the minimum notice period remains 12 weeks.

Section 86 specifies that the notice periods which it sets out are minimum periods. Therefore any agreement that less notice is required will have no effect. If, however, a greater period of notice is agreed then this greater period of notice will be required.

As the employer has no duty to provide work (subject to the exceptions considered above at 20.2.4) an employee cannot insist on a right to work his notice if he is given a payment in lieu of notice.

Section 86(2) specifies that the notice to be given by an employee who has been continuously employed for one month or more to terminate his contract of employment is not less than one week. A greater period of notice could well be required by a term of the contract. If there is no term as to the period of notice, the employee is required to give a reasonable period of notice. Often an employee leaves his employment without giving the required period of notice. In such cases the employer could, theoretically, sue the employee for breach of contract. However, such actions are extremely rare. As the employer would be under a duty to mitigate his loss, his damages would generally be limited to the expense of finding another employee.

If a fixed term contract is terminated by the employer before the end of the term then this will amount to a breach of contract. It will also be a breach of contract if an employee is employed to achieve a particular purpose and is dismissed before this purpose has been achieved. If an employee is employed to achieve one specific purpose and the employment is ended as a consequence of this purpose having been achieved, this will not amount to a dismissal. The contract is discharged by performance.

20.3.2 Summary dismissal

An employee who is summarily dismissed is dismissed with immediate effect, without being given any notice. If the employee's conduct is a sufficient repudiation of the contract then summary dismissal can be justified and the employer will not have committed a breach of contract. However, summary dismissal is an exceptional measure and only in exceptional circumstances will it be justified. Summary dismissal can be justified for refusal to obey a lawful order, as was seen earlier in this chapter in *Pepper* v *Webb*. In that case the head gardener's refusal to obey the lawful order, and the manner of his refusal, caused the employer to summarily dismiss him. The court held that the summary dismissal was justified and so the gardener could not claim wrongful dismissal. Other cases have held that gross misconduct or neglect, or serious breaches of duty can justify summary dismissal. Dishonesty may also justify summary dismissal. In the following case the employee was dishonest, although not dishonest to the point of committing a criminal offence, and summary dismissal was justified.

■ *Sinclair* v *Neighbour* [1967] 2 QB 279 (Court of Appeal)

The claimant was employed as the manager of a bookmaker's shop. He was paid £22 a week and received 5% commission on the shop's net profits. The claimant took £15 out of the till in order to place a bet at a different betting shop. He left an I.O.U. in the till, but knew that if he had asked for permission to borrow the money this would have been refused. The bet won and the claimant returned the £15 to the till the following day. The employer summarily dismissed the claimant.

Held. The summary dismissal was justified. Even if the claimant's behaviour was not dishonest, it was of such a grave and weighty character that it undermined the confidence which should exist between employer and employee.

Whether or not a dismissed employee was given the required period of notice is important for the purposes of wrongful dismissal. But is not important for the purposes of unfair dismissal, except that it might influence the amount of the discretionary compensatory award.

20.3.3 Termination by agreement

The employer and employee may agree to end the contract at any time, with or without notice. If this is a genuine agreement, freely entered into by the employee, then the contract of employment will be discharged and the employee will have no claim for wrongful dismissal, as there will have been no dismissal. A contract might be terminated by agreement if it was agreed at the outset that the employment was to last merely until some purpose was achieved. However, if the agreement to terminate the contract was entered into as a result of pressure by the employer, the courts may well find that there was no true agreement but rather a dismissal by the employer.

Even if the parties agree that the employment should end on the happening of a certain event this may be a dismissal for the purposes of unfair dismissal and redundancy, although not for the purposes of wrongful dismissal. Section 203 ERA 1996 provides that any provision in an agreement (whether a contract of employment or not) is void in so far as it purports to exclude or limit the operation or provision of any part of ERA 1996. (The ERA confers redundancy rights and the right not to be unfairly dismissed.) In *Igbo* v *Johnson, Matthey Chemicals Ltd* [1986] IRLR 215 the employee wanted leave to visit Nigeria and it was agreed that if she should fail to return to work on a certain date, for whatever reason, her contract would be terminated. She did not return on the specified date because she was ill. The employer therefore treated the contract as terminated. The Court of Appeal held that the agreement was rendered void by what is now s.203 and so the employee was dismissed for the purposes of unfair dismissal.

20.3.4 Termination by frustration

In Chapter 7 at 7.1.3 we saw that a contract will be frustrated if it becomes impossible to perform, illegal to perform or radically different from what the parties contemplated when they made the contract. We also saw that the frustrating event must not be the fault of either of the parties. If a contract of employment is frustrated it is terminated from the moment of the frustrating event, and the employee is not regarded as dismissed. As a consequence the employee will not be able to claim either unfair or wrongful dismissal. Imprisonment of the employee, or long-term sickness of the employee, may both amount to frustration of the contract. Even though it could be argued that it is the employee's fault that he was imprisoned, the courts have held that the imprisonment of the employee frustrates the contract. If the contract was not frustrated the employer would either have to keep the job open or terminate the contract. Such a termination would amount to a dismissal by the employer and would therefore put the imprisoned employee in a better position than if the contract was not frustrated. (The employee would be able to claim wrongful dismissal and perhaps unfair dismissal.) The argument that imprisonment could not frustrate the contract was described by the Court of Appeal in *Shepherd* v *Jerrom* [1986] ICR 802 as an 'affront to common sense'.

In *Egg Stores (Stamford Hill) Ltd* v *Leibovici* [1977] ICR 260 an employee of 15 years' standing was off work for five months after having been injured in a car crash. The employer continued to pay the employee's wages for two months, but stopped paying when they got another employee to take over his work. When the employee returned to work he was told that his position had been filled. The EAT held that the employer could claim that the contract was frustrated if the employee's injury was such that further performance of his obligations under the contract would be impossible or radically different from what the parties contemplated when they made the contract. As regards a long-standing employee, the question to be asked was 'has the time arrived when the employer can no longer reasonably be expected to keep the absent employee's post open for him?' Phillips J identified nine factors to be taken into account in deciding whether the contract had been frustrated.

(1) the length of the previous employment;
(2) how long it had been expected that the employment would continue;
(3) the nature of the job;
(4) the nature, length and effect of the illness or disabling event;
(5) the need of the employer for the work to be done, and the need for a replacement to do it;
(6) the risk to the employer of acquiring obligations to the replacement employee in respect of redundancy payments or compensation for unfair dismissal;
(7) whether wages have continued to be paid;
(8) the acts and the statements of the employer in relation to the employment, including the dismissal of, or failure to dismiss, the employee; and
(9) whether in all the circumstances a reasonable employer could be expected to wait any longer.

20.3.5 Repudiation of the contract

In Chapter 7 we saw that if one party acts in a way which shows that he no longer intends to be bound by the contract, this amounts to a repudiation of the contract and the other party is entitled to accept this repudiation and regard his own contractual obligations as discharged. If, therefore the employer's behaviour amounts to a repudiation of the contract the employee is entitled to accept this, regard himself as dismissed, and bring a claim for wrongful dismissal. As regards unfair dismissal, an employee who resigns on account of the employer's behaviour may claim to have been constructively dismissed. (Constructive dismissal is examined below at 20.4.2.3.) An employee who resigns otherwise than in response to a repudiatory breach by the employer will have no claim to damages for wrongful dismissal and, unless constructive dismissal can be proved, will not be regarded as dismissed for the purposes of unfair dismissal. Nor will the employee be regarded as dismissed for the purposes of redundancy.

If the employee's behaviour amounts to a repudiation of the contract, and the employer in response dismisses the employee then this will amount to a dismissal. However, if the dismissal is justifiable then the employee will have no claim to damages, as we saw when considering summary dismissal. If the dismissal was fair then there will be no claim for unfair dismissal. (See, however, *London Transport Executive* v *Clarke*, below at 20.4.2.6.)

A dismissal also occurs if an employer dismisses an employee without going through the contractually agreed dismissal procedures or makes an employee redundant in breach of contractually agreed redundancy procedures. An example of wrongful dismissal caused by failure to observe the correct procedures was seen earlier in this chapter in *Gunton* v *London Borough of Richmond upon Thames*.

20.3.6 Remedies for wrongful dismissal

An action for wrongful dismissal is an action for breach of contract. The employee does not need to prove that the employer acted unreasonably, but only that the contract was in fact breached. As an action for wrongful dismissal is an action for breach of contract, the common law rules on quantification of damages apply. As we saw in Chapter 7, contract damages are designed to put the injured party in the position which he would have been in if the breach of contract had not occurred. Damages will be assessed as the payment of the wages and other contractual benefits which would have been received if the employee had been given the proper period of notice. Discretionary payments will not be included. Furthermore, the employee will have an obligation to mitigate his loss. If the employer can prove that the employee could have mitigated his loss by earning money at other employment, but has failed to do so, the damages will be reduced accordingly. However, the dismissed employee is only expected to take reasonable steps to mitigate and would therefore only be expected to take a similar type of job at a similar level.

Damages for wrongful dismissal may take into account other matters such as lost pension rights, lost holiday pay, lost share options, lost bonuses or tips, as these would be matters within the two rules in *Hadley* v *Baxendale*. In *Malik* v *BCCI SA* [1997] IRLR 462 the House of Lords held that damages for loss of reputation caused by breach of contract may be recoverable, provided that there was a relevant breach of contract and the requirements of causation, remoteness and mitigation were satisfied.

Damages paid for wrongful dismissal are not taxable unless they exceed £30 000, and so the employer only has to pay the net sum which the employee would have received after the payment of tax and national insurance contributions. If the employee receives benefits, such as unemployment benefit, then the net amount of benefits received will be deducted from the damages. In very limited circumstances, an employee may be entitled to an injunction restraining the employer from breaching the contract of employment. As we saw in Chapter 7, an injunction is only ordered at the court's discretion and would not be ordered to effect specific performance in cases where specific performance would not be ordered. Specific performance is never ordered to enforce a contract of personal service.

The employment tribunal has the power to award up to £25 000 for wrongful dismissal. However, it would be unusual for an employment tribunal to hear a case of wrongful dismissal if the case could be brought as a claim for unfair dismissal, as the compensatory award available for unfair dismissal would take account of wages lost between the times of dismissal and the hearing. (The two claims are based on different legal rights, but the basis of the complaint often overlaps.) In some limited circumstances it might be possible to bring an action for unfair dismissal at an employment tribunal and an action for wrongful dismissal in the High Court. If this were the case the court could stay one of the actions until the outcome of the other was decided, and the action stayed could only proceed as far as was necessary to resolve matters undecided by the first action. An award made by one court would generally be deducted from any award made by the other court to prevent double recovery. An action for wrongful dismissal must be brought within the usual six year limit laid down by the Limitation Act 1980.

Test your understanding

1 What is the essential difference between wrongful and unfair dismissal?

2 If an employee is dismissed without having been given the notice to which he was entitled, will damages to compensate for this be awarded on the basis of wrongful or unfair dismissal?

3 How much notice will an employee be entitled to?

4 What is summary dismissal? Can it ever be justified?

5 If an employee agrees to leave the employment, can there be a claim for wrongful dismissal?

6 Can a claim for wrongful dismissal be made if the employer or employee repudiates the contract?

7 How are damages for wrongful dismissal calculated?

Answers

1 Wrongful dismissal is a common law action for breach of contract. Unfair dismissal is a statutory concept and if unfair dismissal is substantiated compensation is awarded on a statutory basis.

2 An employee dismissed without having been given the proper amount of notice will be entitled to sue for damages for wrongful dismissal.

3 Employees will be entitled to the notice agreed with their employers or, if there was no agreement, to a reasonable period of notice. Statute lays down minimum periods of notice, which may well exceed the amount agreed or the amount which the common law would require. The minimum periods are one week for every year's continuous employment where the employee has worked for between two and 12 years. Where the employee has worked for more than 12 years the statutory minimum remains 12 weeks. Employees who have worked for more than one month but less than two years are entitled to one week's statutory minimum notice.

4 An employee is summarily dismissed if he is dismissed on the spot, without notice. This can be justified if the employee's behaviour was a sufficient repudiation of the contract of employment.

5 If the agreement to leave was freely entered into by the employee there can be no claim for wrongful dismissal. If the employee left in response to the employer's repudiation of the contract, there could be a claim for wrongful dismissal.

6 If the employer's conduct amounts to a repudiation of the contract, the employee is entitled to accept this, leave the job and claim wrongful dismissal. An employee who repudiates the contract cannot claim wrongful dismissal.

7 Damages for wrongful dismissal are calculated on ordinary contract principles. The employee can claim for foreseeable losses and has a duty to mitigate.

20.4 · Unfair dismissal

Section 94(1) ERA 1996 gives a statutory right not to be unfairly dismissed to employees who have been continuously employed for at least one year. (In addition, certain dismissals are regarded as automatically unfair, in which case there is no qualifying period of continuous employment) (see below at 20.4.3.2). However, certain types of employees are excluded from claiming unfair dismissal. The circumstances in which a person is dismissed, for the purposes of unfair dismissal, are laid down by ERA 1996. The Act also lays down rules for deciding whether or not a dismissal can be regarded as 'unfair', and sets out a formula for calculating the basic award of compensation. The dismissal will only be unfair if the reason for the dismissal was outside one of the 'fair' reasons set out by the Act and the employer acted unreasonably in deciding to dismiss the employee. It is also necessary that the dismissal is procedurally fair. Section 98A ERA 1996 provides that a dismissal will be procedurally unfair if the statutory dispute resolution procedure contained in Schedule 2 to the Employment Rights Act 2002 is not followed. Schedule 2 sets out a standard minimum procedure for dismissal and disciplinary procedures and a modified procedure. The standard procedure has three steps.

It will be seen that unfair dismissal is quite different from wrongful dismissal and is not based on the general law of contract. Even a person who has been dismissed without any breach of contract may have a claim for unfair dismissal.

20.4.1 Employees excluded from claiming unfair dismissal

Only employees have the right to claim unfair dismissal. Self-employed workers have no such right.

Employees who have reached the age of 65 are excluded from claiming unfair dismissal by s.109 ERA 1996. If the undertaking where the employee is employed has a normal retirement age for an employee holding the position in question, and the normal retiring age was the same whether the employee was a man or a woman, an employee who has reached this normal retiring age cannot claim unfair dismissal. This is the case even if the normal retiring age is not 65. If the normal retiring age discriminates between men and women, the right to claim unfair dismissal exists until the employee reaches the age of 65.

Fishermen who are paid by taking a share of the catch are excluded. If employees are covered by a dismissal procedure designated and approved by the Secretary of State they may not claim unfair dismissal. Such agreements would be made between the employer and the trade unions, substituting their own dismissals procedure. There have been few such agreements.

Employees are not generally entitled to claim unfair dismissal unless they have at least one year's continuous employment. This period was set at two years until it was reduced in 1999 by the Unfair Dismissal and Statement of Reasons for Dismissal (Variation of Qualifying Period) Order 1999 (SI 1999 No. 1436). Where a dismissal is regarded as automatically unfair then there is no qualifying period of continuous employment. The grounds on which a dismissal is regarded as automatically unfair are set out below at 20.4.3.2.

20.4.1.2 Continuous employment

The concept of continuous employment is important not only because those who have less than one year's continuous employment will not be able to claim unfair dismissal, but also because the amount of the basic award for unfair dismissal will be calculated by reference to the length of the complainant's continuous employment.

Section 212(1) ERA 1996 states that:

> 'Any week during the whole or part of which an employee's relations with his employer are governed by a contract of employment counts in computing the employee's period of employment.'

As continuous employment is only of relevance in a statutory context, it is always calculated according to s.212(1). Any agreement by the parties to count employment as continuous employment will not affect the employee's statutory rights. Section 212(1) does not require that the employee works continuously in the same capacity or at the same place, merely that the employee works for the employer under a continuing contract of employment. In order for continuous employment to be broken the employee must fail to work for the employer for at least one week. Weeks when an employee is off work on account of pregnancy, childbirth, sickness or injury count as continuous employment. Time off for a temporary cessation of work also counts. If an employee is on strike this does not break the continuity of employment, but the period on strike does not count as continuous employment. It is presumed that a person's employment is continuous unless the contrary is proved.

Part-time workers are treated in the same way as full-time workers for the purposes of calculating continuous employment, regardless of how many hours a week they work.

If the employer changes, so that the employee becomes employed by a different employer, continuity of employment may be preserved. Section 218 ERA 1996 provides that employment with the old employer will count as continuous employment with the new employer, and there will be no break in the continuity of the employment, if a trade or business is transferred from one employer to another employer as a going concern. The same is true where the employer dies and his personal representatives carries on the business or where there is a change in the partners who constitute the employer. The Transfer of Undertakings (Protection of Employment) Regulations 1981 are considered in the following chapter. Where the Regulations apply, continuity of employment would be preserved despite the transfer.

If an employee is unfairly dismissed and a tribunal orders that the employee be reinstated or re-engaged, the continuity of employment is preserved and the period when the employee was absent after the dismissal will count as continuous employment.

20.4.1.3 The effective date of termination (EDT)

In order to calculate the amount of compensation, and in order to know whether or not there is sufficient continuous employment for a claim to be made, it is necessary to know the precise date on which the employment ended. It is also important to know this date because a claim for unfair dismissal must be brought within three months of the termination of the employment. This date is known as the effective date of termination. Section 97 ERA 1996 defines the effective date of termination as being:

(a) Where the contract is terminated by notice, whether given by the employer or the employee, the date on which the notice expires.
(b) Where the contract is terminated otherwise than by notice, the date on which the termination takes effect.
(c) Where the employee is employed under a contract for a fixed term, which expires without being renewed under the same contract, the date on which the fixed term expires.

Where an employee accepts wages in lieu of notice, the effective date of termination will be the date on which the employment ended, not the date on which the notice would have expired. Section 97(2) provides that where a contract of employment is terminated by the employer, the effective date of termination is the date on which the employee's statutory notice would have expired. However, this is only the case for the purpose of seeing if the employee has the necessary one year's continuous employment and for the purpose of calculating the basic award for unfair dismissal. So an employee dismissed after 51 weeks, without notice, would be entitled to one week's statutory notice and the effective date of termination would be one week after his actual dismissal. He would therefore have one year's continuous employment. (Section 97(2) only applies as regards statutory notice, not as regards any longer notice agreed by the parties.) If the employee commits a repudiation of the contract which would justify his dismissal without notice the period of notice to which he would otherwise have been entitled will not be regarded as continuous employment, as the provision in s.97(2) will not apply.

Time limits

Section 111 ERA 1996 requires a claim for unfair dismissal to be brought within three months of the effective date of termination. The tribunal has an option to extend this limit to such period as it considers reasonable where it was satisfied that it was not reasonably practicable for the complaint to be presented within the three-month period. The time limit is not often extended. Even if the late claim is brought in consequence of poor legal advice, this is unlikely to be a sufficient reason to extend the limit. If, however, the lateness was caused by incorrect advice from the Central Office of Industrial Tribunals this may be a good reason for extending the limit.

20.4.2 What amounts to a dismissal?

ERA 1996 provides a statutory definition of dismissal, for the purposes of unfair dismissal. Section 95 provides that an employee is dismissed if: (a) the employer terminates the contract, with or without notice; or (b) a fixed term contract expires; or (c) the employee is constructively dismissed; or (d) an employee who has been given notice by the employer, himself gives the employer a shorter period of notice to end the contract. An employee can also be deemed to have been dismissed. The various methods of dismissal need to be examined individually. It is up to the employee to prove that he was dismissed.

20.4.2.1 Termination by the employer

If the employer terminates the contract unilaterally, with or without notice, then this amounts to a dismissal. If the employee either resigns or agrees to terminate the employment then this will generally not amount to a dismissal. However, if an employee resigns because he is told that if he does not resign he will be dismissed, this amounts to a dismissal. An example can be seen in *Robertson* v *Securicor Transport Ltd* [1972] IRLR 70, where a guard who had broken the rules by signing for a package he did not have was given the choice of resigning or being sacked. He chose to resign and was held to have been unfairly dismissed.

If the employer radically and unilaterally changes the conditions of employment then this may amount to a dismissal, as it did in the following case.

■ *Alcan Extrusions* v *Yates* [1996] IRLR 327

The employees worked 37 hours a week on a shift system. Work done at the weekend or bank holidays was overtime. The employers introduced a new rolling shift system, which caused the employees to lose money because weekend and holiday work was no longer regarded as overtime. Negotiations with the union failed to achieve acceptance of the new scheme, so the employer imposed it unilaterally. Letters were sent to the employees telling them that the new system would be adopted. The complainant and others stipulated that they would work the new system under protest, reserving their rights to claim unfair dismissal and redundancy. They later lodged unfair dismissal claims, while continuing to work.

Held. The employees had been expressly dismissed by their employers.

COMMENT The dismissal took effect when the employer unilaterally imposed the new conditions. This seems somewhat strange as the complainant continued to work for the employer after this. The explanation is that the old contract was terminated and the complainant then worked under a different inferior contract.

If the employer's words or actions are ambiguous, so that they might or might not amount to a termination of the contract, the court will ask what the reasonable person would have made of the words. In reaching a decision as to whether or not the employer intended to terminate the employment, the court will consider the context of the employment and the context in which the words were spoken. Words spoken after the dismissal are only relevant in so far as they shed light upon the employer's intention at the time of the dismissal. Once the dismissal has been made it cannot be unilaterally withdrawn, although words spoken in the heat of the moment may sometimes be withdrawn if this is done quickly enough.

20.4.2.2 Expiry of fixed term contract

A fixed term contract of employment has definite dates for both the commencement and the termination of the employment. If such a fixed term contract expires without being renewed under the same contract then the employee is regarded as dismissed, for the purposes of unfair dismissal. Since October 1999 employees can no longer waive their rights to claim unfair dismissal on the expiry of a fixed term contract. However, as regards fixed term contracts entered into before 25 October 1999 an agreement to waive the right to claim unfair dismissal on the expiry of the contract continues to be effective.

20.4.2.3 Constructive dismissal

Section 95(1)(c) ERA 1996 states that an employee is dismissed by his employer, for the purposes of unfair dismissal, if the employee terminates the contract under which he is employed (with or without notice) in circumstances in which the employee is entitled to terminate it without notice by reason of the employer's conduct. This is often known as constructive dismissal. Lord Denning MR gave an explanation of constructive dismissal in *Western Excavating* v *Sharp* [1978] 1 All ER 713:

'If the employer is guilty of conduct which is a significant breach going to the root of the contract of employment, or which shows that the employer no longer intends to be bound by one or more of the essential terms of the contract, then the employee is entitled to treat himself as discharged from any further performance. If he does so, then he terminates the contract by reason of the employer's conduct. He is constructively dismissed. The employee is entitled in those circumstances to leave at the instant without giving notice at all or, alternatively, he may give notice and say he is leaving at the end of the notice. But the conduct must in either case be sufficiently serious to entitle him to leave at once. Moreover, he must make up his mind soon after the conduct of which he complains: for, if he continues for any length of time without leaving, he will lose his right to treat himself as discharged. He will be regarded as having elected to affirm the contract.'

If the employer unilaterally imposes a change in the essential terms of the contract, the employee is entitled to regard himself as constructively dismissed. It is up to the employee to show that he was constructively dismissed.

Breach of any term of the contract of employment, if sufficiently serious to go to the root of the contract and therefore justify the employee's resignation, will enable the employee to claim constructive dismissal. It is relatively easy to deduce whether or not an express term of the contract has been breached, but can be very difficult to say whether or not an implied term has been breached.

If the conduct of the employer is within the contract of employment then it cannot give rise to a constructive dismissal. However, if the employer invokes a contract term in an unreasonable way then this may be a breach of the implied term of mutual respect and confidence.

The fact that an employee has been constructively dismissed does not necessarily mean that the dismissal was unfair.

There is generally no implied term that an employee will be entitled to an annual pay rise. However, if the employer arbitrarily and capriciously refuses to give an employee a pay rise this may be enough to enable the employee to claim constructive dismissal.

When an employer commits an act which would justify constructive dismissal the employee must leave the employment reasonably soon afterwards. If the employee does not leave reasonably soon, he will be regarded as having waived the right to treat the contract as repudiated.

20.4.2.4 Employee gives notice, having already received notice

Section 95(2) provides that an employee shall be taken to be dismissed for the purposes of unfair dismissal if the employer gives notice to terminate the contract and the employee gives notice to terminate on a date earlier than the date on which the employer's notice was to expire. The reason for the dismissal is taken to be the reason for which the employer's notice was given.

20.4.2.5 Deemed dismissal

Section 96 ERA 1996 provides that a woman who is not permitted to return to work after childbirth is deemed to have been dismissed, for the purposes of unfair dismissal. The woman must have properly exercised her right to return to work. The employment is regarded as continuous up until the date on which she would have been due to return to work, and is regarded as terminated from that date.

20.4.2.6 Situations in which there is no dismissal

There will be no dismissal if the contract is frustrated. Nor will there be a dismissal if the employee resigns, unless constructive dismissal can be claimed. (These circumstances in which the contract is frustrated, and in which there is a genuine resignation by the employee were examined above at 20.3.4 and 20.3.5.) Nor will there be a dismissal if the parties mutually agree to end the employment (see above at 20.3.3) nor if the contract is discharged by performance when the employee completes the specific task which he was employed to perform. Nor will there be a dismissal if a woman fails to return to work after maternity leave, although the contract will be terminated.

In the following case the Court of Appeal considered the position where the employer claimed that the contract was terminated by reason of the employee's breach of the contract. (This situation is sometimes referred to as constructive resignation.)

■ *London Transport Executive* v *Clarke* [1981] IRLR 166 (Court of Appeal)

The complainant, a bus mechanic who had been born in Jamaica, applied for unpaid leave to go back to Jamaica. This request was turned down because he had already exhausted the amount of unpaid leave which the employers allowed. He again applied for leave and was again refused. He asked what would happen if he went without permission and was informed that there was a laid down procedure which would be followed and that this procedure would result in his being removed from the books. The complainant took the leave anyway. The employers wrote to the complainant's London address, asking for an explanation. One week later they wrote to say that if he did not respond within 14 days he would be removed from their books. The complainant did not reply within the period. Two weeks later the employers wrote to the complainant, telling him that his name had been permanently removed from the books on that day. When the complainant returned to England he presented himself at work, with a medical certificate which covered the precise period for which he had been absent from work. He claimed that he had sent a medical certificate to the employers, although they did not receive one. The employers refused to take him back and the complainant claimed unfair dismissal.

Held. The contract of employment was not terminated by the complainant's conduct. The complainant had repudiated the contract, but the contract was terminated by the employers when they accepted this repudiation. (They did this when they wrote to him telling him that he had been permanently removed from the books.) Therefore, the employers had dismissed the complainant. If an employee walks out of his job and does not thereafter claim to be entitled to resume work, he repudiates his contract of employment and the employer accepts this. There can then be no claim for unfair dismissal unless the worker claims that he was constructively dismissed. But where the worker repudiates his contract, by walking out of his job or otherwise, and later claims to be entitled to resume work, then his contract is only terminated if the employer expressly or impliedly accepts the repudiation. This acceptance of the repudiation by the employer amounts to a dismissal, and refusing to allow the worker to return would be such an acceptance of the repudiation.

COMMENT The dismissal was not unfair. The employment tribunal had held that it was. The Court of Appeal overturned this, regarding the tribunal as having erred in law. The Court of Appeal described the tribunal's finding as to unfairness as one which outraged common sense, being a conclusion which no reasonable tribunal could have reached.

20.4.3 Fair and unfair dismissals

After deciding that an employee has been dismissed, the next step is to consider whether or not the dismissal was unfair.

Section 98 ERA 1996 states that in determining whether or not the dismissal of an employee is fair or unfair, it is for the employer to show the reason for the dismissal, or the principal reason for the dismissal if there was more than one. Section 98 also provides that it is for the employer to show that the reason for the dismissal was either one of the four matters listed, or was for some other substantial reason of a kind such as to justify the dismissal of an employee holding the position which the employee held. The four matters listed are:

(a) the reason for the dismissal relates to the capability or qualifications of the employee for performing work of the kind which he was employed by the employer to do;
(b) the reason for the dismissal relates to the conduct of the employee;
(c) the reason for the dismissal is that the employee was made redundant; or
(d) the reason for the dismissal is that the employee could not continue to work in the position which he held without contravention, either by him or by his employer, of a duty or restriction imposed by or under a statute.

20.4.3.1 Grounds on which dismissal may be fair

As we have seen, the burden of proof is on the employer to show the reason for the dismissal, and that the reason fell within one of the matters listed. We therefore need to consider each of the matters listed. The fact that the dismissal was made on the grounds of one of the matters listed does not necessarily mean that the dismissal was fair. However, if the dismissal was made not on the grounds of one of the matters listed then it will always amount to an unfair dismissal.

Lack of capability or qualifications to do the job

It is obviously fair to dismiss an employee who is inherently incapable of performing the job which he was employed to do. However, the employer is still required to act reasonably and should therefore take steps such as: finding out why the employee has difficulty; providing remedial training; providing warnings in appropriate cases and perhaps offering the employee alternative employment. In *Davison* v *Kent Meters Ltd* [1975] IRLR 145, for example, an employee who had incorrectly assembled a large number of components in the wrong way was held to have been unfairly dismissed because she had not been shown how to do the job properly. Generally, a dismissal on the grounds of lack of capability will require more than one act of incompetence.

An employer can dismiss an incompetent employee if, subjectively, the employer considers that the employee was incompetent. There must also be reasonable grounds for such a belief. It is not necessary to prove, objectively, that the employee actually was incompetent. Before dismissing the employee the reasonable employer should first consider other steps, such as warnings. However, a warning is only appropriate if it has some chance of achieving a change in the employee's behaviour.

Earlier in this chapter we considered *Egg Stores (Stamford Hill) Ltd* v *Leibovici* and the circumstances in which a contract of employment is frustrated, rather than terminated by a dismissal, on the grounds of long-term sickness or injury. When an employee is dismissed on the grounds of long-term illness or injury the employer should also consider the Disability Discrimination Act 1995, which is considered in the following chapter.

In *International Sports Co Ltd* v *Thomson* [1980] IRLR 340 the EAT considered the position where an employee is off sick due to minor ailments. This case might be better classified as absenteeism, rather than as genuine long-term illness. Over the previous 18 months the complainant had been absent from work for about 25% of the time. She always provided a medical certificate to cover her absences. She suffered from various complaints, including 'dizzy spells, anxiety and nerves, bronchitis, virus infection, althruigra of the left knee and dyspepsia and flatulence'. The employers' medical adviser said that there was no point in examining the complainant because her complaints were all unconnected and none of them amounted to a chronic illness. After several warnings and a final warning, the complainant was dismissed. The EAT held that the dismissal was fair. The EAT held that the procedure required in cases of intermittent absence through minor ailments is similar to the procedure for misconduct. First, the employer should conduct a fair review of the employee's attendance record and the reasons for it. Second, appropriate warnings should be given after the employee has been given an opportunity to make representations. If there is no subsequent improvement in the attendance record, in most cases the employer will be justified in treating the persistent absences as a sufficient reason for dismissing the employee. On the facts of the case the EAT held that this was a case where the reasonable employer was entitled to say 'enough is enough'.

There are very few cases concerning dismissal for lack of qualifications. Generally, those who are not qualified to do the job are not given the job in the first place. If an aptitude test is introduced for all employees, it may be that an employee can be fairly dismissed on account of not being able to pass the test.

Dismissal on the grounds of the employee's conduct

An employee's conduct, either while at work or outside work, may be sufficiently bad for the employer to fairly dismiss the employee. Some misconduct is of such a serious nature that a summary dismissal would be justified. Minor misconduct would not justify a dismissal without warnings and a final warning having been issued. In all cases of misconduct except those which would obviously justify summary dismissal, the employer should not dismiss the employee without giving the employee the chance to explain himself, without gaining evidence as to what happened and without conducting an enquiry into what happened.

Examples of conduct while at work which have been held to justify dismissal include fighting, swearing, theft, dangerous conduct, dishonesty, immorality and refusing to obey orders, to name but a few. Everything depends upon all the facts of the case. A schoolteacher swearing at young children might be fairly dismissed for using language which would not raise an eyebrow if used by one labourer on a building site to another. Again, the question is whether the employer acted reasonably in dismissing the employee.

Conduct outside the employment can be enough to justify dismissal, but only if it would have an sufficiently adverse effect on the employer's business. In *Gardiner* v *Newport County Council Borough* [1974] IRLR 262, for example, a lecturer at a college of art and design, who taught students aged 16–18, was fairly dismissed after having been convicted of gross indecency with another man in a public lavatory.

Dismissal on the grounds of redundancy

Below, at 20.5, we shall consider the circumstances in which a person is made redundant. A person who is made redundant will not be regarded as having been unfairly dismissed. In *Williams* v *Compair Maxam Ltd* [1982] ICR 156 Browne Wilkinson J set down five principles which a reasonable employer would be expected to adopt in choosing which employees should be made redundant, when a large number of redundancies were inevitable. The principles were as follows: first, the employees should be given as much warning of redundancy as possible; second, the employer should consult the union to see how the redundancies could be achieved fairly and with as little hardship to the employees as possible; third, criteria which can be objectively checked, such as attendance records, efficiency, experience and length of service should be used rather than subjective criteria; fourth, the employer should consider union representation as to the appropriate criteria; fifth, the employer should consider whether instead of dismissing the employee he could offer him alternative employment.

The principles laid down in *Williams* v *Compair Maxam Ltd* are less appropriate in relation to small employers. In all cases the employer should consider alternatives to redundancy, should observe the Code of Practice relating to redundancies and should ensure that a proper selection procedure is used.

Conflict with a statute

An employee might be dismissed fairly on account of the continuing employment conflicting with a statutory provision. For example, if the employee was a driver who was banned from driving, or if a newly passed statute made the employee's further employment unlawful. The employer must still act reasonably. In *Mathieson* v *Noble & Sons Ltd* [1972] IRLR 76 a salesman, whose job required him to drive, was banned from driving. At his own expense the salesman arranged for a chauffeur to drive him around until his disqualification was over. His employer was not prepared to give this arrangement a try and dismissed him. The dismissal was held to be unfair. The employers had acted unreasonably.

Some other substantial reason

The four factors examined above are not exhaustive. A dismissal may be fair although outside the matters specified if it was for some other substantial reason of a kind such as to justify the dismissal of an employee holding the position which he held. There is no closed list of what might amount to some other substantial reason, but employees have been fairly dismissed under this heading in the following circumstances: a teacher failing to forgo a pay rise when all the other teachers at the school had agreed to this, on account of the financial difficulties which the school was experiencing; deliberate concealment of a history of mental illness by an insurance inspector who had to visit clients' homes; refusing to accept a variation in the terms of the employment which was reasonably made in the commercial interest of the employer; refusing to accept a wage cut which has been negotiated by a trade union; being one of several employees at an off-licence, one of whom had stolen £4 600, where a thorough investigation could not reveal which employee was responsible; being an employee who could not get along with another employee, serious efforts to resolve the situation without the need for a dismissal having been considered.

20.4.3.2 Automatically unfair dismissals

Certain reasons for dismissal are automatically regarded as unfair. These include the following:

Dismissal for claiming a statutory right (ERA 1996 s.104)

Section 104 ERA 1996 provides that an employee is unfairly dismissed if the reason for the dismissal (or the principal reason if there was more than one) was that the employee brought proceedings against the employer to enforce a statutory right, or alleged that the employer had infringed a statutory right. It does not matter whether or not the employee actually had the statutory right, or whether or not it was actually infringed. The statutory rights to which this section applies include all those conferred by ERA 1996.

Leave for family reasons (ERA 1996 s.99)

An employee is automatically unfairly dismissed if the reason for the dismissal, or the principal reason, was a reason relating to: (a) pregnancy, childbirth or maternity; (b) maternity or adoption leave; (c) parental or paternity leave; or (d) statutory time off for dependants.

Health and safety cases (ERA 1996 s.100)

An employee is automatically unfairly dismissed if the reason for the dismissal was that he carried out duties, which the employer had designated him to carry out, in connection with preventing or reducing risks to health and safety at work. If there is no health and safety representative or committee, a dismissal on the grounds of the employee carrying out health and safety duties will similarly be automatically unfair. No qualifying period of employment is necessary. Section 103 makes a similar provision in respect of a dismissal for carrying out duties in connection with the employee's role as trustees of an occupational pension scheme.

Working time cases (ERA 1996 ss.101 and 101A)

A worker who is dismissed for insisting on his rights under the Working Time Regulations 1998 is unfairly dismissed. (These Regulations are considered in the following chapter.) Employees who work in shops or betting offices are automatically unfairly dismissed if they are dismissed for refusing to work on a Sunday.

Trade union membership (TULRCA 1992 s.137)

It is automatically unfair to dismiss a person either because he is a member of a trade union or because he is not. There is no qualifying time of employment. If an employee is dismissed on account of having taken official strike action, during the first eight weeks of such action, this is automatically an unfair dismissal.

Transfer of undertakings

Employees who have at least one year's continuous employment, and who are dismissed in connection with a transfer of undertaking which falls within the 1981 Regulations are automatically unfairly dismissed. (The circumstances in which employees are protected is considered in Chapter 21.)

Failure to comply with a statutory dismissal or disciplinary procedure

Section 98A(1) ERA 1996, considered below, makes it automatically unfair for an employer to dismiss an employee without going through one of the dismissal and disciplinary procedures set out in Part 1 of Schedule 2 to the Employment Act 2002, if the non-completion was caused mainly or wholly by the employer's failure to comply with the procedure's requirements.

20.4.3.3 Was the dismissal actually unfair?

If the employer cannot prove that the reason for the dismissal was within the matters listed above at 20.4.3.1, the employee will have been unfairly dismissed. If the employer can show that the employee was dismissed for one of the matters listed, it then needs to be considered whether or not the dismissal actually was unfair. Section 98(4) ERA 1996 states that:

> 'Where the employer has fulfilled the requirements of [s.98(1),] the determination of the question whether the dismissal is fair or unfair (having regard to the reason shown by the employer) –
> (a) depends on whether in the circumstances (including the size and administrative resources of the employer's undertaking) the employer acted reasonably or unreasonably in treating it as a sufficient reason for dismissing the employee, and
> (b) shall be determined in accordance with equity and the substantial merits of the case.'

The burden of proof as to whether or not the dismissal actually was unfair is neutral. This is a matter for the tribunal to decide in the light of s.98(4) and all the evidence.

The tribunal is likely to consider the dismissal unfair if the employer cannot show that he went through the proper procedures and then that he acted reasonably, that is to say whether he acted as a reasonable employer would have done. Whether or not the employer actually did act as a reasonable employer would have done is a question to be decided by the tribunal in the light of all the circumstances. An appellate court can only overrule the tribunal's finding if it was perverse or made as a consequence of an error of law.

The band of reasonable responses

In *Iceland Frozen Foods* v *Jones* [1983] ICR 17 Browne-Wilkinson J summarised the law in this way:

> 'We consider that the authorities establish that in law the correct approach for the employment tribunal to adopt in answering the question posed by [s.98(4) ERA 1996] is as follows: (1) the starting point should always be the words of [s.98(4) ERA 1996] themselves; (2) in applying the section an employment tribunal must consider the reasonableness of the employer's conduct, not simply whether they (the members of the employment tribunal) consider the dismissal to be fair; (3) in judging the reasonableness of the employer's conduct an employment tribunal must not substitute its decision as to what was the right course to adopt for that of the employer; (4) in many, though not all, cases there is a band of reasonable responses to the employee's conduct within which one employer might reasonably take one view, another quite reasonably take another; (5) the function of the employment tribunal, as an industrial jury, is to determine whether in the particular circumstances of each case the decision to dismiss the employee fell within the band of reasonable responses which a reasonable employer might have adopted. If the dismissal falls within the band the dismissal is fair: if the dismissal falls outside the band the dismissal is unfair.'

This test seems very favourable to the employer. Only if the employer's decision to dismiss could not have been within the band of reasonableness will it be unfair. It will thus be fair even if many employers would have considered the decision to dismiss the employee as an unreasonable response. The band of reasonableness responses seems preferable to allowing the tribunal to decide if they, as reasonable employers, would have dismissed the employee. To do this would be to allow a subjective review by the tribunal members to replace the subjective decision of the employer who dismissed the employee. At times the band of reasonable responses test has been doubted, but its validity was approved by the Court of Appeal in *Post Office* v *Foley* [2000] IRLR 827.

Procedural unfairness

Even if a dismissal was for one of the fair reasons specified, and even if it was within the band of reasonable responses, it will be automatically unfair if one of the statutory dismissal and disciplinary procedures was not complied with.

Section 98A(1) ERA 1996 now provides:

'An employee who is dismissed shall be regarded for the purposes of this Part as unfairly dismissed if –
(a) one of the procedures set out in Part 1 of Schedule 2 to the Employment Act 2002 (dismissal and disciplinary procedures) applies in relation to the dismissal,
(b) the procedure has not been completed, and
(c) the non-completion of the procedure is wholly or mainly attributable to failure by the employer to comply with its requirements.'

(As regards dismissal procedures other than the ones set out in Part 1 of Schedule 2 to the Employment Act 2002, s.98A(2) provides that failure to follow such an other dismissal procedure shall not be regarded for the purposes of s.98(4)(a) as by itself making the employer's action unreasonable if he shows that he would have decided to have dismissed the employee if he had followed the procedure.)

20.4.3.4 Part 1 Statutory dismissal and disciplinary procedures

Part 1 of Schedule 2 to the Employment Act 2002 sets out standard and modified dismissal and disciplinary procedures, which are to be part of all employees' contracts of employment, as follows.

Standard dismissal and disciplinary procedure

'1 Step 1: statement of grounds for action and invitation to meeting
(1) The employer must set out in writing the employee's alleged conduct or characteristics, or other circumstances, which lead him to contemplate dismissing or taking disciplinary action against the employee.
(2) The employer must send the statement or a copy of it to the employee and invite the employee to attend a meeting to discuss the matter.

2 Step 2: meeting
(1) The meeting must take place before action is taken, except in the case where the disciplinary action consists of suspension.
(2) The meeting must not take place unless –
  (a) the employer has informed the employee what the basis was for including in the statement under paragraph (1)(1) the ground or grounds given in it, and
  (b) the employee has had a reasonable opportunity to consider his response to that information.
(3) The employee must take all reasonable steps to attend the meeting.
(4) After the meeting, the employer must inform the employee of his decision and notify him of the right to appeal against the decision if he is not satisfied with it.

3 Step 3: appeal
(1) If the employee does wish to appeal, he must inform the employer.
(2) If the employee informs the employer of his wish to appeal, the employer must invite him to attend a further meeting.
(3) The employee must take all reasonable steps to attend the meeting.

(4) The appeal meeting need not take place before the dismissal or disciplinary action takes effect.

(5) After the appeal meeting, the employer must inform the employee of his final decision.'

Modified dismissal and disciplinary procedure

The modified procedure is to be used where it would be illegal to continue to employ the employee or in the rare cases where the employee commits such gross misconduct that it would be futile to carry out an investigation. It has only two steps. In other gross misconduct cases the employee might be suspended while the standard procedure was followed. Proposed regulations suggest that the new Disciplinary and Dismissal Procedures should not apply if the disciplinary action is less than dismissal, such as a written or oral warning because it would be senseless to write a letter threatening disciplinary action before taking such action.

'4 Step 1: statement of grounds for action

The employer must –

(a) set out in writing –

    (i) the employee's alleged misconduct which has led to the dismissal,

    (ii) what the basis was for thinking at the time of the dismissal that the employee was guilty of the alleged misconduct, and

    (iii) the employees' right to appeal against dismissal, and

(b) send the statement, or a copy of it, to the employee.

5 Step 2: appeal

(1) If the employee does wish to appeal, he must inform the employer.

(2) If the employee informs the employer of his wish to appeal, the employer must invite him to attend a meeting.

(3) The employee must take all reasonable steps to attend the meeting

(4) After the appeal meeting, the employer must inform the employee of his final decision.'

If the employer fails to comply with the Dismissal and Disciplinary Procedures the employee will be automatically unfairly dismissed.

Schedule 2 also sets out a standard **grievance procedure**, as follows. (Failure by the employer to comply with the grievance procedure requirements will not automatically amount to unfair dismissal.)

'6 Step 1: statement of grievance

The employee must set out the grievance in writing and send the statement or a copy of it to the employer.

7 Step 2: meeting

(1) The employer must invite the employee to attend a meeting to discuss the grievance.

(2) The meeting must not take place unless-

    (a) the employee has informed the employer what the basis for the grievance was when he made the statement [under Step 1], and

    (b) the employer has had a reasonable opportunity to consider his response to that information.

(3) The employee must take all reasonable steps to attend the meeting.

(4) After the meeting, the employer must inform the employee of his decision as to his response to the grievance and notify him of the right to appeal against the decision if he is not satisfied with it.

8 Step 3: appeal

(1) If the employee does wish to appeal, he must inform the employer.

(2) If the employee informs the employer of his wish to appeal, the employer must invite him to attend a further meeting.

(3) The employee must take all reasonable steps to attend the meeting.

(4) After the appeal meeting, the employer must inform the employee of his final decision.'

The following modified grievance procedure is also set out.

'Modified procedure

9 Step 1: statement of grievance
The employee must–
(a) set out in writing–
    (1) the grievance, and
    (2) the basis for it, and
(b) send the statement, or a copy of it, to the employer.

10 Step 2 response
The employer must set out his response in writing and send the statement or a copy of it to the employee.'

The standard procedure should apply in all cases where the employment continues. Even where the employment has ended the standard procedure should apply unless it is not reasonably practicable. (For example if the ex-employee had left the area.)

Section 32 of the Employment Act 2002 provides that an employee cannot present a case of unfair dismissal to the employment tribunal if he has not gone through Step 1 of the Grievance Procedure. After Step 1 has been complied with the employee must then wait another 28 days, to give the employer time to respond. If the employee claims unfair dismissal the usual three-month time limit for applying to an employment tribunal is extended by a further three months if the employee sends Step 1 of the grievance procedure, or tries to submit Form IT1 within the initial three month period.

If either the Dismissal and Disciplinary Procedure, or the Grievance Procedure, was not complied with the employment tribunal has the power, under s.31 of the Employment Act 2002, to increase or reduce the compensation payable. If the failure to comply was wholly or mainly due to the employer, the employee will automatically be entitled to an increase of 10% in any award made. If the tribunal considers it just and equitable the award could be increased by more than 10%, up to a maximum of 50%. If the failure to comply was wholly or mainly due to the employee then the award must be reduced by 10% and could be reduced by more, up to a maximum of 50%, if this is just and equitable. In wholly exceptional circumstances there could be no increase or reduction.

20.4.4 Remedies for unfair dismissal

ERA 1996 specifies the remedies available for unfair dismissal. These are reinstatement, re-engagement or compensation.

20.4.4.1 Re-engagement and reinstatement

Section 113 ERA 1996 lists re-engagement and reinstatement as remedies for unfair dismissal. If an employee is reinstated he is given his old job back. The employer must treat the complainant in all respects as if he had not been dismissed. The tribunal will specify the amount of back pay he should receive, any rights and privileges (including seniority and pension rights) which must be restored to the employee and the date by which the order must be complied with. If the employee is re-engaged he is taken back in a capacity comparable to that in which he was previously employed, on the terms which the tribunal thinks fit. The tribunal will specify the nature of the employment, the remuneration of the employment, any back pay to which the employee might be entitled, any rights and privileges (including seniority and pension rights) which must be restored to the employee and the date by which the order must be complied with. As regards either type of award the tribunal takes into account any payments made by the employer, and any social security benefits received by the employee, in deciding upon the amount of back pay. Neither of these remedies is awarded very often. Generally, the implied term as to mutual trust and respect has been irrevocably breached by the time of the hearing. For this reason the tribunal is loath to make an order of re-engagement or reinstatement. If an employee is re-engaged or reinstated his continuous employment is not broken and the period for which he was absent from work counts as part of his continuous employment.

20.4.4.2 Compensation awards

The basic award

This award is calculated according to a formula set out by s.119 ERA 1996. The formula multiplies the employee's relevant years of continuous employment by his weekly wage. For each year of continuous employment below the age of 22 the employee is awarded half a week's pay. For each year during which the employee was 22 or more but below the age of 41 he gets one week's pay, and for each year of continuous employment during which the employee was 41 or more he gets one and a half weeks' pay. The week's pay is the normal week's pay. Overtime is not included unless there is a contractual provision for the employer to provide it and for the employee to work it. The amount awarded is often severely restricted by two limits. First, an applicant cannot claim for more than 20 years' continuous employment, even if he has worked more. Second, the week's pay which can be claimed is limited to a maximum of £270 per week, no matter how much the employee actually earns. The maximum award is therefore $20 \times 1.5 = 30 \times £270 = £8\,100$. The number of relevant years in each category is calculated by working backwards from the effective date of termination. Only whole years count. The statutory restriction on the maximum week's pay is periodically increased.

If the complainant has reached the age of 64, the basic award is reduced by one twelfth for each month that he is over 64 and is therefore extinguished altogether if at the effective date of termination the complainant had reached the age of 65.

The following example shows how the basic award is calculated.

■ **Example**

Both Fred and Jill are unfairly dismissed. Fred has 16 years' continuous employment, six of these having been worked since he reached the age of 41. His weekly wage is £200. Jill has 20 years' continuous employment, ten of these having been worked since she reached the age of 41. Jill's weekly wage is £660.

Fred's entitlement will be calculated as 19 weeks' pay, for the purpose of calculating the basic award. (The six years after attaining the age of 41 counting as nine weeks. The ten years before he reached the age of 41 counting as one week per year.) Fred will get a basic award of $19 \times £200 = £3\,800$.

Jill's entitlement will be calculated as 25 weeks' pay for the purpose of calculating the basic award. (The ten years worked after she was 41 count as 15 weeks. The ten years worked before attaining the age of 41 count as one week each.) Jill earns more than the maximum weekly wage of £270, so her weekly wage will be set at £270. Jill will therefore receive a basic award of $25 \times £270 = £6\,750$.

The basic award can be reduced in three circumstances. First, if the employer has made an offer of re-engagement or reinstatement which the employee has refused to take up. The refusal must be unreasonable, in which case the tribunal can reduce the award by the amount which it sees fit. Second, the tribunal may reduce the award if the complainant's conduct before the dismissal was such as to make the reduction equitable. This is similar to contributory negligence, although the conduct of the complainant does not need to have contributed to the employer's decision to dismiss. The award can be dismissed on the grounds of conduct committed before the dismissal, even if this conduct was not discovered until after the dismissal. Third, if the employer claimed that the complainant was dismissed on the grounds of redundancy, when in fact the complainant was unfairly dismissed, the amount of any redundancy payment received by the complainant will be deducted from the basic award for unfair dismissal. This will only make a difference in respect of continuous service worked before the age of 18. Such service is counted when calculating the basic award for unfair dismissal but is not counted when assessing a redundancy payment.

As the basic award is not an award of damages, the complainant has no duty to mitigate the loss.

Automatic entitlement to basic award

Section 138 ERA 1996 provides that an employee who is made redundant, having refused an offer of suitable alternative employment, will not be entitled to a redundancy payment. He will however, be entitled automatically to a basic award of two weeks' pay. (The £270 maximum applies.)

Section 141 ERA 1996 entitles an employee who chooses not to accept a renewal of his contract or a re-engagement under a new contract to regard himself as dismissed and take a basic award calculated as two weeks' pay. (Subject to the £270 maximum.) The employee would not be entitled to a redundancy payment, on account of having refused the renewal or re-engagement.

Section 120(1) provides that the amount of the basic award shall be not less than £3100 where the reason, or principal reason, for a dismissal or for selecting a person for redundancy is membership or non-membership of a trade union.

Compensatory awards

Section 123(1) provides that the amount of the compensatory award shall be such amount as the tribunal considers just and equitable in all the circumstances, having regard to the loss sustained by the employee in consequence of the dismissal in so far as that loss is attributable to action taken by the employer. The maximum compensatory award which can be awarded is currently £53500. (However, in cases where discrimination is proved there is no upper limit on the amount of damages.)

This award is in addition to the basic award. As the purpose of the compensatory award is to compensate the complainant, not to punish the employer, it is only given in respect of financial losses. The tribunal has a wide discretion but should set out the ways in which the award was made up. The usual headings are: immediate and future loss of earnings (the burden of proof as regards these losses is on the complainant but the tribunal speculates as to how long the employee is likely to remain unemployed. There is no upper limit on the weekly pay. The immediate loss of earnings will be the amount lost between the dates of termination and the hearing. If wages were paid in lieu of notice the tribunal will take account of this); expenses; loss of statutory rights, bearing in mind that rights such as not to be unfairly dismissed will not arise until there has been one year's continuous employment; loss of pension rights; and a supplementary amount if the employer failed to go through an established appeal procedure.

The compensatory award will be reduced in respect of losses which the employee could have mitigated. If he therefore turned down suitable employment the amount will be reduced. It is up to the employer to prove that the employee failed to mitigate. It will also be reduced by the amount of job seeker's allowance which the applicant has received. Section 123(6) provides that where the tribunal finds that the dismissal was to any extent caused or contributed to by any action of the employee, it shall reduce the amount of the compensatory award by such proportion as it considers just and equitable having regard to that finding. Again, this is similar to contributory negligence.

Additional awards

If an employer refuses to comply with a re-engagement or reinstatement order the tribunal may make an additional award. This additional award should be of between 13 and 26 weeks' pay, unless the dismissal was on the grounds of sex or racial discrimination, in which case it could be of between 26 and 52 weeks' pay. (The week's pay is still subject to the £270 maximum.)

Test your understanding

1 What period of continuous employment must an employee have worked in order to claim unfair dismissal?

2 What is the effective date of termination? In what three ways is it significant?

3 On what grounds may an employee be regarded as having been dismissed, for the purposes of unfair dismissal?

4 On what five grounds might a dismissal be fair, for the purposes of unfair dismissal?

5 On what grounds can a dismissal be automatically unfair?

6 If the employer establishes that the dismissal was for one of the specified fair reasons, does this automatically mean that the dismissal was fair?

7 Can a dismissal be rendered unfair merely because the employer did not follow the correct procedures?

8 What remedies can be awarded for unfair dismissal?

9 How are the basic award and the compensatory award assessed?

Answers

1 Except as regards dismissals which are automatically unfair, only employees with at least one year's continuous employment will be able to claim unfair dismissal.

2 The effective date of termination is the date at which the employment is taken to have ended, for the purposes of unfair dismissal and redundancy. In relation to unfair dismissal, it is significant in deciding: whether or not a claimant has enough continuous employment to make a claim; whether the claim is made in time; and the amount of the complainant's basic award.

3 An employee can only be regarded as having been dismissed, for the purposes of unfair dismissal if: (a) the employer terminates the contract, with or without notice; or (b) a fixed term contract expires; or (c) the employee is constructively dismissed; or (d) an employee who has been given notice by the employer, himself gives the employer a shorter period of notice to end the contract. An employee who is not allowed to return to work after childbirth can be deemed to have been dismissed. There is a dismissal if the employer accepts a repudiatory breach by the employee (because the employer terminates the contract by accepting the breach) but not if the contract is frustrated.

4 The employee's dismissal can only be regarded as fair if the employer shows that the dismissal was for one of the four following reasons: (a) the reason for the dismissal relates to the capability or qualifications of the employee for performing work of the kind which he was employed by the employer to do; (b) the reason for the dismissal relates to the conduct of the employee; (c) the reason for the dismissal is that the employee was made redundant; or (d) the reason for the dismissal is that the employee could not continue to work in the position which he held without contravention, either by him or by his employer, of a duty or restriction imposed by or under a statute. A dismissal can also be regarded as fair if the employer shows that the dismissal was for some other substantial reason of a kind such as to justify the dismissal of an employee holding the position which the employee held.

5 A dismissal can be automatically unfair if it was: on the grounds of the employee claiming a statutory right; or in connection with pregnancy and childbirth; or for pursuing health and safety issues; or for causing shop assistants to work on Sundays; or connected with trade union membership or because the employer's statutory dismissal and disciplinary procedures were not complied with.

6 Even if the employer proves that the dismissal was for one of the specified fair reasons, the dismissal may still be unfair. This will depend upon whether in the circumstances the employer acted reasonably or unreasonably in treating the reason shown for the dismissal as a sufficient reason for dismissing the employee. This matter will be determined by the tribunal in accordance with equity and the substantial merits of the case.

7 Even if a dismissal is for one of the fair reasons specified, and was within the band of reasonable responses, it will be rendered unfair if the employer's statutory dismissal and disciplinary procedures were not complied with.

8 The possible remedies for unfair dismissal are: re-engagement or reinstatement; a basic award; and a compensatory award.

9 The basic award is calculated according to a formula set out in the ERA. The complainant has no duty to mitigate his loss. The compensatory award is at the tribunal's discretion. It is designed to compensate the complainant for financial losses and therefore the complainant has a duty to mitigate these.

20.5 · Redundancy

An employee with at least two years' continuous employment who is made redundant is entitled to a statutory payment, as compensation for the loss of his job. Lord Denning MR gave the following explanation of redundancy and the nature of redundancy payments in *Lloyd* v *Brassey* [1969] 2 QB 98.

'It is as well to remind ourselves of the policy of this legislation [the Redundancy Payments Act 1965, which has been consolidated into the ERA 1996.] ... a worker of long standing is now recognised as having an accrued right in his job; and his right gains in value with the years. So much so that if the job is shut down he is entitled to compensation for loss of the job – just as a director gets compensation for loss of office. The director gets a golden handshake. The worker gets a redundancy payment. It is not unemployment pay. I repeat "not". Even if he gets another job straightaway, he nevertheless is entitled to full redundancy payment. It is, in a real sense, compensation for long service. No man gets it unless he has been employed for at least two years by the employer; and then the amount of it depends solely upon his age and length of service.'

A redundancy payment is therefore aimed at cushioning the blow when workers lose their jobs. Before 1972 there was no statutory payment for unfair dismissal. Employees were therefore keen to prove that a dismissal amounted to redundancy. We saw earlier in this chapter that an employee who is properly made redundant will not be able to claim unfair dismissal. These days, employees commonly argue that they have not been made redundant, as this will entitle them to claim unfair dismissal, which may result in a higher payment being made.

20.5.1 Dismissal by reason of redundancy

Section 139(1) ERA 1996 sets out the circumstances in which an employee will have been made redundant.

'(1) For the purposes of this Act an employee who is dismissed shall be taken to be dismissed by reason of redundancy if the dismissal is wholly or mainly attributable to –
(a) the fact that his employer has ceased or intends to cease –
    (i) to carry on the business for the purposes of which the employee was employed by him, or
    (ii) to carry on that business in the place where the employee was so employed, or
(b) the fact that the requirements of that business –
    (i) for employees to carry out work of a particular kind, or
    (ii) for employees to carry out work of a particular kind in the place where the employee was employed by the employer,
have ceased or diminished or are expected to cease or diminish.'

It can be seen for s.139(1) that the meaning of redundancy is not the same as the everyday meaning. Both employers and employees often refer to any dismissal as a redundancy. In fact the situations in which an employee can be dismissed by reason of redundancy are specific. A little needs to be said about each of the possible types of dismissals which can be by reason of redundancy.

20.5.1.1 Cessation of the business

The employees of a business will be dismissed by reason of redundancy if they are dismissed on account of the employer either ceasing or intending to cease to carry on the business for the purposes of which the employee was employed. This is one of the most common redundancy situations, with which most people are probably familiar. It is commonly reported in the newspapers that a particular company has gone into receivership and that all of the employees have been made redundant.

20.5.1.2 The employer moves the place of the business

If the employer moves the place of work from one place to another the employees may have been made redundant. Whether they have been made redundant is a question of fact, and will depend amongst other things upon the distance moved and the level of inconvenience caused to the employees by the move.

The true place of work of the employee may well cause difficulty if the employee's contract contains a 'mobility clause' requiring him to work anywhere in the country. Is the employee's place of work to be ascertained by the contract test, which would regard the place of work as the place where the employee could be required within his contract to work? Or is it to be ascertained by the geographical test, which would regard the place of work as the place where the employee actually worked? In the following case the Court of Appeal strongly favoured the geographical test.

■ *High Table Ltd* v *Horst* [1997] IRLR 513 (Court of Appeal)

The three applicants worked as waitresses for a firm which provided catering services in London. They were dismissed and the company claimed that this was by reason of redundancy, on the grounds that the employees were no longer needed at the place where they worked. The applicants' contracts of employment contained a mobility clause and so they could therefore have been employed elsewhere. The applicants claimed that as they had not been employed elsewhere they had been unfairly dismissed.

Held. The applicants were made redundant.

Peter Gibson LJ: 'The question [s.139(1)] poses – where was the employee employed by the employer for the purposes of the business? – is one to be answered primarily by a consideration of the factual circumstances which obtained until the dismissal. If an employee has worked in only one location under his contract of employment for the purposes of the employer's business, it defies common sense to widen the extent of the place where he was so employed, merely because of the existence of a mobility clause. Of course, the refusal by the employee to obey a lawful requirement under the contract of employment for the employee to move may constitute a valid reason for dismissal, but the issues of dismissal, redundancy and reasonableness in the actions of an employer should be kept distinct. It would be unfortunate if the law were to encourage the inclusion of mobility clauses to defeat genuine redundancy claims.'

20.5.1.3 The employer sheds surplus labour

An employer's need to employ workers may diminish either because there is less work to be done or because the existing work can be performed by fewer employees. Many innovations and new technologies have had the effect of reducing the need for workers of a particular kind. Often a reorganisation by the employer requires employees to work at a different time of day. Employees who refuse to do this and are consequently dismissed will not be entitled to a redundancy payment.

Difficulties have been caused by the meaning of 'work of a particular kind'. Several tests have been used by the courts to discover the meaning of 'work of a particular kind'. In the following case the Employment Appeal Tribunal formulated what has become known as the statutory test.

■ *Safeway Stores plc* v *Burrell* [1997] IRLR 200

A petrol station manager at a Safeway supermarket was dismissed when Safeway carried out a nationwide re-organisation. The post of petrol station manager disappeared and a new post of petrol filling station controller was created. Some redundancies of management employees were inevitable, as there were to be fewer new posts than old posts. The applicant did not apply for the new job of petrol filling station controller as the pay was only £11 000 p.a., whereas previously he had earned £13 052 p.a. The applicant agreed to take a redundancy payment and pay in lieu of notice. Subsequently he claimed unfair dismissal, on the grounds that he had not been made redundant.

Held. The applicant was made redundant. The statutory framework of s.139(1)(b) involved the following three-stage process:
(i) Was the employee dismissed? If so
(ii) Had the requirements of the employer's business for employees to carry out work of a particular kind ceased or diminished, or were they expected to cease or diminish? If so
(iii) Was the dismissal of the employee caused wholly or mainly by the state of affairs identified at stage 2?

COMMENT The test applied in the case is known as the statutory test. Two other tests, the function test and the contract test have also been used. The statutory test now seems to be the correct one. In *Murray* v *Foyle Meats* [1999] IRLR 562 the House of Lords strongly approved the decision in *Safeway Stores plc* v *Burrell*. Lord Irvine of Lairg LC, giving the leading judgment, said that he entirely agreed with the clear reasoning and conclusions of the case. The decision seems to allow for what is known as 'bumping' where one employee, who would otherwise have been made redundant, replaces another and the employee replaced is regarded as having been made redundant. This seems to be allowed because the stage 2 question asks whether the requirements of the employer's business for employees has ceased or diminished, rather than asking whether the need to employ the particular employee had ceased or diminished.

In many cases the fact that a dismissed employee was not replaced will indicate that he was made redundant.

20.5.2 Who can claim redundancy?

Only employees with at least two years' continuous employment since reaching the age of 18 are entitled to claim redundancy. Continuous employment before the age of 18 does not count. Share fishermen and Crown employees are excluded from claiming redundancy, as are employees who have reached 65 or the normal retiring age. Those ordinarily employed outside Great Britain cannot usually claim. They can, however, claim if they were present in Great Britain on the employer's instructions, on the date when they were made redundant.

We examined the meaning of continuous employment earlier in this chapter at 20.4.1.2. Section 139(2) ERA 1996 provides that for the purposes of redundancy the business of the employer together with the business or businesses of his associated employers shall be treated as one. Associated employers would include companies who control the business of the main employer company or are controlled by it. Two employers are treated as associated if both are companies controlled directly or indirectly by a third person.

Section 218(2) ERA 1996 provides that if a trade or business or undertaking is transferred from one person to another, this does not break the continuity of employment.

Section 163(2) ERA 1996 states that an employee who has been dismissed by his employer shall, unless the contrary is proved, be presumed to have been so dismissed by reason of redundancy.

If upon leaving the employment the employee is immediately entitled to payments under an occupational pension scheme which amount to at least one third of the final salary, the employer may serve notice that he is excluding the right to a redundancy payment. For these purposes the annual salary is set at a maximum of £14 040 (52 weeks × £270). If the amount payable is less than one third of the final salary, or if it is payable not immediately but within 90 weeks, the redundancy payment can be reduced proportionately.

20.5.3 Offer of suitable alternative employment

If an employee is offered suitable alternative employment, and unreasonably refuses to accept it, then he cannot claim to have been dismissed. Whether alternative employment offered is suitable or not is a question to be determined in the light of all the circumstances. Even if the offer of alternative employment is suitable, the employee can still reject it and claim redundancy if this is reasonable in all of the circumstances. The suitable alternative employment must take effect within four weeks of the expiry of the old employment.

20.5.3.1 Trial period of new employment

An employee is entitled to a trial period of four weeks if he is offered employment on terms and conditions which differ from those of the previous employment. If the employer terminates the contract during this four-week period, for a reason connected with the new contract, the employee is regarded as dismissed on the date when the old contract ended and is dismissed for the reason which caused the old contract to end. The same is true if the employee ends the contract within the four-week period unless the employee terminated it unreasonably, in which case he will not be entitled to a redundancy payment. After the statutory four-week period the employee is deemed to have accepted alternative terms regardless of any agreement with the employer and therefore the redundancy claim would be defeated.

20.5.4 Procedure for redundancy

Earlier in this chapter we considered *Williams* v *Compair Maxam Ltd*, in which Browne-Wilkinson J set out the principles which a large employer should adopt for deciding who to make redundant when a large number of redundancies was inevitable. We also considered the statutory dismissal and disciplinary procedures with which an employer must comply before making a dismissal. If these procedures are not followed the dismissal will be unfair.

20.5.5 Redundancy payments

A redundancy payment is calculated in the same way as a basic award for unfair dismissal except that: years of continuous employment worked while the employee was under 18 years old do not count, and the award cannot be reduced on account of the employee's contributory conduct.

The employee must be given a written statement explaining how the redundancy payment was calculated. Failure to do this can result in the employer being fined. The time limit for presenting a claim is six months from the effective date of termination. The tribunal has a discretion to allow a claim to be made within 12 months of the effective date of termination, if it considers it just and equitable to do so, but no claim can be made after 12 months.

If the employer has become insolvent the employee may make a claim to the Department of Employment, which will pay the statutory redundancy due.

20.5.6 Consultation on redundancies

Section 188 of the Trade Union and Labour Relations (Consolidation) Act 1992 (TULRCA 1992) provides that where an employer is proposing to dismiss as redundant 20 or more employees at one establishment within a period of 90 days or less, the employer shall consult about the dismissals all the persons who are appropriate representatives of any of the employees who may be so dismissed.

These consultations must begin at least 30 days before the dismissals take effect, unless 100 or more dismissals are proposed when they must begin at least 90 days before the dismissals take effect. The consultations must consider ways of avoiding the dismissals, ways of reducing the number of employees to be dismissed and ways of mitigating the consequences of the dismissals. The employer must undertake the consultations with a view to reaching agreement with the appropriate representatives.

The employer has to disclose in writing:

(a) the reason for his proposals,
(b) the number and description of the employees he proposes to make redundant,
(c) the total number of such employees of any such description employed by the employer at the establishment in question,
(d) the proposed method of selecting the employees who are to be dismissed,
(e) the proposed method of carrying out the dismissals, with due regard to any agreed procedure, including the period over which the dismissals are to take effect,
(f) the proposed method of calculating the amount of any redundancy payments to be made to employees who may be dismissed.

The employer has a duty to allow the appropriate representatives access to the employees whom it is proposed to dismiss as redundant and to provide for the representatives such accommodation and other facilities as may be appropriate.

If there are special circumstances which render it not reasonably practicable for the employer to comply with these requirements, the employer must take all steps towards compliance as are reasonably practicable in all the circumstances.

If the employer does not comply with these requirements, a complainant may present a case to an employment tribunal. The tribunal may make a protective award if it considers the case well founded. This award is made in respect of employees dismissed or employees whose dismissal is proposed. The employer is ordered to pay remuneration for the protected period. This period begins on the date when the first of the dismissals to which the complaint relates takes effect, or the date of the award, whichever is earlier. It is of such length as the tribunal considers just and equitable in all the circumstances, having regard to the employer's default in not complying with the requirements to consult. If the employer failed in his duty to consult about avoiding the dismissal, the protected period may not exceed 90 days. In other cases the protected period may not exceed 30 days.

An employer proposing to dismiss as redundant 100 or more employees at one establishment within a period of 90 days or less must **notify the Secretary of State**, in writing, of his proposal at least 90 days before the first of the dismissals take effect. The time limit is 30 days where the redundancy of at least 20 employees is proposed. Failure to give such notification is a criminal offence.

Test your understanding

1 In what three circumstances will a dismissal be by reason of redundancy?

2 How much continuous employment does an employee need to have in order to claim redundancy?

3 What is the effect of an employer not following the correct procedures when making employees redundant?

4 How is a redundancy payment calculated?

5 In what circumstances will an employer making employees redundant need to consult representatives of the employees concerned?

6 What are the purposes of the consultations?

Answers

1 A dismissal will be by reason of redundancy if it is wholly or mainly attributable to: (a) the employer ceasing to carry on the business; or (b) the employer moving the place of business; or (c) the employer shedding surplus labour.

2 Only employees with at least two years' continuous employment since the age of 18 can claim redundancy.

3 If the employer's statutory dismissal and disciplinary procedures are not followed an employee will have been unfairly dismissed, rather than made redundant.

4 Redundancy payments are calculated on the same basis as the basic award for unfair dismissal, except that years of continuous employment worked before the age of 18 do not count, and the payment will not be reduced on account of the employee's contributory conduct.

5 An employer proposing to make 20 or more employees at one establishment redundant within a 90 day period must consult appropriate representatives of any of the employees who may be made redundant.

6 The consultations must consider ways of avoiding the dismissals, reducing the number of employees to be dismissed and mitigating the consequences of the dismissals. Also, the employer must undertake the consultations with a view to reaching agreement with the appropriate representatives.

Key points

■ Although many statutes relate to employment law, and although there is a significant EC element to employment law, the law of contract underpins the employment relationship.

■ Almost all employment cases are heard by an employment tribunal. From there an appeal lies to the Employment Appeal Tribunal and from there to the Court of Appeal and House of Lords.

■ Any UK court can refer an employment case to the European Court of Justice for an opinion on a matter of EC law. The European Court of Justice gives the opinion and the case is then sent back to the court which referred it so that the decision can be applied.

■ Decisions of the European Court of Justice are binding upon all UK courts. The decisions of an employment tribunal are not binding upon other courts. The decisions of the Employment Appeal Tribunal are binding upon employment tribunals but not upon subsequent sittings of the Employment Appeal Tribunal.

Employees and independent contractors distinguished

■ Employees are said to be employed under a contract of service. Independent contractors are said to work under a contract for services.

■ There is no list of tests to be used in distinguishing employees and independent contractors. Generally, the question is one of fact and must be determined by considering all of the relevant facts.

Written particulars and employment terms

■ Employees must be given a written statement of particulars of the employment not later than two months after the commencement of the employment.

■ If expressly agreed as the terms of the contract, the matters set out in the written particulars will be the terms. If not expressly agreed as the terms they are only very strong evidence of the terms of the contract of employment.

■ Collective agreements are made between employers and trade unions. The terms of collective agreements may be expressly accepted by an individual employee as the terms of his contract of employment. The terms of a collective agreement may be impliedly accepted by union members, but not by non union members.

■ Employees have duties to: show mutual respect; give faithful service; obey lawful and reasonable orders; use reasonable care and skill; not to accept bribes; not to reveal confidential information; and to disclose the shortcomings of their subordinates.

■ Employers have duties to: show mutual respect; pay wages (but not generally to provide work); observe confidentiality; indemnify the employee; ensure the safety of employees; and insure the employee. There is generally no duty to provide references.

■ Terms may be implied into a contract by custom and practice. Such terms are becoming of less importance.

■ A works rule book may provide some of the terms of the contract of employment if there has been an agreement to this effect between employer and employee. Such agreed terms could only be altered by mutual consent.

■ A works rule book may unilaterally impose some of the employees' duties, as long as this is not in conflict with their contract of employment. A unilaterally imposed works rule book could be unilaterally varied by the employer as long as this did not amount to a breach of contract.

■ Failure to observe agreed disciplinary and grievance procedures would amount to a breach of contract and might allow the employee to claim constructive dismissal.

■ Failure to comply with the statutory dismissal, disciplinary or grievance procedures will mean that any award made to the employee for unfair dismissal will be increased by between 10% and 50%.

- The procedures do not apply in certain circumstances, including circumstances where the violent or unreasonable behaviour of the employee make them unreasonable, factors beyond either party's control (such as long-term illness) make them unreasonable, the employee misses at least two meetings, or the dismissal was because of industrial action.
- The terms of a contract of employment can only be varied by agreement between employer and employee. The contract of employment itself might allow for variation.

Termination of employment

- Either employer or employee can terminate a contract of employment by giving notice.
- The amount of notice required may be agreed between the parties, or may be the amount which is reasonable. It cannot be less than the statutory minimum period of notice.
- The statutory minimum period of notice is one week after the employee has been employed for one month. After the employee has been employed for two years this period increases to one week for every year worked. The statutory minimum cannot exceed 12 weeks' notice.
- An employee is summarily dismissed if he is dismissed without notice. This will only be justifiable in exceptional circumstances where the employee repudiated the contract.
- If the contract of employment is genuinely terminated by agreement there will be no dismissal.
- If the contract is frustrated there will be no dismissal.
- If the employer's behaviour amounts to a repudiation of the contract, the employee is entitled to accept the repudiation and claim to have been wrongfully dismissed.
- Wrongful dismissal is a common law action for breach of contract and damages are therefore assessed on ordinary contract principles.

Unfair dismissal

- Employees with at least one year's continuous employment have the right not to be unfairly dismissed.
- The effective date of termination is the date on which the employment ended. It can be important in determining whether or not the employee has sufficient continuous employment to make a claim for unfair dismissal, in deciding whether the employee has made a claim within the three month time limit and in determining the amount of the employee's basic award. The effective date of termination is also significant in redundancy.
- For the purposes of unfair dismissal, the employee must show that he was dismissed because the employer terminated the contract, or because a fixed term contract expired without being renewed, or because he was constructively dismissed. A woman who is not allowed to return to work after childbirth is deemed to have been dismissed.
- An employee who resigns, and who cannot claim constructive dismissal, will not have been dismissed. Nor will there have been a dismissal if the contract of employment is frustrated.
- The ERA sets out five circumstances in which a dismissal can be fair.
- Even if the dismissal was on the grounds of one of the five specified circumstances, the dismissal will still be unfair unless the employer acted reasonably in treating the reason for the dismissal as a sufficient reason for dismissing the employee and unless the employer adhered to the statutory dismissal and disciplinary procedures.
- Remedies for unfair dismissal include re-engagement, reinstatement and compensation. Re-engagement and reinstatement are rarely ordered.

■ The basic award of compensation is calculated according to a statutory formula. The compensatory award is at the discretion of the tribunal, and is designed to compensate the employee for losses sustained as a consequence of having been unfairly dismissed. It cannot exceed £53 500.

Redundancy

■ An employee will have been dismissed by reason of redundancy if the reason for the dismissal was wholly or mainly attributable to: (a) the employer ceasing to carry on the business; or (b) the employer moving the place of business; or (c) the employer shedding surplus labour.

■ Redundancy can only be claimed by those who have two years' continuous employment since the age of 18.

■ If the employer does not follow the correct procedures when making employees redundant then the dismissals are likely to have been unfair, rather than dismissals by reason of redundancy.

■ A redundancy payment is the same as a basic award for unfair dismissal except that: years of continuous employment worked while under the age of 18 do not count; and the payment cannot be reduced on account of the employee's contributory conduct.

■ If more than 20 employees at one establishment are to be dismissed as redundant within a 90 day period, the employer must consult representatives of the employees concerned about the redundancies.

■ The consultations must consider ways of avoiding the dismissals, reducing the numbers to be dismissed and mitigating the consequences of the dismissals.

Summary questions

1   Brian, a building labourer, has worked for Bigga Builders for the past six years. When Brian took the job he was told that he was self-employed and that he had to look after his own tax and national insurance. Brian's work is not skilled and he uses the tools provided by Bigga Builders. On three occasions when Brian could not work personally his brother did the day's work instead. This situation was accepted, reluctantly, by the foreman. About half of the money which Brian receives from Bigga Builders is by way of bonus. The other half is paid at a flat hourly rate. Consider whether or not Brian is likely to be an employee of Bigga Builders.

2   Charlene has worked as a sales representative of Fancy Products Ltd for 15 years. Every three months the sales representative with the best sales has been given a bonus of £250. The office manager has now stuck a notice on the sales representatives' office wall, stating that the bonus will no longer be payable. To what extent will the sales representatives be bound by the provisions of the notice?

3   David, who is 21 years old, has worked as a cocktail barman at a hotel which is part of a large national chain of hotels for the past ten months. His weekly wage is £150 and he averages about £35 a week in tips. Last night, upon arrival for work, David was told by the head waiter that he would not be allowed to work and that he was dismissed with immediate effect. On asking why this has been decided, David is told that one of the tills which he operates was £45 light and that the other three workers with access to the till have worked for years without any problem. After the hotel manager has confirmed that David is dismissed and will not be allowed to work, David swears at both the manager and the head waiter. He is forcibly removed from the hotel premises. The following day the hotel posted a letter to David explaining that he has been dismissed because he is suspected of stealing money and because he assaulted the hotel manager and the head waiter. The letter tells David that he has a right to appeal against this decision but David does not reply to it. Advise David as to whether or not he will have any rights against the hotel.

4   Elaine has worked as a machinist for 22 years at a local factory. She began work on her 18th birthday and earns £250 for a 45 hour week. Two months ago Elaine's supervisor said that Elaine's pay would be subject to a deduction of £40 because a whole batch of clothes which she was meant to stitch had been ruined by

Elaine's negligence. Such deductions had been made from other employees' wages, but very rarely. Elaine insists that there was nothing wrong with her work and that she can prove it. She sees the manager who says that he is not prepared to get into arguments about whose defective work caused the problem. Elaine says that she knows whose work it was, but she isn't going to say. The manager says that unless Elaine says whose work it was, the deduction from her wages will stand. In front of all the other machinists, Elaine shouts, 'You know where you can stick your bleeding job' and walks out. The following day Elaine returns and says that she is ready to carry on with her job. The manager, who has subsequently discovered that it was not Elaine's negligence which caused the problem, refuses to take her back. Advise Elaine of any claim which she might make against the employer.

5   Bossco Ltd dismissed two employees, George and Harry, claiming that they had become redundant. Both were dismissed without notice and were given the correct amount of redundancy pay. The employer had no occupational pension scheme. Now a tribunal has held that the workers were unfairly dismissed, not made redundant. At the effective date of termination Harry was aged 64 years and 10 months and had 46 years' continuous employment. His wage as a supervisor was £320 a week. He had intended to keep working until he was 67 the age at which the employer insisted that employees retire. George, aged 53, had 16 years' continuous employment. His weekly wage was £230 a week. Harry, aged 40 had 10 years' continuous employment and had a weekly wage of £180. How much redundancy pay would each of the workers have received? How would a finding of unfair dismissal help them?

Multiple choice questions

1   Which **one** of the following statements is true?

   a   As all employment law is regarded as having an element of EC law, any national court may refer any question of employment law to the European Court of Justice for a ruling.
   b   ACAS and other bodies issue Codes of Practice concerning employment law and these Codes have the same legal effect as a statute.
   c   It is possible for the two lay members sitting in an employment tribunal to outvote the legally qualified chairman.
   d   Legal aid is available to an employee making a claim in an employment tribunal, but is not available to the employer defending the case.

2   Which **one** of the following statements is **not** true?

   a   There is no single test which is capable of distinguishing employees from independent contractors.
   b   The question as to whether or not a worker is an employee is, in all but exceptional cases, a question of fact rather than a question of law.
   c   If an employer has no obligation to employ a casual worker, and the worker has no obligation to accept work offered, the worker is unlikely to be regarded as an employee when not actually working.
   d   Independent contractors are never protected by employment legislation and can never bring a case alleging discrimination.

3   Which **one** of the following statements is **not** true?

   a   Unless the matters set out in the written particulars are agreed to be the terms of the contract of employment, they are not the terms but only very strong evidence of the terms.
   b   If a collective agreement is made between an employer and a trade union, all the terms of the agreement will automatically become the terms of all employees.
   c   Employees have a duty to perform their employment using reasonable care and skill.
   d   An employee whose negligence causes loss to the employer may be required to pay damages to compensate for the loss.

4   Which **one** of the following statements is **not** true?

   a   An employee who has a valid claim for unfair dismissal must pursue this claim in preference to a claim for wrongful dismissal.
   b   If a contract of employment is frustrated the employee will not be regarded as having been dismissed.
   c   Damages for wrongful dismissal are calculated on ordinary common law principles as damages for breach of contract.

d An employee who resigns, otherwise than in response to a repudiation of the contract by the employer, will not be able to claim wrongful dismissal.

5 Which **one** of the following statements is **not** true?

a An employee who has less than one year's continuous employment can never claim unfair dismissal.

b Weeks when an employee is off work on account of pregnancy, childbirth, sickness or injury count as continuous employment.

c Even if the employee leaves the job in a manner which amounts to a definite repudiation of the contract, the employer may have dismissed the employee if he is not allowed to return to work.

d If an employee consistently works in a manner which is inconsistent with the express terms of his contract for a considerable time, then an implied variation of the contract can possibly be inferred.

6 Which **one** of the following statements is **not** true?

a In some circumstances an employer's conduct is bad enough to entitle the employee to leave the job and nevertheless claim to have been dismissed.

b If an employer has given notice to an employee, and the employee gives counter-notice to expire before the employer's notice would have done so, the employee is taken to be dismissed for the reason for which the employer's notice was given.

c If the employer can prove that the employee's dismissal was within one of the fair reasons specified by the ERA, the dismissal cannot have been unfair.

d If the employer fails to follow the correct procedures when dismissing an employee, a dismissal which would otherwise have been fair will be rendered unfair.

7 John has worked in continuous employment for 22 years and six months. He was unfairly dismissed, the effective date of termination being one week after his 51st birthday. At the time of the dismissal John's weekly wage was £312. How much will John's basic award for unfair dismissal be?

a £8 424.

b £8 100.

c £7 500.

d £7 290.

8 Which **one** of the following statements is **not** true?

a An employee can be entitled to a redundancy payment even if he gets another job straightaway.

b A redundancy payment is always calculated according to precisely the same principles as those used to calculate a basic award for unfair dismissal.

c An employee who unreasonably rejects an offer of suitable alternative employment will not be entitled to claim a redundancy payment.

d A claim for a redundancy payment must be made within six months of the effective date of termination. The tribunal has a discretion to allow a claim to be made within 12 months, but cannot allow a claim after that.

Task 20

A friend of yours visiting the country from the USA has a keen interest in employment rights. Your friend has asked you if you would draw up a report dealing briefly with the following matters.

a How the courts distinguish between employees and independent contractors.

b How the terms of a contract of employment are determined.

c The ways in which a contract of employment can be terminated.

d The differences between unfair and wrongful dismissal and the remedies available for them.

e The meaning of redundancy and the statutory remedies available to an employee who is made redundant.

f The courts and tribunals to which an employment dispute could be taken and the lines of appeal if the case should be appealed as far as possible.

Chapter 21

EMPLOYMENT 2 – DISCRIMINATION · HEALTH AND SAFETY · RIGHTS OF EMPLOYEES

Introduction

In the previous chapter we began the study of employment law. We considered the distinction between employees and independent contractors, the express and implied terms of the employment contract, and two important rights of employees; the right not to be unfairly dismissed and the right to a statutory payment if made redundant. In this chapter we consider discrimination in employment, the health and safety responsibilities of employers, and other miscellaneous rights which employees have.

Over the past 35 years several important statutes have been enacted with the object of preventing discrimination. The Equal Pay Act 1970 provides that men and women who work for the same employer should receive the same employment benefits if they do like work, work rated as equivalent or work of equal value. The Sex Discrimination Act 1975 attempts to prevent discrimination (whether it is direct, indirect or victimisation) on the grounds of a person's sex or marital status. The Race Relations Act 1976 is modelled on the Sex Discrimination Act and seeks to prevent discrimination on racial grounds. Other statutes outlaw discrimination against disabled persons, part-time workers, fixed-term workers or on the grounds of religious belief. The Rehabilitation of Offenders Act 1974 recognises that those with criminal records can be discriminated against and attempts to counter this by allowing some convictions to become 'spent'. Once a conviction is spent then in most circumstances an employee can deny that he has been convicted and the employer may not discriminate against the employee on the grounds of the spent conviction.

Employers have serious health and safety responsibilities to their employees. The Health and Safety at Work etc. Act 1974 attempts to raise the standards of safety in employment by imposing criminal sanctions on employers who neglect health and safety. The Act also sets up a system of inspectors who have wide powers to enforce the law. The Act does not confer the right to sue upon an injured employee, but the law of negligence will provide a remedy where the injury arose in consequence of the employer breaching a common law duty of care which he owed.

At the end of this chapter we consider the following miscellaneous rights which employees enjoy: maternity rights; the right to be paid at least the national minimum wage; rights given to employees when their employer's undertaking is transferred to another employer; rights on working hours; and various rights to time off work for public duties. We conclude the chapter by considering in outline the procedure for bringing a claim before an employment tribunal.

21.1 · The Equal Pay Act 1970

The Equal Pay Act 1970 requires that men and women in the same employment should be treated equally by their employer, regardless of their sex, as regards pay and other benefits. It is generally women who have been discriminated against and so when describing the effect of the Act it is convenient to assume that a claim under the Act is brought by a woman. (This is merely as matter of convenience and there is no reason why a man should not bring a claim.) Under the Act there are three grounds on which a woman can claim that she should receive equal treatment to that afforded to a man in the same employment. These grounds are: that she does like work with that of the man; that the work she does is rated as equivalent with that of the man; or that her work is of equal value to that of the man. The equal treatment which the Act requires means not only that the woman should receive equal pay, but also that the other benefits of the job, such as pension rights and sick pay, should be equally beneficial. The employer does not need to give equal treatment in so far as he can prove that the difference in treatment was genuinely due to a material factor other than the woman's sex.

21.1.1 The sources of law

The Equal Pay Act 1970 is the main source of law on equal pay. However, Article 141 of the Treaty of Rome (which was formerly Article 119) provides that: 'Each Member State shall ensure that the principle of equal pay for male and female workers for equal work or work of equal value is applied.' The Article states that 'pay' includes not only the ordinary basic minimum wage or salary, but also any other consideration, whether in cash or in kind, which the worker receives directly or indirectly, in respect of his employment, from his employer. Two EU Directives passed in 1975 and 1976 (Directives 75/117 and 76/207) make it plain that the Equal Pay Act should be interpreted positively with the intention of ending discriminatory treatment of women as regards the conditions of their employment terms. As equal pay is a matter which involves EU law, the European Court of Justice may consider an application that either Article 141 or one of the Directives is not being given effect. If there is a conflict between the UK legislation and Article 141 or the Directives, it is the latter which will prevail.

However, in *Pickstone and others* v *Freemans plc* [1988] IRLR 357 the House of Lords held that if national legislation gives a sufficient remedy then there is no room for the matter to be pursued through the alternative route of the direct application of European law.

21.1.2 The need for a male comparator

An applicant can only claim equal treatment with a male working in the same employment. The Act does not require that a woman employed by one employer should be treated as favourably as a man doing identical work, or the same type of work, for another employer. In order to gain a remedy under the Act, the woman will therefore need to find a male comparator, that is to say a male working for the same employer who is being treated more favourably. It is not possible to claim equal treatment with a person of the same sex.

Section 1(6) of the Equal Pay Act allows comparison with male employees working for associated employers. (The meaning of this was considered in the previous Chapter 20 at 20.5.2; that one is a company which controls the other, or both are companies controlled by the same third party.) Section 1(6) requires equal treatment not only if the man and the woman are employed at the same establishment, but also if they are employed at different establishments in Great Britain, as long as common terms and conditions apply or are observed at the different establishments. Applying s.1(6), in *Leverton* v *Clwyd County Council* [1989] ICR 33 the House of Lords held that a nursery nurse employed by the county council could validly compare herself with male clerks who worked for the council in different establishments. The nurse worked 32.5 hours a week and had 70 days' holiday a year, the higher paid male comparators worked 37 hours a week and had 30 days' holiday a year. (The nurse's claim did not succeed because the House of Lords found that the difference in treatment of her and the men was justified on the grounds of a genuine material factor. However, the principle that the men could be used as comparators was established.) In *British Coal Corporation* v *Smith* [1996] IRLR 404 the House of Lords allowed female canteen workers and cleaners who were employed at 47 different establishments to compare themselves with male surface workers and clerical staff who worked at four different establishments. The Coal Board's argument that local bargaining accounted for the differences in some terms, as it also accounted for differences between the treatment of miners and clerical workers at different establishments, was rejected. The terms and conditions would be common terms and conditions for the purposes of s.1(6) if they were substantially comparable on a broad basis. They did not have to be identical.

The choice of comparator is a matter for the woman bringing the claim. If the employer were allowed to choose the comparator this would raise the possibility of employers having a 'token man' employed on inferior terms so that the treatment of female employees could be compared with the treatment of the token man. The woman is not confined to one comparator, but may choose multiple comparators.

A former employee may be used as the comparator. In *Macarthys Ltd* v *Smith* [1980] ICR 672 the European Court of Justice held that a female stockroom manager who was paid £50 a week could compare herself to the male who had previously done the same job at £60 a week. However, it was held that there is a need for a real comparator, the woman cannot compare herself to a hypothetical comparator by asking how a hypothetical man would have been treated.

21.1.3 Like work

In order to succeed under the Act the claimant will need to prove that she does like work, work rated as equivalent, or work of equal value to that of the comparator. Each of these matters needs to be examined in turn.

Section 1(4) of the Equal Pay Act provides that a woman is to be regarded as employed on like work with men if, but only if, her work and theirs is of the same or a broadly similar nature, and the differences (if any) between the things she does and the things they do are not of practical importance in relation to terms and conditions of employment. Section 1(4) also provides that in deciding whether the work is like work regard shall be had to the frequency or otherwise with which any such differences occur in practice as well as to the nature and extent of the differences.

■ *Capper Pass Ltd* v *Lawton* [1977] ICR 83 (House of Lords)

The claimant worked 40 hours a week preparing lunches for about 10 to 20 of the company's directors and their guests. She was responsible to the catering manager and was the only cook who worked in the kitchen. The two male comparators were assistant chefs who worked under a head chef in a different kitchen which provided breakfast, lunch and tea in two sittings for the company's workers. The assistant chefs provided about 350 meals each day. They worked 40 hours a week, 5.5 hours overtime and one Saturday in three. When the head chef or catering manager was away, the assistant chefs deputised for the head chef.

Held. The work done by the claimant was like work to that done by the assistant chefs. Work is like work if it is of the same nature as, or of a broadly similar nature to, the work done by the man. In deciding whether work was like work consideration should be given to the type of work involved and the skill and knowledge required to do that work. If there were differences the tribunal should decide whether or not these were of practical importance in relation to the terms and conditions of employment.

In *Shields* v *E. Coombes (Holdings) Ltd* [1978] ICR 1159, the Court of Appeal demonstrated that practical differences between the duties of the female and the comparators had to be real rather than merely theoretical. The claimant was a counterhand in a betting shop, being paid 92p per hour. The male comparator working in the same shop was a counterhand receiving £1.06 per hour. The employers claimed that the work was not of a broadly similar nature because the shop was in an area where robbery or trouble from customers was expected, and in the event of any such trouble the male was supposed to sort it out, whereas the claimant was not. This argument failed because there had been no trouble for the male to sort out in the previous three years and so the male's additional responsibilities were of no practical importance.

A man can be paid at a higher rate than a woman who does similar work if the man has genuine greater responsibilities than the woman. So in *Eaton Ltd* v *Nuttall* [1977] IRLR 71 a man who handled packages worth between £5 and £1000 could be paid more than a woman who did the same work but only handled packages worth less than £2.50. The man had greater responsibilities because if he made a mistake a much greater loss would be caused to the employer than if the woman did.

If the men and women work different hours, as where only the men work a night shift, this is not a good reason for the basic rate of pay to differ. The men can receive a shift allowance, which will mean that they actually earn more than the women, but this allowance reflects the fact that they worked the night shift. If, however, both men and women work different hours then the basic pay of those working shifts can be higher than the basic pay of those who do not.

21.1.4 Work rated as equivalent

Work is rated as equivalent if a properly conducted job evaluation scheme has been carried out and has found that the work is equivalent. Such a scheme must be analytical in approach, rather than impressionistic. In *Eaton Ltd* v *Nuttall* Philips J reviewed the principal methods of evaluation. He considered the most commonly used system to be one of points assessment, where the job was broken down into component factors with points awarded for each factor according to a predetermined scale. Whatever the method used, the tribunal cannot override the results of a properly conducted job evaluation scheme.

21.1.5 Work of equal value

In considering whether the work done by a woman is of equal value to that of a male comparator, regard must be had to the demands made on the woman, for instance under such headings as effort, skill and decision-making, compared with the demands made on the comparator. When faced with a claim based on work of equal value the employment tribunal will first decide whether or not there can be grounds for such a complaint. If there cannot, the case will be dismissed. Having decided that there can be grounds, the tribunal can either itself decide whether or not the work was of equal value, or can refer the case for expert evaluation. If the case is referred for expert evaluation, the tribunal cannot come to a decision until the report it has commissioned is received. However, the tribunal can reject part or all of the report's conclusions.

The requirement that a woman should be treated equally for doing work of equal value was introduced by the Equal Pay (Amendment) Regulations 1983. The following case was one of the first major cases to consider the requirements of an equal value claim.

■ *Hayward* v *Cammell Laird Shipbuilders Ltd* [1988] 2 All ER 257 (House of Lords)

The claimant worked as a cook at a shipyard. She claimed that her work was of equal value to that of a painter, a joiner and an insulation engineer, all of whom worked at the same shipyard. The employers argued that the claimant was treated as favourably as the men. They claimed that although her basic pay and overtime rates were lower than those of the male comparators her contract as a whole was equally favourable because she enjoyed better sickness benefits, paid meal breaks and better holiday pay. The employment tribunal, the EAT and the Court of Appeal all held that the claim failed because the claimant's conditions were no less favourable when the contract was viewed as a whole. An appeal was made to the House of Lords.

Held. Where the woman did equal work to that of a male comparator all the terms of her contract had to be as favourable as the equivalent term in the comparator's contract. This was the case even if she was treated as favourably as the man overall when the whole contract was compared.

COMMENT　The House of Lords did recognise that this would involve an element of leapfrogging. The claimant's contract was improved so that her basic rate and overtime rates were as favourable as those of the men. The men could then claim the improved sickness, meal and holiday benefits enjoyed by the claimant. In the case the employers did not argue the defence of genuine material factor, which is considered immediately below.

21.1.6　Defence of genuine material factor

Even if a woman has proved that she does like work with that of a male comparator (or work rated as equivalent or work of equal value) the employer has a defence if he can prove that the variation in treatment was due to a genuine material factor which was not the difference of sex.

A wide variety of matters can amount to genuine material factors which would justify different treatment. These matters would include long service increments, academic qualifications, different places of work, perhaps different hours of work, responsibility allowances, and protection of pay for those who were demoted (as long as this treatment was not based on the employee's sex). In the following case the EAT held that 'red-circling', whereby a man's wages were protected when he was downgraded, could amount to a genuine material factor, but not if the red-circling was done in a discriminatory way.

■ *Charles Early & Marriott (Witney) Ltd* v *Smith* [1977] ICR 700

A male warehouseman was downgraded to the job of ticket writer in 1966. He was red-circled, so that his wages were not reduced. In 1973 female ticket writers who were paid less than the downgraded man claimed that they did like work and ought therefore to be paid the same as the man.

Held. Where wages were protected for causes which were neither directly nor indirectly due to a difference of sex, a difference in pay might be justifiable on the grounds that there was a genuine material difference.

COMMENT　In *Snoxell* v *Vauxhall Motors Ltd*, which the EAT considered at the same time, women were not red-circled because they were women. They compared themselves with males, all of whom had been red-circled. The defence of genuine material difference failed because it was not genuine, clear and convincing. Red-circling will not be a genuine material factor where past discrimination had contributed to its being applied.

It is not easy to state the extent to which market forces will permit the different treatment of female employees. If the difference in treatment is caused by sound economic reasons then the defence of genuine material difference may succeed. In *Rainey* v *Greater Glasgow Health Board* [1987] 1 All ER 65 the Scottish Health Department employed prosthetists on civil service pay. Twenty employees, who all happened to be men, had previously worked for private contractors. These private contractors paid well above the health service rates. These 20 men were therefore taken on by the Health Department at their old, private practice, rates. The claimant later joined the health service as a prosthetist and was taken on at the health service rate. This meant that she was paid about 72% of the salary paid to the 20 men. The House of Lords held that the employer's defence of genuine material difference succeeded. The 20 men had to be offered their old rates of pay in order to attract them into the Health Department. It was merely fortuitous that the 20 employees taken from private contractors had all been men.

However, in *Enderby* v *Frenchay Health Authority* [1994] 1 All ER 495 the ECJ held that the objective of Article 119 of the Treaty of Rome (now Article 141) was equal pay for men and women for work of equal value. Where statistics showed that there were appreciable differences in pay between two jobs of equal value, one of these jobs being carried out exclusively by women and the other predominantly by men, this was *prima facie* discrimination. The onus was therefore on the employer to show that the difference was based on objectively justified factors which were not related to any discrimination on grounds of sex. This was the case even though the rates of pay had been arrived at by a process of collective bargaining. It was for the national courts to decide whether and to what extent the shortage of candidates for a job, and the need to attract them by higher pay, constituted objectively justified economic grounds for the difference in pay between the jobs in question. The case was brought by a speech therapist working for a health authority on an annual salary of £10 106. She was held to be entitled to compare herself to a clinical psychologist earning £12 527 and to a pharmacist earning £14 106 p.a.

In *Ratcliffe* v *North Yorkshire County Council* [1995] IRLR 439 the House of Lords held that when women dinner ladies had their wages reduced by a county council, in order that the county council could compete with commercial contractors who paid women employees less than the local government rate, the tribunal could find that this was not a genuine material difference which justified paying the women less than that paid to men engaged on work rated as equivalent. It is plain from this decision that the market forces defence will not be allowed to become too wide.

21.1.7 Remedies

Where a woman does like work, work rated as equivalent or work of equal value with that of a man, s.1(1) of the Equal Pay Act provides that if the terms of the contract under which the woman is employed do not include **an equality clause** they shall be deemed to include one. An equality clause is a provision which requires that any terms of a woman's contract shall be modified so as to be no less favourable than a term of a similar kind in the contract of a male comparator. It also requires that if the woman's contract does not include a term corresponding to a term benefiting the man included in the contract under which he is employed, the woman's contract shall be treated as including such a term.

Generally, a claim must be brought before an employment tribunal within six months of the woman leaving the employment, or while she is still in the employment. Back pay and damages can be awarded to a successful complainant. In *Levez* v *TH Jennings (Harlow Pools) Ltd (No 2)* [1999] IRLR 764 the European Court ruled that up to six years' arrears of pay could be awarded. Before this ruling a claimant could not be awarded more than two years' arrears of pay. The six-year period was necessary to bring the remedies under the Equal Pay Act into line with the remedies under the Race Relations Act and the Disability Discrimination Act. Under both of these Acts unlawful deductions of pay could be claimed for six years before proceedings were begun.

The following matters have all been held to be 'pay' and therefore within the provisions of Article 141: sick pay; compensation for unfair dismissal; redundancy payments; occupational pensions; pay for attending courses; and concessionary travel benefits for employees who have retired.

Test your understanding

1 Is the Equal Pay Act 1970 restricted to claims for equal wages and salary?

2 What is the male comparator?

3 On what three grounds can the applicant claim to be treated as favourably as a male comparator?

4 What defence might an employer have?

5 What is the effect of an equality clause?

6 What remedies can be awarded by the employment tribunal in respect of a claim under the 1970 Act?

Answers

1 The Equal Pay Act 1970 is not restricted to claims for equality of wages and salary. If a woman is employed on like work etc. with a male in the same employment, all of her terms of employment should be as beneficial as the terms of the comparator's terms.

2   The male comparator is the man with whom the woman wishes to compare herself. He must be employed by the same employer or by an associated employer.

3   Under the Act, a woman can claim equal treatment to that afforded the male comparator if she does like work to his work, or work rated as equivalent or work of equal value.

4   The employer will have a defence if he can prove that the unequal treatment was due to a genuine material factor which was not the difference of sex.

5   An equality clause modifies the terms of the applicant's contract of employment so that any term of that contract is no less favourable than a similar term in the contract of the male comparator.

6   The employment tribunal can award arrears of pay, backdated for six years, and damages.

21.2 · The Sex Discrimination Act 1975

The Sex Discrimination Act 1975, as amended by the Sex Discrimination Act 1986, outlaws discrimination on the grounds of a person's sex or on the grounds that a person is married. The Act defines discrimination in the employment field broadly, but the special treatment afforded to women in connection with childbirth or pregnancy is not regarded by the Act as discrimination. The vast majority of complaints are made by women, although the Act does of course also outlaw discrimination against men.

The issue of 'positive discrimination' has caused considerable difficulty. In areas of employment where women are considerably under-represented employers sometimes positively discriminate in favour of women, that is to say they give preference to women when taking on new employees. In *Kalanke* v *Freie Hansestadt Bremen* [1996] All ER (EC) 66 the European Court of Justice held that a law which provided that an equally qualified woman should be promoted in preference to promoting a male was unlawful discrimination contrary to the Equal Treatment Directive (76/207). However, the Treaty of Amsterdam amended the Treaty of Rome with effect from May 1999. Article 141(4) of the amended Treaty provides that,

'With a view to ensuring full equality in practice between men and women in working life, the principle of equal treatment shall not prevent any Member State from maintaining or adopting measures providing for specific advantages in order to make it easier for the under-represented sex to pursue a vocational activity or to prevent or compensate for disadvantages in professional careers.'

This seems to indicate a tolerance for positive discrimination. In *Application by Badeck and others* Case C-158/97 [2000] All ER (EC) 289 the European Court of Justice held that measures giving preference to women for employment in public service sectors where they were under-represented did not contradict Community equal treatment principles. However, this was only the case where (a) the measures did not automatically and unconditionally prefer women over equally qualified men, and (b) where the candidates were subjected to an objective assessment which considered their specific personal situations.

The Sex Discrimination Act offers protection not only to employees, but also to those who contract personally to provide any work or labour. The Act outlaws direct discrimination, indirect discrimination and victimisation. Each of these matters needs to be considered in turn.

21.2.1 Direct discrimination

Direct discrimination occurs if an employer treats a woman less favourably than he treats or would treat a man on the grounds of her sex. Discrimination against a married person is direct if the married person is treated less favourably than an unmarried person of the same sex on the grounds of his or her marital status. Discrimination on the grounds that a person is not married is not within the Act.

A fairly early example of direct discrimination contrary to the Act was provided by *Batisha* v *Say* [1977] IRLIB where Miss Batisha applied for a job as a cave guide at the Cheddar caves and was not taken on because she was a woman. The manager in charge of making the appointment told the tribunal that he had no intention of appointing a woman, because he did not think the work was suitable for a woman. The tribunal could find no reason why a woman should not be employed and that Miss Batisha had therefore been directly discriminated against.

In *James* v *Eastleigh Borough Council* [1990] 2 All ER 607 the House of Lords held that the appropriate question to ask to discover whether or not discrimination was on the grounds of sex was objective rather than subjective. That is to say that the motive for the discrimination is not relevant. The case concerned a married couple, both aged 61. The local council had a policy of allowing those who could claim the State old age pension free access to their swimming pools. The wife therefore gained free access but the man did not. The House of Lords held that the man was discriminated against. The question to ask is whether the man would have received the same treatment as his wife but for his sex. As he plainly would, the policy, however well-intentioned, was discriminatory.

If different dress codes apply to male and female employees this can amount to discrimination but does not necessarily do so.

In *Smith* v *Safeways plc* [1996] IRLR 456 a male delicatessen assistant was dismissed because his ponytail was too long to stay under his hat. Male employees were required to have tidy hair which was not below shirt-collar length, whereas female employees were allowed shoulder length hair if it was tied back. The Court of Appeal held that the man had not been discriminated against. Discrimination between the sexes is permissible whereas discrimination against one or other sex is not. An appearance code which applies a standard of what is conventional is not discriminatory as long as it applies an even-handed approach between men and women.

Section 5(3) provides that a comparison can only be made with a person of a different sex, or different marital status, if the relevant circumstances in the one case are the same as, or not materially different from, the relevant circumstances in the other. If the circumstances are not the same, or are materially different, then no comparison can be made. Therefore, in *Bullock* v *Alice Ottley School* [1993] ICR 138 the Court of Appeal held that it was not discriminatory for an employer to require teaching and domestic staff at a girls' school to retire at 60, whereas gardeners and maintenance staff retired at 65. All of the gardeners and maintenance staff were male, but there was no policy of recruiting only males, and the different retirement age applied because gardeners and maintenance staff were difficult to recruit.

Even rules which apply equally to men and women can be directly discriminatory if they adversely affect pregnant women. In *Brown* v *Rentokil Ltd* [1998] IRLR 445 the ECJ considered that a woman had been discriminated against when she was dismissed for having been absent from work for more than 26 weeks. The employer had a policy that all employees who were absent for more than 26 weeks on the grounds of illness should be dismissed. However, much of the absence of the woman in question was due to illness related to her pregnancy and so she had been directly discriminated against.

In 1991 the EU Commission issued a Code of Practice, the European Commission recommendation No. 92/131/EEC on the protection of the dignity of women and men at work. The Code requires Member States to promote awareness that conduct of a sexual nature, or other conduct based on sex affecting the dignity of women and men at work, including conduct of superiors and colleagues, is unacceptable if:

(a) such conduct is unwanted, unreasonable and offensive to the recipient;

(b) a person's rejection of, or submission to, such conduct on the part of employers or workers (including superiors or colleagues) is used explicitly or implicitly as a basis for a decision which affects that person's access to vocational training, access to employment, continued employment, promotion, salary or other employment decisions; and/or

(c) such conduct creates an intimidating, hostile or humiliating work environment for the recipient.

The Code also provides that conduct in contravention of it may, in certain circumstances, be contrary to the principle of equal treatment set out in the Equal Treatment Directive.

If sufficiently serious, even a single act of harassment can be enough to constitute discrimination.

21.2.2 Indirect discrimination

Section 1(1)(b) provides that indirect discrimination against a woman arises if the employer applies to her a requirement or condition which he applies or would equally apply to a man, but:

(i)   which is such that the proportion of women who can comply with it is considerably smaller than the proportion of men who can comply with it; and

(ii) which he cannot show to be justifiable irrespective of the sex of the person to whom it is applied, and

(iii) which is to her detriment because she cannot comply with it.

An example would be a job advertisement for a van driver which said that applicants must have large beards or must be keen boxers. These requirements would apply equally to male and female applicants for the job, but the proportion of females who could comply with them is considerably smaller than the proportion of men who could. The requirements could not be shown to be justified, they operate to the detriment of women, and would therefore amount to indirect discrimination against women. Section 3(1)(b) makes a description of indirect discrimination against married persons which is virtually identical to the description in s.1(1)(b).

The question as to whether or not a requirement is justifiable is objective rather than subjective. That is to say that it is not enough that the employer genuinely believed it to be justifiable if, on an objective analysis of the facts, it was not. In order to establish indirect discrimination the claimant will need to identify a pool of comparators who can comply with the requirement.

The applicant in *London Underground* v *Edwards* [1995] IRLR 355 was a female single-parent train operator with a young child who usually worked between 8 a.m. and 4.30 p.m., with Saturday as a rest day. This allowed her to be at home with her son in the mornings and evenings. As part of a cost saving plan the employers introduced a new flexible shift system. This required train operators to begin work at 4.45 a.m. and to work on Sundays. Employees could avoid these unsocial hours but only if they took a drop in pay. The claimant resigned and claimed unfair dismissal. The EAT held that the correct question was not whether a smaller proportion of female single parents than male single parents could comply with the new requirements. It was wrong to take as the pool of comparators only those train operators who were single parents. The correct pool of comparators was all train operators affected by the new arrangement. The proper question was whether the new requirements were such that a considerably smaller proportion of women qualified to be train operators could comply than of men qualified to be train operators. (The EAT referred the case back to another employment tribunal for it to decide, as a matter of fact, whether the proportion of female qualified drivers who could comply with the new requirements was smaller than the proportion of male qualified drivers.) However, the EAT awarded the applicant compensation anyway, on the grounds that the employers had failed to show that the requirement was justifiable. The requirement was not justifiable because London Underground could have catered for the needs of single parents without detriment to their objective of saving costs. As they knew of the undesirable consequences for single parents, they could be taken as having had an intention to produce those consequences.

In *Jones* v *University of Manchester* [1993] IRLR 218 (Court of Appeal) Ralph Gibson LJ said that in order to compare the proportion of women who can comply with a requirement with the proportion of men who can comply with it, it is necessary to determine the relevant total of all people to whom the employer would apply the requirement. Then one would consider what proportion of this total were men and what proportion were women. The total number of men and women who could comply with the requirement was not relevant. For example, let us assume that are 3 000 opticians in the country, male opticians outnumbering female opticians by two to one. If a requirement was made of opticians who might apply for a particular job that they had to have a driving licence, the correct procedure would be first to consider the total number of opticians who could comply with this requirement, and second to see what proportion of this number were men and what proportion were women. If the total number of opticians who could comply was 2 700 and 1 800 of these were male and 900 female, the proportion of male and female opticians who could comply would be the same for both sexes. The requirement would not therefore be discriminatory, even though the number of male opticians who could comply was twice the number of female opticians who could comply. If the figure of 2 700 opticians who could comply was made up of 1 950 males and 750 females the proportion of females who could comply would be smaller than the proportion of men (75% compared with 97.5%) and if it was held to be considerably smaller this would amount to indirect discrimination. It would not be significant that considerably more men than women in the population at large hold driving licences. The employer is not intending to apply the requirement to the population at large, but only to opticians.

In *Price* v *Civil Service Commission* [1978] ICR 27 it was held that a 36-year-old woman was indirectly discriminated against when applying for a job which required applicants to be aged between $17\frac{1}{2}$ and 28. The decision accepted that between those ages many women were unable to work because they were looking after young children, and there was no justifiable reason for making the age requirement.

In *Mandla* v *Dowell Lee* [1983] ICR 385 (House of Lords) Lord Fraser considered the meaning of 'can comply' in s.1(1)(b)(i). The case concerned the Race Relations Act, but the description of indirect discrimination in that Act is virtually identical to the section of indirect discrimination in the Sex Discrimination Act. Lord Fraser said: 'The word "can" is used with many shades of meaning ... it must, in my opinion, have been intended by Parliament to be read not as meaning "can physically", so as to indicate a theoretical possibility, but as meaning "can in practice" or "can consistently with the customs and cultural conditions of the racial group". Therefore the conditions with which a woman can comply will take account of the reality of the situation and will not be based on theoretical possibility of compliance.'

It has therefore been held that the inclusion of a mobility clause in a contract of employment can be indirectly discriminatory. As women are more often the secondary wage earners in a family, the number of women who 'can' move is significantly fewer than the number of men who could. In *Meade-Hill* v *British Council* [1995] IRLR 478 the Court of Appeal held that a mobility clause in the contract of a middle manager employed by the British Council, which required her to work anywhere in the UK, was indirect discrimination unless justifiable irrespective of her sex.

21.2.3 Victimisation

A person is victimised under the Act if he or she is treated less favourably by the employer (the discriminator) than in the same circumstances he would treat any other person, by reason that the victimised person has:

(a) brought legal proceedings against the employer under the Sex Discrimination Act, or the Equal Pay Act 1970, or the provisions of the Pensions Act 1995 which relate to equal treatment;
(b) given evidence or information in proceedings brought under any of the Acts; or
(c) done anything under, or by reference to, any of the Acts in relation to the discriminator or any other person; or
(d) alleged that the discriminator or any other person has committed an act which amounts to a contravention of any of the Acts.

It is similarly victimisation if the employer treats the victim less favourably because he knows that the victim intends to do any of these things, or suspects that the victim has done, or intends to do, any of these things. The correct test to use in deciding whether or not there has been victimisation is the 'but for' test. If the applicant would have been treated differently but for his having brought proceedings etc under the Act, he has been victimised.

21.2.3.1 Vicarious liability

Section 41 fixes an employer with vicarious liability by providing that anything done by a person in the course of his employment shall be treated for the purposes of this Act as done by his employer as well as by him, whether or not it was done with the employer's knowledge or approval. However, in respect of proceedings against an employer in respect of an act alleged to have been done by an employee of his it is a defence for the employer to show that he took such steps as were reasonably practicable to prevent the employee from doing the act, or from doing in the course of his employment acts of that description.

In *Chief Constable of the Lincolnshire Police* v *Stubbs* [1999] IRLR 81 it was held that the Chief Constable of Lincolnshire Police was vicariously liable for sex discrimination against a female police officer by a male police officer. For the purposes of s.41, the EAT held that work-related social functions could fall within the meaning of 'in the course of his employment'.

21.2.4 Discrimination in the employment field

Part II of the Act is entitled 'Discrimination in the Employment Field'. However, the definition of employment would include independent contractors who agree to provide services personally.

Section 6 of the Act specifies that an employer must not discriminate against a woman in the employment field in any of the following ways:

(a) in the arrangements he makes for the purposes of determining who should be offered employment; or

(b) in the terms on which he offers her employment; or

(c) by refusing or deliberately omitting to offer her employment; or

(d) in the way he affords her access to opportunities for promotion, transfer or training, or to any other benefits, facilities or services, or by refusing or deliberately omitting to afford her access to them; or

(e) by dismissing her or subjecting her to any other detriment.

21.2.5 Permissible discrimination

Section 7 of the Act allows discrimination where sex is a genuine occupational qualification. The circumstances in which being a man is a genuine occupational qualification for a job are only the following:

(a) The essential nature of the job calls for a man for reasons of physiology (excluding physical strength or stamina) or in dramatic performances or other entertainment, for reasons of authenticity, so that the essential nature of the job would be materially different if carried out by a woman. So, for example, it is permissible to insist that a man be taken on to play the role of Macbeth in the theatre.

(b) The job needs to be held by a man to preserve decency or privacy, because (i) it is likely to involve physical contact with men in circumstances where they might reasonably object to its being carried out by a woman, or (ii) the holder of the job is likely to do his work in circumstances where men might reasonably object to the presence of a woman because they are in a state of undress or using sanitary facilities. So, it would be permissible to insist that an assistant in a men's Turkish bath was a man.

(c) The job is likely to involve the holder of the job doing his work, or living, in a private home and needs to be held by a man because objection might reasonably be taken to allowing a woman,

THE SEX DISCRIMINATION ACT 1975 669

(i) the degree of physical or social contact with a person living in the home, or (ii) the knowledge of intimate details of such a person's life, which the job would be likely to entail. This exception would make it permissible to insist that a male nurse be employed to nurse a man in his own house.

(d) The nature or location of the establishment makes it impracticable for the holder of the job to live elsewhere than in premises provided by the employer, and (i) the only available premises for the workers are normally lived in by men and are not equipped with separate sleeping and sanitary facilities which could be used by women in privacy from men, and (ii) it is not reasonable to expect the employer either to equip the premises with sleeping and sanitary facilities suitable for women, or to provide other suitable premises for women. This exception might make it permissible to discriminate in favour of a man to work at a particularly remote site where there were no facilities for women.

(e) The nature of the establishment may require the work to be done by a man if (i) it is, or is part of, a hospital, prison or other establishment for persons requiring special care, supervision or attention, and (ii) all of those persons are men (disregarding any women whose presence is exceptional), and (iii) it is reasonable, having regard to the essential characteristics of the establishment, that the job should not be held by a woman. An obvious example would be that it might be permissible to insist that a nurse at a secure psychiatric hospital for men should be a male.

(f) The holder of the job provides individuals with personal services promoting their welfare or education, or similar personal services, and those services can most effectively be provided by a man. For example, it might be permissible to insist that certain social workers were male.

(g) The job needs to be held by a man because it is likely to involve the performance of duties outside the United Kingdom in a country whose laws or customs are such that the duties could not, effectively, be performed by a woman. It would therefore, currently, be permissible to insist that a travel guide who was to drive across Afghanistan should be a male.

(h) The job is one of two to be held by a married couple.

The Act does not apply to employment wholly outside Great Britain. Nor does it require that the State pension should be payable to men and women at the same age.

21.2.6 Enforcement and remedies

Section 63A of the Act provides if the complainant proves facts which could, in the absence of an adequate explanation from the employer, lead the tribunal to conclude that the employer had committed a discriminatory act, then the tribunal will uphold the complaint unless the employer proves that he did not commit the discriminatory act.

A complaint of discrimination must be presented to the tribunal within three months of the act complained of, although the tribunal has a discretion to extend this period if it considers it just and equitable to do so. If the discrimination is continuing the period is three months from the end of the discrimination. A conciliation officer attempts conciliation before a case brought by an individual reaches an employment tribunal. If the complainant is successful before the tribunal it may:

(a) make an order declaring the complainant's rights;
(b) order the payment of damages;
(c) order the employer to take action to reduce or obliterate the effect of the discrimination.

Damages awarded can take account of injured feelings and there is no upper limit on the amount of damages which can be awarded.

The Equal Opportunities Commission can carry out investigations into discrimination and can require persons to give written evidence or require them to attend and give evidence. It has the power to issue non-discrimination notices to prevent discriminatory practices. These notices can be enforced by county court injunction. The Commission also has the power to bring cases before the tribunal, even on behalf of a person who has not made a complaint and to give legal assistance to a complainant.

The Sex Discrimination Act makes several other acts unlawful, as follows:

(a) Applying or operating discriminatory practices.
(b) Publishing discriminatory advertisements, or causing these to be published. A job description with a sexual connotation (such as 'waiter', 'salesgirl', 'postman' or 'stewardess') is taken to indicate an intention to discriminate, unless the advertisement contains an indication to the contrary.
(c) Instructing or pressurising another to discriminate.
(d) Aiding unlawful acts.

Test your understanding

1 On what two grounds does the Sex Discrimination Act 1975 outlaw discrimination?

2 In what three ways may this discrimination occur?

3 How does indirect discrimination arise?

4 In what way is an employer made vicariously liable for discrimination?

5 Is discrimination on the grounds of sex ever permissible in employment?

Answers

1 The Sex Discrimination Act 1975 outlaws discrimination on the grounds of a person's sex, or on the grounds that a person is married.

2 The discrimination may be direct discrimination, indirect discrimination or victimisation.

3 Indirect discrimination occurs when a condition is imposed, without justification, and this operates to the detriment of women because a smaller proportion of otherwise suitably qualified females than otherwise suitably qualified males can comply with the condition.

4 Section 41 of the Act makes an employer vicariously liable for acts of discrimination committed by employees in the course of their employment. It is a defence for the employer to show that he took reasonable steps to prevent the employee from doing the act.

5 The Act does allow certain permissible discriminations. These include requiring an actor to be a man for reasons of authenticity, requiring a man on the grounds of decency, requiring that certain social workers should be men, and requiring a man for a job which require the employee to travel to countries which might object to a woman doing the job.

21.3 · The Race Relations Act 1976

The Race Relations Act outlaws discrimination on racial grounds. The Act is closely modelled on the Sex Discrimination Act, and decisions as to the meaning of words in one of the Acts can be precedents when considering the meaning of the equivalent words in the other Act. The Act seeks to prevent racial discrimination by outlawing direct discrimination, indirect discrimination and victimisation.

21.3.1 Direct discrimination, indirect discrimination and victimisation

The Act's definitions of the three methods of discrimination are, for all practical purposes, the same as the definitions of the three methods which we have already considered in relation to sex discrimination. There is therefore little point in examining these definitions in detail, as their meaning can be gained by reading the text above at 21.2.1 to 21.2.3. However, one difference is that s.1(2) provides that segregating a person from other persons on racial grounds is treating him less favourably than others are treated. This would therefore amount to direct discrimination. Despite the three types of discrimination being defined in virtually identical terms, a little needs to be said about all three in a racial context.

People can be directly discriminated against on racial grounds no matter what their race. In *Showboat Entertainment Centre* v *Owens* [1984] 1 WLR 384 for example, a white manager of an entertainment centre was directly discriminated against on racial grounds when he was dismissed for refusing to obey an instruction to exclude all black customers from the centre. An employee is not necessarily discriminated against racially just because he is treated differently than some employees of a different race, it must also be shown that the employee alleging discrimination was treated less favourably on racial grounds.

Indirect discrimination arises if an employer applies a requirement or condition which is such that the proportion of suitably qualified persons of one racial group who can comply with it is considerably smaller than the proportion of suitably qualified persons of another racial group. This must cause detriment to the person belonging to the group which has a lower proportion of persons able to comply with the requirement. The employer must not be able to show that the requirement was justifiable on grounds other than racial grounds.

The application of a particular requirement can only amount to indirect discrimination if it is a requirement which **must** be complied with. In *Meer* v *London Borough of Tower Hamlets* [1988] IRLR 399 a solicitor of Indian origin applied for a vacancy as head of the employer's legal department. There were 23 applicants and 12 were put on a long list of candidates. The claimant was not on the list. The employer had drawn up the list according to 12 criteria. One of these was previous Tower Hamlets experience. The claimant did not have such experience and claimed that this was indirect discrimination against those of Indian origin. The Court of Appeal rejected this claim because Tower Hamlets experience was not a 'must', and was not therefore a 'requirement or condition' within the meaning of the Act's definition of indirect discrimination.

We saw when considering indirect sex discrimination that if the employer can show that the requirement or condition is justifiable then it will not amount to indirect discrimination. The correct procedure for deciding whether a condition was justifiable was laid down by Wood J in *St Mathias Church of England School* v *Crizzle* [1993] IRLR 472. First the tribunal should consider whether the objective which was trying to be achieved was legitimate. Then it should consider whether the means used to achieve the objective were reasonable in themselves. Finally, it should consider whether the means were justified when balanced on the principles of proportionality between the discriminatory effect upon the claimant's racial group and the reasonable needs of those applying the condition. Applying this procedure the EAT held that it was not indirect discrimination for a Church of England school in Hackney to require the head teacher to be a 'committed communicant Christian' even though half of the school's pupils were of Bengali origin.

A new section of the Act, s.1(1)(A), provides that a person also discriminates against another in relation to discrimination in employment if he applies to that other a provision, criterion or practice which he applies or would apply equally to persons not of the same race or ethnic or national origins as that other, but: (a) which puts or would put persons of the same race or ethnic or national origins as that other at a particular disadvantage when compared with other persons; (b) which puts that other at that disadvantage; and (c) which he cannot show to be a proportionate means of achieving a legitimate aim. An example might be an employer insisting that all employees who want advancement should drink alcohol at the Christmas party. Members of ethnic groups which do not drink alcohol would be disadvantaged and the policy would not be a proportionate means of achieving a legitimate aim.

Victimisation arises if a person is treated less favourably because

(a) he has brought proceedings under the Race Relations Act; or
(b) he has given evidence or information in proceedings brought under the Act; or
(c) otherwise done anything under or by reference to the Act; or
(d) alleged that a person has contravened the Act.

In *Chief Constable of West Yorkshire Police* v *Khan* [2000] ICR 1169 the Court of Appeal considered how the correct comparator should be identified when a claim of victimisation was brought. The applicant had brought proceedings against the employer, alleging direct discrimination. Shortly afterwards he applied for a promotion with another police force. The employer refused to give him a reference because they claimed that to do so would prejudice their defence to the claim of direct discrimination. The employer argued that the correct comparator was a person who had brought proceedings against the employer under some Act other than the Race Relations Act. Upholding a finding of victimisation, the Court of Appeal rejected this argument. The correct comparator was anyone else who had applied for a reference from the employer.

21.3.2 Meaning of 'racial grounds' and 'racial group'

The Act outlaws discrimination on racial grounds. Section 3(1) states that in the Act 'racial grounds' means any of the following grounds, namely colour, race, nationality or ethnic or national origins. The section also states that 'racial group' means a group of persons defined by reference to colour, race, nationality, or ethnic or national origins.

The meaning of 'ethnic' was clarified in the following case.

■ *Mandla v Dowell Lee* [1983] ICR 385 (House of Lords)

A Sikh boy was refused entry to a school because the boy and his father would not agree that the son should cut his hair and cease to wear a turban. The judge who heard the case dismissed the complaint on the grounds that Sikhs were not a racial group.

Held. Sikhs are a racial group defined by ethnic origins and the boy had been indirectly discriminated against.

Lord Fraser thought that in order for a group to constitute an ethnic group in the sense of the Act, it must regard itself, and be regarded by others, as a distinct community by virtue of certain characteristics. Two of the characteristics are essential. Another five characteristics are not essential, but will commonly be found and will help to distinguish the group from the surrounding community.

The two **essential** characteristics are:

(1) A long shared history of which the group is conscious as distinguishing it from other groups, and the memory of which it keeps alive.
(2) A cultural tradition of its own, including family and social custom and manners, often but not necessarily associated with religious observance.

The five **relevant** characteristics are:

(1) Either a common geographical origin, or descent from a small number of ancestors.
(2) A common language, not necessarily peculiar to the group.
(3) A common literature peculiar to the group.
(4) A common religion different from that of neighbouring groups or from the general surrounding community.
(5) Being a minority or being an oppressed or dominant group within a larger community. For example, a conquered people and their conquerors might both be ethnic groups, as would have been the case in England shortly after the Norman Conquest.

A group is not to be regarded as an ethnic group merely on account of its religion (except in Northern Ireland). It follows that Rastafarians are not an ethnic group, as they do not seem to satisfy the first essential requirement of a long shared history. Jews have been held to constitute an ethnic group, as have the Welsh. There is yet to be an authoritative case on whether or not Muslims constitute an ethnic group. However, this question may now be of little importance in the light of the Employment Equality (Religion or Belief) Regulations 2003 (SI 2003 No. 1660), which outlaw discrimination against employees or those who contract to provide work personally on the grounds of religion, religious belief, or similar philosophical belief. The Regulations are considered below at 21.4.8.

21.3.2.1 Harassment

Section 3A(1) now defines harassment. It states that a person subjects another to harassment where, on grounds of race or ethnic or national origins, he engages in unwanted conduct which has the effect of: (a) violating that other person's dignity; or (b) creating an intimidating, hostile, degrading, humiliating or offensive environment for him. The test to see whether conduct amounts to harassment, as defined, is to see whether it reasonably should be considered to have the effect specified in s.3A(1), having regard to all of the circumstances, in particular the perception of the person claiming to be harassed.

21.3.3 Discrimination in the employment field

Part II of the 1976 Act is concerned solely with discrimination in the employment field. As was the case with sex discrimination, workers who contract personally to provide any services are included, whether they provide these services as employees or not. Section 4 sets out the ways in which such discrimination can occur. As regards selecting employees, it is unlawful to discriminate against another:

(a)   in the arrangements made for the purpose of determining who should be offered employment;
(b)   in the terms on which employment is offered;
(c)   by refusing or deliberately omitting to offer employment.

Placing a discriminatory advertisement is not enough to give an applicant a ground for complaint, even if the advertisement does indicate an intention to discriminate. However, the Commission for Racial Equality could take action against the person who placed the advertisement.

Section 4(2) sets out three ways in which it is unlawful to discriminate against an existing employee. These ways are:

(a)   in the terms of the employment; or
(b)   in the way the employee is afforded access to opportunities for promotion, transfer, training, or to any other benefits, facilities or services, or by refusing or deliberately omitting to afford him access to them; or
(c)   by dismissing him or subjecting him to any other detriment.

Section 4A provides that the dismissal can include, where the discrimination is on grounds of race or ethnic or national origins, either constructive dismissal or not renewing a fixed term contract.

The examples which we studied in relation to sex discrimination would indicate how the various methods of discrimination might be committed.

21.3.4 Genuine occupational qualifications

Section 5 of the Act does allow racial discrimination in employment if being of a particular racial group is a genuine occupational qualification for some or all of the duties of the job. It states that being of a particular racial group is a genuine occupational qualification for the job only in the following circumstances:

(a)   Where the job involves participation in a dramatic performance, or other entertainment, in a capacity for which a person of that racial group is required for reasons of authenticity. For example, in a play about Nelson Mandela it would be permissible to insist that the person to play Mandela was black and the person to play Prime Minister Botha was white.
(b)   Where the job involves participation as an artist's or photographic model in the production of a work of art, and a person of that racial group is required for reasons of authenticity. For

example, if a series of photographs depicting the murder of Thomas à Becket were to be made it could be stipulated that the model to be photographed as Becket was white.

(c) Where the job involves working in a place where food or drink is (for payment or not) provided to and consumed by members of the public, in a particular setting where a person of that racial group is required for reasons of authenticity. For example, it would be permissible to require that waiters in a Chinese restaurant were Chinese.

(d) The holder of the job provides persons of a certain racial group with personal services promoting their welfare, and those services can most effectively be provided by a person of that racial group. Many of the social work jobs advertised in the newspapers provide examples.

The Race Relations Act 1976 (Amendment) Regulations 2003 have substituted a different test where the alleged discrimination is on the grounds of race or ethnic or national origins (as opposed to colour or nationality). The new test is that having regard to the nature of the employment, and the context of where it is performed, being of a particular race or particular ethnic or national origins is a genuine and determining requirement and that requirement is applied in a proportionate manner, and either the person to whom that requirement is applied does not meet it or the employer is not satisfied, and in all the circumstances it is reasonable for him not to be satisfied, that the person meets it.

Section 32 of the Act provides that employers can be vicariously liable for the actions of their employees in the same way as they can in respect of sex discrimination. The following case, recently overruled, used to provide an example.

■ *Burton and Rhule v De Vere Hotels* [1996] IRLR 596

Two black women worked as casual waitresses at a hotel. The work was performed at a function organised by the Round Table, which had booked Bernard Manning as the speaker. On the evening in question a manager and two assistant managers were on duty. Mr Manning made a series of very racist and very sexually racist remarks against the two women. The women carried on working. Later they complained to the hotel manager, who apologised for what had happened.

Held. The women had been subjected to a detriment within the meaning of the Race Relations Act, and the employer had subjected them to this detriment. It would have been good employment practice for the manager to have warned the two women to keep a look out for Mr Manning and to withdraw the waitresses if things became unpleasant. As this practice had not been followed, the employers had subjected the women to the racial harassment which they had suffered. Mr Manning's behaviour would now amount to harassment, as defined by s.3A(1). However, the employer would no longer be vicariously liable for it. In *MacDonald v Advocate General for Scotland* [2003] UKHL 34 the House of Lords said that the case was wrongly decided because the hotel would have treated white women in the same way.

Contract workers are protected by the Act. In *Harrods Ltd v Remick* [1998] 1 All ER 52 the Court of Appeal held that Harrods had racially discriminated against a member of a sales force who was employed by a third party but subject to Harrods' approval.

The Act only applies to discrimination within Great Britain. Other discriminatory acts are outlawed in the same way as they were in respect of sex discrimination. Thus it is unlawful to apply discriminatory practices, to discriminate in advertisements, to instruct to discriminate and to pressurise to discriminate. Section 27A makes it unlawful for an employer to discriminate or harass after the employment relationship has come to an end. This might be done, for example, by refusing to supply a reference.

21.3.5 Enforcement of the Act

A complaint of discrimination must be brought before the tribunal within three months of the discrimination, although the tribunal has a discretion to extend the period if it considers it just and equitable to do so. If the discrimination is continuing the period is three months from the end of the discrimination. The case will only proceed to a tribunal hearing if a conciliation officer cannot promote a settlement between the parties. Section 54A provides that if an employee presents evidence to a tribunal which could show that the employer has committed discrimination or harassment then the burden of proof shifts to the employer to show that he did not.

The tribunal may award three remedies:

(1) Declare the rights of the complainant.
(2) Order the payment of damages.
(3) Recommend that action to obviate or reduce the discrimination should be taken within a certain time.

As was the case with sex discrimination, the damages may take account of injured feelings and there is no upper limit on the amount awarded. In *Essa v Laing Ltd* [2004] EWCA Civ 62 the Court of Appeal held, Rix LJ dissenting, that if there was a causal link between the act of discrimination and the injury alleged it was not necessary that the injury should have been reasonably foreseeable. Damages should be awarded to cover any injury which flowed directly and naturally from the wrong, as in the case of the torts of assault and battery. Applying this test the Court of Appeal upheld an award of £5 000 to a building labourer of Somali ethnicity. His foreman had made racially abusive comments about him and this had caused him to suffer severe depression. Consequently, he lost interest in his hobby of boxing, lost interest in finding another job and fell into debt. It was thought that the absence of a need to prove foreseeability would not open the floodgates to claims because tribunals would use good sense in finding facts and drawing conclusions from them.

The Commission for Racial Equality has similar powers to the Equal Opportunities Commission to carry out formal investigations, serve non-discriminatory notices and gain injunctions to prevent further discrimination.

21.4 · The Disability Discrimination Act 1995

The Disability Discrimination Act 1995 seeks to prevent discrimination against disabled persons, that is to say against persons who have a disability. Section 1 of the Act states that for the purposes of the Act, a person has a disability if he has a physical or mental impairment which has a substantial and long-term adverse effect on his ability to carry out normal day-to-day activities. Persons who have had a disability in the past are also covered by the Act.

21.4.1 Methods of discriminating by employers

Section 4 of the Act is modelled very closely on s.6 of the Sex Discrimination Act 1975 and s.4 of the Race Relations Act 1976. It makes it unlawful to discriminate in the same ways as previously considered above at 21.2.4 and 21.3.3. Thus as regards potential employees it is unlawful to do any of the following:

(a) make discriminatory arrangements for the purposes of deciding who should be offered employment; or
(b) offer disabled persons inferior terms; or
(c) refuse to offer, or deliberately not offer a disabled person employment.

As regards existing disabled employees, it is unlawful to discriminate against them by:

(a) employing them on inferior terms; or

(b) refusing to afford them access to promotion, transfer, training or any other benefit; or

(c) dismissing them or subjecting them to any other detriment.

21.4.2 Meaning of discrimination

Section 3A defines discrimination and harassment:

'**3A Meaning of "discrimination"**

(1) For the purposes of this Part, a person discriminates against a disabled person if –

    (a) for a reason which relates to the disabled person's disability, he treats him less favourably than he treats or would treat others to whom that reason does not or would not apply, and

    (b) he cannot show that the treatment in question is justified.

(2) For the purposes of this Part, a person also discriminates against a disabled person if he fails to comply with a duty to make reasonable adjustments imposed on him in relation to the disabled person.

(3) Treatment is justified for the purposes of subsection (1)(b) if, but only if, the reason for it is both material to the circumstances of the particular case and substantial.

(4) But treatment of a disabled person cannot be justified under subsection (3) if it amounts to direct discrimination falling within subsection (5).

(5) A person directly discriminates against a disabled person if, on the ground of the disabled person's disability, he treats the disabled person less favourably than he treats or would treat a person not having that particular disability whose relevant circumstances, including his abilities, are the same as, or not materially different from, those of the disabled person.

(6) If, in a case falling within subsection (1), a person is under a duty to make reasonable adjustments in relation to a disabled person but fails to comply with that duty, his treatment of that person cannot be justified under subsection (3) unless it would have been justified even if he had complied with that duty.

3B Meaning of "harassment"

(1) For the purposes of this Part, a person subjects a disabled person to harassment where, for a reason which relates to the disabled person's disability, he engages in unwanted conduct which has the purpose or effect of –

    (a) violating the disabled person's dignity, or

    (b) creating an intimidating, hostile, degrading, humiliating or offensive environment for him.

(2) Conduct shall be regarded as having the effect referred to in paragraph (a) or (b) of subsection (1) only if, having regard to all the circumstances, including in particular the perception of the disabled person, it should reasonably be considered as having that effect.'

Section 6 of the Act creates a positive duty on an employer to make adjustments to cater for the needs of disabled workers.

Section 6(1) provides that where (a) any arrangements made by or on behalf of an employer, or (b) any physical feature of premises occupied by the employer, place the disabled person concerned at a substantial disadvantage in comparison with workers who are not disabled, it is the duty of the employer to take such steps as it is reasonable, in all the circumstances of the case, for him to have to take in order to prevent the arrangement or feature having that effect. This positive duty applies in relation to (a) arrangements for determining to whom employment should be offered, or (b) any terms, conditions or arrangements on which employment or other benefits such as training, transfer or promotion are offered. It also applies in relation to working conditions during employment. Section 6(3) of the Act gives examples of steps which an employer might have to take to comply with the duty to make adjustments. The steps specified are:

(a) adjusting premises;

(b) allocating some of a disabled person's duties to someone else;

(c) transferring a disabled person to fill an existing vacancy;

(d) altering a disabled person's working hours;

(e) sending a disabled person to a different place of work;

(f) allowing a disabled person time during working hours for rehabilitation, assessment or treatment;
(g) giving a disabled person training or arranging training;
(h) acquiring or modifying equipment;
(i) modifying manuals or procedures;
(j) providing a reader or interpreter; and
(k) providing supervision.

Section 6(4) requires that particular regard must be had to the following five matters in determining whether it is reasonable for an employer to have to take a particular step in order to comply with the duty to make adjustments:

(a) The extent to which taking the step would prevent the disabled person from being placed at a considerable disadvantage.
(b) The extent to which it is practicable for the employer to take the step.
(c) The financial and other costs which would be incurred by the employer in taking the step and the extent to which taking it would disrupt any of his activities.
(d) The extent of the employer's financial and other resources.
(e) The availability to the employer of financial and other assistance with respect to taking the step.

The duty to make adjustments applies not only in respect of existing employees, but also in respect of applicants for employment. However, the duty is not imposed if the employer does not know, and could not reasonably be expected to know, that a disabled person is applying for a job. Nor does it apply as regards either existing or potential employees if the employer does not know that the employee has a disability and that he is likely to be affected by the employer's arrangements or the physical features of the premises.

Apart from the duty to make adjustments set out in s.6, there is no requirement for an employer to treat a disabled person more favourably than he would treat others. Nor does the duty to make adjustments apply in relation to benefits payable on:

(a) termination of service;
(b) retirement, old age or death; or
(c) accident, injury, sickness or invalidity.

Victimisation as a consequence of having tried to utilise or enforce the Act is outlawed in the same way as it was outlawed in the cases of sex and race discrimination.

21.4.3 Procedure to be followed

In *Morse* v *Wiltshire County Council* [1998] IRLR 352 the EAT considered the procedure to be followed when considering whether the requirements of the Act had been followed. The case concerned an applicant who was made redundant. The applicant had been in a car crash which left him disabled and unable to drive. Redundancies were necessary for financial reasons, and one of the factors used by the employer in determining who should be made redundant was whether or not the employee could drive. The employment tribunal found that the applicant had been made redundant and that although he had been treated less favourably on the grounds of his disability this less favourable treatment was justified. The tribunal also held that no reasonable adjustment could have been made by the employer. Bell J, giving the judgment of the EAT, held that deciding whether or not the employer had fulfilled the s.6 duty to make adjustments involved going through the following steps. First, the tribunal should decide whether or not s.6 imposes a duty on the employer in the particular case. If so, the tribunal must decide whether the employer has taken such steps as is reasonable, in all the circumstances of the case, for him to have to take to prevent the arrangements or physical features of premises putting the disabled person at a substantial disadvantage as regards persons who are not disabled. This involves the tribunal objectively asking whether the employer could reasonably have taken any steps, including those set out in s.6(3). The purpose of these s.6(3) steps is to focus the mind of the employer on the steps he might take and to focus the mind of the tribunal in considering whether the employer had failed in the duty to take positive steps. At the same time the tribunal should have regard to the matters set out in s.6(4). Only if the tribunal, after following all of these steps, finds that the employer has failed to comply with the s.6 duty in respect of the disabled applicant does the tribunal have to decide whether or not the failure to comply with the s.6 duty is justified. This will involve objectively considering whether the reason for the failure to comply is both material to the circumstances of the particular case and substantial.

21.4.4 Remedies and enforcement

A claim of discrimination may be brought before an employment tribunal by an individual. First ACAS will perform its statutory duty to conciliate and only if conciliation is not achieved will the case proceed. The tribunal may:

(a) Make a declaration as to the complainant's rights.
(b) Order the payment of unlimited damages, which may take account of injury to feelings.
(c) Recommend that certain action be taken within a specified time.

The concept of vicarious liability applies in the same way as it does in respect of sex and race discrimination. If an advertisement indicated an intention to discriminate the tribunal shall assume, unless the contrary is shown, that the employer's reason for refusing to offer employment to a disabled person was related to the complainant's disability.

In April 2000 the Disability Rights Commission was set up to perform a role similar to that of the EOC and the CRE.

21.4.5 Discrimination against persons with criminal records

The Rehabilitation of Offenders Act 1974 allows people whose convictions have become **spent** to deny that they have ever been convicted. Furthermore, if a person is dismissed because of a spent conviction this will amount to unfair dismissal. It is, however, permissible for an employer to refuse to employ a person on account of that person's criminal record or to discriminate in other ways such as to refuse promotion. In certain jobs some types of spent convictions will justify dismissal. However, it is up to the employer to check the nature of the spent conviction and whether or not it would make the employee unfit to hold his job.

■ *Brooks* v *Ladbroke Lucky Seven Entertainment* (1977) IRLIB

Ladbrokes dismissed a gaming club employee when they discovered that he had a conviction. They did not know that the conviction was spent and argued that the nature of the work would have justified dismissal anyway. The man claimed unfair dismissal.

Held. The dismissal was unfair. The employer should have considered the nature of the conviction and whether or not it made the applicant unsuitable to do the job.

A conviction becomes spent after a length of time which varies with the severity of the sentence passed. The times are:

Over 2.5 years imprisonment	Never spent.
6 months–2.5 years	Spent after 10 years.
Less than 6 months	Spent after 7 years.
Youth custody	Spent after 7 years
Fined/Community Service Order	Spent after 5 years.

Detention Centre	Spent after 3 years.
Probation/Binding Over	Spent after 1 year.
Care/Supervision order	Spent after 1 year.
Absolute discharge	Spent after 6 months.

The amount of time actually served in prison is not relevant. The time periods begin when the sentence is passed, not when the prisoner is released.

21.4.6 Discrimination against part-time workers

The Part-time Workers (Prevention of Less Favourable Treatment) Regulations 2000 (SI 2000 No. 1551) came into force in July 2000. The main provisions of the Regulations are set out in Regulation 5(1):

'A part-time worker has the right not to be treated by his employer less favourably than the employer treats a full-time worker –
(a) as regards the terms of his contract; or
(b) by being subjected to any other detriment by any act, or deliberate failure to act, of his employer.'

However, these rights only apply if the treatment of the part-time worker is on the grounds that he is a part-time worker. Nor will the rights apply if the treatment is justified on objective grounds (Reg.5(2)(b)).

In assessing whether or not a part-time worker has been treated less favourably the pro-rata principle should be applied unless it is inappropriate. This principle requires that the part-time worker should receive the appropriate proportion of the pay and benefits enjoyed by the full-time worker with whom he compares himself. Part-timers will not be entitled to overtime rates until they have worked for longer than normal full-time hours. Contractual sick pay and maternity pay are covered by the Regulations. Part-timers must have equal access to occupational pension schemes, to training and career breaks. Holiday entitlement should be pro rata the holiday entitlement of full-timers.

Where a part-time worker is given less favourable treatment Reg.6 entitles him to a written statement of the reasons for the less favourable treatment. If a worker is dismissed for bringing proceedings under the Regulations, or otherwise in connection with the Regulations, this amounts to automatic unfair dismissal.

A complaint under the Regulations is made to the employment tribunal in the usual way. The tribunal can make a declaration of the claimant's rights, order the employer to pay compensation or recommend that the employer take reasonable action to prevent the discrimination. Compensation cannot include an amount for injured feelings, and the complainant has a duty to mitigate any loss. The Regulations were passed to give effect to EC Directive 98/23/EC.

21.4.7 Discrimination on the grounds of sexual orientation

The Employment Equality (Sexual Orientation) Regulations 2003 (SI 2003 No. 1661) outlaw discrimination on the grounds of sexual orientation.

Regulation 2(1) defines 'sexual orientation' as meaning an orientation towards persons of the same sex, the opposite sex or both sexes. The Regulations are modelled closely on the Sex Discrimination Act and outlaw direct discrimination, indirect discrimination and victimisation. Regulation 5 provides that a person is subjected to harassment where, on the grounds of sexual orientation, another engages in unwanted conduct which has the purpose or effect of: (a) violating the person's dignity; or (b) creating an intimidating, hostile, degrading, humiliating or offensive environment for the harassed person. Regulation 6 sets out unlawful discrimination practices which are very close to those found in s.6 of the Sex Discrimination Act (considered above at 21.2.4). Regulation 7 sets out two genuine occupational qualifications, on which discrimination is permitted. The first is that being of a particular sexual orientation is a genuine and determining occupational requirement and that it is proportionate to apply the requirement in the particular case. The second is that the employment is for the purposes of an organised religion and the requirement as to sexual orientation is to avoid conflicting with the strongly held religious beliefs of a significant number of the religion's followers.

The Regulations apply not only to persons with a particular sexual orientation but also to persons who are perceived to have a particular sexual orientation. If discrimination is alleged the procedures and remedies are the same as if the case had been one of sex discrimination.

21.4.8 Discrimination on grounds of religious belief

The Employment Equality (Religion or Belief) Regulations 2003 outlaw discrimination against employees or those who contract to provide work personally on the grounds of religion, religious belief, or similar philosophical belief. The belief can be real or perceived. The Regulations also outlaw discrimination on the grounds of the belief of others with whom the worker associates. Strong political views, or strong associations with a political party or a sports club are not regarded as religious beliefs. Earlier in this chapter we saw that Rastafarians and Jehovah's Witnesses have been held not to be ethnic groups for the purposes of the Race Relations Act 1976. Both groups would be protected by the 2003 Regulations.

The Regulations are modelled very closely on the Sex Discrimination Act 1975. So they outlaw direct discrimination, indirect discrimination, harassment and victimisation. The procedures will be the same as for a complaint under the Sex Discrimination Act and the remedies which an employment tribunal can award will also be the same.

21.4.9   Discrimination against fixed term workers

The Fixed-term Employees (Prevention of Less Favourable Treatment) Regulations 2002 (SI 2002 No. 2034) seek to prevent discrimination against employees working on fixed term contracts. Regulation 3(1) provides that a fixed term employee has the right not to be treated by his employer less favourably than the employer treats a comparable permanent employee: (a) as regards the terms of his contract; or (b) by being subjected to any other detriment by any act, or deliberate failure to act, of his employer. However, these rights apply only if the different treatment was on the grounds that the worker was a fixed term worker and if it was not justified on objective grounds.

Regulation 3(2) specifies that in particular this includes the right not to be treated less favourably in relation to any period of service qualification, the opportunity to receive training or the opportunity to secure any permanent job. In determining whether treatment was less favourable, the pro rata principle is used, as explained above in relation to discrimination against part-time workers. If fixed term workers are treated less favourably as regards particular terms of their contracts, this can be justified on objective grounds if their contracts as a whole are at least as favourable as the terms of the comparable permanent employee's contract of employment (Reg.4).

A fixed term employee who thinks that he is being treated less favourably is entitled to a written statement of the reasons for the less favourable treatment and this is admissible as evidence in any proceedings under the regulations. It will be automatically unfair dismissal to dismiss an employee on the grounds that he has requested a written statement or brought proceedings under the regulations. Complaints are made to the tribunal in the usual way. Compensation cannot cover damages for injured feelings. An employee who works on a fixed term contract which is renewed is to be regarded as a permanent employee once he has been continuously employed for at least four years, unless the failure to renew can be justified on objective grounds. However, for this purpose employment before 10 July 2002 does not count as continuous employment.

Test your understanding

1 On what grounds does the Race Relations Act 1976 outlaw discrimination? In what three ways might this discrimination occur?

2 What is the meaning of discrimination 'on racial grounds'?

3 What are the two essential characteristics which a group must possess in order to constitute an ethnic group?

4 In what circumstances can being a member of a particular racial group be a genuine occupational qualification?

5 On what grounds does the Disability Discrimination Act prevent discrimination? On what grounds does the Act regard a person as being disabled?

6 What is the meaning of discrimination under the Act?

7 Are any positive duties imposed on the employer by the Disability Discrimination Act?

8 What protection against discrimination is provided to those who have been convicted of criminal offences?

9 What is the main effect of the Part-time Workers (Prevention of Less Favourable Treatment) Regulations 2000?

10 Is discrimination on the grounds of sexual orientation permissible in employment?

11 On what grounds do the Employment Equality (Religion or Belief) Regulations 2003 outlaw discrimination?

12 What rights are given to fixed term employees by the Fixed-term Employees (Prevention of Less Favourable Treatment) Regulations 2002?

Answers

1 The Race Relations Act outlaws discrimination on racial grounds. Such discrimination might be direct discrimination, indirect discrimination or victimisation.

2 Discrimination is on racial grounds if it is on the grounds of colour, race, nationality or ethnic or national origins.

3 In order to constitute an ethnic group, the group must have a long shared history and a cultural tradition of its own.

4 Being a member of a particular racial group can be a genuine occupational qualification for reasons of authenticity in works of drama, entertainment or art; to provide authenticity in places where food or drink is served; or in certain social work jobs.

5 The Disability Discrimination Act outlaws discrimination against disabled persons. A person is regarded as disabled if he has a physical or mental impairment which has a substantial and long-term adverse effect on his ability to carry out normal day-to-day activities.

6 A person is discriminated against if he is treated less favourably than he otherwise would be and the employer cannot show that this less favourable treatment is justified.

7 The employer has a positive duty to take such steps as are reasonable to see that arrangements and physical features do not have a discriminatory effect.

8 A person whose conviction is spent can deny having been convicted. If dismissed on account of the conviction this will amount to unfair dismissal. However, several types of employment are exempted from these provisions.

9 The Regulations insist that part-time workers should be treated no less favourably than comparable full-time workers unless the less favourable treatment is justified on objective grounds.

10 The Employment Equality (Sexual Orientation) Regulations 2003 forbid discrimination on the grounds of sexual orientation by outlawing direct discrimination, indirect discrimination and victimisation.

11 The Employment Equality (Religion or Belief) Regulations 2003 seek to prevent discrimination against employees, or those who contract to provide work personally, on the grounds of religion, religious belief, or similar philosophical belief by outlawing direct discrimination, indirect discrimination and victimisation.

12 The Fixed-term Employees (Prevention of Less Favourable Treatment) Regulations 2002 provide that a fixed term employee has the right not to be treated by his employer less favourably than the employer treats a comparable permanent employee.

21.5 · Health and safety

The Health and Safety at Work etc. Act 1974, as amended, imposes duties on employers. Breach of these duties constitutes a criminal offence, but does not necessarily give rise to any civil action. An employee who is injured by an employer's breach of a duty of care can sue in the tort of negligence. Therefore, for two quite different reasons employers should ensure the health and safety of their workers. First, if they do not they might be convicted of an offence under the Health and Safety at Work Act. Second, they might, additionally or alternatively, be liable to pay compensation to workers who are injured or whose health is adversely affected. First we consider the Act, then the civil position.

In *R (Junttan Oy) v Bristol Magistrates' Court* [2003] UKHL 55 the House of Lords held that the Health and Safety Executive could choose to prosecute under the 1974 Act rather than under one of the 'six-pack' Regulations considered below at 21.5.6. The maximum sentence under the Act was considerably heavier than that under the Regulations.

21.5.1 The Health and Safety at Work etc. Act 1974

21.5.1.1 Enforcement of the Act

The Health and Safety Commission (HSC), which consists of a chairman and nine other members, presides over health and safety at work. The Act is enforced both by the Health and Safety Executive (HSE), which consists of the Director and two assistant Directors, and by local authority enforcement officers. The HSE carries out functions as directed by the Health and Safety Commission. Inspectors are given powers to do the following things:

(a) enter premises where there is a dangerous situation at any reasonable time;
(b) make whatever examinations and investigations as may be necessary;
(c) take samples from within premises or from the atmosphere;
(d) test articles and substances;
(e) dismantle dangerous articles;
(f) take away dangerous articles or substances for examination;
(g) require that books and records are produced;
(h) require that people answer questions and sign a declaration that their answers are true;
(i) require that they are not obstructed in the execution of their powers; and
(j) use any other power necessary to exercise the powers previously listed.

Section 21 allows an inspector to issue an **improvement notice**. Such a notice would be served on an employer, and would require the employer to stop contravening one of the Act's provisions within a period which may not be less than 21 days.

Prohibition notices can be issued under s.22 to prevent, with immediate effect, the carrying on of an activity which involves a risk of serious personal injury. Failure to comply with either an improvement notice or with a prohibition notice is a criminal offence. Where the employee is the Crown, as in many government departments, improvements and enforcement notices are called **Crown notices**. Breach of these is not a criminal offence, as the Crown cannot be prosecuted, but the publicity engendered would ensure that remedial action is taken.

Section 25 gives an inspector the **power to deal with a cause of imminent danger**. This power allows an inspector to seize and render harmless any article or substance found on any premises which he has the power to enter. The power arises if the inspector has reasonable cause to believe that, in the circumstances in which he finds it, the article or substance is a cause of imminent danger of serious personal injury.

21.5.2 Duties of the employer

Section 2(1) of the Act states that it shall be the duty of every employer to ensure, so far as is reasonably practicable, the health, safety and welfare at work of all his employees. Without prejudice to this general duty, s.2(2) sets out five matters to which the duty particularly extends. The matters are:

(a) the provision and maintenance of safe plant and safe systems of work;
(b) arrangements for ensuring the safe use, handling, storage and transport of articles and substances;
(c) providing information, instruction, training and supervision as is necessary to ensure the health and safety of employees;
(d) maintaining any place under the employer's control in a safe condition and maintaining safe ways in and out; and
(e) providing and maintaining an overall safe working environment for employees.

It should be emphasised that none of these matters are absolute duties. The employer only has a duty to comply with them so far as is reasonably practicable. However, if a duty is practicable then it will be very likely that failure to carry it out was unreasonable. If the employer argues that it was not reasonably practicable for him to carry out any of his duties under the Act then the burden of proof is on him to prove this.

Section 2(3) provides that it shall be the duty of every employer employing five or more persons to prepare a written statement of his general policy with respect to health and safety at work of his employees. This statement must also be revised as often as is appropriate. The written statement must also set out the organisation and arrangements for the time being in force for carrying out that policy. It is also the duty of the employer to bring the statement and any revision of it to the notice of all of his employees.

Employers may be required to consult with recognised trade unions in order to cooperate effectively in promoting and developing measures to ensure the health and safety at work of the employees, and in checking the effectiveness of such measures. The employer may also be required to set up a safety committee to keep matters under review.

Section 3 requires that employers conduct their undertakings in such a way as to ensure, as far as is reasonably practicable, that non-employees who may be affected by the undertaking are not exposed to risks to their health and safety. Section 4 imposes a similar duty on employers in respect of non-employees who may use the employer's premises.

When we considered unfair dismissal, in the previous chapter, we saw that a dismissal connected with having carried out activities in connection with health and safety could be automatically unfair (ERA ss.44 and 100).

21.5.3 Duties of manufacturers, designers, importers and suppliers

Section 6(1) imposes a number of duties on employers who design, manufacture, import or supply any article for use at work. The manufacturer etc must:

(a) ensure, so far as is reasonably practicable, that the article is so designed and constructed that it will be safe and without risk to health at all times when it is being set, used, cleaned or maintained by a person at work;
(b) carry out, or arrange to have carried out, such tests and examinations as are necessary to ensure compliance with requirement (a);
(c) make sure that persons supplied with any article are provided with adequate information about the use for which it is designed and about any conditions required to make sure its use is safe; and

(d) provide revised information to make sure that duty (c) is complied with, as far as is reasonably practicable.

Section 6(4) imposes very similar duties on those who import or supply any substance, rather than manufacture etc any article.

Section 6(2) imposes a duty upon designers and manufacturers to carry out research with a view to discovering and eliminating risks to health and safety.

Section 6(3) requires those who erect and install equipment at work to ensure, as far as is reasonably practicable, that nothing about the way this is done should make the article unsafe or a risk to health.

The duties imposed by s.6 only extend to things done in the course of a trade or business (whether for profit or not) and also only to matters within the control of the person on whom the duty is imposed.

21.5.4 Employees' duties at work

Section 7 provides that it shall be the duty of every employee while at work:

(a) to take reasonable care for the health and safety of himself and of other persons who may be affected by his acts or omissions at work; and
(b) as regards any duty imposed on his employer or anyone else by a statute, to co-operate with him so far as necessary to enable that duty or requirement to be performed or complied with.

21.5.5 Other aspects of the Act

Section 8 imposes a duty on all persons not to interfere with or misuse anything provided in the interests of health, safety or welfare in pursuance of the relevant statutory provisions. Both intentional and reckless interference are prohibited.

Section 9 makes it illegal for an employer to charge, or permit to be charged, any employee in respect of anything done or provided in pursuance of any specific requirement of the relevant statutory provisions.

Section 36 provides that where any person commits an offence under the Act due to the act or default of some other person, that other person shall be guilty of the offence. This other person can be convicted even if proceedings are not brought against the person who committed the offence.

Section 37 provides that if a company commits an offence under the Act with the consent or connivance of any director, manager or secretary or other similar officer of the company then both the company and the company officer shall be guilty of the offence. The same is true if the offence was caused by the neglect of the company officer.

The Act also allows regulations to be made by the Secretary of State or the Health and Safety Commission. There are many regulations applying either generally or to particular hazards and risks. It is beyond the scope of this book to examine these.

21.5.6 European law

Article 137 of the Treaty of Rome, which used to be Article 118, allows the passing of Directives to improve the working environment to protect workers' health and safety and working conditions. Six new sets of Regulations were passed in 1992. It is probable that these merely state clearly requirements which were previously imposed on employers by the old law. The new law spells out that employers must actively take steps to ensure the health and safety at work of their employees. The six Regulations in question are as follows.

The **Management of Health and Safety at Work Regulations 1992** require all employers to make an assessment of the risk to health and safety of their employees while at work. An employer must make health and safety arrangements, provide appropriate health surveillance and appoint assistants to help him comply with his statutory duties. The employer must also have procedures to deal with serious and imminent danger and for dealing with danger areas. Information must be given to employees, who must cooperate with the employer. There is also a duty on the employer to provide adequate training of employees.

The **Workplace (Health Safety and Welfare) Regulations 1992** require that employers provide clean, efficient places of work. Sanitary facilities should be provided, safe seats if the workers are to sit down, and also rest facilities where non-smokers are protected from smokers. Suitable facilities for eating meals should also be provided.

The **Provision and Use of Work Equipment Regulations 1992** require equipment used at work to be maintained and repaired. They also provide that the equipment must conform to any legislation and that employees should be trained in the use of equipment. In *Stark v The Post Office* (2000) Times, 29 March the Post Office were found to be in breach of these regulations when a postman suffered injury as a consequence of the front brake of his delivery bike breaking. The duty set out in Reg.6(1), that every employer shall ensure that work equipment is maintained in an efficient state, in efficient working order and good repair was held to be an absolute duty. The Court of Appeal also held that although the EC Directive which gave rise to the Regulations imposed minimum standards to be observed they did not prevent higher standards from being introduced if the Member State chose to introduce higher standards.

The **Personal Protective Equipment at Work Regulations 1998** provide that personal protective equipment must be supplied to employees where appropriate. The equipment must be kept clean and well repaired and employees must be instructed and trained in the use of it.

The **Manual Handling Operations Regulations 1992** seek to minimise the risk from employees manually handling things in a way which involves the risk of injury.

The **Health and Safety (Display Screen Equipment) Regulations 1998** require that users of work stations must be trained, must be given eye tests and treatment if they request them and must be given breaks and changes of activity.

The Health and Safety Commission may issue **Codes of Practice** in relation to any statutory duties or duties imposed by regulations. Breach of such a code does not automatically mean that a criminal offence has been committed, but will almost always mean that it has. Adherence to the code will mean that an offence has not been committed.

The Control of Substances Hazardous to Health Regulations 2002 (COSHH Regulations 2002), as amended by the COSHH Regulations 2003, replace the 1999 Regulations of the same name. The duties imposed on employers by the regulations apply not only in respect of employees but also in respect of any person who might be affected by the work carried on by the employer.

The Regulations prohibit the importation or supply for use at work of certain substances. These substances include benzene, sand containing free silica, ground flint or quartz, white phosphorus and certain types of oil. They also require employers to carry out an assessment of the risk to health created by work involving any substances hazardous to health and to make sure that the exposure of his employees to substances hazardous to health is prevented.

21.5.7 Common law health and safety

A term is implied into a contract of employment requiring an employer to take reasonable care to ensure the safety of his employees. Breach of this term could enable an employee to sue for breach of contract. Generally, however, where an employee is injured at work he will seek to sue the employer in the tort of negligence. As was seen in Chapter 12, a successful claim in negligence will require the claimant to prove three things:

(a) that the defendant (employer) owed the claimant (employee) a duty of care;

(b) that the defendant breached this duty; and

(c) that this breach resulted in the claimant suffering foreseeable injury.

21.5.7.1 The duty of care

The duty of care owed by an employer is generally thought to be made up in particular of three matters: to provide safe plant and equipment, to provide a safe system of work and to provide reasonably competent fellow employees. The duty is not an absolute one to see that the employee is not injured, but only a duty to take such care as an ordinary prudent employer would take in all the circumstances. The duty is owed personally by the employer and therefore he cannot escape liability by passing the duty to another person. The duty is also owed to employees personally, rather than to all of the employees collectively. So if the employee has a particular weakness, or is particularly inexperienced, account must be taken of this. An example can be seen in *Paris* v *Stepney Borough Council* [1951] 1 All ER 42. An employee with the use of only one eye was asked to work on the underneath of a vehicle and was not given protective goggles. A shard of metal flew into his good eye and blinded him as he hammered a bolt in an attempt to remove it. The employer was liable for this injury and it was a relevant factor that the employee had the use of only one eye and was therefore particularly vulnerable.

As the general law of negligence is applicable, it is only necessary here to say a little about each of the three matters which apply especially to employers.

21.5.7.2 Safe plant and equipment

An example of an employer being liable in consequence of not providing safe equipment can be seen in the following case.

■ *Bradford* v *Robinson Rentals* [1967] 1 All ER 267

The claimant, a 57-year-old man, was employed as a radio service engineer. He generally travelled short distances between customers' houses. In January 1963, when the employer knew that the weather was likely to be very severe, he was ordered to do a round journey of 500 miles to change a colleague's van. This involved about 20 hours' driving. (Motorways were a thing of the future.) Both of the vans were unheated. The employee said that he thought the journey should not be undertaken as it was hazardous. He was ordered to go and suffered frostbite, a very unusual condition in England.

Held. The employee was entitled to damages. The employers had exposed him to a reasonable risk of injury. Injury from exposure to cold was foreseeable and so it did not matter that the exact nature of the injury was unusual.

21.5.7.3 Safe system of work

The employer's duty to provide a safe system of work involves all matters relating to the way the work is done. These matters would commonly include whether training was provided, whether the system used was inherently safe, and whether the employee was given special instructions or protective clothing. Problems often arise, as in the case which follows, when employees are provided with protective equipment but choose not to use it.

■ *MacWilliams* v *Sir William Arrol & Co Ltd* [1962] 1 All ER 623 (House of Lords)

A steel erector was killed when he fell 70 feet from a steel tower which he was helping to build. His widow sued the employer for negligence. If the worker had been wearing a safety belt he would not have been killed by the fall. The employer had provided safety belts on the site in question until two or three days before the accident when they had been removed. The dead worker was an experienced steel erector and would probably not have worn a safety belt if one had been provided. The employer had never instructed the dead worker to wear a safety belt and it was only in exceptional circumstances that any of the workers did wear them.

Held. The employers were not liable to pay damages. Their breach of duty in not supplying safety belts was not the cause of the damage suffered because the evidence showed that the deceased would not have worn a safety belt and the employer had no duty to exhort or instruct the employee to wear a safety belt.

21.5.7.4 Duty to provide reasonably competent fellow employees

Workers often rely on the competence of other workers for their safety. Several cases, such as the one which follows, have been concerned with injury caused by a practical joker.

■ *Hudson v Ridge Manufacturing Co Ltd* [1957] 2 QB 348

The claimant was injured by a fellow employee, one Chadwick, who the judge described as 'not over-intelligent and [who] appears to have grown to manhood with childish pranks still part of his make-up'. For some years Chadwick frequently engaged in horseplay and skylarking and often tripped people up. Chadwick frequently teased the claimant. He grabbed the claimant, who was crippled, from behind and forced him down to the ground. The claimant put out his arm to save himself and his wrist was broken in the fall. Chadwick had been warned by the foreman not to indulge in horseplay on many occasions but no further steps had been taken against him.

Held. The employers were liable to pay damages to the claimant. They had known about the potentially dangerous behaviour for some time and had failed to prevent it. They had therefore failed to take proper care of the claimant's safety.

An employer who takes all reasonable precautions will not have been negligent and will not therefore be liable to the employee. An example can be seen in *Latimer* v *AEC Ltd* [1953] AC 643. The floors of a factory became flooded during an unusually heavy rainstorm. The flood caused oil, which normally ran along a channel in the floor, to mix with the flood water on the factory floor. The factory floor was therefore in a slippery state when the flood subsided. Sawdust was spread where possible, but some areas of the floor were still slippery. An employee who was working in an area not treated with sawdust was trying to lift a heavy barrel onto a trolley when he slipped and injured his ankle. The House of Lords held that the employers were not negligent. Having regard to the degree of risk to employees, they had done all that a reasonable employer could be expected to do. The only way to have made sure that the accident did not happen would have been to close the factory down, and this was not reasonable in all the circumstances.

In Chapter 12 at 12.2.6.2 we saw that *volenti non fit injuria* provides a complete defence to negligence and that the contributory negligence of the claimant may result in his damages being reduced to the extent which is just and equitable.

In *ICI Ltd* v *Shatwell* [1965] AC 656 the employer was able to rely on *volenti non fit injuria* as a complete defence. Experienced and qualified shot firers had been given proper instructions as to how to test detonators. These instructions involved retreating into a shelter before making the tests. In complete contravention of these instructions the claimant and others tested detonators. The claimant was badly injured when testing detonators without retreating to the shelter. The House of Lords held that *volenti non fit injuria* provided the employer with a complete defence.

Test your understanding

1 Does the Health and Safety at Work etc. Act 1974 impose civil or criminal sanctions against employers who neglect the health and safety of their employees?

2 How is the Act enforced?

3 How is the Act supplemented by European law?

4 What will an injured employee need to prove in order to sue the employer for negligence?

5 What are the three particular aspects of the employer's duty of care to employees?

Answers

1   The Health and Safety at Work etc. Act 1974 imposes criminal sanctions on employers who neglect the health and safety of their employees.

2   The Act is enforced by the Health and Safety Executive and by local authority enforcement officers.

3   Article 137 of the Treaty of Rome allows the passing of directives to improve the working environment and to protect workers' health and safety and working conditions. Six important Regulations were passed in 1992.

4   The employee will need to prove that the employer owed him a duty of care, that this duty was breached and that he suffered a foreseeable type of damage as a consequence.

5   The three particular aspects of the employer's duty of care are to provide safe plant and equipment, a safe system of work and reasonably competent fellow employees.

21.6 · Maternity rights

Female employees are given several rights in connection with childbirth and pregnancy. The Pregnant Workers Directive (92/85/EEC) required changes to existing law and these changes have been superimposed on the old law. When used in the Employment Rights Act 1996, 'childbirth' means the birth of a living child or the birth of a child whether living or dead after 24 weeks of pregnancy.

21.6.1 Time off for ante-natal care

Section 55(1) ERA 1996 provides that an employee who is pregnant, and who has made an appointment to attend any place for the purpose of receiving ante-natal care, must be given time off by the employer to keep the appointment. The appointment in question must have been made on the advice of a registered medical practitioner, a registered midwife or a registered health visitor. The employee is also entitled to be paid the appropriate hourly rate for the period when she is absent.

This right is given whether the pregnant employee is full or part-time, and no matter how short her period of continuous employment. If the employee is unreasonably refused the time off work, or is not paid the appropriate amount, she can bring a case before an employment tribunal. The case must be brought within three months of the appointment concerned, although the tribunal has the power to extend this period. The tribunal can make a declaration that the complaint is well founded, and order that the employer pays the amount he should have paid.

Except as regards the first appointment, the pregnant employee must produce a statement from the registered medical practitioner etc stating that she is pregnant, and an appointment card or some other document showing that an appointment has been made.

21.6.2 Time off for dependants

Section 57A ERA 1996 allows employees to take a reasonable amount of time off, during working hours, to provide assistance to a dependant who gives birth or in other specified circumstances. A dependant is defined as a spouse, a child, a parent or a person who is a live-in lover, as well as any person who reasonably relies on the employee to make arrangements for the provision of care. The entitlement is available if it is necessary:

(1)   to make arrangements to provide care for a dependant who is ill, giving birth, injured or assaulted;
(2)   in consequence of the death of a dependant;
(3)   because of the unexpected disruption or termination of arrangements for the care of a dependant; or
(4)   to deal with an incident which involves a child of the employee and which occurs unexpectedly during school hours.

In all these cases the employee must tell the employer the reason for his absence as soon as reasonably practicable. Illness includes mental illness. There is no right to be paid during time off work to look after dependants.

A complaint that time off has not been allowed can be made to an employment tribunal within three months of the refusal. The tribunal has the usual power to extend this period. It can declare the complainant's rights and award compensation, which can take account of any loss to the complainant which is attributable to the matter complained of.

21.6.3 Parental leave

The Maternity and Parental Leave Regulations 1999 give all employees who have one year's continuous employment the right to take parental leave to care for their children. Thirteen weeks' unpaid leave will be allowed in respect of each child. The leave must be taken before the child's fifth birthday, unless the child is disabled, in which case the leave must be taken before the child's 18th birthday. The employee must give at least four weeks' notice of taking the leave and the notice must always be at least twice the length of the leave which is to be taken. So if three weeks' leave is to be taken, six weeks' notice of this must be given. The employer can postpone the leave, for up to six months, if the needs of the business make this necessary and if it is reasonable to do so.

The employee remains employed during the period of leave and has a right to return to the same job after the leave has ended. Where the leave taken is more than four weeks the employer may offer a similar job instead of the previously held job, as long as the conditions of service are at least as favourable. There is no right to be paid during parental leave.

The Regulations' fallback scheme requires leave to be taken in blocks or multiples of one week and that only four weeks may be taken in any one year. If the employer prevents the employee from taking the leave, or attempts to do so, a complaint can be made to an employment tribunal.

21.6.4 Suspension on maternity grounds

An employee is regarded as suspended from work on maternity grounds if, in consequence of any legislation or official code of practice, the employer suspends her on the ground that she is pregnant, has recently given birth or is breastfeeding a child. However, the woman is only regarded as suspended for as long as she continues to be employed by the employer but is not provided with work or does not perform the work she normally performed before the suspension. The employee has a right to be offered suitable alternative work if the employer has such work available. Such suitable alternative work must be given on equally favourable terms, must be suitable in relation to the employee, and must not be substantially less favourable than her previous terms. An employee who is suspended on maternity grounds is entitled to be paid the normal weekly wage while she is suspended, unless she unreasonably refused the offer of suitable alternative employment.

Earlier in this chapter we saw that the Management of Health and Safety at Work Regulations 1992 required employers to carry out a risk assessment of the health and safety of employees while they are at work. Such a risk assessment could require the employer to suspend an employee on maternity grounds.

21.6.5 Right to maternity leave of absence

In addition to the two weeks' compulsory maternity leave after the birth of a child, all pregnant employees have the right to at least 26 weeks' maternity leave. The employee may choose the date on which the maternity leave period starts. During the maternity leave the employee is entitled to all the benefits of her terms and conditions of employment, except wages or salary, which would have applied if she had not been absent. An employee who has been continuously employed for one year at the beginning of the eleventh week before the expected date of childbirth, has the right to return to work after the maternity leave with all seniority rights intact. At the same time the employee is bound by the obligations arising under the terms and conditions of her contract of employment.

The Maternity and Parental Leave Regulations 1999 make the following, rather technical, rules.

An employee is entitled to **ordinary maternity leave** if at least 21 days before the maternity leave is to start (or if that is not reasonably practicable, as soon as is reasonably practicable) she notifies her employer of: (i) her pregnancy; (ii) the expected week of childbirth; and (iii) the date on which she intends her maternity leave to start. In addition, if requested to do so by the employer, the employee must produce a certificate from a registered medical practitioner or a registered midwife stating the expected week of childbirth.

The employee may not begin the maternity leave earlier than the eleventh week before the expected date of childbirth.

An employee is entitled to **additional maternity leave** if she has been continuously employed for at least one year at the beginning of the eleventh week before the expected date of childbirth. Ordinary maternity leave continues for 26 weeks after its commencement. But if any statutory provision prevents the employee from returning to work on account of her having given birth, the ordinary maternity leave extends until this provision allows her to return to work. Additional maternity leave starts when ordinary maternity leave finishes. It can continue for a further 26 weeks. If an employee is dismissed during either maternity leave period the leave period ends at the time of the dismissal. The employee is not entitled to remuneration during maternity leave unless her contract provides that she is. However, **statutory maternity pay** is payable for 18 weeks. The woman's earnings must be enough for her to pay national insurance contributions (she must have earned at least £66 a week) and she must have been continuously employed for 26 weeks by the end of the 14th week before the baby is due. The first six weeks' statutory maternity pay are calculated as 90% of gross average weekly earnings. The other twenty weeks are paid at a minimum of £100 per week, unless the employee does not usually earn this much. Employers pay the SMP but get a rebate on their national insurance contributions. The rebate is 92%, unless the employer is a small employer paying less than £20 000 p.a. in National Insurance, when it is 100% plus a 7% handling charge.

A woman who wants to come back to work before the end of her maternity leave can do so but must give the employer 21 days' notice.

Maternity allowance is payable to women who earn at least £30 a week, but who do not qualify for maternity pay from their employer. The amount is 90% of the woman's weekly earnings.

21.6.5.1 Right to return after maternity leave

If the maternity leave taken was for a period of four weeks or less, the employee has a right to return to the same job. If the employee takes maternity leave of more than four weeks, the employer may provide a suitable alternative job instead if it is not reasonably practicable for the employee to return to her old job. The terms and conditions of this alternative employment must be no less favourable than the terms and conditions of the previous employment.

An employee is **automatically unfairly dismissed** if the reason for the dismissal was connected with pregnancy, childbirth, or the fact that she took or tried to take maternity leave. When calculating a week's pay for the purposes of ERA 1996, any lesser amount paid to an employee who was off work on maternity or parental leave should not be used. Instead the amount the employee would actually have earned if she had worked should be used.

21.6.6 Paternity leave and pay

Section 80A of the Employment Act 2002, as expanded by the Paternity and Adoption Leave Regulations 2002 (SI 2002 No. 2788), gives rights to paternity leave and paternity pay. In order to qualify for paternity leave, the employee must satisfy three conditions. First, the employee must have responsibility for the new child's upbringing or expect to have this responsibility. Second, he must either be the biological father of the child or he must be the husband or partner of the child's mother. Third, he must have had at least 26 weeks' continuous employment 15 weeks before the baby is due to be born.

Paternity leave can either be for one week or for two consecutive weeks. It cannot be for parts of a week but it can begin midweek. The leave can begin either from the date of the child's birth or at some later date, but it must be completed 56 days after the child was born. If the mother gives birth to twins no extra paternity leave is available. The rate of statutory paternity pay is currently either £100 a week or, if the average weekly earnings are less than £100, 90% of average weekly earnings. Other contractual benefits must also be received. Employees who do not earn enough to pay any national insurance contributions are not entitled to statutory paternity pay.

Employees intending to take statutory paternity leave must inform their employers at least 15 weeks before the baby is expected. They must say when the baby is due, when they want the leave to start, and whether they want one week's leave or two weeks' leave. Employees are obliged to give the employer a completed self-certificate which provides evidence of their entitlement to statutory paternity pay. A model certificate can be found on the DTI website, www.dti.gov.uk. Employees who take statutory paternity leave are entitled to return to work afterwards and must not be discriminated against for having taken the leave. Employers can reclaim from the government about 90% of the amount which they have paid in statutory paternity pay.

21.7 · Adoption leave and pay

When a couple adopt a child, s.75A of the Employment Act 2002 entitles one member of the couple to time off work with statutory adoption pay. In addition, the other member of the couple, or a partner of an individual who adopts, may be entitled to paternity leave and pay.

In order to claim adoption leave the employee must have worked continuously for the employer for 26 weeks and be newly matched with a child by an adoption agency. Such employees are entitled to 26 weeks' **ordinary adoption leave**, during which they are entitled to statutory adoption pay, and an additional 26 weeks' **additional adoption leave**. The leave can start either on the date of the child's placement or 14 days before the expected date of the placement. The rate of statutory adoption pay is £100 a week or 90% of the normal weekly wage if this is less than £100. Adopters have to give notice of their intention to take adoption leave. Employers can also ask for a matching certificate from the adoption agency. Those taking time off are entitled to contractual benefits other than pay which they would normally receive and have a right to return to work after the adoption leave. Employers can reclaim about 90% of money paid in adoption leave from the Government. The statutory rates of maternity pay, paternity pay and adoption pay increase periodically.

21.8 · Time off for dependants

All employees are entitled under s.57A ERA 1996 to take time off work to look after dependants in an emergency. The right can arise in the following circumstances: if assistance is needed when a dependant gives birth, is injured or assaulted; to provide care for a dependant who is ill or injured; when a dependant dies; when there is an unexpected disruption or ending of arrangements for the care of a dependant; or when an incident involving the employee's child arises unexpectedly during school hours. Dependants include spouses, children, parents and people who live in the same house as the employee. It also includes people who reasonably rely on the employee. There is no entitlement to pay during the time off.

21.9 · Flexible working for parents

Section 80F of the Employment Act 2002 has introduced a right for parents with children under six years old to apply for flexible working. In the case of disabled children the age limit is 18. Employers will have a statutory duty to consider these applications seriously but there is no automatic right to work flexibly.

Only employees with at least 26 weeks' continuous employment can apply. They must either be the child's mother, father, adopter, guardian or foster parent or be married to such a person. They must be making the application so that they can care for a child for whom they have, or expect to have, responsibility for bringing up. Only one application can be made every 12 months and agency workers cannot apply.

The application can ask for a change of hours, a change to the times of work or to work from home. If the application is accepted then the change will be permanent unless the parties agree otherwise. As a change in working pattern might involve a drop in pay, applicants need to think things through carefully before applying. Once the employer receives a written application, a meeting with the employee must be arranged within 28 days. At this meeting the application, and other possible solutions, are considered. Within 14 days of the meeting the employer has to write to the employee either agreeing to a new date on which a new work pattern starts or giving reasons why the application has been refused.

21.10 · The national minimum wage

The National Minimum Wage Act 1998 provides that workers aged 20 or over should be paid a minimum wage of £4.50 an hour, while workers between 18 and 20 are entitled to a minimum wage of £3.80 an hour. Workers aged 22 or over, and who are receiving accredited training, have a minimum level of £3.80 an hour for six months after starting to work for a new employer. (After six months these workers are entitled to the national minimum wage.) These rates were set by the Government on the advice of the Low Pay Commission, which consulted various organisations.

The employer is required to keep records relating to pay, and workers are given a right of access to those records. Workers may require the employer to produce the records, and may inspect, examine and copy them. However, these rights are only available if the worker believes, on reasonable grounds, that there has been or will be a breach of the requirement to pay the minimum wage, and the rights are necessary to establish whether or not this is the case. The worker is entitled to exercise the rights accompanied by any other person he sees fit. If the worker is not allowed access to the records an employment tribunal may declare a complaint well founded and award the complainant 80 hours' pay at the minimum wage rate. The burden of proof is on the employer to show that the national minimum wage is being paid. The worker has the right not to suffer any detriment on the grounds of his having taken any action under the Act. A worker who alleges that he has suffered such a detriment may take the case to an employment tribunal. The usual three-month period applies in respect of bringing a claim and the tribunal has the usual power to extend this period. The tribunal can award a payment to an individual to bring the amount he was paid up to the amount he ought to have been paid.

The Act protects all workers, whether they work under a contract of employment or not and no matter what the size of the business for which they work. Apprentices are protected by the Act, but not if they are under 19 or for the first 12 months of their contracts if they are under 26. Workers who do not work under a contract of employment are protected if they contract to perform personally any work or services for another, as long as the other is not a client or customer of any profession or business undertaking carried on by the individual. Those who are genuinely self-employed are therefore not covered by the Act. A worker who is not an employee, but who is dismissed on the grounds of having taken action under the Act, is entitled to a payment which would equal the payment of a basic award for unfair dismissal if the worker had been an employee.

A worker's hourly rate is calculated by reference to a 'relevant pay reference period', which is usually one month. Matters such as incentive bonuses and performance-related pay do count when calculating the hourly rate. But matters such as overtime or shift allowances, do not. Therefore, a 22-year-old paid a basic hourly rate of £4.50 per hour plus 20% shift allowance would be being paid less than the minimum wage, even though his pay for hours worked would be £5.40. But a 23-year-old salesman paid a basic rate of £3 an hour would not be paid less than the minimum wage if he always earned an additional £100 commission every week. The only benefit in kind which can be used in calculating the hourly rate is accommodation. Any attempt to contract out of the provisions of the Act is void.

The Inland Revenue will be able to enforce the Act on behalf of individual workers and can serve penalty notices on employers who are not complying with the provisions of the Act. These penalty notices fine the employer £9 a day, per worker, as regards workers who were being paid less than the minimum wage. The employer has four weeks to appeal against such a notice. The amount of the financial penalty for failure to pay the minimum wage is twice the hourly amount of the national minimum wage in respect of each worker to whom the failure to comply relates for each day during which the failure to comply has continued in respect of the worker. The burden of proof is on the employer to show that he did pay the minimum wage.

The Act protects not only employees, but also agency workers, home workers and Crown employees. Those serving in the armed forces are not protected, nor are voluntary workers, religious and other community workers, prisoners or employees such as au pairs who work and live as part of a family. Perhaps the biggest gap is that employees under the age of 18 are not protected.

If a worker is dismissed because he has become entitled to the national minimum wage, or to a higher rate of the national minimum wage, this may be unfair dismissal even if the worker has not served the usual qualifying period of one year's continuous employment.

An employer who breaches the Act commits a criminal offence, the maximum fine for which is £5 000.

21.11 · The Transfer of Undertakings (Protection of Employment) Regulations 1981 (TUPE)

At common law the contract of employment is personal between the employer and the employee, and so a worker is dismissed if the employer transfers the undertaking to another employer. The TUPE Regulations were passed to give effect to the Acquired Rights Directive (77/187/EEC). This provided that when a business undertaking is transferred the rights of its employees should be protected and be enforceable against the new employer, the transferee.

The TUPE Regulations apply when an undertaking situated in the UK is transferred to another person and the undertaking retains its identity after the transfer. The Regulations do not apply when a company's shares are bought by new shareholders, because the company continues to be the employer and there is therefore no transfer of the business undertaking. An 'undertaking' includes any trade or business, and non-profit-making organisations such as charities could be included. Regulation 5(1) provides that a relevant transfer shall not terminate the contract of employment of any person employed by the transferor. The contract continues in effect as if originally made between the employee and the person to whom the undertaking is transferred, the transferee. Regulation 5(2) provides that all the transferor's rights, duties, powers and liabilities are transferred to the transferee. Anything done by the transferor before the transfer is deemed to have been done by the transferee.

Regulations 4A and 4B allow the employee to object to being transferred. If the employee does object, the contract of employment will be terminated but the employee will not be regarded for any purpose as having been dismissed. However, if substantial and detrimental changes are made in the employee's working conditions the employee can terminate the contract without notice and claim unfair dismissal. The mere fact that the identity of the employer has changed is not enough to amount to a substantial and detrimental change in working conditions.

The only rights which are not transferred are occupational pension rights. Pension rights already accrued are protected but the new employer's occupational pension scheme might be less beneficial than that of the transferor. However, if this is the case it might mean that the overall terms and conditions of the transferee were inferior and the employee might therefore have a claim of unfair dismissal. The new employer can worsen conditions of employment if this is possible under the terms of the contract of employment, but not if this worsening is connected with the transfer of the undertaking.

If an employee is dismissed, either before or after a relevant transfer, this will amount to an unfair dismissal as long as the reason or principal reason for the dismissal is the transfer or a reason connected with it. However, this is not the case if the reason for the dismissal, or the principal reason, is an economic, technical or organisational reason entailing changes in either the workforce of the transferor or the transferee before or after a relevant transfer. In such a case the dismissal is regarded as having been for a substantial reason of a kind such as to justify the dismissal of an employee holding the position which the employee held. Continuous employment is preserved, despite the transfer, but an employee will need to have at least one year's continuous employment in order to make a claim for unfair dismissal.

Where a collective agreement exists between the transferor and any trade union which the transferor recognises, then after the transfer the agreement shall be regarded as having been made by the transferee and the trade union. If a trade union is recognised to any extent by the transferor before the transfer then the union will be deemed to have been recognised to the same extent by the transferee. The transferor has a duty to inform employee representatives about the transfer and to consult them about the transfer. If this is not done a complaint may be made to an employment tribunal, which may make a declaration that it has not been done and order the payment of compensation to affected employees.

The Regulations have helped preserve the pay of many groups of employees whose pay was reduced as a result of compulsory competitive tendering and the contracting out of services. It is not possible to make an agreement to contract out of the main provisions of the Regulations.

21.12 · The Working Time Regulations 1998

These Regulations were passed to give effect to the Working Time Directive (93/104/EEC) and the Young Workers Directive (94/33/EC).

21.12.1 Maximum weekly working time

The main provision of the Regulations is that a worker's working time, including overtime, shall not exceed 48 hours for each seven days, averaged out over any period of 17 weeks' employment. The employer has a duty to take all reasonable steps, in keeping with the need to protect the health and safety of workers, to ensure that the limit is complied with. This duty arises in respect of every worker employed by him. Days taken off as annual leave, periods of sick leave and maternity leave are regarded as excluded days. In assessing the average working time of a worker for each seven day period, an appropriate number of days is added on to cater for excluded days. Young workers (aged under 18) are not allowed to work more than 8 hours a day or 40 hours a week.

■ Example

Jim worked in a factory for 50 hours a week for 15 straight weeks. He then took two weeks annual leave and came back to work, doing 46 hours a week for the next two weeks. The days taken as annual leave are excluded. Jim has therefore 750 hours + 92 hours = 842 hours in a 17-week period. This averages out at slightly over 49.5 hours a week and so the Regulations have been breached.

The 48-hour limit does not apply if the worker agrees in writing that it should not. So if in the above example Jim had agreed that the 48-hour limit should not apply, the Regulations would not have been breached.

21.12.2 Protection of night workers

The normal hours of night workers in any 17-week period should not exceed an average of eight hours for each 24 hours. Rest periods do not count as working days.

An employer has a duty to ensure that no night worker employed by him whose work involves special hazards, or heavy physical or mental strain, works for more than eight hours in any 24-hour period in which the worker performs the night work. This differs from the approach on general working hours and general night time working hours in that there is no averaging out over a 17-week period. As regards special hazards or work involving heavy strain, the Regulations are breached if the worker ever works more than eight hours in any 24. Work is to be regarded as involving special hazards or heavy strain if a collective agreement or workforce agreement identifies it as such work.

The employer must not assign a worker to night work unless: (a) the employer has ensured that the worker has the opportunity of a free health assessment before going on to the night work; or (b) the worker has already had an assessment and the employer has no reason to believe that the assessment is no longer valid. In addition, the employer has a duty to ensure that all night workers employed by him have the opportunity of a free health assessment at regular intervals. Young workers, that is to say those under the age of 18, are not allowed to work between 10 p.m. and 6 a.m.

21.12.3 Entitlement to daily and weekly rest

Where the **pattern of work** is such as to put the health and safety of a worker at risk, in particular because the work is monotonous or the work-rate is predetermined, the employer must ensure that the worker is given adequate rest breaks.

The employer has a duty to keep records to show that the provisions of the Regulations are being complied with, and to keep such records for two years from the date on which they were made.

An adult worker is entitled to a rest period of at least 11 consecutive hours in each 24-hour period during which he works for the employer. As regards young workers (those under 18 years of age) the entitlement is 12 consecutive hours. The rest periods are not applicable where people work split-shifts or work periods of short duration.

An adult worker is entitled to an uninterrupted rest period of not less than 24 hours in each seven-day period during which he works for his employer. However, the employer can determine that instead an adult worker is entitled to two uninterrupted periods of at least 24 hours in each 14 days, or one uninterrupted period of at least 48 hours in each 14-day period. Young workers are entitled to a rest period of at least 48 hours in each seven-day period. The entitlement of young persons may be interrupted if they work split-shifts or work for periods of short duration. They may also be reduced to 36 consecutive hours where this is justified by technical or organisational reasons.

21.12.4 Entitlement to rest breaks

Where an adult worker's daily working time is more than six hours he is entitled to a rest break. This period, which the employee can spend away from his work station if he has one, must not be of less than 20 minutes. It can be for longer if a collective or workforce agreement provides that it should be. Young workers are entitled to a rest break of 30 minutes, which should be consecutive if possible, if their daily working time is more than 4.5 hours.

21.12.5 Entitlement to annual leave

Workers are entitled to annual leave of at least four weeks. If the worker does not work for a full year entitlement is proportional, and any fraction of a day's leave is to count as a full day's leave. However, those with less than 13 weeks' continuous service have no entitlement to annual leave. The leave may be taken in instalments. However, it can only be taken in respect of the leave year in which it becomes due, and can only be replaced by a payment in lieu where the employment is terminated. If the employment is terminated and the worker has taken less leave than had proportionately become due to him, the employer has to make a payment in lieu of leave.

As a general principle, a worker may take his leave entitlement when he wishes. The worker must give the employer notice of when the leave is to be taken. However, the employer may require that leave is taken, or is not taken, on particular days by giving the worker notice of this before the relevant date. This date is calculated as twice the number of days in advance of the beginning of the leave as the number of days to which the notice relates. In other words, if either an employer or an employee is giving notice of the taking of 15 days' leave, the notice must be given 30 days before the date on which the leave is to commence. The rights as to dates on which leave is to be taken may be varied or excluded by a relevant agreement. (An agreement which is part of a collective agreement, or which is in writing and legally enforceable between the worker and the employee.) The worker is entitled to be paid while on leave.

21.12.6 Who is protected

The definition of a worker is the same as the definition in the National Minimum Wage Regulations 1998. However, the Regulations do not apply to doctors in training, the police or the armed forces. Domestic servants are protected only as regards daily and weekly rest periods, rest breaks and annual leave. Those who work in transport, or sea fishing, or other activity at sea only gain protection in respect of health assessment for night workers, a safe pattern of work and annual leave.

If the worker's time is not measured or predetermined, most of the Regulations do not apply. The Regulations suggest that this exemption might apply to: (a) managing executives or other persons with autonomous decision-taking powers; or (b) family workers; or (c) workers officiating at religious ceremonies in churches and religious communities.

The Regulations contain miscellaneous other special exemptions, including:

(a) where the worker works at separate places of work which are distant from one another;
(b) where security and surveillance activities require a permanent presence;
(c) where a worker's continuity of presence is needed in relation to hospital services, airport or dock work, media or postal work, work in the industries which provide services to households, industries where there cannot be an interruption for technical reasons, research and development activities and agriculture;
(d) where there is a foreseeable surge of activity in relation to agriculture, tourism or postal services;
(e) where the worker's activities are affected by an occurrence beyond the control of the employer, or exceptional events which could not have been foreseen or an accident or the imminent risk of an accident.

21.12.7 Enforcement of the Regulations

The Health and Safety Executive and local authority inspectors may enforce the Regulations by prosecuting employers who breach them. Employees may bring infringements before an employment tribunal with the usual protection against victimisation on account of having taken action under the Regulations. If an employee is dismissed for having taken action under the Regulations this is automatically unfair dismissal.

21.13 · Authorised deductions from wages

There is no requirement that employees should be paid in cash, rather than into a bank account or by cheque. The way in which an employee is paid is determined by the terms of the contract. However, ERA 1996 ss.13–27 make provisions about protection of wages, and an outline of those provisions is set out below.

21.13.1 Right not to suffer unauthorised deductions

An employer is not allowed to make a deduction from a worker's wages unless: (a) it is authorised or required by a statutory provision or a relevant provision of the worker's contract; or (b) the worker has previously signified in writing his agreement or consent to the making of the deduction. If the deduction is allowed by a written term of the employee's contract, the employee must be given a copy of the term before the deduction is made by the employer. If the deduction is authorised by an implied term of the contract (whether written or not) the existence and effect of the term must be notified to the employee before the deduction is made. Such a notification would usually be in the worker's wage packet. The statutorily allowed deductions will include matters such as tax, national insurance and deductions made under the Child Support Act 1991.

Whenever the worker is paid less than he should be paid, the missing amount of money is to be treated as a deduction. However, this does not apply if the deficiency was caused by an error, or on account of the employee's conduct, or was in respect of a sum of money which cannot be classed as 'wages'.

The reclaiming of the accidental overpayment of wages is regarded as an excepted deduction and the general provisions do not apply. Deductions made because the employee has been on strike or in consequence of any disciplinary proceedings are also excluded.

21.13.2 The meaning of 'wages'

Section 27(1) ERA 1996 states that 'wages' in relation to a worker, means any sum payable to the worker in connection with his employment, including:

(a) any fee, bonus, commission, holiday pay or other emoluments referable to his employment, whether payable under his contract or otherwise;
(b) statutory sick pay;
(c) statutory maternity pay;
(d) a guarantee payment;
(e) any payment for time off for carrying out trade union activities;
(f) remuneration on suspension on medical or maternity grounds;
(g) any sum payable under a reinstatement or re-engagement order; and
(h) payment under an order for continuance of employment under s.130 of the Act, or under s.164 of the Trade Union and Labour Relations (Consolidation) Act 1992 (TULRCA 1992).

Some of these matters are self-explanatory but others need to be explained. Category (a) is very broad, including overtime pay, shift allowances and bonuses. It does not include payments in lieu of wages, which are damages rather than wages.

A **guarantee payment** entitles an employee to be paid for a day during any part of which he would normally be required to work but on which he is not provided with work due to: (a) a falling off of the employer's need for work to be done; or (b) any other occurrence relating to the employer's business in relation to the need for work of the type in question to be done. The payment is only due to workers who have at least one month's continuous employment. Those employed on a fixed term contract of less than three months' duration are excluded. Seasonal workers are also excluded, as the payment is not due if the employment is expected to last for less than three months. The amount of the payment cannot exceed £17.30 a day and an employee cannot be entitled to be paid for more than five days in any three month period. There is no entitlement if the employer provides suitable alternative employment.

Suspension on maternity grounds was dealt with above at 21.6.4. Section 64 ERA 1996 provides that an employee who is suspended from work by his employer **on medical grounds** is entitled to be paid while he is suspended for a period not exceeding 26 weeks. The suspension must have arisen as a result of a requirement of a statute or statutory instrument or a recommendation of an approved code of practice. The length of service qualifications are the same as for employees to receive a guarantee payment. The employee is only entitled to the payment if he is fit for work. The provision may seem strange but it applies when a worker is not allowed to work because he has been too exposed to lead, radiation or other specified hazardous substances.

Reinstatement and re-engagement orders were considered in the previous chapter when we considered the remedies for unfair dismissal. We saw that the orders are infrequently made.

An order for **continuance of employment** under s.130 of the Act is a form of interim relief which is applicable when an employee has been unfairly dismissed for an inadmissible reason. The inadmissible reasons in question concern having carried out health and safety duties, or duties as trustee of an occupational pension scheme or as a trade union representative. A similar right exists under TULRCA s.192 when a protective award is made in a redundancy situation.

21.14 · Time off work

21.14.1 Time off for public duties

Section 50 ERA 1996 provides that an employee who is a magistrate must be given time off during working hours to perform the duties of his office. Time off to attend meetings and otherwise discharge their duties must also be given to employees who are members of the following: a local authority; a statutory tribunal; a police authority; a Service Authority for National Crime prevention; a board of prison visitors or a prison visiting committee; a relevant health authority; a relevant education body; the Environment Agency; or the Scottish Environment Protection Agency.

The amount of time allowed to be taken is the amount reasonable in all the circumstances. These circumstances include: (a) how much time is needed to perform the duties in question; (b) how much time the employee has already had off for public duties or trade union duties and activities; and (c) the circumstances of the employer's business and the effect which the time off has on the running of that business.

A complaint that time off has not been allowed can be presented to an employment tribunal within the usual time limits. The tribunal may declare the complaint well founded and award the complainant compensation. The amount of compensation should be whatever is just and equitable in all the circumstances, having regard to: (a) the employer's default in not allowing the employee to take the time off; and (b) any loss sustained by the employee which is attributable to the matters to which the complaint relates. The employer does not need to pay the employee for time taken off under s.50.

21.14.2 Time off to look for work or training

Section 52 ERA 1996 allows an employee who is made redundant reasonable time off during the employer's working hours, before the end of his notice, to look for new employment or make arrangements for training for future employment. In order to be afforded this right, the employee must have had two years' continuous employment by the time his notice would have ended. During the time off the employee is entitled to be paid at the usual hourly rate. An employee who is not afforded this right can bring a claim before an employment tribunal in the usual way. The tribunal may declare his complaint well founded and order the employer to pay the employee the amount due to him.

21.14.3 Time off for pension scheme trustees and employee representatives

Employees who are members of a relevant occupational pension scheme are allowed time off, with pay, for performing any of their duties as trustees or undergoing training relevant to the performance of those duties. A very similar right is extended to those employees who are, or who have been elected, employee representatives. The compensation as regards employees not allowed time off for duties as occupational pension scheme trustees is the amount which the tribunal considers just and equitable. As regards employee representatives it is the amount of pay which he would have been entitled to if the employer had allowed him time off with pay. In both cases the tribunal may declare the complaint well founded.

21.14.4 Right to time off for young people for study or training

Employees aged 16 or 17 who are not in full-time education and who have not reached educational standards laid down by the Secretary of State, are entitled to time off, with pay, during working hours, to reach the relevant standard (Level 2). Employees aged 18 or over have the right to time off to complete study or training leading to a relevant qualification if they begun the training before reaching the age of 19. The amount of time is the amount which is reasonable in all of the circumstances having particular regard to: (a) the requirement of the employee's study or training; and (b) the circumstances of the employer's business and the effect of the employee's time off on the running of that business. An employment tribunal can declare the complaint well founded and award the employee the amount of pay he would have been entitled to if he had been given the time off.

21.14.5 Jury service

If an employee is called up for jury service then he has to attend unless he is in one of the excluded categories. The employer must allow the employee time off work to perform jury service. Jurors can be exempted from jury service if they can show a good reason for being excused. The courts are reluctant to allow exemption but if an employee's presence at work was particularly vital this could amount to a good reason.

21.15 · Procedure for bringing a claim before an employment tribunal

21.15.1 Time limits

A claim to gain a remedy or to enforce a statutory right must be made to an employment tribunal within the appropriate time limit. Generally, this time limit is three calendar months from the date of

the act complained of. So if the act complained of occurred on 20 January, the claim would have to be received by the tribunal on or before 19 April. However, where it is not reasonably practicable to present the claim within this period the tribunal can extend the period by the length of time which it considers reasonable. Where the act complained of continues over a period of time, the claim must be brought within three months of the end of this period. However, in cases of unfair dismissal the time limit is extended by a further three months if the employee sends Step 1 of the grievance procedure, or tries to submit Form IT1 within the initial three-month period. The time limit for a claim to a redundancy payment is six months from the relevant date. Again, the tribunal has a discretion to extend this limit.

21.15.2 Presenting a complaint and conciliation

A complaint must be presented in writing. Most complaints are made by completing Form IT1, which can be obtained from Job centres or from the offices of employment tribunals. This relatively short form requires details of the parties involved, the type of complaint being made, the name of anybody representing the employee, the type of work done by the employee, his normal hours and earnings and a brief description of the complaint. If the employer wishes to contest the case he must reply on Form IT3 within 14 days. Form IT3 requires the employer to indicate the grounds on which he intends to resist the application.

Copies of the complaint are sent to the employer and to a conciliation officer. The conciliation officer is an ACAS official, who has a statutory duty to try to promote a settlement between the employer and employee without the need for a tribunal hearing. Either party can ask for an attempt at conciliation, either before or after the complaint is presented. Even if neither party does request this, the conciliation officer will attempt conciliation unless he believes that there is no reasonable prospect of success. Any information revealed to the conciliation officer is inadmissible in subsequent tribunal proceedings unless the person who revealed it consents to it being admissible. It is not part of the conciliation officer's duties to inform employees of their rights and so a conciliation officer should not interfere with an agreement reached between employer and employee, even if he thinks the employee could have done better.

The tribunal may conduct a pre-hearing review, either at the request of one of the parties or on its own initiative. At this review a party can be ordered to pay a deposit of £150 if the tribunal considers that he has no reasonable prospect of success. If the party still pursues the case and loses it, he may forfeit the deposit and be ordered to pay costs.

21.15.3 Procedure at the tribunal

The tribunal sets its own procedure but tries to avoid a highly legalistic procedure. It can order a party to produce documents and to reveal more details of his position. The burden of proof is generally upon the applicant. The standard of proof is on a balance of probabilities. Strict rules of evidence may be relaxed. The tribunal's job is to apply the law. The system is adversarial, with the employer and the employee trying to prove their case, but the tribunal members adopt an interventionist approach and may themselves ask questions of witnesses or the parties.

The decisions of employment tribunals are almost always unanimous. When they are not unanimous it is almost always the case that one of the lay men sided with the legally qualified chairman. Very occasionally, the two laymen outvote the chairman. Generally, the tribunal gives an oral decision at the end of the case and follows this up with a written decision at a later date. The written decision should be full enough for the parties to know why they won or lost and for the EAT to see whether a question of law, which might be appealed against, arises.

Generally, the two sides pay their own costs. Costs can be awarded against a party who brought a vexatious or frivolous claim, or if it was that party's fault that the proceedings were postponed. In these circumstances an employment tribunal can award costs of up to £10 000.

21.15.4 Appeals

An appeal can be made to the EAT. Generally, such an appeal must be lodged within 42 days of receiving the full written decision of the employment tribunal. Legal aid may be available for such an appeal. With permission of either the EAT or the Court of Appeal, a further appeal may be made to the Court of Appeal. With permission of the Court of Appeal or the House of Lords, a further appeal may be made to the House of Lords. Where the outcome of an appeal will depend upon the correct application of EC law, and the meaning of the EC law is unclear, any court or tribunal may refer the matter to the ECJ. If the court is the final court of appeal it must make such a reference. Over the next few years it is proposed that Employment Tribunals and the EAT will be part of a unified Tribunal Service.

Test your understanding

1 What rights in respect of leave and time off work does a pregnant woman have?

2 Do women have the right to be paid while on maternity leave?

3 What is the national minimum wage for adult workers and for those under 20?

4 What are the main rights given to workers by the TUPE Regulations 1981?

5 What is the main provision of the Working Time Regulations 1998?

6 What rights does a worker have in relation to deductions from wages?

7 On what grounds do employees have a right to time off work?

8 In what circumstances will an employee be entitled to paternity leave and pay?

9 In what circumstances will an employee be entitled to adoption leave and pay?

10 What rights does an employee have in respect of flexible working?

Answers

1 A pregnant woman is entitled to paid time off work to attend ante-natal appointments. In addition, all pregnant employees are entitled to up to 26 weeks' maternity leave. Additional maternity leave is available to women who have been continuously employed for one year by the beginning of the eleventh week before the expected date of childbirth.

2 Women on maternity leave are entitled to all the benefits of their contract of employment except pay. However statutory maternity pay can be claimed for the 26 week ordinary maternity leave period.

3 For adult workers the national minimum wage is £4.50 an hour. For those between 18 and 20 it is £3.80 an hour. There is no entitlement to the minimum wage for those under the age of 18.

4 The TUPE Regulations provide that where a business undertaking is transferred to a transferee and it retains its identity, the contractual right of the workers should be enforceable against the transferee. In addition, continuous service worked for the transferor should be regarded as having been worked for the transferee.

5 Although they can be contracted out of, the Working Time Regulations provide that workers should not work more than 48 hours a week, averaged out over a 17-week period. Other rights relating to rest breaks and annual leave are conferred. Special rights are conferred on night workers.

6 Unauthorised deductions cannot be made from a worker's wages.

7 Workers must be allowed time off work for public duties. Those made redundant must be allowed a reasonable amount of time off work to look for work or training. Pensions scheme trustees and employee representatives must be given time off work to perform their duties. Young people are allowed time off for study and training if they have not reached the Level 2 educational standard. Workers are also allowed time off for jury service. Time may also be taken off to look after dependants or as parental leave.

8 Employees with 26 weeks' continuous employment are entitled to paternity leave and pay if they are responsible for the child's upbringing, are the biological father of the child or the partner of the child's mother.

9 When a couple adopt a child, one of them, if he or she has 26 weeks' continuous employment, is entitled to 26 weeks' paid adoption leave and another 26 weeks' additional adoption leave.

10 Parents of children under six have the right to apply for flexible working and the employer has a duty to consider such an application seriously.

Key points

Equal Pay

- The Equal Pay Act requires that if a woman does like work, or work rated as equivalent to that of a male comparator her contract of employment should be deemed to include an equality clause.

- Men can claim equal treatment with a female comparator, but neither men nor women can claim equal treatment with a person of the same sex.

- An equality clause would modify the woman's contract of employment so that any of the terms of her contract were no less favourable than a similar term in the contract of the male comparator.

- The male comparator must be a man working for the same employer or an associated employer. The woman's work must be like work to that of the male comparator, or work rated as equivalent or work of equal value.

- Like work means that the work is broadly similar to that done by the male comparator. Work is rated as equivalent if a properly conducted job evaluation scheme has found it to be equivalent. Work is of equal value if the demands which the work places on the woman are similar to the demands which the male comparator's work places upon him.

- The employer has a defence if the variation in treatment is due to a genuine material factor which was not the difference in sex.

- If an applicant's claim is successful under the Act, an employment tribunal can award arrears of pay, backdated for six years, and damages.

Sex Discrimination Act

- The Sex Discrimination Act 1986 outlaws discrimination on the grounds of a person's sex or on the grounds that a person is married.

- The Act outlaws direct discrimination, indirect discrimination and victimisation.

- Direct discrimination occurs when an employer treats a woman less favourably on the grounds of her sex.

- Indirect discrimination occurs when the employer imposes a requirement which can be complied with by a considerably smaller proportion of women to whom the employer applies it than the proportion of men to whom the employer applies it.

- Victimisation occurs if a woman is treated less favourably on account of having enforced or taken other actions in respect of the Equal Pay Act 1970, the Sex Discrimination Act 1986 or the provisions of the Pensions Act 1995 which relate to equal treatment.

- An employer can be vicariously liable for acts of discrimination committed by employees in the course of their employment. However, the employer has a defence if he shows that he took reasonable steps to prevent the act of discrimination or to prevent acts of that description.

- It is permissible to discriminate: if the nature of the job calls for a man for reasons of physiology; for reasons of authenticity in dramatic entertainment; to preserve decency; because of the nature of the establishment where the work is done; where the location of the job requires that the employee lives in and the employer cannot reasonably provide sleeping and sanitary premises for women; in certain social work jobs; in certain jobs which involve travelling abroad; and where the job is one of two held by a married couple.

- A tribunal has the power to declare the complainant's rights, to award unlimited damages and to order the employer to end the discrimination.

- The Equal Opportunities Commission can carry out investigations, require people to give evidence, issue non-discrimination notices and bring individual cases before an employment tribunal.

■ It is unlawful to apply or operate discriminatory practices, publish discriminatory advertisements, instruct or pressurise others to discriminate or aid unlawful acts.

Race Relations Act

■ The Race Relations Act outlaws discrimination on racial grounds. Such discrimination can consist of direct discrimination, indirect discrimination or victimisation.

■ Discrimination is on racial grounds if it is on the grounds of colour, race, nationality or ethnic or national origins.

■ Being of a particular racial group can be a genuine occupational qualification for a job, but only on the grounds of authenticity in works of drama or art; authenticity where the job involves working in a place where food or drink are served; or in certain social work jobs.

■ Employers can be vicariously liable for discriminatory acts committed by their employees.

■ A tribunal has the power to declare the complainant's rights, to award unlimited damages and to order the employer to end the discrimination.

Disability Discrimination Act

■ The Disability Discrimination Act outlaws discrimination against disabled persons.

■ The Act regards a person as disabled if he has a physical or mental impairment which has a substantial and long-term adverse effect on his ability to carry out normal day-to-day activities.

■ Disabled persons are discriminated against if they are treated less favourably on account of being disabled and the employer cannot show that this is justified.

■ Employers have a positive duty to make adjustments and arrangements to cater for the needs of disabled employees.

■ Upon finding that a disabled person has been unlawfully discriminated against, a tribunal has the power to declare the complainant's rights, to award unlimited damages and to order the employer to end the discrimination.

■ As regards most types of employment, a person whose conviction has become spent can deny having been convicted, and if the person is dismissed on account of a spent conviction this will amount to unfair dismissal.

■ The Part-Time Workers (Prevention of Less Favourable Treatment) Regulations 2000 prevent discrimination against part-time workers by applying the pro-rata principle.

■ The Employment Equality (Sexual Orientation) Regulations 2003 outlaw discrimination on the grounds of sexual orientation, which means an orientation towards persons of the same sex, the opposite sex or both sexes.

■ The Equality (Religion or Belief) Regulations 2003 outlaw discrimination against employees, or those who contract to provide work personally, on the grounds of religion, religious belief, or similar philosophical belief.

■ The Fixed-term Employees (Prevention of Less Favourable Treatment) Regulations 2002 prevent discrimination against fixed term workers.

Health and safety at work

■ The Health and Safety at Work etc. Act 1974 imposes criminal sanctions on employers who do not look after the health and safety of their employees.

■ The Act is enforced by the Health and Safety Executive and by local authority enforcement officers.

■ The Act imposes particular duties on employers, manufacturers, designers, importers, suppliers and employees.

- Six directives, all passed in 1992, supplement the Act.
- An employee will be able to sue his employer in negligence if the employer breached a duty of care owed to that employee and if this breach caused a foreseeable type of loss.
- The employer's duty of care to employees particularly involves providing safe plant and equipment, a safe system of work and reasonably competent fellow employees.

Maternity rights and rights to time off work

- Pregnant employees are entitled to paid time off work to attend ante-natal care appointments.
- Employees are entitled to unpaid time off work to provide necessary assistance to dependants who are ill, giving birth, injured or assaulted. Time off can also be taken in consequence of a dependant's death, or because of unexpected disruption of care arrangements for a dependant, or to deal with an incident which involves the employee's child and which occurs unexpectedly during school hours.
- Employees are entitled to up to 13 weeks' parental leave in respect of each of their children.
- An employee who is suspended from work on maternity grounds is entitled to be paid during the period of suspension.
- All pregnant women are entitled to 26 weeks' maternity leave. This may not begin before the 11th week before the expected date of childbirth. Statutory maternity pay can be claimed during this leave.
- Women with one year's continuous employment are entitled to an additional 26 weeks maternity leave. This begins after the ordinary maternity leave has ended.
- Women have an entitlement to return to work after their maternity leave.

Other rights to leave or flexible working

- Employees with 26 weeks' continuous employment are entitled to paternity leave and pay if they are responsible for the child's upbringing, are the biological father of the child or the partner of the child's mother.
- When a couple adopt a child, one of them, if he or she has 26 weeks' continuous employment, is entitled to 26 weeks' paid adoption leave and another 26 weeks' additional adoption leave.
- An employee with at least one year's continuous employment can take 13 weeks' parental leave, in respect of each child under five, to look after the child or make arrangements for the child's welfare.
- Parents of children under six have the right to apply for flexible working and the employer has a duty to consider such an application seriously.

National minimum wage

- Workers aged 20 or over have a right to be paid the national minimum wage of £4.50 an hour. The rate is £3.80 an hour for those under 20.
- The hourly rate is calculated by reference to a one-month period.
- Employers must keep records showing that the national minimum wage is being paid. In certain circumstances employees have a right to access to these records.
- Workers who are not being paid the national minimum wage can bring a claim before an employment tribunal. In addition, the National Minimum Wage Act 1998 can be enforced by the Inland Revenue.

TUPE

■ When a business undertaking is transferred, and yet retains its identity, employees who work for the undertaking have the same employment rights against the transferee as they had against the transferor.

■ Continuous service worked for the transferor is regarded as having been worked for the transferee.

■ If the employee is dismissed for a reason connected with the transfer this will be an unfair dismissal.

■ Union agreements between the transferor and a trade union which the employer recognised are binding upon the transferee.

Working Time Regulations

■ The normal working week should not exceed 48 hours, averaged out over a 17-week period.

■ Night workers should not work more than eight hours in any 24, averaged out over a 17-week period.

■ Workers are entitled to daily and weekly rest periods.

■ Employees are entitled to four weeks' paid annual leave a year.

Time off work

■ Workers must be given time off work to perform their public duties.

■ Workers who have been made redundant are allowed time off work to look for work or training.

■ Young people who have not reached the Level 2 educational standard are allowed time off to reach this standard.

■ Employees must be allowed time off for jury service. However, it is possible that a court will excuse an employee from jury service if his presence at work is so vital as to amount to a good reason to be excused.

Bringing a claim to a tribunal

■ Generally, a claim to an employment tribunal must be made within three months of the act complained of.

■ The complaint is generally filed by filling in Form IT1. The employer replies on Form IT3 within 14 days if he wishes to contest the claim.

■ ACAS conciliation officers have a duty to attempt conciliation and settlement of the claim before it proceeds to a tribunal hearing.

■ Proceedings at an employment tribunal are relatively relaxed. Each side usually pays their own costs and legal aid is not available.

■ An appeal from the decision of an employment tribunal can be made to the EAT.

Summary questions

1 Alice works as a computer operator for Acme Ltd in Nottingham. She is paid £4.80 an hour. Brian who has worked in the same office as a computer operator for ten years is paid £6.20 an hour. If any of the computer operators experience a problem Brian is required to provide assistance, although such assistance is very rarely in fact required. Alice has heard that computer technicians employed by Acme Ltd in London earn £10 an hour and that female computer operators employed by a subsidiary company of Acme Ltd earn £5.90 an hour.

Advise Alice as to whether or not there are grounds on which she might bring a claim of equal pay and of any defences which Acme Ltd might have. Advise Alice also of the procedure which she would need to follow in order to bring a claim before an employment tribunal.

2 Old Co Ltd have advertised for an office administrator and a night time security guard. The advertisement states that the office staff must wear ties and that the security guards must have a driving licence. Belinda applied for the job as an office administrator. She did not wear a tie to the interview but did wear a smart business outfit. She did not get the job, which was given to a man. Caroline applied for the job as a night time guard. She was not given the job, which went to a man, despite her having had five years' experience in a similar job. The man had no experience. At the interview Caroline was asked if she had a driving licence. She enquired whether the job ever entailed driving and was told it did not, but that the employer preferred to take people with a driving licence as he thought this indicated a degree of general competence. Caroline has seen statistics that the percentage of women who hold a driving licence is considerably lower than the percentage of men who do.
Advise Belinda and Caroline as to whether or not they could bring a claim of sex discrimination. If either of the two women did successfully bring such a claim, what remedies could the employment tribunal award?

3 Benjamin, who is of Jamaican origin, is a Rastafarian. Three years ago Benjamin was injured in a car crash and this has confined him to a wheelchair. Benjamin works as an accounts clerk at a local college. As part of a major reorganisation, the college is moving the accounts department onto the third floor from the ground floor where it is currently situated. The college does not have a lift. Benjamin tells his office manager that he will not be able to work on the third floor as he will not be able to negotiate the stairs. The manager says that if Benjamin could not get to the third floor he would have to leave the job. Benjamin was considering applying for a job advertised by a different employer. However, the advertisement said 'Must be of smart appearance, no dreadlocks, ear-rings etc.' Benjamin applied for the job anyway. He was invited for an interview but when the employer saw his dreadlocks he refused to interview him.
Advise Benjamin as to any rights he might have against his current employer or against the employer who refused to interview him.

4 Charlie has worked in a bakery for seven years. The work is somewhat monotonous and Charlie seeks to enlighten the atmosphere by playing practical jokes. Charlie climbed into one of the mixing machines so that he could leap out and give a fellow employee, David, a surprise. Charlie has done this type of thing fairly frequently over the years. The foreman has often told him not to, but rather half-heartedly as he too seems to enjoy Charlie's antics. David is not working on the particular morning when Charlie hides in the mixing machine. Eric, a worker transferred from the cake department, turns on the mixing machine and Charlie is killed. All of the employees in Charlie's department know of the rule that the mixing machines must never be turned on unless they have been checked to see that no one is cleaning them or otherwise too near them. The transferred employee had not been told this. As a result of the accident the transferred employee suffers nervous shock and depression which keep him off work for eight months.
Advise the employers of any civil or criminal liability which they might have incurred.

5 Elaine has been continuously employed for three years. She has recently discovered that she is pregnant. Explain the rights to time off work to which Elaine will become entitled and the benefits which she is entitled to receive during this time off. Explain also any rights to time off work, and the benefits payable, which Elaine's husband might have in connection with the pregnancy, the child birth and becoming a parent.

6 At Gradgrind Ltd's factory workers work long hours. None of the workers have agreed to give up their rights under the Working Time Regulations. Jim who is 46 works five consecutive 12-hour day shifts for four weeks in a row and then has a week off. John works five 12-hour night shifts a week every week for five consecutive weeks and then has a week off. The time off taken by John and Jim is not annual leave, but is to compensate for the long hours worked in the previous weeks. Explain whether or not the Regulations have been breached and any entitlement to rest breaks which the two workers are entitled to.

Multiple choice questions

1 Consider the following statements made in relation to the Equal Pay Act 1970:

i The applicant can choose the comparator, but the comparator must work for the same employer or for an associated employer.

ii If a male comparator working shifts is paid a higher basic hourly rate than a woman in the same employment (ignoring any shift allowance) the woman will always be able to claim that she is doing like work.

iii If a woman does like work to the work done by a male comparator, all of her contract terms must be as beneficial as the equivalent terms in the comparator's contract, even if the woman's contract is more beneficial overall than that of the comparator.

iv The male comparator must be an existing employee. A woman cannot compare herself to a hypothetical male comparator.

Which of the above statements are true?

a i and iii only.

b i, ii and iii only.

c ii, iii and iv only.

d All of the statements.

2 Consider the following statements made in relation to the Sex Discrimination Act 1975.

i A rule can be discriminatory, even though it is applied equally to men and women, if it adversely affects pregnant women.

ii If a woman is sexually harassed she can have been sexually discriminated against even though a man, although not sexually harassed, would have been harassed to the same extent.

iii In deciding whether a requirement is indirectly discriminatory, a tribunal should consider the proportion of women in the working population as a whole who can comply with the requirement seeing if this is considerably smaller than the proportion of men in the working population as a whole who can comply with it.

iv An employer will be vicariously liable for the discriminatory acts of employees during the course of their employment, even if the employer took reasonable steps to prevent the employee from doing the discriminatory act.

v If a man was not promoted because he had given evidence against the employer in a case concerning a woman's complaint of sexual harassment, which was dismissed, the man would have been victimised.

Which of the above statements are true?

a i, ii and iii only.

b i, ii and v only.

c ii, iii and iv only.

d All of the statements.

3 Which one of the following statements, made in relation to the Race Relations Act 1976, is not true?

a If a white person was dismissed for refusing to discriminate against black people, the white person could claim direct discrimination.

b The application of a particular requirement can only amount to indirect discrimination if the requirement is one which must be complied with.

c In England discrimination against Scots could amount to discrimination because Scots are an ethnic group.

d Those who provide a personal service otherwise than as employees are not protected by the Race Relations Act.

4 Which one of the following statements is not true?

a Employers have a positive duty to make sure that arrangements and physical features do not place employees who they know to be disabled at a disadvantage.

b Apart from the positive duty set out in (a), employers have no duty to treat disabled persons more favourably than employees who are not disabled.

c It will always be unfair dismissal to dismiss an employee on account of a spent conviction.

d If a person sentenced to three years' imprisonment was released after 18 months, his conviction will never become spent.

5 Which one of the following statements is not true?

    a All employers must prepare a written statement on their general policy with respect to the health and safety at work of their employees.

    b Employees have a duty to take reasonable care for the health and safety of themselves and others who may be affected by their acts and omissions at work.

    c The six Regulations passed in 1992 supplement the Health and Safety at Work etc. Act 1974, rather than replace it.

    d The common law duty of care owed by employers is owed to individual employees and therefore account must be taken of their particular weaknesses and inexperience.

6 Which one of the following statements is not true?

    a Women must be allowed paid time off work to attend ante-natal care appointments.

    b Employees are allowed paid time off work if this is necessary to provide care for a dependant who is ill.

    c Parents are allowed up to 13 weeks' unpaid leave in respect of each of their children. If the child is not disabled the leave must be taken before the child's fifth birthday.

    d Parents have no statutory right to flexible working.

7 Which one of the following statements is not true?

    a All workers aged 20 or over, even those receiving accredited training, are entitled to the national minimum wage of £4.50 an hour.

    b A worker dismissed for claiming the national minimum wage can be unfairly dismissed even if he has not been continuously employed for one year.

    c The TUPE Regulations only apply where the undertaking retains its identity after the transfer.

    d When the TUPE Regulations apply continuous employment worked for the transferor is regarded as having been worked for the transferee.

8 Which one of the following statements is not true?

    a A person who has not contracted out of the Working Time Regulations could work 50 hours a week for 10 consecutive weeks and yet the Regulations might not have been breached.

    b Young workers who work more than 4.5 consecutive hours are entitled to a 30 minute rest break.

    c The Working Time Regulations do not apply to workers such as managers whose working time is not measured or predetermined.

    d The Working Time Regulations entitle a worker who has been continuously employed for at least four years to six week's paid annual leave.

Task 21

A friend of yours visiting the country from Japan has a keen interest in employment rights. Your friend has asked you if you would draw up a report dealing briefly with the following matters.

a The effect of the laws which outlaw discrimination in employment.

b The civil and criminal liability which an employer might be under as regards the health and safety of his employees.

c The maternity rights available to pregnant employees and their relatives.

d Any new types of rights acquired by employees in the past five years.

Chapter 22

REGULATION OF BUSINESS BY THE IMPOSITION OF CRIMINAL LIABILITY

Introduction

First in this chapter we consider, in outline, the nature of criminal liability. We then consider three areas in which the law regulates business by the imposition of criminal liability.

The Trade Descriptions Act 1968 creates two criminal offences relating to the false description of goods and two offences relating to the false description of services, accommodation or facilities. All four of the offences can be committed only by a person acting in the course of a trade or business. Liability in respect of the offences relating to services, accommodation or facilities arises only if the person making the statement knows that it is false or recklessly makes a statement which is false. The offences relating to goods are offences of strict liability. However, certain defences can be invoked as regards all four of the offences.

The Consumer Protection Act 1987 Part III creates two offences in relation to misleading price indications. Both offences can only be committed by a person acting in the course of his own business. The first offence is to give a consumer a misleading indication as to the price at which goods, services, accommodation or facilities are available. The second offence is committed by failing to take reasonable steps to correct a price indication which becomes misleading after it was given to consumers. A Code of Practice supplements the statutory provisions. Breach of the Code does not automatically give rise to any civil or criminal liability, but compliance with the Code can be relied upon to show that an offence has not been committed.

Criminal liability regarding the supply of unsafe products is imposed by the Consumer Protection Act 1987 Part II and by the General Product Safety Regulations 1994. To a large extent the 1994 Regulations have replaced the effect of the 1987 Act. However, the Act can still be of some significance and so its effect is considered in outline. The main offence created by the Regulations is one of strict liability and is committed by a producer placing an unsafe product on the market.

22.1 · The nature of a crime

It is not the purpose of this book to examine the nature of criminal liability in any degree of detail. However, in order to understand the liability imposed by the legislation considered in this chapter we do need to have some idea of the elements of a crime.

Generally, criminal offences are made up of two elements, an *actus reus* and a *mens rea*. The *actus reus* is often defined as the guilty act, whereas the *mens rea* is defined as the guilty mind. The *actus reus* of each offence is different. The definition of the *actus reus* as the guilty act is essentially correct, but rather too brief. It would be more correct to say that the *actus reus* of an offence is the external element of the definition of the offence which is objectively required before the offence can be committed. It might be committed either by mere conduct or by bringing about a prohibited outcome. For example, the *actus reus* of reckless driving is committed by mere conduct, whereas the *actus reus* of causing death by dangerous driving also requires an outcome, namely that a death is caused. *Mens rea* might be more fully defined as the mental state of the accused which the prosecution will need to prove in order to establish that the offence was committed. Generally, the *mens rea* of a crime will require an intention to do the act which a statute or the common law made illegal, although recklessness as to the circumstances and consequences which amount to the *actus reus* is enough as regards some crimes. The prosecution must prove both the *actus reus* of an offence and the *mens rea* beyond a reasonable doubt.

Homicide provides an easily understood example of what is meant by *actus reus* and *mens rea*. The *actus reus* of both murder and manslaughter is the same. For both crimes the accused must voluntarily and unlawfully cause the death of another human being. It is the different *mens rea* of the two crimes which distinguishes them. The *mens rea* of murder is that the accused either intended to kill or intended to cause grievous bodily harm. The *mens rea* of involuntary manslaughter is that the death was caused by the accused acting in a grossly negligent or reckless manner, but without the *mens rea* necessary for murder. (There are also several defences which reduce murder to voluntary manslaughter.)

So if an accused kills another person by shooting him with a gun, the *actus reus* of both murder and manslaughter is established. Which crime, if either, the accused will have committed will depend upon the accused's state of mind when he pulled the trigger. If the accused intended to kill the victim or intended to cause serious injury then he will be guilty of murder. If the accused was grossly negligent, perhaps pointing the gun at a friend in the grossly negligent belief that it was unloaded, then he will be guilty of manslaughter. If the accused has neither *mens rea* he will not be guilty of either offence. This would be the case, for example, if he shot the victim on a firing range, not knowing that the victim was hiding behind one of the targets.

22.1.1 *Actus reus* and *mens rea* must coincide

A person can only be guilty of a crime if he commits the *actus reus* of that crime at the same time as he has the *mens rea*. A person who today accidentally ran over his enemy would not be guilty of murder on account of his having unsuccessfully attempted to run him over yesterday. Such a person would have had the *mens rea* of murder yesterday and have committed the *actus reus* today, but that is not enough. The two must coincide.

Similarly, an accused must intend to commit the *actus reus* in the manner in which he did commit it. If an accused was driving around to his enemy's house, with the intention of shooting him dead, he would not be guilty of murder if he accidentally ran over his enemy on the way.

The doctrine of transferred malice holds that a person can be guilty of a crime even if the outcome of his actions was not quite what he expected. If A shoots a gun at B intending to kill him, but misses and kills C, he will still be guilty of murder. He is guilty because he had the *mens rea* for murder at the same time as he had the *actus reus* for murder. Transferred malice will only apply where the accused has the *actus reus* and *mens rea* of the same crime.

■ *R v Pembliton* (1874) 17 QBD 359

The defendant and his friends had been thrown out of a pub. They then fought with a crowd of people. After the fight the defendant threw a large stone at the people he had been fighting with, intending to hurt them. The stone missed the people, but broke a large window. The defendant was charged with maliciously damaging the window contrary to the Malicious Damage Act 1861.

Held. The defendant was not guilty of the offence. He had the *actus reus* of malicious damage to property (he broke the window) but he did not have the *mens rea* (he did not intend to break it). Nor would he have been guilty of maliciously wounding the people he threw the stone at. He had the *mens rea* for that crime, but not the *actus reus*.

■ *R v Latimer* (1874) LR 2 CCR 119

The defendant had a fight with another man in a pub. Having got the worst of the fight, the defendant went out into the pub yard. He came back into the pub with his belt in his hand and swung it at the man with whom he had been fighting. The belt only grazed this man but it bounced off him and severely wounded the woman he was talking to. The defendant was charged with maliciously wounding the woman.

Held. The defendant was guilty of malicious wounding. He had committed the *actus reus* of that crime (by wounding the woman) at the same time as he had the *mens rea* (by intending to wound the man).

Mens rea will generally consist of either an intention to do the act which is made criminal, or recklessness as to the circumstances and consequences of the action which constitutes the *actus reus* of the crime.

Parliament has created a number of crimes of **strict liability** where the prosecution do not need to prove *mens rea* in respect of one or more elements of the *actus reus*. The two offences set out by s.1 of the Trade Descriptions Act 1968, considered below at 22.2.1, provide an example of strict liability offences. It is not the case that strict liability offences are offences of absolute liability. Defences may be available, as they are to the s.1 Trade Descriptions Act offences. It is also the case that the accused must know that the acts which he commits are capable of leading to the behaviour which constitutes the offence. Generally, it is presumed that *mens rea* is required in respect of any crime. When it is not required this is because the wording of a statute rebuts this presumption.

22.2 · The Trade Descriptions Act 1968

The Trade Descriptions Act 1968 created four main offences, two of these relating to the misdescription of goods and two to the misdescription of services.

22.2.1 False trade descriptions of goods

Section 1(1)(a) of the 1968 Act makes it an offence to apply a false trade description to goods. Section 1(1)(b) makes it an offence to supply, or offer to supply, any goods to which a false trade description is applied. The offence created by s.1(1)(a) is the more serious of the two. Both of the offences relating to the misdescription of goods are crimes of strict liability and both offences can only be committed by a person acting in the course of a trade or business.

22.2.1.1 When is a person 'acting in the course of a trade or business'?

Apart from the 'by-pass' offence, which is considered below at 22.2.3.2, only a person acting in a course of a trade or business can commit an offence under the Trade Descriptions Act. In the following case the House of Lords considered the circumstances in which a business asset could be regarded as having been sold in the course of a trade or business.

■ *Davies v Sumner* [1984] 3 All ER 831 (House of Lords)

A self-employed courier traded in his old car for a new one. The car's odometer read 18 100 miles, but should have read 118 100 as it had gone right around the clock. There was no doubt that the defendant applied a false trade description to the car when he traded it in. However, the car which the courier traded in was the first car he had bought for use in his business, and was therefore the first car which he had traded in. The courier had used other cars in his business but he had rented these.

Held. Although the car traded in was a business asset which had been sold, and although it had been sold in a way which was reasonably incidental to the carrying on of the business, the defendant was not guilty. The Act only intended to catch such sales when they occurred with some regularity.

COMMENT The case provided an example of the long title of an Act being used as an aid to statutory interpretation. Lord Keith of Kinkel said: 'The expression "in the course of a trade or business" in the context of an Act having consumer protection as its primary purpose conveys the concept of some degree of regularity, and it is to be observed that the long title to the Act refers to "misdescription of goods, services, accommodation or facilities provided in the course of trade".' (See Aids to construction of statutes in Chapter 1 at 1.3.1.4.)

In *Davies* v *Sumner* Lord Keith considered *Havering London Borough* v *Stevenson* [1970] 3 All ER 609 in which the Divisional Court had convicted a car-hire firm which regularly sold off cars after about two years. None of the cars was ever sold at a profit. Lord Keith regarded this case as correctly decided. It could be distinguished because the regularity of the sales made them an integral part of the business of a car-hire firm.

When a business buys an item with the intention of reselling it at a profit, this can amount to a one-off adventure in the nature of trade even if the business has never before traded in this kind of item. Such a transaction could clearly be committed in the course of a trade or business. For example, if a business bought an item at an auction and then renovated the item and sold it at a good profit, the sale would have been made in the course of a trade or business even if the transaction was not of a type which the business usually conducted.

Although it is almost always a seller of goods who applies a false trade description, a buyer of goods can be guilty of the s.1(1)(a) offence of applying a false trade description to goods.

■ *Fletcher* v *Budgen* [1974] 1 WLR 1056

A motor dealer who was considering buying a car made several disparaging remarks about it. He said that the car could not be repaired and was fit only for scrap. The owner of the car was persuaded by these remarks to sell it to the dealer for £2. The dealer, who knew when he made the disparaging remarks that they were false, spent £56 on the car and then offered it for sale for £136.

Held. The buyer was guilty of an offence under s.1(1)(a) of the Act. However, Lord Widgery noted that it would be unusual for a buyer to be guilty of an offence under the Act and that the decision did not mean that every buyer who made derogatory or disparaging remarks about the goods ran the risk of committing an offence under the Act.

If the false trade description is not made in connection with any supply or offer to supply goods then the defendant will not have committed an offence under s.1, even if the defendant made the description while conducting his business.

■ *Wycombe Marsh Garages Ltd* v *Fowler* [1972] 1 WLR 1152

The defendant company conducted an MOT test on a car. A foreman mechanic examined the car and decided that it failed the MOT because the car's tyres suffered from tread lift. The tyres were then examined by their manufacturer who decided, after eight days of tests by an expert, that the tyres suffered from mould drip. Unlike tread lift, mould drip would not cause tyres to fail their MOT. Having been convicted under s.1(1)(a) of applying a false trade description to the tyres the defendant appealed to the Divisional Court.

Held. The defendant was not guilty of any offence. Lord Widgery, applying the mischief rule, said, 'It seems to me that one must have regard here to the undoubted mischief which prompted the passing of this Act and so far as the Act deals with goods the mischief was that goods might be provided for sale or otherwise with a misleading trade description applied to them … I do not believe Parliament meant to apply [s.1 of the Act] to the description of goods given incidentally in the performance of the service of advising in regard to some matter affecting those goods.' (The Mischief Rule of statutory interpretation is considered in Chapter 1 at 1.3.1.4.)

Section 20 provides that when a company commits an offence under the Act with the consent or connivance of a company officer, or any person purporting to act as a company officer, then the officer can be prosecuted as well as the company.

Those who carry on a profession, such as vets, can be regarded as carrying on a trade or business for the purposes of the Act.

22.2.1.2 The s.1(1)(a) offence: applying a false trade description to any goods

The main offence relating to the misdescription of goods, the s.1(1)(a) offence, is committed by applying a false trade description to goods. Goods are not defined by the Act, although s.39(1) says that 'goods' includes ships and aircraft, things attached to the land and growing crops.

The meaning of applying a false trade description was considered in the following case.

■ *Cavendish Woodhouse Ltd* v *Wright* (1985) 149 JP 497

The defendant was charged with several offences under s.1(1)(a) and s.1(1)(b) of the Act, the offences concerning several different customers. Miss Crawley, who had visited the defendant's shop and looked at bedroom furniture, was told that identical furniture was in stock and that this furniture could be supplied to her. In fact there was no identical furniture in stock. The furniture which was eventually supplied to Miss Crawley was far from identical. At no time did the defendant change Miss Crawley's notion that the furniture supplied would be identical. Mr and Mrs Mayo, who examined a suite in the defendant's shop, were told that all the cushions were reversible and that the suite was perfect. Having checked that this was the case, they ordered such a suite. However, the suite supplied to them had one cushion which was not reversible. Mr and Mrs Stewart bought a corner table, having seen one in the defendant's shop which did not have a glass top. The table was plainly meant to have a glass top. Mr and Mrs Stewart were told that the table supplied to them would have a glass top. However, due to an error made in the course of supply, it did not.

Held. As regards the bedroom furniture, the defendant had committed an offence under both s.1(1)(a) and s.1(1)(b) of the Act. The s.1(1)(a) offence (applying a false trade description to goods) was committed when the defendant stated that identical furniture was in stock and could be supplied. As no attempt was made to correct this statement by the time of supply, the statement was carried along to the time of supply. The s.1(1)(b) offence (supplying or offering to supply goods to which a false trade description is applied) was therefore committed at the time of supply. The same reasoning was applied to the statements about the suite, and again the two offences were committed. However, no offence was committed in respect of the table. There had been no attempt to misdescribe the table which the Stewarts received, but rather an accident had occurred in the course of supply.

No offence will be committed if the false trade description is made after the goods have been supplied. In *Hall* v *Wickens Motors Ltd* [1972] 1 WLR 1418, for example, motor dealers sold a car saying nothing about the steering. When the customer complained about the steering, 40 days later, the dealers said that there was nothing wrong with it. In fact the steering was defective and had been defective at the time of the sale. The Divisional Court held that no offence had been committed because Parliament had only intended to create an offence where the description was associated with the actual sale or supply of the goods.

Definition of a false trade description relating to goods

Section 2(1) gives an exhaustive definition of a trade description.

'A trade description is an indication, direct or indirect, and by whatever means given, of any of the following matters with respect to any goods or parts of goods, that is to say –
(a) quantity, size or gauge;
(b) method of manufacture, production, processing or reconditioning;
(c) composition;
(d) fitness for purpose, strength, performance, behaviour or accuracy;
(e) any physical characteristics not included in the preceding paragraphs;
(f) testing by any person and results thereof;
(g) approval by any person or conformity with a type approved by any person;
(h) place or date of manufacture, production, processing or reconditioning;
(i) person by whom manufactured, produced, processed or reconditioned;
(j) other history, including previous ownership or use.'

It can be seen that s.2(1)(a)–(e) deal with physical characteristics, whereas s.2(1)(f)–(j) deal with past history. All of the matters listed are matters of fact and so a matter or mere opinion cannot amount to a false trade description. A statement which is sufficiently a statement of fact to amount to a misrepresentation should be enough of a statement of fact to amount to a false trade description. (For the circumstances in which a statement is sufficiently a statement of fact to amount to a misrepresentation see Chapter 6 at 6.1.1.1.) When considering the meaning of words which are alleged to amount to a false trade description the primary question for consideration by the court is the impression or impact which was likely to be made on the mind of the ordinary person by the words used. Thus in *Robertson v Dicicco* [1972] RTR 431 a dealer who described a car which was in very poor condition as a 'beautiful' car was guilty of an offence, even though the purchaser of the car thought that the physical appearance of the car was very pleasing.

Section 3(1) provides that a false trade description is a description which is false to a material degree. Applying s.3(1), in *Kent County Council v Price* (1993) 157 JP 1161 the Divisional Court held that a defendant who supplied brand copies of goods was not guilty of an offence under s.1(1)(b). The defendant had a stall selling six types of T-shirts which were identical except for bearing different names, such as 'Reebok' and 'Puma'. A notice on the stall said 'Brand Copy' and the defendant pointed out to customers that he was selling the shirts for £1.99 whereas the genuine items would cost at least £12. No offence under the Act was committed because members of the public would have realised that they were not buying genuine T-shirts and so the descriptions were not false to a material degree.

Section 3(2) tells us that a trade description which is not literally false but which is misleading shall be deemed to be false, and that a misleading trade description is one which is likely to be taken for such an indication of any of the matters specified in s.2 of the Act as would be false to a material degree. An example of this was provided by *Robertson v Dicicco* above, where the unroadworthy car was described as a 'beautiful car'. As we saw earlier, the Divisional Court convicted the defendant. Applying s.3(2), the court considered that the description was a false indication in respect of the car's performance, within s.2(1)(d).

Section 3(3) states: 'Anything which, though not a trade description, is likely to be taken for an indication of any of those matters [set out in s.2(1)] and, as such an indication, would be false to a material degree, shall be deemed to be a false trade description.' In *Cottee v D. Seaton Ltd* [1972] 1 WLR 1408 the Divisional Court considered whether s.3(3) meant that a trade description could be implied from the defendant's conduct. A private motorist, who had effected an obvious and amateurish repair on the bodywork of his car surrounding the engine, had sold the car to the defendants, who were motor dealers. The defendants had undertaken work to hide the repair because they found that they could not sell the car. The defendants then sold the car to another dealer, Warry. Warry, who knew nothing about the repair, sold the car to a private motorist. The defendants were charged with an offence under s.23 of the Act. However, this offence could only be established if it was proved that Warry, who was not charged, had committed an offence under s.1(1)(b) of the Act. It was held that Warry was not guilty of an offence under s.1(1)(b) because he did not even know that a trade description had been applied to the car. However, the defendants could have committed an offence under s.1(1)(a) of the Act. They had effected the repairs to make it appear that the bodywork surrounding the engine was sound when it was not. They had therefore given an indication of the matters set out in s.2(1)(d) of the Act.

Section 4(1) provides that a false trade description can be applied in the following ways: by fixing it or annexing it either to the goods themselves or to anything in which the goods are supplied; by placing the goods in, on or with anything to which a false trade description has been affixed or annexed; or by using the trade description in any manner likely to be taken as referring to the goods. Section 4(2) tells us that an oral statement may amount to the use of a trade description.

Section 4(3) provides that where goods are supplied in pursuance of a request in which a false trade description is used, and the circumstances are such as to make it reasonable to infer that the goods are supplied as goods corresponding to that trade description, the person supplying the goods shall be deemed to have applied the trade description to the goods. For example, if a customer in a shop asked for a quarter of Darjeeling tea, a shopkeeper who supplied a quarter of Assam tea, without explaining that this is what he was doing, would be deemed to have described the tea as Darjeeling.

No special offence relating to advertisements is created by the Act. But the use of an advertisement can create liability under either s.1(1)(a) or 1(1)(b) of the Act. Advertisers who publish material supplied by another are given a defence by s.25 if they did not know, and had no reason to suspect, that an offence was being committed under the Act.

22.2.1.3 The s.1(1)(b) offence: supplying or offering to supply goods to which a false trade description is applied

The s.1(1)(b) offence of supplying or offering to supply goods to which a false trade description is applied is less serious than the s.1(1)(a) offence. Those who commit the s.1(1)(a) offence were described by Lord Lane CJ in *R* v *Southwood* [1987] 3 All ER 556 as unscrupulous, whereas those who committed the s.1(1)(b) offence were described as irresponsible.

The offence is committed by supplying or offering to supply goods rather than by merely selling or offering to sell them. Although a sale is clearly a supply, so is a contract of hire. In *Formula One Autocentres Ltd* v *Birmingham City Council* (1998) *Times*, 28 December, it was held that when a car taken in for a service is returned to its owner then this too amounts to a supply of the goods.

As the Act is concerned with the supply of goods in the course of a trade or business, an unincorporated association cannot commit an offence under the Act. Section 6 states that a person exposing goods for supply or having in his possession goods for supply shall be deemed to offer to supply them. This makes it plain that the difficulty experienced in *Partridge* v *Crittenden* (set out in Chapter 3 at 3.1.2) will not be experienced in respect of s.1(1)(b) offences.

Cavendish Woodhouse Ltd v *Wright*, considered earlier in this chapter, provides an example of the s.1(1)(b) offence being committed.

Disclaimers

Later in this chapter we consider defences available under the Act. A disclaimer is not a defence as such, but rather may prevent a trade description from arising in the first place. The Act makes no mention of disclaimers. They are a creation of the courts and have been applied almost exclusively to cases concerning false odometer readings. However, it is clear that a defendant who himself turns the clock back on a car cannot rely on a disclaimer to escape liability under s.1(1)(a).

■ *R* v *Southwood* [1987] 3 All ER 556 (Court of Appeal)

The defendant deliberately turned back the odometer on a number of cars which he had bought. Purchasers of the cars were given invoices, which stated 'We do not guarantee the accuracy of the recorded mileage.' Stickers saying 'We do not guarantee the accuracy of the recorded mileage. To the best of our knowledge and belief, however, the reading is incorrect' were stuck on the odometers of the cars. A notice in the sales office stated 'All mileage on cars offered are incorrect and sold and offered on this understanding.'

Held. The disclaimers did not prevent the defendant from committing the strict liability s.1(1)(a) offence. The very act of turning the odometers back was the application of a false trade description contrary to s.1(1)(a). It was immaterial that no one was likely to be misled by a second-hand car which had an odometer reading of zero.

The s.1(1)(a) offence can be committed by copying a false odometer reading onto an invoice, as this act is in itself an application of a false trade description. In *R* v *Bull* (1996) 160 JP 240 it was held that a disclaimer could provide a defence to a car dealer who innocently copied the false odometer reading onto an invoice. The dealer had not turned the odometer back himself. In *R* v *Bull* there was a disclaimer on the odometer itself and on the invoice. When the dealer copied the odometer reading onto the invoice he highlighted with an asterisk the words: 'We have been unable to confirm the mileage recorded on this odometer and therefore it must be considered incorrect.' It was held that the disclaimer could be effective, even for a s.1(1)(a) offence, if it prevented a reasonable person from regarding the odometer reading as accurate.

Disclaimers are far more likely to be effective as regards the s.1(1)(b) offence of supplying or offering to supply goods to which a false trade description is applied. In *Norman v Bennett* [1974] 1 WLR 1229 Lord Widgery said that to be effective the disclaimer must be 'as bold precise and compelling as the description itself' and 'must equal the trade description in the extent to which it is likely to get home to anyone interested in receiving the goods'.

In *Waltham Forest London Borough Council v TG Wheatley (Central Garage) Ltd* [1978] RTR 157 Lord Widgery CJ said that: 'The cases show that, in order for such a disclaimer to be effective, it must be of equal power and penetration as the statement on the odometer which it seeks to counter … in developing this doctrine of the disclaimer notice we never contemplated that a motor trader could put up a notice on the wall of his office and then forget all about his responsibility in this regard.'

In *Farrand v Lazarus* [2002] EWHC 226 (Admin) the Divisional Court held that where a dealer knew that odometer readings were incorrect, a generalised disclaimer could not prevent the commission of the s.1(1)(b) offence. The defendants were second-hand car dealers who had left a general disclaimer near the odometer of all the cars they were offering for sale. These disclaimers said that the defendants did not guarantee the accuracy of the recorded mileage but to the best of their belief the mileage displayed was incorrect. Two of these cars had been bought at auction where it was made plain that they had done more than 100 000 miles. However, as the odometers had only five figures the mileages displayed were 100 000 miles below the true mileages. The Divisional Court recognised that, in general, dealers had no obligation to point out defects and disadvantages attaching to goods sold. However, they held that dealers had to tell the truth, if they knew it, with regard to inaccurate odometer readings. The dealers knew that the recorded mileages were very misleading. This, coupled with the fact that the same disclaimer was applied to all the other cars, meant that the disclaimer were far short of the necessary emphatic indication that the recorded mileage was incorrect.

To be effective a disclaimer must be made before the goods are supplied. Goods are supplied at the time the deal is struck, not at the time when the goods are delivered.

22.2.2 Offences relating to the misdescription of services, accommodation or facilities

Section 14 of the Act creates two offences relating to the misdescription of services, accommodation or facilities. Section 14(1)(a) makes it an offence, in the course of any trade or business, to make a statement which is known to be false. Section 14(1)(b) makes it an offence, in the course of any trade or business, to recklessly make a statement which is false. It can be seen that, unlike the s.1 offences relating to goods, both of these offences require a *mens rea*.

Both of the s.14 offences can only be committed by a defendant who is acting in the course of a trade or a business. Both of the s.14 offences require that a false statement is made, a matter considered by the Court of Appeal in the following case.

■ *R v Thomson Holidays Ltd* [1974] 2 WLR 371 (Court of Appeal)

In 1972 the defendants pleaded guilty to contravening s.14(1)(b) of the Act, in that they had recklessly made false statements in their travel brochure about a particular hotel in Greece. The defendants had falsely claimed that the hotel had a children's paddling pool, a private swimming pool and a nightclub on the beach. In 1973 the defendants were charged with three new charges under s.14(1)(b). These new charges related to a complaint by a second person who had booked a holiday at the same hotel. This second person had relied on the same edition of the brochure in respect of which the first conviction had been secured. The brochure described the same amenities at the same hotel. The defendants entered a plea of *autrefois convict* (that they had already been convicted of the offence and could not therefore be convicted of it again). Whether or not this defence would be successful would depend upon whether a statement in a brochure is made once, when the brochure is published, or whether it is made every time a reader reads the brochure.

Held. False statements in brochures were made on each occasion when the brochure was read by the people for whom it was intended. There were therefore as many offences as there were readers. Lord Lawton said: 'with the printed word the information would be given when the statements were read. In our judgment that was when the false statements were made, and they were made to each reader.' The defence of *autrefois convict* therefore failed.

The House of Lords considered this matter in the following case.

■ *Wings Ltd* v *Ellis* [1985] 1 AC 272 (House of Lords)

Wings Ltd published a brochure which falsely described a hotel in Sri Lanka as being air-conditioned. At the time of publication no one within the company knew that the description was false. After the brochure had been issued to travel agents, the error was discovered and Wings Ltd made strenuous efforts to rectify matters. In June 1981 all staff of Wings Ltd were told to amend their brochures to remove the false description. Sales staff were also told to inform travel agents and customers of the error when holidays were booked. Those customers who had already booked were informed by letter. On 13 January 1982 the complainant read a brochure which had not been amended and in reliance on it booked a holiday through a travel agent. This customer, who could only be contacted through the travel agent, was not told of the error. When he returned from Sri Lanka this customer complained to a trading standards officer that the hotel was not air-conditioned, as the brochure had described it. Wings Ltd were charged with making a statement which they knew to be false, on 13 January 1982, as to the nature of the accommodation at the hotel. The House of Lords therefore had to consider whether or not a defendant could be guilty of the s.14(1)(a) offence of making a statement which is known to be false when he did not know of the falsity of the statement at the time of publication, but did know of the falsity at the time when the statement was read by the complainant.

Held. The offence had been committed because at the time the statement was made it was known by the company to be false. It was made by the company when it was read by the complainant, an interested member of the public doing business with the company on the basis of the statement. There was no requirement that the company should have known that the statement was false when they first made it.

COMMENT   The Law Lords were unanimous in thinking that the defendants might have been better off relying on one of the defences set out in the Act, rather than in trying to show that no offence had been committed.

The false statement about the services, accommodation or facilities does not need to induce a contract, but it must be connected to the supply of the services, accommodation or facilities.

■ *R* v *Bevelectric* (1992) 157 JP 323

A company which carried on a business repairing washing machines told all customers whose washing machines were not working that a new motor would be needed. This was done even as regards very minor faults and even where the expense of having a new motor fitted could not be justified.

Held. The company was guilty of an offence under s.14(1)(b) even though the false statement was about a service provided in the past. (Examining the washing machines and ascertaining that a new motor would be needed.) The statements were clearly connected with the supply of a service.

22.2.2.1 The *mens rea*

In *Wings* v *Ellis* the House of Lords classified the s.14(1)(a) offence as an offence of semi-strict liability. By this it was meant that the defendant must know that the statement he makes is false, but he does not need to know this at the time the statement is first published. When a statement is made many times, the defendant will have the necessary *mens rea* as regards every making of the statement after he knows it to be false. It is not necessary that the defendant knows that the statement is being made.

The s.14(1)(b) offence can only be committed by a statement made recklessly. Section 14(2)(b) states that: 'A statement made regardless of whether it is true or false shall be deemed to be made recklessly, whether or not the person making it had reasons for believing that it might be false.'

In Chapter 6 at 6.1.2 we considered the states of mind necessary to commit the three types of misrepresentations. Both the state of mind necessary to give rise to a fraudulent misrepresentation and the state of mind necessary to give rise to a negligent misrepresentation will be enough for the statement to have been made recklessly for the purposes of s.14 of the Trade Descriptions Act.

■ *MFI Warehouses Ltd* v *Nattrass* [1973] 1 WLR 307

The defendants advertised louvre doors for sale by mail order, making it plain that a carriage charge of 25p was to be made for each door supplied. The advertisement also offered folding door gear for sale, stating that in respect of these carriage was free. The defendants intended that the folding door gear could only be bought along with the louvre doors. Before publication the defendants' chairman had studied the advertisement for five or ten minutes. However, he did not appreciate that the folding door gear could be bought separately. A customer who bought some folding door gear separately, was charged for carriage.

Held. The defendants were guilty of an offence under s.14(1)(b) because the statement about free carriage of folding door gears was made recklessly. The statement had been made without regard to its truth or falsity even though the chairman had not had any kind of dishonest mind or deliberately closed his eyes to the truth. The chairman had not had regard to whether the advertisement was true or false, because he had not examined the advertisement with this end in view. Consequently, the advertisement was issued 'regardless of whether it is true or false'.

22.2.2.2 Services, accommodation or facilities

None of the three words in respect of which the s.14 offences can be committed are defined by the Act.

In *Newell and another* v *Hicks* [1984] RTR 125 the Divisional Court held that the supply of goods would not fall within 'services' or 'facilities', except in the most exceptional circumstances. The defendant had offered a free video to anyone who bought a car. In fact the videos were not free as the price of them was either added onto the price of the car sold or deducted from the amount allowed on any car traded in. (The defendants might have been more appropriately charged with giving a misleading price indication, contrary to what is now Part III of the Consumer Protection Act 1987. See below at 22.3.) Goff LJ said that 'services' in this context should be regarded as doing something for somebody, whereas facilities gave someone the opportunity to do something for himself.

In the following case the Divisional Court considered this matter again.

■ *Ashley* v *Sutton London Borough Council* (1994) 156 JP 631

Ten people received unsolicited mailshots from the appellant. These offered for sale a book which gave a strategy to profit from betting on fixed odds football pools. The advertisement said that if the customers were not satisfied with the book which explained the strategy then they could have all of their money back. The ten people sent the defendant between £55 and £179 for the book. All ten returned the book, but none were sent their money back.

Held. The extravagant language of the mailshot, and the inflated price of the book, indicated that what was being sold was not the book itself but the information in the book (i.e. the strategy to profit from the fixed odds football pools). Therefore, the defendants were properly convicted under s.14(1)(b).

COMMENT This decision can be criticised on the basis that the Divisional Court was asked to decide whether or not the statement that the purchase price of the book would be refunded was a statement about the provision of a service. But Scott-Baker J read the question as asking whether or not the provision of the book itself was the provision of a service. The decision is unfortunate, because generally the mere supply of goods will not amount to the provision of a service. (Although a supply of goods is within the provision of a service where it is ancillary to the provision of a service, such as changing the oil when a car is serviced.) It may be important to know whether the supply of goods also amounts to the provision of a service because, as we have seen, the *mens rea* requirements for s.1 and s.14 are different.

■ *R v Breeze* [1973] 1 WLR 994

A potential customer engaged the defendant to draw up plans because the defendant falsely claimed to be a qualified architect. The Crown Court convicted the defendant of making a statement about the provision of a service which he knew to be false, in the course of any trade or business, contrary to s.14(1)(a). The defendant appealed to the Court of Appeal, putting forward two arguments. First, that the services he provided were professional services and were not therefore provided in the course of a trade or business. Second, the false statement related to professional qualifications and not to the provision of any services.

Held. Neither argument was successful. First, the defendant could not claim that he was conducting an activity of a professional character when he did not have the qualifications to carry on that profession. Second, the statement that he was qualified as an architect would affect the likely quality of the service to be provided. It therefore amounted to a statement as to the provision of services.

This case was followed by the Divisional Court in the following case.

■ *R v David Martin Holland* [2002] EWCA Crim 2022

The defendant had invited members of the public to join a holiday club, membership of which gave them holidays for life at a reduced rate. The defendant had greatly exaggerated the size and financial assets of the club. The defendant argued that the false statements were not about the provision of the service but about the person who would provide the service.

Held. The defendant was convicted. The holiday club was not only advertising that holidays would be provided, but also that it was a club of far greater substance than in fact it was, and an organisation in which members could safely place their trust.

Accommodation includes short-term accommodation, as has already been made plain by cases such as *Wings* v *Ellis*. In *Westminster City Council* v *Ray Allan Manshops Ltd* [1982] 1 WLR 383 Ormrod LJ said that 'the word facilities in s.14 should be construed *ejusdem generis* with the preceding words "services" and "accommodation"'. It should therefore be construed in relation to these two words. (The *ejusdem generis* rule of statutory interpretation is explained in Chapter 1 at 1.3.1.4.) Ormrod LJ said of the words 'services' and 'facilities': 'Perhaps one can illustrate the difference in this way. Hotels or businesses of all kinds provide services, meaning that they do something for their customer. Others provide facilities in the sense that various things are made available to customers to use if they are so-minded in a more passive sense than the activities implied in the word "services".'

22.2.2.3 Making a false statement

As regards both offences, the *actus reus* requires that a false statement is made as to one of the matters listed in s.14(1). These matters are as follows:

(i) the provision in the course of any trade or business of any services, accommodation or facilities;
(ii) the nature of any services, accommodation or facilities provided in the course of any trade or business;
(iii) the time at which, manner in which or persons by whom any services, accommodation or facilities are so provided;
(iv) the examination, approval or evaluation by any person of any services, accommodation or facilities so provided:
(v) the location or amenities of any accommodation so provided.

In *R* v *John Killian* [2002] EWCA Crim 404 the Court of Appeal considered whether a company which offered remortgages to house owners had committed an offence under s.14. Costs of about £4 000 were usually incurred and added to the mortgages of the house owners. However, the house owners were assured, falsely, that this money could be recouped by means of an insurance based cash-back. Although this cash-back was said to be unconditional, in fact so many conditions were attached that no cash-back was ever offered. It was held that the defendant was rightly convicted under s.14, as the benefits from the cash-back were properly characterisable as the provision of services or facilities.

In *R* v *Piper* (1995) JP 116 it was held that the prosecution must establish as regards which of the five matters specified the statement was false. It was not enough to prove that it was false as regards one or other of them.

Section 14(4) provides that a statement is false if it is false to a material degree. Drawings and visual representations which are not literally statements can be regarded as statements. Section 14(2)(a) says that for the purposes of s.14: 'anything (whether or not a statement as to any of the matters specified in s.14(1)) likely to be taken for such a statement as to any of those matters as would be false shall be deemed to be a false statement as to that matter'.

Parliament did not intend to make a criminal offence out of what is really a breach of warranty. This can cause difficulties as regards statements about services etc to be provided in the future, as the following two cases show.

■ *R* v *Sunair Holidays Ltd* [1973] 1 WLR 1105 (Court of Appeal)

The defendants advertised a hotel in their 1970 summer brochure in the following way: ' ... swimming pool. Modern restaurant: the food is good, with English dishes also available – as well as special meals for children ... push chairs for hire.' The hotel was closed over the winter of 1969–70 in order that the swimming pool could be built. A customer booked a holiday in the hotel, in reliance on the brochure, in January 1970. The customer stayed at the hotel at the end of May 1970. He was dissatisfied because during his family's stay at the hotel the swimming pool could not be used. His family were also dissatisfied with the other services promised. The Crown Court convicted the defendants of an offence under s.14(1)(b).

Held. The conviction should be quashed. Section 14(1) did not apply to the statements which amounted to promises with regard to the future and which, when they were made, could not have the character of being either true or false. However, a promise about the future could be within s.14 if it was an implied statement of present intention, means or belief, which was false at the time of making and was made recklessly or knowingly.

■ *R* v *Avro plc* (1993) 157 JP 759 (Court of Appeal)

A customer of the defendant airline booked a return flight from Gatwick to Alicante and on the outward flight he was given a replacement ticket for the return flight. This replacement ticket was for a flight leaving at 12 noon on 17 April and was to arrive at Southend, whereas the original return ticket had been for a flight at 12.55 p.m. on 17 April and was for a return to Gatwick. When he found out that the original flight did not exist, the customer felt obliged to take the 12 noon flight to Southend.

Held. The defendants were guilty of an offence contrary to s.14 because two statements as to existing fact were made by implication. First there was a statement that there was a flight which was timed to leave Alicante at 12.55. Second, there was a statement that the customer was booked on that flight. Lloyd LJ made the point that the important question was whether the statement was likely to be taken by a member of the public as a statement of fact and that it was therefore a question of fact for the jury or the magistrates.

22.2.3 Defences

Even though the s.1 offences are offences of strict liability, the Act sets out defences which can apply to both the s.1 and the s.14 offences. These defences do not operate in the way that disclaimers do. They do not prevent an offence from having been committed in the first place. They provide an excuse which exonerates the defendant from liability.

22.2.3.1 Defence of mistake, accident etc

Section 24(1) states that:

'In any proceedings for an offence under this Act it shall, subject to subsection (2) of this section, be a defence for the person charged to prove –

(a) that the commission of the offence was due to a mistake or to reliance on information supplied to him or to the act or default of another person, an accident or some other cause beyond his control; and
(b) that he took all reasonable precautions and exercised all due diligence to avoid the commission of such an offence by himself or any person under his control.'

This defence is available in respect of any of the four main offences. However, it is not available in respect of the s.1(1)(a) offence if the defendant himself applied the false trade description.

The defendant needs to prove both elements of the defence on a balance of probabilities. If the defence is that the offence was committed due to a mistake then the mistake must be one made by the person charged, not by any other person. In *Birkenhead Co-operative Society* v *Roberts* [1970] 1 WLR 1497 the defendants had supplied a customer with a piece of lamb described as English lamb. This was caused by a mistake of one of the supermarket assistants, who had inadvertently used the wrong label on a piece of New Zealand lamb. As the mistake was not their own, the Co-op could not rely on the defence of mistake and were therefore convicted of an offence under s.1(1). However, it is a defence to prove that the offence was committed in reliance on information supplied by another or on account of the act or default of another person. If either of these two defences are invoked, s.24(2) requires the defendant to give the prosecution seven days' clear notice identifying this other person. If this is not done the defences cannot be relied upon. (The prosecution might prosecute the other person under s.1, s.14 or under the by-pass provision which is considered below.) As regards companies, it can be difficult to decide which employees can be regarded as another person and which can be regarded as the company itself.

In *Tesco Supermarkets* v *Nattrass* [1971] 2 All ER 127 the House of Lords held that the very senior managers of a company might be regarded as the controlling mind and will of the company, and therefore as its alter ego. A mere supermarket manager could not be so regarded and was therefore another person. The defendants, Tesco Ltd, were charged under a section of the Act concerning the giving of misleading price indications, which has since been repealed. The offence had been committed when a shop assistant had put out ordinary packets of Radiant washing powder, which cost 3s 11d. Posters in the shop stated that 'flash packs' of Radiant were available at 2s 11d. The shop assistant did not tell the supermarket manager that the wrong packets had been put out and a customer paid 3s 11d for a packet of Radiant. The responsibility of seeing that the correct packets were put out was that of the supermarket manager, who had been trained to do this properly. The defendants argued that the offence was committed because of the act of another person, the supermarket manager. Holding that the offence had been committed on account of the act of another person, the supermarket manager, the House of Lords recognised that very senior managers might be regarded as the alter ego of the company.

Whichever of the aspects of the s.24 defence is being relied upon, the defendant will always need to prove that he took all reasonable precautions and exercised all due diligence to prevent the commission of the offence. Whether or not this has been done will be an objective question of fact, to be decided by examining all the circumstances of the case. In *Tesco Supermarkets Ltd* v *Nattrass* Lord Morris thought that a company would have satisfied the requirement if it had created a system which could be rationally said to be so designed that the commission of offences would be avoided.

As already mentioned, the s.24(1) defence cannot be invoked by a defendant charged under s.1(1)(a) if he has deliberately applied the false trade description in question. In *R* v *Southwood* Lord Lane CJ said: 'It seems to us to be absurd to suggest that the actual falsifier could, by any stretch of the imagination, be said to have taken all reasonable precautions to attempt to avoid the commission of an offence merely by issuing a disclaimer, however expressed. By his initial actions in falsifying the instrument he has disqualified himself from asserting that he has taken any precautions, let alone all reasonable precautions.'

However, the defence may be available to a defendant charged with the s.1(1)(b) offence of supplying or offering to supply a car with a false odometer reading.

■ *Ealing London Borough Council* v *Taylor* (1996) 159 JP 460

A motor dealer was charged with two offences under s.1(1)(b). First, that he offered to supply a car to which a false trade description had been applied. Second, that he actually did supply a car with a false trade description applied to it. The car in question had a true mileage of over 55 000, but the recorded mileage was only 32 000. A written disclaimer had been attached to the car. The justices found that, although the disclaimer had not been displayed prominently enough to be an effective disclaimer which would prevent the commission of an offence, the defendant had done enough to establish a defence under s.24(1). The defendant had bought the car from another dealer who had provided no service record, although he did guarantee the 32 000 mileage. The condition of the car was such that the defendant's belief that it had done only 32 000 miles was reasonable. The defendant did not try to contact any other previous owners to check the mileage because he had in the past made attempts to do this, but had never had any success.

Held. The magistrates' finding that the defendant had satisfied the requirements of the s.24(1) defence should not be overturned. Buckley J made it plain that it was difficult to lay down hard and fast rules in such cases, all of which had to be decided on their own facts: 'It cannot be a matter of law that in every case where a defendant seeks to make good a defence under s.24 that a disclaimer has to be placed on the car, or that inquiries have to be made of the previous owner. What precautions it is reasonable to take in any particular case must depend upon all the circumstances of the case.'

A **supplier's defence** is provided by s.24(3):

> 'In any proceedings for an offence under this Act of supplying or offering to supply goods to which a false trade description is applied it shall be a defence for the person charged to prove that he did not know, and could not with reasonable diligence have ascertained, that the goods did not conform to the description or that the description had been applied to the goods.'

The defendant must prove this defence on a balance of probabilities. Reasonable diligence is the equivalent of due diligence in s.24(1). Whether or not the defendant has taken reasonable precautions is not relevant. The defence is concerned with the steps which the defendant did not take, rather than with the steps which he did take.

22.2.3.2 **The by-pass provision**

Section 23 deals with the situation where the offence was committed due to the act or default of another person:

> 'Where the commission by any person of an offence under this Act is due to the act or default of some other person that other person shall be guilty of the offence, and a person may be charged with and convicted of the offence by virtue of this section whether or not proceedings are taken against the first-mentioned person.'

Even a person who does not conduct any trade or business can be guilty of an offence under s.23. In *Olgeirsson* v *Kitching* [1986] 1 All ER 764 a private motorist sold a car to a garage saying that it had done 38 000 miles, even though he knew that this was not true. The owner of the garage sold the car on, applying the 38 000 mile description. The purchaser found out that the description was false. The private motorist was guilty of an offence under s.23, even though he could not have been guilty of an offence under s.1.

Section 23 requires that the first person is guilty of an offence. However, s.23 is used when the first person has established that he has a defence under s.24. In *Coupe* v *Guyett* [1973] 1 WLR 669 Lord Widgery CJ said: 'The solution of the conflict is that, when the first mentioned person in section 23 has no defence to the charge except the statutory defence under section 24, he or she can properly still be regarded as having committed "the offence" for the purpose of section 23.'

Section 25 gives a **defence to an advertiser** who receives an advertisement in the ordinary course of business and did not know and had no reason to suspect that the publication of the advertisement would amount to an offence under the Act.

Test your understanding

1 What is meant by *actus reus* and *mens rea*?

2 What is a crime of strict liability?

3 What are the two offences created by s.1 of the Trade Descriptions Act 1968?

4 Section 2(1) of the Act defines the meaning of a trade description. Into what two broad categories do such descriptions fall?

5 What is the effect of disclaimers used in cases concerning false odometer readings?

6 What are the two offences created by s.14 of the Act, in relation to the misdescription of services, accommodation or facilities?

7 Why is the s.14(1)(a) offence regarded as an offence of 'semi-strict' liability?

8 In order to convict a defendant of the s.14(1)(b) offence, is it necessary to show the mental requirement which would be needed to establish that the defendant had committed fraudulent misrepresentation?

9 What will a defendant need to prove in order to establish a defence under s.24 of the Act?

10 What is the effect of the by-pass provision set out in s.23 of the Act?

Answers

1 *Actus reus* and *mens rea* are the two elements of a criminal offence. The *actus reus* is the external element of the definition of an offence which is objectively required before the crime can be committed. The *mens rea* is the mental state of the accused which the prosecution will need to prove in order to establish that the crime was committed.

2 A crime of strict liability is one where the prosecution do not need to prove *mens rea* in respect of one or more elements of the *actus reus*.

3 Section 1(1)(a) of the Act makes it an offence to apply a false trade description to goods. Section 1(1)(b) makes it an offence to supply or offer to supply any goods to which a false trade description is applied. Both can only be committed by a person acting in the course of a trade or business.

4 A trade description is an indication, direct or indirect, and by whatever means given of matters relating either to the physical characteristics of the goods or to their past history.

5 A disclaimer is not a defence as such, but may prevent a false description from having been applied and may therefore prevent a s.1 offence from having been committed.

6 The two offences created by s.14 of the Act in relation to the misdescription of services, accommodation or facilities are: making a statement which is known to be false; or recklessly making a statement which is false. As regards either offence the statement must be made in the course of a trade or business.

7 The s.14(1)(a) offence of making a statement which is known to be false is regarded as an offence of semi-strict liability because although the defendant needs to know that the statement is false when it is made, he does not need to know that the statement is being made or need to know that the statement was false when it was first published.

8 As regards the s.14(1)(b) offence of recklessly making a statement which is false, the mental requirement needed to establish either negligent or fraudulent misrepresentation will be enough to mean that the offence is committed.

9 In order to establish a defence under s.24 of the Act the defendant will first need to prove, on a balance of probabilities, that the offence was committed either due to his own mistake, or to reliance on information supplied to him, or to the act or default of another person, or to some accident or other cause beyond his control. In addition, the defendant will need to prove that he took all reasonable precautions and exercised all due diligence to prevent the commission of the offence.

10 The by-pass provision allows a person who has caused another to be guilty of an offence under the Act to be charged with and convicted of the offence, whether or not proceedings are taken against the other person.

22.3 · Misleading price indications

The Consumer Protection Act 1987 Part III creates two offences concerning misleading price indications. The law had previously been contained in s.11 of the Trade Descriptions Act 1968 which outlawed three types of price indications relating to goods. The first offence is defined by s.20(1):

'A person shall be guilty of an offence if, in the course of any business of his, he gives (by any means whatever) to any consumers an indication which is misleading as to the price at which any goods, services, accommodation or facilities are available (whether generally or from particular persons).'

Section 20(2) defines the second offence:

'A person shall be guilty of an offence if –
(a) in the course of any business of his, he has given an indication to any consumers which, after it was given, has become misleading as mentioned in subsection (1) above; and
(b) some or all of those consumers might reasonably be expected to rely on the indication at a time after it has become misleading; and
(c) he fails to take all such steps as are reasonable to prevent those consumers from relying on the information.'

It can be seen that the s.20(1) offence, which is the main offence, is committed by giving to a consumer a misleading indication as to price, whereas the s.20(2) offence is committed by failing to correct an indication as to price which has become misleading after it has been given to consumers. The following case illustrates the difference between the two offences.

■ *Toys 'R' Us* v *Gloucestershire County Council* (1994) 158 JP 338

Two customers each bought a pair of swimming goggles at the defendants' store. A price sticker was attached to each pair of goggles. When the cashier on the till scanned the bar code on the first pair of goggles this caused a higher price to be displayed on the till than was shown on the stickers attached to the goggles. The discrepancy was pointed out to the cashier. The cashier voided the till and manually entered the lower price on the sticker. As regards the second pair of goggles, the cashier then manually entered the lower price on the sticker attached to the goggles. The assistants had been instructed always to do this in the event of any discrepancy between the prices shown on the stickers and those rung up on the till. The defendants pleaded guilty to a s.20(1) charge as regards the first pair of goggles. They pleaded not guilty as regards the second pair. Later on enforcement officers seized 12 specimen items on which the price on the stickers was lower than the prices which were caused to be rung up on the till by the bar codes. When enforcement officers subsequently visited the shop they found further discrepancies in the prices displayed on the stickers and those which the bar codes caused to be rung up. The defendants contested 34 offences with which they were charged, but pleaded guilty to two charges where enforcement officers made test purchases and were charged the higher bar code prices.

Held. The defendants were not guilty of any of the offences which they contested. The prices which they intended to charge were the prices on the stickers. The goods were displayed bearing these prices and were available at these prices, as these were the prices which customers would have to pay. The relevant time for the purposes of s.20(1) is the time at which the indication as to price is given, and in this case that time was when the item was on the shelf with the price attached to it. If no-one had noticed that a higher price was rung up by the bar code and this price was therefore paid, an offence under s.20(1) would have been committed as to the price at which the goods were available. In such a case the court could regard the goods as not available at the sticker prices, even when the goods were on the shelves. The s.20(2) offence was not committed because the prices on the stickers did not become misleading when the bar codes caused a higher price to be rung up on the till. Kennedy LJ said: 'Section 20(2) ... is intended to deal with a quite different situation – the advertisement or shelf barker which ceases to be accurate because of some event which takes place after it was displayed. For example, if an advertisement claims that the vendor's price is less than that of a competitor, who then reduces his price.'

The case shows us that the Act is not concerned with whether or not goods are sold at the correct price.

The s.20 offences can only be committed by a person acting 'in the course of a business of his'. In *Warwickshire County Council* v *Johnson* [1993] 1 All ER 299 the House of Lords held that this meant any business in which the defendant had a controlling interest or of which he was the owner. A shop manager of a Dixons retail shop was not within the definition and therefore could not commit either offence under s.20. Although services provided by an employee as part of his contract of employment are excluded from the provisions of the Act, s.20(3) allows an agent who carries on business on his own account to be guilty of either of the offences when selling on behalf of another.

A notice which is not on the face of it misleading can become misleading on account of a refusal to honour its terms. In *Warwickshire County Council* v *Johnson* the branch manager of a Dixons shop had put up a notice saying: 'We will beat any TV HiFi and Video price by £20 on the spot.' A customer showed the manager another shop at which a certain television set was priced at £159.95. The manager of the Dixons shop refused to sell such a television to the customer for £139.95. The notice displayed was held by the House of Lords to be misleading. The notice constituted a continuing offer and the only way to discover whether or not it was misleading was to try to take advantage of it.

Section 20(6) requires that a misleading price indication be given to a consumer. A consumer in this context is a person who wants the goods, services or accommodation for his private purposes rather than for business purposes. A trading standards officer is to be regarded as a consumer because the Act's lengthy definition of a consumer includes a 'person who might wish to be supplied with goods for his own private use or consumption'.

Section 20(6) defines price as the aggregate sum required to be paid by a consumer or any method which has been applied for the purpose of determining that aggregate. It is not necessary that a consumer actually makes a purchase. Article 2.2.6 of the Code of Practice requires that all price indications given to consumers by any means whatever be given inclusive of VAT.

The Act only applies to the prices at which goods, services or accommodation are available. If the price is in respect of discontinued stock, or stock which is otherwise unavailable, no offence is committed. A person who agrees to provide a service for a certain price and then puts in a bill for more than the agreed price will not have committed an offence under the Act.

Both offences can be committed only if a misleading price indication is given to a consumer. Section 21 defines misleading:

> 'For the purposes of section 20 above an indication given to any consumers is misleading as to a price if what is conveyed by the indication, or what those consumers might reasonably be expected to infer from the indication or any omission from it, includes any of the following, that is to say –
> (a) that the price is less than in fact it is;
> (b) that the applicability of the price does not depend on facts or circumstances on which its applicability does in fact depend;
> (c) that the price covers matters in respect of which an additional charge is in fact made;
> (d) that a person who in fact has no such expectation –
>   (i) expects the price to be increased or reduced (whether or not at a particular time or by a particular amount); or
>   (ii) expects the price, or the price as increased or reduced, to be maintained (whether or not for a particular period); or
> (e) that the facts or circumstances by reference to which the consumers might reasonably be expected to judge the validity of any relevant comparison made or implied by the indication are not what in fact they are.'

Section 21(2) sets out a very similar list in respect of misleading indications as to the method of determining the price.

In *R* v *Kettering Magistrates' Court, ex parte MRB Insurance Brokers Ltd* [2000] JPR 164 the Divisional Court held that when the contract price was payable by instalments the APR could be an indication as to the price. The defendants had told a customer who was paying his motor insurance premiums by instalments that the APR was 28.3%, whereas in fact it was over 64%. This was a misleading indication as to the price because the APR was used in calculating the total amount payable under the contract.

22.3.1 Defences

Section 24 sets out four defences to the s.20 offences. These are:

(1) that the acts or omissions in question were authorised by Regulations passed by the Secretary of State under s.26 of the Act;
(2) that as regards price indications published in books, newspapers, magazines, films, or radio or television broadcasts, the indications were not contained in an advertisement;
(3) that an advertiser has a defence in the same circumstances as an advertiser's defence as was available under the Trade Descriptions Act 1968; and
(4) that the offence was caused by a recommended price given to all suppliers not being followed, and that it was reasonable for the person who gave the recommended price to assume that the recommendation was for the most part being followed.

Section 39 provides a defence of taking all reasonable precautions and exercising all due diligence to avoid committing the offence. If this involves blaming a third party then the prosecution must be given details of the third party, who may be prosecuted under the s.40 by-pass provision.

An offence can only be prosecuted within three years of it having been committed, or within one year of the day on which the person bringing the prosecution discovered that the offence had been committed, whichever is the earlier.

22.3.2 The Code of Practice

The Consumer Protection (Code of Practice for Traders on Price Indications) Approval Order 1988 (SI 1988 No. 2078) (the Code) works in conjunction with the Act. Section 25(2) of the Act provides that a contravention of the Code does not of itself give rise to any civil or criminal liability. Section 25(2)(a) provides that if a person contravenes the Code this may be relied upon either for the purpose of establishing that the person committed an offence or for the purpose of negativing any defence. In addition, s.25(2)(b) provides that compliance with the Code may be relied upon to show that the commission of an offence has not been established or that a person has a defence.

The paragraphs of the Code deal with the following matters:

Part 1 Price comparisons

1.1   Price comparisons generally;
1.2   Comparisons with the trader's own previous selling price;
1.3   Introductory offers, after-sale or after-promotion prices;
1.4   Comparisons with price related to different circumstances;
1.5   Comparison with another trader's prices;
1.6   Comparison with 'Recommended Retail Price' or similar;
1.7   Pre-printed prices;
1.8   Reference to value or worth;
1.9   Sales or special events;
1.10 Free offers.

Part 2 Actual price to the consumer

2.1   Indicating two different prices
2.2   Incomplete information and non-optional extras.

Part 3 Price indications which become misleading after they have been given

3.1   General
3.2   Newspaper and magazine advertisements
3.3   Mail order advertisements, catalogues and leaflets
3.4   Selling through agents
3.5   Changes in the rate of value added tax.

Part 4 applies to the sale of new homes

The Code is easy to read and understand, being aimed at traders, as the following extract shows:

'**1.2 Comparisons with the trader's own previous price**

1.2.1 General In any comparison between your present selling price and another price at which you have in the past offered the product, you should state the previous price as well as the new lower price.

1.2.2 In any comparison with your own previous price:
(a) the previous price should be the last price at which the product was available to consumers in the previous 6 months;
(b) the product should have been available to consumers at that price for at least 28 consecutive days in the previous 6 months; and
(c) the previous price should have applied (as above) for that period at the same shop where the reduced price is now being offered.

1.2.3 If the previous price in a comparison does not meet one or more of the conditions set out in 1.2.2 above:
(i) the comparison should be fair and meaningful; and
(ii) give a clear and positive explanation of the period for which and the circumstances in which the higher price applied. For example 'these goods were on sale here at the higher price from 1 February to 26 February' or 'these goods were on sale at the higher price in 10 of our 95 stores only'. The explanation should be displayed as clearly, and as prominently as the price indication. You should *not* use general disclaimers saying for example that the higher price used in comparisons have not necessarily applied for 28 consecutive days.'

In the following case the Divisional Court, although primarily considering the meaning of the Act, also considered the meaning of paras 1.2.2. and 1.2.3 of the Code.

■ *AG Stanley Ltd (T/A Fads)* v *Surrey County Council* (1994) 159 JP 691

On 2 April 1992 the defendants priced a table at £7.99. In a special promotion, which ran from 14 October 1992 to March 1993, the price of the tables was reduced to £4.99. In the meantime, on 10 November 1992 the tables were advertised as: 'Occasional table was £7.99. Now only £4.99.' This price was advertised as a 13-day event which must end on 24 November. The price of the tables remained at £4.99 until March 1993. On 21 December 1992 the table was still on sale at £4.99 when a point of sale notice stated: 'Sale, round occasional table, now £4.99 was £7.99.' The justices convicted the defendants of two offences under s.20 of the 1987 Act. The offences related to the advertisement of 10 November and the point of sale notice on 21 December. The defendants appealed to the Divisional Court.

Held. The defendants were guilty of both offences. The facts or circumstances by reference to which the consumers might reasonably be expected to judge the validity of any relevant comparison made or implied by the indications were not in fact what they were. It could easily be inferred that the price would revert to the higher price once the event or offer was over. The defendants had also contravened paras 1.2.2. and 1.2.3 of the Code. The 'last price' mentioned in para 1.2.2 was the higher price immediately before the commencement of the special event or offers. It was not the last numerically different price, as the appellants had argued.

Test your understanding

1 What are the two offences relating to misleading prices created by s.20 of the Consumer Protection Act 1987?

2 As regards both offences, to whom must a misleading price indication have been given?

3 What is the legal status of the Code of Practice which is used in conjunction with the Consumer Protection Act 1987 Part III?

Answers

1 The two offences created by s.20 are: giving any consumers a misleading indication as to the price at which goods, services, accommodation or facilities are available; and failing to correct a price indication which has become misleading after it was given to any consumers. Both offences can only be committed by a person acting in the course of any business of his.

2 Both offences require that a misleading price indication be given to consumers, but this can include a trading standards officer.

3 The Code of Practice does not have the force of law. However, establishing that the Code has been contravened may be relied upon for establishing that a person has committed an offence or for the purpose of negativing a defence. Conversely, compliance with the Code may be relied upon to show that an offence has not been committed or that a person has a defence.

22.4 · Product safety

Criminal liability as regards unsafe products is imposed both by the Consumer Protection Act 1987 Part II and by the General Product Safety Regulations 1994. To a considerable extent the 1994 Regulations have replaced the measures in the 1987 Act. However, the Act is not rendered completely ineffective and so first we consider the Act and then the 1994 Regulations.

22.4.1 The Consumer Protection Act 1987 Part II

Part II of the 1987 Act introduced the 'general safety requirement' making it an offence to supply consumer goods which are not reasonably safe. It also gives the Secretary of State the power to make safety regulations, to serve prohibition and warning notices and to require a person to furnish information. Enforcement authorities have the power to issue suspension notices and order the forfeiture of goods.

22.4.1.1 The general safety requirement

Section 10(1) of the Act sets out the general safety requirement:

'A person shall be guilty of an offence if he –
(a) supplies any consumer goods which fail to comply with the general safety requirement; or
(b) offers or agrees to supply any such goods; or
(c) exposes or possesses any such goods for supply.'

The 'general safety requirement' is an objective standard. Section 10(2) tells us that goods fail to comply with it if they are not reasonably safe having regard to all of the circumstances, including:

(a) the manner in which, and purposes for which, the goods are being or would be marketed, the get-up of the goods, the use of any mark in relation to the goods and any instructions or warnings which are given with respect to the keeping, use or consumption of the goods;
(b) any relevant published safety standards;

(c) the existence of any means by which it would have been reasonable (taking into account the cost, likelihood and extent of any improvement) for the goods to have been made safer.

Section 19(1) explains the meaning of 'safe' in this context:

' "safe" in relation to any goods, means that there is no risk, or no risk apart from one reduced to a minimum, that any of the following will (whether immediately or after a definite or indefinite period) cause the death of, or any personal injury to, any person whatsoever, that is to say –

(a) the goods;
(b) the keeping, use or consumption of the goods;
(c) the assembly of any of the goods which are, or are to be supplied, unassembled;
(d) any emission or leakage from the goods or, as a result of keeping, use or consumption of the goods, from anything else, or;
(e) reliance on the accuracy of any measurement, calculation or other reading made by or by means of the goods

and "safer" and "unsafe" shall be construed accordingly.'

Factor (a) deals with the situation where the goods are inherently unsafe. Examples of the four factors (b) to (e) might be as follows: (b) a gas canister explodes whilst in storage; (c) self-assembly shelves contain very sharp edges which injure a consumer who is assembling the shelves; (d) a car battery leaks corrosive acid onto a consumer; (e) a faulty meat thermometer gives a false reading which leads a consumer to falsely believe that his roast chicken is correctly cooked.

The Act requires only that risk should be kept to a minimum. If the Act insisted that there was no risk in relation to goods then a huge number of goods could not be supplied at all. For example, cars, cookers, aeroplanes etc are all inherently unsafe to some degree or other. Therefore, it is necessary to require that the risk should be reduced to a minimum rather than to require that it be non-existent.

Section 10(7) describes 'consumer goods' as any goods ordinarily intended for private use or consumption, not being growing crops or things comprised in land by virtue of being attached to it. The following types of goods are excluded, but only because they are covered elsewhere by more detailed regulations: water, food, feeding stuff, fertilisers, gas from an authorised supplier, aircraft, motor vehicles, controlled drugs, licensed medicinal products or tobacco.

'Supply' is defined widely by s.46 to include sale, hire, loan, and hire-purchase. However, the supply must be made in the course of a business (whether or not a business dealing in the goods in question) and can be made either as principal or agent.

Three special defences are set out in s.10(4):

(a) It is a defence for a defendant to show that he reasonably believed that the goods would not be used or consumed in the United Kingdom.
(b) As regards a retailer, it is a defence to show that at the time he supplied the goods or offered or agreed to supply them or exposed or possessed them for supply, he neither knew nor had reasonable grounds for believing that the goods failed to comply with the general safety requirement.
(c) It is a defence for a defendant to show that the goods were not supplied or to be supplied as new goods (s.10(4)(c)).

Section 39(1) provides a defence of due diligence and s.40 provides for the possibility of a prosecution under the by-pass procedure, as considered above in relation to misleading price indication offences.

Section 11 of the Act also empowers the Secretary of State to make such regulations as he considers appropriate to ensure that goods are safe, that unsafe goods are not made generally available, and that appropriate information is supplied with goods. Section 11(5) requires the Secretary of State to consult such organisations as appear to him to be representative of interests substantially affected by the proposal.

Section 13 of the Act gives the Secretary of State the power to serve 'prohibition notices' and 'warning notices'. Prohibition notices prohibit a particular person from supplying, offering to supply or possessing for supply goods which the Secretary of State considers to be unsafe. The Secretary of State may also serve a 'notice to warn' requiring the person upon whom it is served to publish a warning at his own expense. The warning must give a relevant warning about goods which the Secretary of State considers unsafe which the person supplies or has supplied. Notices to warn are generally used when unsafe goods have already been supplied to the public. Warning notices are often voluntarily published in the national press by manufacturers or importers of unsafe products.

If an enforcement authority has reasonable grounds to believe that any safety precaution has been contravened in relation to any goods, it may serve a suspension notice. Such a notice will prohibit the person upon whom it is served, for a period of up to six months, from supplying the goods, offering to supply them, agreeing to supply them or exposing them for supply without the consent of the authority. Section 15 gives any person having an interest in any goods in respect of which a suspension order is in force a right to appeal against the order.

Section 16 gives an enforcement authority the right to apply for an order for the forfeiture of any goods on the grounds that there has been a contravention in relation to the goods of a safety provision.

Section 18 gives the Secretary of State the power to serve a notice on a person requiring that person to furnish him with information to help him decide whether to make, vary or revoke safety regulations or serve, vary or revoke prohibition or warning notices. It is an offence to refuse to supply this information without reasonable cause.

22.4.1.2 The General Product Safety Regulations 1994

The Regulations are separate from the Act. What is an offence under the Act is not necessarily an offence under the Regulations, and vice versa. Regulation 5 provides that, for the purposes of the Regulations, s.10 of the Act is disapplied. So the general safety requirement set out in s.10 of the Act has no effect where the Regulations apply. However, s.10 of the Act can apply in circumstances where the Regulations do not apply and is not therefore rendered wholly redundant.

The general safety requirement

Regulation 7 sets out the main offence, which is one of strict liability: 'No producer shall place a product on the market unless the product is a safe product.'

Regulation 2(1), the interpretation regulation, defines a 'producer' as:

'(a) the manufacturer of the product, when he is established in the [European] Community, and includes any person presenting himself as the manufacturer by affixing to the product his name, trade mark or other distinctive mark, or the person who reconditions the product;
(b) when the manufacturer is not established in the Community –
   (i) if the manufacturer does not have a representative established in the Community, the importer of the product;
   (ii) in all other cases, the manufacturer's representative; and
(c) other professionals in the supply chain, insofar as their activities may affect the safety properties of a product placed on the market.'

It should be noted that retailers are not included in this definition, unless their activities affect the safety of a product placed on the market. Retailers can be guilty of an offence under s.10 of the Consumer Protection Act 1987, subject to the defence specific to retailers set out in s.10(4). However, distributors can commit two separate offences under the Regulations, as we shall see.

Regulation 2(1) defines 'product' as:

'any product intended for consumers or likely to be used by consumers, supplied whether for consideration or not in the course of a commercial activity and whether new, used or reconditioned; provided, however, a product which is used exclusively in the context of a commercial activity even if it is used for or by a consumer shall not be regarded as a product for the purposes of these Regulations provided always and for the avoidance of doubt this exception shall not extend to the supply of such a product to a consumer.'

This definition is wider than that contained in s.10 of the Act and could include products which are not new, products designed for export and the types of goods, such as tobacco, which are excluded from the ambit of the Act.

Regulation 2(1) also defines a 'safe product':

' "safe product" means any product which, under normal or reasonably foreseeable conditions of use, including duration, does not present any risk or only the minimum risks compatible with the product's use, considered as acceptable and consistent with a high level of protection for the safety and health of persons, taking into account in particular –

(a) the characteristics of the product, including its composition, packaging, instructions for assembly and maintenance;

(b) the effect on other products, where it is reasonably foreseeable that it will be used with other products;

(c) the presentation of the product, the labelling, any instructions for its use and disposal and any other indication or information provided by the producer; and

(d) the categories of consumers at serious risk when using the product, in particular children;

and the fact that higher levels of safety may be obtained or other products presenting a lesser degree of risk may be available shall not of itself cause the product to be considered other than a safe product.'

Regulation 3 states that the Regulations do not apply to:

(a) antiques;

(b) products supplied for repair or reconditioning before use, provided the supplier clearly informs the person to whom he supplies the product to that effect; or

(c) any product where there are specific provisions in rules of European Community law governing all aspects of the safety of the product.

Regulation 8 requires a producer, within the limits of his activity, to:

(a) provide consumers with the relevant information to enable them to assess the risks inherent in a product throughout the normal or reasonably foreseeable period of its use, where such risks are not immediately obvious without adequate warnings, and to take precautions against those risks; and

(b) adopt measures commensurate with the characteristics of the products which he supplies, to enable him to be informed of the risks which those products might present and to take appropriate action, including, if necessary, withdrawing the product in question from the market to avoid those risks. The appropriate measures might include, whenever appropriate –

  (i) marking of their products or product batches in such a way that they can be identified;

 (ii) sample testing of marketed products;

(iii) investigating complaints; and

(iv) keeping distributors informed of such monitoring.

Regulation 9 requires that distributors act with due care in order to help ensure compliance with Reg. 7, the general safety requirement. (A distributor is defined as any professional in the supply chain whose activity does not affect the safety properties of a product. It would generally therefore include retailers.) In particular distributors are required not to supply products which they know, or should have presumed on the basis of information in their possession as a professional, are dangerous products. It is an offence for a distributor to do this. Distributors are also particularly required, within the limits of their activities, to participate in monitoring the safety of products placed on the market, in particular by passing on information on the product risks and cooperating in the action taken to avoid those risks.

As we have seen, Reg.7 relates only to placing an unsafe product on the market. Regulation 13 therefore creates two more offences of strict liability;

'No producer or distributor shall –
(a) offer or agree to place on the market any dangerous product or expose or possess any such product on the market; or
(b) offer or agree to supply any dangerous product or expose or possess any such product for supply.'

Regulation 14 sets out the standard defence of due diligence. Regulation 15 sets out a by-pass procedure.

Test your understanding

1 In what circumstances will a person commit an offence by breaching the general safety requirement which is set out in s.10(1) of the Consumer Protection Act 1987?

2 What powers in respect of product safety does the Consumer Protection Act Part 2 confer upon the Secretary of State?

3 What is the general safety requirement set out in Reg.7 of the General Product Safety Regulations?

4 What persons are regarded by the General Product Safety Regulations as producers of a product?

5 What two offences are created by Reg.13 of the General Product Safety Regulations?

Answers

1 A person will commit an offence by breaching s.10(1) of the Consumer Protection Act 1987 if he (a) supplies any consumer goods which fail to comply with the general safety requirement; or (b) offers or agrees to supply any such goods; or (c) exposes or possesses any such goods for supply.

2 The Consumer Protection Act Part 2 confers upon the Secretary of State the powers to make regulations to ensure that goods are safe, to ensure that unsafe goods are not made generally available and to ensure that appropriate information is supplied with goods. The Secretary of State may also serve prohibition notices, warning notices and notices requiring a person to supply him with information.

3 The general safety requirement, set out in Reg.7 of the General Product Safety Regulations, requires that no producer shall place a product on the market unless it is a safe product.

4 The General Product Safety Regulations primarily regard the manufacturer of the product as the producer of the product. Other professionals in the chain of supply can be regarded as producers of a product, insofar as their activities may affect the safety properties of a product placed on the market.

5 Reg.13 makes it an offence for a producer or distributor to: (a) offer or agree to place on the market any dangerous product or expose or possess any such product on the market; or (b) offer or agree to supply any dangerous product or expose or possess any such product for supply.

22.5 · The Computer Misuse Act 1990

The Computer Misuse Act 1990 was passed to deal with computer hacking. Since 1968 the Theft Act could deal adequately with computer crime where money was stolen or where property or a pecuniary advantage were obtained by deception. But no statute dealt with computer hacking, that is to say with accessing another's computer system without that person's express or implied permission. The need for a new statute was made plain by the House of Lords decision in *R v Gold* [1988] 2 WLR 984. In that case two journalists gained access to BT's computer network and altered some data. One of the journalists also gained access to the Duke of Edinburgh's PC and left the message: 'GOOD AFTERNOON. HRH DUKE OF EDINBURGH'. The journalists, who claimed to have acted to demonstrate how easy hacking was, were charged with an offence under the Forgery and Counterfeiting Act 1981. The House of Lords held that the defendants had committed no offence under that Act and so the need for new legislation was made apparent.

22.5.1 **The unauthorised access offence**

Section 1(1) of the Computer Misuse Act makes hacking a criminal offence. It provides that:

'A person is guilty of an offence if –
(a) he causes a computer to perform any function with intent to secure access to any program or data held in any computer;
(b) the access he intends to secure is unauthorised; and
(c) he knows at the time when he causes the computer to perform the function that this is the case.'

The *actus reus* of the s.1 offence is causing a computer to perform any function, which could merely meaning turning a computer on. Section 1(1)(c) makes it plain that *mens rea* is needed and s.1(2) provides that:

'The intent a person has to have to commit an offence under this section need not be directed at –
(a) any particular program or data;
(b) a program or data of any particular kind; or
(c) a program or data held in any particular computer.'

The s.1 offence is punishable by six months' imprisonment. The offence does not require that the defendant succeeds in securing unauthorised access, it is enough that he intends to do this.

Section 17(2) defines securing access to a program or data as causing a computer to perform any function so as to alter or erase the program or data, or copy or move it, or use it or have it output from the computer. So downloading music or copying software would be within s.1 as long as this was unauthorised. Although hackers generally use one computer to gain access to another, this is not necessary. In *Attorney-General's Reference (No.1 of 1991)* [1992] 3 WLR 432 a customer who had been left alone in a shop caused the shop owner's computer to give him a discount on the goods he was buying. The Court of Appeal held that he was rightly convicted under s.1.

Section 17(5) defines the meaning of unauthorised access:

'Access of any kind by any person to any program or data held in a computer is unauthorised if –
(a) he is not entitled to control access of the kind in question to the program or data; and
(b) he does not have consent to access by him of the kind in question to the program or data from any person who is so entitled.'

This definition was interpreted in a very limited way in *DPP v Bignell* [1988] 1 Cr App R 1. In that case two police officers who did have authorised access to the national police computer used a computer operator to gain information for personal purposes, misrepresenting the reason why they wanted the information. The Divisional Court held that the officers were not guilty, as 'access of the kind in question' (in s.17(5)(a)) meant only the type of access defined in s.17(2), that is to say altering, erasing, copying or moving it. The court thought that the Act was designed to protect the integrity of computer systems themselves rather than to protect the integrity of the information stored on such computer systems. In *R v Bow Street Magistrates and Allison, ex parte US Government* [1999] 3 WLR 620 the House of Lords agreed that the decision in *Bignell* was correct on the grounds that the computer operator did not exceed his authority. (This seems somewhat surprising, as it would be easy to regard the computer operator as an innocent agent through whom the police officers exceeded their authority.) However, their Lordships indicated that the Divisional Court had been wrong to interpret s.17(5) as it did. Lord Hobhouse said that s.1 was concerned with authority to access the actual data involved, rather than with authority to access kinds of data. In *Bignell* the Divisional Court thought that there was no problem in acquitting the officers as they would anyway have committed an offence under the Data Protection Act. However, this would not have been the case if the information retrieved had not been personal data (see Chapter 23 at 23.5.1).

A circuit judge who is satisfied that there are reasonable grounds for believing that a s.1 offence has been or is about to be committed in any premises can issue a search warrant for those premises to be searched. The police can then seize any article if they believe that it is evidence that a s.1 offence has been or is about to be committed. So a computer could be seized in order that its hard disk could be examined.

22.5.2 Intent to commit a further offence

The second offence under the Act is contained in s.2(1). This section makes it an offence to commit the s.1 offence with the intention of committing, or facilitating the commission of murder or a further offence which carries a sentence of at least five years' imprisonment.

There is no requirement that the further offence should be committed at the same time as the s.1 offence. Indeed, the s.2 offence can be committed even though it was impossible to commit the further offence. The sentence for the s.2 offence is five years' imprisonment. So the s.2 offence will not generally be used where the defendant succeeds in committing the further offence, because the defendant could anyway be sentenced to at least five years for having committed that offence. The s.2 offence is therefore useful when the defendant does not succeed in committing the further offence. For example, it would be useful where a defendant hacked into a computer to try to commit blackmail but failed so abysmally that he could not be convicted of blackmail or attempted blackmail.

22.5.3 Unauthorised modification of computer material

Section 3 makes it an offence to modify computer material without authorisation, by providing that:

'A person is guilty of an offence if –
(a) he does any act which causes an unauthorised modification of the contents of any computer; and
(b) at the time when he does the act he has the requisite intent and the requisite knowledge.'

The requisite intent is defined by s.3(2) as an intent to cause a modification of the contents of any computer program and by so doing: impair the operation of any computer; or prevent or impair access to any program or data held on any computer; or impair the operation of any such program or reliability of such data. The requisite knowledge is defined by s.3(4) as knowledge that any modification the defendant intends to cause is unauthorised. Section 3(3) provides that the intent does not need to be directed at any particular computer, program, data or modification.

Section 17(7) defines modification as using any computer so as to alter, add to or erase any program or data. Therefore, sending computer viruses is clearly within s.3. The maximum sentence is five years.

22.6 · Enforcement of consumer law

The Enterprise Act 2002 has replaced the Stop Now Orders Regulations 2001 and Part III of the Fair Trading Act 1973 by setting up an enforcement procedure which is based on the one created by the 2001 Regulations. The powers set out in the Act can be exercised by the OFT and other bodies responsible for enforcing consumer legislation. However, before seeking an enforcement order against a trader, the enforcing body will always give the trader a chance to respond to allegations against him and the option of giving a binding undertaking instead of being taken to court.

The OFT has a coordinating role to see that it is the most appropriate enforcement authority which takes action in any particular case. There are three types of enforcer. First, there are general enforcers, namely the OFT, trading standards departments and The Department of Enterprise, Trade and Investment in Northern Ireland. Second, there are EC based community enforcers. Third, there are bodies designated by the Secretary of State. At the time of writing these are the Civil Aviation Authority, the Director General of Electricity Supply for Northern Ireland, the Director General of Gas for Northern Ireland, the Director General of Telecommunications, the Director General of Water Services, the Information Commissioner and the Office of the Rail Regulator. However, enforcers other than the OFT must consult the OFT before taking any action to prevent a breach of consumer protection law.

Before taking action against a business any enforcer must give the business a notice period during which the business can give written undertakings, to either the OFT or a court, that it will voluntarily stop the offending behaviour and in future comply with the law. This notice period is generally two weeks but can be a short period if the interests of consumers are threatened to the extent that a shorter period is appropriate. An enforcement order will indicate the nature of the conduct which amounts to an infringement and direct the perpetrator not to continue with the conduct or repeat it. The court can also order that a corrective statement be published by the perpetrator in order to eliminate any continuing effects of the infringement. If undertakings are given but then ignored, action can be taken for contempt of court.

A domestic infringement of consumer law occurs when an act or omission is done or made by a person in business and this harms the collective interests of consumers within the UK. However, the act or omission in question must be a criminal offence, a breach of contract or some other civil wrong with a remedy which would be legally enforceable. It must also be within a certain range of trading activities. The OFT gives the following examples: misleading advertising, lotteries, credit, underage sales, sale of goods laws, misleading health claims, trade descriptions and mock auctions. A community infringement is an act or omission which harms the collective interests of consumers and which contravenes a Directive which has been given effect by a European Economic Area State. The OFT gives as examples: timeshare, unfair terms in consumer contracts, doorstep selling, distance selling, package travel and consumer credit. The OFT has the power to take action in other EC States but if a business in another country harms the collective interests of UK consumers then, generally, the OFT would ask the appropriate community enforcer to take enforcement action. If it is a UK-based business which is harming the collective interest of consumers in another EC State then a community enforcer could either ask the OFT to take action in the UK courts or could take such action himself, in consultation with the OFT.

Test your understanding

1 What three offences are created by the Computer Misuse Act 1990?

2 What powers does the OFT have to ensure that consumer protection legislation is complied with?

Answers

1 Section 1 of the Computer Misuse Act makes it an offence to cause a computer to perform any function with the intention of securing access to a program or data where this access is known to be unauthorised. Section 2 of the Computer Misuse Act makes it an offence to commit the s.1 offence with the intention of committing, or facilitating the commission of, an offence which carries a sentence of at least five years' imprisonment. Section 3 of the Computer Misuse Act makes it an offence to intentionally modify computer material while knowing that this is unauthorised.

2 The OFT has a coordinating role to ensure that the most appropriate enforcement authority takes action against a trader who is breaching consumer protection legislation. The OFT itself might be the most appropriate authority, in which case it could seek an enforcement order against a trader.

Key points

The nature of criminal liability

- The *actus reus* of an offence is the external element of the definition of the offence which is objectively required before the crime can be committed. The *mens rea* is the mental state of the accused which the prosecution will need to prove in order to establish that the offence was committed.

- A crime of strict liability is one which does not require the prosecution to prove *mens rea* in respect of one or more elements of the *actus reus*.

The Trade Descriptions Act 1968

- Section 1(1)(a) of the Trade Descriptions Act makes it an offence, in the course of a trade or business, to apply a false trade description to goods.

- Section 1(1)(b) of the Act makes it an offence, in the course of a trade or business, to supply or offer to supply any goods to which a false trade description is applied.

- Both of the s.1 offences are offences of the strict liability.

- False trade descriptions must relate either to the physical characteristics of the goods or to their past history.

- A trade description is false if it is false to a material degree.

- A disclaimer may prevent a trade description from arising.

- Section 14(1)(a) of the Act makes it an offence, in the course of a trade or business, to knowingly make a statement which is false about services, accommodation or facilities.

- As long as the defendant knows that the statement he makes is false, the s.14(1)(a) offence can be committed in respect of a statement which the defendant does not know is being made.

- Section 14(1)(b) of the Act makes it an offence, in the course of a trade or business, to recklessly make a statement which is false about services, accommodation or facilities.

- Section 24 of the Act gives a defence if the defendant can prove, on a balance of probabilities:
  (a) that the offence was committed either due to his own mistake, or to reliance on information supplied to him, or to the act or default of another person, or to some accident or other cause beyond his control; and
  (b) that he took all reasonable precautions and exercised all due diligence to prevent the commission of the offence.

- Section 23 of the Act sets out a by-pass provision, which allows a person who has caused another to be guilty of an offence under the Act to be charged with and convicted of the offence, whether or not proceedings are taken against the other person.

Misleading price indications

- Section 20 of the Consumer Protection Act 1987 creates two offences relating to misleading price indications. Both offences can only be committed by a person acting in the course of a business of his.

- The more serious offence, set out in s.20(1) of the Act, is committed by giving any consumers a misleading indication as to the price at which goods, services, accommodation or facilities are available.

- The less serious offence, set out in s.20(2) of the Act, is committed by failing to correct a misleading price indication which has been given to consumers.

■ Special defences are provided for publishers, advertisers and those who give a recommended price to all retailers. Section 39 of the Act provides a general defence of taking all reasonable precautions and exercising all due diligence to avoid committing the offence.

Product safety

■ Section 10 of the Consumer Protection Act 1987 sets out the general safety requirement which makes it an offence for a person to:

(a) supply any consumer goods which fail to comply with the general safety requirement; or

(b) offer or agree to supply any such goods; or

(c) expose or possess any such goods for supply.

■ The Consumer Protection Act 1987 confers power on the Secretary of State to make regulations and serve prohibition or warning notices in order to ensure product safety.

■ For the purposes of the General Product Safety Regulations 1994, s.10 of the Consumer Protection Act 1987 is disapplied.

■ Regulation 7 of the General Product Safety Regulations 1994 sets out the general safety requirement which requires that no producer shall place a product on the market unless it is a safe product.

■ A product is defined by the General Product Safety Regulations 1994 as any product intended for consumers or likely to be used by consumers and which was supplied in the course of a commercial activity. However, products used exclusively in the context of a commercial activity are excluded.

■ Regulation 13 of the General Product Safety Regulations 1994 makes it an offence for a producer or distributor to:

(a) offer or agree to place on the market any dangerous product or expose or possess any such product on the market; or

(b) offer or agree to supply any dangerous product or expose or possess any such product for supply.

Misuse of computers

■ Section 1 of the Computer Misuse Act makes it an offence to cause a computer to perform any function with the intention of securing access to a program or data where this access is known to be unauthorised.

■ Section 2 of the Computer Misuse Act makes it an offence to commit the s.1 offence with the intention of committing, or facilitating the commission of, an offence which carries a sentence of at least five years' imprisonment.

■ Section 3 of the Computer Misuse Act makes it an offence to intentionally modify computer material while knowing that this is unauthorised.

Summary questions

1 Last Monday Dicey Motors Ltd sold two cars. The first car, an Aston Martin, had an odometer reading of 21 000 miles because the managing director of Dicey Motors, Mr David Icey, had rewound the car's odometer from its true reading of 74 000 miles. The second car, a Bentley, also had a false odometer reading but Mr Icey was unaware of this both when he supplied the car to the purchaser and when he recorded the false reading onto an invoice, immediately prior to the customer signing the contract. Both of the cars sold had a sticker next to the odometer, reading 'THE MILEAGE ON THIS VEHICLE IS NOT GUARANTEED'. In the sales office of Dicey Motors Ltd a prominently displayed sign said: 'YOU SHOULD TAKE IT THAT ALL MILEOMETER READINGS DISPLAYED ARE INCORRECT, AS THIS IS THE BASIS ON WHICH ALL CARS ARE SOLD.' Mr Icey pointed this notice out to both purchasers before they bought their respective cars. Advise Dicey Motors Ltd of any liability they may have under the Trade Descriptions Act 1968.

2   In February 1999 Jim booked a holiday in Scotland with AB Holidays Ltd. The holiday was booked after Jim read AB's 1998 holiday brochure. This brochure stated that the hotel which Jim had chosen was 'within a stone's throw of the beach' and a 'sedate, contemplative spot, invoking the peaceful spirit of ancient Celtic mysteries'. The brochure also said that the hotel had its own 18-hole golf course, and that this was reserved solely for the hotel's guests.

When he returned from his holiday Jim complained to his local trading standards department that the hotel was at the top of a sheer 300 foot cliff, that it took 35 minutes to walk to the beach, that the noise from a local oil refinery carried on 24 hours a day, making it difficult to sleep at night, and that the golf course was closed while its greens were being re-laid. At the time when Jim booked the holiday, AB Holidays Ltd knew that the golf course greens were to be re-laid but it was believed that the job would have been completed by the time of Jim's holiday.

Advise AB Holidays Ltd of any liability they may have under the Trade Descriptions Act 1968.

3   Stores Ltd have a shop in a local shopping centre. Last week the shop was visited by trading standards officers, following complaints from customers. While at the shop the officers discovered that the goods in the shop had labels attached to them which indicated the price of the goods, but that there was occasionally a discrepancy between the prices indicated and those rung up on the till when the cashiers scanned the bar codes attached to the goods. The officers made several test purchases, and on two occasions they were charged the higher prices which were rung up on the till. On ten more occasions the cashier substituted the lower price written on the labels attached to the goods, voiding the price rung up on the till. The officers also discovered that on three items VAT was added by the cashier, although there had been no indication that VAT was not included in the price. The prices of all the other goods in the shop were inclusive of VAT. The officers also discovered that a conspicuous notice which said that the price of CDs was due to increase the following week has proved to be inaccurate as the price had remained the same. The store manager said that he had forgotten to increase the price because he had been worried about the health of his dog.

Explain whether or not Stores Ltd have committed any offences under the Consumer Protection Act 1987 Part 3.

4   Susan buys an electric hedge-cutter from Blunder Ltd DIY store. The hedge-cutters are part of a consignment which were manufactured in the UK by Cutcost Co Ltd. Blunder's manager saw a documentary on television which revealed that two people in Scotland have been severely electrocuted while using this type of hedge-cutter on damp hedges. As the documentary made clear, the instructions which come with the hedge-cutters clearly state that they should never be used on wet hedges and never used without a circuit breaker. Blunder Ltd do not make any attempt to recall hedge-cutters already sold, but do decide not to order any more.

While cutting the hedge after a heavy shower Susan's gardener, Henry, is electrocuted by the hedge-cutter and suffers severe burns.

Explain any criminal liability which either Blunder Ltd or Cutcost Co Ltd might be under.

Multiple choice questions

1   Which one of the following statements is not true?

a An offence is one of strict liability if the prosecution do not need to prove *mens rea* as regards one or more elements of the *actus reus*.

b The two offences created by s.1 of the Trade Descriptions Act 1968 can only be committed by a person acting in the course of a trade or business.

c As regards the Trade Descriptions Act 1968, whenever a business asset is sold, the sale will necessarily have been made in the course of a trade or business.

d A defendant will not commit the offence of applying a false trade description to goods, contrary to s.1 of the Trade Descriptions Act 1968, unless the false description is made in connection with a supply or an offer to supply goods.

2 Which one of the following statements, all of which are made in relation to the Trade Descriptions Act 1968, is not true?

  a A buyer of goods cannot be guilty of the s.1(1)(a) offence of applying a false trade description to goods.

  b The s.1(1)(a) offence cannot be committed if the false trade description was made after the goods had been supplied.

  c A false trade description must be false to a material degree, but a trade description which is not literally false, but is misleading, shall be deemed to be false.

  d A false trade description can be applied merely by supplying goods in pursuance of a request in which a false trade description is used.

3 Which one of the following statements, all of which are made in relation to the Trade Descriptions Act 1968, is not true?

  a A disclaimer, whilst not a defence as such, can prevent a trade description from being applied.

  b A person who innocently copies a false odometer reading onto an invoice applies a false trade description to goods.

  c A person can be guilty of the s.14(1)(a) offence even as regards a statement which he did not know had been made.

  d The s.14 offences can only be committed if the false statement induces the making of a contract.

4 Which one of the following statements, all of which are made in relation to the Trade Descriptions Act 1968, is not true?

  a The Act makes no mention of disclaimers, which are a creation of the courts.

  b The defences set out in s.24 of the Act cannot exonerate a defendant from liability for one of the s.1 offences of strict liability.

  c As regards the defences set out in s.24 of the Act, the defendant needs to prove both elements of the defences on a balance of probabilities.

  d Even a person who does not engage in any trade or business can be guilty of an offence under the by-pass provision, set out in s.23 of the Act.

5 Which one of the following statements is not true?

  a Part 3 of the Consumer Protection Act 1987 attempts to ensure that goods are sold at the correct price.

  b A notice relating to price which does not appear to be misleading can become misleading on account of a refusal to honour the terms of the notice.

  c No offence will be committed under s.20 of the Consumer Protection Act 1987 if a misleading price indication is given in respect of goods which are not available.

  d If misleading price indications have been given solely to persons who cannot be regarded as consumers then no offence will have been committed under s.20 of the Consumer Protection Act 1987.

6 Which one of the following statements is not true?

  a The general safety requirement set out in s.10(1) of the Consumer Protection Act 1987 is disapplied for the purposes of the General Product Safety Regulations 1994.

  b Regulation 7 of the General Product Safety Regulations 1994 sets out the main offence under the Regulations, namely that no producer shall place a product on the market unless it is a safe product.

  c For the purposes of Regulation 7 of the General Product Safety Regulations 1994, a retailer is not regarded as a producer unless the retailer's activities may affect the safety properties of a product placed on the market.

  d The General Product Safety Regulations 1994 do not set out any defences to the offence created by Regulation 7.

Task 22

A friend of yours who works as a market trader wants to ensure that he does not commit any criminal offences whilst running his business. He knows that you have some understanding of the way in which businesses are regulated by the imposition of criminal liability. Your friend has asked you to draft a report, briefly explaining the following matters:

a The offences created by the Trade Descriptions Act 1968, and any defences which may be available in respect of these offences.

b The offences relating to misleading price indications created by the Consumer Protection Act 1987, and any defences which may be available in respect of these offences.

c The offences relating to the supply of unsafe products created by the Consumer Protection Act 1987 and the General Product Safety Regulations 1994, and any defences which may be available in respect of these offences.

Chapter 23

BUSINESS PROPERTY

Introduction

We begin this chapter by classifying the different types of property and by explaining some fundamental legal concepts relating to property. We shall see that business property might be broadly classified into three types: land, goods or intangible rights. It is beyond the scope of this book to consider the law relating to the ownership of land. The law relating to ownership of goods was set out in Chapter 9. In this chapter therefore the emphasis is on the law relating to intangible property rights.

23.1 · Legal concepts of property

The common law categorises all property as either real property or as personal property. Real property is comprised of all freehold interests in land. Personal property is comprised of all other property, including leasehold interests in land. This distinction arose because in the Middle Ages a person who was dispossessed of real property could bring what was known as a real action to regain possession of the land. A person dispossessed of personal property could only bring a personal action, that is to say that he could only bring an action against the person who had dispossessed him, rather than an action which gave him a right to recover the property itself. Although leasehold interests in land are classed as personal property rather than as real property, most businesses would regard freehold and leasehold interests in land as much the same type of property. For most practical purposes leasehold interests in land have much more in common with real property than with other types of personal property (such as goods) or intangible rights (such as copyright).

Personal property is itself classified as either chattels real or chattels personal. Chattels real consist of leasehold interests in land. Chattels personal consist of all the remaining types of personal property. Chattels personal are divided into choses in possession, choses in action and intangible personal property. Choses in possession are moveable things of which physical possession can be taken, for example goods. Choses in action are intangible property rights which can only be enforced by taking legal action, for example the rights attaching to shares in a company. Finally, choses in action may be split into documentary and non-documentary choses in action. Documentary choses in action are represented by documents, such as bills of lading, which give a tangible form to a right to money or goods. The rights represented by the document can be transferred to a third party by delivering the document to him, and if necessary by endorsing the document. Choses in action other than documentary choses are non-documentary choses and consist of absolutely intangible rights such as a debt. These rights can be transferred to another by assignment. Intellectual property such as patents, copyright and trade marks are best regarded as intangible personal property, as various statutes indicate that they are not choses in action.

The different types of property can be seen in Figure 23.1.

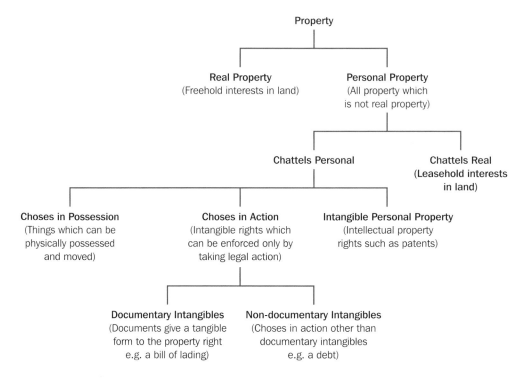

Figure 23.1   The legal classification of property

At common law personal property can either be owned or possessed. No other rights regarding property are recognised. But equity recognises other rights, such as a beneficiary's rights under a trust. Equity also recognises powers concerning property, these powers only being exercisable against certain other people. A good example is provided by the power of a person to rescind a voidable contract and thereby regain ownership of property which passed under the contract. (Rescission is examined in Chapter 6 at 6.1.3.) It should also be realised that property rights are not absolute. For example, we saw in Chapter 9, at 9.3.8, that until January 1995 a person who bought goods in good faith in a market overt could defeat any claim to ownership by a person from whom the goods had been stolen. The person from whom the goods had been stolen might have considered his ownership total, but his inability to regain the goods would reveal that this was not in fact the case.

Generally, a person who owns property will have both legal and equitable ownership. However, this is not necessarily the case. For example, when a trust exists the trustees have legal ownership of the property whilst the beneficiaries have equitable ownership.

Both the common law and equity recognise co-ownership of personal chattels. The common law recognises that a chattel might be co-owned either by joint tenants or by tenants in common. Equity has always recognised that chattels may be the subject of several equitable interests. Statutes too recognise co-ownership. For example, in Chapter 9 at 9.1.3, we saw that s.20A of the Sale of Goods Act 1979 allows a person who has bought a specified quantity of unascertained goods which form part of a bulk to become an owner in common of the bulk, even though his share of the bulk has not been ascertained.

The major intellectual property rights are fairly well known. These would include copyright, patents, trade marks, rights in performance, design rights, and the law of passing-off. The law of passing-off was considered briefly in Chapter 15 at 15.4.1.3. In this chapter we consider the law relating to copyright, patents and trade marks. We also consider the Data Protection Act 1998, which seeks to ensure that data relating to identifiable living individuals are not misused.

23.2 · Copyright

The law relating to copyright is governed by the Copyright, Designs and Patents Act 1988, referred to in this section of the book as the Act. The Act has been amended by the Copyright and Related Rights Regulations 2003, which implemented the Information Society Directive (2001/39) and fulfilled a number of international obligations.

Section 1(1) of the Act defines copyright:

'Copyright is a property right which subsists ... in the following descriptions of work –
(a) original literary, dramatic, musical or artistic works,
(b) sound recordings, films, or broadcasts and
(c) the typographical arrangements of published editions.'

Copyright protects the way in which ideas are expressed, rather than the ideas themselves. The matters listed in s.1(a) must be original. In *University of London Press Ltd* v *University Tutorial Press Ltd* [1916] 2 Ch 601 Peterson J said: 'The word original does not in this connection mean that the work must be the expression of original or inventive thought. Copyright Acts are not concerned with the originality of ideas, but with the expression of thought, and in the case of a literary work, with the expression of thought in print, writing or recorded spoken words. The originality which is required relates to the expression of the thought.' In the case it was decided that mathematics exams which drew on the stock of knowledge common to mathematicians were literary works.

It is not essential that the work must have taken a long time to complete, but the *de minimis* principle will prevent single words, such as brand names, or very small numbers of words from being regarded as artistic works, within the meaning of s.1(1)(a).

23.2.1 The types of work in which copyright can exist

We have seen that s.1(1) of the Act sets out the types of work in which copyright can exist. In order to understand the boundaries of copyright we need to examine the nature of these types of work in some detail. The Act sets out specific definitions of the various matters and the definitions need to be examined in turn.

Section 1(1)(a) refers to original literary, dramatic, musical or artistic works. Section 3(1) defines both 'literary work' and 'musical work'. This rather lengthy definition tells us that a literary work might be written, spoken or sung and therefore classifies song lyrics as literary works. It also tells us that databases, computer programs, tables and compilations are literary works. Although not specifically mentioned in the definition, a street directory has been held to be a literary work. It is therefore plain that a literary work does not have to be what most people would regard as a work of literature.

A database is defined by s.3A(1) as a collection of independent works, data or other material which (a) are arranged in a systematic or methodical way, and (b) are individually accessible by electronic or other means. However, a database can only be regarded as an original literary work if the way its contents were selected or arranged constituted the author's own intellectual creation. This requirement would debar an alphabetical list of names.

A musical work is defined as a work consisting of music, exclusive of any words or action intended to be sung, spoken or performed with the music. A dramatic work is not defined, but includes a work of dance or mime as well as the more obvious example of a script for a play. Artistic work is not concerned with artistic quality at all where photographs, graphic works, sculptures and collages are concerned. However, works of architecture and of artistic craftsmanship do require artistic quality.

Section 3(2) of the 1988 Act provides that copyright does not exist in a literary, dramatic or musical work until it is recorded, in writing or otherwise. However, the recording does not need to be done by the author or with the author's permission.

The matters set out in s.1(1)(a) need to be original works in the sense that they must involve an original expression of an idea. The matters listed in s.1(1)(b) and (c) are derivative. They are based upon and derived from an original work. For example, most popular films are derivative works which are based upon an original work, the film script.

Sound recordings are defined by s.5A(1) of the Act. They mean (a) a recording of sounds, from which the sounds may be reproduced, or (b) a recording of the whole or any part of a literary, dramatic or musical work, from which sounds reproducing the work or part may be produced. Recordings can be sound recordings regardless of the medium on which they are made or the method by which the sounds are reproduced or produced. Copyright does not exist to the extent that a sound recording is a copy taken from a previous sound recording. The use of the word 'sound' means that speech and other noises are included, and that any musical quality or other quality of the sounds is not a factor.

Films are defined by s.5B(1) as recordings on any medium from which a moving image may by any means be reproduced. An accompanying sound track is treated as part of the film. Copyright does not exist in a film to the extent that it is a copy of a previous film.

Section 6 has been amended by the 2003 Regulations to give a new definition of 'broadcasts':

'A broadcast is an electronic transmission of visual images, sounds or other information which –
(a) is transmitted for simultaneous reception by members of the public and is capable of being lawfully received by them, or
(b) is transmitted at a time determined solely by the person making the transmission for presentation to members of the public.'

Section 6(1A) provides that internet transmissions are not broadcasts unless they are one of the following:

(a)   a transmission taking place simultaneously on the internet and by other means;
(b)   a concurrent transmission of a live event; or
(c)   a transmission of recorded moving images or sounds forming part of a programme service offered by the person responsible for making the transmission, being a service in which programmes are transmitted at scheduled times determined by that person.

Section 6(2) provides that an encrypted transmission (such as pay-per-view tv) shall be regarded as capable of being lawfully received by members of the public only if decoding equipment has been made available to members of the public by or with the authority of the person making the transmission or the person providing the contents of the transmission.

Section 1(1)(c) provided that copyright could subsist in the typographical arrangements of published editions. Typography is the art of planning and setting out type so that a work may be printed. Section 8(1) states that 'published edition' in the context of copyright in the typographical arrangement of a published edition, means a published edition of the whole or any part of one or more literary, dramatic or musical works. Although most readers of a book would recognise that the author had copyright in the words, they might not realise that the publisher has copyright in the typographical arrangement of the book.

23.2.2 Authorship and ownership of copyright

The Act defines the author of a work as the person who created it. In the case of a film the authors will be taken to be the producer and principal director, who will be joint owners if they are not the same person. As regards the typographical arrangements of published editions, the publisher is regarded as the author. The author of a work will be the first owner of it. However, s.11(2) provides that where a literary, dramatic, musical or artistic work, or a film, is made by an employee in the course of his employment, the employer is the first owner of any copyright in the work subject to any agreement to the contrary.

23.2.3 Duration of copyright

Copyright exists for different lengths of time, depending upon the type of work concerned. As regards the copyright in literary, dramatic, musical or artistic works, the copyright expires at the end of 70 years from the end of the calendar year in which the author dies. However, if the work is computer-generated, copyright expires at the end of the period of 50 years from the end of the calendar year in which the work was made. A work will not be a computer-generated work merely because it was produced on a word processor. Section 178 provides that a work is computer-generated if it is generated by computer in circumstances such that there is no human author of the work. There is considerable debate as to the circumstances in which this might happen. One possible example might be provided by weather reports produced by a computer which automatically took information from various weather centres.

Section 13A provides that copyright in a sound recording expires:

'(a) at the end of the period of 50 years from the end of the calendar year in which the recording is made, or
(b) if during that period it is published, 50 years from the end of the calendar year in which it is first published; or
(c) if during that period the recording is not published but is made available to the public by being played in public or communicated to the public, 50 years from the end of the calendar year in which is first so made available,

but in determining whether a sound recording has been published, played in public or communicated to the public, no account shall be taken of any unauthorised act.'

It would therefore be possible for the copyright in a sound recording to exist for 100 years after it was made, if the sound recording was not published until 50 years after it was made.

The copyright in films expires 70 years from the end of the calendar year in which the death occurs of the last to die of:

(a) the principal director;
(b) the author of the screenplay;
(c) the author of the dialogue; or
(d) the composer of music specially created for and used in the film.

Copyright in a broadcast expires at the end of the period of 50 years from the end of the calendar year in which the broadcast was made. Copyright in typographical arrangements of published editions expires at the end of 25 years from the end of the calendar year in which the edition was first published.

Special rules apply to Crown and Parliamentary copyright. As regards literary, dramatic, musical or artistic work, Crown or Parliamentary copyright does not expire until 125 years from the end of the calendar year in which the work was created. As regards Acts of Parliament, copyright expires 50 years after the end of the year in which the Act was given the Royal Assent.

23.2.4 Rights of copyright owners

Section 16(1) gives the copyright owner the exclusive right to:

(a) copy the work;
(b) issue copies of the work to the public;
(c) rent or lend the work to the public;
(d) perform, show or play the work in public;
(e) communicate the work to the public;
(f) make an adaptation of the work or do any of the above in relation to an adaptation.

If any person does any of the above restricted acts without the licence of the copyright holder, or authorises anyone else to do this, copyright in the work is infringed. It is important to remember that what is protected is not an idea, but the way in which an idea is expressed. It is also important to realise that infringement does not need to be intentional and can be committed subconsciously. There must, however, be a causal connection. The work must be copied.

A little needs to be said about the various matters in respect of which the copyright owner has exclusive rights. Copying the work can be done by storing the work electronically, for example by down-loading material onto a computer. In relation to a film or broadcast, copying can be done by making a photograph of the whole or any substantial part of any image forming part of the film or broadcast. Making a video recording of a film would probably be the most common way in which this is done. In relation to typographical arrangements of published editions, copying can only be done by making a facsimile copy of the arrangement, for example by photocopying it.

A new section, s.28A, allows the making of temporary copies in certain circumstances such as browsing on the Internet. It provides that copyright in a literary work, other than a computer program or a database, or in a dramatic, musical or artistic work, the typographical arrangement of a published edition, a sound recording or a film, is not infringed by the making of a temporary copy which is transient or incidental, which is an integral and essential part of a technological process and the sole purpose of which is to enable: (a) a transmission of the work in a network between third parties by an intermediary; or (b) a lawful use of the work; and which has no independent economic significance.

Section 16(3)(a) provides that restricted acts must relate to the work as a whole or to any substantial part of it. This creates a difficulty in that the Act does not define what is meant by a substantial part. Each case is decided on its own facts, and there is no given percentage above which a substantial part is reached. It is not the quantity of the work copied which is relevant, but the quality. If the most 'important' part of a work was copied this might be a substantial part even if it was not a large percentage of the work. An important factor for consideration, but only a factor, is whether the work alleged to have been copied is in competition with the copyrighted work.

Infringement by issuing copies to the public would be committed by putting into circulation copies which had not previously been put into circulation by or with the consent of the copyright owner. The right of the copyright owner to issue works to the public for the first time is known as the 'distribution right'. Once copies have been put on the market in the EEA, this right is exhausted.

Copyright can be infringed by renting the work for commercial gain. Lending of the work to the public without gaining any commercial advantage can also infringe copyright. The performance of a literary, dramatic or musical work in public includes delivery in a lecture or speech and any mode of visual or acoustic presentation. If the copyright is infringed by being shown by electronic means, the person by whom the visual images or sounds are sent is not regarded as responsible for the infringement. Section 182 of the Act now includes a 'making available right'. It provides that a performer's rights are infringed if someone makes available to the public a recording of the whole or a substantial part of a performance by electronic transmission so that the public can access it from a place or time which they choose.

Section 16(1)(e) gives the copyright owner the exclusive right to make an adaptation of a literary, dramatic or musical work. Adaptations of works include translations, conversions of a dramatic work into a non-dramatic work and vice versa, and conveying the work in pictures. In relation to computer programs and databases, adaptation includes making an arrangement or altered version of the work. A computer program is regarded as having been translated if it is converted into or out of a computer language or code, or into a different computer language or code.

Section 23 provides that:

'The copyright in a work is infringed by a person who, without the licence of the copyright owner –

(a) possesses in the course of a business;
(b) sells or lets for hire, or offers or exposes for sale or hire;
(c) in the course of a business exhibits in public or distributes; or

(d) distributes otherwise than in the course of a business to such an extent as to affect prejudicially the owner of the copyright,

an article which is, and which he knows or has reason to believe is, an infringing copy of the work.'

This is known as secondary infringement, whereby the perpetrator does not himself copy the work but rather he exploits it commercially. It can be seen from the definition that secondary infringement can only be committed when the perpetrator knows or has reason to believe that copyright is being infringed. This is in contrast to primary infringement which, as we have seen, can be committed subconsciously.

The Act lists at great length various acts which are permitted in relation to copyright works. The more important of these relate to the following: 'Fair dealing with a literary work (other than a database), or a dramatic, musical or artistic work for the purposes of research or private study does not infringe copyright.' The Act does not define the meaning of fair dealing. In *Hubbard* v *Vosper* [1972] 2 QB 84 at 94 Lord Denning MR said:

> 'It is impossible to define what is "fair dealing". It must be a question of degree. You must consider first the number and extent of the quotations and extracts. Are they altogether too many and too long to be fair? Then you must consider the use made of them. If they are used as a basis for comment, criticism or review, that may be fair dealing. If they are used to convey the same information as the author, for a rival purpose, that may be unfair. Next, you must consider the proportions. To take long extracts and attach short comments may be unfair. But short extracts and long comments may be fair. Other considerations may come to mind also. But, after all is said and done, it must be a matter of impression.'

As regards a database, fair dealing for the purposes of research and private study will not infringe copyright as long as the source is indicated. In the cases of criticism, review and news reporting, fair dealing does not infringe copyright provided that it is accompanied by a sufficient acknowledgement. Where a work is incidentally included in an artistic work, sound recording, film, broadcast or cable programme, copyright in the work is not infringed.

As well as these generally permitted acts, special exemptions also apply as regards things done for the purpose of education, as regards libraries and archives, and as regards things done for the purposes of parliamentary or judicial proceedings.

If the copyright is transferred by the author to another by way of assignment then the transferee takes over from the author all rights in respect of infringement. The assignment may be partial, in that it may apply to only some of the things which the copyright holder has the exclusive right to do. It may also be partial in that it may be for a shorter period of time than that for which the copyright is to exist. An assignment of copyright will only be effective if it is signed by or on behalf of the assignor.

As an alternative to assignment, the proprietor might grant a licence in respect of the work. This licence might be exclusive, in which case the assignee is granted rights in the work to the exclusion of all other people, including the person granting the licence. An exclusive licence can only be transferred in writing signed by or on behalf of the copyright owner. A licence granted by a copyright owner will bind all successors in title to his interest in the copyright, except a purchaser in good faith for valuable consideration who had no actual or constructive notice of the assignment, or a person deriving title from such a purchaser. At first sight this seems a major exception. However, once a work has been exploited commercially by the licensee it will be very difficult for anyone to argue that he had no constructive notice of the licence.

23.2.4.1 Moral rights

Authors are given several moral rights in respect of their works. If these rights are infringed then a remedy for breach of statutory duty will be available. Damages are therefore available. An injunction will be the appropriate remedy to prevent derogatory treatment of the work.

There are four moral rights. First, an author who asserts his right to be identified as the author of a literary, dramatic, musical or artistic work has the moral right to be identified as the author of the work whenever the work is performed commercially, performed in public or communicated to the public (the paternity right). Regardless of whether or not the author asserted any rights, he is also given a second moral right to object to any derogatory treatment of the work, and a third right not to have literary, dramatic, musical or artistic works falsely attributed to him as author. (This particular right subsists only for 20 years after the author's death, the other moral rights subsist for as long as the copyright itself subsists.) A fourth and final moral right gives a person who commissions the taking of a photograph or the making of a film for private purposes not to have the work, or copies of it, exhibited, broadcast or shown in public. A fifth moral right, the artist's resale right or droit de suite, is to take effect in 2006.

Generally, copyright can be transmitted by assignment, by leaving it in a will, by operation of law or as personal or moveable property. The moral rights cannot be assigned, but some moral rights can be inherited. (The paternity right, the right to object to derogatory treatment and the right to privacy regarding photographs or films.) The moral rights cannot be infringed if the author has consented to the infringement or has waived his moral rights.

23.2.5 Remedies for infringement

Section 96 provides that an infringement of copyright is actionable by the copyright owner, and that all the remedies which would be available in respect of the infringement of any other property right should be available. However, the remedy of damages is not available if the defendant, at the time of infringement, did not know, and had no reason to believe, that copyright subsisted in the work. The other remedies, such as injunction would be available. When a court does award damages it may award additional damages if the justice of the case so requires. In assessing this, s.97 requires the court to have regard to all the circumstances, but particularly to (a) the flagrancy of the infringement, and (b) any benefits accruing to the defendant by reason of that infringement.

An owner of copyright may apply for a court order that a person deliver up an infringing copy of a work in his possession, custody or control. This right also exists in respect of articles specifically designed or adapted for making copies of a particular copyright work. An owner of copyright may seize and detain infringing copies of works which are exposed for sale or hire. A court order is not necessary, but the owner, or a person authorised by him to do the seizing, must notify a local police station of the time and place of the proposed seizure. Where a person has been granted an exclusive licence in respect of the work he has the same rights as the copyright owner.

Various criminal offences are created in relation to articles which are, and which the defendant knows or has reason to believe are, infringements of copyright. These offences relate to making copies of the work for sale or hire, importing them for business purposes, possessing them for business purposes with a view to committing a copyright infringement and selling, exhibiting or distributing them. The criminal law here is enforced by local weights and measures authorities. The 2003 Regulations have created new criminal offences of infringing a work by communicating it to the public to such an extent as to affect prejudicially the owner of the copyright (while knowing or believing that by so doing he is infringing copyright in the work) and infringing a performer's 'making available' rights (considered above). It is also now an offence to manufacture or import, sell, advertise, possess or distribute any device which is primarily designed to facilitate the circumvention of technological measures which are designed to protect copyright holders against infringement and unauthorised use.

Copyright licensing schemes exist whereby the owners of copyright give permission to do certain acts on standard terms. An example is provided by the Authors' Licensing and Collecting Society Limited. This society runs a scheme which raises money, to be distributed to authors, when copies of works are made by licensees.

Civil copyright cases are heard in the county court or the Chancery Division of the High Court. If the infringement of copyright constitutes a criminal offence a case can be brought in either the magistrate's court or the Crown Court.

Test your understanding

1 What are choses in action?

2 What is the difference between a documentary intangible and a non-documentary intangible?

3 What three descriptions of work in which copyright might subsist are set out s.1(1)(a) to (c) of the Copyright, Designs and Patents Act 1988?

4 To what extent is copyright concerned with the protection of ideas?

5 For how long does copyright in a literary, dramatic, musical or artistic work subsist?

6 Does copyright have to be registered?

7 What are the four moral rights given to an author of copyright?

Answers

1 A chose in action is an intangible form of personal property which cannot be physically possessed or touched.

2 A documentary intangible is a form of intangible property represented by and embodied in a document. A non-documentary intangible is an intangible property right which is not represented by and embodied in a document.

3 The three types of work in which copyright may exist, as set out by s.1(1) of the Act are: (a) original literary, dramatic, musical or artistic works; (b) sound recordings, films or broadcasts; and (c) the typographical arrangements of published editions.

4 Copyright is not concerned with the protection of ideas themselves, but with the protection of the way in which ideas are expressed.

5 Copyright in a literary, dramatic, musical or artistic work subsists for 70 years after the end of the calendar year in which the author died.

6 Copyright does not have to be registered.

7 The four moral rights given to an author of copyright are: the right to be identified as the author of the work; the right to object to derogatory treatment of the work; the right not to have literary, dramatic, musical or artistic work falsely attributed to him; and the right of a person who commissions the taking of a photograph or making of a film for private purposes not to have the work or copies of it exhibited, broadcast or shown in public.

23.3 · Patents

Patents can be taken out only in respect of inventions which are capable of having industrial application. A patent must be applied for and, as we shall see, is not easily granted. Patents law is governed by the Patents Act 1977, which in this section of this book is referred to as the Act. Patents have a twofold purpose. They encourage innovation by granting monopoly rights in respect of inventions, while at the same time making access to technological advances publicly available.

23.3.1 Patentable inventions

Section 1(1) of the Patents Act 1977 provides that a patent can only be granted for an invention in respect of which four conditions are satisfied. These conditions are:

(a) that the invention is new;
(b) that it involves an inventive step;
(c) that it is capable of industrial application;
(d) that the grant of a patent is not excluded by s.1(2) or s.1(3).

Section 1(2) provides that the following matters are not inventions and that there can therefore be no patenting of them:

(a) discoveries, scientific theories or mathematical methods;
(b) aesthetic creations and literary, dramatic, musical or artistic work;
(c) ways of performing a mental act, playing a game, or doing business;
(d) a program for a computer; or
(e) the presentation of information.

The European Commission has published a Draft Directive on the patenting of software, which would apply if the software operates in tandem with an apparatus, if it does 'more' than a mental act and with the apparatus it makes a 'technical contribution' to the state of the art.

Section 1(3) provides that a patent shall not be granted for an invention the commercial exploitation of which would be contrary to public policy or morality (which means that the exploitation is prohibited by any law in force in the UK or part of it). Section 1(3) also provides that animals and plants are excluded, as are essentially biological processes for the production of animals or plants if they are not a microbiological process or the product of such a process. However, plant varieties are protected by the Plant Varieties and Seeds Act 1964, as amended.

An invention can only be regarded as new if it does not form part of the state of the prior art, which includes all matters that have at any time before the date of the invention been made available to the public in any way. This can include matters contained in an application for another patent.

A step can only be regarded as an inventive step if it was not obvious to a person who was skilled in the art. An invention is capable of having industrial application if it can be made or used in any kind of industry, including agriculture. New methods of surgery, therapy or diagnosis which are to be practised on humans or animals cannot be taken to be of industrial application.

A patent does not have to apply to a new item, it can apply to the way an existing item is used or to the way in which an existing item is produced. For example, a new way of manufacturing paper could be patentable.

23.3.2 Making an application

Applications for a patent are made to the Patent Office, to whom a fee must be paid. The application must contain a specification containing a description of the invention, as well as a claim for the patent and any drawing referred to in the description or the claim. An abstract, meaning a concise summary of the specification, must also be submitted. Generally, a specification would contain complex drawings.

Section 14(3) provides that the specification must disclose the invention in a manner which is clear enough and complete enough for the invention to be performed by a person skilled in the art. It must therefore be comprehensive and exact enough to be capable of being used by a person skilled in the art to produce the invention. Section 14(5) provides that the claim must: (a) define the matter for which the applicant seeks protection; (b) be clear and concise; (c) be supported by the description; and (d) relate to one invention or to a group of inventions which are so linked as to form a single inventive concept.

The date of filing an application will arise as soon as the documents filed at the Patent Office contain an indication that a patent is being sought. These documents must identify the applicant and a description of the invention, and the date will not arise until the fee is paid.

Once the application has acquired a date of filing it is then referred to an examiner for a preliminary application and search. The purpose of this examination is to determine whether or not the application complies with the Act's requirements. If this stage is satisfied, the application then goes for a substantive examination. If this substantive examination reveals that any of the Act's requirements have not been met the applicant is given an opportunity, within a specified time, to make observations on the report and to amend the application. If the examiner is not satisfied with the amendments the application for a patent may be refused. If the examiner is satisfied that the application does satisfy the Act's requirements then a patent can be granted.

An applicant has a general power to amend an application of his own volition before a patent is granted. A patent must comply with all of the Act's requirements within a prescribed period or the application will be regarded as having been refused.

If a patent is granted this fact is published as soon as is practicable in a notice in the Official Journal (*Patents*). The notice contains the name of the inventor, the names of the proprietor and any other matters which the comptroller thinks it desirable to publish. A patent can continue in force for 20 years from the date of filing the application for the patent. Initially patents last for four years. After this they can be renewed annually on payment of a fee.

Patent agents commonly act for people applying for a patent. A patent agent's role is to prepare the specification and the claim. Only those who are registered with the Chartered Institute of Patents Agents can call themselves patent agents.

23.3.3 Property in patents

The proprietor of a patent has a monopoly right to exploit it. This is the case even if it could be shown that someone else had independently reached the same inventive step. Both patents and applications for patents are personal property but s.30(1) of the Act states that they are not things in action. This seems surprising but it is a technicality which allows patents to be reached in bankruptcy proceedings. Anyway, it is of little importance as patents can be transferred by way of assignment or mortgaged. A patent may also be inherited in the same way as any other personal property. When two or more people are granted a patent they are granted equal co-ownership unless there is an indication to the contrary.

A patent can be licensed to another so that this other may exploit the patent without infringing the rights of the proprietor. Rights are commonly granted in this way.

23.3.4 Employees' inventions

Section 39(1) states that an invention made by an employee shall be taken as belonging to his employer in two circumstances. These circumstances are that:

(a) the invention was made in the course of the normal duties of the employee, or in the course of other duties which were specifically assigned to him, and the circumstances in either case were such that an invention might reasonably be expected to result from the carrying out of his duties; or

(b) the invention was made in the course of the duties of the employee and, at the time of making the invention, because of the nature of his duties and the particular responsibilities arising from the nature of his duties, he had a special obligation to further the interests of the employer's undertaking.

Where the conditions in s.39(1) are not satisfied, s.39(2) provides that any other invention made by an employee shall be taken as belonging to the employee.

Section 40 allows a court or the comptroller to award compensation to an employee who makes an invention belonging to the employer for which a patent has been granted. This will be done if the patent is (having regard amongst other things to the employer and the size and nature of the employer's undertaking) of outstanding benefit to the employer and that by reason of those facts it is just that the employee should be paid compensation by the employer. Section 41 provides that the amount of the compensation should be such as will secure for the employee a fair share, having regard to all the circumstances, of the benefits which the employer has derived or can be expected to derive from the patent. The court or comptroller also has the power to award compensation where the patent was assigned by the employee to the employer for less than it was worth. Contract terms which seek to restrict these rights will be unenforceable.

23.3.5 Compulsory licences

Subject to provisions of EC law, three years after a patent has been granted, any person may apply to the comptroller for a licence under the patent on the following grounds:

(a) that the patented invention is not being worked commercially in the UK, although it could be, or is not being worked to the fullest extent that is reasonably practicable;
(b) in the case of a patented product, that UK demand for the product is either not being met on reasonable terms, or is being met to a substantial extent by imports;
(c) in the case of patented inventions, that they are not being commercially worked in the UK, although they could be, and that they are being prevented or hindered from being so worked by imports;
(d) that on account of the proprietor's refusal to grant a licence on reasonable terms, an export market for the patented product is not being supplied, or that commercial or industrial activities in the UK are unfairly prejudiced from being established or developed, or that the working in the UK of any other patented invention is prevented or hindered;
(e) that the manufacture, use or disposal of materials which are not protected by the patent, or commercial or industrial development in the UK, is unfairly prejudiced by conditions imposed by the proprietor of the patent.

If satisfied that any of these conditions are being fulfilled the comptroller may either grant a licence in respect of the patent on any terms which he sees fit, or may make an entry in the register to the effect that licences under the payment are available as of right. The Secretary of State may also make such an entry on the register if the Competition Commission lay a report before Parliament to the effect that a monopoly situation exists. When a compulsory licence is granted the patentee will generally be compensated.

Section 55 allows any government department to take over a patent for the services of the Crown. When the Crown exercises this right compensation is payable to the proprietor of the patent. The compensation is for any loss resulting from the proprietor not being awarded a contract to supply the patented product or to perform the patented process or supply a thing made by means of the patented process.

23.3.6 Infringement of patents

Section 60(1) sets out three ways in which a patent can be infringed. These are as follows:

(a) In respect of patented products infringement is committed by making, disposing of, offering to dispose of, using or importing the product or keeping it whether for disposal or otherwise.
(b) In respect of patented processes, infringement is committed by using the process or offering it for use in the UK when the person who does this knows, or where it is obvious to a reasonable person in the circumstances, that its use there without the consent of the proprietor would be an infringement of the patent.
(c) In respect of patented process infringement can be committed by disposing of, offering to dispose of, using or importing any product obtained directly by means of that process or by keeping any such product whether for disposal or otherwise.

Section 60(5) provides that acts done privately and for purposes which are not commercial will not constitute infringement, nor will acts done for purely experimental purposes.

Section 61(1) provides that the following civil remedies may be claimed for infringement:

(a) an injunction restraining the defendant from any apprehended act of infringement;
(b) an order to destroy or deliver up any patented product or any product in which a patented product is incorporated;
(c) damages;
(d) an account of the profits derived from the infringement;
(e) a declaration that the patent is valid and has been infringed.

A court will not award both damages and an order for an account of profits. A person who was not aware, and had no reasonable grounds to suppose, that the patent existed will not be ordered to pay damages or ordered to make an account of profits. It is up to the defendant relying on either of these two matters to prove them. The word patent on the product will not be enough to mean that the defendant should have been aware that a patent existed unless it is accompanied by the appropriate patent number.

If a patentee brings groundless claims for infringement then any aggrieved person who has suffered more than minimal damage may sue for a declaration that the threats are groundless, or an injunction to prevent further groundless threats and damages to compensate for losses caused by the groundless threats.

The court or comptroller may revoke a patent for an invention on grounds which equate approximately to the grounds on which an application for a patent could have been refused in the first place. The comptroller can exercise this power on his own initiative.

It is a criminal offence either to represent falsely that a thing disposed of for value is a patented product, or to claim falsely that a patent has been applied for in respect of any article disposed of for value.

23.4 · Trade marks

The Trade Marks Act 1994 (which in this section of the book is called 'the Act') replaced the Trade Marks Act 1938. The Act, and the accompanying Trade Mark Rules 1994, have updated the law and given effect to an EC Directive which sought to harmonise the law throughout the EC.

23.4.1 Meaning of trade marks and registration of trade marks

A trade mark is given a wide definition by s.1(1):

> 'In this Act a "trade mark" means any sign capable of being represented graphically which is capable of distinguishing goods or services of one undertaking from those of another undertaking. A trade mark may, in particular, consist of words (including personal names), designs, letters, numerals or the shape of goods or their packaging.'

It can be seen that a trade mark is widely defined and can consist of almost any visual representation, including a shape. The only two requirements in s.1(1) are that the sign should be capable of being represented graphically and that it should be capable of distinguishing one person's products from another person's. However, registration of a trade mark can be refused on either absolute or relative grounds.

The absolute grounds for refusal of registration, set out in s.3, are as follows:

(a) the sign does not satisfy the definition set out in s.1(1);
(b) that the trade mark is devoid of any distinctive character;
(c) that the trade mark consists exclusively of signs which may serve in trade to indicate matters such as kind, quality, quantity, intended purpose, value, geographical origin, the time of production or other characteristics of goods or services;

(d) that the trade mark consists exclusively of signs or indications which have become customary in the current language or established practices of the trade;

(e) that it consists exclusively of a shape which results from the very nature of the goods, or a shape necessary to obtain technical results, or a shape which gives substantial value to the goods;

(f) that the trade mark is contrary to public policy or is of a nature intended to deceive the public;

(g) that the trade mark is illegal or the application was made in bad faith.

The matters set out in (b), (c) and (d) will not prevent registration if the trade mark has acquired a distinctive character as a result of the use which is made of it. A large number of national and international emblems are prohibited from being trade marks by s.4.

The relative grounds for refusing registration, set out in s.5, are as follows:

(a) identical marks on identical goods and services;

(b) identical marks on similar goods and services (and there exists a likelihood of confusion on the part of the public, which includes the likelihood of association with the earlier mark);

(c) similar marks on identical or similar goods and services (and there exists a likelihood of confusion on the part of the public, which includes the likelihood of association with the earlier mark);

(d) identical or similar marks on goods and services which are not similar, if the use of the mark without due cause would take unfair advantage of the earlier mark or be detrimental to it.

An identical or similar trade mark can be registered for goods or services which are not similar to those for which the earlier trade mark is protected. However, even here registration will not be allowed to the extent that the earlier mark has a reputation in the UK and the use of the later mark would take unfair advantage of this or be detrimental to it. An earlier trade mark is one which has been registered in the UK or the EC or has an earlier date of application to be registered.

The rights under the Act are only conferred once the trade mark, which is a property right, is registered. As regards an unregistered trade mark an action for passing off may lie, but the Act will provide no remedies.

23.4.2 Effect of registered trade mark

The proprietor of a registered trade mark is given exclusive rights in the trade mark. If the trade mark is used in the UK without his consent these rights are infringed. Section 10 sets out the various ways in which infringement might occur. These might be summarised as:

(a) using a sign in the course of a trade or business which is identical to the trade mark and is used in relation to identical goods or products;

(b) using a sign which is similar to the trade mark, in relation to similar or identical goods, thereby creating the likelihood of confusion on the part of the public;

(c) using a sign which is similar or identical to a trade mark, in relation to goods or services which are not similar to the goods or services protected by the trade mark, where the trade mark has a reputation in the UK and the use of the sign takes unfair advantage of, or is detrimental to, the distinctive character or the repute of the trade mark.

A sign is used in various ways, including by: fixing it onto a package; putting goods under the sign; importing or exporting under the sign; or using the sign on business paper or in advertising.

Trade marks are not infringed by a person using his own name and address as long as the use is in accordance with honest practices in industrial or commercial matters. This is an objective test and is not the same as asking whether or not the defendant acted honestly.

An action for infringement is brought by the proprietor of the trade mark and all remedies which would be available in respect of any other property right are available. In addition the court may: order offending signs to be erased or removed; order infringing goods, materials or articles to be delivered up to the proprietor; and order that these may be destroyed or forfeited to such person as the court thinks fit. If a groundless threat of infringement proceedings is made any aggrieved person who has suffered more than minimal damage may apply to a court for a declaration that the threats are unjustifiable or for damages or for an injunction.

A registered trade mark is personal property which can be co-owned or assigned to another. Licences permitting their use may be granted to others.

23.4.3 Procedure for registration

An application for registration of a trade mark has to include the following four matters: a request for registration; the name and address of the applicant; a statement of the goods or services to which the trade mark is to apply; and a representation of the trade mark itself. A system of classification exists, for more than 40 classes of goods and services, under which the applicant applies for registration.

The registrar decides whether or not an application should be granted. In order to make this decision he will carry out a search of earlier trade marks. If the registrar decides that the requirements are met he will accept the application. If the registrar decides that the requirements are not met he will give the applicant an opportunity to amend the application within a given period. Failure to amend the application adequately within this period will mean that the registrar will refuse the application.

Where the registrar decides that the application for registration has been accepted he publishes this in the *Trade Marks Journal*. Any person may then make a written objection or make written observations to the registrar. The applicant may amend or withdraw his application at any time. If, after considering any objections and observations, the registrar is satisfied, and if the appropriate fee has been paid, the trade mark is registered as of the date when the application was filed.

Initially, trade marks are registered for a ten-year period from the date of registration. Registration may be renewed for further periods of ten years if the proprietor so requests and pays the appropriate fee. Generally, trade marks cannot be altered in the register either during the period of registration or renewal. However, if the trade mark includes the proprietor's name an address alteration of this may be allowed as long as this does not substantially affect the identity of the trade mark.

A trade mark may be surrendered by the proprietor. It may also be revoked on the following grounds:

(a) it has, without good reason, not been put to genuine use in the UK within five years of completion of the registration procedure;
(b) that its use has become suspended for a five-year period, without good reason;
(c) that the proprietor's acts or omissions have allowed it to become the common name in the trade for a service or product for which it is registered;
(d) that the way it has been used, or been allowed to be used, by the proprietor has made it liable to mislead the public.

A trade mark can be declared invalid on the ground that it was wrongly registered. If the proprietor of a trade mark acquiesces in another's use of the trade mark for a continuous period of five years he loses any entitlement to oppose the use of that trade mark by the other or to apply for a declaration that its registration is invalid. However, this is not the case if the later registration was applied for in bad faith.

Collective marks, which distinguish the goods or services of members of an association, are covered by the Act.

A register of trade mark agents is kept. These agents act for others for the purpose of obtaining the registration of trade marks. Once a person's name is on the register he is known as a 'registered trade mark agent'. It is an offence for any other person to claim to be a registered trade mark agent.

In any civil proceedings the burden of proof is on the proprietor to show any use to which a registered trade mark has been put.

The unauthorised use of a trade mark can amount to a criminal offence. It is also a criminal offence to falsely represent that a trade mark has been registered. Counterfeit goods which misuse trade marks can be forfeited and destroyed.

Test your understanding

1 How is a patent acquired?

2 What three conditions relating to an invention must be satisfied before a patent can be granted?

3 How can a person other than the patentee acquire the right to exploit the patent?

4 What rights are available if a patent is infringed?

5 What is a trade mark?

6 Does a trade mark have to be registered?

7 What rights does registration give to the proprietor of a trade mark?

Answers

1 Patents are granted by the Patent Office if they approve an application for a patent.

2 A patent can be granted only if the invention is new, if the invention involves an inventive step and if the invention is capable of industrial application.

3 Patents may be assigned to another or a licence to exploit the patent may be granted.

4 If a patent is infringed the following remedies are available: an injunction, an order to destroy or deliver up any patented product, damages, an account of profit, and a declaration that the patent is valid and has been infringed.

5 A trade mark is a sign capable of being represented graphically which is capable of distinguishing goods or services of one undertaking from those of another undertaking.

6 No rights under the Trade Marks Act 1994 are gained until a trade mark is registered. Prior to registration a passing-off action may be possible.

7 The proprietor of a registered trade mark is given exclusive rights in the trade mark. If these rights are infringed the proprietor may bring an action for any civil remedy which would be available in respect of infringement of any other property right.

23.5 · The Data Protection Act 1998

The Data Protection Act 1998 was passed to give effect to the EC Data Protection Directive (94/46/EC), which strengthened the regime imposed by the Data Protection Act 1984. The 1998 Act (which in this section of the book is called 'the Act'), applied the rules on data protection to some manual files and strengthened the rights available to individuals. The Act imposes criminal liability on those who breach its provisions.

The holding of data banks has increased in a way which was unimaginable 40 years ago. The Younger Committee's Report in 1972 found that the public felt very concerned about the possible misuse of data. Without protective legislation these fears would have increased as the amount of data held multiplied and became a commodity. There are nowadays few businesses which do not hold and process personal data.

23.5.1 The definitions in the Act

The Act begins with certain definitions. These definitions need to be considered carefully because the provisions of the Act can only be understood in the light of the definitions.

Section 1(1) defines 'data' as information which:

'(a) is being processed by means of equipment operating automatically in response to instructions given for that purpose,

(b) is recorded with the intention that it should be processed by means of such equipment,

(c) is recorded as part of a relevant filing system or with the intention that it should form part of a relevant filing system, or

(d) does not fall within paragraph (a), (b) or (c) but forms part of an accessible [health, educational or publicly accessible] record.'

A data controller is defined by s.1(1) as a person who determines the purposes for which and the manner in which any personal data are, or are to be, processed.

In relation to personal data, a 'data processor' is defined as any person (other than an employee of the data controller) who processes the data on behalf of the data controller. A 'data subject' is an individual who is the subject of personal data.

Personal data must relate to a living individual who can be identified either from the data itself or from the data and other information which is, or which is likely to come into, the possession of the data controller. Both expressions of opinion about the individual and indications of the intentions of the data controller or other person are included.

'Processing' in relation to information or data is defined as obtaining, recording or holding the information or data or carrying out any operation or set of operations on the information or data. Specifically included are:

(a) organising, adapting or altering the information or data;

(b) retrieving, consulting or using the information or data;

(c) disclosing the information or data by transmitting it, disseminating it or otherwise making it available;

(d) aligning, combining, blocking, erasing or destroying the information or data. There is no requirement that processing should be done electronically. The Act will apply even if it is done manually.

Special rules apply to 'sensitive personal data' which is defined as personal data consisting of information as to:

(a) the racial or ethnic origin of the data subject,

(b) his political beliefs,

(c) his religious beliefs or other beliefs of a similar nature,

(d) whether he is a member of a trade union,

(e) his physical or mental health or condition,

(f) his sexual life,

(g) the commission or alleged commission by him of any offence, or

(h) any proceedings for any offence committed or alleged to have been committed by him, the disposal of such proceedings or the sentence of any court in such proceedings.

The Act changes the name of the Data Protection Registrar to the Data Protection Commissioner, referred to in the Act as 'the Commissioner'. Registration with the Commissioner has been renamed as notification.

23.5.2 The rights conferred on data subjects

Section 7 of the Act gives individuals the right of access to their personal data. This right entitles individuals to be informed by a data controller whether personal data of which the individual is a data subject is being processed by or on behalf of the data controller. If this is happening the individual is entitled to a description of the data, the purpose for which it was processed and the recipients to whom it was disclosed. The individual is also entitled to be given a copy of any personal data of which the individual is a data subject and any information which the data controller has as to the source of those data. If personal data relating to the individual are processed automatically in order to evaluate the individual (perhaps in relation to his work, creditworthiness, reliability or conduct) and this is the sole basis of any decision taken in respect of him, the individual is entitled to be informed of the logic involved in the decision-taking. The data controller is only obliged to supply the information described above if he receives a request in writing and a fee. Nor is the data controller obliged to comply unless he is given enough information as he may reasonably require to satisfy himself as to the identity of the person making the request and to locate the information which that person requests. In certain circumstances the data controller can refuse the request if it would be impossible to comply with it without revealing information about another identifiable person.

Section 10 gives an individual the right to give a data controller written notice requiring the data controller to stop processing personal data of which the individual is the data subject. This right only arises if the processing of the data, or the way in which it is processed, is likely to cause substantial unwarranted damage or distress to the individual. The data controller then has 21 days in which to give the individual notice either that he has complied or the reasons why he considers compliance unjustified.

Section 11 gives an individual the right to give written notice requiring the data controller, at the end of a reasonable period, to stop processing personal data for the purposes of direct marketing.

Section 12 gives an individual a right to give written notice to a data controller preventing him from taking an evaluating decision which significantly affects the individual if the decision is based solely on the processing by automatic means of personal data in respect of which that individual is the data subject. Even where no notice is given by the individual, a data controller who takes an evaluating decision which significantly affects an individual, and which was based solely on the processing by automatic means of personal data, must as soon as is reasonably practicable notify the individual that the decision was taken on that basis. The individual then has 21 days in which to require the data controller to reconsider the decision. If the individual does this the data controller has 21 days in which to give a written notification of the steps which he intends to take in order to comply with the request.

If any of the requirements of the Act are contravened by a data controller, an individual who suffers damage as a consequence is entitled to damages.

Section 14 gives a court, upon application by a data subject, the power to order inaccurate personal data to be rectified, blocked, erased or destroyed.

Subject to certain exceptions, personal data must not be processed unless an entry in respect of the data controller is included in the register maintained by the Commissioner. Data controllers who want to be included in the register give a notification to the Commissioner. A person who processes personal data without an entry in respect of the data being included in the register commits an offence. Data does not have to be notified unless it is in relation to personal data, or if it appears to the Secretary of State that processing of a particular description is unlikely to prejudice the rights and freedoms of data subjects and regulations have done away with the need to notify. Nor is there a need to notify in relation to any processing whose sole purpose is the maintenance of a public register. The Secretary of State may also make regulations under which a data controller may appoint a person to act as data protection supervisor to monitor the data controller's compliance with the Act in an independent manner. A data controller who did this might then be able to take advantage of exemptions or other modifications such as the regulations might specify.

23.5.3 The data protection principles

Schedule 1 to the Act sets out eight data protection principles, which apply to all non-exempt processing. The eight principles are as follows:

THE DATA PROTECTION ACT 1998

(1) Personal data shall be processed fairly and lawfully and, in particular, shall not be processed unless:

    (a) at least one of the conditions in Schedule 2 is met, and

    (b) in the case of sensitive personal data, at least one of the conditions in Schedule 3 is also met.

    (Schedules 1 and 2 are considered after the eight data protection principles are set out.)

(2) Personal data shall be obtained only for one or more specified and lawful purposes, and shall not be further processed in any manner incompatible with that purpose or those purposes.

(3) Personal data shall be adequate, relevant and not excessive in relation to the purpose or purposes for which they are processed.

(4) Personal data shall be accurate and, where necessary, kept up to date.

(5) Personal data processed for any purpose or purposes shall not be kept for longer than is necessary for that purpose or those purposes.

(6) Personal data shall be processed in accordance with the rights of data subjects under this Act.

(7) Appropriate technical and organisational measures shall be taken against unauthorised or unlawful processing of personal data and against accidental loss or destruction of, or damage to, personal data.

(8) Personal data shall not be transferred to a country or territory outside the European Economic Area unless that country or territory ensures an adequate level of protection for the rights and freedoms of data subjects in relation to the processing of data.

The European Economic Area is made up of the member states of the EC and Iceland, Norway and Liechtenstein.

Schedule 2 provides that for the purposes of the first data principle, in regard to determining whether personal data are fairly processed, regard should be had to the method by which the data are obtained, including in particular whether any person from whom they were obtained was deceived or misled as to the purposes for which they were to be processed. It also provides that, as regards the first principle, data are not to be treated as fairly processed unless the data subject is provided with information as to the identity of the controller and the purposes for which the data are to be processed, or unless this information is made readily available to him. The first principle is not breached if the data subject has given his consent to the processing. Nor is it breached if the processing is necessary for: functions of a judicial or public nature; or for the performance of a contract to which the data subject is a party; or to comply with a legal obligation to which the data controller is subject; or to protect the vital interests of the data subject.

The fourth principle is not to be regarded as having been contravened by reason of inaccuracy in personal data which accurately record information obtained by the data controller where the data controller had taken reasonable steps to ensure the accuracy of the data. Where the data subject has notified the data controller that the data are inaccurate the data must either be made accurate or indicate that this notification has been made.

The sixth principle can only be committed by a person who breaches ss.7, 10, 11 or 12.

As regards the seventh principle, in order to decide whether the measures ensure a level of security appropriate to the harm which might be done and the nature of the data to be protected, regard must be had to the technological development and the cost of implementing any measures. The data controller must take reasonable steps to ensure the reliability of any employees of his who have access to personal data. He must also take reasonable steps to ensure that any data processor he appoints gives sufficient guarantees in respect of organisational security measures governing the processing to be carried out and also take reasonable steps to ensure compliance with those measures. The seventh principle also requires that a data controller employing a data processor must ensure that the processing is carried out under a contract which is evidenced in writing and under which the data processor is to act only on instructions from the data controller. In addition, the contract must require the data processor to comply with obligations equivalent to those which the seventh principle imposes on a data controller.

As regards the eighth principle an adequate level of protection is a level which is adequate in all the circumstances of the case. The nature of the data and the the laws of the countries of destination and origin are particularly important. Schedule 4 provides that the eighth principle does not apply if the transfer is necessary for the performance of a contract between the data subject and the data controller, or where the transfer is necessary for reasons of substantial public interest. Nor does it apply where the transfer is necessary in respect of legal proceedings, or to protect the vital interests of the data subject or where the transfer is authorised by the Commissioner as being made in a manner which will ensure adequate safeguards for the rights and freedoms of data subjects.

As regards sensitive personal data, Schedule 3 provides that the following are relevant conditions for assessing the extent to which the first principle's requirements that data should be processed fairly and lawfully have been met:

(1) The data subject has given his explicit consent to the processing of the personal data.
(2) The processing is necessary for the data controller to exercise or perform a right or obligation conferred or imposed on him in connection with employment.
(3) The processing is necessary to protect the vital interest of the data subject.
(4) The processing is carried out in the course of legitimate activities by a non-profit-making body which exists for political, philosophical, religious or trade union purposes. The processing must be carried out with appropriate safeguards for the rights and freedoms of data subjects and relate only to members of the body or association in question and must not involve disclosure of the personal data to a third party without the consent of the data subject.
(5) The information in the personal data has been made public as a result of steps deliberately taken by the data subject.
(6) The processing is necessary for the purposes of legal proceedings or the administration of justice.
(7) The processing is necessary for medical purposes and is undertaken by a health professional or some other person who owes a duty of confidentiality which is the equivalent of that owed by a health professional.
(8) The processing is of sensitive data relating to racial or ethnic origin and is necessary to make sure that unequal treatment in these fields does not occur.
(9) The processing is necessary for other purposes set out in regulations made by the Secretary of State.

The Act contains various exemptions in respect of: confidential references given by the data controller; the armed forces; judicial appointments and honours; Crown employment and Ministerial appointment; management forecasts; corporate finance; exam marks and scripts; legal professional privilege; and self-incrimination.

Exemptions in respect of the data protection principles, or the data protection rights, or the need to register also exist in relation to: national security; crime and taxation; health education and social work; journalism, literature or art; and domestic purposes.

Transitional relief may be available against non-compliance with the Act. Before 24 October 2001 some manual data are exempt from the data protection principles. They are also exempt from the rights of data subjects and the rules on notification to the registrar. Exemptions are available until 24 October 2007 in respect of eligible manual data which were held immediately before 24 October 1998. These exemptions are in respect of the first, second, third, fourth and fifth data protection principles and some of the rules on blocking, rectifying, erasing and blocking data. Other exemptions apply to historical research.

A circuit judge can issue a search warrant to the Commissioner if the Commissioner satisfies him that there are reasonable grounds for suspecting that a data controller has contravened, or is contravening, any of the data protection principles or that an offence under the Act has been or is being committed. Intentionally obstructing a person executing such a warrant is an offence. It is also an offence to fail to give any person executing a warrant such assistance as he may reasonably require, without reasonable excuse. The main offences created by the Act are: failure to specify changes in contravention of a notice to do this; failure to comply with an enforcement notice; deliberately or recklessly making a false statement while purporting to comply with an enforcement notice; and unlawfully obtaining, selling or offering to sell personal data.

The Commissioner has the power to serve enforcement notices which give a person a reasonable time to stop contravening the data protection principles. The Commissioner also has the function of promoting good practice by data controllers and ensuring that data controllers comply with the Act.

Test your understanding

1 What rights does the Data Protection Act 1998 confer on data subjects?

2 What are the eight data protection principles?

Answers

1 The 1998 Act confers upon data subjects the following rights: to access to personal data; to prevent processing which is likely to cause distress or damage; to prevent processing for the purposes of direct marketing; to prevent evaluation by automatic decision taking; to compensation if certain requirements are not complied with; and to have inaccurate data rectified or erased.

2 The eight data protection principles are that: personal data should be processed lawfully and fairly; that personal data should be obtained for one or more specified and lawful purposes and not be used for other purposes; that personal data should be adequate, relevant and not excessive; that personal data should be accurate and kept up to date; that personal data should not be kept for longer than is necessary to process it; that personal data should be processed in accordance with the rights which the Act gives to data subjects; that appropriate measures should be taken against unauthorised processing and against loss or destruction of personal data; and that personal data should not be transferred to a country outside the EEA, unless its laws are sufficiently robust to ensure protection for the rights and freedoms of data subjects.

Key points

The nature of property

■ Intellectual property rights are concerned with rights in intangible property.

■ Choses in action may be documentary or non-documentary. The documentary rights can be transferred to another by delivering the document which embodies the right. Non-documentary rights can be transferred to another by assignment.

Copyright

■ Copyright is concerned with protecting the expression of ideas, rather than with protecting ideas themselves.

■ There is no need to register copyright.

■ Copyright may exist in: (a) original literary, dramatic, musical or artistic works; (b) sound recordings, films, broadcasts or cable programmes; and (c) the typographical arrangements of published editions.

■ As regards literary, dramatic, musical and artistic works, copyright subsists for 70 years after the end of the calendar year in which the author dies.

■ Authors of copyright are given moral rights in respect of the work. These rights are the paternity right; the right to object to derogatory treatment of the work; the right not to have work falsely attributed to them; and a right of privacy relating to photographs and films.

- If copyright is infringed the copyright holder will have all the remedies available to him which would be available in respect of infringement of any other property right.

Patents

- A patent can only exist if it is granted by the Patent Office.
- An invention can only be patented if it is new, involves an inventive step and is capable of industrial application.
- Animals and plants may not be patented.
- Patents may be assigned or mortgaged. Licences to exploit a patent may be granted.
- Inventions made by employees will belong to the employer if they were made in the normal course of the employment.
- A compulsory licence may be granted if a patent is not being fully exploited in the UK.
- A person whose patent is being infringed can bring an action for an injunction, an order to deliver up or destroy a product, damages, an account of profits or a declaration that the patent has been infringed.

Trade marks

- A trade mark is a sign capable of being represented graphically which is capable of distinguishing the goods or services of one undertaking from those of another.
- The Trade Marks Act 1994 gives the proprietor of a registered trade mark exclusive rights in the trade mark. Before a trade mark is registered the Act will confer no rights, although a passing-off action may be possible.
- There are a number of absolute and relative grounds for refusing registration of a trade mark.
- If the rights of a proprietor of a trade mark are infringed any civil remedy which would ordinarily be available for infringement of a property right will be available to the proprietor.

The Data Protection Act 1998

- The 1998 Act confers upon data subjects the rights to:
  - access to personal data;
  - prevent processing which is likely to cause distress or damage;
  - prevent processing for the purposes of direct marketing;
  - prevent evaluation by automatic decision taking;
  - compensation if certain requirements are not complied with; and
  - have inaccurate data rectified or erased.
- The eight data protection principles are as follows:
  - that personal data should be processed lawfully and fairly;
  - that personal data should be obtained for one or more specified and lawful purposes and not be used for other purposes;
  - that personal data should be adequate, relevant and not excessive;
  - that personal data should be accurate and kept up to date;
  - that personal data should not be kept for longer than is necessary to process it;
  - that personal data should be processed in accordance with the rights given to data subjects by the Act;
  - that appropriate measures should be taken against unauthorised processing, and against loss or destruction of personal data;
  - that personal data should not be transferred to a country outside the EEA, unless that country ensures an adequate level of protection for the rights and freedoms of data subjects.

Summary questions

1 In 2001 Angus MacSpiers wins the most prestigious prize for any work of art, the Rembrandt prize, with his photograph of two haggises in a butcher's shop. The photograph is lavishly praised by the Rembrandt prize judges as a highly significant comment on the pressures of 21st-century life. John Doe writes an article in a national newspaper which is highly critical of MacSpiers' work. This article falsely shows a variety of every-day photographs and claims that they are 'other works of genius by Angus MacSpiers'. A University lecturer photocopies Doe's article and gives a copy to 250 of his students. A local printer incorporates a copy of the prize-winning photograph into a poster which also shows a piece of tripe. The poster is entitled, 'Spot the difference'. The printer sells this poster in several newsagents. Advise the parties as to whether or not any of them have infringed copyright and of any remedies which may be available.

2 John thinks he has invented a new mousetrap which is superior to any mousetrap he has ever seen or heard of. Explain to John what a patent is, the steps which he will need to take in order to acquire a patent and the rights which a patent would confer upon him.

3 Acme Ltd, a manufacturer of footballs, wants to register a trade mark under which its goods are sold. Explain the process of registration, the tests the mark will have to satisfy in order to be capable of being a trade mark and the benefits of registering the mark as a trade mark.

4 Try to think of two persons who hold personal data on you or a member of your family. Is the data held personal data? Outline the data protection principles which would apply in respect of this data and the rights conferred on the data subject.

Multiple choice questions

1 Which one of the following statements is not true?

   a Copyright does not exist in a literary, dramatic, or musical work until that work is recorded.

   b Copyright in a literary, dramatic, musical or artistic work subsists for 70 years after the end of the calendar year in which the author died.

   c The mere act of down-loading work from the Internet could amount to an infringement of copyright.

   d The four moral rights can be enforced by injunction but damages cannot be claimed in respect of a breach of a moral right.

2 Which one of the following statements is not true?

   a A patent can only be granted in respect of an invention which is new, which involves an inventive step and which is capable of industrial application.

   b If a patent is registered the patentee is granted an absolute right to prevent the use of the patented invention for 20 years.

   c A person can be sued for bringing a groundless claim for infringement of a patent.

   d A patent can be assigned to another person, and another person can be granted a licence to exploit a patent.

3 Which one of the following statements is not true?

   a Only a sign which is capable of being represented graphically can be a trade mark.

   b Shapes cannot be registered as trade marks.

   c A court may order the destruction of goods which infringe a trade mark.

   d Trade marks are initially registered for a 10-year period and registration can be renewed at 10-yearly intervals.

4 Which one of the following statements is not true?

   a The Data Protection Act 1998 applies only to electronically processed data.

   b Upon making a written request and paying a fee, individuals have a right to receive a copy of personal data relating to them.

   c Personal data held by a data controller must be accurate and, where necessary, kept up to date.

   d A circuit judge has the power to issue a search warrant if the Commissioner satisfies him that a person is contravening any of the data principles.

Task 23

Your employer has recently become concerned with the infringement of intellectual property rights. Write a report for him, briefly explaining the following matters:

a The meaning of copyright, the ways in which copyright is created and the remedies available for infringement of copyright.

b The meaning of a patent, how a patent is acquired and the remedies of infringement of a patent.

c The meaning of a trade mark, the way in which a trade mark is acquired and the remedies for infringement of a trade mark.

d The effect of the Data Protection Act 1998.

BIBLIOGRAPHY

Chapters 1 and 2

Smith, Bailey and Gunn on the Modern English Legal System (4th edition) Sweet and Maxwell deals very comprehensively with all the matters considered in these two chapters. Despite the scope of the book and the detailed approach, the book remains fairly easy to read.

Chapter 3

The Law of Contract by Paul Richards (6th edition) Financial Times/Pitman Publishing is a detailed book which is easy to read. A short chapter is devoted to the evolution and definition of a contract. A lengthy chapter deals with offer, acceptance, termination of offers and certainty. Despite being aimed primarily at LLB students, this is a useful book for anyone who wants a good understanding of the law of contract.

Chapter 4

Richards has a lengthy chapter on consideration and shorter chapters on intention to create legal relations, capacity and formalities. Again, plenty of detail while remaining easily readable.

Chapter 5

In *Richards* one chapter deals with terms generally (express and implied terms and the classification of terms) while another chapter is devoted to exemption clauses, which are considered in considerable detail.

Chapter 6

Richards devotes a chapter to misrepresentation, another to mistake, another to duress, undue influence and inequality of bargaining power and yet another to illegality. The detail here might be excessive for readers other than LLB students. *Davies on Contract by Robert Upex (9th edition) Sweet and Maxwell* might be preferable. *Davies* is very easy to read, but lacks the detailed analysis to be found in *Richards*.

Chapter 7

Again *Richards* might be too detailed here. Three separate chapters deal with discharge of contracts while three more deal with remedies for breach of contract. Again, *Davies* is an excellent alternative. *Contract Law, Text, Cases and Materials by Professor Ewan McKendrick (1st edition) Oxford University Press* is an outstanding case book on the whole of the law of contract. The materials reproduced are well chosen and the author's detailed comments are very useful.

Chapter 8

Commercial Law by Robert Bradgate (3rd edition) LexisNexis UK has one chapter devoted to the classification of transactions and another to the substance of the statutory implied terms to be found in the Sale of Goods Act 1979. Yet another chapter deals with contracts for the supply of services. *Bradgate* is a well-written book which deals with the various matters convincingly. Some students might find it rather difficult to read, but it is much easier to read than most of its competitors.

Chapter 9

Bradgate considers the matters covered in this chapter in great detail, taking four chapters to do so. Again, preferable to most of its competitors.

Chapter 10

The matters covered in this chapter are dealt with more briefly by *Bradgate*. Complex issues are not avoided, and yet the style remains readable.

Chapter 11

Bradgate deals with agency over four relatively short chapters, providing an excellent treatment of the subject, once the basic concepts have been mastered. *An Outline of the Law of Agency by Markesinis and Munday (4th edition) LexisNexis UK* is a short but interesting book which deals with some of the more complex aspects of the law of agency. However, at times this book can be rather difficult to read.

Chapters 12 and 13

The Law of Torts Learning Text by John Hodgson and John Lewthwaite (2nd edition) Blackstone Press leads the reader through this difficult subject. The text is designed to be used with a companion text containing Cases and Materials. The complexity of the subject is never avoided and yet the style remains clear and readable. For those who prefer a more conventional approach, *Street on Torts (10th edition) LexisNexis UK* is an excellent book.

Chapter 14

The law on credit is highly complex and maintaining a readable style is a struggle for any author dealing with the subject. *Bradgate* explores the subject in great detail and is as readable as any other book which does so.

Chapter 15

There are few books which deal convincingly with the law of partnership. *Partnership Law by Geoffrey Morse (5th edition) Oxford University Press* is probably the best. The book is academic in its approach but remains reasonably easy to read.

Chapter 16

Mayson, French and Ryan on Company Law (21st edition) Blackstone Press is an excellent book. It deals with all aspects of Company Law in great detail and yet remains clear, practical and comprehensible. Several chapters are devoted to corporate personality and the registration of companies.

Chapters 17 to 19

Again, *Mayson, French and Ryan* seems the pick of the bunch. It is updated annually and is therefore always up to date. Much of company law is changing rapidly and the book explains these changes in a readable style. The policy behind the law is also considered critically and convincingly.

Chapters 20 and 21

Selwyn's Law of Employment (12th edition) LexisNexis UK is an excellent conventional textbook. The text is broken down into easily manageable chunks and the style of the writing is clear. Employment law is changing at a phenomenal rate and the DTI Website (www.dti.gov.uk) provides excellent summaries of all new legislation. *Tolley's Employment Handbook by Elizabeth Slade (18th edition) LexisNexis UK* is the most authoritative book on employment law. It is clear and accurate, but very expensive.

Chapter 22

Textbook on Consumer Law by David Oughton and John Lowry (2nd edition) Blackstone Press provides an excellent treatment of the subjects covered in this chapter. The text is detailed and authoritative but reasonably easy to read.

Chapter 23

Intellectual Property by David Bainbridge (5th edition) Financial Times/Pitman Publishing is a comprehensive work which deals with all aspects of intellectual property. The book is well written and detailed.

INDEX